Lecture Notes in Computer Science 2470

Edited by G. Goos, J. Hartmanis, and J. van Leeuwen

Springer
Berlin
Heidelberg
New York
Hong Kong
London
Milan
Paris
Tokyo

Pascal Van Hentenryck (Ed.)

Principles and Practice of Constraint Programming– CP 2002

8th International Conference, CP 2002
Ithaca, NY, USA, September 9-13, 2002
Proceedings

Springer

Series Editors

Gerhard Goos, Karlsruhe University, Germany
Juris Hartmanis, Cornell University, NY, USA
Jan van Leeuwen, Utrecht University, The Netherlands

Volume Editor

Pascal Van Hentenryck
Brown University
Box 1910, Providence, RI 02912, USA
E-mail: pvh@cs.brown.edu

Cataloging-in-Publication Data applied for

Die Deutsche Bibliothek - CIP-Einheitsaufnahme

Principles and practice of constraint programming : 8th international
conference ; proceedings / CP 2002, Ithaca, NY, USA September 9 - 13, 2002.
Pascal Van Hentenryck (ed.). - Berlin ; Heidelberg ; New York ; Barcelona ;
Hong Kong ; London ; Milan ; Paris ; Tokyo : Springer, 2002
  (Lecture notes in computer science ; Vol. 2470)
  ISBN 3-540-44120-4

CR Subject Classification (1998): D.1, D.3.2-3, I.2.3-4, F.3.2, F.4.1, I.2.8

ISSN 0302-9743
ISBN 3-540-44120-4 Springer-Verlag Berlin Heidelberg New York

Springer-Verlag Berlin Heidelberg New York,
a member of BertelsmannSpringer Science+Business Media GmbH

http://www.springer.de

© Springer-Verlag Berlin Heidelberg 2002
Printed in Germany

Typesetting: Camera-ready by author, data conversion by DA-TeX Gerd Blumenstein
Printed on acid-free paper   SPIN: 10871314   06/3142   5 4 3 2 1 0

Preface

This volume is the conference record for the Eighth International Conference on Principles and Practice of Constraint Programming (CP 2002) held at Cornell University, Ithaca (USA) on September 9-13, 2002. The series of CP conferences deals with original papers on all aspects of computing with constraints. After a few annual workshops, the conferences were held at Cassis (France) in 1995, at Cambridge (USA) in 1996, in Schloss Hagenberg (Austria) in 1997, at Pisa (Italy) in 1998, at Alexandria (USA) in 1999, at Singapore in 2000, and at Paphos (Cyprus) in 2001.

One of the most appealling features of constraint programming is its multi-disciplinary nature, which gives rise to a unique combination of theoretical and experimental research and which provides bridges between areas that are often thought of as separate and remote. The theme of CP 2002, which was chosen together with Carla Gomes (the conference chair), was to emphasize this multi-disciplinary nature. CP 2002 tried to broaden the audience of the CP series and to reach out to a number of communities which are increasingly interested in CP, but do not (yet) participate in the CP conferences. The objective was to encourage cross-fertilization of ideas from various fields which have been looking at related problems from different, often complementary, angles. This theme was present in many aspects of the conference, including the program committee, the invited talks and tutorials, the computational symposium on graph coloring and generalizations and, of course, the papers that truly capture the wide variety of research encompassed under the umbrella of constraint programming.

About 146 papers were submitted in response to the call for papers. After the reviewing period and some online discussion, the program committee met physically at Brown University on June 14 and 15. The program committee decided to accept two types of papers: technical and innovative application papers. Both types of papers were reviewed rigourously and held to very high standards. The separation into two tracks crystallizes two fundamental ways to make significant advances to the field as it matures; it also acknowledges that the evaluation criteria ought to be different for each type of contribution. In particular, innovative application papers advance the state of the art by presenting innovative applications and systems, by providing insightful evaluations of constraint programming technology, and/or by enhancing and extending existing ideas to solve complex industrial problems. At the end of the two days, the program committee accepted 44 papers (6 of which are innovative applications), which is an acceptance ratio of around 30%. In addition, the program committee also accepted 16 posters, which were allocated 5 pages in these proceedings. In general, these posters were selected because the program committee felt that they contain a very promising, although somewhat premature, idea. Finally, CP 2002 continued the wonderful doctoral program initiated in previous years. This program makes it possible for students to present their work and receive feedback from more senior members of the community. CP 2002 featured 25 of these young promising researchers, each of whom was given one page in the proceedings to describe their ongoing research.

CP 2002 has been fortunate to attract outstanding invited talks and tutorials. Professors Edward Clarke, Rina Dechter, Jean-Louis Lassez, George Nemhauser, and David Schmoys all kindly accepted our invitation to speak at CP 2002. Nicolas Beldiceanu and Jean-Charles Régin, Frédéric Benhamou, Mats Carlsson and Christian Schulte, and John Hooker kindly agreed to give tutorials on global constraints, interval reasoning, constraint programming languages and systems, and the integration of constraint and integer programming. In addition, the doctoral program also featured a number of tutorials about research and career issues. Finally, we were lucky to have David Johnson, Anuj Mehrotra, and Michael Trick organize the symposium on graph coloring and generalizations in conjunction with the conference.

As constraint programming grows and matures, so does the organization of its conferences. I have been fortunate to work with many talented and dedicated individuals who made outstanding contributions to the conference. I am extremely grateful to Carla Gomes, the conference chair. In addition to her organization skills and her unlimited energy and passion, she helped define, shape, and implement the theme of the conference. She truly was an amazing ambassador for the conference. I also would like to thank the outstanding program committee who worked very hard under tight deadlines, Francesca Rossi for chairing the wonderful doctoral program whose integration in the technical program was as smooth as humanly possible, Peter van Beek for chairing and orchestrating the successful workshop program, Helmut Simonis for chairing the innovative applications program, and Ramon Bejar, the publicity chair. And, last but not least, I am deeply grateful to Lori Agresti and Laurent Michel for their work in the trenches in preparing, running, and concluding the PC meeting at Brown.

July 2002   Pascal Van Hentenryck

Organization

Conference Chair:	Carla Gomes, Cornell University, USA
Program Chair:	Pascal Van Hentenryck, Brown University, USA
Innovative Applications:	Helmut Simonis, Parc Technologies, UK
Doctoral Program:	Francesca Rossi, University of Padova, Italy
Workshop Chair:	Peter van Beek, University of Waterloo, Canada
Publicity Chair:	Ramon Bejar, Cornell University, USA
Local Arrangements:	Beth Howard, Cornell University, DK

Program Committee

Slim Abdennadher, University of Munich, Germany
Fahiem Bacchus, University of Toronto, Canada
Pedro Barahona, Universidade Nova de Lisboa, Portugal
Nicolas Beldiceanu, SICS, Sweden
Frederic Benhamou, University of Nantes, France
Alexander Bockmayr, LORIA, France
Mats Carlsson, SICS, Sweden
Philippe Codognet, University of Paris 6, France
Hubert Comon, ENS, France
Maria Garcia de la Banda, Monash University, Australia
Ian Gent, University of St. Andrews, UK
Hector Geffner, Universitat Pompeu Fabra, Spain
Carla Gomes, Cornell University, USA
Martin Henz, National University of Singapore, Singapore
John Hooker, CMU, USA
Richard Korf, UCLA, USA
Pedro Meseguer, IIIA-CSIC, Spain
George Nemhauser, Georgia Tech., USA
Barry O'Sullivan, University College Cork, Ireland
Gilles Pesant, University of Montreal, Canada
Jochen Renz, Vienna University of Technology, Austria
Francesca Rossi, University of Padova, Italy
Michel Rueher, University of Nice, France
Christian Schulte, Saarland University, Germany
Bart Selman, Cornell University, USA
Pascal Van Hentenryck, Brown University, USA
Moshe Vardi, Rice University, USA
Gerard Verfaillie, ONERA, France
Mark Wallace, IC-PARC, UK
Joachim Walser, I2 Technologies, USA
Brian Williams, MIT, USA
Makoto Yokoo, NTT, Japan

Referees

Slim Abdennadher
F. Ajili
Paula Amaral
Matthieu Andre
Ola Angelsmark
Alexis Anglada
Fahiem Bacchus
Pedro Barahona
Tania Bedrax-Weiss
Ramon Bejar
Nicolas Beldiceanu
Frederic Benhamou
Christian Bessière
Stefano Bistarelli
Alexander Bockmayr
Patrice Boizumault
Lucas Bordeaux
James Bowen
Pascal Brisset
Mathias Broxvall
Mats Carlsson
Manuel Carro
Carlos Castro
Martine Ceberio
Philippe Codognet
Dave Cohen
Hubert Comon
Jorge Cruz
Joseph Culberson
Romuald Debruyne
Joerg Denzinger
Yannis Dimopoulos
Carmel Domshlak
Olivier Dubois
Torsten Fahle
Boi Faltings
Cesar Fernandez
Filippo Focacci
Thom Fruehwirth
Philippe Galinier
Maria Garcia de la Banda
Hector Geffner
Ian Gent
Yan Georget

Alfonso Gerevini
Carla Gomes
Frederic Goualard
Jean Goubault-Larrecq
Laurent Granvilliers
Martin Grohe
Martin Henz
Katsutoshi Hirayama
Petra Hofstedt
John Hooker
Holger Hoos
Wuh Hui
Joxan Jaffar
Vipul Jain
Ari Jonsson
Peter Jonsson
Narendra Jussien
Jin-Kao Hao
Thomas Kasper
George Katsirelos
Alexander Knapp
Richard Korf
Per Kreuger
Ludwig Krippahl
Bhaskar Krishnamachari
Arnaud Lallouet
Arnaud Lalourt
Javier Larrosa
Yahia Lebbah
Jimmy Lee
M. Lema
Michel Lemaitre
Jonathan Lever
Olivier Lhomme
James Little
Pierre Lopez
Carsten Lutz
Ines Lynce
Arnold Maestre
Vicky Mak
Felip Manya
Kim Marriott
Michael Marte
Lionel Martin

Bart Massey
Iain McDonald
Pedro Meseguer
Bernd Meyer
Laurent Michel
Michela Milano
Eric Monfroy
J. Moura Pires
Guy Narboni
George Nemhauser
Bertrand Neveu
Barry O'Sullivan
Maria Osorio
Greger Ottosson
Andrew Parkes
Gilles Pesant
Thierry Petit
Evgueni Petrov
Nicolai Pisaruk
Steven Prestwich
Patrick Prosser
Alessandra Raffaeta
Jean-Charles Régin
Jochen Renz
Christophe Rigotti
Jussi Rintanen
Francesca Rossi
Louis-Martin Rousseau
Andrew Rowley
Michel Rueher
Harald Ruess
Irena Rusu
Frederic Saubion
Thomas Schiex
Joachim Schimpf
Craig Schmidt
Christian Schulte
Dale Schuurmans
Evgeny Selensky
Bart Selman
Helmut Simonis
Daniel Singer
Barbara Smith
Harald Sondergaard

Finnegan Southey	Marc van Dongen	Brian Williams
Peter Stuckey	Pascal Van Hentenryck	Thorsten Winterer
Peter Szeredi	Moshe Vardi	Armin Wolf
Armagan Tarim	Gerard Verfaillie	Quanshi Xia
Sven Thiel	Thierry Vidal	Roland Yap
Carme Torras	Razvan Voicu	Makoto Yokoo
Erlendur Torsteinsson	Mark Wallace	Tallys Yunes
Michael Trick	Richard Wallace	Hantao Zhang
Gilles Trombettoni	Paul Joachim Walser	Weixiong Zhang
Beek van Peter	Toby Walsh	Yuanlin Zhang

CP Organizing Committee

Alan Borning, University of Washington, USA
Alex Brodsky, George Mason University, USA
Jacques Cohen, Brandeis University, USA
Alain Colmerauer, University of Marseille, France
Rina Dechter, University of California at Irvine, USA
Eugene Freuder, chair, University of Cork, Ireland
Hervé Gallaire, Xerox, USA
Joxan Jaffar, National University of Singapore, Singapore
Jean-Pierre Jouannaud, University of Paris Sud, France
Jean-Louis Lassez, New Mexico Tech, USA
Michael Maher, Griffith University, Australia
Ugo Montanari, University of Pisa, Italy
Anil Nerode, Cornell University, USA
Jean-François Puget, ILOG, France
Francesca Rossi, University of Padova, Italy
Vijay Saraswat, AT&T Research, USA
Gert Smolka, Univ. des Saarlandes, Germany
Ralph Wachter, Office of Naval Research, USA
Toby Walsh, University of Cork, Ireland
Roland Yap, National University of Singapore, Singapore

Sponsoring Institutions

We gratefully acknowledge the support of AAAI, the Association for Logic Programming (ALP), CoLogNet, Cosytec, ILOG, and the Intelligent Information Systems Institute (IISI) at Cornell University.

Table of Contents

Innovative Applications

Posters

Doctoral Program

Reduced Cost-Based Ranking
for Generating Promising Subproblems

Michela Milano[1] and Willem J. van Hoeve[2]

[1] DEIS, University of Bologna
Viale Risorgimento 2, 40136 Bologna, Italy
mmilano@deis.unibo.it
http://www-lia.deis.unibo.it/Staff/MichelaMilano/
[2] CWI, P.O. Box 94079, 1090 GB Amsterdam, The Netherlands
w.j.van.hoeve@cwi.nl
http://www.cwi.nl/~wjvh/

Abstract. In this paper, we propose an effective search procedure that interleaves two steps: subproblem generation and subproblem solution. We mainly focus on the first part. It consists of a variable domain value ranking based on reduced costs. Exploiting the ranking, we generate, in a Limited Discrepancy Search tree, the most promising subproblems first. An interesting result is that reduced costs provide a very precise ranking that allows to almost always find the optimal solution in the first generated subproblem, even if its dimension is significantly smaller than that of the original problem. Concerning the proof of optimality, we exploit a way to increase the lower bound for subproblems at higher discrepancies. We show experimental results on the TSP and its time constrained variant to show the effectiveness of the proposed approach, but the technique could be generalized for other problems.

1 Introduction

In recent years, combinatorial optimization problems have been tackled with hybrid methods and/or hybrid solvers [11,18,13,19]. The use of problem relaxations, decomposition, cutting planes generation techniques in a Constraint Programming (CP) framework are only some examples. Many hybrid approaches are based on the use of a relaxation R, i.e. an easier problem derived from the original one by removing (or relaxing) some constraints. Solving R to optimality provides a bound on the original problem. Moreover, when the relaxation is a linear problem, we can derive *reduced costs* through dual variables often with no additional computational cost. Reduced costs provide an optimistic esteem (a bound) of each variable-value assignment cost. These results have been successfully used for pruning the search space and for guiding the search toward promising regions (see [9]) in many applications like TSP [12], TSPTW [10], scheduling with sequence dependent setup times [8] and multimedia applications [4].

We propose here a solution method, depicted in Figure 1, based on a two step search procedure that interleaves (i) subproblem generation and (ii) subproblem

P. Van Hentenryck (Ed.): CP 2002, LNCS 2470, pp. 1–16, 2002.

solution. In detail, we solve a relaxation of the problem at the root node and we use reduced costs to rank domain values; then we partition the domain of each variable X_i in two sets, i.e., the *good* part D_i^{good} and the *bad* part D_i^{bad}. We search the tree generated by using a strategy imposing on the left branch the branching constraint $X_i \in D_i^{good}$ while on the right branch we impose $X_i \in D_i^{bad}$. At each leaf of the *subproblem generation tree*, we have a subproblem which can now be solved (in the *subproblem solution tree*).

Exploring with a Limited Discrepancy Strategy the resulting search space, we obtain that the first generated subproblems are supposed to be the most promising and are likely to contain the optimal solution. In fact, if the ranking criterion is effective (as the experimental results will show), the first generated subproblem (discrepancy equal to 0) $P^{(0)}$, where all variables range on the good domain part, is likely to contain the optimal solution. The following generated subproblems (discrepancy equal to 1) $P_i^{(1)}$ have all variables but the i-th ranging on the good domain and are likely to contain worse solutions with respect to $P^{(0)}$, but still good. Clearly, subproblems at higher discrepancies are supposed to contain the worst solutions.

A surprising aspect of this method is that even by using low cardinality good sets, **we almost always find the optimal solution in the first generated subproblem**. Thus, reduced costs provide extremely useful information indicating for each variable which values are the most promising. Moreover, this property of reduced costs is independent of the tightness of the relaxation. Tight relaxations are essential for the proof of optimality, but not for the quality of reduced costs. Solving only the first subproblem, we obtain a very effective incomplete method that finds the optimal solution in almost all test instances.

To be complete, the method should solve all subproblems for all discrepancies to prove optimality. Clearly, even if each subproblem could be efficiently solved, if all of them should be considered, the proposed approach would not be applicable. The idea is that by generating the optimal solution soon and tightening the lower bound with considerations based on the discrepancies shown in the paper, we do not have to explore all subproblems, but we can prune many of them.

In this paper, we have considered as an example the Travelling Salesman Problem and its time constrained variant, but the technique could be applied to a large family of problems.

The contribution of this paper is twofold: (i) we show that reduced costs provide an extremely precise indication for generating promising subproblems, and (ii) we show that LDS can be used to effectively order the subproblems. In addition, the use of discrepancies enables to tighten the problem bounds for each subproblem.

The paper is organized as follows: in Section 2 we give preliminaries on Limited Discrepancy Search (LDS), on the TSP and its time constrained variant. In Section 3 we describe the proposed method in detail. Section 4 discusses the implementation, focussing mainly on the generation of the subproblems using LDS. The quality of the reduced cost-based ranking is considered in Section 5.

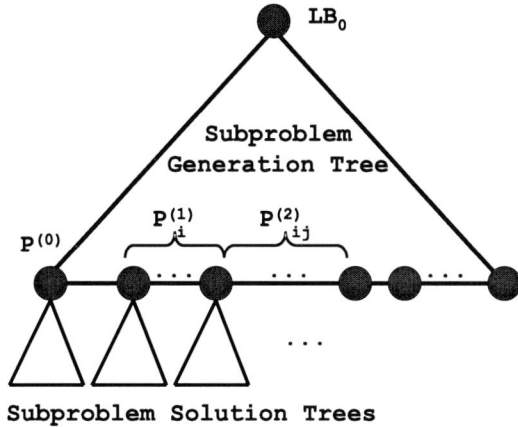

Fig. 1. The structure of the search tree

In this section also the size of subproblems is tuned. Section 6 presents the computational results. Conclusion and future work follow.

2   Preliminaries

2.1   Limited Discrepancy Search

Limited Discrepancy Search (LDS) was first introduced by Harvey and Ginsberg [15]. The idea is that one can often find the optimal solution by exploring only a small fraction of the space by relying on tuned (often problem dependent) heuristics. However, a perfect heuristic is not always available. LDS addresses the problem of what to do when the heuristic fails.

Thus, at each node of the search tree, the heuristic is supposed to provide the *good* choice (corresponding to the leftmost branch) among possible alternative branches. Any other choice would be *bad* and is called a *discrepancy*. In LDS, one tries to find first the solution with as few discrepancies as possible. In fact, a perfect heuristic would provide us the optimal solution immediately. Since this is not often the case, we have to increase the number of discrepancies so as to make it possible to find the optimal solution after correcting the mistakes made by the heuristic. However, the goal is to use only few discrepancies since in general good solutions are provided soon.

LDS builds a search tree in the following way: the first solution explored is that suggested by the heuristic. Then solutions that follow the heuristic for every variable but one are explored: these solutions are that of discrepancy equal to one. Then, solutions at discrepancy equal to two are explored and so on.

It has been shown that this search strategy achieves a significant cutoff of the total number of nodes with respect to a depth first search with chronological backtracking and iterative sampling [20].

2.2   TSP and TSPTW

Let $G = (V, A)$ be a digraph, where $V = \{1, \ldots, n\}$ is the vertex set and $A = \{(i, j) : i, j \in V\}$ the arc set, and let $c_{ij} \geq 0$ be the cost associated with arc $(i, j) \in A$ (with $c_{ii} = +\infty$ for each $i \in V$). A *Hamiltonian Circuit (tour)* of G is a partial digraph $\bar{G} = (V, \bar{A})$ of G such that: $|\bar{A}| = n$ and for each pair of distinct vertices $v_1, v_2 \in V$, both paths from v_1 to v_2 and from v_2 to v_1 exist in $\bar{G}$ (i.e. digraph $\bar{G}$ is *strongly connected*).

The Travelling Salesman Problem (TSP) looks for a Hamiltonian circuit $G^* = (V, A^*)$ whose cost $\sum_{(i,j) \in A^*} c_{ij}$ is a minimum.

A classic Integer Linear Programming formulation for TSP is as follows:

$$v(TSP) \;\; = \min \sum_{i \in V} \sum_{j \in V} c_{ij}\, x_{ij} \tag{1}$$

$$\text{subject to} \sum_{i \in V} x_{ij} = 1, \qquad j \in V \tag{2}$$

$$\sum_{j \in V} x_{ij} = 1, \qquad i \in V \tag{3}$$

$$\sum_{i \in S} \sum_{j \in V \setminus S} x_{ij} \geq 1, \qquad S \subset V,\ S \neq \emptyset \tag{4}$$

$$x_{ij} \text{ integer}, \;\; i, j \in V \tag{5}$$

where $x_{ij} = 1$ if and only if arc (i, j) is part of the solution. Constraints (2) and (3) impose in-degree and out-degree of each vertex equal to one, whereas constraints (4) impose strong connectivity.

Constraint Programming relies in general on a different model where we have a domain variable $Next_i$ (resp. $Prev_i$) that identifies cities visited after (resp. before) node i. Domain variable $Cost_i$ identifies the cost to be paid to go from node i to node $Next_i$.

Clearly, we need a mapping between the CP model and the ILP model: $Next_i = j \Leftrightarrow x_{ij} = 1$. The domain of variable $Next_i$ will be denoted as D_i. Initially, $D_i = \{1, \ldots, n\}$.

The Travelling Salesman Problem with Time Windows (TSPTW) is a time constrained variant of the TSP where the service at a node i should begin within a time window $[a_i, b_i]$ associated to the node. Early arrivals are allowed, in the sense that the vehicle can arrive before the time window lower bound. However, in this case the vehicle has to wait until the node is ready for the beginning of service.

As concerns the CP model for the TSPTW, we add to the TSP model a domain variable $Start_i$ which identifies the time at which the service begins at node i.

A well known relaxation of the TSP and TSPTW obtained by eliminating from the TSP model constraints (4) and time windows constraints is the *Linear Assignment Problem* (AP) (see [3] for a survey). AP is the graph theory problem of finding a set of *disjoint* subtours such that all the vertices in V are visited and the overall cost is a minimum. When the digraph is complete, as in our case, AP always has an optimal integer solution, and, if such solution is composed by a single tour, is then optimal for TSP satisfying constraints (4).

The information provided by the AP relaxation is a lower bound LB for the original problem and the reduced cost matrix $\bar{c}$. At each node of the decision tree, each $\bar{c}_{ij}$ estimates the additional cost to pay to put arc (i, j) in the solution. More formally, a valid lower bound for the problem where $x_{ij} = 1$ is $LB|_{x_{ij}=1} = LB + \bar{c}_{ij}$. It is well-known that when the AP optimal solution is obtained through a *primal-dual* algorithm, as in our case (we use a C++ adaptation of the AP code described in [2]), the reduced cost values are obtained without extra computational effort during the AP solution. The solution of the AP relaxation at the root node requires in the worst case $O(n^3)$, whereas each following AP solution can be efficiently computed in $O(n^2)$ time through a single augmenting path step (see [2] for details). However, the AP does not provide a tight bound neither for the TSP nor for the TSPTW. Therefore we will improve the relaxation in Section 3.1.

3   The Proposed Method

In this section we describe the method proposed in this paper. It is based on two interleaved steps: subproblem generation and subproblem solution. The first step is based on the optimal solution of a (possibly tight) relaxation of the original problem. The relaxation provides a lower bound for the original problem and the reduced cost matrix. Reduced costs are used for ranking (the lower the better) variable domain values. Each domain is now partitioned according to this ranking in two sets called the *good* set and the *bad* set. The cardinality of the good set is problem dependent and is experimentally defined. However, it should be significantly lower than the dimension of the original domains.

Exploiting this ranking, the search proceeds by choosing at each node the branching constraint that imposes the variable to range on the good domain, while on backtracking we impose the variable to range on the bad domain. By exploring the resulting search tree by using an LDS strategy we generate first the most promising problems, i.e., those where no or few variables range on the bad sets.

Each time we generate a subproblem, the second step starts for optimally solving it. Experimental results will show that, surprisingly, even if the subproblems are small, the first generated subproblem almost always contains the optimal solution. The proof of optimality should then proceed by solving the remaining problems. Therefore, a tight initial lower bound is essential. Moreover, by using some considerations on discrepancies, we can increase the bound and prove optimality fast.

The idea of ranking domain values has been previously used in incomplete algorithms, like GRASP [5]. The idea is to produce for each variable the so called Restricted Candidate List (RCL), and explore the subproblem generated only by RCLs for each variable. This method provides in general a good starting point for performing local search. Our ranking method could in principle be applied to GRASP-like algorithms.

Another connection can be made with iterative broadening [14], where one can view the breadth cutoff as corresponding to the cardinality of our good sets. The first generated subproblem of both approaches is then the same. However, iterative broadening behaves differently on backtracking (it gradually restarts increasing the breadth cutoff).

3.1   Linear Relaxation

In Section 2.2 we presented a relaxation, the Linear Assignment Problem (AP), for both the TSP and TSPTW. This relaxation is indeed not very tight and does not provide a good lower bound. We can improve it by adding cutting planes. Many different kinds of cutting planes for these problems have been proposed and the corresponding separation procedure has been defined [22]. In this paper, we used the Sub-tour Elimination Cuts (SECs) for the TSP. However, adding linear inequalities to the AP formulation changes the structure of the relaxation which is no longer an AP. On the other hand, we are interested in maintaining this structure since we have a polynomial and incremental algorithm that solves the problem. Therefore, as done in [10], we relax cuts in a Lagrangean way, thus maintaining an AP structure.

The resulting relaxation, we call it AP^{cuts}, still has an AP structure, but provides a tighter bound than the initial AP. More precisely, it provides the same objective function value as the linear relaxation where all cuts are added defining the sub-tour polytope. In many cases, in particular for TSPTW instances, the bound is extremely close to the optimal solution.

3.2   Domain Partitioning

As described in Section 2.2, the solution of an Assignment Problem provides the reduced cost matrix with no additional computational cost. We recall that the reduced cost $\bar{c}_{ij}$ of a variable x_{ij} corresponds to the additional cost to be paid if this variable is inserted in the solution, i.e., $x_{ij} = 1$. Since these variables are mapped into CP variables $Next$, we obtain the same esteem also for variable domain values. Thus, it is likely that domain values that have a relative low reduced cost value will be part of an optimal solution to the TSP.

This property is used to partition the domain D_i of a variable $Next_i$ into D_i^{good} and D_i^{bad}, such that $D_i = D_i^{good} \cup D_i^{bad}$ and $D_i^{good} \cap D_i^{bad} = \emptyset$ for all $i = 1, \ldots, n$. Given a ratio $r \geq 0$, we define for each variable $Next_i$ the good set D_i^{good} by selecting from the domain D_i the values j that have the $r * n$ lowest $\bar{c}_{ij}$. Consequently, $D_i^{bad} = D_i \setminus D_i^{good}$.

The ratio defines the size of the good domains, and will be discussed in Section 5. Note that the *optimal* ratio should be experimentally tuned, in order to obtain the optimal solution in the first subproblem, and it is strongly problem dependent. In particular, it depends on the structure of the problem we are solving. For instance, for the pure TSP instances considered in this paper, a good ratio is 0.05 or 0.075, while for TSPTW the best ratio observed is around 0.15. With this ratio, the optimal solution of the original problem is indeed located in the first generated subproblem in almost all test instances.

3.3   LDS for Generating Subproblems

In the previous section, we described how to partition variable domains in a good and a bad set by exploiting information on reduced costs. Now, we show how to explore a search tree on the basis of this domain partitioning. At each node corresponding to the choice of variable X_i, whose domain has been partitioned in D_i^{good} and D_i^{bad}, we impose on the left branch the branching constraint $X_i \in D_i^{good}$, and on the right branch $X_i \in D_i^{bad}$. Exploring with a Limited Discrepancy Search strategy this tree, we first explore the subproblem suggested by the heuristic where all variable range on the good set; then subproblems where all variables but one range on the good set, and so on.

If the reduced cost-based ranking criterion is accurate, as the experimental results confirm, we are likely to find the optimal solution in the subproblem $P^{(0)}$ generated by imposing all variables ranging on the good set of values. If this heuristic fails once, we are likely to find the optimal solution in one of the n subproblems ($P_i^{(1)}$ with $i \in \{1, \ldots, n\}$) generated by imposing all variables but one (variable i) ranging on the good sets and one ranging on the bad set. Then, we go on generating $n(n-1)/2$ problems $P_{ij}^{(2)}$ all variables but two (namely i and j) ranging on the good set and two ranging on the bad set are considered, and so on.

In Section 4 we will see an implementation of this search strategy that in a sense *squeezes* the subproblem generation tree shown in Figure 1 into a constraint.

3.4   Proof of Optimality

If we are simply interested in a good solution, without proving optimality, we can stop our method after the solution of the first generated subproblem. In this case, the proposed approach is extremely effective since we almost always find the optimal solution in that subproblem.

Otherwise, if we are interested in a provably optimal solution, we have to prove optimality by solving all sub-problems at increasing discrepancies. Clearly, even if all subproblems could be efficiently solved, generating and solving all of them would not be practical. However, if we exploit a tight initial lower bound, as explained in Section 3.1, which is successively improved with considerations on the discrepancy, we can stop the generation of subproblems after few trials since we prove optimality fast.

An important part of the proof of optimality is the management of lower and upper bounds. The upper bound is decreased as we find better solutions, and the lower bound is increased as a consequence of discrepancy increase. The idea is to find an optimal solution in the first subproblem, providing the best possible upper bound.

The ideal case is that all subproblems but the first can be pruned since they have a lower bound higher than the current upper bound, in which case we only need to consider a single subproblem.

The initial lower bound LB_0 provided by the Assignment Problem AP^{cuts} at the root node can be improved each time we switch to a higher discrepancy k. For $i \in \{1, \ldots, n\}$, let $\bar{c}_i^*$ be the lowest reduced cost value associated with D_i^{bad}, corresponding to the solution of AP^{cuts}, i.e. $\bar{c}_i^* = \min_{j \in D_i^{bad}} \bar{c}_{ij}$. Clearly, a first trivial bound is $\mathrm{LB}_0 + \min_{i \in \{1, \ldots, n\}} \bar{c}_i^*$ for all problems at discrepancy greater than or equal to 1. We can increase this bound: let L be the nondecreasing ordered list of $\bar{c}_i^*$ values, containing n elements. $L[i]$ denotes the i-th element in L. The following theorem achieves a better bound improvement [21].

Theorem 1. *For $k \in \{1, \ldots, n\}$, $\mathrm{LB}_0 + \sum_{i=1}^{k} L[i]$ is a valid lower bound for the subproblems corresponding to discrepancy k.*

Proof. The proof is based on the concept of additive bounding procedures [6,7] that states as follows: first we solve a relaxation of a problem P. We obtain a bound LB, in our case LB_0 and a reduced-cost matrix $\bar{c}$. Now we define a second relaxation of P having cost matrix $\bar{c}$. We obtain a second lower bound $LB^{(1)}$. The sum $LB + LB^{(1)}$ is a valid lower bound for P. In our case, the second relaxation is defined by the constraints imposing in-degree of each vertex less or equal to one plus a linear version of the k-discrepancy constraint: $\sum_{i \in V} \sum_{j \in D_i^{bad}} x_{ij} = k$. Thus, $\sum_{i=1}^{k} L[i]$ is exactly the optimal solution for this problem. $\qquad \square$

Note that in general reduced costs are not additive, but in this case they are. As a consequence of this result, optimality is proven as soon as $\mathrm{LB}_0 + \sum_{i=1}^{k} L[i] >$ UB for some discrepancy k, where UB is the current upper bound. We used this bound in our implementation.

3.5   Solving Each Subproblem

Once the subproblems are generated, we can solve them with any complete technique. In this paper, we have used the method and the code described in [12] and in [10] for the TSPTW. As a search heuristic we have used the one behaving best for each problem.

4   Implementation

Finding a subproblem of discrepancy k is equivalent to finding a set $S \subseteq \{1, \ldots, n\}$ with $|S| = k$ such that

$$Next_i \in D_i^{bad} \quad \text{for } i \in S, \text{ and}$$
$$Next_i \in D_i^{good} \quad \text{for } i \in \{1, \ldots, n\} \setminus S.$$

The search for such a set S and the corresponding domain assignments have been 'squeezed' into a constraint, the *discrepancy constraint* discr_cst. It takes as input the discrepancy k, the variables $Next_i$ and the domains D_i^{good}. Declaratively, the constraint holds if and only if exactly k variables take their values in the bad sets.

Operationally, it keeps track of the number of variables that take their value in either the good or the bad domain. If during the search for a solution in the current subproblem the number of variables ranging on their bad domain is k, all other variables are forced to range on their good domain. Equivalently, if the number of variables ranging on their good domain is $n - k$, the other variables are forced to range on their bad domain.

The subproblem generation is defined as follows (in pseudo-code):

```
for (k=0..n) {
  add(discr_cst(k,next,D_good));
  solve subproblem;
  remove(discr_cst(k,next,D_good));
}
```

where k is the level of discrepancy, next is the array containing $Next_i$, and D_good is the array containing D_i^{good} for all $i \in \{1, \ldots, n\}$. The command solve subproblem is shorthand for solving the subproblem which has been considered in Section 3.5.

A more traditional implementation of LDS (referred to as 'standard' in Table 1) exploits tree search, where at each node the domain of a variable is split into the good set or the bad set, as described in Section 3.3. In Table 1, the performance of this traditional approach is compared with the performance of the discrepancy constraint (referred to as discr_cst in Table 1). In this table results on TSPTW instances (taken from [1]) are reported. All problems are solved to optimality and both approaches use a ratio of 0.15 to scale the size of the good domains. In the next section, this choice is experimentally derived. Although one method does not outperform the other, the overall performance of the discrepancy constraint is in general slightly better than the traditional LDS approach. In fact, for solving all instances, we have in the traditional LDS approach a total time of 2.75 with 1465 fails, while using the constraint we have 2.61 seconds and 1443 fails.

5   Quality of Heuristic

In this section we evaluate the quality of the heuristic used. On the one hand, we would like the optimal solution to be in the first subproblem, corresponding to discrepancy 0. This subproblem should be as small as possible, in order to be able to solve it fast. On the other hand, we need to have a good bound to prove optimality. For this we need relatively large reduced costs in the bad domains, in order to apply Theorem 1 effectively. This would typically induce a larger first subproblem. Consequently, we should make a tradeoff between finding a

Table 1. Comparison of traditional LDS and the discrepancy constraint

	standard		discr_cst			standard		discr_cst	
instance	time	fails	time	fails	instance	time	fails	time	fails
rbg016a	0.08	44	0.04	44	rbg021.2	0.13	66	0.13	66
rbg016b	0.15	57	0.10	43	rbg021.3	0.22	191	0.20	158
rbg017.2	0.05	14	0.05	14	rbg021.4	0.11	85	0.09	40
rbg017	0.10	69	0.09	47	rbg021.5	0.10	45	0.16	125
rbg017a	0.09	42	0.09	42	rbg021.6	0.19	110	0.2	110
rbg019a	0.06	30	0.06	30	rbg021.7	0.23	70	0.22	70
rbg019b	0.12	71	0.12	71	rbg021.8	0.15	88	0.15	88
rbg019c	0.20	152	0.19	158	rbg021.9	0.17	108	0.17	108
rbg019d	0.06	6	0.06	6	rbg021	0.19	152	0.19	158
rbg020a	0.07	5	0.06	5	rbg027a	0.22	53	0.21	53

good first solution and proving optimality. This is done by tuning the ratio r, which determines the size of the first subproblem. We recall from Section 3.2 that $|D_i^{good}| \leq rn$ for $i \in \{1, \ldots, n\}$.

In Tables 2 and 3 we report the quality of the heuristic with respect to the ratio. The TSP instances are taken from TSPLIB [23] and the asymmetric TSPTW instances are due to Ascheuer [1]. All subproblems are solved to optimality with a fixed strategy, as to make a fair comparison. In the tables, 'size' is the actual relative size of the first subproblem with respect to the initial problem. The size is calculated by $\frac{1}{n}\sum_{i=1}^{n}|D_i^{good}|/|D_i|$.

The domains in the TSPTW instances are typically much smaller than the number of variables, because of the time window constraints that already remove a number of domain values. Therefore, the first subproblem might sometimes be relatively large, since only a few values are left after pruning, and they might be equally promising.

The next columns in the tables are 'opt' and 'pr'. Here 'opt' denotes the level of discrepancy at which the optimal solution is found. Typically, we would like this to be 0. The column 'pr' stands for the level of discrepancy at which

Table 2. Quality of heuristic with respect to ratio for the TSP

	ratio=0.025				ratio=0.05				ratio=0.075				ratio=0.1			
instance	size	opt	pr	fails	size	opt	pr	fails	size	opt	pr	fails	size	opt	pr	fails
gr17	0.25	0	1	2	0.25	0	1	2	0.32	0	1	7	0.32	0	1	7
gr21	0.17	0	1	1	0.23	0	1	6	0.23	0	1	6	0.28	0	1	14
gr24	0.17	0	1	2	0.21	0	1	2	0.21	0	1	2	0.26	0	1	39
fri26	0.16	0	1	1	0.20	0	1	4	0.24	0	1	327	0.24	0	1	327
bayg29	0.14	1	2	127	0.17	0	1	341	0.21	0	1	1k	0.21	0	1	1k
bays29	0.13	1	6	19k	0.16	0	2	54	0.20	0	1	65	0.20	0	1	65
average	0.17	0.33	2	22	0.20	0	1.17	68	0.24	0	1	68	0.25	0	1	75

optimality is proved. This would preferably be 1. The column 'fails' denotes the total number of backtracks during search needed to solve the problem to optimality.

Concerning the TSP instances, already for a ratio of 0.05 all solutions are in the first subproblem. For a ratio of 0.075, we can also prove optimality at discrepancy 1. Taking into account also the number of fails, we can argue that both 0.05 and 0.075 are good ratio candidates for the TSP instances.

For the TSPTW instances, we notice that a smaller ratio does not necessarily increase the total number of fails, although it is more difficult to prove optimality. Hence, we have a slight preference for the ratio to be 0.15, mainly because of its overall (average) performance.

An important aspect we are currently investigating is the dynamic tuning of the ratio.

6   Computational Results

We have implemented and tested the proposed method using ILOG Solver and Scheduler [17,16]. The algorithm runs on a Pentium 1Ghz, 256 MB RAM, and uses CPLEX 6.5 as LP solver. The two sets of test instances are taken from the TSPLIB [23] and Ascheuer's asymmetric TSPTW problem instances [1].

Table 4 shows the results for small TSP instances. Time is measured in seconds, fails again denote the total number of backtracks to prove optimality. The time limit is set to 300 seconds. Observe that our method (LDS) needs less number of fails than the approach without subproblem generation (No LDS). This comes with a cost, but still our approach is never slower and in some cases considerably faster. The problems were solved both with a ratio of 0.05 and 0.075, the best of which is reported in the table. Observe that in some cases a ratio of 0.05 is best, while in other cases 0.075 is better. For three instances optimality could not be proven directly after solving the first subproblem. Nevertheless the optimum was found in this subproblem (indicated by objective 'obj' is 'opt'). Time and the number of backtracks (fails) needed in the first subproblem are reported for these instances.

In Table 5 the results for the asymmetric TSPTW instances are shown. Our method (LDS) uses a ratio of 0.15 to solve all these problems to optimality. It is compared to our code without the subproblem generation (No LDS), and to the results by Focacci, Lodi and Milano (FLM2002) [10]. Up to now, FLM2002 has the fastest solution times for this set of instances, to our knowledge. When comparing the time results (measured in seconds), one should take into account that FLM2002 uses a Pentium III 700 MHz.

Our method behaves in general quite well. In many cases it is much faster than FLM2002. However, in some cases the subproblem generation does not pay off. This is for instance the case for `rbg040a` and `rbg042a`. Although our method finds the optimal solution in the first branch (discrepancy 0) quite fast, the initial bound LB_0 is too low to be able to prune the search tree at discrepancy 1. In those cases we need more time to prove optimality than we would have needed if we

Table 3. Quality of heuristic with respect to ratio for the asymmetric TSPTW

	ratio=0.05				ratio=0.1				ratio=0.15				ratio=0.2			
instance	size	opt	pr	fails	size	opt	pr	fails	size	opt	pr	fails	size	opt	pr	fails
rbg010a	0.81	1	2	7	0.94	0	1	5	0.99	0	1	7	0.99	0	1	7
rbg016a	0.76	1	4	37	0.88	0	2	41	0.93	0	2	44	0.98	0	1	47
rbg016b	0.62	1	4	54	0.72	0	3	54	0.84	0	2	43	0.91	0	2	39
rbg017.2	0.38	0	1	2	0.49	0	1	9	0.57	0	1	14	0.66	0	1	27
rbg017	0.53	1	9	112	0.66	1	5	70	0.79	0	3	47	0.89	0	2	49
rbg017a	0.64	0	1	10	0.72	0-	1	13	0.80	0	1	42	0.88	0	1	122
rbg019a	0.89	0	1	17	0.98	0	1	27	1	0	1	30	1	0	1	30
rbg019b	0.68	1	3	83	0.78	1	3	85	0.87	0	1	71	0.95	0	1	71
rbg019c	0.52	1	4	186	0.60	1	3	137	0.68	1	2	158	0.76	0	2	99
rbg019d	0.91	0	2	5	0.97	0	1	6	1	0	1	6	1	0	1	6
rbg020a	0.78	0	1	3	0.84	0	1	3	0.89	0	1	5	0.94	0	1	5
rbg021.2	0.50	0	2	23	0.59	0	1	48	0.66	0	1	66	0.74	0	1	148
rbg021.3	0.48	1	5	106	0.55	1	4	185	0.62	0	3	158	0.68	0	3	163
rbg021.4	0.47	1	4	152	0.53	0	3	33	0.61	0	3	40	0.67	0	2	87
rbg021.5	0.49	1	3	160	0.55	0	2	103	0.61	0	2	125	0.67	0	2	206
rbg021.6	0.41	1	2	8k	0.48	1	2	233	0.59	0	2	110	0.67	0	1	124
rbg021.7	0.40	1	3	518	0.49	0	2	91	0.59	0	1	70	0.65	0	1	70
rbg021.8	0.39	1	3	13k	0.48	1	2	518	0.56	0	1	88	0.63	0	1	88
rbg021.9	0.39	1	3	13k	0.48	1	2	574	0.56	0	1	108	0.63	0	1	108
rbg021	0.52	1	4	186	0.60	1	3	137	0.68	1	2	158	0.76	0	2	99
rbg027a	0.44	0	3	15	0.59	0	2	35	0.66	0	1	53	0.77	0	1	96
average	0.57	0.67	3.05	1725	0.66	0.38	2.14	114	0.74	0.10	1.57	69	0.80	0	1.38	81

	ratio=0.25				ratio=0.3				ratio=0.35			
instance	size	opt	pr	fails	size	opt	pr	fails	size	opt	pr	fails
rbg010a	1	0	1	8	1	0	1	8	1	0	1	8
rbg016a	1	0	1	49	1	0	1	49	1	0	1	49
rbg016b	0.97	0	1	36	0.99	0	1	38	1	0	1	38
rbg017.2	0.74	0	1	31	0.84	0	1	20	0.90	0	1	20
rbg017	0.95	0	2	58	0.99	0	1	56	1	0	1	56
rbg017a	0.93	0	1	143	0.97	0	1	165	1	0	1	236
rbg019a	1	0	1	30	1	0	1	30	1	0	1	30
rbg019b	0.97	0	1	72	1	0	1	72	1	0	1	72
rbg019c	0.82	0	2	106	0.92	0	1	112	0.95	0	1	119
rbg019d	1	0	1	6	1	0	1	6	1	0	1	6
rbg020a	0.99	0	1	5	1	0	1	5	1	0	1	5
rbg021.2	0.80	0	1	185	0.91	0	1	227	0.95	0	1	240
rbg021.3	0.78	0	2	128	0.90	0	2	142	0.94	0	1	129
rbg021.4	0.74	0	2	114	0.88	0	1	67	0.94	0	1	70
rbg021.5	0.74	0	1	193	0.88	0	1	172	0.94	0	1	173
rbg021.6	0.73	0	1	132	0.89	0	1	145	0.95	0	1	148
rbg021.7	0.71	0	1	71	0.82	0	1	78	0.89	0	1	78
rbg021.8	0.71	0	1	89	0.83	0	1	91	0.90	0	1	95
rbg021.9	0.71	0	1	115	0.83	0	1	121	0.90	0	1	122
rbg021	0.82	0	2	106	0.92	0	1	112	0.95	0	1	119
rbg027a	0.83	0	1	245	0.90	0	1	407	0.96	0	1	1k
average	0.85	0	1.24	92	0.93	0	1.05	101	0.96	0	1	139

Table 4. Computational results for the TSP

instance	No LDS		LDS			first subproblem		
	time	fails	time	fails	ratio	obj	time	fails
gr17	0.12	34	0.12	1	0.05	-	-	-
gr21	0.07	19	0.06	1	0.05	-	-	-
gr24	0.18	29	0.18	1	0.05	-	-	-
fri26	0.17	70	0.17	4	0.05	-	-	-
bayg29	0.33	102	0.28	28	0.05	-	-	-
bays29*	0.30	418	0.20	54	0.05	opt	0.19	36
dantzig42	1.43	524	1.21	366	0.075	-	-	-
hk48	12.61	15k	1.91	300	0.05	-	-	-
gr48*	21.05	25k	19.10	22k	0.075	opt	5.62	5.7k
brazil58*	limit	limit	81.19	156k	0.05	opt	80.3	155k

* Optimality not proven directly after solving first subproblem.

did not apply our method (No LDS). In such cases our method can be applied as an effective *incomplete* method, by only solving first subproblem. Table 6 shows the results for those instances for which optimality could not be proven directly after solving the first subproblem. In almost all cases the optimum is found in the first subproblem.

7   Discussion and Conclusion

We have introduced an effective search procedure that consists of generating promising subproblems and solving them. To generate the subproblems, we split the variable domains in a good part and a bad part on the basis of reduced costs. The domain values corresponding to the lowest reduced costs are more likely to be in the optimal solution, and are put into the good set.

The subproblems are generated using a LDS strategy, where the discrepancy is the number of variables ranging on their bad set. Subproblems are considerably smaller than the original problem, and can be solved faster. To prove optimality, we introduced a way of increasing the lower bound using information from the discrepancies.

Computational results on TSP and asymmetric TSPTW instances show that the proposed ranking is extremely accurate. In almost all cases the optimal solution is found in the first subproblem. When proving optimality is difficult, our method can still be used as an effective incomplete search procedure, by only solving the first subproblem.

Some interesting points arise from the paper: first, we have seen that reduced costs represent a good ranking criterion for variable domain values. The ranking quality is not affected if reduced costs come from a loose relaxation.

Table 5. Computational results for the asymmetric TSPTW

instance	FLM2002 time	fails	No LDS time	fails	LDS time	fails	instance	FLM2002 time	fails	No LDS time	fails	LDS time	fails
rbg010a	0.0	6	0.06	6	0.03	4	rbg021.7	0.6	237	0.19	45	0.21	43
rbg016a	0.1	21	0.04	10	0.04	8	rbg021.8	0.6	222	0.09	30	0.10	27
rbg016b	0.1	27	0.11	27	0.09	32	rbg021.9	0.8	310	0.10	31	0.11	28
rbg017.2	0.0	17	0.04	14	0.04	2	rbg021	0.3	81	0.07	17	0.14	74
rbg017	0.1	27	0.06	9	0.08	11	rbg027a	0.2	50	0.19	45	0.16	23
rbg017a	0.1	22	0.05	8	0.05	1	rbg031a	2.7	841	0.58	121	0.68	119
rbg019a	0.0	14	0.05	11	0.05	2	rbg033a	1.0	480	0.62	70	0.73	55
rbg019b	0.2	80	0.08	37	0.09	22	rbg034a	55.2	13k	0.65	36	0.93	36
rbg019c	0.3	81	0.08	17	0.14	74	rbg035a.2	36.8	5k	5.23	2.6k	8.18	4k
rbg019d	0.0	32	0.06	19	0.07	4	rbg035a	3.5	841	0.82	202	0.83	56
rbg020a	0.0	9	0.07	11	0.06	3	rbg038a	0.2	49	0.37	42	0.36	3
rbg021.2	0.2	44	0.09	20	0.08	15	rbg040a	738.1	136k	185.0	68k	1k	387k
rbg021.3	0.4	107	0.11	52	0.14	80	rbg042a	149.8	19k	29.36	11k	70.71	24k
rbg021.4	0.3	121	0.10	48	0.09	32	rbg050a	180.4	19k	3.89	1.6k	4.21	1.5k
rbg021.5	0.2	55	0.14	89	0.12	60	rbg055a	2.5	384	4.39	163	4.50	133
rbg021.6	0.7	318	0.14	62	0.16	50	rbg067a	4.0	493	26.29	171	25.69	128

Table 6. Computational results for the first subproblem of the asymmetric TSPTW

instance	opt	obj	gap (%)	time	fails	instance	opt	obj	gap (%)	time	fails
rbg016a	179	179	0	0.04	7	rbg021.5	169	169	0	0.10	19
rbg016b	142	142	0	0.09	22	rbg021.6	134	134	0	0.15	49
rbg017	148	148	0	0.07	5	rbg021	190	202	6.3	0.10	44
rbg019c	190	202	6.3	0.11	44	rbg035a.2	166	166	0	4.75	2.2k
rbg021.3	182	182	0	0.09	29	rgb040a	386	386	0	65.83	25k
rbg021.4	179	179	0	0.06	4	rbg042a	411	411	0	33.26	11.6k

Second, the tightness of the lower bound is instead very important for the proof of optimality. Therefore, we have used a tight bound at the root node and increased it thus obtaining a discrepancy-based bound.

Third, if we are not interested in a complete algorithm, but we need very good solutions fast, our method turns out to be a very effective choice, since the first generated subproblem almost always contains the optimal solution.

Future directions will explore a different way of generating subproblems. Our domain partitioning is statically defined only at the root node and maintained during the search. However, although being static, the method is still very effective. We will explore a dynamic subproblem generation.

Acknowledgements

We would like to thank Filippo Focacci and Andrea Lodi for useful discussion, suggestions and ideas.

References

1. N. Ascheuer. ATSPTW - Problem instances.
   http://www.zib.de/ascheuer/ATSPTWinstances.html.
2. G. Carpaneto, S. Martello, and P. Toth. Algorithms and codes for the Assignment Problem. In B. Simeone et al., editor, *Fortran Codes for Network Optimization - Annals of Operations Research*, pages 193–223. 1988.
3. M. Dell'Amico and S. Martello. Linear assignment. In F. Maffioli M. Dell'Amico and S. Martello, editors, *Annotated Bibliographies in Combinatorial Optimization*, pages 355–371. Wiley, 1997.
4. T. Fahle and M. Sellman. Cp-based lagrangean relaxation for a multi-media application. In [13], 2001.
5. T. A. Feo and M. G. C. Resende. Greedy randomized adaptive search procedures. *Journal of Global Optimization*, 6:109–133, 1995.
6. M. Fischetti and P. Toth. An additive bounding procedure for combinatorial optimization problems. *Operations Research*, 37:319–328, 1989.
7. M. Fischetti and P. Toth. An additive bounding procedure for the asymmetric travelling salesman problem. *Mathematical Programming*, 53:173–197, 1992.
8. F. Focacci, P. Laborie, and W. Nuijten. Solving scheduling problems with setup times and alternative resources. In *Proceedings of the Fifth International Conference on Artificial Intelligence Planning and Scheduling (AIPS2000)*, 2000.
9. F. Focacci, A. Lodi, and M. Milano. Cost-based domain filtering. In *CP'99 Conference on Principles and Practice of Constraint Programming*, pages 189–203, 1999.
10. F. Focacci, A. Lodi, and M. Milano. A hybrid exact algorithm for the TSPTW. *INFORMS Journal of Computing*, to appear. Special issue on *The merging of Mathematical Programming and Constraint Programming*.
11. F. Focacci, A. Lodi, M. Milano, and D. Vigo Eds. Proceedings of the International Workshop on the Integration of Artificial Intelligence and Operations Research techniques in Constraint Programming, 1999.
12. F. Focacci, A. Lodi, M. Milano, and D. Vigo. Solving TSP through the integration of OR and CP techniques. *Proc. CP98 Workshop on Large Scale Combinatorial Optimisation and Constraints*, 1998.
13. C. Gervet and M. Wallace Eds. Proceedings of the International Workshop on the Integration of Artificial Intelligence and Operations Research techniques in Constraint Programming, 2001.
14. M. L. Ginsberg and W. D. Harvey. Iterative broadening. *Artificial Intelligence*, 55(2):367–383, 1992.
15. W. D. Harvey and M. L. Ginsberg. Limited Discrepancy Search. In C. S. Mellish, editor, *Proceedings of the Fourteenth International Joint Conference on Artificial Intelligence (IJCAI-95); Vol. 1*, pages 607–615, 1995.
16. ILOG. ILOG Scheduler 4.4, Reference Manual, 2000.
17. ILOG. ILOG Solver 4.4, Reference Manual, 2000.
18. U. Junker, S. Karisch, and S. Tschoeke Eds. Proceedings of the International Workshop on the Integration of Artificial Intelligence and Operations Research techniques in Constraint Programming, 2000.

19. F. Laburthe and N. Jussien Eds. Proceedings of the International Workshop on the Integration of Artificial Intelligence and Operations Research techniques in Constraint Programming, 2002.
20. P. Langley. Systematic and nonsystematic search strategies. In *Proceedings of the 1st International Conference on AI Planning Systems*, pages 145–152, 1992.
21. A. Lodi. Personal communication.
22. M. Padberg and G. Rinaldi. An efficient algorithm for the minimum capacity cut problem. *Mathematical Programming*, 47:19–36, 1990.
23. G. Reinelt. TSPLIB - a Travelling Salesman Problem Library. *ORSA Journal on Computing*, 3:376–384, 1991.

Integrating Constraint and Integer Programming for the Orthogonal Latin Squares Problem

Gautam Appa[1], Ioannis Mourtos[1], and Dimitris Magos[2]

[1] London School of Economics
London WC2A 2AE, UK
{g.appa,j.mourtos}@lse.ac.uk
[2] Technological Educational Institute of Athens
12210 Athens, Greece
dmagos@teiath.gr

Abstract. We consider the problem of Mutually Orthogonal Latin Squares and propose two algorithms which integrate Integer Programming (IP) and Constraint Programming (CP). Their behaviour is examined and compared to traditional CP and IP algorithms. The results assess the quality of inference achieved by the CP and IP, mainly in terms of early identification of infeasible subproblems. It is clearly illustrated that the integration of CP and IP is beneficial and that one hybrid algorithm exhibits the best performance as the problem size grows. An approach for reducing the search by excluding isomorphic cases is also presented.

1 Introduction and Definitions

A *Latin* square of *order* n is a square matrix of order n, where each value $0, .., (n-1)$ appears exactly once in each row and column. Latin squares are multiplication tables of *quasigroups* ([5]). Two Latin squares of order n are called *orthogonal (OLS)* if and only if each of the n^2 ordered pairs $(0,0), ..., (n-1, n-1)$ appears exactly once in the two squares. A pair of *OLS* of order 4 appears in Table 1. This definition is extended to sets of $k > 2$ Latin squares, which are called *Mutually Orthogonal (MOLS)* if they are pairwise orthogonal. There can be at most $n - 1$ MOLS of order n ([10]).

A related concept is that of a *transversal*. A transversal of a Latin square is defined as a set of n cells, each in a different row and column, which contain pairwise different values. As an example, consider the bordered cells of the second square in Table 1. It is easy to prove that a Latin square has an orthogonal mate if and only if it can be decomposed into n disjoint transversals.

MOLS are closely related to finite algebra, in particular to theories of hypercubes, affine & projective planes and (t, m, s)-nets ([5]). Apart from their theoretical properties, they also possess interesting applications, mainly in multivariate statistical design and optimal error-correcting codes. Recently, they have been applied to problems related to tournament design and conflict-free access to parallel memories (see [10]).

P. Van Hentenryck (Ed.): CP 2002, LNCS 2470, pp. 17–32, 2002.

Table 1. A pair of *OLS* of order 4

0	1	2	3
1	0	3	2
2	3	0	1
3	2	1	0

0	1	2	3
2	3	0	1
3	2	1	0
1	0	3	2

This work aims at identifying pairs of OLS for orders up to 12 and triples of MOLS of orders up to 10. Infeasible and unsolved problem instances are included. For example, it is well known that a pair of OLS of order 6 does not exist, whereas it remains unknown whether a triple of MOLS of order 10 exists. Both *Integer Programming* (IP) and *Constraint Programming* (CP) methods are applied. We report on the comparative performance of CP and IP on this feasibility problem, along with two algorithms that integrate both methods. This defines our broader aim, which is to investigate the potential of integrating CP and IP. Propositional reasoning has been successfully applied to solve open quasigroup problems ([17]), while recent work ([7]) has tested a CP/LP algorithm on the problem of quasigroup completion, commenting on the comparative superiority this scheme.

IP has, in the main, been developed within the discipline of Operational Research, while CP is an "offspring" of the computer science community, mainly articulated within the field of Artificial Intelligence. Having developed separately, CP and IP often use analogous techniques under a different terminology. The necessity to solve large scale optimisation problems ([6]), together with the revelation of strong links between logic and optimisation ([3]), have stimulated a strong interest in successfully integrating IP and CP.

The combinatorial optimisation problems (COP) targeted by both methods are of the following generic form, hereafter called $COP(x, f, C, D)$:

$$min\{f(x) : x \in C, x \in D\} \qquad (1)$$

In this formulation, x is the vector of variables, f the objective function, D the external product of variable domains and C a set of constraints, restricting the possible values that the variables can take simultaneously. The variable domains can be integers, symbols or intervals of real numbers. A *relaxation* of (1), called $REL(x, f, C', D')$, is defined as:

$$min\{f(x) : x \in C', x \in D'\} \qquad (2)$$

where $C' \subseteq C$ and $D' \supseteq D$, i.e. (2) is derived by dropping at least one constraint or by enlarging the domain of at least one variable. This implies that the set of feasible solutions of (2) includes that of (1). Hence, a solution to (2) is not necessarily a solution to (1). If, however, (2) has no solution, neither does (1).

Every algorithmic method for solving (1) adopts further assumptions about the form of f, C and D. IP requires that both the objective function f and the set of constraints C are linear. This fact highly restricts its declarative power, but allows it to produce efficient problem relaxations. In CP, constraints can be of arbitrary type, although there is a broadening menu of specific constraint types, which are universally used in the CP literature. An example is the *all_different* predicate, which states that certain variables must be assigned pairwise different values (see [13, 15]).

The rest of this paper is organised as follows. Section 2 exhibits the IP and CP modes for the MOLS problem. Section 3 discusses a generic scheme for integrating CP and IP. An outline of all the algorithms is presented in Section 4. Computational results are discussed in Sections 5 and 6.

2   CP and IP Models for the MOLS Problem

Consider 4 n-sets I, J, K, L and let I be the row set, J the column set and K, L the sets of values for the two squares. Let the binary variable x_{ijkl} be 1 if the pair of values (k, l) appears in cell (i, j) and 0 otherwise. Since each pair must occur exactly once, it follows that $\sum\{x_{ijkl} : i \in I, j \in J\} = 1$, for all (k, l). Five more constraints of this type are formed by taking into account that the roles of the 4 sets are interchangeable. The result is the following IP model (also in [4]):

$$\sum\{x_{ijkl} : i \in I, j \in J\} = 1, \forall k \in K, l \in L \tag{3}$$

$$\sum\{x_{ijkl} : i \in I, k \in K\} = 1, \forall j \in J, l \in L \tag{4}$$

$$\sum\{x_{ijkl} : i \in I, l \in L\} = 1, \forall j \in J, k \in K \tag{5}$$

$$\sum\{x_{ijkl} : j \in J, k \in K\} = 1, \forall i \in I, l \in L \tag{6}$$

$$\sum\{x_{ijkl} : j \in J, l \in L\} = 1, \forall i \in I, k \in K \tag{7}$$

$$\sum\{x_{ijkl} : k \in K, l \in L\} = 1, \forall i \in I, j \in J \tag{8}$$

$$x_{ijkl} \in \{0, 1\} \forall i \in I, j \in J, k \in K, l \in L$$

This is a $0-1$ IP model consisting of $6n^2$ constraints and n^4 binary variables, which also defines the *planar 4-index assignment problem* ($4PAP_n$) (in [1]).

The CP formulation of the OLS problem is easier to devise. Let the two squares be denoted as X, Y and X_{ij}, $Y_{ij} \in \{0, ..., n-1\}$ be the variables denoting the value assigned to the cell (i, j) in the two squares. For each square, an *all_different* predicate on the n cells of every row and column ensures that the squares are Latin. To express the orthogonality condition we define the variables $Z_{ij} = X_{ij} + n \cdot Y_{ij}$, for $i, j = 0, 1, \ldots, n-1$. There are n^2 possible values for Z_{ij}, i.e. $Z_{ij} \in \{0, \ldots, n^2 - 1\}$, which have a $1-1$ correspondence with all n^2 ordered pairs (i, j), for $i, j = 0, 1, \ldots, n-1$. The two squares are orthogonal iff all Z_{ij}s are pairwise different. The CP model for the OLS problem is exhibited below.

$$all\_different\{X_{ij} : i \in I\}, \ \forall \ j \in J \tag{9}$$

$$all\_different\{X_{ij} : j \in J\}, \ \forall \ i \in I \tag{10}$$

$$all\_different\{Y_{ij} : i \in I\}, \ \forall \ j \in J \qquad (11)$$
$$all\_different\{Y_{ij} : j \in J\}, \ \forall \ i \in I \qquad (12)$$
$$all\_different\{Z_{ij} : i \in I, j \in J\} \qquad (13)$$
$$Z_{ij} = X_{ij} + n \cdot Y_{ij}, \ \forall \ i \in I, j \in J \qquad (14)$$
$$X_{ij}, Y_{ij} \in \{0, ..., n-1\}, \ Z_{ij} \in \{0, ..., n^2 - 1\}, \ \forall \ i \in I, j \in J$$

It is not difficult to establish the equivalence between the constraint sets of the two models. For example, (9) is the equivalent of constraint set (5). Clearly, the CP model is more compact, requiring $3n^2$ variables and $n^2 + 4n + 1$ constraints. The extensions of these models to the problem of identifying sets of k MOLS ($k \leq n-1$) results in an IP model of n^{k+2} variables and $\binom{k+2}{2} \cdot n^2$ constraints, whereas the CP model still requires only $O(n^2)$ variables and constraints. It follows that IP alone is impractical to handle large instances of the MOLS problem.

3   Integrating CP and IP

CP and IP models are solved using analogous algorithmic schemes. Both methods apply the "Divide & Conquer" paradigm: the initial problem is recursively divided into subproblems by partitioning the domain of at least one variable. A search tree is formed, where each node corresponds to a subproblem, the top node representing the initial problem. Both methods are *exact*, in the sense that they guarantee a complete search.

IP can be efficiently used to solve logic structures, as discussed in [3], while it is also possible to embed logic within a classical optimisation framework (see [9]). However, the integration of the two approaches poses a different task, *viz.* that of using the tools of both CP and IP for modelling and solving COP of general form. The prospect of integration will be discussed with respect to the next generic algorithm.

Algorithm 1 *At each node/subproblem:*
    Preprocess $COP(x, f, C, D)$;   **(I)**
    if *(feasible)*
      repeat
      {
          Solve $REL(x, f, C', D')$;   **(II)**
          Infer additional constraints;   **(III)**
      }
      until *($x \in D$)* **or** *(infeasible)* **or** *(no inference)*
    if *(no inference)* **and** **not**$((x \in D)$ *or (infeasible))*
      Create subproblems;   **(IV)**
    return;

Concerning IP, step (I) involves preprocessing of variables ([14]). By using logical relations among the variables and information from the variables already fixed, additional variable fixing is attempted. Step (II) implies solving the *LP-relaxation* of the problem, derived by dropping the integrality constraints. The advantage of this relaxation is that it provides an assignment of values to all variables and, if infeasible, it implies infeasibility for the original (sub)problem. If an LP-feasible but non-integer solution is produced, IP can proceed further by introducing additional inequalities, which cut-off this fractional solution and restrict further the feasible region D' of the relaxation. These additional constraints, called *cutting planes*, are derived from the initial set of linear constraints C by enforcing the fact that a subset of the variables must be integer. This process of solving the relaxation and extracting further inference in the form of cutting planes is repeated until the problem becomes infeasible or a feasible integer solution is found or no additional constraints can be generated. Identifying a cutting plane, which cuts off a certain fractional point, constitutes the *separation problem*. Although this can generally be a task as difficult as the original problem, i.e. they can both be $\mathcal{NP}$-complete, it is possible to separate certain classes of cutting planes in polynomial time (see [12]).

For CP, steps (I) & (III) are essentially parts of the same process: the domains of uninstantiated variables are reduced in order to avoid examining values that will lead to infeasible subproblems. The central notion in this approach is that of *k-consistency* (see [15] for definitions). Although domain reduction can be efficiently performed to achieve 1- & 2-consistency, higher consistency levels require considerable computational effort. Exceptions occur in the case of structured constraints, e.g. the *all_different* predicate, for which *full hyperarc-consistency* ([9]) can be accomplished in reasonable time (in [13]). Again, domain reduction may have further repercussions, therefore the process is repeated until no more domain values can be removed. CP lacks a proper relaxation for step (II), although recent work (in [9]) explores the potential of discrete relaxations. For both methods, Step (IV) is conducted by selecting an uninstantiated variable and splitting its domain to create two or more subproblems.

The foregoing discussion suggests that CP & IP can be integrated, at least in an algorithmic sense. For step (I), logical preprocessing conducted by IP is a subset of the sophisticated tools available for CP. IP can contribute by providing the powerful relaxation lacking from CP. The inference step (III) can still be performed by both methods. The complementarity exists in the fact that CP directly reduces the discrete solution space of the original problem in contrast to IP, which reduces the continuous solution space of the relaxation (see also [2] and [8]). Finally, one of the two, or both, methods can be applied at step (IV) to determine the partition of the subproblem.

Note that the theoretical connections and equivalences between CP & IP do not guarantee a beneficial integration; they primarily illustrate the feasibility of the project. The virtue of integration can be justified only if the inference generated by the two methods can be viewed as complementary. In other words, it has to be concluded that one approach succeeds in cases where the other fails. So far, evidence for this fact remains mostly empirical. In theory, CP is much faster in searching the solution space, since it does not have to solve a relaxation.

However, it is exactly the LP-relaxation, which gives IP its global perspective and allows for a solution to be found without extensive branching.

4   Hybrid Algorithms

This section presents an outline of the algorithms implemented to solve the OLS problem. In total, five algorithms were examined, namely BB, BC, FC, IPC and CPI. The first three employ either IP or CP techniques. Algorithm *BB* is a simple *Branch & Bound* scheme. Algorithm *BC* is a *Branch & Cut* scheme and algorithm *FC* is a *Forward Checking* scheme, which implements various levels of constraint propagation.

The last two algorithms, namely *IPC* and *CPI*, integrate both methods. Note that, in accordance with Algorithm 1, the form of integration is basically determined by which method implements step (IV). This choice determines the form of the search tree. Hence, step (IV) can be implemented by:

(A) only CP, embedding IP within the CP search tree;
(B) only IP, embedding CP within the IP search tree;
(C) either IP or CP, switching between CP and IP search trees.

Algorithm CPI follows option (A), while algorithm IPC follows option (B).

We discuss the components of the CP and IP solver, i.e. the form of algorithms BC and FC, in 4.1 and 4.2, respectively. Preliminary variable fixing, which exploits problem symmetry, is illustrated in 4.3. In 4.4, we present the branching rule, which is common to all schemes for assessment purposes. Finally, the exact form of the algorithms is presented in 4.5.

4.1   CP Components

A node of the CP search tree is created whenever an uninstantiated variable is assigned a value still existing in its domain. The algorithm selects a certain cell (i_0, j_0) such that $X_{i_0 j_0}$ is not instantiated. It then selects the smallest value $x \in D_{X_{i_0 j_0}}$ not already examined, sets $X_{i_0 j_0} = x$ and repeats this process for $Y_{i_0 j_0}$ if it is still uninstantiated. Thus it fixes a pair of cells, creating up to 2 successive nodes in the search tree. The orthogonality constraint is checked by maintaining auxiliary $0-1$ variables C_{kl}, in addition to variables Z_{ij}. Each such variable is initially 0 and is set to 1 whenever the pair (k, l) is assigned to a particular pair of cells.

Concerning domain reduction, setting $X_{i_0 j_0} = k_0$ requires the deletion of value k_0 from the domains of all variables $\{X_{i_1 j_1} : i_1 = i_0 \text{ or } j_1 = j_0\}$. This reflects the fact that each value must appear exactly once in every row and column of each Latin square. The same procedure is applied when setting $Y_{i_0 j_0} = l_0$. Value l_0 is also removed from the domain of any $Y_{i_1 j_1}$ such that $X_{i_1 j_1} = k_0$. This enforces the orthogonality constraint.

In CP terms, this procedure achieves 2-consistency in $O(n)$ steps. If the cardinality of a domain becomes one, the variable is instantiated to this single remaining value and the propagation routine is recursively called until no more variables can be fixed. If a domain is annihilated the node is declared infeasible, whereas if all variables are instantiated the algorithm terminates and returns the solution.

An additional level of consistency can be achieved by utilising the following lemma, presented here for the rows of square X.

Lemma 1. *Let* $S_{i_0} = \{X_{ij} : i = i_0 \text{ and } X_{ij} \text{ uninstantiated}\}$ *and* $D_{i_0} = \{\bigcup D_{ij} : X_{ij} \in S_{i_0}\}$, $i_0 = 0, \ldots, n-1$. *A necessary condition for the existence of a feasible solution, at any subproblem, is that* $|S_{i_0}| \leq |D_{i_0}|$ *for each* $i_0 \in I$.

This lemma is valid for the variable set of an arbitrary *all_different* constraint. Computing the union of domains at each step, could pose a significant amount of work. For the problem in hand, the conditions of the above lemma are checked by introducing the notion of "degrees of freedom". For square X, the degrees of freedom for a certain row i and value k, denoted by $XRDF_{ik}$, are the number of cells in this row, which still have value k in their domains. The degrees of freedom for columns of X ($XCDF_{jk}$) and for rows and columns of Y are defined similarly. It is easy to see that $XRDF_{i_0k_0} = 0$ for some k_0, if and only if $|S_{i_0}| > |D_{i_0}|$ or $X_{i_0j} = k_0$ for some j. Consider the example of $D_{X_{11}} = D_{X_{12}} = D_{X_{13}} = \{1,2\}$, where X_{11}, X_{12}, X_{13} are the only uninstantiated variables of the row 1 of square X. Although no domain is empty, the problem is clearly infeasible. Since the remaining $n-3$ cells of row 1 have been instantiated to $n-3$ different values, there must exist a value k_0, not appearing in any cell, such that $XRDF_{1k_0} = 0$. Degrees of freedom can be updated in $O(n)$ time in each node. Again, if $XRDF_{i_0k_0} = 1$, the single variable in row i_0, which has value k_0 in its domain, is assigned this value, no matter which other values are still in its domain.

As noted in Section 3, the particular structure exhibited by the *all_different* predicate allows for additional consistency checks to be performed. For example, let $D_{X_{11}} = D_{X_{12}} = \{1,2\}$ and $D_{X_{13}} = D_{X_{14}} = \{1,2,3,4\}$ be the only uninstantiated variables/cells of row 1. It is easy to see that values $1,2$ must be deleted from $D_{X_{13}}, D_{X_{14}}$. Such cases are captured by the filtering algorithm presented in [13]. This algorithm runs in $O(p^2d^2)$ steps for a constraint on p variables with domains of cardinality at most d. Hence, we need $O(n^4)$ steps for each of the constraints (9)-(12), i.e. $O(n^5)$ steps in total, and $O(n^8)$ steps for constraint (13). Being significantly more expensive, this filtering scheme is applied periodically, i.e. only after a certain number of variables have been fixed.

4.2   IP Components

The IP algorithm divides the initial problem recursively into subproblems by incorporating the concept of *Special Ordered Sets of type I (SOS-I)*. Observe that the IP model consists entirely of equalities. Let S represent the set of variables appearing on the left-hand side of a particular equality. Exactly one variable in S will be 1 at any feasible $0-1$ vector. Assume $S_1, S_2 \subset S$ such that $S_1 \cap S_2 = \emptyset$ and $S_1 \cup S_2 = S$. Then the single variable of S set to 1 will be either in S_1 or in S_2. Thus the problem can be partitioned into two subproblems, each defined by setting the variables of either S_1 or S_2 to 0. The set S is called an *SOS-I*. By recursively partitioning sets S_1 and S_2, eventually a subproblem will be left with a single variable of S not set to 0, which is bound to be 1. If $|S_1| = |S_2| = \frac{n}{2}$, this occurs at most after $\lceil 2log_2 n \rceil$ partitions (levels of the tree), since each constraint involves n^2 variables. The search then proceeds by selecting another equality, whose left-hand side has at least one variable still not set to 0. It can be proved that, by branching on *SOS-I* instead of single $0-1$ variables, the depth of the search tree is reduced by a logarithmic factor (see also [11]).

Integer preprocessing is performed at each node in order to fix the values of additional variables before the LP is solved. Note that each variable appears in exactly 6 constraints. If $x_{i_0 j_0 k_0 l_0}$ is set to 1, all variables appearing in the same constraints as $x_{i_0 j_0 k_0 l_0}$ are set to 0, i.e. a total of $6(n-1)^2$ variables. Although this would also be enforced by the LP, implementing this "redundant" variable fixing can detect an infeasible node prior to solving the corresponding LP. It also accelerates the solution of the LP. Observe that the LP can also detect infeasibility arising from an empty domain or from a degree of freedom becoming 0. For example, if $D_{X_{i_0 j_0}} = \emptyset$, the constraint (i_0, j_0) of (8) is violated, while $XCDF_{j_0 k_0} = 0$ implies that the constraint (j_0, k_0) of (5) is violated. The only types of infeasibility not detected by the LP are some cases captured exclusively by the filtering algorithm for the *all_different* constraints.

Polyhedral analysis has been successfully applied to the OLS problem and has provided families of strong cutting planes. The convex hull of all $0-1$ vectors satisfying (3)-(8) is the OLS polytope $P_I = \text{conv}\{x \in \{0,1\}^{n^4} : Ax = e\}$. The LP-relaxation of P_I is the polytope $P_L = \{x \in \mathbb{R}^{n^4} : Ax = e, 0 \leq x \leq 1\}$. An inequality satisfied by all points in P_I is called *valid*. A valid inequality, which is not dominated by any other valid inequality, is called a *facet*. Thus, facets are the strongest possible inequalities in a polyhedral sense. Valid inequalities are not satisfied by all points of P_L. Therefore, their addition to the initial constraint set restricts further the feasible region of the LP-relaxation. Adding all known facets is impractical because it increases dramatically the size of the LP. In contrast, adding them "on demand", i.e. only when violated by the current (fractional) LP solution is more efficient. In [1], two non-trivial classes of facets induced by *cliques* are identified. The term "clique" stands for a *maximal* set of variables, at most one of which can be set to 1. Whether such an inequality is violated by the current LP solution can be determined in $O(n^4)$ steps, i.e. in time linear in the number of variables, which is the lowest possible. Two more classes of valid inequalities are also linearly separable: lifted 5-hole and lifted antiweb inequalities. An important thing to note is that a lifted antiweb inequality essentially states that a pair of OLS does not exist for $n = 2$ or, equivalently, any 2×2 subsquares of a set of OLS of order n must contain at least 3 distinct values.

Violated cutting planes are added at the top node of the IP search tree and then every $\lceil (n-1)log_2 n \rceil$ levels, i.e. every time at least $\frac{(n-1)}{2}$ variables have been fixed to value 1. Violated cutting planes are repetitively added for up to

$\frac{n}{2}$ iterations. Within each iteration, clique inequalities are separated first and lifted 5-hole and antiweb inequalities are examined only if no violated cliques emerge. This happens because clique inequalities are, on average, cheaper to generate. The process terminates if (i) an integer solution is found or (ii) infeasibility is detected or (iii) the maximum number of iterations is reached. In case (iii), cutting planes, which are not satisfied as equalities by the last fractional solution, are deleted in order to reduce the matrix size. The remaining ones are retained at the descendant nodes.

4.3 Dealing with Symmetry

Algorithms searching for a feasible solution should reduce redundant search by excluding symmetrical subproblems. The set theoretical definition of isomorphy is applicable to Latin squares, viewed as multiplication tables of quasigroups. Hence, two Latin squares are *isomorphic* if one can be obtained from the other by permuting its rows, columns and elements. Extending this concept to OLS, we call two pairs of OLS *isomorphic* if one can be derived from the other by applying certain permutations to the rows, columns, elements of the first and elements of the second square. According to our notation, this is equivalent to permuting the sets I, J, K and L respectively. The following analysis reduces the solution space of the original problem by proving that any subproblems not examined are isomorphic to a subproblem included in the reduced solution space.

Consider a random pair of OLS of order n, represented by point $u \in P_I$. The simplest isomorphism is the interchange of the roles of any two elements of a single set, e.g. the swapping of rows 0 and 1. The *interchange operator* ($\longleftrightarrow$), introduced in [1], facilitates this process. Writing $u^1 = u(0 \longleftrightarrow 1)_I$ implies that point u^1 represents a new pair of OLS derived from u by interchanging the roles of members 0 & 1 of set I. In general, we can write $u^1 = u(m_1 \longleftrightarrow m_2)_M$, where $M = I, J, K, L$. Interchanges can be applied sequentially.

The first observation is that, by properly permuting the elements of sets K and L, we can have the cells of the first row of both squares containing the integers $0, ..., n-1$ in natural order. Given this arrangement of the first row, we can permute the elements of set $I \backslash \{0\}$ in such a way that the first column of square X is also in natural order. A pair of OLS of this form is called *standardised*. Fixing these $3n - 1$ cells already reduces the problem size by a factor of $(n!)^2 \cdot (n-1)!$ ([10]).

Our approach allows for further reduction. Consider cell Y_{10} and observe that $D_{Y_{10}} = \{2, ..., n-1\}$, i.e. $Y_{10} \neq 0, 1$, since $Y_{00} = 0$ and pair $(1, 1)$ already appears in position $(0, 1)$. Assume a pair of OLS having $Y_{10} = w$, where $w \in \{3, .., n-1\}$, and let $u \in P_I$ be the corresponding integer vector. Construct point $u^1 = u(2 \longleftrightarrow w)_L (2 \longleftrightarrow w)_K (2 \longleftrightarrow w)_J (2 \longleftrightarrow w)_I$ and observe that $u^1_{1012} = 1$, i.e. $Y_{10} = 2$, and u represents a standardised pair of OLS. It follows that if a solution having $Y_{10} = w$, $w \in \{3, .., n-1\}$, exists, a solution having $Y_{10} = 2$ must also exist. Therefore, we can fix pair $(1, 2)$ in position $(1, 0)$, which reduces the solution space by an additional factor of $(n - 2)$.

Table 2. Variable fixing and domain reduction

0	1	$\cdots$	n-2	n-1
1				
2				
$\vdots$				
i				
$\vdots$				
n-2				
n-1				

0	1	$\cdots$	n-2	n-1
2				
{1,3}				
$\vdots$				
{1,3,4,..,i-1,i+1}				
$\vdots$				
n-1				
{1,3,..,n-2}				

Using the same approach, it can be proved that $D_{Y_{20}} = \{1,3\}$, i.e. if there exists a solution with $Y_{20} = w$, $4 \leq w \leq n-1$, there exists also a standardised solution with $Y_{20} = 3$, having also $Y_{10} = 2$. In general, $D_{Y_{i0}} = \{1,3,4,...,i-1,i+1\}$ for $i \in \{3,...,n-1\}$. Given these reduced domains, observe that value $n-1$ appears only in $D_{Y_{(n-2)0}}$. Therefore, we can also set $Y_{(n-2)0} = n-1$. The final form of the pair of OLS after this preliminary variable fixing, is depicted in Table 2.

4.4   Branching Rule

We present an efficient branching strategy used in both CP and IP. Recall first that CP creates subproblems by fixing a cell of the square X and then fixing the same cell in square Y. There are two systematic methods for selecting the next cell to be examined. One is to examine all cells in a certain row (or column). The alternative is to always select a cell in a different row and column. The first method fixes rows (columns) of the squares, therefore selecting each time a different value for a cell in the current row. The second method does not need to select a different value each time, since, pairwise, all cells are in different rows and columns. Therefore, it can set all cells of square X to the same value and, according to the orthogonality constraint, set all cells of square Y to pairwise different values. Hence, by definition, this method fixes transversals of square Y.

A common criterion for branching, is to select the next variable in the way that maximises the domain reduction achieved. If the search proceeds by fixing the remaining $n-1$ cells of the second row in both squares, $n-1$ different values will appear in each square. Setting $X_{1j_0} = k_0$ implies the deletion of value k_0 from the domains of all variables $X_{i_0j_0}$ for $2 \leq i_0 \leq n-1$, except for $i_0 = k_0$ (having fixed $X_{k_00} = k_0$ implies that $k_0 \notin D_{k_0j_0}$). Hence, $(n-3)$ domain members are removed for each value k_0 appearing in the second row, the only exception being value $k_0 = 1$ which results in removing $n-2$ domain members. In total, $(n-2) \cdot (n-3) + (n-2)$ domain values are removed. Similarly, $(n-2)^2 + (n-3)$ domain values are removed from square Y. The total number of values removed from the domains of the uninstantiated variables/cells is $\alpha(n) = 2(n-2)^2 + (n-3)$.

Using an analogous argument, it can be proved that by fixing a transversal of square Y along with fixing the corresponding cells of square X with the same value 0, $(n-1)(n-2)$ domain values are removed from square X and $2n(n-3)$ domain values are removed from square Y. The total number of domain values removed is $\beta(n) = (n-1)(n-2) + 2n(n-3)$. It turns out that $\alpha(n) \leq \beta(n)$ for $n \geq 2$. Therefore, fixing transversals is computationally more beneficial, a fact also supported by experimental results.

For IP to employ an equivalent branching scheme, it is sufficient to always select the *SOS-I* among the equalities of constraint set (7). Fixing, for example, value 0 in row 1 is implemented by recursively partitioning the variable set of equality $(1,0)$ of (7). In the worst case, after branching on all n^2 *SOS-I* emanating from (7), a solution is bound to be constructed. Given this branching rule, the maximum depth of the search trees created by CP and IP is $O(n^2)$ and $O(n^2 log_2 n)$, respectively.

4.5   The Algorithms

Algorithm BB involves no problem specific features and is considered in order to compare our results with those of a commercial IP solver, namely XPRESS-MP [16]. The IP solver uses its own cutting planes and all tuning parameters are set to their default values. No general purpose CP software has been used. Algorithm BC incorporates all the IP components and the branching rule described in the previous sections. Algorithm FC maintains 2-consistency and updates all "degrees of freedom" at each node. Each *all_different* constraint is made full hyperarc-consistent only whenever a transversal has been fixed. Again, this procedure is applied for up to $\frac{n}{2}$ iterations or until no more domain filtering is achievable.

Algorithm IPC embeds CP within IP by propagating on *all_different* constraints as an additional preprocessing step at each node. The technical details are as follows: observe first that the constraint set (3) is equivalent to the constraint *all_different*$\{W_{(i+n \cdot j)} : i \in I, j \in J\}$, where $D_{W_{i+n \cdot j}} = \{0, ..., n^2 - 1\}$. This is valid since each ordered pair (k,l) is uniquely mapped to a number $(k + n \cdot l) \in \{0, ..., n^2 - 1\}$. An analogous constraint arises from each of the five constraint sets (4)-(8), i.e. in total, 6 *all_different* predicates are formed. Let V denote the set of the n^4 $0-1$ variables. At a certain node of the IP search tree, let $F \subseteq V$ be the set of fixed variables. Define $W = \{W_{i+n \cdot j} : x_{ijkl} \in V \backslash F$ for some $k \in K, l \in L\}$ and $D_{W_{i+n \cdot j}} = \{(k+n \cdot l) : x_{ijkl} \in V \backslash F\}$. The preprocessing step for (3) is the application of the filtering algorithm of [13] to the predicate *all_different*(W). If value $(k + n \cdot l)$ is removed from $D_{W_{i+n \cdot j}}$, x_{ijkl} is set to 0.This procedure is then applied to constraint sets (4)-(8) for up to $\frac{n}{2}$ iterations. The objective of this preprocessing is to fix additional variables and to detect infeasibility without having to solve the LP.

The second hybrid scheme, embedding IP within CP, is Algorithm CPI. It is based on the FC algorithm, the additional step being to call the IP solver whenever a transversal has been fixed. The current status of the variables' domains in CP is passed to IP in the form of variable fixing. Obviously, $x_{ijkl} = 0$

iff $k \notin D_{X_{ij}}$ or $l \notin D_{Y_{ij}}$ and $x_{ijkl} = 1$ iff $X_{ij} = k$ and $Y_{ij} = l$. Note that, before calling the IP solver, all possible domain reduction by CP has been achieved. The reason is not only to avoid solving an infeasible IP but also to detect cases where IP can prove infeasibility although CP cannot. The IP solver deals with a single node, adding cutting planes for up to n iterations. The initial LP is solved by the Primal Simplex algorithm, whereas all other iterations use the Dual Simplex algorithm. This is the standard approach because adding violated inequalities makes the solution of the previous iteration infeasible for the primal problem but feasible for the dual. Although an objective function is meaningless, a random objective function is introduced, in order to avoid degeneracy in the dual problem. No branching is performed by IP, the aim being to either extend a partial solution to a complete one or to prune a branch as infeasible.

Note that both CP and IP models are active in both hybrid algorithms, i.e. there has been no decomposition of the problem. The rationale is to achieve the best possible inference by both methods and also to compare their performance. The cost of maintaining both models is easily seen to be negligible.

5   Computational Experience

The callable libraries of XPRESS-MP have been used to codify the IP components ([16]). The code for the CP components has been written in Microsoft C++ environment and is mainly problem specific. All experiments were conducted on a PC under WinNT, with a PentiumIII processor at 866MHz and 256Mb of main memory. The experiments presented in this section concern the identification of a pair of OLS for orders $n = 3, ..., 12$. The number of variables in the IP model range from 81 ($n = 3$) to 20736 ($n = 12$), while the number of constraints ranges between 54 and 864. The CP model starts with 27 variables for $n = 3$ and ends up with 432 variables for $n = 12$ (see Section 2). Each algorithm returns a solution or proves that the problem is infeasible for the case of $n = 6$, where a complete search is required. For this reason, this instance is also particularly interesting for assessing the performance of the algorithms.

Table 3 illustrates two performance indicators: the number of nodes created during the search and the time in seconds taken to solve each problem. The number of nodes is illustrated in logarithmic scale. All schemes present the same general behaviour, with complexity exploding after $n = 9$. FC creates significantly more nodes than BB, which itself is much worse than BC. Algorithm IPC constantly creates fewer nodes that IP, although the difference is not significant. The striking difference appears between FC and CPI, with the hybrid algorithm creating considerably fewer subproblems. This indicates that CPI prunes infeasible branches much earlier by complementing CP's inference strength with that of IP. Note that CPI's performance is always between those of FC and BC.

In terms of time, the first comment is that BB is the slowest. Algorithm FC is the fastest for orders up to 9, providing the fastest enumeration of the whole solution space for $n = 6$. For larger values of n, however, it is outperformed by BC. Again IPC is slightly better than BC. It appears that the extra overhead of

Table 3. Performance indicators

NODES (log)						TIME (sec)					
n	BB	BC	FC	IPC	CPI	n	BB	BC	FC	IPC	CPI
3	0.00	0.00	0.00	0.00	0.00	3	3.2	3.2	0.0	3.2	0.00
4	0.00	0.00	0.00	0.00	0.00	4	5.8	3.7	0.0	3.7	0.00
5	2.32	0.00	7.50	0.00	5.58	5	12.4	9.6	0.0	9.6	0.57
6	14.88	12.39	18.13	12.33	14.65	6	1,843	553	43	532	376
7	14.36	8.13	20.58	7.87	19.02	7	7,689	3,325	523	2,937	854
8	10.08	5.58	11.36	5.39	10.37	8	294	252	2.7	231	112
9	18.24	15.01	28.27	18.22	22.45	9	32,341	17,854	12,745	15,826	14,439
10	22.44	19.72	32.88	19.70	26.95	10	37,065	20,561	20,935	19,306	17,842
11	27.20	22.37	35.16	22.20	29.85	11	46,254	24,812	29,423	23,538	21,651
12	29.32	23.17	39.49	23.09	32.78	12	59,348	31,642	37,161	29,213	26,983

Table 4. Percentage of nodes pruned

n	3	4	5	6	7	8	9	10	11	12
INFI	0.0	0.0	0.532	0.657	0.416	0.227	0.321	0.315	0.264	0.250
INFC	0.0	0.0	0.0	0.046	0.052	0.059	0.032	0.032	0.048	0.024

preprocessing at each node is counteracted by the smaller number of subproblems created. Once more, the more consistent and robust performance is exhibited by algorithm CPI, which lies between BC and FC up to $n = 9$ and outperforms both thereafter, i.e. as problem size grows.

Table 4 provides further insights on the performance of the hybrid algorithms. It depicts the percentage of infeasible nodes pruned by IP in algorithm CPI and the percentage of infeasible nodes pruned by CP in algorithm IPC. Hence, indicator INFC is the percentage of infeasible nodes in the search tree of IPC which were detected by CP during preprocessing, without having to solve them. On the other hand, INFI denotes the percentage of infeasible nodes in the search tree of CPI which were pruned only by solving the corresponding IP. These nodes correspond to subproblems made already consistent by CP alone. Thus INFI also indicates the percentage of cases where the inference generated by IP could achieve what CP alone could not, except by further branching. In other words, INFC and INFI are indicators of the usefulness of incorporating CP within the IP search tree and IP within the CP search tree, respectively. Hence, only up to 6% of the nodes in the IP search tree are pruned as infeasible during preprocessing. On the contrary, at least 25% of nodes in the CP search tree are pruned by IP. Note that for $n = 6$, INFI rises to 66%. This explains the significant improvement accomplished by incorporating IP within CP (algorithm CPI) in terms of nodes. CP is also useful within IP but to a smaller extent.

Another measurement of the inference strength is the early identification of infeasible branches. A representative criterion, independent of the actual tree form, is the number of transversals fixed before pruning a node. We report on algorithms BC, FC, IPC, CPI only for the infeasible case of $n = 6$. Algorithms BC, IPC and CPI need to fix at most one transversal before proving that a specific branch is infeasible, i.e. all of them generate approximately the same quality of inference. In contrast, algorithm FC is able to prune a node as infeasible, after fixing a single transversal, only in around 10% of the cases; in the remaining ones it has to fix up to 4 transversals before proving infeasibility. Analogous results appear for larger values of n and explain the fact that algorithm FC creates the largest number of nodes. Algorithm CPI is faster than algorithms BC and IPC for $n = 6$, exactly because it solves a much smaller number of linear programs and employs IP only after the problem has been restricted enough for cutting planes to become capable of proving infeasibility. On the contrary, BC and IPC keep on solving LPs and adding cutting planes in between without pruning any further branches.

These observations have obvious implications for more general COP. Given that a combinatorial problem is in $\mathcal{NP}$, obtaining a complete polyhedral description is as hopeless as finding a polynomial algorithm. Partial polyhedral description can be efficiently used to reduce the search, but usually cannot become effective unless the problem has been sufficiently restricted. For example, obtaining an integer solution or a certificate of infeasibility at the top node of a Branch & Cut tree is possible only for very small problem instances. For larger instances, CP can provide substantial improvement by enumerating all partial assignments of a certain number of variables. IP can then be applied to the restricted problem and attempt to extend the partial solution to a complete one or prune the partial solution without any further enumeration. If IP fails to do either, CP can again be used to extend the partial solution by instantiating further variables before IP is called again. The point where the algorithm must "switch" between CP and IP is, most probably, problem specific. In the case of OLS, the notion of transversal offers such a convenient criterion.

6   Triples of MOLS

We conclude by briefly presenting the algorithm implemented for triples of MOLS. Having already discussed the superiority of hybrid algorithms, we apply this approach to triples of MOLS. Since the IP model would require n^5 binary variables, we have to decompose the problem. Assume Latin squares X, Y and U of order n, where X, Y are as in Table 2 and the first row of U contains integers $0, ..., n-1$ in natural order.

CP fixes a certain number of $t(< n-1)$ values in square U, each in $n-1$ cells of different rows and columns, and performs the appropriate domain reduction. The IP model for the pair X, Y of OLS is then used, after adding $2tn$ extra equality constraints to ensure orthogonality with the partially completed square U. The IP model is handled by algorithm IPC and returns an integer solution or proves infeasibility. If no integer solution is found, the CP solver backtracks and provides the next partial instantiation of square U before the IP solver is called again. If an integer solution is returned, the CP solver instantiates the

Table 5. Time to identify triples of MOLS of order n

n	4	5	6	7	8	9	10
TIME (sec)	2.34	11.83	n/a	685	1457	13873	*

remaining cells of square U, under the additional constraints for orthogonality with squares X, Y. If it succeeds, a solution for the overall problem is found and the algorithm terminates. If not, the IP solver is called again and the search in the IP tree is resumed. Hence, the algorithm interchanges between the two solvers and retains both search trees active. Since both CP and IP control the creation of subproblems in different stages, this hybrid scheme implements option (C) (see Section 4). Table 5 illustrates preliminary results about the time (seconds) taken to identify a triple of MOLS of order n, using $t = 1$. Note that no triple of MOLS exists for $n = 6$, therefore this instance was not examined. For $n = 10$, the algorithm was interrupted after $40,000$ seconds, having explored at least 0.00538% of the solution space.

References

[1] Appa G., Magos D., Mourtos I., Janssen J. C. M.: On the Orthogonal Latin Squares polytope. Submitted to Discrete Mathematics (2001). (URL: http://www.cdam.lse.ac.uk/Reports/reports2001.html)
[2] Bockmayr A., Casper T.: Branch and infer: a unifying framework for integer and finite domain constraint programming. INFORMS Journal on Computing, **10** (1998) 187-200.
[3] Chandru V., Hooker J. N.: Optimization methods for logical inference. J.Wiley (1999).
[4] Dantzig G. B.: Linear Programming and extensions. Princeton Univ. Press (1963).
[5] Dénes J., Keedwell A. D.: Latin squares and their applications. Acad. Press (1974).
[6] Freuder E. C., Wallace R. J. (ed.): Constraint Programming and Large Scale Discrete Optimization. DIMACS Series in Discrete Mathematics and Theoretical Computer Science, **57**, Amer. Math. Soc (1998).
[7] Gomes C., Shmoys D.: The Promise of LP to Boost CSP Techniques for Combinatorial Problems, CP-AI-OR'02, 291-305, Le Croisic, France (2002).
[8] Hooker J. N., Osorio M. A.: Mixed logical/linear programming. Discrete Applied Mathematics, **96-97** (1994) 395-442.
[9] Hooker J. N.: Logic-Based Methods for Optimization: Combining Optimization and Constraint Satisfaction. J.Wiley (2000).
[10] Laywine C. F., Mullen G. L.: Discrete Mathematics using Latin squares. J.Wiley (1998).
[11] Magos D., Miliotis P.: An algorithm for the planar three-index assignment problem. European Journal of Operational Research **77** (1994) 141-153.
[12] Nemhauser G. L., Wolsey L. A.: Integer and Combinatorial Optimization. J.Wiley (1988).
[13] Regin J. C.: A filtering algorithm for constraints of difference in CSPs. Proceedings of National Conference on Artificial Intelligence (1994), 362-367.

[14] Savelsbergh M. W. P.: Preprocessing and Probing for Mixed Integer Programming Problems. ORSA J. on Computing, **6** (1994) 445-454.
[15] Tsang E.: Foundations of Constraint Satisfaction, Acad. Press (1993).
[16] Dash Associates: XPRESS-MP Version 12, Reference Manual (2001).
[17] Zhang H., Hsiang J.: Solving open quasigroup problems by propositional reasoning, Proc. of International Computer Symposium, Hsinchu, Taiwan (1994).

On Optimal Correction
of Inconsistent Linear Constraints

Paula Amaral[1] and Pedro Barahona[2]

[1] Department of Mathematics UNL
paca@fct.unl.pt
[2] Department of Computer Science UNL
pb@di.fct.unl.pt

Abstract. In practice one has often to deal with the problem of inconsistency between constraints, as the result, among others, of the complexity of real models. To overcome these conflicts we can outline two major
actions: removal of constraints or changes in the coefficients of the model.
This last approach, that can be generically described as "model correction" is the problem we address in this paper. The correction of the right
hand side alone was one of the first approaches. The correction of both
the matrix of coefficients and the right hand side introduces non linearity
in the constraints. The degree of difficulty in solving the problem of the
optimal correction depends on the objective function, whose purpose is
to measure the closeness between the original and corrected model. Contrary to other norms, the optimization of the important Frobenius was
still an open problem. We have analyzed the problem using the KKT conditions and derived necessary and sufficient conditions which enabled us
to unequivocally characterize local optima, in terms of the solution of the
Total Least Squares and the set of active constraints. These conditions
justify a set of pruning rules, which proved, in preliminary experimental
results, quite successful in a tree search procedure for determining the
global minimizer.

1 Introduction

The wide application of constraints solvers to solve real problems is for itself
a good motivation for developing a study in the correction of linear systems.
Inconsistency in linear models is often a consequence of the complexity of the
problem, conflicting goals in different groups of decision makers, lack of communication between different groups that define the constraints, different views over
the problem, partial information, wrong or inaccurate estimates, over optimistic
purposes, errors in data, integration of different formulations and actualization
of old models. If models are sometimes meant to describe existing real situations,
many others are used as preferences regarding the "a posteriori" construction
of a physical system. In the first situation and specially in the second situation
modifications of a model can be necessary for sake of plausibility. The modifications of the model, to render it feasible, can be overcome by considering some

P. Van Hentenryck (Ed.): CP 2002, LNCS 2470, pp. 33–46, 2002.
© Springer-Verlag Berlin Heidelberg 2002

constraints as "soft" in the sense that they can be removed, or, more generally, corrected by changes in the coefficients of the constraints.

A variety of frameworks have been proposed in Constraint Programming to deal with soft constraints. In the Partial Constraint Satisfaction formalism [FrWa92], constraints are removed if they cannot be satisfied and one is interested in solutions that violate the least number of soft constraints. This is an appropriate formalism when all preferences have the same "weight" and the amount of violation is not taken into consideration, but its expressive power is quite limited. In practice, preferences are often of unequal importance and more expressive formalisms have been proposed to model these problems, namely by assigning different weights to the soft constraints. The quality of a solution is then measured by some aggregation of the weights of unsatisfied constraints, as done in hierarchical constraint solving [BoBe89].

The above formalisms do not take into account the degree in which a constraint is unsatisfied. More expressive models, namely the semi-ring and Valued-CSP [Ball96], and Fuzzy CSP models [DuFP93] allow in different ways to assign "degrees of unsatisfaction" among tuples of the domain of the variables of a constraint that do not satisfy it, so that the aggregated violation of the constraints is minimized. Many algorithms have been proposed to handle these approaches, but they are largely limited to finite domains variables.

The formalisms may be adapted to mixed and continuous domains, and among these to linear constraints over the rationals/reals. Some theoretical results have been developed related to the removal of constraints. Van Loon [VLoo81] addressed the identification of Irreducible Inconsistent Systems (IIS) - a set of non-solvable relations, where each of its proper subsystems is solvable. Detection of IIS is an important tool for analyzing inconsistencies, and to identify constraints that can be removed in order to obtain a consistent system, and the work was later extended [WaHu92] [ChDr91]. Chakravatty [Chak94] proved that the identification of Minimum Cardinality Infeasibility Sets (MCIS) is NP-Hard. Given a set of relations C a Minimum Cardinality Infeasibility Set M is a subset of C such that $C \setminus M$ is feasible and, among sets that verify this condition, M has smallest cardinality. This work is thus closely related to Partial Constraint Satisfaction in finite domains. In the context of Hierarchical Constraint Logic Programming, Holzbaur, Menezes and Barahona [HoMB96] showed how to find minimal conflict sets (equivalent to IISs), upon the addition to a set of feasible constraints of a further constraint, that makes the new set infeasible.

Much less work was developed, to our knowledge, regarding the correction of linear constraints. Roodman [Rood79] developed one of the first known approaches, which accounted only for changes in the right-hand side of constraints. A method based on the analysis of the final Phase I solution in the Simplex method allowed to estimate lower bounds on the amount of change in the RHS of each constraint to attain feasibility. Some additional results based on the analysis of the final solution in the Dual Simplex were also presented. Insights on how to work with multiple changes in constraints were given, in a sort of parametric approach although guided by one parameter alone.

In analogy with finite domains, the degree of unsatisfaction of a system of linear constraints of the form

$$\sum_{j=1}^{m} a_{ij}x_j \leq b_i, \ i = \ldots, m$$

may be done by adding an extra non-negative variable p_i to the RHS and minimizing an aggregation of the p_i's. In the simplest case, where the aggregation is the sum of the p_i's, the minimization problem is mapped into straightforward linear programming.

With the usual interpretation of linear constraints, changing the RHS alone aims at minimizing the amount of resources needed (the b_i terms) to make all the tasks feasible. However, the tasks may become feasible not only by an increase of the resources available, but also by an increased efficiency in their use, which require changes in the a_{ij} terms.

Vatolin [Vato92] was the first to propose a study for the correction of both the coefficient matrix and the RHS for a special category of objective function as the correction criteria, which did not include the Frobenius norm. He proved that for a system of equations and inequations, with non negativity constraints for variables, and for such class of cost functions the optimal correction of the model could be solved by a finite number of linear programming problems.

In this paper we address a general approach to model the correction of over-constrained linear problems, minimum discrepancy, whereby one aims at minimizing all the changes in the coefficients of the linear constraints, to make them feasible. The paper is organized as follows. In section 2 we formalize our minimal discrepancy approach and present a number of variants of it, as well as algorithms appropriate to solve some of these variants. In section 3, we focus on the Frobenius variant and present the key result that relates local minima solutions with the well known Total Least Square problem. In section 4, we refer to a simple method to finding local optima, by means of unconstrained minimization and show how to speed up the search. In section 5 we propose a tree-search approach to obtain global optima, as well as criteria to prune the search. We conclude with some remarks on the experimental results of the previous two sections, as well as some directions for future research.

2   The Correction of Linear Inequalities

Consider a system of linear inequalities:

$$Ax \leq b, x \in \Re^n,$$

where A and b are respectively, a real matrix of size $m \times n$ and a real vector of dimension m. Assuming that this system is inconsistent, we want to find a matrix $H \in \Re^{m \times n}$ and a vector $p \in \Re^m$ such that the corrected system:

$$(A + H)x \leq (b + p), x \in \Re^n.$$

is feasible. Since the corrected model should be close to the original one, H and p must be the solution of the nonlinear problem:

$$\hat{f} = \inf \Psi(H,p)$$
$$\text{s.t. } (A+H)x \le b+p \tag{1}$$
$$H \in \Re^{m\times n}, \quad p \in \Re^m, \quad x \in \Re^n.$$

For $\Psi = \|\cdot\|_{l_1}$, $\Psi = \|\cdot\|_{l_\infty}$, or $\Psi = \|\cdot\|_\infty$, we have proved in [AmPa01] that a result of Vatolin [Vato92] can be applied and the optimal solution can be obtained through the solution of a finite number of linear programming problems all having the base formulation:

$$PL(s)$$
$$v_s = \min \theta$$
$$\text{s.t. } \sum_{j=1}^{n} a_{ij} y_i - b_i y_{n+1} \le t_i \,, i = 1, \dots, m$$
$$\sum_{j=1}^{n+1} w_j^s y_j = -1 \tag{2}$$
$$y_{n+1} > 0, \; t_i \ge 0, i = 1, \dots, m$$

where for the norm l_∞, $s \in \mathcal{L} = \{1, \dots, 2^n\}$ and for the norms l_1 and ∞, $s \in \mathcal{L} = \{1, \dots, 2n+1\}$. Correspondingly, w^s is a vector that varies according to the norm we are using. For norm l_∞ each component can take values 1 or -1, except for the $(n+1)$−th component which must be 1 ($w^s = (\pm 1, \pm 1, \dots, \pm 1, 1)^T$). For the norm l_1 and ∞, $w^s = (0, \dots, 1, \dots, 0)^T$ where the 1 component can appear in any of the $n+1$ positions in the vector, or $w^s = (0, \dots, -1, \dots, 0)^T$ where the -1 value can appear in any of the n positions in the vector.

In (2) additional constraints:

$$t_1 \le \theta, \dots, t_m \le \theta$$

must be introduced for the l_∞ and ∞ norms, and

$$\sum_{i=1}^{m} t_i \le \theta$$

for the l_1 norm. If $s^* = \arg\min_{s \in \mathcal{L}} v_s$ and (y^*, t^*, w^{s^*}) are the optimal solution of problem $PL(s^*)$, then the optimal correction in each row is given by $[H_i, p_i] = t_i w^{s^*}$ and $x = [y_1^*, \dots, y_n^*]^T / y_{n+1}^*$. Analyzing the structure of w^{s^*} we observe that for the norms l_1 and ∞ only one column of matrix $[H, p]$ is corrected, while for l_∞ the corrections of the coefficients in each row differ only in sign. In these three cases the structure of the correction matrix has a rigid pattern. This is one more reason to investigate the minimization of the Frobenius norm, expecting to find a matrix of corrections without a predefined pattern. It seems to us that this option is more natural in some practical situations.

3   For the Frobenius Norm

For $\Psi = \| \cdot \|_F$ we obtain the following problem:

$$\hat{f} = \inf \ \|(H, p)\|_F$$
$$\text{s.t.} \ (A + H)x \leq b + p \tag{3}$$
$$H \in \Re^{m \times n}, \quad p \in \Re^m, \quad x \in \Re^n.$$

This norm is not only an interesting open problem from a theoretical point of view, but it is also important in practice, since the square of this norm is the sum of the euclidian norm for the row vectors. It is well-known the importance of the euclidian norm in geometrical applications.

Vatolin was the first to approach this problem, presenting a result with necessary and sufficient conditions for local minimizers. Unfortunately the direct application of these results is impracticable for large problems, since they depend on a convenient choice of a submatrix, but no indication is given on how to find it. A complete search would require the study of a large number of possible combinations of rows and columns, impracticable for large problems. We showed that the sufficient conditions are not necessary and under failure of the conditions imposed by the result of Vatolin, for a "guessed" subset of rows and columns, we are left without any clue on how to proceed, since no information can be driven from that.

If instead of inequalities we were dealing with equalities, the problem is well studied and known as the "Total Least Squares" (TLS). Given an infeasible system $Ax = b$, the optimal solution (H^*, p^*, x_{TLS}) of the TLS is unique if $\sigma_n(A) > \sigma_{n+1}(C)$ $(C = [A, -b])$ and is given by:

$$[H^*, p^*] = -u_{n+1}\sigma_{n+1}(C)v_{n+1}^T \tag{4}$$

$$\begin{bmatrix} x_{TLS} \\ 1 \end{bmatrix} = \frac{v_{n+1}}{v_{n+1,n+1}}, \tag{5}$$

where $\sigma_n(A)$ and $\sigma_{n+1}(C)$ are respectively the smaller singular value of A and C, and u_{n+1} and v_{n+1} are the left and right singular vectors associated to $\sigma_{n+1}(C)$. For convenience x_{TLS} will be designated as the optimal solution, while (H^*, p^*) will be referred as the optimal correction.

In [AmPa01] we presented results that related the TLS with the problem of correction of inequalities. This relation is the outcome of the application of the KKT conditions to (3). The following relations were obtained:

$$H = -\lambda x^T; \tag{6}$$
$$p = -\lambda; \tag{7}$$
$$\lambda^T(A + H) = 0; \tag{8}$$
$$\lambda^T\left((A + H)x + p - b\right) = 0; \tag{9}$$
$$\lambda \geq 0. \tag{10}$$

Based on (6) to (10) it was possible to obtain necessary and sufficient conditions for local optima, and we proved that if the problem has a minimum, then a correction corresponds to a local optima iff the solution of the corrected system is the TLS solution for the set of active constraints, and is feasible for the non active constraints. An inequality constraint is active at a point if it holds with equality at that point. Let $CC \subseteq \{1, 2, \ldots, m\}$ be a candidate set of active constraints to which the TLS will be applied, yielding the TLS solution $x_{TLS}(CC)$ and the matrix of corrections (H^*, p^*). We were able to prove in [AmPa01] that all local optima depend on a convenient choice of the set CC for which the following facts are true:

F1- The TLS solution for CC exists; (11)

F2- $x_{TLS}(CC)$ must be feasible for the set $\{1, 2, \ldots, m\} \setminus CC$; (12)

F3- x_{TLS} must be unfeasible for the non degenerate constraints
   in CC; (13)

F4- The size of CC must be no less then $n + 1$. (14)

4   Local Minimizers

In practice, these relations not only ensure whether CC is in fact an active set of constraints, but also provide hints regarding changes in the chosen set of active constraints. In a previous work [AmBa99], we have use the TLS as a framework in an heuristic approach, to which these results gave support. The basic idea was an iterative update of set CC, in such a way that condition (14) was always true and in case of failure of conditions (11),(12) or (13) at least one direct cause of failure was removed. To initialize we made $CC = \{1, \ldots, m\}$. Since we could not guarantee that in the next iterations no other failures would appear, there was no proved convergence to a local optima, although the results were quite satisfactory.

In [AmTB00], using substitutions (6) and (7) in (3) an equivalent formulation was obtained in x and λ. The authors proved that the problem could be further reduced to the unconstrained formulation:

$$\min \frac{(Ax - b)^{+T}(Ax - b)^+}{x^T x + 1},$$ (15)

where $(Ax-b)_i^+ = \max(0, (Ax-b)_i)$ $(i = 1, \ldots, m)$. Using this formulation (15), the authors used a combination of the gradient projection method to identify the set of active constraints, followed by an algebraic step using the TLS on the active set, in order to find local optima. The convergence towards a local optima using the gradient projection can be quite slow. If we are close enough to a local optima, so that the set of active constraints can be identified, then a local minimizer can be found in one algebraic step .

Example 41 *Consider the following inconsistent linear system presented in [AmTB00]:*

$$
\begin{bmatrix}
-0.1043 & -0.3350 \\
-2.3176 & -2.0354 \\
-0.6778 & 0.6547 \\
1.0524 & -0.4328 \\
0.0145 & -1.9312 \\
0.2438 & 0.5537
\end{bmatrix}
x \le
\begin{bmatrix}
-2.2440 \\
0.7579 \\
0.4303 \\
2.5747 \\
-2.2600 \\
0.4285
\end{bmatrix}
$$

The following table shows (in the first column) the number of iterations of the gradient projection, followed by the coordinates of x after these iterations, and the value of the slack variables (f_i), $(i_1, \ldots, 5)$.

Iteration	x	f_1	f_2	f_3	f_4	f_5	f_6
10	(3.0646 , 3.3476)	0.8030	-14.6740	-0.3159	-0.7983	-4.1605	2.1720
20	(3.9942, 2.7514)	0.9057	-15.6150	-1.3364	0.4381	-2.9956	2.0685
30	(3.9470, 2.6061)	0.9593	-15.2099	-1.3995	0.4513	-2.7157	1.9766
40	(3.9284, 2.5619)	0.9760	-15.0769	-1.4159	0.4510	-2.6305	1.9476
50	(3.9231, 2.5490)	0.9809	-15.0383	-1.4207	0.4509	-2.6057	1.9391

After iteration 20 the active set is perfectly identified as constraints $\{1, 4, 6\}$. We could then apply the TLS and obtain the local optima. By so doing, the solution $x^T = (3.9210, 2.5439)$ with cost 0.2152 is obtained. Only after about 100 iterations of the gradient projection method this solution is obtained. If the conditions early described failed, we could allow for some more for iterations of the gradient method and apply again the TLS to the set of active constraints.

Since the problem can have many local optima, we are interested in developing methods for global optimization. A local optima gives only a tenuous guarantee of the quality of the solution, and we aim to identify, if not global optimum, at least a very good solution among the several local optima.

5   Global Minimizers

We know that the key factor in the search for local optima is the identification of the active set of constraints, so it seems natural to developed a binary tree search procedure, based on the construction of this set. In each node at level q a branching occurs, corresponding to the decisions of introducing, or not, constraint q in CC. If no more then this were done, then we were dealing with a very inefficient complete search of order $2^{|M|}$. We proved some additional results to prune this search tree. Considere the following definitions:

$B \subseteq \{1, 2, \ldots, m\}$;

$\overline{B} = \{1, 2, \ldots, m\} \setminus B$;

R(I) = Set of constraints whose indexes are in $I \subseteq \{1, 2, \ldots, m\}$;

$\ddot{\text{R}}(I)$ = Constraints obtained from R(I), where the inequalities are replaced by an equality sign;

$\tilde{R}(I) =$ Constraints obtained from R(I), where the inequalities $\leq$ are replaced by an inequality sign $\geq$;

$F(X) =$ Set of feasible solutions of constraints X.

Lemma 51 *If $F(\mathrm{R}(\overline{B})) = \emptyset$, then $\forall\, CC \subseteq B$, R(CC) cannot represent a set of active constraints for a local minimizer.*

Proof- If $CC \subseteq B$ then $\overline{B} \subseteq \overline{CC}$. Since $F(\mathrm{R}(\overline{B})) = \emptyset$, then $F(\mathrm{R}(\overline{CC})) = \emptyset$, so $x_{TLS}(CC)$ cannot be feasible for R($\overline{CC}$). $\Diamond$

Lemma 52 *If $F(\tilde{R}(B)) = \emptyset$, then $\forall CC : B \subseteq CC$, R(CC) cannot represent a set of active constraints for a local minimizer.*

Proof- If $F(\tilde{R}(B)) = \emptyset$, then, $\forall CC : B \subseteq CC$, $F(\tilde{R}(CC)) = \emptyset$. Since $x_{TLS}(CC)$ must be unfeasible for all constraints whose indexes are in CC, the system:

$$A_i x > b_i,\ i \in CC \tag{16}$$

must be feasible. If $\tilde{R}(B)$ is inconsistent, so is (16), and R(CC) cannot represent a set of active constraints for a local minimizer.$\Diamond$

Lemma 53 *If $F(\ddot{R}(B)) \neq \emptyset$, then $\forall\, CC \subseteq B$, R(CC) cannot represent a set of active constraints for a local minimizer.*

Proof- Since $F(\ddot{R}(B)) \neq \emptyset$ then $F(\ddot{R}(CC)) \neq \emptyset$, for all $CC \subseteq B$, which contradicts the inconsistency of $\ddot{R}(CC)$. If the system of constraints $\ddot{R}(CC)$ is feasible then the correction of the constraints in CC is a matrix of zeros and if $x_{MQT(CC)}$ is feasible for the constraints in $\overline{CC}$ then the original problem is feasible. $\Diamond$

Lemma 54 *If R(CC) is feasible and f(CC) is the global optimal value of problem (3) where only constraints CC are considered then, if there is a global optima for (3), its optimal value is f(CC) and the optimal solution is $x_{MQT}(CC)$.*

Proof - f(CC) is a lower bound because R($\overline{CC}$) is consistent. Since it is also an upper bound, then the proof is completed.

Corolary 51 *Let f(CC) be the optimal value of the TLS applied to CC. If $\#CC = n+1$, and R(CC) is inconsistent, then if a global minimizer exists, its value must be f(CC) and $x_{MQT}(CC)$ is the optimal solution.*

Given the above lemmas, we can in each node perform some tests aiming at pruning the search from this node. For node k, let:

- CC_F^k be the set of constraints introduced in CC so far;

- $\overline{CC}_F^k$ be the set of constraints introduced in $\overline{CC}$;
- $S^k = \{1, 2, \ldots, m\} \setminus (CC_F^k \cup \overline{CC}_F^k)$

A node is unequivocally identified by the level of the tree k and CC_F^k or $\overline{CC}_F^k$. At each node in level k, the branching rule is:

Br1- $CC_F^k = CC_F^{k-1} \cup \{k\}$;
Br2- $\overline{CC}_F^k = \overline{CC}_F^{k-1} \cup \{k\}$.

In order to apply results (11) to (14) we need the definition of CC. Yet, given lemmas (51) to (54) we know that it is possible to eliminate CC as an active set for a local minimizer, upon some properties of a subset B of CC. The same for $\overline{CC}$. In each node if we apply the TLS to CC_F^k it is possible to investigate whether it is worth to continue search from this node. More specifically, the following rules can be applied to eliminate the search from a node k:

Cut1- For $CC = CC_F^k$ and $\overline{CC} = \overline{CC}_F^k \cup S^k$ a local optima is obtained;
Cut2- $\overline{CC}_F^k$ is unfeasible.
Cut3- The cost of the TLS solution applied to CC_F^k is greater or equal of a known upper bound;
Cut4- The set of constraints $\tilde{R}(CC_F^k)$, is feasible;
Cut5- $|CC_F^k| + |S^k| < n + 1$.

From lemma 51 letting $\overline{B} = \overline{CC}_F^k$ we obtain Cut2. If in lemma 51 we let $B = CC_F^k$ we obtain Cut4.

Example 51 *Let us consider the system of inequalities:*

$$\begin{bmatrix} 1 & -1 \\ -1 & 1 \\ 1/3 & -1 \\ 1 & 1 \\ 0 & -1 \end{bmatrix} \begin{bmatrix} x_1 \\ x_2 \end{bmatrix} \leq \begin{bmatrix} -1 \\ 0 \\ -1 \\ 2 \\ -1/4 \end{bmatrix}$$

graphically displayed in figure 1. The tree in figure 2 illustrates the search for global minimizer of the correction problem. We will describe in detail the actions taken in certain nodes.

Node 1
- $CC_F^1 = \{1\}$
- $\overline{CC}_F^1 = \{\}$
- $S^1 = \{2, 3, 4, 5\}$

It was not possible to apply any of rules Cut1 to Cut4. Cut5 is not efective. Since $|CC_F^1| < n + 1 = 3$ then we proceed without applying the TLS to $CC_F^1 = \{1\}$

Node 2
- $CC_F^1 = \{1, 2\}$
- $\overline{CC}_F^1 = \{\}$
- $S^2 = \{3, 4, 5\}$

Cut1 to Cut3 can not be applied. Cut4 and Cut5 are not efective. Since $|CC_F^2| < n + 1 = 3$ then we proceed without applying the TLS to $CC_F^2 = \{1\}$

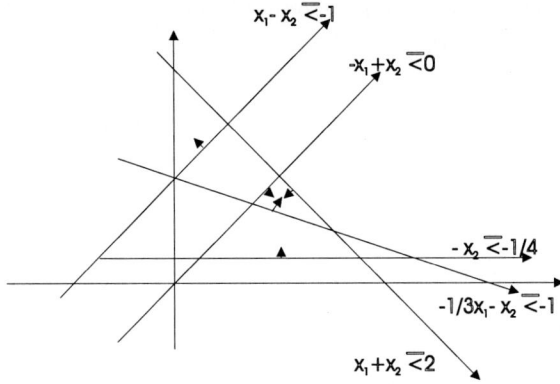

Fig. 1. Graphical representation

Node 3
- $CC_F^3 = \{1,2,3\}$
- $\overline{CC}_F^3 = \{\}$
- $S^3 = \{4,5\}$

We can not apply Cut2.
Cut4 and Cut5 are not effective.
Using the TLS on $CC = CC_F^3 = \{1,2,3\}$ and $\overline{CC} = \overline{CC}_F^3 \cup S^3 = \{4,5\}$, we do not obtain a local optimum since for $r = Ax - b$, it not true that $r(i) \geq 0$ for $i \in CC$ and $r(i) \leq 0$ for $i \in \overline{CC}$
The application of Cut3 is not successful, $LS = 0,1959$.

Node 4
- $CC_F^4 = \{1,2,3,4\}$
- $\overline{CC}_F^4 = \{\}$
- $S^4 = \{5\}$

Cut4 is effective, constraints $1,2,3,4$, in particular $2,3,4$, changing the sign for " $\geq$ " are inconsistent.

Skipping intermediate nodes we shall analyze node 8.

Node 8
- $CC_F^8 = \{1,2,4\}$
- $\overline{CC}_F^8 = \{3\}$
- $S^8 = \{5\}$

The application of Cut2, Cut4 and Cut5 do not allow to eliminate the search from this node.
Applying the TLS to $CC = CC_F^8 = \{1,2,4\}$ and $\overline{CC} = \overline{CC}_F^8 \cup S^8 = \{3,5\}$ a local optima is obtained with value $0,1518$ and the upper bound UB is updated to $\min(0,1959,0,1518)$. By Cut1 the search is eliminated.

Going to node 20:

Node 20
- $CC_F^{20} = \{1\}$
- $\overline{CC}_F^{20} = \{2,3,4\}$
- $S^{20} = \{5\}$

By Cut5 the search from this node is abandoned.

Finally we shall analyze node 31.

Node 31
- $CC_F^{31} = \{\}$
- $\overline{CC}_F^{31} = \{1,2\}$
- $S^{31} = \{3,4,5\}$

Using Cut2 the search from this node on is eliminated.
Constraints 1 and 2 are inconsistent.

So we can conclude that the optimal value is 0.1518 and was obtained is node 8.

We tested the tree search described in three sets of ramdomly generated inconsistent problems (when a consistent set was generated it was eliminated). In

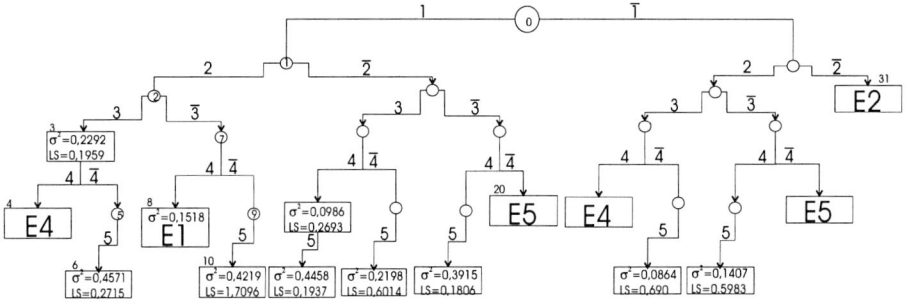

Fig. 2. Tree Search

the first set, all problems had 6 constraints on 2 variables, in the second set, 10 constraints and 5 variables, and in the last set 12 constraints on 3 variables. Table 1 shows the experimental results obtained. The first five columns represent the number of cuts obtained with each of our five cutting rules. The following columns represent the total number of leaves and total nodes that were generated. The next two columns show, respectively, the local minimizers obtained by our previous method (TLS applied on the active constraints hinted at by local search) and the global minimizer obtained. The last column indicate the computation time required in the search (on a Pentium III, 500 MHz, 128 MB memory).

The results show a significant use of the pruning rules and the subsequent pruning of the search space (the complete search space would be of the order of 2^{m+1}, where m is the number of constraints).

The results also shown that for problems instances of this size, the procedure is quite effective, being able to obtain global optimizers in about 1 minute in the worst case and usually in much less time. Of course, these results were obtained without the use of any heuristics to direct the search, which may improve the procedure very significantly.

Table 1. Experimental results

m	Prob.	Cut1	Cut12	Cut13	Cut4	Cut5	leafs	t.nodes	UB	opt.value	time (s)
	P1	1	2	8	3	10	6	78	22,5093	22,5093	0,55
	P5	1	2	8	3	10	4	74	7,6496	7,6496	0,71
	P6	2	0	14	5	15	2	72	2,8849	0,2245	0,50
6	P8	1	0	10	11	15	2	76	1,3099	0,0564	0,50
	P9	1	1	6	10	14	3	72	17,4400	9,1006	0,49
	P10	1	2	5	11	11	6	78	32,9654	20,6406	0,55
	Pro1	1	0	92	0	252	74	1122	0,0069	0,0069	16,86
	Pro2	1	0	161	24	252	38	1022	0,0049	0,0046	15,76
10	Pro3	1	0	191	33	252	58	1104	0,0022	0,0003	19,05
	Pro4	1	0	54	20	252	70	1106	0,0509	0,0504	17,76
	Pro5	1	0	188	13	252	15	972	≈0	≈0	15,05
	P11	1	117	216	283	62	277	2322	28,3931	28,3931	40,15
	P12	2	941	93	519	103	407	5124	236,7480	6,8689	94,53
	P14	1	151	263	431	84	272	2682	21,2997	21,2997	44,60
12	P16	1	86	285	124	66	353	2504	22,6909	22,6909	41,80
	P17	1	208	211	368	19	264	2352	32,7234	32,7234	40,75
	P18	1	70	331	441	185	575	3584	37,5627	0,1521	63,72
	P20	1	673	22	453	65	576	4870	82,7502	82,7502	90,41

6 Conclusion and Further Work

In this paper we studied the problem of the optimal correction of an infeasible set of linear inequalities, according to the Frobenius norm. For the other norms (l_1, l_∞ and ∞) the optimal correction can be found through the solution of a set of linear programming problems. The structure of the correction matrix for these norms has a fixed pattern that may be undesirable in practical situations. This was one of the reasons for studying the minimization of the Frobenius norm. For this norm although a result on this problem regarding necessary and sufficient conditions is mentioned on a previous work, we were able to complete this work with an approach using the KKT conditions and relating to the similar problem with only equalities constraints, known as the TLS problem. We proved that if the solution exists then it must be a TLS solution for a set of active constraints of size no less then $n + 1$.

We then extended our previous work on finding local optima, and present a tree search for global optimization, which is based on choosing a correct set of active constraints. Clearly this search has worst case exponential complexity, but we defined sound and effective rules to prune the search tree.

So far, the method was only tested in artificial problem instances, producing quite encouraging results. In the future we intend to apply it in real life problems in order to assess how effective the pruning rules might be as well as exploiting different heuristics to speed up the search. On more theoretical grounds, we intend to investigate extensions of the models to make it more expressive in two related directions. On the one hand, we would like to select, "a priori", some constraints as hard in order to guarantee that only coefficients of the "soft" constraints are corrected. On the other hand, we would like to assign weights to the coefficients of the model, so that the corrections of these coefficients are aggregated taking into account these weights. In practice, by considering very large weights in some of the constraints, we turn them into hard constraints.

References

[AmPa01] Paula Amaral, Contribuições para o Estudo de Sistemas Lineares Incon-sistentes, Ph.D. dissertation, Faculty of Science and Thecnology, UNL, Lisbon, 2001.

[AmBa99] Paula Amaral, Pedro Barahona, About infeasibility in the constraints of a linear model, Ricerca Operativa, Vol. 92, pp 49-67, 1999.

[AmTB00] P. Amaral, M. W. Trosset, P. Barahona, Correcting an Inconsistent Sys-tem of Linear Inequalities by Nonlinear Programming, Technical Report 00-27, Department of Computational & Applied Mathematics, Rice Uni-versity, Houston, TX 77005, 2000.

[Ball96] S. Bistarelli, H. Fargier, U. Montanari, F. Rossi, T. Schiex and G. Ver-faillie, Semiring -based CSPs and Valued CSPs: basic properties and comparison, in Overconstrained Systems, M. Jampel, E. C. Freuder and M. Maher(Eds.), LNCS vol. X, Springer, 1996.

[BDMo91]   Bart L. R. De Moor, Total linear least squares with inequality con-
            straints, ESAT-SISTA Report 1990-02,March 1990, Department of Elec-
            trical Engineering, Katholieke Universiteit Leuven, 1990.
[BoBe89]   A. Borning, B. Freeman-Benson and M. Wilson, Constraint Hierarchies
            and Logic Programming, Procs. International Conference on Logic Pro-
            gramming, ICLP'89, MIT Press, 1989
[Chak94]   N. Chakravarti, Some results concerning post-infeasibility analysis,
            EJOR, Vol. 73, pp. 139-143, 1994.
[ChDr91]   J. W Chinneck and E. W Dravnieks, Locating Minimal Infeasible Con-
            straint Sets in Linear Programs, ORSA Journal on Computing, Vol. 3,
            No. 2, pp. 157-168, 1991.
[Demm87]   James Weldon Demmel, The smallest perturbation of a submatrix which
            lowers the rank and constrained total least squares problems, Siam Jour-
            nal Numerical Analysis, Vol. 24, N° 1, pp. 199-206, 1987.
[DuFP93]   D. Dubois, H. Fargier and H. Prade, The Calculus of Fuzzy Restrictions
            as a Basis for Flexible Constraint Satisfaction, Proc. IEEE International
            Conference on Fuzzy Systems, IEEE, pp. 1131-1136, 1993
[Elst93]   Karl-Heinz Elster (Edt) Modern Mathematical Methods of Optimiza-
            tion, Akademie Verlag, 1993.
[FrWa92]   E. C. Freuder and R. J. Wallace, Partial Constraint Satisfaction, Artifi-
            cial Intelligence, Vol. 58, No. 1-3, 21-70, 1992
[GoLo83]   G. H. Golub and C. F. Van Loan, Matrix Computations,
[Gree93]   H. J. Greenberg, How to Analyse the Results of Linear Programs- Part
            3: Infeasibility Diagnoses, Interfaces, Vol 23, No 6, pp. 120-139, 1993.
[HoMB96]   C. Holzbaur, F. Menezes and P. Barahona, Defeasibility in CLP(Q)
            through Generalised Slack Variables, Proceedings of CP'96, 2nd Int.
            Conf. in Principles and Practice of Constraint Programming, E. C.
            Freuder(ed.), Lecture Notes in Computer Science, Vol. 1118, Springer-
            Verlag, pp. 209-223, 1996.
[HoJo85]   oger A. Horn, Charles R. Johnson, Matrix Analysis, Cambridge Univer-
            sity Press, 1985
[Pena00]   Javier Pena, Understanding the geometry of infeasible perturbations of
            a conic linear system, Siam J. Optimization, Vol. 10, No. 2, pp 534-550,
            2000.
[Rene94]   James Renegar, Some perturbation theory for linear programming,
            Mathematical Programming, Vol. 65, pp 73-91, 1994.
[Rene95]   James Renegar, Linear programming, complexity theory and elementary
            functional analysis, Mathematical Programming, Vol. 70, pp 279-351,
            1995.
[Rood79]   G. M. Roodman, Post-Infeasibility Analysis in Linear Programming,
            Management Science, Vol. 25, No. 9, pp. 916-922, 1979.
[StSo96]   Stephen G. Nash, Ariela Sofer, Linear and Nonlinear Programming,
            McGraw-Hill, 1996.
[SVHu91]   Sabine van Huffel, The total least squares problem: computational as-
            pects and analysis, Frontiers in applied mathematics, 9, Siam, 1991.
[VLoo81]   J. N. M. Van Loon, Irreducibly inconsistent systems of linear inequalities,
            EJOR, Vol. 8, pp. 282-288, 1981.
[Vato92]   A. A. Vatolin, An Lp-Based Algorithm for the Correction of Inconsistent
            Linear Equation and Inequality Systems, Optimization, Vol. 24, pp 157-
            164, 1992.

[Vato86]   A. A. Vatolin, Parametric approximation of inconsistent systems of linear equations and inequalities. Seminarber., Humboldt-Univ. Berlin, Sekt. Math. 81, pp 145-154, 1986.

[Vera96]   Jorge R. Vera, Ill-posedness and the complexity of deciding existence of solutions to linear programs, Siam J. Optimization, Vol. 6, No. 3, pp 549-569, 1996.

[WaHu92]   Hsiao-Fan Wang, Chen-Sheng Huang, Inconsistent structures of linear systems, Int. J. General Systems, Vol. 21, pp 65-81, 1992.

Temporal Planning through Mixed Integer Programming: A Preliminary Report

Yannis Dimopoulos[1] and Alfonso Gerevini[2]

[1] Department of Computer Science, University of Cyprus
P.O. Box 20537, CY-1678 Nicosia, Cyprus
yannis@cs.ucy.ac.cy
[2] DEA – Università degli Studi di Brescia
Via Branze 38, I-25123 Brescia, Italy
gerevini@ing.unibs.it

Abstract. Temporal planning is an important problem, as in many real world planning domains actions have different durations and the goals should be achieved by a specified deadline, or as soon as possible. This paper presents a novel approach to temporal planning that is based on Mixed Integer Programming. In the new framework, a temporal planning domain is modeled by two sets of linear inequalities. The first set involves integer variables and is a Graphplan-like encoding of a simplification of the original problem where the duration of the actions is ignored. The second set involves both integer and real valued variables, and models the temporal aspects of the problem. The two sets interact through the common integer variables, and their combination can be solved by using available Mixed Integer Programming software. The new method aims at generating good solutions quickly, under different minimization objectives. Preliminary experimental results illustrate the effectiveness of our approach.

1 Introduction

Over the last years there has been a remarkable progress in solving STRIPS planning problems [16]. However, for many interesting applications the STRIPS language is inadequate. We need to solve problems that involve actions that have different durations, consume resources and must be executed by certain deadlines. We need to generate plans that optimize complex combinations of different criteria, including completion time, resource utilization, action costs and others.

Such advanced application domains involve *numeric* variables, constraints, and complex objective functions. Mixed Integer Programming (MIP), and its language of linear inequalities, can easily accommodate these key features and therefore seems to provide a rich representational framework for such applications. However, there are relatively few works that apply IP to planning problems with numeric constraints [17], [11].

In the original STRIPS language actions are instantaneous and time is implicitly represented. Several domain-independent systems have been proposed to

P. Van Hentenryck (Ed.): CP 2002, LNCS 2470, pp. 47–62, 2002.

handle a richer notion of time (e.g., [1, 14, 12]). However, these approaches scale up poorly, and can deal with only very simple problems. The success of recent approaches to STRIPS planning, such as planning graphs and heuristic search, has motivated the application of these techniques to temporal planning. For instance, TGP [13] uses a generalization of Graphplan mutual exclusion reasoning to handle actions with durations, while TP4 [10] applies heuristic search to solve problems with action durations and resources.

In this paper we apply MIP to temporal planning, by developing models for domains that contain actions with different durations. Our approach decomposes a planning domain into two interacting sets of linear inequalities referred to as the *logical* and the *temporal* part respectively.

The logical part is an encoding of the planning graph of the STRIPS problem that is obtained from the original problem by ignoring action durations. For this encoding we use the method developed by [15] and improved by [3]. This approach formulates the planning graph of a STRIPS planning domain as an Integer Programming problem and then uses branch-and-bound for solution extraction.

The temporal part associates with every action a real-valued variable that represents the start time of the action. The linear inequalities of this part ensure the correctness of the start times that are assigned to the actions taking into account their durations.

The combination of the logical and temporal parts can be solved in a uniform, integrated way by well-known MIP software like CPLEX. Since the two sets of constraints interact, this is much more effective than a naive approach in which the logical part is iteratively solved first, and each potential solution is checked against the constraints of the temporal part (which may include a constraint on the overall duration of the plan), until a valid (i.e., a solution for both the sets of constraints) or optimal temporal plan is found.

In order to increase the efficiency of the representation, the structure of the domain is exploited. In particular, we propose some techniques that use ideas from domain analysis tools [5, 7, 8] to reduce the number of constraints and variables of the temporal part of a planning problem, leading to stronger MIP formulations.

In contrast to TGP and TP4 that generate plans of minimum duration, the new approach does not provide optimality guarantees. However, apart from the overall duration of the plan, the MIP models can easily accommodate different optimization criteria and any constraint that can be expressed as a linear inequality. Furthermore, the new method is capable of generating high quality plans early in the computation.

The rest of the paper is organized as follows. First we briefly give the necessary background; then we present our basic temporal model, i.e., the set of inequalities forming the temporal part of the problem encoding (while for the logical part we will use some known encoding); then we describe how planning problems can be solved in the new approach; then we give some preliminary experimental results; finally, we give our conclusions and mention future work.

2   Preliminaries

The planning language we consider is propositional STRIPS extended with time. Actions have (positive) preconditions, (add and delete) effects and constant duration that can be any real number. Our assumptions for the execution of actions are the same as those used in [13] and [10]:

- The preconditions of an action must hold in the beginning and during the execution of the action.
- Add and delete effects take place at some point during the execution of an action and can only be used at the end of the execution of the action.

The above assumptions require that the preconditions and effects of an actions are protected during their execution. Therefore, the linear inequalities of the MIP models we develop, enforce that actions with contradictory effects or with contradictions between their effects and preconditions do not overlap in time.

A MIP problem [18] comprises of a mixture of real-valued and integer variables, a set of linear inequalities on these variables, and an objective function. The models developed in the paper are 0/1 MIP models i.e., integer variables can only assume the values 0 and 1. We assume that the reader is familiar with the basics of MIP.

Our modeling techniques utilize some ideas developed in the context of the domain analysis tool DISCOPLAN [8]. In particular, they exploit *single-valuedness* (sv) constraints and binary XOR-constraints, which are automatically inferred by DISCOPLAN. An sv-constraint states that the value of a certain predicate argument is unique for any given values of the remaining arguments. An example of an sv-constraint in blocks-world is $on(x, *y)$, stating that any object is on at most one thing ("$*$" indicates the single-valued argument). An example of XOR-constraint is (XOR $on(x, y)$ $clear(y)$) stating that any object is either clear or has something on it.

3   The Basic Temporal Model

Let P be a temporal planning problem, let P^S be its STRIPS simplification (i.e., actions are instantaneous), and assume a planning graph representation of P^S. For each action (instantiated operator) A of the problem and each level l of the graph, there is a corresponding node in the planning graph, denoted by A^l, that can be understood as a binary variable. A plan for P^S is essentially a value assignment to the action variables such that the value 1 is assigned to variable A^l iff action A at level l is included in the plan.

Our goal now is to find a set of linear inequalities for problem P that, given a plan for P^S, assign start times to the actions in the plan. The inequalities that model the temporal part of P involve, apart from the binary action variables A^l, a set of real valued variables as follows. For every action A and level l of the graph, we introduce a variable A^l_{st} (also denoted as $st(A^l)$) that represents the start time of action A at level l, i.e., the time when the execution of the action starts. Similarly, for every fluent f of the domain, and every level l of the graph, we introduce a variable f^l_{st} (also denoted as $st(f^l)$) that represents the time at which fluent f becomes true. In the following, $dur(A)$ denotes the duration of action A, which is a real number.

The first set of inequalities of the temporal model is used to enforce the constraint that actions can not start before their preconditions become true. If f is a precondition of A, the following set of inequalities is included in the model, for each level l of the planning graph

$$(1) \quad A^l_{st} \geq f^l_{st}$$

The next set of inequalities represents the contraint that a fluent can become true after the execution of an action that adds it. Therefore, if f is an add effect of action A the model includes (A^l is a 0/1 variable)

$$(2) \quad f^{l+1}_{st} \geq A^l_{st} + dur(A) \cdot A^l$$

Note that if fluent f was true at level l before the execution of action A, the above constraint causes f^{l+1}_{st} to take a value that can not be smaller than the end time of A. In combination with the previous constraint (1) this causes all actions that have f as their precondition, and appear in levels higher than l, to start after the end time of A. Although there is a way to overcome this restriction, in this paper we assume that there is no reachable state s such that a fluent f is true in s, and an action that adds f can be executed in s (the blocks world and rocket are examples of such domains).

The temporal model prevents contradictory actions from overlaping in time. For every pair of actions A and B such that A deletes the preconditions of B, the following constraints are added to the model

$$(3) \quad A^{l+1}_{st} \geq B^l_{st} + dur(B) \cdot B^l$$

For every pair of actions A and B such that A deletes an add effect of B, the model includes the following inequalities

$$(4.1) \quad A^{l+1}_{st} \geq B^l_{st} + dur(B) \cdot B^l$$

$$(4.2) \quad B^{l+1}_{st} \geq A^l_{st} + dur(A) \cdot A^l$$

For every fluent f, the following constraints propagate the start time of f through the levels of the planning graph

$$(5) \quad f^{l+1}_{st} \geq f^l_{st}$$

Similarly, for each action A, its start time is propagated through the following constraints

$$(6) \quad A^{l+1}_{st} \geq A^l_{st}$$

Finally, plans start at time 1, which is stated by

(7) $f_{st}^1 \geq 1$

The following theorem states that any valid Graphplan-style plan satisfying constraints (1)–(7) is temporally sound.

Theorem 1 (Soundness). *For every action A that is in a plan and satisfies the constraints above, the following holds: If p is precondition of A, then there exists an action A_p such that p is an add effect of A_p, and*

a) $st(A_p) + dur(A_p) \leq st(A)$;
b) *if B is an action that has p as a delete effect, $st(B) + dur(B) \leq st(A_p)$ or $st(A) + dur(A) \leq st(B)$.*

Furthermore, if q is an add effect of A, then

c) *for every action C in the plan that deletes q, $st(C) + dur(C) \leq st(A)$ or $st(A) + dur(A) \leq st(C)$.*

Proof: The correctness of the underlying non-temporal planning algorithm guarantees that if A is an action in the plan and p is a precondition of A, there will be another action A_p in the plan that has p as an add effect. Moreover, if l is the level of A and l' the level of A_p, it must be the case that $l' < l$, and there is no action that deletes p and occurs in any level l'' with $l'' \geq l'$ and $l'' \leq l$.
In order to prove (a), observe that because of inequality (2), $st(p^{l'+1}) \geq st(A_p^{l'}) + dur(A_p)$. Moreover, the set of inequalities (5) will enforce $st(p^l) \geq st(A_p^{l'}) + dur(A_p)$ (because $l' < l$). Finally, because of inequality (1), we have $st(A^l) \geq st(p^l)$, which together with the previous constraint give $st(A^l) \geq st(A_p^{l'}) + dur(A_p)$.
In order to prove (b), let B be any action that has p as delete effect, and let l'' be its level. As noted earlier, the correctness of the non-temporal plan implies that either $l'' < l'$ or $l'' > l$ must hold. Assume $l'' < l'$. Since B deletes an add effect of A_p, inequality (4.2) will enforce the constraint $st(A_p^{l''+1}) \geq st(B^{l''}) + dur(B)$. This constraint, together with the set of inequalities (6), impose $st(A_p^{l'}) \geq st(B^{l''}) + dur(B)$. Assume that $l'' > l$. Since B deletes a precondition of A, inequality (3) will enforce $st(B^{l+1}) \geq st(A^l) + dur(A)$ which together with inequalities (6) ensure that $st(B^{l''}) \geq st(A^l) + dur(A)$. Thus it is indeed the case that $st(B) + dur(B) \leq st(A_p)$ or $st(A) + dur(A) \leq st(B)$ is true.
In order to prove (c), assume that an action $C^{l'}$ in the plan deletes q, and that q is an add effect of A^l. Clearly $l' < l$ or $l' > l$ (because of the correctness of the non-temporal plan). If $l' < l$, since constraints (4) will enforce $st(A^{l'+1}) \geq st(C^{l'}) + dur(C)$, by constraints (6) we have $st(A^l) \geq st(C^{l'}) + dur(C)$. Similarly, if $l' > l$, since constraints (4) ensure that $st(C^{l+1}) \geq st(A^l) + dur(A)$, by constraints (6) we have $st(C^{l'}) \geq st(A^l) + dur(A)$. Therefore, it is indeed the case that $st(C) + dur(C) \leq st(A)$ or $st(A) + dur(A) \leq st(C)$ is true. $\square$

4 Improved Temporal Model

When a planning problem is modeled as a set of linear inequalities, the number of constraints and variables that are included in the model can significantly affect the performance of the solver that is used for generating plans. The previously described model of temporal planning problems can generate a large number of constraints and variables, but it can be substantially improved if certain features of the domain structure are taken into account. The improvements that we will discuss aim at reducing the number of temporal constraints, as well as the number of temporal variables that are required to correctly model a planning domain. The reduction of the number of temporal constraints is based on the notions of *persistent fluent, persistent pair of fluents* and *strong interference* that we give for binary fluents, and that can be computed by exploiting existing domain analysis tools like DISCOPLAN [8].[1]

Definition 1 (Persistent fluent). *Let f be a binary fluent such that $f(x, *y)$ holds, and every action (instantiated operator) that has an instance of f in its add effects has another instance of f with the same first argument but different second argument in its preconditions. We say that f is persistent on its first argument.*

Persistence on the second argument of a fluent is defined similarly. We now define argument persistence on the first argument for a pair of binary fluents. Persistence on other arguments, or between a binary and a unary fluent can be defined in a similar way. In the following, X, Y, Z and W indicate any constant, x, y and z universally quantified variables, x, y and z operator parameters. Moreover, we assume that no action has any literal as both precondition and add effect.

Definition 2 (Persistent pair of fluents). *Let $f1$ and $f2$ be two binary fluents such that $f1(x, *y)$, $f2(x, *z)$ and (XOR $f1(x,y)$, $f2(x,z)$) hold. We say that $f1$ and $f2$ is a persistent pair of fluents on their first argument, if every action that has $f1(X, Y)$ or $f2(X, Z)$ as an add effect, also has $f1(X, W)$ or $f2(X, W')$ as a precondition, where $W \neq Y, Z$ and $W' \neq Y, Z$.*

Now we can define the notion of *strong interference* between actions that will be used to improve the temporal model.[2]

Definition 3 (Strong interference). *A pair of actions A and B strongly interfere if*

---

[1] We restrict our analysis to binary fluents, which are the most common in many existing domain formalizations. Work on an extension to fluents of higher arity is in progress.

[2] For the sake of clarity, the definition is given for the case of persistence on the first argument of binary fluents, but it can be easily generalized to the cases where persistence is on the second argument, and f, $f1$, $f2$ are unary fluents.

- $f(X, Y)$, B has a precondition $f(X, Z)$, and either $Y \neq Z$, or $Y = Z$ and A and B have an instance of f as add effect with X as the same first argument and different second argument; or
- $f1, f2$ is a persistent pair of fluents on their first argument, and A has a precondition $f1(X, Y)$ and B a precondition $f2(X, Z)$, or (a) they have a common precondition $f1(X, Y)$ or $f2(X, Y)$ which they both delete and (b) they have an instance of $f1$ or $f2$ as add effect with X as the first argument and different second argument (if they are instances of the same fluent).

For instance, under the assumptions of the previous definition, A and B strongly interfere when

- $f1(a, b)$ is a precondition of A and $f2(a, c)$ is a precondition of B, or
- when $f1(a, b)$ is a precondition of A and B, $\neg f1(a, b)$ is an effect of A and B, $f2(a, b)$ is an effect of A, and $f1(a, c)$ an effect of B.

It turns out that for pairs of actions that strongly interfere, all constraints of the form (3) and (4) can be omitted from the temporal model, because actions that strongly interfere can not overlap in time. We call such models *reduced temporal models*. An example of a reduced model is given at the end of this section. The following theorem states the soundness of the reduced temporal models.

Theorem 2. *For any two actions A and B that strongly interfere and are both included in a plan, a reduced temporal model satisfies either $st(A) \geq st(B) + dur(B)$ or $st(B) \geq st(A) + dur(A)$.*

Proof (sketch): Assume that both actions A and B are included in a plan generated by the underlying non-temporal planning algorithm, and let l be the level of A and l' the level of B. Since by Definition 3 the two actions have mutually exclusive preconditions or mutually exclusive effects, the soundness of the non-temporal algorithm implies $l' \neq l$.

We first consider the case in which $l < l'$, and $f(X, a)$ is a precondition of A and $f(X, b)$ a precondition of B, where f is a persistent fluent on its first argument, and a, b any pair of different constants.[3] Assume that A has $f(X, b)$ as an add effect. Consequently, because of constraint (2), $st(f(X, b)^{l+1}) \geq st(A^l) + dur(A)$ will hold. Then the set of constraints (5) will enforce that $st(f(X, b)^{l'}) \geq A_{st}^l + dur(A)$. Since $f(X, b)$ is a precondition of B, constraints (1) will enforce $st(B^{l'}) \geq st(f(X, b)^{l'})$ and therefore $st(B^{l'}) \geq st(A^l) + dur(A)$.

Assume now that either A does not have any add effect of the form $f(X, Y)$, or it has an add effect $f(X, Y)$ with $Y \neq b$. Then there will be a sequence of actions $A_1, ..., A_n$ in the plan, at levels $l_1, ..., l_n$ respectively, with $n > 1$, $l_i > l$ and $l_i < l'$, such that $f(X, b_i)$ is an add effect of A_i and a precondition of A_{i+1} for some constant b_i, $b_n = b$ and $l_{i+1} > l_i$. Since f persists on its first argument, if $f(X, b_i)$ is an add effect of A_i, then, for some d, $f(X, d)$

---

[3] For clarity the proof is given considering only persistence on first arguments; generalization to persistence on different arguments is straightforward.

must be a precondition of A_i. Hence, it must be the case that $d = b_{i-1}$, where b_{i-1} is an add effect of action A_{i-1}. Therefore, the combination of constraints (1), (2) and (5) implies, along the sequence of actions $A_1, .., A_n$, a set of constraints $st(A_{i+1}^{l_i+1}) \geq st(A_i^{l_i}) + dur(A_i)$, for every $i \geq 1$, which implies that $st(A_n^{l_n}) \geq st(A_1^{l_1}) + \sum_{1 \leq i \leq n-1} dur(A_i)$. Then, by constraints (6) $st(B^{l'}) \geq st(A_1^{l_1}) + \sum_{1 \leq i \leq n-1} dur(A_i)$.

We now consider the temporal relation between actions A and A_1. Assume first that action A has an add effect $f(X,c)$ for some constant $c \neq b$. Then, $f(X,c)$ must be a precondition of A_1. Therefore $st(A_1^{l_1}) \geq st(A^l) + dur(A)$. Assume now that action A does not have any instance of fluent f in its add effects with X as its first argument. Then, by Definition 1 and the assumed soundness of the non-temporal plan, $f(X,a)$ must be a precondition of A_1, and A, A_1 do not strongly interfere, provided that they do not have other preconditions or effects that could cause strong interference. Moreover, note that $f(X,a)$ must be a delete effect of A_1. Since A_1 deletes a precondition of A, constraint (4) applies, and $st(A_1^{l_1}) \geq st(A^l) + dur(A)$ must hold. Hence, it is again the case that $st(A_1^{l_1}) \geq st(A^l)+dur(A)$. This constraint, together with $st(B^{l'}) \geq st(A_1^{l_1})+ \sum_{1 \leq i \leq n-1} dur(A_i)$, give us $st(B^{l'}) > st(A^l) + dur(A)$.

Assume now that actions A and B, have both precondition $f(X,c)$ and that A adds $f(X,a)$ and B adds $f(X,b)$, for some different constants a, b and c. Then again there will be a sequence of actions $A_1, ..., A_n$ in the plan, such that A_n adds $f(X,c)$, and by an analogous argument the constraints $st(A_1) \geq st(A^l)+dur(A)$ and $st(B^{l'}) \geq st(A_1^{l_1})+\sum_{1 \leq i \leq n-1} dur(A_i)$ will hold, enforcing $st(B^{l'}) \geq st(A^l)+ dur(A)$.

Now let again $l < l'$, and assume that A has a precondition $f1(X,a)$ and B has a precondition $f2(X,b)$, where $f1$ and $f2$ is a persistent pair on the first argument, and a and b is any pair of different constants. If A has $f2(X,b)$ as an add effect, then using arguments similar to the one given above we can prove that $st(B^{l'}) \geq st(A^l) + dur(A)$. Otherwise, there will be a sequence of actions $A_1, ..., A_n$ in the plan, at levels $l_1, ..., l_n$ respectively, with $n > 1$, $l_i > l$ and $l_i < l'$, such that $f1(X,b_i)$ or $f2(X,b_i)$ is an add effect of A_i for some constant b_i, and $f2(X,b)$ is an add effect of A_n. By arguments similar to those used above, we can prove that $st(B^{l'}) \geq st(A_1^{l_1}) + \sum_{1 \leq i \leq n-1} dur(A_i)$ and $st(A_1^{l_1}) \geq st(A^l) + dur(A)$ will hold. Thus $st(B^{l'}) \geq st(A^l) + dur(A)$ will also hold.

Finally, if $l > l'$, we can use symmetric arguments to those above to prove $st(A^l) \geq st(B^{l'}) + dur(B)$. □

We now discuss some improvements that reduce the number of temporal variables in the model of a problem. More importantly, they achieve more effective propagation of the start times of actions and fluents. We note that some of these improvements also reduce the number of constraints that are included in the model of a planning domain.

Let f be a binary fluent for which the sv-constraint $f(x, *y)$ holds. We can replace in the model all temporal variables $st(f(X,Y)^l)$ that refer to the different values of Y and same value of X with one new variable $st(fn(X)^l)$, for each level l. Similarly, if $f(*x, y)$ holds. Moreover, if $f1(x, y)$ and $f2(x, z)$ are two fluents related with a XOR constraint (XOR $f1(x, y)$ $f2(x, z)$), we can replace their corresponding temporal variables referring to the different values of y and z by, but same value X for x, with a single variable $st(f12(X)^l)$. Similarly, if (XOR $f1(y, x)$ $f2(z, x)$) or (XOR $f1(x, y)$ $f2(x)$) holds. We call this new set of variables *abstract temporal fluent variables*. Note that it can be the case that several different sv or XOR constraints hold for the same fluent, giving rise to different models depending on the particular abstract variables that are choosen. We handle such cases in an ad-hoc manner, but here we do not discuss this issue further.

In domains that involve operators with more than two arguments that can be instantiated by many objects, the technique of splitting action start time variables can be used. Let $A(\mathbf{x}, \mathbf{y}, \mathbf{z})$ be an operator such that, for every possible value of parameter $\mathbf{x}$, all actions that have different values for the pair of parameters $\mathbf{y}$ and $\mathbf{z}$ are mutually exclusive. We denote such an operator by $A(\mathbf{x}, *\mathbf{y}, *\mathbf{z})$. Moreover, assume that all preconditions and effects of $A(\mathbf{x}, *\mathbf{y}, *\mathbf{z})$ are unary or binary fluents, none of which has the pair $\mathbf{y}, \mathbf{z}$ in its parameters. If this is the case, we can split each variable $st(A(X, Y, Z)^l)$ into two variables $st(A_1(X, Y)^l)$ and $st(A_2(X, Z)^l)$, and add the constraint $st(A_1(X, Y)^l) = st(A_2(X, Z)^l)$ to the model. In the constraints (1) and (2) of the temporal model, in which $st(A(X, Y, Z)^l)$ occurs along with a start time variable that refers to a fluent of the form $f(X)$, $f(Y)$ or $f(X, Y)$, variable $st(A(X, Y, Z)^l)$ is replaced by $st(A_1(X, Y)^l)$. Similarly, if the start time fluent variables that occurs in such a constraint is on a fluent of the form $f(X, Z)$, variable $st(A(X, Y, Z)^l)$ is replaced by $st(A_2(X, Z)^l)$. In constraints (3) and (4) one of $st(A_1(X, Y)^l)$ and $st(A_2(X, Z)^l)$ replaces variable $st(A(X, Y, Z)^l)$, depending on the fluent that gives rise to the conflict.

Let again $A(\mathbf{x}, *\mathbf{y}, *\mathbf{z})$ be an operator as defined above. It may be the case that the duration of the instances of $A(\mathbf{x}, *\mathbf{y}, *\mathbf{z})$ does not depend on all its parameters, but only on a subset of them. In the blocks world for example, it is possible that the duration of the move actions depends on the block that moves and the destination of the block, but not the origin of the block. Assume that the duration of a given operator $A(\mathbf{x}, *\mathbf{y}, *\mathbf{z})$ does not depend on the values of parameter $*\mathbf{z}$. Then, we can replace all occurences of $dur(A(X, Y, Z)) \cdot A(X, Y, Z)^l$ in constraints (1)–(4) of the temporal model by $dur(A(X, Y, Z)) \cdot \sum_z A(X, Y, z)^l$, where $\sum_z$ denoted the sum over all possible values of parameter $\mathbf{z}$. If the duration of $A(\mathbf{x}, *\mathbf{y}, *\mathbf{z})$ depends only on the values of parameter $\mathbf{x}$ we can replace $dur(A(X, Y, Z)) \cdot A(X, Y, Z)^l$ by $dur(A(X, Y, Z)) \cdot \sum_y \sum_z A(X, y, z)^l$. We call this technique, *compact duration modeling*. In some domains this technique combined with start time variable splitting may lead to tight MIP formulations.

For instance, suppose that $\mathbf{z}$ can assume two values, say $Z1$ and $Z2$, and that $A(X, Y, Z1)^l$ and $A(X, Y, Z2)^l$ are mutually exclusive. When the branch and bound algorithm solves the relaxed MIP problem using the Simplex algorithm, it is very likely that some real values different from zero are assigned to

$A(X, Y, Z1)^l$ and $A(X, Y, Z2)^l$ (e.g., $A(X, Y, Z1)^l = 0.5$ and $A(X, Y, Z2)^l = 0.5$). Suppose in addition that the action $B(X, Y)$ deletes an effect of both $A(X, Y, Z1)$ and $A(X, Y, Z2)$. The basic temporal model would then contain the following inequality

$$B(X, Y)_{st}^{l+1} \geq A(X, Y, Z1)_{st}^l + d \cdot A(X, Y, Z1)^l$$

where d is the duration of $A(X, Y, Z1)$. In the improved model this inequality is replaced by the following stronger constraint

$$B(X, Y)_{st}^{l+1} \geq A(X, Y, Z1)_{st}^l + d \cdot (A(X, Y, Z1)^l + A(X, Y, Z2)^l).$$

Example. Consider the Rocket domain with the usual ld (load) and ul (unload) actions for packages and fl (fly) for airplanes. Assume that these actions have different durations. The basic temporal model for this domain includes all constraints that have been described in the previous section. Consider for example $ld(p1, pl1, l1)$, which represents the action of loading package $p1$ to plane $pl1$ at location $l1$. The constraints of type (1) for this action are $st(ld(p1, pl1, l1)^l) \geq st(at(p1, l1)^l)$ and $st(ld(p1, pl1, l1))^l \geq st(at(pl1, l1)^l)$ for each level l. There is one constraint of type (2) for each level l, namely $st(at(p1, l1)^{l+1}) \geq st(ld(p1, pl1, l1))^l + dur(ld(p1, pl1, l1)) \cdot x_{ld}^l$, where x_{ld}^l is a 0/1 variable that takes the value 1 if the action $ld(p1, pl1, loc1)$ is included in the plan, and 0 otherwise.

The temporal overlap of actions deleting preconditions of $ld(p1, pl1, l1)$ is prohibited by constraints (3), namely, $st(ld(p1, X, l1)^{l+1}) \geq st(ld(p1, pl1, l1)^l) + dur(ld(p1, pl1, l1)) \cdot x_{ld}^l$ and $st(fly(pl1, l1, Y)^{l+1}) \geq st(ld(p1, pl1, l1)^l) + dur(ld(p1, pl1, l1)) \cdot x_{ld}^l$, where X stands for any plane different from $pl1$ and Y for any location different from $l1$. Since $at(p1, l1)$ and $in(p1, Z)$ is a persistent pair for any plane Z, and the two load-actions of the first inequality strongly interfere (they share the precondition $at(p1, l1)$, but add different instances of in with $p1$ as first argument), by Theorem 2 the first constraint is not included in the reduced model. However, the second constraint is included, since the load and fly actions that are involved do not strongly interfere. The only action that deletes the add effect of $ld(p1, pl1, l1)$ is "blocked" through a pair of constraints of type (4), which are $st(ul(p1, pl1, l1)^{l+1}) \geq st(ld(p1, pl1, l1))^l) + dur(ld(p1, pl1, l1)) \cdot x_{ld}^l$ and its symmetric. Note that by Theorem 2 these constraints are not included in the reduced model, because of the persistent pair $in(p1, pl1)$, $at(p1, l1)$ appearing in the preconditions of the two interfering actions.

Since $at(x, *y)$ holds for any plane x and location y, all occurrences of $st(at(p1, l1)^l)$ can be replaced by the variable $st(at1(p1)^l)$. Moreover, since (XOR $at(x, y)$ $in(x, y)$) holds, $st(at(p1, X)^l)$ and $st(in(p1, Y)^l)$ can be replaced by $st(atin(p1)^l)$.

5   Solving Planning Problems

When considered alone, the temporal model that we have described could find feasible start times for the actions of a plan that is produced by any algorithm

solving planning graphs. This STRIPS planner would ignore completely the duration of the actions, and the temporal part would not need to know how the
planner generates the plans. The two parts would be "glued" together through
the 0/1 action variables that are shared by the two parts.

This separation of the logical and the temporal part of a planning problem facilitates the use of a different algorithm for each of these parts, e.g., propositional
satisfiability for the first and linear programming for the second, in an architecture similar to LPSAT [17]. However, in the approach taken here we represent
both parts by a set of linear inequalities and use standard branch-and-bound on
the *union* of the two parts. The potential benefit of such a unified algorithmic
framework is the possibility of exploiting the strong interaction between the two
parts, which may lead to extensive value propagation.

For the formulation of a logical part of a temporal planning problem as a
set of linear inequalities, we use the method developed by [15] and improved
by [3]. This approach essentially translates the planning graph of a STRIPS
problem into an Integer Programming model, and then uses branch-and-bound
for solution extraction.

The role of the logical part is to order actions in such a way that dependencies
and interactions between them are respected, and consistent states are generated.
If an action appears at some level i of the planning graph, this means that it can
be executed only after the completion of the execution of some other actions at
lower levels of the graph.

The overall duration of the plan is represented by the variable mks (for
makespan) and a set of constraints of the form $(a_{st}^l + dur(a) \cdot a^l \leq mks)$, for
every action a and level l. The objective function that is used in the problem
formulation depends on the optimization objective. If the objective is the minimization of the makespan of the plan the objective function is $min(mks)$. If
there is a deadline for the overall execution of the plan, mks is constrained to be
less than or equal to this value, and in the objective function any other quantity
can be used. For instance, if each action a_i has an associated cost c_i the overall
cost of the plan is minimized through the objective function $min(\sum_{a_i^l} c_i \cdot a_i^l)$.

The algorithm starts with the encoding of the planning graph of length 1 (i.e,
with one level), and then it extends the encoding by increasing the number of
levels in the underlying graph, until a feasible solution for both the logical and
the temporal parts of the encoding is found. Let l be the level of the first solution,
and let opt^l denote the value of the optimal solution for that level, under the
optimization objective. After the problem for the l levels is solved to optimality,
the encoding is extended by considering an extra level of the underlying graph,
and a new search starts for a solution with an objective function value less than
opt^l.[4] If a new, improved, solution is found, the procedure repeats by extending
again the encoding (i.e, by considering an extra level for the underlying planning
graph). If at some level no better solution is found, the algorithm terminates. Of
course, the solutions found are not guaranteed to be optimal, as it is possible that

---

[4] When we extend the encoding, both the logical and the temporal parts of encoding
are extended.

better solutions can be extracted if the underlying planning graph is extended further.

An improvement of the incremental process is to estimate a lower bound κ on the size of the underlying planning graph, that is likely to be higher than one. κ can then be used to generate the initial MIP encoding, and this could same a significant amount of time because there is no need to run the MIP solver for determining that the encodings of size less than κ do not admit a feasible solution. An obvious possibility for estimating the value of κ is to construct the planning graph using a Graphplan-style algorithm and set κ to the level (if any) were all goals of the problem are reached and are not mutually exclusive. However, in the experimental results that we present in the next section we have not exploited this possibility (the initial size of the encoding in terms of underlying graph levels is one).

6   Experimental Results

We ran some initial experiments with the new temporal planning approach. The models were generated by hand, using the algebraic modeling system PLAM (Pro-Log and Algebraic Modeling) [2], and solved by CPLEX 7.1 with the following parameters. Dual Simplex was used with steepest-edge pricing, the variable selection strategy was set to pseudo reduced costs, while probing was set to 1 or 2 depending on the domain. In order to gain some insight about the difficulty of the problems, and the quality of the solution that are generated by the new method, the makespan minimization problem were also solved with TP4 and TGP. TP4 and CPLEX were run on a Sun Ultra-250 with 1 GB RAM, and an UltraSparcII 400MHz processor. TGP was run on a Pentium 500MHz machine running under Linux. Table 6 presents some of the experimental results. The bw rows refer to blocks world problems, and the r rows refer to rocket problems. All blocks world problems are instances with 8 blocks and the duration of each action depends on which block is moved and where. The rocket problems involve 4 locations, 2 or 3 planes, and 9 to 11 packages. The duration of a fly-action depends on which airplane is used and on which are the cities connected by the flight; the duration of a load/unload-action depends on which airplane is used by the action. All run times reported are in seconds. A time limit of 7200 seconds was used for all systems.

For TP4 and TGP, the entries t/d/a in the table are respectively the run time (t), plan duration (d) and number of actions (a) of the generated plan. A -/d/- entry indicates that the system was searching for a solution of duration d, when the time limit was reached, and execution was aborted.

The data for the MIP method are presented under the MIP-full column in the t/d/a/l format, with the following meaning. The number in position l is the first planning graph level at which a feasible solution is found. The data t/d/a refer to the optimal solution of the problem that corresponds to graph length l. The duration of this optimal solution is presented in d, and the number of actions in the solution in a. The number in position t is the run time,

Table 1. TP4, TGP and MIP on makespan minimization problems

Problem	TP4 t/d/a	TGP t/d/a	MIP-full t/d/a/l	tt	MIP-reduced tf	tt
bw1	3/11/11	-/10/-	37/11/11/5	817	1563	–
bw2	51/11/14	-/9/-	32/11/12/5	653	2045	–
bw3	423/8/10	1231/8/9	9/8/9/4	276	1412	–
bw4	-/13/-	-/12/-	65/14/13/6	–	–	–
r1	288/14/30	140/14/24	87/14/24/7	2064	218	–
r2	-/14/-	3306/15/28	94/15/28/7	2840	212	–
r3	6252/9/36	5692/9/29	969/10/29/6	–	2540	–
r4	-/9/-	-/9/-	415/11/34/6	–	2530	–

and includes both the time needed for proving the infeasibility of the problems associated with planning graphs of length less than l, as well as finding the optimal solution for the graph of length l. The last column in the table, labeled with tt, presents the overall run time needed for solving the problem on all different levels, up to the level where the solution does not improve further. A dash "–" in this column denotes that CPLEX reached the time limit before completing the search of the last level.

We note that in all problems, except bw4, the best solution that was found by the method, was at the same planning graph level with the first feasible solution. In problem bw4, the first solution was found at level 6. The optimal solution for this level is 14, the graph was expanded, and a better solution with duration 13 was found after 3032 seconds. Regarding the rocket problems, the first MIP solutions for r1 and r2 are optimal solutions, while the first solutions for the other problems are good quality solution but are not the best ones. However, in all cases except the easiest problem the first MIP solutions are computed more efficiently than the optimal solutions of TP4 and TGP (MIP was up to two orders of magnitude faster).

While column MIP-full refers to the fully optimized MIP models, column MIP-reduced presents experimental results with the reduced temporal fluent models that do not incorporate any of the additional improvements described in section 4, such as abstract fluent variables, start time variable splitting and compact duration modeling. The tf entries are the run times for solving the makespan minimization problem for the first level of the planning graph where a feasible solution exists (they do not include the time needed for proving the infeasibility of planning graphs with fewer levels). The tt entries have the same meaning as in MIP-full. Note that the additional improvements lead to substantial speed-up in the computation, especially in the case of the blocks world problems. In this domain, these improvements reduce the number of temporal variables, but also cause a dramatic reduction of the number of constraints. Indeed, it seems that in the blocks world domain, the inefficiency of the reduced model is mainly due to the large number of constraints that make extremely hard the problem of solving the linear relaxation at each node of the branch and bound tree. The basic model contains even more constraints that further degrade the performance of the method, making it impractical for domains such as the blocks world. Therefore, we do not present experimental results for the basic model.

It is important to note that the improvements to the reduced temporal models also lead to tighter MIP formulations. For instance, the solution of the initial relaxation (at the root node of the branch and bound tree) of problem bw1 (r1) with the reduced model is 5.399 (1.898), while the solution of the same problem with the additional improvements is 6.647 (2.535).

Table 5 presents experimental results on planning problems with deadlines and different minimization objectives. The columns under "action min." correspond to planning problems where the number of actions is minimized. The deadline for each of these problems was set to the minimum makespan as it is computed in the experiments that are reported in Table 6. Data are given for the first and the best solution found by MIP, in the t/a/l format. The run time is presented by t, the number of actions in the plan by a, and the planning graph length by l. A dash "—" in the optimal solution column denotes that the first solution that was found was also the best.

It appears that the problem of generating plans with minimum number of actions (even with tight deadlines as those used in our experiments) can be solved more effectively than that of finding plans that minimize makespan. Moreover, as one might expect, with the new objective function, MIP generates plans that contain fewer actions than those generated when minimizing makespan.

The second set of experiments that are reported in Table 5 appear under "action and makespan min.", and corresponds to optimization problems where the objective function is $min(\sum_{a_i^l} a_i^l + 2 \cdot mks)$. This is a simple example of optimization with multiple criteria that can be competing, since makespan minimization may introduce more actions in the generated plans. The particular objective function that has been used in these experiments, assigns slightly higher preference to plan duration minimization through the higher weight of variable mks. A typical example that shows the effects of competing optimization criteria is bw4 in Table 5, where the decrease in plan duration from 14 to 13, comes with an increase in the number of actions from 12 to 13.

As in the previous experiments, a deadline is used for each problem, with the difference that this deadline is now two time units higher[5] than the makespan computed in the makespan minimization experiments. The experimental results are presented in the t/d/a/l format, with the same interpretation as in Table 6. Note that CPLEX performs better on these combined action and makespan optimization problems than on optimizing makespan alone. Therefore, it seems that action minimization provides strong guidance in the search for good solutions.

---

[5] The value 2 that has been selected, seems on the one hand to provide a fairly tight deadline for the generated plans, and on the other hand to allow for further improvement of the makespan of the plans. However, it is only indicative, and other values could have been used.

Table 2. MIP on action minimization and combined action and makespan minimization problems with deadlines

Problem	action min.			action and makespan min.		
	First t/a/l	Best t/a/l	tt	First t/d/a/l	Best t/d/a/l	tt
bw1	15/10/5	—	103	18/11/10/5	—	388
bw2	14/10/5	—	87	18/11/10/5	—	277
bw3	5/8/4	—	25	12/8/8/4	—	222
bw4	310/13/7	740/12/8	1555	31/14/12/6	974/13/13/7	-
r1	35/24/7	—	136	49/14/24/7	—	877
r2	53/28/7	—	215	81/15/28/7	—	1027
r3	138/29/6	1736/27/7	-	375/10/29/6	2475/10/27/7	-
r4	215/32/6	1903/29/7	-	330/11/32/6	—	-

It appears that the new MIP temporal planning method performs well in providing good solutions early in the computation, regardless of the optimization objective that is used. Of course there can be cases, such as problem r3 in Table 6, where the method fails to find the optimal solution within a reasonable time. Nevertheless, in all problems considered, it quickly found high quality solutions.

7   Conclusions and Current Work

We have presented a novel approach to temporal planning that relies on an explicit representation of the temporal constraints present in a planning problem. We have showed how the structure of a domain can be exploited in the MIP formulations, and presented some encouraging preliminary results from an experimental analysis of the new method.

Currently we are extending our experiments to consider several additional domains, and compare our method to other recent planners that may also generate non-optimal solution such as SAPA [4] and LPG [9]. At the same time we are investigating ways of improving our method. One promising direction is to exploit further the interaction between the logical and temporal part of a planning problem by relaxing the former and tightening the latter. Another direction concerns modeling more expressive planning languages capable, for instance, of dealing with level 3 of PDDL 2.1, the language of the AIPS-2002 planning competition [6]. Features of such languages include actions with preconditions/effects involving numerical quantities, resources, and temporal conditions that are required to hold at some point during the execution of an action, at its beginning or at its end. It appears that all such features can be accommodated by a simple extension of our model.

Finally, we are investigating the use of domain knowledge in the form of valid linear inequalities, which in our approach can be easily incorporated into the representation and used by the MIP solver.

References

[1] J. Allen. Temporal reasoning and planning. In J. Allen, H. Kautz, R. Pelavin, and J. Tenenberg, editors, *Reasoning about Plans*, San Mateo, CA, 1991. Morgan Kaufmann.
[2] P. Barth and A. Bockmayr. Modelling discrete optimisation problems in constraint logic programming. *Annals of Operations Research*, 81, 1998.
[3] Y. Dimopoulos. Improved integer programming models and heuristic search for AI planning. In *Proceedings of ECP-01*. Springer Verlag, 2001.
[4] M. B. Do and S. Kambhampati. Sapa: A domain-independent heuristic metric temporal planner. In *Proceedings of ECP-01*. Springer Verlag, 2001.
[5] M. Fox and D. Long. The automatic inference of state invariants in TIM. *JAIR*, 9:367–421, 1998.
[6] M. Fox and D. Long. PDDL2.1: An extension to PDDL for expressing temporal planning domains. Technical report, University of Durham, UK, 2001.
[7] A. Gerevini and L. Schubert. Inferring state constraints for domain-independent planning. In *Proceedings of AAAI-98*, 1998.
[8] A. Gerevini and L. Schubert. Discovering state constraints in DISCOPLAN: Some new results. In *Proceedings of AAAI-00*, 2000.
[9] A. Gerevini and I. Serina. LPG: a planner based on planning graphs with action costs. In *Proceedings of AIPS'02*, 2002.
[10] P. Haslum and H. Geffner. Heuristic planning with time and resources. In *Proceedings of ECP-01*. Springer Verlag, 2001.
[11] H. Kautz and J. Walser. State-space planning by integer optimization. In *Proceedings of AAAI-99*, 1999.
[12] J. Penberthy and D. Weld. Temporal planning with continuous change. In *Proceedings of AAAI-94*, pages 1010–1015, Seattle, WA, 1994. Morgan Kaufmann.
[13] D. Smith and D. Weld. Temporal planning with mutual exclusive reasoning. In *Proceedings of IJCAI-99*, 1999.
[14] E. Tsang. Plan generation in a temporal framework. In *Proceedings of ECAI-96*, pages 479–493, 1986.
[15] T. Vossen, M. Ball, A. Lotem, and D. Nau. On the use of integer programming models in AI planning. In *Proceedings of IJCAI-99*, 1999.
[16] D. Weld. Recent advances in AI planning. *AI Magazine*, 20(2), 1999.
[17] S. Wolfman and D. Weld. The LPSAT engine and its application to resource planning. In *Proceedings of IJCAI-99*, 1999.
[18] L. Wolsey. *Integer Programming*. John Wiley and Sons, 1998.

A New Multi-resource *cumulatives* Constraint with Negative Heights

Nicolas Beldiceanu and Mats Carlsson

SICS
Lägerhyddsvägen 18, SE-75237 Uppsala, Sweden
{nicolas,matsc}@sics.se

Abstract. This paper presents a new *cumulatives* constraint, which generalizes the original *cumulative* constraint in different ways. The two most important aspects consist in permitting multiple cumulative resources as well as negative heights for the resource consumption of the tasks. This allows modeling in an easy way workload covering, producer-consumer, and scheduling problems. The introduction of negative heights has forced us to come up with new filtering algorithms and to revisit existing ones. The first filtering algorithm is derived from an idea called *sweep*, which is extensively used in computational geometry; the second algorithm is based on a combination of *sweep* and *constructive disjunction*; while the last is a generalization of *task intervals* to this new context. A real-life crew scheduling problem originally motivated this constraint which was implemented within the SICStus finite domain solver and evaluated against different problem patterns.

1   Introduction

Within the constraint community, the *cumulative* constraint was originally introduced in [1] in order to model scheduling problems where one has to deal with a single resource of limited capacity. It has the following definition:

$$\text{cumulative}([Origin_1,..,Origin_n],[Duration_1,..,Duration_n],[Height_1,..,Height_n],Limit), \qquad (1)$$

where $[Origin_1,..,Origin_n]$, $[Duration_1,..,Duration_n]$ and $[Height_1,..,Height_n]$ are non-empty lists of non-negative domain variables[1], and *Limit* is a non-negative integer. The *cumulative* constraint holds if the following condition is true:

$$\forall i \in \text{IN} \qquad \sum_{j | Origin_j \le i < Origin_j + Duration_j} Height_j \le Limit . \qquad (2)$$

From an interpretation point of view, the *cumulative* constraint matches the single resource-scheduling problem [14], where $Origin_1,..,Origin_n$ correspond to the start of

---

[1] A domain variable x is a variable that ranges over a finite set of integers. dom(x), min(x), and max(x) denote respectively the set of possible values, smallest possible value, and greatest possible value of x.

P. Van Hentenryck (Ed.): CP 2002, LNCS 2470, pp. 63–79, 2002.

each task, $Duration_1,..,Duration_n$ to the duration of each task, and $Height_1,..,Height_n$ to the amount of resource used by each task. The *cumulative* constraint specifies that, at any instant i, the summation of the amount of resource of the tasks that overlap i, does not exceed *Limit* .

Over the past years the *cumulative* constraint was progressively integrated within most of the current constraints systems [10], [11], [20], and extended by introducing elastic [11] or continuous [16] resource consumption. It was also used with success as an essential component of a large number of real-life applications involving resource constraints. However, feedback resulting from handling industrial problems has pointed out several serious modeling limitations. Perhaps the most serious limitation concerns the fact that quite often we have more that one cumulative resource [2] as well as tasks that are not yet assigned to a cumulative resource. Planning problems [3], [5] also require dealing with tasks for which we don't know the resource in advance. A second major restriction concerns the fact that the amount of resource used by each task is non-negative. By allowing both negative and positive values for the amount of resource used by a task we open the *cumulatives* constraint to producer-consumer problems where a given set of tasks has to cover another set of tasks (i.e. a demand profile). A major modeling advantage comes from the fact that the profile to cover does not necessarily need to be completely fixed in advance which is actually the case for current approaches.

For all the above mentioned reasons, we present a new constraint, called *cumulatives* , which generalizes the original *cumulative* constraint in 4 different ways:

- It allows expressing the fact that we have several cumulative resources and that each task has to be assigned to one of these resources.
- The amount of resource used by each task is a domain variable, which can take positive or negative values.
- One can either enforce the cumulated consumption to be less than or equal, or greater than or equal to a given level.
- On a given resource, the constraint on the cumulated resource consumption holds only for those time-points that are overlapped by at least one task.

The next section introduces the *cumulatives* constraint as well as several typical utilizations. Sect. 3.1 provides a detailed description of the main filtering algorithm while Sect. 3.2 gives the flavor of an algorithm, which combines *sweep* and *constructive disjunction* in order to derive additional pruning. Sect. 3.3 shows how to generalize *task intervals* to this new constraint. Finally the last section presents the first experimental results on a large selection of typical patterns of the *cumulatives* constraint.

2   The *cumulatives* Constraint

The *cumulatives* constraint has the form cumulatives$(Tasks, Resources, Op)$, where:

- *Tasks* is a collection of tasks where each task has a *Machine* , an *Origin* , a *Duration*, a *Height* and an *End* attribute; *Duration* is a non-negative domain variable, while *Machine* , *Origin* , *Height* and *End* are domain variables which may be negative, positive or zero.

-    *Resources* is a collection of resources where each resource has an *Identifier* and a given *Limit* ; the *Identifier* and *Limit* attributes are fixed integers which may be negative, positive or zero; Moreover, the *Identifier* is a unique value for each resource; the *Machine* attribute of a task is a domain variable for which the possible values correspond to values of the *Identifier* attribute.
-    *Op* is the less or equal (i.e. ≤) or the greater or equal (i.e. ≥) relation.

In the rest of this paper, we denote by $|C|$ the number of items of a collection C and $a[i]$ the value of the attribute a of the ith item of collection C. The *cumulatives* constraint holds if the following two conditions are both true:

$$\forall t \in [1, |Tasks|]: Origin[t] + Duration[t] = End[t]. \tag{3}$$

$\forall t \in [1, |Tasks|], \ \forall i \in [Origin[t], End[t]-1]:$

Let m be the unique value such that: $Machine[t] = Identifier[m]$,

$$\sum_{j \begin{cases} Origin[j] \leq i < End[j] \\ Machine[j] = Machine[t] \end{cases}} (Height[j]) \ Op \ Limit[m]. \tag{4}$$

Condition (3) imposes for each task t the fact that its end be equal to the sum of its origin and its duration. When *Op* is ≤ (≥), Condition (4) enforces that, for each instant i that is over-lapped by at least one task t , such that t is assigned to resource m , the sum of the *Height* attribute of all tasks j , that are both assigned on resource m and overlap instant i, be less or equal (respectively greater or equal) than the *Limit* attribute of resource m . When *Op* is ≥ (≤), the *Limit* attribute should be interpreted as the *minimum level* to reach on a given re-source (the *maximum capacity* of a given resource).

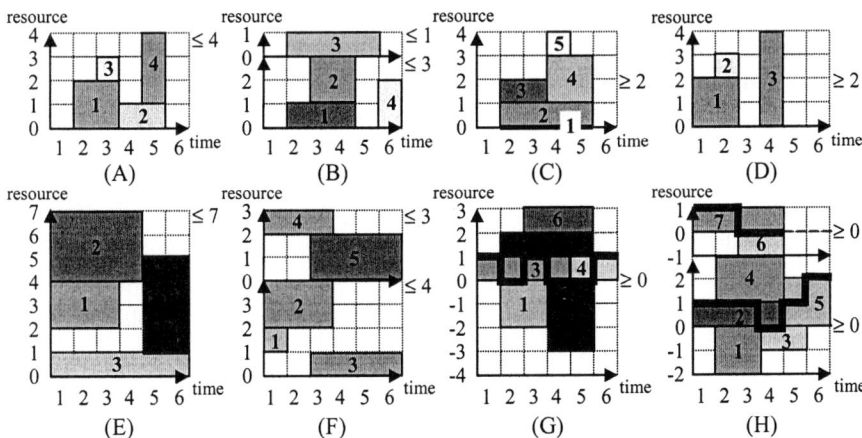

Fig. 1. Typical uses of the *cumulatives* constraint

Fig. 1 gives 8 ground instances, corresponding to solutions, of *cumulatives* , all re-lated to a typical utilization of the constraint. Bear in mind that all the attributes of a task may not be fixed when the constraint is posted. Each resource is represented as a drawing where the horizontal and the vertical axes respectively correspond to the time and to the amount of used resource. A task is represented as a rectangle for which the length and the height respectively match the duration and the absolute value of the amount of resource used by the task. The position of the leftmost part of a rectangle on the time axis is the start of the task. Tasks with positive or negative heights are respectively drawn on top or below the time axis, so that we can look both to the cumulated resource consumption of the tasks with a positive height and to the cumulated consumption of the tasks with a negative height. Finally, the *Op* parameter and the *Limit* attribute are mentioned to the right of each resource.

- Part (A) is the classical original *cumulative* constraint described in [1]. In the *Resources* parameter we have introduced one single resource, which has value 1 as identifier and 4 as its maximum capacity.
- Part (B) is an extension of the original *cumulative* constraint where we have more than one single resource.
- Part (C) is the *at least* variant of the *cumulative* constraint available in CHIP. This variant enforces to reach a minimum level between the earliest start of any task and the latest end of any task using the resource. In order to express this condition, we create a dummy task of height 0 (represented by the thick line between instants 2 and 5) for which the start and the end respectively correspond to the earliest start and to the latest end of the different tasks to schedule. For this purpose, we respectively use a *minimum* and a *maximum* constraint [6]. The $minimum(M,\{X_1,...,X_n\})$ $(maximum(M,\{X_1,...,X_n\}))$ constraint holds if M is the minimum (maximum) value of variables $X_1,...,X_n$.
- Part (D) is a new variant of the previous case where the „at least" constraint applies only for the instants that are overlapped by at least one task.
- Part (E) is a producer-consumer problem [18] where tasks 1,2 represent producers, while tasks 3,4 are consumers. On one side, a producer task starts at the earliest start and produces a quantity equal to its height at a date that corresponds to its end. On the other side, a consumer task ends at the latest end and consumes a quantity equal to its height at a date that matches its start. The resource can be interpreted as a tank in which one adds or removes at specific points in time various quantities. The *cumulatives* constraint enforces that, at each instant, one does not consume more than what is currently available in the tank.
- Part (F) is a generalization of the previous producer-consumer problem where we have two tanks. As for the previous example, the *cumulatives* constraint enforces no negative stocks on both tanks.
- Part (G) describes a covering problem where one has to cover a given workload by a set of tasks. The workload can be interpreted as the number of persons required during specific time intervals, while a task can be interpreted as the work performed by a group of persons. The height of the initially fixed tasks (i.e. tasks 1 and 2) that represent the workload is modelled with negative numbers, while the height of the tasks related to the persons (i.e. tasks 3,4,5,6) is positive. The covering constraint is imposed by the fact that, at each point in time, the *cumulatives* constraint enforces the cumulated height, of the tasks that

overlap this point, to be greater than or equal to 0: at each point in time the number of available persons should be greater than or equal to the required demand expressed by the work-load to cover. A thick line indicates the cumulated profile resulting from the negative and positive heights.

- Finally, part (H) generalizes (G) by introducing 2 distinct workloads to cover.

3   Filtering Algorithms

The purpose of this section is to introduce three algorithms used for implementing the *cumulatives* constraint. The first algorithm, based on the idea of *sweep*, is required for checking the constraint and for doing some basic pruning. It is based on a necessary condition, which is also sufficient when all the attributes of the different tasks are fixed. The second algorithm performs additional pruning by using *constructive disjunction* [12], [19]. The third algorithm generalizes *task intervals* [4], [11], [13] to the case where negative resource consumption (i.e. production of resource) is also allowed. Since the „at least" and „at most" sides of the *cumulatives* constraint are symmetric, we only focus on the „at least" side where the constraint enforces for each resource to reach a given minimum level. To get the algorithm for the „at most" side, one has to replace in the forthcoming algorithms „max($Height[t]$)" by „min($Height[t]$)", „max($Height[t]$)<" by „min($Height[t]$)>", „<$Limit[r]$" by „>$Limit[r]$", „$\geq Limit[r]$" by „$\leq Limit[r]$", „ADJUSTMINVAR($Height[t]$)" by „ADJUSTMAXVAR($Height[t]$)" and „max($0,Limit[r]$)" by „min($0,Limit[r]$)".

Before going further into the presentation of the algorithms, let us first introduce some notions, which will be used in the different algorithms. A task t of origin $Origin[t]$ and end $End[t]$ has a *compulsory part*[2] [15] if its latest start max($Origin[t]$) is strictly less than it earliest end min($End[t]$). For such a task, we call *support of the compulsory part* the interval $[\max(Origin[t]), \min(End[t])-1]$.

Within the different algorithms, this set of functions access domain variables:

- ISINT(*var*) returns 1 if the variable *var* is fixed, and 0 otherwise.
- FIXVAR(*var, val*) fixes variable *var* to value *val* .
- REMOVEVALUEVAR(*var, val*) removes value *val* from the domain variable *var* .
- ADJUSTMINVAR(*var, val*) and ADJUSTMAXVAR(*var, val*) respectively adjust the minimum and maximum value of a given domain variable *var* to value *val* .
- PRUNEINTERVALVAR(*var, low, up*) removes the interval of values $[low, up]$ from a given domain variable *var* .

These functions return fail if a contradiction was found (i.e. the domain of the pruned variable *var* becomes empty), or return delay otherwise.

---

[2] When *Op* is $\geq$ ($\leq$), the *compulsory part* of a task t is the maximum (minimum) resource consumption of that task together with the interval [max(Origin[t]),min(End[t])−1].

3.1   The *Sweep* Algorithm

The *sweep* algorithm is based on an idea that is widely used in computational geometry and that is called sweep [8, page 22], [17, pages 10-11]. Within constraint programming, *sweep* has also been used in [7] for implementing different variants of the non-overlapping constraint.

In dimension 2, a plane *sweep* algorithm solves a problem by moving a vertical line from left to right. The algorithm uses two data structures:

- A data structure called the *sweep-line status*, which contains some information related to the current position Δ of the vertical line,
- A data structure named the *event point series*, which holds the events to process, ordered in increasing order according to the abscissa.

The algorithm initializes the sweep-line status for the starting position of the vertical line. Then the line „jumps" from event to event; each event is handled and inserted or removed from the sweep-line status. In our context, the sweep-line scans the time axis on a given resource r in order to build an optimistic[3] cumulated profile (i.e. the sweep-line status) for that resource r and to perform check and pruning according to this profile and to the limit attribute of resource r. This process is repeated for each resource present in the second argument of the *cumulatives* constraint. Before going further into any detail, let us first give the intuition of the *sweep* algorithm on the simple case where all tasks are fixed.

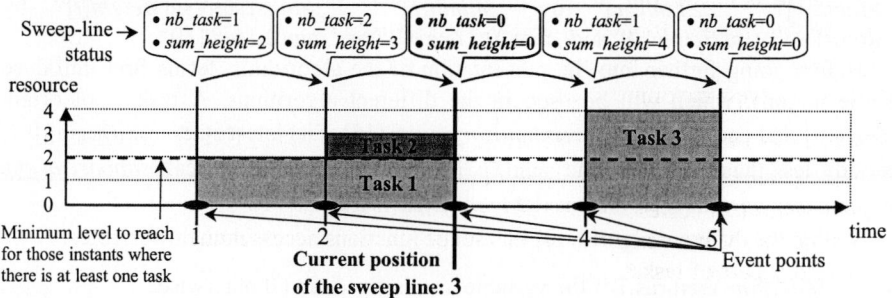

Fig. 2. Illustrative example of the *sweep* algorithm when all tasks are fixed

Consider the illustrative example given in Fig. 2, which is associated to instance (D) of Fig. 1. Since all the tasks of that instance are fixed, we want to check that, for each time point i where there is at least one task, the cumulated height of the tasks that overlap i is greater than or equal to 2. The sweep-line status records the following counters *sum_height* and *nb_task*, which are initially set to 0; *sum_height* is the sum of the height of the tasks that overlap the current position Δ of the sweep-line, while *nb_task* is the number of such tasks.

Since we don't want to check every time-point, the event points correspond only to the start and to the end of each task:

---

[3] Since the constraint enforces to reach a given minimum level, we assume that hopefully, each task will take its maximum height.

- For the start of each task t, we generate a start-event, which will respectively increment by $Height\lfloor t \rfloor$ and 1 the counters sum_height and nb_task.
- For the end of each task t, we generate an end-event, which will respectively decrement by $Height\lfloor t \rfloor$ and 1 sum_height and nb_task.

We initially generate all these events, sort them in increasing order and finally handle them as explained before. Each time we finish to handle all the events associated to a given date, and only when nb_task is strictly greater than 0, we check that sum_height is greater than or equal to the required minimum level.

The next paragraph introduces the sweep-line status and the event points we consider when the tasks are not yet fixed, while Sect. 3.1.2 explains how to prune the attributes of the tasks according to the sweep-line status.

3.1.1 Checking for Failure

Given that we want to catch situations where, for sure there is no solution to the *cumulatives* constraint, the *sweep* algorithm assumes that each task will take its maximum height[4] in order to facilitate to reach the required minimum level. For a given resource r, let us first introduce the following sets that will be used later on:

- $CHECK_r$ is the set of tasks that simultaneously have a compulsory part, are assigned to r, and have a maximum height that is strictly less than $\max(0, Limit\lfloor r \rfloor)$.
- BAD_r is the set of tasks that have a compulsory part, are assigned to resource r, and have a strictly negative maximum height.
- $GOOD_r$ is the set of tasks that may be, or are actually, assigned to resource r and have a maximum height that is strictly greater than 0.

Time-Points to Check Since the *cumulatives* constraint considers only those instants where there is at least one task, the *sweep* algorithm has to perform a check only for those instants that correspond to the support of the compulsory part of a task assigned to resource r. Moreover, no check is required for those instants where we only have a compulsory part of tasks for which the maximum height is greater than or equal to $\max(0, Limit\lfloor r \rfloor)$. This is because the cumulated maximum height of such tasks will always be greater than or equal to the minimum required level $Limit\lfloor r \rfloor$. A first counter called nb_task_r is associated to the sweep-line status of resource r. It gives the number of tasks of the set $CHECK_r$ for which the compulsory part intersects the current value of Δ.

Building the Optimistic Profile For a given resource r, the optimistic cumulated profile is obtained by considering two kinds of contributions:

- The contributions of the tasks that belong to the set BAD_r; since their maximum height is strictly negative, the contribution of these tasks in the cumulated profile is bad from the point of view of the minimum level to reach. This is why

---

[4] Remember that we present the „at least" side where, for each resource, the *cumulatives* constraint enforces to reach a given minimum level.

we count such contribution only for those instants where it occurs for sure, that is for the support of the compulsory part of such tasks.

- The contributions of the tasks that belong to $GOOD_r$; since it is strictly positive, the contributions in height of these tasks in the cumulated profile can help to reach the required minimum level. This is why it is counted for all instants where such a task can be placed, that is between its earliest start and its latest end.

The sum of these contributions is recorded in a second counter, denoted sum_height_r, which is also associated to the status of the sweep-line corresponding to resource r. It gives for the current position of the sweep-line, the sum of the maximum height of the tasks t that satisfy one of the following conditions:

- Task t belongs to BAD_r and $\max(Origin[t]) \le \Delta < \min(End[t])$,
- Task t belongs to $GOOD_r$ and $\min(Origin[t]) \le \Delta < \max(End[t])$.

Recording the Tasks to Prune In order to prepare the pruning phase, we store the tasks that can intersect in time the current value of Δ. For this purpose, the sweep-line status contains an additional counter top_prune_r and stack $stack\_prune_r[1..top\_prune_r]$ which records these tasks. A LIFO stack discipline is not critical; we could just as well have chosen a FIFO queue.

Table 1. Summary of the different types of events. There is no event for removing the tasks that can't be pruned any more (i.e. the tasks that can't intersect the current position of the sweep-line); this is achieved by the pruning procedure itself by compacting the stack $stack\_prune_r$

Conditions for Generating an Event	Generated Events
$\max(Origin[t]) < \min(End[t])$ **and** $\max(Height[t]) < \max(0, Limit[r])$ **and** $\min(Machine[t]) = \max(Machine[t]) = r$	$\langle$**check**, t, $\max(Origin[t])$, $1\rangle$ $\langle$**check**, t, $\min(End[t])$, $-1\rangle$
$\max(Origin[t]) < \min(End[t])$ **and** $\min(Machine[t]) = \max(Machine[t]) = r$ **and** $\max(Height[t]) < 0$	$\langle$**profile**, t, $\max(Origin[t])$, $\max(Height[t])\rangle$ $\langle$**profile**, t, $\min(End[t])$, $-\max(Height[t])\rangle$
$r \in Machine[t]$ **and** $\max(Height[t]) > 0$	$\langle$**profile**, t, $\min(Origin[t])$, $\max(Height[t])\rangle$ $\langle$**profile**, t, $\max(End[t])$, $-\max(Height[t])\rangle$
$r \in Machine[t]$ **and** $\neg(ISINT(Origin[t])$ **and** $ISINT(End[t])$ **and** $\qquad\qquad ISINT(Machine[t])$ **and** $ISINT(Height[t]))$	$\langle$**pruning**, t, $\min(Origin[t])$, $0\rangle$

Updating the Sweep-Line Status Table 1 depicts the events that update the different constituents of the sweep-line status introduced so far. We respectively call *check*, *profile* or *pruning* event, an event modifying nb_task_r, sum_height_r or $stack\_prune_r[1..top\_prune_r]$. We choose to encode these events by using the following fields $\langle type, task, date, increment \rangle$, where:

- *type* tells whether we have a *check*, a *profile* or a *pruning* event; in case of a *pruning* event the content of the slot *increment* is irrelevant,
- *task* indicates the task that generates the event,
- *date* specifies the time of the event,
- *increment* gives the quantity to add to nb_task_r or to sum_height_r.

The *Sweep* Algorithm The events are initially generated and sorted in increasing order of their respective date. For each date, Algorithm 1 (lines 9, 10) processes all the corresponding events; in addition when nb_task_r is different from 0 it checks that the height sum_height_r of the optimistic cumulated profile is greater than or equal to the minimum level of resource r (lines 7, 12).

1	Set nb_task_r, sum_height_r and top_prune_r to 0.
2	Extract the next event $\&\langle type,task,date,increment\rangle$.[5]
3	Set d to *date*.
4	**while** $\langle type,task,date,increment\rangle \neq$NULL **do**
5	**if** *type*≠*pruning* **then**
6	**if** $d\neq date$ **then**
7	**if** nb_task_r>0 **and** sum_height_r<$Limit[r]$ **then fail**.
8	Set d to *date*.
9	**if** *type*=*check* **then** Add *increment* to nb_task_r **else** Add *increment* to sum_height_r
10	**else** Set top_prune_r to top_prune_r+1 and set $stack\_prune_r[top\_prune_r]$ to *task*.
11	Extract the next event $\&\langle type,task,date,increment\rangle$.
12	**if** nb_task_r>0 **and** sum_height_r<$Limit[r]$ **then fail**.

Alg. 1. Main loop of the *sweep* algorithm on a resource r

1	**if** nb_task_r≠0 **and** sum_height_r−$contribution[t]$ < $Limit[r]$ **then**.
2	**if** FIXVAR($Machine[t]$, r)=fail
3	**or** ADJUSTMINVAR($Origin[t]$, up−max($Duration[t]$)+1)=fail
4	**or** ADJUSTMAXVAR($Origin[t]$, low)=fail
5	**or** ADJUSTMAXVAR($End[t]$, low+ max($Duration[t]$))=fail
6	**or** ADJUSTMINVAR($End[t]$, up+1)=fail
7	**or** ADJUSTMINVAR($Duration[t]$, min(up−max($Origin[t]$)+1, min($End[t]$)−low))=fail **then fail**.

Alg. 2. Pruning the attributes of task t in order to enforce to cover an interval $[low,up]$ *contribution[t]* stands for the saved maximum height of task t that was added to sum_height_r

---

[5] We assume that we get a pointer to an event.

3.1.2   Pruning the Attributes of a Task

Let *low* denote the current value of Δ and let *up* denote the next value of Δ-1. For each value of Δ related to resource r we perform three kinds of pruning[6] of the attributes of the tasks that can both be assigned to resource r and overlap the interval [*low*,*up*]:

-   A first pruning is tried out for tasks with a maximum height greater than 0 (Algorithm 2). It consist in pruning the *Machine*, *Origin*, *End* and *Duration* attributes of those tasks that are absolutely required (line 1) in order to reach a given minimum level $Limit\lfloor r \rfloor$ on interval [*low*,*up*]. More precisely we fix the *Machine* attribute to resource r (line 2), and prune the minimum and maximum values of the *Origin* and *End* attributes (lines 3-6) in order to remove values for which there is no way to cover all instants of interval [*low*,*up*]. We also adjust the minimum duration (line 7) for a similar reason.
-   A second pruning is undertaken for tasks with a maximum height strictly less than $\max(0, Limit\lfloor r \rfloor)$ (Algorithm 3). It consists in pruning the *Machine*, *Origin*, *End* and *Duration* attributes of those tasks that would prevent to reach the minimum required level (line 1) on interval [*low*,*up*] if they would simultaneously overlap that interval and utilize resource r. For such tasks we first forbid to assign them on resource r if they overlap for sure interval [*low*,*up*] (lines 2-3). Conversely, if they are assigned to r we prune the *Origin*, *End* and *Duration* attributes in order to prevent any overlap with interval [*low*,*up*] (lines 4-9).
-   Finally, a third pruning (Algorithm 4) is performed for all tasks that are assigned to resource r (line 1) and that overlap for sure interval [*low*,*up*] (line 2). It consists in removing from the *Height* attribute those values which would prevent to reach the minimum required level on interval [*low*,*up*] (line 3).

1	**if** *sum_height$_r$–contribution*[*t*]+ max(*Height*[*t*]) < *Limit*[*r*] **then**
2	**if** min(*End*[*t*])>low **and** max(*Origin*[*t*])≤ *up* **and** min(*Duration*[*t*])>0 **then**
3	**if** REMOVEVALUEVAR(*Machine*[*t*], *r*)=fail **then fail**.
4	**else if** ISINT(*Machine*[*t*])[7] **then**
5	**if** min(*Duration*[*t*])>0 **then**
6	**if** PRUNEINTERVALVAR(*Origin*[*t*], *low*–min(*Duration*[*t*])+1, *up*)=fail
7	**or** PRUNEINTERVALVAR(*End*[*t*], *low*+1, *up*+min(*Duration*[*t*]))=fail **then fail**.
8	Set *maxd* to max(*low*–min(*Origin*[*t*]), max(*End*[*t*])–*up*–1, 0).
9	**if** ADJUSTMAXVAR(*Duration*[*t*]), *maxd*)=fail **then fail**.

Alg. 3. Pruning the attributes of task *t* in order to forbid to intersect an interval [*low*,*up*]

---

[6] These three types of pruning are inserted just after line 7 and line 12 of Algorithm 1.

[7] Since by hypothesis we only try to prune tasks that can be assigned to resource r, the test ISINT(*Machine*[*t*]) means that task *t* is actually assigned to resource r.

1   **if**   ISINT(*Machine*[*t*])
2   **and** min(*End*[*t*])>*low* **and** max(*Origin*[*t*])<*up* **and** min(*Duration*[*t*])>0 **then**
3   **if** ADJUSTMINVAR(*Height*[*t*], *Limit*[*r*]−(*sum_height_r*−*contribution*[*t*]))=fail
then return fail.

Alg. 4. Pruning the minimum resource consumption of task *t* according to interval [*low,up*]

Complexity of the *Sweep* Algorithm   Let m be the number of resources, n the total number of tasks and p the number of tasks for which at least one attribute is not fixed. First note that updating the sweep-line status and performing the pruning actions (Algorithms 2, 3 and 4)[8] is done in $O(1)$. Second, given that a task can generate at most 7 events (see Table 1), the total number of events is proportional to the number of tasks n. Since we first sort all these events and scan through them in order to update the sweep-line status, the complexity of the check procedure on a resource is $O(n \cdot \log n)$. As the total number of calls to the pruning algorithms is less than or equal to the total number of events and since during a pruning step we consider at most p tasks, the complexity of the pruning on a resource is $O(n \cdot p)$. As we have m resources, the overall complexity of the *sweep* algorithm is $O(m \cdot n \cdot \log n + m \cdot n \cdot p)$.

3.2   Using Constructive Disjunction within the Sweep Algorithm

A second algorithm based on *constructive disjunction* [12], [19] and on some of the propagation rules (lines 5-9 of Algorithm 3 and lines 2-3 of Algorithm 4) of the previous pruning algorithms was implemented. For a not yet assigned task, it consists first in making the hypothesis that it is assigned on its possible resources and in performing the mentioned pruning rules. In a second phase we remove those values that were rejected under every hypothesis.

3.3   Adapting Task Intervals

The main difficulty for adapting the task intervals method [11] of the *cumulative* constraint comes from the fact that now the constraint on the cumulated consumption holds only for those time-points that are overlapped by at least one task. We restrict ourselves to the essential point of the method, namely the description of a necessary condition on an interval [*low,up*] and a set of machines M for the feasibility of the new *cumulatives* constraint. For this purpose we introduce several quantities. The *minimum possible intersection* and *maximum possible intersection* in time of a task *t* with   an   interval   [*low,up*] ,   respectively   denoted $min\_inter(low,up,t)$ and $max\_inter(low,up,t))$, are respectively given by expression **(5)** and Algorithm 5.

$$\max(0, \min(Duration[t], up - low + 1, \min(End[t]) - low, up - \max(Origin[t]) + 1)) \quad (5)$$

---

[8] We assume that all operations on domain variables are performed in $O(1)$.

1	**if** $\max(Origin[t])<low-\max(Duration[t])+1$ **or** $\min(Origin[t])>up$
	or $\max(Duration[t])=0$ **then return** 0.
2	**if** $up-low+1>\max(Duration[t])$ **then** Set *maxinter* to $\max(Duration[t])$ and
	start_maxinter to *low*.
3	**else** Set *maxinter* to $up-low+1$ and *start_maxinter* to $up-\max(Duration[t])+1$.
4	**if** $\max(Origin[t])<start\_maxinter$
	then return $maxinter-(start\_maxinter-\max(Origin[t]))$.
5	Set *end_maxinter* to $up-maxinter+1$.
6	**if** $\min(Origin[t])>end\_maxinter$
	then return $maxinter-(\min(Origin[t])-end\_maxinter)$ **else return** *maxinter*.

Alg. 5. Computing the maximum possible intersection of a task t with an interval $[low,up]$

The *contribution* of a task t on an interval $[low,up]$ and on a set of machines M, denoted *contribution*(low,up,t,M), is:

- if $\max(Height[t])<0$ and $\mathrm{dom}(Machine[t])\subseteq M$ then
  $min\_inter(low,up,t)\cdot\max(Height[t])$; if the contribution of t on $[low,up]$ is for sure harmful for reaching a minimum level then we take its smallest possible value.
- if $\max(Height[t])\geq 0$ and $\mathrm{dom}(Machine[t])\cap M\neq\varnothing$ then
  $max\_inter(low,up,t)\cdot\max(Height[t])$; if the contribution of t on $[low,up]$ may be helpful for reaching a minimum level then we take its largest possible value.
- otherwise 0.

The *minimum use in time* of an interval $[low,up]$ according to a given machine m, denoted $min\_use(low,up,m)$, is equal to the cardinality of the set:

$$\bigcup_{t:\{m\}=\mathrm{dom}(Machine[t])\wedge min\_inter(low,up,t)>0}([\max(Origin[t]),\min(End[t])-1]\cap[low,up])$$

Similarly, the *maximum use in time* of an interval $[low,up]$ according to a given machine m, denoted $max\_use(low,up,m)$, is equal to the cardinality of the set:

$$\bigcup_{t:m\in\mathrm{dom}(Machine[t])\wedge max\_inter(low,up,t)>0}([\min(Origin[t]),\max(End[t])-1]\cap[low,up])$$

The *minimum use in time* is the size of the union of the support of the compulsory parts which intersect interval $[low,up]$, while the *maximum use in time* is the number of instants of interval $[low,up]$ which may be intersected by at least one task. The *slack* of a machine m according to an interval $[low,up]$, denoted $slack(low,up,m)$ is:

- if $Limit[m]\geq 0$ then $slack(low,up,m)=min\_use(low,up,m)\cdot Limit[m]$; *slack* is the minimum surface to fill on interval $[low,up]$.
- if $Limit[m]<0$ then $slack(low,up,m)=max\_use(low,up,m)\cdot Limit[m]$; $-slack$ is the maximum available surface on interval $[low,up]$.

Theorem 1. Let T be the set of tasks present in *cumulatives* , M a subset of machines, and [*low,up*] an interval. In order to fulfill the *cumulatives* constraint, the following condition must hold: $\sum_{t \in T} contribution(low, up, t, M) \geq \sum_{m \in M} slack(low, up, m)$.

Finally, after checking this necessary condition on an interval [*low,up*], we try to
prune the different attributes of the tasks, which can intersect [*low,up*], in order to
avoid this necessary condition to be false. This leads to force (forbid) some task to use
more (less) than a given amount of resource within [*low,up*] .

4   Experimental Results

Benchmark Description As it was already shown in Sect. 2, the *cumulatives* constraint can model a large number of situations. Rather than focusing on a specific
problem type, we tried to get some insight of the practical behavior of the sweep
algorithm[9] on a large spectrum of problem patterns. For this purpose we generated
576 different problems patterns by combining the possible ways to generate a problem instance as shown by Table 2.

For each problem pattern we generated 20 random instances with a fixed density
for the resource consumption and computed the median time for running a limited
discrepancy search of order 1 for 50, 100, 150 and 200 tasks. Benchmarks were run
on a 266 MHz Pentium II processor under Linux with a version of SICStus Prolog
compiled with gcc version 2.95.2 (-O2). Our experiments were performed by fixing
the tasks according to their initial ordering; within a task, we successively fixed the
resource consumption, the machine, the origin and the duration attributes.

Analysis Parts (A) and (B) of Fig. 4 report on the best, median and worst patterns
when most of the tasks are not fixed as well as when most of the tasks are fixed. A
problem pattern is denoted by a tuple ⟨*Origin, Duration, Resource, Machine*⟩ where each
position indicates the way to generate the corresponding characteristic. For instance
part (A) tells us that, when all tasks are nearly free, the combination „random earliest
start", „variable small or large duration", „positive or negative resource consumption"
and „full set of machines" is the most time-consuming one.

Finally parts (C) to (F) show for each way to generate a task attribute the total median time over all problem patterns that effectively use this given method divided by
the number of problem patterns. For example, (D) gives the following ordering (in
increasing time) for the different way to generate the duration attribute: „fixed small
duration", „variable small duration", „fixed small or large duration", „variable small
or large duration".

---

[9] For space limitation reasons, we only benchmark the first algorithm.

Table 2. Generation of the characteristics of a problem pattern (assuming ≤ constraint). min and max stand for the minimum and maximum values of the domain variable for which we generate the initial domain; random(*low,up*) stands for a random number r such that *low≤r≤up*

Characteristic	Ways to Generate the Different Characteristic of a Problem Pattern

Origin	1 **(full origin):** min=1, max=horizon.
	2 **(random earliest start):**
	    min=random(1,0.9×horizon) max=horizon.
	3 **(fixed origin):** min=max=random(1,0.9×horizon).
	    horizon = $h_1 \cdot h_2$ (average minimum duration)
	    h_1 = 50 if one machine, 5 otherwise h_2 = 0.5 if exist tasks with negative height, 1 otherwise

Duration	1 **(fixed small duration):** min=max=random(0,10). 2 **(fixed small or large duration):** min=max=random(0,200). 3 **(variable small duration):** min=random(0,10), max=min+random(0,5) 4 **(variable small or large duration):** min=random(0,100), max=min+random(0,100)
Resource consumption	1 **(fixed consumption):** min=max=random(0,10). 2 **(variable consumption):** min=random(0,7), max=min+random(0,5) 3 **(variable positive or negative consumption):** min=random(-10,0), max=min+random(0,10)
Machine	1 **(single machine):** min=max=1 2 **(full set of machines):** min=1, max=10 3 **(subset of machines):** min=random(1,10), max=min+random(0,10) 4 **(fixed machine with several machines):** min=max=random(1,10)
Task	1 **(nearly fixed):** at most 5 tasks are not completely fixed 2 **(nearly free):** nearly all tasks are not fixed

5   Conclusion

A first contribution of this paper is the introduction and definition of the *cumulatives* constraint, which for the first time completely unifies the „at most" and „at least" sides of the constraint. Surprisingly, different variants of the „at least" side of the *cumulative* constraint were introduced in different constraint systems but, to our best knowledge, nothing was published on this topic, and one may assume that distinct algorithms were used for the „at least" and the „at most" sides. In contrast, our approach allows the use of a single algorithm for both sides. Moreover, this algorithm assumes neither the duration nor the resource consumption to be fixed, and provides pruning for all the different types of attributes of a task. A second major contribution from the modeling point of view, which was never considered before, neither in the constraint nor in the operation research community [9], [14], is the introduction of negative heights for the quantity of resource used by the tasks. This opens the *cumulatives* constraint to new producer consumer problems [18] or to new problems where a set of tasks has to cover several given profiles, which may not be completely fixed initially.

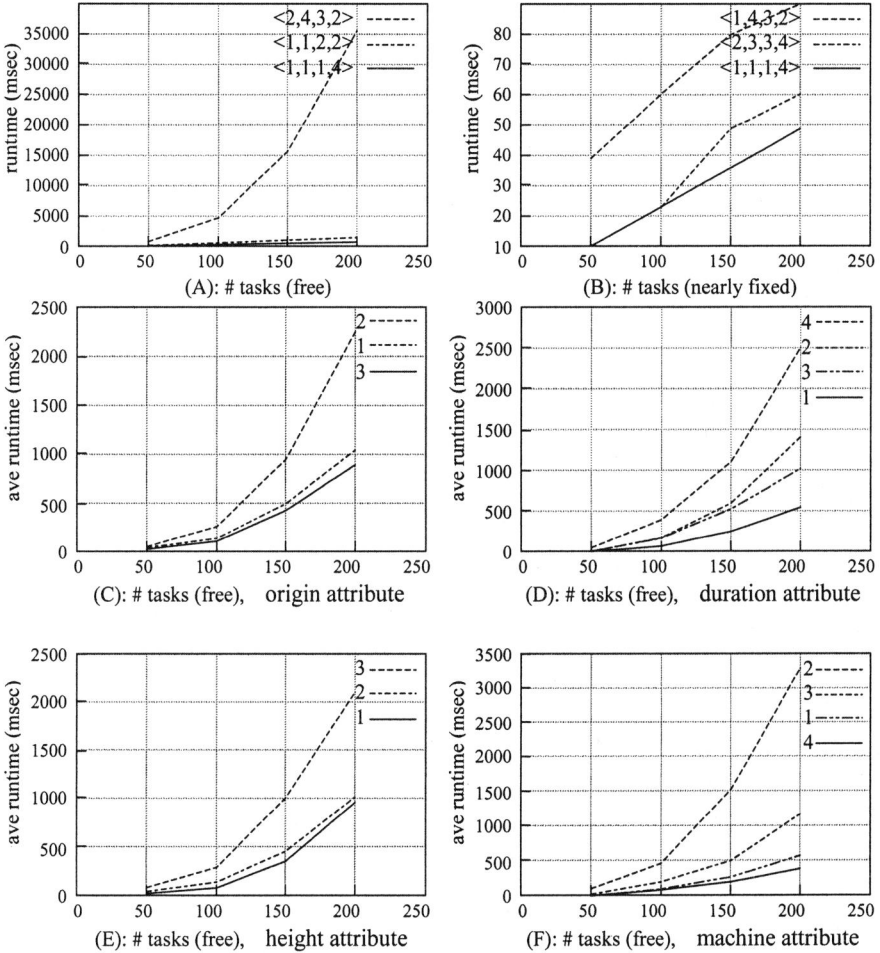

Fig. 4. Performance evaluation of the sweep algorithm (each legend is ordered by decreasing runtime)

References

1. Aggoun, A., Beldiceanu, N.: Extending CHIP to solve Complex Scheduling and Packing Problems. Mathl. Comput. Modelling, 17(7), pages 57-73, (1993).
2. Artigues, C., Roubellat, F.: A polynomial activity insertion algorithm in a multi-resource schedule with cumulative constraints and multiple modes. In *European Journal of Operational Research (EJOR)*, 127, pages 297-316, (2000).

3.   Barták, R.: Dynamic Constraint Models for Planning and Scheduling Problems. In *New Trends in Constraints* (Papers from the Joint ERCIM/Compulog-Net Workshop, Cyprus, October 25-27, 1999), LNAI 1865, Springer Verlag, (2000).
4.   Baptiste, P., Le Pape, C., Nuijten, W.: *Constraint-based Scheduling*. Kluwer Academic Publishers, International Series in Operations Research & Management Science, (2001).
5.   Beck, J. C., Fox, M. S.: Constraint-directed techniques for scheduling alternative activities. In *Artificial Intelligence 121*, pages 211-250, (2000).
6.   Beldiceanu, N.: Pruning for the minimum Constraint Family and for the number of distinct values Constraint Family. In *Proc. of the 7th CP*, 211-224, Paphos, (2001).
7.   Beldiceanu, N., Carlsson, M.: Sweep as a Generic Pruning Technique Applied to the Non-Overlapping Rectangles Constraint. In *Proc. of the 7th CP*, 377-391, Paphos, (2001).
8.   de Berg, M., van Kreveld, M., Overmars, M., Schwarzkopf, O.: *Computational Geometry – Algorithms and Applications*. Springer, (1997).
9.   Brucker, P., Drexl, A., Möhring, R., Neumann, K., Pesch, E.: Resource-constrained project scheduling: Notation, classification, models and methods, in *EJOR 112*, pages 3-41, (1999).
10.   Carlsson, M., Ottosson G., Carlson, B.: An Open-Ended Finite Domain Constraint Solver. *Proc. Programming Languages: Implementations, Logics, and Programs*, vol. 1292 of Lecture Notes in Computer Science, pages 191-206, Springer-Verlag, (1997).
11.   Caseau, Y., Laburthe, F.: Cumulative Scheduling with Task Intervals. In *Proceedings of the Joint International Conference and Symposium on Logic Programming*, MIT Press, (1996).
12.   De Backer, B., Beringer, A.: A CLP Language Handling Disjunctions of Linear Constraints. In *Proc. 10th International Conference on Logic Programming*, pages 550-563, (1993).
13.   Erschler, J., Lopez, P.: Energy-based approach for task scheduling under time and resources constraints. In *2nd International Workshop on Project Management and Scheduling*, pages 115-121, Compiègne (France), June 20-22, (1990).
14.   Herroelen, W., Demeulemeester, E., De Reyck, B.: A Classification Scheme for Project Scheduling Problems. in: Weglarz J. (Ed.), *Handbook on Recent advances in Project Scheduling*, Kluwer Academic Publishers, (1998).
15.   Lahrichi, A.: Scheduling: the Notions of Hump, Compulsory Parts and their Use in Cumulative Problems. in: C. R. Acad. Sc. Paris, t. 294, pages 209-211, (1982).
16.   Poder, E., Beldiceanu, N., Sanlaville, E.: Computing the Compulsory Part of a Task with Varying Duration and Varying Resource Consumption. Submitted to *European Journal of Operational Research (EJOR)*, (February 2001).
17.   Preparata, F. P., Shamos, M. I.: *Computational geometry. An introduction.* Springer-Verlag, (1985).
18.   Simonis, H., Cornelissens, T.: Modelling Producer/Consumer Constraints. In *Proc. of the 1st CP*, 449-462, Cassis, (1995).

19. Van Hentenryck, P., Saraswat, V., Deville, Y.: Design, Implementation and Evaluation of the Constraint Language cc(*FD*). In *A. Podelski, ed., Constraints: Basics and Trends*, vol. 910 of Lecture Notes in Computer Science, Springer-Verlag, (1995).
20. Würtz, J.: Oz Scheduler: A Workbench for Scheduling Problems. In *Proceedings of the 8th IEEE International Conference on Tools with Artificial Intelligence*, Nov16--19 1996, IEEE Computer Society Press, (1996).

On the Sum Constraint:
Relaxation and Applications

Tallys H. Yunes*

Graduate School of Industrial Administration
Carnegie Mellon University, Pittsburgh, PA 15213-3890, USA
tallys@cmu.edu

Abstract. The global constraint *sum* can be used as a tool to implement summations over sets of variables whose indices are not known in advance. This paper has two major contributions. On the theoretical side, we present the convex hull relaxation for the sum constraint in terms of linear inequalities, whose importance in the context of hybrid models is then justified. On the practical side, we demonstrate the applicability of the sum constraint in a scheduling problem that arises as part of the development of new products in the pharmaceutical and agrochemical industries. This problem can be modeled in two alternative ways: by using the sum constraint in a natural and straightforward manner, or by using the element constraint in a trickier fashion. With the convex hull relaxation developed earlier, we prove that the linear relaxation obtained from the former model is tighter than the one obtained from the latter. Moreover, our computational experiments indicate that the CP model based on the sum constraint is significantly more efficient as well.

1   Introduction

The global constraint *sum* can be used as a tool to implement summations over sets of variables whose indices are not known in advance. These are referred to as *variable index sets*. When studying a scheduling problem in the context of the development of new products in the agrochemical and pharmaceutical industries, we were faced with a subproblem where the sum constraint appears as a natural modeling candidate. We baptize this problem as the *Sequence Dependent Cumulative Cost Problem* (SDCCP), and we describe it in more detail in Sect. 2.1. The difficulties faced by previous attempts to solve the original main problem [5,9] indicate that a combination of Mathematical Programming and Constraint Programming methodologies might produce improved results.

The contributions of this paper are twofold. Firstly, from a hybrid modeling perspective, we give a first step toward better understanding the set of feasible solutions of the sum constraint by presenting its convex hull relaxation in terms of linear inequalities. Building on this result, we look at two alternative formulations of the SDCCP: one using the sum constraint and another using the

---

* Supported by the William Larimer Mellon Fellowship.

P. Van Hentenryck (Ed.): CP 2002, LNCS 2470, pp. 80–92, 2002.

element constraint. We then show that the former is better than the latter in a well defined sense, i.e. its linear relaxation gives a tighter bound. Secondly, on the purely Constraint Programming side, our computational results for the SDCCP indicate that a model that uses the sum constraint also has the advantage of being more natural, more concise and computationally more efficient than the alternative model with the element constraint alone.

The remainder of this text is organized as follows. In Sect. 2, we describe the semantics of the sum constraint and we present a real-world example of its applicability. In Sect. 3, we analyze the importance of having a linear relaxation for the sum constraint, and for any global constraint in general, from the viewpoint of a hybrid modeling paradigm. Given this motivation, in Sect. 4 we present the best possible linear relaxation of the sum constraint, i.e. its convex hull. Within the idea of obtaining better dual bounds for optimization problems addressed by a combination of solvers, it then makes sense to assess the relative strengths of relaxations provided by alternative models of a given problem. Section 5 presents such a comparison for the SDCCP. Computational results on some randomly generated instances of that problem are given in Sect. 6. Finally, Sect. 7 summarizes our main conclusions.

2   The Sum Constraint and Its Applications

The main purpose of the sum constraint is to implement variable index sets, as defined below.

Definition 1. *Let $S_{j_1}, \ldots, S_{j_d}$ be sets of indices in $\{1, \ldots, n\}$, and let $c_1, \ldots, c_n$ be constants. If y is a variable with domain $D_y = \{j_1, \ldots, j_d\}$, the constraint $sum(y, (S_{j_1}, \ldots, S_{j_d}), (c_1, \ldots, c_n), z)$ states that*

$$z = \sum_{j \in S_y} c_j . \tag{1}$$

That is, the c_i's on the right hand side of (1) are not know a priori. They are function of the variable y. An extended version of this constraint exists where each constant c_i is replaced by a variable x_i. One can think of the well known element constraint as a special case of the sum constraint in which we have $S_j = \{j\}$ for all $j \in \{1, \ldots, n\}$. Algorithms for achieving hyper arc consistency for the sum constraint with constant terms, and a slightly weaker version of bounds consistency for the case with variable terms are presented in [6].

The next section introduces a scheduling problem that turns out to be a natural application of the sum constraint.

2.1   The Sequence Dependent Cumulative Cost Problem

Let us define the *Sequence Dependent Cumulative Cost Problem* (SDCCP) as follows. Suppose we are given a set of n tasks that have to be scheduled so that each task is assigned a unique and distinct position in the set $\{1, \ldots, n\}$.

Let q_i be the position assigned to task $i \in \{1, \ldots, n\}$, and let p_j contain an arbitrary value associated to the task assigned to position j. We are interested in computing

$$v_i = \sum_{1 \leq j < q_i} p_j \ , \ \forall \, i \in \{1, \ldots, n\} \ . \tag{2}$$

Two possible ways of computing v_i are: by using variable subscripts

$$v_i = \sum_{j=1}^{n} p_{\max\{0,\, q_i - q_j\}} \quad \text{(with } p_0 = 0\text{)} \tag{3}$$

or by using variable index sets in a more natural way

$$v_i = \sum_{j=1}^{q_i - 1} p_j \ . \tag{4}$$

Apart from these constraints, we also have upper and lower bounds on the value of q_i, for every i. In job-shop scheduling terminology, these can be thought of as release dates and due dates. Finally, we are interested in minimizing $\sum_{i=1}^{n} c_i v_i$, where c_i is the cost of performing task i.

This problem appears in the context of scheduling safety/quality tests under resource constraints. It is part of the *New Product Development Problem* (NPDP), which arises in the pharmaceutical and agrochemical industries and has been studied by many authors [3,5,9,10]. In the NPDP, a given set of products (e.g. newly created drugs) have to pass a series of tests enforced by law before being allowed to reach the market. A stochastic component is present in the sense that each test has a probability of failure. In case one of the tests for a certain product fails, all subsequent tests for that same product are canceled and rescheduling is often necessary in order to make better use of the available resources. The expected cost of test i is given by the probability of executing the test times the cost of performing it. In turn, this probability equals the product of the success probabilities of every test that finishes before test i starts. Another relevant issue is that we usually have technological precedences among the tests, which enforce an initial partial sequencing and contribute to the initial lower and upper bounds on the q_i variables, as mentioned earlier. The objective function of the NPDP seeks to minimize the total cost of performing all the required tests, while satisfying constraints on the number of available laboratories and capacitated personnel. The total cost also takes into account other factors such as a decrease in income due to delays in product commercialization, and the possibility of outsourcing the execution of some tests at a higher price. As reported in [9], the NPDP is a very hard problem to solve, even when the number of products is small.

Although the objective function of the NPDP turns out to be nonlinear, Jain and Grossmann [9] show that it can be accurately approximated by a piecewise linear function after using a logarithmic transformation. In this approximation, which we are going to consider here, one needs to calculate, for each test i, an expression of the form (2), where p_j equals the logarithm of the success probability of the test assigned to position j. As was done in [9], an immediate Mixed Integer Programming (MIP) formulation of (2) would look like

$$v_i = \sum_{j=1,\, j\neq i}^{n} y_{ji} p_j \ , \ \forall\, i \in \{1,\ldots,n\} \ , \tag{5}$$

where $y_{ji} = 1$ if test j precedes test i and $y_{ji} = 0$ otherwise. We are unaware of any previous work that addresses the SDCCP alone via an MIP approach. In this paper, we will only use CP to tackle the SDCCP and we will not explicitly evaluate MIP models for it.

3   The Logic-Based Modeling Paradigm

The concept of logic-based modeling is far more general and powerful than what is presented in this paper. In [6], Hooker gives a lot of illustrative examples and develops the topic to a large extent. The basic philosophy of this paradigm is very similar to the one behind the Branch-and-Infer [4], Mixed Logical/Linear Programming [7] or Branch-and-Check [11] frameworks. That is, a problem can be modeled with the Mixed Integer Programming (MIP) language of linear inequalities and also with the more expressive language of Constraint Programming (CP). Then, each type of constraint is handled by its specific solver in a collaborative effort to find an optimal solution to the original problem. That collaboration can be done in a myriad of ways and the best choice will depend on the structure of the problem being studied.

In real world situations, one can usually identify substructures or smaller parts of a problem that possess nice or well studied properties. These can even be parts of other known problems that, when put together, define the problem under consideration. When trying to write an MIP model, the modeler is aware of the structure of the problem and how its different parts are connected. However, given the limited expressive power of the vocabulary of linear inequalities, much of this structure will be lost during the translation phase. Many state-of-the-art MIP softwares have algorithms that try to identify some structure inside the linear programs in order to take advantage of them. For example, they can try to use some valid cuts that have been developed for that particular class of problems and improve the quality of the Linear Programming (LP) relaxation, or even apply a different, more specialized, algorithm such as the Network Simplex. But this is not always effective. The more localized view of the problem substructures is usually lost or becomes unrecognizable, and the solver can only work with the global picture of a linear (integer) program. Moreover, a significant portion of the cutting plane theory developed so far is not a default component of current MIP packages.

On the other hand, the Constraint Programming (CP) community has done a lot of work on special purpose algorithms tailored to solve Constraint Satisfaction Problems [12] through local inference inside global constraints.

Looking at the CP and Operations Research (OR) worlds, it is not hard to see that they can benefit from each other if the local and global views are combined properly. In the logic-based modeling framework, the modeler is able to write the problem formulation with both linear inequalities and more expressive global constraints or logic relations that can better capture and exploit some local structure in the problem. Obviously, this hybrid formulation needs both an LP solver and a constraint solver in order to be useful. But, in principle, this would be transparent to the end-user. In essence, the whole mechanism works as follows. The linear constraints in the logic-based formulation are posted to the LP solver, as usual, and some of them may also be posted to the constraint solver. The constraint solver handles the constraints that cannot be directly posted to the LP solver (e.g. global constraints). When applicable, the continuous relaxation of some global constraints is also sent to the LP solver so as to strengthen the overall relaxation, providing better dual bounds. These linear relaxations of global constraints are sometimes referred to as *dynamic linear relaxations*, because they are supposed to change according to the way the search procedure evolves. This idea also plays a key role behind increasing the performance of hybrid decomposition procedures like Benders decomposition [2] or, more generally, Branch-and-Check, as argued by Thorsteinsson [11].

It is important to notice that some global constraints have known continuous relaxations that can be added to the set of linear inequalities that are sent to the LP solver. Nevertheless, there are also global constraints for which a continuous relaxation is either not known or too large for practical purposes. In these cases, when building the linear relaxation of the entire logic-based formulation, these global constraints are simply removed and the LP solver ignores their existence. The overall linear relaxation derived from a logic-based formulation is often smaller and weaker than what would be obtained from a pure MIP formulation. On one hand, this allows for a faster solution of the associated linear programs. On the other hand, if we make use of an implicit enumeration algorithm like branch-and-bound, the weaker bounds can result in a larger search tree. Domain reductions resulting from constraint propagation at each node of the tree may help compensate for that.

Given this motivation, the next two sections develop the strongest possible linear relaxation for the sum constraint and theoretically assess its effectiveness when applied to the SDCCP.

4   The Convex Hull Relaxation of the Sum Constraint

When dealing with linear optimization problems over disjunctions of polyhedra (see [1]), the convex hull relaxation is the best that one can hope for. More precisely, if Q is the union of a number of nonempty polyhedra and $\max\{f(x) : x \in Q\}$ is attained at an extreme point x^* of Q, there exists an extreme point x' of the convex hull of Q such that $f(x') = f(x^*)$.

From now on, we assume that $z \geq 0$, $x_i \geq 0$ for all $i \in \{1, \ldots, n\}$, and y is an integer variable whose domain has size $|D_y| = d$. For each $j \in D_y$, $S_j \subseteq$

$\{1, \ldots, n\}$ is a set of indices. We will denote by $\mathrm{conv}(Q)$ the convex hull of an arbitrary set $Q \in \mathbb{R}^m$, for any $m \in \mathbb{N}$. Also, x and $\bar{x}$ are n-dimensional vectors whose elements are referred to by subscripts, e.g. x_i and $\bar{x}_i$.

4.1   The Constant Case

For all $i \in \{1, \ldots, n\}$, let c_i be integer constants. Then, the sum constraint

$$\mathrm{sum}(y, (S_{j_1}, \ldots, S_{j_d}), (c_1, \ldots, c_n), z) \tag{6}$$

represents the disjunction

$$\bigvee_{j \in D_y} \left(z = \sum_{i \in S_j} c_i \right) . \tag{7}$$

Proposition 1. *The convex hull of (7) is given by*

$$\min_{j \in D_y} \left\{ \sum_{i \in S_j} c_i \right\} \leq z \leq \max_{j \in D_y} \left\{ \sum_{i \in S_j} c_i \right\} .$$

Proof. For each $j \in D_y$, let $t_j = \sum_{i \in S_j} c_i$. Notice that (7) is a one-dimensional problem in which z can take one of $|D_y|$ possible values $t_j \in \mathbb{R}$. The convex hull of these points is simply the line segment connecting all of them. □

4.2   The Variable Case

The interesting case is when the list of constants is replaced by a list of variables. This other version of the sum constraint, $\mathrm{sum}(y, (S_{j_1}, \ldots, S_{j_d}), (x_1, \ldots, x_n), z)$, represents the disjunction

$$\bigvee_{j \in D_y} \left(z = \sum_{i \in S_j} x_i \right) . \tag{8}$$

Lemma 1. *Let $I = \bigcap_{j \in D_y} S_j$ and, for every $j \in D_y$, let $S_j' = S_j \setminus I$. If $I \neq \emptyset$, (8) is the projection of (9)–(10) onto the space of z and x. Moreover, the convex hull of (9)–(10) is given by (9) and the convex hull of (10), together with the non-negativity constraints $z \geq 0$, $x \geq 0$ and $w \geq 0$.*

$$z = \sum_{i \in I} x_i + w \tag{9}$$

$$\bigvee_{j \in D_y} \left(w = \sum_{i \in S_j'} x_i \right) . \tag{10}$$

Proof. Clearly, for any point $(\bar{z}, \bar{x}) \in \mathbb{R}^{1+n}$ satisfying (8), it is easy to find a $\bar{w} \in \mathbb{R}$ such that $(\bar{z}, \bar{x}, \bar{w}) \in \mathbb{R}^{1+n+1}$ satisfies (9)–(10). For instance, if $(\bar{z}, \bar{x})$ satisfies the rth disjunct in (8) (i.e. the one with $j = r$), take $\bar{w} = \sum_{i \in S'_r} x_i$. Conversely, let $(\bar{z}, \bar{x}, \bar{w})$ satisfy (9) and the rth disjunct in (10). Then, $(\bar{z}, \bar{x})$ satisfies the rth disjunct in (8). For the last part, let conv(10) denote the convex hull of (10). Also, let A be the set of points in $\mathbb{R}^{1+n+1}$ defined by (9)–(10) and let B be the set of points in $\mathbb{R}^{1+n+1}$ defined by the intersection of (9) and conv(10). We want to show that $\text{conv}(A) = B$.

conv$(A) \subseteq B$: Any point in A is built in the following way: pick a point $(\bar{x}, \bar{w})$ that satisfies one of the disjuncts in (10) and then set $\bar{z} = \sum_{i \in I} \bar{x}_i + \bar{w}$. Any point $p_3 \in \text{conv}(A)$ can be written as $p_3 = \lambda p_1 + (1 - \lambda) p_2$, for some $\lambda \in [0, 1]$ and some $p_1 = (\bar{z}_1, \bar{x}^1, \bar{w}_1)$ and $p_2 = (\bar{z}_2, \bar{x}^2, \bar{w}_2)$ from A, built as indicated before. To see that $p_3 = (\bar{z}_3, \bar{x}^3, \bar{w}_3) \in B$, notice that $p_3 \in \text{conv}(10)$ because both p_1 and p_2 satisfy (10). Finally, p_3 also satisfies (9) because $\bar{z}_3 = \lambda \bar{z}_1 + (1 - \lambda) \bar{z}_2 = \sum_{i \in I} \bar{x}_i^3 + \bar{w}_3$.

$B \subseteq \text{conv}(A)$: Any point in conv(10) can be written as $(\bar{z}, \bar{x}, \bar{w}) = \lambda(\bar{z}_1, \bar{x}^1, \bar{w}_1) + (1 - \lambda)(\bar{z}_2, \bar{x}^2, \bar{w}_2)$, where $p_1 = (\bar{z}_1, \bar{x}^1, \bar{w}_1)$ and $p_2 = (\bar{z}_2, \bar{x}^2, \bar{w}_2)$ satisfy some disjuncts in (10). When $\bar{z} = \sum_{i \in I} \bar{x}_i + \bar{w}$, then $p = (\bar{z}, \bar{x}, \bar{w}) \in B$. To see that $p \in \text{conv}(A)$, simply notice that p_1 and p_2 can always be chosen with $\bar{z}_1 = \sum_{i \in I} \bar{x}_i^1 + \bar{w}_1$ and $\bar{z}_2 = \sum_{i \in I} \bar{x}_i^2 + \bar{w}_2$, i.e. points in A. $\qquad \square$

Before stating the main theorem of this section, we mention an auxiliary result that can be easily proved with standard arguments from Convex Analysis.

Lemma 2. *Let S be an arbitrary set in $\mathbb{R}^{\ell+m}$ and let $\text{Proj}_{\ell}(S)$ be the projection of S onto the $\mathbb{R}^{\ell}$ space. Then, $\text{Proj}_{\ell}(\text{conv}(S)) = \text{conv}(\text{Proj}_{\ell}(S))$.*

Theorem 1. *Let I and S'_j, for all $j \in D_y$, be defined as in Lemma 1. Let $U = \bigcup_{j \in D_y} S'_j$. The convex hull of (8) is given by the projection of (9) and (11) onto the space of z and x, with $z \geq 0$ and $x \geq 0$.*

$$0 \leq w \leq \sum_{i \in U} x_i \ . \tag{11}$$

Proof. By lemmas 1 and 2, it suffices to show that (11) is the convex hull of (10). Clearly, every point that satisfies (10) also satisfies (11). To complete the proof, we need to show that any point that satisfies (11) is a convex combination of points satisfying (10). Let $(\bar{x}, \bar{w})$ satisfy (11), and let $K = |U| + 1$. The role of K is to ensure that the sum of the multipliers in (12) is equal to 1. From (11), there exists $\alpha \in [0, 1]$ such that $\bar{w} = \alpha \sum_{i \in U} \bar{x}_i$. We can write $(\bar{x}, \bar{w})$ as

$$\begin{pmatrix} \bar{x} \\ \bar{w} \end{pmatrix} = \frac{\alpha}{K} \sum_{i \in U} \begin{pmatrix} K\bar{x}_i e^i \\ K\bar{x}_i \end{pmatrix} + \frac{(1-\alpha)}{K} \sum_{i \in U} \begin{pmatrix} K\bar{x}_i e^i \\ 0 \end{pmatrix} + \frac{1}{K} \begin{pmatrix} K\bar{u} \\ 0 \end{pmatrix} , \tag{12}$$

where e^i is the ith unit vector, and $\bar{u}_i = \bar{x}_i$ for every $i \in \{1, \ldots, n\} \setminus U$ and $\bar{u}_i = 0$ otherwise. Notice that every point $(K\bar{x}_i e^i, K\bar{x}_i)$ satisfies the jth disjunct for some j such that $i \in S'_j$. Also, since $\bigcap_{j \in D_y} S'_j = \emptyset$, for every $i \in U$ there exists a disjunct k that is satisfied by the point $(K\bar{x}_i e^i, 0)$. Namely, any k such that $i \notin S'_k$. Finally, $(K\bar{u}, 0)$ trivially satisfies any disjunct in (10) by construction. $\qquad \square$

After Fourier-Motzkin elimination of w, we get

$$\sum_{i \in I} x_i \leq z \leq \sum_{i \in I \cup U} x_i \ .$$

For the special case when $I = \emptyset$, we have $z = w$ and the previous proof shows that the convex hull of (8) is given by (11) with w replaced by z, and the non-negativity constraints $z \geq 0$ and $x \geq 0$.

5 Comparing Alternative Formulations for the SDCCP

Some parts of the NPDP described in Sect. 2.1 present clearly recognizable substructures that could be explored in the context of a logic-based modeling framework. For instance, besides the SDCCP, it is possible to model the influence of the resource limitations on the final schedule of tests by using the global constraint cumulative in a very natural way. In this paper, however, we will only concentrate on the role of the sum constraint as a tool to model the SDCCP.

Let $p_0 = 0$. We can implement the variable subscripts in (3) with (13)–(15).

$$y_{ij} = q_i - q_j + n, \quad \forall j = 1, \ldots, n, \ \ j \neq i \tag{13}$$

$$\text{element}(y_{ij}, [\overbrace{p_0, \ldots, p_0}^{n \ \text{times}}, p_1, \ldots, p_{n-1}], z_{ij}), \quad \forall j = 1, \ldots, n, \ \ j \neq i \tag{14}$$

$$v_i = \sum_{j=1, j \neq i}^{n} z_{ij} \ . \tag{15}$$

From (13), the domain of y_{ij} is $D_{y_{ij}} \subseteq \{1, \ldots, 2n - 1\}$. The values between 1 and n represent the situations when $q_i \leq q_j$, which are of no interest. That is why the first n variables in the second argument of (14) are set to zero. The variable index sets in (4) can be implemented as

$$\text{sum}(q_i, [\{1\}, \{2\}, \{2,3\}, \{2,3,4\}, \ldots, \{2, \ldots, n\}], [p_0, p_1, \ldots, p_{n-1}], v_i) \ . \tag{16}$$

The next result states that, from the viewpoint of a Linear Programming relaxation, we only need to consider the variable index set formulation (16).

Theorem 2. *For each $i \in \{1, \ldots, n\}$, let the initial domain of q_i be $D_i = \{1, \ldots, n\}$. If we impose the constraint alldifferent$(q_1, \ldots, q_n)$, the bounds on v_i given by the relaxation of (16) are at least as tight as the bounds given by the relaxation of (13)–(15).*

To prove this theorem, we need an auxiliary result that follows from the pigeon-hole principle.

Lemma 3. *Let $A = \{a_1, \ldots, a_k\} \subseteq \{1, \ldots, n\}$, and let $q_1, \ldots, q_n$ have initial domains $D_1 = \cdots = D_n = \{1, \ldots, n\}$, respectively. When we require the constraint alldifferent$(q_1, \ldots, q_n)$, there exist at least k distinct variables $q_{i_1}, \ldots, q_{i_k}$ such that $a_1 \in D_{i_1}, \ldots, a_k \in D_{i_k}$.*

Proof of Theorem 2. The convex hull relaxation of (14) gives $0 \leq z_{ij} \leq \sum_{k \in D_{y_{ij}}, k \geq n} p_{k-n}$, for all $j = 1, \ldots, n$, $j \neq i$ (see [6] for a proof). Therefore, we can write

$$0 \leq v_i \leq \sum_{j=1}^{n} \left(\sum_{k \in D_{y_{ij}}, k \geq n} p_{k-n} \right) . \tag{17}$$

Let $S_1 = \{0\}$ and $S_j = \{1, \ldots, j-1\}$, for all $j = 2, \ldots, n$. As before, let $U = \bigcup_{j \in D_i} S_j$. By Theorem 1, the convex hull relaxation of (16) is given by

$$0 \leq v_i \leq \sum_{k \in U} p_k . \tag{18}$$

We want to show that the RHS of (18) is always less than or equal to the RHS of (17). We divide the proof in 3 sub-cases.

$q_i = 1$: Clearly, both (17) and (18) give $v_i = 0$.

$q_i = b > 1$: In this case, the RHS of (18) reduces to $\sum_{k=1}^{b-1} p_k$. Notice that, for any j, $D_{y_{ij}}$ will contain values larger than n if and only if D_j contains values smaller than b. But, by Lemma 3, for every number $a \in \{1, \ldots, b-1\}$ there exists at least one variable q_j such that $a \in D_j$. Hence, the RHS of (17) reduces to $\sum_{k=1}^{b-1} c_k p_k$, where $c_k \geq 1$.

$|D_i| = d \geq 2$: Let $D_i = \{b_1, \ldots, b_d\}$, with $b_1 < \cdots < b_d$. The RHS of (18) reduces to $\sum_{k=1}^{n} c_k p_k$, where $c_k = 1$ if $k \in U$, and $c_k = 0$ otherwise. We will show that the RHS of (17) reduces to $\sum_{k=1}^{n} \bar{c}_k p_k$, with $\bar{c}_k \geq c_k$ for every $k = 1, \ldots, n$. Let us start by calculating $\bar{c}_1$, that is, the number of variables q_j for which $n + 1 \in D_{y_{ij}}$. Notice that, for every j, $n + 1 \in D_{y_{ij}}$ if and only if D_j contains at least one of $b_1 - 1, b_2 - 1, \ldots, b_d - 1$. By Lemma 3, there exist at least d such D_j's ($d - 1$ if $b_1 = 1$). Hence, $\bar{c}_1 \geq d$ ($d - 1$ if $b_1 = 1$). Analogously, for $k = 2, \ldots, b_1 - 1$, we want to know how many distinct D_j's contain at least one of the numbers $b_1 - k, b_2 - k, \ldots, b_d - k$. This will be equal to the number of distinct $D_{y_{ij}}$'s that contain the value $n + k$. By the same reasoning, we have that $\bar{c}_k \geq d$ whenever $1 \leq k < b_1$. If $b_1 \leq k < b_2$, $b_1 - k \leq 0$ and we need only consider the $d - 1$ positive numbers $b_2 - k, b_3 - k, \ldots, b_d - k$. Again, there are at least $d - 1$ distinct q_j variables whose domains contain at least one of these numbers. So, $\bar{c}_k \geq d - 1$ for $k = b_1, \ldots, b_2 - 1$. We can now repeat this argument until $k = b_d - 1$. □

To see that (18) can be strictly stronger than (17), let us consider the following example. Let $n = 3$ and $q_1, q_2, q_3 \in \{1, 2, 3\}$. Then, when we look at v_1, y_{12}, $y_{13} \in \{1, \ldots, 5\}$. From (17) we get $v_1 \leq 2p_1 + 2p_2$, whereas from (18) we get the inequality $v_1 \leq p_1 + p_2$, which strictly dominates the previous one, since p_1 and p_2 are non-negative.

6   Implementation of the Alternative Models

In order to describe the two CP models for the SDCCP, we will recall some of the notation introduced in Sect. 2.1. Let $\text{prob}(i)$ denote the probability of success of task $i \in \{1, \ldots, n\}$. Since we have been assuming that all variables are non-negative, the variable p_j will represent $-\log(\text{prob}(\text{task assigned to position } j))$, for every $j \in \{1, \ldots, n\}$. In this fashion, we can state the SDCCP as a maximization problem with $v_i \geq 0$ for each task i. Let q_i represent the position assigned to task i and let c_i be the cost of performing it. The CP formulation of the SDCCP can be written as

$$\max \sum_{i=1}^{n} c_i v_i \qquad (19)$$

$$\text{element}(q_i, [p_1, \ldots, p_n], -\log(\text{prob}(i))), \ \forall i \in \{1, \ldots, n\} \qquad (20)$$

$$< \text{relationship between } p_i, q_i \text{ and } v_i > \qquad (21)$$

$$L_i \leq q_i \leq U_i, \ \forall i \in \{1, \ldots, n\} \ , \qquad (22)$$

where L_i and U_i are, respectively, lower and upper bounds on the value of q_i.

The two alternative models differ in the way they represent constraints (21). In the element constraint model (Model 1), we replace (21) by (13)–(15). In the sum constraint model (Model 2), we replace (21) by (16), for all $i \in \{1, \ldots, n\}$.

Using the ECL^{i}PS^e [8] constraint logic programming system version 5.3, we implemented an algorithm that achieves a slightly weaker version of bounds consistency for the sum constraint with variable terms. We also implemented a hyper arc consistency algorithm for the version of the element constraint that indexes a list of variables, as needed for (20). For the details regarding the propagation algorithms and the strategies for incremental maintenance, we refer the reader to [6]. The computational times reported in this section are given in CPU seconds of a Sun UltraSPARC-II 360MHz running SunOS 5.7.

6.1   Computational Results

To test the performance of the two models described above, we generated random instances of the SDCCP[1]. The size of the instances n, given as the number of tasks, varies from 5 to 10. The values of c_i are randomly picked from a discrete uniform distribution in the interval $[10, 100]$. To control the percentage of tasks with uncertainty in the completion, as well as the percentage of tasks with release dates and due dates, we divided the instances in four classes. Each class is characterized by two numbers a and b that denote, respectively, the percentage of tasks with $\text{prob}(i) < 1$, and the percentage of tasks with non-trivial release dates and due dates. The (a, b) pairs chosen for our experiments are: $(33\%, 33\%)$, $(50\%, 33\%)$, $(50\%, 50\%)$ and $(75\%, 50\%)$. The rationale behind this choice is to try to evaluate the behavior of the models under different problem configurations.

---

[1] The instance generator can be made available upon request.

Table 1. Comparison of the two CP models for the SDCCP (33%, 33%)

		Model 1		Model 2	
Size	Optimum	Backtracks	Time	Backtracks	Time
5	312.88	2	0.10	2	0.04
6	427.04	14	1.58	7	0.37
7	572.93	67	7.75	36	1.22
8	1,163.76	149	79.10	63	8.18
9	1,183.07	1,304	518.38	328	44.33
10	1,102.39	31,152	6,293.25	4,648	308.60

For example, for problems of size 6 in class (50%, 33%), 50% of the tasks have prob(i) chosen randomly from a uniform distribution in the interval $[0, 1]$. The other half of the prob(i) values are set to 1. Also, for 33% of the tasks, L_i and U_i are randomly chosen from a discrete uniform distribution in the interval $[1, 6]$. For the remaining 67% of the tasks, $L_i = 1$ and $U_i = 6$.

For each one of the four classes of instances, the numbers reported in tables 1 through 4 are the average values over 10 different runs for each instance size ranging from 5 to 9, and average values over 3 runs for instances of size 10.

Our results indicate that, as the instance size increases, Model 1, which is based on the element constraint, requires a significantly larger number of backtracks than Model 2, which uses the sum constraint. In terms of computational time, solving Model 2 tends to be roughly one order of magnitude faster than solving Model 1. One reason for this behavior can be attributed to the fact that Model 2, besides being more compact, also provides more efficient pruning, since Model 1 is essentially simulating the sum constraint with a number of element constraints.

Table 2. Comparison of the two CP models for the SDCCP (50%, 33%)

		Model 1		Model 2	
Size	Optimum	Backtracks	Time	Backtracks	Time
5	180.39	4	0.15	3	0.05
6	367.76	18	1.07	10	0.24
7	898.01	41	6.25	24	1.06
8	1,435.72	303	52.47	91	4.96
9	1,595.03	1,803	187.27	881	19.41
10	1,505.62	67,272	8,605.18	15,345	561.90

Table 3. Comparison of the two CP models for the SDCCP (50%, 50%)

Size	Optimum	Model 1		Model 2	
		Backtracks	Time	Backtracks	Time
5	330.01	3	0.13	3	0.04
6	444.10	7	0.67	5	0.17
7	995.88	28	6.44	14	0.94
8	1,488.54	121	68.04	48	6.28
9	995.72	1,216	293.11	358	31.74
10	2,207.05	973	524.69	121	21.15

Table 4. Comparison of the two CP models for the SDCCP (75%, 50%)

Size	Optimum	Model 1		Model 2	
		Backtracks	Time	Backtracks	Time
5	670.65	5	0.20	4	0.05
6	825.83	8	0.47	4	0.10
7	1,241.32	46	4.05	23	0.59
8	1,713.76	96	24.19	46	3.14
9	2,346.90	1,943	233.54	869	19.86
10	2,512.04	4,025	1,794.19	1,311	155.76

7   Conclusions

We study a scheduling problem that appears as a substructure of a real-world problem in the agrochemical and pharmaceutical industries called the New Product Development Problem (NPDP) [5,9]. We refer to that subproblem as the Sequence Dependent Cumulative Cost Problem (SDCCP).

Given the description of the SDCCP, the sum constraint is identified as a natural tool, simplifying the modeling effort and making it more intuitive. Apart from these advantages, our computational experiments show that the sum constraint exhibits a significantly improved performance over an alternative model that uses the element constraint. From a more theoretical point of view, we study the characteristics of the set of feasible solutions of the sum constraint. We provide the representation of the convex hull of this set of feasible solutions and we prove that this linear relaxation gives tighter bounds than the linear relaxation of the aforementioned alternative model. The relevance of this result is related to hybrid modeling efforts. One promising idea is to use linear relaxations of global constraints to help in the process of solving optimization problems through a combination of solvers. These linear relaxations, or at least some of their valid inequalities, may contribute to speed up the solution process by improving the bounds on the optimal solution value.

As an extension of this work, one can try to look at different contexts in which the sum constraint also fits well as a modeling device, and then compare its performance against other modeling possibilities. Finally, the impact of modeling the SDCCP with the sum constraint while solving the more general NPDP is another topic that deserves further investigation.

Acknowledgments

The author would like to thank Professor John N. Hooker for his many helpful comments during the development of this work.

References

1. E. Balas. Disjunctive programming: Properties of the convex hull of feasible points. *Discrete Applied Mathematics*, 89:3–44, 1998.
2. J. F. Benders. Partitioning procedures for solving mixed-variables programming problems. *Numerische Mathematik*, 4:238–252, 1962.
3. G. Blau, B. Mehta, S. Bose, J. Pekny, G. Sinclair, K. Keunker, and P. Bunch. Risk management in the development of new products in highly regulated industries. *Computers and Chemical Engineering*, 24·659–664, 2000.
4. A. Bockmayr and T. Kasper. Branch and infer: A unifying framework for integer and finite domain constraint programming. *INFORMS Journal on Computing*, 10(3):287–300, 1998.
5. S. Honkomp, G. Reklaitis, and J. Pekny. Robust planning and scheduling of process development projects under stochastic conditions. Presented at the AICHE annual meeting, Los Angeles, CA, 1997.
6. J. N. Hooker. *Logic-Based Methods for Optimization*. Wiley-Interscience Series in Discrete Mathematics and Optimization, 2000.
7. J. N. Hooker and M. A. Osorio. Mixed logical/linear programming. *Discrete Applied Mathematics*, 96–97(1–3):395–442, 1999.
8. IC-Parc, Imperial College, London. The ECL^{i}PS^e Constraint Logic Programming System. http://www.icparc.ic.ac.uk/eclipse.
9. V. Jain and I. Grossmann. Resource-constrained scheduling of tests in new product development. *Industrial and Engineering Chemistry Research*, 38(8):3013–3026, 1999.
10. C. Schmidt and I. Grossmann. Optimization models for the scheduling of testing tasks in new product development. *Industrial and Engineering Chemistry Research*, 35(10):3498–3510, 1996.
11. E. S. Thorsteinsson. Branch-and-Check: A hybrid framework integrating mixed integer programming and constraint logic programming. In Toby Walsh, editor, *Proceedings of the Seventh International Conference on Principles and Practice of Constraint Programming*, volume 2239 of *Lecture Notes in Computer Science*, pages 16–30. Springer-Verlag, November 2001.
12. E. Tsang. *Foundations of Constraint Satisfaction*. Academic Press, 1993.

Global Constraints for Lexicographic Orderings[*]

Alan Frisch[1], Brahim Hnich[1], Zeynep Kiziltan[2], Ian Miguel[1], and Toby Walsh[3]

[1] Department of Computer Science, University of York
Heslington, York, United Kingdom
{frisch,ianm}@cs.york.ac.uk
[2] Computer Science Division
Department of Information Science, Uppsala University
Uppsala, Sweden
{Brahim.Hnich,Zeynep.Kiziltan}@dis.uu.se
[3] Cork Constraint Computation Center, University College Cork
Ireland
tw@4c.ucc.ie

Abstract. We propose some global constraints for lexicographic orderings on vectors of variables. These constraints are very useful for breaking a certain kind of symmetry arising in matrices of decision variables. We show that decomposing such constraints carries a penalty either in the amount or the cost of constraint propagation. We therefore present a global consistency algorithm which enforces a lexicographic ordering between two vectors of n variables in $O(nb)$ time, where b is the cost of adjusting the bounds of a variable. The algorithm can be modified very slightly to enforce a strict lexicographic ordering. Our experimental results on a number of domains (balanced incomplete block design, social golfer, and sports tournament scheduling) confirm the efficiency and value of these new global constraints.

1 Introduction

Global (or non-binary) constraints are one of the most important and powerful aspects of constraint programming. Specialized propagation algorithms for global constraints are vital for efficient and effective constraint solving. A number of consistency algorithms for global constraints have been developed by several researchers (see [1] for examples). To continue this line of research, we propose a new family of efficient global constraints for lexicographic orderings on vectors of variables.

[*] We are very thankful to Warwick Harvery, Nicolas Beldiceanu, the members of the APES research group (especially Ian Gent, Patrick Prosser, and Barbara Smith), and Pierre Flener for valuable discussions on this work. The algorithm described herein is the subject of British Patent Application No. 0205606.7. This research was made possible by VR grant 221-99-369, EPSRC grant GR/N16129 and an EPSRC advanced research fellowship.

P. Van Hentenryck (Ed.): CP 2002, LNCS 2470, pp. 93–108, 2002.
© Springer-Verlag Berlin Heidelberg 2002

These global constraints are especially useful for breaking a certain kind of symmetry arising in matrices of decision variables. Dealing efficiently and effectively with symmetry is one of the major difficulties in constraint programming. Symmetry occurs in many scheduling, assignment, routing and supply chain problems. These can often be modelled as constraint programs with matrices of decision variables [6] in which the matrices have symmetry along their rows and/or columns [5]. For instance, a natural model of the sports tournament scheduling problem has a matrix of decision variables, each of which is assigned a value corresponding to the match played in a given week and period [10]. In this problem, weeks and periods are indistinguishable so we can freely permute rows and columns. To break this symmetry, we can add an additional constraint that the rows and columns are lexicographically ordered [5]. These global constraints can also be used in multi-criteria optimization problems where the objective function consists of features which are ranked [4].

2   Formal Background

A constraint satisfaction problem (CSP) consists of a set of variables, each with a finite domain of values, and a set of constraints that specify the allowed values for given subsets of variables. The solution to a CSP is an assignment of values to the variables which satisfies all the constraints. To find such solutions, constraint solvers often explore the space of partial assignment enforcing some level of consistency like (generalized) arc-consistency or bounds consistency. A CSP is generalized arc-consistent (GAC) iff, when a variable in a constraint is assigned any of its values, there exist compatible values for all the other variables in the constraint. When the constraints are binary, we talk about arc-consistency (AC). For totally ordered domains, like integers, a weaker level of consistency is bounds consistency. A CSP is bounds consistent (BC) iff, when a variable in a constraint is assigned its maximum or minimum value, there exist compatible values for all the other variables in the constraint. If a constraint c is AC or GAC then we write $AC(c)$ or $GAC(c)$ respectively.

In this paper, we are interested in lexicographic ordering constraints on vectors of distinct variables and having the same length. Throughout, we assume finite integer domains, which are totally ordered. Given two vectors, $\bar{x}$ and $\bar{y}$ of n variables, $\langle x_0, x_1, \ldots, x_{n-1} \rangle$ and $\langle y_0, y_1, \ldots, y_{n-1} \rangle$, we write a lexicographical ordering constraint as $\bar{x} \leq_{\text{lex}} \bar{y}$ and a strict lexicographic ordering constraint as $\bar{x} <_{\text{lex}} \bar{y}$. Indexing is from left to right with the most significant index for the lexicographic ordering at 0. The lexicographic ordering constraint $\bar{x} \leq_{\text{lex}} \bar{y}$ ensures that: $x_0 \leq y_0$; $x_1 \leq y_1$ when $x_0 = y_0$; $x_2 \leq y_2$ when $x_0 = y_0$ and $x_1 = y_1$; $\ldots$; $x_{n-1} \leq y_{n-1}$ when $x_0 = y_0$, $x_1 = y_1$, $\ldots$, and $x_{n-2} = y_{n-2}$. The strict lexicographic ordering constraint $\bar{x} <_{\text{lex}} \bar{y}$ ensures that: $\bar{x} \leq_{\text{lex}} \bar{y}$; and $x_{n-1} < y_{n-1}$ when $x_0 = y_0$, $x_1 = y_1$, $\ldots$, and $x_{n-2} = y_{n-2}$.

We are also interested in multiple lexicographic ordering constraints. For example, all rows or columns in a matrix of variables might be lexicographically ordered. We denote m vectors of n domain variables by:

$$\bar{x}_0 = \langle x_{0,0}, \quad x_{0,1}, \quad \cdots \quad, x_{0,n-1} \rangle$$
$$\bar{x}_1 = \langle x_{1,0}, \quad x_{1,1}, \quad \cdots \quad, x_{1,n-1} \rangle$$
$$\vdots$$
$$\bar{x}_{m-1} = \langle x_{m-1,0}, x_{m-1,1}, \cdots, x_{m-1,n-1} \rangle$$

We write $\bar{x}_0 \leq_{\text{lex}} \bar{x}_1 \ldots \leq_{\text{lex}} \bar{x}_{m-1}$ for the single global constraint on these $m.n$ variables which ensures that each pair of vectors is in lexicographic order. Also, we write $\bar{x}_0 <_{\text{lex}} \bar{x}_1 \ldots <_{\text{lex}} \bar{x}_{m-1}$ for the single global constraint on the $m.n$ variables which ensures that each pair of vectors is in strict lexicographic order.

We need the following additional notation. The sub-vector of $\bar{x}$ with start index a and last index b inclusive is denoted by $\bar{x}_{a \to b}$. The minimum element in the domain of x_i is denoted by $min(x_i)$, and the maximum by $max(x_i)$. Given a binary constraint c, if any assignment of values to x_i and y_i guarantees that c holds then we write $x_i \, c^* y_i$, otherwise we write $\neg(x_i \, c^* y_i)$. Hence, $x_i \leq^* y_i$ is equivalent to $max(x_i) \leq min(y_i)$, $x_i <^* y_i$ to $max(x_i) < min(y_i)$, $x_i >^* y_i$ to $min(x_i) > max(y_i)$, and $\neg(x_i >^* y_i)$ to $min(x_i) \leq max(y_i)$. If x_i and y_i are ground and equal then we write $x_i \doteq y_i$, otherwise we write $\neg(x_i \doteq y_i)$. Finally, the function $\texttt{floor}(\bar{x})$ assigns all unassigned variables in a vector $\bar{x}$ to their minimum values, whilst $\texttt{ceiling}(\bar{x})$ assigns all to their maximum values.

3   GAC Algorithms for Lexicographic Ordering

We sketch the main features of a family of linear time algorithms for enforcing GAC on a (strict or non-strict) lexicographic ordering constraint. Consider the lexicographic ordering constraint $\bar{x} \leq_{\text{lex}} \bar{y}$ with:

$$\bar{x} = \langle \{2\}, \quad \{1,3,4\}, \{1,2,3,4,5\}, \{1,2\}, \{3,4,5\} \rangle$$
$$\bar{y} = \langle \{0,1,2\}, \quad \{1\}, \quad \{0,1,2,3,4\}, \{0,1\}, \{0,1,2\} \rangle$$

The key idea is to have two pointers, α and β which save us from repeatedly traversing the vectors. The pointer α points to the index such that all variables above it are ground and equal. The pointer β points either to the most significant index starting from which the sub-vectors are lexicographically ordered the wrong way whatever the remaining assignments are (that is, $\texttt{floor}(\bar{x}_{\beta \to n-1}) >_{\text{lex}}$ $\texttt{ceiling}(\bar{y}_{\beta \to n-1})$), or (if this is not the case) to infinity. As variables are assigned, α and β are moved inwards, and we terminate when $\beta = \alpha + 1$. The algorithm restricts domain prunings to the index α, and as α is strictly increasing and bounded by n, the algorithm runs in $O(nb)$ time where b is the cost of adjusting the bounds of a variable.

In this example, we initialize α to point to the index 0 since y_0 is not ground. We initialize β to the index 3 since the sub-vectors starting at index 3 are ordered the wrong way round (i.e. $\bar{x}_{3 \to 4} >_{\text{lex}} \bar{y}_{3 \to 4}$):

$$\bar{x} = \langle \{2\}, \quad \{1,3,4\}, \{1,2,3,4,5\}, \{1,2\}, \{3,4,5\} \rangle$$
$$\bar{y} = \langle \{0,1,2\}, \quad \{1\}, \quad \{0,1,2,3,4\}, \{0,1\}, \{0,1,2\} \rangle$$
$$\phantom{\bar{y} = \langle} \alpha \uparrow \phantom{\{0,1,2\}, \quad \{1\}, \quad \{0,1,2,3,4\},} \uparrow \beta$$

Since α is at 0, the start of the vectors, there can be no support for any value in the domain of y_α which is less than the minimum value in the domain of x_α. We can therefore remove 0 and 1 from the domain of y_α and increment α to 1:

$$\bar{x} = \langle \{2\}, \{1,3,4\}, \{1,2,3,4,5\}, \{1,2\}, \{3,4,5\} \rangle$$
$$\bar{y} = \langle \{2\}, \quad \{1\}, \quad \{0,1,2,3,4\}, \{0,1\}, \{0,1,2\} \rangle$$
$$\qquad \quad \alpha \uparrow \qquad\qquad\qquad \uparrow \beta$$

As the vectors above α are ground and equal, there can be no support for any value in the domain of x_α which is more than the maximum value in the domain of y_α. We can therefore remove 3 and 4 from the domain of x_α and increment α to 2:

$$\bar{x} = \langle \{2\}, \{1\}, \{1,2,3,4,5\}, \{1,2\}, \{3,4,5\} \rangle$$
$$\bar{y} = \langle \{2\}, \{1\}, \{0,1,2,3,4\}, \{0,1\}, \{0,1,2\} \rangle$$
$$\qquad\qquad\quad \alpha \uparrow \qquad\quad \uparrow \beta$$

Since α has now reached $\beta - 1$, there can be no support for any value in the domain of x_α (resp. y_α) which is greater (resp. less) than or equal to the maximum (resp. minimum) value in the domain of y_α (resp. x_α). We must therefore strictly order the index α. That is, we can remove 4 and 5 from the domain of x_α, and also 0 and 1 from the domain of y_α:

$$\bar{x} = \langle \{2\}, \{1\}, \{1,2,3\}, \{1,2\}, \{3,4,5\} \rangle$$
$$\bar{y} = \langle \{2\}, \{1\}, \{2,3,4\}, \{0,1\}, \{0,1,2\} \rangle$$
$$\qquad\qquad\quad \alpha \uparrow \quad \uparrow \beta$$

We now terminate as $\beta = \alpha + 1$. Note that we also terminate when any value assignment to x_α and y_α gurantees that $x_\alpha < y_\alpha$.

3.1   GAC on $\leq_{\text{lex}}$

We now define more formally the algorithm for enforcing GAC on the constraint $\bar{x} \leq_{\text{lex}} \bar{y}$. As we have seen, the pointers α and β play a central role in the algorithm. The pointer α points to an index of $\bar{x}$ and $\bar{y}$ such that for all $j < \alpha$ we have $x_j \doteq y_j$, and $\neg(x_\alpha \doteq y_\alpha)$. The pointer β points either to the most significant index starting from which the sub-vectors are lexicographically ordered the wrong way whatever the remaining assignments are:

$$\texttt{floor}(\bar{x}_{\beta \to n-1}) >_{\text{lex}} \texttt{ceiling}(\bar{y}_{\beta \to n-1})$$
$$\forall i \ 0 \leq i < \beta . \ \neg(\texttt{floor}(\bar{x}_{i \to n-1}) >_{\text{lex}} \texttt{ceiling}(\bar{y}_{i \to n-1}))$$

or (if this is not the case) to ∞. Consider two vectors $\bar{x}$ and $\bar{y}$ of length 1 and x_0 and y_0 both have the domain $\{0,1\}$. The pointer α is set to 0 and if we set the pointer β to 1, then our rule would assign 0 to x_α and 1 to y_α, which is wrong. To avoid such situations, the pointer β is set to a value bigger than the length of the vectors. It is not hard to show that generalised arc-inconsistent values can exist only in the interval $[\alpha, \beta)$ where $\beta < n$. Indeed, we can restrict pruning to the index α, and show that GAC($\bar{x} \leq_{lex} \bar{y}$) iff: AC($x_\alpha < y_\alpha$) when $\beta = \alpha + 1$, and $AC(x_\alpha \leq y_\alpha)$ when $\beta > \alpha + 1$. The algorithm also has a flag, *consistent* which indicates that all possible assignments satisfy the lexicographic ordering constraint. That is, `ceiling`$(\bar{x}) \leq_{\text{lex}}$ `floor`$(\bar{y})$.

We first give the procedure to initialise the two pointers (α and β) and the flag (*consistent*). Line 4 of **Initialise** traverses $\bar{x}$ and $\bar{y}$, starting at index 0, until either it reaches the end of the vectors (all pairs of variables are ground and equal), or it reaches an index where the pair of variables are not ground and equal.

1. **Procedure Initialise()**
2. *consistent* $:= false$
3. $i := 0$
4. **WHILE** $(i < n \ \wedge \ x_i \doteq y_i) \ i := i + 1$
5. **IF** $(i = n)$ *consistent* $:= true$, **Return**
6. **ELSE** $\alpha := i$
7. **IF** (**Check_Lex**(i)) *consistent* $:= true$, **Return**
8. $\beta := -1$
9. **WHILE** $(i \neq n \wedge \neg(x_i >^* y_i))$
10.   **IF** $(min(x_i) = max(y_i))$
11.   **IF**$(\beta = -1) \ \beta := i$
12.   **ELSE** $\beta := -1$
13.   i:=i+1
14. **IF** $(i = n) \ \beta := \infty$
15. **ELSE IF** $(\beta = -1) \ \beta := i$
16. **IF** $(\alpha \geq \beta)$ **FAIL**
17. **GACLexLeq**(α)

In the first case, `ceiling`$(\bar{x}) \leq_{\text{lex}}$ `floor`$(\bar{y})$. Hence, *consistent* is set to *true* and the algorithm returns (line 5). In the second case, α is set to the most significant index where the pair of variables are not ground and equal (line 6). In line 7, *consistent* is set to *true* if the call to **Check_Lex**(i) succeeds. This call checks whether the lexicographic ordering constraint is satisfied for all possible assignments:

1. **Boolean Check_Lex**(i)
2. **IF** $(i = n - 1)$ **Return**$(x_i \leq^* y_i)$
3. **ELSE Return**$(x_i <^* y_i)$

Line 9 traverses $\bar{x}$ and $\bar{y}$, starting at index α, until either it reaches the end of the vectors (none of the pairs of variables satisfy $x_i >^* y_i$), or it reaches an index i where the pair of variables satisfy $x_i >^* y_i$. In the first case, β is set to ∞ (line 14). In the second case, β is guaranteed to be at most i (line 15). If, however, there exist a pair of sub-vectors, $\bar{x}_{h \to i-1}$ and $\bar{y}_{h \to i-1}$ such that $min(x_j) = max(y_j)$ for all $h \leq j \leq i - 1$, then β can be revised to h (lines 10-11).

The complexity of the initialisation is $O(n)$ since both vectors are traversed in the worst case. Initialization terminates either with failure (if $\alpha \geq \beta$) or by calling GACLexLeq(α). GACLexLeq(i) is also called by the event handler whenever the minimum or the maximum value of a variable at index i changes.

In the **GACLexLeq** procedure, lines 2, 3-5, 6-9, and 10-12 are mutually exclusive, and will be referred as parts A, B, C, and D respectively.

Part A: Generalised arc-inconsistent values exist only in $[\alpha, \beta)$ where $\beta < n$. Therefore, no inconsistent value can exist at an index greater than or equal to β. Hence, if $i \geq \beta$, the vectors are already GAC and the algorithm returns. If the flag *consistent* is true, `ceiling`$(\bar{x}) \leq_{\text{lex}}$ `floor`$(\bar{y})$ so the algorithm returns. The complexity of this step is constant.

1. **Procedure GACLexLeq(i)**
2. **IF** $(i \geq \beta \vee consistent)$ **Return**
3. **IF** $(i = \alpha \ \wedge \ i + 1 = \beta)$
4.   **AC**$(x_i < y_i)$
5.   **IF** (**Check_Lex**(i)) $consistent := true$, **Return**
6. **IF** $(i = \alpha \ \wedge \ i + 1 < \beta)$
7.   **AC**$(x_i \leq y_i)$
8.   **IF** (**Check_Lex**(i)) $consistent := true$, **Return**
9.   **IF** $(x_i \doteq y_i)$ **UpdateAlpha**$(i + 1)$
10. **IF** $(\alpha < i < \beta)$
11.   **IF** $(\ (i = \beta - 1 \ \wedge \ min(x_i) = max(y_i)\ ) \vee x_i >^* y_i)$
12.   **UpdateBeta**$(i - 1)$

Part B: **AC**$(x_i < y_i)$ stands for maintaining arc-consistency on $x_i < y_i$. This is implemented as follows: If $max(x_i)$ (resp. $min(y_i)$) is supported by $max(y_i)$ (resp. $min(x_i)$) then all the other elements in the domain of x_i (resp. y_i) are supported. Otherwise, the upper (resp. lower) bound of the domain of x_i (resp. y_i) is tightened. The worst-case complexity of maintaining arc-consistency on $x_i < y_i$ is thus $O(b)$, where b is the cost of adjusting the bounds of a variable. If $\beta = \alpha + 1$ then we need to ensure that $AC(x_\alpha < y_\alpha)$. If a domain wipe-out occurs then the algorithm fails, and the vectors cannot be made GAC. Otherwise, the vectors are now GAC. After the propagation carried out by maintaining arc-consistency, **Check_Lex**(i) is called. This part of the algorithm thus has an $O(b)$ complexity.

Part C: If $\beta > \alpha + 1$ then we need to ensure $AC(x_\alpha \leq y_\alpha)$. If a domain wipe-out occurs then the algorithm fails, and the vectors cannot be made GAC. Otherwise, the vectors are now GAC. After the pruning carried out by maintaining arc-consistency, **Check_Lex**(i) is called and α updated if necessary.

1. **Procedure UpdateAlpha(i)**
2. **IF** $(i = \beta)$ **FAIL**
3. **IF** $(i = n)$ $consistent := true$, **Return**
4. **IF** $\neg(x_i \doteq y_i)$
5. $\alpha := i$
6.   **GACLexLeq**(i)
7. **ELSE UpdateAlpha**$(i + 1)$

In lines 4 and 7 of **UpdateAlpha**(i), the vectors are traversed until the most significant index k where $\neg(x_k \doteq y_k)$ is found. If such an index does not exist, $\texttt{ceiling}(\bar{x}) \leq_{\text{lex}} \texttt{floor}(\bar{y})$, so *consistent* is set to true (line 3). Otherwise, α is set to k (line 5). **GACLexLeq** is then called with this new value of α. In the worst case, α moves one index at a time, and on each occasion AC is enforced. Hence, this part of the algorithm gives an $O(nb)$ complexity, where b is the cost of adjusting the bounds of a variable.

Part D: β is updated by calling **UpdateBeta**($i-1$) when we set a variable at an index i between α and β, and either x_i now must be greater than y_i (i.e $x_i >^* y_i$), or i is adjacent to β (i.e. $i = \beta - 1$) and y_i can at best only equal x_i.

1. **Procedure UpdateBeta(i)**
2. **IF** $(i + 1 = \alpha)$ **FAIL**
3. **IF** $(\ min(x_i) < max(y_i)\ )$
4. $\beta := i + 1$
5.   **IF** $\neg(x_i <^* y_i)$ **GACLexLeq**(i)
6. **ELSE IF** $(\ min(x_i) = max(y_i)\ )$ **UpdateBeta**($i - 1$)

In lines 3 and 6 of **UpdateBeta(i)**, the vectors are traversed until the most significant index k where $min(x_k) < max(y_k)$ is found. The pointer β is set to $k + 1$ (line 4). **GACLexLeq**($\beta - 1$) is then called in case $\beta = \alpha + 1$, and we need to ensure $AC(x_\alpha < y_\alpha)$. If $\beta = \alpha + 1$ and $x_\alpha <^* y_\alpha$ then *consistent* would already have been set to *true*. The algorithm, however, always terminates after one more step. The worst case complexity of the algorithm remains $O(nb)$.

When updating α or β, failure is established if these pointers meet. This situation can only arise if the event queue contains several domain prunings due to other constraints, for the following reasons. After initialisation, the constraint is GAC. Hence, we can find a single consistent value for all variables. If after every assignment we enforce GAC on this constraint, this property persists. Therefore, we can only fail when the queue contains a series of updates which must be dealt with simultaneously.

3.2   GAC on $<_{\text{lex}}$

With very little effort, **GACLexLeq()** can be adapted to give an algorithm, **GACLexLess()** that enforces GAC on a strict lexicographic ordering constraint between two vectors. The reason that the two algorithms are so similar is that, as soon as β is assigned a value other than ∞, **GACLexLeq()** enforces strict inequality in subvectors above β. In the **GACLexLess()** algorithm, β again points either to the most significant index starting from which the sub-vectors must be ordered the wrong way:

$$\texttt{floor}(\bar{x}_{\beta \to n-1}) \geq_{\text{lex}} \texttt{ceiling}(\bar{y}_{\beta \to n-1})$$
$$\forall i\ 0 \leq i < \beta\ .\ \neg(\texttt{floor}(\bar{x}_{i \to n-1}) \geq_{\text{lex}} \texttt{ceiling}(\bar{y}_{i \to n-1}))$$

or (if this is not the case) to n (so that equality of the vectors is not allowed). There are only two other changes. When α is initialized, we fail if α gets set to n

(as the vectors are ground and equal so cannot be strictly ordered). Finally, for obvious reasons, all calls to **Check_Lex**(i) are replaced by $(x_i <^* y_i)$.

Given two vectors $\bar{x}$ and $\bar{y}$ with non-empty domains, executing the two algorithm **GACLexLeq** and **GACLexLess** maintain generalised arc-consistency on $\bar{x} \leq_{\text{lex}} \bar{y}$ and $\bar{x} <_{\text{lex}} \bar{y}$, respectively.

Theorem 1. *Given a pair of vectors $\bar{x}$ and $\bar{y}$ of domain variables,* **GACLexLeq** *(resp.* **GACLexLess***) either establishes failure if $\bar{x} \leq_{\text{lex}} \bar{y}$ (resp. $\bar{x} <_{\text{lex}} \bar{y}$) is unsatisfiable, or prunes elements from $\bar{x}$ and $\bar{y}$ such that $GAC(\bar{x} \leq_{\text{lex}} \bar{y})$ (resp. $GAC(\bar{x} <_{\text{lex}} \bar{y})$) and the set of solutions is preserved.*

Proof. For reasons of space, we are unable to give the correctness proofs of the algorithms. These can, however, be found in an accompanying technical report [8].

4   Alternative Approaches

There are at least two other ways of posting global lexicographic ordering constraints: by decomposing them into smaller constraints, or by posting an arithmetic inequality constraint. We show here that such decomposition usually increases the runtime or decreases the amount of constraint propagation. The experimental results in Section 6 support this observation.

A lexicographic ordering constraint $\bar{x} \leq_{\text{lex}} \bar{y}$ can be decomposed it into n non-binary constraints:

$$\{x_0 \leq y_0, \ x_0 = y_0 \rightarrow x_1 \leq y_1, \ x_0 = y_0 \ \wedge \ x_1 = y_1 \rightarrow x_2 \leq y_2, \ldots,$$
$$x_0 = y_0 \ \wedge \ x_1 = y_1 \ \wedge \ldots \wedge \ x_{n-2} = y_{n-2} \rightarrow x_{n-1} \leq y_{n-1}\}$$

Similarly a strict lexicographic ordering constraint $\bar{x} <_{\text{lex}} \bar{y}$ can be decomposed into n non-binary constraints:

$$\{x_0 \leq y_0, \ x_0 = y_0 \rightarrow x_1 \leq y_1, \ x_0 = y_0 \ \wedge \ x_1 = y_1 \rightarrow x_2 \leq y_2, \ldots,$$
$$x_0 = y_0 \ \wedge \ x_1 = y_1 \ \wedge \ldots \wedge \ x_{n-2} = y_{n-2} \rightarrow x_{n-1} < y_{n-1}\}$$

As the following theorem shows, such decompositions do not affect the pruning of GAC. However, in many solvers (e.g. Solver 5.0), only nFC0 [1] is enforced on such non-binary decompositions. Our linear time GAC algorithm will clearly do more propagation. In addition, the experiments in Section 6 show that, despite enforcing a weaker consistency like nFC0, a state of the art system like ILOG's Solver 5.0 handles such decompositions inefficiently.

---

[1] Forward checking (FC) has been generalised to non-binary constraints [2]. nFC0 makes every k-ary constraint with $k-1$ variables instantiated AC. nFC0 usually denotes the search algorithm, but we overload notation here to use nFC0 to describe the level of local consistency that it enforces at each node in its search tree.

Theorem 2. *GAC($\bar{x} \leq_{\text{lex}} \bar{y}$) is equivalent to GAC on the decomposition, but strictly stronger than nFC0 on the decomposition. Similarly, GAC($\bar{x} <_{\text{lex}} \bar{y}$) is equivalent to GAC the decomposition, but strictly stronger than nFC0 on the decomposition.*

Proof. (Outline) We just consider GAC($\bar{x} \leq_{\text{lex}} \bar{y}$) as the proof for GAC($\bar{x} <_{\text{lex}} \bar{y}$) is entirely analogous. Clearly GAC on $\bar{x} \leq_{\text{lex}} \bar{y}$ is as strong as GAC on the decomposition. To show the reverse, suppose that every constraint in the decomposition is GAC but that the undecomposed constraint is not. There is some index α such that for all $j < \alpha$ we have $x_j \doteq y_j$ and $\neg(x_\alpha \doteq y_\alpha)$, and x_α or y_α has a value that is not GAC. The two cases are dual so we just consider the first. There exists a value a in the domain of x_α that has no support in the domain of y_α. Hence, all values in the domain of y_α are smaller than a. However, this is not possible if the decomposed constraint, $x_0 = y_0 \wedge x_1 = y_1 \wedge \ldots \wedge x_{\alpha-1} = y_{\alpha-1} \rightarrow x_\alpha \leq y_\alpha$ is GAC.

Clearly GAC on the decomposition is as strong as nFC0. To show strictness, consider $\langle\{0,1\},\{1\}\rangle \leq_{\text{lex}} \langle\{0,1\},\{0\}\rangle$. This problem is not GAC. However, nFC0 leaves the problem unchanged as more than one variable is uninstantiated. □

Note that naively enforcing GAC on the decomposition of a global lexicographic ordering constraint will usually be expensive as the decomposition contains non-binary constraints, some of which are large in size. Suppose we use an optimal algorithm like GAC-schema [3]. For e constraints of arity k and variables with domains of size d, GAC-schema takes $O(ed^k)$ time. As the decomposition introduce n constraints with arity up to $2n$, GAC-schema on the decomposition takes $O(nd^{2n})$ time, making especially long vectors difficult to deal with.

A second way of enforcing a lexicographic ordering is via an arithmetic constraint. To ensure that $\bar{x} \leq_{\text{lex}} \bar{y}$ with domains of size d, we post the arithmetic constraint:

$$d^{n-1} * x_0 + d^{n-2} * x_1 + \ldots + d^0 * x_{n-1} \leq d^{n-1} * y_0 + d^{n-2} * y_1 + \ldots + d^0 * y_{n-1}$$

And to ensure that $\bar{x} <_{\text{lex}} \bar{y}$ we post the arithmetic constraint:

$$d^{n-1} * x_0 + d^{n-2} * x_1 + \ldots + d^0 * x_{n-1} < d^{n-1} * y_0 + d^{n-2} * y_1 + \ldots + d^0 * y_{n-1}$$

Maintaining BC on such arithmetic constraints does the same pruning as GAC.

Theorem 3. *GAC($\bar{x} \leq_{\text{lex}} \bar{y}$) and GAC($\bar{x} <_{\text{lex}} \bar{y}$) are equivalent to BC on the corresponding arithmetic constraints.*

Proof. (Outline) We just consider GAC($\bar{x} \leq_{\text{lex}} \bar{y}$) as the proof for GAC($\bar{x} <_{\text{lex}} \bar{y}$) is entirely analogous. Suppose that the arithmetic constraint is BC, but that $\bar{x} \leq_{\text{lex}} \bar{y}$ is not GAC. There is some index α such that for all $j < \alpha$ we have $x_j \doteq y_j$ and $\neg(x_\alpha \doteq y_\alpha)$, and x_α or y_α has a value that is not GAC. The two cases are analogous so we just consider the first. There exits a value a in the domain of x_α that has no support in the domain of y_α. Hence, all the values in the domain of y_α are smaller than a. However, this contradicts the arithmetic constraint being BC. □

Maintaining BC on such arithmetic constraints can be achieved in $O(ndc)$ where n is the length of the vectors, d is the domain size, and c is the time required to check that a particular (upper or lower) bound of a variable is BC. At best, c is a constant time operation. However, when n and d get large, d^{n-1} will be much more than the word size of the computer and computing BC will be significantly more expensive. Hence, this method is only feasible when the vectors and domain sizes are small. For instance, on the BIBD problem in Section 6 with vectors of length 120 and domain size 2, the coefficients in the arithmetic constraint would exceed 2^{31}, the maximum integer size allowed in Solver 5.0.

5   Extensions

We often have multiple lexicographic ordering constraints. For example, all rows or columns in a matrix of decision variables might be lexicographically ordered. We can treat such a problem as a single global ordering constraint over the whole matrix. Alternatively, we can decompose it into lexicographic ordering constraints between all pairs of vectors. We can decompose this further by posting lexicographic ordering constraints just between immediate pairs of vectors (and calling upon the transitivity of the orderings). The following theorems demonstrate that such decompositions hinder constraint propagation in general. However, we identify the special case of a (non-strict) lexicographical ordering on 0/1 variables where it does not.

Theorem 4. $GAC(\bar{x}_0 \leq_{lex} \bar{x}_1 \ldots \leq_{lex} \bar{x}_{m-1})$ is strictly stronger than $GAC(\bar{x}_i \leq_{lex} \bar{x}_j)$ for all $i < j$. Similarly, $GAC(\bar{x}_0 <_{lex} \bar{x}_1 \ldots <_{lex} \bar{x}_{m-1})$ is strictly stronger than $GAC(\bar{x}_i <_{lex} \bar{x}_j)$ for all $i < j$.

Proof. Consider the following 3 vectors:

$$\bar{x}_0 = \langle \{0,2\}, \{1\} \rangle \quad \bar{x}_1 = \langle \{1,2\}, \{0,3\} \rangle \quad \bar{x}_2 = \langle \{2\}, \{0,2\} \rangle$$

Although $GAC(\bar{x}_i \leq_{lex} \bar{x}_j)$, and $GAC(\bar{x}_i <_{lex} \bar{x}_j)$ for all $i < j$, neither $GAC(\bar{x}_0 \leq_{lex} \bar{x}_1 \leq_{lex} \bar{x}_2)$ nor $GAC(\bar{x}_0 <_{lex} \bar{x}_1 <_{lex} \bar{x}_2)$ holds as $x_{0,0} = \{2\}$ cannot be consistently extended. □

A simple corollary is that enforcing GAC on (strict) lexicographic ordering constraints between neighbouring pairs of vectors does less pruning than enforcing GAC on a single global ordering constraint. Indeed, GAC on neighbouring pairs does less pruning than GAC on each pair of vectors.

Theorem 5. $GAC(\bar{x}_i \leq_{lex} \bar{x}_j)$ for all $i < j$ is strictly stronger than $GAC(\bar{x}_i \leq_{lex} \bar{x}_{i+1})$ for all i. Similarly, $GAC(\bar{x}_i <_{lex} \bar{x}_j)$ for all $i < j$ is strictly stronger than $GAC(\bar{x}_i <_{lex} \bar{x}_{i+1})$ for all i.

Proof. Consider the following 3 vectors:

$$\bar{x}_0 = \langle \{0,1\}, \{1\}, \{0,1\} \rangle \quad \bar{x}_1 = \langle \{0,1\}, \{0,1\}, \{0,1\} \rangle \quad \bar{x}_2 = \langle \{0,1\}, \{0\}, \{0,1\} \rangle$$

Although $GAC(\bar{x}_i \leq_{lex} \bar{x}_{i+1})$, and $GAC(\bar{x}_i <_{lex} \bar{x}_{i+1})$ for all i, neither $GAC(\bar{x}_0 \leq_{lex} \bar{x}_2)$ nor $GAC(\bar{x}_0 <_{lex} \bar{x}_2)$ holds as $x_{0,0} = \{1\}$ cannot be consistently extended.   □

In the special case that the domains of the vectors are 0/1, enforcing GAC on lexicographic ordering constraints between *every* pair of vectors achieves global consistency. This is not true, however, for the strict lexicographic ordering constraint, nor for non-strict lexicographic ordering constraints between neighbouring pairs of vectors.

Theorem 6. *For 0/1 variables, $GAC(\bar{x}_i \leq_{lex} \bar{x}_j)$ for all $i < j$ is equivalent to $GAC(\bar{x}_0 \leq_{lex} \bar{x}_1 \ldots \leq_{lex} \bar{x}_{m-1})$.*

Proof. (Outline) We assume that we have a problem in which $GAC(\bar{x}_0 \leq_{lex} \bar{x}_1 \ldots \leq_{lex} \bar{x}_{m-1})$ does not hold and show that there exist $i < j$ such that $GAC(\bar{x}_i \leq_{lex} \bar{x}_j)$ does not hold. As $GAC(\bar{x}_0 \leq_{lex} \bar{x}_1 \ldots \leq_{lex} \bar{x}_{m-1})$ does not hold, there is variable with a value which lacks support. With this value of the variable, there exist indices p, q, and k such that $p < q, x_{p,k} = 1$, and $x_{q,k} = 0$. Also, for all $k' < k$ any assignment of values to the variables guarantees that either $x_{0,k'} = x_{1,k'} \ldots = x_{m-1,k'}$, or there exist two indices p' and q' such that $p' < q'$, $x_{p',k'} = 1$, and $x_{q',k'} = 0$. Hence, there exist a pair of vectors $\bar{x}_i$ and $\bar{x}_j$ such that $\text{floor}(\bar{x}_i) >_{lex} \text{ceiling}(\bar{x}_j)$.   □

This result, however, does not hold for a strict lexicographical ordering.

Theorem 7. *For 0/1 variables, $GAC(\bar{x}_0 <_{lex} \bar{x}_1 \ldots <_{lex} \bar{x}_{m-1})$ is strictly stronger than $GAC(\bar{x}_i <_{lex} \bar{x}_j)$ for all $i < j$.*

Proof. Consider 5 vectors $\bar{x}_0, \ldots, \bar{x}_4$, where $\bar{x}_i = \langle \{0,1\}, \{0,1\} \rangle$ for all $i \in [0,4]$. Although $GAC(\bar{x}_i <_{lex} \bar{x}_j)$ for all $i < j$ there is no globally consistent solution as there are only 4 possible distinct vectors.   □

6   Experimental Results

We tested our global constraints on three problem domains: the balanced incomplete block design (prob028 in CSPLib: www.csplib.org), the social golfer (prob010 in CSPLib), and the sports tournament scheduling (prob026 in CSPLib). Each is naturally modelled by matrices of decision variables which exhibit a high degree of symmetry. The rows and columns of these matrices can therefore be ordered lexicographically to break much of this symmetry. Throughout, we compare the performance of the global constraints developed here with FC on the decomposed form described in Section 4 using ILOG's Solver 5.0 on a 750Mhz PentiumIII, 128Mb RAM, but not with GAC-schema as it is computationally expensive.

When using symmetry-breaking constraints, the variable and value ordering (VVO) is very important. In particular, if the VVO moves right to left along the rows, it will increasingly conflict with the lexicographic ordering constraints. We can then expect to gain from both the lower complexity and increased pruning

Table 1. BIBDs: Time is in seconds and a dash means no result is obtained in 1 hour

Problem v, b, r, k, λ	GACLexLeq (Adjacent Pairs)			GACLexLeq (All Pairs)			Decomposition		
	Fails	Choice-points	Time	Fails	Choice-points	Time	Fails	Choice-points	Time
6,50,25,3,10	2738	2787	1.7	2738	2787	1.8	2758	2807	10.7
6,60,30,3,12	5924	5982	4.6	5924	5982	4.9	5959	6017	45
6,70,35,3,10	11731	11798	11.4	11731	11798	11.7	11787	11854	137.6
10,90,27,3,6	90610	90827	111	90610	90827	120.4	90610	90827	742.2
9,108,36,3,9	2428	2619	8.4	2428	2619	7.6	2428	2619	73.3
15,70,14,3,2	2798	3080	6.2	2798	3080	8.4	2798	3080	20.7
12,88,22,3,4	139988	140236	249	139988	140236	317	139988	140236	1153.6
9,120,40,3,10	1646	1858	8	1646	1858	7.2	1646	1858	81.5
10,120,36,3,8	577280	577532	1316.3	577280	577532	1132.3	—	—	—
13,104,24,3,4	114666	114999	397.6	114666	114999	448.3	114666	114999	1666.9

achieved by our global constraints. Given a VVO that agrees with the lexicographic ordering constraints, we can expect to gain more from the lower complexity of our global constraint than from the increased pruning.

6.1   The Balanced Incomplete Block Design Problem

Balanced Incomplete Block Design (BIBD) generation is a standard combinatorial problem from design theory with applications in cryptography and experimental design. A BIBD is specified by a binary matrix of b columns and v rows, with exactly r ones per row, k ones per column, and a scalar product of λ between any pair of distinct rows. Our model consists of sum constraints on each row and each column as well as the scalar product constraint between every pair of rows. Trivially, we can exchange any pair of rows, and any pair of columns of a solution to obtain another symmetrical solution. We therefore impose lexicographic ordering constraints on rows and columns.

We used a static variable ordering, tuned by initial experimentation, which gives the best results we have found so far on this problem. This ordering begins by filling the first row left to right. Our value ordering is to try 0 then 1. Hence, this gives a first row with $b - r$ 0's followed by r 1's (by the row sum constraint). We then fill from top to bottom, the rightmost r columns from right to left. This is the most constrained part of the problem due to the λ constraints. Finally we fill the remaining rows alternately right to left, then left to right from top to bottom. Alternating directions favours the updating of α and β in **GACLexLeq**, and pruning in the decomposition.

Results presented in Table 1 indicate a substantial gain in efficiency on the long vectors by using **GACLexLeq** in preference to the decomposition. The similar size of the search trees explored indicates that the variable ordering is highly compatible with lexicographic ordering, and it is rare for the global constraint to be able to prune more than the decomposition. However, we report lower runtimes due to the increased efficiency of our **GACLexLeq** algorithm.

Although we have shown that, in theory, enforcing lexicographic ordering between all pairs of rows or columns can increase pruning, we do not see any evidence of it on these problems. In most cases, the increased overhead results in increased run-times. However, in three cases, enforcing lexicographic ordering between all pairs reduces the run-time. Since the size of the search tree remains the same, we conjecture that this is a result of a complex dead-end being detected more quickly with the extra global constraints.

6.2   The Social Golfer Problem

The social golfer problem is to schedule a golf tournament over w weeks. In each week, the golfers must be divided into g groups of size s. Every golfer must play once in every week, and every pair of players can meet at most once. Our model consists of a 3-dimensional 0/1 matrix of groups × weeks × golfers. Assigning 1 to an entry at index $[g, w, p]$ means that golfer p plays in group g in week w. Sum constraints ensure that every golfer plays once in every week and that every group contains s players. A constraint similar in form to the λ constraint described above ensures that every pair of players meet only once.

Each of the weeks, golfers and groups are symmetrical and cannot be equal. In the first two cases, we impose a strict lexicographic ordering constraint between the planes of the matrix that represent weeks and the planes of the matrix that represent golfers. However, the contents of a group from one week to the next are independent of each other. Hence, we impose a strict lexicographic ordering between groups within each week. A static variable ordering was again used, filling the matrix a player at a time, assigning each week in turn. The results are presented in Table 2.

The more complex interactions resulting from 3-dimensional symmetry breaking result in more pruning with the global constraint than with the decomposition. Hence, we observe a reduction in the size of the search tree in many cases. As expected, this leads to an even larger reduction in run-times. Given the size of the vectors involved, the machine on which these experiments were run started to run low on memory using the decomposition. Better run times may be possible using a machine with more memory, but as we try to model larger problems this is a clear disadvantage of using decompositions.

Again, we see no evidence that enforcing lexicographic ordering between all pairs of vectors leads to increased pruning. Indeed, given the relatively large size of the vectors compared to those found in the BIBD models, we usually observe a small increase in overhead.

6.3   The Sports Tournament Scheduling Problem

In the sports tournament scheduling problem we have n teams playing over $n-1$ weeks. Each week is divided into $n/2$ periods, and each period divided into two slots. The first team in each slot plays at home, whilst the second plays the first team away. Every team must play once a week, every team plays at most twice in the same period over the tournament and every team plays every other team. We use a model consisting of two matrices proposed by Van Hentenryck et al. [10]. The first matrix, *teams* is a 3-dimensional matrix of periods × (extended) weeks

Table 2. Golfers: Time is in seconds and a dash means no result is obtained in 1 hour

Problem w,g,s	GACLexLess (Adjacent Pairs)			GACLexLess (All Pairs)			Decomposition		
	Fails	Choice-points	Time	Fails	Choice-points	Time	Fails	Choice-points	Time
11,6,2	166	305	0.7	116	305	0.8	314	453	7
13,7,2	1525	1792	9.7	1525	1792	10.4	16584	16851	547.2
5,6,3	2090342	2090435	2976.1	2090342	2090345	3120.6	—	—	—
4,7,3	248	371	0.7	248	371	0.8	340	463	8.2
5,8,3	625112	625328	2450.9	625112	625328	2655	—	—	—
4,5,4	1410774	1410825	1675	1410774	1410825	1865.3	—	—	—
3,6,4	2777416	2777486	2771.7	2777416	2777486	3073	—	—	—
3,7,4	646124	646235	1147.9	646124	646235	1173.7	—	—	—
9,8,4	27	380	3.3	27	380	3.6	32	385	68.9
2,7,5	32944	33029	53.2	32944	33029	55.7	58512	58597	959.1
2,8,5	42008	42123	93.2	42008	42123	91.2	122271	122386	3462.5
9,8,8	19	373	16	19	373	18.7	—	—	—

Table 3. Sports: Time is in seconds

n	GACLexLess (Adjacent Pairs)			GACLexLess (All Pairs)			Decomposition		
	Fails	Choice-points	Time	Fails	Choice-points	Time	Fails	Choice-points	Time
6	285	295	0.2	285	295	0.2	285	295	0.2
8	53	81	0.2	53	81	0.2	53	81	0.2
10	4931	4979	0.6	4931	4979	0.6	4933	4982	0.9
12	433282	433357	38.6	433282	433357	48.2	433283	433358	92.7
14	20404472	20404581	2016.7	20404472	20404581	2643.7	20439055	20439164	6516.8

× slots, each element of *teams* can take a value between 1 and n expressing that a team plays in a particular period in a particular week, in the home or away slot. Weeks are extended to include a dummy week to makes posting some constraints easier. The second matrix, *games* is a 2-dimensional matrix of periods × weeks, each element of which has a domain in $[1, n^2]$, recording a particular unique combination of home and away teams. All-different and occurrence constraints are then used to enforce the problem constraints.

Symmetry on the slots is broken by specifying that the home team must be less than the away team (this is in fact essential for the *game* matrix to work correctly). In addition, the periods and the weeks are symmetrical and cannot be equal. Hence, we post a strict lexicographic ordering constraint between periods and weeks in *teams*. A static variable ordering on *teams*, tuned by initial experiments, is used as follows. We fill the first row left to right. We fill the 2nd row right to left. We fill the 1st column top to bottom. From then on we fill the remainder of the rows left to right, right to left from top to bottom. Again, alternating directions appears to help both the global constraint and the decomposition.

The results are presented in Table 3. They show that **GACLexLess** maintains a significant advantage over the decomposition on multi-valued domains. The variable ordering chosen is compatible with lexicographic ordering, so there is no difference in the size of the search tree. However, the benefits of having an efficient global constraint are again apparent.

7   Related Work

Beldiceanu has classified many global constraints in terms of simple graph properties [1]. This classification provides hints at ways to implement pruning algorithms for the global constraints. However, our algorithms are developed by taking a different approach.

For ordering constraints, Gent et al. show that, GAC on a global monotonicity constraint on n variables (e.g. $x_0 < x_1 < \ldots < x_{n-1}$) is equivalent to AC on its decomposition into binary ordering constraints [9]. This is based on a result of Freuder as the decomposed constraint graph is a tree [7]. As arc-consistency can be efficiently enforced on the decomposed binary ordering constraints, there is no need for global consistency algorithms for simple orderings like monotonicity constraints. However, our results show both theoretically and empirically the value of global consistency algorithms for more complex orderings.

The ECLiPSe constraint solver provides a global constraint for lexicographically ordering two vectors. However, it is not documented what level of consistency is enforced with this constraint, nor the complexity of enforcement. It does no pruning on $\langle \{0,1\}, \{0,1\}, \{1\} \rangle \leq_{\text{lex}} \langle \{0,1\}, \{0\}, \{0\} \rangle$, even though the problem is not GAC.

8   Conclusions

We have proposed some global constraints for lexicographic orderings. We show that decomposing such global constraints carries a penalty either in the amount or the cost of constraint propagation. We have therefore developed an $O(nb)$ global consistency algorithm which enforces a lexicographic ordering between two vectors of n variables, where b is the cost of adjusting the bounds of a variable. The algorithm can be modified very slightly to enforce a strict lexicographical ordering. Our experimental results confirm the efficiency and value of these new global constraints which are very useful for breaking symmetry. The motivation of the need of such constraints in the presence of other approaches to handling symmetries can be found in [5].

In our future work, we plan to use our global constraints in multi-criteria optimization problems. We also hope to develop algorithms for GAC on $\bar{x}_0 \leq_{\text{lex}} \bar{x}_1 \ldots \leq_{\text{lex}} \bar{x}_{m-1}$ and GAC on $\bar{x}_0 <_{\text{lex}} \bar{x}_1 \ldots <_{\text{lex}} \bar{x}_{m-1}$. The example in the proof of Theorem 7 suggests that this may be quite challenging. Such algorithms need to be able to perform sophisticated counting arguments and solve pigeonhole problems quickly. Global constraints for lexicographic orderings simultaneously along both rows and columns of a matrix would also present a significant challenge. Finally, we intend to look at global constraints for other orderings like the multiset ordering. Such orderings are also very useful for breaking symmetry.

References

[1] N. Beldiceanu. Global constraints as graph properties on a structured network of elementary constraints of the same type. In *Proc. of CP'2000*, pages 52–66. Springer, 2000.

[2] C. Bessière, P. Meseguer, E. C. Freuder, and J. Larrosa. On forward checking for non-binary constraint satisfaction. In *Proc. of CP'99*, pages 88–102. Springer, 1999.

[3] C. Bessière and J. C. Régin. Arc consistency for general constraint networks: Preliminary results. In *Proc. of IJCAI'97*, pages 398–404. Morgan Kaufmann, 1997.

[4] M. Ehrgott and X. Gandibleux. A survey and annotated bibliography of multi-objective combinatorial optimization. *OR Spektrum*, 22:425–460, 2000.

[5] P. Flener, A. Frisch, B. Hnich, Z. Kiziltan, I. Miguel, J. Pearson, and T. Walsh. Breaking row and column symmetries in matrix models. In *Proc. of CP'2002*. Springer, 2002.

[6] P. Flener, A. Frisch, B. Hnich, Z. Kiziltan, I. Miguel, and T. Walsh. Matrix modelling. Technical Report APES-36-2001, APES group, 2001. Available from http://www.dcs.st-and.ac.uk/~apes/reports/apes-36-2001.ps.gz. Presented at Formul'01, CP'2001 post-conference workshop.

[7] E. Freuder. A sufficient condition for backtrack-bounded search. *Journal of the Association for Computing Machinery*, 32(4):755–761, 1985.

[8] A. Frisch, B. Hnich, Z. Kiziltan, I. Miguel, and T. Walsh. Global constraints for lexicographical orderings. Technical Report APES-51-2002, APES group, 2002. Available from http://www.dcs.st-and.ac.uk/~apes/reports/apes-51-2001.ps.gz.

[9] I. P. Gent, K. Stergiou, and T. Walsh. Decomposable constraints. *Artificial Intelligence*, 123(1-2):133–156, 2000.

[10] P. Van Hentenryck, L. Michel, L. Perron, and J. C. Régin. Constraint programming in OPL. In *Proc. of PPDP'99*, pages 98–116. Springer, 1999.

A Global Filtering Algorithm for Handling Systems of Quadratic Equations and Inequations

Yahia Lebbah[2], Michel Rueher[1], and Claude Michel[1]

[1] Université de Nice–Sophia Antipolis, I3S–CNRS
930 route des Colles, B.P. 145, 06903 Sophia Antipolis Cedex, France
{cpjm,rueher}@essi.fr
[2] Université d'Oran, Département d'Informatique
31000 Oran, Algeria
ylebbah@yahoo.fr

Abstract. This paper introduces a new filtering algorithm for handling systems of quadratic equations and inequations. Such constraints are widely used to model distance relations in numerous application areas ranging from robotics to chemistry. Classical filtering algorithms are based upon *local* consistencies and thus, are unable to achieve a significant pruning of the domains of the variables occurring in quadratic constraints systems. The drawback of these approaches comes from the fact that the constraints are handled independently. We introduce here a *global* filtering algorithm that works on a tight linear relaxation of the quadratic constraints. First experimentations show that this new algorithm yields a much more effective pruning of the domains than local consistency filtering algorithms.

1 Introduction

This paper introduces a new filtering algorithm for handling systems of quadratic equations and inequations over the reals[1]. Such *quadratic continuous constraints* can be formulated as follows :

$$\sum_{(i,j) \in M} C_{i,j}^k x_i * x_j + \sum_{i \in N} C_i^k x_i^2 + \sum_{i \in N} d_i^k x_i = b_k \tag{1}$$

where $C_{i,j}^k, C_i^k, d_i^k \in I\!R$ for all $(i,j) \in M$ and $k \in 1..K$; M and N being sets of indices.

Quadratic constraints are widely used to model distance relations in numerous application areas ranging from robotics to chemistry. Thus, an efficient filtering of quadratic constraint systems is a key issue for solving many non linear constraint systems.

---

[1] For sake of simplicity, we will only consider equations in the rest of this paper; handling of inequations is straightforward in our framework since it is based on the simplex algorithm.

P. Van Hentenryck (Ed.): CP 2002, LNCS 2470, pp. 109–123, 2002.
© Springer-Verlag Berlin Heidelberg 2002

Classical filtering algorithms are based upon *local* consistencies such as 2B–consistency [16] or Box–consistency [7]), and thus, are unable to achieve a significant pruning of the domains of the variables occurring in quadratic constraints systems. The drawback of these approaches comes from the fact that the constraints are handled independently.

$3B$–consistency and kB–consistency are partial consistencies which can achieve a better pruning since they are "less local" [12]. However, they require numerous splitting steps to find the solutions of a system of quadratic constraints; so, they may become rather slow.

We introduce here a *global* filtering algorithm that works on a tight linear relaxation of the quadratic constraints. This relaxation is adapted from a classical linearization method, the "Reformulation-Linearization Technique (RLT)" [22, 21]. The simplex algorithm is then used to narrow the domain of each variable with respect to the subset of the linear set of constraints generated by the relaxation process. The coefficient of these linear constraints are updated with the new values of the bounds of the domains and the process is restarted until no more significant reduction can be done.

First experimentations show that this new algorithm yields a much more effective pruning of the domains than filtering algorithms based upon local consistencies. It outperforms systems like Numerica [24] on the classical *Gough-Stewart platform*[11] benchmark.

Before going into the details, let us illustrate our framework on a short example.

1.1   An Illustrative Example

Consider the constraint system $\mathcal{C} = \{2x * y + y = 1, x * y = 0.2\}$ which represent two intersecting curves (see figure 1).

Suppose that $D_x = Dy = [-10, +10]$. Interval $[\underline{x}, \overline{x}]$ denotes the set of reals $S = \{r : \underline{x} \le r \wedge r \le \overline{x}\}$.

The reformulation-linearization technique (see section 3) yields the following constraints system:

$$
(a) \begin{cases}
y + 2 * xy = 1, \quad xy = 0.2 \\
y * x + \underline{x} * y - xy \le \underline{x} * y, \quad \overline{y} * x + \underline{x} * y - xy \ge \underline{x} * \overline{y}, \\
y * x + \overline{x} * y - xy \ge \overline{x} * y, \quad \overline{y} * x + \overline{x} * y - xy \le \overline{x} * \overline{y} \\
x \ge \underline{x}, x \le \overline{x}, \quad y \ge \underline{y}, y \le \overline{y} \\
xy \ge \min\{\underline{x} * \underline{y}, \overline{x} * \underline{y}, \overline{x} * \overline{y}, \underline{x} * \overline{y}\}, \quad xy \le \max\{\underline{x} * \underline{y}, \overline{x} * \underline{y}, \overline{x} * \overline{y}, \underline{x} * \overline{y}\}
\end{cases}
$$

where xy is a new variable that stands for the product $x * y$.
Substituting $\underline{x}, \underline{y}, \overline{x}$ and $\overline{y}$ by their values and minimizing (resp. maximizing) of x, y and xy with the simplex algorithm yields the following new bounds: $D_x = [-9.38, 9.42], D_y = [0.6, 0.6], D_{xy} = [0.2, 0.2]$.
By substituting the new bounds of x, y and xy in the constraint system (a), we

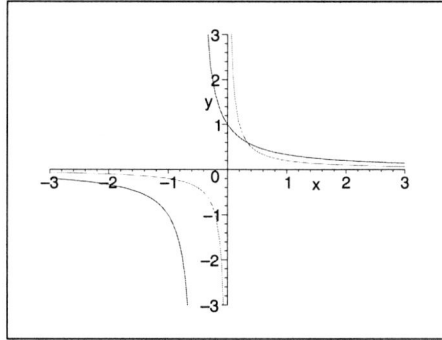

Fig. 1. Geometrical representation of $\{2xy + y = 1, xy = 0.2\}$

obtain the following linear constraint system :

$$(b) \begin{cases} y + 2xy = 1, \quad xy = 0.2 \\ 0.6 * x - 9.38 * y - xy \leq -5.628 \quad 0.6 * x - 9.38 * y - xy \geq -5.628 \\ 0.6 * x + 9.42 * y - xy \geq 5.652, \quad 0.6 * x + 9.42 * y - xy \leq 5.652 \\ x \geq -9.38, x \leq 9.42, \quad y \geq 0.6, y \leq 0.6, \quad xy \geq 0.2, xy \leq 0.2 \end{cases}$$

Two more minimizing (resp. maximizing) steps of x, y and xy are required to obtain the bounds displayed in figure 2. Note that several splitting operations are required to find the unique solution of the problem with a 3B-consistency filtering algorithm. The proposed algorithm solves the problem by generating 5 linear constraints and with 18 calls to the simplex algorithm. It finds the same solution than a solver based on 3B–consistency but without splitting and in less time (especially on more complex problem, see section 5).

1.2   Outline of the Paper

Section 2 introduces the notations and recalls the basics on local consistencies that are needed in the rest of the paper. Section 3 gives an overview of our frame-

	$2B$	Box	$3B$	$quad$
$x \in$	$[0, 10]$	$[0, 10]$	$[0.333372, 0.333379]$	$[0.333333, 0.333333]$
$y \in$	$[-10, 10]$	$[-10, 10]$	$[0.599917, 0.599930]$	$[0.599999, 0.599999]$
$splits$	$-$	$-$	2	0
$time(sec)$	2	1	3	1

Fig. 2. Filtering of $\{2xy + y = 1, xy = 0.2\}$

work and introduces different relaxation classes. Section 4 details the filtering process while section 5 provides some experimental results.

2   Preliminaries

2.1   Notations

This paper focuses on CSPs where the domains are intervals and the constraints are continuous. A n-ary continuous constraint $C_j(x_1, \ldots, x_n)$ is a relation over the reals. $\mathcal{C}$ stands for the set of constraints.

D_x denotes the domain of variable x, that's to say, the interval $[\underline{x}, \overline{x}]$ of allowed values for x. $\mathcal{D}$ stands for the set of domains of all the variables of the considered constraint system.

We also use the "reformulation-linearization technique" notations introduced in [22, 4] with slight modifications.

2.2   Projection Functions

The algorithms used over numeric CSPs typically work by narrowing domains and need to compute the projection $\Pi_{C_j, x_i}(\mathcal{D})$, or also $\Pi_{j,i}(\mathcal{D})$, of a constraint $C_j(x_1, \ldots, x_n)$ over each variable x_i in the space delimited by $D_1 \times \ldots \times D_n$.

$$\Pi_{j,i}(\mathcal{D}) = \{d_i | d_i \in D_i, \exists d_{j_1}, \ldots, d_{i-1}, d_{i+1}, \ldots, d_{j_k}$$
$$(d_{j_1} \in D_{j_1}, \ldots, d_{i-1} \in D_{i-1}, d_{i+1} \in D_{i+1}, \ldots, d_{j_k} \in D_{j_k}, \quad (2)$$
$$\langle d_{j_1}, \ldots, d_i, \ldots, d_{j_k} \rangle \in C_j)\}.$$

Such a projection cannot be computed exactly due to several reasons : (1) the machine numbers are floating point numbers and not real numbers so round-off errors occur; (2) the projection may not be representable as floating point numbers; (3) the computations needed to have a close approximation of the projection of only one given constraint may be very expensive; (4) the projection may be discontinuous whereas it is much more easy to handle only closed intervals for the domains of the variables.

Thus, what is usually done is that the projection of the constraint C_j over the variable x_i is approximated. Let $\pi_{C_j, x_i}(\mathcal{D})$ denote such an approximation. All that is needed is that $\pi_{C_j, x_i}(\mathcal{D})$ includes the exact projection; this is possible thanks to interval analysis [17, 19].

$$\pi_{j,i}(\mathcal{D}) \supseteq [min(\Pi_{j,i}(\mathcal{D})), max(\Pi_{j,i}(\mathcal{D}))] \supseteq \mathcal{D}.$$

$\pi_{C_j, x_i}(\mathcal{D})$ hides all the problems seen above. In particular, it allows us not to go into the details of the relationships between floating point and real numbers (see for example [3] for those relationships) and to consider only real numbers.

For example, most of the numeric CSPs systems (e.g., BNR-prolog [20], CLP(BNR) [8], PrologIV [9], UniCalc [5], Ilog Solver [13] and Numerica [24]) compute an approximation of the projection functions. They are based on the two most popular local consistencies: $2B$-consistency [16], *Box*-consistency [7] and the associated higher consistencies[2].

2.3   Limits of Local Consistencies

Formal definitions of $2B$-consistency and *Box*-consistency can be found in [12]. We will just recall here the basic idea of these local consistencies.

$2B$-consistency [16] states a local property on the bounds of the domains of a variable at a single constraint level. Roughly speaking, a constraint c is $2B$-consistent if, for any variable x, there exist values in the domains of all other variables which satisfy c when x is fixed to $\underline{x}$ and $\overline{x}$.

Box-consistency [7] is a coarser relaxation of *Arc*-consistency than $2B$-consistency. It mainly consists of replacing every existentially quantified variable but one with its interval in the definition of $2B$-consistency.

Different approximations are introduced in the implementations of the corresponding filtering algorithms:

- $2B$-filtering decomposes the initial constraints in ternary basic constraints for which it is trivial to compute the projection [10, 16].
- *Box*-filtering generates a system of univariate interval functions which can be tackled by numerical methods such as Newton. Contrary to $2B$-filtering, *Box*-filtering does not require any constraint decomposition of the initial constrain systems.

The success of $2B$-consistency depends on the precision of the projection function $\pi_{j,i}$. In this paper, we introduce an efficient way to handle quadratic constraints without using direct projection functions. Indeed, the difficulty when solving quadratic equations comes from the quadratic terms $f(x) = x^2$ and $g(x_i, x_j) = x_i * x_j$. f is a convex function whereas g is neither concave nor convex. It is easy to underestimate convex functions such as f, whereas it is difficult to handle non-convex and non-concave functions. That is why we will define tight approximations of these constraints.

3   Quadratic Constraint Filtering Based on Linear Programming

The problem of quadratic terms linearization has been studied in quadratic optimization; for a deeper overview see [1, 21]. We introduce here a simplification of these linearizations adapted to our purpose.

The proposed approach is based on Reformulation-Linearization Technique (RLT) [21] for filtering efficiently a quadratic constraints systems:

---

[2] In the same way that *arc*-consistency has been generalized to higher consistencies (e.g. path-consistency), $2B$–consistency can be generalized to $3B$-consistency and *Box*–consistency can be generalized to Bound-consistency [12].

$$\sum_{(i,j)\in M} C^k_{i,j} x_i * x_j + \sum_{i\in N} C^k_i x_i^2 + \sum_{i\in N} d^k_i x_i = b_k$$

where $C^k_{i,j}, C^k_i, d^k_i \in I\!R$ for all $(i,j) \in M$ et $k \in 1..K$.

3.1   An Overview of the Proposed Framework

The goal is to transform the quadratic constraints system into a linear program to be able to approximate the upper and lower bounds of the variables with the simplex algorithm.

Quadratic constraints may be approximated by linear constraints in the following way :

– create a new variable for each quadratic term : y for x^2 with a domain $[\underline{x}, \overline{x}]$; $y_{i,j}$ for $x_i * x_j$ with a domain $[\min\{\underline{x_i} * \underline{x_j}, \underline{x_i} * \overline{x_j}, \overline{x_i} * \underline{x_j}, \overline{x_i} * \overline{x_j}\}, \max\{\underline{x_i} * \underline{x_j}, \underline{x_i} * \overline{x_j}, \overline{x_i} * \underline{x_j}, \overline{x_i} * \overline{x_j}\}]$
– linearize each quadratic constraint of the constraint system (1) by using the previous new variables; we denote the produced system

$$[\sum_{(i,j)\in M} C^k_{i,j} x_i * x_j + \sum_{i\in N} C^k_i x_i^2 + \sum_{i\in N} d^k_i x_i = b_k]_l$$

where $(i,j) \in M$ and $k \in 1..K$; $[E]_l$ denotes E where the quadratic terms are replaced by their variables.

A tight linear (convex) relaxation, or outer-approximation to the convex and concave envelope[3] of the quadratic terms over the constrained region, is built by generating new linear inequalities.

So, we obtain a first naive linear relaxation of the quadratic constraints (1). We denote it LP1. Of course, if no quadratic terms occurs in the initial constraints, LP1 is an exact relaxation. As stated before, we have to introduce a new linear relaxation to take into account quadratic terms. In the next subsections we introduce two tight linear relaxation classes that preserves equations $y = x^2$ and $y_{i,j} = x_i * x_j$ and that provide a better approximation than interval arithmetic. In section 4, we give an overview of the whole filtering algorithm of quadratic constraints.

---

[3] "Let $f : S \rightarrow E_1$, where $S \subseteq E_n$ is a nonempty convex set. Then, the **convex envelope** of f over S, denoted $f_s(x), x \in S$, is a convex function such that : (1) $f_s(x) \leq f(x)$ for all $x \in S$, (2) if g is any other convex function for which $g(x) \leq f(x)$ for all $x \in S$, then $f_s(x) \geq g(x)$ for all $x \in S$. Hence, $f_s(x)$ is the component-wise supremum over all convex underestimation of f over S. **Concave envelope** is defined in a similar way, and defines component-wise infemum over all convex overestimation of f over S" [6],page 125.

3.2   Linearization of x^2

Proposition 1 introduces the simplest and straightforward linearizations.

Proposition 1 (class I: linearizations for $f(x) = x^2$).
Consider the function $f(x) = x^2$ and suppose that $\underline{x} \leq x \leq \overline{x}$, then the following relations preserve all values (x, y) satisfying $y = f(x)$:

$$L1(y, \alpha) \equiv [(x - \alpha)^2 \geq 0]_l \ \text{where} \ \alpha \in [\underline{x}, \overline{x}] \tag{3}$$

and

$$L2(y) \equiv (\underline{x} + \overline{x})x - y - \underline{x} * \overline{x} \geq 0 \tag{4}$$

Proof : Inequality (3) is straightforward.
The second inequality (4), stated by [2], comes from the valid inequality :

$$0 \leq [(x - \underline{x})(\overline{x} - x)]_l = -y + (\underline{x} + \overline{x})x - \underline{x} * \overline{x}$$

□

Note that $[(x - \alpha_i)^2 = 0]_l$ generates the tangent line to the curve $y = x^2$ at the point $x = \alpha_i$. Consider for instance the quadratic term x^2 with $x \in [-4, 5]$. Figure 3 displays the initial curve (i.e., D_1), and the lines corresponding to the equations generated by the relaxations: D_2 for $L1(y, -4) \equiv y + 8x + 16 \geq 0$, D_3 for $L1(y, 5) \equiv y - 10x + 25 \geq 0$, and D_4 for $L2(y) \equiv -y + x + 20 \geq 0$. We may note that $L1(y, -4)$ and $L1(y, 5)$ are an underestimations of y whereas $L2(y)$ is an overestimation.

The following proposition shows that Class I relaxations respect the interval square as defined in interval arithmetic [17].

Proposition 2 (interval square).
Consider the function $f(x) = x^2$ and suppose that $\underline{x} \leq x \leq \overline{x}$, then it results from relations $L1(y, \underline{x})$, $L1(y, \overline{x})$ and $L2(y)$ that

$$y \in [min(\underline{x}^2, \overline{x}^2), max(\underline{x}^2, \overline{x}^2)] \ \text{if} \ 0 \notin [\underline{x}, \overline{x}]$$

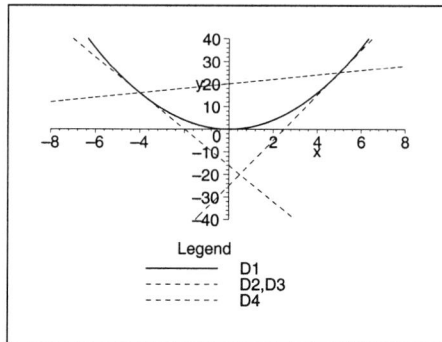

Fig. 3. Illustration of class I relaxations

and

$$y \in [0, max(\underline{x}^2, \overline{x}^2)] \ otherwise$$

Proof : Relations $L1(y, \underline{x})$, $L1(y, \overline{x})$ and $L2(y)$ state that

$$y - 2\underline{x} * x + \underline{x}^2 \geq 0 \Rightarrow y \geq 2\underline{x} * x - \underline{x}^2$$

$$y - 2\overline{x} * x + \overline{x}^2 \geq 0 \Rightarrow y \geq 2\overline{x} * x - \overline{x}^2$$

$$(\underline{x} + \overline{x})x - y - \underline{x} * y \geq 0 \Rightarrow y \leq (\underline{x} + \overline{x})x - \underline{x} * y$$

Suppose that $x \geq \underline{x} \geq 0$, then the first inequation entails $y \geq \underline{x}^2$ and the second one implies $y \leq \overline{x}^2$. The other cases can be proven in a similar way. $\square$

3.3 Linearization of $x_i * x_j$

Now, consider the function $g(x_i, x_j) = x_i x_j$ over $[\underline{x_i}, \overline{x_i}] \times [\underline{x_j}, \overline{x_j}]$. Proposition 3 has been stated by [2, 1]. It introduces a linear outer approximations of the function g on the hyper-rectangle $[\underline{x_i}, \overline{x_i}] \times [\underline{x_j}, \overline{x_j}]$.

Proposition 3 (Class II : linearization of $g(x_i, x_j) = x_i x_j$).
Consider $g(x_i, x_j) = x_i x_j$ *with* $\underline{x_i} \leq x_i \leq \overline{x_i}$ *and* $\underline{x_j} \leq x_j \leq \overline{x_j}$, *then for all* $x_i \in [\underline{x_i}, \overline{x_i}]$ *and* $x_j \in [\underline{x_j}, \overline{x_j}]$, *the following relations preserve all values* $(x_i, x_j, y_{i,j})$ *satisfying* $y_{i,j} = g(x_i, x_j)$:

$$L3(y_{i,j}) \equiv [(x_i - \underline{x_i})(x_j - \underline{x_j}) \geq 0]_l \tag{5}$$

$$L4(y_{i,j}) \equiv [(x_i - \underline{x_i})(\overline{x_j} - x_j) \geq 0]_l \tag{6}$$

$$L5(y_{i,j}) \equiv [(\overline{x_i} - x_i)(x_j - \underline{x_j}) \geq 0]_l \tag{7}$$

$$L6(y_{i,j}) \equiv [(\overline{x_i} - x_i)(\overline{x_j} - x_j) \geq 0]_l \tag{8}$$

Proof : Relations $L3(y_{i,j})...L6(y_{i,j})$ are of the form $AB \geq 0$, where A and B are always positive. $\square$

These relations define respectively the concave and convex envelopes of $g(x_i, x_j)$. Consider for instance the quadratic term $x * y$ with $x \in [-5, 5]$ and $y \in [-5, 5]$. The work done by the linear relaxations of the 3D curve $z = x * y$ is well illustrated in 2D by fixing z. Figure 4 displays the 2D shape, for the level $z = 5$, of the initial curve (i.e., Cu), and the lines corresponding to the equations generated by the relaxations (where $z = 5$): D_1 for $L3(z) \equiv z + 5x + 5y + 25 \geq 0$, D_2 for $L4(z) \equiv -z + 5x - 5y + 25 \geq 0$, D_3 for $L5(z) \equiv -z - 5x + 5y + 25 \geq 0$, and D_4 for $L6(z) \equiv z - 5x - 5y + 25 \geq 0$. We may note that these relaxations are the optimal linear relaxations of $z = x * y$.

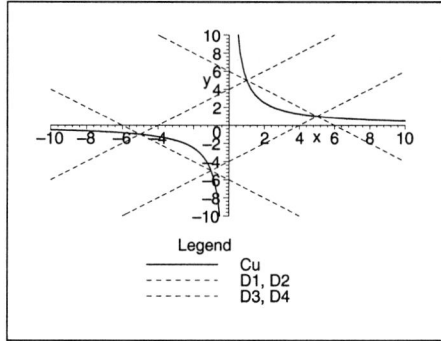

Fig. 4. Illustration of class II relaxations

Proposition 4 (Convex/concave envelopes of g [2, 1]). $L3(y_{i,j})$ and $L6(y_{i,j})$ are the convex envelope of g. $L4(y_{i,j})$ and $L5(y_{i,j})$ are the concave envelope of g.

Proof : See [2, 1]. $\square$

Thus with Class II, we have the tightest linear relaxations of the function g.

The following proposition shows that Class II relaxations respect interval multiplication as defined in interval arithmetic [17].

Proposition 5 (interval multiplication).
Consider $g(x_i, x_j) = x_i * x_j$ with $\underline{x_i} \leq x_i \leq \overline{x_i}$ and $\underline{x_j} \leq x_j \leq \overline{x_j}$, then for all $x_i \in [\underline{x_i}, \overline{x_i}]$ and $x_j \in [\underline{x_j}, \overline{x_j}]$. It results from relations $L3(y_{i,j})$, $L4(y_{i,j})$, $L5(y_{i,j})$ and $L6(y_{i,j})$ that

$$y_{i,j} \in [min(\underline{x_i} * \underline{x_j}, \underline{x_i} * \overline{x_j}, \overline{x_i} * \underline{x_j}, \overline{x_i} * \overline{x_j}), max(\underline{x_i} * \underline{x_j}, \underline{x_i} * \overline{x_j}, \overline{x_i} * \underline{x_j}, \overline{x_i} * \overline{x_j})]$$

Proof : According to the sign of $\underline{x_i}, \overline{x_i}, \underline{x_j}$ and $\overline{x_j}$: $L3(y_{i,j})$ or $L6(y_{i,j})$ yields the interval multiplication lower bound whereas $L4(y_{i,j})$ or $L5(y_{i,j})$ provides the interval multiplication upper bound. $\square$

Many other relaxations have been proposed by [21, 4]. For simplicity, we prefer to restrict the presentation to only these two classes which are sufficient to achieve a better filtering than $2B$-consistency and *Box*-consistency do.

4   Quad, The New Filtering Algorithm

Now, we are in position to define LRQ, the set of linear relations we use to approximate quadratic constraints:

$$LRQ \equiv \begin{cases} [\sum_{(i,j)\in M} C_{i,j}^k x_i * x_j + \sum_{i\in N} C_i^k x_i^2 + \sum_{i\in N} d_i^k x_i = b_k]_l \\ L1(y, \underline{x_i}), L1(y, \overline{x_i}) \text{ for all } i \in N \\ L2(y) \text{ for all } i \in N \\ L3(y_{i,j}), L4(y_{i,j}), L5(y_{i,j}), L6(y_{i,j}) \text{ for all } (i,j) \in M \end{cases}$$

LRQ will be embedded in a linear program (LP) for filtering *quad*-constraints.

The filtering process is shown in Algorithm 1.

Algorithm 1 The `Quad` algorithm

Function *quad−filtering*(IN: $\mathcal{D}$, Q, ϵ) **return** $\mathcal{D}'$
% $\mathcal{D}$: input domains; Q: quadratic constraints (1)
% ϵ: minimal reduction
$\mathcal{D}' := \mathcal{D}$
do
    $\mathcal{D} := \mathcal{D}'$
    for all $x_i \in vars(Q)$ **do**
        Construct and solve the following LP
        $\begin{cases} Z = minimize(x_i) \\ LRQ \text{ from the quadratic constraints } Q \end{cases}$
        $\underline{x_i}' := max(\underline{x_i}, Z)$
        Solve the same LP with $Z = maximize(x_i)$
        $\overline{x_i}' := min(\overline{x_i}, Z)$
    endfor
while the reduction amount of some bound is greater than ϵ **and** $\emptyset \notin \mathcal{D}'$

Since *LRQ* is a safe approximation of the initial constraint system, `Quad` achieves a safe pruning of the domains[4].

At each iteration step, the reduction achieved by the simplex must be greater than ϵ for at least one bound of some variable. The iteration process is stopped as soon as the domain of some variable becomes empty. So, the algorithm converges and terminated if ϵ is greater than zero.

Next section shows that this algorithm behaves well on different benchmarks.

5   Experimentations

To evaluate the contribution of the `Quad` algorithm we have compared its performances with classical filtering algorithms (i.e., 2B-filtering, *Box*-filtering and 3B-filtering) and with the `Numerica` system [24] on two benchmarks : the Gough-Stewart platform [11] and a Kinematics application, named "kin2" [18, 23]. We have performed the following experimentations:

– Filtering initial domains containing exactly one solution;

---

[4] Provided that the computation done by the simplex algorithm are corrects, that's to say that the rounding problem are properly handled in the implementation of the simplex algorithm; actually a safe rounding can also be achieved after calling an LP-solver (see 'Safe bounds in linear and mixed-integer programming' http://www.mat.univie.ac.at/ neum/papers.html#mip)

- Filtering initial domains containing many solutions;
- Combining of filtering and splitting to isolate all the solutions.

Experimentations concerning $2B$-filtering, Box-filtering and $3B$-filtering have been performed with the implementation of iCOs [14, 15], one of the most efficient library for this kind of algorithms.

Quad has been implemented with the linear programming solver "SOPLEX" [25]. Quad and Numerica use the same splitting strategies to isolate the different solutions. Experimentations with Numerica have been run on a Sun Enterprise 4000 with two Ultrasparc II at 336Mhz whereas all other experimentations have been done on PC-Notebook/1Ghz. CPU times are given in seconds.

5.1   The Gough-Stewart Platform Benchmark

The first benchmark [11] comes from robotics and describes the kinematics of a Gough-Stewart platform.

Problem 1 (Gough-Stewart [11]).
$$\begin{cases} x_1^2 + y_1^2 + z_1^2 = 31; x_2^2 + y_2^2 + z_2^2 = 39; x_3^2 + y_3^2 + z_3^2 = 29; \\ x_1x_2 + y_1y_2 + z_1z_2 + 6x_1 - 6x_2 = 51; \\ x_1x_3 + y_1y_3 + z_1z_3 + 7x_1 - 2y_1 - 7x_3 + 2y_3 = 50; \\ x_2x_3 + y_2y_3 + z_1z_3 + x_2 - 2y_2 - x_3 + 2y_3 = 34; \\ -12x_1 + 15y_1 - 10x_2 - 25y_2 + 18x_3 + 18y_3 = -32; \\ -14x_1 + 35y_1 - 36x_2 - 45y_2 + 30x_3 + 18y_3 = 8; \\ 2x_1 + 2y_1 - 14x_2 - 2y_2 + 8x_3 - y_3 = 20; \\ x_1 \in [-2.00, 5.57]; y_1 \in [-5.57, 2.70]; z_1 \in [0, 5.57] \\ x_2 \in [-6.25, 1.30]; y_2 \in [-6.25, 2.70]; z_2 \in [-2.00, 6.25] \\ x_3 \in [-5.39, 0.70]; y_3 \in [-5.39, 3.11]; z_3 \in [-3.61, 5.39] \end{cases}$$

Table 1 shows the results of the different filtering algorithms for some initial domains containing only one solution. The symbol "−" means that no reduction has been done. Quad is the only algorithm who isolates the unique solution. These results outline the advantage of the global view of Quad over the local or partial view of the other filtering algorithms.

Table 2 shows that the different algorithms yield almost the same pruned domains for some initial domains containing several solutions.

Table 3 provides the execution timing for finding all the solutions on the domains of 2. Quad outperforms Numerica and "interval Newton" on this problem. Numerica was run with Box–consistency, the default consistency; results where worst with $Bound$–consistency.

More than 3 hours CPU time are required to isolate the solutions when using $3B$–consistency filtering and a splitting process.

The results of "interval Newton" are those published by [11]; the computations where done on a Pentium 90 computer, more than 10 time slower than our computer. Removing multiple occurrences of the variables, enables [11] to solve the problem in about three hours. Didrit [11] solves in 24 minutes an other formulation of that problem which is far from being obvious and where three

Table 1. Filtering results on the Gough-Stewart problem for some domain containing only one solution

	Initial domains	2B	Box	3B	Quad
x_1	[0.00, 5.57]	[0.00, 5.56]	[0.00, 5.56]	[0.55, 4.68]	[2.93, 2.93]
y_1	[0.00, 2.70]	-	-	-	[0.45, 0.45]
z_1	[0.00, 5.57]	[0.00, 5.56]	[0.00, 5.56]	[1.14, 5.54]	[4.70, 4.70]
x_2	[-6.00, 0.00]	[-4.50,-0.15]	[-4.50,-0.15]	[-4.07,-0.84]	[-1.81,-1.81]
y_2	[-2.00, 0.00]	-	-	-	[-0.48,-0.48]
z_2	[0.00, 6.25]	[3.83, 6.24]	[3.83, 6.24]	[4.43, 6.17]	[5.95, 5.95]
x_3	[-5.39,-1.00]	[-5.38,-1.00]	[-5.38,-1.00]	[-5.05,-1.00]	[-1.66,-1.66]
y_3	[-5.39, 0.00]	[-5.29, 0.00]	[-5.29, 0.00]	[-4.38, 0.00]	[-0.20,-0.20]
z_3	[0.00, 5.39]	[0.00, 5.29]	[0.00, 5.29]	[0.91, 5.29]	[5.11, 5.11]

Table 2. Filtering results on the Gough-Stewart problem for some domain containing many solutions

	Initial domains	2B	Box	3B	Quad
x_1	[-2.00, 5.57]	[-2.00, 5.56]	[-2.00, 5.56]	[-2.00, 5.44]	-
y_1	[-5.57, 2.70]	[-5.56, 2.70]	[-5.56, 2.70]	[-5.56,2.70]	-
z_1	[0.00, 5.57]	[0.00, 5.56]	[0.00, 5.56]	[0.00,5.56]	-
x_2	[-6.25, 1.30]	[-6.19, 1.30]	[-6.19, 1.30]	[-5.64, 0.75]	[-5.17, 0.34]
y_2	[-6.25, 2.70]	[-6.24, 2.70]	[-6.24, 2.70]	[-6.24, 2.70]	[-1.77, 2.70]
z_2	[-2.00, 6.25]	[-2.00, 6.24]	[-2.00, 6.24]	[-2.00, 6.24]	-
x_3	[-5.39, 0.70]	[-5.38, 0.69]	[-5.38, 0.69]	[-5.38, 0.69]	[-5.38, 0.69]
y_3	[-5.39, 3.11]	[-5.38, 3.10]	[-5.38, 3.10]	[-5.38, 3.10]	[-5.39, 3.10]
z_3	[-3.61, 5.39]	[-3.60, 5.38]	[-3.60, 5.38]	[-3.60, 5.38]	[-3.60, 5.38]

variables are removed. Note that Quad requires very few splittings to find the four solutions of this problem.

5.2   The Kinematics Benchmark

Now, let us consider a kinematics application, named " kin2" [18, 23]. This second benchmark describes the inverse position for a six-revolute-joint problem. The results obtained with the different algorithms are similar to the previous one.

Table 4 shows the results of the different filtering algorithms for some initial domains containing only one solution. Quad is again the only algorithm who isolates the unique solution.

Once again, the pruning achieved by $2B/Box/3B$-filtering and Quad is not significant when the initial domains contain several solutions (see table 5).

Table 6 shows that the performances of Quad and Numerica are comparable but that Quad requires much less splittings than Numerica to find the solutions. The speed of Quad could probably be improved by using a more efficient simplex algorithm like CPLEX .

Table 3. Filtering performance for Gough-Stewart problem

	Interval Newton	Numerica	Quad
CPU time	14400	4480	183
splittings	?	122469	24
narrowings	10^6	10470159	27255

Table 4. Filtering results on the kinematics problem for some domain containing a single solution

	Initial domains	$2B$	Box	$3B$	Quad
x_1	[0.00, 1.00]	-	-	-	[0.97, 0.97]
x_2	[0.00, 1.00]	-	-	-	[0.20, 0.20]
x_3	[0.00, 1.00]	-	-	[0.00, 0.95]	[0.02, 0.02]
x_4	[0.00, 1.00]	-	-	[0.29, 1.00]	[0.99, 0.99]
x_5	[-1.00, 0.00]	-	-	-	[-0.09,-0.09]
x_6	[0.00, 1.00]	-	-	-	[0.99, 0.99]
x_7	[0.00,1.00]	-	-	[0.00, 0.96]	[0.07, 0.07]
x_8	[-1.00, 0.00]	-	-	[-1.00,-0.27]	[-0.99,-0.99]

Table 5. Filtering results on the kinematics problem for some domain containing many solutions

	Initial domains	$2B$	Box	$3B$	Quad
x_1	[-1.00, 1.00]	-	-	-	-
x_2	[-1.00, 1.00]	-	-	-	-
x_3	[-1.00, 1.00]	-	-	-	-
x_4	[-1.00, 1.00]	-	-	-	-
x_5	[-1.00, 1.00]	-	-	-	-
x_6	[-1.00, 1.00]	-	-	-	-
x_7	[-1.00, 1.00]	-	-	-	[-0.99, 1.00]
x_8	[-1.00, 1.00]	-	-	-	[-1.00, 0.98]

6   Conclusion

This paper has introduced a new algorithm for handling systems of quadratic constraints. This algorithm performs a global filtering on a linear relaxation of the initial constraint system. First experimentations are very promising and show the capabilities of this framework.

Further works concern the integration of Quad in a general interval solver to tackle non-polynomial problems with a significant subset of quadratic constraints. So, Quad could play the role of global constraint in many geometric or robotics applications where numerous distance constraints often occur.

Table 6. Filtering performance for the kinematics problem

	Numerica	*quad*
CPU time	169	61
splittings	5421	33
narrowings	105704	12267

Acknowledgments

Thanks to Prof. Arnold Neumaier who suggested us to explore the capabilities of linearization techniques for a global handling of distance relations. Thanks also to Bertrand Neveu for his careful reading of an earlier draft of this paper.

References

[1] F. A. Al-Khayyal. Jointly constrained biconvex programming and related problems: An overview. *Computers and Mathematics with Applications*, pages Vol.19, No.11, 53–62, 1990.

[2] F. A. Al-Khayyal and J. E. Falk. Jointly constrained biconvex programming. *Mathematics of Operations Research*, pages Vol.8, No.2, 273–286, 1983.

[3] G. Alefeld and J. Hezberger, editors. *Introduction to Interval Computations.* Academic press, 1983.

[4] C. Audet, P. Hansen, B. Jaumard, and G. Savard. Branch and cut algorithm for nonconvex quadratically constrained quadratic programming. *Mathematical Programming*, pages 87(1), 131–152, 2000.

[5] O. P. Babichev, A. B.and Kadyrova, T. P. Kashevarova, A. S. Leshchenko, and Semenov A. L. Unicalc, a novel approach to solving systems of algebraic equations. *Interval Computations 1993 (2)*, pages 29–47, 1993.

[6] M. S. Bazaraa, H. D. Sherali, and C. M. Shetty. *Nonlinear Programming : Theory and Algorithms.* John Wiley & Sons, 1993.

[7] F. Benhamou, D. McAllester, and P. Van-Hentenryck. Clp(intervals) revisited. In *Proceedings of the International Symposium on Logic Programming*, pages 124–138, 1994.

[8] F. Benhamou and W. Older. Applying interval arithmetic to real, integer and boolean constraints. *Journal of Logic Programming*, pages 32(1):1–24, 1997.

[9] A. Colmerauer. Spécifications de prolog iv. Technical report, GIA, Faculté des Sciences de Luminy,163, Avenue de Luminy 13288 Marseille cedex 9 (France), 1994.

[10] E. Davis. Constraint propagation with interval labels. *Journal of Artificial Intelligence*, pages 32:281–331, 1987.

[11] O. Didrit. *Analyse par intervalles pour l'automatique : résolution globale et garantie de problèmes non linéaires en robotique et en commande robuste.* PhD thesis, Université Parix XI Orsay, 1997.

[12] M. Rueher H.Collavizza, F.Delobel. Comparing partial consistencies. *Reliable Computing*, pages Vol.5(3),213–228, 1999.

[13] Ilog, editor. *ILOG Solver 4.0, Reference Manual.* Ilog, 1997.

[14] Y. Lebbah. *Contribution à la résolution de contraintes par consistance forte*. PhD thesis, Ecole des Mines de Nantes, France, 1999.

[15] Y. Lebbah and O. Lhomme. Accelerating filtering techniques for numeric csps. *Journal of Artificial Intelligence*, page Forthcoming, 2002.

[16] O. Lhomme. Consistency techniques for numeric csps. In *Proceedings of IJCAI'93*, pages 232–238, 1993.

[17] R. Moore. *Interval Analysis*. Prentice Hall, 1966.

[18] A. P. Morgan. Computing all solutions to polynomial systems using homotopy continuation. *Appl. Math. Comput.*, pages 24:115–138, 1987.

[19] A. Neumaier. *Introduction to Numerical Analysis*. Cambridge Univ. Press, Cambridge, 2001.

[20] W. J. Older and A. Velino. Extending prolog with constraint arithmetic on real intervals. In *Proc. of IEEE Canadian conference on Electrical and Computer Engineering*, pages 14.1.1–14.1.4. IEEE Computer Society Press, 1990.

[21] H. D. Sherali and W. P. Adams. *A Reformulation-Linearization Technique for Solving Discrete and Continuous Nonconvex Problems*. Kluwer Academic Publishing, 1999.

[22] H. D. Sherali and C. H. Tuncbilek. A global optimization algorithm for polynomial using a reformulation-linearization technique. *Journal of Global Optimization*, pages 7, 1–31, 1992.

[23] P. Van-Hentenryck, D. Mc Allester, and D. Kapur. Solving polynomial systems using branch and prune approach. *SIAM Journal on Numerical Analysis*, pages 34(2):797–827, 1997.

[24] P. Van-Hentenryck, L. Michel, and Y. Deville. *Numerica : a Modeling Languge for Global Optimization*. MIT press, 1997.

[25] R. Wunderlings. *Paralleler und Objektorientierter Simplex-Algorithmus (in German)*. PhD thesis, Berlin, 1996.

Amplification of Search Performance through Randomization of Heuristics

Vincent A. Cicirello and Stephen F. Smith

The Robotics Institute, Carnegie Mellon University
5000 Forbes Avenue, Pittsburgh, PA 15213
{cicirello,sfs}@cs.cmu.edu

Abstract. Randomization as a means for improving search performance in combinatorial domains has received increasing interest in recent years. In optimization contexts, it can provide a means for overcoming the deficiencies of available search heuristics and broadening search in productive directions. In this paper, we consider the issue of amplifying the performance of a search heuristic through randomization. We introduce a general framework for embedding a base heuristic within an iterative sampling process and searching a stochastic neighborhood of the heuristic's prescribed trajectory. In contrast to previous approaches, which have used rank-ordering as a basis for randomization, our approach instead relies on assigned heuristic value. Use of heuristic value is important because it makes it possible to vary the level of stochasticity in relation to the discriminatory power of the heuristic in different decision contexts, and hence concentrate search around those decisions where the heuristic is least informative. To evaluate the efficacy of the approach, we apply it to a complex, weighted-tardiness scheduling problem. Taking a state-of-the-art heuristic for this scheduling problem as a starting point, we demonstrate an ability to consistently and significantly improve on the deterministic heuristic solution across a broad range of problem instances. Our approach is also shown to consistently outperform a previously developed, rank-ordering based approach to randomizing the same heuristic in terms of percentage of improvement obtained.

1 Introduction

A fundamental design challenge for search procedures in combinatorial domains concerns how to promote good coverage of higher-valued points of the solution space in a computationally efficient manner. Search heuristics provide a basis for managing search efficiency in many domains. But since heuristics are not infallible, an optimizing search process must in many cases balance adherence to their advice against the possibility of missing better solutions.

Randomization provides a natural approach to hedging on this trade-off. One general schema that has gained increasing attention in recent years follows an iterative sampling framework - solutions (or partial solutions) are generated using a base search procedure with some amount of non-determinism and this procedure is repeatedly re-started to explore different solution paths. In constraint

P. Van Hentenryck (Ed.): CP 2002, LNCS 2470, pp. 124–138, 2002.
© Springer-Verlag Berlin Heidelberg 2002

satisfaction problem-solving (CSP) domains, the observed heavy-tailed nature of search runtime distributions across different solution trajectories provides a conceptual rationale for adopting this approach [6]. By cutting off search at specified computational time-limits (in essence, abandoning trials that belong to the heavy-tail) and repeatedly restarting along different solution paths, the overall search process can reach more productive regions of this search space sooner. In practice, this is precisely the behavior observed; the approach has been shown to significantly reduce the run-times of complete search procedures on hard problem instances across a range of problem domains [6, 10].

In the realm of combinatorial optimization, randomization and iterative sampling have similarly yielded productive results [13, 2, 3, 6, 5], although the underlying rationale is somewhat different. The concern in this case is more than minimizing the time required to obtain a feasible solution; it is instead to find the best possible solution as quickly as possible. Given this optimizing search focus, research has tended to place greater reliance on strong, domain-specific heuristics and emphasize randomization of incomplete search approaches. The rationale starts from the assumption that a good heuristic is available and argues that the neighborhood around its preferred solution path is a good one to search.[1] In essence, randomization serves to amplify the performance of the heuristic by allowing search to compensate for its occasional misstep.

One crucial aspect of any iterative sampling search procedure is the approach taken to randomizing the base search heuristic. Conceptually, the goal is to perturb the choice order prescribed by the heuristic at a given decision point in a way that preserves much of the heuristic's original bias. A simple, non-interfering strategy is to simply break ties randomly in those decision contexts where two or more top choices are ranked equivalently (i.e., making random decisions only when the heuristic fails to make a selection). A somewhat more aggressive approach, called heuristic equivalency [6], chooses randomly among all choices having a heuristic value within $H\%$ of the highest. Bresina [2] defined a more general framework called Heuristic-Biased Stochastic Sampling (HBSS), which utilizes a specified bias function as a basis for deviating from the choice order given by the base heuristic. Through use of different bias functions, a wide range of randomization strategies can be realized, including the two basic strategies just mentioned.

In this paper, we propose an alternative approach to randomizing search heuristics within an iterative sampling framework. Our approach has much in common with the HBSS approach of Bresina [2], but with one important difference. Instead of operating with respect to the rank ordering of choices that is implied by application of the heuristic, our approach biases selection on the actual values assigned by the heuristic to each possible choice. Like Oddi and Smith [10], we assume that the heuristic can be more or less discriminating in different decision contexts and argue that the heuristic's degree of preference for one choice over another should impact the random selection process. Our

---

[1] This rationale also underlies the design of some recent deterministic search procedures such as discrepancy search [7, 12].

approach is inspired by a stochastic model of how wasp colonies self-organize (or order themselves) into dominance hierarchies. However, the technique is lifted from the Biological context and reformulated as a general framework for randomizing heuristics. Borrowing from HBSS, we designate our approach Wasp beHavior Inspired STochastic sampLING (WHISTLING).

We demonstrate the advantage of this "value-based" approach to randomization through application to a class of sequence-dependent, weighted-tardiness scheduling problems. This domain is interesting in two respects. On one hand, it presents a difficult combinatorial optimization challenge. On the other, it is a practical problem and significant prior effort has gone into the development of good heuristics. Taking a state-of-the-art heuristic for this problem class as a starting point, we show that our technique consistently improves the quality of the solution obtained by straight deterministic application of the heuristic, and consistently outperforms HBSS in terms of percentage of improvement obtained. Further, as a consequence of relying directly on the values assigned to different choices by the heuristic, our approach is an inherently more efficient computational process. Before describing our approach, we first summarize the earlier developed HBSS framework.

2 Heuristic-Biased Stochastic Sampling

As just indicated, Bresina's HBSS framework provides a general basis for amplifying heuristic performance through randomization. HBSS operates within a global search paradigm, where partial solutions are extended by adding one new decision at each step of the search. A random choice process is invoked to make each decision, and this process is biased according to a pre-specified heuristic for the problem at hand. Specifically, the heuristic is used to first prioritize the alternatives that remain feasible at a given decision point, and then a bias function is superimposed over this ranking to stochastically select from this ranked set. Once a complete solution is generated, it is evaluated according to overall optimization criteria. The search process is then repeated some number of times and the best solution generated is taken as the final result.

The specific problem considered by Bresina was the scheduling of observations on a telescope. Given a set of potential observation tasks and an objective criterion (e.g., maximize viewing time), the problem is to produce a schedule (i.e., a sequence of tasks) for execution during the next period. Formulated within HBSS, generation of a schedule proceeds in a forward dispatching manner, by repeatedly ranking the subset of tasks that remain "unscheduled", and then choosing the next task to append to the current (partial) schedule.[2] This process iterates until either all potential tasks have been scheduled or the time

---

[2] Re-ranking is necessary at each step because the state (e.g., the position of the telescope and current time), and thus the heuristic ordering, change each time a new task is added to the tentative schedule. Also contributing to the context-dependent nature of the ranking is the fact that some observation tasks are only schedulable within specific time windows and thus are not always feasible choices.

Algorithm 1: Heuristic-Biased Stochastic Sampling (HBSS)
Input: Number of iterations I; a "heuristic" function; a "bias" function; an "objective" function; and a set of tasks T_j to schedule.
Output: A schedule S.
HBSS(I, heuristic, bias, objective, tasks T_j)
(1)   bestsofar ← DISPATCHSCHEDULING(T_j, heuristic)
(2)   **repeat** I times
(3) S ← the empty schedule
(4)   **while** not all tasks scheduled
(5)   **foreach** unscheduled task T
(6)   score[T] ← heuristic(T, S)
(7)   sort all tasks T according to score[T]
(8)   **foreach** unscheduled task T
(9)   rank[T] ← sort position of T
(10)   weight[T] ← bias(rank[T])
(11)   totalweight ← totalweight + weight[T]
(12)   **foreach** unscheduled task T
(13)   prob[T] ← weight[T] / totalweight
(14)   **select** randomly the next task biased according to prob[T]
(15)   add this selected task to the candidate schedule S
(16)   remove this selected task from the set of unscheduled tasks
(17)   evaluate[S] ← objective(S)
(18)   **if** evaluate[S] is superior to evaluate[bestsofar]
(19)   bestsofar ← S
(20)   **return** bestsofar

Fig. 1. The HBSS Algorithm

frame has been exhausted.[3] The resulting schedule is then evaluated globally and the search process is restarted. The HBSS algorithm is illustrated in the context of this scheduling problem in Algorithm 1.

The ability to use different bias functions within HBSS provides a means of placing more or less emphasis on following the advice of the base heuristic. In Bresina's HBSS framework [2] a number of polynomial bias functions of the form r^{-n} and an exponential bias function of the form e^{-r}, are proposed and explored, where r is the rank of the choice in question. As pointed out by Bresina [2], the choice of bias function can and should be made based on overall confidence in the base heuristic. If the heuristic is deemed strong, then it makes sense to follow it more often; if the heuristic is weak, then a more disruptive bias is called for. The potential problem is that heuristics are typically more or less informed in different decision contexts; and it is not possible to calibrate the degree of randomness allowed according to this dynamic aspect of problem solving

---

[3] In most cases, it is not possible to schedule all desired observations in Bresina's domain within the allotted time window.

state. This capability requires movement away from an approach to random bias based strictly on rank order. We introduce such an approach in the next section.

3   Wasp Behavior Inspired Stochastic Sampling (WHISTLING)

Our stochastic search framework makes its random decisions using a value-based bias rather than a rank-based bias. Random decisions are made in a manner equivalent to spinning a roulette wheel, where each choice is given a section of the wheel proportional in size to the value given by the heuristic to making that choice.

Our approach to computing this roulette wheel decision derives from a naturally-inspired computational model of the self-organization that takes place within a colony of wasps [11]. In nature, a hierarchical social order among the wasps of the colony is formed through interactions among individual wasps of the colony. This emergent social order is a succession (or prioritization) of wasps from the most dominant to the least dominant. In the model of Theraulaz *et al.*, the results of these interactions are determined stochastically based on the "force" variables of the wasps involved. The probability of wasp 1 winning a dominance contest against wasp 2 is defined based on the force variables, F_1 and F_2, of the wasps as:

$$P(F_1, F_2) = \frac{F_1^2}{F_1^2 + F_2^2} \ . \tag{1}$$

After such an interaction, the value of the force variable of the winner is increased and the value of the force variable of the loser is decreased. Over time, through many such interactions, a hierarchical social order is formed.

We can map the above model to the problem of randomizing heuristic choices by associating a wasp as a proxy for each possible choice in a decision context, and defining the force of a given wasp to be a function of the heuristic value assigned to its corresponding choice.

More precisely, we define the force of a wasp as:

$$F_w = \text{bias}(\text{heuristic}(\text{Choice}_w)) + D \ , \tag{2}$$

where Choice_w is the choice represented by wasp w, heuristic() is a function that returns the heuristic value of the given choice, and bias() is a bias function (as in the HBSS framework). D is a variable that is initialized to 0 and varies according to the results of dominance contests during a run of the algorithm (see below). It mimics the fluctuations that occur in the force variable values as dominance contests between real wasps are won and lost in nature.

Given that our definition of F_w includes an explicit bias factor, we are able to generalize, as well as simplify, the stochastic rule for choosing the winner of a dominance competition (Equation 1) as follows:

$$P(F_1, F_2) = \frac{F_1}{F_1 + F_2} \ . \tag{3}$$

Algorithm 2: Wasp beHavior Inspired STochastic sampLING (WHISTLING)
Input: Number of iterations I; a "heuristic" function; a "bias" function; an "objective"
function; and a set of tasks T_j to schedule.
Output: A schedule S.
WHISTLING(I, heuristic, bias, objective, tasks T_j)
(1)   bestsofar ← DISPATCHSCHEDULING(T_j, heuristic)
(2)   **repeat** I times
(3) S ← the empty schedule
(4)   **while** not all tasks scheduled
(5)   **foreach** unscheduled task T
(6)   force[T] ← bias(heuristic(T, S))
(7)   WinnerSoFar ← arbitrary task T from the unscheduled tasks
(8)   Challengers ← the set of unscheduled tasks − WinnerSoFar
(9)   **foreach** task T in the set Challengers
(10)   **with** probability P(force[T], force[WinnerSoFar]) (see Eq. 3)
(11)   force[T] ← force[T] + force[WinnerSoFar]
(12)   WinnerSoFar ← T
(13)   **otherwise**
(14)   force[WinnerSoFar] ← force[WinnerSoFar] + force[T]
(15)   Add WinnerSoFar to the candidate schedule S
(16)   Remove WinnerSoFar from the set of unscheduled tasks
(17)   evaluate[S] ← objective(S)
(18)   **if** evaluate[S] is superior to evaluate[bestsofar]
(19)   bestsofar ← S
(20)   **return** bestsofar

Fig. 2. The WHISTLING Algorithm

By coupling this new definition in Equation 3 with an appropriate bias function
in the force definition of Equation 2 (i.e., p^2) we can express the original rule
given in Equation 1. However, like HBSS, our reformulation allows the expression of a range of bias functions. Bonabeau *et al.* generalize their definition as
$P(F_1, F_2) = \frac{F_1^a}{F_1^a + F_2^a}$ where a is a parameter [1]. However, their motivation is
somewhat different. They discuss how this formula models the behavior of real
insect societies and how different values for a may more closely model a particular society's behavior. Furthermore, force is a variable in their model that adapts
according to wins and losses of dominance contests and is not explicitly defined
functionally as we do here. Our definition allows for the spectrum of polynomials as does Bonabeau *et al.*'s; but it also allows expression of many others
(e.g., exponentials and logarithms) that cannot be expressed by Bonabeau *et
al.*'s generalization.

  Given the above definitions of $P(F_1, F_2)$ and F_w, we can make the sampling algorithm concrete by defining a specific competition structure. In what
follows, we assume the following style of tournament. An initial wasp (choice)
is selected arbitrarily and proceeds to engage in successive competitions with
all other wasps (other choices). The initial wasp continues to compete as long

as it wins. If it is defeated, the new winner takes its place and proceeds to face
the remaining candidates. Upon winning a competition, the winning wasp's D
variable is updated to accumulate the force variable value of the loser, and the
loser drops out. The wasp (choice) remaining at the end of the tournament is
returned as the final selection.

It can be shown that this computation is equivalent to selecting according to
a standard roulette wheel decision, with each possible choice Choice$_w$ taking a
chunk of the wheel proportional to bias(heuristic(Choice$_w$)). The advantage of
this method of computing a roulette wheel decision over the usual one is that
a single pass through the set of choices is required. The alternative would be
to make one initial pass to compute $\sum_j$ bias(heuristic(Choice$_j$)) followed by a
second pass to choose w with probability $\frac{\text{bias(heuristic(Choice}_w))}{\sum_j \text{bias(heuristic(Choice}_j))}$. A proof
of the equivalence of the tournament of dominance contests to a roulette wheel
decision is provided in Appendix A.

The WHISTLING algorithm is presented in Algorithm 2, expressed in the
same scheduling problem context used earlier to describe HBSS. Line 6 of the
algorithm is the initial definition of the force of the scheduling wasps with $D = 0$
(see Equation 2). Line 11 and line 14 represent the increase in the value of D
in Equation 2 for the winning wasp. The dominance contests (see Equation 3)
take place in line 10 of the algorithm.

Computationally, the WHISTLING algorithm selects the next task to schedule in $O(T)$ time where there are T tasks to be scheduled. Since it must do
this T times, the core sampling procedure has an overall algorithmic complexity of $O(T^2)$. In fact, the complexity of a corresponding deterministic dispatch
scheduling procedure is also $O(T^2)$. Hence, WHISTLING adds only a constant
factor to the computational time required for strict deterministic application
of the heuristic. If we compare this complexity to that of the HBSS algorithm
of Algorithm 1, we can see that WHISTLING is asymptotically more efficient.
Since HBSS biases its stochastic decisions according to a rank-ordering of the
tasks, it necessarily sorts the tasks according to their heuristic values each time a
task is scheduled – an $O(T \log T)$ operation.[4] And with T tasks to schedule, the

[4] It has been pointed out that the worst-case complexity of choosing the i-th largest
element from an unsorted list is $O(n)$. Thus, in theory, this stochastic selection
operation can be done in linear time. Under an assumption that the n choices have
ranks 1 through n, we can select the winning rank without looking at the actual
elements themselves. And then use the winning rank and the linear time selection
algorithm to make the decision. One problem with this is that the assumption that
the n elements have ranks 1 through n does not hold if more than one element
may have the same heuristic value and thus the same rank. This assumption can
cause one or more choices to be ranked differently than they should be as well as
it can cause choices which should be ranked equivalently to be ranked differently.
Furthermore, the linear time algorithm for the selection operation itself is more of
a theoretical interest than of practical interest. It has a large constant factor that
results in the $O(n \log n)$ sort-first-then-select algorithm dominating for all but very
large problem instances [4].

algorithmic complexity of HBSS is $O(T^2 \log T)$. In the next Section, we will see how WHISTLING and HBSS compare experimentally in a particular scheduling domain.

4   Experiments

4.1   Experimental Design

To demonstrate and experimentally evaluate the WHISTLING framework, we turn to the domain of factory scheduling and the fairly broad body of work in the area of dispatch scheduling heuristics (c.f., [9]). In dynamic factory environments, dispatch scheduling heuristics provide a practical, robust basis for managing execution. Scheduling decisions such as which job to assign to a machine next are made in an online manner only as needed, based on the current state of the factory. Dispatch heuristics make use of information about jobs such as expected processing time, setup time, due date, priority, etc., and are typically designed to optimize a given performance objective. Their virtue is their simplicity and insensitivity to environmental dynamics and for these reasons they are commonly employed. At the same time, the localized and myopic nature by which decisions are made under such schemes make them inherently susceptible to sub-optimal decision-making.

We focus specifically on a weighted tardiness scheduling problem with sequence-dependent setups. The objective of this problem is to sequence the set of jobs J on a machine so as to minimize the total weighted tardiness:

$$T = \sum_{j \in J} w_j T_j = \sum_{j \in J} w_j \max\left(f_j - d_j, 0\right), \tag{4}$$

where T_j is the tardiness of job j; w_j, f_j, d_j are the weight, finish time, and due-date of job j. The problem is complicated by the fact that it takes variable amounts of time to reconfigure (or setup) the machine when switching between any two jobs.

To address this problem within our stochastic framework, we take as our starting point the *Apparent Tardiness Cost with Setups (ATCS)* dispatch heuristic [8]. ATCS builds on earlier research into the weighted tardiness problem and is arguably the current best performing dispatch policy for this class of scheduling problem. ATCS is defined as follows:

$$\mathrm{ATCS}_j(t, l) = \frac{w_j}{p_j} \exp\left(-\frac{\max\left(d_j - p_j - t, 0\right)}{k_1 \bar{p}} - \frac{s_{lj}}{k_2 \bar{s}}\right), \tag{5}$$

where t is the current time; l is the index of the job just completed (or the last job added to the schedule); w_j, p_j, d_j are the weight, processing time, and due-date of job j (the job for which we are computing the heuristic value), respectively; $\bar{p}$ is the average processing time of all jobs; $\bar{s}$ is the average setup time; s_{lj} is the amount of setup time needed if job j is sequenced after job l.

Table 1. Comparison of average percent improvement of 1 iteration of WHISTLING to 1 iteration of HBSS over the deterministic heuristic solution of ATCS for different classes of problem instance. n is the number of instances in the problem class. "Lee" shows the results of Lee *et al.*'s hill climber

				Lee	HBSS Bias Function		WHISTLING Bias Function		
τ	R	η	n		p^{-4}	p^{-5}	p^6	p^7	p^8
0.3	0.25	0.25	10	**19.60**	10.21	7.36	15.07	4.60	8.94
0.3	0.25	0.75	10	**24.26**	7.92	9.48	22.29	23.81	11.83
0.3	0.75	0.25	10	**50.09**	27.23	14.54	21.81	20.18	26.97
0.3	0.75	0.75	10	**40.15**	14.09	8.92	21.98	18.89	28.34
0.6	0.25	0.25	10	0.17	2.01	1.47	**2.95**	1.96	1.81
0.6	0.25	0.75	10	1.12	3.16	0.98	2.39	3.05	**3.51**
0.6	0.75	0.25	10	0.23	0.30	0.65	**1.31**	1.12	0.52
0.6	0.75	0.75	10	0.65	0.40	2.04	1.88	5.36	**6.06**
0.9	0.25	0.25	10	0.00	**0.39**	0.33	0.00	0.00	0.00
0.9	0.25	0.75	10	0.00	**0.25**	0.03	0.16	0.22	0.00
0.9	0.75	0.25	10	0.04	0.00	**0.35**	0.00	0.12	0.00
0.9	0.75	0.75	10	0.00	0.21	0.04	0.00	0.29	**0.65**
0.3	*	*	40	**33.53**	14.86	10.08	20.29	16.87	19.02
0.6	*	*	40	0.54	1.47	1.29	2.13	2.87	**2.98**
0.9	*	*	40	0.01	**0.21**	0.19	0.04	0.16	0.16
*	0.25	*	60	**7.53**	3.99	3.28	7.14	5.61	4.35
*	0.75	*	60	**15.19**	7.04	4.42	7.83	7.66	10.42
*	*	0.25	60	**11.69**	6.69	4.12	6.86	4.66	6.37
*	*	0.75	60	**11.03**	4.34	3.58	8.12	8.60	8.40
*	*	*	120	**11.36**	5.51	3.85	7.49	6.63	7.39

k_1 and k_2 are parameters for tuning the heuristic. In the experiments reported below, we set the values of these parameters according to Lee *et al.*'s original recommendations [8]. When applied deterministically, the next job j added to the schedule using the ATCS heuristic is simply:

$$j = \arg\max_j \text{ATCS}_j(t, l) \ . \tag{6}$$

The problem instances that we consider are generated according to Lee *et al.*'s procedure [8]. That is, each problem instance is characterized by three parameters: the due-date tightness factor τ; the due-date range factor R; and the setup time severity factor η. We, specifically, consider problem sets characterized by the following parameter values: $\tau = \{0.3, 0.6, 0.9\}$; $R = \{0.25, 0.75\}$; and $\eta = \{0.25, 0.75\}$. For each of the twelve combinations of parameter values, we generate 10 problem instances with 60 jobs each. Generally speaking, these 12 problem sets cover a spectrum from loosely to tightly constrained problem instances.

With regard to configuration of the WHISTLING and HBSS search procedures, we consider runs with polynomial bias functions of degree $d = 1 \ldots 8$ and

Table 2. Comparison of average percent improvement of 10 iterations of WHISTLING to 10 iterations of HBSS over the deterministic heuristic solution of ATCS for different classes of problem instance. n is the number of instances in the problem class. "Lee" shows the results of Lee *et al.*'s hill climber

Problem τ	R	η	n	Lee	HBSS Bias Function p^{-4}	p^{-5}	WHISTLING Bias Function p^6	p^7	p^8
0.3	0.25	0.25	10	19.60	18.57	25.34	28.85	25.46	**32.09**
0.3	0.25	0.75	10	24.26	32.07	29.00	**44.74**	41.47	40.30
0.3	0.75	0.25	10	**50.09**	41.84	48.41	49.68	40.80	49.22
0.3	0.75	0.75	10	40.15	44.36	53.18	54.85	53.60	**58.96**
0.6	0.25	0.25	10	0.17	3.63	4.84	3.63	4.20	**5.21**
0.6	0.25	0.75	10	1.12	9.21	7.00	8.85	**13.04**	11.19
0.6	0.75	0.25	10	0.23	3.03	1.86	**4.51**	3.68	4.21
0.6	0.75	0.75	10	0.65	6.99	11.88	11.07	12.91	**12.92**
0.9	0.25	0.25	10	0.00	**1.25**	0.86	0.30	0.39	1.14
0.9	0.25	0.75	10	0.00	1.26	1.08	0.97	0.73	**1.49**
0.9	0.75	0.25	10	0.04	**0.64**	0.48	0.00	0.13	0.23
0.9	0.75	0.75	10	0.00	1.01	1.10	0.87	**1.26**	0.76
0.3	*	*	40	33.53	34.21	38.98	44.53	40.33	**45.14**
0.6	*	*	40	0.54	5.72	6.40	7.02	**8.46**	8.38
0.9	*	*	40	0.01	**1.04**	0.88	0.54	0.63	0.91
*	0.25	*	60	7.53	11.00	11.35	14.56	14.22	**15.24**
*	0.75	*	60	15.19	16.31	19.49	20.16	18.73	**21.05**
*	*	0.25	60	11.69	11.49	13.63	14.50	12.44	**15.35**
*	*	0.75	60	11.03	15.82	17.21	20.23	20.50	**20.94**
*	*	*	120	11.36	13.66	15.42	17.36	16.47	**18.14**

number of iterations $I = 1, 10, 100$.[5] The heuristic and objective are as indicated above. We benchmark both WHISTLING and HBSS in terms of average percent improvement over the deterministic heuristic solution of ATCS.

4.2   Results

The average percent improvement of HBSS and WHISTLING over the deterministic dispatch scheduling policy of ATCS is shown in Table 1, Table 2, and Table 3 for one iteration, ten iterations, and 100 iterations of HBSS, respectively. The tables show the results obtained with the best-performing bias functions for each approach (i.e., p^{-4} and p^{-5} for HBSS; p^6, p^7, and p^8 for WHISTLING).[6]

---

[5] Negative polynomials are used in the case of HBSS since bias here is defined with respect to rank (where a lower rank is preferred). For WHISTLING, we use positive polynomials since bias is instead defined with respect to heuristic value (where a higher value is preferred).

[6] The authors can be contacted for the equivalent data for all bias functions considered during experimentation - lack of space prohibits their inclusion here.

Table 3. Comparison of average percent improvement of 100 iterations of WHISTLING to 100 iterations of HBSS over the deterministic heuristic solution of ATCS for different classes of problem instance. n is the number of instances in the problem class. "Lee" shows the results of Lee *et al.*'s hill climber

				Lee	HBSS Bias Function		WHISTLING Bias Function		
τ	R	η	n		p^{-4}	p^{-5}	p^6	p^7	p^8
0.3	0.25	0.25	10	19.60	37.19	31.43	37.67	**38.92**	35.78
0.3	0.25	0.75	10	24.26	49.52	52.39	55.04	**55.93**	54.85
0.3	0.75	0.25	10	50.09	59.15	59.02	61.37	61.70	**63.97**
0.3	0.75	0.75	10	40.15	63.66	62.61	**65.28**	64.83	63.61
0.6	0.25	0.25	10	0.17	7.42	7.62	7.82	**9.18**	8.24
0.6	0.25	0.75	10	1.12	12.27	14.37	15.56	**17.18**	15.94
0.6	0.75	0.25	10	0.23	7.01	8.13	8.19	9.16	**9.32**
0.6	0.75	0.75	10	0.65	16.20	16.46	19.03	19.40	**19.94**
0.9	0.25	0.25	10	0.00	1.68	**1.76**	0.70	1.28	1.66
0.9	0.25	0.75	10	0.00	2.36	2.11	2.15	2.52	**3.01**
0.9	0.75	0.25	10	0.04	1.10	**1.27**	0.44	0.73	1.07
0.9	0.75	0.75	10	0.00	2.19	2.08	1.45	2.29	**2.58**
0.3	*	*	40	33.53	52.38	51.36	54.84	**55.35**	54.55
0.6	*	*	40	0.54	10.73	11.65	12.65	**13.73**	13.36
0.9	*	*	40	0.01	1.83	1.81	1.19	1.71	**2.08**
*	0.25	*	60	7.53	18.41	18.28	19.82	**20.84**	19.91
*	0.75	*	60	15.19	24.89	24.93	25.96	26.35	**26.75**
*	*	0.25	60	11.69	18.93	18.21	19.37	**20.16**	20.01
*	*	0.75	60	11.03	24.37	25.00	26.42	**27.03**	26.66
*	*	*	120	11.36	21.65	21.60	22.89	**23.59**	23.33

We also show, as a basis for comparison, the average percent improvement over the deterministic solution obtained by the hill climber designed by Lee *et al.* to improve the solutions found by their heuristic [8]. After sequencing the jobs according to the heuristic, this hill climber greedily selects the job that contributes the most to the weighted tardiness objective. It then considers swapping this job with each of the twenty nearest jobs in the sequence.[7] If any of these swaps improve the objective score of the sequence, it takes the one that improves it the most. The algorithm continues until no further improvement can be made through this method. In the tables, the results of this method are listed as "Lee".

The first 12 rows of each table show the results for each the 12 problem classes individually. The next three rows show the results of aggregating these classes according to the τ (due-date tightness) parameter. This is followed in the next two rows by the results of aggregating the classes according to the R (due-

---

[7] It considers only the twenty nearest jobs rather than all jobs because through experimentation Lee *et al.* found that considering jobs sequenced further apart by the heuristic for this swap did not buy them much.

date range) parameter. The next two rows show the results of aggregating the problem classes by the η (setup time severity) parameter. The final row of each table then gives the average results across all problem instances. The first four columns of each table describe the problem class by the three aforementioned parameters as well as the number of problem instances in the class. For each of the 12 classes there are 10 instances (the aggregate classes have more instances).

Interpreting these results, we can make several observations:

- At all number of iterations considered, WHISTLING exhibits a greater overall average percentage improvement over the deterministic ATCS strategy than does HBSS. In fact, all three top WHISTLING configurations outperform the best HBSS configuration over all problem instances (see last row of tables).
- The hill climber of Lee *et al.* outperforms both a single iteration of HBSS as well as WHISTLING. But for 10 and 100 iterations, the stochastic sampling algorithms begin finding better solutions than the hill climber. It may be interesting to investigate using WHISTLING to generate starting points for a random restart variation of Lee *et al.*'s hill climber, but this has not been done.
- All three WHISTLING configurations equal or outperform the best HBSS configuration in all aggregated problem categories (rows 13 - 19) except for the $\tau = 0.9$ class (row 15). In this one particular problem category, only for 100 iterations does WHISTLING do better than HBSS. However, for all other categories, WHISTLING dominates.
- Perhaps the strongest comparative advantage can be seen on the 100 iteration runs (see Table 3). Here, the WHISTLING configuration with bias function p^7 alone produces a greater percent improvement than both HBSS configurations for every problem class (individual and aggregated) except 3. These results are statistically significant according to paired t-tests.

All of these results can be strengthened by considering computation time. Recall that the HBSS algorithm requires a rank-ordering step that adds to the computational complexity. For the problems considered here with 60 jobs, on a Sun Ultra 1, HBSS requires on average 0.16 seconds for one iteration, 1.59 seconds for ten iterations, and 15.46 seconds for 100 iterations; while WHISTLING only requires 0.016 seconds for one iteration, 0.16 seconds for ten iterations, and 1.50 seconds for 100 iterations. So ten iterations of WHISTLING can be performed in approximately the same amount of CPU time as one iteration of HBSS (and similarly 100 iterations of WHISTLING in the same CPU time as ten iterations of HBSS).

5   Conclusion

In this paper, we have presented a new iterative sampling framework for searching a stochastic neighborhood of an ordering heuristic. This algorithm, which we call WHISTLING, is defined in much the same spirit as the earlier developed

HBSS framework - to provide a general means for overcoming the potential mis-step that any given search heuristic is prone to take. However, the WHISTLING approach differs from that of HBSS in one crucial respect: it bases its stochastic decisions on assigned heuristic values instead of a rank-ordering of alternatives. This value-based approach allows the WHISTLING procedure to take into account the discriminating power of the heuristic in different decision contexts, and to better concentrate search around those decisions where the heuristic provides less guidance. As a beneficial side-effect of the use of heuristic value rather than rank order, there is no longer the need to sort the set of choices at each step of the search, and hence WHISTLING is also an inherently more efficient computational process than HBSS.

In our experimental analysis of the performance of WHISTLING, we have focused on a weighted tardiness scheduling problem with sequence-dependent se-tups. Taking a state-of-the-art dispatch heuristic (ATCS) for this class of problem as a starting point, we tested several configurations of WHISTLING and HBSS over a broad range of problem instances. With relatively few iterations, WHISTLING was shown to consistently and significantly improve on the deterministic ATCS solution. HBSS is also seen to produce significantly better solutions than ATCS alone. However, on runs covering varying numbers of iterations and over problem classes of varying degrees of difficulty and constraint tightness, WHISTLING's performance is seen to dominate HBSS's in terms of average percentage of improvement. The advantage for stochastic search of an ability to vary the degree of randomness as a function of the discriminatory power of the heuristic (or the lack thereof) in specific decision contexts is clearly evident in this domain.

These results suggest several directions for future research. On one front, we are interested in exploring application of the WHISTLING framework in other combinatorial optimization contexts. Another interest is in exploiting the observed anytime characteristics of our stochastic search framework to enhance online decision-making in dynamic domains such as scheduling. Finally, we are interested in developing a better understanding of how aspects of problem structure affect the ability of stochastic search to amplify heuristic performance in optimization domains.

Acknowledgements

This work has been funded in part by the Department of Defense Advanced Research Projects Agency and the U.S. Air Force Rome Research Laboratory under contracts F30602-97-2-0066 and F30602-00-2-0503 and by the CMU Robotics Institute. The views and conclusions contained in this document are those of the authors and should not be interpreted as necessarily representing the official policies or endorsements, either expressed or implied, of the Air Force or U.S. Government.

References

[1] E. Bonabeau, M. Dorigo, and G. Theraulaz. *Swarm Intelligence: From Natural to Artificial Systems*. Santa Fe Institute Studies in the Sciences of Complexity. Oxford University Press, 1999.

[2] J. L. Bresina. Heuristic-biased stochastic sampling. In *Proceedings of the Thirteenth National Conference on Artificial Intelligence and the Eighth Innovative Applications of Artificial Intelligence Conference, Volume One*, pages 271–278. AAAI Press, 1996.

[3] A. Cesta, A. Oddi, and S. F. Smith. An iterative sampling procedure for resource constrained project scheduling with time windows. In *Proceedings of the Sixteenth International Joint Conference on Artificial Intelligence*, pages 1022–1029. Morgan Kaufmann, 1999.

[4] T. H. Cormen, C. E. Leiserson, and R. L. Rivest. *Introduction to Algorithms*. McGraw-Hill, 1990.

[5] M. Dorigo and G. Di Caro. The ant colony optimization meta-heuristic. In D. Corne, M. Dorigo, and F. Glover, editors, *New Ideas in Optimization*. McGraw-Hill, 1999.

[6] C. Gomes, B. Selman, and H. Kautz. Boosting combinatorial search through randomization. In *Proceedings of the Fifteenth National Conference on Artificial Intelligence and Tenth Innovative Applications of Artificial Intelligence Conference*, pages 431–437. AAAI Press, 1998.

[7] W. Harvey and M. Ginsberg. Limited discrepency search. In *Proceedings of the Fourteenth International Joint Conference on Artificial Intelligence*, pages 607–613. Morgan Kaufmann, 1995.

[8] Y. H. Lee, K. Bhaskaran, and M. Pinedo. A heuristic to minimize the total weighted tardiness with sequence-dependent setups. *IIE Transactions*, 29:45–52, 1997.

[9] T. E. Morton and D. W. Pentico. *Heuristic Scheduling Systems: With Applications to Production Systems and Project Management*. John Wiley and Sons, 1993.

[10] A. Oddi and S. F. Smith. Stochastic procedures for generating feasible schedules. In *Proceedings of the Fourteenth National Conference on Artificial Intelligence and Ninth Innovative Applications of Artificial Intelligence Conference*, pages 308–314. AAAI Press, 1997.

[11] G. Theraulaz, S. Goss, J. Gervet, and J. L. Deneubourg. Task differentiation in polistes wasp colonies: A model for self-organizing groups of robots. In *From Animals to Animats: Proceedings of the First International Conference on Simulation of Adaptive Behavior*, pages 346–355. MIT Press, 1991.

[12] T. Walsh. Depth-bounded discrepency search. In *Proceedings of the Fifteenth International Joint Conference on Artificial Intelligence*. Morgan Kaufmann, 1997.

[13] J. P. Watson, L. Barbulescu, A. E. Howe, and L. D. Whitley. Algorithm performance and problem structure for flow-shop scheduling. In *Proceedings, Sixteenth National Conference on Artificial Intelligence (AAAI-99), Eleventh Innovative Applications of Artificial Intelligence Conference (IAAI-99)*, pages 688–695. AAAI Press, 1999.

A   Proof: Dominance Tournament = Roulette Wheel Decision

Dominance Tournament = Roulette Wheel Decision: The structure of the tournament of dominance contests within the WHISTLING algorithm is such that Choice$_w$ is chosen with probability $\dfrac{\text{bias(heuristic(Choice}_w))}{\sum_{j=1}^{k}\text{bias(heuristic(Choice}_j))}$. That is, the tournament is such that each Choice$_w$ is chosen according to a roulette wheel decision where each Choice$_w$ takes a chunk of the wheel proportional to bias(heuristic(Choice$_w$)).

Proof (by induction): In this proof, $F_w = $ bias(heuristic(Choice$_w$)) is the initial value of the force of Choice$_w$. Further F'_w is the force of Choice$_w$ including the accumulation of the force variables of other choices which it has defeated in the tournament.

Base Case: Dominance tournament of two choices.

- Choice$_1$ wins with probability $\frac{F_1}{F_1+F_2}$. If it wins, its new force is $F'_1 = F_1+F_2$.
- Choice$_2$ wins with probability $\frac{F_2}{F_1+F_2}$. If it wins, its new force is $F'_2 = F_1+F_2$.
- Therefore, for the base case of two choices we have the equivalent of a roulette wheel decision.

Inductive Step:

- Assume that for the case of a tournament of dominance contests of $k-1$ choices that this tournament is equivalent to a roulette wheel decision.
- Further assume that upon the completion of this tournament that the winning choice Choice$_w$ has a force value of $F'_w = \sum_{j=1}^{k-1} F_j$.
- Now consider the addition of a k-th choice Choice$_k$ at the end of the list of choices with an initial force F_k. The winner Choice$_w$ of the sub-tournament consisting of the first $k-1$ choices would then compete in a dominance contest against Choice$_k$.
- Choice$_k$ wins this dominance contest and thus the tournament of contests among the k choices with probability $\frac{F_k}{F_k+F'_w} = \frac{F_k}{F_k+\sum_{j=1}^{k-1} F_j} = \frac{F_k}{\sum_{j=1}^{k} F_j}$. If it wins, its new force is $F'_k = F_k + F'_w = \sum_{j=1}^{k} F_j$.
- Choice$_w$ wins this dominance contest against Choice$_k$ with probability $\frac{F'_w}{F_k+F'_w}$. Further, since it had a probability of $\frac{F_w}{F'_w}$ of winning the sub-tournament of the first $k-1$ choices, it therefore wins the overall tournament of k choices with probability $\frac{F_w}{F'_w}\frac{F'_w}{F_k+F'_w} = \frac{F_w}{\sum_{j=1}^{k} F_j}$. Its new force if it wins is $F''_w = F_k + F'_w = \sum_{j=1}^{k} F_j$.
- Therefore, for the case of a tournament of k choices, we have the equivalent of a roulette wheel decision.

Computing the Envelope
for Stepwise-Constant Resource Allocations

Nicola Muscettola

NASA Ames Research Center
Moffett Field, California 94035-1000
mus@email.arc.nasa.gov

Abstract. Computing tight resource-level bounds is a fundamental problem in the construction of flexible plans with resource utilization. In this paper we describe an efficient algorithm that builds a resource envelope, the tightest possible such bound. The algorithm is based on transforming the temporal network of resource consuming and producing events into a flow network with nodes equal to the events and edges equal to the necessary predecessor links between events. A staged maximum flow problem on the network is then used to compute the time of occurrence and the height of each step of the resource envelope profile. Each stage has the same computational complexity of solving a maximum flow problem on the entire flow network. This makes this method computationally feasible and promising for use in the inner loop of flexible-time scheduling algorithms.

1 Resource Envelopes

Retaining temporal flexibility in activity plans is important for dealing with execution uncertainty. For example, flexible plans allow explicit reasoning about the temporal uncontrollability of exogenous events [11] and the seamless incorporation of execution countermeasures. Fixed-time schedules (i.e., the assignment of a precise start and end time to all activities) are brittle and it is typically very difficult to exactly follow them during execution. For an example of the effect of fixed-time schedules in an intelligent execution situation, consider the "Skylab strike" [6], when during the Skylab 4 mission, astronauts went on a sit-down strike after 45 days of trying to catch up with the exact demands of a fast paced schedule with no flexibility for them to adjust to the space environment.

A major obstacle to using flexible schedules, however, remains the difficulty of computing the amount of resources needed across all of their possible executions. This problem is particularly difficult for multiple-capacity resources (such as electrical power) that can be both consumed and produced in any amount by concurrent activities. Techniques have been developed [5] [10] for giving conservative estimates of the resource levels needed by a flexible schedule, yielding both an upper bound and a

P. Van Hentenryck (Ed.): CP 2002, LNCS 2470, pp. 139-154, 2002.
© Springer-Verlag Berlin Heidelberg 2002

lower bound profile on the resource level over time. In the context of a systematic search method to build flexible plans, resource-level bounds can be used at each search step as follows: a) as a backtracking test, i.e., to determine when the lower/upper bound interval is outside of the range of allowed resource levels at some time and therefore no fixed-time instantiations of the plan is resource-feasible; and b) as a search termination test, i.e., to determine when the lower/upper bound range is inside the range of allowed resource levels at all times and therefore all fixed-time instantiations of the plan are resource-feasible.

Bound tightness is extremely important computationally since a tight bound can save a potentially exponential amount of search (through early backtracking and solution detection) when compared to a looser bound. In this paper, we discuss how to compute the *resource-level envelope*, i.e., the measure of maximum and minimum resource consumption at any time for all fixed-time schedules in the flexible plan. At each time the envelope guarantees that there are two fixed-time instantiations, one producing the minimum level and the other the maximum. Therefore, the resource-level envelope is the tightest possible resource-level bound for a flexible plan since any tighter bound would exclude the contribution of at least one fixed-time schedule. If the resource-level envelope can be computed efficiently, it could substitute looser bounds that are currently used in the inner core of constraint-posting scheduling algorithms (Laborie 2001) with the potential for great improvements in performance.

To appreciate the difficulty of computing the resource level, we can compare the cases of a fully flexible plan with that of a plan with a single fixed-time instantiation. In the fixed-time case, the envelope degenerates to the resource profile that is used in the inner loop of traditional scheduling algorithms [2][15]. Computing from scratch a resource profile is cheap. It is easy to see that its worst cast time complexity is $O(N \lg N)$ where N is the number of activities in the flexible plan. Consider now a fully flexible plan and assume that we naively wanted to compute the resource-level envelope for a flexible plan by simply enumerating all schedules and taking the maximum/minimum of all resource levels at all times. Since a flexible activity plan has a number of possible instantiated fixed-time schedules that is exponential in the number of events, such naïve method is clearly impractical in most cases.

Note that "resource-level envelope calculation" is *not* equivalent to "scheduling with multiple capacity", an NP-hard problem. For example, note that a reduction of the envelope calculation to scheduling is not straightforward. Consider the interval between minimum and maximum envelope at a given time. It is true that a solution to the scheduling problem can be obtained in polynomial time if the envelope interval is always completely contained within resource availability (in which case all fixed-time instantiations are legal schedules). However, if at least two times the envelope interval is partly outside the availability bound, one can generate examples in which the envelope cannot tell us whether there is a fixed-time schedule that is within availability at all times or whether for all schedules the resource level is outside availability at some time. Discriminating between these two cases still requires search.

This paper presents a polynomial algorithm for the computation of resource-level envelopes based on a novel combination of the theory of shortest-paths in the temporal constraint network for the flexible plan, and the theory of maximum flows for a flow network derived from the temporal and resource constraints. We develop the theory, show that the algorithm is correct, and that its asymptotic complexity is **O(N O(maxflow(N)))**, where **N** is the number of start/end times of the activities in the plan, which is at most twice the number of activities, and **O(maxflow(N))** is the complexity of a maximum flow algorithm applied to an auxiliary flow network with **N** nodes. We believe that this method will be efficient in practice, since experimental analysis [1] show the practical cost of maxflow to be as good as **O (N $^{1.5}$)**. However this paper is a theoretical contribution and a definitive answer to its practical complexity will require further experimental work.

In the rest of the paper we introduce some notation and describe the formal model of activity networks with resource consumption. Then we review the literature on resource contention measures and show an example in which the current state of the art is inadequate. The discussion of our algorithm follows. Some informal examples to establish an intuitive understanding of our method are first given. Then we establish the connection between maximum flow problems and finding sets of activities that have the optimal contribution to the resource level. These sets are then shown to compute an envelope. Finally, we describe a simple envelope algorithm and its complexity, and conclude discussing future work.

2   Resource Envelopes

Figure 1 shows an activity network with resource allocations. Our notation is equivalent to that of previous work on flexible scheduling with multiple-capacity resources [5][10]. The network has two time variables per activity, a start event and an end event (e.g., e_{1s} and e_{1e} for activity A_1), a non-negative flexible activity duration link (e.g., **[2, 5]** for activity A_1), and flexible separation links between events (e.g., **[0, 4]** from e_{3e} to e_{4s}). A time origin, T_s, corresponds to time **0** and supports separation links to other events. Without loss of generality we assume that all events occur after T_s and before an event T_e rigidly connected to T_s. The interval $T_s T_e$ is the *time horizon* **T** of the network.

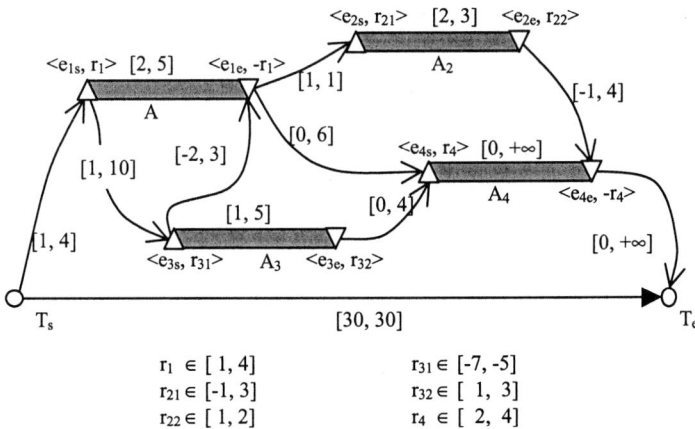

$$r_1 \in [1, 4] \qquad r_{31} \in [-7, -5]$$
$$r_{21} \in [-1, 3] \qquad r_{32} \in [1, 3]$$
$$r_{22} \in [1, 2] \qquad r_4 \in [2, 4]$$

Fig. 1. An activity network with resource allocations

Time origin, events and links constitute a Simple Temporal Network (STN) [8]. Unlike regular STNs, however, each event has an associated *allocation variable* with real domain (e.g., r_{31} for event e_{3s}) representing the amount of resource allocated when the event occurs. We call this augmented network **R** a piecewise-constant Resource allocation STN (cR-STN). In the following we will assume that all allocations refer to a single, multi-capacity resource. The extension of the results to the case of multiple resources is straightforward. An event e^- with negative allocation is a *consumer,* while an e^+ with positive allocation is a *producer.*

This formalization covers many of the usual models for resource allocations. For example, note that an event can be either a consumer or a producer in different instantiations of the allocation variables (e.g., event e_{2s} for which the bound for r_{21} is **[-1,3]**). This allows reasoning about dual-use activities (e.g., the activities of starting a car and running it make use of the alternator as either a power consumer or producer). Moreover, some events can have resource allocations that are opposite to each other (e.g., e_{1e} vs. e_{1s}). This allows modeling allocations that last only during an activity's occurrence, such as power consumption. Note, however, that this model does not cover continuous accumulation such as change of energy stored in a battery over time. A conservative approximation can be achieved by accounting for the entire resource usage at the activity start or end.

We will always assume that the cR-STN is temporally consistent. From the STN theory [8], this means that the shortest-path problem associated with **R** has a solution. Given two events e_1 and e_2 we denote with $|e_1e_2|$ the shortest-path from e_1 to e_2. We will call a full instantiation of the time variables in **R** a *schedule* **s(.)** where **s(e)** is the time of occurrence of event **e** according to schedule **s**. The set **S** contains all possible consistent schedules for **R**. Each event **e** has a time bound **[et(e), lt(e)]**, with **et(e)** and **lt(e)** respectively the earliest and latest time for **e**. The time bound represents the range of possible time values **s(e)** for all $s \in$ **S**. From the STN theory, we know that **et(e)** = − $|eT_s|$ and **lt(e)** = $|T_se|$. Finally, given three events, e_1, e_2 and e_3, the triangular inequality among shortest paths $|e_1e_3| \le |e_1e_2| + |e_2e_3|$ holds.

A fundamental data structure used in the rest of the paper is the *anti-precedence graph,* **Aprec(R)**, for a cR-STN **R**. The anti-precedence graph is similar to the precedence graph of [10] with the following differences: a) the links are in reverse order; 2) it does not distinguish between the set of strict precedence edges, $E_<$, and the set of precedence edges that allow time equality, $E_\le$; and 3) several possible kinds of precedence graphs are allowable for a network **R**. Formally, **Aprec(R)** is a graph with the same events as **R** and such that for any two events e_1 and e_2 with $|e_1 e_2| \le 0$ there is a path from e_1 to e_2 in **Aprec(R)**. Alternatively, we can say that an event e_1 precedes another e_2 in the anti-precedence graph if e_1 cannot be executed before e_2. A way to build an anti-precedence graph is to run an all-pairs shortest-path algorithm on **R** and retain only the edges with non-positive shortest distance. Smaller graphs can also be obtained by eliminating dominated edges. The choice of precedence graph type may affect performance but not the correctness of the algorithm described here.

The cost of computing **Aprec(R)** is therefore bound by the cost of computing the all-pairs shortest path graph for **R**, i.e., it is $O(NE + N^2 \lg V)$ where **N** is the number of events (at most twice the number of activities in the plan) and **E** is the number of temporal distance constraints in the original cR-STN [7].

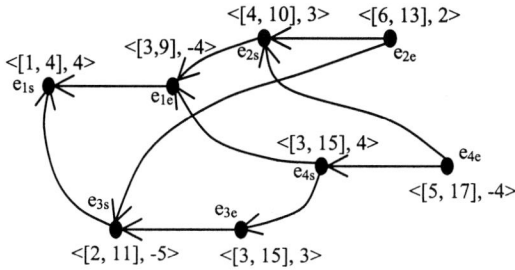

Fig. 2. Anti-precedence graph with time/resource usage

Figure 2 depicts one of the anti-precedence graphs of the network in Figure 1 with the time bound and the maximum allowed resource allocation labeling each event.

3   Resource Contention Measures

Safe execution of a flexible activity networks needs to avoid resource contention, i.e., the possibility that for some consistent time assignment to the events there is at least one time at which the total amount of resource allocated is outside the availability bounds. There are essentially two methods for estimating resource contention: heuristic and exact. Most of the heuristic techniques [14] [12] [3] measure the probability of an activity requesting a resource at a certain time. This probability is estimated either analytically on a relaxed constraint network or stochastically by sampling time assignments on the full constraint network. The occurrence probabilities are then combined in an aggregate demand on resources over time, the contention measure. Probabilistic contention can give a measure of likelihood of a conflict. However, it is not a safe measure, i.e., the lack of detected conflicts does not exclude that a variable instantiation for the cR-STN could cause an inconsistent resource allocation.

Exact methods avoid this problem. They compute sufficient conditions for the lack of contention. [10] has a good survey of such methods. Current exact methods operate on relaxations of the constraint network. For example, edge-finding techniques [13] analyze how an activity can be scheduled relative to a subset of activities, comparing the sum of all durations with a time interval derived from the time bounds of all the activities under consideration. Relying solely on time bounds ignores much of the inter-activity constraints and is effective only when the time bounds are relatively tight. Therefore algorithms using these contention measures tend to eliminate much of the flexibility in the activity network. Some recent work [5] [10] goes further in exploiting inter-activity constraints. For example, [10] proposes a *balance constraint* that is based on conservative upper and lower bounds on the resource level immediately before and after each event **e**. These bounds precisely estimate the contribution of events that must precede **e** and overestimate the contribution of events that may or may not precede **e**. The over-estimate assumes that only the events with the worst contribution (producers for upper bounds and consumers for lower bounds) happen before **e**. The balance constraint appears to work well in a flexible scheduling algorithm [10] but the bounds on which it is based may be very loose for networks with significant amounts of parallelism.

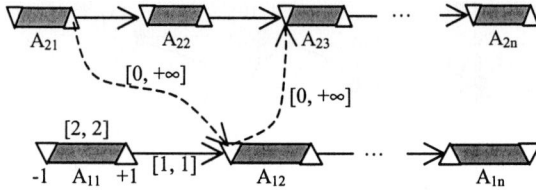

Fig. 3. Over-constraining a flexible activity network

For example, consider the activity graph in Figure3, consisting of two rigid chains of **n** activities with the same fixed duration and the same fixed activity separation. Assume that the horizon **T** is wide enough to allow any feasible ordering among them. Each activity consumes one unit during its occurrence and the resource has two available units of capacity over time. It is clear that the maximum resource level requested by the flexible plan at any time cannot exceed two, and therefore all schedules obtained by merging any schedule of the two chains are feasible. A scheduling algorithm using a resource-level envelope will therefore recognize that the initial problem is already a feasible flexible plan and will terminate immediately. In contrast, a scheduler using the balance constraint will always detect an over-allocation until it somehow constrains the network (e.g., by systematic or local search) with constraints that are at least as tight as the two following cases: a) the start activity **n** of one chain occurs no later than the start of the second activity of the other; or b) more than two activities overlap and there is an activity **k** on one chain that must start between the end of activity **i** and the start of activity **i+2** on the other chain. The dashed arrows in Figure 3 represent the constraints posted in case b. The balance constraint cannot correctly handle this situation because it cannot account for the constraint structure of all possible parallel chains *simultaneously*. The rest of this paper shows that the full constraint structure can be efficiently exploited in calculating the resource-level envelope.

4   Resource Envelopes

As discussed in the introduction, we are seeking the maximum and minimum possible resource production (consumption) among all possible schedules of **R**. Note that the maximum (minimum) overall resource level induced by **R** for any possible schedule can always be obtained by assigning each allocation variable to its maximum (minimum) possible value. For any specific value assignment to the allocation variables, each event has a constant weight: positive, $c(e^+)$, for a producer and negative, $-c(e^-)$, for a consumer. Given a schedule $s \in S$ and a time $t \in T$, $E_s(t)$ is the set of events e such that $s(e) \leq t$. For any subset A of the set of events in R, $E(R)$, we define the *resource-level increment* as $\Delta(A) = 0$ if $A = \varnothing$, and $\Delta(A) = \Sigma_{e^+,e^- \in A} c(e^+) - c(e^-)$ if $A \neq \varnothing$. The following functions of time rigorously define the resource-level envelope:

- *Resource level due to schedule s*: $L_s(t) = \Delta(E_s(t))$.
- *Maximum resource envelope* : $L_{max}(t) = max_{s \in S}(L_s(t))$.
- *Minimum resource envelope*: $L_{min}(t) = min_{s \in S}(L_s(t))$.

The *resource level envelope* that we seek is the interval bound function of time $[L_{min}(t), L_{max}(t)]$. Since the methods to compute L_{min} and L_{max} can be obtained from each other with obvious term substitutions, we only develop the algorithm for L_{max}.

Before we formally discuss our algorithm, we want to introduce some examples to give an intuitive feel of the foundations of the method. First consider an activity network consisting of a single activity that produces or consumes resource capacity during its occurrence (Figure 4(a)). We could build L_{max} by asking at each time $t \in T$ whether A_1 can happen before, after or can overlap t. If the activity starts with a resource production (Figure 4(b)), then the resource level will be maximum at t if A_1 starts, contains or ends at t. This is always possible between $et(e_{1s})$ and $lt(e_{1e})$. Within this interval $L_{max}(t) = 1$, while outside $L_{max}(t) = 0$. Conversely, if A_1 starts with a consumer (Figure 4(c)), then the maximum resource level can be zero at time t only if A_1 can start after t or can end before t for some schedule. This is possible only before $lt(e_{1s})$ and after $et(e_{1e})$. Therefore, $L_{max}(t) = -1$ between $lt(e_{1s})$ and $et(e_{1e})$, and $L_{max}(t) = 0$ everywhere else. This example suggests a strategy for computing L_{max} that looks at each event and considers the incremental contribution of the event's weight to the maximum resource envelope at the earliest time for producers or at the latest time for consumers.

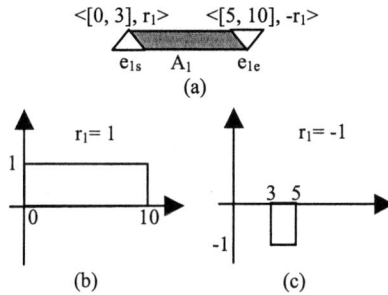

Fig. 4. Maximum resource-level envelope for a single activity

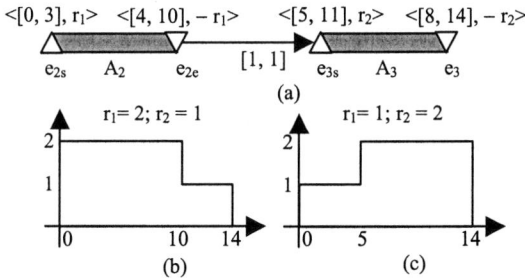

Fig. 5. Maximum level envelope for two chained activities

For a complex network, however, this simple strategy is insufficient. Consider a rigidly linked pair of activities with a reusable resource allocation (Figure 5(a)). In this case, the time of occurrence of e_{2e} and e_{3s} are bound together. Looking at the contribution to the envelope of each event in isolation, we would want to add the contribution of e_{2e} as late as possible since it is a consumer, and the contribution of e_{3s} as early as possible, since it is a producer. The decision of which time to choose depends on the total contribution of *both* events. The total contribution will be added at $lt(e_{2e})$ if the total contribution is a consumption (Figure 5(b)) or at $et(e_{3s})$ if the total contribution is a production (Figure 5(c)). Note that in both cases e_{2s} and e_{3s} are *pending* at the selected time, i.e., their contribution has not been added yet to the envelope but they both could occur at the selected time. This suggests revising the strategy for computing L_{max} as follows: at the earliest or latest time of each event, select the set of pending events whose resource-level increment is maximum, eliminate these events from the pending events and declare the increment for L_{max} at that time to be their resource-level increment.

Now consider the network in Figure 1 and the event time bounds, maximum resource allocation and precedence graph in Figure 2. Assume that we want to compute $L_{max}(3)$. The set of events that may be scheduled before, at or after time **3** is $\{e_{1s}, e_{1e}, e_{3s}, e_{3e}, e_{4s}\}$. However, of these only $\{e_{1e}, e_{3s}, e_{3e}, e_{4s}\}$ are pending since the contribution to L_{max} of e_{1s} occurs at its earliest time **1**. The subset of pending events that we need to consider at time **3** to compute the increment on L_{max} are all those that are forced to occur at or before **3** assuming that some pending event occurs at **3**. These subsets are $\{e_{1e}\}, \{e_{3s}\}, \{e_{3s}, e_{3e}\}$ and $\{e_{1e}, e_{3s}, e_{3e}, e_{4s}\}$. Unfortunately, each of these subsets has a negative weight and therefore none of them is selected at time **3** since, from the definition of resource-level increment, the empty event set has the maximum (zero) increment. At time **4** the set of pending events is augmented with e_{2s} and a new subset of pending events with positive weight, $\{e_{1e}, e_{2s}, e_{3s}, e_{3e}, e_{4s}\}$, is possible. This generates the increment that, added to $L_{max}(3)$, gives us $L_{max}(4)$.

The selection of the pending events subset of maximum resource-level increment is the key source of complexity in calculating L_{max}. An exhaustive enumeration of all subsets is intractable in the general case. Fortunately, it turns out that this selection problem is equivalent to a maximum flow problem for an appropriate flow network derived from **Aprec(R)**. We discuss this rigorously in the rest of the paper.

5   Calculating Maximum Resource-Level Increments

Consider an interval $H \subseteq T$. We can partition all events in **R** into three sets depending on their relative position with respect to **H**: 1) the *closed events* C_H with all events that must occur strictly before or at the start of **H**, i.e., such that that $lt(e) \leq start(H)$; 2) the *pending events* R_H with all events that can occur within or at the end of interval **H**, i.e., such that $lt(e) > start(H)$ and $et(e) \leq end(H)$; and 3) the *open events* O_H with all events that must occur strictly after **H**, i.e., such that $et(e) > end(H)$.

The set R_H could contain events that can be scheduled both inside and outside **H**. If **H=T**, then $C_T = \varnothing$, $R_T = E(R)$ and $O_H = \varnothing$. If **H** is a single instant of time, i.e., **H=[t,t]**, we will use the simplifying notation $C_t = C_{[t, t]}$, $R_t = R_{[t, t]}$ and $O_t = O_{[t, t]}$.

Assume that we want to compute the resource-level increment for a schedule **s** at a time $t \in H$. This will always include the contribution of all events in C_H and none of those in O_H irrespective of **s** and **t**. With respect to the events in R_H, if an event is scheduled to occur at or before **t,** then all of its predecessors (according to **Aprec(R)**) will also have to occur at or before **t.** In other words, it is possible to find a set of events $X \in R_H$ such that the events $e_p \in R_H$ that are scheduled no later than **t** in **s** are those in X or those $e_p \in R_H$ such that $|e_x e_p| \leq 0$ for some $e_x \in X$. We call this the *predecessor set* P_X of X. Therefore, the resource level at time **t** for a given schedule **s** is the sum of the weights of events in C_H and in $P_X \subseteq R_H$. Since we are trying to maximize the resource level, we will look for the sets P_X with the maximum total weight.

An important property that we will exploit later is that given two predecessor sets P_X and P_Y, $P_X \cap P_Y$ and $P_X \cup P_Y$ are also predecessor sets.

5.1   Resource-Level Increments and Maximum Flow

We know that to compute L_{max} we want to look for sets P_X with maximum weight. We find these by computing a maximum flow for an auxiliary flow network built from R_H and **Aprec(R)**. For a complete discussion of maximum flow problems see [7]. Here we only highlight some concepts and relations that we will use.

First let us define the auxiliary flow problem that we will us to compute L_{max}.

Resource Increment Flow Problem: Given a set of pending events R_H for a cR-STN **R,** we define the resource increment flow problem $F(R_H)$ with source σ and sink τ as follows:

1. For each event $e \in R_H$ there is a corresponding node $e \in F(R_H)$.
2. For each event $e^+ \in R_H$, there is an edge $\sigma \rightarrow e^+$ with capacity $c(e^+)$.
3. For each event $e^- \in R_H$, there is an edge $e^- \rightarrow \tau$ with capacity $c(e^-)$, i.e., the opposite of e^-'s weight in **R**.
4. For each pair of e_1 and e_2 with an edge $e_1 \rightarrow e_2$ in the anti-precedence graph **Aprec(R)**, there is a corresponding link $e_1 \rightarrow e_2$ in $F(R_H)$ with capacity $+\infty$.

Figure 6 shows the auxiliary flow problem for the anti-precedence graph in Figure 2, with every edge labeled with its capacity.

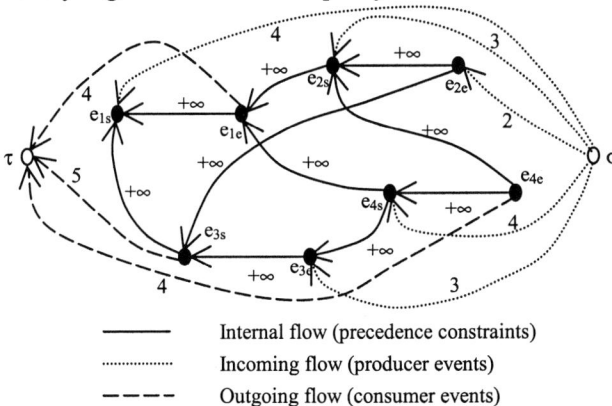

Fig. 6. Resource increment flow problem

Consistent with the theory of maximum flows, we will indicate $f(e_1, e_2)$ as the flow associated to a link $e_1 \rightarrow e_2$ in $F(R_H)$. The flow function has, by definition, several properties. It is skew-symmetric, i.e., $f(e_2, e_1) = - f(e_1, e_2)$. Each flow has to be not greater than the capacity of the link to which it is associated. For example, referring to the flow network in Figure 6, $f(\sigma, e_{2e}) \leq 2$, while $f(e_{2e}, \sigma) \leq 0$ since there is no edge from e_{2e} and σ, a situation equivalent to the capacity of the edge $e_2 \rightarrow \sigma$ being zero. We also use the implicit summation notation $f(A, B)$, where B and A are disjoint event sets in $F(R_H)$, to indicate the flow $f(A, B) = \Sigma_{a \in A} \Sigma_{b \in B} f(a, b)$. Consider now any subset of events $A \subseteq R_H$ and let us call A^c the set of events $A^c = R_H - A$. >From the final property defining a flow function, flow conservation, we can obtain the following: $f(\{\sigma\}, A) = f(A, \{\tau\}) + f(A, A^c)$. The total network flow is defined as $f(\{\sigma\}, R_H) = f(R_H, \{\tau\})$. The maximum flow of a network is a flow function f_{max} such that the total network flow is maximum.

A fundamental concept in the theory of flows is the *residual network*. This is a graph with an edge for each pair of nodes in $F(R_H)$ with positive *residual capacity*, i.e., the difference between edge capacity and flow. Each edge in the residual network has capacity equal to the residual capacity. For example, considering the network in Figure 6, assume that $f(e_{1e}, \tau) = 3$ and $f(\sigma, e_{2e}) = 2$. The residual network for that flow will have the following edges: $e_{1e} \rightarrow \tau$ with capacity 1, $\tau \rightarrow e_{1e}$ with capacity 3, and $e_{2e} \rightarrow \sigma$ with capacity 2. Also note that any residual network for any flow of $F(R_H)$ will always have an edge of infinite capacity for each edge in the precedence graph $Aprec(R)$. An *augmenting path* is a path connecting σ to τ in the residual network. The existence of an augmenting path indicates that additional flow can be pushed from σ to τ. Alternatively, the lack of an augmenting path indicates that a flow is maximum. A resource-level increment $\Delta(A)$ for an event set $A \subseteq R_H$ is related to a flow in $F(R_H)$ as follows. We define the producer weight in A as $c(A^+) = \Sigma_{e+ \in A} c(e^+)$ and the consumer weight in A as $c(A^-) = \Sigma_{e- \in A} c(e^-)$. We also define the *producer residual* in A for a flow f of $F(R_H)$ as $r(A^+) = c(A^+) - f(\{\sigma\}, A)$, i.e., the total residual capacity of the edges from σ to A, and the *consumer residual* in A as $r(A^-) = c(A^-) - f(A, \{\tau\})$.

Lemma 1: $\Delta(A) = r(A^+) - r(A^-) + f(A, A^c)$.
Proof: $\Delta(A) = c(A^+) - c(A^-) = (c(A^+) - f(\{\sigma\}, A)) - (c (A^-) - f(\{\sigma\}, A)) = r(A^+) - (c(A^-) - f(A, \{\tau\}) - f(A, A^c)) = r(A^+) - r(A^-) + f(A, A^c).\square$

We now focus on predecessor sets such as P_X.

Lemma 2: $f(P_X, P^c_X) \leq 0$. Moreover, $f(P_X, P^c_X) = 0$ if and only if $f(e_1, e_2) = 0$ for each $e_1 \in P^c_X$ and $e_2 \in P_X$.
Proof: From the definition of predecessor set there is no edge $e_2 \rightarrow e_1$ in $F(R_H)$ with $e_1 \in P^c_X$ and $e_2 \in P_X$. Therefore, $f(e_2, e_1) \leq 0$ and $f(P_X, P^c_X) \leq 0$. The second condition can be demonstrated by observing that the sum of any number of non-positive numbers is 0 if and only if each number is $0.\square$

Corollary 1: $\Delta(P_X) \leq r(P_X^+) - r(P_X^-)$.

Proof: Immediate from Lemma 1 and Lemma 2.

5.2   Maximum Flows and Maximum Resource-Level Increments

We can now find the maximum resource-level increment set $P_{max} \subseteq R_H$. Since $P_{max} = \varnothing$ may be true, the maximum resource-level increment is always non-negative. The computation of the set uses a maximum flow f_{max} of $F(R_H)$. We indicate with $r_{max}(A)$ the producer/consumer residual of A computed for f_{max}. The following fundamental theorem holds.

Theorem 1: Given a partial plan R_H, consider the (possibly empty) set P_{max} of events that are reachable from the source σ in the residual network of some f_{max} of $F(R_H)$. P_{max} is the predecessor set with maximum $\Delta(P_{max}) \geq 0$.
Proof: Assume that $r_{max}(e^+) = 0$ for each $e^+ \in F(R_H)$. In this case no event is reachable from σ in the residual network, thus $P_{max} = \varnothing$ and $\Delta(P_{max}) = 0$. From Corollary 1, for any predecessor set P_X it is $\Delta(P_X) \leq -r_{max}(P_X^-) \leq 0 = \Delta(P_{max})$ and therefore $\Delta(P_{max})$ is maximum.

Assume now $r_{max}(e^+) > 0$ for some $e^+ \in F(R_H)$, in which case P_{max} is not empty. The following three properties hold.

1. P_{max} is a predecessor set.
    If not, there will be an event $e_2 \notin P_{max}$ such that $|e_1e_2| \leq 0$ for some event $e_1 \in P_{max}$. From the definition of **Aprec(R)**, however, we know that there must be a path in **Aprec(R)** from e_1 to e_2. Since this path will be present in $F(R_H)$ with all links having infinite capacity, the path will also always be present in any residual network for any flow. Therefore there is a path in the residual network going from σ to e_1 (by definition of P_{max}) and then to e_2. Therefore, $e_2 \in P_{max}$, which is a contradiction.

2. $r_{max}(P_{max}^-) = 0$.
    If not, there will be an event $e^- \in P_{max}$ such that $r_{max}(e^-) > 0$. We can therefore build an augmenting path of $F(R_H)$ as follows: 1) a path from σ to e^- with positive residual capacity which exists by definition of P_{max}; and 2) an edge $e^- \to \tau$ with positive residual capacity $r_{max}(e^-)$. The existence of the augmenting path means that f_{max} is not a maximum flow, which is a contradiction.

3. $f_{max}(P_{max}, P^c_{max}) = 0$
    Since P_{max} is a predecessor set, from the proof of Lemma 2 we know that $f_{max}(P_{max}, P^c_{max}) \leq 0$. If $f_{max}(P_{max}, P^c_{max}) < 0$, then there is a pair of events $e_1 \in P_{max}$ and $e_2 \in P^c_{max}$ such that $f_{max}(e_1, e_2) < 0$. This means that the residual capacity from e_1 to e_2 is positive and therefore there is an edge $e_1 \to e_2$ in the residual network. But by definition of P_{max}, this means that $e_2 \in P_{max}$, which is a contradiction.

Applying the properties of P_{max} to Lemma 1, $\Delta(P_{max}) = r_{max}(P_{max}^+) - r_{max}(P_{max}^-) + f_{max}(P_{max}, P^c_{max}) = r_{max}(P_{max}^+) > 0$.
To prove the maximality of P_{max}, observe from Corollary 1 that a non-empty predecessor set P_X has $\Delta(P_X) > 0$ only if $r_{max}(e^+) > 0$ for some $e^+ \in P_X$. It is easy to see that P_X is the set of events reachable in the residual graph from $P_X^+ \subseteq P_{max}^+$ and that the properties at points 2 and 3 above also hold for P_X. Therefore, $\Delta(P_X) = r_{max}(P_X^+) \leq r_{max}(P_{max}^+) = \Delta(P_{max})$, which proves the maximality of P_{max}.□
The construction of P_{max} discussed before does not guarantee its uniqueness since it depends on a specific maximum flow among potentially many for $F(R_H)$. The follow-

ing theorem proves, however, that $\mathbf{P}_{max}$ is indeed unique for all maximum flows of $\mathbf{F(R_H)}$ and that it contains the minimum number of events among all predecessor sets with maximum positive resource-level increment.

Theorem 3: The predecessor set $\mathbf{P}_{max}$ with maximum resource-level increment $\Delta(\mathbf{P}_{max})$ and with minimum number of events is unique across all maximum flows of $\mathbf{F(R_H)}$.

Proof: Consider two maximum flows $\mathbf{f}_{max,j}$ and $\mathbf{f}_{max,\,k}$ among all maximum flows of $\mathbf{F(R_H)}$ and assume that they produce two distinct maximum resource-level increment predecessor sets, $\mathbf{P}_{max,\,j}$ and $\mathbf{P}_{max,\,k}$. From the maximality of their increment, it must be $\Delta(\mathbf{P}_{max,k}) = \Delta(\mathbf{P}_{max,j}) = \Delta_{max}$. We can rewrite one maximum predecessor set as $\mathbf{P}_{max,j} = \mathbf{P}_{j \cap k} \cup \mathbf{P}_{k-j}$ where $\mathbf{P}_{j \cap k} = \mathbf{P}_{max,j} \cap \mathbf{P}_{max,k}$ and $\mathbf{P}_{k-j} = \mathbf{P}_{max,k} - \mathbf{P}_{max,j}$. The hypothesis of distinction of $\mathbf{P}_{max,\,j}$ and $\mathbf{P}_{max,\,k}$ yields $\mathbf{P}_{k-j} \neq \emptyset$.

First we observe that $\Delta(\mathbf{P}_{j \cap k}) = \Delta_{max}$. If not, $\Delta(\mathbf{P}_{j-k}) > 0$ and $\Delta(\mathbf{P}_{k-j}) > 0$. But this means that $\mathbf{P}_{j \cup k} = \mathbf{P}_{max,j} \cup \mathbf{P}_{max,k}$ is a predecessor set such that $\Delta(\mathbf{P}_{j \cup k}) > \Delta_{max}$, which is a contradiction. Consider now $\mathbf{P}_{max,j}$ and let us call $r_j(e)$ the residual $r_{max}(e)$ computed in flow $\mathbf{f}_{max,j}$. Since $\Delta(\mathbf{P}_{j \cap k}) = \Delta_{max}$, it must be $r_j(e^+) = 0$ if $e^+ \in \mathbf{P}_{j-k}$. Also, $r_j(e^-) = 0$ for each $e^- \in \mathbf{P}_{max,j}$. From Lemma 1, $\Delta(\mathbf{P}_{j-k}) = \mathbf{f}_{max,j}(\mathbf{P}_{j-k}, \mathbf{P}^c_{j-k}) = 0$. >From Lemma 2 it follows that $\mathbf{f}_{max,j}(\mathbf{P}_{j-k}, \mathbf{P}_{j \cap k}) = 0$. Hence, there cannot be a link in the residual network from an event in $\mathbf{P}_{j \cap k}$ to one in $\mathbf{P}_{j-k}$. Therefore, $e \in \mathbf{P}_{j-k}$ is not reachable from σ in the residual network and $\mathbf{P}_{j-k} = \emptyset$. Since this is true for any pair $<j, k>$, $\mathbf{P}_{max}$ is unique.

The same argument applied to $\mathbf{P}_{max}$ and $\mathbf{P}^{\emptyset} \subseteq \mathbf{P}_{max}$ proves the minimality of $\mathbf{P}_{max}$, where $\mathbf{P}^{\emptyset}$ is a predecessor set such that $\Delta(\mathbf{P}^{\emptyset}) = \Delta_{max}$. $\square$

6   Building Resource Envelopes

So far we know that the resource level for a schedule s at time $t \in \mathbf{H}$ is equal to $\mathbf{L}_s(t) = \Delta(\mathbf{C_H}) + \Delta(\mathbf{P_X})$ for some predecessor set $\mathbf{P_X}$. However, it is not immediately obvious that the converse also applies. Given any predecessor set $\mathbf{P_X}$, we want to be able to determine a time $t_X \in \mathbf{H}$, the *separation time*, and a schedule s_X, the *separation schedule*, such that all and only the events in $\mathbf{C_H} \cup \mathbf{P_X}$ are scheduled at or before time t_X. The existence of a separation schedule and a separation time is not obvious because of the upper-bound constraints in the STN, i.e., the metric links between events that do not contribute to the construction of $\mathbf{Aprec(R)}$. If some event occurs too early with respect to t_X, an upper-bound constraint may force some event to occur before time t_X even if it is not a successor in $\mathbf{Aprec(R)}$. We now show that indeed we can find a separation time and schedule for *any* $\mathbf{P_X}$ and therefore also for $\mathbf{P}_{max}$. For the latter, we show that t_X is one of the times at which the resource level is maximum over $\mathbf{H}$ for any schedule. This yields the maximum resource envelope $\mathbf{L}_{max}$ if $\mathbf{H} = [t, t]$ and we scan t over the horizon $\mathbf{T}$.

6.1   Latest Events

First we find the events in P_X that will be scheduled at time t_X. We say that e is a *latest event* of P_X if it is not a strict predecessor of any other event in P_X, i.e., for any $e' \in P_X$, $|e'\ e| \geq 0$. We will call $P_{X,late}$ the set of all latest events in P_X. Also, we define $P_{X,early} = P_X - P_{X,late}$.

The following property holds between events in $P_{X,late}$ and $P_{X,early}$.

Property 1: Any event $e_1 \in P_{X,early}$ is a strict predecessor of some event $e_2 \in P_{X,\ late}$, i.e., $|e_2 e_1| < 0$.

Proof: Since $e_1 \in P_{X,early}$, there must be an event $e_{11} \in P_X$ such that $|e_{11}e_1| < 0$. If $e_{11} \in P_{X,\ late}$, the property is proven. Otherwise, we can find a finite chain of events $e_2 \rightarrow e_{1k} \rightarrow ... \rightarrow e_{11} \rightarrow e_1$ with $e_2 \in P_{X,\ late}$ and $|e_2 e_{1k}| < 0$, $|e_{1j}e_{i\ j-1}| < 0$ and $|e_{11}e_1| < 0$, yielding $|e_2 e_1| < 0$ for the triangular inequality of the shortest paths. If we could not find an $e_2 \in P_{X,\ late}$ to start such a finite chain, the chain would have to become a cycle of events in $P_{X,early}$, which contradicts the temporal consistency of **R**.   □

6.2   Separation Time for Latest Events

We can construct a separation time t_X at which we will schedule all latest events.

Lemma 3: There is a time interval $[t_{X,min}, t_{X,max}]$ that intersects all time bounds

$$[et(e), lt(e)] \text{ with } e \in P_{X,late} \text{ and such that } start(H) \leq t_{X,max}.$$

Proof: There must be a time value in common among all time bounds in $P_{X,late}$. If not, there would be two events $e_1, e_2 \in P_{X,late}$ such that $et(e_1) > lt(e_2)$ and, from the triangular inequality, $|e_1 e_2| \leq - et(e_1) + lt(e_2) < 0$, which is inconsistent with the definition of $P_{X,late}$. Observe that there must be an event $e \in P_{X,late}$ such that $lt(e) = t_{X,\ max}$. If $start(H) > t_{X,\ max}$, then $lt(e) < start(H)$, which contradicts $e \in R_H$.□

We define the separation time as $t_X = max\ (start(H), t_{X,min})$, with $t_X = start(H)$ if $P_X = \emptyset$. We can then show that each event in P^c_X can be scheduled after t_X.

Lemma 4: For any event $e \in P^c_X$, $lt(e) > t_X$

Proof: By definition of R_H it must be $lt(e) > start(H)$. So we only need to consider the case in which $t_X = t_{X,min} > start(H)$. In this case there is at least one event $e_1 \in P_{X,late}$ such that $et(e_1) = t_{X,min}$. For this event it is $|e_1\ e| \leq - et(e_1) + lt(e)$. Since $e \in P^c_X$, it must be that $|e_1\ e| > 0$, otherwise e would follow in **Apred(R)** an event in P_X. Therefore, $lt(e) \geq et(e_1) + |e_1\ e| > et(e_1) = t_{X,\ min}$.   □

6.2   Separation Schedule for Predecessors

We now build the separation schedule s_X for P_X and t_X, i.e., a schedule such that $s_X(e) \leq t_X$ for $e \in C_H \cup P_X$ and $s_X(e) > t_X$ for $e \in P^c_X \cup O_X$. Note that the following discussion holds also if $P_X = \emptyset$ and $t_X = start(H)$.

The following algorithm builds the separation schedule.

1.   Schedule all $e \in \mathbf{P}_{X, \text{late}}$ at t_X, i.e., $s_X(e) = t_X$.
2.   Propagate time through $\mathbf{R}$ obtaining new time bounds $[et'(e), lt'(e)]$ for each $e \in \mathbf{E(R)}$.
3.   Schedule all events $e \in \mathbf{E(R)} - \mathbf{P}_{X,\text{late}}$ at their new latest time, i.e., $s_X(e) = lt'(e)$.

For s_X to be a schedule, it must be consistent with respect to $\mathbf{R}$. We see that step 1 is consistent since: 1) t_X belongs to the intersection of all latest event time bounds; and 2) since for any pair of latest events $|e_1 e_2| \geq 0$, scheduling one at t_X does not prevent any other latest events to be also scheduled at time t_X. Step 3 above is also consistent because it is always possible to schedule all events at their latest times without temporal repropagation.

Now we need to show that the property defining a separation schedule is satisfied for s_X. Note that we already know that it is satisfied for events in $\mathbf{P}_{X,\text{late}}$. By definition it is also satisfied for events in $\mathbf{C_H}$ and $\mathbf{O_H}$. Therefore, we need to show that it is satisfied for $\mathbf{P}_{X,\text{early}}$ and $\mathbf{P^c}_X$.

(a) $lt'(e) \leq t_X$ for all $e \in \mathbf{P}_{X,\text{early}}$
       According to Property 1 we can pick an event $e_1 \in \mathbf{P}_{X,\text{ late}}$ such that $|e_1 e| < 0$. From the triangular inequality we have $lt'(e) \leq lt'(e_1) + |e_1 e| < lt'(e_1) = t_X$.
(b) $lt'(e) > t_X$ for all $e \in \mathbf{P^c}_X$.
       From Lemma 4 we know that before temporal repropagation it was $lt(e) > t_X$. After it, either $lt'(e) = lt(e)$, in which case the condition is satisfied, or $lt'(e)$ has changed due to a propagation that starts from some event $e_1 \in \mathbf{P}_{X,\text{ late}}$. So it must be $lt'(e) = t_X + |e_1 e|$. Since $e \in \mathbf{P^c}_X$, it must be $|e_1 e| > 0$, otherwise e would follow in $\mathbf{Apred(R)}$ an event in $\mathbf{P_X}$. Hence, $lt'(e) > t_X$.

We can now compute the maximum resource level for any schedule within the interval $\mathbf{H}$. In the following, we indicate with $\mathbf{P}_{\max}(\mathbf{R_H})$ the $\mathbf{P}_{\max}$ computed over $\mathbf{F(R_H)}$.

Theorem 4: The maximum resource level for any schedule of $\mathbf{R}$ over an interval $\mathbf{H} \subseteq \mathbf{T}$ is given by $\Delta(\mathbf{C_H}) + \Delta(\mathbf{P}_{\max}(\mathbf{R_H}))$.

Proof: We know that at any time $t \in \mathbf{H}$ the events in $\mathbf{R_H}$ that are scheduled before t are a predecessor set $\mathbf{P_X}$. For the resource level at time t it is always $\Delta(\mathbf{C_H}) + \Delta(\mathbf{P_X}) \leq \Delta(\mathbf{C_H}) + \Delta(\mathbf{P}_{\max}(\mathbf{R_H}))$, the latter being the resource level at the separation time t_X for the separation schedule s_X.   □
There are two interesting special cases of Theorem 4.

Corollary 2: The maximum possible resource consumption for $\mathbf{R}$ over $\mathbf{T}$ is equal to $\Delta(\mathbf{P}_{\max}(\mathbf{R_T}))$.
This means that estimating the maximum possible resource consumption for a flexible plan over the entire time horizon has the same complexity as a maximum flow problem.

Corollary 3: $L_{\max}(t) = \Delta(\mathbf{C_t}) + \Delta(\mathbf{P}_{\max}(\mathbf{R_t}))$.

The last formula tells us how to compute the resource-level envelope at a specific time. We now need to find an efficient algorithm to compute the resource-level envelope over the entire horizon $\mathbf{T}$.

7   Efficient Computation of Resource Envelopes

From Corollary 3, the naïve approach to compute a resource-level envelope would be to iterate over all possible $t \in T$. However, we only need to compute L_{max} at times when either C_t or R_t changes. This can only happen at $et(e)$ or $lt(e)$ for any $e \in E(R)$. Therefore we need to compute new levels for L_{max} only $2N$ times, where N is the number of start/end events in the original activity network. For each such computation, we need to: a) compute $P_{max}(R_t)$ by running a maximum flow on a network with at most N nodes; and 2) collect and sum the events in C_t and $P_{max}(R_t)$. The total complexity of the algorithm is therefore $O(N \ O(maxflow(N)) + N^2)$, where $O(maxflow(N))$ is the complexity of finding a maximum flow with an arbitrary maximum flow algorithm. For modern algorithms using the "preflow push" method [9], the worst case complexity can be $O(N^3)$. Extensive empirical studies show that the practical complexity of variations of the method can be as fast as $O(N^{1.5})$ [1]. This suggests that resource-level envelopes could operate in the inner loop of scheduling search algorithms, especially if they can be computated incrementally.

8   Conclusions

In this paper we describe an efficient algorithm to compute the tightest exact bound on the resource level induced by a flexible activity plan. This can potentially save exponential amounts of work with respect to currently available looser bounds. Future work will pursue two directions. The first is developing more incremental algorithms for the computation of the envelope. Using a temporal scanning of the events in the temporal network, it should be possible to significantly reduce the size of the networks on which the maximum flow algorithm needs to be run. This could significantly speed up the envelope calculation. The second direction will test the practical effectiveness of resource envelopes in the inner loop of search algorithms for multi-capacity resource scheduling, such as those used in (Laborie, 2001). This includes inner-loop backtracking and termination tests and variable and value ordering heuristics that exploit more directly the properties of the resource envelopes.

Acknowledgements

Ari Jonsson and Jeremy Frank were instrumental in pushing me to focus on this problem. During a dinner discussion at possibly the worst tourist restaurant in Paris, Grigore Rosu convinced me that the key of the resource-level envelope problem lies with the maximum-flow problem. Paul Morris gave me several helpful comments and suggested a simplification of the proof of theorem 1. Finally, Amedeo Cesta, Mary Bernardine Dias, Gregory Dorais, Paul Tompkins, an anonymous reviewer of a previous, unsuccessful submission, and a reviewer of the current successful one, gave several comments that helped me improve the presentation.

This work was performed with the support of the Intelligent Systems project of the Computing, Information and Communication Technologies research program of the National Aeronautics and Space Administration.

References

1. R.K. Ahuja, M. Kodialam, A.K. Mishra, J.B. Orlin. Computational Investigations of Maximum Flow Algorithms, *European Journal of Operational Research*, Vol 97(3), 1997.
2. K.R. Baker. Introduction to Sequencing and Scheduling. Wiley, New York, 1974.
3. J.C. Beck, A.J. Davenport, E.D. Davis, M.S. Fox. Beyond Contention: Extending Texture-Based Scheduling Heuristics. in *Proceedings of AAAI 1997*, Providence, RI, 1997.
4. A., Cesta, A. Oddi, S.F. Smith, A Constraint-Based Method for Resource Constrained Project Scheduling with Time Windows, CMU RI Technical Report, February 2000.
5. A. Cesta, C. Stella. A time and Resource Problem for Planning Architectures. *Proceedings of the 4th European Conference on Planning (ECP 97)*. Toulouse, France, 1997.
6. H. S.F. Cooper Jr., The Loneliness of the Long-Duration Astronaut, *Air & Space/Smithsonian*, June/July 1996, available at http://www.airspacemag.com/ASM/Mag/Index/1996/JJ/llda.html
7. T.H. Cormen, C.E. Leiserson, R.L. Rivest. *Introduction to Algorithms*. Cambridge, MA, 1990.
8. R. Dechter, I. Meiri, J. Pearl. Temporal Constraint Networks. *Artificial Intelligence*, 49:61-95, May 1991.
9. A.V. Goldberg, R.E. Tarjan. A New Approach to the Maximum-Flow Problem. *Journal of the ACM*, Vol. 35(4), 1988.
10. P. Laborie, Algorithms for Propagating Resource Constraints in AI Planning and Scheduling: Existing Approaches and New Results, *Proceedings of ECP 2001*, Toledo, Spain, 2001.
11. P. Morris, N. Muscettola, T. Vidal. Dynamic Control of Plans with Temporal Uncertainty, in *Proceedings of IJCAI 2001*, Seattle, WA, 2001
12. N. Muscettola. On the Utility of Bottleneck Reasoning for Scheduling. in *Proceedings of AAAI 1994*, Seattle, WA, 1994.
13. W.P.M. Nuijten. Time and Resource Constrained Scheduling: a Constraint Satisfaction Approach. PhD Thesis, Eindhoven University of Technology, 1994.
14. N. Sadeh. Look-ahead techniques for micro-opportunistic job-shop scheduling. PhD Thesis, Carnegie Mellon University, CMU-CS-91-102, 1991.
15. M. Zweben, M.S. Fox. *Intelligent Scheduling*. Morgan Kaufmann, San Francisco, 1994.

Local Probing Applied to Scheduling

Olli Kamarainen and Hani El Sakkout

IC-Parc
Imperial College of Science, Technology and Medicine
London SW7 2AZ, UK
{ok1,hhe}@icparc.ic.ac.uk

Abstract. This paper describes *local probing*, an algorithm hybridization form that combines backtrack search enhanced with local consistency techniques (BT+CS) with local search (LS) via probe backtracking. Generally BT+CS can be effective at finding solutions for (or proving the infeasibility of) tightly constrained problems with complex and overlapping constraints, but lacks good optimization characteristics. By contrast, LS can be superior at optimizing problems that are loosely constrained, or that have constraints which are satisfiable by simple neighbourhood procedures, but it also has several weaknesses of its own. It is weaker on problems with a complex constraint satisfaction element, and cannot prove problem infeasibility, causing prolonged execution times and ambiguous search outcomes for even trivially infeasible problems. We show these divergent characteristics on a general resource constrained scheduling problem class, extended with a widely applicable objective function. We then detail a local probing hybrid that marries the strengths of constraint satisfaction techniques, including good satisfaction characteristics and proofs of problem infeasibility, with the superior optimization characteristics of LS. This local probing hybrid achieves *sat-completeness*, without incorporating all the constraints into the LS neighbourhood function. Finally, we discuss the principal questions that must be answered in creating local probing hybrids for other problems.

1 Introduction

1.1 Paper Overview

The paper is structured as follows. This section motivates the paper, and introduces the hybrization form and the application domain. Section 2 details local probing's application to scheduling. Experimental results and comparisons to other algorithms are described in Sect. 3. In Sect. 4, the key questions that must be answered in creating a new local probing hybrid are listed and discussed. Lastly, Sect. 5 gives the conclusions of this study.

1.2 Motivation

Backtrack search supported by local consistency techniques (BT+CS) is often good at solving tight problems with complex constraints. However, it is generally less suitable for optimization.

P. Van Hentenryck (Ed.): CP 2002, LNCS 2470, pp. 155–171, 2002.

In this paper, local search (LS) is hybridized with BT+CS. In LS, typically one or more complete but partially consistent or sub-optimal assignments are improved at each search step. This gives rise to LS's strengths vis-a-vis conventional constraint satisfaction methods. Firstly, its search moves are more "informed" than those of backtrack search, since the quality of a complete assignment is more easily measurable, by comparison with the quality of BT+CS's partial assignments.[1] This is particularly valid when assessing the quality of the assignment w.r.t. a global optimization function. Secondly, the absence of systematicity allows assignments to be modified in any order, and so early search moves do not necessarily skew search to focus only on particular sub-spaces. This avoids a principal pitfall of BT+CS, where early search moves can skew the search by restricting it to particular sub-spaces, until they are exhaustively investigated.[2]

However, a traditional LS algorithm suffers from a number of drawbacks. Firstly, its lack of "search memory" can mean that it constantly returns to the same search sub-spaces, causing it to get trapped in local optima.[3] Secondly, it lacks a natural way in which the effective local consistency procedures of constraint satisfaction can be easily integrated, since these work best in combination with hard search decisions (such as variable assignments) that lead to further local-consistency deductions. This is a disadvantage when solving complex constraints, i.e. ones that cannot be adequately captured by simple LS neighbourhood procedures, nor adequately dealt with by LS violation-minimization optimization criteria. Thirdly, when the problem is infeasible, it cannot prove infeasibility, and continues to search unsuccessfully for a solution, eventually timing-out or giving up without informing the user whether the problem is infeasible or not, even when infeasibility is trivial to determine. This characteristic is unacceptable when, for instance, the algorithm must be applied to a large batch of problems in a reasonable amount of time, or if proofs of infeasibility are valuable to the user.

The above considerations lead many researchers to conclude that the different characteristics of conventional LS and BT+CS algorithms are complementary. It is reasonable to assume that the hybridization of these methods can be fruitful for certain problems.

1.3   Hybridization Form: Probe Backtracking

In the literature, various approaches to hybridizing BT+CS and LS, have been investigated (e.g. [2, 4, 17, 23, 24, 25, 27, 28]).[4] Here the focus is the hybridization

---

[1] Informedness was discussed in [21].

[2] Moreover, if we consider as a measure of search move informedness the length of the partial assignment undergoing extension, early BT+CS search decisions are even less informed than decisions deeper in the search tree, greatly increasing the chance that search is skewed to unproductive areas.

[3] Many variations of basic LS strategies have tried to tackle this defect (e.g. tabu search [11] and guided local search [26]).

[4] See [10] for a general survey.

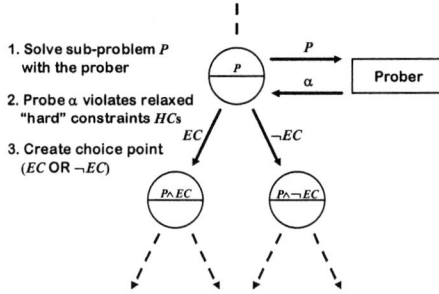

1. Solve sub-problem *P* with the prober

2. Probe α violates relaxed "hard" constraints *HCs*

3. Create choice point (*EC* OR ¬*EC*)

Fig. 1. An illustration of probe backtrack search

of the two by means of *probe backtrack search* [7, 9]. Probe backtracking (PBT) is a general hybridization form that has been shown to yield efficient hybrid algorithms for problem classes similar to the one investigated here. Previously though probe backtracking was used to hybridize BT+CS with linear and mixed integer solvers, rather than with LS [1, 9].[5]

In probe backtracking, a constraint satisfaction and optimization problem is solved by a high-level BT+CS algorithm that hybridizes another algorithm. All the problem constraints are classified into two sets: "easy" and "hard". The "easy" constraints are those constraints that are easily solved by the hybridized algorithm, known as the *prober*. At any search node, the backtrack search applies the prober to a sub-problem consisting of the "easy" constraints and an objective function. The prober will generate a complete assignment that satisfies all the "easy" constraints, and is good (and, for some probers, *super-optimal*) with respect to the objective function.[6] If the assignment also happens to satisfy all the "hard" constraints, a solution has been generated, and the search may terminate, or continue with a tighter cost bound if better solutions are sought as part of the branch and bound process. If the assignment has been found to violate one or more "hard" constraints, then a new "easy" constraint is identified and posted to the prober. This "easy" constraint is chosen to force the prober to generate a different assignment that reduces the violation of one of the violated "hard" constraints. The posting of this constraint moves the backtrack search to a new node, and the process repeats. On backtracking, the negation of this "easy" constraint is posted (the negation must also be an "easy" constraint). Figure 1 illustrates the behaviour of probe backtracking when the prober returns an assignment that violates one or more "hard" constraints. A pseudo-code description can be found in [9].

---

[5] A similar evolution from integrating LP-based methods towards other solvers has been discussed in [15].

[6] A *super-optimal* assignment is a complete, partially consistent assignment that is no worse w.r.t. the objective function than any optimal solution.

1.4   Application to Scheduling

Different versions of probe backtrack search have been applied to commercial dynamic scheduling problems [9], to earliness/tardiness scheduling problems [3], and to a generic scheduling problem extended with a piecewise linear objective function [1]. The latter is selected here as a testbed for the technique that is developed, because it generalizes the first two.

The selected problem is a scheduling problem that is based on the kernel resource feasibility problem (KRFP) [6, 9]. The KRFP generalizes most scheduling benchmarks, including job shop scheduling, ship loading, bridge building, and resource constrained project scheduling.

In the KRFP, we have several types of resources and a given quantity of each. We have also a fixed number of non-preemptive activities. Each activity requires a quantity of a specific resource type during its execution. An arbitrary set of metric temporal constraints relate the start and end times of activities. The aim is to schedule activities so that all the temporal constraints are satisfied, and the demand on any resource does not exceed its resource quantity at any time on the scheduling horizon.

While the KRFP itself represents only a constraint satisfaction problem, an objective function is often needed. Many real world optimization criteria such as revenue and cost optimization in transportation can be approximated by a piecewise linear function. In the problem we investigate, a piecewise linear function maps the start time (or end) of each of the activities of the KRFP to an activity cost. The objective function is then a minimization of the sum of the values of these functions. The kernel resource feasibility problem with a piecewise linear objective function is abbreviated by PL-KRFP.

Like many large scale combinatorial optimization problems (LSCO's), the PL-KRFP can be clearly divided into different sub-problems. The probe backtrack approach presented in [9] keeps temporal constraints within the sub-problem addressed by the prober, while relaxing the resource constraints and handling them at the backtrack search level. If the solution to the sub-problem does not satisfy the relaxed resource constraints, additional temporal precedence constraints are added to the sub-problem in order to relieve violations. This approach was also used in several algorithms described in [1]. In all these algorithms, the probers are based on linear programming (LP) or mixed-integer programming (MIP).

1.5   Overview of Approach

In *local probing*, an LS algorithm is used as the prober instead. Here, simulated annealing (SA, [19]) is the LS algorithm that is hybridized to illustrate the potential of this form.[7]

---

[7] Note that most other LS algorithms including hill climbing, tabu search ([11]), guided local search ([26]), and genetic algorithms ([12, 14]) could have been hybridized in an analogous fashion. SA is selected for this preliminary study because of its simplicity. Arguably, the results of SA are representative since a more sophisticated LS algorithm would also lead to a better hybrid.

By comparison with the earlier probe backtracking hybrids based on LP and MIP, which rely on the prober solving a sub-problem that is linear, or highly linear, local probing hybrids are widely applicable, because the prober can solve sub-problems with arbitrary objective functions and arbitrary "easy" constraints.

However, one disadvantage of local probing hybrids is that, because an LS prober is normally incomplete, the overall algorithm loses completeness. We distinguish though two levels of completeness for constraint satisfaction and optimization problems:

- *sat-completeness*, where the algorithm returns a solution, or proves no solution exists, in a finite number of steps; and
- *opt-completeness*, where the algorithm returns an *optimal* solution, or proves no solution exists, in a finite number of steps.

We show how *sat-complete* local probing hybrids can be constructed.

The local probing algorithm that is presented here solves the PL-KRFP, and uses an LS prober that utilizes a generic neighbourhood operator. The operator is capable of satisfying an arbitrary set of "easy" temporal constraints. It needs to do so because neighbourhood is dynamic, i.e. the set of temporal constraints that must be satisfied by LS changes from one backtrack search node to the next. This neighbourhood operator has been found to be much more effective than other tested alternatives [18]. It uses a linear solver to find temporally feasible neighbours in the proximity of the current node by solving an LP problem with a linear *minimal perturbation* objective function.

Our local probing hybrid is compared with (1) a different, LP-based, probe backtracking hybrid previously specialized for the PL-KRFP, and (2) a "pure" SA algorithm tuned for the same problem. The results show that applying local probing can lead to better overall algorithm performance by comparison with the other hybrid algorithm. They also show that local probing improves the SA algorithm by addressing its weaknesses: it forces SA to escape from infeasible local optima by dynamically reshaping its neighbourhood function; it supports it by applying local consistency methods where they are more effective; and it restores algorithm *sat-completeness*. Finally, the paper discusses the broader potential of local probing.

2   Local Probing for Scheduling

2.1   Overview

The constraints of the PL-KRFP consist of three classes: resource constraints, temporal constraints and constraints linking the objective function to the temporal decision variables. The neighbourhood operator of the LS algorithm can be designed such that it satisfies certain constraint classes, thereby guaranteeing that the probes never violate these classes. It is possible to take any subset of the problem constraints into the neighbourhood operator, and thus, ensure probe feasibility with respect to that subset. The question is which kind of sub-problem

```
 1.  begin local_probing
 2.       if not(solve temporal sub-problem by LS prober)
 3.           then return FALSE
 4.           else if not(find violated resource constraints)
 5.               then return TRUE
 6.               else begin
 7.                       select violated resource constraint HC;
 8.                       select temporal constraint EC that reduces violation of HC;
 9.                       post EC;
10.                       if local_probing
11.                           then return TRUE;
12.                       remove EC;
13.                       post not(EC);
14.                       if local_probing
15.                           then return TRUE;
16.                       remove not(EC);
17.                       return FALSE;
18.                   end;
19.  end local_probing
```

Fig. 2. Local probing algorithm

is "easy" for the neighbourhood operator to satisfy and makes the overall algorithm efficient at the same time. This is important since the class of constraints satisfied by the neighbourhood operator includes the ones that will be posted by probe backtracking as it drives the search towards globally feasible solutions.

In this paper, the *temporal constraints* are dealt with by the neighbourhood operator while the LS objective function aims to minimize the overall cost, and penalizes the violation of the "hard" resource constraints. The local probing procedure is summarized in Fig. 2. If the algorithm returns a solution, a cost bound constraint is posted and the algorithm is repeated. The cost bound is not dealt with in the neighbourhood operator; rather, before returning a probe, LS prober checks that the cost bound is satisfied (and fails if it is not).

In probe backtracking, different types of constraint propagation and search ordering heuristics can be applied. When making the decision on which constraint to post to the sub-problem in order to repair the violations, we select first the resource constraint that is violated the most, then we select a temporal constraint that would reduce violation (by reducing resource overlap), but which would cause minimal change to the proposed schedule. On backtracking, the negation of this constraint is posted instead. Posting the temporal constraint triggers local consistency procedures which reduce the domains of the variables further. The details are described in [9]. The implementation relies on the hybridization facilities of the ECLiPSe constraint logic programming platform, e.g. *attributed variables*, *tentative values* and *waking priorities* [16].

2.2   Simulated Annealing as an LS Prober

As an LS strategy, we use simulated annealing (SA) [19], which is easy to implement and may avoid local minima. It starts from an initial assignment[8], and, at each search step, the neighbourhood operator suggests for the sub-problem a candidate solution that satisfies all the temporal sub-problem constraints.

Search continues until a termination condition is satisfied. In SA, a worse neighbour may be accepted. The acceptance is randomized and depends on the quality of a neighbour and a *temperature* parameter, which is decreased during the search depending on the selected *cooling strategy*. The probability of moving to worse neighbours decreases with the temperature parameter.

"Hard" resource constraints are treated as soft constraints by adding a penalty component to the objective function, namely, the resource utilization area that exceeds the resource limit over the time horizon, multiplied by a constant. The results presented suggest that this approach works well together with the repair-based search capability of probe backtracking.

2.3   Minimal Perturbation Neighbourhood Operator

We require an efficient neigbourhood operator, which finds feasible neighbour solutions. It should be generic and capable of satisfying different classes of constraints, especially temporal constraints in our scope. In order to utilize the efficiency benefits of LP within the neighbourhood operator of local probing, an operator based on minimal perturbation search [7, 9] is introduced. First, it assigns a value to only one randomly selected variable[9]. This value selection is backtrackable and all the feasible values in the domain of the selected variable can be explored. Once the variable has been instantiated, the remaining variables are solved as a *minimal perturbation problem* by LP. In a minimal perturbation problem the aim is to find the temporally feasible solution which minimizes the changes to the previous assignment. The objective function and the minimal perturbation constraints are modelled as follows:

$$\min \sum_{i=1}^{N} d_{x_i}, \qquad \text{s.t.} \tag{1}$$

$$d_{x_i} \geq x_i - c_i, \qquad i = 1, \ldots, N \tag{2}$$

$$d_{x_i} \geq c_i - x_i, \qquad i = 1, \ldots, N \tag{3}$$

The absolute change between variable x and its initial value c is a non-linear expression. It is represented by a new variable $d_x = |x - c|$, and the total change

---

[8] The initial assignment in the very beginning is the initial schedule. Subsequently, the previously generated probe is used.

[9] The domain of the selected variable is divided into two sets, by randomly selecting a value x and placing values better than x in the "better" set S_1 and worse (or equal) values in the "worse" set S_2. S_1 is explored first by using random value selection, before exploring S_2.

over all the N non-instantiated variables can be minimized by adding linear constraints (2) and (3). The objective function (1) of the minimal perturbation problem is linear and the solution can be produced by a Simplex-based LP solver extremely quickly.

2.4   Sat-completeness

Probe backtrack search will guarantee to satisfy any constraints that are monitored for violation and repaired within its backtrack procedure, provided that a number of conditions are met. Specifically: (1) if a constraint is violated, it must be detected and scheduled for repair by probe backtracking within a finite number of steps; (2) the probe backtrack procedure must identify all "easy" constraints whose satisfiability will determine whether the "hard" constraint can be satisfied; (3) it must systematically post these "easy" constraints (and on backtracking, their negations, to fully partition the search space) to the prober until either the constraint is satisfied, or it is proved impossible to satisfy; and (4) the prober must guarantee to satisfy the posted "easy" constraints if this is possible.

We do not refer to the first three conditions in the context of the KRFP resource constraints and their relationship with temporal precedence constraints, since they have been fully described in the context of previous complete probe backtracking hybrids [9].

Condition (4) is satisfied because the neighbourhood operator will always find a temporally feasible assignment if one exists. The neighbourhood operator will select a variable and systematically attempt each of its values. If a temporally feasible solution exists with the variable set to a particular value, the LP solver will find one. Thus the neighbourhood operator ensures that the LS prober guarantees to satisfy the set of "easy" constraints if they are satisfiable.

Thus local probing is *sat-complete*: it finds a solution if one exists, and proves infeasibility if no solutions exist. However, the algorithm is not *opt-complete* since the assignments it returns are not *super-optimal*.

3   Empirical Study

3.1   Algorithms Used for Comparison

We compared a tuned local probing hybrid (denoted Probe(Loc)) with two other algorithms: an LP-based probe backtracking hybrid from [1] (Probe(LP)), and a "pure" SA algorithm (SA).

Probe(LP). The best performing LP-based probe backtracking algorithm from [1] was chosen (we refer you to this paper for a full algorithm description). The algorithm is similar to our local probing instance in that it is a probe backtracking hybrid specialized for solving the PL-KRFP, but differs in that its prober is LP-based and *opt-complete*. The prober of Probe(LP) applies an LP solver to a linear relaxation of the piecewise linear objective function. Possible discrepancies between the linearly relaxed objective and the allowed values of the true piecewise linear function are resolved by a small search procedure which branches over the temporal variables' domains, until this discrepancy has been eliminated. This allows the prober to return assignments that satisfy all the "easy" temporal constraints, and are *super-optimal*. Note that Probe(LP) does not include any resource constraint violation penalties within the prober's objective function, resulting in a prober that has a "greedy" characteristic: it finds the best quality prober solution from the cost point of view, independent of how many "hard" resource constraints it violates.[10]

SA. SA was selected to represent "pure" LS because SA is used as our local probing prober, allowing fair comparisons of performance: the SA implementation utilizes precisely the same neighbourhood operator and objective function that are used in the prober.

A manual tuning process was applied to refine SA's parameters until it produced good quality results: the parameters applied in SA were those that produced the best results on a representative sample of PL-KRFP instances, w.r.t. both the number of solved problems, and the quality of the generated solutions. SA starts with the initial temperature of 100000, and after every 10000 neighbour candidate evaluations the temperature is lowered by multiplying it with constant 0.85 (geometric reduction).[11] This search continues until it times-out.

Probe(Loc). The SA prober of Probe(Loc) was tuned in a similar fashion, but the best parameters in this case were different because resource satisfaction is supported by the backtrack search component. The best combination are used in Probe(Loc), and they comprise: a cooling factor of 0.9; a cooling step every 10 neighbour candidate evaluations; and an SA procedure that terminates after 100 cooling steps.

3.2   Test Problems

The tests were carried out on 1200 PL-KRFP benchmark problems. Each instance contains an initial schedule, comprising scheduled activities which all use the same type of resource. The initial schedule needs to be changed because (a) it is made infeasible by a reducing the number of available resources, and

---

[10] There are no easy ways to penalize resource violation in an LP objective function, due to the limited constraint and objective function classes it can deal with. Therefore, in the hybrids of [1], resource constraint satisfaction was handled completely at the probe backtracking level.

[11] A neighbour candidate is accepted if it is better than the current assignment or $p < exp^{(C_{curr}-C_{new})/T}$ where: p is a random number between 0 and 1; C_{new} is the cost of the neighbour candidate; C_{curr} is the cost of the current assignment; and T is the temperature.

Table 1. Results over all instances

Method	Proved infeasible	Solution found	Timeout w/o solution
SA	0 (0.0%)	417 (34.8%)	783 (65.3%)
Probe(LP)	299 (24.9%)	313 (26.1%)	588 (49.0%)
Probe(Loc)	285 (23.8%)	429 (35.8%)	486 (40.5%)

(b) it needs to be optimized with respect to a piecewise linear objective function. The problem instances contain randomly-generated temporal constraints
between arbitrary activity start and end points. The temporal constraints are
always satisfied by the initial schedule, but must continue to be enforced as
the schedule changes. A *temporal constraint density* parameter controls their
density, and is proportional to the probability of a temporal constraint existing
between any pair of start/end time variables.[12] Each activity is associated with
a piecewise linear function containing at least five local minima. The function
represents the varying cost of the activity as its start time takes different values.
The objective is to minimize the sum of the activity costs.

The tests were run over 300 different schedule and temporal constraint density combinations. The number of activities varied over $\{50, 100\}$, and the temporal constraint densities over $\{0.3, 0.6, 0.9\}$. Each combination was the basis
for four problem instances: different time window constraints were used for the
activities, allowing them to change by no more than $\{\pm 10, \pm 20, \pm 50, \pm 100\}$
time units from their initial position. The number of available resources was
40 per cent lower than the number used by the input schedule. The scheduling
horizon was limited to 200 time units.[13]

The test were run on Pentium II 450 MHz PCs, and the algorithms timed-
out after 1800 seconds of CPU time. The three algorithms were implemented on
ECLiPSe 5.3, and the LP sub-problems were solved using the default settings of
CPLEX 6.5.

3.3   Results

Any algorithm run on a problem instance results in one of the following outcomes:
search completion with an infeasibility proof; search completion with a solution,
or a time-out with a solution; or, finally, a time-out without a solution.

Table 1 presents, for each algorithm, the number of instances (out of 1200)
for which it (a) obtained an infeasibility proof; (b) found a solution (whether or
not the search completed); or (c) timed-out without a solution.

The results for *proofs of infeasibility* show the trivial result that SA is not
able to prove that a solution cannot be found, while the other two algorithms
do. Interestingly though, they also seem to indicate that Probe(LP) is slightly

---

[12] The probability is equal to $density/(2N - 1)$, where N is the number of activities.
[13] See http://www.icparc.ic.ac.uk/~ok1/pl-krfp_benchmarks.html for the benchmarks.

better at proving infeasibility than Probe(Loc) within the selected time limit. This must be due to the fact that the LP-based prober of Probe(LP) is faster at generating probes than the SA prober of Probe(Loc). Nevertheless, the two algorithms remain comparable overall, because the former's prober returns assignments that generally violate more "hard" resource constraints (its objective function is unable to penalize resource constraint violation).

By the *solutions found* measure, the results show that Probe(Loc) slightly outperforms SA and is clearly better than Probe(LP). For SA and Probe(Loc), the resource-violation penalty term seems to work well on solvable problems, giving them a clear advantage over Probe(LP), whose prober is unable to recognize resource violations and does not incrementally improve a partially consistent solution. The greater flexibility of LS over linear programming when modelling disjunctive constraints and objective criteria is the source of this advantage.

The third measure, *timeout w/o solution*, seems to be one of the best overall indicators of algorithm performance, since it quantifies the problem instances where the algorithm was unable to generate a meaningful answer. By this measure Probe(Loc) is the best of the three algorithms (40.5% by comparison with 49.0% for Probe(LP), and 65.3% for SA).

A different measure of performance is solution quality. Probe(Loc) or Probe(LP) proved that no solution exists for 356 instances out of the 1200, and in 399 cases, all three algorithms timed-out without a solution. However, at least one algorithm found a solution for the remaining 445 cases, and of these, 300 were solved by all three. These 300 instances, even though they represent only 25 per cent of the whole problem set, provide us with a vehicle to compare fairly the cost minimization abilities of the three algorithms.

Table 2 shows the average cost improvement relative to the cost of the initial (input) schedule, expressed as a percentage change.[14] Even though the differences between algorithms are not great, by this measure Probe(LP) clearly outperforms both Probe(Loc) and SA. Of course, the 300 instances that were solved by each algorithm represent the "easiest" part of the problem set, where the hard resource constraints are less relevant, and Probe(LP)'s greedy, *super-optimal* probes are most effective. This advantage though must be weighed against the fact that Probe(LP) solves by far the fewest problems (out of the 445 problems solved by at least one algorithm, it fails to solve 132, versus 28 for SA, and 16 for Probe(Loc)).

Table 3 presents the average CPU times needed to get a first solution or prove infeasibility. Where an algorithm timed-out, the time-out period was used instead.[15] For each algorithm, the first column covers all 1200 instances. The second column covers just the "easy" 300 instances that were solved by all three algorithms. It seems that Probe(Loc) not only finds solutions more often, but is faster at doing so than Probe(LP) and SA.

---

[14] Recall that the initial input schedule is infeasible due to the imposed 40% resource utilization reduction, and so some returned solutions are associated with a rise in cost.

[15] We preferred to use the time-out period rather than some arbitrary penalty.

Table 2. Average cost improvement relative to initial schedule cost, for problem instances solved by all three algorithms

Method	Improvement (%)
SA	-21.31
Probe(LP)	-24.57
Probe(Loc)	-22.81

Table 3. Average CPU time in secs. needed to get a first solution over all instances (CPU-all), and over the instances solved by all three algorithms (CPU-easy)

Method	CPU-all	CPU-easy
SA	1228	70
Probe(LP)	924	43
Probe(Loc)	839	35

Finally, Fig. 3 shows how the algorithm performance measures vary as the problem tightness varies.[16] Problem tightness is inversely proportional to time-window size, and directly proportional to temporal constraint density. It is clear from these figures that Probe(Loc) shadows the performance of SA on feasible, loose problems and that of Probe(LP) on tight and infeasible problems, leading to better overall performance.

4   Discussion

4.1   Discussion on Experimental Results

Constraint Satisfaction Characteristic The results demonstrate that local probing can improve SA's performance by addressing its three principal weaknesses: it forces SA to escape from infeasible local optima by dynamically reshaping its neighbourhood function; it supports it by applying local consistency methods where they are more effective; and it restores algorithm *sat-completeness*. Addressing the first two weaknesses leads to improved performance on medium tightness problems (e.g. in the tests, instances where density=0.6). Addressing the last enables proofs of infeasibility, and eliminates SA's needless timeouts on infeasible problems (e.g. where density=0.9).

The results also show the benefits of LS's flexibility by comparison with LP-based probers — the ability to easily penalize violations of "hard" constraints in the objective function means that local probing is able to capitalize on SA's

---

[16] Please note that the directions of the axes have been changed for different measures to improve the observation angle.

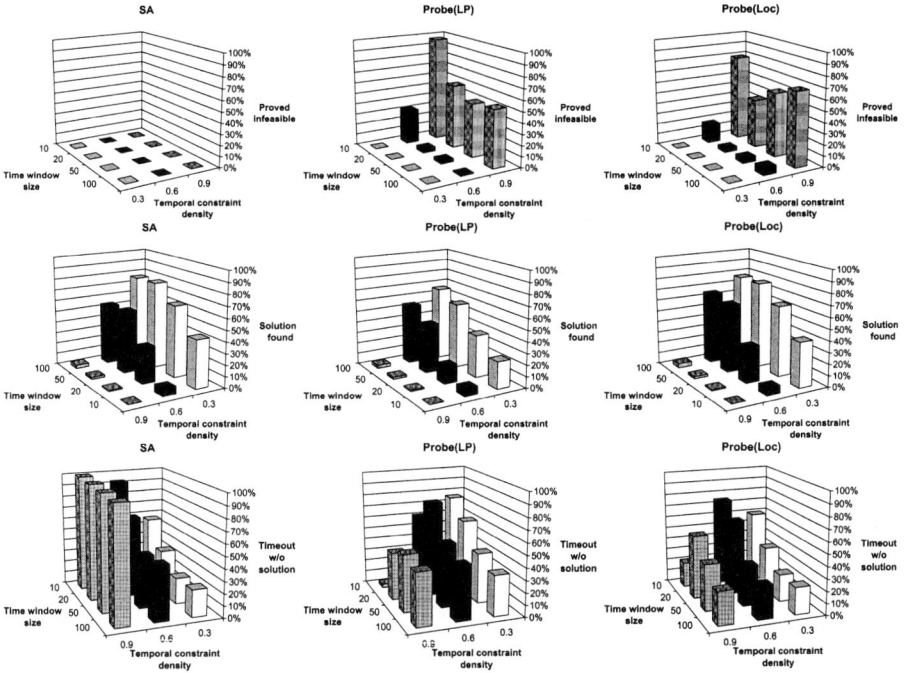

Fig. 3. Infeasibility proofs, solutions found, and time-outs without a solution over temporal constraint density and time-window size

ability to solve relatively loosely-constrained problems more often (e.g. where density=0.3). This results in a large increase in the number of solutions found within the timeout, and a shorter time to the first solution. Nevertheless the LP-based prober's speed enabled it to prove infeasibility slightly more often.

Optimization Characteristic Although LP-based probers are not as widely applicable as LS probers, when they are applicable their ability to quickly generate *super-optimal* assigments can enable a high-quality optimization characteristic. The results support this statement, showing that the LP-based prober returned better quality solutions for those problems that it was able to solve. For such loosely-constrained problems, the time spent in each call of the prober of Probe(Loc) is too short to enable it to find the best quality solutions. However, it cannot be increased dramatically though without impacting the performance on more tightly-constrained problems. This trade-off indicates that a dynamic prober termination condition, that varies the time spent in the LS prober according to the number of violated "hard" constraints, might prove very effective.

This is also true when comparing Probe(Loc) to SA. While the results show that the local probing hybrid is on average slightly better at optimization, for problems where constraint satisfaction is less of an issue, it makes sense to fully utilize the computation time for optimization, by allowing the prober to take more time.

4.2 Building Other Local Probing Algorithms

Given the performance improvements obtained on the PL-KRFP, it is likely that other problems could also be solved better by applying a local probing hybrid. However, in building a local probing hybrid, the algorithm creator faces many design dimensions. As for other probe backtracking approaches these include the backtrack search **heuristics**, the **local consistency** techniques, and the **branch and bound procedure** that is applied at the backtrack search level of probe backtracking.

The creator of local probing hybrids faces many other choices though. Such choices mostly relate to the LS strategy, and include the basic **algorithm** type, e.g. *hill climbing, tabu search* [11], or *genetic algorithm* [12, 14]; its **initialization procedure**, e.g. heuristic or randomized; and the applied **neighbourhood operator**, e.g. *first improvement, steepest descent*.[17] The operator might also be expanded systematically in order to find feasible neighbours, e.g. variable neighbourhood search in [22], large neighbourhood search in [25] and the neighbourhood operators in [18]. Other algorithmic dimensions include **learning**: e.g. the tabu lists of tabu search, or the penalty terms of *guided local search* (GLS, [26]); the **iteration structure**, e.g. SA's temperature schedules, and the selection processes of genetic algorithms; and lastly the **termination condition**: perhaps a maximum run-time; a best solution quality (optimal, gap-to-lower-bound, improvement-too-slow); or a maximum number of neighbour candidate evaluations.

However, among the most critical choices in a local probing hybrid are the constraint classes that must be satisfied by the neighbourhood operator, and those classes modelled by the LS prober's objective function. These choices distribute the responsibility for solving the problem constraints, sharing them between the LS prober, and the higher level BT+CS algorithm.

Recall that in probe backtracking, the problem constraints are divided into "easy" and "hard" constraint sets, as explained in the introduction. Here LS is the prober that solves "easy" sub-problem. Thus it must be capable of: (1) satisfying the "easy" constraints, while seeking to (2) optimize the objective function, and possibly (3) minimize the violation of "hard" constraints.

Achieving (1) depends on finding neighbourhood operators that can satisfy the "easy" constraints, since these are normally the only constraints that an LS algorithm guarantees to satisfy.

Achieving (2) is possible by including the problem's objective criteria in the LS objective function. To achieve (3), it is necessary to extend the objective function to penalize "hard" constraint violation. This reduces the risk of "hard" constraint violation, but clearly the probe backtracking procedure must

---

[17] N.B. the genetic algorithm cross-over and mutation operators can be viewed as specialized neighbourhood operators.

still monitor and repair such constraints to remain *sat-complete*, as there is no guarantee that they will all be satisfied by the LS prober.

4.3   Related Work

In this paper, the resource constraints of the scheduling problem are relaxed, and a temporal sub-problem which is easy to satisfy is solved separately. The approach was used in [8], and elsewhere (e.g. [5]). Here, the neighbourhood operator of LS satisfies the temporal constraints, and the cost function and the resource constraints are modelled in an extended objective function. In [18], the LS probers did not penalize "hard" constraint violation, but some were able to satisfy the cost bound constraint.

Local probing belongs to the class of LS/BT+CS hybridizations where LS is performed in search nodes of the global search tree. In [24], a constructive approach continues until a dead-end is reached, then an LS algorithm modifies the current partial solution passing it back to the construction routine. In [4], a vehicle routing problem with side constraints is solved by performing LS after each insertion of a customer during the construction process (Incremental Local Optimization). In [28], a two-phase algorithm applies LS to generate a partial solution and uses BT to extend it to a complete one, repeating this process until a solution is found. In one approach presented in [27], an LS procedure, utilizing special constraints based on *invariants* of Localizer [20], is run at each node in the constructive search tree to select the next variable to be instantiated.

The minimal perturbation neighbourhood operator used to satisfy the temporal constraints in the LS prober of Probe(Loc) is related to a hybridization class where BT+CS is used in neighbourhood exploration. For instance, in [25], *limited discrepancy search* ([13]) is applied to incrementally explore the neighbourhood. In the genetic algorithm approach presented in [2], instead of values, sub-domains of original variables are used as meta-variables, which are evaluated by solving the corresponding sub-CSPs by BT+CS. In [23], obtaining a neighbour is a constrained optimization problem that is solved by a branch and bound algorithm. In [17], a complete solution is constructed by tabu search using BT+CS to choose neighbours from sets of alternative partial assignments.

5   Conclusion

This paper demonstrated that local probing hybrids can marry the strengths of constraint satisfaction techniques, including good satisfaction characteristics and proofs of problem infeasibility, with the superior optimization characteristics of local search. The paper detailed a local probing algorithm that solved a highly generic scheduling problem class, and showed it to be more effective than an LP-based hybrid, and a traditional "pure" local search algorithm, both of which were specialized for this class.

Acknowledgements

The authors would like to thank Farid Ajili and Neil Yorke-Smith for their help and valuable feedback on this work.

References

[1] F. Ajili and H. El Sakkout. LP probing for piecewise linear optimization in scheduling. In *Proc. of CP-AI-OR'01*, pages 189–203, 2001.

[2] N. Barnier and P. Brisset. Combine & conquer: Genetic algorithm and CP for optimization. In *Proc. of CP98*, page 436, 1998.

[3] C. Beck and P. Refalo. A hybrid approach to scheduling with earliness and tardiness costs. In *Proc. of CP-AI-OR'01*, pages 175–188, 2001.

[4] Y. Caseau and F. Laburthe. Heuristics for large constrained vehicle routing problems. *Journal of Heuristics*, 5(3):281–303, 1999.

[5] A. Cesta, A. Oddi, and S. Smith. A constraint-based method for project scheduling with time windows. *Journal of Heuristics*, 8(1):109–136, 2002.

[6] A. El-Kholy and B. Richards. Temporal and resource reasoning in planning: The *parc*PLAN approach. In *Proc. of ECAI96*, pages 614–618, 1996.

[7] H. El Sakkout. *Improving Backtrack Search: Three Case Studies of Localized Dynamic Hybridization*. PhD Thesis, Imperial College, London, 1999.

[8] H. El Sakkout, T. Richards, and M. Wallace. Minimal perturbation in dynamic scheduling. In *Proc. of ECAI98*, pages 504–508, 1998.

[9] H. El Sakkout and M. Wallace. Probe backtrack search for minimal perturbation in dynamic scheduling. *Constraints*, 5(4):359–388, 2000.

[10] F. Focacci, F. Laburthe, and A. Lodi. Local search and constraint programming. In *Handbook on Metaheuristics*, Kluwer, 2002. To be published.

[11] F. Glover. Future paths for integer programming and links to artificial intelligence. *Computers & Operations Research*, 5:533–549, 1986.

[12] D. E. Goldberg. *Genetic Algorithms in Search, Optimization, and Machine Learning*. Addison-Wesley, 1989.

[13] W. D. Harvey and M. L. Ginsberg. Limited discrepancy search. In *Proc. of IJCAI95*, pages 607–615, 1995.

[14] J. H. Holland. *Adaptation in Natural and Artificial Systems*. University of Michigan Press, Ann Arbor, 1975.

[15] J. N. Hooker, Hak-Jin Kim, and G. Ottosson. A declarative modeling framework that integrates solution methods. *Annals of Operations Res.*, 104:141–161, 2001.

[16] IC-Parc. *ECLiPSe User manual.* http://www.icparc.ic.ac.uk/eclipse/, 2001.

[17] N. Jussien and O. Lhomme. Local search with constraint propagation and conflict-based heuristics. In *Proc. of AAAI-00*, pages 169–174, 2000.

[18] O. Kamarainen, H. El Sakkout, and J. Lever. Local probing for resource constrained scheduling. In *Proc. of the CP01 Workshop on Cooperative Solvers*, 2001.

[19] S. Kirkpatrick, C. Gelatt Jr., and M. Vecchi. Optimization by simulated annealing. *Science*, 220:671–680, 1983.

[20] L. Michel and P. Van Hentenryck. Localizer: A modeling language for local search. In *Proc. of CP97*, pages 237–251, 1997.

[21] S. Minton, M. D. Johnston, A. B. Philips, and P. Laird. Minimizing conflicts: a heuristic repair method for constraint satisfaction and scheduling problems. *Artificial Intelligence*, 58:161–205, 1992.

[22] N. Mladenovic and P. Hansen. Variable neighbourhood search. *Computers & Operations Research*, 24:1097–1100, 1997.

[23] G. Pesant and M. Gendreau. A constraint programming framework for local search methods. *Journal of Heuristics*, 5(3):255–279, 1999.

[24] A. Schaerf. Combining local search and look-ahead for scheduling and constraint satisfaction problems. In *Proc. of IJCAI97*, pages 1254–1259, 1997.

[25] P. Shaw. Using constraint programming and local search methods to solve vehicle routing problems. In *Proc. of CP98*, pages 417–431, 1998.

[26] C. Voudouris and E. Tsang. Partial constraint satisfaction problems and guided local search. In *Proc. of PACT96*, pages 337–356, 1996.

[27] M. Wallace and J. Schimpf. Finding the right hybrid algorithm - a combinatorial meta-problem. *Annals of Math. and Artificial Intelligence*, 34(4):259–269, 2002.

[28] J. Zhang and H. Zhang. Combining local search and backtracking techniques for constraint satisfaction. In *Proc. of AAAI96*, pages 369–374, 1996.

A Hybrid Approach for SAT[*]

Djamal Habet[1], Chu Min Li[2], Laure Devendeville[2], and Michel Vasquez[1]

[1] Centre LGI2P, école des Mines d'Alès, Site EERIE
Parc Scientifique Georges Besse, 30035, Cedex 01, Nîmes, France
{Djamal.Habet,Michel.Vasquez}@ema.fr
[2] LaRIA, Université de Picardie Jules Verne
5, Rue du Moulin Neuf, 80000, Amiens, France
{cli,devendev}@laria.u-picardie.fr

Abstract. Exploiting variable dependencies has been shown very useful in local search algorithms for SAT. In this paper, we extend the use of such dependencies by hybridizing a local search algorithm, Walksat, and the DPLL procedure, Satz. At each node reached in the DPLL search tree to a fixed depth, we construct the literal implication graph. Its strongly connected components are viewed as equivalence classes. Each one is substituted by a unique representative literal to reduce the constructed graph and the input formula. Finally, the implication dependencies are closed under transitivity. The resulted implications and equivalencies are exploited by Walksat at each node of the DPLL tree. Our approach is motivated by the power of the branching rule used in Satz that may provide a valid path to a solution, and generate more implications at deep nodes. Experimental results confirm the efficiency of our approach.

1 Introduction

Consider a propositional formula $\mathcal{F}$ in Conjunctive Normal Form (CNF) on a set of boolean variables $\{x_1, x_2, \ldots, x_n\}$, the satisfiability problem (SAT) consists in testing wether all clauses in $\mathcal{F}$ can be satisfied by some consistent assignment of truth values to variables.

SAT is the first known [3] and one of the most well-studied NP-complete problem. It has many applications like graph coloring, circuit designing or planning, since such problems can be encoded into CNF formulas in a natural way.

Stochastic Local Search (SLS) approaches for SAT became prominent, when independently Selman, Levesque, and Mitchell [25] as well as Gu [12] introduced algorithms based on stochastic local hill-climbing. They are considered as the most powerful incomplete methods for solving large and hard SAT instances. However, such algorithms can get stuck in the local minima of the search space, and do not integrate the structural relations between variables in their resolution. On the other hand, the complete methods, based on the Davis-Putnam-Logemann-Loveland procedure (DPLL) [5], depend on the choice of the variable to branch on. One of the best recent implementations of DPLL procedure,

---

[*] This work is partially supported by French CNRS under grant number SUB/2001/0111/DR16

P. Van Hentenryck (Ed.): CP 2002, LNCS 2470, pp. 172–184, 2002.
© Springer-Verlag Berlin Heidelberg 2002

Satz [19,20], uses a branching heuristic based on examining the amount of unit propagations that reduces the largest clause's number in the input SAT formula.

Improving stochastic local search on structured problems by efficiently handling variable dependencies is one of the ten challenges proposed by Selman, Kautz, and McAllester [24]. In this aim, combining systematic and stochastic search was suggested. Ginsberg and McAllester [10] have combined GSAT [25], a local search algorithm for SAT, and a dynamic backtracking [9]. The resulted algorithm allows substantial freedom of a movement in the search space but enough information is retained to ensure systematicity. Jussien and Lhomme [14] proposed a hybrid approach, for the Constraint Satisfaction Problem (CSP), performing an overall local search, based on the tabu mechanism, and using a systematic search, by filtering techniques, either to select a candidate neighbor or to prune the search space. Mazure, Saïs, and Grégoire [21] use a local search to implement the variable ordering heuristic for a systematic search. By the unit propagation process, Devendeville, Saïs, and Grégoire [2] extract variable implications, that are integrated to the tabu search mechanism of TSAT. Hirsch and Kojevnikov [13] developed a SAT solver, UnitWalk, by combining a local search and unit clause elimination.

In this paper, we extend the use of variable dependencies to a full construction of implications and equivalencies between literals (a literal is either a variable or its negation). This is performed by combining two main algorithms, Walksat [22] and Satz [19,20]. At each node of the DPLL search tree, we first construct an implication graph which is ensured consistent by propagating every instantiation. Secondly, we reduce the implication graph to its collapse strongly connected components, where each component is an equivalency class represented by an unique literal. Thirdly, because of the transitivity property of the implication, we generate its transitive closure. At the end, considering these implications, we apply Walksat to the reduced formula where a tabu list is added to forbid any cycling. This process terminates if either a solution is found or a maximal fixed depth of the Satz tree is reached. These treatments allow the DPLL procedure to support the local search mechanism, strengthened by the variable dependencies.

This paper is organized as follows: sections 2 and 3 respectively present the two combined algorithms Walksat and Satz. Section 4 describes the different steps of our approach. Section 6 discusses the experimental results presented in section 5, and section 7 concludes.

2   Walksat

Originally introduced in [23], Walksat performs a greedy local search for a satisfying assignment of a set of propositional clauses in SAT format. The procedure starts with a randomly generated truth assignment. It then changes (flips) the assignment of a variable chosen under the heuristic described in algorithm 2 below. Flips are repeated until either a satisfying assignment is found or a preset maximum number of flips, *Max-Flips*, is reached. This process is repeated up to a maximum number of *Max-Tries* times.

Algorithm 1: Walksat

Input: SAT-formula $\mathcal{F}$, Max-Tries,Max-Flips
Output: A satisfying truth assignment T of $\mathcal{F}$, if found
begin
> **for** *try=1* **to** *Max-Tries* **do**
> > $T \leftarrow$ randomly generated truth assignment;
> > **for** *flip=1* **to** *Max-Flips* **do**
> > > **if** T *satisfies* $\mathcal{F}$ **then** return T;
> > > $c \leftarrow$ randomly selected clause violated under T;
> > > $v \leftarrow$ Heuristic($\mathcal{F}$,c);
> > > $T \leftarrow T$ with v flipped;
>
> return "Solution not found";
end;

Algorithm 2: Heuristic

Input: SAT-formula $\mathcal{F}$, violated clause c
Output: Selected variable to flip, v
begin
> **for** *each variable u appearing in c* **do**
> > Calculate $score(u)$ equal to the violated clause number in $\mathcal{F}$ if u is flipped;
>
> **if** *there are variables with null score* **then**
> > $v \leftarrow$ randomly select one **(zero-damage-flip)**;
>
> **else**
> > **switch** *a probability value (noise setting)* **do**
> > > **case** wp : $v \leftarrow$ variable with minimal score **(minimal-damage-flip)**;
> > > **otherwise** $v \leftarrow$ randomly select a variable from c **(random walk)**;
>
> return v ;
end;

Compared to its predecessors, like GSAT, Walksat differs in one important aspect. In fact, while GSAT architecture is characterized by a static neighborhood relation between assignments with Hamming distance one, Walksat's one is based on a dynamically determined subset of the GSAT neighborhood relation. Effectively, the experimental results show that Walksat outperforms the existing SLS algorithms proposed before, and it is proved Probabilistically Approximately Complete (PAC property) with a noise setting $wp > 0$ [13].

3   Satz

Despite its simplicity and seniority, the Davis-Putnam-Logemann-Loveland procedure (DPLL) remains one of the best complete procedures for SAT. It essentially constructs a binary search tree and its nodes are results of recursive calls. While a solution is not found, all leaves represent a dead-end where a contradiction (empty clause) is found.

Algorithm 3: DPLL

Input: SAT-formula $\mathcal{F}$
Output: SAT-decision
begin
    if $\mathcal{F}$ *is empty* **then** return "Satisfiable";
    $\mathcal{F} \leftarrow$ UnitPropagation(F);
    if $\mathcal{F}$ *contains an empty clause* **then** return "Unsatisfiable";
    Select a variable x in $\mathcal{F}$ according to a heuristic H (**Branching rule**);
    if *DPLL($\mathcal{F} \cup \{x\}$) return "Satisfiable"* **then** return "Satisfiable";
    else return the result of calling DPLL($\mathcal{F} \cup \{\bar{x}\}$);
end;

Algorithm 4: UnitPropagation

Input: SAT-formula $\mathcal{F}$
Output: $\mathcal{F}$ simplified by unit propagations
begin
    while *there is no empty clause and a unit clause l exists in $\mathcal{F}$* **do**
        Assign *true* to l and simplify $\mathcal{F}$;
    return $\mathcal{F}$;
end;

DPLL procedure performance is closely related to the selection of the branching variable. In fact, this selection affects the search tree size, and consequently the required time to solve $\mathcal{F}$. A popular and a cheap branching heuristic is the MOM[1] heuristic [8], which picks the variable that occurs the most often in the minimal size clauses. However, work realized in Posit [7,8], Tableau [4], and Satx [19] have suggested to integrate unit propagations to the heuristic H. It results in an UP[2] heuristic which examines the variable x by respectively adding the unit clauses x and $\bar{x}$ into $\mathcal{F}$, and independently making two unit propagations. The real effect of those propagations is then used to weigh x. However, since examining variables by two unit propagations is time consuming, it is necessary to reduce the number of variables examined by the UP heuristic. Taking into account the number of binary occurrences of variables, Satz gets the best restrictions on the number of examined variables. In that way, combining the MOM and UP heuristics, Satz reduces the size of the search tree by detecting failed literals as early as possible.

---

[1] Maximum Occurrences of clauses of Minimum size
[2] Unit Propagation

4 Hybrid Approach

4.1 Variable Dependencies

SAT encodings of structured problems, such as planning and diagnosis, often contain large numbers of variables whose values are constrained to be a simple boolean function of other variables. These variables are then dependent. Variables whose values cannot be easily determined to be a simple function of other variables are independent. For a given SAT problem, there may be many different ways to classify the variables as dependent. In this work, we use the *dependency definition* given in [17] as follows:

Definition 1. *Let Σ be a set of clauses, V the related variables, C finite conjunctions of literals such that $V_C \subseteq V$, and a variable y such that $\Sigma \models (y \Rightarrow C)$. Then we say that the variables of V_C depend on the variable y. Roughly speaking, if y is instantiated then all variables of V_C are instantiated too.*

Example 1. Consider the set of clauses $\Sigma = \{\neg l \vee a, \ \neg l \vee \neg b, \ b \vee \neg c\}$. If l is fixed then the literals a, $\neg b$, $\neg c$ are fixed too. So we have the dependencies $l \rightarrow \{a, \neg b, \neg c\}$. Such dependencies are *implications*.

The implications are naturally constructed by unit propagations, performed by Satz when looking for the variable to branch on, and are represented by a directed graph, where nodes are literals and edges relate two dependent literals. This construction is done in linear time.

Favorably, two literals mutually implied are *equivalent*. An equivalency is a stronger dependency than a simple implication. A set of equivalent literals, constituting a class, is a strongly connected component of the implication graph, where a representative literal, chosen randomly, substitutes the other element of its class. Consequently, the input formula is reduced and the implication graph is also reduced and becomes acyclic.

4.2 Dependencies Consistency

In the preprocessing of a SAT formula or when a branching occurs, Satz fixes some variables and their states become *passive*. To maintain the implications coherent, this state must be propagated through the implication graph for the satisfied literals, and through its transposed graph for the falsified literals. Those propagations are performed by a Depth-First-Search procedure in a linear time, which is also used to construct the equivalency classes restricted to the *active* variables. On the other hand, the implication relation is transitive. Once again, by the Depth-First-Search procedure, the implication closure is constructed from the reduced implication graph. At this stage, the implications are fully enumerated and are consistent.

4.3 Proposed Algorithm: *WalkSatz*

After applying the enumerated processes to each sub-formula obtained in a current node of the Satz tree, Walksat is then applied by considering the equivalency classes rather than original variables. The class to flip is selected as described in the section 2. The implications are to be integrated advantageously in the Walksat resolution. In fact, three cases are distinguished when Walksat chooses a variable to flip: a zero-damage-flip, a minimal-damage-flip, and a random walk. It is then possible to merge the implication constraint in one, two, or all the three cases, i.e., in any case, if a class is flipped then the implied ones are flipped too. We have tested the eight possible combinations under a large variety of problems, and the best integration was observed in the case of a minimal-damage-flip. Such result can be interpreted by:

1. The zero-damage-flip is the best case, but flipping the implied classes may increase the violated clause number.
2. The random walk is incompatible with the deterministic behavior of implications, and integrating the implication relation to all levels, without any improved mechanism, the search may be trapped easily in the local minima.

We should remark that a large reduction of an instance size may cause, in the undesirable cases, a cancellation of successive actions (flips) applied to a same class. To avoid this, a tabu list [11] of a tenure fixed empirically to 1, is used as follows: each flipped class, as well as the related ones by the implication relation (if flipped), are forbidden to any change during one iteration. The full steps of the hybrid approach are resumed in the developed algorithm, **WalkSatz**, which is incomplete because of the restriction on the depth of the Satz tree.

Algorithm 5: WalkSatz

Input: SAT-formula $\mathcal{F}$
Output: A satisfying truth assignment T of $\mathcal{F}$, if found
begin

    for *each node reached by Satz, down to a fixed depth* **do**
        if *$\mathcal{F}$ is empty* **then** return "Solution T found, by Satz";
        Construct for $\mathcal{F}$, the implication graph I and its transposed I^t;
        Propagate variables state under I and I^t;
        Construct the equivalency classes and reduce $\mathcal{F}$, I, and I^t;
        Construct the implication closure for the reduced graphs I and I^t;
        Apply Walksat to $\mathcal{F}$ reduced to its equivalency classes, taking into account the reduced graphs I and I^t when minimizing the total number of violated clauses (minimal-damage-flip);
        if *the last step returns "Solution T found"* **then**
            return "Solution T, by Walksat";
    return "Solution not found";
end;

---

5   Experimental Results

The hybrid approach is the result of combining a systematic method and a local search one. Consequently, it is not so evident to give comparative criteria between such families. However, in order to evaluate the performances of WalkSatz, we compare it with Walksat and Satz on a broad range of benchmarks[3]. WalkSatz is coded in Linux/C++ and compiled with g++ compiler. Comparative parameters used in our experiments[4] are:

	WalkSatz	Walksat
Max-Tries	1	100
Max-Flips	10^5	15×10^5
Number of runs	100	1
Noise setting	0.5	0.5

Despite the importance of the noise parameter, no optimization is made on. However, its value is fixed to an identical value, 0.5, to both algorithms. The depth of the Satz tree is limited to 3, the root being at level 0, at most fifteen nodes are then developed, and the total number of the authorized flips is identical for WalkSatz and Walksat. The columns T%, # flips, and sec. correspond respectively to the success rate, average flips, and average run time in second. # flips and sec. are calculated for the successful executions, and the running time for Satz is limited to 7200 seconds. All the used instances are satisfiable.

5.1   Latin Square

Given a set S, a Latin square indexed by S is an $|S| \times |S|$ array such that each row and each column of the array are a permutation of the elements in S. $|S|$ is called the order of the Latin square. These instances have been contributed by H. Zhang [27].

Table 1. Experimental results for the "qg" instances

Latin square			WalkSatz			Walksat			Satz
Instance	# Vars.	# Cls.	T%	# flips.	sec.	T%	# flips.	sec.	sec.
qg1-08	512	148957	6	1307271	1499.446	0	-	-	125.220
qg2-07	343	68083	100	39719	0.901	25	693660	694.622	24.340
qg3-08	512	148957	100	238622	1.505	9	628604	148.794	0.210
qg4-09	512	10469	83	701706	9.169	1	328792	3226.650	0.750
qg5-11	1331	64054	8	277167	370.769	0	-	-	4.830
qg6-09	729	21844	100	368	0.664	0	-	-	0.830
qg7-09	729	22060	100	81	0.824	0	-	-	0.970

---

[3] http://www.satlib.org
[4] All experiments are on a Duron 800 Mhz machine with 256 MB of RAM.

Table 2. Experimental results for the "aim" instances

AIM			WalkSatz			Walksat			Satz
Instance	# Vars.	# Cls.	T%	# flips.	sec.	T%	# flips.	sec.	sec.
aim-50-1-6-yes1-1	50	300	100	1	0.001	6	920684	44.422	0.020
aim-50-1-6-yes1-2	50	300	100	1	< 0.001	1	64016	148.600	0.030
aim-50-1-6-yes1-3	50	300	100	1	< 0.001	34	685077	6.378	0.010
aim-50-1-6-yes1-4	50	300	100	1	< 0.001	0	-	-	0.010
aim-50-2-0-yes1-1	50	100	100	1	< 0.001	2	702	83.125	0.010
aim-50-2-0-yes1-2	50	100	100	1	< 0.001	97	22170	0.094	0.020
aim-50-2-0-yes1-3	50	100	100	1	< 0.001	100	151431	0.287	0.020
aim-50-2-0-yes1-4	50	100	100	1	< 0.001	100	137124	0.237	0.020
aim-100-1-6-yes1-1	100	160	100	1	< 0.001	0	-	-	0.020
aim-100-1-6-yes1-2	100	160	100	1	< 0.001	0	-	-	0.030
aim-100-1-6-yes1-3	100	160	100	1	< 0.001	0	-	-	0.030
aim-100-1-6-yes1-4	100	160	100	1	< 0.001	0	-	-	0.030
aim-100-2-0-yes1-1	100	200	100	1	< 0.001	0	-	-	0.020
aim-100-2-0-yes1-2	100	200	100	1	0.001	0	-	-	0.030
aim-100-2-0-yes1-3	100	200	100	1	< 0.001	0	-	-	0.030
aim-100-2-0-yes1-4	100	200	100	1	< 0.001	0	-	-	0.020
aim-200-1-6-yes1-1	200	360	100	1	0.003	0	-	-	0.050
aim-200-1-6-yes1-2	200	360	100	1	0.003	0	-	-	0.090
aim-200-1-6-yes1-3	200	360	100	1	< 0.001	0	-	-	0.050
aim-200-1-6-yes1-4	200	360	100	1	0.001	0	-	-	0.050
aim-200-2-0-yes1-1	200	400	100	1	0.001	0	-	-	0.050
aim-200-2-0-yes1-2	200	400	100	1	0.001	0	-	-	0.040
aim-200-2-0-yes1-3	200	400	100	1	0.001	0	-	-	0.100
aim-200-2-0-yes1-4	200	400	100	1	0.001	0	-	-	0.070

5.2   DIMACS Benchmarks

"aim" instances: proposed by Iwama and *al.* [1], the instances are all generated with a particular random 3-SAT instance generator.

"ssa" instances: contributed by A.V. Gelder and *al.*, the instances correspond to single-stuck-at-faults problem in circuit analysis. The used instances are selected formulas from those generated by *N*emesis [6,18], which is a test-pattern generation program.

Table 3. Experimental results for the "ssa" instances

SSA			WalkSatz			Walksat			Satz
Instance	# Vars.	# Cls.	T%	# flips.	sec.	T%	# flips.	sec.	sec.
ssa7552-160	1391	3126	100	385	2.270	100	30875	0.061	0.080
ssa7552-159	1363	3032	100	344	2.265	100	22006	0.433	0.080
ssa7552-158	1363	3034	100	255	2.218	100	26738	0.052	0.070
ssa7552-038	1501	3575	100	991	2.581	100	80673	0.167	0.120

Table 4. Experimental results for the "par8" instances

PAR			WalkSatz			Walksat			Satz
Instance	# Vars.	# Cls.	T%	# flips.	sec.	T%	# flips.	sec.	sec.
par8-1-c	64	254	100	12062	0.024	100	10628	0.025	0.02
par8-1	350	1149	100	68175	0.180	4	977367	79.366	0.01
par8-2-c	68	270	100	1	0.003	100	15504	0.036	0.02
par8-2	350	1157	100	120942	0.356	2	483886	160.791	0.02
par8-3-c	75	298	100	35293	0.069	100	37213	0.089	0.02
par8-3	350	1171	100	96110	0.272	3	538312	107.811	0.02
par8-4-c	67	266	100	1	0.000	100	41423	0.098	0.02
par8-4	350	1155	100	22966	0.681	0	-	-	0.02
par8-5-c	75	298	100	12843	0.027	100	34534	0.084	0.02
par8-5	350	1171	100	77604	0.284	1	304169	330.066	0.03

"par8" instances: contributed by J. Crawford and suggested by M. Kearns, these instances are propositional versions of the parity learning problem.

5.3 Superscalar Processor Verification

Defined by M.N. Velev [26], these instances result from the verification of exceptions, multicycle functional units, and branching prediction in superscalar microprocessors, DLX.

5.4 Beijing-Challenge Benchmarks

This set comprises the instances which have been proposed for the International Competition on SAT Testing in Beijing, 1996, including planning and scheduling problems [15,16].

Table 5. Experimental results for the "dlx_cc" instances

DLX2_CC			WalkSatz			Walksat			Satz
Instance	# Vars.	# Cls.	T%	# flips.	sec.	T%	# flips.	sec.	sec.
dlx2_cc_bug01	1515	12808	100	989391	49.607	79	603523	24.857	> 7200
dlx2_cc_bug02	1515	12808	100	858251	43.818	80	517174	21.958	> 7200
dlx2_cc_bug03	1515	12808	100	1013661	51.013	71	723533	33.193	> 7200
dlx2_cc_bug14	1516	12811	100	458607	26.524	98	381390	10.122	> 7200
dlx2_cc_bug16	1516	12811	100	461816	25.555	92	417319	13.432	> 7200
dlx2_cc_bug33	1516	12798	100	636107	23.721	99	265186	6.820	> 7200
dlx2_cc_bug34	1516	12718	100	965240	43.048	98	369863	9.282	> 7200
dlx2_cc_bug38	1515	12783	100	652728	35.267	63	516764	1.404	> 7200
dlx2_cc_bug39	1482	12111	93	1141143	49.067	66	640518	33.861	> 7200
dlx2_cc_bug40	1520	12811	100	629230	33.210	98	358702	9.688	> 7200

Table 6. Experimental results for the Beijing instances

Beijing			WalkSatz			Walksat			Satz
Instance	#Vars.	# Cls.	T%	# flips.	sec.	T%	# flips.	sec.	sec.
3blocks	370	13732	100	26768	0.222	100	49960	0.626	0.060
4blocks	900	59285	34	519608	102.429	0	-	-	0.060
4blocksb	540	34199	100	264532	3.655	19	694517	210.913	0.650
e0ddr2-10-by-5-1	19500	108887	100	246496	1067.484	0	-	-	137.820
e0ddr2-10-by-5-4	19500	104527	98	463371	3116.833	18	1202849	132.465	185.900
enddr2-10-by-5-1	20700	111567	97	292415	2352.466	0	-	-	112.960
enddr2-10-by-5-8	21000	113729	100	261973	1463.593	2	1329010	1448.225	105.230
ewddr2-10-by-5-1	21800	118607	97	252841	1119.552	0	-	-	401.460
ewddr2-10-by-5-8	22500	123329	100	205542	846.741	1	1456023	3136.267	120.640

Table 7. Experimental results for the Kautz & Selman planning problem

Planning			WalkSatz			Walksat			Satz
Instance	# Vars.	# Cls.	T%	# flips.	sec.	T%	# flips.	sec.	sec.
logistics.a	828	6718	100	21508	0.088	100	133275	0.469	2.750
logistics.b	843	7301	100	36783	0.142	100	249287	0.887	0.090
logistics.c	1141	10719	100	77653	0.334	87	490317	2.896	0.420
logistics.d	4713	21991	100	286041	155.530	74	624500	6.990	507.490
bw_large.a	459	4675	100	5146	0.199	100	14359	0.057	0.070
bw_large.b	1087	13772	100	96838	1.899	86	564590	6.249	0.240
bw_large.c	3016	50157	100	198672	22.738	0	-	-	2.740

5.5   Kautz & Selman Planning Problems

Proposed by H. Kautz and B. Selman [15,16], these instances correspond to the planning logistic problem.

6   Experimental Result Discussion

Globally and when Compared to Walksat, WalkSatz largely reduces the required flips number to get a solution, and has a good behavior when solving hard instances. These statements may be justified as follows:

1. The equivalency classes reduce the problem size and eliminate the cyclic implications. On the other side, the implication transitive closure permit to enumerate all the dependent literals, and so, exploit fully their advantage.
2. The implication relation can be viewed as a tabu which restricts the visited neighborhood by the local search. Furthermore, checking the implication consistency allows to verify implicit constraints, then reduce the number of flips required to reach a solution.
3. The branching rule used by Satz gives two sub-formulas completely disjoint. So, the space search explored by Walksat is diversified.

Excepting "qg1-08", "qg5-11", and "4blocks" instances, the high rate success of
WalkSatz shows the robustness of this hybrid algorithm. Furthermore, whenever
Satz works well, WalkSatz takes advantage in robustness, and when Satz works
less well, for example for the "dlx2_cc" instances, there is a small improvement
in robustness at the expense of computation time. On random SAT problems
containing few variable dependencies, Walksatz and Walksat essentially have the
same behavior. The experimental results are not presented here.

As said in the section 5, it is less evident to make an adjusted comparison,
and the used parameters are retained to compare the behavior of WalkSatz and
WalkSat with a same number of authorized flips. However, other parameters
are to underline: in the above experiments, if WalkSatz fails in a given node
of the Satz tree, no restart is done on (only one try is authorized), but other
experiments show that WalkSatz works better with more tries: a restart is an
useful aspect in a local search. The depth of the Satz tree is also prominent,
and its optimized value can be found for each problem class. However, a tarde-
off should be respected: it is look not so interesting to develop many nodes, in
the Satz tree, to let the local search reaching a solution. At the end, the tabu
tenure and list, used by WalkSatz, are to be well handled: because of the instance
reduction, these tabu parameters can be a function of the number/size of the
equivalency classes.

The main weakness of WalkSatz is the computation time requirements. It is
mainly caused by the repeated Depth-First-Search procedures at every node of
the Satz search tree. In fact, the version elaborated in this paper is not optimized.
This lack is easily improved by an incremental construction of the implications
and equivalencies at each branching and backtracking done by Satz. Despite this
drawback, the experimental results prove the efficiency of our approach.

7   Conclusion

In this paper, we presented a hybrid approach between two efficient algorithms
Walksat and Satz. Our work is motivated by the performances of such algorithms. In fact, by its powerful branching rule, Satz provides an optimal search
tree, and by its variable selection heuristic, Walksat outperforms the precedent
SLS algorithms. On the other hand, SAT formulas contain implicit variable dependencies that are so useful in a SAT resolution, especially in a local search
process. To well exploit those elements, WalkSatz was elaborated. It is the result
of numerous experiments in the aim to get a good hybridization that increases
the contribution of implication and equivalency relationships in the resolution
mechanism. The obtained results support our approach.

As perspective works, more powerful variants of Walksat, such as Novelty and
R-Novelty [22], are also indicated for such approach. The variable dependencies,
as well as tabu, noise setting, and other WalkSatz parameters, are to be further
studied to increase their effects. Finally, to improve the computation time, these
dependencies must be constructed *incrementally*.

References

1. Y. Asahiro, K. Iwama, and E. Miyano. Random Generation of Test Instances with Controlled Attributes. In *D. S.Johnson and M. A.Trick, editors, Cliques, Coloring, and Satisfiability; The Second DIMACS Implementation Challenge*, volume 26, pages 377–394, 1996.
2. L. Brisoux Devendeville, L. Saïs, and E. Grégoire. Recherche locale: vers une exploitation des propriétés structurelles. In *proceedings of JNPC'2000*, pages 243–244, Marseille, France, 2000.
3. S. Cook. The Complexity of Theorem Proving Procedures. In *Proceeding oh the Third Annual ACM Symp. on Theory of Computing*, pages 151–158, 1971.
4. J. M. Crawford and L. D. Auton. Experimental Results on the Crosover Point in Random 3-SAT. *Artificial Intelligence Journal*, 81(1-2):31–57, 1996.
5. M. Davis, G. Logemann, and D. Loveland. A Machine Program for Theorem Proving. In *Communication of ACM Journal*, volume 5(7), pages 394–397, July 1962.
6. F. J. Ferguson and T. Larrabee. Test Pattern Generation for Realistic Bridging Faults in CMOS ICS. In *Proceedings of the International Testing Conference*, pages 492–499, 1991.
7. J. W. Freeman. *Improvements to Propostional Satisfiability Search Algorithms*. PhD thesis, Departement of Computer and Information Science, University of Pennsylvania, Philadelphia, PA, 1995.
8. J. W. Freeman. Hard Random 3-SAT Problems and the Davis-Putnam Procedure. In *Artificial Intelligence Journal*, pages 81:183–198, 1996.
9. M. L. Ginsberg. Dynamic backtracking. *Journal of Artificial Intelligence Research*, 1:25–46, 1993.
10. M. L. Ginsberg and D. A. McAllester. GSAT and Dynamic Backtracking. In P. Torasso, J. Doyle, and E. Sandewall, editors, *Proceedings of the 4th International Conference on Principles of Knowledge Representation and Reasoning KR'94*, pages 226–237. Morgan Kaufmann, 1994.
11. F. Glover and M. Laguna. *Tabu Search*. Kluwer Academic Publishers, 1997.
12. J. Gu. Efficient Local Search for Very Large-Scale Satisfiability problems. In *ACM SIGART Bulletin*, pages 3(1):8–12, 1992.
13. H. H. Hoos and T. Stutzle. Local search algorithms for SAT: An empirical evaluation. *Journal of Automated Reasoning*, 24(4):421–481, 2000.
14. N. Jussien and O. Lhomme. Local search with constraint propagation and conflict-based heuristics. In *Proceedings of the Seventh National Conference on Artificial Intelligence (AAAI'2000)*, pages 169–174, Austin, TX, USA, August 2000.
15. H. Kautz, D. McAllester, and B. Selman. Encoding Plans in Propositional Logic. In *Proceedings of the 4th International Conference on the Principle of Knowledge Representation and Reasoning, KR'96*, pages 374–384, 1996.
16. H. Kautz and B. Selman. Pushing the Envelope: Planning, Propositional Logic, and Stochastic Search. In Howard Shrobe and Ted Senator, editors, *Proceedings of the 13th National Conference on Artificial Intelligence and the 8th Innovative Applications of Artificial Intelligence Conference*, pages 1194–1201, Menlo Park, California, 1996.
17. J. Lang and P. Marquis. Complexity Results for Independence and Definability in Propositional Logic. In A. G. Cohn, L. K. Schubert, and S. C. Shapiro, editors, *Proceedings of the Sixth International Conference on Principles of Knowledge Representataion and Reasoning, KR'98*, pages 356–367, 1998.

18. T. Larrabee. Test Pattern Generation Using Boolean Satisfiability. In *IEEE Transactions on Computer-Aided Design*, pages 11(1):6–22, 1992.

19. C. M. Li. Exploiting Yet More the Power of Unit Clause Propagation to solve 3-SAT Problem. In *ECAI'96 Workshop on Advances in Propositional Deduction*, pages 11–16, Budapest, Hungray, 1996.

20. C. M. Li and Anbulagan. Heuristic Based on Unit Propagation for Satisfiability. In *Proceedings of CP'97, Springer-Verlag, LNCS 1330*, pages 342–356, Austria, 1997.

21. B. Mazure, L. Saïs, and E. Grégoire. Boosting Complete Techniques Thanks to Local Search. *Annals of Mathematics and Artificial Intelligence*, 22(3-4):319–331, 1998.

22. D. McAllester, B. Selman, and H. Kautz. Evidence for Invariants in Local Search. In *Proceedings of the 14th National Conference on Artificial Intelligence, AAAI'97*, pages 321–326, Providence, Rhode Island, 1997. MIT Press.

23. B. Selman, H. Kautz, and B. Cohen. Noise Strategies for Improving Local Search. In MIT press, editor, *Proceedings of the 12th National Conference on Artificial Intelligence AAAI'94*, volume 1, pages 337–343, 1994.

24. B. Selman, H. Kautz, and D. McAllester. Ten Challenges in Propositional Reasoning and Search. In *Proceedings of IJCAI'97*, pages 50–54, Nagoya, Aichi, Japan, August 1997.

25. B. Selman, H. J. Levesque, and D. Mitchell. A New Method for Solving Hard Satisfiability Problems. In Paul Rosenbloom and Peter Szolovits, editors, *Proceedings of the 10th National Conference on Artificial Intelligence, AAAI'92*, pages 440–446, Menlo Park, California, 1992.

26. M. N. Velev and R. E. Bryant. Superscalar processor verification using efficient reductions of the logic of equality with uninterpreted functions to propositional logic. In *Correct Hardware Design and Verification Methods, CHARME'99*, 1999.

27. H. Zhang and M. E. Stickel. Implementing the davis-putnam method. *Journal of Automated Reasoning*, 24(1):277–296, 2000.

Recovering and Exploiting Structural Knowledge from CNF Formulas

Richard Ostrowski, Éric Grégoire, Bertrand Mazure, and Lakhdar Saïs

CRIL CNRS – Université d'Artois
rue Jean Souvraz SP-18, F-62307 Lens Cedex France
{ostrowski,gregoire,mazure,sais}@cril.univ-artois.fr

Abstract. In this paper, a new pre-processing step is proposed in the resolution of SAT instances, that recovers and exploits structural knowledge that is hidden in the CNF. It delivers an hybrid formula made of clauses together with a set of equations of the form $y = f(x_1, \ldots, x_n)$ where f is a standard connective operator among $(\vee, \wedge, \Leftrightarrow)$ and where y and x_i are boolean variables of the initial SAT instance. This set of equations is then exploited to eliminate clauses and variables, while preserving satisfiability. These extraction and simplification techniques allowed us to implement a new SAT solver that proves to be the most efficient current one w.r.t. several important classes of instances.

Keywords: SAT, Boolean logic, propositional reasoning and search

1 Introduction

Recent impressive progress in the practical resolution of hard and large SAT instances allows real-world problems that are encoded in propositional clausal normal form (CNF) to be addressed (see e.g. [20,10,27]). While there remains a strong competition about building more efficient provers dedicated to hard random k-SAT instances [8], there is also a real surge of interest in implementing powerful systems that solve difficult large real-world SAT problems. Many benchmarks have been proposed and regular competitions (e.g. [6,1,22,23]) are organized around these specific SAT instances, which are expected to encode structural knowledge, at least to some extent.

Clearly, encoding knowledge under the form of a conjunction of propositional clauses can flatten some structural knowledge that would be more apparent in a full propositional logic representation, and that could prove useful in the resolution step [21,12].

In this paper, a new pre-processing step is proposed in the resolution of SAT instances, that extracts and exploits some structural knowledge that is hidden in the CNF. It delivers an hybrid formula made of clauses together with a set of equations of the form $y = f(x_1, \ldots, x_n)$ where f is a standard connective operator among $\{\vee, \wedge, \Leftrightarrow\}$ and where y and x_i are Boolean variables of the initial SAT instance. Such an hybrid formula exhibits a twofold interest. On the one hand, the structural knowledge in the equations could be exploited by the SAT

P. Van Hentenryck (Ed.): CP 2002, LNCS 2470, pp. 185–199, 2002.
© Springer-Verlag Berlin Heidelberg 2002

solver. On the other hand, these equations can allow us to determine equivalent variables and implied ones, in such a way that clauses and variables can be eliminated, while preserving satisfiability. These extraction and simplification techniques allowed us to implement a new SAT solver that proves to be the most efficient current one w.r.t. several important classes of instances.

The paper is organized as follows. After some preliminary definitions, it is shown how such a kind of equations can be extracted from the CNF, using a graph of clauses. Then, the task of simplifying the set of clauses using these equations is addressed. Experimental results showing the efficiency of the proposed approach are provided. Finally, promising paths of research are discussed in the conclusion.

2   Technical Preliminaries

Let $\mathcal{L}$ be a Boolean (i.e. propositional) language of formulas built in the standard way, using usual connectives ($\vee$, $\wedge$, $\neg$, $\Rightarrow$, $\Leftrightarrow$) and a set of propositional variables. A *CNF formula* is a set (interpreted as a conjunction) of *clauses*, where a clause is a disjunction of *literals*. A literal is a positive or negated propositional variable. An *interpretation* of a Boolean formula is an assignment of truth values $\{true, false\}$ to its variables. A *model* of a formula is an interpretation that satisfies the formula. Accordingly, SAT consists in finding a model of a CNF formula when such a model does exist or in proving that such a model does not exist. Let c_1 be a clause containing a literal a and c_2 a clause containing the opposite literal $\neg a$, one *resolvent* of c_1 and c_2 is the disjunction of all literals of c_1 and c_2 less a and $\neg a$. A resolvent is called *tautological* when it contains opposite literals. Let us recall here that any Boolean formula can be translated thanks to a linear time algorithm in CNF, equivalent with respect to SAT (but that can use additional propositional variables). Most satisfiability checking algorithms operate on clauses, where the structural knowledge of the initial formulas is thus flattened.

Other useful definitions are the following ones. An *equation* or *gate* is of the form $y = f(x_1, \ldots, x_n)$ where f is a standard connective among $\{\vee, \wedge, \Leftrightarrow\}$ and where y and x_i are propositional variables. An equation is satisfied iff the left and right hand sides of the equation are simultanously *true* or *false*. An interpretation of a set of equations is a model of this set iff it satisfies each equation of this set.

The first technical goal of this paper is to extract gates from a CNF formula. A propositional variable y (resp. $x_1, \ldots, x_n$) is an *output variable* (resp. are *input variables*) of a gate of the form $y = f(x_1, \ldots, x_n)$. An output variable is also called *definable*.

A propositional variable z is an *output variable of a set of gates* iff z is an output variable of at least one gate in the set. An *input variable of a set of gates* is an input variable of a gate which is not an output variable of the set of gates.

Clearly, the truth-value of an y output variable depends on the truth value of the x_i input variables of its gate. Moreover, the set of definable variables of a CNF formula is a subset of the so-called *dependent* variables as defined in [15]. Knowing output variables can play an important role in solving the consistency status of a CNF formula. Indeed, the truth value of such variables can be obtained by propagation, and *e.g.* they can be omitted by selection heuristics of DPLL-like algorithms [4]. In the general case, knowing n' output variables of a CNF formula using n variables allows the size of the set of interpretations to be investigated to decrease from 2^n to $2^{n-n'}$.

Unfortunately, extracting gates from a CNF formula can be a time-consuming operation in the general case, unless some depth-limited search resources or heuristic criteria are provided. Indeed, showing that $y = f(x_1, \ldots, x_i)$ (where $y, x_1, \ldots, x_i$ belong to Σ), follows from a given CNF Σ, is coNP-complete [15].

3   Gates Extraction

To the best of our knowledge, only equivalent gates were subject of previous investigation. Motivated by Selman et-al. challenge [24] about solving the parity-32 problems, Warners and van Maaren [26] have proposed an approach that succeeds in solving such class of hard CNF formulas. More precisely, a two steps algorithm is proposed: in the first one, a polynomially solvable subproblem (a set of equivalent gates) is identified thanks to a linear programming approach. Using the solution to this subproblem, the search-space is dramatically restricted for the second step of the algorithm, which is an extension of the well-known DPLL procedure [4]. More recently, Chu Min Li [18] proposed a specialised DPLL procedure called EqSatz which dynamically search for lists of equivalent literals, lists whose length is lower or equal to 3. Such an approach is costly as it performs many useless syntactical tests and suffers from restrictions (*e.g.* on the length of the detected lists).

In this paper, in order to detect hidden gates in the CNF formula, it is proposed to make use of an original concept of partial graph of clauses to limit the number of syntactical tests to be performed. Moreover, this technique allows gates $y = f(x_1, \ldots, x_n)$ (where $f \in \{\Leftrightarrow, \vee, \wedge\}$ and where no restriction on n is *a priori* given) to be detected.

Definition 1 (Graph of clauses)
*Let Σ be a CNF formula. A **graph of clauses** $\mathcal{G} = (\mathcal{V}, \mathcal{E})$ is associated to Σ s.t.*
- *each vertex of $\mathcal{V}$ corresponds to a clause of Σ;*
- *each edge (c_1, c_2) of $\mathcal{E}$ corresponds to a pair of clauses c_1 and c_2 of Σ exhibiting a resolvent clause;*
- *each edge is labeled either by $\mathbb{T}$ (when the resolvent is tautological) or $\mathbb{R}$ (when the resolvent is not tautological).*

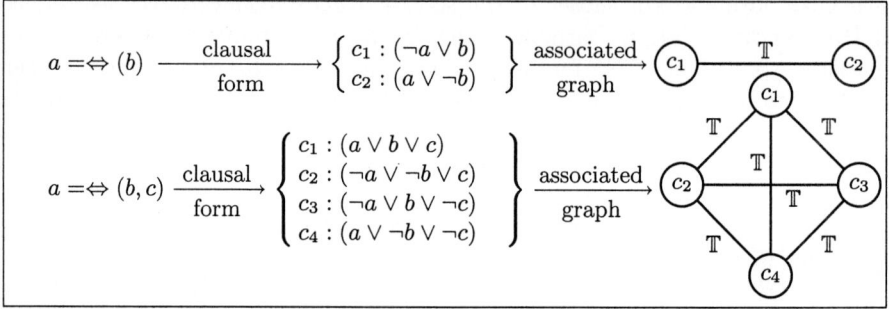

Fig. 1. Clausal and graphical representations of $\Leftrightarrow$ gates

Example 1 (Graph of clauses)

$$\Sigma = \left\{ \begin{array}{l} c_1 : (a \vee b \vee \neg c) \\ c_2 : (\neg a \vee b \vee d) \\ c_3 : (\neg a \vee b \vee \neg c) \\ c_4 : (a \vee c \vee \neg e) \end{array} \right\} \xrightarrow{\text{graph of clauses}} \mathcal{G} =$$

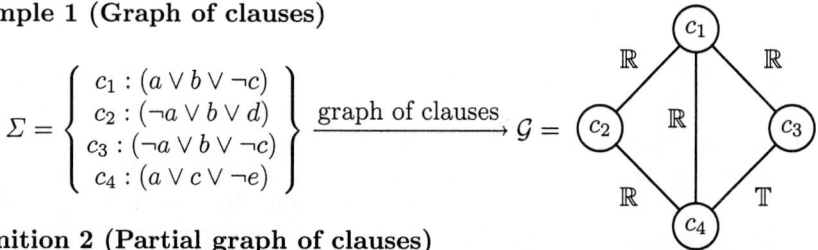

Definition 2 (Partial graph of clauses)
A **partial graph of clauses** $\mathcal{G}'$ of a CNF formula Σ is the graph of clauses $\mathcal{G}$ of Σ that is restricted to edges labelled by $\mathbb{T}$.

Example 2 (Partial graph of clauses)

$$\Sigma = \left\{ \begin{array}{l} c_1 : (a \vee d \vee e) \\ c_2 : (\neg a \vee \neg b \vee \neg c) \\ c_3 : (a \vee b \vee \neg c) \\ c_4 : (\neg a \vee b \vee c) \end{array} \right\} \xrightarrow[\text{of clauses}]{\text{partial graph}} \mathcal{G}' =$$

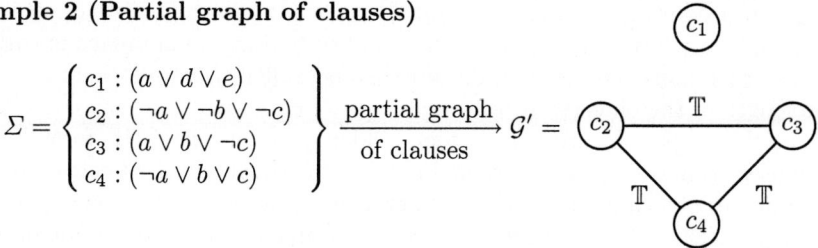

In Figure 1, both graphical and clausal representations of an equivalence gate $y = \Leftrightarrow (x_1, \ldots, x_n)$ ($n = 1$ and $n = 2$) are given. In the general case an equivalence gate will be represented by a partial graph that is a clique since any pair of clauses gives rise to a tautological resolvent.

In Figure 2, both graphical and clausal representations of gates $a = \wedge(b, c, d)$ and $a = \vee(b, c, d)$ are provided.

Let us note that graphical representations of gates $\vee$ and $\wedge$ are identical since their clausal representations only differ by the variables signs. We also note that one clause plays a pivotal role and exhibits tautological resolvents with all clauses in the clausal representation of a $\vee$ or $\wedge$ gate. This property also applies for gates whose number of involved literals is greater than 3:

$$a = \wedge(b, c, d) \xrightarrow[\text{form}]{\text{clausal}} \begin{cases} c_1 : (a \vee \neg b \vee \neg c \vee \neg d) \\ c_2 : (\neg a \vee b) \\ c_3 : (\neg a \vee c) \\ c_4 : (\neg a \vee d) \end{cases}$$

$$a = \vee(b, c, d) \xrightarrow[\text{form}]{\text{clausal}} \begin{cases} c_1 : (\neg a \vee b \vee c \vee d) \\ c_2 : (a \vee \neg b) \\ c_3 : (a \vee \neg c) \\ c_4 : (a \vee \neg d) \end{cases}$$

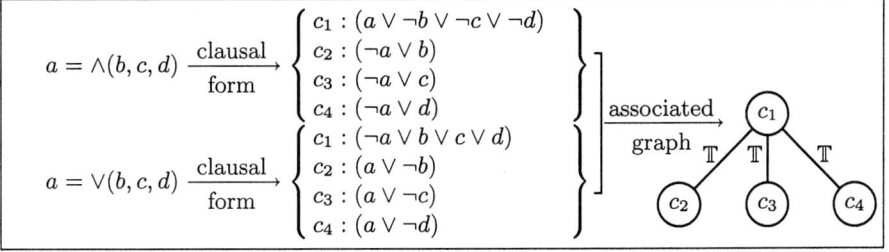

Fig. 2. Clausal and graphical representations of $\wedge$ and $\vee$ gates

$$y = \vee(x_1, \ldots, x_n) \xrightarrow[\text{form}]{\text{clausal}} \begin{cases} (\neg y \vee x_1 \cdots \vee x_n) \\ (y \vee \neg x_1) \\ \cdots \\ (y \vee \neg x_n) \end{cases}$$

It is also easy to check that any resolvent from any pair of clauses from a same gate is tautological. Accordingly, the clauses from a same gate ($\Leftrightarrow$, $\vee$ and $\wedge$) are connected in the partial graph of clauses. Thus, a necessary (but not sufficient) condition for clauses to belong to a same gate is to form a connected subgraph. An example showing that such a condition is not sufficient is given in Example 2.

Building the graph of clauses is quadratic in the size of the set of clauses Σ but the representation of the graph can be too much space-consuming. Accordingly, finding gates will be performed in a dynamic manner (without representing the graph explicitly) by checking for each clause c which clauses of Σ exhibit tautological resolvents with c. This step can be achieved using two stacks:

- a stack of clauses sharing literals with c;
- a stack of clauses containing opposite literals to the literals of c.

At this step, the initial CNF formula is reduced to an hybrid formula, *i.e.* a set of equations together with initial clauses not taking part in these equations. For the uniformity of the representation each such remaining clause $c : (x_1 \vee \cdots \vee x_n)$ can be interpreted as a or gate of the form $true = \vee(x_1, \ldots, x_n)$ with its output variable assigned the value $true$ (but we shall sometimes still call them clauses, indifferently).

4   Exploiting Structural Knowledge

In this section, it is shown how such an obtained representation can even be simplified, and how its intrinsic properties can lead to more efficient satisfiability checking algorithms (by eliminating variables and clauses).

First of all, the n' output variables of the set of gates are clearly fixed by the remaining input variables. Accordingly, DPLL-like satisfiability algorithms [4] can restrict their search to input variables only.

Moreover, in the following it is shown how some properties of gates can allow even more variables and equations to be eliminated.

4.1 Equivalence Gates

First, let us recall that when only equivalence gates are involved, then they can be solved in polynomial time [9]. These classes of formulas are known as chains of biconditionals. In the following, some basic properties of equivalence gates are presented. For more details, see, Dunham and Wang's paper [9]. For commodity, we use chains of biconditionals instead of equivalences gates.

Property 1 (about $\Leftrightarrow$ gates [9])
1. $\Leftrightarrow$ *is commutative and associative.*
2. $(a \Leftrightarrow a \Leftrightarrow B)$ *(resp.* $(\neg a \Leftrightarrow a \Leftrightarrow B))$ *with B a chain of biconditionnals is equivalent to B (resp $\neg B$).*
3. $\neg(a \Leftrightarrow b \Leftrightarrow c)$ *is equivalent to* $(\neg a \Leftrightarrow b \Leftrightarrow c)$
4. $(\neg a \Leftrightarrow \neg b \Leftrightarrow \neg c)$ *is equivalent to* $(\neg a \Leftrightarrow b \Leftrightarrow c)$.
5. $(l \Leftrightarrow A_1), (l \Leftrightarrow A_2), \ldots, (l \Leftrightarrow A_m)$ *is SAT iff* $(A_1 \Leftrightarrow A_2), \ldots, (A_{m-1} \Leftrightarrow A_m)$ *is SAT.*

It is easy to see that the first four equivalence gates properties apply on hybrid formulas.

As a consequence of the first property, any variable in an equivalence gate can play the role of the output variable of this gate. Currently, we have selected a very simple way for choosing output variables of equivalence gates. An output variable of an equivalence gate is selected among the set of output variables already defined for other gates. When the intersection of this set and the set of variables of the equivalence gate is empty, the output variable is selected in a random way in the set of variables involved in the equivalence gate. Properties 1.2. and 1.5. can lead to the elimination of variables and thus to a reduction of the search space. Property 1.4. shows that negation can be eliminated in pairs in chains of biconditionals (i.e. at most one literal of a chain of biconditionals is a negative one).

Let us now give new simplification properties of equivalent gates in the context of hybrid formulas (set of gates).

Property 2
Let Σ be a set of gates (i.e. an hybrid formula), $B \subset \Sigma$ a set of equivalence gates, $b \in B$ s.t. its output variable y occurs only in B and Σ' the set of gates obtained by the substitution of y with its definition and removing b from Σ, then Σ is satisfiable iff Σ' is satisfiable

Remark 1
The previous property is a simple extension of property 1.5 to set of gates.

Property 3
Let Σ be a set of gates, any equivalence gate of Σ containing a literal which does not occur elsewere in Σ, can be removed from Σ without loss of satisfiability.

Consequently, each literal in an equivalence gate must occur at least twice in the formula.

4.2 "And" & "or" Gates

In the case of $\vee$ and $\wedge$ gates, the following property can be used to achieve useful simplifications.

Property 4 ($\vee$ and $\wedge$ gates)
 - $a = f(b, c, b)$ *with* $f \in \{\vee, \wedge\}$ *is equivalent to* $a = f(b, c)$
 - $a = \vee(b, c, \neg b)$ *(resp.* $a = \wedge(b, c, \neg b)$*) is equivalent to* a *(resp.* $\neg a$*)*
 - $\neg a = \vee(b, c, d)$ *(resp.* $\neg a = \wedge(b, c, d)$*) is equivalent to* $a = \wedge(\neg b, \neg c, \neg d)$ *(resp.* $a = \vee(\neg b, \neg c, \neg d)$*)*
 - *Property 2 and 3 hold for $\vee$ and $\wedge$ gates.*

4.3 Simplification of the Remaining Set of Clauses

Let Γ be the remaining set of clauses (that can be interpreted as $true = \vee(x_1, \ldots, x_n)$ equations). Many practical approaches to SAT focus on the reduction of the number of variables of the instance to be solved, in order to reduce the size of the search space. In this paper, we also try to reduce the number of involved clauses. As we shall show it, this can lead to the elimination of variables, too. Interestingly, reducing the number of clauses and variables involved in Γ, leads to a reduction of the number of input variables.

In the following, two types of simplification are proposed. The first one is derived from an extension of the definition of blocked clauses, as proposed in [13,14,9]. The second one takes its roots in the pre-processing step of many efficient implementations of the DPLL algorithm [4]: the introduction of constant-length resolvents in a C-SAT-like spirit [7]. Let us note that, we can use other useful simplification techniques (see for example recent works by Brafman [3] and Marques-Silva [19]) to achieve further reduction on the CNF part of the formula.

Generalization of the Blocked Clause Concept

Definition 3 (Blocked clause [13])
*A clause c of a CNF formula Σ is **blocked** iff there is a literal $l \in c$ s.t. for all $c' \in \Sigma$ with $\neg l \in c'$ the resolvent of c and c' is tautological.*

From a computational point of view, a useful property attached to the concept of blocked clause is the following one.

Property 5 (Blocked clause [13])
Let c be a clause belonging to a CNF formula Σ s.t. c is blocked. Σ is satisfiable iff $\Sigma \backslash \{c\}$ is satisfiable.

Example 3 (Blocked clause)
The following clause c_1 is blocked by the literal a.

$$\Sigma = \left\{ \begin{array}{l} c_1 : (a \vee b \vee c) \\ c_2 : (\neg a \vee \neg b) \\ c_3 : (\neg b \vee c) \\ c_4 : (b \vee \neg c) \end{array} \right\} \text{ is SAT iff } \Sigma \backslash \{c_1\} = \left\{ \begin{array}{l} c_2 : (\neg a \vee \neg b) \\ c_3 : (\neg b \vee c) \\ c_4 : (b \vee \neg c) \end{array} \right\} \text{ is SAT}$$

The concept of blocked clause can be generalized as follows, using the definition of non-fundamental clause.

Definition 4 (Non-fundamental clause)
*A clause c belonging to a CNF formula Σ is **non-fundamental** iff c is either tautological or is subsumed by another clause from Σ.*

From this, the concept of blocked clause is extended to *nf-blocked* clause.

Definition 5 (nf-blocked clause)
*A clause c belonging to a CNF formula Σ is **nf-blocked** iff there exists a literal l from c s.t. there does not exist any resolvent in l, or s.t. all resolvents are not fundamental.*

Property 5 can be extended to nf-blocked clauses.

Property 6 (nf-blocked clause)
Let c be a clause belonging to a CNF formula Σ s.t. c is nf-blocked. Σ is satifiable iff $\Sigma \backslash \{c\}$ is satisfiable.

Corollary 1
Blocked clauses and clauses containing a pure literal are nf-blocked.

The following example illustrates how the elimination of clauses can allow the consistency of a CNF formula to be proved.

Example 4 (nf-blocked)

$$\left\{ \begin{array}{l} c_1 : (a \vee b \vee c) \\ c_2 : (\neg a \vee b \vee d) \\ c_3 : (b \vee c \vee d) \\ c_4 : (\neg b \vee c \vee \neg d) \\ c_5 : (a \vee b \vee \neg c) \end{array} \right\} \xrightarrow[\text{nf-blocked clause}]{c_1 \text{ nf-blocked by } a} \left\{ \begin{array}{l} c_2 : (\neg a \vee b \vee d) \\ c_3 : (b \vee c \vee d) \\ c_4 : (\neg b \vee c \vee \neg d) \\ c_5 : (a \vee b \vee \neg c) \end{array} \right\}$$

$$\left\{ \begin{array}{l} c_2 : (\neg a \vee b \vee d) \\ c_3 : (b \vee c \vee d) \\ c_4 : (\neg b \vee c \vee \neg d) \\ c_5 : (a \vee b \vee \neg c) \end{array} \right\} \xrightarrow[\text{blocked clause}]{c_2 \text{ nf-blocked by } b} \left\{ \begin{array}{l} c_3 : (b \vee c \vee d) \\ c_4 : (\neg b \vee c \vee \neg d) \\ c_5 : (a \vee b \vee \neg c) \end{array} \right\}$$

$$\left\{\begin{array}{l} c_3 : (b \lor c \lor d) \\ c_4 : (\neg b \lor c \lor \neg d) \\ c_5 : (a \lor b \lor \neg c) \end{array}\right\} \xrightarrow[\text{blocked clause}]{c_3 \text{ nf-blocked by } d} \left\{\begin{array}{l} c_4 : (\neg b \lor c \lor \neg d) \\ c_5 : (a \lor b \lor \neg c) \end{array}\right\}$$

$$\left\{\begin{array}{l} c_4 : (\neg b \lor c \lor \neg d) \\ c_5 : (a \lor b \lor \neg c) \end{array}\right\} \xrightarrow[\text{pure literal}]{c_4 \text{ nf-blocked by } d} \left\{ c_5 : (a \lor b \lor \neg c) \right\}$$

$$\left\{ c_5 : (a \lor b \lor \neg c) \right\} \xrightarrow[\text{pure literal}]{c_5 \text{ nf-blocked by } a} \text{SAT}$$

As it can be done when pure literals are involved, this technique can lead to the elimination of variables. Indeed, it is always possible to nf-block a clause. To this end, we just have to add to the CNF all resolvents of the clause w.r.t. a given literal of this clause.

Property 7
Any clause c from a CNF formula Σ can be nf-blocked, introducing additional clauses in Σ.

In order to eliminate a variable, we just have to nf-block all clauses where it occurs. From a practical point of view, such a technique should be limited to variables giving rise to a minimum number of resolvents (*e.g.* variables which do not occur often). This idea is close to the elimination technique proposed in [5] and has been revisited in [25].

More generally, a concept of *redundant clause* can be defined as follows.

Definition 6 (Redundant clause [2])
*A clause c belonging to a CNF formula Σ is **redundant** iff $\Sigma \backslash \{c\} \models c$.*

From a practical computational point of view, looking for redundant clauses amounts to proving that $\Sigma \land \neg c$ is inconsistent. Accordingly, it should not be searched for such clauses in the general case. However, it is possible to limit the search effort, *e.g.* by looking for implicates clauses or literals by unit propagation [16].

Definition 7 (u-redundant clause)
*A clause c from a CNF formula Σ is **u-redundant** iff the unsatisfiability of $\Sigma \land \neg c$ can be obtained using unit propagation, only (i.e. $\Sigma \backslash \{c\} \models_{Unit} c$).*

Clearly, the set of u-redundant clauses of a CNF formula is a subset of the set of redundant clauses of this formula. Using Example 4, the relationship between both nf-blocked and u-redandant clauses can be illustrated :

- nf-blocked clauses can be non u-redundant. (See clause c_1 in Example 4)
- u-redundant clauses can be non nf-blocked. (In the same example, if the initial CNF formula is extended with a clause $c_6 : (a \lor \neg d)$ and $c_7 : (\neg a \lor \neg d)$, then clause c_1 becomes u-redundant but is not nf-blocked anymore).
- Clauses can be u-redundant and nf-blocked at the same time. (In the same example, extending the initial CNF formula with both clauses $c_6' : (b \lor c)$ and $c_7' : (b \lor \neg c)$, clause c_1 remains nf-blocked and becomes u-redundant)

Limited Form of Resolution Many recent efficient implementations of DPLL
[4] contain a preprocessing step introducing limited-length resolvents (the maximal length being generally fixed to 2), which increases the performance of the
solver. However, the number of resolvents possibly introduced in this way can
be prohibitive. Accordingly, we propose to limit the introduction of clauses to
resolvents allowing clauses to be eliminated.

Definition 8 (Subsuming resolvent)
Let Σ be a CNF formula, a **subsuming resolvent** *is a resolvent from two
clauses from Σ that subsumes at least one clause of Σ.*

Taking subsuming resolvents into account entails at least two direct useful
consequences from a computational point of view. First, the subsuming resolvent
is a shorter clause. Indeed, a subsuming clause is shorter than the subsumed one.
From a practical point of view, we just need to eliminate one or some literals
from the subsumed clause to get the subsuming one. Secondly, the elimination
of such literals in the clause can lead to the suppression of a variable, or make
it a unit literal or a pure literal. In all three cases, the search space is clearly
reduced accordingly.

Example 5
Clauses $(a \vee b \vee c)$ and $(a \vee \neg c)$ generate the resolvent $(a \vee b)$, which subsumes
the ternary clause and allows the literal c to be eliminated.

5   Implementation and Experimental Results

In this section, some preliminary -but significant- experimental results are presented. All algorithms have been programmed in C under Linux. All experimentations have been conducted using a 1 Ghz Pentium III processor, with 256 MB
RAM, under Mandrake Linux 8.2.

Before we implemented the solver, we addressed the *a priori* feasibility of
the equations extraction technique, at least w.r.t. standard benchmarks. Indeed,
although it is naturally expected that gates do exist in such benchmarks, these
gates have never been exhibited. Moreover, despite the fact that the use of
the partial graphs limits the number of syntactical tests to be performed, the
extraction technique could appear too much time-consuming from a practical
point of view.

The results given in Table 1 answer these issues for benchmarks from the last
SAT competitions [6,1,22,23]. For every tested instance, we have listed:
- the number of clauses ($\#C$) and of variables ($\#V$) of the initial instance;
- the number of discovered gates, using two separate categories: equivalence
  ($\# \Leftrightarrow$) and $\vee$ and $\wedge$ gates ($\# \vee \wedge$);
- the size of the set Γ of remaining clauses ($\#C_\Gamma$ & $\#V_\Gamma$);
- the time spent by the extraction process.

Table 1. Number of extracted equations and time spent for the extraction

instance	#C	#V	# ⇔	# ∨ ∧	#C_Γ	#V_Γ	time(s)
par8-1-c	254	64	56	15	30	31	0.00
par8-1	1149	350	135	15	30	31	0.07
par16-1-c	1264	317	270	61	184	124	0.08
par16-1	3310	1015	560	61	184	124	0.25
par32-1-c	5254	1315	1158	186	622	375	0.38
par32-1	10277	3176	2261	186	622	375	0.64
barrel5	5383	1407	1065	152	1163	430	0.3
barrel6	8931	2306	1746	254	2013	821	0.53
barrel7	13765	3523	2667	394	3195	1337	0.96
barrel8	20083	5106	3864	578	4763	2158	1.80
ssa7552-125	3523	1512	1033	154	1270	501	0.33
ssa2670-130	3321	1359	859	254	1352	530	0.26
ssa0432-001	1027	435	225	43	244	124	0.1
bf1355-348	7271	2286	1082	383	3533	962	0.46
dubois100	800	300	200	0	0	0	0.05
2dlx_cc_mc_ex_bp_f2_bug091	55424	5259	0	4053	7575	5214	4.50
dlx1_c	1592	295	0	209	139	291	0.01
dlx2_cc_bug18	19868	2047	0	1567	1312	2039	0.92
dlx2_cc	12812	1516	0	1063	1137	1508	0.39
1dlx_c_mc_ex_bp_f	3725	776	0	542	378	755	0.05
2dlx_ca_mc_ex_bp_f	24640	3250	0	2418	1627	3223	0.94
2dlx_cc_mc_ex_bp_f	41704	4583	0	3534	2159	4538	2.88

The results from Table 1 are really promising since they show that there exist many gates in many classes of benchmarks and that the time spent to find them is negligible (far less than 1 second, including the time spent to load the instance). Moreover, the size of the set Γ of remaining clauses after the extraction process is reduced in a significant manner (on average, the number of clauses is divided by a factor ranging from 2 to 10) and can even be zero for certain types of instances (*e.g.* Dubois100).

However, the set of variables from Γ and of the equations are not disjoint. We thus then focused on determining the number of variables that are really non defined, i.e. the variables that are never output ones. Table 2 provides the number of non defined variables (or input variables #V_{nd}) for several instances, notably for "parity" instances. These instances were selected because solving them is recognized as a challenge in the research community about SAT [24]. The results are quite surprising since only 32 variables are not defined w.r.t. the 3176 ones in the par32-1 instance. This means that the truth value of the 3144 other variables depends only on these 32 variables obtained by the extraction technique. Accordingly, the search space is reduced from 2^{3176} to 2^{32} !

These abstraction and simplification techniques have been grafted as a preprocessing step to the DPLL procedure [4], using a branching heuristics *à la* Jeroslow-Wang [11]. This algorithm, called **LSAT** runs a DPLL-like algorithm on Γ and checks during the search process if the current interpretation being built does not contradict any detected gate. In the positive case, a backtrack step is performed. This new algorithm has been compared with the last versions

Table 2. Number of undefinable variables

instance	#C	#V	#Vr	#Vnd	time(s)
par8-1	1149	350	31	8	0.00
par16-1	3310	1015	124	16	0.05
par32-1	10277	3176	375	32	0.10
ssa0432-001	1027	437	106	63	0.00
ssa2670-140	3201	1327	444	196	0.01
ssa7552-001	3614	1534	408	246	0.02
bf2670-001	3434	1393	439	210	0.02
bf1355-160	7305	2297	866	526	0.06
bf0432-001	3668	1040	386	294	0.02
2dlx_cc_mc_ex_bp_f2_bug091	55424	5259	5214	1170	4.45
dlx1_c	1592	295	291	82	0.01
dlx2_cc_bug18	19868	2047	2039	477	0.92
dlx2_cc	12812	1516	1508	448	0.38
1dlx_c_mc_ex_bp_f	3725	776	755	214	0.0
2dlx_ca_mc_ex_bp_f	24640	3250	3223	807	0.97
2dlx_cc_mc_ex_bp_f	41704	4583	4538	1012	2.87

of the most efficient SAT solvers, namely Satz [17], EqSatz [18], Zchaff [27]. The obtained results are given in Table 3 (time is given in seconds)[1].

These results show that LSAT is really more efficient that those solvers for many instances. Moreover, LSAT solves some instances in less than 1 second, whereas the other solvers took more than 16 minutes to give an answer.

6   Future Work

This work opens promising paths for future research. Indeed, the current version of the LSAT solver is just a basic prototype that runs a DPLL procedure on the remaining clauses and checks that the current interpretation does not contradict the other equations. Clearly, such a basic prototype can be improved in several directions. First, it would be interesting to develop DPLL-specific branching heuristics that take all the equations into account (and not only the remaining clauses). It would also be interesting to explore how the algorithm could exploit the intrinsic properties of each type of equation.

In this paper, the simplification process of ∧, ∨ gates and clauses has been described, but not yet implemented in the current LSAT version. On many classes of formulas (*e.g.* formal verification instances) containing a large part of such gates, we attempt further improvements using such simplification properties. More generally, it might be useful to extend this work to the simplification and resolution of general Boolean formulas. Finally, this work suggests that to model real-world problems, one might directly use more general and extended boolean formulas.

---

[1] In the table, $> n$ means that the instance could not be solved within n seconds.

Table 3. Comparison of LSAT, Satz, EqSatz and Zchaff

instance	#C	#V	SAT	Satz	EqSatz	Zchaff	LSAT
par8-1	1149	350	yes	0.05	0.01	0.01	0.01
par8-2	1149	350	yes	0.04	0.01	0.01	0.01
par8-3	1149	350	yes	0.07	0.01	0.01	0.01
par8-4	1149	350	yes	0.09	0.01	0.01	0.01
par8-5	1149	350	yes	0.05	0.01	0.01	0.01
par16-1	3310	1015	yes	8.96	0.19	0.47	0.05
par16-2	3310	1015	yes	0.48	0.20	0.88	0.05
par16-3	3310	1015	yes	16.79	0.22	4.07	0.02
par16-4	3310	1015	yes	11.15	0.17	0.82	0.06
par16-5	3310	1015	yes	1.59	0.18	0.41	0.03
par32-1-c	5254	1315	yes	¿1000	540	¿1000	6
par32-2-c	5254	1315	yes	¿1000	24	¿1000	28
par32-3-c	5254	1315	yes	¿1000	1891	¿1000	429
par32-4-c	5254	1315	yes	¿1000	377	¿1000	16
par32-5-c	5254	1315	yes	¿1000	4411	¿1000	401
par32-1	10227	3176	yes	¿1000	471	¿1000	27
par32-2	10227	3176	yes	¿1000	114	¿1000	7
par32-3	10227	3176	yes	¿1000	4237	¿1000	266
par32-4	10227	3176	yes	¿1000	394	¿1000	3
par32-5	10227	3176	yes	¿1000	5645	¿1000	471
barrel5	5383	1407	no	86	0.38	1.67	0.19
barrel6	8931	2306	no	853	0.71	8.29	0.55
barrel7	13765	3523	no	¿1000	0.96	21.55	6.23
barrel8	20083	5106	no	¿1000	1.54	53.76	412
dubois10	80	30	no	0.03	0.08	0.01	0.01
dubois20	160	60	no	26.53	0.03	0.01	0.01
dubois30	240	90	no	¿1000	0.05	0.01	0.01
dubois50	400	150	no	¿1000	0.08	0.01	0.01
dubois100	800	300	no	¿1000	0.06	0.06	0.01
Urquhart3	578	49	no	¿1000	¿1000	190	0.02
Urquhart4	764	81	no	¿1000	¿1000	¿1000	0.03
Urquhart5	1172	125	no	¿1000	¿1000	¿1000	0.06
Urquhart15	11514	1143	no	¿1000	¿1000	¿1000	0.42
Urquhart20	18528	1985	no	¿1000	¿1000	¿1000	0.64
Urquhart25	29670	3122	no	¿1000	¿1000	¿1000	1.05

7   Conclusion

In this paper, a technique of extraction of equations of the form $y = f(x_1, \ldots, x_n)$ with $f \in \{\vee, \wedge, \Leftrightarrow\}$ from a CNF formula has been presented. This extraction technique allows us to rewrite the CNF formula under the form of a conjunction of equations. These equations classify variables into defined ones and undefined ones. The defined variables can be interpreted as the output of the logical gates discovered by the extraction process, and allow us to reduce the search space in a significant way very often. Another contribution of this paper was the introduction of various simplification techniques of the remaining equations. In their turn, these latter techniques allow us to eliminate variables, reducing the search space again. These new techniques of extraction and simplification have been grafted as a pre-processing step of a new solver for SAT: namely, LSAT. This solver proves extremely competitive w.r.t. the best current techniques for several classes of structured benchmarks.

198   Richard Ostrowski et al.

Acknowledgements

We are grateful to the anonymous referees for their comments on the previous version of this paper. This work has been supported in part by the CNRS, the "Conseil Régional du Nord/Pas-de-Calais", by the EC under a FEDER program, the "IUT de Lens" and the "Université d'Artois".

References

1. First international competition and symposium on satisfiability testing, March 1996. Beijing (China).
2. Yacine Boufkhad and Olivier Roussel. Redundancy in random sat formulas. In *Proceedings of the Seventeenth National Conference on Artificial Intelligence (AAAI'00)*, pages 273–278, 2000.
3. Ronen I. Brafman. A simplifier for propositional formulas with many binary clauses. In *Proceedings of the Seventeenth International Joint Conference on Artificial Intelligence (IJCAI'01)*, 2001.
4. M. Davis, G. Logemann, and D. Loveland. A machine program for theorem proving. *Journal of the Association for Computing Machinery*, 5:394–397, 1962.
5. Martin Davis and Hilary Putnam. A computing procedure for quantification theory. *Journal of the Association for Computing Machinery*, 7:201–215, 1960.
6. Second Challenge on Satisfiability Testing organized by the Center for Discrete Mathematics and Computer Science of Rutgers University, 1993. http://dimacs.rutgers.edu/Challenges/.
7. Olivier Dubois, Pascal André, Yacine Boufkhad, and Jacques Carlier. Sat versus unsat. In D. S. Johnson and M. A. Trick, editors, *Second DIMACS Challenge*, DIMACS Series in Discrete Mathematics and Theorical Computer Science, American Mathematical Society, pages 415–436, 1996.
8. Olivier Dubois and Gilles Dequen. A backbone-search heuristic for efficient solving of hard 3–sat formulae. In *Proceedings of the Seventeenth International Joint Conference on Artificial Intelligence (IJCAI'01)*, volume 1, pages 248–253, Seattle, Washington (USA), August 4–10 2001.
9. B. Dunham and H. Wang. Towards feasible solution of the tautology problem. *Annals of Mathematical Logic*, 10:117–154, 1976.
10. E. Giunchiglia, M. Maratea, A. Tacchella, and D. Zambonin. Evaluating search heuristics and optimization techniques in propositional satisfiability. In *Proceedings of International Joint Conference on Automated Reasoning (IJCAR'01)*, Siena, June 2001.
11. Robert G. Jeroslow and Jinchang Wang. Solving propositional satisfiability problems. *Annals of Mathematics and Artificial Intelligence*, 1:167–187, 1990.
12. Henry A. Kautz, David McAllester, and Bart Selman. Exploiting variable dependency in local search. In *Abstract appears in "Abstracts of the Poster Sessions of IJCAI-97"*, Nagoya (Japan), 1997.
13. Oliver Kullmann. Worst-case analysis, 3-sat decision and lower bounds: Approaches for improved sat algorithms. In *DIMACS Proceedings SAT Workshop*, DIMACS Series in Discrete Mathematics and Theorical Computer Science, American Mathematical Society, 1996.
14. Oliver Kullmann. New methods for 3-sat decision and worst-case analysis. *Theoretical Computer Science*, pages 1–72, 1997.

15. Jérome Lang and Pierre Marquis. Complexity results for independence and definability in propositional logic. In *Proceedings of the Sixth International Conference on Principles of Knowledge Representation and Reasoning (KR'98)*, pages 356–367, Trento, 1998.

16. Daniel Le Berre. Exploiting the real power of unit propagation lookahead. In *Proceedings of the Workshop on Theory and Applications of Satisfiability Testing (SAT2001)*, Boston University, Massachusetts, USA, June 14th-15th 2001.

17. Chu Min Li and Anbulagan. Heuristics based on unit propagation for satisfiability problems. In *Proceedings of the Fifteenth International Joint Conference on Artificial Intelligence (IJCAI'97)*, pages 366–371, Nagoya (Japan), August 1997.

18. C. M. Li. Integrating equivalency reasoning into davis-putnam procedure. In *Proceedings of the Seventeenth National Conference on Artificial Intelligence (AAAI'00)*, pages 291–296, 2000.

19. Joao P. Marques-Silva. Algebraic simplification techniques for propositional satisfiability. In *Proceedings of the 6th International Conference on Principles and Practice of Constraint Programming (CP'2000)*, September 2000.

20. Shtrichman Oler. Tuning sat checkers for bounded model checking. In *Proceedings of Computer Aided Verification (CAV'00)*, 2000.

21. Antoine Rauzy, Lakhdar Saïs, and Laure Brisoux. Calcul propositionnel : vers une extension du formalisme. In *Actes des Cinquièmes Journées Nationales sur la Résolution Pratique de Problèmes NP-complets (JNPC'99)*, pages 189–198, Lyon, 1999.

22. Workshop on theory and applications of satisfiability testing, 2001. http://www.cs.washington.edu/homes/kautz/sat2001/.

23. Fifth international symposium on the theory and applications of satisfiability testing, May 2002. http://gauss.ececs.uc.edu/Conferences/SAT2002/.

24. Bart Selman, Henry A. Kautz, and David A. McAllester. Computational challenges in propositional reasoning and search. In *Proceedings of the Fifteenth International Joint Conference on Artificial Intelligence (IJCAI'97)*, volume 1, pages 50–54, Nagoya (Japan), August 1997.

25. A. Van Gelder. Extracting (easily) checkable proofs from a satisfiability solver that employs both preorder and postorder resolution. *Annals of Mathematics and Artificial Intelligence*, 2002. to appear.

26. Joost P. Warners and Hans van Maaren. A two phase algorithm for solving a class of hard satisfiability problems. *Operations Research Letters*, 23(3–5):81–88, 1999.

27. L. Zhang, C. Madigan, M. Moskewicz, and S. Malik. Efficient conflict driven learning in a boolean satisfiability solver. In *Proceedigns of ICCAD'2001*, pages 279–285, San Jose, CA (USA), November 2001.

Towards a Symmetric Treatment of Satisfaction and Conflicts in Quantified Boolean Formula Evaluation

Lintao Zhang and Sharad Malik

Department of Electrical Engineering, Princeton University
Princeton, NJ 08544
{lintaoz,sharad}@ee.princeton.edu

Abstract. In this paper, we describe a new framework for evaluating Quantified Boolean Formulas (QBF). The new framework is based on the Davis-Putnam (DPLL) search algorithm. In existing DPLL based QBF algorithms, the problem database is represented in Conjunctive Normal Form (CNF) as a set of clauses, implications are generated from these clauses, and backtracking in the search tree is chronological. In this work, we augment the basic DPLL algorithm with conflict driven learning as well as satisfiability directed implication and learning. In addition to the traditional clause database, we add a cube database to the data structure. We show that cubes can be used to generate satisfiability directed implications similar to conflict directed implications generated by the clauses. We show that in a QBF setting, conflicting leaves and satisfying leaves of the search tree both provide valuable information to the solver in a symmetric way. We have implemented our algorithm in the new QBF solver Quaffle. Experimental results show that for some test cases, satisfiability directed implication and learning significantly prunes the search.

1   Introduction

A Quantified Boolean Formula is a propositional logic formula with existential and universal quantifiers preceding it. Given a Quantified Boolean Formula, the question whether it is satisfiable (i.e. evaluates to 1) is called a Quantified Boolean Satisfiability problem (QBF). In the rest of the paper, we will use QBF to denote both the formula and the decision problem, with the meaning being clear from the context. Many practical problems ranging from AI planning [1] to sequential circuit verification [2] [3] can be transformed into QBF problems. QBF is P-Space Complete, thus placing it higher in the complexity hierarchy than NP-Complete problems. It is highly unlikely that there exists a polynomial time algorithm for QBF. However, because of its practical importance, there is interest in developing efficient algorithms that can solve many practical instances of QBF problems.

Research on QBF solvers has been going on for some time. In [4], the authors present a resolution-based algorithm and prove that it is complete and sound. In [5],

P. Van Hentenryck (Ed.): CP 2002, LNCS 2470, pp. 200–215, 2002.

the authors proposed another QBF evaluation method that is essentially a resolution-based procedure. Both of these resolution-based algorithms suffer from the problem of space explosion; therefore, they are not widely used as practical tools. Other efforts have resulted in some QBF solvers that will not blow up in space (e.g. [7] [8] [10] [17]). These solvers are all based on variations of the Davis Logemann Loveland (sometimes called DPLL) algorithm [6]. Most of these methods can be regarded as a generalization of the algorithms commonly used to evaluate Boolean propositional formulas (called the Boolean Satisfiability Problem or SAT). SAT can be regarded as a restricted form of QBF. In SAT, only existential quantifiers are allowed. SAT differs from QBF in that when a satisfying assignment is found, the algorithm will stop, while QBF may need to continue the search because of the universal quantifiers. Because the above-mentioned QBF algorithms are by and large based on SAT algorithms (even though they may incorporate some QBF specific rules and heuristics), they all operate on a clause database, and use clauses to generate implications and conflicts. In SAT, a conflict is the source of more information for the future, while a satisfying assignment is the end of the search. As a result QBF solvers based on a SAT search inherit this characteristic and focus on conflicts for deriving further information for search progress. However, as far as QBF is concerned, a satisfying assignment is not the end of the search and, as we will show, can also be used to derive further information to drive the search. A symmetric treatment of satisfaction and conflict is highly desirable (and useful) and is the focus of this paper.

Due to its importance, significant research effort has been spent on finding fast algorithms for SAT. Recent years have seen major advances in SAT research, resulting in some very efficient complete SAT solvers (e.g. GRASP [12], SATO [14], rel_sat [13], Chaff [15]). These solvers are also based on the DPLL algorithm, and all of them employ conflict driven learning and non-chronological backtracking techniques (e.g. [12] [13]). Experiments shows that conflict driven learning is very effective in pruning the search space for structured (in contrast of random) SAT problems. Recently, Zhang and Malik [17] have developed method to incorporate Conflict Driven Learning in a QBF solver. Their experiments show that conflict driven learning, when adapted in a QBF solver, can speed up the search process greatly. However, just like other DPLL based QBF solvers mentioned above, the solver they have developed is not able to treat satisfiable leaves and conflicting leaves symmetrically. The solver has to use chronological backtracking on satisfying leaves.

In this paper, we describe our work that augments the solver described in [17]. Our framework is still based on the DPLL algorithm; therefore, it will not suffer from the memory explosion problem encountered by the resolution-based algorithms [4] [5]. We introduce the notion of Satisfiability Directed Implication and Learning, and show how to augment the widely used CNF database with *cubes* to make this possible. In our framework, the solver will operate on an *Augmented CNF* database. Because of this, our solver will have an almost symmetric (or dual) view for Satisfying Leaves as will as Conflicting Leaves encountered in the search.

A closely related work to this paper is presented by E. Giunchiglia *et al.* recently in [11]. In that paper, the authors demonstrate how to add backjumping into their QBF solving process. Our work differs from this in that we keep the knowledge from conflicts as learned clauses and the knowledge of satisfying branches as learned cubes. Backjumping (or sometimes called non-chronological backtracking) is a direct result of the learned clauses and cubes. Because of learning, the knowledge obtained from some search space can be utilized in other search spaces. In contrast, in [11] learning is not possible. Our framework also has the notion of satisfiability directed implication, which is not available in their work.

2   Problem Formulation

A QBF has the form

$$Q_1x_1......Q_nx_n \; \varphi \tag{1}$$

Where φ is a propositional formula involving propositional *variables* x_i (i=1…n). Each Q_i is either an existential quantifier $\exists$ or a universal quantifier $\forall$. Because $\exists x \exists y$ $\varphi = \exists y \exists x \; \varphi$ and $\forall x \forall y \; \varphi = \forall y \forall x \; \varphi$, we can always group the quantified variables into disjoint sets where each set consists of adjacent variables with the same type of quantifier. Therefore, we can rewrite (1) into the following form:

$$Q_1X_1......Q_nX_n \; \varphi \tag{2}$$

X_i's are mutually disjoint sets of variables. Each variable in the formula must belong to one of these sets. We will call the variables existential or universal according to the quantifier of their respective quantification sets. Also, each variable has a quantification level associated with it. The variables belonging to the outermost quantification set have quantification level 1, and so on.

A *literal* is the occurrence of a variable in either positive or negative *phase*. A *clause* is a disjunction (logic *or*) of literals. A *cube* is a conjunction (logic *and*) of literals (this term is widely used in logic optimization, see e.g. [18]). In the rest of the paper, we will use concatenation to denote conjunction, and "+" to denote disjunction. A propositional formula φ is said to be in Conjunctive Normal Form (CNF) if the formula is a conjunction of clauses. When φ is expressed in CNF, the QBF becomes

$$Q_1X_1......Q_nX_n \; C_1 \; C_2...C_m \tag{3}$$

Here, the C_i's are clauses. In the following, we will call the QBF in form (3) a QBF in Conjunctive Normal Form (CNF).

It is also possible to express a propositional formula φ in the Sum of Product (SOP) form, or sometimes called Disjunctive Normal Form (DNF). In that case, the formula is a disjunction of cubes. A QBF formula in DNF looks like:

$$Q_1X_1......Q_nX_n \; (S_1 + S_2 +...+ S_{m'}) \tag{4}$$

Here, the S_i's are cubes. We will call a QBF in this form a QBF in Disjunctive Normal Form (DNF). CNF and DNF are not the only representations for propositional formulas and QBF. Suppose we have

$$\varphi = C_1....C_m = \; S_1 + S_2 +......+ S_{m'}$$

Then

$$Q_1X_1......Q_nX_n \; \varphi = Q_1X_1......Q_nX_n \; C_1 \, C_2...C_m$$
$$= Q_1X_1......Q_nX_n \; (S_1 + S_2 +......+ S_{m'})$$
$$= Q_1X_1......Q_nX_n \; (C_1 \, C_2...C_m + S_1 + S_2 +......+ S_{m'})$$
$$= Q_1X_1......Q_nX_n \; C_1 \, C_2...C_m(S_1 + S_2 +......+ S_{m'})$$
$$= Q_1X_1......Q_nX_n \; (C_1 \, C_2...C_m + \Sigma AnySubset\{ S_1, S_2...,S_{m'}\}) \qquad (5)$$
$$= Q_1X_1......Q_nX_n \; (\Pi AnySubset\{ C_1 ,C_2...,C_m\})(S_1 + S_2 +...+ S_{m'}) \; (6)$$

Here we use $\Sigma\omega$ to denote disjunction of elements in set ω, and $\Pi\omega$ to denote conjunction of the elements in the set ω. We use AnySubset(ω) to denote any set υ s.t. $\upsilon \subseteq \omega$. We will call the QBF in form (5) a QBF in *Augmented Conjunctive Normal Form (ACNF)* and QBF in form (6) a QBF in *Augmented Disjunctive Normal Form (ADNF)*. Because we will use ACNF extensively in our future discussion, we will define it here.

Definition 1: A Propositional formula φ is said to be in *Augmented CNF (ACNF)* if

$$\varphi = C_1C_2...C_m + S_1 + S_2 +......+ S_k$$

Where C_i's are clauses, and S_j's are cubes. Moreover, each S_j is contained in the term $C_1 \, C_2...C_m$. i.e.

$$\forall i \in \{1,2...k\}, \; S_i \Rightarrow C_1 \, C_2...C_m$$

A Quantified Boolean Formula in form (2) is said to be in *Augmented CNF* if the propositional formula φ is in Augmented CNF. We will call all the conjunction of clauses $C_1 \, C_2...C_m$ in the ACNF the *clause term*. By definition, in an ACNF all the cubes are contained in the clause term. Deleting any or all of the cubes will not change the propositional Boolean function φ or the Quantified Boolean Function F.

Traditionally, QBF problems are usually presented to the solver in CNF. The QBF solver operates on a clause database that corresponds to the CNF clauses. All the theorems and deduction rules are valid under the assumption that the QBF is in CNF. In this paper, our discussion will concentrate on QBF in ACNF. CNF is a special case of ACNF. The conclusions that are drawn from QBF in ACNF will be applicable to QBF in CNF as well.

3   The QBF Solver Framework

3.1   Algorithm Overview

Our framework for solving QBF is based on the well-known Davis-Putnam-Logemann-Loveland (DPLL) algorithm. The DPLL procedure is a branch and search procedure on the variables. Therefore, in the rest of the paper, many of the statements will have the implicit "with regard to the current assignment of variable values" as a suffix. For example, when we say "the clause is conflicting", we mean that "the clause is conflicting in the context of the current variable assignments". We will omit this suffix for concise presentation when no confusion can result. The value assignment to the variables may be a partial assignment. We will call variables (and literals) that have not been assigned *free*. Each branch in the search has a *decision level* associated with it. The first branch variable has decision level 1, and so on. All of the variables implied by a decision variable will assume the same decision level as the decision variable. In the rest of the paper, we may use terms like "in the current branch". This has the same meaning as "in the partial variable assignment resulting from the implication of the current branching variables' assignments".

The top-level algorithm for our framework is described in Fig. 1. It is an iterative (instead of recursive) version of the DPLL algorithm similar to many Boolean SAT solvers (e.g. [12] [15]) and many other QBF solvers (e.g. [7] [8] [10]). The difference between our framework and them is the actual meaning of each of the functions.

```
while(1) {
  decide_next_branch();
  while (true) {
    status = deduce();
    if (status == CONFLICT) {
      blevel = analyze_conflict();
      if (blevel == 0)
        return UNSAT;
      else backtrack(blevel);
    }
    else if (status == SATISFIABLE) {
      blevel = analyze_SAT();
      if (blevel == 0)
        return SAT;
      else backtrack(blevel);
    }
    else break;
  }
}
```

Fig. 1. The top level DPLL algorithm for QBF evaluation

Unlike a regular SAT solver, the decision procedure `decide_next_branch()` in Fig. 1 needs to obey the quantification order. A variable can be chosen as a branch variable if and only if all variables that have smaller quantification levels are already assigned. This is similar to other QBF solvers.

Unlike other QBF solvers, the solver database is in ACNF; thus, the function `deduce()` will have different rules and can generate different implications. We will describe these rules in the following sections. The status of deduction can have three values: UNDETERMINED, SATISFIABLE or CONFLICT. The status is SATISFIABLE (CONFLICT) if we know that φ must evaluate to 1 (0) under the current partial variable assignment, otherwise, the status is UNDETERMINED. The purpose of function `deduce()` is to prune the search space. Therefore, any rules can be incorporated in the function without affecting the correctness of the algorithm as long as the rules are valid (e.g. the function will not return SATISFIABLE when the problem is CONFLICT, and vice-versa). Some algorithms use the unit literal rule [7], some may add pure literal rule [7] [10], and some add failed literal detection [8] and sampling [8] to `deduce()`. As long as the rules are valid, the algorithm is correct.

When deduction finds that the current branch is satisfiable, in Boolean SAT, the solver will return immediately with the satisfying assignment. In a QBF solver, because of the universal quantifiers, we need to make sure that both branches of a universal variable lead to a satisfiable solution. Therefore, the solver needs to backtrack and continue the search.

When the status of deduction is CONFLICT, we say that a conflicting leaf is reached. When the status of deduction is SATISFIABLE, we say that a satisfying leaf is reached. The functions analyze_conflict() and analyze_SAT() will analyze the current status and bring the search to a new space by backtracking (and possibly do some learning). The most simplistic DPLL algorithm will backtrack chronologically with no learning (see e.g. [17] for a description of non-chronological backtracking). Many QBF solvers, such as [7] [8], use this backtracking method.

In [11], the authors demonstrated a method for conflict-directed and satisfiability-directed non-chronological backjumping. In their approach, when the current assignment leads to a satisfying leaf or conflicting leaf, the reason for the result is constructed, and the solver will backjump to the decision level that is directly responsible for the conflicting or satisfiable leaf. However, the constructed reason will not be used to generate implications in future reasoning; thus learning is not possible. In [17], the authors demonstrated that conflict driven learning can be adapted and incorporated into QBF solvers. When a conflicting leaf is encountered, a learned clause is constructed and added to the clause database. The learned clause can be used in future search, thus enabling conflict driven learning. However, the algorithm is limited to chronological backtracking when satisfying leaves are encountered. In this work, we will show how to augment [17] by introducing satisfiability directed implication and learning. More specifically, we will keep the function analyze_conflict() in [17] intact and improve analyze_SAT(). When a satisfying leaf is encountered, analyze_SAT() will construct a *learned cube*, and add it to the database, which consists of both clauses and cubes that corresponding to an ACNF formula. The cubes may help search in the future, just as learned clauses do.

3.2   Motivation for Augmenting CNF with Cubes

Traditionally, for SAT, the DPLL algorithm requires that the problems be in CNF. The reason for that is because of the two important and useful rules that are direct results for formulas in CNF: the unit literal rule and the conflicting rule. The unit literal rule states that if a clause has only one free literal, then it must be assigned to value 1. The conflicting rule states that if a clause has all literals that evaluate to 0, then the current branch is not satisfiable. The function of these two rules is to direct the solver away from searching space with an obvious outcome. In the SAT case, the obvious outcome is that there is no solution in that space. For example, if there exists a conflicting clause, then any sub-space consistent with the current assignment will not have any solution in it, so we better backtrack immediately. If there exists a unit clause, we know that assigning the unit literal with value 0 will lead to a search space with no solution, so we better assign it 1. In SAT we are only interested in finding one solution, so we only need to prune the search space that has no solution. We call the implication by unit clauses *conflict directed implications* because the purpose of the implication is to avoid conflict (i.e. a no-solution space).

A QBF solver is different from SAT because it usually cannot stop when a single satisfying branch is found. In fact, it needs to search multiple combinations of assignments of the universal variables to declare satisfiability. Therefore, we are not only interested in pruning the space that obviously has no solution, we are also interested in pruning the space that obviously *has* a solution. Most of the DPLL based QBF solvers are based on [7], which in turn is based on SAT procedures and requires the database in CNF. Even though the implication rule and conflicting rule of QBF is a little different from SAT, these rules are still *conflict directed*, i.e. they bring the search away from an obviously no-solution space. There is no mechanism in these algorithms to bring the search away from an obviously has-solution space.

To cope with this obvious asymmetry, we introduce the Augmented CNF in our framework. In ACNF, cubes are *or*-ed with the clause term. Whenever a cube is satisfied, the whole propositional formula evaluates to 1. Similar to unit clauses, we have the notion of *unit cubes*. A unit cube will generate an implication, but the implication's purpose is to bring the search away from space that obviously *has* solutions. Similar to conflicting clauses, we have the notion of *satisfying cubes*. Whenever a satisfying cube is encountered, we can declare the branch is satisfiable and backtrack immediately. We will describe the rules for the cubes in next sections.

Most frequently the QBF problem is presented to the solver in CNF form. Therefore, initially there is no cube in the database. We need to generate cubes during the solving process. ACNF requires that the generated cubes be contained in the clause term. Therefore, the satisfiability of the QBF will not be altered by these cubes.

3.3   Implication Rules

In this section, we will show the rules used in the deduce () function in Fig. 1. These rules are valid for QBF in ACNF forms. Therefore, they can be directly applied to the database the solver is working on.

A note on the notation used. We will use C, C_1, C_2 ... to represent clauses, S, S_1, S_2... to represent Cubes. We use $E(C), E(S)$ for the set of existential literals in the clause and cube respectively, and $U(C), U(S)$ for the set of universal literals in the clause and cube respectively. We use a, b, c... (letters appearing in the early part of the alphabet) to denote existential literals, and x, y, z ... (letters appearing in the end of the alphabet) to denote universal literals. We use $V(a), V(b)$... to denote the value of the literals. If literal a is free, $V(a) = X$. We use $L(a), L(b)$... to denote the quantification level of the variables corresponding to the literals.

Definition 2. A *tautology clause* is a clause that contains both a literal its complement. An *empty cube* is a cube that contains both a literal and its complement.

Proposition 1. Conflicting Rule for Non-Tautology Clause: For QBF F in ACNF, if in a certain branch, there exists a non-tautology clause C, s.t. $\forall a \in E(C)$, $V(a) = 0$, and $\forall x \in U(C)$, $V(x) \neq 1$, then F cannot be satisfied in the branch. We call such a clause a *conflicting clause*.

Proposition 2. Implication Rule for Non-Tautology Clause: For QBF F in ACNF, if in a certain branch, a non-tautology clause C has literal a s.t.

1. $a \in E(C)$, $V(a) = X$. For any $b \in E(C)$, $b \neq a$; $V(b)=0$.
2. $\forall x \in U(C)$, $V(x) \neq 1$. If $V(x) = X$, then $L(x) > L(a)$

Then the formula F can be satisfied in the branch if and only if $V(a)=1$. We will call such a clause a *unit clause*, and the literal *a* the *unit literal*. Notice that the unit literal of a unit clause is always an existential literal. By this proposition, to avoid exploring an obviously no-solution space, we need to assign *a* with 1 to continue search.

Proposition 3. Satisfying Rule for Non-Empty Cube: For QBF F in ACNF, if in a certain branch, there exists a non-empty cube S, s.t. $\forall x \in U(S)$, $V(x) = 1$, and $\forall a \in E(S)$, $V(a) \neq 0$, then F is satisfied in the branch. We call such a cube a *satisfying cube*.

Proposition 4. Implication Rule for Non-Empty Cube: For QBF F in ACNF, if in a certain branch, a non-empty cube S has literal *x* s.t.

1. $x \in U(S)$, $V(x) = X$. For any $y \in U(S)$, $y \neq x$ then $V(y)=1$.
2. $\forall a \in E(S)$, $V(a) \neq 0$. If $V(a) = X$, then $L(a) > L(x)$

Then the formula F is satisfied unless $V(a)=0$. We call such a cube a *unit cube*, and the literal *x* the *unit literal*. Notice that the unit literal of a unit cube is always a universal literal. Similar to Proposition 2, to avoid exploring an obviously has-solution space, we need to assign *x* with 0 to continue search.

Proposition 1 and 2 are the regular conflicting rule and implication rules for QBF if the database is in CNF (see, e.g. [7]). Because the cubes are redundant in ACNF, these rules will also apply for QBF in ACNF. Proposition 3 and 4 are exactly the dual of Proposition 1 and 2. When a unit literal in a clause or cube is forced to be assigned a value because of Proposition 2 or 4, we say that this literal (or the variable corresponding to it) is *implied*. The unit cube or clause where the unit literal is coming from is called the *antecedent* of the literal (or variable). The antecedent of an implied universal variable is a cube, and the antecedent of an implied existential variable is a clause. The implication rules corresponding to Proposition 2 and 4 can be used in the function deduce() in Fig. 1 for deduction. The pseudo code for it is listed in Fig. 2.

```
deduce() {
    while(problem_sat()==false &&
          num_conflicting_clause()==0) {
        if (exist_unit_clause())
            assign_unit_literal_in_clause_to_be_1();
        else if (exist_unit_cube())
            assign_unit_literal_in_cube_to_be_0();
        else
            return UNDETERMINED;
    }
    if (problem_sat()) return SAT;
    return CONFLICT;
}
```

Fig. 2. The deduce() function for both conflict and satisfiability directed implication

3.4   Generating Satisfiability-Induced Cubes

In this section, we will discuss how to generate cubes that are contained by the clause terms in an ACNF database. When the QBF problem is given to the solver, it usually is in CNF and does not have any cubes. To generate cubes that are contained by the clause term, one obvious way is to expand the clause term by the distribution law. Unfortunately, this is not practical since the number of cubes generated is intractable.

Here, we will discuss another way to generate cubes. The main idea is that whenever the search procedure finds that all the clauses are satisfied (i.e. for each clause, at least one literal evaluates to 1), we can always find a set of value 1 literals such that for any clause, at least one of the literals in the set appears in it. We will call such a set a *cover set* of the satisfying assignment. The conjunction of the literals in the cover set is a cube, and this cube is guaranteed to be contained by the clause term.

For example, consider the ACNF:

$$(a + b + x)(c + y')(a + b' + y')(a + x' + y') + xy'$$

The variable assignments of $\{a=1, b=0, c=X, x=0, y=0\}$ is a satisfying assignment. The set of literals $\{a, y'\}$ is a cover set. Therefore, cube ay' is a cube that is contained in the clause term, and can be added to the ACNF. The resulting formula will be:

$$(a + b + x)(c + y')(a + b' + y')(a + x' + y') + ay' + xy'$$

We will call the cube generated from a cover set of a satisfying assignment a satisfiability-induced cube.

For a satisfying assignment, the cover set is not unique. Therefore, we can generate many satisfiability-induced cubes. Which and how many of these cubes should be added to the database is to be determined by heuristics. Different heuristics, while not affecting the correctness of the algorithm, may affect the efficiency. Evaluating different heuristics for generating satisfiability-induced cubes is beyond the scope of this paper. Here we will simply assume that we have some heuristics (for example, a greedy heuristic) to choose a single covering set for each satisfying assignment.

3.5   Conflict-Driven and Satisfiability-Directed Learning

Conflict driven learning in QBF was introduced in [17]. Here we will briefly review it for completeness of discussion. Conflict driven learning occurs when a conflicting leaf is encountered. The pseudo-code for analyzing the conflict as well as generating the learned clauses is shown in Fig. 3. The learning is performed by the function `add_clause_to_database()`. In this function, the solver can throw away all the universal literals that have a higher quantification level than any existential literal in the clause, as pointed out in [4]. The learned clause is generated by the function `resolution_gen_clause()`. Routine `choose_literal()` will choose an implied *existential* variable from the input clause in the reverse chronological order (i.e. variable implied last will be chosen first). Routine `resolve(cl1,cl2,var)` will return a clause that has all the literals appearing in *cl1* and *cl2* except for the literals corresponding to variable *var*. If the generated clause meets some predefined stopping criterion, the resulting clause will be returned, otherwise the resolution process is called recursively. The stopping criterion is that the clause satisfies:

1. Among all its existential variables, one and only one of them has the highest decision level. Suppose this variable is V.
2. V is in a decision level with an existential variable as the decision variable.
3. All universal literals with a quantification level smaller than V's are assigned 0 before V's decision level.

If these criteria are met, after backtracking to a certain decision level (determined by function `clause_asserting_level()`),, this clause will be a unit clause and force the unit literal to assume a different value, and bring the search to a new space. For more details about conflict driven learning in QBF, we refer the readers to [17].

Proposition 5. The learning procedure depicted in Fig. 3 will generate valid clauses that can be added to the database even when the QBF is in ACNF. Moreover, the learned clauses will obey the same implication rule and conflicting rule as regular non-tautology clauses even though some of the learned clauses may be tautologies, i.e. contain universal literals in both the positive and negative phases.

```
resolution_gen_clause( cl ) {
    lit = choose_literal (cl);
    var = variable_of_literal( lit );
    ante = antecedent( var );
    new_cl = resolve(cl, ante, var);
    if (stop_criterion_met(new_cl))
        return new_cl;
    else
        return resolution_gen_clause(new_cl);
}
analyze_conflict(){
    conf_cl = find_conflicting_clause();
    new_cl = resolution_gen_clause(conf_cl);
    add_clause_to_database(new_cl);
    back_dl = clause_asserting_level(new_cl);
    return back_dl;
}
```

Fig. 3. Generating learned clause by resolution

When a satisfying leaf is encountered, similar to conflict driven learning, we can also perform satisfiability directed learning. Conflict driven learning adds (redundant) clauses into the ACNF database; similarly, satisfiability directed learning adds (redundant) cubes into the ACNF database. The procedure for satisfiability directed learning, which is shown in Fig. 4, is very similar to the procedure for conflict driven learning. The only major difference is that when a satisfiable leaf is encountered, there are two scenarios, while in conflicting case there is only one. The first scenario in the satisfying leaf case is that there exists a satisfying cube in the ACNF; this is similar to the conflicting case, where there exists a conflicting clause. The second scenario, which is unique in the satisfying case, is that all the clauses in the ACNF are satisfied (i.e. every clause has at least one literal evaluate to 1) but no satisfying cube exists. In Fig. 4, if function `find_sat_cube()` returns NULL, then the second case is encountered. In that case, we have to construct a satisfiability-induced cube from the current variable assignment. The learned cube is generated by the function `consensus_gen_cube()`. Routine `choose_literal()` will choose an implied universal variable from the input clause in the reverse chronological order. Routine `consensus(S1,S2,var)` will return a cube that has all the literals appearing in S1 and S2 except for the literals corresponding to variable var. If the generated cube meets the following conditions, the recursion will stop:

Among all its universal variables, one and only one of them has the highest decision level. Suppose this variable is V.

V is at a decision level with a universal variable as the decision variable.

All existential literals with quantification level smaller than V's are assigned 1 before V's decision level.

If these criteria are met, the resulting cube will have only one universal literal at the highest decision level. After backtracking to a certain decision level (determined by function `cube_asserting_level()`), this cube will be a unit cube and will force this literal to assume a different value, and bring search to a new space.

```
consensus_gen_cube( s ) {
   lit = choose_literal (s);
   var = variable_of_literal( lit );
   ante = antecedent( var );
   new_cube = resolve(s, ante, var);
   if (stop_criterion_met(s))
     return new_cube;
   else
     return consensus_gen_cube(new_cube);
}

analyze_SAT(){
   cube = find_sat_cube();
   if (cube == NULL)
     cube = construct_sat_induced_cube();
   if (!stop_criterion_met(cube))
     cube = consensus_gen_cube(cube);
   add_cube_to_database(cube);
   back_dl = cube_asserting_level(cube);
   return back_dl;
}
```

Fig. 4. Generating learned cube

Proposition 6. The learning procedure depicted in Fig. 4 will generate valid cubes that are contained by the clause term of the ACNF and can be added to the database. Moreover, the learned cubes will obey the same implication rule and conflicting rule as non-empty cubes even though some of the learned cubes may contain an existential literal in both positive and negative phases.

From the pseudo-code of analyze_conflict() and analyze_SAT() we can see that the DPLL procedure will have an almost symmetric view on satisfying and conflicting leaves in the search tree. Whenever a conflicting leaf is encountered, a clause will be learned to prune the space that obviously has *no* solution. When a satisfying leaf is encountered, a cube will be learned to prune the space that obviously *has* solutions. The only asymmetry that exists is that in our database, the cubes are contained by the clause terms, but not vice-versa. Therefore, the cubes only contain partial information about the propositional formula. Because of this, we may need to generate a satisfiability-induced cube when a satisfying assignment is found but no existing cube is satisfied. On the other hand, the formula need not be in ACNF for QBF. If the original QBF problem is given in DNF form (problem in DNF is trivial for SAT), we may augment it into ADNF. In that case, we need to construct conflict-induced clauses.

4   Experimental Results

We implemented the algorithm described in this paper in the new QBF solver Quaffle, which was first described in [17] to demonstrate the power of conflict driven learning in a QBF environment. We have improved the original Quaffle with a cube database such that the data structure corresponds to an ACNF. We incorporated the new rules on cubes (i.e. Proposition 3 and 4) into the `deduce()` function shown in Fig. 1. We also implemented code corresponding to Fig. 4 in place of `analyze_SAT()`. Because of these improvements, the solver now has the ability to do satisfiability directed implication and learning.

The heuristic we use for generating a cover set from a satisfying assignment is a simple greedy method to minimize the number of universal variables in the set. The decision heuristic we used to decide on the next branching variable is VSIDS [15], with quantification order of the variables being observed. We do not delete learned cubes or learned clauses in all the runs because the benchmarks we tested are mostly time-limited. Both learned clauses and cubes can be deleted in a similar manner as deletion of learned clauses in SAT if memory is limited.

The problem set was obtained from J. Rintanen [19]. We have already reported the performance comparison of Quaffle with other state-of-the-art QBF solvers in [17]. Therefore, in this paper we will only show two versions of Quaffle. One version of Quaffle has satisfiability directed implication and learning turned off. This is the version we reported in [17], we call it Quaffle-CDL to be consistent with our previous work. The other version has satisfiability directed implication and learning turned on. We call this version Quaffle-FULL. All the tests were conducted on a PIII 933 machine with 1G memory. The timeout limit is 1800 seconds for each instance.

Table 1 showed the run time data for the benchmarks (except the ones that cannot be solved by both versions within time limit). From the result table we can see that for some classes of benchmarks such as `impl` and random 3-QBF R3..., Quaffle with satisfiability directed implication and learning is faster when compared with Quaffle with no satisfiability directed implication and learning. For some other benchmarks such as the `CHAIN` and `TOILET` sets, the result is not really good. For others such as `BLOCKS` and `logn`, the results are mixed. To get a better understanding of the performance gain and loss, we show some of the detailed statistics in Table 2.

Table 1. Run time of Quaffle with Satisfiability driven implication turned on and off (time unit is second, we use – to denote timeout)

Testcase	nVar	nCl	T/F	Quaffle-CDL	Quaffle-FULL	Testcase	NVar	nCl	T/F	Quaffle-CDL	Quaffle-FULL
BLOCKS3i.4.4	288	2928	F	0.07	0.09	impl20	82	162	T	15.51	0.02
BLOCKS3i.5.3	286	2892	F	29.03	103.73	logn...A0	828	1685	F	0	0
BLOCKS3i.5.4	328	3852	T	2.88	146.54	logn...A1	1099	62820	F	2.21	2.14
BLOCKS3ii.4.3	247	2533	F	0.05	0.04	logn...A2	1370	65592	T	125.85	193.88
BLOCKS3ii.5.2	282	2707	F	0.13	0.48	logn...B0	1474	3141	F	0	0
BLOCKS3ii.5.3	304	3402	T	0.33	0.48	logn...B1	1871	178750	F	8.26	8.18
BLOCKS3iii.4	202	1433	F	0.03	0.03	logn...B2	2268	183601	F	763.37	750.92
BLOCKS3iii.5	256	1835	T	0.27	0.23	R3...3...50_0.T	150	375	T	1.22	0.02
BLOCKS4i.6.4	779	15872	F	249.09	110.2	R3...3...50_1.F	150	375	F	0.02	0.05
BLOCKS4i.6.3	838	15061	F	367.54	591.95	R3...3...50_2.T	150	375	T	0.81	0.01
BLOCKS4iii.6	727	9661	F	39.33	294.49	R3...3...50_3.T	150	375	T	1.06	0
CHAIN12v.13	925	4582	T	0.31	7.11	R3...3...50_4.T	150	375	T	1.43	0.09
CHAIN13v.14	1080	5458	T	0.66	19.09	R3...3...50_5.T	150	375	T	0.95	0.06
CHAIN14v.15	1247	6424	T	1.45	51.09	R3...3...50_6.F	150	375	F	1.51	0.37
CHAIN15v.16	1426	7483	T	3.15	142.21	R3...3...50_7.F	150	375	F	0.6	0.07
CHAIN16v.17	1617	8638	T	6.82	472.38	R3...3...50_8.F	150	375	F	0.29	0.05
CHAIN17v.18	1820	9892	T	14.85	1794.35	R3...3...50_9.T	150	375	T	0.87	0.02
CHAIN18v.19	2035	11248	T	32.4	–	R3...7...60_0.F	150	390	F	0.14	0.11
CHAIN19v.20	2262	12709	T	71.41	–	R3...7...60_1.T	150	390	T	0.23	0.02
CHAIN20v.21	2501	14278	T	154.86	–	R3...7...60_2.T	150	390	T	1.27	0.02
CHAIN21v.22	2752	15958	T	343.62	–	R3...7...60_3.T	150	390	T	0.34	0.02
CHAIN22v.23	3015	17752	T	747.3	–	R3...7...60_4.T	150	390	T	13.3	0.17
CHAIN23v.24	3290	19663	T	1710.06	–	R3...7...60_5.F	150	390	F	1.3	0.11
impl02	10	18	T	0	0	R3...7...60_6.T	150	390	T	0.51	0.03
impl04	18	34	T	0	0	R3...7...60_7.T	150	390	T	2.21	0.33
impl06	26	50	T	0	0	R3...7...60_8.F	150	390	F	0	0
impl08	34	66	T	0.01	0.01	R3...7...60_9.T	150	390	T	0.23	0.02
impl10	42	82	T	0.02	0.01	TOILET02.1.iv.3	28	70	F	0	0
impl12	50	98	T	0.06	0.01	TOILET02.1.iv.4	37	99	T	0	0
impl14	58	114	T	0.24	0.02	TOILET06.1.iv.11	294	1046	F	39.51	221.45
impl16	66	130	T	0.97	0.02	TOILET06.1.iv.12	321	1144	T	18.23	74.16
impl18	74	146	T	3.88	0.02						

From Table 2 we get some additional insight for the performance difference between Quaffle-CDL and Quaffle-Full. In testcases that have few satisfiable leaves such as logn...B1, logn...A2, BLOCKS4ii.6.3, Quaffle-Full take about the same time or just a little bit more than Quaffle-CDL because the satisfiability induced pruning does not have many chances to work. For problem class CHAIN and

TOILET, though there exist many satisfying leaves, satisfiability induced learning is not able to prune much of the search space. The reason for this is because these testcases all have the property that when a satisfying assignment is found, the satisfiability-induced cover set often includes all of the universal literals. Because of this, the learned cubes will not be able to prune any search space (similar to very long conflict clause in SAT). For testcases R3... and impl, satisfiability directed implication and learning dramatically reduced the number of satisfying leaves need to be visited, therefore, the total run time is reduced significantly.

Table 2. Some detailed statistics of the representative testcases

Testcase	T/F	Quaffle-CDL			Quaffle-Full		
		No. Sat. Leaves	No. Conf. Leaves	Runtime	No. Sat. Leaves	No. Conf. Leaves	Runtime
TOILET06.1.iv.12	F	24119	7212	18.23	17757	8414	74.16
TOILET06.1.iv.11	T	30553	11000	39.51	30419	13918	221.45
CHAIN15v.16	T	32768	43	3.15	32768	43	142.21
CHAIN16v.17	T	65536	46	6.82	65536	46	472.38
CHAIN17v.18	T	131072	49	14.85	131072	49	1794.35
impl16	T	160187	17	0.97	106	17	0.02
impl18	T	640783	19	3.88	124	19	0.02
impl20	T	2563171	21	15.51	142	21	0.02
R3...3...50_8.F	F	11845	374	0.29	59	460	0.05
R3...3...50_9.T	T	33224	87	0.87	35	50	0.02
logn...A2	T	3119	11559	125.85	1937	14428	193.88
logn...B1	F	2	601	8.26	2	609	8.18
BLOCKS4ii.6.3	F	5723	52757	367.54	98	45788	591.95

From the experimental results we find that satisfiability directed implication and learning can help prune the search space for some benchmarks but only induce overhead without much help for other benchmarks. Therefore, the question is when to apply it, and how to reduce the overhead when no pruning of search is possible. Currently, publicly available QBF benchmarks are very scarce, and very few of them are actually derived from real world problems. It is not easy to evaluate the applicability of any heuristic when test cases are limited.

The overhead of satisfiability directed implication and learning mainly comes from two places. The first overhead is that the added cubes will slow down the implication process. This overhead can be reduced by an intelligent clause and cube deletion heuristic. The other overhead arises from generating the learned cubes. This overhead is tightly related to the heuristic to generate the satisfiability-induced cover set, which in turn affects the quality of the generated cube. Determining an effective cover set without introducing a large overhead is an interesting research question.

5   Additional Notes

An anonymous reviewer pointed out that two independent in-submission papers [20] and [21] reached results similar to this work. We briefly review them here. In [20], the author proposed model and lemma caching similar to learning in our work, and dependency-directed backtracking (i.e. non-chronological backtracking in this work). However, it does not have a clean way to deal with tautology clauses and empty cubes, which is an important feature of our framework [17]. Moreover, unlike our work (as well as related results in the SAT domain), learning and non-chronological backtracking are not coupled in [20]. In [21], the authors pointed out that "good" solutions should be represented in DNF form and use a separate set of specially marked clauses to perform the same functions as the cubes in our work do. [21] also has the concept of conflict driven learning. However, their work is not resolution and consensus based, therefore require some special treatment for the assignments (i.e. pre-fix closed) to be able to construct valid reasons.

6   Conclusions

In this paper, we introduce the notion of satisfiability directed implication and learning and show how to incorporate it in a solver framework. In our new framework, the QBF solver works on an Augmented CNF database instead of the traditional CNF database. This enables the solver to have an almost symmetric view of both satisfied leaves and conflicting leaves in the search tree. Implications in the new framework not only prune search spaces with no solution, but also prune search spaces with solutions. We have implemented our idea in the new QBF solver Quaffle. Experiments show that Quaffle with satisfiability directed implication and learning can help prune search for many instances.

References

[1]   J. Rintanen. Constructing conditional plans by a theorem prover. *Journal of Artificial Intelligence Research, 10:323-352, 1999*

[2]   M. Sheeran, S. Singh, G. Stålmark, Checking Safety Properties Using Induction and a SAT-Solver, in *Proceedings of FMCAD, 2000*

[3]   A. Biere, A. Cimatti, E. M. Clarke, and Y. Zhu. Symbolic Model Checking without BDDs, In *Tools and Algorithms for the Analysis and Construction of Systems (TACAS), 1999*

[4]   H. Kleine-Büning, M. Karpinski and A. Flögel. Resolution for quantified Boolean formulas. In *Information and Computation, 117(1):12-18, 1995*

[5]   D. A. Plaisted, A. Biere and Y. Zhu. A Satisfiability Procedure for Quantified Boolean Formulae, To appear in, *Discrete Applied Mathematics*

[6]   M. Davis, G. Logemann, and D. Loveland. A machine program for theorem proving. In *Communications of the ACM, 5:394-397, 1962*

[7]   M. Cadoli, M. Schaerf, A. Giovanardi and M. Giovanardi. An algorithm to evaluate quantified Boolean formulae and its experimental evaluation, in *Highlights of Satisfiability Research in the Year 2000, IOS Press, 2000*

[8]   J. Rintanen, Improvements to the Evaluation of Quantified Boolean Formulae, in Proceedings of International Joint Conference on Artificial Intelligence (IJCAI), 1999

[9]   J. Rintanen, Partial implicit unfolding in the Davis-Putnam procedure for quantified Boolean formulae, in *International Conf. on Logic for Programming, Artificial Intelligence and Reasoning (LPAR), 2001*

[10] E. Giunchiglia, M. Narizzano and A. Tacchella,. Qube: a system for Deciding Quantified Boolean Formulas Satisfiability,. In *Proc. of International Joint Conf. on Automated Reasoning (IJCAR), 2001*

[11] E. Giunchiglia, M. Narizzano and A. Tacchella. Backjumping for Quantified Boolean Logic Satisfiability. In *Proc. of International Joint Conf. on Artificial Intelligence (IJCAI), 2001*

[12] João P. Marques-Silva and Karem A. Sakallah, "GRASP: A Search Algorithm for Propositional Satisfiability, In *IEEE Transactions on Computers, vol. 48, 506-521, 1999*

[13] R. Bayard and R. Schrag. Using CSP look-back techniques to solve real-world SAT instances, in *Proc. of the 14th Nat. (US) Conf. on Artificial Intelligence (AAAI), 1997*

[14] H. Zhang. SATO: An efficient propositional prover, In Proc. of the International Conference on Automated Deduction, 1997

[15] M. Moskewicz, C. Madigan, Y. Zhao, L. Zhang, and S. Malik. Engineering an efficient SAT Solver, In *Proceedings of the Design Automation Conference, 2001*

[16] [16] L. Zhang, C. Madigan, M. Moskewicz, S. Malik, Efficient Conflict Driven Learning in a Boolean Satisfiability Solver, in *Proc. of International Conference on Computer Aided Design (ICCAD), 2001*

[17] [17] L. Zhang and S. Malik, Conflict Driven Learning in a Quantified Boolean Satisfiability Solver, Accepted for publication, *International Conference on Computer Aided Design (ICCAD), 2002*

[18] G. Hachtel and F. Somenzi, *Logic Sysntheiss and Verification Algorithms*: Kluwer Academic Publishers, 1996

[19] J. Rintanen's benchmarks are at http://ww.informatik.uni-freiburg.de/~rintanen/qbf.html

[20] R. Letz, Lemma, Model Caching in Decision Procedures for Quantified Boolean Formulas, in Proc. International Conf. on *Automated Reasoning with Analytic Tableaux and Related Methods, 2002*

[21] E. Giunchiglia, M. Narizzano and A. Tacchella, Learning for Quantified Boolean Logic Satisfiability, in *Proc. of the 18th Nat. (US) Conf. on Artificial Intelligence (AAAI), 2002*

Accelerating Random Walks

Wei Wei and Bart Selman

Department of Computer Science, Cornell University
Ithaca, NY 14853

Abstract. In recent years, there has been much research on local search techniques for solving constraint satisfaction problems, including Boolean satisfiability problems. Some of the most successful procedures combine a form of random walk with a greedy bias. These procedures are quite effective in a number of problem domains, for example, constraint-based planning and scheduling, graph coloring, and hard random problem instances. However, in other structured domains, backtrack-style procedures are often more effective. We introduce a technique that leads to significant speedups of random walk style procedures on structured problem domains. Our method identifies long range dependencies among variables in the underlying problem instance. Such dependencies are made explicit by adding new problem constraints. These new constraints can be derived efficiently, and, literally, "accelerate" the Random Walk search process. We provide a formal analysis of our approach and an empirical validation on a recent benchmark collection of hardware verification problems.

1 Introduction

Local search style methods have become a viable alternative to constructive backtrack style methods for solving constraint satisfaction and Boolean satisfiability problems. Local search techniques were originally introduced to find good approximate solutions to optimization problems [14]. In subsequent years, many refinements have been introduced such as simulated annealing and tabu search. More recently, local search methods have also been used for solving decision style problems, in particular Boolean satisfiability (SAT) problems. We will restrict most of our discussion to the SAT domain. However, many of the insights should carry over to the richer domain of general constraint satisfaction problems.

The first local search methods for SAT, such as GSAT, were based on standard greedy hill-climbing search [26, 10, 8], inspired by heuristic repair techniques as studied for optimization [17]. A major improvement upon these algorithms was obtained by building the search around a so-called random walk strategy, which led to WalkSat and related methods [24]. These algorithms combine a Random Walk search strategy with a greedy bias towards assignments with more satisfied clauses. A random walk procedure for satisfiability is a deceptively simple search technique. Such a procedure starts with a random truth assignment. Assuming this randomly guessed assignment does not already satisfy the formula, one selects one of the unsatisfied clauses at random, and flips the truth

P. Van Hentenryck (Ed.): CP 2002, LNCS 2470, pp. 216–232, 2002.

assignment of one of the variables in that clause. This will cause the clause to become satisfied but, of course, one or more other clauses may become unsatisfied. Such flips are repeated until one reaches an assignment that satisfies all clauses or until a pre-defined maximum number of flips is made. This simple strategy can be suprisingly effective. In fact, Papadimitriou [19] showed that a pure (unbiased) random walk on an arbitrary satisfiable 2SAT formula will reach a satisfying assignment in $O(N^2)$ flips (with probably going to 1). More recently, Schoening [22] showed that a series of short unbiased random walks on a 3-SAT problem will find a satisfying assignment in $O(1.334^N)$ flips (assuming such an assignment exists), much better than $O(2^N)$ for an exhaustive check of all assignments.

In the next section, we will discuss how one can introduce a greedy bias in the Random Walk strategy for SAT, leading to the WalkSat algorithm. WalkSat has been shown to be highly effective on a range of problem domains, such as hard random k-SAT problems, logistics planning formulas, graph coloring, and circuit synthesis problems [24, 12]. However, on highly structured formulas, with many dependent variables, as arise in, for example, hardware and software verification, the WalkSat procedure is less effective. In fact, on such domains, backtrack style procedures, such as the Davis-Putnam-Logemann-Loveland (DPLL) [2, 3] procedure are currently more effective. One of the key obstacles in terms of WalkSat's performance on highly structured problems is the fact that a random walk will take at least order N^2 flips to propagate dependencies among variables. On the other hand, unit-propagation, as used in DPLL methods, handles such dependencies in linear time. With thousands or ten of thousands of variables in a formula, this difference in performance puts local search style methods at a distinct practical disadvantage. Moreover, there are also chains of simple ternary clauses that require exponential time for a random walk strategy, yet can be solved in linear time using unit propagation [21].

We will consider such dependency chains in detail and provide a rigorous analysis of the behavior of a pure random walk strategy on such formulas. This analysis suggest a mechanism for dealing more effectively with long range dependencies. In particular, we will show how by introducing certain implied clauses, capturing the long range dependencies, one can significantly "accelerate" random walks on such formulas. We show how the implied clauses can often reduce quadratic convergence time down to near linear, and, in other cases, reduce exponential time convergence of the random walk to polytime convergence. Moreover, the implied clauses can be derived efficiently.

The speedups obtained on the chain-like formulas are encouraging but leave open the question of whether such an approach would also work on practical instances. We therefore validated our approach on a range of highly structured test problems from hardware verification applications [28, 29]. Our experiments show that after adding certain implied dependencies, WalkSat's overall performance improves significantly, even when taking into account the time for computing the dependencies. This work provides at least a partial response to the challenge

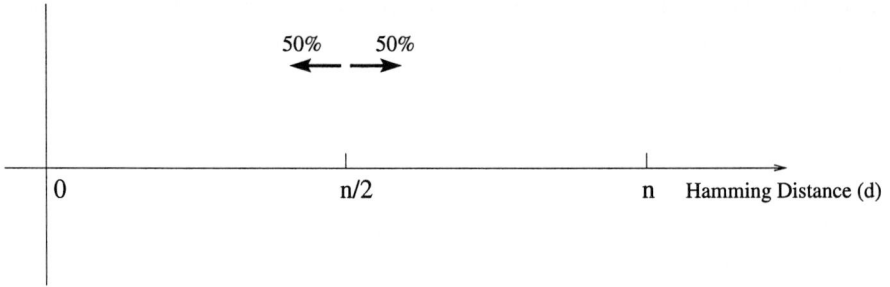

Fig. 1. A Random Walk

in [25] on how to improve local search methods to deal with dependent variables in highly structured SAT problems.

We would also like to stress the benefit from the particular methodology followed in this work. By first analyzing special classes of formulas, which bring out "extreme" behavior of the random walk process, we obtain valuable insights to remedy this behavior. These insights are subsequently used to improve performance on more general formulas. Given the intractability of directly analyzing local search behavior on general classes of formulas, we believe the use of special restricted classes is highly beneficial. There are no doubt many other forms of problem structure that could be studied this way.

The paper is structured as follows. In section 2, we first review Random Walk strategies — biased and unbiased — for SAT. In section 3, we give results on special classes of chain formulas and provide a formal analysis. In section 4, we give an empirical evaluation of our approach. Section 5 contains conclusions and future directions.

2   Random Walk Strategies for SAT

To gain some further insight into the behavior of random walk strategies for SAT, let us briefly consider the very elegant argument introduced by Papadimitriou showing polytime behavior on 2SAT. Consider a satisfiable 2SAT formula F on N variables. Let T denote a satisfying assignment of F. The random walk procedure starts with a random truth assignment, T'. On average, this truth assignment will differ from T on the assignment of $N/2$ letters. Now, consider an unsatisfied clause in F (if no such clause exists, then T' is a satisfying assignment). Without loss of generality, we assume that the unsatisfied clause is of the form $(a \vee \neg b)$. Since this clause is unsatisfied, T' must assign both literals in the clause to False (which means that a is assigned False and b True). Also, the satisfying assignment T is such that at least one of the literals in the clause is assigned to True. Now, randomly select a variable in the clause and flip its truth value in T'. Since we have only two variables in the clause, we have at least a 50% chance of selecting the variable corresponding to the literal set to True in T. (Note that if T satisfied exactly one literal in the clause, we will select that literal with 0.5 probability. If T satisfies both literals, we select the "right" literal with probability 1.0.) It follows that with at least 50% chance, the Hamming distance of our new truth assignment to T will be reduced by 1, and with at most 50% chance, we will have picked the wrong variable and will have increased the Hamming distance to the satisfying assignment. Papadimitriou now appeals to a basic result in the theory of random walks. Consider a one dimensional "random walker" which starts at a given location and takes L steps, where each step is either one unit to the left or one unit to the right, each with probability 0.5 (also called a "drunkards walk"). It can be shown that after L^2 steps, such a walker will on average travel a distance of L units from its starting point. Given that the random walk starts a distance $N/2$ from the satisfying truth assignment T, after order N^2 steps, the walk will hit a satisfying assignment, with probability going to one. Note that although the walk may at first wander away from the satisfying assignment, it will "bounce off" the reflecting barrier at distance N. Also, our analysis is worst-case, *i.e.*, it holds for *any* satisfiable 2SAT formula.

It is instructive to consider what happens on a 3SAT formula, *i.e.*, a conjunctive normal form formula with 3 literals per clauses. In this case, when flipping a variable selected at random from an unsatisfied clause, we may only have 1/3 chance of fixing the "correct" variable (assuming our satisfying assignment satisfies exactly one literal in each clause). This leads to a random walk heavily biased away from the solution under consideration. The theory of random walks tells us that reaching the satisfying assignment under such a bias would take an exponential number of flips. And, in fact, in practice we indeed see that a pure random walk on a hard random 3SAT formula performs very poorly.

However, we can try to counter this "negative" bias by considering the gradient in the overall objective function we are trying to minimimize. The idea is that the gradient may provide the random walk with some additional information "pointing" towards the solution, and thus towards the right variable to flip. In SAT, we want to minimize is the number of unsatisfied clauses. So, in selecting the variable to flip in an unsatisfied clause, we can bias our selection towards a variable that leads to the greatest decrease in the overall number of unsatisfied clauses. Introducing a bias of this form leads us to the WalkSat algorithm and its variants [24, 15].

For reasons of efficiency, WalkSat uses a bias defined by the so-called "break value" of a variable. Given a formula and a truth assignment T, the break value of a variable, x, is defined by the number of clauses that are satisfied by T but become unsatisfied (are "broken") when the truth value of x is changed. In practice, this bias is a good measure of the overall change in number of unsatisfied clauses when x is "flipped".

WalkSat boosts its search by interleaving purely random walk moves and greedily biased moves. The number of random walk moves is controlled by a parameter p. That is, with probability p, we select a random variable from the chosen unsatisfied clause, and with probability $1 - p$, we select a variable in the

Procedure RW
repeat
    c:= an unsatisfied clause chosen at random
    x:= a variable in c chosen at random
    flip the value of x;
until a satisfying assignment is found.

Procedure RWF
repeat
    c:= an unsatisfied clause chosen at random
    if there exists a variable x in c with break value $= 0$
        flip the value of x (freebie move)
    else
        x:= a variable in c chosen at random from c;
        flip the value of x
until a satisfying assignment is found.

Procedure WalkSat
repeat
    c:= an unsatisfied clause chosen at random
    if there exists a variable x in c with break value $= 0$
        flip the value of x (freebie move)
    else
        with probability p
            x:= a variable in c chosen at random;
            flip the value of x
        with probability (1-p)
            x:= a variable in c with smallest break value
            flip the value of x
until a satisfying assignment is found.

Fig. 2. The main loop of the Random Walk (RW), Random Walk with freebie (RWF), and WalkSat procedures

clause with the minimal break value (ties are broken randomly). In practice, one can often identify a (near) optimal value for p for a given class of formulas. (For example, $p = 0.55$ for hard random 3SAT formulas, and $p = 0.3$ for planning problems.)

As a final refinement, WalkSat incorporates one other important feature to speed up its search: when there is a variable in the randomly selected unsatisfied clauses with break value zero, that variable is flipped immediately. Note that such a flip will increase the total number of satisfied clauses by at least one. These flips are called "freebies".

In order to study the introduction of a greedy bias in its minimal form, we will also consider a Random Walk with just "freebie" moves added. This is equivalent to running WalkSat with noise parameter $p = 1.0$. Figure 2 gives the

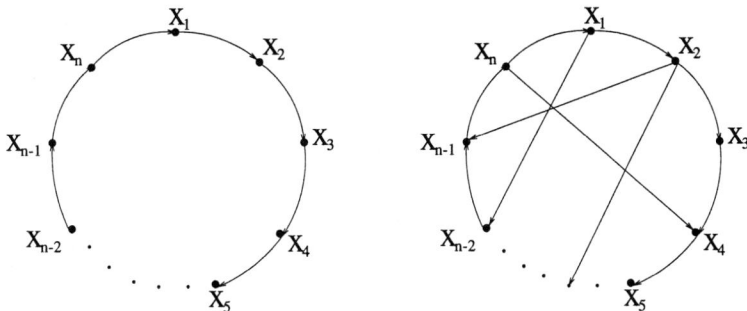

Fig. 3. The left panel shows a graph of a binary chain formula, F_{2chain} on n variables. The right panel shows the formula after adding a number of random implied clauses

main loop of the Random Walk (RW) procedure, the Random Walk with freebie (RWF) procedure, and the WalkSat procedure.[1]

3   Chain Formulas and Theoretical Underpinning

In order to obtain a good understanding of the behavior of pure Random Walk and biased Random Walk strategies on SAT instances, we now consider several families of formulas which demonstrate extreme properties of random walk style algorithms. We elucidate these properties by introducing long chains of dependencies between variables. We consider 2SAT and 3SAT problems. Our 3SAT formulas are motivated by formulas introduced by Prestwich [21].

3.1   Binary Chains

In the previous section, we derived a quadratic upperbound for the number of flips for solving a 2SAT problem using a unbiased Random Walk strategy. In practice, on for example, randomly generated 2SAT problems, Random Walk may take far fewer than N^2 flips. How would one construct a 2CNF formula that exhibits the worst case quadratic behavior? To obtain such a formula we need to create a truly unbiased random walk. (A truly unbiased random walk takes $\Theta(N^2)$ flips to travel a distance N.) As we argued above, when flipping a random variable in a binary clause, we have at least 50% chance of "fixing" the correct variable (on a path to a satisfying assignment). We need to ensure that we have exactly 50% chance of selecting the right variable to flip. We do this by constructing a formula such that a satisfying assignment of the formula satisfies exactly one literal (a variable or its negation) in each clause.

---

[1]   The WalkSat program [35] performs RW when option **-random** is selected. When selecting option **-noise 100 100** (*i.e.*, p = 1.0), we obtain RWF.

This can be achieved by considering the following 2CNF formula, F_{2chain}, consisting of a chain of logical implications: $(x_1 \rightarrow x_2) \wedge (x_2 \rightarrow x_3) \wedge \ldots \wedge (x_N \rightarrow x_1)$. See Figure 3, left panel. This formula has two assignments, namely the all True assignment and the all False assignment. Each clause is of the form $\neg x_i \vee x_{i+1}$). So, each of the two satisfying assignment satisfies exactly one literal in each clause. We therefore obtain a truly unbiased random walk, and we obtain the following result.

Theorem 1. *The RW procedure takes $\Theta(N^2)$ to find a satisfying assignment of F_{2chain}.*

In contrast, DPLL's unit propagation mechanism finds an assignment for F_{2chain} in linear time. Moreover, our experiments show that adding a greedy bias to our random walk does not not help in this case: both the RWF and the WalkSat procedure take $\Theta(N^2)$ flips to reach a satisfying assignment on these formulas.[2]

3.2   Speeding Up Random Walks on Binary Chains

Given the difference in performance between DPLL and random walk style algorithms on the 2SAT chain formulas, the question becomes whether we can somehow speed-up the random walk process on such formulas to perform closer to DPLL.

Intuitively, the random walk process needs to line up the truth values along the chain, but can only do so by literally "wandering" back and forth based on local inconsistencies detected in the chain. One possible remedy is to add clauses that capture longer range dependencies between variables more directly.

We therefore consider adding clauses of the form $x_i \rightarrow x_j$, with i and $j \in \{1, 2, \cdots, n\}$, chosen uniformly at random. A binary chain with redundancy (BCR) formula is composed of all clauses from binary chain F_{2chain} and a fraction of the redundant clauses, generated independently at random. Since any redundant clause is implied by the binary chain, it follows that any BCR formula is equivalent to the chain itself. We define the redundancy rate of a BCR formula as the number of redundant clauses divided by the length of its base binary chain. The right hand side panel of Figure 3 shows a binary chain formula with added random redundancies.[3]

---

[2]   In this paper, we derive rigorous results for the unbiased random walk procedure. Our results for biased random walk strategies are empirical. The reason for this is that the tools for a rigorous analysis of greedy local search methods are generally too weak to obtain meaningful upper- and lower-bounds on run time, as is apparent from the relative paucity of rigorous run time results for methods such as simulated annealing and tabu search (expect for general convergence results).

[3]   For readers familiar with the recent work by Watts and Strogatz [32] on 'small world' graphs, we note the resemblence of our 2SAT chain with redundancies and small world graphs. In fact, the small world topology where long range and short range interactions are combined provided an impetus for this work. We are currently exploring further connections to computational properties of small world graphs. See also [13, 31].

Perhaps somewhat suprisingly, the implied "long-range" clauses do not make any difference for the performance of an unbiased random walk. The reason for this is that the underlying random walk remains completely balanced (*i.e.*, 50% chance of going in either direction). This follows from the fact that each of the added clauses again has exactly one literal satisfied in the two satisfying assignments.

However, the situation changes dramatically for the biased random walk case. The right panel of Figure 4 gives the scaling for RWF for different levels of redundancies. We see that the scaling improves dramatically with increased levels of implied long range clauses. More specifically, with a redundancy rate of 0, we have a scaling of $\Theta(N^2)$, wich improves to $\Theta(N^{1.2})$ for a redundancy rate of 2. (Regression fits with MatLab.) The right panel shows that we get a further improvement when using WalkSat. WalkSat scales as $\Theta(N^{1.1})$ (redundancy rate of 2). So, we note that the performance of WalkSat becomes quite close to that of unit propagation. Interestingly, when we further increase the level of implied clauses, the performance of biased random walk procedures starts to decrease again. See Figure 5. We will encounter a similar phenomenon when considering our benchmark problems from hardware verification.

The clauses added to the binary chain can be understood as results of a series of resolutions. Therefore, we have shown for this basic structure — which brings out the worst case behavior in random walks on 2SAT problems — that the added long distance resolvents, coupled with a greedy bias in the local search algorithm, effectively reduces the run time required to find a solution. Of course, for solving a single 2SAT chain formula in isolation, the process of adding long range resolvents would not make much sense, since the formulas are easily solvable using just unit-propagation. However, if such chains are embedded in much larger formulas, then speeding up the random walk process can be useful because it may speed up the overall solution process by propagating dependency information much more quickly. In fact, we will see in our experimental validation section that this is indeed the case on large-scale practical formulas from the hardware verification domain.

3.3   Ternary Chains

We now consider another class of formulas, involving ternary clauses. As discussed in Section 2, on ternary clauses the Random Walk strategy becomes biased away from the solution, at least in the worst case. When faced with such a bias, a Random Walk would require an exponential number of flips to reach a satisfying assignment. This effect is quite dramatic. For example, in Figure 1, a random walk with just a 0.1% bias in the wrong direction, i.e., 49.9% to the left and 50.1% to the right will take exponential time to reach the origin. We will give a concrete family of chain-like formulas that exhibit such exponential worst-case behavior. However, on the positive side, we will also show how a quite similar family of 3CNF formulas exhibits polynomial time behavior. *By considering the differences between the intractable and the tractable structures, we obtain new insights into methods for speeding up random walk techniques.* To the best of our

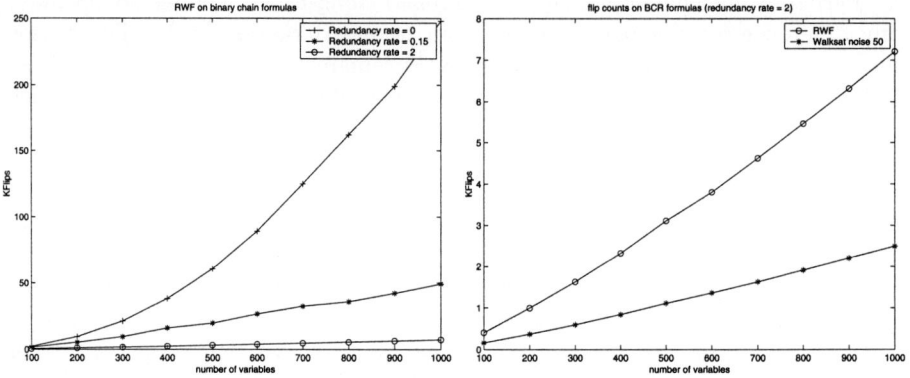

Fig. 4. The left panel shows the number of flips vs. the number of variables in binary chains of different sizes. The right panel shows the curves for RWF and WalkSat algorithms when the redundancy rate is set at 2

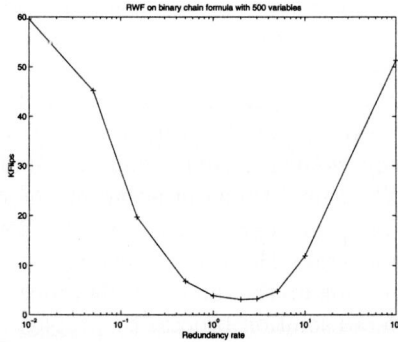

Fig. 5. This figure shows the number of flips RWF makes on the 500-variable binary chain formulas with different redundancy rates

knowledge, our results are the first rigorous results identifying a tractable class of 3CNF problems for a random walk style local search method.

In our analysis, we consider formulas inspired by ternary chain formulas first introduced by Prestwich [21]. Prestwich provided empirical results on such formulas for the WalkSat procedure. Our analysis extends his observations, and provides the first rigorous proofs for the convergence rates of unbiased Random Walk on these formulas. Our results also show that on these formulas the difference between biased and unbiased walks is minimal.

Let $low(i)$ be a function that maps i, with $3 \le i \le n$, into an integer in the range from 1 to $i - 2$. We consider ternary chain formulas, $F_{3chain,low(i)}$, on variables x_1 through x_n consisting of a conjunction of the following clauses:

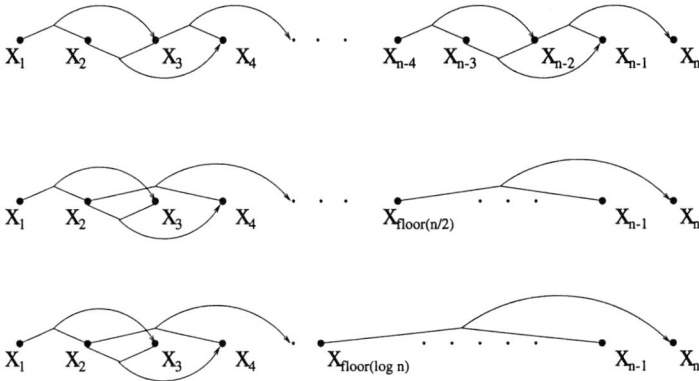

Fig. 6. These three diagrams illustrate our ternary chain formulas. The top panel shows $F_{3chain,i-2}$ which has local links in the form of $x_{i-2} \wedge x_{i-1} \to x_i$ only. The middle panel gives $F_{3chain,\lfloor \frac{i}{2} \rfloor}$ which has longer links of the form $x_{\lfloor \frac{i}{2} \rfloor} \wedge x_{i-1} \to x_i$. The bottom panel shows $F_{3chain,\lfloor \log i \rfloor}$ with even longer links of the form of $x_{\lfloor \log i \rfloor} \wedge x_{i-1} \to x_i$

$$x_1$$
$$x_2$$
$$x_1 \wedge x_2 \to x_3$$
$$\vdots$$
$$x_{low(i)} \wedge x_{i-1} \to x_i$$
$$\vdots$$
$$x_{low(n)} \wedge x_{n-1} \to x_n$$

Depending on our choice of the function $low(i)$, we obtain different classes of formulas. For example, with $low(i) = i - 2$, we get the formula

$$x_1 \wedge x_2 \wedge (x_1 \wedge x_2 \to x_3) \wedge (x_2 \wedge x_3 \to x_4) \wedge \ldots \wedge (x_{n-2} \wedge x_{n-1} \to x_n).$$

Note that the function $low(i)$ determines how the implications in the chain are linked together. We will consider three different ways of linking the left hand side variable in each implication with the earlier variables in the chain. Our choices are:

a) Short range connections: $low(i) = i - 2$.
b) Medium range connections: $low(i) = \lfloor \frac{i}{2} \rfloor$.
c) Long range connections: $low(i) = \lfloor \log i \rfloor$.

Figure 6 illustrates each of these formula classes. We refer to these classes of formulas by given $low(i)$ as a subscript. We thus obtain the classes $F_{3chain,i-2}$, $F_{3chain,\lfloor \frac{i}{2} \rfloor}$, and $F_{3chain,\lfloor \log i \rfloor}$.

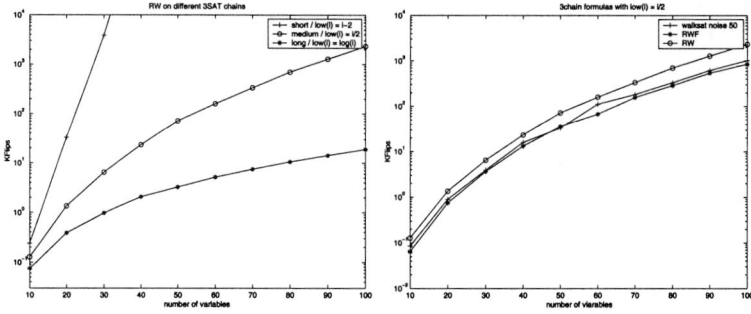

Fig. 7. RW on tenary chains (left). RW, RWF, and WalkSat on ternary chain with low$(i)= \lfloor \frac{i}{2} \rfloor$ (right)

It is clear that each of our ternary chain formulas is trivially solvable by unit propagation since the effect of the first two unit clauses x_1 and x_2 directly propagates through the chain of implications. The only satisfying assignment is the all True assignment.[4] However, it is far from clear how long a Random Walk would take to find the satisfying assignment, when starting from a random initial assignment. This brings us to our main formal results.

We found that the convergence rate of RW differs dramatically between the three formula classes, *ranging from exponential on $F_{3chain,i-2}$ (short range connections), to quasi-polynomial on $F_{3chain,\lfloor \frac{i}{2} \rfloor}$ (medium range connections), and finally to polynomial on $F_{3chain,\lfloor \log i \rfloor}$ (long range connections).*

The tractable cases are especially encouraging, since it has been widely believed that an unbiased RW can hardly solve any 3-SAT formulas in less than exponential time (unless such formulas have an exponential number of assignments). Consider RW on any of our ternary chain formulas after selecting an unsatisfied clause. The procedure now has only a probability of 1/3 of selecting the right variable to fix. To see this, consider a clause in one of our chain formulas that is not satisfied by the current truth assignment, e.g., $x_{low(i)} \wedge x_{i-1} \rightarrow x_i$. This means that the current truth assignment must assign $x_{low(i)}$ and x_{i-1} to True and x_i to False. The "correct" flip to make would be to assign x_i to True. However, with probability 2/3, the RW procedure will flip either $x_{low(i)}$ or x_{i-1} to False. Thus, strongly biasing the walk away from the unique all True solution. This general argument might lead one to conclude that RW should take exponential time on all three of our ternary chain formula classes. However, a much more refined analysis, which also takes into account how variables are shared among clauses and the order in which the clauses become satisfied/unsatisfied during the random walk, shows that on the formulas with medium and long

---

[4] One could argue that, in practice, a local search algorithm would never encounter such a formula, since one generally removes unit clauses before running a local search procedure. However, note that the forced setting of x_1 and x_2 to True could be a hidden consequence of another set of non-unit clauses.

range connections the RW procedure converges much more quickly than one would expect.

Let $f(s)$ denote the random variable that represents the number of flips RW takes before reaching a satisfying assignment when starting from an initial (arbitrary) assignment s. We want to determine the expected value of $f(s)$, *i.e.*, $\mathbf{E}(f(s))$, given any initial starting assignment s.

The following theorems summarize our main formal results.

Theorem 2. *Given a ternary chain formula $F_{3chain,i-2}$, starting at a random assignment s, the expected value of $f(s)$, the number of flips to reach a satisfying truth assignment, scales exponentially in n.*

Theorem 3. *Given a ternary chain formula $F_{3chain,low(i)}$ and let s be an arbitrary truth assignment, we have for the expected number of flips for the RW procedure:*

a) $\mathbf{E}(f(s)) = O(n \cdot n^{\log n})$, *for low(i)= $\lfloor \frac{i}{2} \rfloor$*
b) $\mathbf{E}(f(s)) = O(n^2 \cdot (\log n)^2)$, *for low(i)= $\lfloor \log i \rfloor$.*

The proofs of these theorems require the solution of a series of recurrence relations that characterize the expected time of the random walk process. As noted above, instead of analyzing a single random walk, the random walk process is decomposed into separate subsequences depending on the clauses and variables involved. The proofs are rather involved and are omitted here because of space limitations. The interested reader is referred to the long version of the paper, see www.cs.cornell.edu/home/selman/weiwei.pdf.

Theorems 2 and 3 provide further evidence that links capturing longer range dependencies among variables can dramatically accelerate the convergence of RW procedures, just as we saw for biased RW on the binary chain formulas. The left panel in Figure 7 empirically illustrates our scaling results. Note the logarithmic vertical scale. We see clear exponential scaling for the chain formulas with only short range connections. The other graphs curve down, indicating better than exponential scaling, with the best scaling for the long range dependency links (polynomial). Finally, in the right panel of the figure, we consider the effect of adding a greedy bias in the RW. We consider the formulas with medium range dependency links. We see some improvement for RWF and WalkSat over RW, but no dramatic difference in scaling. So, the range of dependency links (short, medium, or long) in the 3chain formulas is the main factor in determining the scaling both for both biased and unbiased random walks.

4   Empirical Results on Practical Problem Instances

We have shown both theoretically and empirically that the performance of the WalkSat procedure improves when long range connections are added to our chain formulas. Given that chains of dependent variables commonly occur in practical problem instances, we hypothesize that similar performance improvements can be obtained on real-world formulas. In this section, we test this hypothesis on a suite of practical problem instances.

In order to apply our technique to a real-world formula, however, we need to be able to discover the underlying variable dependencies and add long-distance links to the corresponding implication graph. Quite fortunately, Brafman's recent 2-Simplify method [5] looks exactly for such long range dependencies. The procedure improves the performance of SAT solvers by simplifying propositional formulas. More specifically, 2-Simplify constructs a binary implication graph and adds new clauses (links) that are based on the transitive closure of existing dependencies. (In current work, we are extending this process by adding links implied by ternary clause chains.)

We built our preprocessor upon Brafman's implementation. More precisely, his code simplifies a formula in the following steps. First, it constructs an implication graph from binary clauses, and collapses strongly connected components that exist in this graph. Second, it generates the transitive closure from existing links in the graph, which enables the algorithm to deduce some literals through binary resolution and hyper-resolution, and remove the assigned variables from the graph. Third, it removes all transitive redundant links to keep the number of edges in the graph minimal. Finally, the graph is translated back into binary clauses. Note that Brafman's procedure eliminates all the transitively redundant links in the third step. The procedure was designed mainly for speeding up DPLL style procedures, which can easily recover the transitive closure dependencies via unit propagation. However, based on our earlier results on the chain formulas, to speed up local search methods, we need to keep exactly those implied clauses that capture long range dependencies. That is, WalkSat may actually exhibit better performance when working on formulas with a fraction of redundant long range links kept in place. To implement this strategy, we modified the 2-Simplify procedure to remove implied transitive links from the transitive closure graph in a probabilistic manner. More specifically, we introduce a *redundancy parameter*, α, which gives the probability that we keep a redundant link. So, in the third step of the 2-Simplify procedure, we step through the redundant links and removes each one with probability $1 - \alpha$.

We will now show that this rather straightforward approach makes a tremendous difference in WalkSat's ability to find a satisfying truth assignment on structured benchmark problems. (Of course, given our earlier results on the chain formulas, this is not completely unexpected.) We ran WalkSat on the SAT-1.0 benchmarks used recently by Velev [28, 29] to evaluate a collection of 28 state-of-the-art SAT solvers. The suite consists of 100 formulas encoding verification problems for superscalar microprocessors. The instances have been shown to be challenging for both local search methods and DPLL procedures [29]. Moreover, they represent an important practical application. From Velev's results and to the best of our knowledge, no local search methods is able to solve more than 65 instances in under 40 seconds of CPU time per instance.

Our experiments were performed on a 600 MHz Pentium II processor running Linux. See Table 4 for our results. The first row shows the results for the original

Table 1. Number of instances WalkSat (noise $= 50$) solved (averaged over 10 runs) on Velev benchmark [28, 29] (100 instances total). Prepocessing using 2-Simplify; α is the redundancy level

Formulas	< 40 sec	< 400 sec	< 4000 sec
$\alpha = 0.0$	15	26	42
$\alpha = 0.2$	**85**	**98**	**100**
$\alpha = 1.0$	13	33	64

formulas in SSS-SAT-1.0 suite after simplification using Brafman's preprocessor ($\alpha = 0.0$). The second row shows the results when a fraction of redundant clauses is added ($\alpha = 0.2$). (The preprocessing time is included in the total run time.)

It is clear from the table that WalkSat's performance improves dramatically when adding a fraction of redundant clauses: solving 85 instances within 40 seconds with 20% redundancy, compared to just 15 with no redundancy; moreover, 98 instances can now be solved in under 400 seconds, compared to 26 without redundancies. In future work, we will provide a comparison with the performance on the original formulas without any preprocessing. Brafman's current simplifier, unfortunately, leads to theories that are logically slightly weaker than the original theory. This makes a comparison with the performance on the original formulas difficult. Nevertheless, our experiments in Table 4 clearly demonstrate the benefit of adding long range dependencies.

We observed a clear optimal value for the rate of redundancy α. In particular, adding all implied transitivity constraints can be harmful. This is apparent from the third row in Table 4. With $\alpha = 1.0$, we add all redundant transitivity constraints uncovered by the simplifier. Clearly, adding only a randomly selected fraction of implied transitivity constraints (20% in this case) gives us much better performance. Figure 8 shows the number of flips until solution and the run time of the WalkSat algorithm for different α values. These results are consistent with our observations for adding random long range links to our binary chain formula. In that setting, there was also a clear optimal level of redundancy for the biased random walk approach. See Figure 5.

Cha and Iwama [6] also studied the effect of adding clauses during the local search process. They focus on clauses that are resolvents of the clauses unsatisfied at local minima, and their randomly selected neighbors. This meant that the added clauses captured mainly short range information. Our results suggest that long range dependencies may be more important to uncover.

In summary, our experiments show that the insights obtained from our study of the chain formulas can be used to speed up local search methods on SAT problems from practical applications. In particular, we found a clear practical benefit of adding implied clauses that capture certain long range variable dependencies and structure in the formulas. Interestingly, to make this approach work one has to tune the level of redundancy added to the formulas. Somewhat surprisingly,

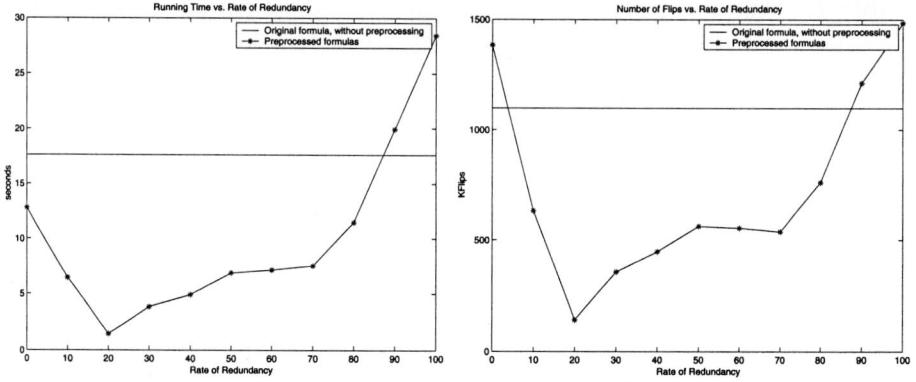

Fig. 8. Different levels of redundancy on instance `dlx2_cc_bug01.cnf` from SAT-1.0 suite [28]. Results are averaged over 100 runs. Noise level WalkSAT set at 50

the total number of added clauses was only about 4% of the original number of clauses.

5   Conclusions

We have provided theoretical and empirical results showing how one can speed up random walk style local search methods. The key idea is to introduce constraints that capture long range dependencies. Our formal analysis for unbiased random walks on ternary chain formulas shows how the performance of RW varies from exponential to polynomial depending on the range of the dependency links, with long range links leading to a tractable sub-case. We believe this is the first tractable 3CNF class identified for unbiased random walks. On the binary chain formulas, we saw how such constraints can also improve the performance of biased random walks. On the binary chains with added implied clauses, biased random walks become almost as effective as unit propagation used in DPLL procedures. Finally, we showed how on practical instances based on hardware verification problems adding a fraction of long range dependencies significantly improves the performance of WalkSat on such formulas.

Our results so far show the promise of our technique for speeding up local search methods on structured benchmarks domains. However, we believe that there is still much room for further improvements. In particular, it should be possible to develop formula preprocessors that uncover other types of dependencies between variables that may be useful for further accelerating random walks. Again, a methodology guided by an analysis of formulas where biased and unbiased random walks exhibit extreme behavior should be helpful.

Acknowledgements

We thank Carla Gomes and Henry Kautz for useful discussions. This research was supported with grants from AFOSR, DARPA, NSF, and the Alfred P. Sloan Foundation.

References

[1] F. Bacchus and P. van Beek. On the Conversion between Non-Binary and Binary Constraint Satisfaction Problems. In *Proceedings of AAAI-98*, pages 311-318, 1998.

[2] M. Davis and H. Putnam. A Computing Procedure for Quantification Theory. *Journal of the ACM*, 7: 201-205, 1960.

[3] M. Davis, G. Logemann, and D. Loveland. A Machine Program for Theorem-Proving. *Communications of the ACM*, 5:394-397, 1962.

[4] B. Bonet and H. Geffner. Planning as Heuristic Search. *Artificial Intelligence, Special issue on Heuristic Search*. Vol 129 (1-2) 2001.

[5] R. I. Brafman. A Simplifier for Propositional Formulas with Many Binary Clauses, In *Proceedings IJCAI-2001*, Seattle, WA, pages 515-520, 2001.

[6] B. Cha and K. Iwama. Adding New Clauses for Faster Local Search. In *Proceedings AAAI-96*, pages 332-337, 1996.

[7] L. Drake, A. Frisch, and T. Walsh. Adding resolution to the DPLL procedure for Satisfiability. In *Proceedings of SAT2002*, pages 122-129, 2002.

[8] I. Gent and T. Walsh. An Empirical Analysis of Search in GSAT. *JAIR*, 1993.

[9] C. P. Gomes, B. Selman, N. Crator, and H. Kautz. Heavy-Tailed Phenomenia in Satisfiability and Constraint Satisfication Problems. *Journal of Automated Reasoning*, Vol 24, No 1-2, February 2000.

[10] J. Gu. Efficient Local Search for Very Large-Scale Satisfiability Problems. *SIGART Bulletin* 3(1): 8-12, 1992.

[11] E. A. Hirsch and A. Kojevnikov. Solving Boolean Satisfiability Using Local Search Guided by Unit Clause Elimination. In Proc. of CP-2001, 2001.

[12] H. Kautz and B. Selman. Unifying SAT-based and Graph-based Planning. In *Proceedings of IJCAI-99*, Stockholm, 1999.

[13] J. Kleinberg. Navigation in a small-world. *Nature*, **406**, 2000.

[14] S. Lin and B. W. Kernighan. An Effective Heuristic Algorithm for the Traveling-Salesman Problem. *Operations Research*, Vol. 21, 2, pages 498–516, 1973.

[15] D. A. McAllester, B. Selman, and H. A. Kautz. Evidence for Invariants in Local Search. In *Proceedings of AAAI-97*, pages 321-326, 1997.

[16] P. Morris. Breakout method for escaping from local minima. *Proc. AAAI-93*, Washington, DC (1993).

[17] S. Minton, M. D. Johnson, A. B. Philips, and P. Laird. Solving Large-Scale Constraint Satisfaction and Scheduling Problems Using a Heuristic Repair Methods. *Artificial Intelligence* 58, pages 161-205, 1990.

[18] M. W. Moskewicz, C. F. Madigan, Y. Zhao, L. Zhang, and S. Malik. Engineering a Highly Efficient SAT Solver. *38th Design Autom. Conference (DAC 01)*, 2001.

[19] C. H. Papadimitriou. On Selecting a Satisfying Truth Assignment. In *Proceedings of the Conference on the Foundations of Computer Science*, pages 163-169, 1991.

[20] A. J. Parkes and J. P. Walser. Tuning Local Search for Satisfiability Testing. In *Proc. AAAI-96*, 1996.

[21] S. Prestwich. SAT Problems with Chains of Dependent Variables. Unpublished technical note, 2001.

[22] U. Schoening. A Probabilistic Algorithm for k-SAT and Constraint Satisfaction Problems. In *Proceeedings of FOCS*, 1999.

[23] D. Schuurmans, F. Southey, and R. C. Holte. The Exponential Subgradient Algorithm for Heuristic Boolean Programming. In *Proc. IJCAI-2001*, 2001.

[24] B. Selman, H. Kautz, and B. Cohen. Local Search Strategies for Satisfiability Testing. *2nd DIMACS Challenge on Cliques, Coloring and Satisfiability*, 1994.

[25] B. Selman, H. Kautz, and D. McAllester. Ten Challenges in Propositional Reasoning and Search. In *Proceedings IJCAI-97*, 1997.

[26] B. Selman, H. J. Levesque, and D. G. Mitchell. A New Method for Solving Hard Satisfiability Problems. In *Proceedings AAAI-92*, pages 440-446, 1992.

[27] T. Suyama, M. Yokoo, and A. Nagoya. Solving Satisfiability Problems on FPGAs Using Experimental Unit Propagation. In *Proceedings of CP-99*, 1999.

[28] M. N. Velev. Benchmark suites SSS-SAT-1.0, SAT-1.0, October 2000. http://www.ece.cmu.edu/~mvelev

[29] M. N. Velev, and R. E. Bryant. Effective Use of Boolean Satisfiability Procedures in the Formal Verification of Superscalar and VLIW Microprocessors. *38th Design Automation Conference (DAC '01)*, June 2001, pp. 226-231.

[30] J. P. Walser, R. Iyer and N. Venkatasubramanyan.An Integer Local Search Method with Application to Capacitated Production Planning. In *Proceedings of AAAI-98*, Madison, WI, 1998.

[31] T. Walsh. Search in a Small World. In *Proceedings of IJCAI-99*, 1999.

[32] D. J. Watts and S. Strogatz. Collective dynamics of 'small-world' networks. *Nature*, **393**, 440-442 (1998).

[33] Z. Wu and B. W. Wah. An Efficient Global-Search Strategy in Discrete Lagrangian Methods for Solving Hard Satisfiability Problems. *Proc. AAAI-2000*, 2000.

[34] H. Zhang. SATO: An Efficient Propositional Prover. *International Conference on Automated Deduction (CADE 97)*, LNAI 1249, Springer-Verlag, 1997.

[35] Available at http://www.cs.washington.edu/homes/kautz/walksat/

Scaling and Probabilistic Smoothing: Efficient Dynamic Local Search for SAT

Frank Hutter, Dave A. D. Tompkins, and Holger H. Hoos*

Department of Computer Science, University of British Columbia
Vancouver, B. C., V6T 1Z4, Canada
mail@fhutter.de
{davet,hoos}@cs.ubc.ca
http://www.cs.ubc.ca/labs/beta

Abstract. In this paper, we study the approach of dynamic local search for the SAT problem. We focus on the recent and promising Exponentiated Sub-Gradient (ESG) algorithm, and examine the factors determining the time complexity of its search steps. Based on the insights gained from our analysis, we developed Scaling and Probabilistic Smoothing (SAPS), an efficient SAT algorithm that is conceptually closely related to ESG. We also introduce a reactive version of SAPS (RSAPS) that adaptively tunes one of the algorithm's important parameters. We show that for a broad range of standard benchmark problems for SAT, SAPS and RSAPS achieve significantly better performance than both ESG and the state-of-the-art WalkSAT variant, Novelty$^+$.

1   Introduction and Background

The Satisfiability problem (SAT) is an important subject of study in many areas of computer science. Since SAT is $\mathcal{NP}$-complete, there is little hope to develop a complete algorithm that scales well on all types of problem instances; however, fast algorithms are needed to solve big problems from various domains, including prominent AI problems such as planning [7] and constraint satisfaction [2]. Throughout this paper, we focus on the model finding variant of SAT: Given a propositional formula the propositional variables in F under which F becomes true. As with most other work on SAT algorithms, we consider only propositional formulae in conjunctive normal form (CNF), *i.e.*, formulae of the form $F = \bigwedge_i \bigvee_j l_{ij}$, where each l_{ij} is a propositional variable or its negation. The l_{ij} are called *literals*, while the disjunctions $\bigvee_j l_{ij}$ are called *clauses* of F.

Some of the best known methods for solving SAT are Stochastic Local Search (SLS) algorithms; these are typically incomplete, *i.e.*, they cannot determine with certainty that a given formula is unsatisfiable, but they often find models of satisfiable formulae surprisingly effectively [5]. Although SLS algorithms for SAT differ in their implementation details, the general search strategy is mostly the same [2]. Starting from an initial, complete assignment of truth values to

---

* Corresponding author

P. Van Hentenryck (Ed.): CP 2002, LNCS 2470, pp. 233–248, 2002.
© Springer-Verlag Berlin Heidelberg 2002

all variables in the given formula F, in each search step, the truth assignment of one variable is changed from true to false or vice versa; this type of search step is also called a *variable flip*. Since the models of F are characterised by the fact that they leave none of F's clauses unsatisfied, variable flips are typically performed with the purpose of minimising an objective function that maps any variable assignment x to the number of clauses unsatisfied under x.

Since the introduction of GSAT [14], a simple best-improvement search algorithm for SAT, much research has been conducted in this area. Major performance improvements were achieved by the usage of noise strategies [12] and the development of the WalkSAT architecture [13]. In each search step, WalkSAT algorithms first choose a currently unsatisfied clause and then flip a variable occurring in this clause. Extensive experiments resulted in the introduction of sophisticated schemes for selecting the variable to be flipped, including the well-known Novelty and R-Novelty algorithms [8]. Further insight into the nature and theoretical properties of these algorithms motivated the more recent Novelty[+] variant [3], which is amongst the state-of-the-art algorithms for SAT.

In parallel to the development of more refined versions of randomised iterative improvement strategies like WalkSAT, another SLS method has become increasingly popular in SAT solving. This method is based on the idea of modifying the evaluation function in order to prevent the search from getting stuck in local minima or other attractive non-solution areas of the underlying search space. We call this approach Dynamic Local Search (DLS). DLS strategies for SAT typically associate weights with the clauses of the given formula, which are modified during the search process. These algorithms then try to minimise the total weight rather than the number of the unsatisfied clauses. GSAT with clause weighting [12] was one of the first algorithms based on this idea, although it changes weights only in connection with restarting the search process. Many variants of this scheme have been proposed: Frank [1] uses a DLS weighting scheme that is updated every time a variable is flipped. Morris' Breakout Method [9] simply adds one to the weight of every unsatisfied clause whenever a local minimum is encountered. The Discrete Lagrangian Method (DLM) [15] is based on a tabu search procedure and uses a similar, but slightly more complicated weight update scheme. Additionally, DLM periodically and deterministically envokes a smoothing mechanism that decreases all clause weights by a constant amount. The Smoothed Descent and Flood (SDF) approach [10] introduced a more complex smoothing method, and the concept of multiplicative weight updates. The most recent and best-performing DLS algorithm for SAT is the Exponentiated Sub-Gradient (ESG) method [11]. ESG, described in more detail in the next section, reaches or exceeds the performance of the best known WalkSAT algorithms in many cases.

In this paper we introduce "Scaling and Probabilistic Smoothing" (SAPS), a new algorithm that is conceptually closely related to ESG, but differs in the way it implements weight updates: SAPS performs computationally expensive weight smoothing probabilistically and less frequently than ESG. This leads to a substantial reduction in the time complexity of the weight update procedure without increasing the number of variable flips required for solving a given SAT instance. Furthermore, different from ESG, SAPS can be implemented efficiently in a rather straight-forward way. We also introduce RSAPS, a partially self-tuning variant of SAPS that robustly reaches and in some cases exceeds the performance of SAPS with manually tuned parameters. As our empirical evaluation shows, SAPS and RSAPS outperform both ESG and Novelty$^+$, two of the best performing SLS algorithms for SAT, on a wide range of random and structured SAT instances, which suggests that these new algorithms might be the best SLS algorithms for SAT currently known.

The remainder of this paper is structured as follows. In Section 2 we review the ESG algorithm and discuss some of its important characteristics. Based on these insights, we present our new SAPS algorithm, a variant of the ESG approach, in Section 3. A self-tuning variant of this algorithm, RSAPS, is introduced in Section 4. In Section 5, we report results from our empirical study of SAPS and RSAPS which illustrate the performance improvements these algorithms achieve as compared to ESG and Novelty$^+$. Finally, Section 6 contains conclusions and points out directions for future work.

2   The ESG Algorithm

The Exponentiated Subgradient (ESG) algorithm by Schuurmans, Southey, and Holte [11] is motivated by established methods in the operations research literature. Subgradient optimisation is a method for minimising Lagrangian functions that is often used for generating good lower bounds for branch and bound techniques or as a heuristic in incomplete local search algorithms.

ESG for SAT works as follows: The search is initialised by randomly chosen truth values for all propositional variables in the input formula, F, and by setting the weight associated with each clause in F to one. Then, in each iteration, a weighted search phase followed by a weight update is performed.

The weighted search phase consists of a series of greedy variable flips ("primal search steps"); in each of these, a variable is selected at random from the set of all variables that appear in currently unsatisfied clauses and when flipped, lead to a maximal reduction in the total weight of unsatisfied clauses. When reaching a local minimum state, *i.e.*, an assignment in which flipping any variable that appears in an unsatisfied clause would not lead to a decrease in the total weight of unsatisfied clauses, with probability η, the search is continued by flipping a variable that is uniformly chosen at random from the set of all variables appearing in unsatisfied clauses. Otherwise, the weighted search phase is terminated.

After each weighted search phase, the clause weights are updated ("dual search step"). This involves two stages: First, the weights of all clauses are multiplied by a factor depending on their satisfaction status; weights of satisfied clauses are multiplied by α_{sat}, weights of unsatisfied clauses by α_{unsat} (scaling stage). Then, all clause weights are pulled towards their mean value using the formula $w \leftarrow w \cdot \rho + (1 - \rho) \cdot \bar{w}$ (smoothing stage), where $\bar{w}$ is the average of all clause weights after scaling, and the parameter ρ has a fixed value between zero and one. The algorithm terminates when a satisfying assignment for F has been found or when a maximal number of iterations has been performed. (For details, see [11].)

In a straight-forward implementation of ESG, the weight update steps ("dual search steps") are computationally much more expensive than the weighted search steps ("primal search steps"), whose cost is determined by the underlying basic local search procedure. Each weight update step requires accessing all clause weights, while a weighted search step only needs to access the weights of the critical clauses, i.e., clauses that can change their satisfaction status when a variable appearing in a currently unsatisfied clause is flipped.[1] Typically, for the major part of the search only few clauses are unsatisfied; hence, only a small subset of the clauses is critical, rendering the weighted search steps computationally cheaper than weight updates.

If weight updates would typically occur very infrequently as compared to weighted search steps, the relatively high complexity of the weight update steps might not have a significant effect on the performance of the algorithm. However, experiments (not reported here) indicate that the fraction of weighting steps performed by ESG is quite high; it ranges from around 7% (for SAT encodings of large flat graph colouring problems) to more than 40% percent (for SAT-encoded all-interval-series problems).

Efficient implementations of ESG therefore critically depend on additional techniques in order to reach the competitive performance results reported in [11]. The most recent publically available ESG-SAT software by Southey and Schuurmans (Version 1.4), for instance, uses $\alpha_{sat} = 1$ (which avoids the effort of scaling satisfied clauses), replaces $\bar{w}$ by 1 in the smoothing step, and utilises a lazy weight update technique which updates clause weights only when they are needed. In Table 1, we compare this algorithm with the WalkSAT variant Novelty$^+$. Especially the step performance of ESG is quite impressive for a variety of problem instances; while it never needs more variable flips, sometimes it outperforms Novelty$^+$ by more than an order of magnitude. In most cases, ESG's time performance is still somewhat better than that of Novelty$^+$, but even with the optimisations in Version 1.4, ESG-SAT does not always reach the performance of Novelty$^+$ in terms of CPU time. Hence, it seems that the complexity of the weight update steps severely limits the performance of ESG in particular and dynamic local search algorithms for SAT in general.

3   Scaling and Probabilistic Smoothing (SAPS)

Based on the observations from the previous section, the most obvious way to improve the performance of ESG would be to reduce the complexity of the weight update procedure while retaining the relatively low number of weighted search steps required to solve a given problem instance. As we will see in this section,

---

[1] The complexity of all other operations is dominated by these operations.

Table 1. Median number of steps and run-time on individual benchmark instances for ESG (Version 1.4) and Novelty[+]; boldface indicates the CPU time of the faster algorithm. For all runs of Novelty[+], $wp = 0.01$, steps for ESG are split into primal and dual steps. Estimates for all instances are based on 100 runs. For details on the experimental methodology and the problem instances, see Section 5

Problem	Novelty[+]			ESG					
Instance	noise	steps	time	α	ρ	noise	pr. steps	d. steps	time
bw_large.a	0.40	7,007	**0.014**	3.0	0.995	0.0015	2,445	282	0.016
bw_large.b	0.35	125,341	0.339	1.4	0.99	0.0005	26,978	4,612	**0.280**
bw_large.c	0.20	3,997,095	**16.0**	1.4	0.99	0.0005	1,432,003	193,700	38.10
logistics.c	0.40	101,670	**0.226**	2.2	0.99	0.0025	9,714	4,664	0.229
flat100-med	0.55	7,632	**0.008**	1.1	0.99	0.0015	6,313	1,154	0.013
flat100-hard	0.60	84,019	0.089	1.1	0.99	0.0015	20,059	2,794	**0.037**
flat200-med	0.60	198,394	**0.208**	1.01	0.99	0.0025	96,585	7,587	0.237
flat200-hard	0.60	18147719	18.862	1.01	0.99	0.0025	2,511,228	213,995	**5.887**
uf100-hard	0.55	29,952	0.046	1.15	0.99	0.001	2,223	638	**0.006**
uf250-med	0.55	9,906	**0.015**	1.15	0.99	0.003	7,006	1,379	0.0195
uf250-hard	0.55	1,817,662	2.745	1.15	0.99	0.003	165,212	26,772	**0.461**
uf400-med	0.55	100,412	**0.160**	1.15	0.99	0.003	100,253	10,016	0.324
uf400-hard	0.55	14,419,948	22.3	1.15	0.99	0.003	3,015,013	282,760	**9.763**
ais10	0.40	1,332,225	4.22	1.9	0.999	0.0004	13,037	9,761	**0.139**

this can be achieved in a rather simple and straight-forward way, leading to our new SAPS algorithm, a simple, yet efficient variant of ESG.

Two key observations provide the basis for the modified weight update scheme underlying SAPS. In the following we let C denote the set of all clauses of a given formula F and U_c the set of all clauses unsatisfied under the current variable assignment. We first note that the scaling operation can be restricted to the unsatisfied clause weights ($\alpha_{sat} = 1$) without affecting the variable selection in the weighted search phase, since rescaling all clause weights by a constant factor does not affect the variable selection mechanism. (As mentioned before, Southey's and Schuurmans' ESG implementation also makes use of this fact.) Based on our previous argument, this reduces the complexity of the scaling stage from $\theta(|C|)$ to $\theta(|U_c|)$. After a short initial search phase, $|U_c|$ becomes rather small compared to $|C|$; this effect seems to be more pronounced for larger SAT instances with many clauses. The smoothing stage, however, has complexity $\theta(|C|)$, and now dominates the complexity of the weight update.

Given this situation, the second key idea is to reduce the time complexity of the weight update procedure by performing the expensive smoothing operation only occasionally. Our experimental results show that this does not have a detrimental effect on the performance of the algorithm in terms of the number

procedure UpdateWeights(F, x, W, α, ρ,P_{smooth})
  input:
    propositional formula F, variable assignment x, clause weights $W = (w_i)$,
    scaling factor α, smoothing factor ρ, smoothing probability P_{smooth}
  output:
    clause weights W
  $C = \{$clauses of $F\}$
  $U_c = \{c \in C \mid c$ is unsatisfied under $x\}$
  for each i s.t. $c_i \in U_c$ **do**
    $w_i := w_i \times \alpha$
  end
  with probability P_{smooth} **do**
    for each i s.t. $c_i \in C$ **do**
      $w_i := w_i \times \rho + (1 - \rho) \times \bar{w}$
    end
  end
  return (W)
end

Fig. 1. The SAPS weight update procedure; $\bar{w}$ is the average over all clause weights

of weighted search steps required for solving a given instance. Towards the end of this section we will provide some intuition into this phenomenon.

Figure 1 shows our novel weight update procedure which is based on these insights. Different from the standard ESG weight update, this procedure scales the weights of unsatisfied clauses, but only smoothes all clause weights with a certain probability P_{smooth}. Thus, we call the corresponding algorithm *Scaling and Probabilistic Smoothing* (SAPS). Compared to ESG, in SAPS the complexity of *UpdateWeights* is reduced from $\Theta(|C|+|U_c|)$ to $\Theta(P_{smooth} \cdot |C|+|U_c|)$. As a result, the amortised cost of smoothing no longer dominates the algorithm's runtime. Obviously, there are other ways of achieving the same effect. For instance, similar to the mechanism found in DLM, smoothing could be performed deterministically after a fixed number of scaling stages. However, the probabilistic smoothing mechanism has the theoretical advantage of preventing the algorithm from getting trapped in cyclic behaviour (see also [3]). Furthermore, it is not clear that the possibility of performing smoothing should be restricted to situations where a local minimum of the evaluation function has been encountered. In fact, preliminary experimental results (not reported here) suggest that decoupling the smoothing operation from local minima results in an approximately optimal setting of P_{smooth} that is more stable over different domains.

Figure 2 shows the main SAPS algorithm and its underlying weighted search procedure; overall, this algorithm is conceptually very similar to ESG, except for the weight update procedure which has substantially smaller time complexity and provides the key for its excellent performance (see Section 5). The SAPS algorithm as described here does not require additional implementation tricks other than the standard mechanism for efficiently accessing critical clauses that is used in all efficient implementations of SLS algorithms for SAT. In particular, different from Southey's and Schuurmans' ESG implementation, SAPS does not replace $\bar{w}$ by one in the smoothing stage, or perform lazy weight updates.

Figure 3 illustrates the effect of varying the smoothing probability, P_{smooth}, on the performance of SAPS, while simultaneously decreasing ρ to compensate for "missed" smoothing stages. Setting P_{smooth} to one results in an algorithm that is very closely related (but still not identical) to ESG. When decreasing P_{smooth} below one, we observe unchanged step performance while the time performance is improving. For some SAT instances, especially from the logistics and blocksworld planning domains, we achieve best time performance for $P_{smooth} = 0$, *i.e.*, when no smoothing is used at all; however, most instances require at least some smoothing. For our computational experiments, unless explicitly noted otherwise, we generally used $P_{smooth} = 0.05$, a setting which resulted in reasonable performance over a broad range of SAT instances. However, in many cases, $P_{smooth} = 0.05$ is clearly not the optimal setting; therefore, in the next section we introduce a scheme for automatically adapting the smoothing probability over the course of the search process.

To gain a deeper understanding of the performance of the ESG and SAPS algorithms and specifically the role of the parameters α, ρ and P_{smooth}, it is useful to study the evolution of clause weights over time. If two clauses were unsatisfied at only one local minimum each, then the relative weights of these clauses depend on the order in which they were unsatisfied. Since the weights are scaled back towards the clause weight average at each smoothing stage, the clause that has been unsatisfied more recently has a larger weight. So scaling and smoothing can be seen as a mechanism for ranking the clause weights based on search history. Clearly, the distribution of clause weights, which is controlled by the settings of α, ρ, and P_{smooth}, has a major impact on the variable selection underlying the primal search steps. Since uniform scaling of weights has no effect on variable selection and hence on the performance of the algorithm, we consider distributions over clause weights that are normalised by multiplying all weights by a constant factor such that clauses that have never been unsatisfied have an adjusted weight of one.

Figure 4 shows typical clause weight distributions (CWDs) for a given SAT instance, *i.e.* all clause weights sorted by weight, for different settings of α, ρ, and P_{smooth} after 400 local minima have been encountered. In our experience, after a certain number of local minima, the CWD converges to a specific distribution that is determined by the problem instance and the settings of α, ρ, P_{smooth}. We hypothesise that the shape of the CWD for a given problem instance determines the performance of ESG and SAPS. In Figure 4, we can see directly the effect of changing the parameters. The smoothing parameter has a significant impact on the shape of the CWD. Intuitively, the basic weighted local search will place greater emphasis on satisfying and keeping satisfied the clauses with higher clause weights. For smaller values of ρ, *i.e.*, more smoothing, fewer clauses

procedure SAPS(F, α, ρ, wp, P_{smooth})
   input:
      propositional formula F, scaling factor α,
      smoothing factor ρ, random walk probability wp,
      smoothing probability P_{smooth}
   output:
      variable assignment x or $\emptyset$
   $x := \mathrm{Init}(F)$
   $W := \mathrm{InitWeights}(F)$
   while not terminate(F, x) **do**
      $x' := \mathrm{WeightedSearchStep}(F, x, W)$
      if $x' = \emptyset$ **then**
         with probability wp **do**
            $x := \mathrm{RandomStep}(F, x)$
         otherwise
            $W := \mathrm{UpdateWeights}(F, x, W, \alpha, \rho, P_{smooth})$
         end
      else
         $x := x'$
      end
   end
   if (F is not satisfied under x) **then**
      $x = \emptyset$
   end
   return (x)
end

procedure WeightedSearchStep(F, x, W)
   input:
      propositional formula F, variable assignment x, clause weights W
   output:
      variable assignment $\hat{x}$ or $\emptyset$
   $U_v = \{$variables of F that appear in clauses unsatisfied under $x\}$
   $X' := \{\hat{x} \mid \hat{x}$ is x with variable $v \in U_v$ flipped$\}$
   $best := \min\{g(F, \hat{x}, W) \mid \hat{x} \in X'\}$
   $X := \{\hat{x} \in X' \mid g(F, \hat{x}, W) = best\}$
   if $best \geq 0$ **then**
      $\hat{x} := \emptyset$
   else
      $\hat{x} := \mathrm{draw}(X)$
   end
   return ($\hat{x}$)
end

Fig. 2. The SAPS Algorithm. 'Init' randomly initialises x, 'InitWeights' initialises all clause weights to 1. 'RandomStep(F,x)' returns an assignment obtained from x by flipping a variable that has been selected uniformly at random from the set of all variables of F; and $g(F, \hat{x}, W)$ denotes the total weight of the clauses in F that are unsatisfied under assignment $\hat{x}$. The function 'draw(X)' returns an element that is uniformly drawn at random from set X

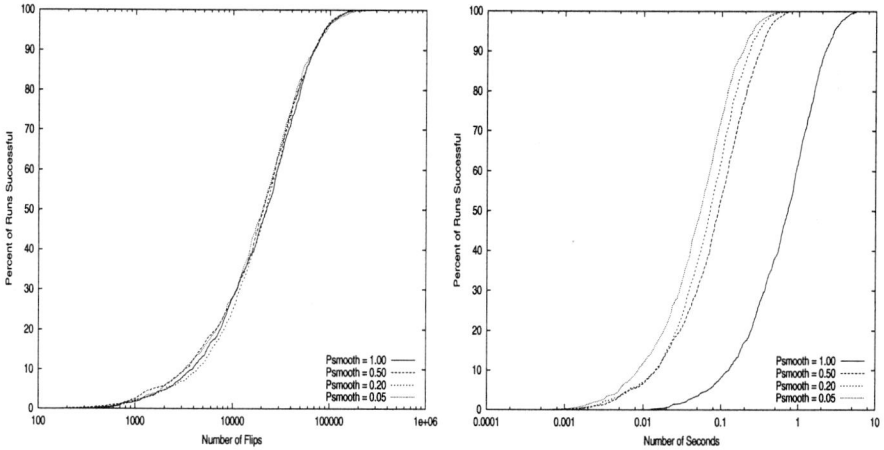

Fig. 3. Flip performance (left) and time performance (right) for SAPS with different values of P_{smooth} for problem instance `ais10`

have high weights, leading to a greedier, more intensified search. Conversely, less smoothing leads to CWDs characteristic for a more diversified search. Interestingly, these effects of the CWDs on the underlying weighted search can be interpreted as that of a soft tabu mechanism on clauses, where clauses with higher weights are "more taboo", *i.e.*, likely to stay satisfied longer.

We also found that if two different $(\alpha, \rho, P_{smooth})$ triplets result in nearly identical CWDs, they will also yield nearly identical performance results. Two such triplets that achieve similar step performance are $(1.3, 0.99, 1.0)$ and $(1.3, 0.80, 0.05)$; as can be seen in Figure 4 (bottom right), the respective CWDs are very similar. In the context of our earlier soft tabu interpretation, this suggests that a clause-based soft tabu algorithm imposing a SAPS- or ESG-like CWD could match the step performance of SAPS and ESG.

4 Reactive SAPS (RSAPS)

As mentioned before, the performance of SAPS depends on the smoothing probability, P_{smooth}, in addition to the three other parameters common to ESG and SAPS. Although we found that, as a rule of thumb, the settings $\alpha = 1.3$, $\rho = 0.8$, $wp = 0.01$, and $P_{smooth} = 0.05$ work reasonably robustly in many cases, there are better parameter settings for almost all problem instances tested here. Determining these settings manually can be difficult and time-consuming; therefore, it would be desirable to automatically find them during the search. In the following, we use a scheme analogous to the one recently applied by Hoos to automatically tuning the noise parameter of Novelty+ [4]. The basic idea is to reactively use higher noise levels, leading to more search diversification, if and

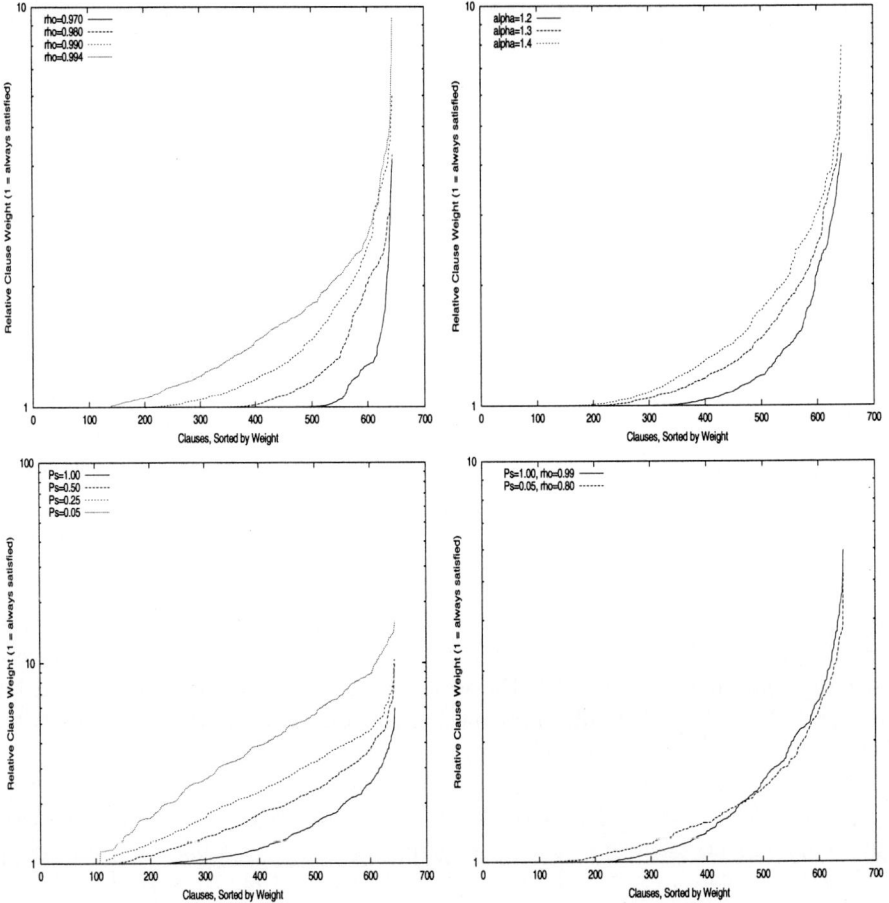

Fig. 4. Clause weight distribution (CWDs) for SAPS after 400 local minima for various values of ρ (top left), α (top right) and P_{smooth} (bottom left). Approximately identical CWDs are obtained for two different $(\alpha, \rho, P_{smooth})$ triplets for which SAPS shows similar step performance (bottom right). All CWDs are measured for Uniform Random 3-SAT instance `uf150-hard`. Unless otherwise noted, $\alpha = 1.3$, $\rho = 0.99$, $P_{smooth} = 1$, and $wp = 0$. All runs were initialised with the same random seed

only if there is evidence for search stagnation, *e.g.* as a result of getting trapped in a local minimum region. Thus, if search stagnation is detected, more noise is introduced; otherwise, the noise value is gradually decreased.

The SAPS algorithm escapes from local minima by scaling the weights of unsatisfied clauses, whereas smoothing the weights back towards uniform values acts as an intensification of the search; complete smoothing ($\rho = 0$) results in basic GSAT behaviour without noise. This suggests that search intensification can be controlled reactively by either adapting ρ or P_{smooth}. At this stage, we neither considered adapting wp nor α, since using fixed values of 0.01 and 1.3, respectively, resulted uniformly and robustly in maximal performance of SAPS in most of our experiments.

Intuitively, it makes much sense to adapt the amount of smoothing since this directly determines the actual extent of search intensification. In order to let changes in ρ effectively control the search, the smoothing probability would have to be rather high. However, in the previous section, we have seen that in order to achieve superior time performance, we need at least a bias towards low smoothing probabilities. Therefore, we decided to use a fixed value of ρ and to control the amount of smoothing by adapting P_{smooth}. By choosing a rather low value for ρ, large amounts of smoothing and high levels of search intensification can still be achieved, while keeping the average smoothing probability low.

It is important to realise the possible gain of adapting the smoothing probability during the search. Besides the obvious advantage of eliminating the need to manually tune P_{smooth}, because of the interdependence of P_{smooth} and ρ, an effective adaptive mechanism for the former parameter should be able to at least partly compensate for suboptimal settings of the latter. Furthermore, when smoothing is performed only in situations where it is actually required, in principle it is possible to obtain better performance than for *optimal* fixed settings of P_{smooth} and ρ. This is due to the fact that optimal settings may differ troughout the course of the search.

Our stagnation criterion is the same as used in Adaptive Novelty$^+$ [4]: if the search has not progressed in terms of a reduction in the number of unsatisfied clauses over the last *(number of clauses)* $\cdot \theta$ variable flips, the smoothing probability is reduced, $\theta = 1/6$ seems to give uniformly good performance. Just like an increase of the noise value in Adaptive Novelty$^+$, this reduction of the smoothing probability leads to a diversification of the search. As soon as the number of unsatisfied clauses is reduced below its value at the last change of the smoothing probability, P_{smooth} is increased in order to intensify exploration of the current region of the search space. The exact mechanism for adapting P_{smooth} is shown in Figure 5. A bias towards low smoothing probabilities is achieved by decreasing P_{smooth} faster than increasing it. Moreover, after each smoothing operation, P_{smooth} is set to zero (this happens in procedure *UpdateWeights*). Together, these two mechanisms help to ensure low average values of P_{smooth} for problem instances that do not benefit from smoothing.

5   Experiments and Results

In order to evaluate the performance of SAPS and RSAPS against ESG as well as Novelty$^+$, we conducted extensive computational experiments on widely used benchmark instances for SAT obtained from SATLIB [6].[2] The benchmark set used for our evaluation comprises SAT-encoded blocksworld and logistics

---

[2] These instances can be found at http://www.satlib.org.

procedure AdaptSmoothingProbability(F, H, P_{smooth})
  input:
    propositional formula F, partial search history H,
    smoothing probability P_{smooth}
  output:
    smoothing probability P_{smooth}
    $C = \{$clauses of $F\}$
    $\theta := 1/6$; $\delta := 0.1$
    if (no improvement has been made for $|C| \cdot \theta$ steps) **then**
      $P_{smooth} := \delta \times P_{smooth}$
      mark the current step as the last improvement
    else if (an improvement has been made in this step) **then**
      $P_{smooth} := P_{smooth} + 2\delta(1 - P_{smooth})$
      mark the current step as the last improvement
    end
    return (P_{smooth})
end

Fig. 5. Procedure for automatically adapting the smoothing probability P_{smooth}; RSAPS calls this procedure after every search step

planning instances, SAT-encoded flat graph colouring problems, critically constrained Uniform Random-3-SAT instances, and SAT-encoded all-interval-series problems. To better assess scaling behaviour, we also used a recently generated test-set of 100 critically constrained, satisfiable Uniform Random-3-SAT instances with 400 variables and 1700 clauses each; this is the same set used in [4]. The instances labelled *-hard and *-med are those instances from the respective test-sets with maximal and median local search cost (*lsc*) for WalkSAT using manually tuned static noise and median *lsc*, respectively (again, these are the same instances as used in [4]).

All computational experiments reported here were executed on a dual 1GHz Pentium III PC with 256KB cache and 1GB RAM, running Red Hat Linux (Version 2.4.9-6smp). Computing times were measured and are reported in CPU seconds. For each problem instance and algorithm, we obtain empirical run-length and run-time distributions (RLDs and RTDs) [5] by solving the problem instance at least 100 times; the cutoff parameter was set to ∞.

In Table 2, for single problem instances from different domains, we present the medians of the RTDs obtained by SAPS and RSAPS. Generally, SAPS and RSAPS achieve superior performance over ESG and Novelty$^+$. In terms of number of search steps, SAPS is performing similar to ESG, with a slight advantage on larger problem instances. Due to the reduced complexity of smoothing, SAPS is outperforming ESG to a factor of up to six (`logistics.c`) in terms of CPU time. For smaller instances, such as `uf100-hard`, the time complexity is roughly the same; SAPS is never slower than ESG. Furthermore, for all problem instances

Table 2. Median run-time and number of steps on individual benchmark instances for our Dynamic Local Search approaches. For all runs, $wp = 0.01$. Estimates are based on 100 runs. Search steps are divided into primal search steps and dual search steps. For SAPS, bold face indicates superior time performance over both ESG and Novelty$^+$, for RSAPS, bold face indicates superior time performance over all the other algorithms. "sf" (speedup factor) denotes the time taken by the faster algorithm of ESG and Novelty$^+$ for the respective instance divided by the time taken by SAPS

Problem Instance	α	ρ	SAPS, $P_{smooth} = 0.05$ pr. steps	d. steps	time	sf	ρ	RSAPS pr. steps	d. steps	time
bw_large.a	1.3	0.8	2,233	331	**0.009**	1.56	0.8	2,413	306	**0.008**
bw_large.b	1.3	0.8	29,452	3,205	**0.179**	1.56	0.8	25,392	2,404	**0.140**
bw_large.c	1.1	0.6	1,866,748	264,211	37.88	0.42	0.9	1,472,480	138,235	**12.66**
logistics.c	1.3	0.9	6,493	2,223	**0.037**	6.10	0.9	6,409	1,077	**0.030**
flat100-med	1.3	0.4	5,437	1,118	0.008	1.00	0.4	6,367	1,292	0.010
flat100-hard	1.3	0.8	22,147	3,501	**0.032**	1.16	0.8	19,627	2,837	**0.029**
flat200-med	1.3	0.4	55,238	4,693	**0.087**	2.39	0.4	71,967	6,183	0.122
flat200-hard	1.3	0.4	1,954,164	215,716	**3.052**	1.93	0.4	3,129,337	308,756	5.162
uf100-hard	1.3	0.8	2,967	811	0.006	1.00	0.8	2,788	865	0.006
uf250-med	1.3	0.4	5,445	1,159	**0.011**	1.36	0.4	5,302	1,253	0.012
uf250-hard	1.3	0.7	144,021	26,348	**0.291**	1.58	0.7	118,960	21,346	**0.249**
uf400-med	1.3	0.7	47,475	5,502	**0.103**	1.55	0.7	46,762	5,579	0.106
uf400-hard	1.3	0.2	900,501	133,267	**1.973**	4.95	0.2	986,621	126,301	2.216
ais10	1.3	0.9	13,482	6,449	**0.051**	2.73	0.9	12,491	6,916	**0.044**

cited in [11] where DLM outperformed ESG, SAPS and RSAPS outperform ESG by a greater margin.

When comparing SAPS to Novelty$^+$, the performance differences are more apparent and the time performance of SAPS is often more than an order of magnitude superior. The big blocksworld planning instance bw_large.c is the only case where Novelty$^+$ performs better than SAPS; RSAPS, however, achieves significantly better performance than Novelty$^+$ for this instance. We have evidence, however, that for the DIMACS graph colouring instances g125.17 and g125.18, Novelty$^+$ performs substantially better than any of the dynamic local search algorithms. SAPS reduces the performance difference but seems unable to outperform Novelty$^+$.

The fact that in many cases, SAPS shows an improvement in step performance over ESG should be emphasised. We attribute this to problems arising from approximations used in efficient implementations of ESG. However, another possible explanation could lie in the additional randomness of SAPS. Since the clause weights in ESG are real numbers, this algorithm becomes almost deterministic after an initial search phase and can be trapped in a cycle, from which it can only escape by means of a random walk step performed in a local minimum.

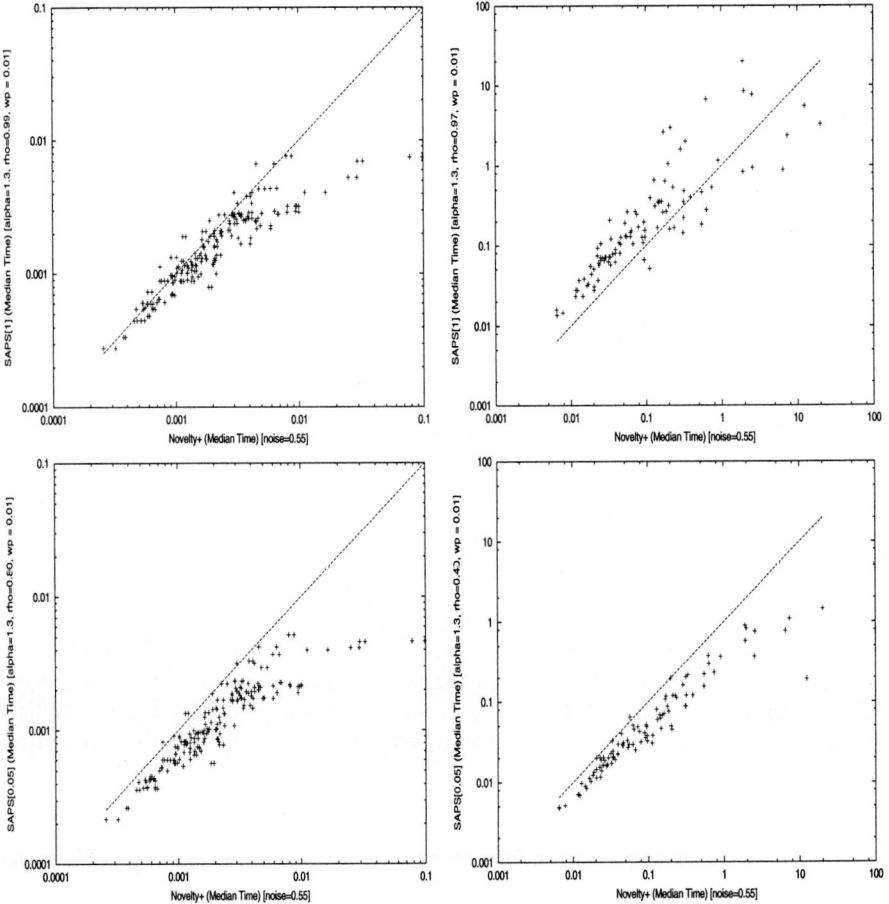

Fig. 6. Correlation between time performance of SAPS and Novelty[+] on Uniform Random 3-SAT test-sets uf100 (left), and uf400 (right); top: Novelty[+] *vs.* SAPS[1], bottom: Novelty[+] *vs.* SAPS[0.05]

In Section 3, we showed how the time complexity of smoothing increases linearly with problem size. This suggests that performance differences between ESG and SAPS should also increase with problem size. To avoid complications arising from different implementations, we use a variant of SAPS with $P_{smooth} = 1$ to illustrate these differences in scaling behaviour.[3] We refer to this variant as SAPS[1] and to regular SAPS as SAPS[0.05]. We demonstrate different scaling properties in time complexity *w.r.t.* problem size for the test sets uf100 and uf400, both of which contain 100 Uniform Random 3-SAT formulae with 100

---

[3] The performance of this variant is very similar to ESG for small instances and seems marginally better for larger instances.

and 400 variables, respectively. In Figure 6 (top), we compare SAPS[1] with Novelty+. We see impressive results for SAPS[1] on test-set uf100, whereas its performance degrades for the instances in test-set uf400. Next, we performed the same comparison for SAPS[0.05] and Novelty+. As can be seen in Figure 6 (bottom), the difference to Novelty+ for test-set uf100 is about the same as for SAPS[1] and Novelty+. However, for the larger instances in uf400 it becomes obvious that the scaling behaviour of SAPS[0.05] is far superior to SAPS[1].

6   Conclusions & Future Work

As we have shown in this work, new insights into the factors underlying the run-time behaviour of the recent and promising Exponentiated Sub-Gradient (ESG) algorithm can lead to variants of this algorithm that show significantly improved performance over both ESG as well as the best known WalkSAT algorithms and hence can be counted amongst the best performing SAT algorithms known to date. Furthermore, reactive search techniques can be used to reduce the need for manual parameter tuning of the resulting algorithms.

In future work, we plan to further investigate the role of the scaling and smoothing stages for ESG and SAPS. By studying clause weight distributions we hope to be able to better understand how these mechanisms interact with the basic weighted search algorithm underlying both algorithms. Ultimately, we are confident that this should lead to further performance improvements. It might even be possible to obtain such improvements with algorithms that are conceptually simpler than ESG or SAPS. Furthermore, it would be interesting to develop completely self-tuning variants of SAPS, which reactively adapt α and ρ as well as the smoothing probability P_{smooth}.

References

[1] J. Frank. Learning Short-term Clause Weights for GSAT. In *Proc. IJCAI-97*, pp. 384–389, Morgan Kaufmann Publishers, 1997.

[2] H. H. Hoos. *Stochastic Local Search — Methods, Models, Applications*, PhD thesis, Darmstadt University of Technology, 1998.

[3] H. H. Hoos. On the Run-time Behaviour of Stochastic Local Search Algorithms for SAT. In *Proc. AAAI-99*, pp. 661–666. AAAI Press, 1999.

[4] H. H. Hoos. An Adaptive Noise Mechanism for WalkSAT. To appear in *Proc.AAAI-02*, AAAI Press, 2002.

[5] H. H. Hoos and T. Stützle. Local Search Algorithms for SAT: An Empirical Evaluation. In *J. of Automated Reasoning*, Vol. 24, No. 4, pp. 421–481, 2000.

[6] H. H. Hoos and T. Stützle. SATLIB: An Online Resource for Research on SAT. In I. P. Gent, H. Maaren, T. Walsh (ed.), *SAT 2000*, pp. 283–292, IOS Press, 2000.

[7] H. Kautz and B. Selman. Pushing the Envelope: Planning, Propositional Logic, and Stochastic Search. In *Proc. AAAI-96*, pp. 1194–1201. AAAI Press, 1996.

[8] D. A. McAllester and B. Selman and H. A. Kautz. Evidence for Invariants in Local Search. In *Proc. AAAI-97*, pp. 321–326, AAAI Press, 1997.

[9] P. Morris. The breakout method for escaping from local minima. In *Proc. AAAI-93*, pp. 40–45. AAAI Press, 1993.

[10] D. Schuurmans, and F. Southey. Local search characteristics of incomplete SAT procedures. In *Proc. AAAI-2000*, pp. 297–302, AAAI Press, 2000.

[11] D. Schuurmans, F. Southey, and R. C. Holte. The exponentiated subgradient algorithm for heuristic boolean programming. In *Proc. IJCAI-01*, pp. 334-341, Morgan Kaufmann Publishers, 2001.

[12] B. Selman and H. A. Kautz. Domain-Independent Extensions to GSAT: Solving Large Structured Satisfiability Problems. In *Proc. IJCAI-93*, pp. 290–295, Morgan Kaufmann Publishers, 1993.

[13] B. Selman and H. A. Kautz and B. Cohen. Noise Strategies for Improving Local Search. In *Proc. AAAI-94*, pp. 337–343, AAAI Press, 1994.

[14] B. Selman, H. Levesque and D. Mitchell. A New Method for Solving Hard Satisfiability Problems. In *Proc. AAAI-92*, pp. 440–446, AAAI Press, 1992.

[15] Z. Wu and B. W. Wah. An Efficient Global-Search Strategy in Discrete Lagrangian Methods for Solving Hard Satisfiability Problems. In *Proc. AAAI-00*, pp . 310–315, AAAI Press, 2000.

Learning and Solving Soft Temporal Constraints: An Experimental Study

Francesca Rossi[1], Alessandro Sperduti[1], Kristen B. Venable[1], Lina Khatib[2,*],
Paul Morris[2], and Robert Morris[2]

[1] Department of Pure and Applied Mathematics, University of Padova, Italy
{frossi,perso,kvenable}@math.unipd.it
[2] NASA Ames Research Center, Moffett Field, CA, USA
{lina,pmorris,morris}@ptolemy.arc.nasa.gov

Abstract. Soft temporal constraints problems allow for a natural description of scenarios where events happen over time and preferences are associated with event distances and durations. However, sometimes such *local* preferences are difficult to set, and it may be easier instead to associate preferences to some complete solutions of the problem, and then to *learn* from them suitable preferences over distances and durations.
In this paper, we describe our learning algorithm and we show its behaviour on classes of randomly generated problems. Moreover, we also describe two solvers (one more general and the other one more efficient) for tractable subclasses of soft temporal problems, and we give experimental results to compare them.

1 Introduction and Motivation

Several real world problems involve the manipulation of temporal information in order to find an assignment of times to a set of activities or events. These problems usually have preferences associated with how long a single activity should last, when it should occur, or how it should be ordered with respect to other activities. For example, an antenna on an earth orbiting satellite such as Landsat 7 must be slewed so that it is pointing at a ground station in order for recorded science or telemetry data to be downlinked to earth. Antenna slewing on Landsat 7 has been shown to occasionally cause a slight vibration to the satellite, which in turn might affect the quality of the image taken by the scanning instrument if the scanner is in use during slewing. Consequently, it is preferable for the slewing activity not to overlap any scanning activity, although because the detrimental effect on image quality occurs only intermittently, this disjointness is best not expressed as a hard constraint. This is only one of the many real world problems that can be cast and, under certain assumptions, solved in our framework.

Reasoning simultaneously with hard temporal constraints and preferences, as illustrated in the example just given, is crucial in many situations. However,

---

* Kestrel Technology

P. Van Hentenryck (Ed.): CP 2002, LNCS 2470, pp. 249–263, 2002.

in many temporal reasoning problems it is difficult or impossible to specify some local preferences on durations. In real world scheduling problems, for example, it is sometimes easier to see how preferrable a solution is, but it may be virtually impossible to specify how specific ordering choices between pairs of events contribute to such global preference value.

This scenario is typical in many cases. For example, it occurs when there is no precise function which describes the assignment of a preference value to a global solution. This may happen for example when we just have an expert, whose knowledge is difficult to code as local preferences, but who can immediately recognize a good (or bad) global solution. Another typical case occurs when the environment in which the solver will work presents some level of uncertainty. In this case, we could have the local preferences, but their effect on a global solution could depend on events which are not modeled within the problem.

On the other hand, if all the knowledge could be coded as local preferences, it could be used as heuristics to guide the scheduler to prefer local assignments that were found to yield better solutions.

We solve this problem by automatically generating local temporal preference information, from global preferences, via a machine learning approach, and using a representation of local preferences in terms of soft constraints.

This paper recalls the current formalism and tractability results for soft temporal constraint problems, and describes the new machinery we have developed for both learning and solving a subclass of soft problems which uses fuzzy constraints [12][1]. The main results of the paper can thus be listed as follows: (1) a learning algorithm which induces local preferences from solution ratings (in Section 4); (2) some new theoretical results on the use of path-consistency in soft temporal constraints (in Section 5.1); (3) a solver based on these results, which solves temporal fuzzy constraint problems from a tractable class (in Section 5.1); (4) another solver based on a "chopping" approach, which is less general but much more efficient (in Section 5.2); (5) a random-problem generator, which extends the usual ones for hard and soft CSPs to deal with temporal constraints (in Section 3); (6) experimental results to show the behaviour of the learning module and of the two solvers, and to compare the solvers (in Section 5.3).

A learning approach related to what we use in this paper has already been used for soft CSPs without temporal information [11, 1], and is here adapted to soft temporal CSPs. Notice that this adaptation is not straightforward, since here we focus on a class of tractable temporal problems, and we build both the solvers and the learning module to work with this class of problems. This poses some restrictions on the learning algorithm which could in principle undermine its ability to learn the preferences over the constraints. Some other preliminary ideas which have led to the development described in this paper have been presented in [9]. However, in [9] the algorithm on which our learning module is based was not present, nor the experimental scenario and results. Another related paper is [8], which contains some of the tractability results for classes of soft temporal problems, which we use in this paper to define both our solvers.

---

[1] Although they could be used also for other classes of soft temporal constraints.

However, additional theoretical results are needed to define one of the two solvers we present here. The solving approach we use in our experiments is related to the literature of fuzzy temporal constraints [5, 10, 15]. Moreover, the translation of a classical CSP into a fuzzy CSP has been explored also in [6].

2   Background

2.1   Temporal Constraint Problems with Preferences

In the Temporal CSP framework (TCSP) [4], variables represent events happening over time, and each constraint gives an allowed range for the distances or durations, expressed as a set of intervals over the time line. Satisfying such a constraint means choosing any of the allowed distances. A solution for a TCSP is an assignment of values to its variables such that all temporal constraints are satisfied.

General TCSPs are NP-hard. However, TCSPs with just one interval for each constraint, called STPs, are polynomially solvable

TCSPs are able to model just *hard* temporal constraints. This means that all constraints have to be satisfied, and that the solutions of a constraint are all equally satisfying. However, in many real-life some solutions are preferred with respect to others. Therefore the global problem is not to find a way to satisfy all constraints, but to find a way to satisfy them optimally, according to the preferences specified. To address such problems, recently [8] a new framework has been proposed, where each temporal constraint is associated with a preference function, which specifies the preference for each distance. This framework is based on a simple merging of TCSPs and soft constraints, where for soft constraints we have taken a general framework based on semirings [3]. The result is a class of problems called Temporal Constraint Satisfaction Problems with Preferences (TCSPPs).

A *soft temporal constraint* in a TCSPP is represented by a pair consisting of a set of disjoint intervals and a preference function: $\langle I = \{[a_1, b_1], \ldots, [a_n, b_n]\}, f \rangle$, where $f : I \to A$ is a mapping of the elements of I^2 into preference values taken from a set A.

Such a set A is ordered (totally or partially), and, following the style of semiring-based soft constraints [3], such an ordering $\leq$ is defined via an operation on elements of A, denoted by $+$, as follows: $a \leq b$ iff $a + b = b$. Informally, $a \leq b$ means that b is better than a.

A *solution* to a TCSPP is a complete assignment to all the variables that satisfies the distance constraints. Each solution has a *global preference value*, obtained by combining the local preference values found in the constraints. This combination operation is usually denoted by $\times$. The two operations ($+$ and $\times$), together with the set of preference values A, form a mathematical structure called a semiring [3], and usually written as a tuple $\langle A, +, \times, \mathbf{0}, \mathbf{1} \rangle$, where 0 and 1 are, respectively, the worst and best preference in the ordering.

---

[2] Here by I we mean the set of all elements appearing in the intervals of I.

The two semiring operations allow for complete solutions to be evaluated in terms of the preference values assigned locally. More precisely, given a solution t in a TCSPP with associated semiring $\langle A, +, \times, \mathbf{0}, \mathbf{1} \rangle$, let $T_{ij} = \langle I_{i,j}, f_{i,j} \rangle$ be a soft constraint over variables X_i, X_j and (v_i, v_j) be the projection of t over the values assigned to variables X_i and X_j (abbreviated as $(v_i, v_j) = t_{\downarrow X_i, X_j}$). Then, the corresponding preference value given by f_{ij} is $f_{ij}(v_j - v_i)$, where $v_j - v_i \in I_{i,j}$. Then the global preference value of t, $val(t)$, is defined to be $val(t) = \times \{ f_{ij}(v_j - v_i) \mid (v_i, v_j) = t_{\downarrow X_i, X_j} \}$. The optimal solutions of a TCSPP are those solutions which have the best global preference value, where "best" is determined by the ordering $\leq_S$ of the values in the semiring.

For example, the semiring $S_{fuzzy} = \langle [0, 1], max, min, 0, 1 \rangle$ is usually used to model fuzzy constraints [12], which we will use in this paper. Preferences are between 0 and 1, the global preference of a solution is the *minimum* of all the preferences associated with the distances selected by this solution in all constraints, and the best solutions are those with the *maximal* preference.

A special case of TCSPPs occurs when each constraint contains a single interval. We call such problems *Simple Temporal Problems with Preferences* (STPPs). These problems are not as general as TCSPPs but can however model many real situations.

We can perform two operations on soft simple temporal constraints: *intersection* and *composition*. Given two such constraints $C_1 = \langle I_1, f_1 \rangle$ and $C_2 = \langle I_2, f_2 \rangle$ the intersection is the constraint $C_1 \oplus C_2 = \langle I_1 \cap I_2, f \rangle$, where $\cap$ is the usual intersection of intervals and $f(a) = f_1(a) \times f_2(a), \forall a \in I_1 \cap I_2$. The composition of the two constraints is again a constraint $C_1 \otimes C_2 = \langle \tilde{I}, \tilde{f} \rangle$, where $\tilde{I} = \{ r | \exists r_1 \in I_1, \exists r_2 \in I_2 r = r_1 + r_2 \}$ and $\tilde{f}(r) = \sum \{ f_1(r_1) \times f_2(r_2) | r = r_1 + r_2, r_1 \in I_1, r2 \in I_2 \}$. We can use these two operations to perform constraint propagation over STPPs. In particular, we can achieve a local consistency notion similar to path-consistency, but adapted to deal with temporal soft constraints. Applying path consistency to an STPP means considering all triangles of constraints, say (C_1, C_2, C_3), composing any two of them, say C_1 and C_2, and then intersecting the resulting constraint with the other, i.e. $(C_1 \otimes C_2) \oplus C_3$. This is performed until stability is reached, that is, until one sweep of path consistency wouldn't result in any changes.

While in general TCSPPs are NP-hard, under certain restrictions on the "shape" of the preference functions and on the semiring, STPPs are tractable. In particular, this happens when the preference functions are semi-convex. A *semi-convex* function f is one such that, for all Y, the set $\{ X$ such that $f(X) \geq Y \}$ forms an interval. It is easy to see that semi-convex functions include linear ones, as well as convex and some step functions. For example, the *close to k* criterion (which gives a higher preference to time points which are closer to k) cannot be coded into a linear preference function, but it can be easily specified by a semi-convex preference function.

STPPs with semi-convex preference functions and a semiring with a total order of preference values and an idempotent multiplicative operation can be solved in polynomial time [8]. Moreover, semi-convex preference functions are closed with respect to path-consistency.

2.2   Learning Soft Temporal Constraints

It is not always easy to specify the preference function in each temporal constraint; sometimes it is easier to specify global preference functions, to be associated to entire solutions. For this reason, and since the whole TCSPP machinery is based on local preference functions, we developed a methodology to induce local preferences from global ones. Here we focus on STPPs, which, as noted above, are tractable, rather than general TCSPPs.

The problem of learning preferences in STPPs, from examples of solutions ratings, can be formally described as an inductive learning problem [14]. Inductive learning can be defined as the ability of a system to induce the correct structure of a map d which is known only for particular inputs. More formally, defining an example as a pair $(x, d(x))$, the computational task is as follows: given a collection of examples of d, i.e., the *training set*, return a function h that approximates d. Function h is called a hypothesis.

A common approach to inductive learning, especially in the context of neural networks, is to evaluate the quality of a hypothesis h (on the training set) through an *error function* [7]. An example of popular error function, that can be used over the reals, is the sum of squares error [7]: $E = \frac{1}{2} \sum_{i=1}^{n} (d(x_i) - h(x_i))^2$, where $(x_i, d(x_i))$ is the i-th example of the training set.

Given a starting hypothesis h_0, the goal of learning is to minimize the error function E by modifying h_0. One popular way of doing this is to use a technique called *gradient descent* [7]. Specifically, the set of parameters W, which define the current hypothesis, is initialized to small random values at time $\tau = 0$ and updated at time $\tau + 1$ according to the following equation: $W(\tau + 1) = W(\tau) + \Delta W(\tau)$, where $\Delta W(\tau) = -\eta \frac{\partial E}{\partial W(\tau)}$, and η is the step size used for the gradient descent. Learning is stopped when a minimum of E is reached. Note that, in general, there is no guarantee that the found minimum is global.

Learning in our context can be used to find suitable preference functions to be associated to the constraints of a given STP. More precisely, let $P = (V, C)$ be an STP where V is a set of variables with domains consisting of time instants, and C is a set of distance constraints of the form $l \leq X - Y \leq u$, where $X, Y, \in V$ and l, u are time points. Let f be a function $f : S \to U$, where S is the set of solutions to P and U is a set of values indicating the "quality" of the solution. The learning task consists of transforming the STP into an STPP, with each constraint $c_{i,j} \in C$ replaced by a soft constraint $\langle c_{i,j}, f_{i,j} \rangle$, where $f_{i,j}$ is the local preference function for $c_{i,j}$.

The examples to be used in the learning task consist of pairs $(s, f(s))$, where s is a solution to the original STP and $f(s)$ is its "score". In the following, we use P to denote an STP and P' to denote a corresponding STPP. Also, $val_{P'}(t)$ is used to indicate the value of a solution t over P'.

Let P and f be as defined above, and suppose a set of examples $TR = \{(t_1, r(t_1)), \ldots, (t_m, r(t_m))\}$ is given. To infer the local preferences, we must also be given the following: a semiring whose element set A contains the values $r(t_i)$ in the examples; and a distance function over such a semiring. For example, if the score values are positive real numbers, we could choose the semiring $\langle \Re^+, min, +, +\infty, 0 \rangle$ and, as distance function, the usual one over reals: $dist(val_{P'}(t), r(t)) = |val_{P'}(t) - r(t)|$. Given all the above, the goal is to define a corresponding STPP P' over the same semiring such that P and P' have the same set of variables, domains and interval constraints, and for each t such that $(t, r(t))$ is an example, $dist(val_{P'}(t), r(t)) < \epsilon$, where $\epsilon > 0$ and small.

If the first condition is true, the only free parameters that can be arbitrarily chosen in order to satisfy the other conditions are the values to be associated to each distance. For each constraint $c_{ij} = \{[a_1, b_1], \ldots, [a_n, b_n]\}$ in P, the idea is to associate, in P', a free parameter w_d, where $d = X_j - X_i$ (note that such a parameter must belong to the set of the chosen semiring), to each element d in $I = \bigcup_i [a_i, b_i]$. This parameter will represent the preference over that specific distance. With the other distances, those outside I, we associate the constant $\mathbf{0}$, (the lowest value of the semiring (w.r.t. $\leq_S$)).

If I contains many time points, we would need a great number of parameters. To avoid this problem, we can restrict the class of preference functions to a subset which can be described via a small number of parameters. For example, linear functions just need two parameters a and b, since they can be expressed as $a \cdot (X_j - X_i) + b$. In general, we will have a function which depends on a set of parameters W, thus we will denote it as $f_W : (W \times I) \to A$.

The value assigned to each solution t in P' is

$$val_{P'}(t) = \prod_{c_{ij} \in P'} [\sum_{d \in \bigcup_{D \in I_{ij}} D} check(d, t, i, j) \times f_W(d)] \tag{1}$$

where $\prod$ generalizes the $\times$ operation, $\sum$ generalizes $+$, I_{ij} is the set of intervals associated to constraint c_{ij}, and $check(d, t, i, j) = \mathbf{1}$ if $d = t \downarrow_{X_j} - t \downarrow_{X_i}$ and $\mathbf{0}$ otherwise. Note that, for each constraint c_{ij}, there is exactly one distance d such that $check(d, t, i, j) = \mathbf{1}$, namely $d = t \downarrow_{X_j} - t \downarrow_{X_i}$. Thus, $val_{P'}(t) = \prod_{c_{ij} \in P'} f_W(t \downarrow_{X_j} - t \downarrow_{X_i})$. The values of the free parameters in W may be obtained via a minimization of the error function, which will be defined according to the distance function of the semiring.

To force the learning framework to produce semi-convex functions, we can specialize it for a specific class of functions with this property. For example, we could choose convex quadratic functions of the form $f(d) = a \cdot d^2 + b \cdot d + c$, where $a \leq 0$. In this case we just have three parameters to consider: $W = \{a, b, c\}$. Of course, by choosing a specific class of semi-convex functions, not all local preference shapes will be representable.

3   The Random Problem Generator

The random generator we have developed focuses on a particular subclass of semi-convex preference functions: convex quadratic functions of the form $ax^2 +$

$bx + c$, with $a \leq 0$. This choice has been suggested by the expressiveness of such a class of functions. In fact, we can notice that this class of functions includes constant, linear, and semi-convex quadratic functions. Moreover, it is easy to express functions in this class: we just need to specify three parameters.

Moreover, the generator generates fuzzy STPPs, thus preference values are between 0 and 1, and they are combined using the max-min approach. A reason for this choice is the fact that the min operator is idempotent, thus the generated problems, according to the results in [8], are tractable. Moreover, the fuzzy approach has been shown to be useful in many real-life problems, as it is demonstrated by the interest in fuzzy theory and by several arguments for its generality.

An STPP is generated according to the value of the following parameters: (1) number n of variables; (2) range r for the initial solution: to assure that the generated problem has at least one solution, we first generate such a solution, by giving to each variable a random value within the range $[0, r]$; (3) density: percentage of constraints that are not universal (that is, with the maximum range and preference 1 for all interval values); (4) maximum expansion from initial solution (max): for each constraint, the bounds of its interval are set by using a random value between 0 and max, to be added to and subtracted from the timepoint identified for this constraint by the initial solution; (5) perturbation of preference functions (pa, pb, pc): we recall that each preference function can be described by three values $(a, b,$ and $c)$; to set such values for each constraint, the generator starts from a standard quadratic function which passes through the end points of the interval, with value 0, and the middlepoint, with value 0.5, and then modifies it according to the percentages specified for a, b, and c.

For example, if we call the generator with the parameters $\langle 10, 20, 30, 40, 20,$ $25, 30 \rangle$, it will generate a fuzzy STPP with 10 variables. Moreover, the initial solution will be chosen by giving to each variable a value between 0 and 20. Among all the constraints, 70% of them will be universal, while the other 30% will be specified as follows: for each constraint, consider the timepoint specified by the initial solution, say t; then the interval will be $[t - t1, t + t2]$, where $t1$ and $t2$ are random numbers between 0 and 40. Finally, the preference function in each constraint is specified by taking the default one and changing its three parameters a, b, and c, by, respectively, 20%, 25%, and 30%.

To compare our generator with the usual one for classical CSPs, we notice that the maximum expansion (max) for the constraint intervals roughly corresponds to the tightness. However, we do not have the same tightness for all constraints, because we just set an upper bound to the number of values allowed in a constraint. Also, we do not explicitly set the domain of the variables, but we just set the constraints. This is in line with other temporal CSP generators, like the one in [13].

4   The Learning Module

We have developed a learning module which can learn fuzzy STPPs where the preference functions are quadratic functions of the form $ax^2 + bx + c$ with $a \leq 0$, which are exactly those functions generated by our random generator.

The input is a set of pairs consisting of a solution and its preference. Part of this set will be used as the training set, and the rest as the test set. The hard version of the problem, that is, the temporal constraints between the variables, is given as input as well.

To each temporal constraint, we then associate three parameters a, b, c, which will specify its preference function. These parameters are initialized to $a = 0$, $b = 0$, and $c = 1$, that is, a constant function.

Learning is performed via a gradient descent technique using an approximated version of the min operation which is continuous and derivable. In words, we approximate the derivative of the min function over each of its arguments, which is a step function, via two sigmoid functions. More precisely, the approximation depends on the value of a parameter, called β: $min^\beta(x_1, \cdots, x_n) = -\frac{1}{\beta}ln(\frac{1}{n}\sum_{i=1}^{n}e^{-\beta x_i})$. Higher beta values give better approximations, but yields an overall slower learning algorithm and with a higher chance of getting into local minima. In our experiments we have used $\beta = 8$, which showed a good trade-off between efficiency and accuracy.

At each learning step, we consider an example from the training set, say $(s, f(s))$, where s is a solution and $f(s)$ is the preference for such a solution. Then we compute the guess for the preference of s, say $g(s)$, according to the current set of temporal soft constraints. Then the error, is computed using the true and the guessed preferences: $E = \frac{1}{2}\sum_{s \in Tr}(f(s) - g(s))^2$. In our fuzzy case this formula becomes: $E = \frac{1}{2}\sum_{s \subset Tr}(f(s) - [min_{i=1,\cdots,\nu}\{a_i s_i^2 + b_i s_i + c_i\}])^2$, where ν is the number of constraints. And, considering the approximation of the min, we have: $E = \frac{1}{2}\sum_{s \in Tr}(f(s) + \frac{1}{\beta}ln(\frac{1}{\nu}\sum_{i=1}^{\nu}e^{-\beta(a_i s_i^2 + b_i s_i + c_i)})])^2$.

The a, b, and c parameters of the function on each constraint are then modified following the gradient descent rule. That is:

$$\tilde{a}_i = a_i - \eta[(f(s) - g(s))(\frac{1}{(\frac{1}{\nu}\sum_{j=1}^{\nu}e^{-\beta(a_j s_j^2 + b_j s_j + c_j)})}(-s_i^2\ e^{-\beta(a_i s_i^2 + b_i s_i + c_i)}))]$$

$$\tilde{b}_i = b_i - \eta[(f(s) - g(s))(\frac{1}{(\frac{1}{\nu}\sum_{j=1}^{\nu}e^{-\beta(a_j s_j^2 + b_j s_j + c_j)})}(-s_i\ e^{-\beta(a_i s_i^2 + b_i s_i + c_i)}))]$$

$$\tilde{c}_i = c_i - \eta[(f(s) - g(s))(\frac{1}{(\frac{1}{\nu}\sum_{j=1}^{\nu}e^{-\beta(a_j s_j^2 + b_j s_j + c_j)})}(-\ e^{-\beta(a_i s_i^2 + b_i s_i + c_i)}))]$$

We recall that η is the step size for the gradient descent, which in our case was set to 5×10^{-5}. Smaller η values yield smaller changes of the parameters, which usually makes local minima less probable.

Table 1. Mean absolute error and number of examples for learning preferences in some STPPs

Max	Mean error (min,max)	Number of examples
20	0.03 (0.02,0.04)	500
30	0.03 (0.02,0.04)	600
40	0.0333 (0.02,0.05)	700

After the updating of the parameters, we compute the absolute mean error over the training set, that is, the mean over the set of differences between $f(s)$ and $g(s)$, for all s. We stop when for 100 consecutive times, the error didn't improve of at least 20% of its previous value.

Once the chosen stopping criterion is met, the constraint network computed by the algorithm is an STPP with preference functions in the shape of convex quadratic functions, whose solutions are ranked very similarly to the original examples in the input. The similarity achieved by the learning algorithm is measured by comparing the solution ratings of the obtained problem with the examples contained in the test set, and by computing the absolute mean error on this set.

Our learning module has been tested on randomly generated problems. Every test involves the generation of an STPP via our generator, and then the generation of some examples of solutions and their rating. Then the STPP, without its preference functions, is given to the learning module, which, starting from the examples, learns new preference functions over the constraints, until the stopping criterion is met.

Table 1 shows the number of examples in the training (and also in the test) set, and the mean error (computed as the average of the mean error for three problems), for learning preferences in STPPs with 20 variables, range $= 40$, density $= 40\%$, and function perturbation parameters 10, 10, and 5. The maximum expansion, which, we recall, is related to the tightness notion, is 20, 30, and 40. What can be noticed is that the mean error increases as the parameter max increases, even if one uses more examples (which should ease the learning process). This is due to the fact that a larger value for max may yields larger intervals, and thus preference functions with larger domains and a larger number of solutions, which require more work from the learning algorithm. This trend seems to be confirmed also by other experimental results not reported here. These results show that it is feasible to learn local preferences from solution ratings, even when no local preference is given. However, it is probable that in many scenarios we will have some local preferences given by the user, and others to be learnt by the system.

5   Solving Soft Temporal Constraints

Once we have an STPP, either after a learning phase or not, we need to solve it, that is, to find an optimal solution according to its preferences. In this section we will describe two solvers for tractable classes of soft temporal constraint problems. The first one, path-solver, is more general, while the other one, called chop-solver, is more efficient. We will also present experimental results over randomly-generated problems to show the difference in performance between the two solvers.

5.1   A Solver Based on Path Consistency

The tractability results for STPPs that are contained in [8] can be translated in practice as follows: to find an optimal solution for an STPP, we can first apply path consistency and then use a search procedure to find a solution without the need to backtrack. More precisely, we can add to the results in [8] (and summarized in Section 2) the following results, whose proofs are omitted for lack of space.

Theorem 1. *Given an STPP P, let us call P' the STPP obtained by applying path-consistency to P. Then, all preference functions in P' have the same best preference level, which is lower than or equal to the original one.*

Theorem 2. *Consider the STP obtained from the STPP P' by taking, for each constraint, the sub-interval corresponding to the best preference level. Then, the solutions of such an STP coincide with the best solutions of the original P (and also of P'). Therefore, finding a solution of this STP means finding an optimal solution of P.*

Our first solver, which we call path-solver, relies on these results. In fact, the STPP solver takes as input an STPP with semi-convex preference functions and fuzzy temporal constraints, and returns an optimal solution of the given problem, working as follows and as shown in Figure 1: first, path consistency is applied to the given problem, by function STPP_PC-2, producing a new problem P'; then, an STP corresponding to P' is constructed, applying REDUCE_TO_BEST to P', by taking the subintervals corresponding to the best preference level and forgetting about the preference functions; finally, a backtrack-free search is performed to find a solution of the STP, specifically the earliest one is returned by function EARLIEST_BEST. All these steps are polynomial, so the overall complexity of solving an STPP with the above assumptions is polynomial. In Figure 1 we show the pseudocode for this solver.

In Figure 2 we show some results for finding an optimal solution for STPPs generated by our generator. Path-solver has been developed in C++ and tested on a Pentium III 1GHz.

As it can be seen, this solver is very slow. The main reason is that it uses a pointwise representation of the constraint intervals and the preference functions. This makes the solver more general, since it can represent any kind of preference functions, even those that don't have an analytical representation via a small set of parameters. In fact, even starting from convex quadratic functions, which need just three parameters, the first solving phase, which applies path consistency, can

```
Pseudocode for path-solver
1. input STPP P;
2. STPP P'=STPP_PC-2(P);
3. if P' inconsistent then exit;
4. STP P"=REDUCE_TO_BEST(P');
5. return EARLIEST_BEST(P").
```

Fig. 1. Path-solver

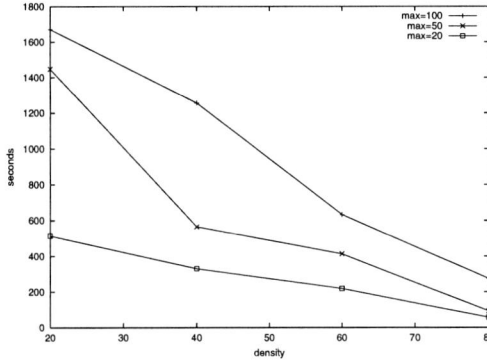

Fig. 2. Time needed to find an optimal solution (in seconds), as a function of density (d). The other parameters are: $n=50$, $r=100$, $pa=20$, $pb=20$, and $pc=30$. Mean on 3 examples

yield new preference functions which are not representable via three parameters only. For example, we could get semi-convex functions which are generic step functions, and thus not representable by giving new values to the initial three parameters.

5.2   A Solver Based on a Chopping Procedure

The second solver for STPPs that we have implemented, and that we will call 'chop-solver', is based on the proof of tractability for STPPs, with semi-convex preference functions and idempotent multiplicative operator of the underlying semiring, described in [8]. Let's briefly recall the main argument of that proof. The first step is to obtain an STP from a given STPP. In order to do this, we reduce each soft constraint of the STPP, say $\langle I, f \rangle$, to a simple temporal constraint without preferences. Consider $y \in A$, a value in the set of preferences. Then, since the function f on the soft constraint is semi-convex, the set $\{x : x \in I, f(x) \geq y\}$ forms an interval, i.e. a simple temporal constraint. Performing this transformation on each soft constraint of the original STPP we get an STP, wich we refer to as STP_y. The proof states that the set of solutions of the STP_{opt},

```
Pseudocode for chop-solver
1. input STPP P;
2. input precision;
3. integer n=0;
4. real lb=0, ub=1, y=0;
5. if(CONSISTENCY(P,y))
6.    y=0.5, n=n+1;
7.    while (n<=precision)
8.    if(CONSISTENCY(P,y))
9.       lb=y, y=y+(ub-lb)/2, n=n+1;
10.   else
11.      ub=y, y=y-(ub-lb)/2, n=n+1;
12.   end of while;
13.   return solution;
14. else exit.
```

Fig. 3. Chop-solver

where *opt* represents the highest level at which the derived STP is consistent, coincides with the set of optimal solutions of the STPP.

This solver works with STPPs with semi-convex quadratic functions (lines and convex parabolas), thus it is less general than path-solver. Preferences are handled via the fuzzy semiring. This means that the set of preferences we are considering is the interval [0,1].

The solver finds an optimal solution of the STPP identifying first STP_{opt} and returning its earliest or latest solution. *Opt* is found by performing a binary search in $[0,1]$. The bound on the precision of a number, that is the maximum number of decimal coded digits, implies that the number of search steps is always finite. Moreover, our implementation allows the user to specify at the beginning of the solving process the number n of digits he or she wants for the optimal solution's preference level.

The search for the optimal preference level starts with $y = 0$. Since STP_0 is the STP we would obtain by considering all the soft constraints as hard constraints, that is, with preference function equal to 1 on the elements of the interval and to 0 everywhere else, the algorithm first checks if the hard version of the problem is consistent. If it is found not to be consistent, the algorithm stops, informing the user that the whole problem is inconsistent. Otherwise the search goes on. Three variables are maintained during the search: *ub*, which contains the lowest level at which an inconsistent STP was found, *lb*, which contains the highest level at which a consistent STP was found, and *y*, which is the current level at which we need to perform the "chopping". It is easy to see that *ub* and *lb* are the upper and lower bound of the portion of the [0,1] interval to which we can restrict our search. The three values are updated depending on the outcome of the consistency test. In Figure 3 we show the pseudocode for this solver.

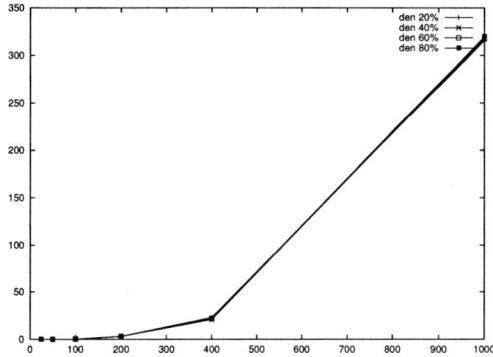

Fig. 4. Time, in seconds, (y-axis) required by chop-solver to solve, varying the number of variables (x-axis) and the density, with r=100000 max=50000, pa=5, pb=5 e pc=5. Mean on 10 examples. (The curves all overlap.)

The actual chopping and the consistency test on the STP obtained are performed by function CONSISTENCY. It receives, as input, the level at which the chop must be performed and the STPP. For each constraint of P, it considers three types of functions: a constant, a line or a semi-convex parabola. It then finds the intersection of the function with the constant function at the chopping level. As it finds the intersection, for each constraint it fills in the distance matrix F. This matrix is $N \times N$, where N is the number of variables of the problem. It represents the distance graph of the STP [4]. This means that if the constraint between variable i and variable j is the interval $[a, b]$, then $F[i][j] = b$ and $F[j][i] = -a$. At this point, we use the fact that an STP is consistent if and only if its distance graph has no negative cycles [4]. In order to accomplish this, we run Floyd-Warshall's all-shortest-paths algorithm on F and then check the diagonal elements. If no diagonal elements are negative, we can conclude that STP_y is consistent. If we have already reached the number of decimal digits the user wanted, then we return either the earliest or the latest solution, respectively corresponding to the assignments $x_i = -F[i][0]$ and $x_i = F[0][i]$. If instead one or more diagonal elements are negative, we can conclude that the STP_y is inconsistent and either return the solution of the last consistent STP or keep searching at lower levels of preference. The solution we return is always made of integers, that is, in the case of the earliest solution, the real numbers found intersecting the preference functions with the chopping level are approximated to the first larger integer while, for the latest, the approximation is to the largest smaller integer.

Figure 4 shows some experimental results for chop-solver. We have used the same random generator used to test path-solver, but with a different representation of the constraints generated, since chop-solver uses a parametric representation while path-solver needs a point-wise representation.

Table 2. Time in seconds, used by path-solver and chop-solver to solve problems with $n = 30, 40, 50$, $r = 100$, $max = 50$, $pa = 10$, $pb = 10$, and $pc = 5$ and varying density D. Results are mean on 3 examples

	D=20	D=40	D=60	D=80
path-solver (n=30)	515.95	235.57	170.18	113.58
chop-solver (n=30)	0.01	0.01	0.02	0.02
path-solver (n=40)	1019.44	516.24	356.71	320.28
chop-solver (n=40)	0.03	0.03	0.03	0.03
path-solver (n=50)	2077.59	1101.43	720.79	569.47
chop-solver (n=50)	0.05	0.05	0.06	0.07

We have tested chop-solver by varying the number of variables, from a minimum of 25 up to a maximum of 1000, and the density from 20% to 80%.

From Figure 4 we can conclude that chop-solver is only slightly sensitive to variations in the density, and it is very sensitive to the number of variables, since a higher number of variables yields an increase of the number of constraints on which the intersection procedure must be performed.

The choice of maintaining a fixed maximum enlargement of the intervals, that can be interpreted as a fixed tightness, is justified by the continuous representation of the constraint this solver uses. In fact, each constraint is represented by only two integers for the left and right ends of the interval and three real numbers as parameters of the function. Increasing max affects this kind of representation of a constraint only making these values bigger in modulo. This change however does not affect any of the operations performed by chop-solver.

5.3   Path-Solver vs. Chop-Solver

In Table 2 we can see a comparison between chop-solver and path-solver.

It appears clear that chop-solver is always much faster than path-solver. It can be noted, however, that chop-solver finds more constrained problems a little more difficult. This fact can be partially explained by the way problems are generated: having a higher density means having more constraints with non trivial parabolas, i.e. $a \neq 0$. The intersection procedure in this case is a little more complicated than in the case of constants or lines. On the other hand, with a higher density, path-solver has to deal with smaller constraints (w.r.t. the default ones), and thus the pointwise representation is less of a problem.

Chop-solver is also more precise, since it can find an optimal solution with a higher precision. It must be kept in mind, though, that path-solver is more general. In fact, the point-to-point representation of the constraints needed by path-solver, to be blamed for its poor performance, allows one to use any kind of semi-convex function, e.g. step functions, that cannot be easily compactly parametrized. Moreover, even wanting to extend the types of parametrized functions in the continuous representation for chop-solver, we must remember that the system deriving from intersecting the constant at chopping level and the function must be solvable in order to find the possible intersections.

6   Future Work

We plan to further test the overall system, composed of the solvers and the learning module, using other classes of randomly generated STPPs and also real-life problem instances such as satellite event scheduling. We also plan to extend our solver to deal with soft temporal problems which are not tractable. Moreover, we believe that the ideas underlying chop-solver can be used also for solving soft constraints in general, not just temporal ones. This would allow for the choice of the precision with which an optimal solution is found. This approach is related to hybrid algorithms based on abstraction of soft constraints, where a series of abstraction and concretization mappings can improve the bounds over an optimal solution [2].

References

[1] A. Biso, F. Rossi, and A. Sperduti. Experimental Results on Learning Soft Constraints. *Proc. KR 2000*, Morgan Kaufmann, 2000.

[2] Abstracting Soft Constraints. S. Bistarelli, P. Codognet, Y. Georget, F. Rossi. *Proc. ERCIM/Compulog Net work. on constraints*, Springer, LNAI 1865, 2000.

[3] S. Bistarelli, U. Montanari, and F. Rossi. Semiring-based Constraint Solving and Optimization. *Journal of the ACM*, 44(2):201–236, March 1997.

[4] R. Dechter, I. Meiri, and J. Pearl. Temporal constraint networks. Artificial Intelligence, Vol. 49, 1991, pp. 61-95.

[5] D. Dubois, H. Prade. Processing Fuzzy Temporal Knowledge. *IEEE Trans. On systems, Man, and Cybernetics*, 19:4,1989.

[6] M. Giacomin. From Crisp to Fuzzy Constraints Networks. *Proc. CP '01 Workshop on Modelling and Solving Problems with Soft Constraints*, 2001.

[7] S. Haykin. *Neural Networks: a comprehensive Foundation*. IEEE Press, 1994.

[8] L. Khatib, P. Morris, R. Morris, F. Rossi. Temporal Constraint Reasoning With Preferences. *Proc. IJCAI 2001*.

[9] L. Khatib, P. Morris, R. Morris, F. Rossi, A. Sperduti. Learning Preferences on Temporal Constraints: A Preliminary Report. *Proc. TIME 2001*, IEEE Comp. Soc. Press, 2001.

[10] R. Marin, M. A. Cardenas, M.Balsa, J. L.Sanchez. Obtaining solutions in Fuzzy Constraint Networks. *Int. Jour. of Approximate Reasoning*, 16:261-288, 1997.

[11] F. Rossi and A. Sperduti. Learning solution preferences in constraint problems. *Journal of Experimental and Theoretical Computer Science*, 1998. Vol 10.

[12] T. Schiex. Possibilistic constraint satisfaction problems, or "how to handle soft constraints?". *Proc. 8th Conf. of Uncertainty in AI*, pages 269–275, 1992.

[13] E. Schwalb, R. Dechter. Coping with disjunctions in temporal constraint satisfaction problems. *Proc. AAAI-93*, 1993.

[14] S. Russell and P. Norvig. *Artificial Intelligence: A Modern Approach*. Prentice Hall, 1995.

[15] L. Vila, L. Godo. On fuzzy temporal constraint networks. *Mathware and Soft Computing*, 3:315-334,1994.

Opportunistic Specialization in Russian Doll Search[*]

Pedro Meseguer[1], Martí Sánchez[1], and Gérard Verfaillie[2]

[1] IIIA-CSIC
Campus UAB, 08193 Bellaterra, Spain
{pedro|marti}@iiia.csic.es
[2] ONERA
2 av. Edouard Belin, BP 4025, 31055 Toulouse Cedex, France
verfaillie@cert.fr

Abstract. Russian Doll Search (RDS) is a clever procedure to solve overconstrained problems. RDS solves a sequence of nested subproblems, each including one more variable than the previous, until the whole problem is solved. Specialized RDS (SRDS) solves each subproblem for every value of the new variable. SRDS lower bound is better than RDS lower bound, causing a higher efficiency. A natural extension is Full Specialized RDS (FSRDS), which solves each subproblem for every value of every variable. Although FSRDS lower bound is better than the SRDS one, the extra work performed by FSRDS renders it inefficient. However, much of the useless work can be avoided. With this aim, we present Opportunistic Specialization in RDS (OSRDS), an algorithm that lies between SRDS and FSRDS. In addition to specialize the values of one variable, OSRDS specializes some values of other variables that look promising to increase the lower bound in the current distribution of inconsistency counts. Experimental results on random and real problems show the benefits of this approach.

1 Introduction

When solving a Constraint Satisfaction Problem (CSP), one has to assign values to variables satisfying a set of constraints. In real applications it often happens that problems are over-constrained and do not have any solution. In this situation, it is desirable to find an assignment that *best respects* the constraints under some preference criterion. Under this view, over-constrained CSPs are optimization problems for which *branch and bound* is a suitable solving method inside a complete search strategy. The efficiency of branch and bound-based algorithms greatly depends on the lower bound used to detect deadends and to avoid the exploration of large regions in the search space. This lower bound should be both as large and as cheap to compute as possible.

---

[*] The first two authors were supported by the IST Programme of the Commission of the European Union through the ECSPLAIN project (IST-1999-11969), and by the Spanish CICYT project TAP99-1086-C03-02.

P. Van Hentenryck (Ed.): CP 2002, LNCS 2470, pp. 264–279, 2002.

An approach [7, 16, 10, 1, 11] for lower bound computation aggregates two main elements: (i) the global contribution of assigned variables, and (ii) the addition of individual contributions of unassigned variables. Another approach [15] keeps (i) but substitutes (ii) by a global contribution of unassigned variables. This is done by the Russian Doll Search (RDS) method: it performs n successive searches on nested subproblems, each one resulting from the addition of one variable to the previous one, to finally solve a problem of n variables.

As RDS solves each subproblem, Specialized RDS (SRDS) [12] solves each subproblem for every value of the new variable, getting a lower bound better than that of RDS and resulting in a higher efficiency.

In this paper we present a natural extension, the *Full Specialized RDS* (FS-RDS), which solves each subproblem for every value of every variable included in the subproblem. The FSRDS lower bound is better than the SRDS one, but the extra effort performed solving subproblems repeatedly makes it inefficient. A detailed analysis shows that much of this work is useless, because many of the subproblem solvings are never used when computing the lower bound during search. To avoid useless work, the main source of inefficiency, we present the *Opportunistic Specialization* approach in RDS (OSRDS), an algorithm that lies between SRDS and OSRDS. In addition to specialize the values of one variable (typically the new variable in the subproblem, as it is done in SRDS), it specializes those values of other variables that look promising to contribute to the lower bound, on the current distribution of inconsistency counts. Clearly, the OSRDS lower bound is better than the SRDS one. Experimental results show that OSRDS strategy is often superior to SRDS, because extra pruning causes substantial savings in global search effort.

In this paper we consider the Weighted CSP model, where constraints can be assigned different weights and the goal is to find the assignment that minimizes the accumulated weight of unsatisfied constraints, considering the Max-CSP model as a particular case where all constraints have the same weight. Both models are tested with with randomly generated problems and radio link frequency assignment problems, respectively. Our approach can also be applied to other frameworks.

This paper is structured as follows. In Section 2 we introduce notations and briefly review previous approaches. In Section 3 we introduce the FSRDS approach, analising the various lower bounds that can be computed. Section 4 presents the FSRDS algorithm. The opportunistic specialization idea is introduced in Section 5, with its corresponding algorithm. In Section 6 we discuss some experimental results. Finally, Section 7 contains some conclusions and directions of further work.

2   Preliminaries

A discrete binary constraint satisfaction problem (CSP) is defined by a finite set of variables $X = \{1, \ldots, n\}$, a set of finite domains $\{D_i\}_{i=1}^n$ and a set of binary constraints $\{R_{ij}\}$. Each variable i takes values in its corresponding domain D_i.

A constraint R_{ij} is a subset of $D_i \times D_j$ which only contains the allowed value pairs for variables i, j [1]. An assignment of values to variables is complete if it includes every variable in X, otherwise it is partial. A *solution* for a CSP is a complete assignment satisfying every constraint. The number of variables is n, the maximum cardinality of domains is d and the number of constraints is e. Letters $i, j, k \ldots$ denote variables, $a, b, c \ldots$ denote values, and a pair (i, a) denotes the value a of variable i.

If a solution does not exist the problem is over-constrained. In this case, it may be of interest to find a complete assignment that best respects all constraints. This moves the problem into the *Soft CSP* framework, for which different theoretical models have been proposed [2, 13]. In this paper, we consider the Weigthed CSP model, where value tuples violating a constraint have associated a weight or cost. The cost of a complete assignment is the sum of all its applicable costs. The solution of an over-constrained CSP is a complete assignment with minimum cost. Note that the sum of costs is the aggregation operator used in this model, which is not idempotent.

There are two main strategies to solve this kind of problems, *inference* and *search*. Inference methods transform the problem into a equivalent one by inferring implicit constraints. The new problem is presumably simpler than the previous one, and the complete process goes on until the whole problem is solved. A good example of this stragegy is the *variable elimination* algorithm [6], which at each step eliminates one problem variable, adding a new constraint that summarizes the effect of the eliminated variable. The problem is trivially solved when all variables have been eliminated. However, this algorithm requires exponential space. The *mini-bucket* approach [5], which approximates the exact method by limiting the space complexity, has been proposed to overcome this difficulty.

Regarding complete search methods, most follow a *branch and bound* schema. These algorithms perform a depth-first traversal on the search tree defined by the problem, where internal nodes represent incomplete assignments and leaf nodes stand for complete ones. At each node, branch and bound computes the *upper bound* (UB) as the cost of the best solution found so far (complete assignment with minimum cost in the explored part of the search tree), and the *lower bound* (LB) as an underestimation of the cost of any leaf node descendant from the current one. When $UB \leq LB$, we know that the current best solution cannot be improved below the current node. In that case, the algorithm prunes all its successors and performs backtracking. In addition, *VarElimSearch* [8] is a hybrid approach that combines inference and search methods. It performs variable elimination when it is not expensive in terms of space, moving to search otherwise.

In this paper, we consider complete search with branch and bound. At each node, assigned variables are called *past* (P), while unassigned variables are called *future* (F). The *cost* of a node is the aggregated cost of the current partial assignment in P. To gain efficiency in branch and bound, the quality of the

---

[1] We assume that for each pair of variables i, j there is only one constraint $R_{i,j}$

lower bound is essential. Because of that many approaches have tried to increase the lower bound in several ways, which can be grouped in two main classes,

1. Direct inconsistency propagation. When the aggregation operator for soft constraints is non-idempotent, inconsistencies cannot be propagated as in the hard case[2], because the resulting problem may not be equivalent to the original one (the process may even not terminate) [3]. However, direct inconsistency propagation (from a constraint to the variables connected by it) can be done. The only caution is to avoid including information from the same constraint more than once in the lower bound. Direct inconsistency propagation has been done in several ways,
   - Inconsistency counts: the inconsistency count of value a of a future variable i, ic_{ia}, is the aggregation of costs that (i, a) has with past variables. This is the basis for the Partial Forward Checking (PFC) [7] lower bound.
   - Directed arc inconsistency counts: constraints among future variables are directed [11]. Costs associated with arc inconsistencies are recorded in the variable where the constraint points to, using directed arc inconsistency counts, which can be combined with inconsistency counts to produce a new lower bound [16, 10, 11].
   - Arc inconsistency counts: constraints among future variables are not directed. Costs associated with arc inconsistencies are recorded using arc inconsistency counts, a fraction of which can be combined with inconsistency counts to produce a new lower bound [1].
   - Russian doll search (RDS): at a point in search, the subproblem formed by future variables and constraints among them has been previously solved to optimality. The optimal cost of this subproblem is added to the PFC lower bound producing a new lower bound [15].
2. Soft propagation. New forms of constraint propagation for soft constraints have been devised [14] [9], adapted to allow for an effective lower bound computation inside a branch and bound algorithm. These approaches have not been fully tested as lower bound generators, although preliminary results show them as very promising in this respect.

3   Full Specialized RDS

To present the different versions of russian doll search in a compact form, we use the following notation. Given a CSP, variables are ordered statically $1, 2, \ldots, n$. The subproblem i is composed by the variables $(i, \ldots, n)$ and the constraints of the original problem among these variables [3]. Subproblems are solved in decreasing index ordering (increasing size ordering), from $n, n-1, \ldots$ until 1, that is the original problem.

---

[2] And also in the fuzzy case, both use the *min* idempotent aggregation operator.

[3] Notice that this subproblem indexing differs from the notation based on the order of subproblem resolution, used in previous papers [15] [12].

For each subproblem i, the different russian doll algorithms work as follows. The original RDS [15] computes rds^i, the optimal cost of subproblem i. Specialized RDS (SRDS) [12] computes rds^i_{ia}, the optimal cost of subproblem i for every value a of the variable i, the first variable of subproblem i. Full Specialized RDS (FSRDS) extends this idea to every variable in the subproblem: it computes rds^i_{ja}, $i \leq j \leq n$, the optimal cost of subproblem i for every value a of every variable j included in the subproblem.

Regarding lower bounds, the lower bound computed by SRDS is higher than the one computed by RDS. Despite the fact that SRDS performs more work per node, its better lower bound allows for a more effective pruning, producing an algorithm clearly more efficient than RDS.

In terms of number of searches, RDS performs n successive searches, one for each subproblem. SRDS performs $n \times d$ searches, since it has to compute the optimal cost for every value of the first variable of each subproblem. FSRDS performs $\frac{n(n-1)d}{2}$ searches, since it has to compute the optimal cost for every value of every variable of each subproblem.

3.1   A New Lower Bound

Let us consider that FSRDS has solved subproblem i, and the sets of past and future variables are $P = \{1, \ldots, i-1\}$ and $F = \{i, \ldots, n\}$. For every $k \in F$ and $a \in D_k$, rds^i_{ka} contains the optimal cost of subproblem i with value a for variable k. ¿From these elements, a new family of lower bounds can be defined as follows,

$$\widehat{LB}^{FS}(P, F, j) = cost(P) + min_a(ic_{ja} + rds^i_{ja}) + \sum_{k \in F, k \neq j} min_a ic_{ka} \quad \forall j \in F$$

Property 1. $\forall j \in F$, $\widehat{LB}^{FS}(P, F, j)$ is a safe lower bound.

Proof. Similar to the proof of Property 1 in [12].

The FSRDS lower bound, $LB^{FS}(P, F)$, is the best lower bound of this family,

$$LB^{FS}(P, F) = max_{j \in F} \widehat{LB}^{FS}(P, F, j)$$

Obviously, $LB^{FS}(P, F)$ is a safe lower bound. In addition, it improves $LB^S(P, F)$, the lower bound of SRDS.

Property 2. Using the same static variable ordering $LB^{FS}(P, F) \geq LB^S(P, F)$

Proof.

$$LB^{FS}(P, F) = cost(P) + max_j[min_a(ic_{ja} + rds^i_{ja}) + \sum_{k \in F, k \neq j} min_a ic_{ka}]$$

$$LB^S(P, F) = cost(P) + max_j[min_a(ic_{ja} + rds^j_{ja}) + \sum_{k \in F, k \neq j} min_a ic_{ka}]$$

Given that $rds^i_{ja} \geq rds^j_{ja}$, we conclude that $LB^{FS}(P, F) \geq LB^S(P, F)$.   □

An example of this property appears in Fig. 1.

	x_1	x_2	x_3	x_4	x_5	x_6
1						
2						
3						

$$P = \{(x_1,1)\}, \quad F = \{x_2,x_3,x_4,x_5,x_6\}, \quad D = \{1,2,3\}$$

ic_{ja}

	x_1	x_2	x_3	x_4	x_5	x_6
1	Q	1	1	1	1	1
2		1	0	0	0	0
3		0	1	0	0	0

rds^j_{ja} (SRDS)

	x_1	x_2	x_3	x_4	x_5	x_6
1		3	2	1	0	0
2		3	2	1	1	0
3		3	2	1	0	0

rds^i_{ja} (FSRDS)

	x_1	x_2	x_3	x_4	x_5	x_6
1		3	3	3	3	3
2		3	4	4	4	3
3		3	3	3	3	3

$$LB^S(P,F) = cost(P) + min_a(ic_{2a} + rds^2_{2a}) + \sum_{k \in F, k \neq 2} min_a(ic_{ka}) = 0+3+0 = 3$$
$$LB^{FS}(P,F) = cost(P) + min_a(ic_{3a} + rds^2_{3a}) + \sum_{k \in F, k \neq 3} min_a(ic_{ka}) = 0+4+0 = 4$$

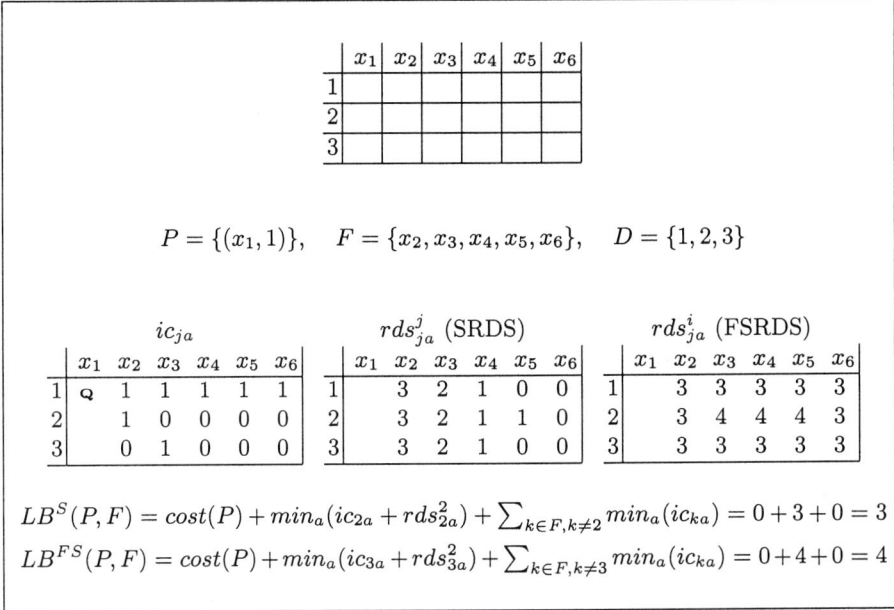

Fig. 1. This example shows the 6-queens problem in a 3×6 chessboard, such that each queen has to be in a different column. It is shown the ic table after assigning $(x_1,1)$, and the tables with the russian doll contribution generated by SRDS and FSRDS. The SRDS lower bound combines ic and rds in variable 2. However, FSRDS takes advantadge of having a more updated information. It combines ic with rds in variable 3, getting a higher lower bound

3.2 Future Value Pruning

A value b of a future variable l can be pruned when the lower bound specialized for that value is greater than or equal to the current UB. In FSRDS there is a family of lower bounds, $LB^{FS}(P,F,j)$, which can be specialized for value b of future variable l as follows,

$$\widehat{LB}^{FS}_{lb}(P,F,j) = \begin{cases} cost(P) + ic_{lb} + min_a(ic_{ja} + rds^i_{ja}) + \sum_{k \in F, k \neq j,l} min_a ic_{ka} & j \neq l \\ cost(P) + ic_{lb} + rds^i_{lb} + \sum_{k \in F, k \neq l} min_a ic_{ka} & j = l \end{cases}$$

The FSRDS lower bound specialized for value b of future variable l is,

$$LB^{FS}_{lb}(P,F) = max_j(\widehat{LB}^{FS}_{lb}(P,F,j))$$

which is always better than the specialized lower bound of SRDS.

Property 3. Using the same static variable ordering $LB^{FS}_{lb}(P,F) \geq LB^S_{lb}(P,F)$.

Proof. Similar to the proof of property 2.

3.3   Initial Adjustment of UB

When solving subproblem i it is very important to start with a good UB, instead of taking $UB = \infty$ by default. In this way, pruning is optimized from the very beginning. Two initial adjustments of UB are considered, as follows,

1. When solving the subproblem $i+1$ and a better solution is found, the current UB is decreased. Then, this new solution is extended to value a of variable i, and the cost of the extended solution is taken as a candidate UB for the subproblem to be solved with (i, a). This strategy is performed for all feasible a of variable i.
2. When solving the subproblem i with (i, a) and a better solution is found, the current UB is decreased. This new solution is modified, substituting a by b in variable i, if b is still unsolved in i. The cost of the modified solution is taken as a candidate UB for the subproblem to be solved with (i, b). This strategy is performed for all unsolved b of variable i.

4   The FSRDS Algorithm

The FSRDS algorithm appears in Figure 2, as an evolved version of the SRDS algorithm [12]. The algorithm solves subproblems in sequence, following a decreasing index ordering. Each subproblem is solved using a branch-and-bound algorithm, where RDS contributions of previously solved subproblems are used to compute the current lower bound at each node.

For each subproblem i the algorithm maintains UB^i and LB^i, two bidimensional (variable, value) tables that contain upper and lower bounds. UB^i_{kc} is an upper bound of the optimal cost of subproblem i that includes the assignment (k, c). It is updated by the $adjustUB()$ procedure, following the criteria given in Section 3.3. LB^i_{kc} is a lower bound of the optimal cost of subproblem i that includes the assignment (k, c). The table of subproblem i is initialized from the table of subproblem $i + 1$, and it is updated by the $updateLB(i, k)$ procedure. It contains either the exact cost of solving subproblem i specialized for (k, c), or a lower bound of it.

The $FullSpecializedRDS$ procedure contains the main differences between FSRDS and SRDS. Each subproblem is solved for each pair (k, c). This is done restricting the domain of the selected variable k to a single value c, and executing the branch-and-bound procedure PFC_SRDS. Once all values of variable k have been specialized, the optimal cost of subproblem i is known, as the $min_c rds^i_{kc}$. This information is updated in the LB^i table, increasing up to this optimum cost all the lower bounds that have not reached it.

The FSRDS algorithm is given for reference purposes only, given that it is not an efficient algorithm. Despite that FSRDS is able to compute better lower bounds than SRDS, it performs too much work when solving subproblems (specially solving big subproblems repeatedly). Because of that, FSRDS is not competitive with SRDS. However, some small changes can produce an efficient algorithm, as explained in the following Section.

procedure $FullSpecializedRDS(\{1,\ldots,n\},\{FD_1,\ldots,FD_n\})$
1 **for** i **from** n **downto** 1 **do**
2   $LB^i \leftarrow LB^{i+1}$;
3   **for** k **from** i **to** n **do**
4   **for all** $c \in FD_k$ **do**
5      $FD'_k \leftarrow \{c\}$;
6      $PFC\_SRDS(k,c,\{\},\{i,\ldots,n\},\{FD_i,\ldots,FD'_k,\ldots,FD_n\})$;
7     $updateLB(i,k)$;

procedure $updateLB(i,k)$
1 **for** l **from** i **to** n **do**
2   **for all** $a \in FD_l$ **do**
3   **if** $(LB^i_{la} < min_c rds^i_{kc})$ **then** $LB^i_{la} \leftarrow min_c rds^i_{kc}$;

procedure $PFC\_SRDS(k,c,P,F,FD)$
1 **if** $(F = \emptyset)$ **then**
2   $Sol \leftarrow assignment(P)$;
3   $UB \leftarrow cost(P)$;
4   $adjustUB()$;
5 **else**
6   $i \leftarrow PopAVariable(F)$;
7   **if** $P = \emptyset$ **then** $UB \leftarrow UB^i_{kc}$;
8   **for all** $a \in FD_i$ **do**
9    $newD \leftarrow cost(P) + ic_{ia}$;
10   **if** $(newD + LB^i_{ia} + \sum_{l \in F} min_b ic_{lb} < UB)$ **then**
11     $lookahead(i,a,F,FD)$;
12   **if** $(newD + max_{j \in F}(min_b(ic_{jb} + LB^i_{jb}) + \sum_{l \in F, l \neq j} min_b ic_{lb}) < UB)$ **then**
13      $newFD \leftarrow prune(F,FD)$;
14      $PFC\_SRDS(k,c,P \cup \{(i,a)\},F,NewFD)$;
15   **if** $P = \emptyset$ **then** $rds^i_{kc} \leftarrow UB$;

procedure $lookahead(i,a,F,FD)$
1 **for all** $l \in F$ **do**
2   **for all** $b \in FD_l$ **do**
3   **if** $(inconsistent(i,a,l,b))$ **then** $ic_{lb} \leftarrow ic_{lb} + 1$;

function $prune(F,FD)$
1 **for all** $l \in F$ **do**
2   **for all** $b \in FD_l$ **do**
3   **if** $(LowerBound^{FS}_{lb}(newD,F) \geq UB)$ **then** $FD_l \leftarrow FD_l - \{b\}$;
4 **return** FD;

function $LowerBound^{FS}_{lb}(newD,F)$
1 $lb_1 \leftarrow newD + ic_{lb} + max_{j \in F}(min_c(ic_{jc} + LB^i_{jc}) + \sum_{p \in F, p \neq j,l} min_c ic_{pc})$;
2 $lb_2 \leftarrow newD + ic_{lb} + LB^i_{lb} + \sum_{p \in F, p \neq l} min_c ic_{pc}$;
3 **if** $(lb_1 > lb_2)$ **return** lb_1 **else return** lb_2;

Fig. 2. Full Specialized Russian Doll Search algorithm

5   Opportunistic Value Specialization

FSRDS has to compute the rds^i_{kc} contribution for every value c of every variable k in the subproblem i. In each tree branch, only one variable j and one value b (the one with minimum sum of ic plus rds contribution) are chosen to contribute to the lower bound. If we could anticipate this pair (j, b) (variable, value), we would specialize this very pair only, saving the useless effort of specializing other values of other variables that finally do not contribute to the lower bound.

In general, unless all rds^i_{kc} contributions are computed, it is impossible to determine the pair (j, b) that offers the best combination between ic and rds in a given tree branch when solving subproblem $i - 1$. However, once variable $i - 1$ has been assigned and its ics have been propagated, it is possible to identify some (variable, value) pairs which look promising to increment the lower bound if their optimum cost would increase their currently recorded cost (which is a lower bound). Then, these (variable, value) pairs are specialized. This idea is called *opportunistic value specialization*, because it specializes those (variable, value) pairs which look promising to increment the lower bound, on the basis of the current ic distribution. It avoids specializing those pairs which will not increment the lower bound, even if their optimum costs were available.

The first step to implement this idea is to find the minimum cost of subproblem i, because it will be used to update the LB^i table (procedure $updateLB(i, k)$ of Fig. 2). Using this updated LB^i, it is possible to identify which (variable, value) pairs look more promising for specialization. This implies specialization of one variable k of subproblem i, in two possible ways,

1. Specialize all values of variable k.
2. Specialize the values of variable k until the minimum cost of solving subproblem i has been found.

Any variable k is suitable for this. An example of this appears in Fig. 3. Once the LB^i table has been updated, subproblem $i - 1$ begins to be solved. After assigning variable $i - 1$ and ics have been propagated, we compute,

$$w = max_j[min_b(ic_{jb} + LB^i_{jb}) + \sum_{k \in F, k \neq j} min_a ic_{ka}]$$

All pairs (j, b) such that,

$$w = min_b(ic_{jb} + LB^i_{jb}) + \sum_{k \in F, k \neq j} min_a ic_{ka} \quad \wedge$$
$$w < ic_{ja} + LB^i_{ja} + \sum_{k \in F, k \neq j} min_a ic_{ka}, \quad \forall a \in D_j - \{b\} \quad \wedge$$
$$rds^i_{jb} = unknown$$

are the candidates to increase the lower bound if their exact rds^i_{jb} costs were known. At this point, the resolution of subproblem $i - 1$ is suspended. The candidates (variable, value) pairs are specialized, one by one, in the subproblem i. As soon as one candidate (j, b) has increased its LB^i_{jb}, no more candidates are

$$LB_{ja}^2$$

	x_1	x_2	x_3	x_4	x_5	x_6
1		**3**	3	3	3	3
2		**3**	3	3	3	3
3		**3**	3	3	3	3

(b)

$$LB_{ja}^2$$

	x_1	x_2	x_3	x_4	x_5	x_6
1		2	2	2	2	2
2		2	2	3	3	2
3		2	2	2	2	2

(a)

	x_1	x_2	x_3	x_4	x_5	x_6
1		3	3	**3**	3	3
2		3	3	3	3	3
3		3	3	**3**	3	3

(c)

$$rds_{ja}^2$$

	x_1	x_2	x_3	x_4	x_5	x_6
1		**3**	**3**	**3**	**3**	**3**
2		**3**	**4**	**4**	**4**	**3**
3		**3**	**3**	**3**	**3**	**3**

(d)

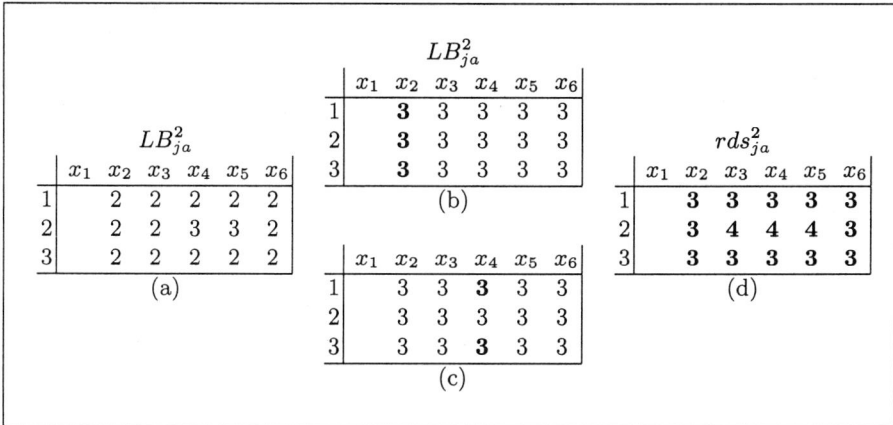

Fig. 3. This example shows how to find the minimum cost of subproblem 2 of the 6-queens on the 3×6 chessboard problem. Before start solving, (a) the LB table is copied from the previous iteration, putting the values of the new variable to the previous minimum. After solving, either (b) specializing all values of variable x_2, or (c) specializing variable x_4 until the minimum cost is found. In both cases, 3 is found as the minimum cost (optimal values are depicted in boldface). All values with costs lower than 3 are updated to 3 (the new minimum cost for subproblem 2, a lower bound for all other values). The optimal values of rds^2 are shown (d)

specialized and the resolution of subproblem $i - 1$ is resumed. An example of this process appears in Fig. 4.

How much can we improve the global lower bound by specializing (j, b)? Let $c \in D_j$ be the value with the next minimum of $ic_{jc} + LB_{jc}^i$. After specialization of (j, b), the maximum increment in lower bound that we can get is $\Delta = ic_{jc} + LB_{jc}^i - ic_{jb} - LB_{jb}^i$, no matter how high rds_{jb}^i could be. Therefore, when a value is specialized opportunistically, we do not ask for the optimum value of the subproblem i with value (j, b). Instead, we pass to the branch and bound the maximum achievable increment of the lower bound as a parameter, and as soon as this increment has been achieved, the specialization process stops.

In fact, when solving subproblem $i - 1$ and pair (j, b) has to be specialized, it is not mandatory to do it in the previous subproblem i. Pair (j, b) can be specialized in any previous subproblem k including j, that is, $i \leq k \leq j$. Obviously, subproblem k has to allow enough room for improvement, that is, $UB_{jb}^k \geq \Delta + LB_{jb}^i$.

Including these ideas in the FSRDS algorithm, we have produced the Opportunistic SRDS (OSRDS) algorithm, which appears in Fig. 5. This algorithm has the following differences with the one presented in Fig. 2,

ic_{ja}

	x_1	x_2	x_3	x_4	x_5	x_6
1	Q	1	1	1	1	1
2		1	0	0	0	0
3		0	1	0	0	0

(a)

LB^2_{ja}

	x_1	x_2	x_3	x_4	x_5	x_6
1		3	3	3	3	3
2		3	<u>3</u>	3	3	3
3		3	3	3	3	3

(b)

	x_1	x_2	x_3	x_4	x_5	x_6
1		3	3	<u>3</u>	3	3
2		3	<u>3</u>	3	3	3
3		<u>3</u>	3	3	3	3

(c)

LB^2_{ja}

	x_1	x_2	x_3	x_4	x_5	x_6
1		3	3	3	3	3
2		3	4	3	3	3
3		3	3	3	3	3

(d)

	x_1	x_2	x_3	x_4	x_5	x_6
1		3	3	<u>3</u>	3	3
2		3	4	3	3	3
3		3	3	<u>3</u>	3	3

(e)

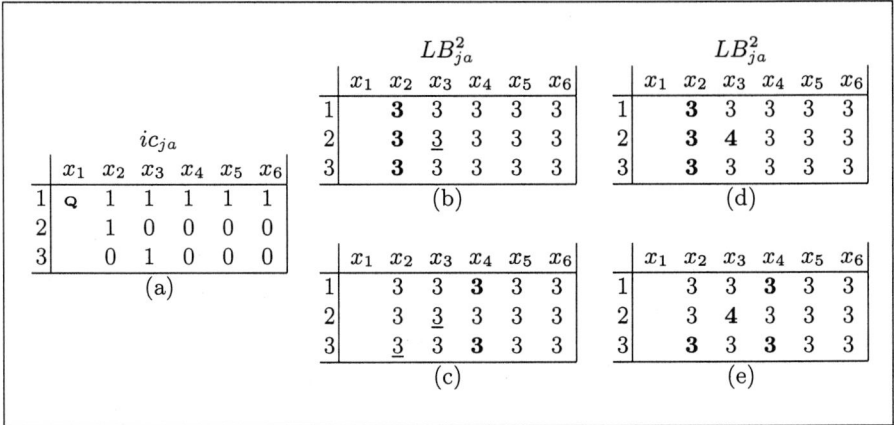

Fig. 4. This example shows the opportunistic value specialization. After finding the minimum cost for subproblem 2 (Fig. 3), there are two possible LB^2 tables. Subproblem 1 is begin to be solved, and the assignment $(x_1, 1)$ causes ic to propagate (a). Combining the ic table with both LB^2 tables, it is easy to realize which values would be good to specialize to obtain an increment in the lower bound, that is, value $(x_3, 2)$ (b) and values $(x_2, 3)$ and $(x_3, 2)$ (c) (candidate values are underlined). Specializing $(x_3, 2)$ increases its rds contribution to 4, which causes an increment in the lower bound (see Fig. 1). Specializing $(x_2, 3)$ does not increase its rds contribution, that remains in 3. The new LB^2 tables are in (d) and (e), respectively

1. Minimum cost of subproblem i. For simplicity, we select variable i as the one to be specialized (line 3 of *OpportunisticSpecializedRDS*). If every value of i is specialized, no other change is needed. If specialization stops when the minimum cost of solving subproblem i has been found, the upper bound has not to be reinitialized for every value of variable i (line 7 of *PFC_SRDS*).
2. Opportunistic specialization. This strategy is performed by the procedure *opportunisticSpecialization*, detailed in Fig. 5. This procedure is called after *lookahead* (see lines 13 to 17 of *PFC_SRDS*). Specialization goes through *candidates* and as soon as one has increased the lower bound, the process terminates (line 10 of *opportunisticSpecialization*).
3. Adjusted increment of the lower bound. To specialize a value, branch and bound is called with the amount required to increment the lower bound. This amount is $UB^i_{kc} - LB^i_{kc}$ when specializing values of variable k (line 6 of *OpportinisticSpecializedRDS*), and it is $\Delta = ic_{jc} + LB^i_{jc} - ic_{jb} - LB^i_{jb}$ for opportunistic value specialization (lines 3 and 4 of *opportunisticSpecialization*).

As in the SRDS case [12], we have developed a limited version of this algorithm. *Limited OSRDS* includes a parameter t that establishes the max-

procedure $OpportunisticSpecializedRDS(\{1,\ldots,n\},\{FD_1,\ldots,FD_n\})$
1 **for** i **from** n **downto** 1 **do**
2   $LB^i \leftarrow LB^{i+1}$;
3   $k \leftarrow i$;
4   **for all** $c \in FD_k$ **do**
5     $FD'_k \leftarrow \{c\}$;
6     $PFC\_SRDS(k,c,UB^i_{kc} - LB^i_{kc},\{\},\{i,\ldots,n\},\{FD_i,\ldots,FD'_k,ts,FD_n\})$;
7     $updateLB(i,k)$;
procedure $PFC\_SRDS(k,c,\Delta,P,F,FD)$
1 **if** $(F = \emptyset)$ **then**
2   $Sol \leftarrow assignment(P)$;
3   $UB \leftarrow cost(P)$;
4   $adjustUB()$;
5 **else**
6   $i \leftarrow PopAVariable(F)$;
7   **if** $P = \emptyset$ **then** $UB \leftarrow \Delta + LB^i_{kc}$;
8   **for all** $a \in FD_i$ **do**
9     $newD \leftarrow cost(P) + ic_{ia}$;
10   **if** $(newD + LB^i_{ia} + \sum_{l \in F} min_b ic_{lb} < UB)$ **then**
11      $lookahead(i,a,F,FD)$;
12   **if** $(newD + max_j(min_b(ic_{jb} + LB^i_{jb}) + \sum_{l \in F, l \neq j} min_b ic_{lb}) < UB)$ **then**
13       $opportunisticSpecialization()$;
14   **if** $(newD + max_j(min_b(ic_{jb} + LB^i_{jb}) + \sum_{l \in F, l \neq j} min_b ic_{lb}) < UB)$ **then**
15        $newFD \leftarrow prune(F,FD)$;
16        $PFC\_SRDS(k,c,\Delta,P \cup \{(i,a)\},F,NewFD)$;
17   **if** $P = \emptyset$ **then** $rds^i_{kc} \leftarrow UB$;
procedure $opportunisticSpecialization()$
1 $candidates \leftarrow findCandidates()$;
2 **for all** $(j,b) \in candidates$ **do**
3   $c \leftarrow argnextmin_a(ic_{ja} + LB^i_{ja})$;
4   $\Delta \leftarrow ic_{jc} + LB^i_{jc} - ic_{jb} - LB^i_{jb}$;
5   find k such that $UB^k_{jb} \geq \Delta + LB^i_{jb}$, $i < k \leq j$
6   $FD'_j \leftarrow \{b\}$;
7   $PFC\_SRDS(j,b,\Delta,\{\},\{k,\ldots,n\},\{FD_k,\ldots,FD'_j,\ldots,FD_n\})$;
8   **if** lower bound has increased **then**
9   **for** l **from** k **downto** i **do** $updateLB(l,j)$;
10   **break**;

Fig. 5. Opportunistic Specialized Russian Doll Search algorithm

imum size of a subproblem k to be solved to specialize a pair (j, b) by the
opportunisticSpecialization procedure.

6   Experimental Results

6.1   Random Problems

We give results on 6 classes of binary random problems. A binary random
problem class is defined by the tuple $\langle n, m, p_1, p_2 \rangle$, where n is the number of variables, m is the number of values per variable, p_1 is the problem connectivity and p_2 is the constraint tightness. We tested the following
six classes $\langle 10, 10, 1, p_2 \rangle$, $\langle 15, 5, 1, p_2 \rangle$, $\langle 15, 10, 50/105, p_2 \rangle$, $\langle 20, 5, 100/190, p_2 \rangle$,
$\langle 25, 10, 37/300, p_2 \rangle$, $\langle 40, 5, 55/780, p_2 \rangle$, increasing the number of variables and
decreasing connectivity. Results are presented in Figure 6, showing mean CPU
time versus tightness. Each point is averaged over 50 executions. The graphics
show the limited OSRDS (for $t = 0$ as a reference and for one t closer to n)
and SRDS algorithms. We observe that limited OSRDS shows a moderated improvement over SRDS, except in the $\langle 40, 5, 55/780, p_2 \rangle$ class. Random problems
do not show the advantages of OSRDS because the homogeneity of values (all
values of a same variable have the same expected cost).

6.2   Frequency Assignment Problems

The Frequency Assignment Problem from CELAR [4] is a widely used binary
overconstrained CSP benchmark. It consists of 11 instances to which different
optimization criteria can be applied. We have centered our efforts in instance
number 6, one of the hardest, which has 200 variables and the optimization
criteria consists of minimizing the accumulated cost of the violated constraints.
Constraints have violation costs that vary from 1 to 1000. A simplification (from
T. Schiex) eliminates all hard equality constraints and reduces the number of
variables by two. We assume this simplification.

We have solved the five subinstances of CELAR instance 6 with an hybrid
strategy. The first 12 variables of a subproblem are solved by FSRDS. From
variable 13 to variable 17, they are solved by OSRDS. ¿From variable 18 to
variable 22, the original RDS approach is used. Results are given in Table 1.
Comparing with the same instances solved by SRDS [12], we observe an speed
up of one order of magnitude in CPU time.

This hybrid strategy is compared with limited SRDS (up to 17 variables)
in Figure 7. We observe that the hybrid is more costly at the beginning, when
subproblems are small, but it shows to be more effective for larger subproblems.
This suggest that, on heterogeneous problems, generalized specialization followed
by opportunistic specialization is an efficient combination of RDS techniques.

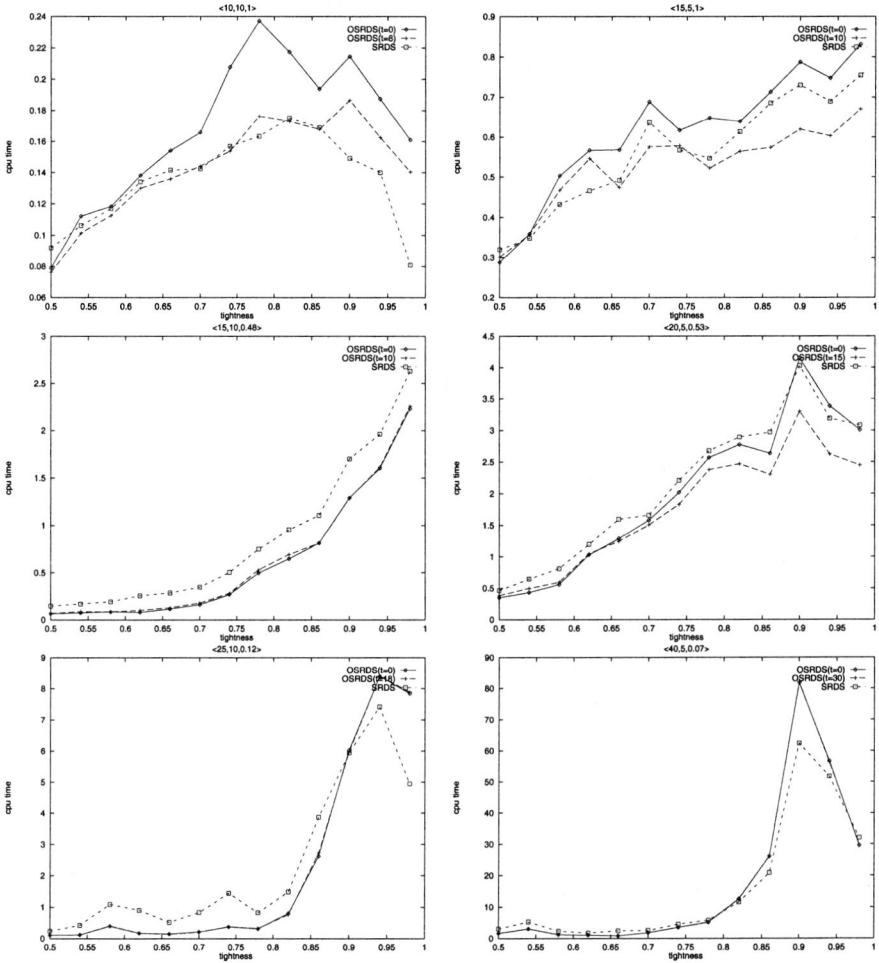

Fig. 6. Average CPU versus tightness for six classes of binary random problems

Table 1. Results on CELAR-6 subinstances. CPU time corresponds to a Pentium IV 1.8GHZ machine with 512M of RAM using GNU g++ compiler

instance	variables	connectivity	optimal cost	cpu time
SUB_0	16	0.47	159	$9.91s$
SUB_1	14	0.82	2669	$92s$
SUB_2	16	0.74	2746	$168s$
SUB_3	18	0.69	3079	$4833s$
SUB_4	22	0.56	3230	$16860s$

278 Pedro Meseguer et al.

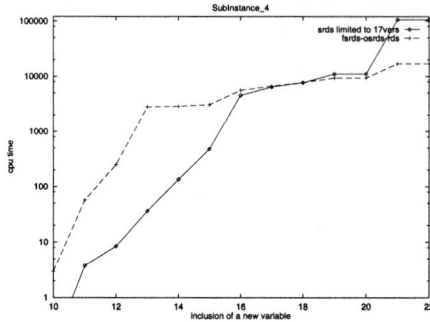

Fig. 7. CPU time versus number of variables in the subproblem for CELAR6-4

7 Conclusions

We have presented the *Opportunistic Specialization RDS* approach and its realization by the OSRDS algorithm. Its main idea consists on specializing only those values that look promising to increase the lower bound, given the current distribution of inconsistency counts. This approach has been shown superior to its predecessor, the *Specialized RDS*, which in turn was superior to the original *RDS*, forming a sequence of RDS-based algorithms of increasing complexity. A future goal is to identify a good policy for combining these different strategies into a single algorithm, able to solve real problems more efficiently than any single RDS-based approach.

References

[1] M. S. Affane and H. Bennaceur. A weighted arc consistency technique for Max-CSP. In *Proc. of the 13th ECAI*, 209–213, 1998.
[2] S. Bistarelli, U. Montanari and F. Rossi. Constraint Solving over Semirings. In *Proc. of the 14th IJCAI*, 1995.
[3] S. Bistarelli, U. Montanari, F. Rossi, T. Schiex, G. Verfaillie and H. Fargier. Semiring-based CSPs and Valued CSPs: Frameworks, Properties and Comparison. *Constraints*, 4:199–240, 1999.
[4] B.Cabon, S. De Givry, L.Lobjois, T.Schiex and J. P.Warners. Radio Link Frequency Assignment *Constraints*, vol. 4, num. 1, 79–89, 1999.
[5] R. Dechter. Mini-buckets: A general scheme for generating approximations in automated reasoning . *Artificial Intelligence*, 113:41–85, 1999.
[6] R. Dechter. Bucket elimination: A unifying framework for reasoning. *Artificial Intelligence*, 113:41–85, 1999.
[7] E. C. Freuder and R. J. Wallace. Partial constraint satisfaction. *Artificial Intelligence*, 58:21–70, 1992.
[8] J. Larrosa. Boosting search with variable elimination. In *Proc. of the 6th CP*, 291–305, 2000.
[9] J. Larrosa. Node and arc consistency in Weighted CSP. In *Proc. of the 18th AAAI*, 2002.

[10] J. Larrosa and P. Meseguer. Exploiting the use of DAC in Max-CSP. In *Proc. of the 2th CP*, 308–322, 1996.

[11] J. Larrosa, P. Meseguer, and T. Schiex. Maintaining reversible DAC for Max-CSP. *Artificial Intelligence*, 107:149–163, 1999.

[12] P. Meseguer, M. Sanchez. Specializing russian doll search. In *Proc. of the 7th CP*, 464–478, 2001.

[13] T. Schiex, H. Fargier and G. Verfaillie. Valued Constraint Satisfaction Problems: hard and easy problems. In *Proc. of the 14th IJCAI*, 631–637, 1995.

[14] T. Schiex. Arc consistency for soft constraints In *Proc. of the 6th CP*, 411–424, 2000.

[15] G. Verfaillie, M. Lemaître, and T. Schiex. Russian doll search. In *Proc. of the 13th AAAI*, 181–187, 1996.

[16] R. Wallace. Directed arc consistency preprocessing. In M. Meyer, editor, *Selected papers from the ECAI-94 Workshop on Constraint Processing*, number 923 in LNCS, 121–137. Springer, Berlin, 1995.

Range-Based Algorithm for Max-CSP

Thierry Petit[1,2], Jean-Charles Régin[1], and Christian Bessière[2]

[1] ILOG, 1681, route des Dolines, 06560 Valbonne, France
{regin, tpetit}@ilog.fr
[2] LIRMM (UMR 5506 CNRS), 161, rue Ada, 34392 Montpellier Cedex 5, France
{bessiere, tpetit}@lirmm.fr

Abstract. A Max-CSP consists of searching for a solution which minimizes the number of violated constraints. The best existing solving algorithm is PFC-MRDAC. It is based on the computation of a lower
bound of the number of violations. To compute this lower bound it is
required to evaluate the violations with respect to each value of each
domain. Unfortunately, some applications imply thousands of variables
with huge domains. In scheduling, it arises that numerous activities have
to be scheduled over several months with a unit of time of a few minutes. In this situation using PFC-MRDAC requires a large amount of
memory which can prevent from using it. In this paper, we propose an
algorithm called the Range-based Max-CSP Algorithm (RMA), based
on the exploitation of bound-based filtering algorithms of constraints.
This technique does not require to study each value of each domain: its
complexity depends only on the number of variables and the number of
constraints. No assumption is made on the constraints except that their
filtering algorithms are related to the bounds of the involved variables,
the general case for scheduling constraints. Then, when the only information available for a variable x w.r.t. a constraint C are the new bounds of
$D(x)$ obtained by applying the filtering algorithm of C, the lower bounds
of violations provided by PFC-MRDAC and RMA are identical.

1 Introduction

A problem is over-constrained when no assignment of values to variables satisfies
all constraints. The simplest theoretical framework for over-constrained problems
is the Maximal Constraint Satisfaction Problem (Max-CSP). A solution of a
Max-CSP is a total assignment of values to variables that minimizes the number
of constraint violations.

The best solving algorithm for Max-CSP, PFC-MRDAC [1], has been extended to the non binary case [4, 5, 3]. Moreover, in [4, 5] it has been shown
that a Max-CSP can be encoded through a global constraint. When we define
a Max-CSP as a global constraint, then we use the PFC-MRDAC algorithm as
the filtering algorithm of the constraint. This formulation is suited to real-life
problems, because generally some parts correspond to Max-CSPs although the
whole problem cannot be expressed as a Max-CSP. Moreover any search algorithm can be used. Therefore we selected it to describe the algorithms presented
in this paper.

P. Van Hentenryck (Ed.): CP 2002, LNCS 2470, pp. 280–294, 2002.
© Springer-Verlag Berlin Heidelberg 2002

For sake of clarity, we consider first that a Max-CSP is solved by a Branch and Bound based search algorithm: successive assignments of values to variables are performed through a depth-first traversal of the search tree, where internal nodes represent incomplete assignments and leaf nodes stand for complete ones. The number of violations to minimize is expressed by an objective variable obj. For any given node, $UB = max(D(obj)) + 1$ corresponds to the number of violations of the best solution found so far. $min(D(obj))$ is the number of violated constraints detected by the solver at the current step of the search. In fact, $min(D(obj))$ can be simply defined as the number of constraints C such that values have been assigned to all variables in the set $var(C)$ of the variables involved in C, and C is violated. This number is generally called the *distance*. If $distance > max(D(obj))$ then the current best solution cannot be improved below the current node. Thus it is not necessary to traverse the sub-tree rooted at the current node.

PFC-MRDAC improves that condition by computing a lower bound LB of the number of violations, equal to *distance* plus an under-estimation of the number of violations entailed by constraints involving some variables which have not yet been instantiated. The new condition of continuation of the search is $LB \leq max(D(obj))$.

When filtering, PFC-MRDAC combines generally LB with a lower bound local to each value, in order to remove this value if it cannot belong to a solution.

All these lower bounds are based on direct violations of constraints by values: they require to maintain for each value a in the domain of a variable x the number of constraints C such that a is not consistent with C. This principle is applicable to a wide number of problems, providing that domain sizes are not too big.

Unfortunately, some applications involve a big number of variables with huge domain sizes.

For instance, consider the problem of scheduling the construction of offices. Some activities, as painting or installing windows, have a short duration and require essentially human resources. They can be performed over a large period. They concern each office of each floor in each building, and they are linked to other activities by precedence rules. Given that the manager has to deal with a large number of workers who express preference constraints with respect to their week schedule, it is mandatory to have a time unit of at most one quarter of hour. If the total duration of the project is one year then for each activity we have 35040 possible start dates. If there exists thousands of activities then it is not realistic to maintain for each possible date of each activity a counter of inconsistencies. Moreover, since scheduling constraints generally propagate on bounds, redundant computations will be made when testing the consistency of each value of a domain with a constraint. Therefore, PFC-MRDAC is not really suited to this case.

In this paper, we propose a new algorithm called the Range-based Max-CSP Algorithm (RMA), which computes a lower bound by exploiting filtering algorithms of constraints. The principle is similar to PFC-MRDAC except concerning the computation of inconsistencies involved by each variable. Instead of evaluating each value of a domain $D(x)$, the RMA stores two entities per constraint C in which x is involved: the new minimum and maximum of $D(x)$ obtained when applying the filtering algorithm of C. For instance, for 100 variables with domains of 35040 values and 100 constraints, the RMA requires to maintain at most 200 minima and maxima per variable (corresponding to a worst-case situation where all constraints imply all variables) instead of 35040 counters in PFC-MRDAC. That is, instead of having a total of 3.5 millions of counters with PFC-MRDAC we have 20000 entities with the RMA.

We show that in the case of constraints which propagate only bounds of domains, the same LB is obtained by using PFC-MRDAC and the RMA.

We compare the complexity of a non incremental implementation with PFC-RDAC:[1] when domain sizes are big the amortized complexity of the RMA is better because it does not depend on the number of values in the domains.

We provide a filtering algorithm based on the same principle, which propagates on bounds. We discuss the incremental version of the RMA and about a filtering algorithm which performs holes in domains. We point out a promising generalization of our algorithm: for general problems, it is possible to take into account ranges of successive values involving the same number of violations to compute the lower bounds.

2   Preliminaries

CSP A *constraint network* $\mathcal{N}$ is defined as a set of n *variables* $\mathcal{X} = \{x_1, \ldots, x_n\}$, a set of *domains* $\mathcal{D} = \{D(x_1), \ldots, D(x_n)\}$ where $D(x_i)$ is the finite set of possible *values* for variable x_i, and a set $\mathcal{C}$ of *constraints* between variables. A *constraint* C on the ordered set of variables $var(C) = (x_{i_1}, \ldots, x_{i_r})$ (also denoted by $C(x_{i_1}, \ldots, x_{i_r})$) is defined by the subset $rel(C)$ of the Cartesian product $D(x_{i_1}) \times \cdots \times D(x_{i_r})$ that specifies the *allowed* combinations of values for the variables $x_{i_1}, \ldots, x_{i_r}$. $D(var(C)) = \cup_{x \in var(C)} D(x)$. An element of $D(x_{i_1}) \times \cdots \times D(x_{i_r})$ is called a *tuple on* $var(C)$. $|var(C)|$ is the *arity* of C. C is *binary* iff $|var(C)| = 2$. A value a for a variable x is denoted by (x, a). A tuple τ on $var(C)$ is *valid* if $\forall (x, a) \in \tau, a \in D(x)$. C is *consistent* iff there exists a tuple τ of $rel(C)$ which is valid. A value $a \in D(x)$ is *consistent with* C iff $x \notin var(C)$ or there exists a valid tuple τ of $rel(C)$ in which a is the value assigned to x. Given $Y \subseteq \mathcal{X}$, an *instantiation* I of Y is an assignment of values to variables Y such that $\forall x \in Y$, the value a assigned to x belongs to $D(x)$. Given $Y \subseteq \mathcal{X}$ and $C \in \mathcal{C}$ such that $var(C) \subseteq Y$, an instantiation I of Y *satisfies* a constraint C iff the projection of I on $var(C)$ belongs to $rel(C)$. If I does not satisfy C, then I *violates* C. The *Constraint Satisfaction Problem* (CSP) consists of finding an instantiation I of X such that $\forall C \in \mathcal{C}$, I satisfies C.

Over-Constrained Problem When a CSP has no solution, we say that the problem is *over-constrained*. $\mathcal{C}_h \subseteq \mathcal{C}$ is the set of *hard* constraints, that is, the

---

[1] PFC-RDAC [2] is the non incremental version of PFC-MRDAC.

constraints that must necessarily be satisfied. $C_s = C \setminus C_h$ is the set of *soft* constraints. Let I be an instantiation of X. If I is a solution of an over-constrained problem then $\forall C \in C_h$, I satisfies C.

Max-CSP The Max-CSP is the problem where $C_h = \emptyset$ and the goal is to find an assignment of values to variables that minimizes the number of violations in $C = C_s$.

Max-CSP as a Global Constraint Let $\mathcal{N} = (\mathcal{X}, \mathcal{D}, \mathcal{C})$ be a constraint network. Constraints in $\mathcal{C}$ can be encapsulated into a single constraint [4, 5], called the Satisfiability Sum Constraint (*ssc*):

Definition 1 *Let $C = \{C_i, i \in \{1, \ldots, m\}\}$ be a set of constraints, and $S[\mathcal{C}] = \{s_i, i \in \{1, \ldots, m\}\}$ be a set of variables and obj be a variable, such that a one-to-one mapping is defined between C and $S[\mathcal{C}]$. A* **Satisfiability Sum Constraint** *is the constraint $ssc(C, S[\mathcal{C}], obj)$ defined by:*

$$[obj = \sum_{i=1}^{m} s_i] \wedge \bigwedge_{i=1}^{m} [((C_i \wedge (s_i = 0)) \vee (\neg C_i \wedge (s_i = 1))]$$

Notation 1 *Given a $ssc(C, S[\mathcal{C}], obj)$, a variable x, $a \in D(x)$ and $\mathcal{K} \subseteq \mathcal{C}$:*
- *$max(D(obj))$ is the highest value of current domain of obj;*
- *$min(D(obj))$ is the lowest value of current domain of obj;*
- *$S[\mathcal{K}]$ is the subset of $S[\mathcal{C}]$ equals to the projection of variables $S[\mathcal{C}]$ on $\mathcal{K}$;*
- *$var(\mathcal{C})$ is the union of $var(C_i)$, $C_i \in \mathcal{C}$.*

The variables $S[\mathcal{C}]$ are used to express which constraints of $\mathcal{C}$ must be violated or satisfied: value 0 assigned to $s \in S[\mathcal{C}]$ expresses that its corresponding constraint C is satisfied, whereas 1 expresses that C is violated. Throughout this formulation, a solution of a Max-CSP is an assignment that satisfies the *ssc* with the minimal possible value of *obj*. Comparing a lower bound of the objective to $max(D(obj))$ leads to a necessary consistency condition of the *ssc*. Domain reduction algorithms for the Max-CSP correspond to specific filtering algorithms of the *ssc*.

Definition 1. *Given a $ssc(C, S[\mathcal{C}], obj)$ and a variable x:*
- *$minObj(C, S[\mathcal{C}])$ is the minimum value of obj consistent with $ssc(C, S[\mathcal{C}], obj)$;*
- *$minObj((x, a), C, S[\mathcal{C}])$ is equal to $minObj(C, S[\mathcal{C}])$ when $x = a$;*

3   Generalized Version of PFC-MRDAC

PFC-MRDAC [1] is one of the best algorithm for solving binary Max-CSPs. This section is a summary of the generalization of this algorithm to non-binary constraints [4, 5, 3]. Basically, PFC-MRDAC is based on counters of violations involved by each value of each domain:

Definition 2 *Let x be a variable, a be a value of $D(x)$, C be a set of constraints, $\#inc((x, a), \mathcal{C}) = |\{C \in \mathcal{C} \text{ s.t. } (x, a) \text{ is not consistent with } C\}|.$*

In a solver, this information can be obtained by applying independently the specific filtering algorithms of the constraints in which x is involved, while the domain of x is reduced to the value a we study.

3.1 Necessary Condition of Consistency

From the definition of $minObj(\mathcal{C}, S[\mathcal{C}])$ we have:

Property 1 *If* $minObj(\mathcal{C}, S[\mathcal{C}]) > max(D(obj))$ *then* $ssc(\mathcal{C}, S[\mathcal{C}], obj)$ *is not consistent.*

A lower bound of $minObj(\mathcal{C}, S[\mathcal{C}])$ provides a necessary condition of consistency of a *ssc*. A possible way for computing it is to perform a sum of independent lower bounds of violations, one per variable. For each variable a lower bound can be defined by:

Definition 3 *Given a variable x and a constraint set $\mathcal{K}$, $\#inc(x, \mathcal{K}) = min_{a \in D(x)} (\#inc((x, a), \mathcal{K}))$.*

The sum of minima $\#inc(x, \mathcal{K})$ over all the variables in $\mathcal{K} = \mathcal{C}$ cannot lead to a lower bound of the total number of violations. Indeed, some constraints can be taken into account more than once. In this case, the lower bound can be overestimated, and an inconsistency could be detected while the *ssc* is consistent.

In the binary case, the constraint graph[2] is used in order to guarantee this independence [1]. Each edge is oriented and for each variable x only the constraints out-going x are taken into account.

This idea was be generalized to the non binary case, by associating with each constraint C one and only one variable x involved in the constraint [4, 5]: C is then taken into account only for computing the $\#inc$ counter of x. Therefore, the constraints are partitioned according to the variables they are associated with:

Definition 4 *Given a set of constraints $\mathcal{C}$, a **var-partition** of $\mathcal{C}$ is a partition $\mathcal{P}(\mathcal{C}) = \{P(x_1), ..., P(x_k)\}$ of $\mathcal{C}$ in $|var(\mathcal{C})|$ sets such that $\forall P(x_i) \in \mathcal{P}(\mathcal{C}) : \forall C \in P(x_i), x_i \in X(C)$.*

Given a var-partition $\mathcal{P}(\mathcal{C})$, the sum of all $\#inc(x_i, P(x_i))$ is a lower bound of the total number of violations, because all sets belonging to $\mathcal{P}(\mathcal{C})$ are disjoint; thus we obtain the following lower bound:

$$LB_{\mathcal{P}(\mathcal{C})} = \sum_{x_i \in var(\mathcal{C})} \#inc(x_i, P(x_i))$$

Property 2 $\forall \mathcal{P}(\mathcal{C}) = \{P(x_1), ..., P(x_k)\}$, $LB_{\mathcal{P}(\mathcal{C})} \leq minObj(\mathcal{C}, S[\mathcal{C}])$.

The necessary condition of consistency of a *ssc* is deduced from this Property:

Corollary 1 $\forall \mathcal{P}(\mathcal{C}) = \{P(x_1), ..., P(x_k)\}$, *If* $LB_{\mathcal{P}(\mathcal{C})} > max(D(obj))$ *then* $ssc(\mathcal{C}, S[\mathcal{C}], obj)$ *is not consistent.*

---

[2] The graph where vertices are variables and edges are binary constraints between pairs of variables.

3.2   Filtering Algorithm

PFC-MRDAC [1] and its extension to the non binary case [4, 5, 3] include a look-ahead procedure used to reduce domains of variables that have not yet an assigned value. From definition of $minObj((x,a),\mathcal{C},S[\mathcal{C}])$ we have:

Theorem 1 $\forall x \in var(\mathcal{C}), \forall a \in D(x)$: if $minObj((x,a),\mathcal{C},S[\mathcal{C}]) > max(D(obj))$ then (x,a) is not consistent with ssc $(\mathcal{C}, S[\mathcal{C}], obj)$.

Any lower bound of $minObj((x,a),\mathcal{C},S[\mathcal{C}])$ can be used to check the consistency of (x,a). An obvious lower bound is $\#inc((x,a),\mathcal{C})$:

Property 3 $\#inc((x,a),\mathcal{C}) \leq minObj((x,a),\mathcal{C},S[\mathcal{C}])$

From this Property and Theorem 1, we obtain a first filtering algorithm. It can be improved by including the lower bound of Property 2. This idea was introduced by Larrosa et al. [1], for binary constraint networks.

It can be applied in the general case [4, 5, 3]. In order to do so, we suggest to split $\mathcal{C}$ into two disjoint sets $P(x)$ and $\mathcal{C} - P(x)$, where $P(x)$ is the subset of constraints associated with x in a var-partition $\mathcal{P}(\mathcal{C})$ of $\mathcal{C}$. Consider the following corollary of Theorem 1:

Corollary 2 Let $\mathcal{P}(\mathcal{C})$ be a var-partition of $\mathcal{C}$, x a variable and $a \in D(x)$, if $minObj((x,a),P(x),S[P(x)]) + minObj((x,a),\mathcal{C} - P(x),S[\mathcal{C} - P(x)]) > max$ $(D(obj))$ then (x,a) is not consistent with $ssc(\mathcal{C},S[\mathcal{C}],obj)$.

Proof: e.g., [5].

Note that $minObj(\mathcal{C} - P(x),S[P(x)]) \leq minObj((x,a),\mathcal{C} - P(x),S[P(x)])$. ¿From this remark and Properties 2 and 3 the following theorem can be deduced:

Theorem 2 $\forall \mathcal{P}(\mathcal{C})$ a var-partition of $\mathcal{C}, \forall x \in var(\mathcal{C}), \forall a \in D(x)$, if $\#inc((x,a),$ $P(x)) + LB_{\mathcal{P}(\mathcal{C}-P(x))} > max(D(obj))$ then a can be removed from $D(x)$.

4   The Range-Based Max-CSP Algorithm

4.1   Principle

PFC-MRDAC algorithm requires to maintain one counter $\#inc\ ((x,a),\ P(x))$ for each value a of each domain $D(x)$. The computation of these counters is sufficient to efficiently compute the consistency of a satisfiability sum constraint (see Corollary 1) and to apply the filtering algorithm associated with it (see Theorem 2). Therefore, the main issue of the PFC-MRDAC algorithm is the computation of these counters, and if this computation is accelerated then the algorithm is improved.

We propose a new algorithm called the Range-based Max-CSP Algorithm (RMA) that does not require one counter per value although the principle is very similar to the non binary PFC-MRDAC: for each variable x we consider a set $P(x)$ of a var-partition of constraints $\mathcal{P}(\mathcal{C})$, in order to compute a lower bound $\#inc(x, P(x))$ of the violations involved by x.

The difference is the way we compute $\#inc(x, P(x))$. In the RMA, there is no need to maintain one counter of violation $\#inc((x, a), P(x))$ for each value a in $D(x)$ as it is the case in PFC-MRDAC (see Definition 3).

The idea exploited in our algorithm is based on the following definition:

Definition 5 *Let $I \subseteq D(x)$ be a range of consecutive values. If $\forall a \in I$, $\forall b \in I$, $\#inc((x, a), P(x)) = \#inc((x, b), P(x))$ then I is homogeneously inconsistent. The number of constraints in $P(x)$ violated if $D(x) = I$ is $\#inc(I, P(x)) = \#inc((x, a), P(x)), a \in I$.*

If any value in a range I violates the same number of constraints of $P(x)$ then we can consider globally the range to evaluate the number of violations, instead of studying the values one by one.

It is possible to take into account only a set of homogeneously inconsistent ranges to compute $\#inc(x, P(x))$, provided that each value of $D(x)$ belongs to one range. More formally, we have:

Definition 6 *A set $\mathcal{I}(P(x)) = \{I_1, ..., I_m\}$ of homogeneously inconsistent ranges such that $\cup_{k=1}^{m} I_k = D(x)$ is called a set of homogeneously inconsistent ranges which covers $D(x)$.*

Property 4 *Let $\mathcal{I}(P(x))$ be a set of homogeneously inconsistent ranges which covers $D(x)$. Then we have: $\#inc(x, P(x)) = min_{I \in \mathcal{I}(P(x))} \#inc(I, P(x))$.*

Proof: from Definition 5

Thus, if we are able to identify such a set $\mathcal{I}(P(x))$ with $|\mathcal{I}(P(x))| < |D(x)|$ then it is possible to improve PFC-MRDAC in two ways:

1. the number of counters required to compute $\#inc(x, P(x))$ is smaller,
2. $\#inc(x, P(x))$ can be computed faster.

The first point is quite important in practice. Indeed, in some problems the number of variables and the size of the domains make methods requiring for each value of each variable some additional data, as $\#inc((x, a), P(x))$, unusable in practice. For instance, this is the case of almost all real world scheduling applications. Moreover, in such problems, the filtering algorithms associated with constraints are range-based filtering algorithms: they reduce only the bounds of the domain. They do not create "holes" in domains.

Such a range-based approach is interesting if some issues can be efficiently solved:

– the number of ranges is small,
– for each range I, $\#inc(I, P(x))$ can be efficiently computed.

In the remaining of this section, we will consider that only range-based filtering algorithms are used. Under this condition, we will prove that:

- the size of $\mathcal{I}(P(x))$ is at most $2 * |P(x)| + 1$,
- the set of all $\#inc(I, P(x))$ can be computed in $O(|P(x)|)$ provided that we have computed $\mathcal{I}(P(x))$.

4.2   Computation of $\#inc$ Counters

The principle is to consider the bounds obtained by applying independently each filtering algorithm of constraints in $P(x)$ on $D(x)$:

Notation 2 *Let $\mathcal{P}(\mathcal{C})$ be a var-partition, x a variable, $P(x) \in \mathcal{P}(\mathcal{C})$ and $C \in P(x)$: $D(x)_C$ is the domain obtained by applying the filtering algorithm of C on $D(x)$.*

For each constraint C we consider the minimum $min(D(x)_C)$ and the maximum $max(D(x)_C)$ of $D(x)_C$. By ordering all these minima and maxima from the lower to the greater, it is possible to divide $D(x)$ in different ranges. Each of them corresponds to a certain number of violations. The following figure illustrates an example where $P(x)$ is the set of constraints $\{C_1, C_2, C_3\}$, which involve four variables x, y, z, t such that $D(x) = D(y) = D(z) = D(t) = [0, 10]$:

- $C_1 = [x - y > 5]$ that leads to $min(D(x)_{C_1}) = 6$, $max(D(x)_{C_1}) = 10$,
- $C_2 = [x - z > 7]$ that leads to $min(D(x)_{C_2}) = 8$, $max(D(x)_{C_2}) = 10$,
- $C_3 = [t - x > 7]$ that leads to $min(D(x)_{C_3}) = 0$, $max(D(x)_{C_3}) = 2$.

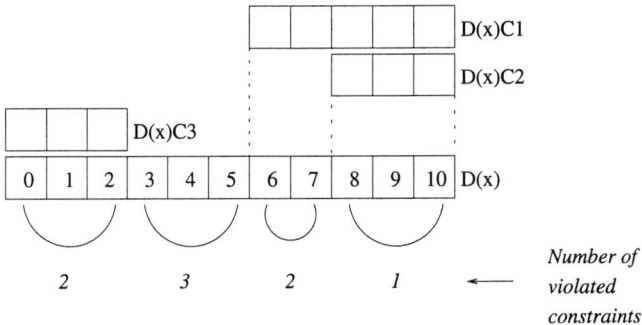

In this example the homogeneously inconsistent ranges are $[0, 3)$, $[3, 6)$, $[6, 8)$, $[8, 11)$ and $\#inc(x, P(x)) = \#inc(x, P(x)) = min_{I \in \mathcal{I}(P(x))} \#inc(I, P(x)) = min(\#inc([0, 3), P(x)) = 2, \#inc([3, 6), P(x)) = 3, \#inc([6, 8), P(x)) = 2, \#inc([8, 11), P(x)) = 1) = 1$.

Definition 7 *Let $B(P(x))$ be the set containing the bounds of $D(x)$ plus the bounds of $D(x)_C$ for all constraints C in $P(x)$, sorted in ascending order. We denote by $\mathcal{I}(B(P(x)))$ the set of ranges such that each range is defined by a pair of two consecutive elements of $B(P(x))$. The kth range of $\mathcal{I}(B(P(x)))$ is denoted by $I_k = [p, q)$, where p is the minimum of I_k and $q - 1$ is the maximum.*

Property 5 *The following properties hold:*

1. *the maximal possible number of ranges in* $\mathcal{I}(B(P(x)))$ *is* $2 * |P(x)| + 1$
2. $\forall a \in D(x)\ \exists I \in \mathcal{I}(B(P(x)))$ *such that* $a \in I$
3. $\forall I \in \mathcal{I}(B(P(x)))\forall C \in P(x) : I \subseteq D(x)_C$ *or* $I \cap D(x)_C = \emptyset$
4. $\forall I \in \mathcal{I}(B(P(x)))$, *I is homogeneously inconsistent.*
5. $\mathcal{I}(B(P(x)))$ *is a set of homogeneously inconsistent ranges which covers* $D(x)$.

Proof:

1. $B(P(x))$ contains at most $2 * |P(x)| + 2$ values, thus the maximum number of ranges is $2 * |P(x)| + 1$.
2. By construction of $\mathcal{I}(B(P(x)))$
3. Suppose that $I \cap D(x)_C = J$ with $J \neq \emptyset$ and $J \neq I$. Then, one bound of J is equal to a bound of $D(x)_C$ and is not equal to a bound of I. So, I contains a bound of $D(x)_C$ which is not one of its bounds. This is not possible by construction of $\mathcal{I}(B(P(x)))$.
4. From 3 $\forall C \in P(x)$ and $\forall a, b \in I$: $a \cap D(x)_C = \emptyset \Leftrightarrow b \cap D(x)_C = \emptyset$. Therefore, $\forall a \in I\ \#inc((x, a), P(x)) = \#inc(I, P(x))$.
5. Immediate from 2 and 4.

The problem is to compute the value $\#inc(I, P(x))$ for each $I \in P(x)$. It is not possible to compute *independently* each $\#inc(I, P(x))$ in $O(1)$, but we will show that all $\#inc(I, P(x))$ can be computed in $O(|P(x)|)$. Therefore, since $|\mathcal{I}(B(P(x)))| \leq 2 * |P(x)| + 1$, the amortized complexity for an $\#inc(I, P(x))$ is $O(1)$. The following property helps us to compute all $\#inc(I, P(x))$ in $O(|P(x)|)$:

Property 6 $\#inc(I, B(P(x))) = |P(x)| - |\{C/D(x)_C \cap I = I\}|$

Proof: $\#inc(I, B(P(x))) = |\{C \text{ s.t. } D(x)_C \cap I = \emptyset\}|$ and by Property 5 (point 3) $|\{C /D(x)_C \cap I = \emptyset\}| + |\{C/D(x)_C \cap I = I\}| = |P(x)|$.

The ranges $\mathcal{I}(B(P(x))$ are traversed w.r.t. the ascending order, applying for each $I_K = [a, b)$ the following rules to determine how many constraints are satisfied:

− if a is a minimum of a domain $D(x)_C$ then we enter in a new $D(x)_C$ and the range I_k satisfies one constraint more than the previous one, I_{k-1}.
− if $a - 1$ is a maximum of a domain $D(x)_C$: we close a domain $D(x)_C$ and I_k satisfies one constraint less than I_{k-1}.

This idea has to be refined, given that a value in $D(x)$ may correspond to minima or maxima of several $D(x)_{C_i}$. Therefore we count the number of minima of domains equal to a, and maxima of domains equal to $a - 1$.

Notation 3 *Given* $a \in D(x)$.

− $nMin(a, B(P(x)))$ *denotes the number of domains* $D(x)_C \in B(P(x))$ *such that* $min(D(x)_C) = a$,

– $nMax(a, B(P(x)))$ denotes the number of domains $D(x)_C \in B(P(x))$ such that $max(D(x)_C) = a$.

Property 7 Given $I_k = [p,q)$. The number of satisfied constraints $\#sat(I_k, P(x))$ of a range $I_k \in \mathcal{I}(B(P(x)))$ can be computed recursively by:

$$\#sat(I_k, P(x)) = \#sat(I_{k-1}, P(x)) + nMin(p, B(P(x))) - nMax(p-1, B(P(x)))$$

with $\#sat(I_{-1}, P(x)) = 0$.

Proof: By induction. The lower bound of I_0 is $min(D(x))$, because all $D(x)_C \subseteq D(x)$. Thus, $\#sat(I_0, P(x)) = \#sat(I_{-1}, P(x)) + nMin(min(D(x)), B(P(x))) - nMax(min(D(x)) - 1, B(P(x))) = nMin(min(D(x)), B(P(x)))$. Therefore the property holds for I_0. Suppose that it is true for I_{k-1}, and $I_k = [p,q)$. By definition of $nMin$ and $nMax$ and from Property 5 (point 3) we have $\#sat(I_k, P(x)) = \#sat(I_{k-1}, P(x)) + nMin(p, B(P(x))) - nMax(p-1, B(P(x)))$

From this proposition and Property 6 the following property holds:

Property 8 Given $I = [p,q)$. Then, $\#inc(I, P(x)) = |P(x)| - \#sat(I, P(x))$.

Consider again the previous example in order to illustrate this principle:

Interval I_k	$\#sat(I_k, P(x))$	$\#inc(I_k, P(x))$
$I_1 = [0,3)$	0 + 1 - 0 = 1	2
$I_2 = [3,6)$	1 + 0 - 1 = 0	3
$I_3 = [6,8)$	0 + 1 - 0 = 1	2
$I_4 = [8,11)$	1 + 1 - 0 = 2	1

We deduce $\#inc(x, P(x)) = min_{I \in P(x)}(\#inc(I_k, P(x))) = 1$. The following algorithm is a possible implementation of the computation of $\#inc$ counters:

```
COMPUTEMININC(x, P(x), B(P(x)), I(B(P(x))))
    #sat ← 0;
    #inc(x, P(x)) ← |P(x)|;
    k ← 1;
    while k ≠ |I(B(P(x)))| do
        let I_k = [p,q) be the k^th range of I(B(P(x)));
        #sat ← #sat + nMin(p, B(P(x))) - nMax(p - 1, B(P(x)));
        if |P(x) - #sat| < #inc(x, P(x)) then
            #inc(x, P(x)) ← |P(x) - #sat|;
        k ← k + 1;
    return #inc(x, P(x));
```

4.3 Necessary Condition of Consistency

The $LB_{\mathcal{P}(C)}$ is computed by performing a sum of all $\#inc(x, P(x))$, following a schema similar to PFC-MRDAC. Note that the LB provided by PFC-RDAC and RMA are the same when filtering algorithms reduce only the bounds of the domains.

Compared with PFC-MRDAC, the computation of the lower bound $LB_{\mathcal{P}(\mathcal{C})}$ of Property 2 remains the same. Thus, we have: $LB_{\mathcal{P}(\mathcal{C})} = \sum_{x_i \in var(\mathcal{C})} \#inc(x_i, P(x_i))$. The difference is the computation of all $\#inc(x_i, P(x_i))$, done trough the COMPUTEMININC presented in above.

Complexity In order to compare the complexity of checking the consistency of a ssc with RMA and with PFC-RDAC (the non incremental version of PFC-MRDAC [2]), we insist on the fact that the principle is the same except for computing the $\#inc(x, P(x))$. Consequently, we compare the procedure COMPUTEMININC with the method used in PFC-RDAC for computing $\#inc(x, P(x))$:

Notation 4 *We denote by :*

- *d the maximal domain size: $max_{x \in \mathcal{X}}(|D(x)|)$,*
- *p the maximal size of a set in the var-partition: $max_{P(x) \in \mathcal{P}(\mathcal{C})}(|P(x)|)$,*
- *f the maximal complexity of a filtering algorithm of a constraint C applied on a domain $D(x)$ (useful either to know if a value $a \in D(x)$ is consistent with a constraint C, in this case we call the algorithm with $D(x) = \{a\}$, or to compute $D(x)_C$).*

In PFC-RDAC, a counter $\#inc((x, P(x), a))$ of violations involved by each value a of $D(x)$ is computed. Thus, for each $a \in D(x)$ the complexity is $O(f * |P(x)|)$; and then we iterate over all counters to determine the minimal one, $\#inc(x, P(x))$. Finally the complexity is $O(|D(x)| * f * |P(x)|)$.

In RMA, the filtering algorithm of each constraint is called only once. That is, $|P(x)| * f$. We sort the $|P(x)| * 2 + 2$ bounds to compute $\mathcal{I}(B(P(x)))$: $O(|P(x)| * log(|P(x)|))$; and we iterate on them to determine $\#inc(x, P(x))$. Finally the complexity is $O(|P(x)| * log(|P(x)|) + f * |P(x)|)$.

To obtain LB, these computations will be performed at most n times (n is the number of variables). Since $\sum_{x_i \in X(\mathcal{C})}(|P(x_i)|) = |\mathcal{C}|$ we have:

	PFC-RDAC	RMA
$\#inc(x, P(x))$	$O(\lvert D(x)\rvert * f * \lvert P(x)\rvert)$	$O(\lvert P(x)\rvert * log(\lvert P(x)\rvert) + f * \lvert P(x)\rvert)$
$LB_{\mathcal{P}(\mathcal{C})}$	$O(\lvert \mathcal{C}\rvert * d * f)$	$O(\lvert \mathcal{C}\rvert * (log(p) + f))$
$LB_{\mathcal{P}(\mathcal{C})}$ when f is negligible	$O(\lvert \mathcal{C}\rvert * d)$	$O(\lvert \mathcal{C}\rvert * log(p))$

Note that $p \leq |\mathcal{C}|$ (if the partition is uniform we have even $p = |\mathcal{C}|/n$). RMA is interesting when the number of values in domains is important w.r.t. the number of constraints. In other terms, in some cases using PFC-MRDAC is almost forbidden because domain sizes are too big, and then the RMA is a good alternative.

4.4   Filtering Algorithm

In this section we propose to apply the principle described in previous sections to filter domains.

It is important to note that if only range based filtering algorithms are associated with the constraints then it is useless to introduce a filtering algorithm which is able to create "holes" in the domains, because these "holes" will not be used by the other algorithms. However, this can have an interest for the search heuristic, which can be based on the number of remaining values in the domains of the variables.

We first propose an algorithm which reduce only the bounds, even if it is also possible to provide an algorithm which creates holes.

Following the schema of PFC-MRDAC (see Theorem 2), we will take into account the lower bound corresponding to all sets in the var-partition $\mathcal{P}(\mathcal{C})$ except $P(x)$: $LB_{\mathcal{P}(\mathcal{C}-P(x))}$. As in PFC-MRDAC, viability of values will be evaluated according to $max(D(obj))$:

Theorem 3 Let $I \in \mathcal{I}(B(P(x)))$. If $\#inc(I, P(x)) + LB_{\mathcal{P}(\mathcal{C}-P(x))} > max (D$ $(obj))$ then all values in I can be removed from $D(x)$.

Proof: I is homogeneously inconsistent thus any value in I violated the same number of constraints. From theorem 2 the proof holds.

The algorithm is based on this theorem: starting from $I = [min(D(x)), q)$, we remove successive ranges while the condition of Theorem 3 is satisfied; and similarly, from the maximum of $D(x)$: starting from $I = [p, max(D(x)) + 1)$, we remove successive ranges while the condition of Theorem 3 is satisfied.

This algorithm can be slightly modified in order to obtain further domain reductions, that is, to create "holes" in the domain: for each range, Theorem 3 is applied and the domain is accordingly modified.

These algorithms have the same worst case complexity, and the gain on PFC-MRDAC is similar as the gain obtained for the consistency checking.

Once again, if the filtering algorithms associated with soft constraints are range based algorithms, the filtering algorithm which makes holes and PFC-MRDAC will lead to the same domain reduction.

4.5   Incremental Version

Until now, we implicitly considered that all the computations are done from scratch. In this section, we study the incremental behavior of RMA. We suggest a technique for maintaining incrementally $\mathcal{I}(B(P(x)))$ during the search.

By propagation, the set of homogeneous ranges $\mathcal{I}(B(P(x)))$ can be modified and consequently $\#inc(x, P(x))$ can also be modified. We distinguish two cases: a modification of $D(x)$ and a modification of $D(x)_C$, $C \in P(x)$.

$D(x)$ Is Modified Assume the minimum of $D(x)$ is increased. We denote by *oldmin* the previous value and *newmin* the new one. To update $\mathcal{I}(B(P(x)))$ it is only required to remove ranges $[p, q) \in \mathcal{I}(B(P(x)))$ such that $q \leq newmin$ and, if $\exists\ [p, q)$ such that $p < newmin$ and $q > newmin$, increase the minimum of such range in order to transform it in a new range $[newmin, q)$.

A Range $D(x)_C$ Is Modified For instance, let x be a variable such that $D(x) = [0, 8]$ and the constraints C_1, C_2, C_3 such that $D(x)_{C_1} = [2, 6]$, $D(x)_{C_2} = [6, 8]$, $D(x)_{C_3} = [0, 3]$. To illustrate the problem we use a bipartite graph $G_{P(x)}$, which represents the link between domains $D(x)_{C_i}$ and each $I \in \mathcal{I}(B(P(x)))$; an edge joins $D(x)_{C_i}$ and I when $I \subseteq D(x)_{C_i}$:

Assume that, due to the propagation process, $D(x)_{C_1}$ is modified to $[5, 6]$ (removed values from $D(x)_{C_1}$ are dashed in the following figure):

We need to update $G_{P(x)}$ according to this modification. We can explain our algorithm by describing its behavior on this example: for the first range previously connected to C_1 (vertex $D(x)_{C_1}$), that is $[2, 3)$, we remove the edge $(D(x)_{C_1}, [2, 3))$, and we decrease the counter $\#sat$ equal to the degree of vertex $D(x)_{C_1}$. The algorithm checks then if the vertex corresponding to the range which precedes $[2, 3)$, that is $[0, 2)$ is connected to the same vertices than $[2, 3)$ in $G_{P(x)}$. The answer is yes, so we perform the union of the two ranges, by grouping the two nodes into a single one: $[0, 3)$.

The process is repeated on next ranges until value 5 is reached. A new range $[5, 6)$ is then created, and the current range $[3, 6)$ is reduced to $[3, 5)$. The $\#sat$ counters are updated (one constraint less than $[3, 6)$ for $[3, 5)$, the same number for $[5, 6)$). $\mathcal{I}(B(P(x)))$ has been updated.

More formally, the following algorithm updates $\mathcal{I}(B(P(x)))$ after a modification of the minimum of $D(x)_C$. In practice, to deal efficiently with unions of ranges we maintain for each $I \in \mathcal{I}(B(P(x)))$ the set $\delta(I)$ of constraints in $P(x)$ that are satisfied exactly by one range among I and the range which precedes I in $\mathcal{I}\,(B(P(x)))$. Implicitly if $\delta(I) = \emptyset$, #sat, values of the two ranges are equal.

UPDATEMODIFMIN $(\mathcal{I}(B(P(x))), D(x)_C = [a, b), D'(x)_C = [newmin, b))$
    $I \leftarrow [p, q) \in \mathcal{I}(B(P(x)))$ such that $p = a$;
    while $q \leq newmin$ **do**
        $\#sat(I, P(x)) \leftarrow \#sat(I, P(x)) - 1$;
        if $\delta(I) = \emptyset$ **then**
            $I \leftarrow I \cup$ predecessor of I in $\mathcal{I}(B(P(x)))$;
            $I \leftarrow$ successor $[p, q)$ of I in $\mathcal{I}(B(P(x)))$;
    if $q < b$ **then**
        $I \leftarrow [p, newmin)$;
        add $[newmin, q)$ in $\mathcal{I}(B(P(x)))$;
        $\#sat([newmin, q), P(x)) \leftarrow \#sat(I, P(x))$;
    $\#sat(I, P(x)) \leftarrow \#sat(I, P(x)) - 1$;
    return $\mathcal{I}(B(P(x)))$;

In PFC-MRDAC an update of the number $\#inc((x, a), P(x))$ of the constraints violated by a value corresponds to one operation: $O(1)$. For k values the worst case complexity is of the order of $|D(x)|$ (when $k \simeq D(x)$). In the algorithm above if a domain $D(x)_C$ is reduced then the worst-case complexity for updating $\mathcal{I}(B(P(x)))$ is bounded by the number of ranges in $\mathcal{I}(B(P(x)))$. Therefore, the computation is faster than PFC-MRDAC when the reduction concerns a number of values greater that the number of ranges in $\mathcal{I}(B(P(x)))$. This number is less than or equal to $|D(x)|$.

5   Discussion

The technique we propose can be used when:

1. domains are not ranges
2. filtering algorithms associated with constraints are not range-based algorithms

Domains Are Not Ranges We can either consider that domains are ranges even if they are not (RMA is then still valid but no longer equivalent to PFC-MRDAC), or directly deal with such domains. When we deal directly with such domains, each domain is an union of ranges. RMA can be applied, but the complexity of this algorithm changes because each range of a domain has to be taken into account. Thus, the number of ranges in $\mathcal{I}(B(P(x)))$ is accordingly changed and also the complexity of the algorithm. We note that the maximal number of ranges in of $\mathcal{I}(B(P(x)))$ is bounded by $min(|P(x)|, |D(x)|)$ and consequently by $|D(x)|$. In PFC-MRDAC, we maintain exactly $|D(x)|$ counters but they have not to be sorted, which is the case in RMA. The choice will then depend on the average number of ranges compared with $|D(x)|$.

Filtering Algorithms Are Not Range-Based Algorithms The application of a filtering algorithm for a constraint may lead to domains which are not ranges. That is, a domain correspond to several ranges. The two possibilities that can be studied are the same of the previous case: either the "holes" are ignored or the algorithm deals with the set of ranges corresponding to each domain.

Acknowledgments

The work of ILOG authors was partially supported by the IST Program of the Commission of the European Union through the ECSPLAIN project (IST-1999-11969). We thank Xavier Nodet for providing us with some feedback about scheduling applications and the reviewers for their helpful comments.

6 Conclusion

We propose an alternative to PFC-MRDAC called the Range-based Max-CSP Algorithm (RMA), based on the exploitation of bound-based filtering algorithms of constraints. An incremental version of the algorithm is provided. This technique does not require to study each value of each domain: its complexity depends only on the number of variables and constraints. It is more suited to problems with large domains than PFC-MRDAC, which requires too much memory. When the only information available for a variable x w.r.t. a constraint C is the values of bounds of $D(x)$ when the filtering algorithm of C is applied, the lower bounds provided by PFC-MRDAC and RMA are identical. In this case, RMA is faster than PFC-MRDAC when domains are large. Some variations of RMA are also studied in order to deal with more general cases, as domains with holes.

References

[1] J. Larrosa, P. Meseguer, and T. Schiex. Maintaining reversible DAC for Max-CSP. *Artificial Intelligence*, 107:149–163, 1999.
[2] J. Larrosa, P. Meseguer, T. Schiex, and G. Verfaillie. Reversible DAC and other improvements for solving Max-CSP. *Proceedings AAAI*, pages 347–352, 1998.
[3] P. Meseguer, J. Larrosa, and M. Sanchez. Lower bounds for non-binary constraint optimization problems. *Proceedings CP*, pages 317–331, 2001.
[4] J.-C. Régin, T. Petit, C. Bessière, and J.-F. Puget. An original constraint based approach for solving over constrained prolems. *Proceedings CP*, pages 543–548, 2000.
[5] J.-C. Régin, T. Petit, C. Bessière, and J.-F. Puget. New lower bounds of constraint violations for over constrained prolems. *Proceedings CP*, pages 332–345, 2001.

Resolution Complexity of Random Constraints

David G. Mitchell

Simon Fraser University
Burnaby, Canada
mitchell@cs.sfu.ca

Abstract. Random instances are widely used as benchmarks in evaluating algorithms for finite-domain constraint satisfaction problems (CSPs). We present an analysis that shows why deciding satisfiability of instances from some distributions is challenging for current complete methods. For a typical random CSP model, we show that when constraints are not too tight almost all unsatisfiable instances have a structural property which guarantees that unsatisfiability proofs in a certain resolution-like system must be of exponential size. This proof system can efficiently simulate the reasoning of a large class of CSP algorithms which will thus have exponential running time on these instances.

1 Introduction

Randomly generated CSP instances are widely used as benchmark instances in the empirical evaluation of algorithms, and have been since the earliest work in the area. They are also used in average case analyses of algorithms, and as combinatorial objects of independent interest. A series of papers beginning with [7] and [20] established that, while random instances are often easy, with suitable choice of generation model and parameters, instances can be generated which are challenging for current complete algorithms. Prosser[23] studied instances from very natural CSP models, which have been further studied in many papers.

Our goal here is to show that many such instances are indeed hard for a large class of algorithms, and to some extent to give an explanation of why. Our approach is inspired by an important result in propositional proof complexity, namely that randomly generated k-CNF formulas with linearly many clauses almost surely have no resolution refutations of less than exponential size [9]. Backtrack-based algorithms for SAT (e.g., DPLL algorithms) can be viewed as constructing resolution refutations for unsatisfiable formulas, so these algorithms will have exponential running time on unsatisfiable random formulas. This suggests that analogous random CSP instances might be similarly hard for backtracking-based CSP algorithms.

To capture as wide a class of algorithms as possible, we take the following two step approach. One step is to show that for some suitable resolution-like proof system for CSPs, random instances require exponential size refutations. The second is to show that the reasoning used in popular CSP algorithms can be efficiently simulated by derivations in this proof system. In this paper we restrict

P. Van Hentenryck (Ed.): CP 2002, LNCS 2470, pp. 295–309, 2002.

our attention to the first step. The interested reader will find some preliminary work on the second step in [17] and a more complete treatment in [18, 19].

1.1   Resolution and Constraint Satisfaction

For a CSP refutation system we employ a natural transformation from CSP to SAT, and regard the (propositional) resolution refutations of the resulting *associated CNF formula* to be (CSP) resolution refutations of the CSP instance. We call this system **C-RES**. The original motivation for its study was de Kleer's paper [10] showing a relationship between CSP local-consistency methods and certain resolution derivations in this CNF encoding. Another notion of resolution for CSP was proposed by Baker [4], and studied in [15, 18]. That system is very natural, but is weaker and cannot account for some basic algorithms [18, 19]

The most-used algorithms in the CSP literature can be viewed as implicitly constructing **C-RES** refutations as they execute. In [18, 19] we call an algorithm **C-RES** *bounded* if its number of steps to execute on an instance $\mathcal{I}$ is greater than the size of the smallest **C-RES** refutation $\mathcal{I}$. The set of **C-RES** bounded algorithms includes all those that can be described in terms of (common variants of) the following methods: backtracking search, including variable and value ordering heuristics; conflict-directed backjumping [22]; forward checking and k-consistency filtering [13, 16]; nogood recording (a.k.a. "learning") [11]. This includes most standard techniques from the CSP literature, for example all algorithms described in [12, 22]. Simulations work roughly as follows. When backtracking returns from a recursive call, it can be viewed as returning a derived clause that rules out the assignment made for that call. When a node is exhausted, several such clauses are combined to derive a clause for the level above. Consistency filtering methods derive new clauses as soon as a local inconsistency is recognized. Backjumping observes which variables occur in derived clauses, and nogood recording caches some derived clauses.

1.2   The Sub-critical Expansion Method

Our method is a generalization to CSPs of existing methods for propositional resolution lower bounds. See, e.g., [5] and [6]. We define a measure $\mathcal{E}(I)$ of a CSP instance $\mathcal{I}$ called the *sub critical expansion*, and show that instances with large $\mathcal{E}(I)$ require large **C-RES** refutations. We then show that random CSP instances, within certain parameter ranges, almost surely have large $\mathcal{E}(I)$.

The intuition is roughly this. The critical size $\mathcal{C}(\mathcal{I})$ is the smallest number of variables in any unsatisfiable sub-instance of $\mathcal{I}$. All "sub-critical" sub-instances are satisfiable. Any **C-RES** refutation of $\mathcal{I}$ must be contain some sub-derivations all of whose input clauses come some sub-critical sub-instance. $\mathcal{E}(\mathcal{I})$ is a measure of how many boundary variables such a sub-instance has. Variable x is a boundary variable if any assignment that satisfies its neighbor variables can be consistently extended to x. If there are many of these, the clause derived from this sub-instance must be large, so in a sense $\mathcal{E}(\mathcal{I})$ is a measure of how much information some clause must carry from a sub-derivation to a refutation of $\mathcal{I}$.

Finally, we can apply a result from [6] relating clause size and refutation size to show that the refutation itself must be large.

Sub-critical expansion is an important structural measure of instances since no **C-RES** refutation can be of size less than $2^{\Omega(\mathcal{E}(\mathbf{I})^2/n)}$. To show that random CSPs have large $\mathcal{E}(I)$, we need to show that they have no small unsatisfiable sub-instances, and that sub-critical sub-instances within a certain size range have large boundaries. Proofs of both of these properties are based on the fact that sub-graphs of random hypergraphs have quite uniform edge density.

1.3   C-RES Complexity of Random CSPs

We consider a class of random CSP models typical of those used in experiments, denoting by $\mathsf{CSP}_{n,\Delta}^{d,k,t}$ the random instance $\mathcal{I}$ with domain $[d]$ and constraint arity k, generated as follows. Select $\lfloor \Delta n \rfloor$ constraints uniformly at random from those constraints with tightness t. Tightness, here, is the number of k-tuples of values the constraint excludes.

We fix all parameters except n, and study $\mathsf{CSP}_{n,\Delta}^{d,k,t}$ as $n \to \infty$. A property holds *almost surely* (a.s.) if it holds with probability tending to 1 as $n \to \infty$. We say $\mathsf{CSP}_{n,\Delta}^{d,k,t}$ exhibits a *phase transition* if there are constants c_1, c_2 such that instances are almost surely satisfiable if $\Delta < c_1$ and a.s. unsatisfiable if $\Delta > c_2$. Models with phase transitions are interesting because empirically challenging instances with a probability of being satisfiable of roughly $1/2$ are often associated with densities at or near c_1, c_2.

We first dispense with some algorithmically easy cases. It is shown in [2], that if $t \geq d^{k-1}$ then $\mathsf{CSP}_{n,\Delta}^{d,k,t}$ is almost surely unsatisfiable, independent of Δ (for any $d, k > 1$), so there is no phase transition. This is because there is a.s. an unsatisfiable sub-instance of size $d(k-1)+1$, from which a **C-RES** refutation of size $O(1)$ can be obtained. These can be found efficiently by standard methods to check for $d(k-1)+1$-consistency. CSPs with $d < 2$ or $k < 2$ are trivial. Results in [8] about random 2-SAT, plus simulation results in [18], show that $\mathsf{CSP}_{n,\Delta}^{2,2,1}$ exhibits a transition and a.s. has a **C-RES** refutation of size $O(\log n)$. More generally, all cases with $d = k = 2$ can be solved in polynomial time, for example by transformation to 2-SAT, and it is not hard to check that all instances have **C-RES** refutations of size at most $O(m^2)$, where m is the number of constraints.

We are left to consider the case when $d, k \geq 2$, $d+k > 4$ and $d^{k-1} > t > 0$. For these values of d,k, the CSP problem is **NP**-complete, and it follows from [21, 14] that when $t <= d^{k-1}$ $\mathsf{CSP}_{n,\Delta}^{d,k,t}$ does exhibit a phase transition (and certainly $c_2 < d^{k(t+2)} \ln d$). So we might expect these problems to be harder for resolution. Since we are studying refutations, our results here will only apply in the case $\Delta > c_2$, when most instances are unsatisfiable. We will leave this assumption implicit in this section. Notice though, that a backtrack-based algorithm can only can only take a long time if it generates an unsatisfiable instance that takes a long time to refute, so this work is not irrelevant in the satisfiable case. Indeed, recent results in [1] suggest that similar, though weaker, results may be obtained for such densities below c_2.

Table 1. Resolution Complexity of Random CSPs: d=2 and $k = 2$ cases

	C-RES($\mathrm{CSP}_{n,\Delta}^{d,2,t}$)		
d	$2^{\Omega(n)}$	?	$O(1)$
3	1	2	3...9
4	1,2	3	4...16
5	1,2,3	4	5...25

(a) Binary CSPs ($k = 2$)

	C-RES($\mathrm{CSP}_{n,\Delta}^{2,k,t}$)		
k	$2^{\Omega(n)}$	?	$O(1)$
3	1	2,3	4...8
4	1,2	3..7	8...16
5	1,2,3	4..15	16...32

(b) Generalized Satisfiability CSPs ($d = 2$)

If we fix $d = 2$, and $t = 1$, we obtain a random CSP equivalent to random k-SAT. The lower bounds for these cases, when $k \geq 3$, can be obtained from the random k-SAT lower bounds of [9], plus simulation arguments given in [18]. So the main question here is to what extent we can extend the range of parameters for which such lower bounds hold.

Our main result is that if $d, k > 1$, $d + k > 4$, and $(d-1)(k-1) > t > 0$ then almost surely **C-RES($\mathrm{CSP}_{n,\Delta}^{d,k,t}$)** $= 2^{\Omega(n)}$. For $d^{k-1} > t \geq (d-1)(k-1)$, resolution complexity remains open. This generalizes the random k-SAT case in the following ways: for $k \geq 3$, to generalized satisfiability (i.e., domain size 2 but constraints with $t > 1$) and to domain sizes larger than two, and to binary CSPs. Table 1 summarizes what we know for the cases $k = 2$ and $d = 2$. Each cell shows a range of values of t for which given **C-RES** complexities hold – "?" denotes unknown. For $k = 2$, a selection of domain sizes is given, whereas for $d = 2$ a selection of constraint arities is given.

The remainder of the paper is organized as follows. Section 2 gives basic definitions, and Section 3 develops the sub-critical expansion method for **C-RES** lower bounds. Section 4 applies this method to obtaining the claimed bounds for random CSPs, and Section 5 makes some concluding remarks.

2   Preliminaries

Since we have fixed domain size and constraint arity, we may adopt a slightly simpler definition of CSP instance than is usual.

Definition 1 (CSP terminology). *Let $d, k, t > 0$ be integers, and $\mathbf{R}$ be the set of all k-ary relations over the domain $[d] = \{1, \ldots, d\}$ having size exactly $(d^k) - t$ (i.e., tightness t). An instance $\mathcal{I}$ of the problem $\mathrm{CSP}^{d,k,t}$ is a set $\mathcal{I} = \{C_1, \ldots C_m\}$ of constraints. Each constraint C_i is an expression $R_i(\boldsymbol{x_i})$, where R_i is a symbol denoting some relation in $\mathbf{R}$, and $\boldsymbol{x_i}$ is a tuple of variable symbols. We denote by $vars(\mathcal{I})$ the set of variable symbols occurring in $\mathcal{I}$. An assignment for $CSP^{d,k,t}$ instance $\mathcal{I}$ is a function $\alpha : vars(\mathcal{I}) \mapsto [d]$. For variable tuple $\boldsymbol{x} = \langle x_1, \ldots, x_i \rangle$, we write $\alpha(\boldsymbol{x})$ for $\langle \alpha(x_1), \ldots, \alpha(x_i) \rangle$. Assignment α satisfies constraint $R(\boldsymbol{x}) \in \mathcal{I}$ if $\alpha(\boldsymbol{x})$ is in the relation denoted by R. Assignment α satisfies $\mathcal{I}$ if it satisfies every constraint of $\mathcal{I}$. $\mathcal{I}$ is satisfiable if there is an assignment that satisfies it. A conflict for instance $\mathcal{I}$ is a partial assignment α, defined on exactly the variables*

x *for some constraint* $R(x) \in \mathcal{I}$ *which does not satisfy that constraint. We write* conflicts$(\mathcal{I})$ *to denote the set of all conflicts for* $\mathcal{I}$.

Definition 2 (propositional resolution). *A* literal *is a propositional variable or its negation, a* clause *is a set of literals, and a (CNF)* formula *is a set of clauses viewed as a conjunction of disjunctions under the usual semantics of propositional logic. The propositional* resolution rule *allows us to infer a clause* $\{X\} \cup \{Y\}$ *from two clauses* $\{X\} \cup \{x\}$ *and* $\{Y\} \cup \{\overline{x}\}$ *by* resolving *them on* x. $\{X\} \cup \{Y\}$ *is called the* resolvent. *A resolution* derivation *of a clause* C *from a set of clauses* ϕ *is a sequence* $C_0, \ldots C_m$ *of clauses, where* $C_m = C$ *and each* C_i *is either an member of* ϕ *or is derived by resolving two clauses* C_j, C_k *with* $j, k < i$. *The derivation is of* length *or* size m. *A resolution derivation of the* empty clause *(denoted* $\square$*) from* ϕ *is called a resolution* refutation *of* ϕ. *We denote the propositional resolution system by* **RES**.

There is a resolution refutation of ϕ if and only if ϕ is unsatisfiable.

Definition 3 (CNF($\mathcal{I}$)). *To any* CSP^{d,k,t} *instance* $\mathcal{I}$ *we associate a formula* CNF$(\mathcal{I})$ *as follows. For each CSP variable* $v \in$ vars$(\mathcal{I})$, *we have* d *propositional variables, one for each value in* $[d]$. *We write* $v{:}a$ *for the propositional variable intended to assert that CSP variable* $v \in$ vars$(\mathcal{I})$ *is assigned value* a. *Two sets of clauses encode properties of a satisfying assignment for* $\mathcal{I}$: *For each CSP variable* $v \in$ vars$(\mathcal{I})$, CNF$(\mathcal{I})$ *has a* domain clause *asserting that* v *must be assigned some value from* $[d]$. *For each constraint* $R(y) \in \mathcal{I}$, *and each partial assignment* α *for exactly the variables in* y *and such that* $\alpha(y) \notin R$, CNF$(\mathcal{I})$ *has a* conflict clause *expressing that* α *is a conflict for* $\mathcal{I}$.

So, the propositional formula associated with $\mathcal{I}$ is

$$\mathrm{CNF}(\mathcal{I}) = \bigcup \left\{ \begin{array}{l} \{\{v{:}a : a \in [d]\} : v \in \mathrm{vars}(\mathcal{I})\} \\ \{\{\overline{x{:}a} : x = a \in \alpha\} : \alpha \in \mathrm{conflicts}(\mathcal{I})\} \end{array} \right.$$

CNF$(\mathcal{I})$ is satisfiable if and only if $\mathcal{I}$ is. Notice there is a one-to-one correspondence between conflict clauses in CNF$(\mathcal{I})$ and elements of conflicts$(\mathcal{I})$. A variant of this encoding includes clauses requiring each CSP variable to be assigned at most one value. All results in this paper are independent of these clauses.

Definition 4 (C-RES). *We define a* **C-RES** refutation *for any* CSP^{d,k,t} *instance* $\mathcal{I}$ *to be a propositional resolution (***RES***) refutation of* CNF$(\mathcal{I})$.

Soundness and refutation completeness of **C-RES** follow from soundness and completeness of **RES**, and the fact that CNF$(\mathcal{I})$ is satisfiable iff $\mathcal{I}$ is.

Definition 5 (resolution complexity). *The* resolution complexity *of a CNF formula* ϕ, *denoted* **RES**(ϕ), *is the minimum number of clauses in any resolution refutation of* ϕ. *The* **C-RES** complexity *a* CSP^{d,k,t} *instance* $\mathcal{I}$, *denoted* **C-RES**$(\mathcal{I})$, *is the minimum number of clauses in any* **C-RES** *refutation of* $\mathcal{I}$.

Note that **C-RES**$(\mathcal{I})$=**RES**$(\text{CNF}(\mathcal{I}))$. We extend **RES**() and **C-RES**() in the natural way to infinite sets. For example, to describe the **C-RES** complexity of a problem $\text{CSP}^{d,k,t}$ we may write **C-RES**$(\text{CSP}^{d,k,t}) = O(f(n))$, denoting by $\text{CSP}^{d,k,t}$ the set of all instances of problem $\text{CSP}^{d,k,t}$ with n variables. Used this way **C-RES**$(\text{CSP}^{d,k,t})$ is implicitly a function of n.

3   C-RES Bounds *via* Sub-critical Expansion

In this section we develop the notion of sub-critical expansion for CSPs, and its use in obtaining **C-RES** lower bounds.

Definition 6 (width, $\mathbf{w}(C)$, $\mathbf{w}(\phi)$, $\mathbf{w}(\pi)$, $\mathbf{W}(\phi)$). *We define the* width $w(C)$ *of clause C, to be the number of literals in C, that is, the size of C. The* width $w(\phi)$ *of formula ϕ, is the size of the largest clause in ϕ. The* width $w(\pi)$ *of resolution refutation π is the width of the largest clause in π. Of special interest for a formula ϕ is the minimum width of any refutation of ϕ, $W(\phi) \stackrel{def}{=} \min\{w(\pi) : \pi$ is a refutation of $\phi\}$, which we call the* refutation width *of ϕ. We extend these functions to infinite families Φ: $w(\Phi) \stackrel{def}{=} \max\{w(\phi) : \phi \in \Phi_n\}$ and $W(\Phi) \stackrel{def}{=} \max\{W(\phi) : \phi \in \Phi_n\}$, where Φ_n is the set of n-variable members of Φ.*

The following result relates refutation width to the minimum refutation size. We give a slightly restricted form of the result sufficient for our context.

Theorem 1 (Ben-Sasson & Wigderson[6]). *For any set of formulas Φ with $w(\Phi)$ bounded by a constant, $\mathbf{RES}(\Phi) = 2^{\Omega((W(\Phi_n))^2/n)}$*

3.1   Width and Sub-critical Expansion

Theorem 1 reduces lower bounds on **RES**(ϕ) to lower bounds on $W(\phi)$. By definition, lower bounds on **C-RES**$(\mathcal{I})$ are shown by proving **RES** lower bounds for $\text{CNF}(\mathcal{I})$. So we could obtain **C-RES**$(\mathcal{I})$ bounds by deriving bounds on $W(\text{CNF}(\mathcal{I}))$. This is less than ideal. For example it requires reasoning over arbitrary sub-formulas of $\text{CNF}(\mathcal{I})$, which is not convenient because of the structure of $\text{CNF}(\mathcal{I})$. So, in this section we reduce lower bounds on **C-RES**$(\mathcal{I})$ to lower bounds on the sub-critical expansion of $\mathcal{I}$. In this way, we also make more transparent the properties of $\mathcal{I}$ that are relevant to intractability for **C-RES**.

To reason about minimum-size refutations, we need to start from minimum-sized unsatisfiable sub-instances.

Definition 7 (sub-instance). *An instance $\mathcal{J}$ is a sub-instance of $\mathcal{I}$ if and only if $\text{vars}(\mathcal{J}) \subseteq \text{vars}(\mathcal{I})$ and the constraint set of $\mathcal{J}$ consists of all the constraints of $\mathcal{I}$ that involve only variables of $\mathcal{J}$.*

Definition 8 (critical size, $\mathcal{C}(\mathcal{I})$). *The* critical size *for instance $\mathcal{I}$, denoted $\mathcal{C}(\mathcal{I})$, is the largest integer such that every sub-instance $\mathcal{J}$ of $\mathcal{I}$ with $\mathcal{C}(\mathcal{I})$ or fewer variables is satisfiable.*

The following definition of a sub-instance implying a clause over the literals of CNF($\mathcal{I}$) makes a direct connection between sub-instances of $\mathcal{I}$ and clauses derived from CNF($\mathcal{I}$).

Definition 9 ($\widehat{\alpha}$, implies). *For any assignment α for $\mathcal{I}$, we denote by $\widehat{\alpha}$ the truth assignment for CNF($\mathcal{I}$) that assigns $x:a$ the value* **true** *iff $\alpha(x) = a$. We say that assignment α for $\mathcal{I}$ satisfies clause C over the literals of CNF($\mathcal{I}$) if $\widehat{\alpha}$ satisfies C. We say instance $\mathcal{J}$ implies clause C if for every assignment α that satisfies $\mathcal{J}$, $\widehat{\alpha}$ satisfies C, in which case we write $\mathcal{J} \models C$.*

A "complex clause", for instance $\mathcal{I}$, is a clause that cannot be derived from CNF($\mathcal{J}$) for any very small sub-instance $\mathcal{J}$ of $\mathcal{I}$.

Definition 10 (clause complexity, $\mu(C)$). *For instance $\mathcal{I}$, and clause C over the literals of CNF($\mathcal{I}$), the* complexity *of C with respect to $\mathcal{I}$, denoted $\mu(C)$, is the size of the smallest sub-instance $\mathcal{J}$ of $\mathcal{I}$ such that $\mathcal{J} \models C$.*

The following lemma establishes that every **C-RES** refutation must contain a complex clause. (Curiously, its statement and proof match almost word-for-word identical those for the propositional case, although the terms actually mean something slightly different.)

Lemma 1. *For any $s \leq \mathcal{C}(\mathcal{I})$, every resolution refutation of CNF($\mathcal{I}$) contains a clause a clause satisfying $s \geq \mu(C) \geq s/2$.*

Proof. Let π be a **RES** refutation of CNF($\mathcal{I}$), and $s \leq \mathcal{C}(\mathcal{I})$. Consider the graph G_π of π. The vertices of G_π are the clauses in π, and there are two directed edges to each non-input clause A, one from each of the two clauses from which A is derived. Search G_π as follows. Let the "current" clause be $\Box$ (the root). Notice that $\mu(\Box) = \mathcal{C}(\mathcal{I})$. As long as at least one of clauses with an edge to the current clause has complexity greater than s, move to such a clause. Stop when both edges to the current clause are from clauses with complexity at most s. This must happen, since every input clause has complexity 1, and since the complexity of clauses on a path from root to leaf must be non-increasing. Now suppose that the current clause A is derived from clauses D and E. It is clear that $\mu(A) \leq \mu(D) + \mu(E)$, so not both of D and E can have complexity less that $s/2$, and one of them must be the desired clause. $\Box$

In discussing instance structure, it is useful to consider the following graph.

Definition 11 (constraint hypergraph/graph). *To every instance $\mathcal{I}$ we associate a hypergraph $G_\mathcal{I} = \langle V, E \rangle$ called the* constraint hypergraph *of $\mathcal{I}$, where $V = vars(\mathcal{I})$, and $E = \{vars(C) \mid C \in \mathcal{I}\}$.*

If $\mathcal{I}$ is binary, $G_\mathcal{I}$ is just a graph. Note that if $\mathcal{J}$ is a sub-instance of $\mathcal{I}$, then the constraint graph of $\mathcal{J}$ is an induced sub-graph of the constraint graph of $\mathcal{I}$.

Next we define the boundary of a sub-instance. Our notion of boundary is more general than that used in proofs for propositional resolution, as there boundary variables must occur only once, whereas our boundary variables may occur more than once, and even with both signs.

Definition 12 (neighborhood, $\mathcal{N}(\mathcal{I})$, boundary, $\mathcal{B}(\mathcal{I})$). *The* neighborhood *of a variable x in $\mathcal{I}$, denoted $\mathcal{N}(x)$, is the set of variables y such that there is a constraint $R(z)$ in $\mathcal{I}$, and both x and y occur in z. The* boundary of $\mathcal{I}$ *is the set of variables x of $\mathcal{I}$ such that every assignment for $\mathcal{N}(x)$ that satisfies the sub-instance of $\mathcal{I}$ whose variables are $\mathcal{N}(x)$ can be extended to an assignment that satisfies the sub-instance with variables $\mathcal{N}(x) \cup \{x\}$. We denote the size of the boundary of $\mathcal{I}$ by $\mathcal{B}(\mathcal{I})$.*

We now draw a connection between boundary size and clause width.

Lemma 2. *Let C be a clause over the literals of CNF($\mathcal{I}$), and $\mathcal{J}$ a minimal sub-instance of $\mathcal{I}$ such that $\mathcal{J} \models C$. Then $w(C) \geq \mathcal{B}(\mathcal{J})$.*

Proof. Let x be any variable in $\mathcal{B}(\mathcal{J})$, and let $\mathcal{J}'$ be the largest sub-instance of $\mathcal{J}$ not including x. By minimality of $\mathcal{J}$ with respect to implying C, there is an assignment α for vars($\mathcal{J}$) such that α satisfies $\mathcal{J}'$ but $\widehat{\alpha}$ does not satisfy C. Denote by $\alpha[x\!=\!a]$ the assignment such that $\alpha[x\!=\!a](x) = a$, and $\alpha[x\!=\!a](y) = \alpha(y)$ if $y \neq x$. Clearly α satisfies the sub-instance of $\mathcal{J}$ whose variables are $\mathcal{N}(x)$, so there is a value a such that $\alpha[x\!=\!a]$ also satisfies $\mathcal{J}$. By choice of $\mathcal{J}$, $\widehat{\alpha[x\!=\!a]}$ satisfies C, so there must be a literal in C that is given different values by $\widehat{\alpha}$ and $\widehat{\alpha[x\!=\!a]}$. This must be a literal mentioning x, that is of the form $x\!:\!i$ or $\overline{x\!:\!i}$ for some value i, so C contains such a literal. Thus $w(C) \geq \mathcal{B}(()\mathcal{J})$. $\square$

Finally, we need a measure for the boundary size of sub-critical sub-instances.

Definition 13 (sub-critical expansion, $\mathcal{E}(\mathcal{I})$). *The* sub-critical expansion *of $\mathcal{I}$, denoted $\mathcal{E}(\mathcal{I})$, is the largest integer such that, for some $s \leq \mathcal{C}(\mathcal{I})$, every sub-instance $\mathcal{J}$ with $s > |vars(\mathcal{J})| \geq s/2$, satisfies $\mathcal{B}(\mathcal{J}) \geq \mathcal{E}(\mathcal{I})$.*

Lemma 3. *For any instance $\mathcal{I}$, $W(\mathcal{I}) \geq \mathcal{E}(\mathcal{I})$.*

Proof. Let π be a **RES** refutation of CNF($\mathcal{I}$), and $s \leq \mathcal{C}(\mathcal{I})$. By Lemma 1 π has a clause C satisfying $s \geq \mu(C) \geq s/2$. By Lemma 2 and the definition of $\mu(C)$, $w(C) \geq \mathcal{B}(\mathcal{J})$ for some sub-instance $\mathcal{J}$ of $\mathcal{I}$ satisfying $s \geq |vars(\mathcal{J})| \geq s/2$. By definition of $\mathcal{E}(\mathcal{I})$, $\mathcal{B}(\mathcal{J}) \geq \mathcal{E}(\mathcal{I})$, so π contains a clause C with $w(C) \geq \mathcal{E}(\mathcal{I})$. $\square$

Finally, the result we wanted in this section now follows immediately from Lemma 3 and Theorem 1.

Theorem 2. *For any set $\mathbf{I}$ of CSP^{d,k,t} instances, $\textbf{C-RES}(\mathbf{I}) = 2^{\Omega(\mathcal{E}(\mathbf{I})^2/n)}$*

4 Random CSP Results

We now apply Theorem 2 to obtain **C-RES** lower bounds for random CSPs.

Definition 14 (CSP$^{d,k,t}_{n,\Delta}$). *Let d, k, t, n be positive integers, with $1 \leq t \leq d^k$, and let $\Delta > 0$ be a real. We denote by CSP$^{d,k,t}_{n,\Delta}$ the random instance of CSP^{d,k,t} with $\lfloor \Delta n \rfloor$ constraints over n variables, selected uniformly at random from all such instances.*

$\mathcal{I} = \mathsf{CSP}^{d,k,t}_{n,\Delta}$ can be seen as being constructed by selecting $\lfloor \Delta n \rfloor$ constraints independently and uniformly at random from all possible constraints for a $\mathsf{CSP}^{d,k,t}$ instance.

Theorem 3. *Let $\Delta > 0$ be constant, and let $d \geq 2$, $k \geq 2$, and $k + d > 4$. Then for $1 \leq t < (d-1)(k-1)$, a random $\mathsf{CSP}^{d,k,t}_{n,\Delta}$ instance $\mathcal{I}$ almost surely satisfies*
$$C\text{-}RES(\mathcal{I}) = 2^{\Omega(n)}$$

The remainder of this section will comprise the proof of this. To obtain **C-RES** lower bounds using Theorem 2, we must show that we have large sub-critical expansion, which entails first showing that the critical size is large, and then that sub-instances not much smaller than the critical size have large boundaries. Both steps use a property of random hypergraphs.

Let k, n, m be positive integers. The random hypergraph denoted $H^k_{n,m}$ is the k-uniform hypergraph on n vertices generated as follows. The vertices of H are $V = [n]$. The edges E of H consist of m edges, selected independently and uniformly at random from the set of $\binom{n}{k}$ possible edges of size k. Notice that the constraint hypergraph of $\mathsf{CSP}^{d,k,t}_{n,\Delta}$ is the random hypergraph $H^k_{n,\Delta n}$.

Definition 15 $(c(\Delta, k, \epsilon))$**.** *For any integer $k > 1$, and reals $\Delta, \epsilon > 0$, we define* $c(\Delta, k, \epsilon) \stackrel{def}{=} \left(3(e^k \Delta)^{\frac{1+\epsilon}{k-1}}\right)^{-1/\epsilon}$ *where* e *denotes the base of the natural logarithm.*

Lemma 4. *Let $\Delta > 0$ be a real number, $k > 0$ an integer, and $H = H^k_{n,\Delta n}$ be the random k-uniform hypergraph with n vertices and $\lfloor \Delta n \rfloor$ edges. Then for any $\epsilon > 0$, a.s. no set of r vertices of H, for any $k \leq r \leq c(\Delta, k, \epsilon)n$, induces more than $(\frac{1+\epsilon}{k-1})r$ edges of H.*

This is a variation on Lemma 1 from [9]. We give a self-contained proof in Appendix A. Using this property, we can bound the critical size as follows.

Lemma 5. *Let $k, d \geq 2$, $1 \leq t < (k-1)(d-1)$, and $0 < \epsilon < 1/t$. Then a.s.* $\mathcal{C}(\mathsf{CSP}^{d,k,t}_{n,\Delta}) \geq c(\Delta, k, \epsilon)n$

A small lemma will be useful in proving this. Recall that a conflict for instance $\mathcal{I}$ corresponds to a conflict clause of $\mathrm{CNF}(\mathcal{I})$.

Definition 16 (minimally unsatisfiable). *A CSP instance $\mathcal{I}$ with n variables is minimally unsatisfiable if $\mathcal{I}$ is unsatisfiable but every sub-instance of $\mathcal{I}$ with fewer than n variables is satisfiable.*

Lemma 6. *Any minimally unsatisfiable instance $\mathcal{I}$ with s variables must have more than $(d-1)s$ conflicts.*

Proof. Suppose $\mathcal{I}$ is a minimally unsatisfiable CSP instance, with s variables and only $s(d-1)$ conflicts, and let ϕ denote $\mathrm{CNF}(\mathcal{I})$. ϕ is unsatisfiable if and only if $\mathcal{I}$ is. ϕ has exactly ds variables and $s(d-1) + s = ds$ clauses. Every minimally unsatisfiable set of clauses has more clauses than variables [3], so ϕ

is not minimally unsatisfiable. Let ψ be a minimally unsatisfiable subset of ϕ. Then ψ is a proper subset of ϕ, and since it has fewer clauses than ϕ, it must also have fewer variables than ϕ. This can only be the case if one of the clauses in $\phi - \psi$ is a domain clause. Suppose that such a domain clause is for the CSP variable x. Any conflict clause involving x contains a literal $\overline{x\colon i}$, and since the only occurrence of $x\colon i$ is in the domain clause, this literal would be a pure literal in ψ. Since pure literals cannot occur in a minimally unsatisfiable clause set, ψ must not contain any conflict clause involving x. Now, let $\mathcal{J}$ be the largest sub-instance of $\mathcal{I}$ that does not have variable x, and let ψ' denote $\mathrm{CNF}(\mathcal{J})$. Then $\psi \subseteq \psi'$, so $\mathcal{J}$ is unsatisfiable, contradicting the assumption that $\mathcal{I}$ is minimally unsatisfiable.   □

Proof. (Lemma 5) By Lemma 6, any unsatisfiable sub-instance of $\mathcal{I}$ with s variables has a sub-instance with $r \leq s$ variables and more than $(d-1)r$ conflicts. So a.s. no sub-instance of $\mathcal{I}$ with $s \leq c(\Delta, k, \epsilon)n$ variables is unsatisfiable unless there is such a sub-instance with more than $(d-1)s$ conflicts, and thus with

$$t(\tfrac{1+\epsilon}{k-1})s > (d-1)s \Rightarrow t(\tfrac{1+\epsilon}{k-1}) > (d-1)$$
$$\Rightarrow t > (d-1)/(\tfrac{1+\epsilon}{k-1})$$
$$\Rightarrow t > (k-1)(d-1)/(1+\epsilon)$$
$$\Rightarrow t \geq (k-1)(d-1), \text{ provided } \epsilon < 1/t.$$

□

The dependence of Lemma 5 on the ratio of clauses to variables implies that this method of bounding critical size cannot work for higher values of t. As we will see below, when $k > 2$ an argument establishing large boundary size works for values of t up to (and indeed above) the value d^{k-1}, above which we have $O(1)$ upper bounds. Thus, extending our lower bounds to larger values of t requires a sharper method for lower bounds on critical size.

We next establish the boundary size for $\mathsf{CSP}_{n,\Delta}^{d,k,t}$. The following simple probabilistic lemma will be useful in doing this.

Lemma 7. *In an experiment in which n independent coins are tossed, each with fixed probability p, $0 < p < 1$, of producing a head, then for any constant $0 < c < 1$, the number of heads is a.s. at least cnp.*

Proof. A standard application of Chernoff bounds.

It will be convenient to treat the cases of $k = 2$ and $k \geq 3$ separately, and we begin with $k \geq 3$, which is slightly simpler.

Lemma 8. *Let $k \geq 3$, $1 \leq t \leq (d-1)d^{k-1}$, $0 < \epsilon < (2(k-1)/k) - 1$, and $0 < r < c(\Delta, k, \epsilon)$, all constant. Then for some $c > 0$, a.s. every sub-instance $\mathcal{J}$ of $\mathsf{CSP}_{n,\Delta}^{d,k,t}$ with rn variables has $\mathcal{B}(\mathcal{J}) \geq cn$.*

Proof. Let $r < c(\Delta, k, \epsilon)$, $s = rn$. Almost surely every size s sub-graph of $H = H_{n,\Delta n}^k$ has at most $s((1 + \epsilon')/(k-1))$ edges, for any $\epsilon' \geq \epsilon$. So the total degree (sum of all vertex degrees) of such a sub-graph is at most $ks((1 + \epsilon')/(k - 1))$. The number of vertices of degree 2 or more must be at most $1/2$ this value, so the number of vertices of degree 0 or 1 is at least

$$s - s\left(\tfrac{k(1+\epsilon')}{2(k-1)}\right) = s\left(1 - \tfrac{k(1+\epsilon')}{2(k-1)}\right)$$
$$= s\left(1 - \tfrac{k}{2(k-1)} - \epsilon'k/2(k-1)\right)$$
$$= s\left(1 - \tfrac{k}{2(k-1)} - \epsilon\right), \text{ where } \epsilon = \epsilon'k/2(k-1) < \epsilon'.$$

This is a positive constant provided that $\epsilon < (2(k-1)/k) - 1$, so for some $c_1 > 0$, a.s. every size-r sub-instance has $c_1 n$ variables with at most one constraint.

Let x be a variable in $\mathcal{J}$ with degree 0 or 1 in $G_{\mathcal{J}}$, the constraint hypergraph for $\mathcal{J}$. Call x good if it is in the boundary of $\mathcal{J}$. If x has degree 0 it is good. If x has degree 1, there is a constant $p > 0$ such that x is good with probability at least p. To see this, let $R(z)$ be the constraint on x, and y be the $k - 1$ variables in z other than x. We need only that at least one choice of t conflicts for R allows any assignment for y to be extended to x, and for this it is sufficient to have $t \le (d-1)d^{k-1}$. This is so, since $(d-1)d^{k-1}$ conflicts can be chosen so that for each of the d^{k-1} assignments for y there are exactly $d - 1$ conflicts agreeing with this assignment on y, leaving one value of x free.

If x, y are two degree-1 variables in $\mathcal{J}$, the events that they are good are dependent only if x and y are in the same constraint. Consider the set of degree-1 variables one-by-one in some order, and for each delete from the set the other at most $k - 1$ variables in the same constraint. We started with at least $c_1 n$ vertices, so are left with at least cn/k degree-1 vertices which are independent with respect to being good. By Lemma 7, for constant $1 > c_2 > 0$, a.s. $c_2 p c_1 n/k$ of these vertices are good. Let $c = c_2 p c_2/k$ and we are done. □

This gives us boundaries of size cn, for constant $c > 0$, for sub-critical sized sub-instances with $\Theta(n)$ variables, for every value of $k \ge 3$. For $k = 2$ (binary problems) this proof gives us nothing. We need a slightly different approach, which takes advantage of the number of vertices of degree 2 or less.

Lemma 9. Let $\epsilon > 0$. Then, in the random graph $H^2_{n,\Delta n}$, a.s. every set of at most $s < c(\Delta, 2, \epsilon)n$ vertices has at least $(1/3 - \epsilon)s$ vertices of degree 2 or less.

Proof. By Lemma 4, a.s. every size $s \le c(\Delta, 2, \epsilon)n$ sub-graph of $H = H^2_{n,\Delta,n}$ has at most $(1 + \epsilon')s$ edges, for any $\epsilon' > \epsilon$. So the total degree of such graphs is at most $2(1 + \epsilon')s$, and the number of vertices with degree 3 or more is at most $2(1 + \epsilon')s/3$. Thus, the number of vertices with degree 2 or less is at least

$$s - \left(\tfrac{2s(1+\epsilon')}{3}\right) = s\left(1 - \tfrac{2(1+\epsilon')}{3}\right)$$
$$= s\left(1 - \tfrac{2}{3} - \tfrac{2\epsilon'}{3}\right)$$
$$= s(1/3 - \epsilon), \text{ where } \epsilon = 2\epsilon'/3 < \epsilon'.$$

□

Not all of these $(1/3 - \epsilon)s$ vertices will be boundary vertices, unless we can guarantee that the constraints on them do not place conflicts on all values. For this, we would require that the total number of conflicts on a variable be strictly less than d, which would require $t < d/2$. However, we can do better by observing that for $t \geq d/2$, while some degree 2 vertices might have more than d conflicts, and therefore not be in the boundary, almost surely some large fraction are.

Lemma 10. *Let $d \geq 3$, $1 \leq t \leq d(d-1)$, $0 < \epsilon < 1/3$, and $0 < r \leq c(\Delta, k, \epsilon)$. Then for some $c > 0$, a.s. every sub-instance $\mathcal{J}$ of $\mathsf{CSP}^{d,2,t}_{n,\Delta}$, with size rn has $\mathcal{B}(\mathcal{J}) \geq cn$.*

Proof. There are at least $(1/3 - \epsilon)rn$ vertices with degree 2 or less. Call such a vertex good if it has degree less than 2 or has degree 2 and at least one value with no conflicts. Suppose x is a degree 2 vertex, with constraints $R_1(x, y)$ and $R_2(x, z)$. The probability that x is good is a positive constant provided there is at least one choice of the t conflicts for each of R_1 and R_2 that leave one value for x without conflicts. This is possible if $t \leq d(d-1)$, since we can pick a value for x to have no conflicts, with the other $d - 1$ values for x having d conflicts with y (one for each value) and d conflicts with z. Therefore, with some fixed probability $p > 0$, each of the $(1/3 - \epsilon)rn$ vertices with degree at most 2 is good. By Lemma 7, for every $0 < c_1 < 1$ a.s. at least $c_1(1/3 - \epsilon)rn$ of these variables are good, and these are in the boundary. Let $c = c_1(1/3 - \epsilon)r$.   □

Notice that this property does not hold for $t > d(d-1)$, since if x has $d(d-1) + 1$ conflicts with some other variable y, at least one value for y has conflicts with every value for x.

Lemma 11. *For any $d, k \geq 2$ with $d + k > 4$, any $\Delta > 0$, and any t, $1 \leq t \leq (d-1)d^{k-1}$, there is a constant $c > 0$ such that a.s. $\mathcal{E}(\mathsf{CSP}^{d,k,t}_{n,\Delta}) \geq cn$.*

Proof. Let $r < c(\Delta, k, \epsilon)$, so that a.s. all instances of size at most rn are satisfiable. Then let $\epsilon > 0$ be small enough to satisfy the conditions of Lemma 5 and Lemma 8, and $c > 0$ satisfy the conditions of either Lemma 8 or Lemma 10, depending on k, and we are done.   □

The lower bounds now follow immediately from Lemma 11 and Theorem 2.

Proof. (Theorem 3) Let $d \geq 2$, $k \geq 2$, be integer constants with $d + k > 4$, and let t satisfy $(d-1)(k-1) > t > 0$. By Lemma 11, for some constant $c > 0$, a.s., $\mathcal{E}(\mathsf{CSP}^{d,k,t}_{n,\Delta}) \geq cn$. By Theorem 2, a.s. $\mathbf{C\text{-}RES}(\mathbf{I}) = 2^{\Omega(\mathcal{E}(\mathbf{I})^2/n)}$. ¿From this it follows that almost surely $\mathbf{C\text{-}RES}(\mathsf{CSP}^{d,k,t}_{n,\Delta}) = 2^{\Omega(c^2 n)}$ □

5   Conclusions

We have presented two important properties for the complexity of CSP refutations in a (useful if not entirely natural) resolution-like system for CSPs. The first is that a (not completely non-intuitive) structural property of CSP instances, the sub-critical expansion, is closely related to the resolution complexity. The second is that for an interesting range of parameters, typical random CSP instances almost surely have linear size sub-critical expansion, and thus almost surely require exponential size refutations.

The refutation system used is interesting mainly because it can efficiently simulate the reasoning implicit in almost all current complete CSP algorithms. Instances which are hard for this refutation system must also be hard for these algorithms. It follows that in certain parameter ranges, almost all CSP instances require exponential time for these algorithms (since a uniformly selected one does!).

We used the sub-critical expansion property in obtaining our random CSP results. However, it should also be applicable to many non-random families of CSPs. Moreover, it provides considerable insight into the structural properties of instances that lead to intractability for current methods. Even for families of instances for which one would not or could not carry out a lower bound proof, it may provide some intuition about when these are likely to be hard for resolution-based algorithms.

References

[1] D. Achlioptas, P. Beame, and M. Molloy. A sharp threshold in proof complexity. In *Proc., 33rd Annual ACM Symp. on the Theory of Computing (STOC-01)*, pages 337–346, 2001.

[2] D. Achlioptas, L. Kirousis, E. Kranakis, D. Krizanc, M. Molloy, and Y. Stamatiou. Random constraint satisfaction: A more accurate picture. *Constraints*, 6(4):329–344, 2001.

[3] R. Aharoni and N. Linial. Minimal unsatisfiable formulas and minimal non-two-colorable hypergraphs. *J. of Combinatorial Theory, Series A*, 43:196–204, 1986.

[4] Andrew B. Baker. *Intelligent Backtracking on Constraint Satisfaction Problems: Experimental and Theoretical Results.* PhD thesis, University of Oregon, 1995.

[5] P. Beame, R. Karp, T. Pitassi, and M. Saks. On the complexity of unsatisfiability proofs for random k-CNF formulas. In *Proc., 30th Annual ACM Symp. on the Theory of Computing (STOC-98)*, pages 561–571, May 1998.

[6] E. Ben-Sasson and A. Wigderson. Short proofs are narrow: Resolution made simple. In *Proc., 31st Annual Symp. on the Theory of Computing (STOC-99)*, pages 517–526, May 1999. (Also appears as ECCC report TR99-022).

[7] P. Cheesman, B. Kanefsky, and W. M. Taylor. Where the really hard problems are. In *Proc., 12th Int'l. Joint Conf. on A. I. (IJCAI-91)*, 1991.

[8] V. Chvátal and B. Reed. Mick gets some (the odds are on his side). In *Proc. of the 33rd Symp. on the Foundations of Comp. Sci. (FOCS-92)*, pages 620–628, 1992.

[9] V. Chvátal and E. Szemerédi. Many hard examples for resolution. *Journal of the ACM*, 35(4):759–768, 1988.

[10] J. De Kleer. A comparison of ATMS and CSP techniques. In *Proc. of the 11th Int'l. Joint Conf. on A. I. (IJCAI-89)*, pages 290–296, 1989.

[11] R. Dechter. Enhancement schemes for constraint processing: Backjumping, learning, and cutset decomposition. *Artificial Intelligence*, 41:273–312, 1990.

[12] R. Dechter and D. Frost. Backtracking algorithms for constraint satisfaction problems. Technical report, Dept. of Inf. & Comp. Sci., U. of California, Irvine, 1999.

[13] J. Gashnig. Experimental case studies of backtrack vs. Waltz-type vs. new algorithms for satisficing assignment problems. In *Proc. of the Canadian Artificial Intelligence Conference*, pages 268–277, 1978.

[14] I. P. Gent, E. MacIntyre, P. Prosser, B. M. Smith, and T. Walsh. Random constraint satisfaction: flaws and structure. *Constraints*, 6(4):345–372, October 2001.

[15] O. Kullmann. Upper and lower bounds on the complexity of generalized resolution and generalized constraint satisfaction problems. Submitted, 2000.

[16] A. K. Mackworth and E. C. Freuder. The complexity of some polynomial network consistency algorithms for constraint satisfaction problems. *Artificial Intelligence*, 25:65–73, 1985.

[17] D. G. Mitchell. Hard problems for CSP algorithms. In *Proc., 15th Nat. Conf. on Artificial Intelligence (AAAI-98)*, pages 398–405, 1998.

[18] D. G. Mitchell. *The Resolution Complexity of Constraint Satisfaction*. PhD thesis, University of Toronto, 2002.

[19] D. G. Mitchell. Constraint satisfaction and resolution. In preparation.

[20] D. G. Mitchell, B. Selman, and H. J. Levesque. Hard and easy distributions of SAT problems. In *Proc. of the 10th Nat. Conf. on A. I. (AAAI'92)*, pages 459–462, 1992.

[21] M. Molloy. Models and thresholds for random constraint satisfaction problems. In *Proc., 34th Annual Symp. on the Theory of Computing (STOC-02)*, pages 209–217. ACM, 2002.

[22] P. Prosser. Hybrid algorithms for the constraint satisfaction problem. *Computational Intelligence*, 9(3):268–299, August 1993.

[23] P. Prosser. An empirical study of phase transitions in binary constraint satisfaction problems. *Artificial Intelligence*, 81:81–109, 1996.

[24] T. J. Schaefer. The complexity of satisfiability problems. In *Proc., 10th Annual ACM Symp. on the Theory of Computing (STOC-78)*, pages 216–226. ACM, 1978.

A   Local Sparsity of Random Hypergraphs

Here we give a proof of Lemma 4: If $c(\Delta, k, \epsilon) = (3(e^k \Delta)^{\frac{1+\epsilon}{k-1}}))^{-1/\epsilon}$, and $\epsilon > 0$ then a.s. $H^k_{n,m}$ has no set of r vertices, for any $k \leq r \leq c(\Delta, k, \epsilon)n$, that induce more than $r(1 + \epsilon)/(k - 1)$ edges. For the remainder, H will always denote the random hypergraph $H^k_{n,m}$. Call H (r, s)-*dense* if some set of r vertices of H induces s or more edges of H.

Lemma 12. *If $r, s \geq 1$, then* $\mathbf{Pr}[H \text{ is } (r, s)\text{-dense}] \leq \left(\frac{en}{r}\right)^r \left(\frac{emr^k}{sn^k}\right)^s$

Proof. Let $H = \langle V, E \rangle$, and $R \subseteq V$ be a set of vertices of H of size r. The probability that a randomly chosen edge on V is also an edge on R is $\binom{r}{k}/\binom{n}{k}$. The probability that at least s edges of H are induced by R is the probability that some size-s subset of E is on R, which is at most the expected number of size-s subsets of E that have all of their vertices in R, so we have

$\mathbf{Pr}[H \text{ has } s \text{ edges in } R] \leq \binom{m}{s} \left(\binom{r}{k}/\binom{n}{k}\right)^s \leq \left(\frac{em}{s}\right)^s \left(\frac{r}{n}\right)^{ks} \leq \left(\frac{emr^k}{sn^k}\right)^s$

Summing over all $\binom{n}{r}$ possible choices for R, we obtain

$$\mathbf{Pr}[H \text{ is } (r,s) - \text{dense}] \leq \binom{n}{r}\left(\frac{emr^k}{sn^k}\right)^s \leq \left(\frac{en}{r}\right)^r \left(\frac{emr^k}{sn^k}\right)^s$$

□

Lemma 13. *Let $z > 0$ be a real, and $s \leq n \in \mathbb{N}$. The probability that, for some r, $1 \leq r \leq s$, $H_{n,m}^k$ is (r,zr)-dense is at most $\sum_{r=1}^{s}\left(en\left(\frac{em}{zn^k}\right)^z r^{z(k-1)-1}\right)^r$*

Proof. $\mathbf{Pr}[\exists r \leq s \text{ s.t. } H \text{ is } (r,zr)\text{-dense}] \leq \sum_{r=1}^{s}$, and

$$\sum_{r=1}^{s}\left(\frac{en}{r}\right)^r\left(\frac{emr^k}{zrn^k}\right)^{zr} = \sum_{r=1}^{s}\left(\frac{en}{r}\left(\frac{emr^k}{zrn^k}\right)^z\right)^r = \sum_{r=1}^{s}\left(en\left(\frac{em}{zn^k}\right)^z r^{z(k-1)-1}\right)^r$$

□

Proof. (Lemma 4) Say that H is bad if for some choice of r, $1 \leq r \leq c(\Delta,k,\epsilon)n$, H is $(r, r(1+\epsilon)/(k-1))$-dense. We need to show H is a.s. not bad. Let z denote $(1+\epsilon)/(k-1)$ and s denote $c(\Delta,k,\epsilon)n$. Then we have

$$\mathbf{Pr}[H \text{ is bad }] \leq \sum_{r=1}^{s}\left(en\left(\frac{e\Delta n}{zn^k}\right)^z r^{z(k-1)-1}\right)^r$$

Now we write A for $en(\frac{e\Delta n}{zn^k})^z$ and write $B(r)$ for $(Ar^{z(k-1)-1})^r$, and have that $\mathbf{Pr}[H \text{ is bad}] \leq \sum_{r=1}^{s} B(r)$, which is a geometric series in r. If $B(r+1)/B(r) \leq 1/2$, the series will be less than twice its largest term, so we have that

$$\begin{aligned}
\mathbf{Pr}[H \text{ is bad }] &\leq 2B(1) \\
&= 2en\left(\frac{e\Delta n}{zn^k}\right)^z \\
&= 2(1/z)^z e(e\Delta)^z n^{z(1-k)+1} \\
&\leq 3e(e\Delta)^{(1+\epsilon)/(k-1)} n^{(1-k)(1+\epsilon)/(k-1)+1} \\
&= 3e(e\Delta)^{(1+\epsilon)/(k-1)} n^{-\epsilon} \\
&= o(1)
\end{aligned}$$

It remains to verify the condition on B:

$$\begin{aligned}
\frac{B(r+1)}{B(r)} &= \frac{(A(r+1)^{z(k-1)-1})^{r+1}}{(Ar^{z(k-1)-1})^r} \\
&= A\left(\left(\frac{r+1}{r}\right)^r (r+1)\right)^{z(k-1)-1} \\
&\leq A\left(e(r+1)\right)^{z(k-1)-1} &&\left(\text{since } \left(\frac{x+1}{x}\right)^x \leq e\right) \\
&= en\left(\frac{e\Delta n}{zn^k}\right)^z (e(r+1))^{z(k-1)-1} \\
&= \left(\frac{1}{z}\right)^z (e^k\Delta)^z n^{z(1-k)+1}(r+1)^{z(k-1)-1} \\
&\leq 1.5\left(e^k\Delta\right)^z \left(\frac{r+1}{n}\right)^{z(k-1)-1} &&(\text{since } \forall z > 0, (1/z)^z < 1.5) \\
&\leq 1.5\left(e^k\Delta\right)^z \left(\frac{c(\Delta,k,\epsilon)n}{n}\right)^{z(k-1)-1} \\
&= 1.5\left(e^k\Delta\right)^z c(\Delta,k,\epsilon)^{z(k-1)-1} \\
&= 1.5\left(e^k\Delta\right)^z \left(\left(3(e^k\Delta)^{\frac{1+\epsilon}{k-1}}\right)^{-1/\epsilon}\right)^{z(k-1)-1} \\
&= 1.5\left(e^k\Delta\right)^{\frac{1+\epsilon}{k-1}}\left(3(e^k\Delta)^{\frac{1+\epsilon}{k-1}}\right)^{-1} \\
&= 1/2
\end{aligned}$$

□

Constraint Satisfaction, Bounded Treewidth, and Finite-Variable Logics

Víctor Dalmau[1], Phokion G. Kolaitis[2] *, and Moshe Y. Vardi[3] **

[1] Universitat Pompeu Fabra, Barcelona
[2] University of California, Santa Cruz
[3] Rice University

Abstract. We systematically investigate the connections between constraint satisfaction problems, structures of bounded treewidth, and definability in logics with a finite number of variables. We first show that constraint satisfaction problems on inputs of treewidth less than k are definable using Datalog programs with at most k variables; this provides a new explanation for the tractability of these classes of problems. After this, we investigate constraint satisfaction on inputs that are homomorphically equivalent to structures of bounded treewidth. We show that these problems are solvable in polynomial time by establishing that they are actually definable in Datalog; moreover, we obtain a logical characterization of the property "being homomorphically equivalent to a structure of bounded treewidth" in terms of definability in finite-variable logics. Unfortunately, this expansion of the tractability landscape comes at a price, because we also show that, for each $k \geq 2$, determining whether a structure is homomorphically equivalent to a structure of treewidth less than k is an NP-complete problem. In contrast, it is well known that, for each $k \geq 2$, there is a polynomial-time algorithm for testing whether a given structure is of treewidth less than k. Finally, we obtain a logical characterization of the property "having bounded treewidth" that sheds light on the complexity-theoretic difference between this property and the property 'being homomorphically equivalent to a structure of bounded treewidth".

1 Introduction and Summary of Results

Constraint satisfaction problems are ubiquitous in several different areas of artificial intelligence, computer science, algebra, logic, and combinatorics. An instance of a constraint-satisfaction problem consists of a set of variables, a set of possible values, and a set of constraints on tuples of variables; the question is to determine whether there is an assignment of values to the variables that satisfies the given constraints. A particularly fruitful way to formalize the above informal

* Supported in part by NSF grant IIS-9907419.
** Supported in part by NSF grants CCR-9988322, IIS-9908435, IIS-9978135, and EIA-0086264, and by BSF grant 9800096.

P. Van Hentenryck (Ed.): CP 2002, LNCS 2470, pp. 310–326, 2002.

description, articulated first by Feder and Vardi [FV98], is to identify the CON-
STRAINT SATISFACTION PROBLEM with the HOMOMORPHISM PROBLEM: given
two relational structures $\mathbf{A}$ and $\mathbf{B}$, is there a homomorphism h from $\mathbf{A}$ to $\mathbf{B}$?
Intuitively, the structure $\mathbf{A}$ represents the variables and the tuples of variables
that participate in constraints, the structure $\mathbf{B}$ represents the domain of values
and the tuples of values that these constrained tuples of variables are allowed
to take, and the homomorphisms from $\mathbf{A}$ to $\mathbf{B}$ are precisely the assignments of
values to variables that satisfy the constraints. For instance, 3-COLORABILITY is
equivalent to the problem of deciding whether there is a homomorphism h from
a given graph $\mathbf{G}$ to $\mathbf{K}_3$, where $\mathbf{K}_3$ is the complete graph with 3 nodes. This identification makes it possible to approach constraint satisfaction problems from an
algebraic perspective [Jea98, FV98]. Moreover, it makes transparent the connection between constraint satisfaction problems and certain fundamental problems
in database theory, such as conjunctive query evaluation and conjunctive query
containment (or implication) [KV00a].

Since in its full generality the HOMOMORPHISM PROBLEM is NP-complete
[GJ79], researchers have intensively pursued tractable cases of this problem, often
referred to as "islands of tractability", that are obtained by imposing restrictions
on the input structures $\mathbf{A}$ and $\mathbf{B}$. If σ is a relational vocabulary, and $\mathcal{A}$, $\mathcal{B}$ are two
classes of finite σ-structures, then $\mathrm{CSP}(\mathcal{A}, \mathcal{B})$ is the following decision problem:
given a structure $\mathbf{A} \in \mathcal{A}$ and a structure $\mathbf{B} \in \mathcal{B}$, is there a homomorphism from
$\mathbf{A}$ to $\mathbf{B}$? In other words, $\mathrm{CSP}(\mathcal{A}, \mathcal{B})$ is the restriction of the HOMOMORPHISM
PROBLEM to inputs from $\mathcal{A}$ and $\mathcal{B}$. If the class $\mathcal{B}$ consists of a single structure
$\mathbf{B}$, then we write $\mathrm{CSP}(\mathcal{A}, \mathbf{B})$ instead of $\mathrm{CSP}(\mathcal{A}, \mathcal{B})$. Furthermore, if $\mathcal{A}$ is the
class $\mathcal{F}(\sigma)$ of all finite σ-structures, then we simply write $\mathrm{CSP}(\mathbf{B})$ instead of
$\mathrm{CSP}(\mathcal{F}(\sigma), \mathbf{B})$.

Note that if $\mathcal{G}$ is the class of all undirected graphs and $\mathbf{K}_3$ is the complete
graph with 3 nodes, then $\mathrm{CSP}(\mathcal{G}, \mathbf{K}_3)$ is the 3-COLORABILITY problem. Consequently, there are fixed structures $\mathbf{B}$ such that constraint satisfaction problems
of the form $\mathrm{CSP}(\mathbf{B})$ are NP-complete. It is a major open problem to characterize those structures $\mathbf{B}$ for which $\mathrm{CSP}(\mathbf{B})$ is tractable. Closely related to this
problem is the Feder-Vardi [FV98] Dichotomy Conjecture, which asserts that for
every fixed structure $\mathbf{B}$ either $\mathrm{CSP}(\mathbf{B})$ is NP-complete or $\mathrm{CSP}(\mathbf{B})$ is solvable in
polynomial time. Although special cases of this conjecture have been confirmed
(see, for instance, [Sch78, HN90]), the full conjecture has not been settled thus
far. Nonetheless, research on these open problems has led to the discovery of
numerous tractable cases of constraint satisfaction (see [Jea98]).

Feder and Vardi [FV98] identified two general sufficient conditions for
tractability of $\mathrm{CSP}(\mathbf{B})$ that are broad enough to account for essentially all
tractable cases of $\mathrm{CSP}(\mathbf{B})$ that were known at that time. One of these two
conditions is group-theoretic, while the other has to do with expressibility of
constraint satisfaction problems in Datalog, the main query language for deductive databases [Ull89]. More precisely, Feder and Vardi [FV98] showed that
for many polynomial-time solvable constraint satisfaction problems of the form

CSP(**B**) there is a Datalog program that defines the complement ¬CSP(**B**) of CSP(**B**).

Tractable constraint satisfaction problems of the form CSP(**B**) represent restricted cases of the HOMOMORPHISM PROBLEM "is there a homomorphism from **A** to **B**?" in which **B** is kept fixed and also required to satisfy certain additional conditions that imply tractability. Tractable cases of constraint satisfaction can also be obtained, however, by imposing conditions on **A** while letting **B** be arbitrary. In particular, an important large "island of tractability" is formed by the class of structures of *bounded treewidth*, where the *treewidth* of a relational structure is a positive integer that measures how "close" to a tree the structure is. Specifically, Dechter and Pearl [DP89] and Freuder [Fre90] have shown that, for every $k \geq 2$, the constraint satisfaction problem $\text{CSP}(\mathcal{T}^k(\sigma), \mathcal{F}(\sigma))$ is solvable in polynomial time, where $\mathcal{T}^k(\sigma)$ is the class of all σ-structures of treewidth less than k (and, as before, $\mathcal{F}(\sigma)$ is the class of all σ-structures). In [KV00b], a different proof of this result was obtained by exploiting the tight connection between the constraint satisfaction and conjunctive query evaluation, as well as the tractability of query evaluation for fragments of first-order logic with a finite number of variables. If **A** is a relational structure, then the *canonical conjunctive query* of $Q^{\mathbf{A}}$ is a positive existential first-order sentence that describes which tuples from **A** are in the various relations of **A**. Chandra and Merlin [CM77] pointed out that, given two structures **A** and **B**, a homomorphism from **A** to **B** exists if and only if **B** satisfies $Q^{\mathbf{A}}$. In general, $Q^{\mathbf{A}}$ requires as many variables as elements in the universe of **A**. In [KV00b], however, it was shown that if **A** is of treewidth less than k, then k variables suffice to express $Q^{\mathbf{A}}$, i.e., $Q^{\mathbf{A}}$ is equivalent to a sentence of L^k, which is the fragment of first-order logic with k variables containing all atomic formulas in these k variables and closed only under conjunction and existential quantification over these variables. The tractability of $\text{CSP}(\mathcal{T}^k(\sigma), \mathcal{F}(\sigma))$ follows then by combining this result with the fact that the evaluation problems for L^k-sentences is polynomial-time solvable, which follows from more general results in [Var95].

Our goal in this paper is to systematically explore the connections between constraint satisfaction problems, structures of bounded treewidth, and definability in logics with a finite number of variables. The first main result asserts that definability in Datalog provides also an explanation for the tractability of constraint satisfaction problems on structures of bounded treewidth. Specifically, we show that, for every $k \geq 2$ and every σ-structure **B**, the complement $\neg\text{CSP}(\mathcal{T}^k(\sigma), \mathbf{B})$ is expressible in k-Datalog, i.e., it is definable by a Datalog program with k variables in the body and the head of each rule. From this it follows that, for every $k \geq 2$, $\text{CSP}(\mathcal{T}^k(\sigma), \mathcal{F}(\sigma))$ is definable in LFP^{2k}, where LFP^{2k} is the fragment of least fixed-point logic with $2k$ variables. Since query evaluation in this fragment is solvable in polynomial time, this result provides another proof of the tractability of the constraint satisfaction problem on structures of bounded treewidth. We also show that testing whether strong k-consistency can be established on **A** and **B** is a sound and complete algorithm for determining whether there is a homomorphism from **A** to **B**, when **A** is a structure of treewidth less than k. The proofs of these results make use of certain connections between constraint satisfaction, finite-variable logics, and combinatorial pebble games that were studied in [KV00b].

After this, we turn attention on the classes $\mathcal{H}(\mathcal{T}^k(\sigma))$, $k \geq 2$, of all σ-structures $\mathbf{A}$ that are *homomorpically equivalent* to a σ-structure $\mathbf{D}$ of treewidth less than k (i.e., there are homorphisms from $\mathbf{A}$ to $\mathbf{D}$ and from $\mathbf{D}$ to $\mathbf{A}$). Clearly, each of these classes properly contains the class $\mathcal{T}^k(\sigma)$. We show that $\mathrm{CSP}(\mathcal{H}(\mathcal{T}^k(\sigma)), \mathcal{F}(\sigma))$ is solvable in polynomial time by establishing that $\neg\mathrm{CSP}(\mathcal{H}(\mathcal{T}^k(\sigma)), \mathbf{B})$ is in k-Datalog, for every σ-structure $\mathbf{B}$. Thus, the classes $\mathcal{H}(\mathcal{T}^k(\sigma))$, $k \geq 2$, constitute new large "islands of tractability" for constraint satisfaction and, moreover, their tractability is once again due to definability in Datalog. We then proceed to characterize $\mathcal{H}(\mathcal{T}^k(\sigma))$ in terms of definability in finite-variable logics by showing that for each $k \geq 2$, a structure $\mathbf{A}$ is homomorphically equivalent to a structure of treewidth less than k if and only if the canonical query $Q^{\mathbf{A}}$ of $\mathbf{A}$ is logically equivalent to an L^k-sentence.

The above properties of the classes $\mathcal{H}(\mathcal{T}^k(\sigma))$, $k \geq 2$, appear to make them large and appealing "islands of tractability". Unfortunately, this expansion of the tractability landscape comes at a price, because accessing these new "islands of tractability" turns out to be a hard problem. Indeed, we show that, for every $k \geq 2$, testing for membership in $\mathcal{H}(\mathcal{T}^k(\sigma))$ is an NP-complete problem. This should be contrasted with the state of affairs for $\mathcal{T}^k$, since it is well known that, for every $k \geq 2$, testing for membership in $\mathcal{T}^k$ is solvable in polynomial time [Bod93].

Our study of the connections between bounded treewidth and finite-variable logics culminates with a logical characterization of bounded treewidth that sheds light on the differences between $\mathcal{T}^k(\sigma)$ and $\mathcal{H}(\mathcal{T}^k(\sigma))$. For this, we analyze a set of *rewriting rules* that are widely used in database query processing and show that, for each $k \geq 2$, a structure $\mathbf{A}$ has treewidth less than k if and only if the canonical query $Q^{\mathbf{A}}$ of $\mathbf{A}$ can be rewritten to an L^k-sentence using these rules.

2   Preliminaries and Background

A *vocabulary* σ is a finite set $\{R_1, \ldots, R_m\}$ of relation symbols of specified arities. A σ-*structure* is a relational structure of the form $\mathbf{A} = (A, R_1^{\mathbf{A}}, \ldots, R_m^{\mathbf{A}})$, where each $R_i^{\mathbf{A}}$ is a relation on the universe A of $\mathbf{A}$ such that the arity of $R_i^{\mathbf{A}}$ matches that of the relation symbol R_i. We write $\mathcal{F}(\sigma)$ for the class of all finite σ-structures, i.e., σ-structures with a finite set as universe. In what follows, we will assume that all structures under consideration are finite; for this reason, the term "σ-structure" should be understood to mean "finite σ-structure" (on a few occasions, however, we will spell out "finite σ-structure" for emphasis). Also, whenever we refer to *undirected graphs* we mean structures of the form $\mathbf{G} = (V, E)$ such that E is a symmetric binary relation on V without self-loops, i.e., E contains no pairs of the form (v, v), where $v \in V$.

2.1   Conjunctive Queries and Homomorphisms

An n-ary *conjunctive query* Q over a vocabulary σ is a query defin-able by a positive existential first-order formula over σ having conjunc-tion as its only propositional connective, i.e., by a formula of the form $(\exists z_1) \cdots (\exists z_s) \psi(x_1, \ldots, x_n, z_1, \ldots, z_s)$, where $\psi(x_1, \ldots, x_n, z_1, \ldots, z_s)$ is a con-junction of atomic formulas over σ. For example, the binary conjunctive query "there is a path of length 3 from x_1 to x_2" is definable by the formula $(\exists z_1)(\exists z_2)(E(x_1, z_1) \wedge E(z_1, z_2) \wedge E(z_2, x_2))$. A *Boolean conjunctive query* is de-finable by a positive existential first-order sentence having conjunction as its only propositional connective, i.e., all variables of ψ have been quantified out.

Every finite σ-structure $\mathbf{A}$ gives rise to a *canonical* Boolean conjunctive query $Q^{\mathbf{A}}$; the positive existential first-order sentence defining $Q^{\mathbf{A}}$ asserts that there exist as many elements as the cardinality of the universe of $\mathbf{A}$ and states all atomic facts satisfied by tuples from the universe of $\mathbf{A}$. For example, if $\mathbf{A} = (A, E)$ is the graph with $A = \{1, 2, 3, 4\}$ and $E = \{(1, 2), (2, 3), (3, 4), (4, 1)\}$, then $Q^{\mathbf{A}}$ is definable by the sentence

$$(\exists x_1)(\exists x_2)(\exists x_3)(\exists x_4)(E(x_1, x_2) \wedge E(x_2, x_3) \wedge E(x_3, x_4) \wedge E(x_4, x_1)).$$

In what follows, we will mildly abuse the notation by using $Q^{\mathbf{A}}$ to denote both the canonical conjunctive query $Q^{\mathbf{A}}$ associated with the structure $\mathbf{A}$ and the positive existential first-order sentence that defines the canonical query $Q^{\mathbf{A}}$.

If $\mathbf{A}$ and $\mathbf{B}$ are σ-structures, then a *homomorphism from* $\mathbf{A}$ *to* $\mathbf{B}$ is a map-ping $h : A \mapsto B$ from the universe A of $\mathbf{A}$ to the universe B of $\mathbf{B}$ such that for every relation symbol R_i of σ and every tuple $(a_1, \ldots, a_n) \in R_i^{\mathbf{A}}$, we have that $(h(a_1), \ldots, h(a_n)) \in R_i^{\mathbf{B}}$. Chandra and Merlin discovered the following funda-mental result.

Theorem 1. [CM77] *The following are equivalent for finite σ-structures $\mathbf{A}$ and $\mathbf{B}$.*

1. *There is a homomorphism h from $\mathbf{A}$ to $\mathbf{B}$.*
2. *$Q^{\mathbf{B}} \models Q^{\mathbf{A}}$, i.e., $Q^{\mathbf{B}}$ logically implies $Q^{\mathbf{A}}$.*
3. *$\mathbf{B} \models Q^{\mathbf{A}}$, i.e., the structure $\mathbf{B}$ satisfies the canonical query $Q^{\mathbf{A}}$ of $\mathbf{A}$.*

To illustrate this result, recall that an undirected graph $\mathbf{G} = (V, E)$ is 3-colorable if and only if there is a homomorphism from $\mathbf{G}$ to $\mathbf{K}_3$. Consequently, Theorem 1 implies that $\mathbf{G}$ is 3-colorable if and only if $\mathbf{K}_3$ satisfies the canonical query $Q^{\mathbf{G}}$ of $\mathbf{G}$.

We say that two σ-structures $\mathbf{A}$ and $\mathbf{B}$ are *homomorphically equivalent* if there is a homomorphism h from $\mathbf{A}$ to $\mathbf{B}$ and a homomorphism h' from $\mathbf{B}$ to $\mathbf{A}$. We write $\mathbf{A} \sim_h \mathbf{B}$ to denote that $\mathbf{A}$ is homomorphically equivalent to $\mathbf{B}$. Clearly, $\sim_h$ is an equivalence relation on the class of all finite σ-structures. Moreover, Theorem 1 implies that $\sim_h$ can be characterized in terms of logical equivalence.

Corollary 1. *The following are equivalent for finite σ-structures $\mathbf{A}$ and $\mathbf{B}$.*

1. *$\mathbf{A} \sim_h \mathbf{B}$.*
2. *$Q^{\mathbf{A}} \equiv Q^{\mathbf{B}}$, i.e., $Q^{\mathbf{A}}$ is is logically equivalent to $Q^{\mathbf{B}}$.*

2.2   Datalog, Pebble Games, and Constraint Satisfaction

Datalog is a database query language that can be succinctly described as logic programming without function symbols. More formally, a *Datalog program* is a finite set of rules of the form $t_0 \leftarrow t_1, \ldots, t_m$, where each t_i is an atomic formula $R(x_1, \ldots, x_n)$. The left-hand side of each rule is called the *head* of the rule, while the right-hand side is called the *body*. In effect, the body of each rule is a conjunctive query such that each variable occurring in the body, but not in the head, is existentially quantified. The relational predicates that occur in the heads of the rules are the *intensional database* predicates (IDBs), while all others are the *extensional database* predicates (EDBs). One of the IDBs is designated as the *goal* of the program. Note that IDBs may occur in the bodies of rules and, thus, a Datalog program is a recursive specification of the IDBs with semantics obtained via least fixed-points of monotone operators, see [Ull89]. Each Datalog program defines a query which, given a set of EDB predicates, returns the value of the goal predicate. If the goal predicate is 0-ary, then the program defines a Boolean query. Note that a Datalog query is computable in polynomial time, since the bottom-up evaluation of the least fixed-point of the program terminates within a polynomial number of steps (in the size of the given EDBs), see [Ull89]. Thus, expressibility in Datalog is a sufficient condition for tractability of a query. As an example, NON-2-COLORABILITY is definable by the goal predicate Q of the Datalog program below, which asserts that the graph $\mathbf{G} = (V, E)$ contains a cycle of odd length:

$$P(x, y) : - \ E(x, y)$$
$$P(x, y) : - \ P(x, z), E(z, w), E(w, y)$$
$$Q : - \ P(x, x)$$

A key parameter in analyzing Datalog programs is the number of variables used. For every positive integer k, let k-Datalog be the collection of all Datalog programs in which the body of every rule has at most k distinct variables and also the head of every rule has at most k variables (the variables of the body may be different from the variables of the head). For instance, the preceding example shows that NON-2-COLORABILITY is definable by a 4-Datalog program (in fact, it is also definable by a 3-Datalog program).

If $\mathcal{A}$ is a class of σ-structures and $\mathbf{B}$ is a σ-structure, then $\neg \mathrm{CSP}(\mathcal{A}, \mathbf{B})$ is the complement (relative to $\mathcal{A}$) of $\mathrm{CSP}(\mathcal{A}, \mathbf{B})$, i.e., it is the class of all σ-structures $\mathbf{A} \in \mathcal{A}$ such that there is *no* homomorphism h from $\mathbf{A}$ to $\mathbf{B}$. Feder and Vardi [FV98] showed that the tractability of many constraint satisfaction problems of the form $\mathrm{CSP}(\mathcal{A}, \mathbf{B})$ is due to the fact that $\neg \mathrm{CSP}(\mathcal{A}, \mathbf{B})$ is expressible in k-Datalog, for some positive integer k. In other words, in many cases in which $\mathrm{CSP}(\mathcal{A}, \mathbf{B})$ is tractable there is a positive integer k and a k-Datalog program P with a 0-ary goal predicate such that, for every σ-structure $\mathbf{A} \in \mathcal{A}$, we have that P on $\mathbf{A}$ evaluates to "true" iff $\mathbf{A} \notin \mathrm{CSP}(\mathcal{A}, \mathbf{B})$. A concrete instance of this phenomenon is 2-COLORABILITY, since it is the same decision problem as $\mathrm{CSP}(\mathcal{G}, \mathbf{K_2})$, where $\mathcal{G}$ is the class of all undirected graphs and $\mathbf{K_2}$ is the undirected graph consisting of a single edge. It should be pointed out that, when linking tractability of constraint satisfaction problems with definability in Datalog, it is necessary to consider the complement $\neg\mathrm{CSP}(\mathcal{A}, \mathbf{B})$ of $\mathrm{CSP}(\mathcal{A}, \mathbf{B})$, because $\mathrm{CSP}(\mathcal{A}, \mathbf{B})$ itself cannot be definable in Datalog. The reason is that Datalog-definable queries are *monotone*, in the sense that they are preserved under the addition of tuples in the relations of the input, while $\mathrm{CSP}(\mathcal{A}, \mathbf{B})$ lacks this monotonicity property.

It is well known that the expressive power of some of the main logical formalisms, including first-order logic and second-order logic, can be analyzed using certain combinatorial two-person games. In particular, the expressive power of k-Datalog can be analyzed using *existential k-pebble games*, which were introduced by Kolaitis and Vardi [KV95] in the context of database theory. These games are played between two players, the *Spoiler* and the *Duplicator*, on two σ-structures $\mathbf{A}$ and $\mathbf{B}$ according to the following rules: a round of the game consists of k moves of each player; on the i-th move of a round, $1 \leq i \leq k$, the Spoiler places a pebble on an element a_i of A, and the Duplicator responds by placing a pebble on an element b_i of B. At the end of the round, if the mapping $a_i \mapsto b_i$, $1 \leq i \leq k$, is not a homomorphim between the corresponding substructures of $\mathbf{A}$ and $\mathbf{B}$ induced by $\{a_1, \ldots, a_k\}$ and $\{b_1, \ldots, b_k\}$, then the Spoiler wins the game. Otherwise, the Spoiler removes one or more pebbles, and a new round of the game begins. The Duplicator wins the existential k-pebble game if he has a *winning strategy*, i.e., a systematic way that allows him to sustain playing "forever", so that the Spoiler can never win a round of the game.

In [KV00a], it was shown that existential k-pebble games can be used to characterize when $\neg\mathrm{CSP}(\mathcal{A}, \mathbf{B})$ is expressible in k-Datalog. Moreover, in [KV00b] it was pointed out that there is a tight connection between existential k-pebble games and strong k-consistency properties of constraint satisfaction problems. Recall that a CSP-instance is *strongly k-consistent* if, for every $i < k$, every partial solution on $i - 1$ variables can be extended to a partial solution on i variables. Moreover, the statement "strong k-consistency can be established for a CSP-instance" means that additional constraints can be added, so that the resulting CSP-instance is strongly k-consistent and has the same solutions as the original one (see [Dec92] for the precise definitions). The following is the key link between existential pebble games and strong consistency properties: given two σ-structures $\mathbf{A}$ and $\mathbf{B}$, it is possible to establish strong k-consistency for the CSP-instance associated with $\mathbf{A}$ and $\mathbf{B}$ ("is there a homomorphism from $\mathbf{A}$ to $\mathbf{B}$?") if and only if the Duplicator wins the existential k-pebble game on $\mathbf{A}$ and $\mathbf{B}$. By combining the results in [KV00a, KV00b], we obtain several different characterizations of when $\neg\mathrm{CSP}(\mathcal{A}, \mathbf{B})$ is expressible in k-Datalog. Before stating these characterizations we note that, whenever we write "strong k-consistency can be established for two σ-structures $\mathbf{A}$ and $\mathbf{B}$", we mean that strong k-consistency can be established for the CSP-instance associated with $\mathbf{A}$ and $\mathbf{B}$ (see [KV00b] for the formal definition of establishing strong k-consistency for $\mathbf{A}$ and $\mathbf{B}$).

Theorem 2. [KV00a, KV00b] *Assume that $\mathcal{A}$ is a class of σ-structures, $\mathbf{B}$ is a σ-structure, and k is a positive integer. Then the following statements are equivalent.*

1. $\neg CSP(\mathcal{A}, \mathbf{B})$ *is expressible in k-Datalog.*
2. $CSP(\mathcal{A}, \mathbf{B})$ *consists precisely of all structures $\mathbf{A} \in \mathcal{A}$ such that the Duplicator wins the existential k-pebble game on $\mathbf{A}$ and $\mathbf{B}$.*
3. *For every structure $\mathbf{A} \in \mathcal{A}$, if the Duplicator wins the existential k-pebble game on $\mathbf{A}$ and $\mathbf{B}$, then there is a homomorphism from $\mathbf{A}$ to $\mathbf{B}$.*
4. *For every structure $\mathbf{A} \in \mathcal{A}$, if strong k-consistency can be established for $\mathbf{A}$ and $\mathbf{B}$, then there is a homomorphism from $\mathbf{A}$ to $\mathbf{B}$.*

When applied to our running example of 2-COLORABILITY, the preceding Theorem 2 implies (among other things) that a graph $\mathbf{G}$ is 2-colorable if and only the Duplicator wins the existential 4-pebble game on $\mathbf{G}$ and $\mathbf{K_2}$. As we will see in the sequel, Theorem 2 is a useful tool for determining when a tractable case of the constraint satisfaction problem is actually definable in Datalog. In addition, it reveals that close links exists between concepts in artificial intelligence and concepts in database theory and logic.

3   Bounded Treewidth and Datalog

Through the efforts of several different researchers, it has been established that many NP-complete problems on graphs become tractable when the input graphs are assumed to have a "tree-like" structure (see [DF99]). The property of being "tree-like" is formalized using the concept of the *treewidth* of a graph [DF99] or, more generally, the concept of the *treewidth* of a structrure, which is defined as follows [FV98]. A *tree decomposition* of a σ-structure $\mathbf{A} = (A, R_1^{\mathbf{A}}, \ldots, R_m^{\mathbf{A}})$ is a labeled tree T such that:

1. Every node of T is labeled by a non-empty subset of V.
2. For every relation $R_i^{\mathbf{A}}$ and every tuple $(a_1, \ldots, a_n) \in R_i^{\mathbf{A}}$, there is a node of T whose label contains $\{a_1, \ldots, a_n\}$.
3. For every $a \in A$, the set X of nodes of T whose labels include a is a subtree of T.

The *width* of a tree decomposition T is the maximum cardinality of a label in T minus 1. The *treewidth* of a σ-structure $\mathbf{A} = (A, R_1^{\mathbf{A}}, \ldots, R_m^{\mathbf{A}})$ is the smallest positive integer k such that $\mathbf{A}$ has a tree decomposition of width k. Several algorithmic problems, including 3-COLORABILITY, that are NP-complete when arbitrary structures are allowed as inputs become solvable in polynomial time, if the inputs are restricted to be structures of treewidth less than k. We write $\mathcal{T}^k(\sigma)$ to denote the class of all finite σ-structures of treewidth less than k. We also write $\mathcal{T}^k$ to denote the class of all structures of treewidth less than k, i.e., $\mathcal{T}^k$ is the union of the classes $\mathcal{T}^k(\sigma)$ over all vocabularies σ.

Dechter and Pearl [DP89] and Freuder [Fre90] were the first to show that bounded treewidth is "an island of tractability" for constraint satisfaction problems. In terms of the notation used here, this means that $CSP(\mathcal{T}^k, \mathcal{F})$ is solvable in polynomial time, where $\mathcal{F}$ is the class of all finite structures. In [KV00a] a different proof of the tractability of $\mathrm{CSP}(\mathcal{T}^k, \mathcal{F})$ was obtained by establishing a connection between bounded treewidth and definability in a certain fragment L^k of first-order logic with k variables. We now describe this fragment and the connection with bounded treewidth.

Let $x_1, \dots, x_k$ be distinct first-order variables. We write L^k to denote the collection of first-order formulas over a vocabulary σ defined by the following conditions:

1. every atomic formula of σ with variables among $x_1, \dots, x_k$ is an L^k-formula;
2. if φ and ψ are L^k-formulas, then $(\varphi \wedge \psi)$ is an L^k-formula;
3. if φ is an L^k-formula, then $(\exists x_i \varphi)$ is an L^k-formula, where $1 \leq i \leq k$.

Note that, although L^k has k distinct variables only, each variable may be reused again and again in an L^k-formula, so that there is no a priori bound on the number of occurrences of variables in L^k-formulas. Reusing variables is the key technique for showing that the expressive power of L^k is not as limited as it may initially appear. For exaple, by judiciously reusing variables, one can show that for every positive integer n, the property "there is a path of length n from a to b" is definable by an L^3-formula.

If $\mathbf{A}$ is a σ-structure with n elements in its universe, then clearly the canonical query $Q^{\mathbf{A}}$ is definable by an L^n-formula. In general, the number of variables needed to define $Q^{\mathbf{A}}$ cannot be reduced. Specifically, if $\mathbf{A}$ is the complete graph $\mathbf{K}_n$ with n nodes, then it can be shown that the canonical query $Q^{\mathbf{A}}$ is not definable by any L^m formula, for $m < n$. The state of affairs is different, however, if $\mathbf{A}$ has bounded treewidth.

Lemma 1. [KV00a] *If $\mathbf{A}$ is a σ-structure of treewidth less than k, then the canonical query $Q^{\mathbf{A}}$ is definable by an L^k-formula, which can be constructed in polynomial time.*

A proof that the constraint satisfaction problem $\mathrm{CSP}(\mathcal{T}^k, \mathcal{F})$ is solvable in polynomial time can be obtained by combining the above result with the fact that the evaluation problem for L^k-formulas is solvable in polynomial time [Var95]. Our goal now is to further explore the connection between bounded treewidth and definability in logics with a bounded number of variables. As described in Section 2, Feder and Vardi [FV98] showed that definability in Datalog provides a unifying explanation for the tractability of constraint satisfaction problems of the form $\mathrm{CSP}(\mathcal{A}, \mathbf{B})$, where $\mathcal{A}$ is a class of σ-structures and $\mathbf{B}$ is a fixed σ-structure. The next result shows that definability in Datalog is also the reason for the tractability of constraint satisfaction problems on constraints of bounded treewidth.

Theorem 3. *Assume that k is a positive integer, σ is a vocabulary, and $\mathbf{B}$ is a σ-structure. Then $\neg\mathrm{CSP}(\mathcal{T}^k(\sigma), \mathbf{B})$ is in k-Datalog, where $\mathcal{T}^k(\sigma)$ the class of all σ-structures of treewidth less than k.*

Proof: (Sketch) In view of Theorem 2, it suffices to show that if $\mathbf{A}$ and $\mathbf{B}$ are two σ-structures such that $\mathbf{A}$ is of treewidth $< k$ and the Duplicator wins the existential k-pebble game on **A** and **B**, then there is a homomorphism h from **A** to **B**. Let **A** and **B** be two such structures and consider the canonical conjunctive query $Q^{\mathbf{A}}$ of **A**. Since the treewidth of **A** is less than k, Lemma 1 implies that $Q^{\mathbf{A}}$ is definable by a sentence ψ of L^k. In particular, ψ is a sentence of $\exists \mathrm{FO}_+^k$, which is the fragment of first-order logic with k variables $x_1, \ldots, x_k$ that contains all atomic formulas involving these variables and is closed under conjunction, disjunction, and existential quantification over these variables. As shown in [KV95], there is a close connection between existential k-pebble games and preservation of $\exists \mathrm{FO}_+^k$-formulas. Specifically, if a σ-structure **A** satisfies an $\exists \mathrm{FO}_+^k$-sentence φ and if the Duplicator wins the existential k-pebble game on **A** and **B**, then **B** satisfies the sentence φ as well. Consider the σ-structures **A** and **B** at hand. Clearly, $\mathbf{A} \models \psi$, because every structure satisfies its canonical query. Since the Duplicator wins the existential k-pebble game on **A** and **B**, it follows that $\mathbf{B} \models \psi$, which means that $\mathbf{B} \models Q^{\mathbf{A}}$. By Theorem 1, a homomorphism from **A** to **B** exists. $\square$

Using Theorem 3, we now derive several additional results concerning the connections between constraint satisfaction, bounded treewidth, and definability in logics with a bounded number of variables. The first one follows from Theorems 2 and 3.

Corollary 2. *Assume that $k \geq 2$, **A** is a σ-structure of treewidth less than k, and **B** is an arbitrary σ-structure. Then the following statements are equivalent:*

1. *There is a homomorphism from **A** to **B**.*
2. *The Duplicator wins the existential k-pebble game on **A** and **B**.*
3. *Strong k-consistency can be established on **A** and **B**.*

Consequently, determining whether strong k-consistency can be established is a sound and complete polynomial-time algorithm for $\mathrm{CSP}(\mathcal{T}^k(\sigma), \mathcal{F}(\sigma))$.

The typical use of strong k-consistency properties in constraint satisfaction problems is to try to establish strong k-consistency for a k that is sufficiently large to guarantee *global consistency*, which is the property that every partial solution can be extended to a solution (see [Dec92]). Corollary 2 yields a different use of strong k-consistency as a sound and complete algorithm for constraint satisfaction problems, when the constraints are of treewidth less than k. Although this result seems to be implicit in other published work, we have not been able to locate an explicit reference to it.

In general, expressibility in k-Datalog is a sufficient condition for tractability of $\mathrm{CSP}(\mathcal{A}, \mathbf{B})$, but it does not provide a method for finding a solution to an instance of $\mathrm{CSP}(\mathcal{A}, \mathbf{B})$, if one exists. This difficulty, however, can be overcome if more stringent definability conditions are satisfied. Specifically, [KV00b] introduced the concept of *k-locality* and showed that it is a sufficient condition for the backtrack-free construction of solutions to constraint satisfaction problems, if such solutions exist.

Let k be a positive integer, $\mathcal{A}$ a class of σ-structures, and **B** a σ-structure. We say that $\mathrm{CSP}(\mathcal{A}, \mathbf{B})$ is *k-local* if $\neg \mathrm{CSP}(\mathcal{A}, \mathbf{B}^*)$ is in k-Datalog for every expansion

$\mathbf{B}^*$ of $\mathbf{B}$ with constants, that is, for every expansion of $\mathbf{B}$ obtained by augmenting $\mathbf{B}$ with a finite sequence of distinguished elements from its universe. Such an expansion can be also viewed as a structure over a relational vocabulary σ^* in which unary relational symbols are used to encode the distinguished elements that form the expansion. We say that $\mathrm{CSP}(\mathcal{A}, \mathcal{B})$ is k-local if $\mathrm{CSP}(\mathcal{A}, \mathbf{B})$ is k-local, for every structure $\mathbf{B} \in \mathcal{B}$.

Theorem 4. [KV00b] *If $\mathrm{CSP}(\mathcal{A}, \mathcal{B})$ is k-local, then there is polynomial-time backtrack-free algorithm such that, given $\mathbf{A} \in \mathcal{A}$ and $\mathbf{B} \in \mathcal{B}$, it finds a homomorphism from $\mathbf{A}$ to $\mathbf{B}$, if one exists, or determines that no such homomorphism exists, otherwise.*

This backtrack-free algorithm builds a homomorphism from $\mathbf{A}$ to $\mathbf{B}$ in a sequence of steps; in each step, one tests whether strong k-consistency can be established for progressively longer expansions $\mathbf{A}^*$ and $\mathbf{B}^*$ of $\mathbf{A}$ and $\mathbf{B}$. Since $\mathrm{CSP}(\mathcal{A}, \mathbf{B})$ is k-local, if strong k-consistency can be established for some such expansions, then a homomorphism between these expansions is guaranteed to exist, which means that there is a homomorphism from $\mathbf{A}$ to $\mathbf{B}$ mapping the distinguished elements of $\mathbf{A}$ to the corresponding distinguished elements of $\mathbf{B}$. Consequently, the algorithm can proceed and construct longer expansions of $\mathbf{A}$ and $\mathbf{B}$ without backtracking, until every element of $\mathbf{A}$ is a distinguished element. Notice that this algorithm makes a quadratic number of calls to the test of whether strong k-consistency can be established.

Corollary 3. $\mathrm{CSP}(\mathcal{T}^k(\sigma), \mathcal{F}(\sigma))$ *is k-local, for every $k \geq 2$ and every σ.*

Proof: (Sketch) If a σ-structure $\mathbf{A}$ has treewidth less than k, then every expansion of it with constants also has treewidth less than k. To see this notice that each such expansion amounts to augmenting the vocabulary with unary predicates, and the addition of unary predicates does not change the treewidth of a structure. The result now follows immediately from Theorem 3.   □

A different polynomial-time backtrack-free algorithm for $\mathrm{CSP}(\mathcal{T}^k(\sigma), \mathcal{F}(\sigma))$ is known in the literature. Specifically, Section 1.4.2 of Hooker [Hoo97]) contains a description of a "zero-step lookahead" algorithm for constructing a homomorphism from $\mathbf{A}$ to $\mathbf{B}$, where $\mathbf{A}$ is of treewidth $< k$. This algorithm is based on Freuder's [Fre90] result that the treewidth of a graph coincides with its *induced width*. Unlike the backtrack-free algorithm based on k-locality, the zero-step lookahead algorithm entails just a single initial test of whether strong k-consistency can be established. It requires, however, the efficient construction of an order of the universe of $\mathbf{A}$ (i.e., of the variables of the CSP-instance) of width $< k$. In turn, for each fixed k, such an order of the universe can be obtained in polynomial time from a tree decomposition of $\mathbf{A}$ of width $< k$, which has to be constructed first in polynomial time [Bod93].

So far, we have established that definability in k-Datalog provides an explanation for the tractability of $\mathrm{CSP}(\mathcal{T}^k(\sigma), \mathbf{B})$, where $\mathbf{B}$ is an arbitrary, but fixed, σ-structure. This, however, does not provide an explanation for the tractability of $\mathrm{CSP}(\mathcal{T}^k(\sigma), \mathcal{F}(\sigma))$ in terms of definability in some tractable logical formalism with a bounded number of variables. Actually, there is a good reason for this, because the monotonicity properties of Datalog, imlpy that neither $\mathrm{CSP}(\mathcal{T}^k(\sigma), \mathcal{F}(\sigma))$ nor $\neg\mathrm{CSP}(\mathcal{T}^k(\sigma), \mathcal{F}(\sigma))$ are expressible in Datalog. There is, however, a well-known logical formalism that is more powerful than Datalog and provides an explanation for the tractability of $\mathrm{CSP}(\mathcal{T}^k(\sigma), \mathcal{F}(\sigma))$. Specifically, *least fixed-point logic* LFP is the extension of first-order logic with least fixed-points of positive first-order formulas. Datalog can be viewed as a fragment of LFP, since Datalog queries are definable using least fixed-points of positive existential first-order formulas. Least fixed-point logic has found numerous applications to database theory and descriptive complexity theory, because of its close connections to polynomial-time computability ([Var82, Imm86, Imm99]). In particular, every LFP-definable query is also computable in polynomial-time. The next result shows that the tractability of $\mathrm{CSP}(\mathcal{T}^k(\sigma), \mathcal{F}(\sigma))$. can be explained via definability in LFP with a bounded number of variables.

Corollary 4. $\mathrm{CSP}(\mathcal{T}^k(\sigma), \mathcal{F}(\sigma))$ *is expressible in* LFP^{2k}, *for every* $k \geq 2$ *and every* σ, *where* LFP^{2k} *is the collection of all LFP-formulas with at most* $2k$ *distinct variables.*

Proof: (Hint) The result is derived by combining Corollary 2 with the fact that determining the winner in the existential k-pebble game on **A** and **B** is expressible in LFP^{2k}, when both structures **A** and **B** are part of the input (see [KV00b]). □

4   Bounded Treewidth and Homomorphic Equivalence

If σ is a vocabulary and $\mathcal{A}$ is a class of σ-structures, then we write $\mathcal{H}(\mathcal{A})$ to denote the class of all σ-structures that are homomorphically equivalent to some structure in $\mathcal{A}$. The first result of this section asserts intuitively that definability of constraint satisfaction problems in Datalog can be extended from a class $\mathcal{A}$ to the class $\mathcal{H}(\mathcal{A})$.

Proposition 1. *Let* $\mathcal{A}$ *be a class of* σ-*structures*, **B** *a* σ-*structure*, *and* k *a positive integer. If* $\neg\mathrm{CSP}(\mathcal{A}, \mathbf{B})$ *is expressible in* k-*Datalog*, *then also* $\neg\mathrm{CSP}(\mathcal{H}(\mathcal{A}), \mathbf{B})$ *is expressible in* k-*Datalog.*

Proof: (Sketch) In view of Theorem 2, it suffices to show that if **A** is a structure in $\mathcal{H}(\mathcal{A})$ such that the Duplicator wins the existential k-pebble game on **A** and **B**, then there is a homomorphis h from **A** to **B**. Assume that **A** is such a structure and let **A**$'$ be a structure in $\mathcal{A}$ that is homomorphically equivalent to **A**. This means that there is a homomorphism h_1 from **A** to **A**$'$, and a homomorphism h_2 from **A**$'$ to **A**. By composing h_2 with the winning strategy for the Duplicator in the existential k-pebble game on **A** and **B**, we obtain a winning strategy for the Duplicator in the existential k-pebble game on **A**$'$ and **B**. Since **A**$'$ is in $\mathcal{A}$ and $\neg\mathrm{CSP}(\mathcal{A}, \mathbf{B})$ is expressible in k-Datalog, Theorem 2 implies that there is a homomorphism h' from **A**$'$ to **B**. Consequently, the composition $h = h_1 \circ h'$ is a homomorphism from **A** to **B**. □

By combining Theorem 3 with Proposition 1, we obtain the following result.

Corollary 5. *Assume that $k \geq 2$ and σ is a vocabulary.*

1. *If $\mathbf{B}$ is a σ-structure, then $\neg \mathrm{CSP}(\mathcal{H}(\mathcal{T}^k(\sigma)), \mathbf{B})$ is expressible in k-Datalog and, hence, it is in PTIME*
2. *$\mathrm{CSP}(\mathcal{H}(\mathcal{T}^k(\sigma)), \mathcal{F}(\sigma))$ is expressible in LFP^{2k} and, hence, it is in PTIME.*

Corollary 5 shows that the classes $\mathcal{H}(\mathcal{T}^k(\sigma))$, $k \geq 2$, give rise to larger "islands of tractability" for constraint satisfaction that those obtained from the classes $\mathcal{T}^k(\sigma)$ of structures of treewidth less than k. In what follows, we will show that the classes $\mathcal{H}(\mathcal{T}^k(\sigma))$, $k \geq 2$, possess also algebraic and logical characterizations that tie together some of the key concepts studied here. To establish this result we need to first bring the concept of a *core* of a structure into the picture.

Let $\mathbf{A}$ be a σ-structure. A substructure $\mathbf{B}$ of $\mathbf{A}$ is called a *core* of $\mathbf{A}$ if there is a homomorphism h from $\mathbf{A}$ to $\mathbf{B}$, but, for every proper substructure $\mathbf{B}'$ of $\mathbf{B}$, there is no homomorphism from $\mathbf{A}$ to $\mathbf{B}'$. A σ-structure $\mathbf{A}$ is a *core* if it is its own core. Altough the study of cores originated in graph theory, the concept has found applications to database theory, as cores play an important role in conjunctive-query processing and optimization (see [CM77]). The following are some well known and easy to establish facts about cores (see [HN92]): (1) Every finite σ-structure $\mathbf{A}$ has a core; (2) If $\mathbf{B}$ is a core of $\mathbf{A}$, then $\mathbf{A}$ is homomorphically equivalent to $\mathbf{B}$; (3) If both $\mathbf{B}$ and $\mathbf{B}'$ are cores of $\mathbf{A}$, then $\mathbf{B}$ is isomorphic to $\mathbf{B}'$. In view of the last fact, we write $\mathrm{core}(\mathbf{A})$ for the unique (up to isomorphism) core of $\mathbf{A}$.

Let us consider some examples that illustrate these concepts and facts. First, the complete undirected graph $\mathbf{K}_2$ with two elements (i.e., the graph that consists of a single edge) is a core. Moreover, an undirected non-empty graph $\mathbf{G}$ has $\mathbf{K}_2$ as its core if and only if $\mathbf{G}$ is 2-colorable. Note that, for $k \geq 3$, this equivalence does not immediately extend to k-colorable graphs and to $\mathbf{K}_k$, because a k-colorable graph need not contain the complete undirected graph $\mathbf{K}_k$ as a subgraph. It is easy to see, however, that for every $k \geq 3$, an undirected graph $\mathbf{G}$ is k-colorable if and only if $\mathbf{K}_k$ is the core of $\mathbf{G} \oplus \mathbf{K}_k$, where $\mathbf{G} \oplus \mathbf{K}_k$ is the *direct sum* of $\mathbf{G}$ and $\mathbf{K}_k$. We are now ready to state and prove the promised characterizations of $\mathcal{H}(\mathcal{T}^k(\sigma))$.

Theorem 5. *Let k be a positive integer, σ a vocabulary, and $\mathbf{A}$ a σ-structure. Then the following statements are equivalent.*

1. *$\mathbf{A} \in \mathcal{H}(\mathcal{T}^k(\sigma))$.*
2. *$\mathrm{core}(\mathbf{A})$ has treewidth less than k.*
3. *The canonical conjunctive query $Q^{\mathbf{A}}$ is logically equivalent to an L^k-formula.*

Proof: (Sketch) We proceed in a round robin fashion. Assume that $\mathbf{A}$ is homomorphically equivalent to a σ-structure $\mathbf{A}'$ of treewidth $< k$. Since $\mathbf{A}$ and $\mathbf{A}'$ are homomorphically equivalent, it is easy to see that $\mathrm{core}(\mathbf{A})$ is isomorphic to $\mathrm{core}(\mathbf{A}')$. At the same time, $\mathrm{core}(\mathbf{A}')$ has treewidth less than k, since it is a substructure of a structure having treewidth less than k. If core($\mathbf{A}$) has treewidth less than k, then Lemma 1 implies that the canonical query $Q^{\text{core}(\mathbf{A})}$ is logically equivalent to an L^k-formula. Since $\mathbf{A}$ is homomorphically equivalent to core($\mathbf{A}$), Corollary 1 implies that $Q^{\mathbf{A}}$ is logically equivalent to $Q^{\text{core}(\mathbf{A})}$. Finally, assume that the canonical query $Q^{\mathbf{A}}$ is logically equivalent to an L^k-sentence ψ. As pointed out in [KV00b, Remark 5.3], if ψ is a an L^k-sentence, then one can construct a σ-structure $\mathbf{B}$ of treewidth less than k such that the canonical query $Q^{\mathbf{B}}$ is logically equivalent to ψ. Consequently, Corollary 1 implies that $\mathbf{A}$ is homomorphically equivalent to such a structure $\mathbf{B}$. □

It is well known that, for each positive integer k, there is a polynomial-time algorithm for determining whether a given structure has treewidth less than k [Bod93]. In other words, for each fixed k, membership in the class $\mathcal{T}^k(\sigma)$ can be tested in polynomial time. Our next result shows that, unfortunately, the state of affairs is dramatically different for the classes $\mathcal{H}(\mathcal{T}^k(\sigma))$, $k \geq 2$.

Theorem 6. *For every $k \geq 2$ and every vocabulary σ containing at least one binary relation symbol, determining membership in $\mathcal{H}(\mathcal{T}^k(\sigma))$ is an NP-complete problem.*

Proof: (Sketch) We first show that if $k \geq 3$ and $\mathbf{G}$ is an undirected graph, then the following are equivalent:

1. $\mathbf{G}$ is k-colorable.
2. core($\mathbf{G} \oplus \mathbf{K}_k$) has treewidth less than k.
3. $\mathbf{G} \oplus \mathbf{K}_k \in \mathcal{H}(\mathcal{T}^k(\sigma))$.

Indeed, if $\mathbf{G}$ is k-colorable, then core($\mathbf{G}\oplus\mathbf{K}_k$) = $\mathbf{K}_k$, which has treewidth $k-1$. If core($\mathbf{G} \oplus \mathbf{K}_k$) has treewidth less than k, then $\mathbf{G} \oplus \mathbf{K}_k$ is certainly homomorphically equivalent to a graph of treewidth less than k, since every graph is homomorphically equivalent to its core. Finally, assume that $\mathbf{G}$ is homomorphically equivalent to a graph H having treewidth less than k. It is known that if a graph has treewidth less than k, then it is k-colorable (this is easy to see using the fact that a graph has treewidth less than k if and only if it is a partial k-tree - see [DF99]). Consequently, $\mathbf{G}$ is k-colorable, because it is homomorphically equivalent to a k-colorable graph.

Next, we consider the case $k = 2$. Let $\mathbf{T}$ be a directed tree. We will exhibit a polynomial-time reduction of CSP($\mathbf{T}$) to $\mathcal{H}(\mathcal{T}^2(\sigma))$. For every σ-structure $\mathbf{G}$, we define $\mathbf{G}^*$ to be $(\mathbf{G} \oplus \mathbf{T})$, if the Duplicator wins the existential 2-pebble game on $\mathbf{G}$ and $\mathbf{T}$, and $\mathbf{K_3}$, otherwise. Clearly, $\mathbf{G}^*$ can be constructed from $\mathbf{G}$ in polynomial time. We claim that, for every $\mathbf{G}$, $\mathbf{G} \in$ CSP($\mathbf{T}$) if and only if $\mathbf{G}^* \in \mathcal{H}(\mathcal{T}^2(\sigma))$. Assume first that $\mathbf{G}$ is in CSP($\mathbf{T}$), which means that there is a homomorphism from $\mathbf{G}$ to $\mathbf{T}$. Consequently, the Duplicator wins the existential 2-pebble game on $\mathbf{G}$ and $\mathbf{T}$. It follows that $\mathbf{G}^* = (\mathbf{G} \oplus \mathbf{T})$ and that $\mathbf{G}^*$ is homomorphically equivalent to $\mathbf{T}$, which has treewidth less than 2. Conversely, assume that $\mathbf{G}^* \in \mathcal{H}(\mathcal{T}^2(\sigma))$. It follows that $\mathbf{G}^* = \mathbf{G} \oplus \mathbf{T}$ is homomorphically equivalent to a σ-structure $\mathbf{H}$ of treewidth less than 2, and that the Duplicator wins the existential 2-pebble game on $\mathbf{G}$ and $\mathbf{T}$. Therefore, the Duplicator also wins the existential 2-pebble game on $\mathbf{G} \oplus \mathbf{T}$ and $\mathbf{T}$. In turn and since $\mathbf{G} \oplus \mathbf{T}$ is homomorphically equivalent to $\mathbf{H}$, it follows that the Duplicator wins the existential 2-pebble game on $\mathbf{H}$ and $\mathbf{T}$. Since $\mathbf{H}$ has treewidth less than k, Corollary 2 implies that there is a homomorphism from $\mathbf{H}$ to $\mathbf{T}$; in turn, this implies that there is a homomorphism from $\mathbf{G} \oplus \mathbf{T}$ to $\mathbf{T}$. By restricting this homomorphism to $\mathbf{G}$, we obtain the desired homomorphism from $\mathbf{G}$ to $\mathbf{T}$. The NP-hardness follows from the existence of particular directed trees $\mathbf{T}$ such that $\text{CSP}(\mathbf{T})$ is an NP-complete problem [GWW92, HNZ96]. $\qquad\square$

Theorem 6 suggests that the logical characterization given in Theorem 5 for the class $\mathcal{H}(\mathcal{T}^k(\sigma))$ is not feasibly effective. It is natural therefore to ask whether the property "$\mathbf{A}$ has treewidth less than k" possesses a logical characterization that might also explain the complexity-theoretic difference between this property and the property "$\mathbf{A}$ is homomorphically equivalent to a structure of treewidth less than k". Clearly, any such characterization should involve a refinement of the property "the canonical query $Q^{\mathbf{A}}$ is logically equivalent to an L^k-formula". We now introduce such a refinement.

Let $\mathbf{A}$ be a σ-structure, let $Q^{\mathbf{A}}$ be the canonical query associated with $\mathbf{A}$. Here, we identify $Q^{\mathbf{A}}$ with its defining formula, i.e., we view $Q^{\mathbf{A}}$ as an existential first-order formula of the form $(\exists z_1) \cdots (\exists z_n) \varphi(z_1, \ldots, z_n)$, where $\varphi(z_1, \ldots, z_n)$ is a conjunction of atomic formulas over σ with variables among $z_1, \ldots, z_n$. We say that a first-order sentence ψ is a *rewriting* of $Q^{\mathbf{A}}$ if there is a finite sequence of formulas $\psi_1, \ldots, \psi_m$ such that ψ_1 is $Q^{\mathbf{A}}$, ψ_m is ψ, and each ψ_{i+1} is obtained from ψ_i by applying one of the following *rewrite rules*:

A-Rule: *Associativity* of conjunction is applied to subformulas of ψ.
C-Rule: *Commutatitivity* of conjunction is applied to subformulas of ψ.
∃-Rule: A subformula of ψ_i of the form $(\exists x(\theta_1 \wedge \theta_2))$ is replaced by the formula $((\exists x \theta_1) \wedge \theta_2)$, provided the variable x is not free in θ_2.
R-Rule: A subformula of ψ of the form $(\exists x \theta)$ is replaced by the fomula $(\exists y)\theta[x/y])$, where y does not occur free in θ and $\theta[x/y]$ is obtained from θ by replacing all free occurrences of x in θ by y.

These four rewrite rules are routinely used in database query processing and optimization in order to transform queries to equivalent, but less-costly-to-evaluate, queries [Ull89]. The final result of this paper asserts that these rules can also be used to obtain a logical characterization of bounded treewidth.

Theorem 7. *Let k be a positive integer, σ a vocabulary, and $\mathbf{A}$ a σ-structure. Then the following statements are equivalent.*

1. $\mathbf{A}$ has treewidth less than k.
2. There is an L^k-sentence ψ that is a rewriting of $Q^{\mathbf{A}}$.

Moreover, if $\mathbf{A}$ has treewidth less than k, then such a rewriting can be constructed in time polynomial in the size of $\mathbf{A}$.

Proof: (Hint) If $\mathbf{A}$ has treewidth less than k, then one can construct in polynomial time a linear order of the universe A of $\mathbf{A}$ of induced width less than k, which means that every element of A has fewer than k smaller neighbors in the traingulation of the constraint graph of $\mathbf{A}$ (see [Fre90]). Using this linear order, it is possible to evaluate the canonical conjunctive query $Q^{\mathbf{A}}$ on every σ-structure $\mathbf{B}$ using intermediate conjunctive queries each of which has at most k variables. Specifically, this evaluation can be carried out by simulating the steps of the "bucket elimination algorithm" for constraint satisfaction in [Dec99]. In turn, each step of this simulation can be translated to rewriting steps that transform the canonical conjunctive query $Q^{\mathbf{A}}$ to an L^k-sentence. For the other direction, one can use the rewriting to build a tree decomposition of width less than k of a σ-structure isomorphic to $\mathbf{A}$.   □

References

[Bod93]   H. L. Bodlaender. A linear-time algorithm for finding tree-decompositions of small treewidth. In *Proc. 25th ACM Symp. on Theory of Computing*, pages 226–234, 1993.

[CM77]   A. K. Chandra and P. M. Merlin. Optimal implementation of conjunctive queries in relational databases. In *Proc. 9th ACM Symp. on Theory of Computing*, pages 77–90, 1977.

[Dec92]   R. Dechter. From local to global consistency. *Artificial Intelligence*, 55(1):87–107, May 1992.

[Dec99]   R. Dechter. Bucket elimination: a unifying framework for reasoning. *Artificial Intelligence*, 113(1–2):41–85, 1999.

[DF99]   R. G. Downey and M. R. Fellows. *Parametrized Complexity*. Springer-Verlag, 1999.

[DP89]   R. Dechter and J. Pearl. Tree clustering for constraint networks. *Artificial Intelligence*, pages 353–366, 1989.

[Fre90]   E.C Freuder. Complexity of k-tree structured constraint satisfaction problems. In *Proc. AAAI-90*, pages 4–9, 1990.

[FV98]   T. Feder and M. Y. Vardi. The computational structure of monotone monadic SNP and constraint satisfaction: a study through Datalog and group theory. *SIAM J. on Computing*, 28:57–104, 1998.

[GJ79]   M. R. Garey and D. S. Johnson. *Computers and Intractability - A Guide to the Theory of NP-Completeness*. W. H. Freeman and Co., 1979.

[GWW92]   W. Gutjahr, E. Welzl, and G. Woeginger. Polynomial Graph Colorings. *Discrete Appl. Math.*, 35:29–46, 1992.

[HN90]   P. Hell and J. Nešetřil. On the complexity of H-coloring. *Journal of Combinatorial Theory, Series B*, 48:92–110, 1990.

[HN92]   P. Hell and J. Nešetřil. The core of a graph. *Discrete Math.*, 109:117–126, 1992.

[HNZ96]   P. Hell, J. Nesetril, and X. Zhu. Complexity of Tree Homomorphism. *Discrete Appl. Math.*, 70:23–36, 1996.

[Hoo97]   J. N. Hooker. Constraint satisfaction methods for generating valid cuts. In *Advances in computational and stochastic optimization, logic programming, and heuristic studies*, pages 1–30. Kluwer, 1997.

[Imm86]   N. Immerman. Relational queries computable in polynomial time. *Information and Control*, 68:86–104, 1986.

[Imm99]   N. Immerman. *Descriptive Complexity*. Springer, 1999.

[Jea98]   P. Jeavons. On the algebraic structure of combinatorial problems. *Theoretical Computer Science*, 200(1–2):185–204, 1998.

[KV95]   Ph. G. Kolaitis and M. Y. Vardi. On the expressive power of Datalog: tools and a case study. *Journal of Computer and System Sciences*, 51(1):110–134, August 1995.

[KV00a]   Ph.G. Kolaitis and M. Y. Vardi. Conjunctive-query containment and constraint satisfaction. *Journal of Computer and System Sciences*, pages 302–332, 2000.

[KV00b]   Ph.G. Kolaitis and M. Y. Vardi. A game-theoretic approach to constraint satisfaction. In *Proc. of the 17th Nat. Conf. on Artificial Intelligence (AAAI 2000)*, pages 175–181, 2000.

[Sch78]   T. J. Schaefer. The complexity of satisfiability problems. In *Proc. 10th ACM Symp. on Theory of Computing*, pages 216–226, 1978.

[Ull89]   J. D. Ullman. *Database and Knowledge-Base Systems, Volumes I and II*. Computer Science Press, 1989.

[Var82]   M. Y. Vardi. The complexity of relational query languages. In *Proc. 14th ACM Symp. on Theory of Computing*, pages 137–146, 1982.

[Var95]   M. Y. Vardi. On the complexity of bounded-variable queries. In *Proc. 14th ACM Symp. on Principles of Database Systems*, pages 266–76, 1995.

Determining the Number of Solutions to Binary CSP Instances

Ola Angelsmark[1], Peter Jonsson[1], Svante Linusson[2], and Johan Thapper[2]

[1] Department of Computer and Information Science, Linköpings Universitet
S-581 83 Linköping, Sweden
{olaan,petej}@ida.liu.se
[2] Department of Mathematics, Linköpings Universitet
S-581 83 Linköping, Sweden
{linusson,jotha}@mai.liu.se

Abstract. Counting the number of solutions to CSP instances has applications in several areas, ranging from statistical physics to artificial intelligence. We give an algorithm for counting the number of solutions to binary CSPs, which works by transforming the problem into a number of 2-SAT instances, where the total number of solutions to these instances is the same as those of the original problem. The algorithm consists of two main cases, depending on whether the domain size d is even, in which case the algorithm runs in $\mathcal{O}(1.3247^n \cdot (d/2)^n)$ time, or odd, in which case it runs in $\mathcal{O}(1.3247^n \cdot ((d^2 + d + 2)/4)^{n/2})$ if $d = 4 \cdot k + 1$, and $\mathcal{O}(1.3247^n \cdot ((d^2 + d)/4)^{n/2})$ if $d = 4 \cdot k + 3$. We also give an algorithm for counting the number of possible 3-colourings of a given graph, which runs in $\mathcal{O}(1.8171^n)$, an improvement over our general algorithm gained by using problem specific knowledge.

1 Introduction

Constraint satisfaction problems (CSPs), first described by Montanari [17], allows for natural descriptions of problems in a wide array of fields. These include such varied areas as machine vision, scheduling, temporal reasoning, graph problems, floor plan design, machine design and manufacturing, and diagnostic reasoning [13]. In particular, it has proven invaluable to artificial intelligence.

Posed with an instance of a CSP problem, one can ask two questions. At first, the question "Does there exist a solution?" might seem the most natural one to ask – and indeed it is the most common one. This is what is usually called the *decision problem*. The second question which might arise is "How many solutions are there?" – known as the *counting problem*. In this paper we will study the latter question.

For (d, l)-CSPs, *i.e.*, CSPs where the variables have domain size d and the constraints have arity l, the decision problem is known to be NP-complete [15], and this may, or may not, imply the non-existence of a polynomial-time algorithm for solving it (depending, as always, on the truth of the equation $P = NP$.) We will avoid making any assumptions about this, since it has no impact on the

P. Van Hentenryck (Ed.): CP 2002, LNCS 2470, pp. 327–340, 2002.
© Springer-Verlag Berlin Heidelberg 2002

results we present. The numerous applications of CSPs have, however, caused intense research, *e.g.*, identifying tractable subclasses of problems [3, 18], and constructing exact algorithms [9, 10, 20].

The corresponding counting problem belongs to a class known as #P (introduced by Valiant [21, 22]) defined as the class of counting problems computable in nondeterministic polynomial time. Computing the number of solutions to a constraint satisfaction problem is, even if we restrict ourselves to binary CSPs, complete for this class of problems [19]. In fact, for every fixed $\varepsilon > 0$, approximating the number of solutions to a binary CSP within $2^{n^{1-\varepsilon}}$ is NP-hard. There exists, however, randomised approximation algorithms which run in polynomial time for certain restricted cases, *e.g.*, finding an estimation of the number of k-colourings of graphs with low degree [12].

Until quite recently, not much attention has been given to the problem of counting solutions. The focus has been on solving the decision problem, rather than the corresponding counting problem, and the algorithms are often probabilistic [9, 10, 20]. Lately, however, several papers have discussed the complexity of counting problems [4, 14], and a number of algorithms have been developed [2, 5, 6, 7]. One reason for this renewed interest for these kinds of problems may be due to the multitude of applications for counting counterparts of several well-studied decision problems. For example, many problems in artificial intelligence can be reduced to counting the number of models to a formula [19]. Solving a CSP instance is equivalent to finding a homomorphism between graphs [11], for instance, finding a k-colouring of a graph G is equivalent to finding a homomorphism from G to a complete graph with k vertices, and determining the number of graph homomorphisms from one graph to another has important applications in statistical physics [12, 23].

Intuitively, it seems reasonable that decision problems which are known to be NP-complete, have corresponding counting problems which are #P-complete, and indeed it has been shown that this is the case for satisfiability problems [4]. However, several decision problems for which polynomial time algorithms are known, also have associated counting problems which are #P-complete. 2-SAT belongs to this class of problems.

In this paper we will focus on *exact, deterministic* algorithms for the following two problems: The counting problem for binary CSPs, denoted $\#(d,2)\text{-CSP}^1$, and the counting problem for 3-colourability of graphs, denoted #3COL.

The $\#(d,2)$-CSP algorithm we present has the following general outline:

1. Create 2-SAT instances corresponding to the original CSP instance.
2. Count the number of solutions to each of these instances.
3. Return the total number of solutions found.

The reason the algorithm looks this way is twofold; First of all, the fastest known algorithm for $(3,2)$-CSP (and $(4,2)$-CSP), suggested by Eppstein [9], works by recursively breaking the problem down into 2-SAT instances. This lead

---

[1] The necessary definitions for the CSP notions used in this paper are found in Section 2, while the graph theoretic notions needed are located in Section 4

us to believe that this approach would work well for the corresponding counting problem. Secondly, by moving over to 2-SAT, we gain access to the fast algorithms developed for #2-SAT [6, 7, 14, 24].

We chose to transform the problem into #2-SAT mainly because of time complexity reasons. Using #3-SAT did not lead to a speed-up, probably due to the rather high time complexity of the #3-SAT algorithm. The fastest known #2-SAT algorithm [6] runs in $\mathcal{O}(1.3247^n)$. Had we instead moved over to #3-SAT, then the fastest known algorithm would have been $\mathcal{O}(1.6894^n)$, which is significantly slower. It is possible that a faster algorithm could be achieved using the #3-SAT algorithm, but if and how this could be done remains an open question.

The running time of the algorithm (we omit polynomial factors here and throughout the paper) is as follows:

- $\mathcal{O}(1.3247^n \cdot (d/2)^n)$, if $d = 2 \cdot k, k > 0$,
- $\mathcal{O}(1.3247^n \cdot ((d^2 + d + 2)/4)^{n/2})$, if $d = 4 \cdot k + 1, k > 0$, and
- $\mathcal{O}(1.3247^n \cdot ((d^2 + d)/4)^{n/2})$, if $d = 4 \cdot k + 3, k \geq 0$.

This division into cases will be explained in detail in Section 3, but in short, the algorithm works by dividing the domain into pairs of values. For even sized domains, this is trivial, but when the domain is of odd size, this can, of course, not be as easily done. One solution would be to add a 'dummy element' to the domain, a value which would then be discarded if found in a solution, but this would give an increased complexity for all odd sized domains, thus we have focused on efficiently dividing the domain. Numerical time complexities for some domain sizes are presented in Table 1, where, for comparative reasons, the results for Eppstein's and Feder & Motwani's algorithms for the corresponding decision problem have been included. If we had chosen to add an element to domains of odd size, the complexities given for, say, 3, 5 and 7, would have been the same as those for 4, 6 and 8.

Table 1. Time complexities for solving the decision problem $(d, 2)$-CSP and the corresponding counting problem $\#(d, 2)$-CSP

d	Eppstein [9]	Feder & Motwani [10]	Our result
3	1.3645^n	1.8171^n	2.2944^n
4	1.8072^n	2.2134^n	2.6494^n
5	2.2590^n	2.6052^n	3.7468^n
6	2.7108^n	2.9938^n	3.9741^n
7	3.1626^n	3.3800^n	4.9566^n
8	3.6144^n	3.7644^n	5.2988^n
10	4.5180^n	4.5287^n	6.6235^n
20	9.0360^n	8.3044^n	13.2470^n

Asymptotically, the algorithm approaches $\mathcal{O}((0.6624d)^n)$, where d is the domain size and n the number of variables. If we compare this to the (probabilistic) algorithm of Eppstein [9], which has a complexity of $\mathcal{O}((0.4518d)^n)$, the gap is not very large. For domain sizes of 10 elements or more, the algorithm presented by Feder & Motwani [10] is faster than Eppstein's. Furthermore, given the modularity of the algorithm, if a faster method for counting the number of solutions to a #2-SAT formula is found, it would be easy to 'plug into' our algorithm, thus improving the time complexity with no extra work.

The second part of this paper contains an algorithm for #3COL, which runs in $\mathcal{O}(1.8171^n)$ time. This is an improvement in complexity compared to our general algorithm, which is gained by using problem specific knowledge, in this case graph-theoretical properties. In particular, rather than transforming the problem into #2-SAT, we move over to #2COL, which is solvable in polynomial time.

The paper has the following organisation: Section 2 contains the basic definitions needed. Section 3 contains the algorithm for counting solutions to a binary CSP, while Section 4 an algorithm for the #3COL problem, together with the graph-theoretic notions it utilises. Section 5 summarises the discussion and suggests future work.

2   Preliminaries

A *binary constraint satisfaction problem ((d,2)-CSP)*, is a triple $\langle V, D, C \rangle$, with V a finite set of variables, D a domain of values, with $|D| = d$, and C a set of constraints $\{c_1, c_2, \ldots, c_q\}$. Each constraint $c_i \in C$ is a triple xRy, where $x, y \in V$, and $R \in D \times D$. To simplify the discussion, we will assume $|V|$ to be an even number, denoted n. A *solution* to a CSP instance is a function $f : V \to D$, such that for each constraint xRy, $(f(x), f(y)) \in R$. Given a CSP instance, the computational problem is to decide whether the instance has a solution, or not. The corresponding *counting problem* is to determine how many solutions the instance has.

A *2-SAT* formula is a sentence consisting of the conjunction of a number of clauses, where each clause contains at most two literals and is of one of the forms $(p \vee q)$, $(\neg p \vee q)$, $(\neg p \vee \neg q)$, (p), $(\neg p)$. The *2-SAT problem* is to decide whether a given 2-SAT formula is satisfiable or not, and this can be done in linear time [1], whereas the *#2-SAT problem* is to decide *how many* solutions a given formula has. The currently best known algorithm runs in $\mathcal{O}(1.3247^n)$ time [6].

3   Algorithm for $\#(d, 2) - \mathrm{CSP}$

The main points of the algorithm, which were mentioned in Section 1, will now be discussed in more detail. To begin with, we give a simplified description, which would give a much worse time complexity than what we eventually will get. This speedup is gained by reducing the number of propositional variables from $2 \cdot n$ to n in the final step.

Assume we have a binary CSP instance P, with domain size d and n variables. The problem can be transformed into a number of instances of 2-SAT, $I_0, I_1, \ldots, I_m$, where m depends on the size of the domain and the number of variables, such that the number of solutions to P equals the total number of solutions to all these instances. In each instance I_k, the propositional variables correspond to an assignment of a value to a variable in the original problem. For a given variable $x \in V$, and a domain value $e \in D$, the propositional variable x_e is true iff x is assigned the value e.

A 2-SAT instance I_k consists of two parts: First, we have clauses corresponding to the constraints in the original problem. For example, say we have the constraint $x \neq y$. Since x and y will never have the same value in a solution, we get the clauses $(\neg x_e \lor \neg y_e)$ for all $e \in D$.

The remaining clauses are constructed by dividing the domain into pairs. For domains of even size, this is straightforward, and we get $d/2$ pairs of values, where each value appears exactly once. Since a solution to the instance implies a certain value for each variable, we know that this value will be represented in one pair. For example, say we have a pair (e_1, e_2), and a variable x. We then add the clauses $(x_{e_1} \lor x_{e_2})$, $(\neg x_{e_1} \lor \neg x_{e_2})$ and, for all $e \in D$ with $e \neq e_1, e \neq e_2$, we add the clause $(\neg x_e)$. This reads as: x can assume exactly one of the values e_1 or e_2, and no other. For each variable, we get $d/2$ possible assignments, or propositional variables, thus we need $(d/2)^n$ instances to cover all of the original problem.

Table 2. The case of $D = \{1, 2, 3\}$, $V = \{x, y\}$. (x_i, x_j is short for $x_i \lor x_j$)

		x_1, x_2	x_1, x_2	x_1, x_2	x_1, x_3	x_1, x_3	x_1, x_3	x_2, x_3	x_2, x_3	x_2, x_3
x	y	y_1, y_2	y_1, y_3	y_2, y_3	y_1, y_2	y_1, y_3	y_2, y_3	y_1, y_2	y_1, y_3	y_2, y_3
1	1	X	X	–	X	X	–	–	–	–
1	2	X	–	X	X	–	X	–	–	–
1	3	–	X	X	–	X	X	–	–	–
2	1	X	X	–	–	–	–	X	X	–
2	2	X	–	X	–	–	–	X	–	X
2	3	–	X	X	–	–	–	–	X	X
3	1	–	–	–	X	X	–	X	X	–
3	2	–	–	–	X	–	X	X	–	X
3	3	–	–	–	–	X	X	–	X	X

A domain of odd size can, naturally, not be divided evenly into pairs. One possible solution to this problem is to simply add a 'dummy element' to the domain, a value we ignore in the subsequent results. However, this would increase the complexity of the algorithm unnecessarily. For instance, it would be equally hard to solve problems with domain size 3 as 4. Instead, we use Proposition 1 to help us with the division of the domain. Note that, unlike the case with even sized domains, where we only considered pairs of propositional variables, we now consider two variables at a time, each with its associated pair of assignments, and we assume we have an even number of variables in the problem. Proposition 1 tells us that we need $(d^2 + d + 2)/4$ such cases to cover all possible assignments if the domain size d is on the form $4 \cdot k + 1$, and $(d^2 + d)/4$, if $d = 4 \cdot k + 3$. Table 2 shows how the situation looks for domains of size 3. The boxed columns in the table clearly cover all possible assignments, but, as can be seen, there are overlaps; some assignments occur in more than one pair of variables. The propositional variables x_1, y_1 occur in columns 2 and 4, x_2, y_3 in columns 2 and 9, and x_3, y_2 are found in both columns 4 and 9. We need to make sure that these assignments are not part of more than one solution, thus to avoid counting these twice, we add the clause $\neg(x_1 \wedge y_1)$, which is equivalent to $(\neg x_1 \vee \neg y_1)$, to one of the instances containing these assignments. In the general case, when an overlap containing the propositional variables x_i and y_j is found, we add the clause $(\neg x_i \vee \neg y_j)$ to all but one of the instances containing this overlap. Had we considered more than two variables at a time, we would have been forced to use more than two propositional variables per clause, thus leaving the 2-SAT setting, and the overall algorithm would have had a much higher time complexity.

For even sized domains, we now have n sets, each containing $d/2$ pairs, while for odd sized domains, we have $n/2$ sets of 4-tuples, with $(d^2 + d + 2)/4$ or $(d^2 + d)/4$ elements, depending on whether $d = 4 \cdot k + 1$ or $d = 4 \cdot k + 3$. By combining the clauses given by one element from each of these sets and the clauses coming from the constraints, we get a set of 2-SAT instances corresponding to the original problem, and each of these instances contains $n \cdot d$ propositional variables. Note that, for even sized domains, each pair give rise to $d - 2$ clauses on the form $\neg x_c$, hence we can in each instance, using unit propagation, remove $n \cdot (d - 2)$ propositional variables, and get $2 \cdot n$ in each instance. For odd sized domains, the situation is similar. Each 4-tuple give rise to $2 \cdot d$ propositional variables, out of which $2 \cdot (d - 2)$ can be removed through unit propagation, leaving 4. Since we have $n/2$ sets to combine elements from, we get $2 \cdot n$ propositional variables per instance for this case too. In all instances, among these $2 \cdot n$ variables, there are n pairs where both cannot be true in a solution, since a variable in the original problem cannot be assigned two different values. For each such pair x_{e_1}, x_{e_2}, take a fresh variable ξ_{x_e}, with the interpretation that ξ_{x_e} is true iff x_{e_1} is true and x_{e_2} is false, and vice versa, and replace all occurrences of x_{e_1} with ξ_{x_e} and all occurrences of x_{e_2} with $\neg \xi_{x_e}$. Through this, we get n propositional variables in each instance, both for even and odd sized domains.

Proposition 1. *Let x, y be a pair of variables taking their values from the domain D, with $|D| = d$. For each odd d, define the set C_d recursively as:*

$$C_1 = \{ (x_1 \vee x_1) \wedge (y_1 \vee y_1)\}$$
$$C_3 = \{ (x_1 \vee x_2) \wedge (y_1 \vee y_3),$$
$$(x_1 \vee x_3) \wedge (y_1 \vee y_2),$$
$$(x_2 \vee x_3) \wedge (y_2 \vee y_3)\}$$

and for $d \geq 5$,

$$C_d = C_{d-4} \cup A_{1,d} \cup A_{2,d} \cup A_{3,d}$$

where

$$A_{1,d} = \bigcup_{i=1}^{(d-3)/2} \{(x_{d-3} \vee x_{d-2}) \wedge (y_{2i-1} \vee y_{2i}), (x_{d-1} \vee x_d) \wedge (y_{2i-1} \vee y_{2i})\}$$

$$A_{2,d} = \bigcup_{j=1}^{(d-3)/2} \{(x_{2j-1} \vee x_{2j}) \wedge (y_{d-3} \vee y_{d-2}), (x_{2j-1} \vee x_{2j}) \wedge (y_{d-1} \vee y_d)\}$$

$$A_{3,d} = \{ (x_{d-2} \vee x_{d-1}) \wedge (y_{d-2} \vee y_d),$$
$$(x_{d-2} \vee x_d) \wedge (y_{d-2} \vee y_{d-1}),$$
$$(x_{d-1} \vee x_d) \wedge (y_{d-1} \vee y_d)\}$$

Then C_d covers all possible assignments of x and y and this can not be done with fewer than $|C_d|$ cases, where

$$|C_d| = \begin{cases} (d^2 + d + 2)/4 & \text{if } d = 4k + 1 \\ (d^2 + d)/4 & \text{if } d = 4k + 3. \end{cases}$$

Proof. C_1 and C_3 are easily verified. Figure 1 shows how the recursive definition of C_d is constructed. Note that in this figure a case '$(x_i \vee x_{i+1}) \wedge (y_j \vee y_{j+1})$' is represented by a 2×2 square covering the values in $[i, i+1] \times [j, j+1]$. $A_{1,d}$ and $A_{2,d}$ then cover the rectangles $[d-3, d] \times [1, d-3]$ and $[1, d-3] \times [d-3, d]$ respectively. $A_{3,d}$ is the same as C_3, but translated to cover the values in $[d-2, d] \times [d-2, d]$. Combined with C_{d-4} this proves that all possible assignments are covered.

For $d = 4k + 1$ we have

$$|C_d| = |C_{d-4}| + |A_{1,d}| + |A_{2,d}| + |A_{3,d}| =$$
$$= |C_{d-4}| + 2(d-3)/2 + 2(d-3)/2 + 3 = |C_{d-4}| + 2d - 3 =$$
$$= \ldots = |C_1| + \sum_{i=1}^{k} (2(4i+1) - 3) = (d^2 + d + 2)/4$$

and for $d = 4k + 3$ we have

$$|C_d| = |C_{d-4}| + 2d - 3 = \ldots = |C_3| + \sum_{i=1}^{k} (2(4i+3) - 3) = (d^2 + d)/4.$$

We finally prove that there can be no smaller set of cases covering all assignments. Every case covers at most 4 different assignments and there are d^2 possible assignments. Since d is odd, we note that for each value of x there must be a value of y such that this assignment is covered by at least two different cases. Therefore there must be at least d assignments which are covered more than once. This shows that $\lceil (d^2 + d)/4 \rceil$ is a lower bound on the number of cases needed to cover all possible assignments. $\square$

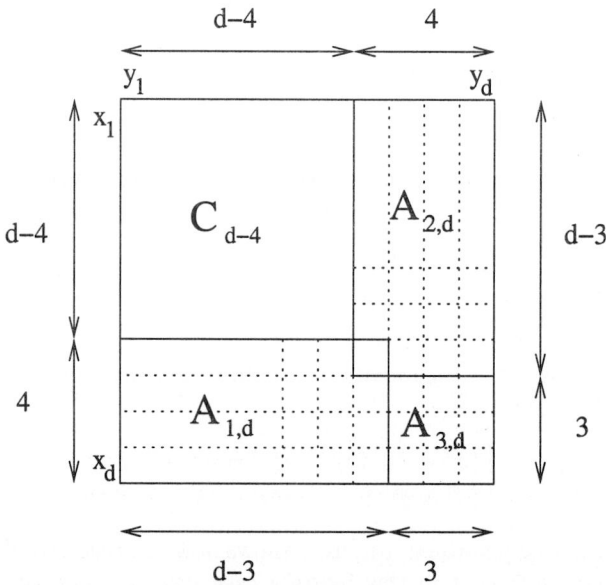

Fig. 1. The construction of C_d

Theorem 1. *Given a binary CSP $P = \langle V, D, C \rangle$, with $|V| = n$ and $|D| = d$, there exists an algorithm for determining the number of solutions in*

- $\mathcal{O}\left(1.3247^n \left(\frac{d}{2}\right)^n\right)$ *time, if $d = 2 \cdot k, k \geq 1$*
- $\mathcal{O}\left(1.3247^n \left(\frac{d^2+d+2}{4}\right)^{\frac{n}{2}}\right)$ *time, if $d = 4 \cdot k + 1$, and*
- $\mathcal{O}\left(1.3247^n \left(\frac{d^2+d}{4}\right)^{\frac{n}{2}}\right)$ *time, if $d = 4 \cdot k + 3$.*

Proof. As was described in the previous discussion, we start with creating the clauses corresponding to the constraints:

$$C_{xRy} = \bigwedge_{i,j \in D, (i,j) \notin R} (\neg x_i \vee \neg y_j)$$

For the value restricting clauses we have two cases.

Case 1: $d = 2 \cdot k, k > 0$

Divide the domain into $d/2$ pairs of values. For each variable x from the original problem instance, and each pair of values $i, i+1$, create the pair x_i, x_{i+1}, and the clauses

$$(x_i \lor x_{i+1}) \land (\neg x_i \lor \neg x_{i+1}) \bigwedge_{c \in D, c \neq i, c \neq i+1} (\neg x_c)$$

Combining these, as was described in the previous discussion, we get $(d/2)^n$ instances, each with $d \cdot n$ propositional variables. In each instance, we have $n \cdot (d-2)$ clauses on the form $\neg x_c$, hence using unit propagation, we arrive at $2 \cdot n$ propositional variables in each instance. Now let $m = 2 \cdot k, k \geq 0$, and, for each pair of propositional variables x_m, x_{m+1}, introduce a fresh variable ξ_{x_m}, with the interpretation that ξ_{x_m} is true iff x_m is true and x_{m+1} is false, and ξ_{x_m} is false iff x_m is false and x_{m+1} is true. Replace all occurrences of x_m and x_{m+1} with the new variable ξ_{x_m}, and $\neg \xi_{x_m}$, respectively, thereby reducing the number of propositional variables in each instance to n.

Case 2: $d = 2 \cdot k + 1, k > 0$

Given a pair of variables from the original problem, each with an associated pair of assignments, Proposition 1 shows that, if $d = 4 \cdot k + 1$, we need $(d^2 + d + 2)/4$, and if $d = 4 \cdot k + 3$, we need $(d^2 + d)/4$ such pairs to cover all possible assignments of values to the variables. To ensure the uniqueness of each solution we count, if there are overlaps between two assignments x_i and y_j, i.e., these assignments occur in more than one pair of variables, we add the clause $(\neg x_i \lor \neg y_j)$ to all but one instance containing these assignments. If we now perform a similar simplification as was done in the previous case, we get n propositional variables in each of the resulting 2-SAT instances.

Summary

Depending on the size of the domain, we now have

- $\left(\frac{d}{2}\right)^n$ instances if $d = 2 \cdot k$,
- $\left(\frac{d^2+d+2}{4}\right)^{\frac{n}{2}}$ instances if $d = 4 \cdot k + 3$, and
- $\left(\frac{d^2+d}{4}\right)^{\frac{n}{2}}$ instances if $d = 4 \cdot k + 1$.

Using the algorithm for #2-SAT presented in Dahllöf *et al.* [6], we can count the number of solutions in each instance in $\mathcal{O}(1.3247^n)$ time, and the result follows. $\square$

4   Algorithm for #3COL

We now present an algorithm for counting the number of 3-colourings of a graph. If we were to use the previously described algorithm, we would get a time complexity of $\mathcal{O}(2.2944^n)$, but as will be seen, this can be improved to $\mathcal{O}(1.8171^n)$ by exploiting problem specific knowledge.

We start with the necessary graph-theoretic preliminaries. A *graph* G consists of a set $V(G)$ of *vertices*, and a set $E(G)$ of *edges*, where each element of E is an unordered pair of vertices. The *size* of a graph G, denoted $|G|$, is the number of vertices. The *neighbourhood* of a vertex v is the set of all adjacent vertices, $\{w \mid (v,w) \in E(G)\}$, denoted $Nbd(v)$ An *independent set* S of G is a subset of $V(G)$, such that for every pair $v, w \in S \to (v,w) \notin E(G)$. A *3-colouring* of G is a function $C : V(G) \to \{R, G, B\}$ such that for all $v, w \in V(G)$, if $C(v) = C(w)$ then $(v,w) \notin E(G)$; that is, no adjacent vertices have the same colour. To *3-assign* $v \in G$ means assigning *colour*(v) a value from the set $\{R, G, B\}$. If G is a graph and $S \subseteq V(G)$, the graph $G|S$ has the vertex set S and

$$E(G|S) = \{(u,v) \in E(G) \mid u, v \in S\},$$

is called the *subgraph* of G *induced by* S. We write $G - S$ to denote the graph $G|(V - S)$.

A *matching* in a graph is a set M of vertices such that each vertex $v \in M$ has an edge to one and only one other vertex in M. The maximum matching (wrt. to the number of matched vertices) of a graph is computable in polynomial time [16]. Let $Match(G)$ be a function that computes a maximum matching of G and returns a pair (G_u, G_m) where $G_u \subseteq V(G)$ contains the unmatched vertices and $G_m \subseteq E(G)$ contains the matched pairs. We say that G is *perfectly matched* if $G_u = \emptyset$.

We consider an arbitrary graph G with n vertices and assume, without loss of generality, that it is connected.

A summary of the algorithm #3C for computing #3COL can be found in Figure 2. The algorithm has two main branches, where the choice of which branch to follow depends on the number of unmatched vertices. Section 4.1 contains the case where the unmatched vertices are less than a third of the total number of vertices in the graph, and Section 4.2 deals with the opposite case. The complexity analysis is done in Section 4.3.

```
1   algorithm #3C
2   (G_u, G_m) = Match(G)
3   c := 0
4   if |G_u| < |G|/3  then
5     for every R{G/B} assignment f of G  do
6       if f is an R{G/B} colouring  then c := c + Count_2(G, f)
7       end if
8     end for
9     return c
10  else
11    for every 3-colouring f of G_m  do
12      c := c + ∏_{v∈G_u} (3 - |{f(w) | w ∈ Nbd(v)}|)
13    end for
14    return c
15  end if
```

Fig. 2. Algorithm #3C

4.1   Case 1: $|G_u| < |G|/3$

We define a $R\{G/B\}$ *assignment* of the graph G as a total function $f : V(G) \to \{R, GB\}$ satisfying the following requirement:

if $v - w$ is a pair in G_m, then $f(v) \neq R$ or $f(w) \neq R$.

We say that an $R\{G/B\}$ assignment f is refineable to a 3-colouring of G iff for each of the vertices v having colour GB, we can assign $v := G$ or $v := B$ in such a manner that we obtain a 3-colouring of G. We call such an assignment an $R\{GB\}$-colouring of G. We note that having an $R\{G/B\}$ assignment for G which is refineable to a 3-colouring of G, is equivalent to the assignment having the following properties:

P1. the vertices with colour R form an independent set;

P2. the induced subgraph of vertices with colour GB is 2-colourable.

Obviously, these conditions can be checked in polynomial time. We can also count the number of possible refinements of an $R\{G/B\}$ assignment: consider the graph $G' = G|\{v \in V(G) \mid f(v) = GB\}$ and note that the number of refinements equals 2^c where c is the number of connected components in G'. Given an $R\{G/B\}$ assignment f, let $Count_2(G, f)$ denote this number (which is easily computable in polynomial time).

Now, let us take a closer look at the algorithm. All $R\{G/B\}$ assignments of G can be efficiently enumerated and there are exactly $2^{|G_u|} \cdot 3^{|G_m|/2}$ such assignments to consider. For each assignment that can be refined to a colouring, the algorithm counts the number of corresponding 3-colourings and adds this number to the variable c. Obviously, c contains the total number of 3-colourings after all assignments have been checked.

4.2   Case 2: $|G_u| \geq |G|/3$

Let $G' = G|\{v \in V; v \text{ appears in } G_m\}$. We begin by noting that G' is perfectly matched and each matched pair $p - q$ can obtain at most six different assignments. Hence, we need to consider at most $6^{|G_m|/2}$ assignments and, in the worst case, $6^{|G_m|/2}$ 3-colourings.

For each 3-colouring f of G, we claim that

$$\prod_{v \in G_u} (3 - |\{f(w) \mid w \in Nbd(v)\}|)$$

is the number of ways f can be extended to a 3-colouring of G. Assume for instance that $v \in G_u$ has three neighbours x, y, z that are coloured with R, G and B, respectively. Then, $3 - |\{f(w) \mid w \in Nbd(v)\}|)$ equals 0 which is correct since f cannot be extended in this case. It is easy to realise that the expression gives the right number of possible colours in all other cases, too. Since G_u is an independent set, we can simply multiply the numbers of allowed colours in order to count the number of possible extensions of f.

4.3   Complexity Analysis

Assume n is the number of vertices in the graph and C satisfies $|G_u| = C \cdot n$.

Case 1: $|G_u| < n/3$ and $C < 1/3$. The number of assignments we need to consider are

$$3^{(n-|G_u|)/2} \cdot 2^{|G_u|} = (3^{(1-C)/2} \cdot 2^C)^n.$$

Since the function $f(C) = 3^{(1-C)/2} \cdot 2^C$ is strictly increasing when $C > 0$, the largest number of assignments we need to consider appears when C is close to $1/3$, i.e., $|G_u|$ is close to $n/3$. In this case, the algorithm runs in $\mathcal{O}((3^{1/3} \cdot 2^{1/3})^n) = \mathcal{O}(6^{n/3}) \approx \mathcal{O}(1.8171^n)$ time.

Case 2: $|G_u| \geq n/3$ and $C \geq 1/3$. The number of assignments we need to consider are

$$6^{(n-|G_u|)/2} = (6^{(1-C)/2})^n.$$

Since the function $f(C) = 6^{(1-C)/2}$ is strictly decreasing when $C > 0$, the largest number of assignments we need to consider appears when $C = 1/3$, i.e., $|G_u| = n/3$. In this case, the algorithm runs in $\mathcal{O}(6^{n/3}) \approx \mathcal{O}(1.8171^n)$ time.

5   Conclusion

We have presented an algorithm for counting the number of solutions to binary constraint satisfaction problem instances. It works by, given a CSP, creating a set of 2-SAT instances, where each instance corresponds to a set of assignments of values to variables. A method for efficiently dividing domains of odd size into pairs of values was given, which makes it possible to avoid an unnecessary increase in time complexity for odd sized domains. The modularity of the algorithm makes it possible to improve the time complexity of the algorithm with no additional work whenever an improved algorithm for the #2-SAT problem is found. Furthermore, as was shown in the proof of Proposition 1, the construction we use cannot be done using fewer instances, thus in order to improve the algorithm, we need to consider a different construction altogether.

We have also shown that using problem specific knowledge, we can improve the complexity of the algorithm, and we give an algorithm for determining the number of possible 3-colourings of a graph.

Several open questions remain, however. We have provided an algorithm for *binary* CSPs, but it is not always the case that an n-ary relation can be represented by binary constraints using n variables [17], thus the problem of counting the number of solutions to a general CSP instance remains. How to deal with the general #k-colouring problem also remains to be investigated.

Can ideas similar to those utilised in our algorithm for #3-colouring be found for the general case?

Numerous tractable subclasses of CSPs have been found [18]. Jeavons *et al.* [11] showed the equivalence between finding graph homomorphisms and solving constraint satisfaction problems. Counting graph homomorphisms is #P-complete in most cases [8], so the existence of polynomial time algorithms for the counting problem for the tractable subclasses is unlikely, but this has not yet been investigated.

Acknowledgments

Ola Angelsmark is supported in part by CUGS – National Graduate School in Computer Science, Sweden. Peter Jonsson is partially supported by the *Swedish Research Council* (VR), under grant 221-2000-361. Johan Thapper is supported by the *Programme for Interdisciplinary Mathematics* at the Department of Mathematics, Linköpings Universitet.

References

[1] B. Aspvall, M. F. Plass, and R. E. Tarjan. A linear time algorithm for testing the truth of certain quantified Boolean formulas. *Information Processing Letters*, 8:121–123, 1979.

[2] R. Bayardo and J. D. Pehoushek. Counting models using connected components. In *Proceedings of the 17th National Conference on Artificial Intelligence and 12th Conference on Innovative Applications of Artificial Intelligence (AAAI/IAAI-2000)*, pages 157–162, 2000.

[3] M. Cooper, D. A. Cohen, and P. G. Jeavons. Characterising tractable constraints. *Artificial Intelligence*, 65(2):347–361, 1994.

[4] N. Creignou and M. Hermann. Complexity of generalized satisfiability counting problems. *Information and Computation*, 125:1–12, 1996.

[5] V. Dahllöf and P. Jonsson. An algorithm for counting maximum weighted independent sets and its applications. In *Proceedings of the 13th Annual ACM-SIAM Symposium on Discrete Algorithms (SODA-2002)*, pages 292–298, 2002.

[6] V. Dahllöf, P. Jonsson, and M. Wahlström. Counting satisfying assignments in 2-SAT and 3-SAT. In *Proceedings of the 8th Annual International Computing and Combinatorics Conference (COCOON-2002), Singapore*, Aug. 2002. To appear.

[7] O. Dubois. Counting the number of solutions for instances of satisfiability. *Theoretical Computer Science*, 81(1):49–64, 1991.

[8] M. Dyer and C. Greenhill. The complexity of counting graph homomorphisms. *Random Structures and Algorithms*, 17:260–289, 2000.

[9] D. Eppstein. Improved algorithms for 3-coloring, 3-edge-coloring, and constraint satisfaction. In *Proceedings of the 12th Annual Symposium on Discrete Algorithms (SODA-2001)*, pages 329–337, 2001.

[10] T. Feder and R. Motwani. Worst-case time bounds for coloring and satisfiability problems. Unpublished manuscript.

[11] P. G. Jeavons, D. A. Cohen, and J. K. Pearson. Constraints and universal algebra. *Annals of Mathematics and Artificial Intelligence*, 24:51–67, 1998.

[12] M. Jerrum. A very simple algorithm for estimating the number of k-colourings of a low-degree graph. *Random Structures and Algorithms*, 7:157–165, 1995.

[13] V. Kumar. Algorithms for constraint-satisfaction problems: A survey. *AI Magazine*, pages 32–44, Spring, 1992.

[14] M. L. Littman, T. Pitassi, and R. Impagliazzo. On the complexity of counting satisfying assignments. Unpublished manuscript, 2001.

[15] A. K. Mackworth. Consistency in networks of relations. *Artificial Intelligence*, 8:99–118, 1977.

[16] S. Micali and V. V. Vazirani. An $O(\sqrt{|v|} \cdot |e|)$ algorithm for finding maximum matching in general graphs. In *21st Annual Symposium on Foundations of Computer Science (FOCS-1980)*, pages 10–16. IEEE Computer Society, 1980.

[17] U. Montanari. Networks of constraints: Fundamental properties and applications to picture processing. *Information Sciences*, 7:95–132, 1974.

[18] J. K. Pearson and P. G. Jeavons. A survey of tractable constraint satisfaction problems. Technical Report CSD-TR-97-15, Royal Holloway, University of London, July 1997.

[19] D. Roth. On the hardness of approximate reasoning. *Artificial Intelligence*, 82:273–302, 1996.

[20] U. Schöning. A probabilistic algorithm for k-SAT and constraint satisfaction problems. In *40th Annual Symposium on Foundations of Computer Science (FOCS-1999)*, pages 410–414. IEEE Computer Society, 1999.

[21] L. G. Valiant. The complexity of computing the permanent. *Theoretical Computer Science*, 8(2):189–201, 1979.

[22] L. G. Valiant. The complexity of enumeration and reliability problems. *SIAM Journal on Computing*, 8(3):410–421, 1979.

[23] E. Vigoda. Improved bounds for sampling colorings. In *40th Annual Symposium on Foundations of Computer Science (FOCS-1999)*, pages 51–59. IEEE Computer Society, 1999.

[24] W. Zhang. Number of models and satisfiability of sets of clauses. *Theoretical Computer Science*, 155(1):277–288, 1996.

Consistency Checking for Qualitative Spatial Reasoning with Cardinal Directions

Spiros Skiadopoulos[1] and Manolis Koubarakis[2]

[1] Dept. of Electrical and Computer Engineering
National Technical University of Athens
Zographou 157 73 Athens, Greece
spiros@dblab.ntua.gr
http://www.dblab.ntua.gr/~spiros
[2] Dept. of Electronic and Computer Engineering
Technical University of Crete
Chania 73100 Crete, Greece
manolis@intelligence.tuc.gr
http://www.intelligence.tuc.gr/~manolis

Abstract. We present a formal model for qualitative spatial reasoning with cardinal directions and study the problem of checking the consistency of a set of cardinal direction constraints. We present the first algorithm for this problem, prove its correctness and analyze its computational complexity. Utilizing the above algorithm we prove that the consistency checking of a set of basic cardinal direction constraints can be performed in $\mathcal{O}(n^5)$ time while the consistency checking of an unrestricted set of cardinal direction constraints is NP-complete. Finally, we briefly discuss some extensions to the basic model.

1 Introduction

Qualitative spatial reasoning has received a lot of attention in the areas of Geographic Information Systems [6, 7, 8], Artificial Intelligence [4, 6, 13, 17], Databases [14] and Multimedia [19]. Qualitative spatial reasoning problems have recently been posed as constraint satisfaction problems and solved using traditional algorithms e.g., path-consistency [18]. One of the most important problems in this area is the identification of useful and tractable classes of spatial constraints and the study of efficient algorithms for consistency checking, minimal network computation and so on [18]. Several kinds of useful spatial constraints have been studied so far e.g., topological constraints [6, 17], cardinal direction constraints [11, 9] and qualitative distance constraints [7].

In this paper we concentrate on *cardinal direction constraints* [9, 11, 14, 20]. Cardinal direction constraints describe how regions of space are placed relative to one another. Typically, direction constraints are of the form $a\,R\,b$, where a is the primary region, b is the reference region and R is a direction relation (e.g., *a north of b*). Earlier qualitative models for cardinal direction relations approximate a spatial region by a representative point (most commonly the centroid) or by a

P. Van Hentenryck (Ed.): CP 2002, LNCS 2470, pp. 341–355, 2002.

representative box (most commonly the minimum bounding box) [7, 8, 11, 13, 14]. Depending on the particular spatial configuration these approximations may be too crude [9]. Thus, expressing direction relations on these approximations can be misleading and contradictory. For instance, with respect to the point-based approximation Spain is northeast of Portugal, but most people would agree that "northeast" does not describe accurately the relation between Spain and Portugal on a map.

Bearing that in mind Goyal and Egenhofer [9], and Skiadopoulos and Koubarakis [20] presented a model that only approximates the reference region (using the minimum bounding box) while using the exact shape of the primary region. Relations in the above model are clearly more expressive than point and box-based models. The model that we will present in this paper is closely related to the model of [9, 20] but there is a significant difference. [9, 20] deal only with extended regions that are connected and with connected boundaries while our approach allows regions to be disconnected and have holes. The regions that we consider are very common in Geography, Multimedia and Image Databases [1, 3, 19]. For example, countries are made up of separations (islands, exclaves, external territories) and holes (enclaves) [3].

We will study the problem of checking the consistency of a given set of cardinal direction constraints in our model. This is a fundamental problem of Logic Programming, Artificial Intelligence and Spatial Reasoning and has received a lot of attention in the literature [11, 14, 18]. Algorithms for consistency checking, are of immediate use in various situations including:

- Propagating relations and detecting inconsistencies in a given set of spatial relations [11, 18].
- Preprocessing spatial queries so that inconsistent queries are detected or the search space is pruned [15].

The technical contributions of this paper can be summarized as follows:

1. We present a formal model for qualitative reasoning about cardinal directions. This model is related to the model of [9, 20] and is currently one of the most expressive models for qualitative reasoning with cardinal directions.
2. We use our formal framework to study the problem of checking the consistency of a given set of cardinal direction constraints in the proposed model. We present the first algorithm for this problem and prove its correctness.
3. We present an analysis of the computational complexity of consistency checking. We show that the consistency checking of a set of *basic* cardinal direction constraints in n variables can be performed in $\mathcal{O}(n^5)$. Moreover, we prove that checking the consistency of an unrestricted set of cardinal direction constraints is NP-complete.
4. Finally, we consider the consistency checking of a set of cardinal direction constraints expressed in some interesting extension of the basic model and outline algorithms for this task.

The rest of the paper is organized as follows. Section 2 presents our model. In Section 3 we discuss the problem of consistency checking, present the main

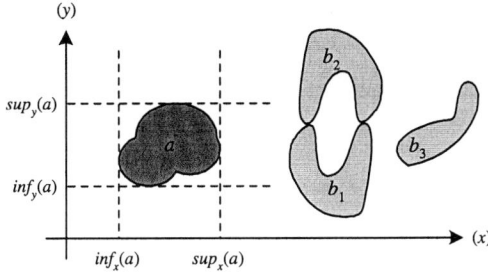

Fig. 1. Regions

algorithm and prove its correctness. Section 4 discusses the computational complexity of consistency checking. Finally, Section 5 concludes the paper by summarizing some interesting extensions of the basic model that we have already completed.

2   A Formal Model for Cardinal Direction Information

We consider the Euclidean space $\Re^2$. *Regions* are defined as non-empty and bounded sets of points in $\Re^2$. Let a be a region. The *greatest lower bound* or the *infimum* [12] of the *projection* of region a on the x-axis (respectively y-axis) is denoted by $inf_x(a)$ (respectively $inf_y(a)$). The *least upper bound* or the *supremum* of the *projection* of region a on the x-axis (respectively y-axis) is denoted by $sup_x(a)$ (respectively $sup_y(a)$). We will often refer to sup and inf as *endpoints*.

Let a be a region. We say that a is a *box* iff a is a rectangular region formed by the straight lines $x = c_1$, $x = c_2$, $y = c_3$ and $y = c_4$ where c_1, c_2, c_3 and c_4 are real constants such that $c_1 \leq c_2$ and $c_3 \leq c_4$. Moreover, iff $c_1 < c_2$ and $c_3 < c_4$ hold, we say that a is a *non-trivial box*. A box is *trivial* if it is a point or a vertical line segment or a horizontal line segment.

The *minimum bounding box* of a region a, denoted by $mbb(a)$, is the box formed by the straight lines $x = inf_x(a)$, $x = sup_x(a)$, $y = inf_y(a)$ and $y = sup_y(a)$ (see Fig. 1). Obviously, the projections on the x-axis (respectively y-axis) of a region and its minimum bounding box have the same endpoints.

We will consider throughout the paper the following types of regions:

– Regions that are homeomorphic to the *closed unit disk* ($\{(x, y) : x^2 + y^2 \leq 1\}$). The set of these regions will be denoted by *REG*. Regions in *REG* are *closed*, *connected* and have *connected boundaries* (for definitions see [2, 12]). Class *REG* excludes disconnected regions, regions with holes, points, lines and regions with emanating lines. Connected regions have been previously studied in [9, 16] and form the first approach to model areas in Geographic Information Systems [7]. Notice that our results are not affected if we consider regions that are homeomorphic to the *open unit disk* (as in [16]).

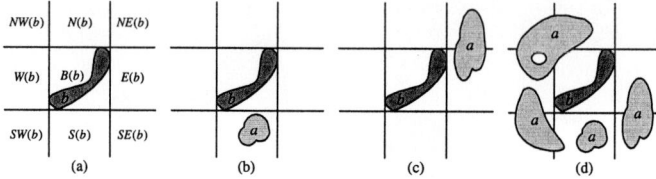

Fig. 2. Reference tiles and relations

- Regions in *REG* cannot model the variety and complexity of geographic entities [3]. Thus, we extend class *REG* in order to accommodate *disconnected regions* and *regions with holes*. The set of these regions will be denoted by REG^*. Set REG^* is a natural extension of *REG* which is useful to model (possibly disconnected) land parcels and countries in Geographic Information Systems [3, 7] or areas of an image containing similar chromatic arrangements [1].

In Fig. 1, regions a, b_1, b_2 and b_3 are in *REG* (also in REG^*) and region $b = b_1 \cup b_2 \cup b_3$ is in REG^*. Notice that region b is disconnected and has a hole.

Proposition 1. *If $a \in REG^*$ then $mbb(a)$ is a non-trivial box. Equivalently, the following inequalities hold:*

$$inf_x(a) < sup_x(a) \ and \ inf_y(a) < sup_y(a).$$

Let us now consider two arbitrary regions a and b in REG^*. Let region a be related to region b through a cardinal direction relation (e.g., a is north of b). Region b will be called the *reference* region (i.e., the region *to* which the relation is described) while region a will be called the *primary* region (i.e., the region *from* which the relation is described). The axes forming the minimum bounding box of the reference region b divide the space into 9 tiles (Fig. 2a). The peripheral tiles correspond to the eight cardinal direction relations *south, southwest, west, northwest, north, northeast, east* and *southeast*. These tiles will be denoted by $S(b)$, $SW(b)$, $W(b)$, $NW(b)$, $N(b)$, $NE(b)$, $E(b)$ and $SE(b)$ respectively. The central area corresponds to the region's minimum bounding box and is denoted by $B(b)$. By definition each one of these tiles includes the parts of the axes forming it. The union of all 9 tiles is $\Re^2$.

If a primary region a is included (in the set-theoretic sense) in tile $S(b)$ of some reference region b (Fig. 2b) then we say that *a is south of b* and we write $a \ S \ b$. Similarly, we can define *southwest (SW), west (W), northwest (NW), north (N), northeast (NE), east (E), southeast (SE)* and *bounding box (B)* relations.

If a primary region a lies partly in the area $NE(b)$ and partly in the area $E(b)$ of some reference region b (Fig. 2c) then we say that *a is partly northeast and partly east of b* and we write $a \ NE{:}E \ b$.

The general definition of a cardinal direction relation in our framework is as follows.

Definition 1. *An atomic cardinal direction relation is an element of the set* $\{B, S, SW, W, NW, N, NE, E, SE\}$. *A basic cardinal direction relation is an atomic cardinal direction relation or an expression* $R_1{:}\cdots{:}R_k$ *where* $2 \le k \le 9$, $R_1, \ldots, R_k \in \{B, S, SW, W, NW, N, NE, E, SE\}$ *and* $R_i \ne R_j$ *for every* i, j *such that* $1 \le i, j \le k$ *and* $i \ne j$.

Example 1. The following are basic cardinal direction relations:
$$S, \quad NE{:}E \text{ and } B{:}S{:}SW{:}W{:}NW{:}N{:}E{:}SE.$$
Regions involved in these relations are shown in Figures 2b, 2c and 2d respectively.

In order to avoid confusion we will write the atomic elements of a cardinal direction relation according to the following order: B, S, SW, W, NW, N, NE, E and SE. Thus, we always write $B{:}S{:}W$ instead of $W{:}B{:}S$ or $S{:}B{:}W$. The readers should also be aware that for a basic relation such as $B{:}S{:}W$ we will often refer to B, S and W as its *tiles*.

2.1 Defining Basic Cardinal Direction Relations Formally

Now we can formally define the atomic cardinal direction relations B, S, SW, W, NW, N, NE, E and SE of our model as follows:

$a\ B\ b$ iff $inf_x(b) \le inf_x(a)$, $sup_x(a) \le sup_x(b)$, $inf_y(b) \le inf_y(a)$ and $sup_y(a) \le sup_y(b)$.

$a\ S\ b$ iff $sup_y(a) \le inf_y(b)$, $inf_x(b) \le inf_x(a)$ and $sup_x(a) \le sup_x(b)$.

$a\ SW\ b$ iff $sup_x(a) \le inf_x(b)$ and $sup_y(a) \le inf_y(b)$.

$a\ W\ b$ iff $sup_x(a) \le inf_x(b)$, $inf_y(b) \le inf_y(a)$ and $sup_y(a) \le sup_y(b)$.

$a\ NW\ b$ iff $sup_x(a) \le inf_x(b)$ and $sup_y(b) \le inf_y(a)$.

$a\ N\ b$ iff $sup_y(b) \le inf_y(a)$, $inf_x(b) \le inf_x(a)$ and $sup_x(a) \le sup_x(b)$.

$a\ NE\ b$ iff $sup_x(b) \le inf_x(a)$ and $sup_y(b) \le inf_y(a)$.

$a\ E\ b$ iff $sup_x(b) \le inf_x(a)$, $inf_y(b) \le inf_y(a)$ and $sup_y(a) \le sup_y(b)$.

$a\ SE\ b$ iff $sup_x(b) \le inf_x(a)$ and $sup_y(a) \le inf_y(b)$.

Using the above atomic relations we can define all non-atomic ones. For instance relation $NE{:}E$ (Fig. 3a) and relation $B{:}S{:}SW{:}W{:}NW{:}N{:}E{:}SE$ (Fig. 3b) are defined as follows:

$a\ NE{:}E\ b$ iff there exist regions a_1 and a_2 in REG^* such that $a = a_1 \cup a_2$, $a_1\ NE\ b$ and $a_2\ E\ b$.

$a\ B{:}S{:}SW{:}W{:}NW{:}N{:}SE{:}E\ b$ iff there exist regions $a_1, \ldots, a_8$ in REG^* such that $a = a_1 \cup \cdots \cup a_8$, $a_1\ B\ b$, $a_2\ S\ b$, $a_3\ SW\ b$, $a_4\ W\ b$, $a_5\ NW\ b$, $a_6\ N\ b$, $a_7\ SE\ b$ and $a_8\ E\ b$.

In general each non-atomic cardinal direction relation is defined as follows.

Definition 2. *If* $2 \le k \le 9$ *then* $a\ R_1{:}\cdots{:}R_k\ b$ *iff there exist regions* $a_1, \ldots, a_k \in REG^*$ *such that* $a_1\ R_1\ b, \ldots, a_k\ R_k\ b$ *and* $a = a_1 \cup \cdots \cup a_k$.

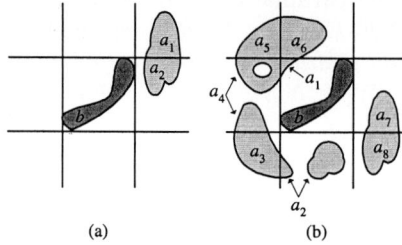

Fig. 3. Relations and component variables

The variables $a_1, \ldots, a_k$ in any equivalence such as the above (which defines a basic cardinal direction relation) will be called the *component variables* corresponding to variable a. Notice that for every i, j such that $1 \le i, j \le k$ and $i \ne j$, a_i and a_j have disjoint interiors but may share points in their boundaries.

The set of basic cardinal direction relations in our model contains $\sum_{i=1}^{9} \binom{9}{i} = 511$ elements. We will use $\mathcal{D}^*$ to denote this set. Relations in $\mathcal{D}^*$ are jointly exclusive and pairwise disjoint. Elements of $\mathcal{D}^*$ can be used to represent *definite information* about cardinal directions, e.g., $a \, N \, b$.

Using the 511 relations of $\mathcal{D}^*$ as our basis, we can define the *powerset* $2^{\mathcal{D}^*}$ of $\mathcal{D}^*$ which contains 2^{511} relations. Elements of $2^{\mathcal{D}^*}$ are called *cardinal direction relations* and can be used to represent not only definite but also *indefinite information* about cardinal directions e.g., $a \, \{N, W\} \, b$ denotes that region a is north *or* west of region b.

The model presented in this section is related to the model of [9, 20] but these proposals deal only with the connected regions of REG. Our approach accommodates a wider set of region (i.e., regions in REG^*) that also allows regions to be disconnected and have holes. As a result we have 511 relations while the model of [9, 20] has 218. This enables us to express several natural spatial arrangements (e.g., $a \, S{:}W \, b$ or $a \, S{:}N \, b$) that are not possible in [9, 20].

3   Constraints and Consistency Checking

In this section we present an algorithm for deciding the consistency of a set of cardinal direction constraints involving only basic relations. Let us first define cardinal direction constraints formally.

Definition 3. *A cardinal direction constraint is a formula $a \, R \, b$ where a, b are variables ranging over regions in REG^* and R is a cardinal direction relation from the set $2^{\mathcal{D}^*}$. Moreover, a cardinal direction constraint is called* atomic *(respectively* basic*) if R is an atomic (respectively basic) cardinal direction relation.*

Example 2. The following are cardinal direction constraints:
$$a_1 \, S \, b_1, \quad a_2 \, NE{:}E \, b_2 \quad \text{and} \quad a_3 \, \{B, S{:}SW\} \, b_3.$$
The constraint $a_1 \, S \, b_1$ is an atomic one (also basic). The constraint $a_2 \, NE{:}E \, b_2$ is a basic one.

Definition 4. *Let C be a set of cardinal direction constraints in variables $a_1, \ldots, a_n$. The* solution set *of C, denoted by $Sol(C)$, is:*

$$\{(o_1, \ldots, o_n) : o_1, \ldots, o_n \in REG^* \text{ and for every } c \in C, (o_1, \ldots, o_n) \text{ satisfies } c\}.$$

Each member of $Sol(C)$ is called a solution *of C. A set of cardinal direction constraints is called* consistent *iff its solution set is non-empty.*

In this paper we will also be interested in special kinds of order constraints which are defined below.

Definition 5. *An* order constraint *is a formula in any of the following forms:*

$$inf_x(a) \sim inf_x(b), \quad sup_x(a) \sim sup_x(b), \quad inf_x(a) \sim sup_x(b),$$
$$inf_y(a) \sim inf_y(b), \quad sup_y(a) \sim sup_y(b), \quad inf_y(a) \sim sup_y(b)$$

where a and b are variables ranging over regions in REG^* and $\sim$ can be any operator from the set $\{<, >, \leq, \geq, =\}$.

Definition 6. *A set of order constraints is called* canonical *iff it includes the constraints $inf_x(a) < sup_x(a)$ and $inf_y(a) < sup_y(a)$ for every region variable a referenced in the set.*

Definition 7. *Let O be a canonical set of order constraints in region variables $a_1, \ldots, a_n$. The* solution set *of O, denoted by $Sol(O)$, is the set of $4n$-tuples $(a_1^{xl}, a_1^{xu}, a_1^{yl}, a_1^{yu}, \ldots, a_n^{xl}, a_n^{xu}, a_n^{yl}, a_n^{yu}) \in \Re^{4n}$ such that the constraints in C are satisfied by assigning*

$$a_i^{xl} \text{ to } inf_x(a_i), \quad a_i^{xu} \text{ to } sup_x(a_i), \quad a_i^{yl} \text{ to } inf_y(a_i), \quad a_i^{yu} \text{ to } sup_y(a_i)$$

for every i, $1 \leq i \leq n$.

According to the above definition when we talk of a solution for a canonical set of order constraints, it is the expressions $sup(\cdot)$ and $inf(\cdot)$ that should interest us and not the region variables of the set. As with cardinal direction constraints, a set of order constraints is called *consistent* if its solution set is non-empty.

3.1   Checking the Consistency of a Set of Basic Cardinal Direction Constraints

The "iff" statements of Definition 2 can be used to equivalently map a set of arbitrary basic cardinal direction constraints C to a set S consisting of the following two types of constraints:

- *atomic* cardinal direction constraints.
- *set-union* constraints.

Example 3. Let C be a set of basic cardinal direction constraints in variables $a_1, \ldots, a_n$. Let us consider an arbitrary constraint $a_i \ R_1 : \cdots : R_k \ a_j$ in C. For this constraint, the mapping of Definition 2 will introduce to S:

- k atomic cardinal direction constraints, i.e., $d_1 \ R_1 \ a_j, \ldots, \ d_k \ R_k \ a_j$ and
- one set-union constraint, i.e, $a_1 = d_1 \cup \cdots \cup d_k$.

where $d_1, \ldots, d_k$ are component variables corresponding to region variable a_i.

If we had an algorithm for deciding the consistency of sets like $\mathcal{S}$, we could use it to solve our problem. Given the unavailability of such an algorithm, we develop Algorithm CONSISTENCY that checks whether C (equivalently $\mathcal{S}$) is consistent. This algorithm proceeds as follows:

1. Initially, Algorithm CONSISTENCY considers each constraint c in C and maps the atomic cardinal direction constraints of its definition into a set of order constraints O. To this end, it uses the definitions of Section 2.1, Page 345. Moreover, the algorithm introduces into set O additional order constraints that are implied by the cardinal direction constraint c. These constraints will be discussed in the sequel.
2. Then Algorithm CONSISTENCY finds a solution of the set of order constraints O or if no solution exists it returns 'Inconsistent'. To this end we use the well-known algorithms of [22, 5]. This solution assigns regions to the regions variables of set C. Moreover, the second step of the algorithm extends the above regions without falsifying any constraint in C.
3. Finally, the algorithm considers the set-union constraints that correspond to every constraint c in C and checks whether they are satisfied by the solution of Step 2. If all set-union constraints are satisfied the algorithm returns 'Consistent'; otherwise it returns 'Inconsistent'.

Let us now describe the 3 steps of Algorithm CONSISTENCY. More details can be found in [21].

Step 1. In this first step, for each cardinal direction constraint $a_i \ R_1 : \cdots : R_k \ a_j$ in C, we consult Definition 2. More specifically, this step introduces new region variables $d_1, \ldots, d_k$ which denote the component variables corresponding to variable a_i. Then, this step introduces order constraints encoding all atomic cardinal direction relations between the reference region a_j and the component variables corresponding to the primary region a_i, i.e., $d_1 \ R_1 \ a_j, \ldots, \ d_k \ R_k \ a_j$ (see Section 2.1, Page 345). We also introduce the obvious order constraints relating the endpoints of the projections of the component variables (Proposition 1). These constraints make the final set O canonical.

Example 4. Let $C = \{a_1 \ S{:}SW \ a_2, \ a_1 \ NW{:}N{:}NE \ a_3\}$ be the given set of basic cardinal direction constraints (see Fig. 5). Step 1.1 considers constraint $a_1 \ S{:}SW \ a_2$ first and introduces component variables d_1 and d_2 representing subregions of a_1 such that $d_1 \ SW \ a_2$ and $d_2 \ S \ a_2$. Then, the definitions of relations SW and S are consulted (see Section 2.1, Page 345) and the following order constraints are added to O:

$$sup_x(d_1) \leq inf_x(a_2), \quad inf_x(a_2) \leq inf_x(d_2), \quad sup_x(d_2) \leq sup_x(a_2),$$
$$sup_y(d_1) \leq inf_y(a_2), \quad sup_y(d_2) \leq inf_y(a_2).$$

The obvious order constraints relating the endpoints of each projection are also added to O during this step (Proposition 1). Similarly, the order constraints corresponding to the second cardinal direction constraint of set C are introduced.

Step 1 also deals with the component variables corresponding to variable a_i. The fact that a variable r is a component variable of a_i implies that r is a subregion of a_i and thus, the constraints $inf_x(a_i) \leq inf_x(r)$, $sup_x(r) \leq sup_x(a_i)$, $inf_y(a_i) \leq inf_y(r)$ and $sup_y(r) \leq sup_y(a_i)$ hold. The above constraints are introduced by Step 1.2 for all component variables corresponding to variable a_i.

Example 5. Let us continue with the set C of Example 4. Since regions d_1 and d_2 are component variable corresponding to a_1, Step 1 adds to O the following constraints for every $r \in \{d_1, d_2\}$:

$$inf_x(a_1) \leq inf_x(r), \ sup_x(r) \leq sup_x(a_1), inf_y(a_1) \leq inf_y(r), \ sup_y(r) \leq sup_y(a_1)$$

The new order constraints corresponding to the second constraint of set C are omitted for brevity.

Finally, in Step 1 we re-examine each constraint $a_i \ R_1{:}\cdots{:}R_k \ a_j$ in C and introduce additional order constraints that establish the *strictest possible* relation between the endpoints of the projections of a_i and a_j on the x and y-axis. In this way, the strictest possible relation between the minimum bounding boxes of a_i and a_j is also established. Notice that these constraints are not implied by the other constraints of Step 1. There are 8 possible cases that need to be considered here. These cases correspond to checking whether the set of relations $\{R_1, \ldots, R_k\}$ is a subset of one or more of the following sets:

$\{SW, S, SE\}, \ \{SW, S, SE, W, B, E\}, \ \{NW, W, SW\}, \ \{NW, W, SW, N, B, S\},$
$\{NW, N, NE\}, \ \{NW, N, NE, W, B, E\}, \ \{NE, E, SE\}, \ \{NE, E, SE, N, B, S\}.$

For example, if the set of relations $\{R_1, \ldots, R_k\}$ is a subset of $\{SW, S, SE\}$, the constraint $sup_y(a_i) \leq inf_y(a_j)$ is introduced by this step (the full version of this paper gives the 7 constraints required by the remaining 7 cases).

Example 6. Let us continue with the set C of Example 4. If we consider the first constraint of C, we notice that relations S and SW are members of $\{SW, S, SE\}$ and $\{NW, W, SW, N, B, S\}$. As a result the constraints $sup_y(a_1) \leq inf_y(a_2)$ and $sup_x(a_1) \leq sup_x(a_2)$ are added to O (see Fig. 5). The new order constraints corresponding to the second constraint of set C are omitted for brevity.

Step 2. In the first step of Algorithm CONSISTENCY we have introduced to set O order constraints which are implied by the spatial configuration that is expressed by the cardinal direction constraints of a given set C. The second step of Algorithm CONSISTENCY uses the well-known algorithms for order constraints to find a solution of set O [22, 5]. If set O is inconsistent obviously set C is also inconsistent. If, on the other hand, a solution of set O exists then this solution assigns values to the *sup*'s and *inf*'s of all region and component variables referenced

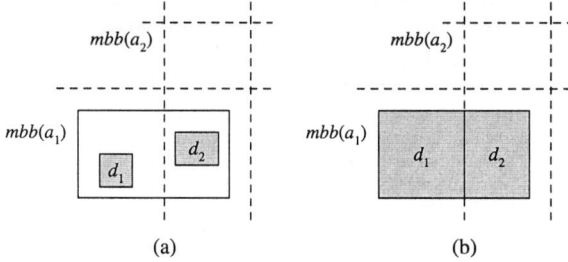

Fig. 4. Extending the solution of O

in set C. Using these values we can draw non-trivial boxes that correspond to the above variables. Then, Step 2 of Algorithm CONSISTENCY extends all these non-trivial boxes as the following example suggests.

Example 7. Let us continue with the set C of Example 4. Using Step 1 we can map C into a set of order constraints O. Let us now assume that set O is consistent and $\bar{x}_0$ is a solution of O. Since O is consistent then $\bar{x}_0$ assigns values to $sup_x(r)$, $inf_x(r)$, $sup_y(r)$ and $inf_y(r)$, for every region variable $r \in \{a_1, a_2, a_3, d_1, d_2\}$. Using the above values, we can form non-trivial boxes that correspond to the minimum bounding boxes of regions a_1, a_2, a_3, d_1 and d_2 respectively.

We can now extend d_1 and d_2 in all directions until they touch whatever line is closer to them from the ones forming the minimum bounding boxes of a_1 and a_2 (see Fig. 4a). For instance, we can extend d_1 to the east to touch the vertical line $y = inf_x(mbb(a_2))$ and to the west to touch the vertical line $y = inf_x(mbb(a_1))$. Fig. 4b illustrates this idea for all regions d_1 and d_2. Now notice that the new regions d_1 and d_2 still satisfy all constraints in O.

The following lemma captures the above observation in its full generality.

Lemma 1. *Let O be the output of Step 1 of Algorithm* CONSISTENCY *when it is called with argument a set of cardinal direction constraints C in variables $a_1, \ldots, a_n$. For each variable a_i $(1 \leq i \leq n)$ let $\{d_1, \ldots, d_l\}$ be the set of component variables corresponding to a_i that have been generated by Step 1 of Algorithm* CONSISTENCY *while considering various constraints $a_i\ R_1: \cdots :R_k\ a_j$, $1 \leq j \leq n$, in C.*

Let $\bar{x}_0$ be a solution of O. Then a new solution $\bar{x}'_0$ of O can be constructed as follows. For every constraint $a_i\ R_1: \cdots :R_k\ a_j$ in C we consider each component variable d_m, $(1 \leq m \leq l)$ in turn.

If $d_m\ S\ a_j$ holds, perform the following substitutions:

$$inf_x(d_m) \text{ by } max\{\ inf_x(a_i),\ inf_x(a_j)\ \},$$
$$sup_x(d_m) \text{ by } min\{\ sup_x(a_i),\ sup_x(a_j)\ \},$$
$$inf_y(d_m) \text{ by } inf_y(a_i),$$
$$sup_y(d_m) \text{ by } min\{\ sup_y(a_i),\ inf_y(a_j)\ \}.$$

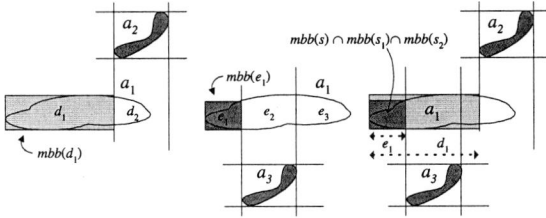

Fig. 5. Example of Constraint (T)

Similar substitutions are performed when d_m SW a_j, d_m W a_j, d_m NW a_j, d_m N a_j, d_m NE a_j, d_m E a_j, d_m SE a_j and d_m B a_j hold (the full version of this paper gives these substitutions [21]).

Example 8. Let us continue with the set C of Example 4 and consider region variable d_2 of Fig. 4a. It is easy to verify that if we perform the substitutions of Lemma 1 then d_2 can be extended as in Fig. 4b. For instance $inf_x(d_2)$ in Fig 4b is $inf_x(a_2) = max\{ inf_x(a_1), inf_x(a_2) \}$.

Let $\bar{x}_0$ be a solution of O. Solution $\bar{x}_0$ is called *maximal* if it is not affected by the substitutions of Lemma 1. The substitutions of Lemma 1 are very useful since they allow us to check rather than enforce the set-union constraint of S.

Step 3. The final step of Algorithm CONSISTENCY checks if the maximal solution of Step 2 satisfies the set-union constraints of S. So far we have dealt only with order constraints, so it would be convenient if we could transform the set-union constraints into a comparable to order constraints from. To do so, we will need the following lemma.

Lemma 2. *Let a be a region in REG^*. Let us now suppose that $S_1 = \{a_1^1, \ldots, a_{k_1}^1\}, \ldots, S_m = \{a_1^m, \ldots, a_{k_m}^m\}$ are sets of subregions of a such that $a_1^1, \ldots, a_{k_1}^1, \ldots, a_1^m, \ldots, a_{k_m}^m \in REG^*$ and $a = a_1^1 \cup \cdots \cup a_{k_1}^1 = \cdots = a_1^m \cup \cdots \cup a_{k_m}^m$ holds. Then, the following constraint also holds.*

Constraint (T): *For all $s \in S_1 \cup \cdots \cup S_m$ there exists a tuple $(s_1, \ldots, s_m) \in S_1 \times \cdots \times S_m$ such that $mbb(s) \cap mbb(s_1) \cap \cdots \cap mbb(s_m)$ is a non-trivial box.*

Example 9. Let us continue with the set C of Example 4. Let $S_1 = \{d_1, d_2\}$ and $S_2 = \{e_1, e_2, e_3\}$ be the set of component variables corresponding to a_1 (see Fig. 5). Since d_1, d_2, e_1, e_2, e_3 are subregions of a_1 such that $d_1, d_2, e_1, e_2, e_3 \in REG^*$ and $a_1 = d_1 \cup d_2 = e_1 \cup e_2 \cup e_3$, the preconditions of Lemma 2 hold. Using Fig. 5, it is not hard to see that Constraint (T) also holds. For instance, for subregion $d_1 \in S_1$ there exists a region $s_1 \in S_1$, namely d_1, and a region in $s_2 \in S_2$, namely e_1, such that $mbb(d_1) \cap mbb(s_1) \cap mbb(s_2)$ is a non-trivial box (the corresponding bounding boxes are depicted in Fig. 5).

Lemma 2 is very important since it provides us with an alternative method to check whether the set-union constraints of S are satisfied. Using Lemma 2

<u>For</u> every region variable a_i in $\{a_1, \ldots, a_n\}$ <u>Do</u>
    Let $\Sigma_1, \ldots, \Sigma_m$ be the sets of boxes that correspond to the sets of component variables $S_1, \ldots, S_m$
    <u>For</u> every s in $\Sigma_1 \cup \cdots \cup \Sigma_m$
        $Q = \{s\}$
        <u>For</u> every Σ' in $\{\Sigma_1, \ldots, \Sigma_m\}$ <u>Do</u>
            $Q' = \emptyset$
            <u>For</u> every s' in Σ' and every q in Q <u>Do</u>
                <u>If</u> $s' \cap q$ is a non-trivial box <u>Then</u> $Q' = Q' \cup \{s' \cap q\}$
            <u>EndFor</u>
            <u>If</u> $Q' = \emptyset$ <u>Then</u> <u>Return</u> 'Inconsistent'
            $Q = Q'$
        <u>EndFor</u>
    <u>EndFor</u>
<u>EndFor</u>

Fig. 6. Step 3 of Algorithm CONSISTENCY

Algorithm CONSISTENCY equivalently checks whether the maximal solution of O satisfies Constraint (T). To this end it proceeds as follows (see also Fig. 6).

First, the algorithm considers every region variable a_i in $a_1, \ldots, a_n$ in turn. Let us assume that the input set C contains m constraints with region a_i as a primary region (i.e., of the form $a_i \, R \, a_j$). Every time each of these m constraints is processed by Step 1 of Algorithm CONSISTENCY a new set of component variables corresponding to a_i is introduced. Let $S_1, \ldots, S_m$ be these sets of component variables corresponding to a_i. The solution of Step 2 assigns non-trivial boxes to all the members of $S_1, \ldots, S_m$. Let $\Sigma_1, \ldots, \Sigma_m$ be the sets of boxes that correspond to $S_1, \ldots, S_m$ after the assignments of Step 2.

For every component variable s in $\Sigma_1 \cup \cdots \cup \Sigma_m$ Algorithm CONSISTENCY checks whether there exists a tuple $(s_1, \ldots, s_m) \in \Sigma_1 \times \cdots \times \Sigma_m$ such that $mbb(s) \cap mbb(s_1) \cap \cdots \cap mbb(s_m)$ is a non-trivial box. To this end, it utilizes set Q. Initially Q contains only the component variable s. Then, the algorithm considers every set of component variables Σ' in $\Sigma_1, \ldots, \Sigma_m$ in turn. Let us now suppose that algorithm has processed sets Σ_1 to $\Sigma_{\mu-1}$ where $1 \leq \mu - 1 < m$. In this case, set Q contains all non-trivial boxes of the form $s \cap \sigma_1 \cap \cdots \cap \sigma_{\mu-1}$ where $\sigma_i \in \Sigma_i$. Then, the algorithm considers the component variables of Σ_μ and the non-trivial boxes of Q. Algorithm CONSISTENCY finds all regions $s' \in \Sigma_\mu$ and $q \in Q$ such that $s' \cap q$ is a non-trivial box and puts them into a new set Q'. In other words set Q' contains all non-trivial boxes of the form $s \cap \sigma_1 \cap \cdots \cap \sigma_\mu$ where $\sigma_i \in \Sigma_i$. Hence, if Q' is empty, Constraint (T) is violated and Algorithm CONSISTENCY returns 'Inconsistent'. Otherwise Q' is assigned to Q and the algorithm continues with the remaining sets of boxes $\Sigma_{\mu+1}, \ldots, \Sigma_m$ that correspond to variable a.

Our discussion has now been completed. The following result summarizes what we have achieved.

Theorem 1. *Let C be a set of basic cardinal direction constraints. Algorithm* CONSISTENCY *correctly decides whether C is consistent.*

Proof. (sketch) Notice that the constraints in O and Constraint (T) are indeed implied by the given set of basic cardinal direction constraints C. This is trivial to see for Step 1; for Step 3, it follows from Lemma 2. Thus, if Algorithm CONSISTENCY returns 'Inconsistent' then C is inconsistent.

If Algorithm CONSISTENCY returns 'Consistent', we start with a solution of O, and form non-trivial boxes (rectangles) that are solutions of the atomic cardinal direction constraints involving only component variables (these atomic constraints are in the set S and have been produced by consulting the righthand sides of "iff" definitions of Section 2.1). Then, for each variable a_i of C we form a family of unions of non-trivial boxes such that each union is a solution of a constraint in C with a_i as the primary region. The constraints introduced by Step 1 can be used here to guarantee that each one of these unions has the same bounding box with the bounding box of a_i. Finally, the intersection of all unions in the family for each a_i results in a region $a_i^0 \in REG^*$ (the constraints introduced by Step 3 are used here). All a_i^0's constructed in this way form a tuple which is a solution of the original constraint set C.

For the details of the proof, the interested reader can consult the full version of this paper [21]. □

4 Complexity of Consistency Checking

We will now turn our attention to the complexity of consistency checking of a set of basic cardinal direction constraints. As we have seen in the previous section checking the consistency of a set of basic cardinal direction constraints can be done using Algorithm CONSISTENCY. The following theorem discusses its complexity.

Theorem 2. *Checking the consistency of a set of* basic *cardinal direction constraints in n variables can be done using Algorithm* CONSISTENCY *in $\mathcal{O}(n^5)$ time.*

Proof. To decide the consistency of a set of basic cardinal direction constraints we can use Algorithm CONSISTENCY introduced above. Let us now calculate its complexity. Let the input to CONSISTENCY be a set C of basic cardinal direction constraints in n region variables. The number of constraints in C is $\mathcal{O}(n^2)$.

The output of Step 1 of Algorithm CONSISTENCY is a set of order constraints O. Algorithm CONSISTENCY introduces at most 9 new variables each time Step 1 is executed. So the total number of region variables is $\mathcal{O}(n^2)$. Step 1 of Algorithm CONSISTENCY adds to O, $\mathcal{O}(n^2)$ atomic order constraints. Therefore, to find a solution of O we have to find a solution of a set of $\mathcal{O}(n^2)$ atomic order constraints in $\mathcal{O}(n^2)$ variables. This can be done in $\mathcal{O}(n^4)$ time using Algorithm CSPAN of [22]. Then Algorithm CONSISTENCY applies Lemma 1. This, can be performed in $\mathcal{O}(n)$ time. Summarizing the first two steps of Algorithm CONSISTENCY can be done in $\mathcal{O}(n^4)$ time.

In the third step, the algorithm checks if Constraint (T) is satisfied. Before we proceed let us measure the size of set Q. For a given variable a_i, $1 \le i \le n$, set C contains $\mathcal{O}(n)$ constraints of the form $a_i \, R \, a_j$, $1 \le i \le n$. Now since a_i participates in $\mathcal{O}(n)$ constraints of C, it follows that the region represented by variable a_i is divided by $\mathcal{O}(n)$ horizontal and $\mathcal{O}(n)$ vertical lines. Thus a_i is divided into $\mathcal{O}(n^2)$ pieces. Now notice that set Q cannot contain more members than the possible pieces of a_i, thus the size of Q is $\mathcal{O}(n^2)$. In order to check whether Constraint (T) is satisfied Algorithm CONSISTENCY performs four nested loops. Each of the outer two loops is executed $\mathcal{O}(n)$ times. Both the inner loops are performed at most $\mathcal{O}(n^3)$ times. Thus checking whether Constraint (T) is satisfied can be done in $\mathcal{O}(n^5)$ time.

Summarizing, the complexity of Algorithm CONSISTENCY is $\mathcal{O}(n^5)$.   □

Now turning our attention to the general problem we have the following result.

Theorem 3. *Checking the consistency of an unrestricted set of cardinal direction constraints is NP-complete.*

Proof. Let C be a set of cardinal direction constraints. Deciding the consistency of C is easily seen to be in NP. To prove NP-hardness use a reduction from 3SAT. To this end, we map each literal of 3SAT to a region variable and each clause of 3SAT to a set of cardinal direction constraints. This proof borrows some ideas form a proof that appears in [23] (like the use of a center region). It differentiates in the way we use relations and auxiliary regions.   □

Following the line of work of [18] for topological constraints, we are currently working on investigating tractable subclasses of cardinal direction relations.

5   Extensions

There are two interesting extensions of the basic model. The first extension is to accommodate any region in $\Re^2$ (i.e., to include points and lines). Points and lines have been excluded carefully from REG^* (they are not homeomorphic to the unit disk). They can be easily included by dividing the space around the reference region into 25 areas (9 two-dimensional areas, 8 semi-lines, 4 line segments and 4 points). This should be contrasted to the model presented in Section 2 that divides the space into 9 areas. The new set contains $\sum_{i=1}^{25} \binom{25}{i} = 33,554,431$ jointly exclusive and pairwise disjoint cardinal direction relations. Algorithm CONSISTENCY can be easily modified to handle this case (details will be given in the long version of the paper). This extension is similar to [10].

The second extension is to modify the framework so that it also covers the case of connected regions as envisioned originally in [9, 20]. This can be done by considering only 218 relations that are possible between connected regions. Algorithm CONSISTENCY also works in this case (details in the long version of the paper [21]).

References

[1] A. Berretti, A. Del Bimbo, and E. Vicario. Modeling Spatial Relationships between Color Sets. In *Proceeding of IEEE Workshop on Content-based Access of Image and Video Libraries (CVPR-2000)*, June 2000.

Consistency Checking for Qualitative Spatial Reasoning   355

[2] W. G. Chinn and N. E. Steenrod. *First Concepts of Topology.* The Mathematical Association of America, 1966.

[3] E. Clementini, P. Di Fellice, and G. Califano. Composite Regions in Topological Queries. *Information Systems,* 7:759–594, 1995.

[4] E. Clementini, P. Di Fellice, and D. Hernandez. Qualitative Representation of Positional Information. *Artificial Intelligence,* 95:317–356, 1997.

[5] J. P. Delgrande, A. Gupta, and T. Van Allen. Point Based Approaches to Qualitative Temporal Reasoning. In *Proceedings of the AAAI-99,* pages 739–744, 1999.

[6] B. Faltings. Qualitative Spatial Reasoning Using Algebraic Topology. In *Proceedings of COSIT-95,* volume 988 of *LNCS,* 1995.

[7] A. U. Frank. Qualitative Spatial Reasoning about Distances and Directions in Geographic Space. *Journal of Visual Languages and Computing,* 3:343–371, 1992.

[8] C. Freksa. Using Orientation Information for Qualitative Spatial Reasoning. In *Proceedings of COSIT-92,* volume 639 of *LNCS,* pages 162–178, 1992.

[9] R. Goyal and M. J. Egenhofer. Cardinal Directions Between Extended Spatial Objects. *IEEE Transactions on Data and Knowledge Engineering,* (in press), 2000. Available at http://www.spatial.maine.edu/~max/RJ36.html.

[10] R. Goyal and M. J. Egenhofer. Consistent Queries over Cardinal Directions across Different Levels of Detail. In *Proceedings of the 11th International Workshop on Database and Expert Systems Applications,* 2000.

[11] G. Ligozat. Reasoning about Cardinal Directions. *Journal of Visual Languages and Computing,* 9:23–44, 1998.

[12] S. Lipschutz. *Set Theory and Related Topics.* McGraw Hill, 1998.

[13] A. Mukerjee and G. Joe. A Qualitative Model for Space. In *Proceedings of AAAI-90,* pages 721–727, 1990.

[14] D. Papadias. *Relation-Based Representation of Spatial Knowledge.* PhD thesis, Dept. of Electrical and Computer Engineering, National Technical University of Athens, 1994.

[15] D. Papadias, N. Arkoumanis, and N. Karacapilidis. On The Retrieval of Similar Configurations. In *Proceedings of 8th International Symposium on Spatial Data Handling (SDH),* 1998.

[16] C. H. Papadimitriou, D. Suciu, and V. Vianu. Topological Queries in Spatial Databases. *Journal of Computer and System Sciences,* 58(1):29–53, 1999.

[17] D. A. Randell, Z. Cui, and A. Cohn. A Spatial Logic Based on Regions and Connection. In *Proceedings of KR'92.* Morgan Kaufmann, October 1992.

[18] J. Renz and B. Nebel. On the Complexity of Qualitative Spatial Reasoning: A Maximal Tractable Fragment of the Region Connection Calculus. *Artificial Intelligence,* 1-2:95–149, 1999.

[19] A. P. Sistla, C. Yu, and R. Haddad. Reasoning About Spatial Relationships in Picture Retrieval Systems. In *Proceedings of VLDB-94,* pages 570–581, 1994.

[20] S. Skiadopoulos and M. Koubarakis. Composing Cardinal Directions Relations. In *Proceedings of the 7th International Symposium on Spatial and Temporal Databases (SSTD-01),* volume 2121 of *LNCS,* pages 299–317, July 2001.

[21] S. Skiadopoulos and M. Koubarakis. Qualitative Spatial Reasoning with Cardinal Directions: Semantics, Algorithms and Computational Complexity. Manuscript in preparation, 2002.

[22] P. van Beek. Reasoning About Qualitative Temporal Information. *Artificial Intelligence,* 58:297–326, 1992.

[23] M. Vilain, H. Kautz, and P. van Beek. Constraint Propagation Algorithms for Temporal Reasoning: A Revised Report. In *Readings in Qualitative Reasoning about Physical Systems,* pages 373–381. Morgan Kaufmann, 1989.

Open Constraint Satisfaction

Boi Faltings and Santiago Macho-Gonzalez

Artificial Intelligence Laboratory (LIA)
Swiss Federal Institute of Technology (EPFL)
IN-Ecublens, CH-1015 Ecublens, Switzerland
boi.faltings|santi.macho@epfl.ch
http://liawww.epfl.ch/

Abstract. Traditionally, constraint satisfaction has been applied in *closed-world* scenarios, where all choices and constraints are known from the beginning and fixed. With the Internet, many of the traditional CSP applications in resource allocation, scheduling and planning pose themselves in *open-world* settings, where choices and constraints are to be discovered from different servers in a network.

We examine how such a distributed setting affects changes the assumptions underlying most CSP algorithms, and show how solvers can be augmented with an information gathering component that allows open-world constraint satisfaction. We report on experiments that show strong performance of such methods over others where gathering information and solving the CSP are separated.

1 Constraint Satisfaction in Distributed Information Systems

Constraint satisfaction has been applied with great success to resource allocation, scheduling, planning and configuration. Traditionally, these problems are solved in a *closed-world* setting: first all variables, domains, constraints and relations are defined, then the CSP is solved by a search algorithm.

With the increasing use of the Internet, many of the problems that CSP techniques are good at now pose themselves in a distributed setting. For example, in personnel allocation, it is possible to obtain additional staff on short notice. In configuration, it is possible to locate additional suppliers of parts through the internet.

This change in setting makes a fundamental difference to the underlying constraint satisfaction problem. Most successful CSP methods, in particular constraint propagation, are based on the closed-world assumption that the domains of variables are completely known and fixed. In an open setting, this assumption no longer holds, making completeness and termination of search algorithms are more complex issue.

In an open world, there are also fundamental questions about the semantics of a CSP. When we combine options for a CSP from different sources, one might suspect that the right way to form the combination would be to form a CSP

P. Van Hentenryck (Ed.): CP 2002, LNCS 2470, pp. 356–370, 2002.
© Springer-Verlag Berlin Heidelberg 2002

whose solutions are the union of the solutions of the CSPs being combined. However, this would not make sense if we are trying to add options to make an unsolvable problem solvable.

Finally, the criteria for performance shift as each information gathering step is orders of magnitude more expensive than searching for solutions themselves. Consequently, good heuristics for information gathering are more important than efficient search heuristics.

In this paper, we define *Open Constraint Satisfaction Problems* (OCSP). We examine relevant related work in the CSP and database communities, and then propose solutions for two major issues: the semantics of combining CSP, and integrating information gathering and solving of OCSP. Finally, we report on some initial experiments that show the strong performance gains that OCSP bring over carrying out information gathering and CSP solving sequentially.

2   Open Constraint Satisfaction Problems

In this section, we define a formal framework for open constraint satisfaction problems.

We consider the setting shown in Figure 1 which reflects the important elements that occur in an open setting. The CSP solver can access an unbounded set of information servers through a mediator. The mediator is a directory that indexes the information that can be found on the information servers. Such directories already exist in unstructured form (Yahoo), and industry is working towards formal models based for example on the UDDI standard. For the purposes of our research, we consider that this technology implements a functionality whereby the CSP solver can obtain additional domain values:

- using the more(vi,...,(vi,vj),...) message, it can request the mediator to gather more values for these variables. The mediator will then contact randomly selected information servers. While servers are selected randomly, any server on the network will eventually be contacted.

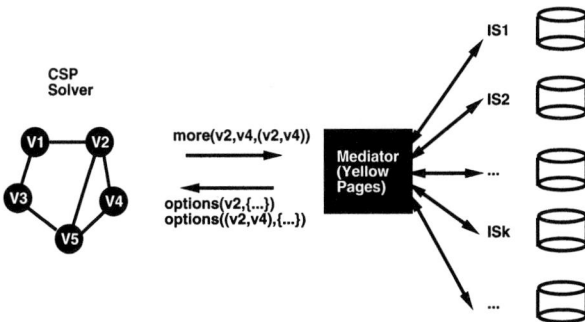

Fig. 1. Elements of an open constraint satisfaction problem

- using `options(vi,...)` and `options((vi,vj),...)` messages, the mediator informs the CSP solver of additional domain values or constraint tuples
  found in the network. This response will return what was found on the
  servers, so it may be empty or not contain any new values.
- when there are no more values to be found, the mediator returns
  `nomore(vi,...)` to inform the problem solver of this.

Note that as we assume an unbounded number of information sources, it
is not even possible to gather all information in a single database and then
start the problem-solving process, as has been implemented in many distributed
information systems ([1, 2, 4]).

We now define:

Definition 1. *An* open constraint satisfaction problem *(OCSP) is a possibly
unbounded, partially ordered set* $\{CSP(0), CSP(1), ...\}$ *of constraint satisfaction
problems, where CSP(i) is defined by a tuple* $< X, C, D(i), R(i) >$ *where*

- $X = \{x_1, x_2, ..., x_n\}$ *is a set of n variables,*
- $C = \{(x_i, x_j, ...), (x_k, x_l, ...), ...\}$ *is a set of m constraints, given by the ordered sets of variables they involve,*
- $D(i) = \{d_1(i), d_2(i), ..., d_n(i)\}$ *is the set of domains for CSP(i), with* $d_k(0) =
  \{\}$ *for all k.*
- $R(i) = \{r_1(i), r_2(i), ..., r_m(i)\}$ *is the set of relations for CSP(i), each giving the list of allowed tuples for the variables involved in the corresponding
  constraints, and satisfying* $r_k(0) = \{\}$ *for all k.*

The set is ordered by the relation $\prec$ *where* $CSP(i) \prec CSP(j)$ *if and only if* $(\forall k \in
[1..n])d_k(i) \subseteq d_k(j), (\forall k \in [1..m])r_k(i) \subseteq r_k(j),$ *and either* $(\exists k \in [1..n])d_k(i) \subset
d_k(j)$ *or* $(\exists k \in [1..m])r_k(i) \subset r_k(j).$

A solution *of an OCSP is a combination of value assignments to all variables
such that for some i, each value belongs to the corresponding domain and all value
combinations corresponding to constraints belong to the corresponding relations
of CSP(i).*

3   Related Work

Within the CSP community, the work that is closest to ours is *interactive constraint satisfaction* (ICSP), introduced in [5]. Similarly to our work, in ICSP
domains are acquired incrementally from external agents. The forward checking
algorithm is modified so that when domains become empty, it launches a specific
request for additional values that would satisfy the constraints on that variable.
In earlier work ([6]), the same authors also show how arc consistency algorithms
can be adapted with the right dependency structures so that consistency can be
adapted to values that might be added later. However, ICSP has a strong focus
on the efficiency of the CSP search algorithm rather than on minimzing information gathering; it typically gathers significantly more values than necessary. It
also does not address the problems of an open environment, in particular it limits

itself to finite domains and assumes that variable domains can be exhaustively retrieved from the information agents.

Open constraint satisfaction bears some ressemblance to the dynamic constraint satisfaction problem (DCSP), where constraints are added and removed over time. Bessiere ([7]) has shown methods for dynamically adapting consistency computations to such changes. However, dynamic CSP methods require that the set of all possible domain values is known beforehand, and thus do not apply to the OCSP problem. Another major difference is that OCSPs are restricted to a monotonic ordering of domains and values, while DCSP allow adding and removing variables in any order.

Another related area is distributed CSP(DisCSP), investigated in particular by Yokoo ([9]) and more recently also other researchers. DisCSP does not require agents to announce the complete variable domains beforehand, so by its formulation it would also allow them to be open. However, all known search algorithms for solving DisCSP rely on closed-world assumptions over variable domains for initiating backtracks. As DisCSP also require each variable to be controlled by a single agent, they also assume that all domain values are known and fixed by a single agent during the search, and so they do not address the context posed by OCSP either.

There has been some research into using constraints as a formalism for representing and integrating information, in particular the KRAFT project ([10]) and the FIPA CCL content language ([11]). These address in particular issues of how to represent constraints in languages such as XML so that it is easy to carry out composition. They will be important for practical implementations of OCSP.

Research in the database community has addressed issues of information gathering and information retrieval, starting with federated databases ([12]), then dynamic information integration ([13, 1]), and finally multi-agent information systems such as InfoSleuth ([2, 3]). Significant work has gone into matchmaking between queries and information sources. In our research, we use an ontology-based classification similar to that of [14]. There are significantly more complex matchmaking techniques such as the Information Manifold ([4]). Decker and Sycara ([15]) investigate the efficiency of middle-agent systems, and Sycara ([16]) elaborates on their use as information agents. Techniques such as LARKS ([17]) show that much more complex classification than simply ontologies are possible. Thus, there is a sufficient technology base for implementing the mediator functionality we assume in this paper.

Recently, researchers in information retrieval have paid more attention to driving information retrieval from the task that users are trying to solve. Systems such as Watson and I2I ([18]) and just-in-time information retrieval ([19]) automatically retrieve information from databases, mail archives and other information sources by matching it with keywords that occur in the current activity of the user - for example, a document being prepared.

4   Using CSP for Information Integration

Solving OCSP implies that CSPs from different sources must be integrated. We assume that the mediator performs the necessary translations so that it returns additional options as domains and relations of a CSP whose variables and constraints are compatible with those of the problem being solved.

There are two different ways that the new domains and relations might be integrated:

- *conjunctive combination*, meaning that the new information represents additional constraints that any solution must satisfy. This occurs for example when we want to schedule a meeting between many participants and need to integrate all their time constraints.
- *disjunctive combination*, meaning that the new information represents additional options and thus enables additional solutions. This occurs for example when a problem-solver obtains schedule information for the same route from different airlines.

Conjunctive combination is a common case in constraint satisfaction algorithms and handled simply by having all relations present simultaneously. Dynamically adding and removing constraints using conjunctive combination has been addressed for example in dynamic constraint satisfaction ([8, 7]). For solving OCSP, we particularly need *disjunctive* combination, which so far has not received much attention in the CSP community (but see [10, 11]).

CSP formulations have commonly been compared through the solutions they admit ([20]). This works well for conjunctive combination, where the solutions of the combined problem is the intersection of the solutions of the components, but is too restrictive for disjunctive combination: when we are looking for additional options to make a scheduling or configuration problem solvable, we are often combining subproblems that have no solutions to obtain a problem that has solutions.

Thus, in accordance with the definition of OCSP, we define the disjunctive combination of two CSP as follows:

Definition 2. *The* disjunctive combination *of $CSP1 = <X_1, D^1, C_1, R^1>$ and $CSP2 = <X_2, D^2, C_2, R^2>$ is $CSP3 = <X_3, D^3, C_3, R^3>$ where*

- $X_3 = X_1 \cup X_2$
- $D^3 = \{d_j^1 | x_j \in X_1 \wedge x_j \notin X_2\} \cup \{d_j^2 | x_j \in X_2 \wedge x_j \notin X_1\} \cup \{d_j^1 \cup d_j^2 | x_j \in X_1 \cap X_2\}$
- $C_3 = C_1 \cup C_2$
- $R^3 = \{r_j^1 | c_j \in C_1 \wedge c_j \notin C_2\} \cup \{r_j^2 | c_j \in C_2 \wedge c_j \notin C_1\} \cup \{r_j^1 \cup r_j^2 | c_j \in C_1 \cap C_2\}$

The difficulty with disjunctive combination is that it is incompatible with the pruning and constraint propagation techniques that have been fundamental to most constraint satisfaction algorithms, and requires additional restrictions on the model in order to give the desired results. The example in Figure 2 illustrates the difficulties.

CSP1

CSP2

CSP3

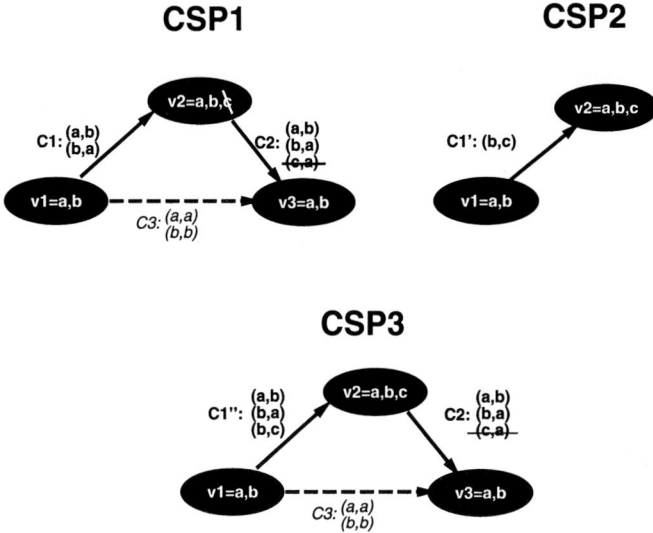

Fig. 2. Possible problems with disjunctive combination of two CSP

In CSP1, we can use constraint propagation to prune values c from variable $x2$ and then tuple (c, a) from constraint $c2$. When we later combine with CSP2, we do not obtain any additional solutions. But if we had combined with CSP1 without pruning, we would have also obtained the solution $x1 = b, v2 = c, v3 = a$. The problem here is that pruning relies on a closed-world assumption: it does not eliminate valid solutions, but only under the condition no additional options are added. While it is easy to recognize this situation when solving a CSP, we have to avoid cases where pruning has already been incorporated in the constraint model. In order to characterize this property, we define:

Definition 3. *A CSP is* redundantly expressed *if it contains a relation or domain whose validity depends on other relations or domains in the CSP.*

A constraint model can also pose problems in the other direction. Consider that CSP1 might have originally had an additional constraint C3. In the database model, this constraint could have been removed as being redundant: it already follows from C1 and C2. When we now combine with CSP2, we would also obtain the new solution $x1 = b, v2 = c, v3 = a$, which would violate the original constraint C3. To avoid this situation, we define:

Definition 4. : *A CSP is* completely expressed *if and only if for any pair of variables x and y and any pair of values x = a and y = b allowed by the constraint (if any) between them, there is a way to change the rest of the CSP so that they become part of a valid solution.*

In order to be composable, CSP models have to be exactly expressed:

Definition 5. *A CSP is* exactly expressed *if and only if it is completely but not redundantly expressed.*

as is shown by the following Theorem:

Theorem 1. *The disjunctive combination of two exactly expressed CSPs is itself exactly expressed.*

Proof. Disjunctive combination does not involve constraint propagation nor elimination of redundancies, so it does not affect the property of being correctly expressed.

This defines a restriction that the CSPs provided by the mediator as well as the CSP representations maintained while solving an OCSP must satisfy. Unfortunately, it turns out that this condition rules out the use of many interesting constraint propagation and preprocessing techniques. However, we will now see that there are other techniques that can be applied.

5   Algorithms for Solving OCSP

We now consider algorithms for actually solving OCSP. The simplest algorithm is the brute-force algorithm: first collect all values from all information sources, and then run an efficient CSP solver to generate a solution to the problem. However, this can be very costly: imagine contacting all PC part manufacturers to figure out how to fix your video card!

It is clearly preferable to only gather information as needed, as shown by function **o-search**(Algorithm 1). If there is a solution within the values available

---

Function **o-search**(CSP)
$s \leftarrow$ **solve**(CSP)
if $s \neq \{\}$ then
    return s as a solution
$CSP_{incr} \leftarrow$ **more**$(X \cup C)$
if **nomore**$(X \cup C)$ then
    return failure
$CSP_{new} \leftarrow$ disjunctive combination of CSP and CSP_{incr}
o-search(CSP_{new})

Algorithm 1: o-search: an incremental algorithm for solving OCSP

---

from the servers, this algorithm will eventually find it, since the mediator will eventually return every value or value combination that the servers can provide. However, it is not very efficient, since it blindly gathers values for any part of the CSP without focussing on those parts that caused the failure.

To reduce the amount of useless server accesses, information gathering must focus on finding additional options for the minimal unsolvable subproblems of the current instantiation of the CSP. Thus, we now show how to improve Algorithm 1 by identifying variables that participate in minimal unsolvable subproblems and gathering values for these individual variables. We then show that the resulting algorithm is complete, and how it can be generalized to the case where values for entire subproblems can be obtained from the information servers.

5.1   Integrating Search and Information Gathering

In order to simplify the algorithms, we make the assumption that all domains of the OCSP are discrete, and that furthermore all constraints (including binary ones) have been encoded using the *hidden variable encoding* ([20, 21]). In this encoding, all constraints are represented as additional variables with tuple-valued domains representing the corresponding relations. The only remaining constraints are then equality constraints that ensure consistency between assignments to the original variables and the corresponding elements of the constraint tuples. Besides the fact that the hidden variable encoding has been shown to have desirable computational properties ([22]), it simplifies the OCSP formulation since now all constraints are fixed, and information gathering only concerns variable domains.

When a CSP has no solution, it is often the case that it contains a smaller subproblem that already has no solution. It will not be possible to create a solution by information gathering unless values are added to variables and relations of that subproblem. This fact can be used to more effectively drive information gathering. The idea is to find a variable that must be part of an unsolvable subproblem as a promising candidate for adding extra values. To develop this into a general and complete algorithm, we need to address two issues: how to identify unsolvable subproblems, and how to select all variables in turn to avoid unbounded information accesses while missing a feasible solution.

The following lemma provides the basis for identifying variables that are part of unsolvable subproblems:

Lemma 1. *Let a CSP be explored by a failed backtrack search algorithm with static variable ordering $(x_1, ..., x_n)$, and let x_k be the deepest node reached in the search with inconsistency detected at x_k. Then x_k, called the* failed variable, *is part of every unsolvable subproblem of the CSP involving variables in the set $\{x_1..x_k\}$.*

Proof. In order to reach x_k, the search algorithm has constructed at least one valid assignment to $x_1, ..., x_{k-1}$, so this set of variables does not contain any unsolvable subproblem. However, there is no consistent assignment to $x_1, ..., x_k$, so this set does contain unsolvable subproblem(s). Since the only difference is x_k, x_k must be part of all of these unsolvable subproblems.   □

On the basis of this proposition, we can use the results of a failed CSP search process to determine for which variable additional values should be collected. These are then passed to the mediator, which will search for relevant information on the network. When there are no additional values for this variable, the mediator returns a `nomore` message, and other variables are then considered. The resulting algorithm **fo-search** (failure-driven open search) is shown in Algorithm 2.

1: Function **fo-search**(X,D,C,R,E)
2: $i \leftarrow 1, k \leftarrow 1$
3: **repeat** {backtrack search}
4:    **if** $exhausted(d_i)$ **then** {backtrack}
5:        $i \leftarrow i - 1, reset - values(d_i)$
6:    **else**
7:        $k \leftarrow max(k, i), x_i \leftarrow nextvalue(d_i)$
8:        **if** $consistent(\{x_1, ..., x_i\})$ **then** {extend assignment}
9:            $i \leftarrow i + 1$
10:        **if** $i > n$ **then**
11:            **return** $\{x_1, ..., x_n\}$ as a solution
12: **until** $i = 0$
13: **if** $e_k = closed$ **then**
14:    **if** $(\forall i \in 1..k - 1)e_k = closed$ **then**
15:        **return failure**
16: **else**
17:    $nv \leftarrow \textbf{more}(x_k)$
18:    **if** $nv = \textbf{nomore}(x_k)$ **then**
19:        $e_k \leftarrow closed$
20:    $d_k \leftarrow nv \cup d_k$
21: reorder variables so that x_k becomes x_1
22: **fo-search**(X,D,C,R,E) {search again}

Algorithm 2: Function **fo-search** for solving OCSP

Algorithm 2 makes the assumption that variables are ordered by the index i. It assumes that no consistency techniques are used in the search, although the chronological backtracking can be replaced with backjumping techniques to make it more efficient.

We are now going to show that **fo-search** is a complete algorithm for solving OCSP. We start by defining:

Definition 6. *An* unsolvable subproblem *of size* k *of an instance* $CSP(i)$ *of an OCSP is a set of variables* $S = \{x_{s1}, x_{s2}, ..., x_{sk}\}$ *such that there is no value assignment* $(x_{s1} \in d_{s1}, ..., x_{sk} \in d_{sk})$ *that satisfies all constraints between these variables.*

and showing the following property:

Lemma 2. *Let* $S = \{S_1, ..., S_m\}$ *bet the set of unsolvable subproblems of instance* $CSP(i)$ *of an OCSP. Then for any instance* $CSP(j), CSP(j) \succ CSP(i)$, *the set of unsolvable subproblems* S' *it contains is a subset of* S.

Proof. Suppose that $CSP(j)$ contains a subproblem $S' \notin S$, and let $S' = \{x_{t1}, ..., xtk\}$. By Definition 1, the domains $d_{t1}(i) \subseteq d_{t1}(j), ..., d_{tk}(i) \subseteq d_{tk}(j)$.

S' is solvable in $CSP(i)$, and the values used in its solution must also be part of the corresponding domains for $CSP(j)$. Thus, S' cannot be unsolvable in $CSP(j)$.   □

This Lemma shows that the set of unsolvable subproblems in successive instances of an OCSP is monotonically non-increasing.

We now consider more closely Algorithm 2, and in particular the sequence of instances it solves in subsequent iterations. We have the following lemma:

Lemma 3. *Assume that the last $k+1$ calls to Algorithm 2 have been with instances $CSP(i_0), ..., CSP(i_k)$, that the algorithm has last searched variables in the order $x_{j1}, ..., x_{jk}$ and identified the k-th variable x_{jk} as the failed variable, and that the each of the instances $CSP(i_0), ..., CSP(i_k)$ has identical unsolvable subproblems. Then:*

- *in the last k calls, Algorithm 2 has called the mediator (function **more**) exactly once for each of the variables $x_{j1}, ..., x_{jk}$;*
- *$S = \{x_{j1}, ..., x_{jk}\}$ is a minimal unsolvable subproblem of $CSP(i_k)$;*
- *the algorithm will continue to call **more** on each of the variables in S in turn until S becomes solvable.*

Proof. As the algorithm always puts the variable for which it has called more values as the first in the search, the first claim follows directly from the function of the algorithm.

Furthermore, S is unsolvable as no solution could be found by complete search. Suppose that it was not minimal, i.e. that there was a variable x_{il} such that $S' = S - x_{il}$ was also unsolvable. x_{il} was the failed variable when **fo-search** was run on $CSP(i_l)$, and that search must have included variable x_k. By Lemma 1, x_{il} was part of every unsolvable subproblem of $CSP(i_l)$ that also involves x_{ik}. But as x_{ik} is the failed variable of subproblem S, by Lemma 1, it is part of every unsolvable subproblem involving variables in S. Consequently, every unsolvable subproblem within S must also involve x_{il}.

The third claim follows from the fact that as long as S is unsolvable, running **fo-search** on $CSP(i_k)$ gives an identical result as running it on $CSP(i_0)$.   □

We can now show completeness of Algorithm 2:

Theorem 2. *Supposed that OCSP is solvable, i.e. by calling **more** on every variable a sufficient number of times we eventually reach an instance $CSP(j)$ such that for all $CSP(m) \succ CSP(j)$, $CSP(m)$ contains no unsolvable subproblems. Then Algorithm 2 will eventually terminate with a solution. Thus, the algorithm is complete.*

Proof. $CSP(1)$ has finitely many variables and thus finitely many unsolvable subproblems of size at most n. Assume that the algorithm never finds a solution; then since by Lemma 2, the set of unsolvable subproblems is monotonically non-increasing, there must exist an infinite sequence of calls to **fo-search** such that the unsolvable subproblems are always identical. By Lemma 3, in such a sequence the algorithm will eventually call for additional values for each variable of the same unsolvable subproblem S. But since the OCSP is solvable, these calls must eventually return values that will make S solvable. Thus, the sequence of calls where subproblems remain unsolvable cannot be infinite.   □

An interesting consequence of Theorem 2 is that if a problem is unsolvable and the set of available values is finite, the algorithm will stop while identifying a minimal unsolvable subproblem. This can be useful when it is possible to obtain information for several variables in parallel.

For efficiency reasons, it may be advantageous for the mediator to obtain values not only for single variables, but entire subproblems with a single query. Algorithm 2 can be modified for this case in two ways:

- it can not gather additional values until a minimal unsolvable subproblem is completely identified, and then call the mediator on that subproblem or subproblems that have a maximal overlap with that subproblem. However, it is important that every variable in the subproblem is eventually queried, for otherwise completeness is no longer ensured.
- it can gather additional values for all subproblems that include the last failed variable. This would preserve completeness of the algorithm, but may be less efficient than focussing search on the minimal unsolvable subproblem itself.

In all cases, it is important that the problem formulation used by the information servers is by CSP that are exactly expressed so that composition will produce correct results.

5.2   Efficiently Integrating New Values

Once additional values have been obtained, the search algorithm can be restarted to see if the problem now has a solution. We would of course like this search to avoid reexploring the search space that had already been explored unsuccessfully earlier. The most obvious solution, reusing the nogoods observed from the earlier search, is not practical since these nogoods may be invalidated by the new values.

The technique of decomposing a CSP into subproblems proposed by Freuder and Hubbe in [24] turns out to be useful here. They proposed to decompose a CSP to factor out unsolvable subproblems, thus limiting search effort to a smaller and solvable part. This idea applies well to OCSP: the new, combined problem can be decomposed into the old problem just searched (which is known to be unsolvable) and a new one based on the values just obtained. However, if we limit subsequent searches only to the newly found values for x_i, we loose the benefit of Lemma 1 and the algorithm is no longer complete. We can nevertheless use the subproblem decomposition to make algorithms more efficient by ordering the values so that the new values are explored first. In this way, the algorithm starts search with the new subproblem, and only revisits earlier assignments when this subproblem has been found to have no solution.

6   Experimental Results

We tested the performance of the techniques we described on synthetic, randomly generated constraint satisfaction problems. As an example, we used resource allocation (equivalent to list coloring), which can be modelled as a CSP whose variable domains are resources and whose constraints are all inequalities (expressing the fact that the same resources cannot be used for different tasks at the same time).

Comparison metrics We compare the algorithms on two aspects. The first is the number of accesses to information sources required to find a solution to the OCSP, and measure the network traffic generated. Several metrics have been developed in the field of database selection ([25]). Since each variable must have at least one value, solving the CSP requires at least one information source access per variable, and this is the theoretical optimum. We measure performance by the ratio:

$$R = \frac{Number\ of\ variables\ of\ the\ CSP}{Number\ of\ access\ to\ IS\ until\ a\ solution\ is\ found}$$

Since each variable must have at least one value, solving the CSP requires at least one information source access per variable, so that the ideal value for R is 1. Smaller values of R mean low efficiency. We consider R a good measure of the relative amount of information gathering effort generated by the different methods, but it does not take into account possible parallization or buffering.

Experiments and results The experiments followed the following steps:

1. Generate a random coloring problem, with between 3 to 10 variables, 3 to 13 values per variable, and random inequality constraints so that the graph is at least connected and at most complete.
2. Distribute the values of the variables in a fixed set of n information sources. The results reported here are for 12 information sources, but do not change substantially when the number of sources is increased or decreased.
3. Use different algorithms to find the first solution to the problem, and measure the efficiency ratio described above.

We compare the performance of different combinations of algorithms in the mediator and the problem solver. For the mediator, we consider the following algorithms:

- *Brute Force:* gather all values from all relevant information sources into a single database, then search for a solution with these values.
- *Random:* The mediator considers only information sources indexed under the given property and concept, and treats them in random order.
- *Size:* The mediator considers the same information sources as above, but in decreasing order of the number of values they carry for the different properties.

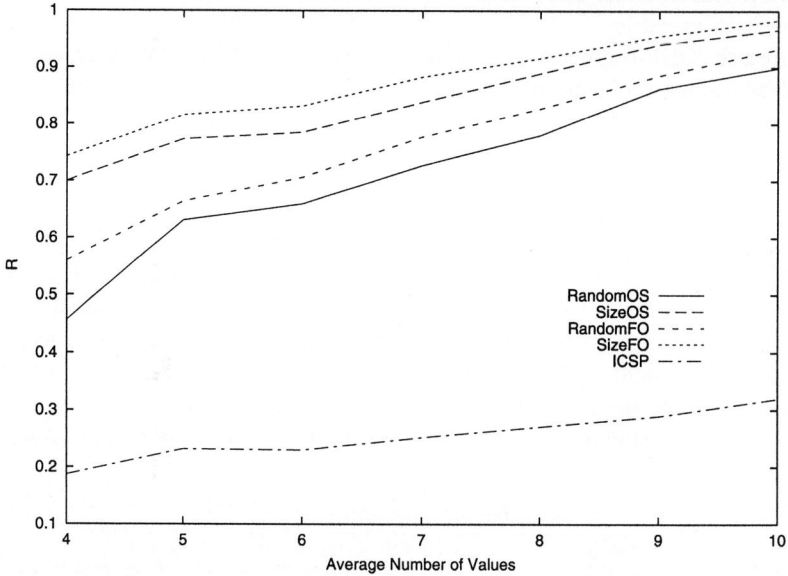

Fig. 3. Efficiency ratio against number of values for several combination of search/mediator algorithms

For the problem solver, we consider the two algorithms given earlier, namely **OS** for `o-search`, obtaining new values for variables randomly, and **FO** for `fo-search`, where search for new values is driven by the failures of backtrack search. Furthermore, we also compare the algorithms with interactive CSP ([5]).

Figure 3 plots the efficiency ratio against the average number of values available for each variable for a setting in which there are a total of 12 information servers. The more values there are for each variable, the easier the problem is to solve, and we can see that the average efficiency in general increases with the number of available values. On the other hand, efficiency can be observed to decrease slightly with the size of the problem. We have not observed any significant dependency of information server accesses on constraint density.

When problem-solving and information gathering are not coupled at all, problem-solving would require accessing all the servers, resulting in an efficiency ratio of 12; this curve is not shown in the graph in Figure 3. Thus, the idea of coupling the two processes definitely provides very large efficiency improvements.

We can also observe a significant improvement over interactive constraint satisfaction as described in [5], which is natural as this algorithm does not provide a method for choosing a variable and preselecting values by constraints is not feasible in an open environment.

The best method is, as expected, a combination of failure-driven open search combined with an indexing of the database on size; this gives an efficiency approaching the theoretical optimum. It appears furthermore that information about the size of information servers plays a bigger role than directing the search for the right variable, as the next runner-up is the algorithm combining size with open-search (OS). In practice, this information is very difficult to provide, so that the improvements obtained by the CSP search algorithm are of great pratical interest.

7 Conclusions

Many new and exciting applications in open information systems, in particular the WWW, address problems which CSP techniques are very good at solving. Such applications will appear increasingly with the emergence of web services and the semantic web. We have defined Open Constraint Satisfaction Problems (OCSP) as a formulation that addresses this open setting.

The first contribution of this paper is the definition of semantic properties that allow incrementally combining values in an OCSP while maintaining a correct solution set. These result in conditions that the problem formulations must satisfy in order to be combinable.

The second contribution is to have shown an effective method for identifying minimal unsolvable subproblems and thus focussing information gathering. Based on this, we have given an algorithm that is provably complete even for unbounded variable domains, and demonstrated that on random coloring problems, it achieves a performance very close to the theoretical minimum as far as accesses to information servers is concerned.

In particular, the gains tend to increase with both the number of information servers and the number of values they provide. Thus, the technique is likely to be particularly useful to improve the scalability of intelligent information systems based on constraint satisfaction techniques.

References

[1] Genesereth, M. R., Keller, A. M., Duschka, O.: "Infomaster: An Information Integration System", Proceedings of 1997 ACM SIGMOD Conference, May 1997.

[2] Marian Nodine, Jerry Fowler, Tomasz Ksiezyk, Brad Perry, Malcolm Taylor and Amy Unruh: Active Information Gathering in InfoSleuth In International Journal of Cooperative Information Systems 9:1/2, 2000, pp. 3-28.

[3] Jerry Fowler, Brad Perry, Marian Nodine, and Bruce Bargmeyer: Agent-Based Semantic Interoperability in InfoSleuth SIGMOD Record 28:1, March, 1999, pp. 60-67.

[4] Alon Y. Levy , Anand Rajaraman , Joann J. Ordille: "Querying Heterogeneous Information Sources Using Source Descriptions," *Proceedings of the 22nd VLDB Conference*, Bombay, India, 1996.

[5] Rita Cucchiara, Marco Gavanelli, Evelina Lamma, Paola Mello, Michela Milano, and Massimo Piccardi: "Constraint propagation and value acquisition: why we should do it interactively," *Proceedings of the 16th IJCAI*, Morgan Kaufmann, pp.468-477, 1999.

[6] R. Cucchiara, E. Lamma, P. Mello, M. Milano: "Interactive Constraint Satisfaction,", Technical Report DEIS-LIA-97-00, University of Bologna, 1997.

[7] Christian Bessière: "Arc-Consistency in Dynamic Constraint Satisfaction Problems," *Proceedings of the 9th National Conference of the AAAI*, pp. 221-226, 1991.

[8] Sanjay Mittal and Brian Falkenhainer: "Dynamic constraint satisfaction problems," *Proceedings of the 8th National Conference of the AAAI*, pp. 25-32, 1990.

[9] Makoto Yokoo: "Asynchronous Weak-commitment Search for Solving Large-Scale Distributed Constraint Satisfaction Problems," *Proceedings of the First International Conference on Multi–Agent Systems*, p. 467, MIT Press, 1995.

[10] Peter M.D. Gray, Suzanne M. Embury, Kit Y. Hui, Graham J.L. Kemp: "The Evolving Role of Constraints in the Functional Data Model", *Journal of Intelligent Information Systems* **12**, pp. 113-137, 1999.

[11] Monique Calisti, Boi Faltings, Santiago Macho-Gonzalez, Omar Belakhdar and Marc Torrens: "CCL: Expressions of Choice in Agent Communication," *Fourth International Conference on MultiAgent Systems (ICMAS-2000)*, Boston MA, USA., July, 2000.

[12] A. Sheth and J.A. Larson: "Federated Database Systems," *ACM Computing Surveys* **22**(3), 1990.

[13] S. Chawathe, H. Garcia Molina, J. Hammer, K.Ireland, Y. Papakostantinou, J. Ullman and J. Widom: The TSIMMIS project: Integration of heterogeneous information sources. In *IPSJ Conference*, Tokyo, Japan, 1994.

[14] José Luis Ambite and Craig Knoblock: "Flexible and scalable cost-based query planning in mediators: A transformational approach," *Artificial Intelligence* **118**, pp. 115-161, 2000.

[15] Keith Decker, Katia Sycara and Mike Williamson: "Middle-Agents for the Internet," *Proceedings of the 15th International Joint Conference on Artificial Intelligence (IJCAI-97)*, Morgan Kaufmann, 1997, pp. 578-583.

[16] Sycara, K. "In-Context Information Management Through Adaptive Collaboration of Intelligent Agents." In Intelligent Information Agents: Cooperative, Rational and Adaptive Information Gathering on the Internet. Matthias Klusch (Ed.), Springer Verlag, 1999.

[17] Katia Sycara, Seth Widoff, Matthias Klusch and Jianguo Lu: "LARKS: Dynamic Matchmaking Among Heterogeneous Software Agents in Cyberspace." Autonomous Agents and Multi-Agent Systems, 5, 173-203, 2002.

[18] J. Budzik, S. Bradshaw, X. Fu, and K. Hammond: "Supporting Online Resource Discovery in the Context of Ongoing Tasks with Proactive Assistants," *International Journal of Human-Computer Studies* **56**(1) Jan 2002, pp. 47-74.

[19] B.J. Rhodes and P. Maes: "Just-in-time information retrieval agents," *IBM Systems Journal* **39**, pp. 685-704, 2000.

[20] F. Rossi, C. Petrie and V. Dhar: "On the equivalence of constraint satisfaction problems," *Proceedings of ECAI-90*, pp. 550-556, 1990.

[21] K. Stergiou and T. Walsh: "Encodings of Non-binary Constraint Satisfaction Problems," *Proceedings of AAAI-99*, ppp. 163-168, AAAI Press, 1999.

[22] N. Mamoulis and K. Stergiou: "Solving Non-binary CSPs Using the Hidden Variable Encoding," *Procceedings of CP 2001*, LNCS 2239, Springer-Verlag, pp. 168-182, 2001.

[23] P. Prosser: "Hybrid Algorithms for Constraint Satisfaction Problems," *Computational Intellligence* **9**(3), pp. 268-299, 1993.

[24] Eugene Freuder and Paul Hubbe: "Extracting Constraint Satisfaction Subproblems," *Proceedings of the 14th International Joint Conference on Artificial Intelligence*, pp. 548-555, 1995.

[25] James C. Freanch and Allison L. Powell :Metrics for Evaluating Database Selection Techniques. 2000.

Beyond NP:
Arc-Consistency for Quantified Constraints

Lucas Bordeaux and Eric Monfroy

Institut de Recherche en Informatique de Nantes (IRIN), France
{bordeaux,monfroy}@irin.univ-nantes.fr

Abstract. The generalization of the satisfiability problem with arbitrary quantifiers is a challenging problem of both theoretical and practical relevance. Being PSPACE-complete, it provides a canonical model for solving other PSPACE tasks which naturally arise in AI.

Effective SAT-based solvers have been designed very recently for the special case of *boolean* constraints. We propose to consider the more general problem where constraints are arbitrary relations over finite domains. Adopting the viewpoint of *constraint-propagation* techniques so successful for CSPs, we provide a theoretical study of this problem. Our main result is to propose *quantified arc-consistency* as a natural extension of the classical CSP notion.

1 Introduction

Many problems arising in Artificial Intelligence or engineering can be modelled as *Constraint Satisfaction Problems* (CSPs), but some are beyond the scope of the usual, existentially quantified satisfiability framework. For instance, a typical problem in game algorithms is to find a winning strategy for a two-player game. Intuitively, the question a player would like answered at any moment is stated as follows:

> Does there exist a move, *s.t.*
>> for any move of the opponent,
>>> there exists a move *s.t.* for any move ...   I win?

This problem can be modelled as a logical formula with alternating quantifiers of the form $\exists x_1 \forall x_2 \exists x_3 \ldots winning(x_1, \ldots, x_n)$, where predicate *winning* is a boolean formula which encodes the rules of the game, and number n bounds the number of moves of the game. Such a problem, where some constraints relate arbitrarily quantified variables ranging over finite domains, shall be referred to as a *Quantified Constraint Problem* (QCP)[1].

The truth value of a QCP can be determined by a straightforward generalization of backtracking. This algorithm runs in polynomial space, but the central question is to prune its computation tree to avoid exponential runtimes.

---

[1] As for CSPs, this name shall be used both for particular instances ("a QCP") and for the general decision problem (*"the* QCP").

P. Van Hentenryck (Ed.): CP 2002, LNCS 2470, pp. 371–386, 2002.

The connections between the QCP and Polynomial-Space are not fortuitous since this problem is indeed complete for PSPACE, a complexity class which contains NP and is a subset of Exponential Time[2] [20, 16]. PSPACE is the natural class for some important problems in AI, some instances being STRIPS-planning search on state graphs [3], as well as many games [19]. Heuristics have been proposed for some of these problems (*e.g.,* A* for graph-search), but the QCP plays a central role. Just as constraint-satisfaction is a good prototypical problem to design algorithms for NP, the QCP is a natural representative of PSPACE (see [11] for recent applications which use a direct encoding of some PSPACE problems as QCPs).

Despite their potential applications, quantified constraints have remained objects of purely theoretical interest for years, and it is only very recently that solvers have been implemented to solve *Quantified Boolean Formulae* (QBF). All of the algorithms we are aware of either rely on or generalize SAT algorithms, such as resolution [5], Davis-Putnam and DLL [7, 18], or backtracking and improvements we do not cite all recent related publications).

In this paper, we propose to study the general problem of quantified constraints over arbitrary finite domains, of which the boolean case is a particular instance. We attempt to apply to this problem some of the tools which have proved successful for CSPs, most notably the notions of *local consistency*. Our main contribution is to propose a notion of *quantified arc consistency*, which generalizes the usual CSP notion. Stronger notions of consistency are also suggested; hence arbitrary levels of filtering can be obtained, at the cost of a higher, but polynomial complexity.

The paper attempts to give a complete overview of the approach and of its similarities and differences with the usual CSP framework. The concepts introduced are exemplified on two classes of problems: Quantified Boolean Formulae, and a class of quantified numerical constraints for which we know of no other published algorithm.

Outline

A presentation of the basic logical material and of the problem considered is given in the next section (2). Section 3 discusses notions of local consistency which are adapted from CSPs. The purpose of local consistency is to define *filtering methods*, on which further details are given in Section 4, and which are exemplified on boolean and numerical domains. Section 5 briefly discusses issues regarding the search algorithm. Section 6 provides additional discussions, and next comes the conclusion (7).

An Illustration of Our Approach

To give a taste of our approach, consider the (rather simple) logical statement $\exists x \in [1..100] \; \forall y \in [1..100] \; (x + y \leq 101)$, which is obviously *true*.

---

[2] These two inclusions are strongly suspected, but not proved, to be strict.

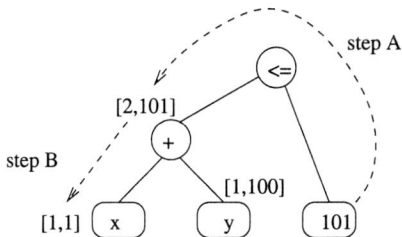

Fig. 1. An example of quantified (interval) propagation

Constraint propagation works in two steps in this example (see Fig 1). In Step A, it deduces from the inequality that the value of the sum must range over the interval $[2, 101]$ — note that this is similar to usual interval propagation. In Step B, it directly deduces that variable x must take value 1.

To propagate information over arbitrary nodes of a quantified expression, one needs to introduce variables using techniques described in Section 2.2. In our example, the statement is "decomposed" into the equivalent one: $\exists x \in [1..100] \ \forall y \in [1..100] \ \exists sum \ (x + y = sum \wedge sum \leq 101)$. The deductions exemplified here are performed locally to each of the "primitive" constraints $\exists x \in [1..100] \ \forall y \in [1..100] \ \exists sum \ (x + y = sum)$ and $\exists sum \ (sum \leq 101)$. The general framework is introduced in Section 3, where the correctness of these local deductions is proved. The use of intervals is just an instance of the framework, which is briefly described in Section 4.3.

2   Logical Basics

A *variable* $(x, y, \ldots,$ possibly subscripted) is an object with an associated finite *domain* D_x, which represents the set of values that the variable may take. A *constraint* C over variables $x_1, \ldots, x_n$ (also noted $C(x_1, \ldots, x_n)$) is a n-ary relation which specifies the combinations of values that these variables may take. A constraint can hence be seen as a *table* of allowed tuples, which is supposed to be easy to compute, and short enough to be explicitly stored.

Definition 1. [QCP] *A* Quantified Constraint Problem *is a statement of the form:*

$$Q_1 x_1 \ldots Q_n x_n \ (C_1, \ldots, C_m)$$

where the Q_is denote quantifiers ($\forall$ or $\exists$) and each C_i is a constraint relating some variables among $x_1, \ldots, x_n$.

Assumption 1. *For the sake of simplicity, we consider only "well-formed" QCPs with no free variable, and where each variable is quantified only once.*

In the list of constraints, commas should be understood as *conjunctions*. We shall often shorten the notation $Q_1 x_1 \ldots Q_n x_n \ (C_1, \ldots, C_m)$ to $Q^\star(C)$, where $Q^\star$ denotes the sequence of quantifiers and C denotes the set of constraints. When the domains need be explicitly stated, we use bounded quantifiers of the form $Qx \in D_x$. Note the restriction to *prenex* formulae, with all quantifiers "on the left" (more general formulae are easily transformed into prenex ones).

2.1   Truth and Falsity

To model the assignment of value $v \in \mathcal{D}$ to variable x, the *selection* $\sigma_{x=v}(C_i)$ (where C_i is a constraint) is the constraint obtained from C_i when keeping only the tuples with value v on x. Given a set of constraints $C = C_1, \ldots, C_m$, we define $\sigma_{x=v}(C)$ as a shorthand for the conjunction $\sigma_{x=v}(C_1), \ldots, \sigma_{x=v}(C_m)$.

The notion of *truth* has a straightforward meaning, but a convenient tool to reason on quantified constraints and to simplify proofs is the following:

Definition 2. [Expanded expression] *The* expanded expression *of a QCP is defined inductively as follows:*

1. *The expanded expression of a quantifier-free QCP is the QCP itself (due to assumption 1, note that it is fully instantiated);*
2. *The expanded expression of* $\forall x \in \{v_1 \ldots v_d\}\ Q^\star(C)$ *is the conjunction of the expanded expressions for* $Q^\star \sigma_{x=v_1}(C),\ \ldots,\ Q^\star \sigma_{x=v_d}(C);$
3. *The expanded expression of* $\exists x \in \{v_1 \ldots v_d\}\ Q^\star(C)$ *is the disjunction of the expanded expressions for* $Q^\star \sigma_{x=v_1}(C),\ \ldots,\ Q^\star \sigma_{x=v_d}(C).$

Example 1. The expanded expression of $\forall x \in \{1,3\}\ \exists y \in \{1,3\}\ (x+y=4)$ is $((1+1=4 \vee 1+3=4) \wedge (3+1=4 \vee 3+3=4))$, which evaluates to *true*.

Clearly, the expanded expression determines the truth of the QCP. Expanded expressions are naturally seen as trees, hence we sometimes talk about their *nodes* and *leaves* (see Fig. 2). Despite their exponential size, it is clear that these

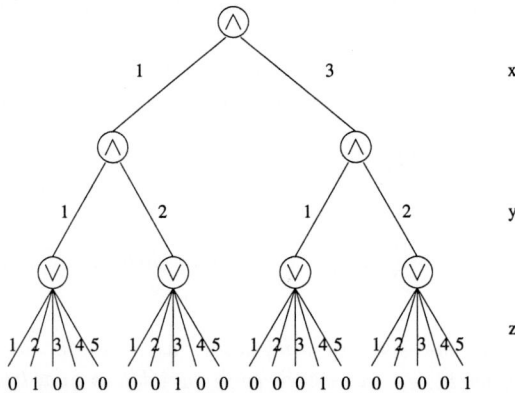

Fig. 2. The expanded expression for $\forall x \in \{1,3\}\ \forall y \in \{1,2\}\ \exists z \in \{1,2,3,4,5\}\ (x+y=z)$, represented as a tree (we have replaced the expressions at the leaves by their values)

expanded trees can be explored by a recursive algorithm which is a generalization of search with both $\wedge$ and $\vee$ nodes, and which works in space linear in the number of variables. PSPACE-completeness follows from the fact that Quantified Boolean Formulae are a special case of QCPs (see next subsection) which is complete [20, 16].

We call two QCPs *equivalent* if their truth is the same. As a straightforward equivalence-preserving transformation, note that a quantifier bounding a variable which is not constrained can be removed (for instance $\forall x \forall y \exists z \ (x + z = 2)$ is equivalent to $\forall x \exists z (x+z = 2)$). In particular, the quantifier for x can be removed from the sequence $Q^\star$ in $Q^\star(\sigma_{x=v}(R))$.

Since our approach shall essentially rely on refutation, we attach special importance to the notion of *falsity*. An essential proposition related to falsity is the following:

Proposition 1. [Monotonicity of falsity] *If $Q^\star(C_1, \ldots, C_m)$ is false, then for any other constraint C_{m+1}, the QCP $Q^\star(C_1, \ldots, C_{m+1})$ is also false.*

Proof. A consequence of the monotonicity of the logical operators $\wedge$ and $\vee$. The truth value of each leaf of the expanded tree of the second QCP is smaller than the truth value of the corresponding leaf in the first tree, due to the additional constraint. □

2.2 Decomposition

Since we have restricted the framework to constraints whose table can be constructed explicitly, we exclude a direct handling of constraints of unbounded arity. This is similar to the restriction usually assumed for CSPs, where most results and techniques are defined for (binary) explicitly-stored constraints, and where a *decomposition* technique is used to transform more general constraints into a convenient form (table[3]).

We temporarily consider the class of quantified statements constructed over a given set of predicates $(P, \ldots)$ and a set of function symbols $(f, g, \ldots)$, each with a given arity (possibly 0). We assume that assumption 1 still holds. Such statements include the usual class of *Quantified Boolean Formulae* (QBF), *i.e.*, quantified constraints built over logical connectives over the domain $\{0, 1\}$. We also define a new class, called *Bounded Arithmetic Formulae* (BAF), as the quantified systems of equalities $(=)$, inequalities $(\leq)$ or disequalities $(\neq)$ between polynomials, where the variables range over a finite subset of the integers. We show that such problems are easily transformed into QCPs. As is done for numerical CSPs, the idea is to replace subexpressions by variables (for instance, $f(x + y)$ can be replaced by the conjunction $f(z)$, $z = x + y$). The following proposition states the exact quantification of these new variables.

---

[3] Of course, this transformation does not necessarily have to be explicitly performed, the information in a row can be computed on demand by a *constraint-check*.

Proposition 2. **[Decomposition of complex formulae]** *Let f and g be two functions of arity ϕ and γ, respectively. Let P be a predicate. The statement:*

$$Q^{\star} \quad P(f(x_1, \ldots, g(\underline{y_1 \ldots y_\gamma}), \ldots, x_\phi)) \tag{1}$$

is equivalent to:

$$Q^{\star} \boxed{\exists x_i} \quad (P(f(x_1, \ldots, \underline{x_i}, \ldots, x_\phi))), \quad x_i = g(y_1, \ldots, y_\gamma) \tag{2}$$

(in other words: additional variables are quantified existentially, and the new quantifiers are inserted "to the end" of the quantifier list)

Proof. Consider the expanded expression associated to the QCP (1); each leaf is a fully instantiated expression of the form $P(f(x_1, \ldots, g(\underline{y_1 \ldots y_\gamma}), \ldots, x_\phi))$, and is hence equivalent to the existentially quantified sentence $\exists x_i(P(f(x_1, \ldots, x_i, \ldots, x_\alpha))), \quad x_i = g(y_1, \ldots, y_\gamma)$. □

We now exhibit a set of constraints which is sufficient to model any BAF and any QBF (or any mix of the two) as a QCP.

QCP	primitive constraints
QBF	The constraint $\{\langle x, y \rangle \mid x = \neg y\}$; each of the constraints $\{\langle x, y, z \rangle \mid x \diamond y = z\}$ and $\{\langle x, y, z \rangle \mid x \diamond y \neq z\}$, where $\diamond$ is any of the binary symbols $\wedge, \vee, =$
BAF	Any of the constraints $\{\langle x, y \rangle \mid x \sim y\}$, where $\sim$ is a comparison symbol ($\leq, <, =, \neq$); Any of the constraints $\{\langle x, y, z \rangle \mid x \diamond y = z\}$ and $\{\langle x, y, z \rangle \mid x \diamond y \neq z\}$, where $\diamond$ is taken among $+, \times$ or among $\leq, <, =, \neq$ (ternary comparison symbols)

The truth table of primitive boolean constraints is known in advance (for instance, disjunction is seen as the table $\{\langle 0, 0, 0 \rangle \langle 0, 1, 1 \rangle \langle 1, 0, 1 \rangle \langle 1, 1, 1 \rangle\}$). The truth table of numerical constraints depends on the considered domain $\mathcal{D}$ but, due to arity 3, it can be constructed in time $|D_x|.|D_y|.|D_z|$. Note that comparison operations $=, \leq, \neq$ can either be seen as binary relations or as ternary relations whose third argument equals 0 or 1 (this is a trick to ease the integration of numerics and booleans).

Corollary 1. *Any BAF/QBF can be transformed into a QCP in time linear in the length of the expressions.*

Example 2. The QBF $\exists x \forall y ((x \wedge y) = y)$ can be encoded as $\exists x \forall y \exists conj ((x \wedge y) = conj, conj = y)$.

The BAF $\forall x, y \in [0, 9] \exists mod \in [0, 9] \exists k \in [0, 1] (x + y - 9.k = mod)$, is decomposed into $\forall x, y \in [0, 9] \exists mod \in [0, 9] \exists k \in [0, 1] \exists sum \in [0, 18] \exists k' \in [0, 9] (x + y = sum, 9.k = k', sum - k' = mod)$ — indeed, the bounds for the new variables may be obtained by propagation; their domain could be overestimated at first.

3   Local Consistency

We now introduce a framework devoted to *deductions* on quantified constraints, with an emphasis on *local* deductions which can be performed efficiently. Here are examples of the deductions we would like to automate, and whose meaning we shall define formally in the following:

(1) $\exists x \in \{0,1\} \; \forall y \in \{0,1\} \; \exists z \in \{1\} \; (x \vee y = z)$ $\leadsto x \neq 0$
(2) $\forall x \in \{0,1\} \; \exists y \in \{1\} \; \exists z \in \{0,1\} \; (x \vee y = z)$ $\leadsto z \neq 0$
(3) $\forall x \in \{1,3\} \; \forall y \in \{1,2\} \; \exists z \in \{1,2,3,4,5\} \; (x + y = z)$ $\leadsto z \neq 1$

The logical interpretation of these deductions is not straightforward. For instance, since the assertion $\exists x \in \{0,1\} \; \exists y \in \{0,1\} \; \exists z \in \{0\} \; ((x \vee y = z) \rightarrow x \neq 1)$ is true whereas $x \neq 1$ is not a valid deduction, logical implications of the form $Q^\star(R \rightarrow x \neq v)$ are not what we look for. Similarly, since the assertion $\forall x \in \{1,3\} \; \forall y \in \{1,2\} \; \exists z \in \{1,2,3,4,5\} \; (x + y = 3)$ is false whereas $x \neq 3$ is not a valid deduction, we are not allowed to deduce $x \neq v$ whenever $Q^\star \sigma_{x=v}(R)$ is false.

3.1   Consistency

Another, more operational approach to consistency is to say that a value is consistent with a variable if it is worth considering this value during the proof construction.

Definition 3. [Promising formulae] *The set of* promising formulae *of a QCP is defined inductively:*

- *If the formula is false then no formula is promising;*
- *Otherwise:*
    - *The set of promising formulae of a true quantifier-free (fully instantiated) QCP is the QCP itself;*
    - *The set of promising formulae of a true QCP of the form $Q_1 x \in \{v_1 \ldots v_d\} \; Q^\star(C)$ contains the formula itself, as well as the union of the promising formulae of each of the QCPs $Q^\star(\sigma_{x=v_1}(C))$ and $\ldots$ and $Q^\star(\sigma_{x=v_d}(C))$.*

The definition is quite technical, but it is best understood using expanded trees as illustrated in Fig. 3. In this interpretation, nodes are identified with subformulae, of which some are promising (circled nodes). For instance, the reason to forsake value $z = 0$ for the 2nd QCP of Fig. 3 becomes clear: this value leads to satisfying assignments in no branch. This is what we now formalize.

Definition 4. [Consistency] *A value v is* consistent *for variable x iff it is the value assigned to x in at least one promising formula of the considered QCP.*

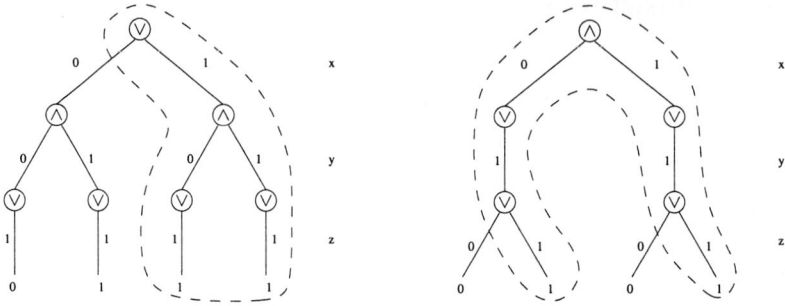

Value $x = 0$ is inconsistent *w.r.t.* the QCP   Value $z = 0$ is inconsistent *w.r.t.* the QCP
$\exists x \in \{0,1\} \forall y \in \{0,1\} \exists z \in \{1\}(x \vee y = z)$ $\forall x \in \{0,1\} \exists y \in \{1\} \exists z \in \{0,1\}(x \vee y = z)$

Fig. 3. Two QCPs and their set of promising formulae

The purpose of local reasoning is, of course, to detect *inconsistent* values. When a value is inconsistent, either its variable is universal, and hence the QCP is false, or the the variable is existential and it is equivalence-preserving to remove the inconsistent value from its domain.

Example 3. Consider the formula $\forall x \in \{1,3\} \, \forall y \in \{1,2\} \, \exists z \in \{1,2,3,4,5\}(x + y = z)$. It can be seen from Fig. 2 that value $z = 1$ is inconsistent. The QCP is hence equivalent to $\forall x \in \{1,3\} \, \forall y \in \{1,2\} \, \exists z \in \{2,3,4,5\} \, (x + y = z)$.

---

consistent (x, v, qcp) :
  if truth_value(qcp) = *false* then
    false
  else if qcp = $Qx \, Q^\star(C)$ then   % x appears under the first quantifier
    truth_value $(Q^\star(\sigma_{x=v}(C)))$
  else   % qcp = $Qy \in D_y \, Q^\star(C)$ for $y \neq x$
    $\bigvee_{w \in D_y}$ consistent $(x, v, Q^\star(\sigma_{y=w}(C)))$

Fig. 4. Algorithm for checking whether value v is consistent for variable x

3.2 Local Conditions for Inconsistency

Detecting inconsistency is costly. The purpose of local consistency techniques is to determine easily checkable, sufficient but non-necessary conditions which ensure inconsistency. The following definition is a natural adaptation of arc-consistency:

Definition 5. [Quantified arc-consistency] *Consider a QCP $Q^\star(C_1, \dots, C_m)$. We call* primitive QCPs *the QCPs $Q^\star(C_1)$ and ... and $Q^\star(C_m)$ which correspond to each constraint. A value v is* arc-consistent *for variable x if it is consistent w.r.t. each of the primitive QCPs.*

Example 4. (Example 2, continued). To check arc-consistency for $\exists x \forall y \,((x \wedge y) = y)$, we have to determine consistency for the two problems $\exists x \forall y \exists conj \,((x \wedge y) = conj)$ and $\forall y \exists conj \,(conj = y)$.

Consider the QCP $\forall x, y \in [0,9]\, \exists mod \in [0,9]\, \exists k \in [0,1]\, (x + y - 9.k = mod)$. To check arc-consistency, we have to consider each of the primitive QCPs: $\forall x, y \in [0,9]\, \exists sum \in [0,18](x + y = sum)$, $\exists k \in [0,1]\, \exists k' \in [0,9]\, (9.k = k')$, and $\exists mod \in [0,9]\, \exists sum \in [0,18]\, \exists k' \in [0,9]\, (sum - k' = mod)$.

Note that the term *arc-consistency* is to be understood in the sense of "consistent *w.r.t.* each constraint", a definition used for instance by [10], and hence somewhat different from the more classical, binary definition. It is also possible to generalize strong consistencies, for instance the following relational consistency (other state-of-the-art techniques could be considered):

Definition 6. [Quantified k-relational-consistency] *Consider a QCP $Q^\star$ $(C_1, \ldots, C_m)$. We call 1-QCP each primitive QCP; we call 2-QCP each QCP of the form $Q^\star(C_i, C_j)$ containing 2 constraints, etc. A value d is k-consistent for variable x if it is consistent w.r.t. each of the k-QCPs.*

Note that when k equals the number of constraints, k-consistency is the same as (global) consistency. Therefore, k-relational-consistency makes it possible to define arbitrary levels of reasoning. The connection between local consistency and global consistency is the following:

Proposition 3. [Correctness of local reasoning] *Inconsistency may be inferred by local means: if a value is not arc-consistent, then it is not consistent.*

Proof. A direct consequence of the fact that the set of promising formulae of $Q^\star(C_i)$ contains the set of promising formulae of $Q^\star(C_1, \ldots, C_i, \ldots, C_m)$. $\square$

4   Filtering

Arc-consistency as it is defined in Section 3.2 allows one to prune the domain of an existential variable by considering one primitive constraint. To each constraint, it is possible to associate the following *filtering operators*:

Definition 7. [Filtering operator] *Given a primitive QCP $Q^\star(C_i)$, the filtering operator associated to variable x is the function which suppresses from the domain of x all values which are not arc-consistent w.r.t. $Q^\star(C_i)$.*

Hence, each QCP defines a set of filtering operators. The method used to obtain domains locally consistent *w.r.t. all* constraints of the problem is called *constraint propagation*; it is defined in subsection 4.1. We also give more concrete details on the compilation of filtering operators on boolean (Subsection 4.2) and numerical (Subsection 4.3) domains.

$Q := \{\text{All primitive QCPs}\}$
while $\neg$ empty(Q) **do**
    $Q := Q - \{c\}$ % c chosen arbitrarily
    for each existential variable x constrained by c **do**
        Remove the arc-inconsistent values from D_x
        if the domain of x was reduced **then** $Q := Q \cup \{c \mid c \text{ constrains } x\}$

Fig. 5. The (constraint-oriented) AC3-like propagation algorithm

4.1   The General Framework

The basic algorithm to perform constraint-propagation is AC3, of which a constraint-oriented presentation is given in Fig. 5. The basic idea is to store every constraint (or every filtering operator) in a queue, and to reinsert constraints only when a domain on which it depends has changed.

Constraint propagation leaves the symbolic expression of a problem unchanged, and simply modifies the *domains* of its existential variables. This process is best understood within Apt's *chaotic iterations* framework [2]. We say that a QCP $A = Q_1 x_1 \in D_1 \ldots Q_n x_n \in D_n(C)$ is *less informative* than $B = Q_1 x_1 \in D_1' \ldots Q_n x_n \in D_n'(C)$ (and we write $A \sqsubseteq_\exists B$) if all the existential domains in B are tighter (for each i in $1..n$, if Q_i is $\exists$, then $D_i \supseteq D_i'$; if Q_i is $\forall$ then $D_i = D_i'$). Note that only (existential) domains differ between A and B. Filtering operators have the following properties, which ensure the correctness, termination and confluence of the propagation algorithm [2].

Proposition 4. [Properties of filtering operators] *A filtering operator* Φ *has the three following properties:*

Inflationarity	$A \sqsubseteq_\exists \Phi(A)$
Monotonicity	$A \sqsubseteq_\exists B \rightarrow \Phi(A) \sqsubseteq_\exists \Phi(B)$
Idempotency	$\Phi(A) = \Phi(\Phi(A))$

Proof. (sketched) Inflationarity means that the operator suppresses values; Monotonicity relies on a monotonicity property of arc-consistency; Idempotency holds because all non arc-consistent values are suppressed by one application of the operator. □

4.2   Boolean Constraints

Boolean filtering operators are easily described using a rule-based framework, like the CHR [12] for instance. For the purpose of our example, it shall be sufficient to consider rules of the form $Guard \Longrightarrow (x \neq val)$, representing the suppression of value val from the domain of variable x. We insist that these rules should *not* be read as logical implications.

A complete implementation of Arc-Consistency filtering for the $\neg$ constraint is detailed in Fig. 6. As an example of deduction made using this table, note that formula $\forall x \in \{0\}\ \forall y \in \{1\}\ (\neg x = y)$ is true; for any larger domain for x and y, the formula becomes false. Note that the case $\exists x \exists y$ is treated as in usual

$$\forall x \forall y \, (\neg x = y) \begin{cases} D_x \supseteq \{0,1\} & \implies fail \\ D_y \supseteq \{0,1\} & \implies fail \\ D_x \supseteq \{0\}, D_y \supseteq \{0\} & \implies fail \\ D_x \supseteq \{1\}, D_y \supseteq \{1\} & \implies fail \end{cases}$$

$$\forall x \exists y \, (\neg x = y) \begin{cases} D_x \supseteq \{0\}, D_y \subseteq \{0\} & \implies fail \\ D_x \supseteq \{1\}, D_y \subseteq \{1\} & \implies fail \end{cases}$$

$$\exists x \forall y \, (\neg x = y) \begin{cases} D_y \supseteq \{0\} & \implies x \neq 0 \\ D_y \supseteq \{1\} & \implies x \neq 1 \end{cases}$$

$$\exists x \exists y \, (\neg x = y) \begin{cases} D_x \subseteq \{1\} & \implies y \neq 1 \\ D_x \subseteq \{0\} & \implies y \neq 0 \\ D_y \subseteq \{1\} & \implies x \neq 1 \\ D_y \subseteq \{0\} & \implies x \neq 0 \end{cases}$$

$$\exists x \forall y \exists z \, (x \vee y = z) \begin{cases} D_x \subseteq \{1\} & \implies z \neq 0 \\ D_z \subseteq \{1\}, D_y \supseteq \{0\} & \implies x \neq 0 \\ D_z \subseteq \{0\}, D_y \supseteq \{1\} & \implies fail \end{cases}$$

Fig. 6. Boolean propagation: rules for $\neg$ and $\vee$

arc-consistency. In the case of this simple constraint, it is clear that the values deleted are exactly those which are not arc-consistent.

To give a flavour of a similar implementation for a ternary constraint, consider the $\exists \forall \exists$ quantification of disjunction (Fig. 6). Due to the number of rules to define, and to the more complicated nature of ternary rules, it becomes less intuitive to define a minimal set of rules which computes arc-consistency. Automated rule generation [1] is an interesting perspective for the generalization of such rules.

4.3   Numerical Constraints

Constraint propagation over numerical domains may be expressed using, for example, the formalism developed by Codognet and Diaz [8]. To conclude our section on filtering, we use a similar framework to suggest how interval constraint-propagation may be adapted to quantifiers. Using the notations of the interval community, we note $\mathbf{x} = [\underline{x}, \overline{x}]$ the interval associated to variable x. Once again, we do not represent the program obtained for each of the 9 combinations of quantifiers:

The reading of these consequences is not as easy as in the boolean case; hence we prove each of them in detail:

– The constraints of the first line of the table ($\forall \forall \exists$) have similar trees to that of Fig. 2. As for this figure, the promising values for z are all those which are sums or the previous branches, i.e., those of the form $\bigcup_x \bigcup_y x + y$. The bounds of this set are exactly what is computed by the interval addition $[\underline{x}, \overline{x}] + [\underline{y}, \overline{y}] = [\underline{x} + \underline{y}, \overline{x} + \overline{y}]$

$$\forall x \forall y \exists z \; (x + y = z) \implies \mathbf{z} = [\underline{x} + \underline{y}, \overline{x} + \overline{y}]$$

$$\exists x \forall y \exists z \; (x + y = z) \implies \begin{cases} \mathbf{z} \subseteq [\underline{x} + \underline{y}, \overline{x} + \overline{y}] \\ \mathbf{x} \subseteq [\underline{z} - \underline{y}, \overline{z} - \underline{y}] \cap [\underline{z} - \overline{y}, \overline{z} - \overline{y}] \end{cases}$$

$$\exists x \forall y \forall z \; (x + y = z) \implies \mathbf{z} \subseteq \begin{bmatrix} \max\{\underline{z} - \underline{y}, \underline{z} - \overline{y}, \overline{z} - \underline{y}, \overline{z} - \overline{y}\}, \\ \min\{\underline{z} - \underline{y}, \underline{z} - \overline{y}, \overline{z} - \underline{y}, \overline{z} - \overline{y}\} \end{bmatrix}$$

Fig. 7. A taste of quantified interval propagation

- The propagation over x for formula $\exists x \forall y \exists z$ is more complicated. The simplest justification for it is that the set of allowed values for x is $\{x \mid \forall y \in [\underline{y}, \overline{y}], \exists z \in [\underline{z}, \overline{z}], x + y = z\}$ which is precisely $\bigcap_y \bigcup_z z - y$. The bounds of this set are computed by $(\bigcup_z z - \underline{y}) \cap (\bigcup_z z - \overline{y})$, which is equal to $([\underline{z}, \overline{z}] - \underline{y}) \cap ([\underline{z}, \overline{z}] - \overline{y})$, which we wrote $[\underline{z} - \underline{y}, \overline{z} - \underline{y}] \cap [\underline{z} - \overline{y}, \overline{z} - \overline{y}]$.
- Last, the values allowed for x in the third constraint ($\exists \forall \forall$) are obtained as the intersection $\cap\{\underline{z} - \underline{y}, \underline{z} - \overline{y}, \overline{z} - \underline{y}, \overline{z} - \overline{y}\}$, which is empty as soon as either $\underline{y} \neq \overline{y}$ or $\underline{z} \neq \overline{z}$.

Much more place would be required to give a full description of a quantified interval arithmetics for constraint propagation, and this will be the subject of some of our future work, but we found it important to show by these examples that the framework developed in this paper is general enough to allow this kind of reasoning. In particular, we now have all elements to explain the computation suggested in example 1.

Example 5. (*cf.* Fig. 1) The formula $\exists x \in [1, 100] \; \forall y \in [1, 100] \; (x + y \leq 101)$ is decomposed into the QCP $\exists x \in [1, 100] \; \forall y \subset [1, 100] \; \exists z \; (x + y = z, z \leq 101)$. Arc-consistency considers the two QCPs (A) $\exists x \in [1, 100] \; \forall y \in [1, 100] \; \exists z \; (x + y = z)$ and (B) $\exists z \; (z \leq 101)$. Using rule 2 of Fig. 7 on QCP A, we get the bounds $[2, 200]$ for z, which we reduce to $[2, 101]$ by existential propagation on QCP B. Using the QCP A to propagate on x, we get $\mathbf{x} = ([2, 101] - 1) \cap ([2, 101] - 100) = [1, 100] \cap [-98, 1] = [1, 1]$.

5 Maintaining Consistency during the Search

The core of the paper was focused on the propagation framework. Local consistency is maintained at each node of the search tree to avoid combinatorial explosion. The search algorithm is straightforward, but two questions remain a little tricky; we briefly discuss them.

5.1 Primal and Dual Consistency

Arc-consistency allows to reduce the domains of existentially quantified variables by proving that some choices are inconsistent. Clearly, we also need to

```
truth_value(q) :
    % (prune the variables by propagation);
    if q is of the form ∀xQ*(C) then ⋀_{v∈D} truth_value (Q*(σ_{x=v}(C)))
    if q is of the form ∃xQ*(C) then ⋁_{v∈D} truth_value (Q*(σ_{x=v}(C)))
    otherwise eval(q)              % no more quantifiers
```

Fig. 8. General algorithm for solving the QCP

define some kind of filtering for *universal* variables, otherwise the runtime shall be exponential in the number of these variables. In particular, we need to be able to detect that a QCP be tautological. The most natural idea is that this pruning can be achieved using classical propagation on a *dual* problem, which models the negation of the statement. This dual problem is easily computed since the negation of a formula $Q_1 x_1 \ldots Q_n x_n (C_1 \wedge \ldots \wedge C_m)$ is defined as $Q'_1 x_1, \ldots Q'_n x_n (\overline{C_1} \vee \ldots \vee \overline{C_m})$, where each quantifier is reversed and $\overline{C_i}$ denotes the complement of C_i. Local inconsistency of the dual proves that the original problem is true. Of course, proving universal statements is not easy, and the *disjunction* obtained can be hard to disprove.

5.2 Incrementality

Incrementality is a well-known desirable feature in constraint-programming. In usual CSPs, incrementality means that when an existential quantifier is eliminated during the search, the information deduced previously still holds, and the propagation can hence be optimized. Questions regarding incrementality are not as easy when universal quantifiers are allowed. Due to lack of space, we just suggest the fact that algorithm 8 *is* actually incremental. The reason is that even for a universal statement, the set of consistent values is the *union* of the consistent values for each leaf. Hence the fact of eliminating a universal quantifier necessarily preserves all the inconsistencies computed previously.

6   Discussion

Since the problem of Quantified Constraints has not been considered in the literature yet, we find it essential to insist on related work and perspectives.

6.1   Connections to Other Works

Though quantifiers have been considered in several research fields, the QCP viewpoint presents some particularities. The QBF problem deals with *propositional* logic (variables are seen as proposition symbols), unlike the more general problem of *first-order* quantified logic with predicate symbols, which is a central issue in the field of automated reasoning. Note that this problem is recursively enumerable, while the QCP is a decidable, and purely combinatorial problem.

In our approach, a key feature is that we propose solutions to handle quantified numerical problems. Closely related is the literature initiated by Tarski's work on the decidability of first-order theorems over the *real numbers*, with such techniques as Cylindrical Algebraic Decomposition. The problem of first-order, real-valued constraints is indeed very different from the discrete constraints discussed in this paper, since the problem is not even solvable in exponential time (at least to our knowledge). Nevertheless, recent effort to mix these techniques with continuous constraint satisfaction [4, 17] could help bridging the two research areas. In particular, the relaxed problem of solving quantified equations over the finite-precision approximations of the real numbers induced by the floating-point machine representation is obviously in PSPACE, and hence closer to our concerns.

Last, quantified constraints have been considered by several independent authors in the CP literature, including a work on quantified rational trees [9] (a problem not even elementary) and a work on a generalization of interval propagation with exotic quantifiers [21].

6.2 Further Developments

This paper has suggested some of the possibilities opened up by constraint-propagation on a new class of problems. Much work remains to be done on both the practical and theoretical sides:

- Our framework defines constraint-propagation in operational terms, using considerations on the search-tree itself to provide pruning. The question of defining consistency in more logical terms is still open;
- We have seen that the definition of constraint propagation rules in Section 4 is a tedious task. This problem legitimates the use of automated solver generation techniques [1], which we plan to experiment;
- Intensive experiments and benchmarking are now needed to determine the practical relevance of the notions of arc-consistency and of stronger consistency; in particular, the comparison to existing, specialized techniques for QBFs shall be informative, since this recent community has already developed a set of benchmarks.

7   Conclusion

In this paper, we have proposed the Quantified Constraint Problem as a generalization of usual CSPs with arbitrary quantifiers. This framework generalizes a class of boolean problems which has recently received a lot of attention.

The technical contribution of the paper was to introduce quantified arc-consistency as a tool to model the propagation of information among quantified variables. We have tried to clarify the theoretical foundations of quantified constraint-propagation, and we have exemplified the class of local deductions obtained on boolean problems and on a new class of numerical problems.

Acknowledgments

This paper received helpful comments from Evgueni Petrov and other colleagues at IRIN. Information provided by A. G. D. Rowley is also gratefully acknowledged. Last, we are indebted to the authors of [13], whose title we somewhat plagiarized.

References

[1] K. Apt and E. Monfroy. Automatic generation of constraint propagation algorithms for small finite domains. In *Proc. of the 5th Int. Conf. on Principles and Practice of Constraint Programming (CP)*, pages 58–72, Alexandria, Virginia, 1999. Springer.

[2] K. R. Apt. The essence of constraint propagation. *Theoretical Computer Science*, 221(1-2):179–210, 1999.

[3] J. L. Balcázar. The complexity of searching implicit graphs. *Artificial Intelligence*, 86(1):171–188, 1996.

[4] F. Benhamou and F. Goualard. Universally quantified interval constraints. In *Proc. of the 6th Int. Conf. on Principles and Practice of Constraint Programming (CP)*, LNCS, pages 67–82, Singapore, 2000. Springer.

[5] H. K. Buening, M. Karpinski, and A. Flogel. Resolution for quantified boolean formulas. *Information and Computation*, 117(1):12–18, 1995.

[6] T. Bylander. The computational complexity of propositional STRIPS planning. *Artificial Intelligence*, 69(1-2):165–204, 1994.

[7] M. Cadoli, A Giovanardi, and M. Schaerf. An algorithm to evaluate quantified boolean formulae. In *Proc. of the 15th Nat. Conf. on AI (AAAI)*, pages 262–267, Madison, USA, 1999. AAAI/MIT Press.

[8] P. Codognet and D. Diaz. Compiling constraints in CLP(FD). *J. of Logic Programming*, 27(3):185–226, 1996.

[9] A. Colmerauer and T. Dao. Expressiveness of full first order constraints in the algebra of finite or infinite trees. In *Proc. of the 6th Int. Conf. on Principles and Practice of Constraint Programming (CP)*, LNCS, pages 172–186, Singapore, 2000. Springer.

[10] R. Dechter and P. van Beek. Local and global relational consistency. *Theoretical Computer Science*, 173(1):283–308, 1997.

[11] U. Egly, T. Eiter, H. Tompits, and S. Woltran. Solving advanced reasoning tasks using quantified boolean formulas. In *Proc. of the 17th Nat. Conf. on AI (AAAI)*, pages 417–422, Austin, TX, 2001. AAAI/MIT Press.

[12] T. W. Fruehwirth. Theory and practice of Constraint Handling Rules. *J. of Logic Programming*, 37(1-3):95–138, 1998.

[13] I. P. Gent and T. Walsh. Beyond NP: the QSAT phase transition. In *Proc. of the 15th Nat. Conf. on AI (AAAI)*, pages 648–653, Madison, USA, 1999. AAAI/MIT Press.

[14] E. Giunchiglia, M. Narizzano, and A. Tacchella. Learning for quantified boolean logic satisfiability. In *Proc. of the 18th Nat. Conf. on AI*, Edmonton, Alberta, 2002. AAAI/MIT Press. To appear.

[15] G. Gottlob. Complexity results for nonmonotonic logics. *J. of Logic and Computation*, 2(3):397–425, 1992.

[16] C. Papadimitriou. *Computational Complexity*. Addison Wesley, 1994.

[17] S. Ratschan. Continuous first-order constraint satisfaction. In *Artificial Intelligence, Automated Reasoning, and Symbolic Computation*, number 2385 in LNCS, Marseille, France, 2002. Springer.

[18] J. Rintanen. Improvements to the evaluation of quantified boolean formulae. In *Proc. of the 16th Int. Joint Conf. on AI (IJCAI)*, pages 1192–1197, Stockholm, Sweden, 1999. Morgan Kaufmann.

[19] T. J. Schaefer. Complexity of decision problems based on finite two-person perfect-information games. *J. of Computer and System Sciences*, 16(2):185–225, 1978.

[20] L. J. Stockmeyer and A. R. Meyer. Word problems requiring exponential time: Preliminary report. In *Conf. Record of the 5th Symp. on the Theory of Computing (STOC)*, pages 1–9, Austin, TX, 1973. ACM.

[21] A. C. Ward, T. Lozano-Perez, and W. P. Seering. Extending the constraint propagation of intervals. In *Proc. of the 11th Int. Joint Conf. on AI (IJCAI)*, pages 1453–1460, Detroit, Michigan, 1989. Morgan Kaufmann.

Secure Distributed Constraint Satisfaction: Reaching Agreement without Revealing Private Information

Makoto Yokoo[1], Koutarou Suzuki[2], and Katsutoshi Hirayama[3]

[1] NTT Communication Science Laboratories, NTT Corporation
2-4 Hikaridai, Seika-cho, Soraku-gun, Kyoto 619-0237, Japan
yokoo@cslab.kecl.ntt.co.jp
http://www.kecl.ntt.co.jp/csl/ccrg/members/yokoo/
[2] NTT Information Sharing Platform Laboratories, NTT Corporation
1-1 Hikari-no-oka, Yokosuka, Kanagawa 239-0847, Japan
koutarou@isl.ntt.co.jp
info.isl.ntt.co.jp/~koutarou/
[3] Kobe University of Mercantile Marine
5-1-1 Fukae-minami-machi, Higashinada-ku, Kobe 658-0022, Japan
hirayama@ti.kshosen.ac.jp
http://www-jo.ti.kshosen.ac.jp/~hirayama/

Abstract. This paper develops a secure distributed Constraint Satisfaction algorithm. A Distributed Constraint Satisfaction Problem (DisCSP) is a CSP in which variables and constraints are distributed among multiple agents. A major motivation for solving a DisCSP without gathering all information in one server is the concern about privacy/security. However, existing DisCSP algorithms leak some information during the search process and privacy/security issues are not dealt with formally. Our newly developed algorithm utilizes a public key encryption scheme. In this algorithm, multiple servers, which receive encrypted information from agents, cooperatively perform a search process that is equivalent to a standard chronological backtracking. This algorithm does not leak any private information, i.e., neither agents nor servers can obtain any additional information on the value assignment of variables that belong to other agents.

1 Introduction

A Distributed Constraint Satisfaction Problem (DisCSP) is a constraint satisfaction problem in which variables and constraints are distributed among multiple agents. Since various application problems in multi-agent systems can be formalized as DisCSPs, there have been many works on this topic in the last decade [5, 7, 10, 13, 14, 15].

One major motivation for solving a DisCSP without gathering all information in one server is the concern about privacy/security, i.e., the knowledge of the problem each agent has is private information and revealing such information

P. Van Hentenryck (Ed.): CP 2002, LNCS 2470, pp. 387–401, 2002.

to a server or other agents is not desirable. Consequently, we cannot gather all information in a single server and solve the problem by using centralized CSP techniques. In a DisCSP, a variable value can be considered as an action/plan that an agent will take. It is natural that an agent does not want to reveal information on possible plans or the final plan it will take to other agents.

For example, a problem of scheduling multiple meetings among multiple participants can be formalized as a DisCSP as follows. Each agent/participant has one variable that corresponds to each meeting. The domain of a variable is possible dates and time slots. There exist equality constraints among variables that represent the same meeting and belong to different agents (i.e., they must meet the same day/time). Also, there exist inequality constraints between multiple variables that belong to the same agent (i.e., a person cannot attend multiple meetings at the same time). Also, an agent has unary constraints on its variables (i.e., he/she has personal schedules that prevent him/her from attending a meeting). In this problem domain, it is clear that a person would not be happy to make such private information public.

However, existing DisCSP algorithms leak some information during the search process and privacy/security issues have not yet been dealt with formally. For example, in the asynchronous backtracking algorithm [14], each agent exchanges a tentative value assignment with each other. If the current assignment does not satisfy constraints, these agents change their assignments and perform backtracking in a certain order. During this search process, an agent can obtain some information on possible values of variables that belong to other agents. Also, an agent can learn the final value assignment of these variables.

When applying this algorithm to the meeting scheduling problem, we can assume each agent makes proposals on the date and time slot of the meeting and negotiates with other agents. The fact that an agent proposes a certain date reveals that he/she does not have any personal schedule on that date. If an agent declines a certain date, this means that he/she has a personal schedule or the date conflicts with some other meeting. Such private information is leaked during the search process.

On the other hand, in the research community on information security and cryptography, there have been many works on multi-party protocols, which deal with performing various computations based on private information of participants, while keeping the private information secret [4, 9]. However, as far as the authors are aware, there has been virtually no work on solving combinatorial optimization problems (including CSPs as a special case) by utilizing information security techniques, with the notable exception of the authors' recent works on secure dynamic programming [12, 16].

In this paper, we develop a secure DisCSP algorithm that utilizes information security techniques. As far as the authors are aware, this is the first research effort that combines the two growing research fields, i.e.. constraint satisfaction and information security.

In this paper, we say that an algorithm does not leak any private information if an agent cannot obtain any additional information on the value assignment of variables that belong to other agents. In a meeting scheduling application, this means that each participant cannot know the scheduled dates of the meetings he/she will not attend. Also, he/she cannot obtain any information on the private schedules of other participants.

In our newly developed secure DisCSP algorithm, multiple computational servers are used to implement a standard chronological backtracking; thus, this algorithm is guaranteed to be complete. Each agent only knows the value assignment of its own variables and cannot obtain any additional information on the value assignment of variables that belong to other agents. Also, computational servers cannot get any information on the value assignment of any variables.

In the rest of this paper, we first show the formal definition of DisCSP and secure algorithms (Section 2). Next, we describe a public key encryption scheme, which is a basic tool used in our secure DisCSP algorithm (Section 3). Then, we describe the details of our newly developed secure DisCSP algorithm (Section 4). Finally, we examine the characteristics of this algorithm (Section 5) and discuss related works (Section 6).

2   Formalization

A DisCSP can be formalized as follows.

- There exist agents $1, 2, \ldots, I$.
- There exist variables $x_1, x_2, \ldots, x_n$. Each variable belongs to one agent. The fact that x_i belongs to agent a is represented as $belongs(x_i, a)$.
- All variables have a common domain $\{1, 2, \ldots, m\}$. This domain of variables is common knowledge among agents.
- There exist unary constraints on one variable and binary constraints between two variables.
- We assume constraints are represented as *nogoods*. A unary nogood $(x_i = d_i)$ represents the fact that the value assignment d_i to variable x_i violates the constraint. A binary nogood $(x_i = d_i, x_j = d_j)$ represents the fact that the assignment of $x_i = d_i$ and $x_j = d_j$ violates the constraint.
- These constraints are the private information of agents. More specifically, the unary constraints on x_i, which belongs to agent a, are known only by agent a. Let us denote a set of these unary constraints as $C_{x_i}^a$. Also, the binary constraints between x_i and x_j, which belong to agent a and agent b, respectively, are distributed between agents a and b. Let us denote the constraints agent a knows as C_{x_i,x_j}^a and the constraints agent b knows as C_{x_i,x_j}^b.
- A solution of DisCSP $D = (x_1 = d_1, x_2 = d_2, \ldots, x_n = d_n)$ is a value assignment of all variables that satisfies all unary and binary constraints.

Let us show an example. Figure 1 shows an example of the well-known n-queens problem, where $n = 4$. If we assume there exists an agent that corresponds to a queen of each row and these queens try to find their positions so that they do not kill each other, this problem can be formalized as a DisCSP. We call this problem the distributed 4-queens problem. More specifically, there are four

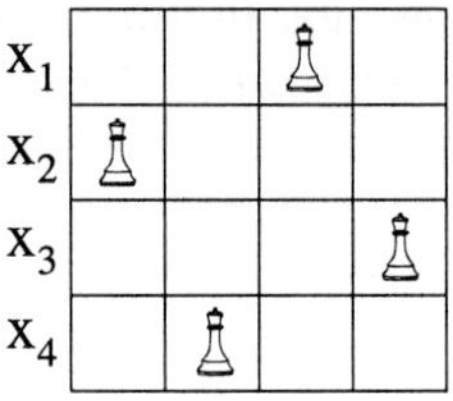

Fig. 1. Distributed 4-Queens Problem

agents $1, 2, 3, 4$. Each agent i has one variable x_i with domain $\{1, 2, 3, 4\}$. In this problem, there is no unary constraint. Let us assume that for $i < j$, $C^i_{x_i,x_j}$, i.e., the constraint agent i knows, consists of diagonal constraints, e.g., $C^2_{x_2,x_3}$ contains nogood $(x_2 = 1, x_3 = 2)$, etc., and $C^j_{x_i,x_j}$ consists of column constraints, e.g., $C^2_{x_1,x_2}$ contains nogood $(x_1 = 1, x_2 = 1)$, etc.

This formalization is based on the traditional definition introduced by [13, 14]. One minor difference is that in [13, 14], it is assumed that the domain of a variable is different and the domain is private information, while in our formalization, the entire domain is common knowledge but an agent can have private unary constraints. These two formalizations are mutually interchangeable and there are no fundamental differences. Another slight difference is that in [13, 14], binary constraints between variables x_i and x_j are assumed to be the common knowledge of agents a and b, who own these variables. This is a special case of our definition where $C^a_{x_i,x_j}$ and $C^b_{x_i,x_j}$ are identical.

In [10], an alternative formalization of DisCSP is presented in which variables and domains are common knowledge and constraints are private information. Our formalization is based on [14], i.e., the constraints an agent has are restricted to the constraints that are related to its own variables.

We define the fact that when solving a DisCSP using a particular algorithm, the algorithm does not leak private information of an agent to other agents as follows.

- After a solution is found, each agent has the same knowledge on the assignment of other agents as the case where the agent obtains (a part of) the solution directly from an oracle without performing the algorithm.
  More specifically, let us denote an assignment of any subset of k variables as $D_k = (x_{j_1} = d_{j_1}, x_{j_2} = d_{j_2}, \ldots, x_{j_k} = d_{j_k})$. Also, let us define $p_a(D_k)$ as the estimated probability of agent a, in that the final solution is a superset of D_k, after a solution is found by performing the algorithm. Also, let us define $p_a^{\mathrm{oracle}}(D_k)$ as the estimated probability of agent a, in that the final solution is a superset of D_k, after obtaining the value assignment of its own variables from the oracle. This definition means $p_a(D_k) = p_a^{\mathrm{oracle}}(D_k)$ for all D_k.

When obtaining the value assignment of its own variables from the oracle, the agent obtains certain information on the value assignment of other variables.

For example, assume x_1 belongs to agent a and x_2 belongs to agent b. If agent a knows there exists an inequality constraint between x_1 and x_2, agent a can infer that $p_a((x_j = d_i)) = 0$ if x_i is assigned to d_i. Also, if there exists an equality constraint, it can infer that $p_a((x_j = d_i)) = 1$. The above condition means that the algorithm does not leak any unnecessary information, i.e., no additional information is leaked besides the information that can be inferred by obtaining a part of the solution.

Basically, the above definition requires that there must be no information leak on unary constraints. It is clear that if a solution is obtained from the oracle, an agent can obtain no information on the unary constraints of other agents. If agent a learns some information on unary constraints, e.g., a learns nogood $(x_j = d_j)$ by performing an algorithm, $p_a((x_j = d_j)) = 0$ cannot be equal to $p_a^{\text{oracle}}((x_j = d_j))$, except when $p_a^{\text{oracle}}((x_j = d_j)) = 0$.

Furthermore, if an algorithm requires a third party other than the agents who originally have variables (we call such an actor a *server*), we define the fact that when solving a DisCSP using a particular algorithm, the algorithm does not leak any private information of an agent to a server as follows. We assume a server does not have any a priori knowledge of the problem.

- A server has no knowledge on the obtained solution after performing the algorithm. More specifically, for an assignment of any subset of k variables $D_k = (x_{j_1} = d_{j_1}, x_{j_2} = d_{j_2}, \ldots, x_{j_k} = d_{j_k})$, let us denote the estimated probability of a server, in that the obtained solution is a superset of D_k, as $p_{\text{server}}(D_k)$. This definition means $p_{\text{server}}(D_k) = 1/m^k$, where k is the number of variables in D_k. This condition means all assignments look equally probable for a server.

This condition requires that a server cannot learn any information on unary/binary constraints.

3   Preliminaries

In this section, we describe a basic tool for our implementation, i.e., an *indistinguishable*, *homomorphic*, and *randomizable* public key encryption scheme. In the rest of this paper, we use ElGamal encryption [2], which has all of these properties, for describing our algorithm. However, our algorithm can be implemented using other encryption methods that also have these properties.

- Public key encryption: In public key encryption, the key used for encryption is public, so anybody can create ciphertext $E(M)$ from plaintext M. On the other hand, the key used for decryption is kept secret and only the one who has the secret key can obtain M from $E(M)$.
- ElGamal encryption: ElGamal encryption is one instance of public key encryption. Let $q, p = 2q+1$ be primes and $G = <g> \subset \mathbf{Z}_p^*$ be a cyclic group of order q generated by g, where $\mathbf{Z}_p$ denotes a set of integers from 0 to $p-1$ and $\mathbf{Z}_p^*$ denotes a set of integers that are in $\mathbf{Z}_p$ and prime to p. The secret key is

$s \in \mathbf{Z}_q$ and the corresponding public key is $g, y = g^s$. ElGamal encryption is based on the assumption of the hardness of the discrete logarithm problem (DLP), i.e., to find s from (g, g^s) is computationally infeasible. Please note that we use modulo p arithmetic.

Anyone can encrypt message $M \in G$ just by using the public key $g, y = g^s$, i.e., choose random number $r \in \mathbf{Z}_q$ and create ElGamal ciphertext $E(M) = (A = g^r, B = y^r M)$.

One who knows the secret key, $s \in \mathbf{Z}_q$, can decrypt ciphertext $E(M) = (A = g^r, B = y^r M)$, i.e., compute $B/A^s = M$.

- Indistinguishable encryption: In ElGamal encryption, $E(M)$ is created using random number r. Thus, if the same plaintext is encrypted twice using different random numbers, these two ciphertexts look totally different and we cannot know whether the original plaintexts are the same or not without decrypting them.

- Homomorphic encryption: Encryption E is homomorphic if $E(M_1)E(M_2) = E(M_1 M_2)$ holds. If we define the product of ciphertexts $E(M_1) = (A_1, B_1)$ and $E(M_2) = (A_2, B_2)$ by $E(M_1)E(M_2) = (A_1 A_2, B_1 B_2)$, ElGamal encryption E is homomorphic encryption. By using this property, we can obtain the product of two plaintexts by taking the product of two ciphertexts without decrypting them.

- Randomization: In ElGamal encryption, one can create a new randomized ciphertext $E(M) = (Ag^{r'}, By^{r'})$ with random value r' from the original ciphertext $E(M) = (A = g^r, B = y^r M)$. This is equivalent to making a product of $E(1) = (g^{r'}, y^{r'})$ and $E(M)$. If we assume that the Decision Diffie-Hellman (DDH) problem is infeasible, one cannot determine whether a ciphertext is a randomized ciphertext of the original ciphertext or not.

- Multiple Servers: By utilizing secret sharing techniques, we can make each server to have only a share of the secret key; thus, any collusion of t (or less than t) servers cannot decrypt E [9].

In the preparation phase, secret key s and public key y are generated in a distributed way [8] and each distributed server has only a share of the secret key. The decryption is performed in a distributed fashion by each distributed server that has a share of the secret key.

For example, let us consider a simplest case where the total number of servers is two and $t = 1$, i.e., there are servers 1 and 2. If these two servers cooperate, they can decrypt E while a single server cannot. Servers 1 and 2 generate their own shares of the secret keys s_1, s_2, respectively. The secret key is $s = s_1 + s_2$, but each server does not know s. They exchange $y_1 = g^{s_1}$ and $y_2 = g^{s_2}$ with each other and obtain public key $y = y_1 \cdot y_2 = g^{s_1 + s_2} = g^s$. When decrypting $E(M) = (A = g^r, B = y^r M)$, these servers calculate A^{s_1} and A^{s_2} and exchange the results with each other. Then, by calculating $B/(A^{s_1} \cdot A^{s_2}) = B/A^{s_1 + s_2} = B/A^s$, these servers can obtain plaintext M. Note that the secret key s is kept secret to these servers even after the decryption; they need to cooperate to decrypt another ciphertext.

4   Secure DisCSP Algorithm

In this section, we show the details of our newly developed algorithm. When describing our algorithm, we put the following assumptions for notation simplicity.

- Each agent i has exactly one variable x_i.
- There exist binary constraints between all pairs of variables.

Relaxing these assumptions and extending the algorithm to general cases is rather straightforward.

4.1   Basic Ideas

In our newly developed secure DisCSP algorithm, computational servers called a search-controller, decryptors, and value-selectors are used. There exist multiple (at least two) decryptors. Each of these decryptors has a share of the secret key of E as described in Section 3, and public key y for E is generated by these decryptors distributedly. There exists one value-selector for each variable/agent. Also, there exists one search-controller.

The main search procedure is performed by the search-controller and value-selectors. Each agent first encodes unary/binary constraints and passes the information to the servers. Then, these servers obtain a solution and return the value assignment to each agent. By utilizing these servers, we can guarantee that the information each agent can get is the same as the case where the agent obtains its value assignment directly from an oracle.

On the other hand, when utilizing servers, we must make sure that these servers do not obtain any information of the obtained solution. The definition introduced in Section 2 is so strict that it requires that a server cannot learn the fact that two variable values are different/equal.

In our secure DisCSP algorithm, this requirement is satisfied by introducing the following methods: 1) constraints are encoded by using a public key encryption scheme, 2) agents cooperatively perform renaming/permutation of variable values, 3) the search procedures are distributed among multiple servers, i.e., a search-controller, decryptors, and value-selectors.

Figure 2 (a) shows the flow of the proposed algorithm. In the rest of this section, we describe the details of these procedures.

4.2   Encoding Constraints

Each agent needs to encode its unary/binary constraints so that subsequent renaming/permutation is possible and so that the search-controller and value-selectors cannot understand but decryptors can cooperatively decrypt.

To satisfy this goal, for each value k of variable x_i, agent i represents its unary/binary constraints using an $n \times m$ constraint matrix. We denote this matrix as $A_{i,k}$. The element of this matrix $A_{i,k}(j,l)$ is defined as follows. $E(1)$ and $E(z)$ denote the encryption of 1 and common public element $z (\neq 1)$, respectively. z is chosen so that $z^c \bmod p \neq 1$ holds for all c, where $0 < c < q$. We also assume $2(n-1) < q$ holds.

394 Makoto Yokoo et al.

- For $j \neq i$:
  - $A_{i,k}(j,l) = E(z)$ if $x_i = k$ and $x_j = l$ are inconsistent, i.e., $\text{nogood}(x_i = k, x_j = l)$ is in $C^i_{x_i,x_j}$, or k violates i's unary constraint, i.e., $\text{nogood}(x_i = k)$ is in $C^i_{x_i}$.
  - $A_{i,k}(j,l) = E(1)$ if $x_i = k$ and $x_j = l$ are consistent.
- For $j = i$ and $l \neq k$: $A_{i,k}(j,l) = E(1)$.
- For $j = i$ and $l = k$: $A_{i,k}(j,l) = E(E_i(k))$, where E_i is i's encryption function. E_i can be any encryption scheme, i.e., it does not need to be a public key encryption scheme. We assume $E_i(k) \in G$ and $E_i(k) \neq 1$.

Figure 2 (b) shows a constraint matrix for value 1 of x_2 encoded by agent 2 in the distributed 4-queens problem. Note that agent 2 knows column constraints with x_1 and diagonal constraints with x_3 and x_4. The j-th row for $j \neq i$ represents binary constraints, i.e., the position that is in conflict with $x_2 = 1$ is filled by $E(z)$ (otherwise filled by $E(1)$). As described in Section 3, E is indistinguishable, which means that each $E(z)$ (or $E(1)$) looks totally different and we cannot know whether the original plaintexts are the same or not without decrypting them.

The i-th row encodes the information that this matrix is on value k. This information is used to obtain the actual value assignment from the solution on renamed/permuted variable values.

4.3 Renaming/Permutation

Next, agents perform the permutation of columns on each constraint matrix. This means that agents transform the original problem into a new problem in which variable values are renamed. More specifically, for each variable value k, k is renamed as $\pi(k)$, where π is a permutation of m elements, i.e., a bijective map from $\{1, 2, \ldots, m\}$ to $\{1, 2, \ldots, m\}$. Note that the domain of all variables is common and agents perform the same permutation for all variables.

To make sure that no agent can know the result of the permutation, each agent sequentially performs the permutation one by one. As a result, no agent knows the result of the total permutation. By utilizing randomization, we cannot know the result of the permutation even if we compare the matrices before and after the permutation.

More specifically, agent j has its own permutation function $\pi_j(\cdot)$. The combined permutation function, i.e., $\pi(\cdot)$ is given by $\pi_n(\pi_{n-1}(\ldots \pi_1(\cdot) \ldots))$.

The detailed procedure is as follows.

- For each k, each agent i makes public $(i, A_{i,k})$.
- From 1 to n, each agent j sequentially applies permutation function π_j to these matrices. More specifically, agent 1 first applies the permutation function $\pi_1(\cdot)$ to columns for all $A_{i,k}$ and makes public the result, where each element of the matrix is randomized by multiplying $E(1)$. Next, agent 2 applies the permutation function $\pi_2(\cdot)$, and so on. Let us denote the final result as $(i, A'_{i,k})$.

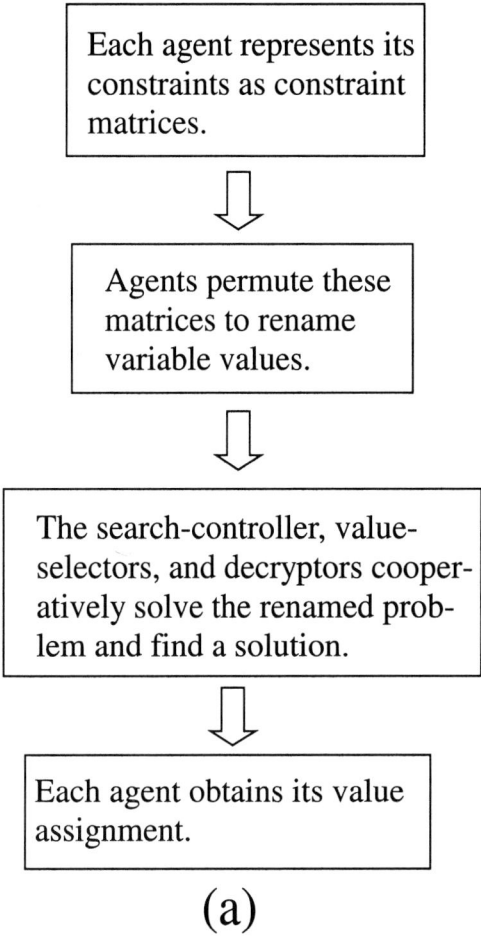

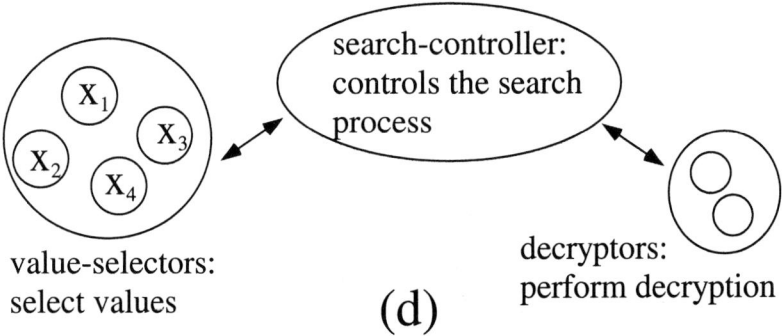

Fig. 2. Overview of Secure DisCSP Algorithm

- Decryptors cooperatively decrypt the i-th row of $A'_{i,k}$. If the k'-th element is not equal to 1, i.e., it is equal to $E_i(k)$, then decryptors send $(k', E_i(k), A'_{i,k})$ to value-selector i. Note that $k' = \pi(k)$.

Figure 2 (c) shows the result of the permutation $1 \rightarrow 2$, $2 \rightarrow 4$, $3 \rightarrow 1$, $4 \rightarrow 3$ for the constraint matrix described in Figure 2 (b).

By using the above procedure, each value-selector i gets the constraint matrices associated with x_i, where variable values are renamed/permuted by $k \rightarrow k'$, where $k' = \pi(k)$.

4.4   Search Procedure

In this section, we show the search procedure performed by the search-controller, decryptors, and value-selectors. The search-controller controls the search process. For each variable x_i, there exists value selector i. Value-selector i selects a renamed variable value for x_i. The decryptors perform decryption (Figure 2 (d)).

$Partial\_Solution \leftarrow \{\}$;
send **start-round** messages to all value-selectors;
wait until receiving all $v(i,j)$;
SELECT-VARIABLE: select variable x_i which is not in $Partial\_Solution$;
if all variables are already included in $Partial\_Solution$
then inform value-selectors that the current assignment is a solution;
    terminate the procedure;
else $pos \leftarrow i$;
    CHECK: $P \leftarrow \prod_j v(pos, j) \cdot v(j, pos)$, where $x_j \in Partial\_Solution$;
    send P to decryptors and wait for the decryption of P.
    if the decryption of P is 1
    then add x_{pos} to $Partial\_Solution$, goto **SELECT-VARIABLE**;
    else
        ASK-NEXT-VALUE: send **set-next-value** message
            to value-selector pos and wait for its reply;
        when received **ok** message do
            send **start-round** messages to all value-selectors;
            wait until receiving all $v(i,j)$; goto **CHECK**; end do;
        when received **backtrack** message do
            if $Partial\_Solution$ is empty
            then announce that there exists no solution;
                terminate the procedure;
            else remove variable $x_{i'}$ that was added to to $Partial\_Solution$
                most recently from $Partial\_Solution$;
                $pos \leftarrow i'$; goto **ASK-NEXT-VALUE**;
            end if; end do; end if; end if;

Fig. 3. Procedure for Search-Controller

Procedure for Search-Controller
Figure 3 shows the procedure for the search-controller. The search-controller performs the described search procedure that is equivalent to a standard chronological backtracking. *Partial_Solution* represents a set of variables that are in a partial solution. All constraints among variables within the partial solution are satisfied. If a variable that is not in the partial solution does not satisfy a constraint with a variable in the partial solution, the search-controller asks the value-selector of the variable to change its current assignment. If the value-selector has no other value, then the value of the variable that was most recently added to the partial solution is changed (backtracking).

In the procedure described in Figure 3, if all constraints are satisfied, then P is $E(1)$, otherwise, P is $E(z^c)$, where c is the number of violated constraints, since E is homomorphic. Also, since z is chosen so that $z^c \bmod p \neq 1$ for all $0 < c < q$ and $2(n-1) < q$, z^c will not be equal to 1.

Procedure for Value-Selector
Figure 4 shows the procedure for a value-selector i. Only this value-selector knows the current assignment of variable x_i. To check the constraints, when value-selector i chooses d_i, it sends a randomized j-th row of $A'_{i,k}$ in $(d_i, E_i(k), A'_{i,k})$ to value-selector j. For example, if value-selector 2 chooses 2, it sends the first row of the matrix of Figure 2 (c), i.e., $[E(1), E(z), E(1), E(1)]$ to value-selector 1. If value-selector j chooses d_j for its variable x_j, it chooses the d_j-th element of the communicated vector. For example, if value-selector 1 chooses 2, it chooses the second element of $[E(1), E(z), E(1), E(1)]$, i.e., $E(z)$. If the decryption of this element (which is performed by decryptors) is 1, this means the current assignment of x_i and x_j satisfies the unary and binary constraints of agent i. In this case, since the decryption is z, the current assignment of x_1 and x_2 does not satisfy the constraints of agent 2.

Procedure for Decryptors
Each decryptor j has a share of secret key s, i.e., s_j, where $s = \sum_j s_j$. The number of decryptors depends on the required level of security, i.e., by using $t + 1$ decryptors, even if t (or less than t) decryptors collude to obtain the private information of agents, they cannot decrypt constraint matrices directly.

If decryptors are asked to decrypt $E(M) = (A, B)$, each decryptor j calculates A^{s_j} and exchanges the results. By calculating $B/\prod_j A^{s_j} = B/A^s$, decryptors can obtain M.

Obtaining a Solution
One instance of a solution obtained under the permutation $1 \rightarrow 2, 2 \rightarrow 4, 3 \rightarrow 1, 4 \rightarrow 3$ is $d_1 = 1, d_2 = 2, d_3 = 3, d_4 = 4$.

When each value-selector is informed by the search-controller that the current assignment is a solution, it sends $E_i(k)$ in $(d_i, E_i(k), A'_{i,k})$, where d_i is the current assignment, to agent i, i.e., $E_1(3)$ to agent 1, $E_2(1)$ to 2, $E_3(4)$ to 3, and $E_4(2)$

Makoto Yokoo et al.

when initialized **do**
    $Done \leftarrow \{\}$, $d_i \leftarrow$ a randomly chosen value from $1, \ldots, m$; **end do**;

when received **start-round** message **do**
    send the following message for all value-selectors $j \neq i$
        $V(i, j)$, where $V(i, j)$ is a randomized j-th row of $A'_{i,k}$ in $(d_i, E_i(k), A'_{i,k})$,
          i.e., $[A'_{i,k}(j, 1), \ldots, A'_{i,k}(j, m)]$; **end do**;

when received $V(j, i)$ from value-selector j **do**
    send $v(j, i)$, which is a randomized d_i-th element of $V(j, i)$,
        to the search-controller; **end do**;

when received **set-next-value** message **do**
    add d_i to $Done$,
    if all values are already included in $Done$,
    then set $Done \leftarrow \{\}$;
        randomly choose new value d_i,
        send **backtrack** message to the search-controller;
    else randomly choose new value d_i that is not in $Done$;
        send **ok** message to the search-controller; **end do**;

Fig. 4. Procedure for Value-Selector i

to 4. By decrypting $E_i(k)$, agent i obtains the value k for its variable x_i, which is a part of the final solution.

5 Algorithm Characteristics

5.1 Security

It is clear that this algorithm does not leak any additional information to other agents. Since constraint matrices are encrypted, an agent cannot get any information during the permutation phase. An agent does not participate in the search phase. Therefore, the information an agent can get is the same as the case where the agent obtains a part of the final solution from an oracle.

    Next, we show that the algorithm does not leak any information to servers, i.e., the search-controller, decryptors, and value-selectors. Since variable values are renamed by permutation, each value-selector cannot know the actual real value it is selecting. Also, the renamed assigned value is known only to one value-selector. Therefore, neither a value-selector, the search-controller, nor an decryptor is able to get any information on whether the values of two variables are the same/different. Also, unless all decryptors collude, decryptors cannot decrypt a constraint matrix directly.

    Although the search-controller observes the search process, this information is useless for updating the estimated probability that a particular assignment is a part of the final solution. For example, let us assume the simplest case, i.e., there exist two variables x_1, x_2, whose domain is $\{1, 2\}$. If the search-controller adds x_1 to *Partial_Solution* first, when a solution is found, there are four possible scenarios, i.e., 1) a solution is obtained immediately, 2) a solution is found after changing x_2's value once, 3) a solution is obtained after changing x_2 twice and performing backtracking, 4) a solution is obtained after changing x_2's value twice and performing backtracking, then changing x_2's value again. Regardless of which pattern is observed, each of the four possible solutions, i.e., $(x_1 = 1, x_2 = 1)$, $(x_1 = 1, x_2 = 2)$, $(x_1 = 2, x_2 = 1)$, and $(x_1 = 2, x_2 = 2)$, is equally probable.

Also, a value-selector observes only partial information of the search process. Even if the value-selector can get the same information as decryptors, it still cannot obtain any additional information on a particular assignment being a part of the final solution.

If we do not perform renaming/permutation, value-selector i can learn the final value assignment of variable x_i. Also, if we do not distribute processing among the search-controller, value-selectors, and decryptors, i.e., solve a problem using a centralized server, although this server cannot know the actual value assignments because of renaming/permutation, the server can tell whether two variable values are the same/different.

5.2 Communication Costs

The search procedure of the secure DisCSP algorithm is equivalent to a standard chronological backtracking. The number of rounds, i.e., the number of times that the search-controller, value-selectors, and decryptors exchange messages, becomes m^n in the worst case.

For each round and for each constraint $C^i_{x_i, x_j}$, value-selector i communicates an m-element vector to value-selector j, and value-selector j communicates one element of the vector to the search-controller. Also, decryptors must communicate with each other to decrypt a ciphertext.

The required communication costs are clearly much larger than existing DisCSP algorithms [5, 7, 10, 13, 14, 15]. However, this seems somewhat inevitable if we wish to preserve the privacy of agents.

6   Discussion

In most of the existing DisCSP algorithms, each agent exchanges the tentative value assignment with other agents, and final value assignments are made public [5, 13, 14, 15]. In [10], an alternative formalization of DisCSP is presented in which variables and domains are common knowledge and constraints are private information. In the algorithm presented in [10], agents obtain a solution by explicitly communicating information on constraints to each other.

In [7], an algorithm called distributed forward-checking algorithm is presented in which an agent communicates possible domains of variables that belong to other agents rather than its own assignments. This is similar to our idea of communicating a row in a constraint matrix. However, in [7], encryption techniques are not used so private information is leaked during the search process.

One promising application field of secure DisCSP algorithms is meeting scheduling. In [3], the trade-off between the efficiency of an algorithm and privacy of agents in meeting scheduling problems is discussed. In [6], a secure meeting scheduling protocol that utilizes information security techniques is developed. However, this protocol is specialized for a meeting scheduling problem in which only a single meeting is scheduled. By applying our newly developed algorithm, multiple meetings can be scheduled simultaneously.

It is well known that any combinatorial circuit can be computed securely by using general-purpose multi-party protocols [1, 4]. Therefore, if we can construct a combinatorial circuit that implements a constraint satisfaction algorithm, in principle, such an algorithm can be executed securely (thus we do not need to develop a specialized secure protocol for DisCSPs). However, implementing a combinatorial circuit that executes a constraint satisfaction algorithm is not easy, and the obtained circuit would be very large. Note that we need to create a general purpose logic circuit to solve CSPs, not specialized hardware to solve a particular problem instance (such as those discussed in [11]).

Furthermore, to execute such a general-purpose multi-party protocol, for each computation of an AND gate in the circuit, the servers must communicate with each other. Using such a general purpose multi-party protocol for a distributed constraint satisfaction problem is not practical at all due to the required communication costs.

7   Conclusions

In this paper, we developed a secure DisCSP algorithm. Our newly developed algorithm utilizes an indistinguishable, homomorphic, and randomizable public key encryption scheme. In this algorithm, multiple servers, which receive encrypted information from agents, cooperatively perform a search process and obtain an encrypted solution. Then, a part of the encrypted solution is sent to each agent. By using this algorithm, the private information of an agent is not leaked during the search process to other agents or servers.

In this paper, we developed an algorithm whose performance is equivalent to a basic chronological backtracking as a first step in developing secure DisCSP algorithms. Our future works include 1) analyzing the robustness of the developed algorithm against collusions of servers and agents, 2) developing new algorithms that are more computationally efficient and require less communication costs without sacrificing security/privacy.

References

[1] Ben-Or, M., Goldwasser, S., and Wigderson, A.: Completeness Theorems for Non-Cryptographic Fault-Tolerant Distributed Computation, *Proceedings of 20th ACM Symposium on the Theory of Computing* (1988) 1–10

[2] ElGamal, T.: A Public Key Cryptosystem and a Signature Scheme Based on Discrete Logarithms, *IEEE Transactions on Information Theory*, Vol. IT-31, No. 4, (1985) 469–472

[3] Freuder, E. C., Minca, M., and Wallace, R. J.: Privacy/Efficiency Tradeoffs in Distributed Meeting Scheduling by Constraint-based Agents, *Proceedings of IJCAI-01 Workshop on Distributed Constraint Reasoning* (2001)

[4] Goldreich, O., Micli, S., and Wigderson, A.: How to Play any Mental Game or A Completeness Theorem for Protocols with Honest Majority, *Proceedings of 19th ACM Symposium on the Theory of Computing* (1987) 218–229

[5] Hamadi, Y., Bessière, C., and Quinqueton, J.: Backtracking in Distributed Constraint Networks, *Proceedings of the Thirteenth European Conference on Artificial Intelligence (ECAI-98)* (1998) 219–223

[6] Herlea, T., Claessens, J., Neven, G., Piessens, F., Preneel, B., and De Decker, B.: On Securely Scheduling a Meeting, Dupuy, M. and Paradinas, P. eds., *Trusted Information - The New Decade Challenge, Proceedings of IFIP SEC* (2001) 183–198

[7] Mesequer, P. and Jiménez, M. A.: Distributed Forward Checking, *Proceedings of CP-00 Workshop on Distributed Constraint Satisfaction* (2000)

[8] Pedersen, T.: A Threshold Cryptosystem without a Trusted Party, *Proceedings of EUROCRYPT '91* (1991) 522–526, Lecture Notes in Computer Science 547

[9] Shamir, A.: How to share a secret, *Communications of the ACM*, Vol. 22, No. 11, (1979) 612–613

[10] Silaghi, M.-C., Sam-Haroud, D., and Faltings, B. V.: Asynchronous Search with Aggregations, *Proceedings of the Seventeenth National Conference on Artificial Intelligence (AAAI-2000)* (2000) 917–922

[11] Suyama, T., Yokoo, M., Sawada, H., and Nagoya, A.: Solving Satisfiability Problems using Reconfigurable Computing, *IEEE Transactions on VLSI*, Vol. 9, No. 1, (2001) 109–116

[12] Suzuki, K. and Yokoo, M.: Secure Combinatorial Auctions by Dynamic Programming with Polynomial Secret Sharing, *Proceedings of Sixth International Financial Cryptography Conference (FC-02)* (2002)

[13] Yokoo, M., Durfee, E. H., Ishida, T., and Kuwabara, K.: Distributed Constraint Satisfaction for Formalizing Distributed Problem Solving, *Proceedings of the Twelfth IEEE International Conference on Distributed Computing Systems* (1992) 614–621

[14] Yokoo, M., Durfee, E. H., Ishida, T., and Kuwabara, K.: The Distributed constraint satisfaction problem: formalization and algorithms, *IEEE Transactions on Knowledge and Data Engineering*, Vol. 10, No. 5, (1998) 673–685

[15] Yokoo, M. and Hirayama, K.: Distributed Breakout Algorithm for Solving Distributed Constraint Satisfaction Problems, *Proceedings of the Second International Conference on Multi-Agent Systems*, MIT Press (1996) 401–408

[16] Yokoo, M. and Suzuki, K.: Secure Multi-agent Dynamic Programming based on Homomorphic Encryption and its Application to Combinatorial Auctions, *Proceedings of the First International Conference on Autonomous Agents and Multiagent Systems (AAMAS-2002)* (2002): (to appear)

A Dual Graph Translation of a Problem in 'Life'

Barbara M. Smith

University of Huddersfield
Huddersfield HD1 3DH, U.K.
b.m.smith@hud.ac.uk

Abstract. Conway's game of Life provides interesting problems in which modelling issues in constraint programming can be explored. The problem of finding a maximum density stable pattern ('still-life') is discussed. A formulation of this problem as a constraint satisfaction problem with 0-1 variables and non-binary constraints is compared with its dual graph translation into a binary CSP. The success of the dual translation is surprising, from previously-reported experience, since it has as many variables as the non-binary CSP and very large domains. An important factor is the identification of many redundant constraints: it is shown that these can safely be removed from a dual graph translation if arc consistency is maintained during search.

1 Introduction

The game of Life was invented by John Horton Conway in the 1960s and popularized by Martin Gardner in his *Scientific American* columns (e.g. [6]). Many variants of the game and problems arising from it have been studied. Here, one such problem is described and its solution using constraint programming is discussed.

Life is played on a squared board, considered to extend to infinity in all directions. Each square of the board is a cell, which at any time during the game is either alive or dead. A cell has eight neighbours, as shown in Figure 1. The configuration of live and dead cells at time t leads to a new configuration at time $t + 1$ according to the rules of the game:

- if a cell has exactly three living neighbours at time t, it is alive at time $t + 1$
- if a cell has exactly two living neighbours at time t, it is in the same state at time $t + 1$ as it was at time t
- otherwise, the cell is dead at time $t + 1$

A *still-life* is a pattern that is not changed by these rules: hence, every cell that has exactly three live neighbours is alive, and every cell that has fewer than two or more than three live neighbours is dead. An empty board is a still-life, but so are more interesting patterns. The question addressed in this paper is: on an $n \times n$ section of the board, with all the rest of the board dead, what is the densest possible still-life pattern, i.e. the pattern with the largest number of live cells? For instance, Figure 2 shows a maximum density 3×3 pattern.

P. Van Hentenryck (Ed.): CP 2002, LNCS 2470, pp. 402–414, 2002.

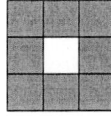

Fig. 1. A cell and its 8 neighbours

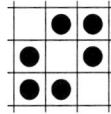

Fig. 2. A maximum density 3 × 3 still-life

Bosch and Trick [4, 3] considered integer programming and constraint programming formulations of the maximum density still-life problem. Their most successful approach [3] used a hybrid of the two. In this paper, pure constraint programming approaches are considered further.

2   A 0-1 Formulation

An obvious way to model the problem as a constraint satisfaction problem (CSP) is to use a 0-1 variable x_{ij} for the cell in row i, column j of the $n \times n$ grid, such that x_{ij} has the value 0 if the cell is dead and 1 if it is alive. Each cell is constrained by its eight neighbouring cells: if the sum of the values assigned to the neighbouring cells is 3, then the cell is alive, and if the sum is less than 2 or more than 3 then the cell is dead. Since all the cells surrounding the $n \times n$ square are dead, we cannot have a sequence of three live cells along the boundary: this is also included as a constraint.

The density of a pattern is the sum of the values of the cell variables. It is maximized by adding a constraint whenever a solution is found, that the density must be greater in any new solution; when no more solutions exist, the last one found is optimal.

The variables are assigned in lexicographic order, row by row and left to right along each row. This may not be the best ordering, but several likely alternatives have proved worse. To find dense solutions quickly, the value 1 is assigned before the value 0.

This formulation has been implemented in ILOG Solver. It is very similar to the basic constraint programming model described in [3].

The first improvement to this model is to deal with the symmetry of the problem. Given any Life pattern, there are up to seven symmetrically equivalent patterns resulting from rotating or reflecting the board. Hence, the search can explore many partial solutions which are symmetrically equivalent to dead-ends that have already been explored. This can be avoided on backtracking by adding

constraints to the new branch of the search tree to forbid the symmetric equivalents of assignments already considered. Gent & Smith [7] have implemented
SBDS (Symmetry Breaking During Search) in Solver to do this. The symmetries
of Life are the same as the symmetries of the n-queens problem, an example discussed in [7]. In this case, all that the SBDS user need do is write seven functions,
each describing the effect of one of the symmetries on an assignment of a value
to a variable. Bosch & Trick added constraints to their constraint programming
formulation to remove some of the symmetry, but SBDS, which removes all of
it, gives a greater reduction in search.

The results of the 0-1 formulation are given in Table 1. Search effort is measured by the number of fails (backtracks) reported by Solver. The table shows
both the effort required to find the optimal solution and the total effort and
running time (on a 600MHz PC). The difference between the number of fails to
find the optimal solution and the total number of fails shows the effort required
to prove optimality, i.e. to prove that there is no solution with greater density.
Using SBDS reduces the number of fails by about a factor of 6, and the running
time by about a factor of 4.

These results are better than those reported by Bosch and Trick for a constraint programming formulation. However, they achieved much better results
from their hybrid approach. The constraint programming approach needs to be
much improved before it is competitive with the hybrid.

Table 1. Search effort and running time to find maximum density still-lifes using
a 0-1 formulation. Value = maximum density; F = number of fails (backtracks)
to find the optimal solution; P = number of fails to prove optimality; sec. =
running time in seconds

n	Value	No symmetry breaking			With SBDS		
		F	P	sec.	F	P	sec.
5	16	3	187	0.03	3	59	0.02
6	18	9	6030	0.88	9	1062	0.22
7	28	617	39561	6.74	607	8436	1.78
8	36	955	811542	135	450	146086	26.6
9	43	*not attempted*			259027	11065129	2140

3   Dual Graph Representation

There are several reasons for the poor performance of the 0-1 model. Firstly,
the constraints between a variable and its 8 neighbouring cell variables are not
helpful in guiding the search. The state of the cell can still be undetermined when
7 of its neighbours have been assigned (if it has exactly 2 or 3 live neighbours

at that point). At best, four of the neighbouring cells must be assigned before a variable's value is determined, and this is only sufficient if all four are live.

Secondly, 0-1 variables do not lend themselves to variable ordering heuristics based on domain size: as soon as a value is removed from the domain of a variable, the alternative value is assigned.

Thirdly, as pointed out in [3], it is difficult to discover whether a partial assignment can be completed to give a higher density than in the incumbent solution. The density is defined as the sum of the variables, and since any unassigned variable has the value 1 in its domain, the upper bound on the density in the unassigned part of the grid is simply the number of cells it contains.

To begin to address these difficulties, we can consider different ways of representing the problem as a CSP. The dual graph representation is a well-known translation of a CSP with non-binary constraints into a binary CSP [5]. As described in [1], for instance, the constraints of the original problem become the variables of the dual representation: the domain of a dual variable is the set of tuples that satisfy the original constraint. There is a binary constraint between two dual variables iff the corresponding constraints in the original problem share at least one variable: the constraint ensures that the dual variables assign the same value to each of the original variables that they share.

In this problem there are two kinds of non-binary constraint: the constraints between each cell and its neighbours, of arity 9, and the objective constraint, ensuring that the number of live cells in any solution is greater than in the incumbent solution. The objective constraint cannot be replaced by a dual variable, since this would require listing all the satisfying tuples and so would entail solving the problem. The dual encoding will only replace the arity 9 constraints, and so will not result in a pure binary CSP.

The variables of the dual encoding correspond to 'supercells' in the grid, i.e. 3×3 squares consisting of a cell and its eight neighbours, as in Figure 1. The supercell variable y_{ij} corresponds to the cell variables $x_{i,j}$, $x_{i,j+1}$, $x_{i,j+2}$, $x_{i+1,j}$, $x_{i+1,j+1}$, $x_{i+1,j+2}$, $x_{i+2,j}$, $x_{i+2,j+1}$ and $x_{i+2,j+2}$.

A possible value of y_{ij} can be represented as a 9-bit number, rather than a 9-tuple, by writing the following constraint between a supercell variable and the variables of its constituent cells:

$$\begin{aligned} y_{ij} = x_{i,j} + 2x_{i,j+1} + 4x_{i,j+2} + 8x_{i+1,j} + 16x_{i+1,j+1} \\ + 32x_{i+1,j+2} + 64x_{i+2,j} + 128x_{i+2,j+1} + 256x_{i+2,j+2} \end{aligned} \tag{1}$$

A supercell variable is therefore an integer variable, with values between 0 and 511.

Each possible value for a supercell variable indicates which of the 0-1 variables in (1) have the value 1, and hence which of the 9 cells are alive. In a still-life many of these values are not allowed: any 3×3 area can contain at most 6 live cells, for instance. The possible values of a supercell variable in the interior of the square just correspond to the 259 tuples satisfying the 9-ary constraint. For supercells on the boundary, the domain has to allow for the neighbouring dead cells. The domains are constructed by finding all the feasible configurations for

a 3×3 square which is within the $n \times n$ square but at the edge. If a value
in the range 0 to 511 represents a feasible assignment for 3×3 square, it will
be consistent with the dead cells beyond the edge, and the value is included in
the domain of the variable; otherwise, this is not a possible value for a supercell
in that position. The supercells in the corners of the grid have fewest possible
values (74), since they must be consistent with the dead cells neighbouring them
on two sides. Supercells along the edges of the grid, but not in a corner, have
148 possible values.

4   Binary Constraints

Following the standard account of the dual encoding given earlier, a constraint
is required between any pair of supercell variables which share a cell variable.
Figure 3 shows the supercell variable y_{33} and the supercells above and to the
left of it that it shares a cell with. y_{33} also shares cells with 18 other supercells,
unless n is small and it is too close to the bottom right corner of the square for
all of these to exist: only one quarter of the possibilities are shown, for space
reasons. In the standard dual encoding, we therefore need binary constraints
between y_{33} and up to 24 other variables.

It was pointed out by Dechter & Pearl [5] that some of the constraints in
the dual graph may be redundant, in the sense that eliminating them does not
change the set of solutions of the problem. A constraint is redundant if there
is an alternative path between the two dual variables involved such that the
variables which they share are also shared by every variable along the path.
The constraints along the alternative path are sufficient to ensure that, in any
solution, the shared variables have the same value in every dual variable along
the path, in particular in the two dual variables at the ends of the redundant
constraint.

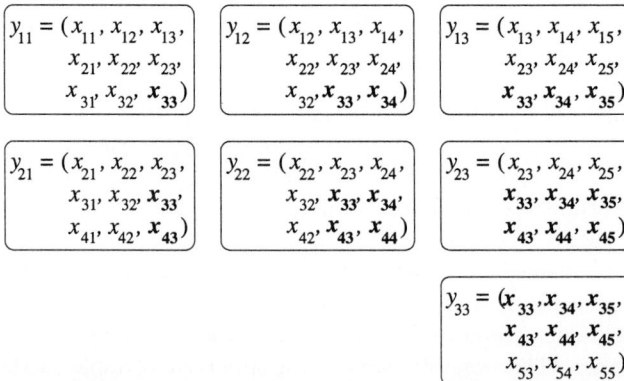

$$y_{11} = (x_{11}, x_{12}, x_{13}, \\ x_{21}, x_{22}, x_{23}, \\ x_{31}, x_{32}, \mathbf{x_{33}})$$
$$y_{12} = (x_{12}, x_{13}, x_{14}, \\ x_{22}, x_{23}, x_{24}, \\ x_{32}, \mathbf{x_{33}}, \mathbf{x_{34}})$$
$$y_{13} = (x_{13}, x_{14}, x_{15}, \\ x_{23}, x_{24}, x_{25}, \\ \mathbf{x_{33}}, \mathbf{x_{34}}, \mathbf{x_{35}})$$

$$y_{21} = (x_{21}, x_{22}, x_{23}, \\ x_{31}, x_{32}, \mathbf{x_{33}}, \\ x_{41}, x_{42}, \mathbf{x_{43}})$$
$$y_{22} = (x_{22}, x_{23}, x_{24}, \\ x_{32}, \mathbf{x_{33}}, \mathbf{x_{34}}, \\ x_{42}, \mathbf{x_{43}}, \mathbf{x_{44}})$$
$$y_{23} = (x_{23}, x_{24}, x_{25}, \\ \mathbf{x_{33}}, \mathbf{x_{34}}, \mathbf{x_{35}}, \\ \mathbf{x_{43}}, \mathbf{x_{44}}, \mathbf{x_{45}})$$

$$y_{33} = (\mathbf{x_{33}}, \mathbf{x_{34}}, \mathbf{x_{35}}, \\ \mathbf{x_{43}}, \mathbf{x_{44}}, \mathbf{x_{45}}, \\ x_{53}, x_{54}, x_{55})$$

Fig. 3. Supercell variable y_{33} and some of the supercell variables which share at
least one cell variable with it

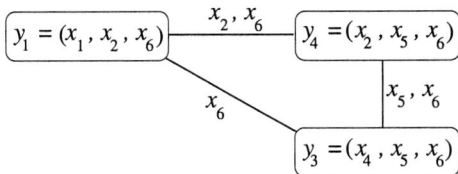

Fig. 4. Binary constraints between three dual variables

All the constraints involving y_{33} shown in Figure 3 are redundant, except for the constraint with y_{23}, which shares 6 cells with y_{33}. The other variables shown share a subset of these 6 cells with y_{33}. If there is a constraint only between pairs of variables that share 6 cells, there will always be a path between pairs of variables sharing at least one cell. For instance, y_{11} and y_{33} have just x_{33} in common: each variable along the path $y_{33} \rightarrow y_{23} \rightarrow y_{13} \rightarrow y_{12} \rightarrow y_{11}$ shares 6 cells with its predecessor and with its successor, and x_{33} is a common cell in them all. If y_{33} is assigned a value, then any consistent assignment to the variables along this path must have each variable assigning the same value to x_{33}, as required.

Although deleting redundant constraints will not change the solutions, it may increase the search effort to find a solution, which is why descriptions of the dual encoding include them. Figure 4 is based on part of a diagram in [1]. There, Bacchus and van Beek discuss using the dual encoding with the forward checking algorithm. Assigning a value to the dual variable y_1 then reduces the domains only of those variables which are constrained by y_1, so that if the redundant constraint between y_1 and y_3 is deleted, the domain of y_3 will not be reduced by an assignment to y_1 and the search may take longer.

However, if arc consistency is maintained after assignments are made, this constraint can safely be deleted: assigning a value to y_1 will still reduce the domain of y_3 appropriately via the other two constraints, because there is an alternative pathway $y_1 \rightarrow y_4 \rightarrow y_3$ with x_6 shared between all three variables. In general, if the search algorithm maintains arc consistency, redundant constraints between dual variables can, and should, be deleted. This has not previously been recognised.

Constraint programming tools such as ILOG Solver can maintain the arc consistency of the binary constraints of the dual encoding during search. The binary constraints for the still-life problem are expressed in Solver using *table constraints*: these implement the general arc consistency schema introduced by Bessière and Régin [2]. A predicate is supplied to the table constraint to evaluate, given a pair of variables and a value for each of them, whether or not the pair of values satisfy the required constraint between the variables.

In the dual representation of the still-life problem, a supercell variable y_{ij} need only be involved in four binary constraints, with $y_{i-1,j}$, $y_{i,j-1}$, $y_{i+1,j}$ and $y_{i,j+1}$. The 20 redundant constraints involving y_{ij} can be omitted. In total, approximately $2n^2$ binary constraints are needed, compared to approximately

$12n^2$ for large n if constraints between all variables sharing a cell are included (precisely, $2(n-2)(n-3)$ compared to $6(n-3)(2n-7)$, e.g. for $n = 8$, 60 constraints compared to a total of 270).

If the redundant constraints were added to the model, it could make no difference to the search, but would greatly increase the running time. Adding just the constraints between each supercell variable y_{ij} and its 'diagonal neighbours' $y_{i+1,j+1}$, $y_{i-1,j-1}$, $y_{i-1,j+1}$ and $y_{i+1,j-1}$ approximately doubles the number of constraints: for the range of problem sizes being considered, the running time increases by roughly 50%. Using all the constraints would more than double their number again, for $n = 8$. Hence, it is essential to remove the redundant constraints in order to achieve good performance.

5   Solving the Dual Model

So far, the dual model has approximately n^2 dual variables, mostly corresponding to interior supercells and so with 259 possible values, and approximately $2n^2$ binary constraints. In principle, in a dual encoding, the original variables are no longer needed. However, the objective constraint still has to be modelled, and the x_{ij} variables are kept for this purpose. The density of a pattern, as before, is the sum of the x_{ij} variables. The constraints (1) ensure that whenever a variable y_{ij} is assigned a value, its constituent x_{ij} variables are bound at the same time. Only the y_{ij} variables are used as search variables.

It is now possible to use the smallest domain variable ordering heuristic, which was not possible in the 0-1 model. This heuristic gives significantly better results than lexicographic ordering; the results given below use this heuristic. As in the 0-1 model, the value ordering used favours dense patterns, by choosing the value for a supercell variable giving the largest number of live cells.

Table 2 shows a comparison between the results of running the 0-1 encoding (repeated from Table 1) and the dual encoding. The dual encoding is doing much less search, but the running time, even without the redundant constraints, is much longer. The much higher ratio of running time to number of fails in the dual representation is because the domains of the dual variables are very large, so that maintaining arc consistency is time-consuming. Further improvements are discussed in the next section.

6   Improved Bounds

One reason for the poor performance of both models is that proving optimality takes a long time. As already noted, given a partial solution, the upper bound on the density of an extension to the rest of the grid assumes that all remaining cells can be alive. Hence, it can appear that even a sparsely populated partial grid can lead to a better solution, and it can take a long time to prove otherwise.

Since a 3×3 square can have at most 6 live cells in a still life, rather than 9, a much better bound on the cost of completing a partial solution can be found by covering the grid with such squares. Bosch & Trick [3] found that this

Table 2. Finding maximum density still-lifes with either the 0-1 encoding or the dual encoding

n	0-1 encoding		Dual encoding		
	P	sec.	F	P	sec.
5	59	0.02	15	51	0.41
6	1062	0.22	0	181	2.23
7	8436	1.78	1321	3510	16.2
8	146086	26.6	18084	53262	264
9	11065129	2140	250401	2091386	10300

gave some improvement in conjunction with their 0-1 model, although not as much as using bounds from the IP formulation. Bounds based on 3 × 3 squares (supercells) are relatively easy to incorporate into the dual representation, so the cost of completing a partial solution can be calculated from a set of supercell variables forming a partition of the unassigned part of the grid.

When n is a multiple of 3, the $n \times n$ grid can be partitioned into disjoint supercells and the density of the grid expressed as the sum of their densities. This defines the objective in terms of a subset of the dual variables. A side-effect is that the original variables are no longer needed; they were kept in the dual encoding only to define the objective. Hence for this special case it is possible to model the problem using just the dual variables, with all binary constraints apart from the objective constraint. However, a comparison of the running time with and without the cell variables shows that having them in the model carries a negligible overhead, when they are used only to access the states of individual cells and not as search variables.

Extending this model to the general case can be done by 'padding' the $n \times n$ grid with dead cells to the right and below it, so that the number of cells on each side is a multiple of 3, as shown in Figure 5. This again allows the density to be defined in terms of a partition of the extended grid into supercells.

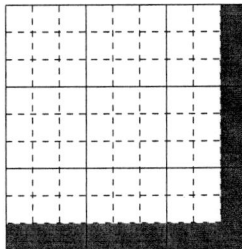

Fig. 5. An 8 × 8 grid, increased to 9 × 9 by adding dead cells

Calculating the density in this way has a dramatic effect on the search effort and the solution time: the 9×9 problem, which previously took over 2 million fails and over 10,000 sec. to solve with the dual encoding, now takes 1555 fails and 73 sec. to solve. This change makes the dual model much faster than the 0-1 model, for problems of this size.

7   Search Strategies & Results

Since the density is now defined in terms of a set of disjoint contiguous supercells, these variables can also be used as the search variables: propagation of the table constraints would assign consistent values to the remaining variables. (A simple way to implement this is to define all the supercell variables as search variables, but allow the variable ordering to select just from those that form a partition of the grid.) This reduces the number of variables to be assigned values from $(n-2)^2$ to $(n/3)^2$, e.g. from 49 to 9 in the 9×9 case. It would be simplistic to expect a similar reduction in search: the domain of each search variable, when it is selected for assignments, is likely to have been much less reduced by previous assignments than before.

With a choice of variable ordering heuristic, we have four possible search strategies: we can use all the supercell variables as the search variables or just a subset that together partition the grid, and we can assign them in lexicographic order, or choose the smallest domain.

The results of these four strategies are compared in Table 3. With lexicographic ordering, using the smaller set of search variables does reduce search,

Table 3. Comparison of four search strategies for the dual encoding

	All variables					
	Lex. ordering			Smallest domain		
n	F	P	sec.	F	P	sec.
5	11	12	1.11	0	2	0.66
6	0	13	0.79	0	13	0.78
7	75	216	7.27	5	54	3.52
8	200	530	33.4	49	206	13.9
9	592	1554	79.4	598	1555	73.4
10	150406	577258	29322	1471	225179	10900

	Partition					
	Lex. ordering			Smallest domain		
n	F	P	sec.	F	P	sec.
5	11	13	0.74	0	2	0.64
6	0	13	0.79	0	13	0.95
7	77	126	7.06	4	45	3.55
8	196	517	32.5	0	125	11.1
9	454	1171	66.7	340	893	56.8
10	102141	369332	21900	89	128905	7780

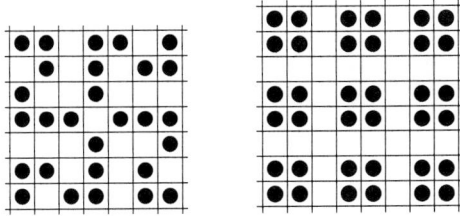

Fig. 6. The maximum density 7×7 and 8×8 still-lifes

especially for the larger problems. Using the partitioning variables in combination with the smallest domain ordering has a much greater effect, however. This ordering strategy will behave very differently depending on the set of search variables. If all the supercell variables are search variables, then after the first variable has been assigned, there will always be at least one variable having at least 6 cells in common with one already assigned, and hence a reduced domain size of at most 8: one of these variables will have the smallest domain. The improved performance of the heuristic when the search variables partition the grid may be because it then has more freedom to choose the variables in different parts of the grid.

Although the 9×9 problem is now easily solved, larger problems are still very difficult, as shown in Table 3 for the 10×10 problem. The optimal solution to this problem and to the 11×11 problem can be found very quickly, and it is proving optimality that is time-consuming. The time to solve the 10×10 problem has been improved to some extent by adding tighter bounds on the cost of completing a partial solution. Problems representing the corner of a larger grid, rather than a complete grid, of sizes 6×6, 6×9, 9×6 and 9×9, were solved optimally. For each corner size, the density of the whole grid is then constrained to be at most the maximum density of the corner plus the maximum densities of supercells covering the rest of the grid. These constraints provide tighter bounds: for instance, a 9×9 corner has maximum density 46, whereas the bound based on supercells suggests that a 9×9 square can hold 54 live cells. With these bounds, the 10×10 problem can be solved optimally in 55550 fails, 3300 sec. The 11×11 problem is still intractable for this approach, however: although the optimal solution (given by Bosch & Trick) is found immediately, with no backtracking, it has not been proved optimal in more than 10 hours running time.

An advantage of using SBDS to eliminate symmetrically-equivalent solutions is that non-isomorphic solutions can be enumerated. There is a unique optimal solution for $n = 3$, 5, 7 and 8; Figure 6 shows two of these. There are 2, 9 and 10 solutions for $n = 4$, 6 and 9 respectively, but many more for $n = 10$ and 12.

When n is too large to solve optimally with current methods, Bosch & Trick proposed finding symmetric solutions, and found optimal horizontally symmetric solutions for $n = 14$ and 15. Restricting solutions to those with 90° rotational symmetry, the dual encoding has found the optimal solution for $n = 18$, which I

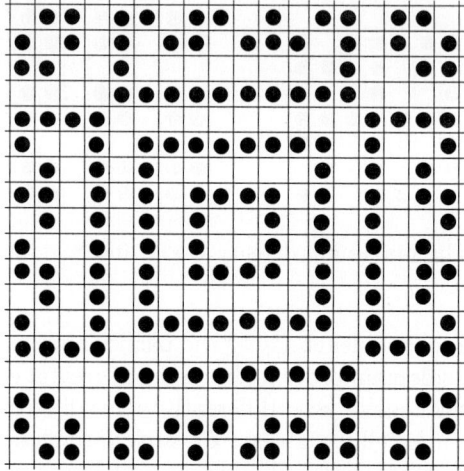

Fig. 7. A maximum density rotationally-symmetric 18 × 18 still-life

believe is new. This solution took 295 fails to find, and 76527 fails, 19900 sec. to prove optimal. It has value 168 and is shown in Figure 7.

8   Discussion & Conclusions

The final version of the dual representation outperforms the 0-1 formulation by two orders of magnitude in running time, and still more in the number of fails. The improvement over the first dual representation is partly due to the better bounding information given by expressing the density in terms of a partition into 3 × 3 squares, corresponding to supercell variables. This could be done by using supercell variables as an adjunct to the 0-1 formulation: Bosch & Trick reported trying this, although it appears that the improvement then was not as dramatic as in the dual encoding. The fact that the dual variables can be identified with 3 × 3 supercells also helps in devising good search strategies for the dual encoding, and the remaining improvement comes from basing the search itself on a subset of the dual variables representing a partition of the $n \times n$ square.

An important factor in the success of the dual representation is that redundant constraints have been removed. They have no pruning effect if arc consistency is maintained during search, and would slow down the search several times over. I believe that it has not previously been noted that redundant constraints in the dual representation should be removed if arc consistency is maintained. Redundant constraints may occur in the dual translations of other problems: a necessary condition is that three dual variables should share a common variable. A problem where this does not occur is the crossword puzzle example considered by Bacchus and van Beek [1]. The original variables correspond to the letter squares in the crossword puzzle grid, and the constraints (and so the dual variables) to sets of consecutive letter squares forming a word. Since any letter square in a crossword grid is the intersection of at most two words, three dual variables cannot have a letter variable in common, and so there are no redundant constraints. An example where they do occur is the Golomb rulers problem, discussed by Stergiou and Walsh [8]: the original CSP has ternary constraints $x_{ji} = x_j - x_i$ for $1 \leq i < j \leq n$, defining the distance between the ith and jth marks on the ruler. The dual variables corresponding to the constraints defining x_{ji}, for $1 \leq j \leq n, j \neq i$, would then all have the variable x_i in common, giving many redundant binary constraints in the dual representation. This shows that redundant constraints can occur in the dual representation of other problems. However, as Bacchus and van Beek noted, there has been little experience reported of the effectiveness of translations into binary representations, so it is hard to say how common redundant constraints are likely to be.

It is surprising that the dual representation of the still-life problem is practicable, since it does not fit the guidelines given by Bacchus and van Beek to indicate when the dual graph representation of a problem might be successful. They suggest that the number of constraints in the original CSP should be small, and the constraints should be tight, i.e. with few of the possible tuples allowed. Hence, the dual CSP will have a small number of variables with small domains. Here the dual representation has about the same number of variables as the non-binary CSP, and the domains are very large, especially in comparison with the original 0-1 variables.

A factor not mentioned by Bacchus and van Beek is the tightness of the binary constraints in the dual translation. Once the redundant constraints have been removed, any constraint of the dual encoding links two dual variables that share 6 cell variables. These are tight constraints: once a dual variable has been assigned a value, any variable it constrains has only three unassigned cells; at most 8 values, out of possibly 259, are still left in the domain. Hence although the domains are initially large, the branching factor of the search tree is manageable. This may be a reason why the dual translation is successful in this case; the tightness of the resulting binary constraints should perhaps be a factor to take into account when considering using the dual translation of a problem.

Compared to Bosch & Trick's results [3], the dual representation solves problems up to 9×9 with much less search: their hybrid of constraint and integer programming takes 46000 choice points (slightly more than the number of fails, in optimization problems) to solve the 9×9 problem, compared with 893 for the dual encoding. On the other hand, the hybrid solves the 11×11 problem with about 10 times the effort required for the 9×9 problem, whereas it is out of reach, so far, for the dual encoding, This suggests that the dual CSP is doing better locally than the hybrid: the effects of an assignment to a supercell variable are quickly propagated to the neighbouring cells. For the smaller problems, local effects are predominant, and so the dual encoding does well. As problems get larger, local information becomes inadequate. The dual encoding does not have good enough bounds to determine the effects of assignments made in one part of the square on the overall density, and the better bounds given by the linear constraints in the CP/IP hybrid become more significant. The two approaches seem to offer complementary advantages, and combining the two could lead to still better results.

The dual representation has so far enabled some new results to be found in the maximum density still-life problem, for instance the 18×18 pattern in Figure 7 and the enumeration of non-isomorphic solutions. It offers the hope of solving further problems in combination with the CP/IP hybrid. It also gives rare practical experience of the successful reformulation of a non-binary CSP using the dual graph translation.

Acknowledgments

I should like to thank Mike Trick for his helpful comments on this work. Thanks are also due to the other members of the APES group for their support: Peter van Beek in particular made encouraging comments on an early version of the paper. I am especially grateful to Ian Gent: the paper has been much improved as a result of his input.

References

[1] F. Bacchus and P. van Beek. On the Conversion Between Non-Binary and Binary Constraint Satisfaction Problems. In *Proceedings AAAI'98*, pages 311–318, 1998.

[2] C. Bessière and J.-C. Régin. Arc consistency for general constraint networks: preliminary results. In *Proceedings IJCAI'97*, volume 1, pages 398–404, 1997.

[3] R. Bosch and M. Trick. Constraint programming and hybrid formulations for three life designs. In N. Jussien and F. Laburthe, editors, *Proceedings of the Fourth International Workshop on Integration of AI and OR Techniques in Constraint Programming for Combinatorial Optimisation Problems (CP-AI-OR'02)*, pages 77–91, 2002.

[4] R. A. Bosch. Maximum density stable patterns in variants of Conway's game of Life. *Operations Research Letters*, 27:7–11, 2000.

[5] R. Dechter and J. Pearl. Tree clustering for constraint networks. *Artificial Intelligence*, 38:353–366, 1989.

[6] M. Gardner. The fantastic combinations of John Conway's new solitaire game. *Scientific American*, 223:120–123, 1970.

[7] I. P. Gent and B. M. Smith. Symmetry Breaking During Search in Constraint Programming. In W. Horn, editor, *Proceedings ECAI'2000*, pages 599–603, 2000.

[8] K. Stergiou and T. Walsh. Encodings of Non-Binary Constraint Satisfaction Problems. In *Proceedings AAAI'99*, pages 163–168, 1999.

Groups and Constraints:
Symmetry Breaking during Search[*]

Ian P. Gent[1], Warwick Harvey[2], and Tom Kelsey[1]

[1] School of Computer Science, University of St Andrews
St Andrews, Fife, KY16 9SS, UK
{ipg,tom}@dcs.st-and.ac.uk
[2] IC-Parc, Imperial College
Exhibition Road, London SW7 2AZ, UK
wh@icparc.ic.ac.uk

Abstract. We present an interface between the ECL^{i}PS^e constraint logic programming system and the GAP computational abstract algebra system. The interface provides a method for efficiently dealing with large numbers of symmetries of constraint satisfaction problems for minimal programming effort. We also report an implementation of SBDS using the GAP-ECL^{i}PS^e interface which is capable of handling many more symmetries than previous implementations and provides improved search performance for symmetric constraint satisfaction problems.

1 Introduction

Dealing with symmetries in constraint satisfaction problems has become quite a popular topic for research in recent years. One of the main areas of recent study has been the modification of backtracking search procedures so that they only return unique solutions. Such techniques currently broadly fall into two main categories. The first involves adding constraints whenever backtracking occurs, so that symmetric versions of the failed part of the search tree will not be considered in future [1, 12]; we will collectively refer to these techniques as SBDS (Symmetry Breaking During Search). The second category involves performing checks at nodes in the search tree to see whether they are dominated by the symmetric equivalent of some state already considered [7, 9]. Note that these two kinds of approaches are closely related; the main difference is when and how the symmetry-breaking conditions are enforced.

The SBDS approach as implemented to date (with one exception) has one main drawback when it comes to problems with large numbers of symmetry: it requires an explicit list of all the symmetries of the problem. It works well if the number of symmetries is small, and has been used effectively with a list of up to about 8000 symmetries, but clearly if a problem has billions of symmetries, a complete explicit list is not practical. Since the symmetries of a problem form

---

[*] This paper is dedicated to Alex Kelsey, 1991–2002

P. Van Hentenryck (Ed.): CP 2002, LNCS 2470, pp. 415–430, 2002.
© Springer-Verlag Berlin Heidelberg 2002

a group, one obvious candidate for representing and manipulating these symmetries implicitly is to use computational group theory (CGT). Modern CGT systems such as GAP [10] are very efficient: they allow rapid calculations to be done on large groups without the need to iterate over or explicitly represent more than a tiny fraction of the group elements. As well as offering a clear benefit in both time and space, using a CGT approach can make the expression of the symmetries by the programmer much easier: typically only a handful of example symmetries are required to generate the full symmetry group, even for very large groups.

Iain McDonald [13] has performed some early experiments using group theory to represent the symmetries in an SBDS implementation, but still only handled a few thousand symmetries. In this paper we present a much more sophisticated approach capable of handling several orders of magnitude more symmetries than any previous SBDS implementation. We interface the constraint logic programming system ECL^{i}PS^e [14] with GAP, running as a sub-process. We use GAP to specify the group and perform stabiliser calculations, passing the results back to ECL^{i}PS^e, which uses them to reduce the computational effort required to solve the problem. Note that while the examples in this paper have integer domain values, our implementation is general, allowing other classes of domain variables to be used.

In Section 2 of this paper we introduce the group theory concepts utilised by our system. These include the definition of symmetries as bijective mappings from an initial subset of the positive integers to itself, groups formed by composition of these maps, subgroups, generators of groups, elements which leave points unchanged (stable), and points which are the image of maps (orbits).

We describe the GAP-ECL^{i}PS^e interface in Section 3 and our SBDS implementation in Section 4. Examples of the use of GAP-ECL^{i}PS^e to improve SBDS are given in Section 5. We discuss our results and highlight future avenues of research in Section 6.

2   Group Theory for CSPs

Consider a constraint satisfaction problem, $\langle C, D \rangle$, consisting of a constraint, C, over variables $x_1, \ldots, x_n$, with finite domains $D(x_i)$. Suppose that the domain elements are also indexed from $D(x_i)_1$ to $D(x_i)_{m_i}$. It is possible that $\langle C, D \rangle$ contains symmetries in either the variables, the domain values, or both. By symmetry, we mean a permutation of either the variables or the domain values, or both, which preserves solutions.

Example 1: Symmetry in Domains. A graph colouring problem $\langle C, D \rangle$ with domain

$$D(x_i)_1 = red, D(x_i)_2 = green, D(x_i)_3 = blue$$

for each variable, has the same solutions as the problem $\langle C, D' \rangle$, where D' is any permutation of the indexing of D. Hence $D'(x_i)_1 = blue, D'(x_i)_2 = green, D'(x_i)_3 = red$ is a symmetric version of D. Since there are $n!$ permutations of n elements in a set, $\langle C, D \rangle$ has $3! = 6$ symmetric variants.

Example 2: Symmetry in Variables. Suppose that we wish to solve

$$\frac{A}{BC} + \frac{D}{EF} + \frac{G}{HI} = 1$$

where each letter is a distinct member of $\{1, \ldots, 9\}$, and BC denotes $10 * B + C$. By the associativity and commutativity of arithmetic over the rationals, if $\{A \mapsto 5, B \mapsto 3, C \mapsto 4, \ldots\}$ is a solution, then so is $\{G \mapsto 5, H \mapsto 3, I \mapsto 4, \ldots\}$. Again we have 3! permutations of the variables which preserve solutions.

Symmetries as Group Elements. A group is a tuple $\langle S, \circ \rangle$ where S is a set and $\circ$ is a closed binary operation over S such that:

1. $\circ$ acts associatively: $(a \circ b) \circ c = a \circ (b \circ c)$ for every $a, b, c \in S$;
2. there is a neutral element, e, such that $a \circ e = e \circ a = a$ for every $a \in S$;
3. each element has an inverse, so that $a \circ a^{-1} = a^{-1} \circ a = e$.

Let $\Omega = \{1, 2, \ldots N\}$ for some N, where each integer might represent (depending on the nature of the symmetries in a given problem) a CSP variable, a value, or a variable/value pair. Our set, S_Ω, is the set of bijective mappings from Ω to itself (i.e. permutations of the elements of Ω), and we take $\circ$ to be the composition of such mappings. $\langle S_\Omega, \circ \rangle$ forms a group since

1. $\circ$ is clearly closed and associative;
2. the identity mapping, denoted by (), is a neutral element: composing () with any other mapping has no effect;
3. by our restriction to bijective mappings, we ensure that each mapping has an inverse.

$\langle S_\Omega, \circ \rangle$ is known as S_N, the symmetric group over N elements. S_N has $N!$ elements (one for each possible bijective permutation), each of which can be represented by the image of the relevant mapping from Ω to Ω. For example, $f(i) = (i + 1) \mod N$ has the image $[2, \ldots, N, 1]$; and g, the swapping of only points 1 and 2, has the image $[2, 1, 3, \ldots, N]$. The inverses of f and g are easy to describe, and their composition $f \circ g$ has the image $[1, 3, \ldots, N, 2]$.

Each member of S_N is a *permutation* of the numbers $\{1, 2, \ldots, N\}$, and each symmetry of a CSP will have an associated permutation. An arbitrary CSP need not have $N!$ symmetries: for example, an N-queens problem has the number of symmetries of a square, which is 8 for any value of N. This motivates a discussion of subgroups of S_N.

Symmetries as Subgroups. The tuple $\langle T, \circ \rangle$ is a subgroup of $\langle S, \circ \rangle$ if T is subset of S which forms a group under the $\circ$ operation. Trivial subgroups are obtained when T consists of only the identity permutation, and when $T = S$. Lagrange's theorem states that the order (number of elements) of a subgroup divides the order of the group. In terms of CSPs, we wish to identify permutations which *generate* the subgroup of S_N which correctly describes the symmetries of a given CSP. The process of subgroup generation involves choosing a small number of permutations, and repeatedly forming other permutations by composition until a closed subset of S_Ω is obtained. For example, consider a CSP involving the symmetries of a 2×2 square, in which we have labelled the cells 1...4 from top left via top right and lower left to lower right. The S_4 elements $p_1 = [3, 1, 4, 2]$ and $p_2 = [3, 4, 1, 2]$ define a rotation by 90° and a flip through the horizontal axis respectively. We see that p_1 and p_2 generate a subgroup of S_4 order 8:

$$p_1 \circ p_1 = [4, 3, 2, 1] \quad \text{rotation by } 180°$$
$$p_1 \circ p_1 \circ p_1 = [2, 4, 1, 3] \quad \text{rotation by } 270°$$
$$p_1 \circ p_1 \circ p_1 \circ p_1 = [1, 2, 3, 4] \quad \text{rotation by } 360° : \text{identity}$$
$$p_2 \circ p_1 = [4, 2, 3, 1] \quad \text{rotate by } 90° \text{ then flip}$$
$$p_1 \circ p_2 = [1, 3, 2, 4] \quad \text{flip then rotate by } 90°$$
$$p_1 \circ p_1 \circ p_2 = [2, 1, 4, 3] \quad \text{flip through vertical axis}$$

It is straightforward to check that any composition involving only p_1 and p_2 gives one of the above elements. The generated group is known as the dihedral group with 8 elements, D_4, and is clearly a subgroup of S_4. Note that 8 divides $4! = 24$ as required by Lagrange's theorem.

In order to identify and deal with symmetries during search, we need to identify the images of points in Ω after permutation by group elements (*orbits* of points), and those elements which leave certain points unchanged after permutation (*stabilisers* of points). The idea is to keep track of the stabilisers of (the identifiers of) forward labelling steps. If a choice is backtracked, we find its orbit in our symmetry group, and add constraints excluding configurations corresponding to each of the points in the orbit. This is justified since points in the orbit are symmetrically equivalent to the choice point, with respect to the current state of our search.

Orbits, Stabilisers and Cosets. Let G be a permutation group acting on N points, so that G is a subgroup of S_N. We define the *orbit*, $O_i(G)$, under G of a point $i \in \{1, \ldots, N\}$ as

$$O_i(G) = \{g(i) \mid g \in G\}.$$

In the above example, $O_3(D_4) = \{1, 2, 3, 4\}$ since p_2 moves 3 to 1, $p_1 \circ p_1$ moves 3 to 2, the identity leaves 3 unchanged, and p_1 moves 3 to 4.

We define the *stabiliser* of point i in G as

$$Stab_G(i) = \{g \in G \mid g(i) = i\}.$$

Using the same example, $Stab_{D_4}(3) = \{(), p_2 \circ p_1\}$, since applying either of these permutations leaves point 3 unchanged (and no others do).

The concepts of orbit and stabiliser can easily be extended to cover more than one point, and it can be shown that any stabiliser of a point acted on by a group is a subgroup of that group. Moreover, the orbit-stabiliser theorem provides the useful result that $|O_i(G)| |Stab_G(i)| = |G|$, i.e. the order of a group is the order of the stabiliser of any point times the size of the associated orbit.

In Section 4 we shall consider chains of stabilisers of points, together with representative permutations of associated orbits. To illustrate this, consider the symmetric group consisting of the 24 permutations of $\{1, 2, 3, 4\}$. We compute a chain of stabilisers of each point, starting arbitrarily with point 1:

$$Stab_{S_4}(1) = \{(), [1, 2, 4, 3], [1, 3, 2, 4], [1, 3, 4, 2], [1, 4, 2, 3], [1, 4, 3, 2]\}.$$

This is the group consisting of the 6 permutations of the set $\{2, 3, 4\}$. We can define a binary relation on the elements of any finite G with subgroup H by setting $a \sim b$ iff $b \circ a^{-1} \in H$. This is an equivalence relation (since $a \sim a$, $a \sim b \Rightarrow b \sim a$, and $a \sim b \wedge b \sim c \Rightarrow a \sim c$), and the equivalence classes are called *right cosets* of H in G. A simple calculation shows that the right cosets of $Stab_{S_4}(1)$ in S_4 are:

$$c_1 = Stab_{S_4}(1)$$
$$c_2 = [2, 1, 4, 3], [2, 1, 3, 4], [2, 4, 3, 1], [2, 3, 4, 1], [2, 4, 1, 3], [2, 3, 1, 4]$$
$$c_3 = [3, 4, 1, 2], [3, 4, 2, 1], [3, 1, 2, 4], [3, 2, 1, 4], [3, 1, 4, 2], [3, 2, 4, 1]$$
$$c_4 = [4, 3, 2, 1], [4, 3, 1, 2], [4, 2, 1, 3], [4, 1, 2, 3], [4, 2, 3, 1], [4, 1, 3, 2]$$

Note that the cosets partition S_4, with c_j consisting of the permutations which send 1 to j. A *right-transversal* of H in G is a list of canonical representatives from the cosets. We only need one representative of each coset, since any member of c_j is equivalent to any other member in terms of where the point fixed by the stabiliser, 1, gets mapped to.

To complete the stabiliser chain we have

$$Stab_{Stab_{S_4}(1)}(2) = \{(), [1, 2, 4, 3]\}$$

which is the subgroup of $Stab_{S_4}(1)$ which leaves point 2 unchanged, and

$$Stab_{Stab_{Stab_{S_4}(1)}(2)}(3) = \{()\}$$

since only the identity permutation leaves point 3 unchanged. Stabiliser chains, in general, collapse quickly to the subgroup containing only the identity since the order of each new stabiliser must divide the order of the stabilisers above it. Once an order 1 stabiliser is reached, all stabilisers further down the chain are trivial.

3   GAP-ECL^{i}PS^e

In this Section we briefly describe the interface between the GAP computational group theory system and the ECL^{i}PS^e Constraint Logic Programming system. The idea is that GAP acts as a black box. While an ECL^{i}PS^e implementation is performing tree search to solve a CSP involving symmetries, GAP is asked to provide group theoretic results such as the symmetry group itself, stabilisers of points, and members of cosets of stabilisers. The ECL^{i}PS^e implementation uses these results to break any symmetries that arise during search.

GAP [10] (Groups, Algorithms and Programming) is a system for computational discrete algebra with particular emphasis on, but not restricted to, computational group theory. GAP includes command line instructions for generating permutation groups, and for computing stabiliser chains and right transversals. Note that GAP does not explicitly create and store each element of a group. This would be impractical for, say, the symmetric group over 30 points, which has 30! elements. Instead group elements are created and used as required by the computation involved, making use of results such as Lagrange's theorem and the orbit-stabiliser theorem to obtain results efficiently. GAP can also be programmed to perform specific calculations in a modular way. GAP is available from http://www.gap-system.org/

ECL^{i}PS^e is a Constraint Logic Programming system which includes libraries for finite domain constraint solving. In addition to its powerful modelling and search capabilities, ECL^{i}PS^e has three important features which we utilise to prune search trees using results from computational group theory.

The first, and most important, feature is efficient communication with subprocesses. It is straightforward to write ECL^{i}PS^e programs which start a GAP subprocess and send and receive information which can be used to prune search. We have implemented an ECL^{i}PS^e module which exports predicates for

- starting and ending GAP processes;
- sending commands to a GAP process;
- obtaining GAP results in a format which is usable by ECL^{i}PS^e;
- loading GAP modules; and
- receiving information such as timings of GAP computations.

The second ECL^{i}PS^e feature is the provision of attributed variables. These allow us to attach extra information to a variable and retrieve it again later. We use this feature to avoid requiring the user to thread extra symmetry-related data through their code: during the search, any symmetry data one needs in relation to any variable (including the global symmetry-breaking state) can be retrieved directly from that variable.

The third feature is the provision of suspended goals. This allows us to evaluate and impose constraints in a lazy fashion, which is a crucial feature of our approach.

4   Using GAP-ECL^{i}PS^e to Break Symmetries

We describe a GAP-ECL^{i}PS^e implementation of SBDS in which symmetric equivalents of assignments are determined by computation within GAP. We assume that the ECL^{i}PS^e user has a constraint satisfaction problem of the form

$$C \wedge x_1 \in D(x_1) \wedge \cdots \wedge x_n \in D(x_n),$$

where C represents the constraints of the problem and $D(x_i)$ is the domain of the ith variable. We first obtain some global symmetry information, and then run a binary backtrack search procedure using SBDS [12]. In the context of a partial assignment A, after the assignment $Var = Val$ fails, SBDS posts the constraint $g(A) \Rightarrow g(Var \neq Val)$ for each element g in the symmetry group. This ensures that if we ever visit a symmetric equivalent of A we never try the equivalent of $Var = Val$.

4.1   Mapping between ECL^{i}PS^e Assignments and GAP Points

Before we can begin describing the symmetries of a CSP, we need to decide on a mapping between the points manipulated by GAP ($1 \ldots N$ for some N) and the constraints imposed by ECL^{i}PS^e during search ($x_i = d_j$, $x_i \neq d_j$). To allow full symmetry generality, one needs to assign a distinct point to each possible assignment; for example, one could assign the points $1 \ldots m$ to the assignments $x_1 = 1, \ldots, x_1 = m$, points $m + 1 \ldots 2m$ to the assignments $x_2 = 1, \ldots, x_2 = m$, etc., but any order will do. Note that we do not have to consider disequality constraints separately since they are affected by symmetries in exactly the same way as the corresponding equality constraint, and the type of constraint (= or $\neq$) will be known from context.

If the problem has only simple variable symmetry (or simple value symmetry), then having one point for each potential assignment is overkill since all assignments involving a given variable (resp. value) are affected by the symmetries in the same way. Instead one can associate points with variables (resp. values), and when computing the symmetric equivalents of assignments retain the value (resp. variable) from the original assignment.

In our implementation, the relevant mapping is encapsulated in a pair of ECL^{i}PS^e predicates. The first takes a variable-value pair and returns the corresponding GAP point. The second takes a GAP point and the original variable-value pair (only used for simple variable or value symmetries), and returns the corresponding variable-value pair.

4.2   Using GAP to Obtain a Symmetry Group

There is no need to explicitly code every symmetry of the CSP. Indeed, this would be impractical for a balanced incomplete block design (henceforth, BIBD) with, say, a 7×7 matrix model, which has full symmetry on both the rows and columns. In other words, any solution matrix is symmetrically equivalent to the same matrix after swapping any number of rows and columns. In this case the symmetry group is $S_7 \times S_7$, the direct product of the row and column symmetry groups, with order $7! \times 7! = 25,401,600$.

A more efficient approach is to identify a small number of symmetries, and use GAP to obtain the generated symmetry group. For example, to generate S_N it is sufficient to provide one permutation that switches exactly two elements, and another permutation that cycles each element by one position. The following GAP session illustrates this for the symmetric group on 7 points:

```
gap> p1 := PermList([2,1,3,4,5,6,7]);;
gap> p2 := PermList([2,3,4,5,6,7,1]);;
gap> g := Group(p1,p2);;
gap> Size(g);
                    5040
```

As a further example we generated the symmetry group of a square from one rotational symmetry and one flip symmetry in Section 2. The greatest number of generators needed is $O(log_2(N))$, and this bound is reached only for a small class of permutation groups. In general, it is sufficient to identify one example of each type of symmetry in the problem for GAP to generate the correct symmetry group. A useful heuristic is to use the first 3 or 4 symmetries that can be easily written down. If this process omits a class of symmetries, then symmetry breaking will still happen, but only for a subgroup of the underlying symmetry group. The CSP practitioner then has the option of identifying other symmetries (so as to generate the largest possible group), or accepting the number of symmetric solutions obtained.

4.3 Symmetry Breaking during Search

We assume that our search algorithm has arrived at a value to variable assignment point. The idea is to try assigning *Val* to *Var*, and if that fails, to exclude all symmetrically equivalent assignments. The procedure takes as argument:

- *Stab*, the member of the stabiliser chain computed at the previous assignment node (i.e. the subgroup of G which stabilises each SBDS point assigned so far) ;
- *A*, the current partial assignment of values to variables;
- *RTchain*, a sequence of the right transversals corresponding to the assignments made so far, $\langle RT_1, \ldots, RT_k \rangle$, where RT_i is a set containing a representative group element for each coset of $Stab_i$ in $Stab_{i-1}$. We define $g \in RTchain$ as any group element g which can be expressed as $g = p_k \circ p_{k-1} \circ \ldots \circ p_1$ where $p_i \in RT_i$. Note that *RTchain* implicitly represents the partial assignments symmetric to A, since any such assignment can be obtained by applying some $g \in RTchain$ to A.

Our implementation is based on the pseudo-code given in Figure 1. We first choose a variable-value pair, and map this pair to a GAP point. The next stage is to use GAP to compute the next member of the stabiliser chain, and the right transversal of this in the previous member of the stabiliser chain. Once this is done, we update *RTchain*. Since *RTchain* is made up of (products of) group elements which appear in the orbits of the points fixed by the current partial assignment, *RTchain* can be thought of as the current set of potentially applicable symmetries. We are now ready to test assignments.

If the assignment *Var = Val* leads to a successful search, we stop searching and the final A is a solution to the CSP which is not symmetric to any other solution found using the same search method. If *Var = Val* leads to a failure, we

```
sbds_search := proc(Stab, A, RTchain)
local Point, NewStab, RT, NewA, BrokenSymms, g;
    choose(Var, Val);
    Point := var_value_to_point(Var, Val);
    NewStab := Stabilizer(Stab, Point);
    RT := RightTransversal(Stab, NewStab);
    NewRTchain = RTchain ^ RT;
    assert(Var = Val);
    if sbds_search(NewStab, A ∧ Var = Val, NewRTchain) = true
    then
        return TRUE
    else
        retract(Var = Val);
        BrokenSymms := lazy_check(NewRTChain, A);
        for g in BrokenSymms do
            assert (g(A) ⇒ g( Var ≠ Val));
        end do;
        return sbds_search(Stab, A, RTchain)
    end if
end proc
```

Fig. 1. SBDS using GAP and ECL^{i}PS^e

backtrack and (effectively) want to impose the constraint $g(A) \Rightarrow g(Var \neq Val)$
for each symmetry g.[1] By symmetry we mean a member of our revised $RTchain$,
which is, perforce, a member of the original symmetry group. However doing
this by iterating over every symmetry would be very inefficient; indeed it would
be completely impractical for large symmetry groups. Instead there are several
observations we can make which allow us to cut down the number of considered
symmetries drastically.

First, there are potentially many symmetries which map $A \wedge Var \neq Val$ to the
same constraint; we need only consider one such g. Indeed, this is where $RTchain$
comes in: each member of $RTchain$ is a representative of the set of symmetries
which agree on what to map each of the variable/value pairs in $A \wedge Var \neq Val$
to. Note that this can be generalised: any members of $RTchain$ which select the
same $p_i \in RT_i$ for $i = 1 \ldots j$ agree on what to map the first j elements of A to.
This also means that the truth value of the first j elements of A is the same for
these members of $RTchain$, suggesting that they should be considered together.

The next observation is that we need not post the constraint for any symmetries for which the precondition $g(A)$ is false. For some g this may be true for the
entire search subtree under consideration; for some it may be true for some part

---

[1] Note that we need not explicitly impose $Var \neq Val$, since the identity permutation
    (or something equivalent) will be one of the symmetries considered.

of the subtree; for others it may never be true. We combine this observation with the previous one to in effect evaluate $g(A)$ lazily, only imposing the constraint $g(\textit{Var} \neq \textit{Val})$ when $g(A)$ is known to be true, sharing as much of the evaluation as possible between different g, and deferring that evaluation until it is known to be needed.

Suppose we have a prefix of $RTchain$ of length $i \geq 0$ (call it $RTchain_i$) and some $p_i \in RTchain_i$ such that the prefix of A of length i is mapped to something which is true for the current point in the search tree. If $RTchain_{i+1} = RTchain_i{}^\wedge\langle RT_{i+1}\rangle$ then we wish to consider $p_{i+1} = rt_{i+1} \circ p_i$ for all $rt_{i+1} \in RT_{i+1}$. All such p_{i+1} map the first i elements of A to the same thing (indeed, the same thing as p_i), but each maps the $i + 1$th element to something different. For each such p_{i+1} we have three cases:

1. The $i + 1$th element of A is mapped to something which is true. In this case, proceed to considering the $i + 2$th element.
2. The $i + 1$th element of A is mapped to something which is false. In this case, do not consider this p_{i+1} any further. (This excludes all symmetries which map the first $i + 1$ elements of A to the same thing from further consideration.)
3. The $i + 1$th element of A is mapped to something which is neither true nor false at this point in the search. In this case we delay further computation based on this p_{i+1} until the truth value is known, and then apply the appropriate case above. We delay in order to avoid considering the next right transversal in $RTchain$ until we know that we must. This is because each time we consider a new right transversal RT for a permutation under consideration, that permutation is expanded into $|RT|$ candidate permutations for the next iteration, and to remain practical we need to minimise the number of such multiplicative expansions.

Whenever the computation determines that $g(A)$ in its entirety is true, $g(\textit{Var} \neq \textit{Val})$ is asserted.

The check on classes of elements of $RTchain$ is crucial to the efficiency of the search procedure, and is made possible by careful use of variable attributes and suspended goals in ECL^iPS^e. It also ensures that we post at most one constraint for each set of symmetries which map A (as a tuple) to the same thing.

4.4 Comparison with [13]

In a prior implementation [13] of SBDS using group theory, on backtracking the orbit of the current partial assignment under the action of the full symmetry group is computed from scratch, and then a constraint is imposed for each member of the orbit, excluding that particular partial assignment. The idea is to ensure that each constraint posted is different, since different symmetries applied to a partial assignment can yield the same constraint. The main drawbacks of this implementation are that the orbit is computed from scratch each time, and no account is taken of whether the constraints are already entailed. The latter is important since it may be that many constraints are posted excluding different partial assignments, but that many of these constraints are useless for the same reason; e.g. because they involve excluding configurations where $X = 1$ when we already know that $X = 2$.

In contrast, our approach is incremental, tries to share computation between symmetries, and exploits knowledge of entailment and disentailment to minimise the work done. On the other hand, our approach can result in the same constraint being imposed more than once because it treats assignments as (ordered) tuples rather than sets; e.g. it might post both $X \neq 1 \wedge Y \neq 2$ and $Y \neq 2 \wedge X \neq 1$. We hope to be able to remove this unnecessary duplication in future.

5   Examples

In this section we present examples of the use of our GAP-ECL^{i}PS^e implementation applied to constraint satisfaction problems having symmetry groups of sizes up to about 10^9. We give CPU times for a 600 MHz Intel PIII processor, version 5.3 of ECL^{i}PS^e and version 4r2 of GAP.

Colouring Dodecahedrons. For our first example we consider the problem of colouring the vertices of a dodecahedron, the regular polyhedron having 12 pentagonal faces and 20 vertices. The variables $x_1, \ldots, x_{20}$ represent the 20 vertices. The values $c_1, \ldots, c_m$ are the m colours in question. It can be shown that the symmetry group of the dodecahedron is isomorphic to the group of even permutations of five objects, known to group theorists as A_5, which has 60 elements. Since any permutation of a colouring is allowed, the symmetry group of the values is S_m. The total number of symmetries is then $60 \times m!$, acting on $20 \times m$ points. We construct this group in GAP from just four generators: one rotation of the vertices about a face, one rotation about a vertex, swapping the first two colour indices, and cycling the colour indices by one place. The constraints of the CSP are of the form $x_i \neq x_j$ whenever vertex i is joined by an edge to vertex j. We seek the number of colourings for a given m, such that no colouring is a symmetric equivalent of another. A standard CSP solver will return all legal assignments. Our approach has the advantage that all symmetries inherent in the problem are dealt with during the initial search.

Table 1. Dodecahedron colouring using GAP-ECL^{i}PS^e

Parameters		GAP-ECL^{i}PS^e			ECL^{i}PS^e		
m	Symms.	Sols.	Time	Backtracks	Sols.	Time	Backtracks
3	360	31	1.0	43	7200	0.2	6840
4	1440	117902	1600	100234	1.7×10^8	5270	1.0×10^8

Table 1 gives a comparison of GAP-ECL^{i}PS^e performance against a standard ECL^{i}PS^e implementation. While the overheads are not repaid for 3-colouring (for so few symmetries one might as well use one of the existing SBDS approaches), we obtain more than a three-fold speedup for 4-colouring.

Alien Tiles. The alien tiles puzzle (http://www.alientiles.com) is Problem 27 in CSPLib (http://www.csplib.org) and consists of an $n \times n$ array of coloured tiles. A click on any tile in the array changes all tiles in the same row and column by one colour in a cycle of m colours. For $n = 4$, $m = 3$, we look at the following two problems, as described in detail in [11]:

1. What is the largest possible number of clicks required in the shortest sequence of clicks to reach any goal state from the start state?
2. How many distinct goal states are there requiring this number?

By distinct we mean not symmetrically equivalent to another sequence. The symmetries of the problem are given by a flip along any diagonal axis (2 symmetries) followed by any permutation of the rows and columns. The total number of symmetries is $2 \times n! \times n!$, for 1152 when $n = 4$. The group is straightforward to generate using three generators: one for a flip and two for permuting the rows (a permutation of the columns can be obtained by doing a flip, permuting the rows and flipping back).

Table 2. Alien tiles comparison: GAP-ECL^{i}PS^e – SBDS – no symmetry breaking

Problem	GAP-ECL^{i}PS^e			ECL^{i}PS^e SBDS		ECL^{i}PS^e	
	Sol.	GCPU	ECPU	ΣCPU	Sol.	Time	Sol.	Time
min. cost		0.95	8.66	9.61		44.95		600.75
dist. sols.	19	0.98	8.51	9.41	19	43.83	11232	862.63

These questions have been answered previously using SBDS with all 1151 non-trivial symmetries explicitly considered [11]: the minimum number is 10 and there are 19 distinct solutions. The use of SBDS led to a 40-fold runtime speedup using ILOG Solver. We implemented the problem in ECL^{i}PS^e with each symmetry explicitly considered, obtaining identical results with slightly less speedup. We then used our GAP-ECL^{i}PS^e system to solve the problem starting from the three generators. This gave a further run-time improvement of a factor of 5 over SBDS without GAP, again obtaining a minimum cost of 10 with 19 distinct solutions. We see an overall speedup by a factor of 60 to 90. We see that the use of GAP-ECL^{i}PS^e leads to a much faster solution with only a small amount of programming effort required to encode the symmetries of the problem.

So far we have used groups up to size 1,440. Our ability to handle groups of this size efficiently and easily is a significant step forward in the application of symmetry breaking in constraint problems. In fact, up to this size there are as many as 49,500,455,063 distinct groups. Each one could arise as the symmetry group of a variety of different constraint problems. However, we can also apply SBDS to problems with symmetry groups several orders of magnitude bigger than could be handled previously, as we now show.

Balanced Incomplete Block Designs. To show that large numbers of symmetries can be dealt with, we consider the problem of finding $v \times b$ binary matrices such that each row has exactly r ones, each column has exactly k ones, and the scalar product of each pair of distinct rows is λ. This is a computational version of the (v, b, r, k, λ) BIBD problem [5]. Solutions do not exist for all parameters, and results are useful in areas such as cryptography and coding theory. A solution has $v! \times b!$ symmetric equivalents: one for each permutation of the rows and/or columns of the matrix.

Table 3. Balanced incomplete block designs using GAP-ECL^{i}PS^e

Parameters	GAP-ECL^{i}PS^e				ECL^{i}PS^e	
v b r k λ	Sols.	GCPU	ECPU	ΣCPU	Sols.	Time
7 7 3 2 1	1	0.71	0.68	1.39	151200	3149.7
6 10 5 3 2	1	0.89	5.57	6.46		$> 4 \times 10^5$

For the $(7, 7, 3, 3, 1)$ problem, GAP-ECL^{i}PS^e finds the unique solution in about one second of combined CPU time. Keen algebraists will note that the number of solutions found by ECL^{i}PS^e with no symmetry breaking is $151,200 = 7!^2/168$. The denominator, 168, is the size of the automorphism group of the projective plane of order 2 defined by the 2-$(7, 3, 1)$ block design. This shows that ECL^{i}PS^e is successfully finding only those solutions which are distinct with respect to the formulation of the problem.

The $(6, 10, 5, 3, 2)$ BIBD has $6! \times 10! = 2,612,736,000$ symmetries. Again, we can find the unique solution in a few seconds. The number of symmetric solutions is so large that an ECL^{i}PS^e program failed to enumerate them after 12 hours elapsed computation time. Taken together, these results demonstrate that many symmetric equivalent solutions are excluded during search in an efficient manner. Both groups were generated from only 4 permutations, and neither group was created as an explicit collection of elements by either ECL^{i}PS^e or GAP, allowing search that is efficient in space as well as time.

For constraint models in the form of a matrix, such as a BIBD, an alternative means of breaking symmetry is to insist that both rows and columns are lexicographically ordered [8]. While this may not break all symmetry, it successfully obtained a unique solution on both BIBDs we studied, in run times at least 10 times faster than our implementation of SBDS.

The lexicographic constraints force only a particular solution to be acceptable. This might conflict with the variable and value ordering heuristics being used, while SBDS will accept the first solution found and remove all symmetric

Table 4. Comparison of symmetry breaking using lexicographic ordering and SBDS in GAP-ECL^{i}PS^e and combinations of heuristics. The variable ordering heuristic + enumerates squares in rows starting from the top left, while - reverses, starting from the bottom right. The value ordering heuristic + tries 0 before 1, while - reverses this

Parameters					Heuristics		Lex-ECL^{i}PS^e		GAP-ECL^{i}PS^e	
v	b	r	k	λ	Var	Val	1st CPU	All CPU	$1^{st}\Sigma$CPU	All ΣCPU
7	7	3	3	1	+	+	0.09	0.13	1.06	1.39
					+	-	0.12	0.13	0.70	0.76
					-	+	1.42	1.62	1.12	1.44
					-	-	0.27	1.62	0.80	0.82
6	10	5	3	2	+	+	0.11	0.17	4.51	6.46
					+	-	0.13	0.16	3.06	4.57
					-	+	126.50	243.29	4.57	6.52
					-	-	116.83	242.85	3.08	4.60

equivalents of it. We investigated this experimentally, with results shown in Table 4. Using the wrong variable ordering heuristic can make a difference of three orders of magnitude in the run time using lexicographic constraints, while we see almost no difference in the run time used by SBDS. We suggest this arises because the reversed heuristic starts with the bottom right corner, and the lexicographic constraints are unable to prune until late in the search tree. We do see a change in run time in both methods when reversing the value ordering. For lexicographic constraints, it makes almost no difference to total time, but it can affect dramatically the time to find the first solution. In the (7,7,3,3,1) BIBD, the reversed value ordering is best with the reversed variable ordering heuristic, because the preferred solution has a 1 in the bottom right square. We do see an improved overall run time with the reversed value ordering heuristic for SBDS. While we do not fully understand this, it seems to be more constraining to choose 1 before 0, and SBDS can exploit this to reduce the size of the overall search tree. We conclude that the low overheads of lexicographic ordering can make it very effective, provided that the programmer is aware of how the constraints will interact with the variable and value ordering heuristics. In comparison, SBDS is relatively unaffected by the choice of variable and value orderings.

6   Discussion

We have shown that constraint logic programming and computational group theory systems can be coupled to provide an efficient mechanism for

A: generating symmetry groups for constraint satisfaction problems, and
B: using group theoretic calculations within search to rule out symmetrically equivalent solutions.

Our implementation utilises features of ECL^{i}PS^e and GAP that allow lazy evaluation of properties of representatives of subsets of the symmetries. We obtain significant increases in computational efficiency for a range of CSP problems with well defined symmetry groups containing as many as 10^9 elements.

There are two areas of future research interest. First, we would like to use the GAP-ECL^{i}PS^e framework to implement another symmetry breaking paradigm. For example, a purely group theoretic approach to symmetry breaking was used to implement efficient backtrack search in [3]. The idea, a precursor of [7], is to perform a backtrack search for broken symmetries within the backtrack search for a solution. It should be possible to implement the subsidiary search in GAP, leaving ECL^{i}PS^e to deal with the resulting (pruned) search tree. It would also be interesting to explore the application of our work to the satisfiability problem, in which Crawford et al [6] successfully applied group theoretic techniques.

The second area is the extension of our approach to more practical CSP problems. In particular the areas of symmetry in model checking [4], and vehicle routing and scheduling [2].

Acknowledgements

The St Andrews' authors are assisted by EPSRC grant GR/R29666. We thank Steve Linton, Ursula Martin, Iain McDonald, Karen Petrie, Joachim Schimpf, Barbara Smith and Mark Wallace for their assistance.

References

[1] R. Backofen and S. Will, *Excluding symmetries in constraint-based search*, Proceedings, CP-99, Springer, 1999, LNCS 1713, pp. 73–87.

[2] J. C. Beck, P. Prosser, and E. Selensky, *On the reformulation of vehicle routing problems and scheduling problems*, Tech. Report APES-44-2002, APES Research Group, February 2002.

[3] C. A. Brown, L. Finkelstein, and P. W. Purdom, Jr., *Backtrack searching in the presence of symmetry*, Proc. AAECC-6 (T. Mora, ed.), no. 357, Springer-Verlag, 1988, pp. 99–110.

[4] M. Calder and A. Miller, *Five ways to use induction and symmetry in the verification of networks of processes by model-checking*, Proc. AVoCS, 2002, pp. 29–42.

[5] C. H. Colbourn and J. H. Dinitz (eds.), *The CRC handbook of combinatorial designs*, CRC Press, Rockville, Maryland, USA, 1996.

[6] J. Crawford, M. Ginsberg, E. Luks, and A. Roy, *Symmetry breaking predicates for search problems*, Proc. KR 96, Morgan Kaufmann, 1996, pp. 148–159.

[7] T. Fahle, S. Schamberger, and M. Sellmann, *Symmetry breaking*, Proc. CP 2001 (T. Walsh, ed.), 2001, pp. 93–107.

[8] P. Flener, A. M. Frisch, B. Hnich, Z. Kızıltan, I. Miguel, J. Pearson, and T. Walsh, *Symmetry in matrix models*, Tech. Report APES-30-2001, APES Research Group, October 2001.

[9] F. Focacci and M. Milano, *Global cut framework for removing symmetries*, Proc. CP 2001 (T. Walsh, ed.), 2001, pp. 77–92.

[10] The GAP Group, *GAP – Groups, Algorithms, and Programming, Version 4.2*, 2000, http://www.gap-system.org.

[11] I. P. Gent, S. A. Linton, and B. M. Smith, *Symmetry breaking in the alien tiles puzzle*, Tech. Report APES-22-2000, APES Research Group, October 2000.

[12] I. P. Gent and B. M. Smith, *Symmetry breaking in constraint programming*, Proceedings of ECAI-2000 (W. Horn, ed.), IOS Press, 2000, pp. 599–603.

[13] I. McDonald, *Unique symmetry breaking in CSPs using group theory*, Proc. SymCon'01 (P. Flener and J. Pearson, eds.), 2001, pp. 75–78.

[14] M. G. Wallace, S. Novello, and J. Schimpf, *ECLiPSe : A platform for constraint logic programming*, ICL Systems Journal **12** (1997), no. 1, 159–200.

Partial Symmetry Breaking

Iain McDonald[1] and Barbara Smith[2]

[1] University of St Andrews
Fife, Scotland
`iain@dcs.st-and.ac.uk`
[2] University of Huddersfield
West Yorkshire, England
`b.m.smith@hud.ac.uk`

Abstract. In this paper we define *partial symmetry breaking*, a concept that has been used in many previous papers without being the main topic of any research. This paper is the first systematic study of partial symmetry breaking in constraint programming. We show experimentally that performing symmetry breaking with only a subset of all symmetries can result in greatly reduced run-times. We also look at the consequences of using partial symmetry breaking in terms of variable and value ordering heuristics. Finally, different methods of selecting symmetries are considered before presenting a general algorithm for selecting subsets of symmetries.

1 Introduction and Motivation

We are now at a point in constraint programming research where there are many methods of both recognizing symmetries and breaking symmetries in CSPs. Backofen and Will [1] described a general method of applying symmetry breaking dynamically during search. Fahle, Schamberger and Sellman [2] recently presented a method of dynamic symmetry breaking which could deal with large groups of symmetries and guarantee unique solutions with large reductions in run-time.

A symmetry breaking **method** for CSPs, can be broken into two parts, the symmetry breaking **technique** and the symmetry **representation**. The technique is how we apply the symmetry breaking. Previous methods of breaking symmetry have involved introducing new constraints to the CSP that break symmetry [3], using heuristics that break symmetry by assigning the most symmetrical variables first [4], forbidding searching subtrees that are symmetrically equivalent to search already done [5, 1] or verifying at each node in search that it is not symmetrically equivalent to search already done [2]. The symmetry representation is concerned with how the descriptions of symmetries are implemented and how we use this implementation to apply the symmetry breaking technique. This was first shown in [6] where Focacci and Milano presented a method of better utilizing the symmetries of the problem independent of the symmetry

P. Van Hentenryck (Ed.): CP 2002, LNCS 2470, pp. 431–445, 2002.

breaking technique. If we are to come up with better symmetry breaking methods we must realize that the overhead for performing symmetry breaking exists in the representations of the symmetries.

Symmetry breaking can be improved by reducing the number of symmetries we need to consider. This affects the *representation* of the symmetries but not the *technique*.

In Section 2 we introduce the definitions and notation used throughout the paper. Section 3 looks more closely at the symmetry representation and some past improvements. This section also defines partial symmetry breaking and how to perform it with respect to the symmetry representation. We present empirical data of partial symmetry breaking experiments in Section 4 and discuss the implications of partial symmetry breaking and symmetry subset selection in Section 5. Finally we present our conclusions and discuss future work in Section 6.

2   Definitions and Notation

We define a CSP L, to be a finite set of variables X where each variable X_i has a finite domain $D(X_i)$. A solution to L is an assignment of all variables: $\{\forall i \exists j \mid X_i = D(X_i)_j\}$ such that a finite set of constraints C are satisfied. A CSP is a *symmetric CSP* if there are symmetries acting on it. A symmetry is defined as follows.

Definition 1. *Given a CSP L, with a set of constraints C, a symmetry of L is a bijective function $f : A \to A$ where A is some representation of a state in search[1] e.g. a list of assigned variables, a set of current domains etc., such that the following holds:*

1. *Given A, a partial or full assignment of L, if A satisfies the constraints C, then so does $f(A)$.*
2. *Similarly, if A is a nogood, then so too is $f(A)$.*

The set of all symmetries of a CSP form, or can be used to form, a **group**. The way in which partial symmetry breaking is performed depends on the symmetry representation. Previous encodings have used group theory techniques to represent a large number of symmetries by listing a small subset of all of them [7, 8, 9]. If it is possible to recreate the entire group of symmetries by reapplying the symmetries in this small subset, we call the subset a *generator set*. Many of the experiments and findings in this paper are based on representations that encode all the symmetries of a CSP and not just the generator set. The content of this paper is still relevant in the general case and modifications are suggested so that partial symmetry breaking can be used for all symmetry breaking techniques.

We now define two classes of symmetric CSPs.

---

[1] Symmetries can act on CSPs regardless of the notation used. Thus for generality, the method of representing an assignment and applying a symmetry is left to the reader.

Definition 2. *Given a CSP L where the number of symmetries of L increases polynomially with respect to the sizes of the variables X and their domains $D(X)$, L is said to be* polynomially symmetric.

Definition 3. *Given a CSP L where the number of symmetries of L increases exponentially with respect to the sizes of the variables X and their domains $D(X)$, L is said to be* exponentially symmetric.

In the polynomially symmetric most perfect squares problem[2] for example, the number of symmetries is $8n^2$ for an $n \times n$ board. Naïve encodings of the exponentially symmetric golfer's problem [10] have $p! \times g! \times w!$ symmetries for p players, g groups and w weeks. Clearly, increasing either the number of players, groups or weeks by even one will greatly increase the number of symmetries.

In group theory there are many groups with common structure and thus they are named e.g. given a set of n objects that can be permuted freely, the group acting on this set is called the symmetric group or S_n which has order $n!$. Most symmetric CSPs that are exponentially symmetric have S_n as part of their group.

3 Partial Symmetry Breaking and Symmetry Representation

There have already been two improvements reported on the representation of symmetries i.e. methods for removing symmetries from consideration from the symmetry representation. The first is found in the symmetry breaking method SET (symmetry excluding trees) developed by Backofen and Will [1] and this removes broken symmetries. Removing broken symmetries from consideration is also in the symmetry breaking method that will be used in the experiments in this paper: SBDS. Therefore, the concept will be explained in terms of the SBDS notation. Symmetry Breaking During Search (SBDS), developed by Gent and Smith [5], works by adding constraints to the current search subtree. After backtracking from a failed assignment $var_i = val_j$, to a point in search with a partial assignment A, we post the constraint:

$$g(A) \ \& \ (var_i \neq val_j) \Rightarrow g(var_i \neq val_j)$$

for every g in the symmetry representation. Symmetries are represented by functions and SBDS removes a function from consideration when it discovers that a pre-condition (i.e. $g(A)$) of the constraint it creates is guaranteed false from the current subtree. For example consider a node k in search, a symmetry function may produce a pre-condition $var_i = val_j$ but if at point k, $var_i \neq val_j$ we can ignore that symmetry function at all children nodes of k.

---

[2] A variation on the magic squares problem. See http://www.geocities.com/~harveyh/ most-perfect.htm for more details

The second improvement is found in [8] where only unique symmetries are considered. McDonald showed how at certain points in search, some sets of symmetries all have the same effect on a partial assignment and so we can discard all but one symmetry from this set e.g. there may be a set of symmetries g and h such that given a partial assignment A, $g(A) = h(A)$. If this is the case we only break symmetry on g or h but not both. These two improvements reduce the number of symmetries to consider without reducing the amount of symmetry breaking possible i.e. they do not introduce non-unique solutions.

We now consider a third optimization. In this paper we show that where there is a large number of symmetries, we can discard some of them and by doing so reduce run-time greatly. If we are trying to solve a problem that is exponentially symmetric we may not be able to fully utilize a given symmetry breaking technique. We cannot apply the dominance check used in SBDD[3] for all symmetries at every node in search for the golfer's problem as it is too expensive. It is still possible to use SBDS if we limit the number of symmetry breaking functions and we can still use SBDD by applying a dominance check under a subgroup of all the symmetries. Describing only a subset of the symmetries does not lose any solutions and may result in redundant search but the overhead of performing symmetry breaking will not be as great. By only describing a subset of symmetries we are performing *partial symmetry breaking* (PSB) i.e. performing some redundant search because the symmetry breaking technique is too costly or even impossible to perform.

An example of PSB can be found in [5] where a restricted method of SBDS is described. It was proved in [1] that if S_n acts on the values of a variable, we can break all symmetry in the values by breaking the symmetry of just the $O(n^2)$ transpositions. In [10] the entire paper used PSB. Finally, in [2] the golfer's problems is solved using SBDD for the most part with only a subgroup of all the possible symmetries[4] since the dominance check on the whole group is too expensive.

As can be seen, previous work has looked at PSB and some small experiments have been completed [2], but this paper is the first to consider systematically what the benefit of PSB is and how its benefit can be maximized.

3.1   Explicit Symmetries and Group Theory

Given a symmetry representation, we perform PSB by only applying the symmetry breaking technique to a subset of the symmetries in the symmetry representation. How the subset of symmetries is generated depends on the symmetry representation. There are two types of symmetry representation:

1. A list of explicit symmetries
2. A generator set of a group

---

[3] Symmetry breaking via dominance detection [2].

[4] Apart from at the leaf nodes where the entire group is used to verify unique solutions.

39

Generating a subset of symmetries from a list of explicit symmetries is trivial, however, the implicit nature of using generators of groups makes it difficult (but still possible) to select a subset of symmetries. Symmetry breaking methods that use generators of groups must still generate elements of the group in order to perform the symmetry breaking technique. When this process of generating group elements takes place, the number of the elements generated should be limited by some global number. By doing so we are performing PSB.

This paper uses the SBDS symmetry breaking method whose symmetry representation uses a list of explicit symmetries. The current thinking in symmetry breaking is that group theory should be more widely used and we will show later that PSB will be easier to extend to symmetry breaking methods that use group theory.

4 Partial Symmetry Breaking Experiments

It is a straightforward assumption that by breaking more symmetries i.e. by increasing the number of symmetries in the representation, we can reduce the search space further up to a certain point.

However, as the number of symmetries represented increases, so does the overhead. Figure 1 illustrates this point by suggesting that there may be a point where the benefit in reducing search from adding more symmetries is out-weighed by the extra overhead

In order to discover how the cpu-time of solving a symmetric CSP varies with the number of symmetries used in the symmetry representation we have constructed the following experiment. Given a symmetric CSP L with n symmetries acting on it, L is solved k times using no symmetry breaking and the cpu-time is recorded. We then solve L another k times - again recording the cpu-time - using some symmetry breaking technique and k different pseudo-random subsets of symmetries of size 1 as the symmetry representation. This pattern is repeated for k pseudo-random subsets of size 2 up to n.

Given the data from the above experiment we can plot graphs of cpu-time *vs* number of symmetries used. We can then use this graph to estimate how

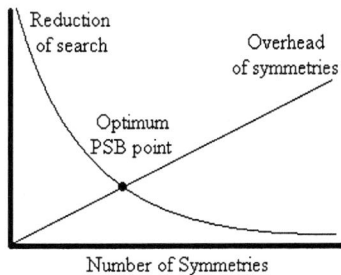

Fig. 1. Finding the optimum point

many symmetries we need to break to minimize cpu-time for SBDS. It should be highlighted though that by doing this we allow duplicate solutions. As was shown in [2] though, using SBDD to break all symmetry on leaf nodes of search is inexpensive and guarantees unique solutions.

4.1   Fractions Puzzle

We consider a very simple problem as an example experiment. Given the following problem:

$$\frac{A}{BC} + \frac{D}{EF} + \frac{G}{HI} = 1$$

Can we find values for each variable such that the equation[5] is satisfied? We can permute the fractions freely, yielding 5 symmetries and the identity e.g. one symmetry is $A \leftrightarrow D$, $B \leftrightarrow E$ and $C \leftrightarrow F$. Since the number of symmetries is so small it is possible to run the experiment with all possible subsets of symmetries. The cpu-times were then averaged for each subset size. Figure 2 contains the graph of the averaged cpu-time with respect to the number of symmetries. As you can see, by adding more symmetries the cpu-time decreases.

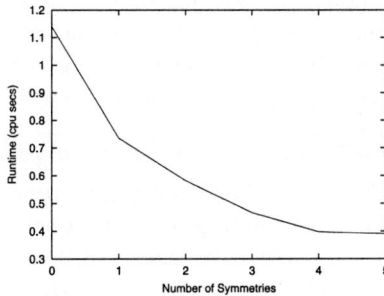

Fig. 2. Fractions Puzzle PSB

4.2   Alien Tiles

SBDS has already been used to solve alien tiles problems with good results [11]. The alien tiles problem can be described with two parameters n and c, the size of the board and the number of colours respectively. An alien tiles board is an $n \times n$ grid of n^2 coloured squares[6]. By clicking on any square on the board, the colour

---

[5] BC does not mean $B \times C$ but rather $(10 \times B) + C$.
[6] Alien tiles puzzles can be found online at http://www.alientiles.com/

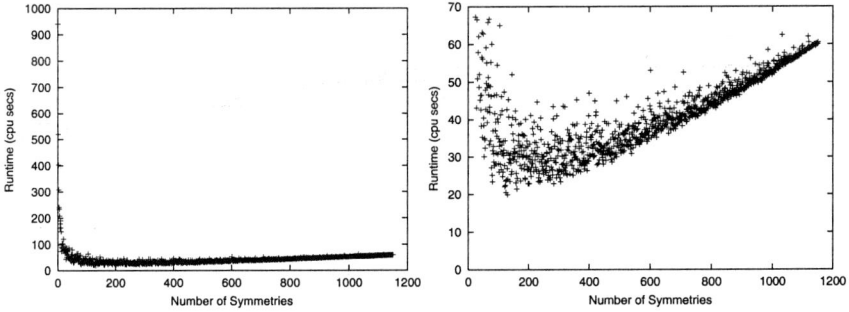

Fig. 3. Random PSB Subsets - Alien Tiles

of the square is changed $+1$ *mod c*. As well as this, the colour of every square in the same row and column is also altered $+1$ *mod c*. Given an initial state and a goal state, the problem is to find the required number of clicks on each square which can be anything between 0 and $c - 1$ (since $0 \equiv c$, $1 \equiv c + 1$ etc). A more challenging problem for constraint programming is finding the most complicated goal state (in terms of the number of clicks needed) and then reaching that goal state in as few clicks as possible and verifying optimality.

The problem we consider is a 4×4 board with 3 colours. The smallest number of clicks that can take us to the most complicated goal state is 10. Proving that 10 clicks is optimal needs a complete traversal of the entire search tree. An instance of the alien tiles problem is exponentially symmetric. Given a solution we can freely permute the rows and columns and flip the board around a diagonal. For a board with n^2 variables, the group acting on the board is $S_n \times S_n \times 2$ which for a 4×4 board is a group of size 1152, or 1151 symmetries and the identity. We derive this number by noting that we have 24 (or 4!) row permutations, which can be used in conjunction with the 24 column permutations, which can be used with the diagonal flip $(2n!^2)$. The reason we are using this symmetric CSP as the main example of PSB is that it is not a trivially easy problem to solve, but with $n = 4$ we can cope with all 1151 symmetry functions so we can compare PSB against breaking all symmetry.

Figure 3 shows the cpu-time to solve the alien tiles problem described above with different sized random[7] subsets of the 1151 symmetries. Figure 3 also shows a magnified version of the same graph so that we can see the results more clearly. By looking at the graphs we can deduce three things. Firstly, most of the run-time improvement from 940.4 seconds and 18751 backtracks with no symmetry breaking to 60.5 seconds and 135 backtracks with all 1151 symmetry functions comes from adding the first 20 or so symmetries. Secondly and perhaps most importantly, we can see that shortest cpu-time comes from using a random subset of size 130. With this subset the problem was solved in 19.9 seconds and with 216 backtracks. The size of this subset is much smaller than the size of the group

---

[7] In this experiment the ECL^{i}PS^e random function was used.

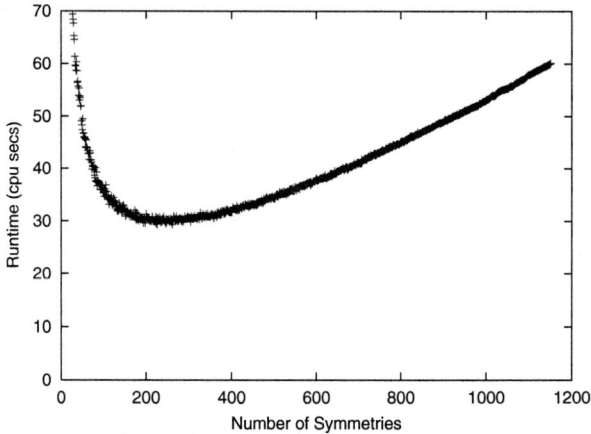

Fig. 4. Average cpu-times - Alien Tiles

acting on the alien tiles CSP. Thirdly, different subsets of a similar size have large differences in cpu-time. This implies that which symmetries we include in our subset is just as important as the size of the subset e.g. another random subset of size 130 yielded a cpu-time of 54.9 seconds (almost as much as breaking all symmetry).

The above experiment was run with 218 different random subsets[8] for each subset size to produce the less scattered curve in Figure 4. It is possible to gain an average factor of 2 improvement over breaking all symmetry and a factor of 32 improvement over no symmetry breaking. In the case of the subset of size 130 mentioned above, we gain a factor of 3 improvement over breaking all symmetry and a factor of 47 improvement over no symmetry breaking. The shape of the curve in Figure 4 is consistent with Figure 1 i.e. the overhead increasing approximately linearly with the number of symmetries, combined with a steep reduction in search as the first few symmetries are added. This reduction tails off as most of the redundant search is pruned, making further symmetries less effective.

4.3   Golfer's Problem

Here we show the existence of similar behaviour for a different problem. This uses Smith's encoding of the golfer's problem taken from [10] with $p!$ symmetries for p players. This well known problem takes three parameters - $golf(p, g, w)$ - the number of players p, the number of groups in each week g where $p \bmod g = 0$ and the number of weeks w. The constraints on this problem are that for each week each player plays golf with the other players in their respective group. Once two players have played golf with one another in one group in one week, they cannot play each other again in any other week. The graph shown in

---

[8] Using ECL^{i}PS^e version 5.3 on a Pentium III 1GHz processor with 512Mb of RAM

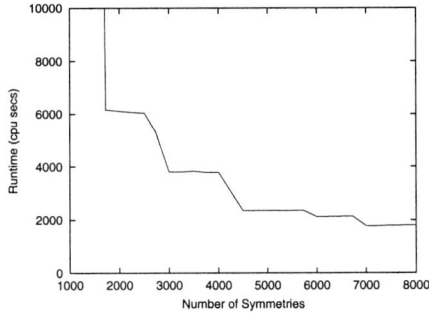

Fig. 5. PSB - Golfer's Problem

Figure 5 shows the results of finding all solutions to $golf(12,4,2)$[9]. Using PSB while finding all solutions will introduce duplicate solutions. Smith's model has $12! - 1$ or 479,001,599 symmetries not including the identity. Using GAP [12] it is possible to produce random elements of the group acting on this problem: S_{12}. GAP was then used to output a random subset of 8000 functions representing 8000 random elements of the group. The same experiment described at the start of this section was run with just one random subset, but due to the complexity of this problem the subsets of symmetries incremented in size in steps of 250. It was not possible to solve the problem with 1500 symmetry breaking functions within 1000 minutes of cpu-time.

The graph in Figure 5 is not as clear as that seen in Figure 3. However, whereas the alien tiles problem needed roughly 20 symmetries to do most of the symmetry breaking, the golfer's problem needs roughly 4500. We need to consider at least 1775 symmetries to be able to solve this problem in reasonable time and the more symmetries we add the smaller the improvement in cpu-time. Using SBDS we are limited by the number of functions we can compile. In this respect it is more advantageous to represent symmetries using groups so that larger subsets of symmetries can be used as was discussed in Section 3.1.

5   Symmetry Subset Selection

In the previous section we saw empirical evidence that using PSB can produce significant improvements. This also highlighted the importance of symmetry subset selection i.e. how we choose the subset of symmetries to break. Figure 6 shows the best and worst cpu-time for different sized subsets of symmetries as well as the absolute difference between them based on the 15 random subsets used in the experiment (described in Section 4.2[10]). The minimum cpu-time we can achieve is 12.61 seconds with a subset of 164 symmetries. However choosing a subset of this size can result in a cpu-time as large as 35.27 seconds. We now look at how

---

[9] Using Ilog Solver version 4.4 on a Pentium II 300MHz processor with 512Mb RAM
[10] Using ECL^{i}PS^e version 5.3 on a dual Pentium III 1GHz processor with 4Gb RAM

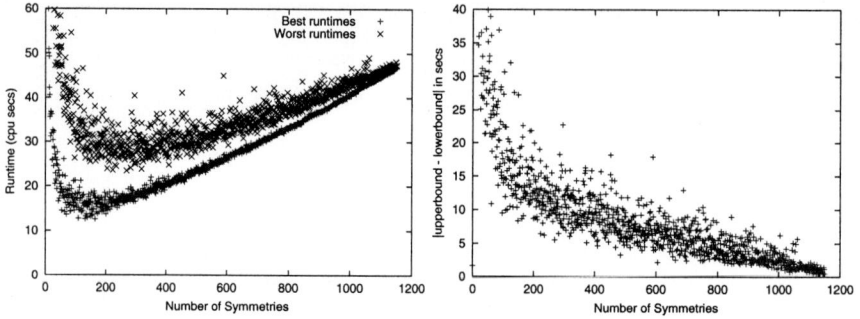

Fig. 6. Best & worst times (left, cut-off at 60secs) and the difference between best & worst times (right, cut-off at 40secs)

the symmetry subset selection effects search and in doing so, hope to find an algorithm to select efficient symmetry subsets.

When solving a symmetric CSP using symmetry breaking techniques there are two types of failure resulting in backtracking. We either fail where we discover a new unique nogood or we fail where we find a nogood symmetrically equivalent to a previously unique nogood.

Definition 4. *Given a complete traversal of the search tree of a CSP L, a list of nogoods found K and a group of symmetries G, acting on L, consider a node in search k which is a nogood. If while traversing the search tree we reach node k and $\not\exists g \in G$ s.t. $g(k) \in K$ then we call k a* unique nogood *else if $\exists g \in G$ s.t. $g(k) \in K$ where $g \neq e$ (the identity element) then we call k a* symmetric nogood. *Unique nogoods result in unique fails and symmetric nogoods result in symmetric fails.*

It is straightforward to see that exponentially symmetric problems can have significantly more symmetric fails than unique fails. By performing symmetry breaking we can eliminate symmetric fails, however if we use PSB some symmetric nogoods persist. Different symmetries can be used to prune different parts of the search tree. The variable and value ordering heuristics and the propagation level dictate how the search space is traversed, therefore the symmetric nogoods pruned are dependent not only on how many symmetries we break but also on the heuristics we use.

In Figure 7 we present experimental evidence of this by performing the same experiment as in Section 4.2 with the same subsets of symmetries but with different variable ordering heuristics[11]. The subsets used in Section 4.2 were randomly chosen for each different size but in this section we have a standard subset that has a random symmetry added to it at the start of each run. The first heuristic (on the left in Figure 7) instantiates the alien tiles squares along the rows from top left to bottom right. The second (on the right) instantiates the

---

[11] Using ECL^{i}PS^e version 5.3 on a dual Pentium III processor 1GHz with 4Gb RAM

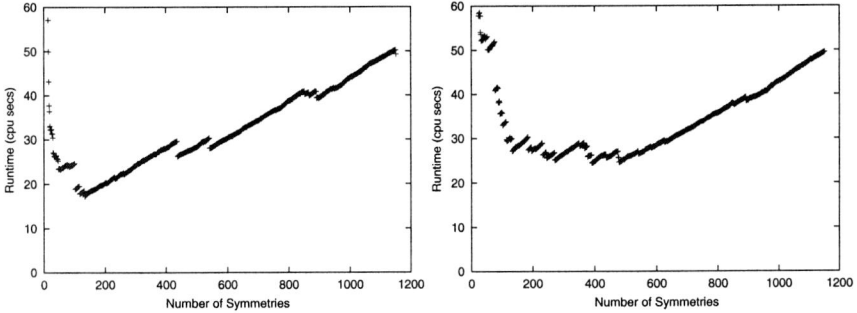

Fig. 7. Identical subsets of symmetries with different variable ordering heuristics (cut-off 60secs). The heuristic used on the left is better up to 376 symmetries after which the heuristic used on the right takes less time

squares along the rows from bottom right to top left. The resulting cpu-times are generally significantly different. On the other hand, changing the value ordering heuristic in solving alien tiles problems makes no difference to the number of symmetric fails we find, since the symmetries in this problem act on just the variables and not the values.

If we want to use PSB with a given symmetry breaking method we need to be aware of the variable and value ordering heuristics when we select a subset of symmetries. We can exploit this fact by choosing heuristics that work well with respect to a subset of symmetries.

5.1   Cats and Dogs

We now look at a problem where it is possible to select a good subset of symmetries with respect to the variable ordering heuristic. The Cats and Dogs problem requires 3 cats and 5 dogs to be placed on a 5×5 chessboard in such a way that no dog can attack any of the cats in a queen's move.

A possible model has a variable for each cat (c_1, c_2, c_3) and a variable for each dog $(d_1, d_2, d_3, d_4, d_5)$. The domain of each variable is the set of squares on the board. There are 15 binary constraints, each between a cat variable and a dog variable, to ensure that no dog and cat are on the same row, column or diagonal. We also have an *all-different* constraint (or one for the cats and one for the dogs, since the constraints already prevent placing a dog and a cat on the same square). The symmetries of the problem are composed of the symmetries of the chessboard, together with the fact that the cat variables are indistinguishable and so are the dog variables. Using this simple model we have $8 \times 3! \times 5!$ or 5760 symmetries. There is only one solution to the problem, ignoring symmetric equivalents. With no symmetry-breaking, there are in fact 5760 solutions: it takes 7046 fails and 4 seconds to find these[12].

---
[12] Using Ilog Solver version 4.4 on a Celeron 600MHz laptop

The model is solved by assigning the variables in the fixed order $c_1, c_2, c_3, d_1, ..$ $, d_5$. In this case, the variable ordering means that the cat symmetries and the dog symmetries have a different effect on search: the cat symmetries are more significant, because the cat variables are assigned first. Ignoring the symmetries of the chessboard, we could clearly eliminate the symmetry due to indistinguishable variables by adding ordering constraints $c_1 < c_2 < c_3$ and $d_1 < ... < d_5$. This suggests that in SBDS we could eliminate these symmetries by describing all transpositions of the c_is and all transpositions of the d_js *independently*. This can be done with 13 SBDS functions (3 for the cat transpositions and 10 for the dog transpositions), and then 8 solutions are found in 1,074 fails with 0.9 seconds. Adding functions for the 7 board symmetries, other than the identity, (20 SBDS functions) reduces the number of solutions to 3 with 513 fails.

Since there is a unique solution, we have not yet eliminated all the symmetry. We continue by combining a board symmetry with a transposition of the cat variables: this gives an additional 21 SBDS functions, 41 in total. Now only one solution is found in 0.3 seconds, and the number of fails is 210. Hence it has been possible in this case to find a small subset of the symmetries (less than 1% of the total) which eliminate all equivalent solutions to the problem.

5.2   Algorithm for Symmetry Selection

The structure in the Cats and Dogs problem means it is possible to construct a variable ordering heuristic that breaks all symmetry with respect to a few hand picked symmetries. For other problems that do not have as much structure as the Cats and Dogs problem, a general purpose algorithm is needed.

If a subset of symmetries is to be used, the symmetries that prune most nogoods should be included in this subset. The symmetries that rule out nodes near the root should prune the most search. Based on this, the following algorithm (Algorithm 5.1) was implemented using GAP's group theoretic capabilities. A symmetry function can be good with respect to variable and value ordering heuristics **and** a failed partial assignment. Therefore, we look at how near to the root the prune is made with respect to every symmetry and every partial assignment. The algorithm orders the symmetries so that those that prune symmetric nogoods near the root are before those that only prune nogoods near the bottom of the tree. To perform PSB with n symmetries, we should use the first n symmetries in the sorted list returned by this algorithm.

This complete algorithm needs to know ahead of time every partial assignment that will be considered e.g. from the variable and value ordering heuristics to be used, and every symmetry of the group. Every symmetry acting on the problem is then applied to these partial assignments. The computation involved in using this algorithm makes it almost unusable for all but the smallest groups and smallest CSPs. Thankfully we can take some random subset of symmetries of size k and find the best n symmetries of this subset (where $k \gg n$). We can also use just a subset of all partial assignments (smaller partial assignments are more preferable).

Algorithm 5.1: SYMMETRYSUBSETSELECTION(*Group, PartialAssignments*)

for each $g \in Group$

do $\begin{cases} \text{for each } pa \in PartialAssignments \\ \quad \text{do} \begin{cases} element.partial\_assignment \leftarrow g(pa) \\ element.symmetry\_used \leftarrow g \\ element.latest \leftarrow \text{latest point in search in } g(pa)^a \\ SymmetricPartialAssignments.add(element) \end{cases} \end{cases}$

for each $i \in SymmetricPartialAssignments$

do $\begin{cases} best \leftarrow i \\ \text{for each } j \in SymmetricPartialAssignments \\ \quad \text{do} \begin{cases} \text{if } j.latest = best.latest \\ \quad \textbf{and } |j.partial\_assignment| < |best.partial\_assignment| \\ \quad \textbf{then } best \leftarrow j \\ \text{if } j.latest < best.latest \\ \quad \textbf{then } best \leftarrow j \end{cases} \\ Symmetries.add(best.symmetry\_used) \\ SymmetricPartialAssignments.remove(best) \end{cases}$

$Symmetries.remove\_duplicate\_symmetries()$

return (*Symmetries*)

---

^{a} Latest $var = val$ assignment to be considered by the heuristics in the partial assignment $g(pa)$.

By using the complete version of this algorithm, it is possible to obtain an ordering of all 1151 symmetries of the alien tiles problem. Also, using a limited version of this algorithm for just partial assignments with 3 or less variables instantiated i.e. we consider just the partial assignments made at depth 3 or less in the search tree, it is possible to obtain a sorted list of 8000 symmetries for the golfer's problem. The experiments in Section 4 were run again with these symmetries. In Figure 8 we compare the results of using this algorithm with respect to previous experiments. The alien tiles problem takes about the same time to solve using the best random subsets in Figure 6 as the symmetries from the complete algorithm.

Even though we can now solve the alien tiles problem in 10.95 seconds with a subset of 92 symmetries, Algorithm 5.1 took 1232 seconds to order the symmetries. However, the extraordinary performance improvement from 1802.53 seconds to 128.1 seconds in solving the golfer's problem warrants the 364 seconds it took to sort the symmetries. This shows that while the complete algorithm is very time consuming for a CSP like the alien tiles problem, using a limited version produces very good results in a reasonable time. This suggests that this algorithm can be used to solve CSPs that cannot be solved with symmetry breaking and random PSB. Future work should reveal a better method of sort-

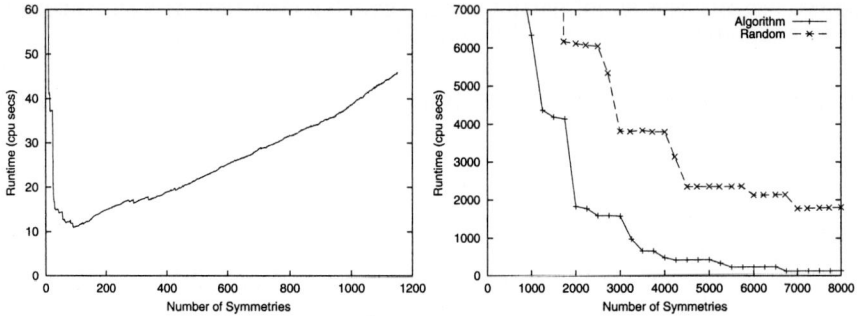

Fig. 8. The alien tiles experiment (left). The golfer's problem (right) is significantly improved over using random symmetries

ing symmetries but this algorithm shows that a generic method of choosing the symmetries that will prune most search is possible.

6   Conclusions and Future Work

This paper is the first systematic study of partial symmetry breaking (PSB) in constraint programming. We have shown that by performing PSB it is possible to significantly decrease run-time in solving symmetric CSPs. Furthermore we have shown that consideration needs to be given to the variable and value ordering heuristics when solving symmetric CSPs suggesting that hand picked symmetries perform better than random symmetries with PSB. Finally we presented a general algorithm for selecting subsets of symmetries. This paper also shows the need for more research into finding general methods for breaking all symmetry with a subset of symmetries.

Future work will look at constructing an efficient symmetry breaking system that implements all three improvements mentioned in Section 3.1. This symmetry breaking system will use group theory to express huge groups, consider non-broken and unique symmetries only and use PSB to minimize run-time.

Acknowledgments

This research is supported by EPSRC grant GR/R29673. The first author is funded by an EPSRC studentship. He would also like to thank his supervisors Ian Gent and Steve Linton as well as Tom Kelsey. Both authors would like to thank all the members of the APES research group, especially Toby Walsh, for their support and helpful comments.

References

[1] Rolf Backofen and Sebastian Will. Excluding symmetries in constraint-based search. In Alex Brodsky, editor, *Principles and Practice of Constraint Programming*, pages 73–87. Springer-Verlag, 1999.

[2] Torsten Fahle, Stefan Schamberger, and Meinolf Sellman. Symmetry breaking. In Toby Walsh, editor, *Principles and Practice of Constraint Programming – CP2001*, pages 93–107. Springer-Verlag, 2001.

[3] James Crawford, Matthew Ginsberg, Eugene Luks, and Amitabha Roy. Symmetry-breaking predicates for search problems. In *Knowledge Representation'96: Principles of Knowledge Representation and Reasoning*, pages 148–159. Morgan Kaufmann, San Francisco, California, 1996.

[4] Pedro Meseguer and Carme Torras. Exploiting symmetries within constraint satisfaction search. In *Artificial Intelligence, Vol 129, No. 1-2*, pages 133–163. 2001.

[5] Ian Gent and Barbara Smith. Symmetry breaking in constraint programming. In W. Horn, editor, *Proceedings of ECAI-2000*, pages 599–603. IOS Press, 2000.

[6] Filippo Focacci and Michaela Milano. Global cut framework for removing symmetries. In Toby Walsh, editor, *Principles and Practice of Constraint Programming – CP2001*, pages 77–92. Springer-Verlag, 2001.

[7] Warwick Harvey. Symmetry breaking and the social golfer problem. In Piere Flener and Justin Pearson, editors, *SymCon'01: Symmetry in Constraints*, pages 9–16, 2001. Available from http://www.csd.uu.se/~pierref/astra/symmetry/index.html.

[8] Iain McDonald. Unique symmetry breaking in CSPs using group theory. In Piere Flener and Justin Pearson, editors, *SymCon'01: Symmetry in Constraints*, pages 75–78, 2001. Available from http://www.csd.uu.se/~pierref/astra/symmetry/index.html.

[9] Cynthia Brown, Larry Finkelstein, and Paul Purdom Jr. Backtrack searching in the presence of symmetry. In *Nordic Journal of Computing*, pages 203–219. Publishing Association Nordic Journal of Computing, 1996.

[10] Barbara Smith. Reducing symmetry in a combinatorial design problem. Technical Report Research Report 2001.01, University of Leeds, January 2001.

[11] Ian Gent, Steve Linton, and Barbara Smith. Symmetry breaking in the alien tiles puzzle. Technical Report APES-22-2000, APES Research Group, October 2000. Available from http://www.dcs.st-and.ac.uk/~apes/apesreports.html.

[12] The GAP Group, Aachen, St Andrews. *GAP – Groups, Algorithms, and Programming, Version 4.2*, 2000.

Symmetry Breaking Revisited

Jean-François Puget

ILOG
9 avenue de Verdun, 94253 Gentilly, France
puget@ilog.fr

Abstract. Symmetries in constraint satisfaction problems (CSPs) are one of the difficulties that practitioners have to deal with. We present in this paper a new method based on the symmetries of decisions taken from the root of the search tree. This method can be seen as an improvement of the nogood recording presented by Focacci and Milano[5] and Fahle, Schamberger and Sellmann[4]. We present a simple formalization of our method for which we prove correctness and completeness results. We also show that our method is theoretically more efficient as the number of dominance checks, the number of nogoods and the size of each nogood are smaller. This is confirmed by an experimental evaluation on the social golfer problem, a very difficult and highly symmetrical real world problem. We are able to break all symmetries for problems with more than 10^{36} symmetries. We report both new results, and a comparison with previous work.

1 Introduction

Symmetries are a prevalent feature of our world, and participate to its beauty. A symmetry is a mapping of an object onto itself that preserves some of its properties. For instance, rotating a cube by 90° along one of its axis does not fundamentally change the cube. Symmetries are also prevalent in CSPs. For instance, in the famous 8 queens' problem, rotating the chess board, or flipping it upside down does not change the nature of the problem. Conversely, rotating a solution or flipping it, yields a new solution.

More generally, symmetries for a CSP are mappings from solutions to solutions. A symmetry also maps infeasible partial assignments into infeasible partial assignments. This is the key reason why symmetries can have an adversary effect on the tractability of a given CSP. If the problem is difficult, it may be the case that all symmetrical variants of every dead end encountered during the search must be explored before a solution can be found. Note that a similar negative effect has also been noticed in mathematical programming for mixed integer problems[16]. Even if the problem is easy, all symmetrical variants of a solution are also solutions, and listing all of them may just be impossible in practice.

A vast variety of algorithms have been devised in the past for solving CSPs. We will focus on complete tree search methods (e.g. MAC, forward checking, etc). In that context, several methods to deal with symmetries have been published :

P. Van Hentenryck (Ed.): CP 2002, LNCS 2470, pp. 446–461, 2002.
© Springer-Verlag Berlin Heidelberg 2002

adding symmetry breaking constraints to the CSP [14] or during search[9][1], removing symmetrical values from a variable's domain upon backtracking[13][17], using symmetry breaking heuristics[13], using all the symmetric variants of a given nogood to prune the search[13], using every completely generated subtree as a nogood to prevent any symmetrical variants from being generated[5][4].

The remainder of the paper is organized as following. Section 2 introduces CSPs, symmetries and tree search. Then, in section 3, we present an improvement of the nogood recording methods presented in[5][4] where the information stored for each nogood is the set of positive decisions taken from the root of the search tree instead of the full description of the search state. We also prove completeness and correctness results using a formalization which is both broader and simpler than previously published ones. In section 4, we explain how symmetry checks can be efficiently implemented with an auxiliary CSP for unary branching constraints. In section 5, we give an extensive experimental comparison of several variants of our method on a highly symmetrical problem, the social golfer. In section 6, we conclude with a comparison with previous work both theoretically and experimentally. This shows that our theoretical improvements result in dramatic performance improvements.

2   Notations

We denote by $\sharp(S)$ the cardinality of set S. We also identify singletons $\{a\}$ with their unique element a whenever appropriate.

2.1   CSP

Constraints can be abstracted as a way to define the set of solutions of the problem in view of this paper.

Definition 1. CSP, assignment, solution, state. *A constraint satisfaction problem $\mathcal{P}$ (CSP) is a triple $\mathcal{P} = (\mathcal{V}, \mathcal{D}, \mathcal{C})$ where $\mathcal{V}$ is a finite set of variables v_i, $\mathcal{D}$ a finite set of finite sets $\mathcal{D}_i$ such that $\sharp(\mathcal{V}) = \sharp(\mathcal{D})$ and $\mathcal{C}$ is a subset of the cross product $\bigotimes_i \mathcal{D}_i$. $\mathcal{D}_i$ is called the* initial domain *of the variable v_i.*

The initial state *of $\mathcal{P}$ is the cross product $\mathcal{S} = \bigotimes_i \mathcal{D}_i$.*

An assignment *A is a member of $\mathcal{S}$, i.e. a set of $\sharp(\mathcal{V})$ values a_i such that $a_i \in \mathcal{D}_i$ for all i, and is denoted $A = \{v_i = a_i\}$.*

A solution *to $(\mathcal{V}, \mathcal{D}, \mathcal{C})$ is an assignment that is a member of $\mathcal{C}$. We denote the set of solutions of $\mathcal{P}$ by $sol(\mathcal{P})$.*

A state *S is a subset of $\mathcal{S}$ s.t. there exists sets $D_i \subset \mathcal{D}_i$ s.t. $S = \bigotimes_i D_i$. By extension, D_i is called the* domain *of v_i in state S.*

Given a state $S = \bigotimes_i D_i$ we denote $sol(S)$ the set of solutions of the form $\{v_i = a_i\}$ s.t. $\forall i, \ a_i \in D_i$

Note that assignments and solutions can be considered as states because we identify singletons with their contents. Note also that the initial state is a state. Last, note that the set of solutions of $\mathcal{P}$ is the set of solutions of its initial state.

Among the constraints we point out decisions, which are elementary constraints used in tree search. An assignment is a set of positive decisions, one for each variable.

Definition 2. Decision. *A positive decision is defined by a variable v_i and an element a_i initial domain of v_i, and is denoted $v_i = a_i$. A negative decision is the opposite $\neg(\delta)$ of a positive decision δ and is denoted as follows*
$$\neg(v_i = a_i) = (v_i \neq a_i)$$

2.2   Symmetries

We define a *symmetry* as being a one to one mapping from states to states that preserves solutions, i.e. that maps solutions to solutions and non solutions to non solutions. Furthermore, we require that symmetries are fully determined by the way they map decisions onto decisions.

Definition 3. Symmetry. *A symmetry σ for $\mathcal{P}$ is a one to one mapping (bijection) from decisions to decisions of $\mathcal{P}$ s.t.*
   (i) For all assignments, $A = \{v_i = a_i\}$, $\sigma(A) = \{\sigma(v_i = a_i)\}$
   (ii) For all assignment A, $A \in sol(\mathcal{P})$ iff $\sigma(A) \in sol(\mathcal{P})$
We denote the set of symmetries of $\mathcal{P}$ by $sym(\mathcal{P})$

Note that our definition of symmetries is broader than what is found in[13][5] as it encompasses $90°$ rotations in the 8 queens' problem for instance. Consider for the classical formulation for this problem, with one variable x_i per row $i \in 1 \ldots 8$, whose value indicates the column j such that there is a queen on square (i, j). Then the the $90°$ degree clockwise rotation can be expressed by :
$$\sigma(x_i = j) = (x_{9-j} = i)$$

2.3   Search Tree and Constraint Propagation

Constraint propagation can be abstracted to its effect on the domains of the variables for the purpose of this paper. This encompasses all the popular methods including, but not limited to, forward checking and all arc-consistency algorithms.

Definition 4. Propagation. *A constraint propagation algorithm for $\mathcal{P}$ is a function Π that takes a set of decisions Δ and a state $S = \bigotimes_i D_i$ and produces another state $S' = \bigotimes_i D'_i$ s.t.*

1. $\forall i,\ D'_i \subset D_i$
2. $(v_i = a_i) \in \Delta \ \Rightarrow\ D'_i = \{a_i\} \lor D'_i = \emptyset$
3. $(v_i \neq a_i) \in \Delta \ \Rightarrow\ a_i \notin D'_i$
4. $sol(S) = sol(S')$.
5. $\Pi(\Delta_1 \cup \Delta_2, S) = \Pi(\Delta_1,\ \Pi(\Delta_2, S))$

We say that Π fails if $\Pi(\Delta, A) = \emptyset$.

Note that the propagation algorithm can fail only when $sol(A) = \emptyset$.
Constraint propagation can deduce new decisions.

Definition 5. Entailment. *We say that a state $S = \bigotimes_i D_i$ entails a decision δ and denote it by $S \vdash \delta$ when one of the following holds.*

$$\bigotimes_i D_i \vdash (v_k = a_k) \quad \textit{iff} \quad D_k = \{a_k\}$$
$$\bigotimes_i D_i \vdash (v_k \neq a_k) \quad \textit{iff} \quad a_k \notin D_k$$

We say that a state S entails a set of decisions Δ iff S entails each element of Δ.

We note $\Delta(S)$ the set of decisions entailed by S.

Lots of variants of tree search have been studied and published, but they can be abstracted as following for the purpose of symmetry detection and removal. In the remainder we will use interchangeably "node" and "state". We also introduce the notion of dominated nodes that will be used later. Such nodes represent nodes where search is stopped because they are symmetrical variants of already explored nodes.

Definition 6. Binary tree *A binary tree is a tree whose nodes have either two children or none. Nodes with two children are called binary nodes. The father node of a node n is noted $f(n)$. The two children of a binary node n are noted $l(n)$ (left child) and $r(n)$ (right child).*

Definition 7. Search tree *A dominance search tree τ for the CSP $\mathcal{P}$ and constraint propagation algorithm Π is a binary tree whose nodes are states of P and arcs are labeled by decisions for $\mathcal{P}$ s.t.*

1. *The root node $root(\tau)$ is the initial state of $\mathcal{P}$.*
2. *For each binary node n there exists a decision δ s.t. the arc $(n, l(n))$ is labeled by δ and the arc $(n, r(n))$ is labeled by $\neg \delta$. Moreover, $l(n) = \Pi(\delta, n)$ and $r(n) = \Pi(\neg \delta, n)$.*
3. *There exist a set of nodes $cut(\tau)$ such that a node n is a leaf iff it is either a solution, an empty node, or a member of $cut(\tau)$.*
4. *Decisions are never repeated along a path from the root to a leaf.*

We denote the set of solution nodes that are not members of $cut(\tau)$ by $sol(\tau)$. A search tree is a dominance tree τ such that $cut(\tau) = \emptyset$.

The non repetition of decisions ensures that search trees are finite, as there is a finite number of decisions.

We consider only binary tree search, but this can be done without any loss of generality. Indeed, given a non binary tree search τ, let us define a binary tree search $bin(\tau)$. All the nodes of τ are nodes of $bin(\tau)$. For each node n whose children are $n_1, n_2, \ldots, n_m$ in τ we create m nodes $n_{j,m}$ in $bin(sp)$ for $j \leq m$. Intuitively, $n_{j,m}$ stands for the set of nodes $\{n_j, n_{j+1}, \ldots, n_m\}$. Node $n_{m,m}$ is the node n_m. The children of n in $bin(\tau)$ are n_1 and $n_{2,m}$. The children of node $n_{j,m}$ in $bin(sp)$ are n_j and $n_{j+1,m}$ if $j < m$. It can be shown that a depth first search of $bin(\tau)$ will explore the nodes of τ in the same order as a depth first search of τ.

The search tree we defined is complete, i.e. it reaches all the solutions of the CSP. Before proving it, let us prove the following lemma.

Lemma 1. *Let τ be a dominance tree search, let n be a binary node in τ and let δ be the decision that labels arc $(n, l(n))$. We have that $sol(n) = sol(l(n)) \cup sol(r(n))$*

Proof: Assume $\delta = (v_i = a_i)$. Let $s \in sol(n)$. A decision $v_i = b_i$ appears in s by definition of solutions. If $a_i = b_i$ then s is a solution of $l(n)$ by properties 2 and 4 of definition 4. If $a_i \neq b_i$ then s is a solution of $r(n)$ by properties 3 and 4 of definition 4.

Conversely, let s be a solution of $l(n)$. Then $s \vdash \delta$ because s only takes values in the domains of state $l(s)$. Moreover, s is also a solution of n. Similarly, solutions of $r(s)$ entail $\neg\delta$ and are solutions of $r(n)$. This concludes the proof.

We can now prove the following.

Proposition 1. Completeness of search
Given a CSP $\mathcal{P}$, a constraint propagation algorithm Π and a search tree τ for $\mathcal{P}$ and Π, then $sol(\tau) = sol(\mathcal{P})$

Proof: By induction on the size of τ using the lemma on the root node.

In the following we will say τ is a search tree as a shorthand for "τ is a search tree for $\mathcal{P}$ and Π" when no ambiguity remains.

We have only considered positive decisions that assign a value to a variable, but this can be done without loss of generality. Indeed, the above definitions can be extended to any other unary constraints. For instance, we could have used the decisions of the form $v_i \leq a_i$ for ordered domains. The entailment relation $\vdash$ is more complex in that case but the results we will prove later still hold.

2.4   An Example

Let us take a simple example that will be used throughout the paper. This example is the same as in [5] section 6. The problem consists in selecting 3 people out of 4, each person being represented by a number in the CSP. This can be represented by three variables v_1, v_2, v_3 subject to an *all different* constraint. The domains of the variables are all equal to $\{1, 2, 3, 4\}$ There are 24 solutions of the problem, including but not limited to the following: $\{v_1 = 1, v_2 = 2, v_3 = 3\}$, $\{v_1 = 1, v_2 = 3, v_3 = 2\}$

These two solutions represent in fact the same solution to the original problem, i.e. the set of selected persons is $\{1, 2, 3\}$. The first solution can be mapped into the second one by the symmetry σ_0 defined as follows. This symmetry is a permutation of the variables v_2 and v_3.

$\sigma_0(v_1 = a) \rightarrow v_1 = a$, for all $a \in \{1, 2, 3, 4\}$
$\sigma_0(v_2 = a) \rightarrow v_3 = a$, for all $a \in \{1, 2, 3, 4\}$
$\sigma_0(v_3 = a) \rightarrow v_2 = a$, for all $a \in \{1, 2, 3, 4\}$

We assume a simple constraint propagation algorithm for the *all different* constraint : Whenever a variable is bound, its value is removed from the domain of all the other variables. Figure 1 shows a part of the tree search that will be explored by a depth first search procedure, assuming decisions are selected in a lexicographic ordering. Nodes are represented by $n : \delta$ where n means the node is the nth node to be expanded by the search procedure, and δ is the decision for the arc between $f(n)$ and n.

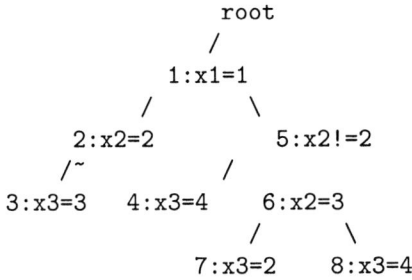

```
                        root
                        /
                    1:x1=1
                   /        \
            2:x2=2            5:x2!=2
           /~                /
    3:x3=3    4:x3=4    6:x2=3
                       /       \
                  7:x3=2     8:x3=4
```

Fig. 1.

The table below gives for each node n the set of decisions taken on the path from the root node to n, as well as the domains of the variables corresponding to its state.

Table 1.

node	decisions	v_1	v_2	v_3	solution
0	-	1,2,3,4	1,2,3,4	1,2,3,4	
1	$v_1 = 1$	1	2,3,4	2,3,4	
2	$v_1 = 1,\ v_2 = 2$	1	2	3,4	
3	$v_1 = 1,\ v_2 = 2,\ v_3 = 3$	1	2	3	yes
4	$v_1 = 1,\ v_2 = 2,\ v_3 = 4$	1	2	4	yes
5	$v_1 = 1,\ v_2 \neq 2$	1	3,4	2,3,4	
6	$v_1 = 1,\ v_2 \neq 2,\ v_2 = 3$	1	3	2,4	
7	$v_1 = 1,\ v_2 \neq 2,\ v_2 = 3,\ v_3 = 2$	1	3	2	yes
8	$v_1 = 1,\ v_2 \neq 2,\ v_2 = 3,\ v_3 = 4$	1	3	4	yes

Four solutions have been obtained so far, at nodes 3, 4, 7 and 8. However the solution found at node 7 is symmetrical with the one found at node 3. Indeed, those solutions are $\{v_1 = 1,\ v_2 = 3,\ v_3 = 2\}$ $\{v_1 = 1,\ v_2 = 2,\ v_3 = 3\}$

The symmetry σ_0 defined above maps each solution into the other. The next section will show how to use such symmetries to prevent the generation of solutions that are symmetrical variants of previously found solutions. Before moving to that, let us introduce a simple, yet effective way to remove symmetries.

2.5   Set Variables

One possible way to reduce symmetries is to reformulate the CSP using sets of binary variables, or finite set variables[15][10].

Definition 8. *A* binary variable *b is a variable whose domain is the set* $\{0, 1\}$. *When the domain of b is reduced to* $\{1\}$ *we say that the variable is* true. *When the domain of b is reduced to* $\{0\}$ *we say that the variable is* false

Definition 9. *A finite set variable s is a set of binary variables* $\{v_i\}$ *s.t. i ranges over an interval* $I(s) = [1..m(s)]$ *such that* $\sum_{i \in I(s)} v_i = \sharp(s)$. *The cardinality* $\sharp(s)$ *can be either another variable of the problem, or a constant.*

We say that the finite set variable s is bound when all the binary variables of s are bound.

A decision on a set variable is a decision on one of its binary variable. If the decision is of the form $v_i = 1$, we note it as $i \in s$. If the decision is of the form $v_i = 0$, we note it as $i \notin s$.

Let us look again at the above example. It can be represented with a finite set variable s s.t. $I(s) = [1..4]$ and $\sharp(s) = 3$. This formulation has no symmetries. Indeed, the two solutions $\{v_1 = 1, v_2 = 2, v_3 = 3\}$ and $\{v_1 = 2, v_2 = 3, v_3 = 1\}$ are now represented by the unique solution $\{1 \in s, 2 \in s, 3 \in s, 4 \notin s\}$

3   Symmetries Removal during Search

In [5] and [4] the author independently developed a method that records the root nodes of all completely expanded subtrees as nogoods, and then check if any new node is not a symmetrical variant from one of the nogoods. In their method, the information stored for the nogood is the state, i.e. the current domains of the variables. We introduce a variant where we store the sets of decisions taken from the tree root to the nogood instead.

3.1   Decision Sequence as Nogoods

Given a node n in a search tree, we will define the nogood w.r.t. n as all the roots of maximal subtrees that are completely traversed by a depth first search before n. Those nogoods can be found by traversing the path from the root node to n as follows. Each time the path goes from a node to its right child, then the left child of that node is a nogood. Indeed, before traversing the right child of a given node a depth first search completely traverses the left subtree of that node. The information stored for a nogood is the set of decisions labeling the path from the root of the tree to the nogood.

Definition 10. Nogood. *Let τ be a search tree and n a node in that tree. We say that node ν is a nogood w.r.t. n if there exists an ancestor n_a of n in τ s.t. $\nu = l(n_a)$ and ν is not an ancestor of n.*

We define the set of decisions $\delta(\nu)$ of nogood ν to be the set of all the decisions that labels the arcs of the path from $root(\tau)$ to ν.

For instance, in the preceding example, node 3 is a nogood w.r.t. node 4, node 2 is a nogood for node 5 and all the nodes in its subtree. The nogoods w.r.t. node 8 are nodes 2 and 7. The information stored for nogood 2 is[1] :
$\delta(2) = \{v_1 = 1, \ v_2 = 2\}$

Note that our definition of nogoods is simpler than previously published ones, as it uniformly handles solutions and dead end nodes. Moreover, it applies to non depth first traversal of the search tree. A similar generalization to non depth first search is also presented in section 2.2. of [4].

3.2   Symmetry Removal

Nogoods are used to prevent the traversal of subtrees symmetrical to subtrees already traversed as following.

Definition 11. Symmetry dominance *We say that a node n is dominated if there exists a nogood ν w.r.t. n and a symmetry σ s.t. $n \vdash \sigma(\delta(\nu))$*

In such a case we say that ν dominates n.

Lemma 2. *Node ν dominates node n iff there exists a symmetry σ s.t. $\sigma(\delta(\nu)) \subset \Delta(n)$.*

Proof. Follows from definitions 5, 10 and 11.

For instance, in our example, nogood 2 dominates node 7. Indeed, $\delta(2) = \{v_1 = 1, v_2 = 2\}$. Using the symmetry σ_0 defined above (σ_0 permutes variables v_2 and v_3), we obtain a symmetrical variant of the nogood $\sigma_0(\delta(2)) = \{v_1 = 1, v_3 = 2\}$ which is a subset of $\Delta(7) = \{v_1 = 1, \ v_3 = 2, v_2 = 3\}$.

Symmetry removal during search is then quite simple : it never generates the children of dominated nodes, and it excludes dominated solutions.

Definition 12. Symmetry removal *A symmetry removal search tree τ is a dominance tree τ as defined in definition 7 such that*

1. *$n \in cut(\tau)$ iff n is dominated.*
2. *nogoods are non dominated nodes.*

Therefore, a node n is a leaf if, and only if, it is either a solution, an empty node, or a dominated node.

Symmetry removal is complete w.r.t. symmetries, i.e. it will reach a symmetrical variant of all the solutions of the CSP.

---

[1] More generally, the column labeled "decisions" in Table 1 give the nogood information corresponding to each node.

Proposition 2. Completeness of symmetry removal *Given a symmetry removal search tree, then* $\forall s \in sol(\mathcal{P})\ \exists \sigma \in sym(\mathcal{P})\ \sigma(s) \in sol(\tau)$

Proof. Let s be a solution of $\mathcal{P}$. By repeated applications of Lemma 1, s is "pushed" down into the tree as much as possible : there exists a leaf node n such that $s \in sol(n)$. This node can either be a solution, or a dominated node. In the former case we are done. In the latter case, there exists a non dominated node ν that dominates n. Then, there exists a symmetry ρ s.t. $n \vdash \rho(\delta(\nu))$. Then $\rho(\delta(\nu)) \subset \Delta(n)$, which entails $\rho(\delta(\nu)) \subset s$ because s is a solution of n. By inverting ρ, we get $\delta(\nu) \subset \rho^{-1}(s)$. Then $\rho^{-1}(s) \in sol(\nu)$. Let $\sigma = \rho^{-1}$: it is the symmetry we are looking for.

Symmetry removal is also correct w.r.t. to symmetries, i.e. it never generates two symmetric solutions.

Proposition 3. Correctness of symmetry removal *Given a symmetry removal search tree* τ, *then*
$$\forall s_1, s_2 \in sol(\tau)\ (\exists \sigma \in sym(\mathcal{P})\ \sigma(s_1) = s_2) \Rightarrow (s_1 = s_2)$$

Proof. Let s_1 and s_2 be two distinct solutions of τ and σ a symmetry s.t. $\sigma(s_1) = s_2$. By definition of solutions, s_1 and s_2 are non dominated leaf nodes of τ. Assume without any loss of generality that s_1 is on the left of s_2 in the tree, and let n be the least common ancestor of s_1 and s_2. Then $l(n)$ is a nogood w.r.t. s_2. Moreover, $l(n)$ is an ancestor of s_1. Then $\delta(l(n)) \subset s_1$. By applying the symmetry we get $\sigma(\delta(l(n))) \subset \sigma(s_1)$. By substituting s_2 we get $\sigma(\delta(l(n))) \subset s_2$. As $l(n)$ is a nogood w.r.t. s_2, node s_2 is dominated, which is a contradiction.

Corollary 1. Nogood unicity *Given a symmetry removal search tree* τ, *and two nogoods* ν_1, ν_2 *w.r.t. node* n, *if there exists a symmetry* σ *s.t.* $\sigma(\nu_1) = \nu_2$ *then* $\nu_1 = \nu_2$

Therefore there is no need to do any check for dominance between two nogoods. This is a significant improvement over[4].

3.3   Getting Rid of Negative Decisions

In our example, the nogoods w.r.t. node 8 are nodes 2 and 7 s.t. $\delta(2) = \{v_1 = 1,\ v_2 = 2\}$ and $\delta(7) = \{v_1 = 1,\ v_2 \neq 2,\ v_2 = 3,\ v_3 = 2\}$. Using $\delta_1 = (v_1 = 1)$, $\delta_2 = (v_2 = 2)$, $\delta_3 = (v_2 = 3)$ and $\delta_4 = (v_3 = 2)$ we have that $\delta(2) = \{\delta_1, \delta_2\}$ and $\delta(7) = \{\delta_1, \neg\delta_2, \delta_3, \delta_4\}$

Node 8 is dominated if there exists a symmetry σ s.t. $n \vdash \sigma(\delta(2)) \vee n \vdash \sigma(\delta(7))$, which is equivalent to $\{\delta_1, \delta_2\} \subset \Delta(8) \vee \{\delta_1, \neg\delta_2, \delta_3, \delta_4\} \subset \Delta(8)$.

By distributivity of disjunction, this can be rewritten into $\delta_1 \in \Delta(8) \wedge (\delta_2 \in \Delta(8) \vee \{\neg\delta_2, \delta_3, \delta_4\} \subset \Delta(8))$.

Using distributivity again, we get $\delta_1 \in \Delta(8) \wedge ((\delta_2 \in \Delta(8) \vee \neg\delta_2 \in \Delta(8)) \wedge (\delta_2 \in \Delta(8) \vee \{\delta_3, \delta_4\} \subset \Delta(8)))$, which can be simplified into $\delta_1 \in \Delta(8) \wedge (\delta_2 \in \Delta(8) \vee \{\delta_3, \delta_4\} \subset \Delta(8))$.

Using distributivity, we get $\{\delta_1, \delta_2\} \subset \Delta(8) \vee \{\delta_1, \delta_3, \delta_4\} \subset \Delta(8)$.

By defining $\delta'(2) = \{\delta_1, \delta_2\}$ and $\delta'(7) = \{\delta_1, \delta_3, \delta_4\}$, this is equivalent to $n \vdash \sigma(\delta'(2)) \vee n \vdash \sigma(\delta'(7))$

In other words 8 is dominated iff it is dominated by the nogoods obtained by removing negative decisions from its nogoods.

This transformation still holds for the general case. From now on, the information stored for nogoods will be the set of positive decisions labeling the path from the tree root to the nogood. A similar generalization of nogoods is described in [5].

For instance, in our example, the information for nogood 7 will be $\{v_1 = 1,\ v_2 = 3,\ v_3 = 2\}$ instead of $\{v_1 = 1,\ v_2 \neq 2,\ v_2 = 3,\ v_3 = 2\}$.

4   Efficient Dominance Checks

Dominance check needs to be done at every node in the search tree. This amounts to search for a symmetry that exhibits some properties. Several authors assume that all possible symmetries are explicitly listed[9][5]. However, when the number of symmetries is extremely large, this is impractical. Other authors have proposed to use a separate CSP to define symmetries[4][11][18]. This latter approach can easily be used in our method.

We are given a node n and a nogood ν w.r.t. n. The problem is to check if there exists a symmetry σ s.t. $\sigma(\delta(\nu)) \subset \Delta(n)$ given lemma 2.

This can be done using a CSP defined as follows : There is one variable x_δ per decision δ in $\delta(\nu)$ whose value will be $\sigma(\delta)$. The initial domains of all those variables are the set of positive decisions from $\Delta(n)$. Those variables are subject to an *all different* constraint because symmetries are bijections. Usually, symmetries are only a subset of all possible mapping of decisions. The restriction to this subset is implemented with problem dependant constraints on the variables x_i such that the CSP has a solution iff a symmetry can be found.

For instance, in our example, the dominance check between nogood 2 and state 7 can be expressed with the following CSP. We have that $\delta(2) = \{v_1 = 1,\ v_2 = 2\}$ and $\Delta(7) = \{v_1 = 1,\ v_3 = 2, v_2 = 3\}$. There are two decision variables $x_{v_1=1}$ and $x_{v_2=2}$, whose domain are $\Delta(7)$, and that are subject to $x_{v_1=1} \neq x_{v_2=2}$.

In this problem variables can be permuted but not values. This is translated using auxiliary variables y_i whose domains are the index of the variables v_i of the original problem. $y_i = j$ means that the symmetry maps v_i to v_j. Those auxiliary variables are linked to the principal variables x_i by the following constraints: $x_{v_i=a_i} = (v_j = a_i)$ iff $y_i = j$

The CSP is then easy to solve and has one solution:
$x_{v_1=1} = (v_1 = 1),\ x_{v_2=2} = (v_3 = 2),\ y_1 = 1,\ y_2 = 3,\ y_3 = 2$

The symmetry is given by the values of the y_i: it permutes variable v_2 and v_3.

More complex symmetries can be expressed that way, as showed by the examples found in section 6.

More generally, the problem is to check if a node is dominated by one of its nogoods ν_i. We construct a global CSP for checking if n is dominated as follows.

For each nogood ν_i we construct a CSP $\mathcal{P}_i$ as explained in the previous section. Then the global CSP is the constructive disjunction of the $\mathcal{P}_i$. This global CSP has a solution iff one of the $\mathcal{P}_i$ has a solution. A similar idea is presented in [11].

5   Computational Results

Many problems have symmetries, but few have been studied as extensively as the social golfer problem (problem 10 in the CSPLib [3]). We have selected this problem because : It is a real problem, it has an extremely high number of symmetries, it has variants of increasing difficulty are easy to generate, and it enables comparison with previously reported methods.

The problem has come up from a question posted to sci.op-research in May 1998. It consists of trying to schedule $g.s$ golfers into g groups of s players over w weeks, such that no golfer plays in the same group as any other golfer more than just once. An instance to the problem is characterized by a triple $g - s - w$. The original question is to find the largest w such that $8 - 4 - w$ has a solution. The current best known solution is a $w = 9$ week schedule. The existence of a solution remains open for $8 - 4 - 10$

Our model for the $g - s - w$ social golfer uses w set variables x_i (one per week) of cardinality g. Its elements are drawn among all the possible groups of s players elements selected among gs. Our model requires the computation of all possible groups. For the $8 - 4 - 10$ problem, there are 35960 such groups. This is large but still tractable. The symmetries in this model are player permutations, and week permutations. The latter corresponds to variable permutations, whereas the former are symmetries on values. Note that values (groups) are not freely permutable. The number of symmetries for this model is equal to $w!(gs)!$. This equal 9.5×10^{41} for $8 - 4 - 10$, which is still extremely large.

The constraints we use are quite straightforward : the groups in each variable x_i must not intersect, and two groups occurring in two different variable x_i and x_j must have at most one player in their intersection. Our implementation uses ILOG Solver, and running times are given for a 833 MHz Pentium III laptop running Windows 2000.

The branching strategy is to label variables one at a time (week per week) and to select first the group containing the most constrained pair of players (i.e. the two players that have the least number of groups left).

Using this model we were able to prove 6-5-7 has no solution and to find the two non symmetrical solutions for 6-5-6.[2] We were also able to find solutions to some problems unsolved so far: 7-3-9, 8-3-10, 9-3-11, 10-3-13, 9-4-8, 10-4-9 and 8-5-5.[3].

In order to assess the relative strength of various symmetry removal methods we compare them not only on a set of examples without solution, but also on the problem of finding all solutions for instances that do have solutions. We have

[2] These result have also been independently found by Meinolf Sellmann
[3] Those solutions can be found on Warwick Harvey's page:
http://www.icparc.ic.ac.uk/~wh/golf/

also tested the finding reported in[18], saying that performing dominance checks less often pays off. Indeed, the cost of dominance checks increases with the depth within the search tree, whereas the number of symmetries decreases on average with the depth.

Table 2 contains the results for examples with $s \geq 3$ and $g \leq 6$ for which all solutions could be found in 5 minutes with our machine. In addition to these, we also report results for the 6-5-7 problem. The problems 3-3-5, 4-4-6, and 5-5-7 were solved immediately, as the propagation procedure detected there are no solutions at the root node. When the program was still running after 5 minutes, we indicate the number of solutions found so far, as well as the number of backtracks. For each instance, we ran our code with the following settings :

– **no**: simple symmetry removal. The first week and the first group of the second week are fixed, and the permutation removal search strategy of [17] is applied.
– **sym**: The symmetry removal strategy discussed in this paper.
– **weeks** The use of the **sym** dominance checks on all choice points within the first three weeks, and only when a week is fully completed for the rest.
– **top** Use of the **sym** matching on all choice points within the first three weeks only. This approach does not ensure unicity of solutions w.r.t. symmetries.

For each of those settings we give the number of solutions found, the number of backtracks needed to find them, as well as the running time. We also provide the number of symmetries in the first column.

We can observe the following on those results.

– With the permutation symmetry removal of [17] the problem is intractable except for the smallest instances.
– The table also shows that matching only on the top of the search tree is useful in practice (compare **weeks** and **sym**).
– It is often better not to remove all symmetries, as shown by **top** result. Moreover, although this is not displayed here because of lack of space, the time needed to get the first solution is also greatly improved in such case, and is comparable to the time without symmetry removal.

6   Comparison with Previous Work

Our method can be related to the cut generation of[5] and the SBDD method of[4]. It shares their advantages over other methods such as SBDS[9][8][12][19]: it can be applied to remove *all* the symmetries of a given CSP when the number of symmetries is too large for being explicitly listed. A recent approach using an algebraic system to implicitly handle symmetries for SBDS[7] does not seem scalable enough for tackling problems with 10^{36} symmetries, although it seems quite promising.

Our method has further advantages.

First of all, previous methods store the state itself, i.e. the domains of the variables. For instance, the nogood information of node 2 in our example will

Table 2. A "−" sign means the program was still running after 5 minutes

size	sym	no			sym			weeks			top		
		sol	bt	time	sol	bt	time	sol	bt	time	sol	bt	time
3-3-2	7.10^5	4	0	0	1	3	0.01	1	3	0.01	1	3	0.01
3-3-3	2.10^6	8	0	0.01	1	4	0.0	1	4	0.0	2	3	0
3-3-4	8.10^6	8	0	0	1	4	0.01	1	4	0.0	2	3	0
4-3-2	9.10^8	48	0	0.01	1	17	0.02	1	17	0.02	1	17	0.02
4-3-3	2.10^9	2688	0	0.53	4	37	0.11	4	37	0.11	14	27	0.05
4-3-4	1.10^{10}	2064	1956	1.0	3	40	0.21	3	40	0.19	15	37	0.06
4-3-5	5.10^{10}	0	612	0.28	0	27	0.03	0	27	0.03	0	27	0.03
4-4-2	4.10^{13}	216	0	0.14	1	40	0.07	1	40	0.07	1	40	0.07
4-4-3	1.10^{14}	5184	0	3.2	2	50	0.2	2	50	0.19	8	44	0.1
4-4-4	5.10^{14}	1512	1296	3.0	1	48	0.14	1	48	0.13	5	44	0.13
4-4-5	2.10^{15}	864	216	1.4	1	43	0.18	1	43	0.18	4	41	0.17
5-3-2	2.10^{12}	2448	0	0.5	2	89	0.13	2	89	0.12	2	89	0.12
5-3-3	7.10^{12}	1372573	0	-	251	1823	35.0	251	1823	34.2	1493	581	14.7
5-3-4	3.10^{13}	1078970	62117	-	13933	39646	3603	13933	61233	2638	353812	20635	105
5-3-5	1.10^{14}	534606	304505	-	9719	60874	5958	9719	78850	4292	528980	290128	298
5-3-6	9.10^{14}	9715	521329	-	49	26669	799	49	33143	407	3765	156042	100
5-3-7	6.10^{15}	15606	307140	-	7	1598	25.5	7	1621	24	102	2134	7.8
5-4-2	4.10^{18}	31104	864	36.1	1	200	0.6	1	200	0.6	1	200	0.6
5-4-3	1.10^{19}	203509	30589	-	40	577	10.1	40	577	10.1	182	435	5
5-4-4	5.10^{19}	44115	157568	-	20	1041	26.6	20	1105	19.4	524	2113	8.1
5-4-5	2.10^{20}	10097	87844	-	10	804	20.4	10	811	19.4	147	1056	7.5
5-4-6	1.10^{21}	0	115045	-	0	549	4.1	0	549	4.1	0	554	3.6
5-5-2	3.10^{25}	25698	0	-	1	460	6.5	1	460	6.5	1	460	6.5
5-5-3	9.10^{25}	18597	0	-	2	516	13.7	2	516	13.5	18	500	12.3
5-5-4	3.10^{26}	3598	10165	-	1	502	25.6	1	502	25.1	5	498	22.0
5-5-5	1.10^{27}	4216	5357	-	1	497	33.3	1	497	33.3	4	494	23.4
5-5-6	1.10^{28}	5528	4684	-	1	477	38	1	477	38.8	12	476	38.2
6-4-2	4.10^{24}	140487	440	-	4	1219	7	4	1219	7	4	1219	7
6-5-6	1.10^{35}							2	154084	21673	30	585372	42811
6-5-7	4.10^{36}				0	52804	5708	0	52804	5690	0	52805	5657

be $v_1 \in \{1\}, v_2 \in \{2\}, v_3 \in \{3, 4\}$. This takes up to $O(nm)$ where n is the number of variables and m the size of the largest domain. The dominance check is also more complex, as a nogood ν dominates a state s if the domains of the variables in s are subsets of the domain of variables in ν. If this is represented as a CSP, we will get $O(nm)$ variables instead of $O(n)$ in our case[11].

Then, it is shown in[5], that a nogood should be generalized (extended cut seeds). We achieve the same effect in a simpler way by getting rid of the negative decisions for nogoods.

Moreover, in[4], every new nogood is compared with all the previously stored nogoods in order to see if one dominates the other. Such checks are not needed in our approach.

Last, we have shown how to match all nogoods using a single CSP. A similar idea is presented for state based nogoods in[11]. However, as noted before, the auxiliary CSP we use is much simpler.

All those advantages should lead to superior performance. This is what we can check on the social golfer problem. We have decided to focus on comparison with methods that aims at removing all symmetries, i.e. the one described in[4][5][18][11]. Those results are compared with the ones we got with the **weeks**

Table 3. (1) means the program was stopped after 3600 seconds

	weeks			[4]			[18]			[5]			[11]	
CP	ILOG Solver			ILOG Solver			ILOG Solver			ILOG Solver			ECL^iPS^e	
CPU	PIII			ultrasparc II			PIII			PII			PII	
MHz	833			450			950			500			450	
size	time	sol	bt	time	sol	bt	time	sol	bt	time	sol	bt	time	sol
4-3-2	0.02	1	17	0.04	1	194		1					0.7	1
4-3-3	0.11	4	37	10	4	28296	0.25	4	76				14.6	4
4-3-4	0.17	3	49	29	3	94843		3		2.9	16	1235	49.1	3
4-3-5	0.03	0	27	36	0	200390	0.26	0	74	3.0	0	1473	29.4	0
4-4-2	0.07	1	40	0.17	1	555		1					2.2	1
4-4-3	0.19	2	50	136	2	43754		2					8.5	2
4-4-4	0.13	1	48	22	1	82634		1					8.5	1
4-4-5	0.19	1	43	26	1	75723		1					12.4	1
4-4-6	0	0	0	30	0	72268		0					21.1	0
5-3-2	0.13	2	89					2					16.7	2
5-3-3	34.1	251	1823				109	251	16396				(1)	220
5-3-4	2638	13933	61233					13933					(1)	356
5-3-5	4792	9719	78850					9719					(1)	47
5-3-6	407	49	33143					49					(1)	0
5-3-7	24	7	1621				393	7	85790				(1)	0
5-4-2	0.6	1	200					1					16.9	1
5-4-3	10.1	40	577				40.1	40	6205				2502	40
5-4-4	19.4	20	1105					20					(1)	14
5-4-5	19.4	10	811					10					(1)	7
5-4-6	4.1	0	549				23.2	0	1770				(1)	0
5-5-2	6.5	1	460										52	1
5-5-3	13.5	2	516										249	2
5-5-4	25.1	1	502										1304	1
5-5-5	33.3	1	497										4027	1
5-5-6	38.8	0	477										(1)	0

settings in Table 3. For each approach, we give the CP system used for the implementation, as well as the CPU and its clock speed to enable a fair comparison.

The greater performance of our code is partly due to the difference in modeling. It would be interesting to compare the methods of [4] and [5] to ours using the same model. However, given the size of the domains of the variables we consider (35960 possible groups for $8 - 4 - 10$), methods based on the full state representation cannot be applied to our model.

We believe the main cause of the difference in performance is the frequency and the efficiency of dominance checks. The greater efficiency allows us to perform them at each choice point, whereas they are only performed at the leaves of the search tree in[4], and every **g** choice points in[18].

7   Conclusion and Future Work

We have presented an improvement of nogood recording methods presented in[5][4] where the information stored for each nogood is the set of positive decisions taken from the root of the search tree. We have formalized this approach using definitions that are broader and simpler than previously published ones. Then we have shown how our method is theoretically more efficient and we explained how dominance checks could be implemented with an auxiliary CSP.

Then, we presented an extensive empirical evaluation on the social golfer problem, where we report new results. We concluded with a comparison with previous work both theoretically and experimentally. Those results showed that our theoretical improvements result in dramatic performance improvements.

One of the possible area for future work is to simplify the definition of the auxiliary CSP used within dominance checks. We could for instance explore how to reuse the symmetry defining functions used in methods tailored for a smaller number of symmetries such as SBDS[9][19]. The use of algebraic systems for generating symmetries seems promising in this context[8][12][7].

Another area is to explore the use of an auxiliary CSP in order to reduce domains instead of merely check for dominance. Preliminary experiments are quite disappointing since the total running time is increased even if the number of backtracks is decreased.

We could also investigate how to extend our results for n-ary branching constraints.

Last, we must admit that even if we report significant performance improvements the original **8-4-10** social golfer problem is still open.

Acknowledgments

We thank Filipo Focacci and Meinolf Sellmann for interesting discussions, as well as Marie Puget, Laurent Perron, Jean-Charles Regin and anonymous referees for their remarks on an earlier draft of this paper.

References

[1]   Backofen, R., Will, S.: Excluding Symmetries in Constraint Based Search. Proceedings of CP'99 (1999).

[2]   Benhamou, B.: Study of Symmetries in Constraint Satisfaction Problems. Proceedings of PPCP'94 (1994).

[3]   Gent, I. P., Walsh, T., Sellmann, B.: CSPlib
      http://www-users.cs.york.ac.uk/~tw/csplib/.

[4]   Fahle, T., Shamberger, S., Sellmann, M.: Symmetry Breaking. Proceedings of CP01 (2001) 93–107.

[5]   Focacci, F., Milano, M.: Global Cut Framework for Removing Symmetries. Proceedings of CP01 (2001) 75–92.

[7]   Gent, I. P., and Harvey, W., and Kelsey, T.: Groups and Constraints: Symmetry Breaking During Search, Technical report APES-48-2002, APES Research Group (2002).

[8]   Gent, I. P., and Linton, S. A., and Smith, B. M.: Symmetry Breaking in the Alien Tiles Puzzle, Technical report APES-22-2000, APES Research Group (1999).

[9]   Gent, I. P., and Smith, B. M.: Symmetry Breaking During Search in Constraint Programming. Proceedings ECAI'2000, pp. 599-603.

[10] Gervet, C.: Interval Propagation to Reason about Sets: Definition and Implementation of a practical language. Constraints, An International Journal, (1997), vol 1. 191-246.

[11] Harvey, W.: Symmetry Breaking and the Social Golfer Problem CP01 Workshop on Symmetries (2001).

[12] McDonald, I., Smith, B.: Partial Symmetry Breaking, Technical report APES-49-2002, APES Research Group (2002).

[13] Meseguer, P., Torras, C.: Exploiting Symmetries Within Constraint Satisfaction Search. Art.Intell. **129** (1999) 133–163.

[14] Puget, J.-F.: On the Satisfiability of Symmetrical Constraint Satisfaction Problems. Proceedings of ISMIS'93 (1993), 350–361.

[15] Puget, J. F.: Finite Set Intervals. Workshop on Set Constraints, CP'96, (1996).

[16] Rothberg, E.: Using cuts to remove symmetry. In proceedings of ISMP 2000, Atlanta.

[17] Roy, P., Pachet, F.: Using Symmetry of Global Constraints to Speed Up the Resolution of Constraint Satisfaction Problems. Proceedings of ECAI'98 workshop on Non Binary Constraints (1998) 27–33.

[18] Sellmann, M., Harvey, W.: Heuristic Constraint Propagation Proceedings of CPAIOR'02 workshop (2002) 191–204.

[19] Smith, B. M.: Reducing Symmetry in a Combinatorial Design Problem Research Report 2001.01, January 2001. Presented at the CP-AI-OR Workshop, April 2001.

Breaking Row and Column Symmetries in Matrix Models

Pierre Flener[1], Alan M. Frisch[2], Brahim Hnich[3], Zeynep Kiziltan[3], Ian Miguel[2], Justin Pearson[1], and Toby Walsh[4]

[1] Dept of Information Tech, Uppsala University
Box 337, 751 05 Uppsala, Sweden
PierreF@csd.uu.se
justin@docs.uu.se
[2] Department of Computer Science, University of York
York YO10 5DD, England
{Frisch,IanM}@cs.york.ac.uk
[3] Dept of Information Science, Uppsala University
Box 513, 751 20 Uppsala, Sweden
Zeynep.Kiziltan,Brahim.Hnich}@dis.uu.se
[4] Cork Constraint Computation Centre, University College Cork
Cork, Ireland
TW@4c.ucc.ie

Abstract. We identify an important class of symmetries in constraint programming, arising from matrices of decision variables where rows and columns can be swapped. Whilst lexicographically ordering the rows (columns) breaks all the row (column) symmetries, lexicographically ordering both the rows and the columns fails to break all the compositions of the row and column symmetries. Nevertheless, our experimental results show that this is effective at dealing with these compositions of symmetries. We extend these results to cope with symmetries in any number of dimensions, with partial symmetries, and with symmetric values. Finally, we identify special cases where all compositions of the row and column symmetries can be eliminated by the addition of only a linear number of symmetry-breaking constraints.

1   Introduction

Modelling is one of the most difficult parts of constraint programming. Freuder has identified it as the "last frontier" [9]. One source of difficulty is dealing with symmetry efficiently and effectively. Symmetry occurs in many assignment, scheduling, configuration, and design problems. Identical machines in a factory, repeat orders, equivalent time periods and equally skilled workers are just a few of the items likely to introduce symmetry into a constraint satisfaction problem (CSP). If we ignore symmetry, a constraint solver will waste time considering symmetric but essentially equivalent assignments. As there are often a (super) exponential number of symmetric solutions, this can be very costly. To help tackle this problem, we identify an important class of symmetries that occur

P. Van Hentenryck (Ed.): CP 2002, LNCS 2470, pp. 462–476, 2002.

frequently in CSPs. These symmetries occur when we have a matrix of decision variables in which rows and/or columns can be swapped. We show how simple lexicographical ordering constraints can be added to such models to break these symmetries. Whilst such ordering constraints break all the row (or column) symmetry when the matrix is symmetric in one dimension, they do not break *all* row and column symmetry when the matrix is symmetric in both dimensions. Nevertheless, our experimental results show that they are effective at eliminating much of the symmetry. We extend these results to deal with matrices with more than two dimensions, with partial symmetries and with symmetric values. We also discuss how to eliminate all symmetry in some special cases.

2   Matrix Models and Symmetry

A *matrix model* is a constraint program that contains one or more matrices of decision variables. For example, a natural model of the round robin tournament scheduling problem (prob026 in CSPlib, at www.csplib.org) has a 2-dimensional (2-d) matrix of variables, each of which is assigned a value corresponding to the match played in a given week and period [21]. In this case, the matrix is obvious in the modelling of the problem: we need a *table* of fixtures. However, many other problems that are less obviously defined in terms of matrices of variables can be effectively represented and efficiently solved using matrix models [6]. For example, the rack configuration problem (prob031) can be modelled with a 2-d 0/1 matrix representing which cards go into which racks (a model with a 3-d matrix is given in [13]).

Symmetry is an important aspect of matrix models. Symmetry often occurs because groups of objects within a matrix are indistinguishable. For example, in the round robin tournament scheduling problem, weeks and periods are indistinguishable. We can therefore permute any two weeks or any two periods in the schedule. That is, we can permute any two rows or any two columns of the associated matrix, whose index sets are the weeks and periods. A *symmetry* is a bijection on decision variables that preserves solutions and non-solutions. Two variables are *indistinguishable* if some symmetry interchanges their rôles in all solutions and non-solutions.

Two common types of symmetry in matrices are row symmetries and column symmetries. The two examples above have row and column symmetries. A *row (column) symmetry* of a 2-d matrix is a bijection between the variables of two of its rows (columns) that preserves solutions and non-solutions. Two rows (columns) are *indistinguishable* if their variables are pairwise indistinguishable due to a row (column) symmetry. Note that the rotational symmetries of a matrix are neither row nor column symmetries. A matrix model *has row (column) symmetry* iff all the rows (columns) of one of its matrices are indistinguishable. A matrix model *has partial row (column) symmetry* iff strict subset(s) of the rows (columns) of one of its matrices are indistinguishable. All these definitions can be extended to matrices with any number of dimensions. A *symmetry class* is an equivalence class of assignments, where two assignments are equivalent if there is some symmetry mapping one assignment into the other. (In group theory, such equivalence classes are referred to as *orbits*.)

Many row and column symmetries have been observed [6], such as in matrix models for the balanced incomplete block design problem (prob028 in CSPlib), the steel mill slab design problem [6], the social golfers problem (prob010), the template design problem (prob002), the progressive party problem (prob013), and (as argued above) the rack configuration problem (prob031) as well as the round robin tournament scheduling problem (prob026). One counter-example is the warehouse location problem [22] because of the unique set of costs of supplying each store from each of the possible warehouses.

3   Breaking Symmetry

There are a number of ways of dealing with symmetry in constraint programming (see Section 7 for a longer discussion). A popular approach is to add constraints that break some of the symmetries [16, 3].

One common method to break symmetry is to impose a constraint that orders the symmetric objects. To break all row (column) symmetries, we can treat each row (column) as a vector and order these vectors lexicographically. The rows (columns) in a 2-d matrix are *lexicographically ordered* if each row (column) is lexicographically smaller (denoted $\leq_{lex}$) than the next (if any), and *anti-lexicographically ordered* if each row (column) is lexicographically larger than the next (if any). As a lexicographic ordering is total, adding lexicographic (or anti-lexicographic) ordering constraints on the rows (columns) breaks all row (column) symmetries.

Whilst breaking all the row symmetries *or* all the column symmetries in a matrix is possible with lexicographic ordering constraints, breaking *both* the row and the column symmetries seems difficult since the rows and columns intersect. Lexicographically ordering the rows will tend to put the columns into lexicographic order. However, it does not always order the columns lexicographically, and lexicographically ordering the columns can then disrupt the lexicographic ordering on the rows.

Example 1. Consider a 3×4 matrix of 0/1 variables, x_{ij}, with the constraints that $\sum_{ij} x_{ij} = 7$ and $\sum_i x_{ij} \cdot x_{ik} \leq 1$ for $j \neq k$ (i.e., the dot product of any two rows is 1 or less). This model has both row and column symmetry. A solution with lexicographically ordered rows is:

$$\begin{pmatrix} 0 & 1 & 0 \\ 0 & 1 & 1 \\ 1 & 0 & 1 \\ 1 & 1 & 0 \end{pmatrix}$$

Lexicographically ordering the columns now gives the solution:

$$\begin{pmatrix} 0 & 0 & 1 \\ 0 & 1 & 1 \\ 1 & 1 & 0 \\ 1 & 0 & 1 \end{pmatrix}$$

However, this destroys the lexicographic ordering on the rows. Reordering the last two rows gives a solution that is lexicographically ordered along both the rows and the columns:

$$\begin{pmatrix} 0\ 0\ 1 \\ 0\ 1\ 1 \\ 1\ 0\ 1 \\ 1\ 1\ 0 \end{pmatrix}$$

One can even construct examples that need several sequential rounds of ordering the rows and then the columns, although the following theorem shows that this process always terminates. During search, both the row and column lexicographic ordering constraints actually work in parallel. The following theorem shows that, whether this ordering is done sequentially or in parallel, there always is a solution with the rows and columns *both* in lexicographic order.

Theorem 1. *For a matrix model with row and column symmetry in some 2-d matrix, each symmetry class of assignments has an element where both the rows and the columns of that matrix are lexicographically ordered.*

Proof: We order 2-d matrices by lexicographically ordering the sequences formed by appending their rows together in top-down order. Lexicographically ordering two rows replaces a larger row at the front of this sequence by a smaller row from further behind. Hence, ordering two rows moves us down the matrix ordering. Lexicographically ordering two columns also moves us down this matrix ordering. Indeed, the two columns have some values (if any) in common at the top and swapping the columns thus does not affect the matrix ordering when just considering the corresponding top rows; also, in the top-most row (if any) where the two columns differ, the value in the left column is then replaced by a smaller value from the right column, as the latter was lexicographically smaller than the left column, making that row lexicographically smaller. This moves us down the matrix ordering, as the first changed row (if any) is replaced in the sequence by a smaller one. Furthermore, the matrix ordering is finite, as there are only a finite number of permutations of the values in a matrix, and bounded below, namely by a matrix whose rows and columns are lexicographically ordered. So we cannot move down the matrix ordering indefinitely, and will find a matrix in which all the rows and columns are lexicographically ordered. □

This result shows that we can always lexicographically order both the rows and the columns. Dually, we can always anti-lexicographically order both the rows and the columns. However, we cannot always lexicographically order the rows and anti-lexicographically order the columns. Lexicographically ordering the rows will tend to push the largest values to the bottom-left of the matrix. Anti-lexicographically ordering the columns will tend to push the larger values to the top-right. For this reason, the two orders can conflict.

Example 2. Consider a 2×2 matrix of $0/1$ variables, x_{ij}, with the constraints that $\sum_i x_{ij} = 1$ and $\sum_j x_{ij} = 1$ (i.e., every row and column has a single 1). This model has both row and column symmetry, and has two symmetric solutions:

$$\begin{pmatrix} 0\ 1 \\ 1\ 0 \end{pmatrix}, \quad \begin{pmatrix} 1\ 0 \\ 0\ 1 \end{pmatrix}$$

The first solution has rows and columns that are lexicographically ordered, whilst the second has rows and columns that are anti-lexicographically ordered. There is thus no solution in which the rows are lexicographically ordered and the columns are anti-lexicographically ordered.

Lexicographically ordering the rows (columns) breaks all the row (column) symmetries. However, lexicographically ordering both the rows and the columns does *not* break all the compositions of the row and column symmetries.

Example 3. Consider a 3×3 matrix of 0/1 variables, x_{ij}, with $\sum_j x_{ij} \geq 1$ and $\sum_{ij} x_{ij} = 4$. This model has both row and column symmetry. The following two symmetric solutions have lexicographically ordered rows and columns:

$$\begin{pmatrix} 0\ 0\ 1 \\ 0\ 1\ 0 \\ 1\ 0\ 1 \end{pmatrix}, \quad \begin{pmatrix} 0\ 0\ 1 \\ 0\ 1\ 0 \\ 1\ 1\ 0 \end{pmatrix}$$

These solutions are symmetric, as one can move from one to the other by swapping the first two rows and the last two columns. Swapping any rows or columns *individually* breaks the lexicographic ordering. Thus, lexicographically ordering both the rows and the columns does not break all the compositions of the row and column symmetries. However, our experimental results (see Section 6) suggest that lexicographically ordering both the rows and the columns breaks enough symmetries to be useful practically.

4   Extensions

We consider a number of extensions that extend the utility of our results considerably.

4.1   Higher Dimensions

Many problems can be effectively modelled and efficiently solved using matrix models with a matrix of more than two dimensions. For example, the social golfers problem can be modelled with a 3-d 0/1 matrix whose dimensions correspond to weeks, groups, and players [17]. A variable x_{ijk} in this matrix is 1 iff in week i player j plays in group k. This matrix model has symmetries along each of the three dimensions: the weeks are indistinguishable, and so are the groups and players. We now generalise the lexicographic ordering constraint to any number of dimensions to break some of these symmetries.

Consider a 2-d matrix. If we look along a particular dimension, we see 1-d vectors at right angles to this axis. To break the symmetries, we order these vectors lexicographically. Now consider a 3-d matrix. If we look along a particular dimension, we see 2-d slices of the matrix that are orthogonal to this axis. To break the symmetries, we need to order these slices. One way is to flatten the slices onto vectors and lexicographically order these. In n dimensions, we see slices that are $n-1$ dimensional hypercubes, which can be compared by flattening onto vectors and lexicographically ordering these.

Definition 1. *An n-dimensional matrix X, with $n \geq 1$, is* multi-dimensionally lexicographically ordered *iff the following conditions hold:*

$$\forall i \; \text{flatten}(X[i][\,]\ldots[\,]) \leq_{lex} \text{flatten}(X[i+1][\,]\ldots[\,])$$
$$\forall j \; \text{flatten}(X[\,][j]\ldots[\,]) \leq_{lex} \text{flatten}(X[\,][j+1]\ldots[\,])$$
$$\ldots$$
$$\forall k \; \text{flatten}(X[\,][\,]\ldots[k]) \leq_{lex} \text{flatten}(X[\,][\,]\ldots[k+1])$$

where $X[\,]\ldots[\,][i][\,]\ldots[\,]$ denotes the $n-1$ dimensional hypercube obtained by taking the slice of X at position i in the dimension where $[i]$ appears in $[\,]\ldots[\,][i][\,]\ldots[\,]$, and where flatten *is used to flatten a slice of a matrix into a 1-d vector and is defined by:*

$$\text{flatten}(X[1..m]) = X[1..m]$$
$$\text{flatten}(X[1..m][\,]\ldots[\,]) = \text{append}(\,\text{flatten}(X[1][\,]\ldots[\,]),$$
$$\ldots,$$
$$\text{flatten}(X[m][\,]\ldots[\,]))$$

with append$(V_1, \ldots, V_n)$ *denoting the left-to-right concatenation of the 1-d vectors $V_1, \ldots, V_n$.*

As in the 2-d case, we can show that this multi-dimensional lexicographic ordering breaks some of the symmetries. Unfortunately, it does not break all the symmetries as the 2-d counter-examples generalise to other numbers of dimensions.

Theorem 2. *For a matrix model with symmetry along each dimension in some n-dimensional matrix, where $n \geq 1$, each symmetry class of assignments has an element where that matrix is multi-dimensionally lexicographically ordered.*

Proof: A proof for the 3-d case is in [5]; it generalises to any number of dimensions. $\square$

4.2 Partial Symmetry

We may only have partial row or column symmetry in a matrix model, namely when only strict subset(s) of the rows or columns of one of its matrices are indistinguishable. We here show through an example how to address this.

Example 4. In a 2-d 0/1 matrix model of the rack configuration problem, only the columns that correspond to racks of the same type are indistinguishable. Suppose there are 10 racks, where the first 4 racks are of a first type, the next 3 racks are of another type, and the last 3 racks are of a third type. Then the following candidate solutions:

```
        ⟶ racks ⟶                      ⟶ racks ⟶
       0 0 0 0  0 1 0  0 0 0           0 0 0 0  0 1 0  0 0 0
       0 0 0 0  1 0 0  0 0 0           1 0 0 0  0 0 0  0 0 0
      ↓0 1 0 0  0 0 0  0 0 0          ↓0 1 0 0  0 0 0  0 0 0
cards 1 0 0 0  0 0 0  0 0 0     cards 0 0 0 0  1 0 0  0 0 0
      ↓0 0 0 0  0 0 0  1 0 0          ↓0 0 0 0  0 0 0  1 0 0
       1 0 0 0  0 0 0  0 0 0           0 0 0 0  1 0 0  0 0 0
```

are not symmetric, because the first and fifth columns have been swapped although they do not pertain to the same rack type. We cannot lexicographically order all the columns in such a situation, as that would here amount to requiring that all the racks are of the same type. However, we can use fewer lexicographic ordering constraints to break some of the underlying symmetries: for each subset of rows (columns) that are indistinguishable, we only state lexicographic ordering constraints between these rows (columns).

We can also extend the 0/1 domain of the decision variables in the matrix, and add a first row for a dummy card that is constrained as follows, say:

```
              ⟶ racks ⟶
             2 2 2 2  3 3 3  4 4 4

             · · · · · · · · · · ·
             · · · · · · · · · · ·
          ↓  · · · · · · · · · · ·
   cards     · · · · · · · · · · ·
          ↓  · · · · · · · · · · ·
             · · · · · · · · · · ·
```

Lexicographically ordering all the columns will now keep the columns pertaining to racks of the same type together and thus only break all the symmetries arising from indistinguishable rack types.

4.3   Value Symmetry

We can deal with symmetric values using the techniques we have developed above for dealing with symmetric variables. A variable x of an n dimensional matrix that takes a value from a domain of indistinguishable values $v_1, \ldots, v_m$ can be replaced by a vector $[x_1, \ldots, x_m]$ of 0/1 variables, with the semantics $x_i = 1 \leftrightarrow v_i = x$. A set variable x taking a set of values from a similar domain of indistinguishable values can also be replaced by a vector of 0/1 variables with the semantics $(x_i = 1 \leftrightarrow v_i \in x)$. Hence, we have introduced $n \times m$ 0/1 variables and constraints. In other words, the (set) variable is replaced by a characteristic function, whose variables take values that are not indistinguishable. This converts indistinguishable values into indistinguishable variables, which become a new dimension in the now $n + 1$ dimensional matrix.

Example 5. Consider a 2-d matrix model of the progressive party problem [19]. A variable x_{ij} in its matrix takes as value the host boat visited by guest i in period j. Now, host boats of the same capacity are indistinguishable. We can turn this partial value symmetry into a partial variable symmetry by channelling into a new 3-d 0/1 matrix that has no value symmetry. A variable y_{ijk} in this new matrix is 1 iff the host boat k is visited by guest i in period j. Channelling constraints of the form $y_{ijk} = 1 \leftrightarrow k = x_{ij}$ can thus link the two matrices. The new matrix model has partial symmetry along the third dimension of its 3-d matrix. We can therefore use lexicographic ordering constraints to break these symmetries. Note that we do not always need to channel between the two matrices and could thus replace the old matrix by the new one. However, it is quite often the case that some constraints are more easily expressed on the original matrix, and this is the case here.

The advantage of this approach is that we can use the multi-dimensional lexicographic ordering to deal simultaneously with symmetric variables and symmetric values. An alternative approach to breaking value symmetry is described in [11], but this method currently assumes that all values in a domain are symmetrical. We can also use the techniques outlined in the previous sub-section to deal with values that are only partially symmetric. Freuder addresses the case of interchangeable values [8], but with respect to individual variables as opposed to symmetries that hold globally between values. Again, we can support this situation by ordering sub-rows or sub-columns.

5   Breaking all the Symmetries

It is always possible to break all the symmetries. In [3], a method is presented for adding a lexicographic ordering constraint for each symmetry of the problem.

Example 6. The set of all compositions of the row and column symmetries of a 3×2 matrix

$$\begin{pmatrix} x_1 & x_2 & x_3 \\ x_4 & x_5 & x_6 \end{pmatrix}$$

can be broken by the following 11 constraints:

$[x_1, x_2, x_3, x_4, x_5, x_6] \leq_{lex} [x_2, x_1, x_3, x_5, x_4, x_6]$, *that is* $[x_1, x_4] \leq_{lex} [x_2, x_5]$

$[x_1, x_2, x_3, x_4, x_5, x_6] \leq_{lex} [x_1, x_3, x_2, x_4, x_6, x_5]$, *that is* $[x_2, x_5] \leq_{lex} [x_3, x_6]$

$[x_1, x_2, x_3, x_4, x_5, x_6] \leq_{lex} [x_4, x_5, x_6, x_1, x_2, x_3]$, *that is* $[x_1, x_2, x_3] \leq_{lex} [x_4, x_5, x_6]$

$[x_1, x_2, x_3, x_4, x_5, x_6] \leq_{lex} [x_6, x_4, x_5, x_3, x_1, x_2]$, *that is* $[x_1, x_2, x_3] \leq_{lex} [x_6, x_4, x_5]$

$[x_1, x_2, x_3, x_4, x_5, x_6] \leq_{lex} [x_5, x_6, x_4, x_2, x_3, x_1]$, *that is* $[x_1, x_2, x_3, x_4] \leq_{lex} [x_5, x_6, x_4, x_2]$

$[x_1, x_2, x_3, x_4, x_5, x_6] \leq_{lex} [x_4, x_6, x_5, x_1, x_3, x_2]$, *that is* $[x_1, x_2, x_3] \leq_{lex} [x_4, x_6, x_5]$

$[x_1, x_2, x_3, x_4, x_5, x_6] \leq_{lex} [x_5, x_4, x_6, x_2, x_1, x_3]$, *that is* $[x_1, x_2, x_3] \leq_{lex} [x_5, x_4, x_6]$

$[x_1, x_2, x_3, x_4, x_5, x_6] \leq_{lex} [x_6, x_5, x_4, x_3, x_2, x_1]$, *that is* $[x_1, x_2, x_3] \leq_{lex} [x_6, x_5, x_4]$

$[x_1, x_2, x_3, x_4, x_5, x_6] \leq_{lex} [x_3, x_2, x_1, x_6, x_5, x_4]$, *that is* $[x_1, x_4] \leq_{lex} [x_3, x_6]$

$[x_1, x_2, x_3, x_4, x_5, x_6] \leq_{lex} [x_2, x_3, x_1, x_5, x_6, x_4]$, *that is* $[x_1, x_2, x_4, x_5] \leq_{lex} [x_2, x_3, x_5, x_6]$

$[x_1, x_2, x_3, x_4, x_5, x_6] \leq_{lex} [x_3, x_1, x_2, x_6, x_4, x_5]$, *that is* $[x_1, x_2, x_4, x_5] \leq_{lex} [x_3, x_1, x_6, x_4]$

The first two constraints arise from the indistinguishability of the first two columns and the last two columns, respectively, whereas the third constraint arises from the indistinguishability of the two rows. The remaining constraints arise from the compositions of these row and column symmetries. These constraints were obtained by first determining the $3! \cdot 2! = 12$ permutations of the vector $[x_1, x_2, x_3, x_4, x_5, x_6]$ obtained by building the 2! concatenations of the row vectors for each of the 3! permutations inside the rows. We then constrained an arbitrary one of these 12 permutations, namely $[x_1, x_2, x_3, x_4, x_5, x_6]$, to be the lexicographically smallest one.

In general, an $m \times n$ matrix has $m! \cdot n! - 1$ symmetries except identity, generating thus a super-exponential number of lexicographic ordering constraints. Hence this approach is not always practical, so we now identify three special cases where all compositions of the row and column symmetries can be broken by a polynomial (and even linear) number of constraints.

First consider the case where all the values in the matrix are distinct. Such matrix models are common. For example, this happens in the single-round tournament scheduling problem, when the matrix entries are ordered pairs of teams.

Theorem 3. *If a matrix model with row and column symmetry in some 2-d matrix, as well as with a constraint requiring all the values in that matrix to be distinct, has a solution, then each symmetry class of solutions has a unique member with the largest value placed in the bottom-right corner as well as the last row and the last column ordered.*

Proof: Given a solution, the row occupied by the largest value contains distinct values that can be permuted by ordering the columns. By ordering this row, we break all possible column symmetries and fix the sequence of the columns. Similarly, the column occupied by the largest value contains distinct values that can be permuted by ordering the rows. By now ordering this column, we break all possible row symmetries, and fix the sequence of the rows, while placing the largest value in the bottom-right corner of the matrix. All the compositions of the row and column symmetries are thus broken, because we have constructed a unique symmetric solution. □

It is therefore the symmetries between identical values that make it difficult to break all the compositions of the row and column symmetries.

In fact, our proof shows that we break all the symmetries even if the other rows and columns contain repeated values. Ordering the row and column with the largest value will fix all the other values in the matrix in a unique way. So we do not need every value in the matrix to be distinct (although this is sufficient to make the row and column with the largest value contain no repeated values).

Next, even when matrices have repeated values, it is still possible in certain situations to break all symmetries by means of a polynomial number of symmetry-breaking constraints. In particular, this is the case for 2-d 0/1 matrices with a single 1 in each row. Such matrix models are quite common. For example, the 2-d matrix we used in the rack configuration problem has this form.

Theorem 4. *If a matrix model with row and column symmetry in some 2-d 0/1 matrix, as well as with a constraint requiring a single 1 in each row of that matrix, has a solution, then each symmetry class of solutions has a unique solution with the rows ordered lexicographically as well as the columns ordered lexicographically and by their sums.*

Proof: Given a solution, by Theorem 1, there is a symmetric solution with the rows and columns lexicographically ordered. In that solution, the top-right corner must contain a 1. Suppose that in the next row down, the 1 occurs to the right of where it does in this row. Then the next row is not lexicographically larger. Suppose that it occurs more than one column across to the left. Then the columns in between are not lexicographically larger. Hence, the 1 in the next row down must occur either directly below or one column to the left. The only freedom is in how many consecutive rows have 1s in the same column. This symmetry is broken by ordering the sums of the columns. All the compositions of the row and column symmetries are broken, because we have constructed a unique symmetric solution. □

Note that we can have the column sums in increasing or decreasing order, depending on which is preferable.

Finally, all the symmetries can be broken with a linear number of constraints when all the rows, seen as multisets, are distinct. We say that a vector v_1 is *multiset-lexicographically smaller than* another vector v_2 if $sort(v_1) \leq_{lex} sort(v_2)$, where $sort(v)$ denotes the ordered permutation of vector v. For instance, the vector $[0, 1, 2, 1, 1]$ is multiset-lexicographically smaller than the vector $[0, 3, 1, 1, 1]$ because $[0, 1, 1, 1, 2] \leq_{lex} [0, 1, 1, 1, 3]$.

Theorem 5. *If a matrix model with row and column symmetry in some 2-d matrix, as well as with a constraint requiring all the rows of that matrix to be distinct as multisets, has a solution, then each symmetry class of solutions has a unique solution with the rows multiset-lexicographically ordered and the columns lexicographically ordered.*

Proof: Given a solution, we can first multiset-lexicographically order the rows. Because the rows are distinct as multisets, this fixes the order of the rows. We can now order the columns lexicographically without changing the multiset of any row. All the compositions of the row and column symmetries are broken, because we have constructed a unique symmetric solution. □

6   Experimental Results

To test the ability of lexicographic ordering constraints to break the compositions of row and column symmetries, we ran some experiments on balanced incomplete block design (BIBD) generation. This is a standard combinatorial problem from design theory. It has applications in experimental design and cryptography (see prob028 at www.csplib.org for more details).

A BIBD is an arrangement of v distinct objects into b blocks, such that each block contains exactly k distinct objects, each object occurs in exactly r different blocks, and every two distinct objects occur together in exactly λ blocks. A BIBD instance is thus determined by its parameters $\langle v, b, r, k, \lambda \rangle$. One way of modelling a BIBD is in terms of its incidence matrix, which is a $b \times v$ 0/1 matrix with exactly r ones per row, k ones per column, and with a scalar product of λ between any pair of distinct rows [6]. This matrix model has row and column symmetry since we can permute any rows or columns freely without affecting any of the constraints. This kind of symmetry is often partially broken by setting the

Table 1. Experimental results on BIBD instances

Instance	distinct #sol	row & col lex #sol	time	set 1st row & col #sol	time	row lex #sol	time	col lex #sol	time
$\langle 7, 7, 3, 3, 1\rangle$	1	1	1.05	216	8	30	3	30	4
$\langle 6, 10, 5, 3, 2\rangle$	1	1	0.95	17,280	332	60,480	3,243	12	2
$\langle 7, 14, 6, 3, 2\rangle$	4	24	10.63	$\geq 90,448$	−	$\geq 68,040$	−	465	55
$\langle 9, 12, 4, 3, 1\rangle$	1	8	28.14	$\geq 5,340$	−	≥ 342	−	840	1,356
$\langle 8, 14, 7, 4, 3\rangle$	4	92	171.00	$\geq 5,648$	−	$\geq 2,588$	−	$\geq 5,496$	−
$\langle 6, 20, 10, 3, 4\rangle$	unknown	21	10.30	$\geq 538,272$	−	$\geq 429,657$	−	73	20

first row and the first column, as this is a cheap but effective method. However, this breaks less symmetry than lexicographically ordering both the rows and the columns, as shown next.

Table 1 shows our experimental results on some BIBD instances. We used the ECLiPSe toolkit as it has a lexicographic ordering constraint. The instances in this table are also used in [14, 15]. We only present a representative sample of our experiments. We enforced a lexicographic ordering between neighbouring pairs of rows and columns (row & col lex). We also include the results when we set the first row and the first column (set 1st row & col), as well as when we impose lexicographic ordering constraints only on the rows (row lex) or only on the columns (col lex). For each instance, we show the number of distinct solutions (distinct #sol), the number of symmetric solutions being always in excess of 2.5 million, as well as the total number of solutions found (#sol) and the run-times (time, in seconds, or a "−" whenever 1 clock hour was exceeded, in which case we report the number of solutions found at that moment) for each of the four symmetry-breaking techniques listed above.

With the row and column lexicographic ordering constraints, we labelled along one row and then down one column, and so on, as this is more efficient than labelling just along the rows or just down the columns, on these instances. However, there are some instances (not shown in the table) where labelling along the rows is much more efficient than labelling along the rows and columns. With the first row and column set, the best labelling strategy varies from instance to instance; we report the best results achieved among the three strategies. Indeed, the objective was to get, within reasonable amounts of time, numbers of solutions that can be compared, rather than to compare the times needed to do so. The times are only indicated to reveal that our symmetry-breaking techniques are cost-effective compared to an existing one. With row lexicographic ordering constraints, the best strategy is to label the columns, and with column lexicographic ordering constraints, the best strategy is to label the rows.

The table reveals that the column lexicographic ordering constraints are much more efficient than the row ones. This is true for many other instances (that are not shown in the table). We conjecture that the scalar product constraint so tightly constrains the rows that little work is left to be done by the row lexicographic ordering constraints. The column lexicographic ordering constraints act orthogonally and so are more constraining. The results also confirm that lexicographically ordering the rows and columns can break most of the compositions of the row and column symmetries.

In [15], a binary CSP model encoded in SAT that breaks symmetries in a different way was proposed to solve several BIBD instances using SATZ, WSAT, and CLS. All its instances could be solved fast enough with our 2-d 0/1 matrix model using row and column lexicographic ordering constraints. For example, our model solves the instance $\langle 8, 14, 7, 4, 3 \rangle$ in 171 seconds, while this instance was not solved in several hours with any algorithm or encoding in [15].

To test the efficacy of channelling to a 0/1 matrix in order to break value symmetry with lexicographic ordering constraints, we experimented with Schur's Lemma (prob 015 in CSPlib). The problem is to put n balls, labelled $\{1,..., n\}$, into 3 boxes so that for any triple of balls (x, y, z) with $x + y = z$, not all are in the same box. A natural model consists of a one-dimensional matrix of variables with domain size 3, each element of which corresponds to a particular box. The boxes, and therefore the values, are symmetrical. We tested this model with no symmetry breaking and with Gent's method [11]. A second model channels to a 0/1 matrix of balls × boxes. In this model, a row corresponds to the contents of a box. Hence, we can use lexicographic row ordering to break the symmetry.

Table 2. Experimental results on Schur's Lemma

n	No Symmetry Breaking				Gent's Method				Lexicographic			
	Fails	Choices	Time	Solns	Fails	Choices	Time	Solns	Fails	Choices	Time	Solns
15	7878	25451	0.6s	17574	1313	4241	0.6s	2929	1317	4245	0.2s	2929
16	10356	25067	0.6s	14712	1726	4177	0.6s	2452	1730	4181	0.2s	2452
17	11970	24029	0.6s	12060	1995	4004	0.7s	2010	1999	4008	0.2s	2010
18	11970	19025	0.6s	7056	1995	3170	0.7s	1176	1999	3174	0.2s	1176
19	12132	16391	0.6s	4260	2022	2731	0.7s	710	2026	2735	0.2s	710
20	11976	14117	0.5s	2142	1996	2352	0.8s	357	2000	2356	0.2s	357
21	10878	11783	0.5s	906	1813	1963	0.7s	151	1817	1967	0.2s	151
22	10206	10397	0.5s	192	1701	1732	0.8s	32	1705	1736	0.2s	32
23	9738	9755	0.5s	18	1623	1625	0.8	3	1627	1629	0.2s	3
24	9072	9071	0.5s	0	1512	1511	0.8	0	1516	1515	0.2s	0

Table 2 summarises the results. Both symmetry breaking methods result in a dramatic reduction in the number of solutions discovered and search tree size. Gent's method appears to propagate slightly before the lexicographic approach, hence the (negligible) difference in terms of fails and choices. Given three boxes, we require just two lexicographic ordering constraints between adjacent rows of the 0/1 matrix. Although Gent's method requires fewer extra variables than the lexicographic approach, each has a relatively large domain. This coupled with $O(n)$ extra constraints results in the gap in overall performance.

7 Related Work

There is currently much interest in symmetry in constraint satisfaction problems. The existing approaches can be broadly categorised into five types.

The first approach, deployed here, adds symmetry-breaking constraints to the model in an attempt to remove some symmetries *before* search starts [16, 3].

A second method breaks adds symmetry-breaking constraints *during* search to prune symmetric branches (e.g., [1], the global cut framework (GCF) [7], and symmetry-breaking during search (SBDS) [12]). A disadvantage of methods like SBDS is that, at each node in the search tree, a constraint for each symmetry is added, but that, for matrix models, there is a super-exponential number of symmetries that have to be treated. Recently, promising results on combining the dynamic SBDS with our static pre-search approach [5] have been reported for matrix models [20], especially for combined methods that break some of the symmetries using row sum ordering and column lexicographic ordering.

Third, in symmetry-breaking via dominance detection (SBDD) [4], the *search procedure* is modified by adding a dominance check that checks if the current assignment is symmetric to a previously encountered assignment. Such a dominance check is problem-specific.

A fourth approach is to break symmetry by means of a *heuristic variable-ordering* that directs the search towards subspaces with a high density of non-symmetric solutions (e.g., [14]).

Lastly, it is sometimes possible to *remodel* a problem to remove some symmetries, for example via the use of set variables. However, this can produce a more complex model [18].

All of these approaches would benefit from an efficient means of automatic symmetry detection. However, symmetry detection has been shown to be graph-isomorphism complete in the general case [2]. Therefore, it is often assumed that the symmetries are known by the user. Since matrices of decision variables are common in constraint programs [6], and since rows and columns in such matrices are often indistinguishable, making matrices first-class objects in the modelling language would give a heuristic symmetry-detection technique obvious clues as to where to look.

8 Conclusions

We have identified an important class of symmetries in constraint models: row and column symmetries. We have shown that we can lexicographically order both the rows and the columns to break some of these symmetries. Whilst lexicographically ordering the rows breaks all the row symmetries and lexicographically ordering the columns breaks all the column symmetries, lexicographically ordering both the rows and the columns fails to break all the compositions of these symmetries. Nevertheless, our experimental results show that this can be effective at dealing with these compositions of the row and column symmetries.

We have extended these results to cope with symmetries in any number of dimensions, with partial symmetries, and with symmetric values. Finally, we have identified a number of special cases where all compositions of the row and column symmetries can be broken by means of adding only a linear number of constraints.

Having established the utility of lexicographic ordering, there is a clear need for efficient methods for establishing generalised arc consistency on constraints that impose this ordering. A first step is to consider lexicographic ordering between a pair of vectors, which is our current focus [10]. We can then consider enforcing generalised arc consistency on sets of such constraints. Furthermore, in Example 6 the choice of which permutation is to be the lexicographically smallest is arbitrary, but the performance of the variable-and-value-ordering depends on this choice. Work on this topic is in progress.

In other future work, we intend to find ways of detecting the row and column symmetries automatically. Also, given several matrices with symmetry and with channelling constraints in-between them, it is not clear how lexicographic orderings on the matrices interact. Finally, we will investigate ways of detecting redundancies among the super-exponential number of lexicographic ordering constraints that are necessary for breaking all the symmetries. For instance, in Example 6, the last three constraints are logically redundant.

Acknowledgements

This work is partially supported by grant 221-99-369 of VR (the Swedish Research Council), by institutional grant IG2001-67 of STINT (the Swedish Foundation for International Cooperation in Research and Higher Education), and grant GR/N16129 of EPSRC (the UK Engineering and Physical Sciences Research Council). The last author was supported by an EPSRC advanced research fellowship. We thank our anonymous referees, Warwick Harvey and the members of the APES research group (www.dcs.st-and.ac.uk/~apes/), especially Barbara Smith, for their helpful discussions.

References

[1] R. Backofen and S. Will, 'Excluding symmetries in constraint-based search', *Proc. CP'99, 5th Int. Conf. on Principles and Practice of Constraint Programming*, ed., J. Jaffar, LNCS 1713, pp. 73–87. Springer-Verlag, (1999).

[2] J. Crawford, 'A theoretical analysis of reasoning by symmetry in first-order logic', *Proc. AAAI'92 workshop on tractable reasoning*, (1992).

[3] J. Crawford, G. Luks, M. Ginsberg, and A. Roy, 'Symmetry breaking predicates for search problems', *Proc. KR'96, 5th Int. Conf. on Knowledge Representation and Reasoning*, pp. 148–159, (1996).

[4] T. Fahle, S. Schamberger, and M. Sellmann, 'Symmetry breaking', *Proc. CP'01, 7th Int. Conf. on Principles and Practice of Constraint Programming*, ed., T. Walsh, LNCS 2239, pp. 93–107. Springer-Verlag, (2001).

[5] P. Flener, A. M. Frisch, B. Hnich, Z. Kiziltan, I. Miguel, J. Pearson, and T. Walsh, 'Symmetry in matrix models', *Proc. SymCon'01, CP'01 Workshop on Symmetry in Constraint Satisfaction Problems*, (2001). Also technical report APES-36-2001 from http://www.dcs.st-and.ac.uk/~apes/reports/apes-36-2001.ps.gz.

[6] P. Flener, A. M. Frisch, B. Hnich, Z. Kiziltan, I. Miguel, and T. Walsh, 'Matrix modelling', *Proc. Formul'01, CP'01 Workshop on Modelling and Problem Formulation*, (2001). Also technical report APES-36-2001 from http://www.dcs.st-and.ac.uk/~apes/reports/apes-36-2001.ps.gz.

[7] F. Focacci and M. Milano, 'Global cut framework for removing symmetries', *Proc. CP'01, 7th Int. Conf. on Principles and Practice of Constraint Programming*, ed., T. Walsh, LNCS 2239, pp. 77–92. Springer-Verlag, (2001).

[8] E. Freuder, 'Eliminating Interchangeable Values in Constraint Satisfaction Problems', *Proc. AAAI'91, 9th Nat. Conf. on AI*, pp. 227–233, (1991).

[9] E. Freuder, 'Modelling: The final frontier', *Proc. PACLP'99, 1st Int. Conf. on Practical Application of Constraint Technologies and Logic Programming*, (1999).

[10] A. M. Frisch, B. Hnich, Z. Kiziltan, I. Miguel, and T. Walsh, 'Global constraints for lexicographic orderings', *Proc. CP'02, 8th Int. Conf. on Principles and Practice of Constraint Programming* (to appear), (2002).

[11] I. P. Gent, 'A symmetry breaking constraint for indistinguishable values', *Proc. SymCon'01, CP'01 workshop on Symmetry in Constraints*, (2001).

[12] I. P. Gent and B. M. Smith, 'Symmetry breaking in constraint programming', *Proc. ECAI'00, 14th Euro. Conf. on AI*, ed., W. Horn, pp. 599–603, IOS, (2000).

[13] Z. Kiziltan and B. Hnich, 'Symmetry breaking in a rack configuration problem', *Proc. IJCAI'01 Workshop on Modelling and Solving Problems with Constraints*, (2001).

[14] P. Meseguer and C. Torras, 'Exploiting symmetries within constraint satisfaction search', *Artificial Intelligence*, **129**(1–2):133–163, (2001).

[15] S. D. Prestwich, 'Balanced incomplete block design as satisfiability', *Proc. 12th Irish Conf. on AI and Cognitive Science*, (2001).

[16] J.-F. Puget, 'On the satisfiability of symmetrical constrained satisfaction problems', *Proc. ISMIS'93*, eds., J. Komorowski and Z. W. Ras, LNAI 689, pp. 350–361. Springer-Verlag, (1993).

[17] B. M. Smith, 'Reducing symmetry in a combinatorial design problem', *Proc. CP-AI-OR'01, 3rd Int. Workshop on Integration of AI and OR Techniques in CP*, (2001). Also Research Report 2001.01, School of Computing, University of Leeds.

[18] B. M. Smith, 'Reducing symmetry in a combinatorial design problem', *Proc. IJCAI'01 workshop on Modelling and Solving Problems with Constraints*, pp. 105–112, (2001).

[19] B. M. Smith, S. C. Brailsford, P. M. Hubbard, and H. P. Williams, 'The progressive party problem: Integer linear programming and constraint programming compared', *Constraints*, **1**:119–138, (1996).

[20] B. M. Smith and I. P. Gent, 'Reducing symmetry in matrix models: SBDS vs. constraints', *Proc. SymCon'01, CP'01 workshop on Symmetry in Constraints*, (2001).

[21] P. Van Hentenryck, L. Michel, L. Perron, and J.-C. Régin, 'Constraint programming in OPL', *Proc. PPDP'99, Int. Conf. on Principles and Practice of Declarative Programming*, ed., G. Nadathur, LNCS 1703, pp. 97–116. Springer-Verlag, (1999).

[22] P. Van Hentenryck *'The OPL Optimization Programming Language'*, The MIT Press, (1999).

Solving the Kirkman's Schoolgirl Problem in a Few Seconds

Nicolas Barnier[1] and Pascal Brisset[2]

[1] Centre d'Études de la Navigation Aérienne
Toulouse, France
[2] École Nationale de l'Aviation Civile
Toulouse, France
{barnier,brisset}@recherche.enac.fr

Abstract. The Social Golfer Problem has been extensively used in recent years by the constraint community as an example of highly symmetric problem. It is an excellent problem for benchmarking symmetry breaking mechanisms such as SBDS or SBDD and for demonstrating the importance of the choice of the right model for one problem. We address in this paper a specific instance of the Golfer Problem well known as the Kirkman's Schoolgirl Problem and list a collection of techniques and tricks to find efficiently all its unique solutions. In particular, we propose SBDD+, an generic improvement over SBDD which allows a deep pruning when a symmetry is detected during the search. Our implementation of the presented techniques allows us to improve previous published results by an order of magnitude for CPU time as well as number of backtracks, and to compute the seven unique solutions of the Kirkman's problem in a few seconds.

Keywords: Symmetry Breaking, Social Golfer Problem, Resolvable Steiner Systems.

1 Introduction

Highly symmetric problems are always challenging for Constraint Programming and breaking, removing, discarding symmetries among solutions has been the subject of much interest among researchers of the CP community in recent years. We focus in this paper on one particular symmetric problem: the Social Golfer Problem[7], also known as resolvable Steiner system in the combinatorial area[12]. Except for small instances, this problem is open and Constraint Programming gives balanced results: formulation is straightforward but far from being sufficiently efficient to solve all instances.

We are interested in breaking as much symmetry as possible, as well as combining and improving previously proposed techniques to find all solutions of one specific instance of the problem. The first important choice concerns the model. We naturally choose a set model [9] which automatically removes one kind of symmetry. The next step is to statically remove symmetries by adding

P. Van Hentenryck (Ed.): CP 2002, LNCS 2470, pp. 477–491, 2002.

constraints. Additional redundant constraints may be added to detect failures as soon as possible. The crucial point is then to be able to find an isomorphism relating two solutions quickly; we propose a "lazy" approach which splits the detection into two phases, building and checking, that provides the required efficiency.

One of the key ideas of the paper is to exploit an isomorphism found between two solutions, or partial solutions, to prune as much as possible of the subsequent search tree. We show that this is possible if the structure of the search tree is intrinsically related to the symmetries; in this case an isomorphism which maps a solution to another one similarly maps also some ancestor nodes. Combined with SBDD [5], we call the technique SBDD+.

Our experiments show that results presented in previous papers[17] can be greatly improved both in number of failures and in CPU time. The problem of finding all solutions to the Kirkman's Problem, which might have been considered hard to solve one year ago using Constraint Programming (two hours of CPU mentioned in [5]) can be solved in few seconds using our approach.

The remainder of the paper is structured as follows: we first define the Social Golfer Problem and model it, giving numerous possible redundant constraints. In the next section, we present our algorithm used to check symmetry and explain extensively our deep pruning technique associated with symmetry finding. Section 4 displays results of our experiments, confirming the approach. We conclude by recalling that many challenges remain.

2   Model

The classical instance of the *Social Golfer Problem* is described in the following terms:

> 32 golfers want to play in 8 groups of 4 each week, in such way that any two golfers play in the same group at most once. How many weeks can they do this for?

The problem may be generalized to w weeks of g groups, each one containing s golfers. This instance will be denoted g-s-w in the sequel of the paper. We note $n = g \times s$ the total number of golfers. The most famous and historical instance is the 5-3-7 for which all 7 unique (non-symmetric) solutions were already computed by Kirkman in the early 1850's [11]. In the combinatorics area, solutions for $s = 3$ are known as *Kirkman triple systems* or *resolvable Steiner systems*. Such systems have been extensively investigated (see for example [2]).

In the context of constraint programming, different models have been proposed in [18] to the Golfer Problem. The integer set model[1] which automatically removes symmetries inside groups is the one we chose for our experiments. In this model, the variables are the groups themselves and constraints are expressed as operations on sets.

---

[1] http://www.icparc.ic.ac.uk/eclipse/examples

The variables $G_{i,j}$, with i index of weeks and j index of groups, are sets and their associated domain is a lattice of sets defined by its greatest lower bound (the necessary elements) and its lowest upper bound (the possible elements) [9]. The $G_{i,j}$'s are subsets of the set of golfers. Each of them contains exactly s elements. All the groups of a week are disjoint and every pair of groups from different weeks share at most one element. All these properties are expressed with the following constraints:

$$1 \le i \le w, \; 1 \le j \le g \;\; G_{i,j} \subset \{1, 2, ..., n\}$$
$$1 \le i \le w, \; 1 \le j \le g \;\; |G_{i,j}| = s \tag{1}$$
$$1 \le i \le w, \; 1 \le j < j' \le g \;\; G_{i,j} \cap G_{i',j} = \emptyset \tag{2}$$
$$1 \le i < i' \le w, \; 1 \le j, j' \le g \;\; |G_{i,j} \cap G_{i',j'}| \le 1 \tag{3}$$

The constraints (2) may be basically implemented as w `all_disjoint` global constraints instead of the $wg(g-1)/2$ binary disjoint constraints. Note that no global consistency is achieved for this global constraint. The number of constraints of type (3) grows quadratically with the number of groups. It may prevent to solve large instances with this model.

According to [18] experiments, the naive set model is not the best one. However, we choose it for several reasons. First it is the simplest one and it uses the highest abstraction level. Second, redundant constraints described in the following section are easy to express with this model. Third, this is the model used in [5, 17] and it allows us to compare our approach with this previous ones.

2.1   Redundant Constraints

Several constraints can be added to the original model. While they may help to solve the hardest instances, the induced overhead is sometimes too large for small instances like Kirkman's one.

The fact that a player plays only once per week is not explicit in the original model, but only entailed by the constraints (1) and (2). The corresponding constraint is written using reified membership constraints:

$$1 \le i \le w, 1 \le p \le n \;\; \sum_{1 \le j \le g} (p \in G_{i,j}) = 1 \tag{4}$$

Warwick Harvey (www.icparc.ic.ac.uk/~wh/golf) proposes to express the fact that the players of a group appear in exactly s groups in other weeks:

$$1 \le i \ne i' \le w, 1 \le j \le g \;\; \sum_{1 \le j' \le g} (G_{i,j} \cap G_{i',j'} \ne \emptyset) = s \tag{5}$$

Taking into account the size of the groups, the global constraint `atmost1` proposed by [16] may also be set on the list of all groups.

$$\texttt{atmost1}(\{G_{i,j}/1 \le i \le w, 1 \le j \le g\}, s) \tag{6}$$

where `atmost1`(S, c) states that sets of S must have cardinal c and must intersect pairwise in atmost one element. The propagation associated with this constraint basically ensures that the possible number of partners of a player p is large enough, i.e. greater or equal to $(c-1)N_p$ where N_p is the number of occurrences of p. In our case, N_p is statically known (equal to w) so the propagation rule of the constraint can be efficiently customized.

2.2   Breaking Symmetries Statically

Our first goal is to compute all the unique non-symmetric solutions to the problem. As described in previous papers[18, 5, 17], the Social Golfer Problem is highly symmetric:

- Players can be exchanged inside groups (ϕ_P);
- Groups can be exchanged inside weeks (ϕ_G);
- Weeks can be ordered arbitrarily (ϕ_W);
- Players can be renamed among $n!$ permutations (ϕ_X).

The symmetry inside groups is inherently removed by modelling groups as sets. The symmetry inside weeks may be handled by ordering the g groups. Because these groups are disjoint, a total order can be achieved by sorting the smallest element of the groups.

$$1 \leq i \leq w,\, 1 \leq j \leq g-1 \quad \min G_{i,j} < \min G_{i,j+1}$$

Note that this implies that the first player is in the first group for each week.

Following the same idea, weeks can be ordered with the first group as key, which can be easily done with the second smallest element:

$$1 \leq i \leq w-1 \quad \min(G_{i,1} \setminus \{1\}) < \min(G_{i+1,1} \setminus \{1\})$$

Symmetries among players are more difficult to handle and only dynamic checks will be able to remove them completely. Statically:

- First week is fixed;
- First group of second week is fixed with smallest possible players
- "Small" players are put in "small" groups: for every week, p^{th} player is in a smaller group than the pth group

$$1 \leq i \leq w,\, 1 \leq p \leq g \quad \bar{G}_{i,p} \leq p$$

where $\bar{G}_{i,p}$ is the number of the group of player p in week i, i.e. the $\bar{G}_{i,p}$ are dual variables defined by

$$1 \leq i \leq w,\, 1 \leq p \leq n \quad \bar{G}_{i,p} = j \text{ iff } p \in G_{i,j}$$

- Players together in a same group in the first week are placed in ordered groups in the second week

$$1 \leq j \leq g,\, p_1, p_2 \in G_{1,j},\, p_1 < p_2 \quad \bar{G}_{2,p_1} < \bar{G}_{2,p_2}$$

- Groups of the first week are ordered in the second week:

$$1 \leq j < j' \leq g \quad \bar{G}_{2,G_{1,j}} <_{lexico} \bar{G}_{2,G_{1,j'}}$$

where $\bar{G}_{i,\{x_1,x_2,...\}}$ is the tuple $(\bar{G}_{i,x_1}, \bar{G}_{i,x_2}, ...)$ and $<_{lexico}$ stands for the lexicographic order on integer tuples.

Unfortunately, the conjunction of all these constraints does not remove all the symmetries among players. For example, for the 5-2-2 instance, the two following solutions are found:

1	2	3	4	5	6	7	8	9	10
1	3	2	4	5	7	6	9	8	10

1	2	3	4	5	6	7	8	9	10
1	3	2	5	4	6	7	9	8	10

Both solutions satisfy all aforementioned breaking symmetry constraints but the second one is isomorphic to the first one through the functions (ϕ_G is the same for the two rounds):

$$\phi_X = \{1 \to 7, 2 \to 8, 3 \to 9, 4 \to 10, 5 \to 1, 6 \to 2, 7 \to 3, 8 \to 4, 9 \to 5, 10 \to 6\}$$
$$\phi_G = \{1 \to 4, 2 \to 5, 3 \to 1, 4 \to 2, 5 \to 3\}$$
$$\phi_W = \{1 \to 1, 2 \to 2\}$$

We notice that even if permutations within weeks and groups may be statically removed by constraints when considered alone, it is still necessary to take them into account when the permutation within players is handled.

Remaining symmetries must be dynamically discarded; we discuss an efficient way to do it in the next section.

2.3   Integer Model with a Cardinality Constraint

We give here another model which allows us to solve efficiently the problem. Its originality comes from the use of a global cardinality constraint [15]. To the best of our knowledge, it is the first time it is proposed.

Decision variables in this model are $\bar{G}_{i,p}$, the number of the group of player p in week i.

$$1 \leq p \leq n \quad \bar{G}_{i,p} \in [1..g]$$
$$1 \leq i \leq w \quad gcc(\{\bar{G}_{i,p}/1 \leq p \leq n\}, < (1, s), ..., (g, s) >)$$

where $gcc(S, < (v_1, c_1), ..., (v_k, c_k), ... >)$ constrains the number of occurrences of elements of S equal to v_k to be equal to c_k.

The "not with the same golfer more than once" is straighforward with reified constraints (whose number is increasing quadratically with the number of golfers):

$$1 \leq p_1 < p_2 \leq n \quad \sum_{1 \leq i \leq w} (\bar{G}_{i,p_1} = \bar{G}_{i,p_2}) \leq 1$$

This model allows for example a short program[2] to solve the classic 8-4-9 instance in half a second and 32 backtracks to find the fist solution. However, as explained earlier, it is not the one used for the experiments in this paper.

3   Handling Symmetries during Search

In this section we present our adaptation to the Social Golfer Problem of a generic symmetry breaking mechanism proposed in [5].

3.1   Generic Techniques for Breaking Symmetries

Symmetry breaking constraints fail to remove statically all symmetries among the players in the Social Golfer problem. Therefore, several solutions have been proposed to prune the search tree taking into account these symmetries dynamically.

Using SBDS [8], which needs to list explicitly the symmetries to remove, Barbara Smith in [18] was able to break most of the symmetries and obtain new results. Later, two generic and similar approaches were proposed in the same time [6, 5]. In the second one, the technique called SBDD (for *Symmetry Breaking via Dominance Detection*) was applied with success to the Social Golfer Problem and allows us to compute all the non-symmetric solutions of small instances.

In SBDD, states during the search (i.e. nodes of the search tree) are compared to previously explored ones modulo a symmetry mapping function. A (new) state P' is *dominated* by an (old) state P if P' is subsumed by $\phi(P)$ where ϕ is a symmetry mapping function. When searching only for non-symmetric solutions, a state which is dominated by an already explored ones is discarded. Then, it requires to store all explored nodes. However, it can be noticed that if P' is dominated by P then it is dominated by the father node of P. It means that when all the sons of a state have been explored, one can remove them from the store and keep only the father. Concretely, in case of depth first search, the store for SBDD can be handled as a stack where states are associated to their depth. When a new state must be added to the store, all the states on top of the stack which have a greater depth may be removed. We will see later that it is worthwhile to store states in a compiled form in order to ease future dominance checks against this state.

One issue of the technique is its efficiency because checking dominance may be very expensive: $w(s!)^g g!$ symmetries to check in the Social Golfer Problem. Some restrictions are necessary to get an effective procedure:

- storage of explored states may be limited;
- checking of dominance may be restricted to some depths.

We propose to specialize the SBDD technique for the Social Golfer Problem, first to be able to check for dominance quickly, second, to better exploit symmetries found.

---

[2] This solution for the Golfer Problem is an example provided in the constraint library we use.

3.2   Filtering Efficiently Symmetric Solutions

It is shown in experiments of [5] that it is not worth to check dominance for every node during search for golfer solutions. For the 4-4-4 instance, authors conclude that checks every 8-th depth give the best result. Results given in the next section show that lazy dominance checking is effective when solving small instances of the Golfer Problem.

General dominance check for the Golfer Problem as described in [5] requires to compute a matching in a bipartite-graph, for which the best algorithm is in $O(n^{5/2})$ [10]. However checking that there exists a symmetric mapping function which maps an old solution (a leaf in the search tree) to a new one is significantly easier.

Actually, it can be noticed that a solution to the Golfer Problem is fully specified by the week number of the pairs of players[3]. Precisely, a solution can be described by the following mapping:

$$(p_1, p_2) \rightarrow i \text{ such that } \bar{G}_{i,p_1} = \bar{G}_{i,p_2} \tag{7}$$

where (p_1, p_2) is a pair of golfers. Note however that the mapping is not total for instances where a player does not play with all others.

A check must be done for each possible symmetry. [5] remarks that the possible symmetries may be easily enumerated looking for a matching from the first week of the first solution (or partial solution) P to any week of the second solution P'. The key idea to compute symmetry checking efficiently is to compute it lazily: instead of choosing a complete matching and checking the other weeks afterward, it is worth checking them *while* the matching is built.

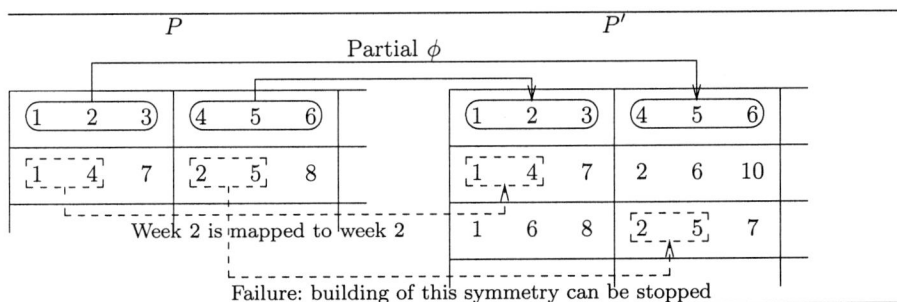

Fig. 1. Partial symmetry between solutions. Solid arrows show isomorphism building while dashed lines show isomorphism checking

Figure 1 illustrates this principle: Suppose a partial isomorphism is built by mapping an exchange of the first two groups of the first week $(1 \leftrightarrow 4, 2 \leftrightarrow 5, 3 \leftrightarrow 6)$. There is enough information in this partial matching to check all pairs

---

[3] Is is the integer model proposed by Barbara Smith in [18].

among other weeks with index of players less than 6. In this example, one can check that pairs $(1,4)$ and $(2,5)$ of the second week would be mapped in the same week of the second solution. Because it is not the case (pair $(1,4)$ is mapped to $(4,1)$ which appears in second week, $(2,5)$ is mapped to $(5,2)$ which does not appear at all), it is not necessary to try to complete this partial matching and we can "backtrack" to consider another mapping for the first two groups of the first week.

The check for pair mapping may be easily performed at a low cost by a precomputation phase:

- Derive the set of pairs of each week i of the first solution P, sorted according to the greatest element of the pair, denoted $C_i(P)$. Note that this precomputation may be done only once when the solution is found and stored.
- Build a table of the week numbers indexed by the pairs of the second solution P' (mapping of equation (7), noted $W_P(c)$).

The complete procedure is detailed in figure 2. The worst case complexity is the same as a naïve approach but experiments show that this checking algorithm, while only applied on leaves of the search tree, is efficient enough to compute all solutions of the Kirkman's problem in a reasonable time (c.f. section 4).

Procedure CheckSymmetry(P, P')
    Compute $C_i(P)$ for $i \in 2..w$ *Usually already computed with P*
    Compute $W_{P'}(c)$ for all pairs c of P'
    for $i' \in 1..w$ *Map first week of P to week i' of P'*
        $\phi_W[1] \leftarrow i$
        for $\phi_G \in \mathcal{P}_g$ *Permute groups within the week*
            for $j \in 1..g$
                for $\phi_P \in \mathcal{P}_s$ *Permute players within the group*
                    Set ϕ_X such that $P'_{i',\phi_G(j)} = \phi_X(\phi_P(P_{1,j}))$
                    try
                        for $i \in 2..w$ *For all other weeks of P*
                            for $c \in C_i(P)$ s.t. $c \leq j\,s$ *For all mapable pairs*
                                if c is the first encountered pair of $C_i(P)$
                                    $\phi_W[i] \leftarrow W_{P'}(\phi_X(c))$ *Store image week of week i*
                                else
                                    if $W_{P'}(\phi_X(c)) <> \phi_W[i]$ *Check if pairs of week i in P are*
                                        continue   *mapped to the same week in P'*
                        return ϕ_X *Symmetry found is returned*
    return NoSymmetry

Fig. 2. Search for symmetry ϕ_X mapping a solution P to P'

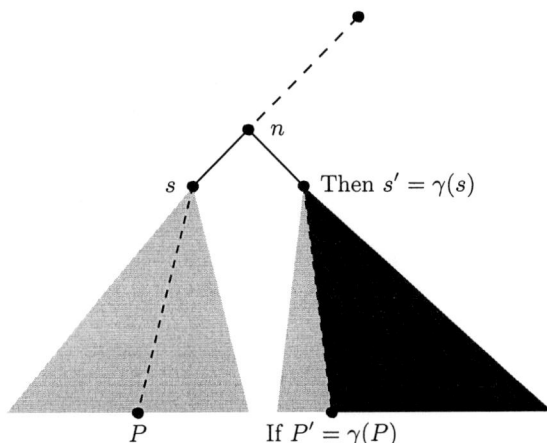

Fig. 3. Illustration of McKay's idea: The dark subtree can be pruned

3.3   Pruning Deeply

An efficient symmetry checking procedure applied on leaves allows us to compute all the unique solutions but does not improve the search itself: no subtrees are removed. However, following an idea of [13] used in an algorithm to compute graph isomorphisms[4], symmetry checking on leaves may be used to prune large subtrees.

The idea is illustrated in figure 3. Let P be a first solution (the tree is explored in depth first search, from left to right) and P' a second solution proved to be isomorphic to P ($P' = \gamma(P)$). We note $n = P \setminus P'$ the lowest node in the search tree which is common to paths from the root to P and P', and s (resp. s') its immediate successor (we suppose that we do only binary branching) leading to P (resp. its immediate successor leading to P'). Under some conditions (which we call "McKay condition" in the sequel), it can be shown that node s' is the image of s by the isomorphism γ (more precisely the canonical extension of γ over partial solutions). In this case, the remaining unexplored subtree of s' is itself the image of an already explored subtree starting from s. Then it can be pruned because it would lead only to solutions that are images by γ of already found solutions.

In order to be able to apply this idea to a search tree, the structure of the tree (i.e. the labelling procedure) must be *compatible* with the symmetric mapping function we consider. For the Golfer Problem, all symmetries but the one on players permutation may be removed simply with constraints. So the

---

[4] The **nauty** software based on McKay ideas is used by combinatorics people to find resolvable Steiner sytems[2].

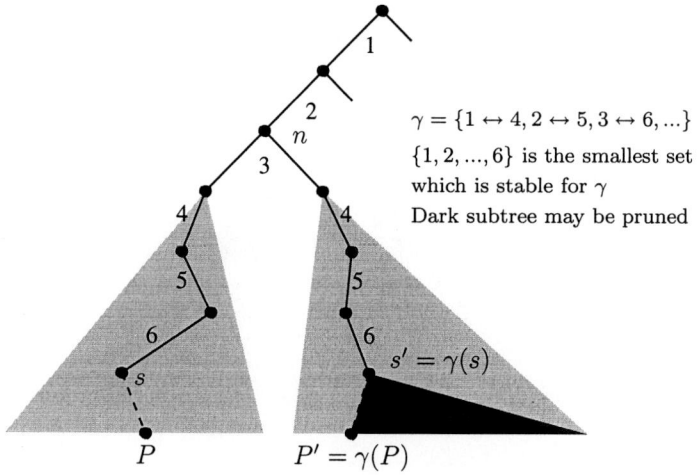

$\gamma = \{1 \leftrightarrow 4, 2 \leftrightarrow 5, 3 \leftrightarrow 6, ...\}$

$\{1, 2, ..., 6\}$ is the smallest set which is stable for γ

Dark subtree may be pruned

Fig. 4. Deep Pruning for the Golfer Problem

symmetries discovered at the leaves concern only ϕ_X. Following these remarks, the right choice is to label golfer by golfer to be able to apply ϕ_X extension on a node of the search tree. Note that a full choice for one golfer p amounts to labelling the w $\bar{G}_{i,p}$ variables.

Unfortunately, this labelling does not ensure the McKay condition if the set of golfers above node n (c.f. figure 4) is not stable through the found isomorphism γ: suppose node n concerns golfer 3 and γ is such that $\gamma(1) = 4$; we clearly cannot have $s' = \gamma(s)$ in this case. The problem in this example is that the choice on golfer 1 for P is mapped to the choice on golfer 4 in P', the latter being *under* the node n. Hence, node n cannot be pruned.

The necessary adaptation of McKay idea for our search tree is to consider two nodes s, s' which are descendants of n, leading respectively to P and P', such that the set of choices above s is mapped by γ to the set of choices above s'. In this case s' can be pruned. Of course, it is better to choose the highest such node in the search tree to prune as much as possible. Figure 4 illustrates the idea; the smallest set of golfers stable for γ which contains 3 (node n) is $\{1, 2, 3, 4, 5, 6\}$.

Results given in next section show that this deep pruning is highly effective.

3.4   SBDD+

We propose in this section an integration of the idea of deep pruning presented in the last section with the symmetry breaking mechanism SBDD. This mechanism computes isomorphism not only on solutions (leaves of the search tree) but on states of the search tree which can be described with the current domains of the

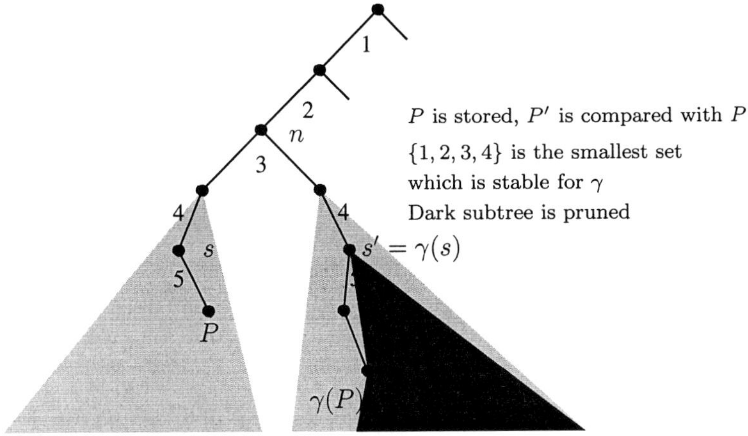

Fig. 5. SBDD+: Deep pruning integrated to SBDD

variables. In SBDD+, we will exploit such isomorphism and try to show that it is applicable on ancestors, leading then to a best pruning.

Based on SBDD, the approach is generic: no hypothesis are required on the nature of the variables (integer or set variables) or the nature of the isomorphism. However, we present here the application of the method only to the Golfer Problem and we did not try to implement it in a generic way.

Fine symmetry checking on leaves improved with deep pruning allows us to solve our problem in a reasonable time. However, better pruning may be obtained if the method is integrated with SBDD approach. It requires first to be able to apply a refinement of the algorithm given in figure 2 to incomplete solutions (nodes of the search tree), second to call the procedure only at the appropriate times.

Experiments show that most of the symmetries found between two complete solutions involve a mapping from the first week to itself[5]. Moreover, incomplete solutions always get a complete first week. This means that the previous symmetry checking algorithm may be easily modified to be applied to incomplete solution if only this kind of symmetry is considered; building of the symmetry can be kept. However, the checking phase of the algorithm remains the same: a symmetry is found if all pairs of P get an image in P'. But it does not mean that the symmetry is necessarily found when it exists, i.e. we possibly do not find all symmetries.

---

[5] For 7 non-symmetric solutions, 927 solutions are found and 603 of them have this property.

Dominance checking remains expensive and it must not be done too often. The check frequency must of course be related to the structure of the problem. A good compromise for the Golfer Problem is to

- Store nodes at every depth of the search tree;
- Check dominance for nodes only against stored nodes of smaller depth;
- Check dominance only for nodes at depth multiple of s.

The maximum size of the node store may be estimated: the depth of the search tree is the number of golfer gs; at each level, there may be g^w (for one golfer, g choices for each week) nodes to store. So the size of the store is bound by gsg^w (12 890 625 for Kirkman's Problem). This bound is a bad upper bound due to numerous symmetries removed by constraints (first week fixed, small golfers fixed, ...). For the Kirkman's Problem, with the detailed previous choices, only 15 nodes are effectively stored in the same time.

SBDD is compatible with the deep pruning mechanism: when a dominance is found, it is usually possible to prune more than the dominated node, just looking for the highest ancestor of the node for which the McKay condition is verified. We call the method SBDD+. It is illustrated in figure 5.

4   Results

We give in this section results of our experiments with the different techniques described in previous sections. The implementation has been done using FaCiLe [1], a functional constraint library written in Objective Caml (`caml.org`). This library provides usual finite domain variables over integers and sets, arithmetic constraints, set constraints[9], global constraints and an extensive mechanism to build search goals. It also includes basic mechanisms to maintain *invariant* expressions. This library, under LGPL license, and its documentation are available at `www.recherche.enac.fr/opti/facile`. CPU times are given for a Pentium 700 MHz running Linux 2.4.5.

The set model has been used with the labelling described earlier, golfer by golfer, choosing a group for each week, in increasing order. Additionally, some simple symmetries are dynamically removed during the search: when a golfer is placed in a group which does not contain any other golfers, this choice is fixed[6]. The refinement of the redundant `atmost1` (c.f. equation (6)) constraint is set in every experiment.

Labeling is slightly improved according to the following remark: the unique solutions of 5-3-7 are extensions of unique solutions of 5-3-2. Let S and S' be isomorphic solutions of 5-3-2 such that $S' = \gamma(S)$. If S is extended into a solution P of 5-3-7, then it is clear that $\gamma(P)$ is an isomorphic solution of 5-3-7 and also is an extension of 5-3-2. Then, our labeling first computes all unique solutions of 5-3-2 and extend them to 7 weeks. There are only 2 unique solutions for 5-3-2 and it takes 0.1 seconds to compute them.

---

[6] A similar idea is used in graph coloring algorithm: if a "new" unused color is tried for a node, there is no need to consider later other new colors for this node.

Table 1 shows the number of created choice points, the number of backtracks, the total number of found solutions, the number of dominance checks and the CPU time for different combinations of methods and tricks presented in this paper to compute all 7 unique solutions to the schoolgirl problem (then 11 found solutions means that isomorphism has been detected only at the leaf of search the tree for 4 of them). First column (Leaves) gives the results for the straightforward search with simple discarding of symmetric solutions at leaves. This time can be compared with the one annouced in [5] (two hours). Next column (McKay) corresponds to the symmetry detection at leaves with deep pruning. We see that the number of failures and the time are smaller by an order of magnitude from the previous ones. Column SBDD uses our incomplete dominance checking; SBDD+ adds deep pruning. It is the best time achieved with our experiments. It can be compared with the result of [17] (400s on a similar CPU).

However, the number of backtracks can still be reduced with redundant constraints: in column "+(4)", the redundant constraint (4) stating that a golfer plays only once per week allows us to further reduce the search but the overhead is too large (with our implementation) and CPU time is not improved. The last column adds redundant constraint (5) which expresses that players of a group are spread among s different groups in other weeks. The overhead is here dissuasive but the number of backtracks is 5 times smaller than what was done in [17].

Our combination of tricks to solve the Golfer Problem allowed us to solve open (at least for constraint programming) instances (6-4-6, 7-3-9, 8-3-7, 7-4-6, 6-5-7, ...). Some of these instances, at the time of writing this paper, are no longer open [14] and last updates of Warwick Harvey's web page include all these results (http://www.icparc.ic.ac.uk/~wh/golf/).

Table 1. Computing the 7 solutions of the Kirkman's Problem

	Leaves	McKay	SBDD	SBDD+	+(4)	+(5)
Choice points	20062206	1845543	107567	29954	18705	18470
Fails	19491448	1803492	104134	28777	16370	16169
Solutions	20640	934	11	11	11	11
Dominance checks			5373	456	456	443
CPU(s)	5925	484	24	7.8	9.4	36

5   Conclusion

We have presented in this paper a combination of techniques which allows us to find efficiently all solutions to the Golfer Problem. The main contribution of the paper is an improvement of the SBDD principle that we call SBDD+. The key idea of the improvement is, while breaking symmetries, to exploit the symmetry function to be able to prune higher in the search tree. Extensive experiments show that this new mechanism can reduce by an order of magnitude the CPU time as well as the number of backtracks on the considered problem.

The deep pruning technique has been applied only to the Golfer Problem but is general. The only restriction is to have a relative compatibility between the structure of the search tree and the considered symmetry mappings in order to be able to prove that a symmetry found between two nodes is also true for ancestors of these two nodes. We believe that the notion of stability through the isomorphism of ancestor nodes, a necessary and sufficient condition for our problem, should be a general property. Further work is needed in this direction.

For the Golfer Problem itself, some instances remain open to constraint programming approaches (even if they are well known by combinatorics, for example 7-3-10 and 7-4-9 are extensively studied). Our model may be improved using the incomplete propagation techniques proposed by [17] in order to attack these instances. Note that SBDD+ must be refined and tuned for larger instances to avoid an explosion of node store and an extreme time overhead due to node dominance checking.

In spite of many efforts from the constraint community, the 8-4-10 instance is still open. This challenge is fascinating and it can be considered with the highest priority to show that constraint technology is really suited for this kind of combinatorial problem.

References

[1] Nicolas Barnier and Pascal Brisset. Facile: a functional constraint library. In *Proceeding of CICLOPS2001*, Paphos, 2001.

[2] M. B. Cohen, C. J. Colbourn, L. A. Ives, and A. C. H. Ling. Kirkman triple systems of order 21 with nontrivial automorphism group. *Mathematics of Computation*, 2001.

[3] *CP'01: 7th International Conference on Principle and Practice of Constraint Programming*, Paphos, Cyprus, 2001.

[4] *CPAIOR'02: Fourth International Workshop on Integration of AI and OR Techniques in Constraint Programming for Combinatorial Optimisation Problems*, Le Croisic, France, 2002.

[5] Torsten Fahle, Stefan Schamberger, and Meinolf Sellmann. Symmetry breaking. In CP'01 [3], pages 93–107.

[6] Filippo Focacci and Michaela Milano. Global cut framework for removing symmetries. In CP'01 [3], pages 77–92.

[7] I. Gent, T. Walsh, and B. Selman. CSPlib: a problem library for constraints. www-users.cs.york.ac.uk/~tw/csplib.

[8] I. P. Gent and Barbara Smith. Symmetry breaking during search in contraint programming. In W. Horn, editor, *EACI'2000*, pages 599–603, 2000.

[9] Carmen Gervet. Interval propagation to reason about sets: Definition and implementation of a practical language. *Constraints*, 1(3):191–244, 1997. www.icparc.ic.ac.uk/~cg6.

[10] J. Hopcroft and R. Karp. An $n^{5/2}$ algorithm for maximum matching in bipartite graphs. *SIAM Journal of Computing*, 2(4):225–231, 1973.

[11] T. P. Kirkman. Note on an unanswered prize question. *Cambridge and Dublin Mathematics Journal*, 5:255–262, 1850.

[12] JR Marshall Hall. *Combinatorial Theory*. Wiley Classics Library, second edition edition, 1983.

[13] Brendan D. McKay. Practical graph isomorphism. *Congressus Numerantium*, 30:45–87, 1981.

[14] Steven Prestwich. Randomised backtracking for linear pseudo-boolean constraint problems. In CPAIOR'02 [4], pages 7–19.

[15] Jean-Charles Régin. Generalized arc consistency for global cardinality constraint. In *Proceedings of the Thirteenth National Conference on Artificial Intelligence*, 1996.

[16] Andre Sadler and Carmen Gervet. Global reasoning on sets. In *Formul'01, Workshop Modelling and Problem Formulation*, 2001.

[17] Meinolf Sellmann and Warwick Harvey. Heuristic constraint propagation. In CPAIOR'02 [4], pages 191–204.

[18] Barbara Smith. Reducing symmetry in a combinatorial design problem. In *CPAIOR'01*, pages 351–359, April 2001. www.icparc.ic.ac.uk/cpAIOR01.

Inferring Constraint Types in Constraint Programming

David Lesaint

Intelligent Systems Lab, BTexact Technologies, BT France
11, place des Vosges, 92061 Courbevoie, France
david.lesaint@bte.bt.com

Abstract. Capturing constraint structure is critical in Constraint Programming to support the configuration and adaptation of domain filtering algorithms. To this end, we propose a software model coupling a relational constraint language, a constraint type inference system, and an algorithm configuration system. The relational language allows for expressing constraints from primitive constraints; the type system infers the type of constraint expressions out of primitive constraint types; and the configuration system synthesises algorithms out of primitive routines using constraint types. In this paper, we focus on the issue of constraint type inferencing, and present a method to implement sound and extendible inference systems.

1   Introduction

Exploiting meta-knowledge on constraints has been a prolific research topic in Constraint Programming (CP), with results ranging from the design of optimal filtering algorithms to the identification of tractable classes of constraints. Domain filtering algorithms, which are the backbone of CP systems, have been repeatedly specialised to handle various types of constraints and domains more efficiently. The most prominent example is arc-consistency computation for which many constraint-specific algorithms have been designed (e.g., [1,2,3,10]).

Yet, CP languages rarely provide constructs and mechanisms to capture and exploit meta-knowledge on constraints be that for configuring filtering algorithms, or conducting other meta-reasoning activities (e.g., asserting satisfiability, restoring local consistency quicker upon constraint retraction, building explanations). The mapping between constraints and filtering algorithms is typically hard-coded [6,7]. Designers program algorithms for built-in constraints that best exploit their properties (e.g., AC-5 for functional constraints). Expert users can do the same for their constraints, while non-expert users have to rely on generic algorithms (e.g., AC-6), which results in poorer performances.

Clearly, we would like a CP system to automatically configure the best possible algorithms for user-defined constraints according to their structure. Algorithms for built-in and user-defined constraints should also be re-configured during propagation (that is, adapted) to take advantage of inferred constraints. The first step towards achieving this objective is to decouple algorithms/routines from constraints and

P. Van Hentenryck (Ed.): CP 2002, LNCS 2470, pp. 492-507, 2002.
© Springer-Verlag Berlin Heidelberg 2002

organise them as software components that can be reused, customised, and composed for different constraints. The second step is to define the mapping between individual constraints and composite algorithms that the configurator will compute.

This is where constraint structure can be instrumental. Since algorithmic routines are engineered for specific constraint types (types are pre-conditions to the applicability of algorithms), a logical approach is to type constraint expressions and use types to drive algorithm configuration. To this end, we propose a software model coupling a relational constraint language, a constraint type inference system, and an algorithm configuration system. The relational language allows for expressing constraints from primitive constraints; the type system infers the type of constraint expressions out of primitive constraint types; and the configuration system synthesises algorithms out of primitive routines from constraint types (see Fig. 1).

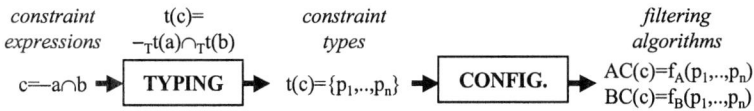

constraint	t(c)=	*constraint*			*filtering*
expressions	$-_T t(a) \cap_T t(b)$	*types*			*algorithms*

$c=a \cap b$ ➡ **TYPING** ➡ $t(c)=\{p_1,..,p_n\}$ ➡ **CONFIG.** ➡ $AC(c)=f_A(p_1,..,p_n)$
$BC(c)=f_B(p_1,..,p_n)$

Fig. 1. Typing constraints for configuring filtering algorithms. *AC(c)* is the arc-consistency algorithm synthesised for the constraint expression c using the routines associated to the primitive types $p_1,...,p_n$ inferred for c

In this paper, we restrict our attention to the issue of constraint type inferencing over finite domains; the design and configuration of filtering algorithms is not discussed here. The main requirements on constraint type inference systems are *soundness* (i.e., any type inference must be logically correct) and *completeness* (i.e., maximum type information should be inferred for any term of the language). In addition, the implementation and extension of inference systems with new constraint types should be as easy and safe as possible.

The paper is organised as follows. We first introduce the relational constraint language and define *constraint properties* as sets of constraints (section 2). We then model the inferencing of properties as morphisms between constraint term algebras and constraint property algebras (section 3). We formalise the notion of *consistency* and *maximum-consistency* between property and term algebras, and show that consistency is necessary and sufficient to assert soundness, while maximum-consistency is necessary but insufficient for completeness. Incompleteness follows from the fact that maximum-consistent property algebras may violate fundamental identities of constraint algebras (e.g., idempotency).

However, implementing property algebras is unrealizable as we require them to be closed by set intersection. To resolve this issue, we represent constraint properties as sets of primitive properties (*constraint types*), and generalise the above results for constraint type inference systems (section 4). Although the maximum-consistent type algebra induces the best possible inference system, implementing its operations remains prohibitive. To this end, we consider recursive type algebras (*decomposable algebras*) that sacrifice maximality for implementability, and we present a concrete example (section 5). Finally, we discuss ways of supporting adaptation through type inferencing (section 6) before concluding (section 7).

2   Constraint Expressions and Constraint Properties

We present the constraint language in the context of COL, a generic object-oriented CP library providing local consistency computation services over finite domains.[1] COL supports *concrete* and *abstract computation domains*. Concrete domains are built-in types of the programming language (e.g., int), while abstract domains are abstract structures (e.g., set, total ordering) to instantiate with compliant data types. Each domain comes with a constraint language where constraints are declared as relational expressions of primitive constraints.

The primitive constraints embody the distinctive relations and operations of the domain. For instance, the language for total orderings $<$ features inequality ($x{<}y$) and succession ($x{=}succ_<(y)$) among other constraints. The user can add primitive constraints by reifying test predicates. Primitive constraints are used as is to declare primitive constraint expressions, or composed to form more complex expressions.

The supported operations are complementation ($-$), intersection ($\cap$), and union ($\cup$) on constraints of identical scope, conversion ($\lrcorner$) for binary constraints, and permutation ($\lrcorner_\sigma$) for n-ary constraints. Aligning the scopes of sub-expressions by conversion or permutation is necessary for the system to correctly compute and type the relations of the resulting constraint expressions. Thus, the expression $<_{(x,y)}\cup<_{(y,x)}$ where $<_{(x,y)}$ is the constraint associating the relation $<$ to the scope (x,y) is incorrect, a correct expression being $<_{(x,y)}\cup\lrcorner(<_{(y,x)})$.

Overall, users can declare constraints in two or three different ways. For instance, one can specify the equality constraint x=y over a total ordering D by (1) instantiating the class for the equality constraint over total orderings with the type D and constructing an object with the scope (x,y), (2) reifying the equality predicate over D into a constraint object over (x,y), or (3) declaring the expression $-(<_{(x,y)}\cup\lrcorner(<_{(y,x)}))$ which is the constraint of scope (x,y) and relation $-(<\cup\lrcorner(<))$ over D^2.

The system will assign optimal filtering routines (AC-5-like) to the first expression. It will assign generic routines that do not exploit the semantics of equality (AC-6-like) to the second, and by default, to the third. What we want is to infer a type for this composite expression using built-in relation properties, so as to synthesise an algorithm out of the routines associated to these properties (e.g., an arc-consistency algorithm mixing routines for reflexive and convex relations).

Constraint relations can indeed be characterised by their mathematical properties over the underlying domain, e.g., reflexivity over sets, min-max-closedness [4] over partial orderings, convexity [9] over total orderings, etc. Given a domain D and an arity n, we call *property* any set of n-ary relations over D. A constraint c *verifies* a property p iff its relation belongs to p. Alternatively, we say that a property p is *valid for* a constraint c, and we denote c:p. A property p is *stronger than* a property q iff $p{\subseteq}q$. Alternatively, we say that p *subsumes* q.

Fig. 2 presents a set of properties for binary relations over a total ordering (D,$<$). *convex* (denoted $\diamond_P$) is the set of row- and column-convex relations defined in [9]. *monotonic* ($\leq_P$) and *functional* ($=_P$) are the sets of monotonic and functional relations defined in [10]. *universal* (1_P) is the singleton property $\{D^2\}$. *concave* ($\asymp_P$) is the

---

[1] COL is implemented in C++ and Java, and is part of BT's optimisation toolkit iOpt [11].

"complement" of *convex*, that is, the set of relations whose complements are convex. *anti-functional* ($\neq_P$) and *empty* (0_P) are the complements of *functional* and *universal*, respectively. *co-monotonic* ($\geq_P$) is both the complement and "converse" of *monotonic*. Finally, *convex-concave* ($<<_P$) is the set of convex and concave relations.

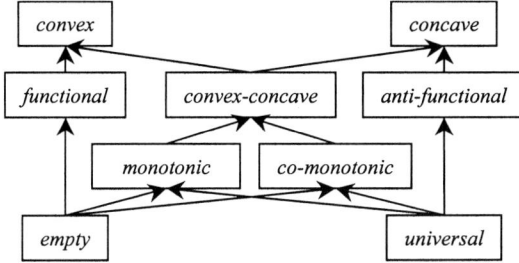

Fig. 2. A set of binary relation properties over a total order. $\subset$ is the transitive closure of $\rightarrow$

3   Inferring Constraint Properties

Our approach relies on the provision of an algebra of properties $<S_P, \neg_P, \dashv_P, \cap_P, \cup_P>$. Thus, we can associate to every constraint expression a property expression that we evaluate over S_P to produce the *inferred property*. For instance, the constraint expression $-(<_{(x,y)} \cup \dashv(<_{(y,x)}))$ admits the relation expression $-(< \cup \dashv(<))$ from which we derive the property expression $-_P(q \cup_P \dashv_P(q))$, where q is the built-in property of the primitive relation $<$ (its typing). The property obtained after evaluation solely depends on the definition of the property algebra and the typing of primitive relations.

These definitions and typings are incumbent on designers and users. Designers must implement a property algebra for each computation domain and each arity. In fact, three algebras suffice: one for the unary case, one for the binary case, and a generic algebra for the n-ary case with n>2. These algebras must also support the addition of properties. Ideally, new properties should be integrated without having to revise the definition of operations on existing properties.

To illustrate property inferencing, consider the program P in Fig. 3. Assume the primitive expressions c_1, c_2, c_3, c_4 inherit their types from their relations (e.g., *anti-functional* for c_1). The best possible typings for the composite expressions are *functional* for c_5, *empty* for c_6, *concave* for c_7, and *anti-functional* for c_8. This is achievable for c_5 if the property operations enforce that complements of anti-functional (resp., monotonic) relations are functional (resp., co-monotonic), and intersections of functional and co-monotonic relations are functional.

On the other hand, inferring that c_6 is the empty constraint involves reasoning with individual relations by recognising that the intersection of the equality and strictly-greater-than relations is empty. Since property algebras work at the property level, *functional* is the maximum type we can expect for c_6. We shall present a model to compute such typings in a systematic way. Before, we formalise and study inference systems, starting with binary constraints.

$c_1 = (\neq_{(x,y)})$; $c_2 = (<_{(x,y)})$; $c_3 = (\text{grtSuc})_{(x,y)}$; $c_4 = (<_{(y,x)})$; // primitive expressions, c_3 is

$\qquad\qquad\qquad\qquad\qquad\qquad\qquad\qquad\qquad\qquad\qquad\qquad (x > \text{succ}_<(y))$

$c_5 = -c_1 \cap -c_2$;   // c_5 is $(x=y) \wedge (x \geq y)$ and is equivalent to $(x=y)$

$c_6 = -c_1 \cap c_2$;   // c_6 is $(x=y) \wedge (x<y)$ and is equivalent to the empty constraint

$c_7 = c_2 \cup c_3$;   // c_7 is $(x<y) \vee (x > \text{succ}_<(y))$

$c_8 = c_2 \cup \lrcorner c_4$;   // c_8 is $(x<y) \vee (x>y)$ and is equivalent to $(x \neq y)$

Fig. 3. A constraint program P. The built-in relations $\neq$ and $<$, and the user-defined relation grtSuc are assumed to be typed *anti-functional, monotonic,* and *co-monotonic,* respectively

A signature is a set of sorts S and a set Σ of function symbols, each of fixed arity over S. We restrict our attention to mono-sorted signatures, and directly denote a signature by its set of function (operation) symbols Σ. A Σ-algebra is a set A provided with a mapping $f_A : A^n \to A$ for each operation symbol f in Σ of arity n. A Σ-morphism $e : A \to B$ between two Σ-algebras is a mapping preserving each operation in Σ, that is, for all $f \in \Sigma$, for all $a_1, \ldots, a_n \in A$, $e(f_A(a_1, \ldots, a_n)) = f_B(e(a_1), \ldots, e(a_n))$. $H_\Sigma(A,B)$ is the set of Σ-morphisms from a Σ-algebra A to a Σ-algebra B.

We consider the signature of binary relations over a finite computation domain D where $\Sigma = \{-, \lrcorner, \cap, \cup\}$. Any set Δ of constant operation symbols representing primitive binary relations induces a binary relation language over D. This language is the term algebra $T_{\Delta \cup \Sigma}$ for the signature $\Delta \cup \Sigma$. Developers encode the interpretation of the set T_Δ of primitive expressions ($T_\Delta \subseteq T_{\Delta \cup \Sigma}$) over the set S_C of binary relations over D ($S_C = \wp(D^2)$). This mapping extends into a unique $\Delta \cup \Sigma$-morphism $e_C \in H_{\Delta \cup \Sigma}(T_{\Delta \cup \Sigma}, S_C)$, which is the interpretation of the whole language $T_{\Delta \cup \Sigma}$.

Given a Σ-algebra $<S_P, -_P, \lrcorner_P, \cap_P, \cup_P>$ of binary relation properties over D, we model the typing of any binary relation language $T_{\Delta \cup \Sigma}$ as a Σ-morphism between $T_{\Delta \cup \Sigma}$ and S_P. Developers type the primitive expressions of T_Δ (built-in and user-defined relations). This mapping extends into a unique Σ-morphism $e_P \in H_{\Delta \cup \Sigma}(T_{\Delta \cup \Sigma}, S_P)$, which defines the typing for the whole language. Each constraint expression then gets the type of its relation expression, e.g., the property mapped to $-c_1 \cap c_2$ in the program P is $\neg_P(e_P(\neq)) \cap_P e_P(<)$ with $e_P(\neq) = \neq_P$ and $e_P(<) = \leq_P$. In an abuse of terminology, we will just refer to $T_{\Delta \cup \Sigma}$ as a *constraint language* and to *relations* as *constraints.*

Typing is implemented with a property inference system I_P that applies the rules of Σ-morphisms between $T_{\Delta \cup \Sigma}$ and S_P:

$$\frac{\vdash c{:}q}{\vdash -c{:}-_P(q)} \qquad \frac{\vdash c{:}q}{\vdash \lrcorner c{:}\lrcorner_P(q)} \qquad \frac{\vdash c1{:}q1,\ c2{:}q2}{\vdash c1 \cap c2{:}q1 \cap_P q2} \qquad \frac{\vdash c1{:}q1,\ c2{:}q2}{\vdash c1 \cup c2{:}q1 \cup_P q2}$$

The system is *sound* if it computes a valid property in S_P for any expression in any binary constraint language whose primitive expressions are assigned valid properties. It is *complete* if it computes the strongest (valid) property in S_P for any expression in any language whose primitive expressions are assigned their strongest properties.

A prerequisite to soundness is that any constraint in S_C admits a valid property in S_P. This requirement is met if S_P includes the universal property $T = S_C$. A prerequisite to completeness is that the set of valid properties for any constraint in S_C admits a $\subseteq$-minimum element. This requirement is met if S_P is closed by set intersection. We will assume that S_P satisfies these two conditions (the set of Fig. 2 does not since T and combinations such as *functional*$\cap$*monotonic* are missing).

Soundness and completeness formulate as follows:

Definition 1: I_P is sound iff for all $T_{\Delta\cup\Sigma}$, $e_C\in H_{\Delta\cup\Sigma}(T_{\Delta\cup\Sigma},S_C)$, $e_P\in H_\Sigma(T_{\Delta\cup\Sigma},S_P)$, $(\forall\varphi\in T_\Delta, e_C(\varphi):e_P(\varphi))\Rightarrow(\forall\varphi\in T_{\Delta\cup\Sigma}, e_C(\varphi):e_P(\varphi))$. I_P, sound, is complete iff for all $T_{\Delta\cup\Sigma}$, $e_C\in H_{\Delta\cup\Sigma}(T_{\Delta\cup\Sigma},S_C)$, the mapping $e_{Pm}:T_{\Delta\cup\Sigma}\rightarrow S_P$ defined by $e_{Pm}(\varphi)=\cap\{p\in S_P: e_C(\varphi):p\}$ belongs to $H_\Sigma(T_{\Delta\cup\Sigma},S_P)$.

Completeness requires that equivalent constraint expressions be typed identically. Therefore, property algebras should be designed to validate all identities of constraint (relation) algebras. For instance, the algebra $S_P=\{T\}\cup\{\{c\}: c\in S_C\}$ defined over $S_P\backslash\{T\}$ by $\lrcorner_P(\{c\})=\{\lrcorner c\}$, $\neg_P(\{c\})=\{\neg c\}$, $\cap_P(\{c_1\},\{c_2\})=\{c_1\cap c_2\}$ and $\cup_P(\{c_1\},\{c_2\})=\{c_1\cup c_2\}$ induces a complete inference system. However, it has no practical interest since it enforces a one-to-one mapping between constraints and properties. What we seek is easy-to-implement property algebras that truly abstract constraints while ensuring structural consistency with constraint algebras. Binary constraint algebras being boolean algebras augmented with conversion [5], we will restrict our attention to the following identities:

1. $-$, $\lrcorner$, $\cap$ and $\cup$ are isotone   [$q\subseteq r\Rightarrow\neg q\subseteq\neg r$, $q\subseteq s\wedge r\subseteq t\Rightarrow q\cap r\subseteq s\cap t$].
2. -2, $\lrcorner 2$, $\cap$ and $\cup$ are extensive   [$\neg\neg q\supseteq q$, $\lrcorner\lrcorner q\supseteq q$, $q\cap q\supseteq q$, and $q\cup q\supseteq q$].
3. $\cap$ and $\cup$ are commutative   [$q\cap r=r\cap q$, $q\cup r=r\cup q$].
4. $-$ and $\lrcorner$ commute   [$\lrcorner(\neg q)=\neg(\lrcorner q)$].
5. $\cap$ and $\cup$ are dual for $-$ [$\neg q\cap\neg r=\neg(q\cup r)$, $\neg q\cup\neg r=\neg(q\cap r)$].
6. $\lrcorner$ distributes over $\cap$ and $\cup$ [$\lrcorner(q\cap r)=\lrcorner q\cap\lrcorner r$, $\lrcorner(q\cup r)=\lrcorner q\cup\lrcorner r$].
7. $-$ and $\lrcorner$ are involutive   [$\neg\neg q=q=\lrcorner\lrcorner q$].
8. $\cap$ and $\cup$ are idempotent   [$q\cap q=q=q\cup q$].
9. $\cap$ and $\cup$ are associative   [$(q\cap r)\cap s=q\cap(r\cap s)$, $(q\cup r)\cup s=q\cup(r\cup s)$].
10. $\cap$ and $\cup$ are semi-absorbant   [$q\cap(q\cup r)\supseteq q$ and $q\cup(q\cap r)\supseteq q$].
11. $\cap$ and $\cup$ are absorbant   [$q\cap(q\cup r)=q=q\cup(q\cap r)$].
12. $\cap$ and $\cup$ are distributive   [$q\cap(r\cup s)=(q\cap r)\cup(q\cap s)$, $q\cup(r\cap s)=(q\cup r)\cap(q\cup s)$].

We formalise the notion of consistency using a map Π that associates to every n-ary operation $f\in\Sigma$ the function $\Pi(f):S_P{}^n\rightarrow\wp(S_P)$ defined by $\Pi(f)(p_1,...,p_n)=\{p\in S_P: \forall c_1,...,c_n\in S_C, c_1:p_1\wedge...\wedge c_n:p_n\Rightarrow f(c_1,...,c_n):p\}$. Using $\Pi(f)$ to define the property operation f_P guarantees that I_P's inference rule for f is sound.

Definition 2: A n-ary property operation ϕ defined over S_P is consistent with a n-ary constraint operation f defined over S_C iff $\phi(p_1,...,p_n)\in\Pi(f)(p_1,...,p_n)$ for all $p_1,...,p_n\in S_P$.

$<S_P,\neg_P,\lrcorner_P,\cap_P,\cup_P>$ is said to be $<S_C,-,\lrcorner,\cap,\cup>$-consistent if $\neg_P$, $\lrcorner_P$, $\cap_P$ and $\cup_P$ are consistent with $-$, $\lrcorner$, $\cap$ and $\cup$, respectively. Consistency is necessary and sufficient to assert soundness:

Theorem 1: I_P is sound iff $<S_P,\neg_P,\lrcorner_P,\cap_P,\cup_P>$ is $<S_C,-,\lrcorner,\cap,\cup>$-consistent.

Note that the trivial algebra evaluating any property expression to the universal property (that is, $\neg_P=\lrcorner_P=S_P\rightarrow\{T\}$ and $\cap_P=\cup_P=S_P\times S_P\rightarrow\{T\}$) induces a sound inference system. We extend set inclusion over properties to property operations as follows:

$g \leq h$ iff $g(p_1,...,p_n) \supseteq h(p_1,...,p_n)$ for all $p_1,...,p_n \in S_P$. The set of property operations that are consistent with a constraint operation admits a $\leq$-maximum element:

Lemma 1: Let f be a n-ary operation defined over S_C. The n-ary operation ϕ defined over S_P by $\phi(p_1,...,p_n)=\cap\Pi(f)(p_1,...,p_n)$ is the $\leq$-maximum f-consistent operation.

$<S_P,\neg_P,\lrcorner_P,\cap_P,\cup_P>$ is said to be $\leq$-maximum $<S_C,-,\lrcorner,\cap,\cup>$-consistent if $\neg_P$, $\lrcorner_P$, $\cap_P$ and $\cup_P$ are $\leq$-maximum-consistent with $-$, $\lrcorner$, $\cap$ and $\cup$, respectively. An operation f_P is said to be maximum f-consistent over a subset P of S_P if its restriction to P is that of the maximum f-consistent operation. By extension, $<S_P,\neg_P,\lrcorner_P,\cap_P,\cup_P>$ is maximum-consistent over $P \subseteq S_P$ if its operations are maximum-consistent over P. Completeness requires maximum-consistency over a subset of properties:

Theorem 2: I_P is complete only if $<S_P,\neg_P,\lrcorner_P,\cap_P,\cup_P>$ is maximum-consistent over $S_P'=\{p \in S_P: p \neq \cup\{q \in S_P: q \subset p\}\}$.

S_P' is the set of properties that are the strongest for some constraints. Its complement is the set of properties that are covered by their descendants (e.g., partitioned) in the semi-lattice $<S_P,\cap>$. Such properties are "redundant" with their covering, and can never be inferred if the system is complete. In theory, it is then pointless to specify both a property and one of its coverings in S_P.

Theorem 3: The maximum-consistent property algebra satisfies the identities (1-3). It satisfies (4-6) if it satisfies (7).

The maximum-consistent algebra does not necessarily satisfy idempotency, associativity, absorption, and distributivity. For instance, no idempotent intersection operation $\cap_P$ can be defined over a set of properties including *concavity*, since the intersection of concave constraints is not concave in general. One can identify various conditions on consistent property algebras to satisfy the missing identities, e.g.,

1. (7) holds iff $\neg_P(q)=\{c \in S_C: -c:q\}$ and $\lrcorner_P(q)=\{c \in S_C: \lrcorner c:q\}$ for all $q \in S_P$.
2. (7,8,11) hold only if $q \cap \neg_P(q)=\varnothing$ for all $q \in S_P \setminus \{T\}$.
3. (7,8,11) hold only if $q \cup \neg_P(q) \subseteq r \Rightarrow r=T$, for all $q \in S_P \setminus \{\bot\}$, $r \in S_P$.

Condition (a) is easily satisfiable: the set of properties must include the complement and converse of each property in the sense of $\neg_P$ and $\lrcorner_P$. Condition (b) forces the exclusion of properties like *convex*, whose set intersection with the complement property is not empty. Condition (c) forces the exclusion of any pair of properties $<q,r>$ such that q and $\neg_P(q)$ are stronger than r (e.g., *<universal,monotonic>*). Yet, such properties are pervasive in real-life problems and give rise to efficient filtering algorithms. Hence, practical property inference systems are bound to be incomplete.

4   Implementing Constraint Property Inference Systems

Implementing a property algebra involves encoding a set of properties that is closed by set intersection, and, if possible, by property complementation and conversion in the sense of (a). Given a set of n primitive properties, the closed set will contain a maximum of 16^n properties. Besides, the developer must encode property intersection for all possible pairs - a $16^n \times 16^n$ matrix in the worst case. Such encodings are clearly unworkable. To this end, we propose a set-based representation of properties.

Given a set of primitive properties S_P and its closure $\hat{S}_P$ by set intersection, every property of $\hat{S}_P$ can be encoded by the set of primitive properties it is the intersection of. We call such sets *constraint types*, and denote S_T their set ($S_T = \wp(S_P)$). Since types can be interpreted as properties, we propose to build constraint type inference systems following the model of the previous section. Given a Σ-algebra $<S_T, \neg_T, \lrcorner_T, \cap_T, \cup_T>$ of constraint types, we denote I_T the type inference system implementing the laws of Σ-morphisms between constraint languages and S_T.

By convention, the set of primitive properties S_P is assumed not to contain the universal and empty properties (the former is always verified, and the latter can never be assigned nor inferred). We adopt the interpretation function $\pi: S_T \to \hat{S}_P \cup \{T\}$ that maps a type to the intersection of its properties: $\pi(t) = \cap t$ for all $t \in S_T \setminus \{\varnothing\}$ and $\pi(\varnothing) = T$. A constraint $c \in S_C$ *verifies* $t \in S_T$ iff $c : \pi(t)$, and we denote $c : t$. We also define the pre-ordering $\leq$ on types: $s \leq t \Leftrightarrow \pi(s) \subseteq \pi(t)$. $\leq$ induces an equivalence relation $\equiv$ ($s \equiv t \Leftrightarrow \pi(s) = \pi(t)$), and it contains the set-inclusion relation $\supseteq$ since $\subseteq$-incomparable types may be equivalent. We extend $\leq$, $\subseteq$, and $\equiv$ to type operations as follows: $g \leq h$ (resp., $\subseteq$, $\equiv$) iff $g(t_1,...,t_n) \leq h(t_1,...,t_n)$ (resp., $\subseteq$, $\equiv$) for all $t_1,...,t_n \in S_T$.

Consider the set of types induced by the set of primitive properties of Fig. 2. The type *{functional,convex}* contains the singleton type *{functional}*, and both are equivalent since functional constraints are convex. On the other hand, the type *{functional}* is smaller than (i.e., $\leq$) *{convex}* and both are incomparable for $\subseteq$ and $\equiv$. In the following, we use the interpretation π and the ordering $\subseteq$ to generalise the definitions and results related to soundness, completeness, and maximum-consistency to type inference systems.

Definition 3: I_T is sound iff for all $T_{\Delta \cup \Sigma}$, $e_C \in H_{\Delta \cup \Sigma}(T_{\Delta \cup \Sigma}, S_C)$, $e_T \in H_{\Sigma}(T_{\Delta \cup \Sigma}, S_T)$, $(\forall \varphi \in T_{\Delta}, e_C(\varphi) : e_T(\varphi)) \Rightarrow (\forall \varphi \in T_{\Delta \cup \Sigma}, e_C(\varphi) : e_T(\varphi))$. I_T, sound, is complete iff for all $T_{\Delta \cup \Sigma}$, $e_C \in H_{\Delta \cup \Sigma}(T_{\Delta \cup \Sigma}, S_C)$, the mapping $e_{Tm} : T_{\Delta \cup \Sigma} \to S_T$ defined by $e_{Tm}(\varphi) = \cup \{t \in S_T : e_C(\varphi) : t\}$ belongs to $H_{\Sigma}(T_{\Delta \cup \Sigma}, S_T)$.

Definition 4: A n-ary type operation ϕ is consistent with a n-ary constraint operation f iff $\phi(t_1,...,t_n) \in \{t \in S_T : \forall c_1,...,c_n \in S_C, c_1:t_1 \wedge ... \wedge c_n:t_n \Rightarrow f(c_1,...,c_n):t\}$ for all $t_1,...,t_n \in S_T$.

Theorem 4: I_T is sound iff $<S_T, \neg_T, \lrcorner_T, \cap_T, \cup_T>$ is $<S_C, \neg, \lrcorner, \cap, \cup>$-consistent.

The $\subseteq$-maximum-consistent type operations follow from the $\leq$-maximum-consistent property operations:

Lemma 2: Let f be a n-ary constraint operation over S_C, f_P be the $\leq$-maximum f-consistent property operation over $\hat{S}_P \cup \{T\}$, and $\tau : \hat{S}_P \cup \{T\} \to S_T$ defined by $\tau(p) = \cup \{t \in S_T : \pi(t) = p\}$. The n-ary type operation f_T defined over S_T by $f_T(t_1,...,t_n) = \tau(f_P(\pi(t_1),...,\pi(t_n)))$ is the $\subseteq$-maximum f-consistent operation.

Theorem 5: I_T is complete only if $<S_T, \neg_T, \dashv_T, \cap_T, \cup_T>$ is $\subseteq$-maximum-consistent over $S_T' = \{t \in S_T : \pi(t) \neq \cap \{\pi(s) : s \in S_T \text{ and } s \supset t\}\}$.

We give below a parameterised version of Theorem 3. By equating S and T with S_T, we obtain the counterpart of Theorem 3 for the $\subseteq$-maximum-consistent type algebra, the only difference being that extensivity does not necessarily hold.

Theorem 6: Let $S \subseteq T \subseteq S_T$ and $<S_T, \neg_T, \dashv_T, \cap_T, \cup_T>$ be $\subseteq$-maximum-consistent over S and consistent over T. If S is closed under $\neg_T$ and $\dashv_T$, and T is closed under all operations, (1,3) hold over S, and (4-6) hold over S if (7) holds over T.

The prime benefit of types is to enable an intensional implementation of the closure of the set of properties by set intersection. Still, implementing the type operations remains challenging. To this end, we consider operations that distribute over set union. By definition, such operations are recursively defined from their restriction to the set of singleton types. Therefore, developers only have to encode their restrictions, the complete definition coming for free.

Of course, $\cup$-distributive operations approximate the $\subseteq$-maximum-consistent type operations. This is partly due to the presence of $\subset$-comparable primitive properties. Consider two primitive properties p and q such that $p \subset q$. If a type t includes p but not q, the evaluation of a $\cup$-distributive operation involving t will not integrate any computation on q, and is likely to be suboptimal. In addition, such approximations may escalate during typing if operation outputs stand as other operations' inputs.

A solution consists of completing every type that is input to or output by an operation with the missing properties that its properties subsume. For instance, the type t above would be completed with the property q. The subsumed properties of a type can be identified by traversing the set-inclusion ordering over primitive properties starting from its properties (e.g., the completion of {*monotonic,co-monotonic*} in Fig. 2 will add *convex*, *concave*, and *convex-concave*). This approach requires encoding efficient traversal strategies for the graph of properties.

Equivalent types are the real source of approximation. The evaluation of $\cup$-distributive operations on types that are not $\subseteq$-maximum in their equivalence class is bound to be suboptimal. One approach is to promote each operation input/output to its $\subseteq$-maximum type. This requires encoding every equivalence class beforehand in a format that guarantees fast look-up. Still, this is only feasible in the rare case where equivalence classes are few, easily identifiable, and admitting small-sized encodings.

Therefore, we forsake this approach and just consider $\cup$-distributive operations that normalise their outputs through graph-based completion. We call such operations *decomposable*. For all $p \in S_P$, $t \in S_T$, [p] denotes the set $\{q \in S_P : p \subset q\}$ of properties subsumed by p, and [t] the type $\cup_{p \in t}[p]$ subsumed by t. t is *normalised* (completed) iff t=[t].[2] t is *primitive* iff it is the normalisation of a singleton type, that is, t=[p] for some $p \in S_P$. S_{TN} is the set of normalised types and $S_{TP} \subseteq S_{TN}$ that of primitive types.

Definition 5: A n-ary type operation ϕ is decomposable if it distributes over $\cup$ and $\phi(S_T^n) \subseteq S_{TN}$.

---

[2] $t \subseteq [t]$, $t \equiv [t]$, $[[t]]=[t]$, and $[s \cup t]=[s] \cup [t]$ for all $s,t \in S_T$.

A type algebra is said to be decomposable if its operations are decomposable. By construction, decomposable algebras are insulated from the presence of $\subset$-comparable properties if primitive expressions are assigned normalised types. They are also completely defined by their restrictions to the set of singleton types since each operation ϕ verifies $\phi(t_1,...,t_n)=\cup_{p1\in t1,...,pn\in tn}\phi(\{p_1\},...,\{p_n\})$. Besides, consistency and some identities hold over normalised types when they hold over primitive types:

Lemma 3: Every decomposable type algebra that is consistent over S_{TP} is consistent. Every decomposable type algebra satisfies (1), and it satisfies (3-7,9) over S_{TN} if it satisfies these identities over S_{TP}.

The $\subseteq$-maximum-consistent algebra is itself decomposable but only over the set of primitive types. So the "best" decomposable algebra $S_{Tdm}=<S_T,\neg_{Tdm},\dashv_{Tdm},\cap_{Tdm},\cup_{Tdm}>$ is the one that is $\subseteq$-maximum-consistent over primitive types. The previous result can be applied to it in combination with Theorem 6 (with $S=S_{TP}$ and $T=S_{TN}$):

Corollary 1: S_{Tdm} is consistent. If S_{TP} is closed under $\neg_{Tdm}$ and $\dashv_{Tdm}$, S_{Tdm} satisfies (1,3) over S_{TN}, and it satisfies (4-6) over S_{TN} if it satisfies (7) over S_{TP}.

S_{Tdm} satisfies the same identities as the $\subseteq$-maximum-consistent type algebra over the set of normalised types, provided the set of primitive types is closed under type conversion and complementation. To satisfy this condition, it suffices to impose that the set of primitive properties be closed by complementation and conversion according to (a), and to make the unary type operations involutive.

5   A Constraint Type Inference System

We propose a decomposable algebra S_{Td} that exploits meta-knowledge on properties. First, the set of primitive properties must be closed by property complementation and conversion using $\neg_P$ and $\dashv_P$ given in (a). Second, the stability by restriction, extension, set intersection and set union must be specified for all primitive properties.[3] For $t\in S_T$, $Sr(t)$ (resp., $Se(t)$, $Si(t)$, $Su(t)$) is the set of properties of t that are stable by restriction (resp., extension, intersection, union). $S_{Td}=<S_T,\neg_{Td},\dashv_{Td},\cap_{Td},\cup_{Td}>$ is defined by:

- $\neg_{Td}(t)=[\cup_{q\in t}\{\neg_P(q)\}]$ and $\dashv_{Td}(t)=[\cup_{q\in t}\{\dashv_P(q)\}]$.
- $s\cap_{Td}t=[Sr(s)\cup Sr(t)\cup Si(s\cap t)]$.
- $s\cup_{Td}t=[Se(s)\cup Se(t)\cup Su(s\cap t)]$.

S_{Td} enforces the fact that properties involved in operations they are stable for can safely appear in the output. S_{Td} is indeed consistent and decomposable. It also validates extensivity, associativity and semi-absorption, as opposed to the $\subseteq$-maximum-consistent type algebra.

---

[3] $p\in S_P$ is stable by restriction (resp., extension) iff $c_1:p\wedge c_1\supseteq c_2\Rightarrow c_2:p$ (resp., $c_1:p\wedge c_1\subseteq c_2\Rightarrow c_2:p$) for all $c_1,c_2\in S_C$. p is stable by set intersection (resp., set union) if it is closed under set intersection (resp., set union).

Theorem 8. S_{Td} is decomposable, consistent, and it satisfies (1-7,9-10) over S_{TN}.

Since $\cap_{Td} \subseteq \cup \leq \cap_{Tm} \supseteq \cap_{Td}$ and $\cup_{Td} \subseteq \cup \leq \cup_{Tm} \supseteq \cup_{Td}$ over S_{TN}, equality or equivalence with $\subseteq$-maximum-consistent operations is achieved over a subset of the language, eg.

- $\neg_{Td} = \neg_{Tm}$ and $\dashv_{Td} = \dashv_{Tm}$ over S_{TN}.
- $\cap_{Td} = \cup \equiv \cap_{Tm}$ over $\{(s,t) \in S_{TN}^2 : Sr(s \oplus t) = s \oplus t \text{ and } Si(s \cap t) = s \cap t\}$.[4]
- $\cup_{Td} = \cup \equiv \cup_{Tm}$ over $\{(s,t) \in S_{TN}^2 : Se(s \oplus t) = s \oplus t \text{ and } Su(s \cap t) = s \cap t\}$.

The definition of S_{Td}'s operations being generic, users just have to specify the graph of primitive properties, the stability information for each, as well as $\neg_p$ and $\dashv_p$. If types are encoded as bitsets, stability operations can be coded as bitsets too, and set-inclusion over properties as a vector of bitsets. Since S_{Td}'s operations just perform set unions, intersections and normalisations of types, they boil down to bitset operations with a complexity linear in the size of their input types. For instance, $s \cap_T t$ involves a maximum of $|s|+|t|$ bitset operations.

We illustrate this system for the program P based on the graph of primitive properties of Fig. 2 and the user-information provided in Table 1. We assume that the primitive expressions c_1, c_2, c_3 and c_4 are typed maximally in S_{TN}, as recommended. That is, $t_1=[\neq_P]$, $t_2=t_4=[\leq_P]$ and $t_3=[\geq_P]$ where t_i is the type of c_i. The system types $c_5 = \neg c_1 \cap \neg c_2$ by constructing and evaluating the expression $t_5 = \neg_{Td}(t_1) \cap_{Td} \neg_{Td}(t_2)$ as follows. $\neg_{Td}(t_1) = \neg_{Td}([\neq_P]) = [=_P]$ and $\neg_{Td}(t_2) = \neg_{Td}([\leq_P]) = [\geq_P]$, so $t_5 = [=_P] \cap_{Td} [\geq_P] = [Sr([=_P]) \cap Sr([\geq_P]) \cap Si([=_P] \cap [\geq_P])]$. $Sr([=_P]) = \{=_P\}$, $Sr([\geq_P]) = \varnothing$, $[=_P] \cap [\geq_P] = [\diamond_P]$ and $Si([\diamond_P]) = \{\diamond_P\}$, so $t_5 = [\{=_P\} \cup \{\diamond_P\}] = [\{=_P, \diamond_P\}] = [=_P]$. c_5 is then typed functional. It is indeed equivalent to $(x=y)$, which admits $[=_P]$ for $\subseteq$-maximum type. Thus, the system achieves an optimal typing and, in some ways, recognises that c_2 is redundant in c_5. It also types c_7 as concave ($t_7=[\gtrless_P]$), which is optimal again.

However, it only infers $t_6=[=_P]$, which is suboptimal since c_6 is the empty constraint. In fact, it can never identify inconsistent expressions because it cannot infer the property *empty* unless the empty constraint appears in the expression - a pathological case. It also types c_8 as *concave*, which is sub-optimal as c_8 is anti-functional and equivalent to $\neq$. The maximum-consistent type algebra does not yield a better result because no consistent algebra can enforce the equivalence $(x<y) \vee (x>y+1) \Leftrightarrow x \neq y$. Indeed, the union of monotonic and co-monotonic relations is not anti-functional in general.

$\cap_{Td}$ and the $\subseteq$-maximum-consistent operation $\cap_{Tm}$ differ on 6 combinations of primitive types out of 81. All involve the universality property, and as such, have no practical incidence. $\cap_{Tm}$ basically exploits the neutrality of the universal constraint for set intersection, e.g., $\cap_{Tm}([1_P],[\neq_P]) = [\neq_P]$ whereas $\cap_{Td}([1_P],[\neq_P]) = \varnothing$. Note finally that distributivity does not hold, e.g., $r \cap_{Td}(s \cup_{Td} t) = [=_P]$ while $(r \cap_{Td} s) \cup_{Td}(r \cap_{Td} t) = \varnothing$ with $r=[=_P]$, $s=[<_P]$, $t=[\neq_P]$.

---

[4] $s \oplus t$ is the symmetric difference between s and t.

Table 1. Complementation, conversion, and stability of primitive properties. Definitions for the complement properties $\{\geq_P, 1_P, \neq_P, ><_P\}$ follow from the fact that $\neg_P$ commutes stability by restriction (resp., intersection) into stability by extension (resp., union) and vice-versa

q	$\diamondsuit_P$	$=_P$	0_P	$\ll_P$	$\leq_P$
$\neg_P(q)$	$><_P$	$\neq_P$	1_P	$\ll_P$	$\geq_P$
$\lrcorner_P(q)$	$\diamondsuit_P$	$=_P$	0_P	$\ll_P$	$\geq_P$
Sr({q})	$\varnothing$	$\{=_P\}$	$\{0_P\}$	□	□
Se({q})	□	□	□	□	□
Si({q})	$\{\diamondsuit_P\}$	$\{=_P\}$	$\{0_P\}$	□	$\{\leq_P\}$
Su({q})	□	□	$\{0_P\}$	$\varnothing$	$\{\leq_P\}$

1.1   Extensions

The optimality of our system (i.e., the quality of its approximation of the maximum-consistent algebra) relies on the stability of primitive properties. The worst case occurs when no primitive property is stable by restriction or intersection as the system systematically infers the empty type. Arguably, this is a rare situation since interesting properties (that is, properties enhancing bound- or arc-consistency computations) are typically stable by restriction (e.g., functionality), extension (e.g., reflexivity), intersection (e.g., min-max-closedness), or union (e.g., symmetry).

An inherent source of suboptimality is due to properties that are stable for a subset of the constraints they cover. Consider the intersection of an irreflexive constraint with a functional and min-max-closed constraint. The resulting constraint is irreflexive and functional as expected, but it is also min-max-closed since *functional∩ min-max-closed* is stable by restriction. Still, our computation will not retain min-max-closedness (as it is unstable by restriction) if *functional∩min-max-closed* has not been declared as a primitive property. This problem can be addressed by overriding the output of stability operators, e.g., the type {*functional*} output by Sr({*functional,min-max-closed*}) should be overriden by {*functional,min-max-closed*}. This approach requires identifying the critical combinations of properties beforehand, and implementing the corresponding promotion rules.

Another extension consists of running a constraint rewriting system to simplify constraint expressions before typing. Here, the goal is to insulate the inference system from the categories of expressions that generate typing discrepancies. The rewriting system should be designed to enforce the identities that the type algebra violates so that stronger types be inferred for critical expressions. In this way, we may achieve (simulate) superior inferencing capabilities without restricting the constraint language.

1.2   Generalisation

All definitions and results extend to unary constraints since the constraint language is just stripped from the conversion operation. For the n-ary case ($n > 2$), conversion is replaced by a generic permutation operation $\lrcorner$ and its counterparts $\lrcorner_P$ and $\lrcorner_T$. Let $\sigma = <\sigma_1,..,\sigma_n>$ be a permutation of $<1,..,n>$,

- $\lrcorner(\sigma)(c)(v_1,..,v_n)=c(v_{\sigma 1},..,v_{\sigma n})$ for all $c\in \wp(D^n)$, $<v_1,..,v_n>\in D^n$.
- $\lrcorner_P(\sigma)(p)=p^\sigma=\{c\in \wp(D^n) \text{ s.t. } \exists c':p \text{ and } c=\lrcorner(\sigma)(c')\}$ for all $p\in S_P$.
- $\lrcorner_T(\sigma)(t)=[\cup_{p\in t}\{p^\sigma\}]$ for all $t\in S_T$.

Each operation $\lrcorner(\sigma)$ is involutive (of a certain rank) and commutes with complementation, so results related to type conversion generalise. Explicitly implementing the set of primitive properties is prohibitive since it must be closed by property permutation. We propose an approach where developers only encode a set R_n of representative properties of S_P and the restrictions of $\neg_P$, Sr, Se, Si, Su, and $\subset$ to this subset. We just require that all properties of R_n be different modulo permutation, and we define S_P as the closure of R_n by permutation.

Thus, each property $q\in S_P$ is the permutation σ of a representative property $p\in R_n$ ($q=p^\sigma$). This allows us to encode all properties of S_P as pairs $<p,\sigma>$. We also provide the pair $<p,*>$ to represent the permutation class $\{p^\sigma: \sigma \text{ permutation of } <1,..,n>\}$. Finally, we impose a parametric definition for set-inclusion. Developers have three exclusive options/assertions to define set-inclusion for a pair (p,q): $A_1(p,q)=(\forall \sigma 1,\sigma 2, p^{\sigma 1}\subset q^{\sigma 2}\Leftrightarrow \sigma 1=\sigma 2)$, $A_2(p,q)=(\forall \sigma 1,\sigma 2, p^{\sigma 1}\subset q^{\sigma 2})$ and $A_3(p,q)= (\forall \sigma 1,\sigma 2, p^{\sigma 1}\not\subset q^{\sigma 2})$. For instance, one would select A_1 for the pair (*row-functional,row-convex*), A_2 for (*convex,row-convex*) and A_3 for (*convex,concave*).

On this basis, types are coded as lists of pairs $(...,<p,\tau>,...)$ where τ is either * or a permutation σ. Set union on types amounts to merging the corresponding lists and deleting any pair $<p,\sigma>$ from the resulting list if it already contains $<p,*>$. Set intersection has a dual implementation. Normalisation, stability, permutation and complementation obey the following rules:

- $Sr((<p_1,\tau_1>,...,<p_s,\tau_s>))=Sr(<p_1,\tau_1>)\cup_{list}...\cup_{list}Sr(<p_s,\tau_s>)$ (same for Se, Si and Su).
- $Sr(<p,\sigma>)=(<p,\sigma>)$ and $Sr(<p,*>)=(<p,*>)$ iff p is stable by restriction.
- $[(<p_1,\tau_1>,...,<p_s,\tau_s>)]=[<p_1,\tau_1>]\cup_{list}...\cup_{list}[<p_s,\tau_s>]$.
- $[<p,\sigma>]=(<p,\sigma>)\cup_{list}(<q,\sigma>: A_1(p,q))\cup_{list}(<q,*>: A_2(p,q))$.
- $[<p,*>]=(<p,*>)\cup_{list}(<q,*>: A_1(p,q)\vee A_2(p,q))$.
- $\lrcorner_T(\sigma)((<p_1,\tau_1>,...,<p_s,\tau_s>))=[\lrcorner_T(\sigma)(<p_1,\tau_1>)\cup_{list}...\cup_{list}\lrcorner_T(\sigma)(<p_s,\tau_s>)]$.
- $\lrcorner_T(\sigma 2)(<p,\sigma 1>)=(<p,\sigma 2(\sigma 1)>)$ and $\lrcorner_T(\sigma)(<p,*>)=(<p,*>)$.
- $\neg_T((<p_1,\tau_1>,...,<p_s,\tau_s>))=[\neg_T(<p_1,\tau_1>)\cup_{list}...\cup_{list}\neg_T(<p_s,\tau_s>)]$.
- $\neg_T(<p,\sigma>)=(<\neg_P(p),\sigma>)$ and $\neg_T(<p,*>)=(<\neg_P(p),*>)$.

The constraint language and type inference system can also accomodate scope extension and restriction. Developers just have to encode the mappings that model the "extension" of primitive unary constraint properties (resp., binary) into binary constraint types (resp., n-ary). For instance, {*row-convex,column-concave*} could be mapped to *concave* to reflect the extension of unary concave constraints over a scope (x) into binary constraints over a scope (x,y).

6   Adaptation

In CP systems, the adaptation logic is usually hard-coded and consists of switching between filtering routines during propagation (see [8] for an implementation model). Since routines are enslaved to daemons that trap the unary constraints inferred by the system, we can elicit these constraints and use them to rewrite problem constraints on the fly. Thus, problem constraints can be retyped and their algorithms reconfigured through a standard process without having recourse to hard-coded switches.

Consider for instance the computation of arc-consistency. This is a fixpoint computation where each step transforms a CSP into an equivalent CSP by making explicit entailed unary constraints. Such constraints are usually enforced and monitored as variable assignments ($x=u$), bound reductions (e.g., $x<u$), and general domain reductions (e.g., $x \in U$). They trigger the filtering routines associated to the problem constraints, which, in turn, produce new unary constraints. This process is iterated until the fixpoint is reached, or inconsistency is detected.

Since each step preserves global equivalence, every constraint expression $c(x,y)$ of the problem can be replaced by $c(x,y) \cap \Gamma(x,y)$ when a set $\Gamma(x,y)$ of unary constraints has been accumulated on x and y. Thus, $c(x,y)$ can be retyped and reconfigured by typing $\Gamma(x,y)$ and type-intersecting the result with its original type. Typing inferred unary constraints is trivial, e.g., variable assignments can be typed as functional, bound-reductions as monotonic, and general domain-reductions as row- or column-convex.

Still, dynamic typing is pointless if $\Gamma(x,y)$ adds no property to $c(x,y)$. This is the case with our system if the type of $\Gamma(x,y)$ contains no property that is stable by restriction. A complementary approach consists of rewriting/simplifying the original constraint expressions using the inferred constraints to trigger (re-)typing. Another alternative is to let filtering routines directly retype "their" relations during execution, as advocated in [8].

7   Conclusion

We have modeled constraint property inferencing for relational constraint languages as the computation of morphisms between constraint term algebras and constraint property algebras. Soundness is achieved by enforcing consistency between algebras, while completeness requires maximum-consistency. However, maximum-consistent property algebras do not guarantee completeness, and their implementation is prohibitive. An alternative is to represent constraint properties as sets of primitive properties (constraint types), and to adopt normalising type operations that are recursively defined from primitive properties (decomposable operations).

We have proposed a generic consistent decomposable algebra that developers must instantiate with their domain and properties of choice. They just have to complement, inverse, and tag with stability information any primitive property. The definition of operations automatically follows. Besides, previously stated information need not be updated when new properties are added. As far as complexity is concerned, typing is virtually cost-free if bitset encodings are used.

This algebra approximates the maximum-consistent algebra and the maximum-consistent decomposable algebra. In return, it satisfies the laws of involution, associativity, and semi-absorption. Besides, the approximation is minimum for certain categories of expressions, and it can be reduced further by rewriting constraints before typing and/or promoting types during typing.

Our overall objective is to exploit types to drive the configuration of domain filtering algorithms for user-defined constraints (static and dynamic configuration) and built-in constraints (dynamic configuration). The same way types are composed out of primitive properties, algorithms can be composed out of primitive routines. The idea is to configure algorithms for individual constraints by selecting and assembling the filtering routines associated to their primitive properties. One approach is to adopt algorithmic inference schemes such as AC-inference [3], which allows the specialisation of arc-consistency algorithms. However, this scheme does not handle the combinatorial aspect of configuration and provides no means to compose multiple routines. We are currently investigating another approach.

References

[1]   Bessière C., "Arc-consistency and arc-consistency again", Artificial Intelligence, Vol. 65, pp. 179-190, 1994.

[2]   Bessière C., E.C. Freuder, and J.C. Regin, "Using inference to reduce arc consistency computation", in Proc. of 14th Int. Joint Conf. on AI, Montreal, pp. 592-598, 1995.

[3]   Bessière C., E.C. Freuder, and J.C. Regin, "Using constraint metaknowledge to reduce arc-consistency computation", Artificial Intelligence, Vol. 107, pp. 125-148, 1999.

[4]   Jeavons P.G., and M.C. Cooper, "Tractable constraints on ordered domains", Artificial Intelligence, Vol. 79, No. 2, pp. 327-339, 1995.

[5]   Jonsson B., "The Theory of Binary Relations", Colloq. Math. Soc. Janos Bolyai, Budapest, Hungary, Algebraic Logic (North Holland), Vol. 54, pp. 245-292, 1988.

[6]   Laburthe F., "Choco: implementing a CP kernel", Workshop on Techniques for Implementing Constraint programming Systems (TRICS-2000), 6th Int. Conf. on Principles and Practice of Constraint Programming (CP-2000), Singapore, 2000.

[7]   Puget J.F., and M. Leconte, "Beyond the glass box: constraints as objects", in Proc. of International Logic Programming Symposium (ILPS'95), Portland, pp. 513-527, 1995.

[8]   Savean P., "Constraint Reduction at the Type Level", Workshop TRICS-2000, 6th Int. Conf. on Principles and Practice of Constraint Programming (CP-2000), Singapore, 2000.

[9]   Van Beek P., "On the minimality and decomposability of constraint networks", in Proc. of 10th National Conference on Artificial Intelligence (AAAI-92), pp. 447-452, 1992.

[10]   Van Hentenryck P., Y. Deville, and C. Teng, "A generic arc-consistency algorithm and its specializations", Artificial Intelligence, Vol. 57, pp. 291-321, 1992.

[11]   Voudouris C., R. Dorne, D. Lesaint, and A. Liret, "iOpt: a software toolkit for Heuristic Search methods", in Proc. of 7th Int. Conf. on Principles and Practice of Constraint Programming (CP-2001), Paphos, Cyprus, pp. 716-719, 2001.

Model-Based Programming: Controlling Embedded Systems by Reasoning About Hidden State

Brian C. Williams and Michel D. Ingham

Space Systems and Artificial Intelligence Laboratories
Massachusetts Institute of Technology
77 Massachusetts Ave., Cambridge, MA 02139
{williams,ingham}@mit.edu

Abstract. Programming complex embedded systems involves reasoning through intricate system interactions along paths between sensors, actuators and control processors. This is a time-consuming and error-prone process. Furthermore, the resulting code generally lacks modularity and robustness. *Model-based programming* addresses these limitations, allowing engineers to program by specifying high-level control strategies and by assembling common-sense models of the system hardware and software. To execute a control strategy, model-based executives reason about the models "on the fly", to track system state, diagnose faults and perform reconfigurations. This paper describes the *Reactive Model-based Programming Language (RMPL)* and its executive, called *Titan*. RMPL provides the features of synchronous reactive languages within a constraint-based modeling framework, with the added ability of being able to read and write to state variables that are hidden within the physical plant.

1   Introduction

We envision a future with large networks of highly robust and increasingly autonomous embedded systems. These visions include intelligent highways that reduce congestion, cooperative networks of air vehicles for search and rescue, and fleets of intelligent space probes that autonomously explore the far reaches of the solar system.

Many of these systems will need to perform robustly within extremely harsh and uncertain environments, or operate for years with minimal attention. To accomplish this, these embedded systems will need to radically reconfigure themselves in response to failures, and then accommodate these failures during their remaining operational lifetime. We support the rapid prototyping of these systems by creating embedded programming languages that are able to reason about how to control hardware from engineering models. This approach, which combines constraint-based and Markov modeling with the features of reactive programming, is called *model-based programming*.

P. Van Hentenryck (Ed.): CP 2002, LNCS 2470, pp. 508–524, 2002.

In the past, high levels of robustness under extreme uncertainty was largely the realm of deep space exploration. Billion dollar space systems, like the Galileo Jupiter probe, have achieved robustness by employing sizable software development and operations teams. Efforts to make these missions highly capable at dramatically reduced costs have proven extremely challenging, producing notable losses, such as the Mars Polar Lander and Mars Climate Orbiter failures[1]. A primary contributor to these failures was the inability of the small software team to think through the large space of potential interactions between the embedded software and its underlying hardware.

Our objective is to support future programmers with embedded languages that avoid common-sense mistakes by automatically reasoning from hardware models. Our solution to this challenge has two parts. First, we have created increasingly intelligent, embedded systems that automatically diagnose and plan courses of action at reactive timescales, based on models of themselves and their environment[2, 3, 4, 5, 6]. This paradigm, called *model-based autonomy*, has been demonstrated in space on NASA's Deep Space One probe[7], and on several subsequent space systems[8, 9]. Second, we elevate the level at which an engineer programs through a language, called the *Reactive Model-based Programming Language (RMPL)*, which enables the programmer to tap into and guide the reasoning methods of model-based autonomy. This language allows the programmer to delegate, to the language's compiler and run-time kernel, tasks involving reasoning through system interactions, such as low-level commanding, monitoring, diagnosis and repair. The model-based execution kernel for RMPL is called *Titan*.

This paper begins by describing the model-based programming paradigm in more detail (Section 2). Section 3 then goes on to demonstrate model-based programming as applied to a simple example. Section 4 introduces the RMPL language. Section 5 presents the semantics of model-based program execution. Section 6 describes Titan's control sequencer, which translates a control program written in RMPL into a sequence of state configuration goals, based on the system's estimated state trajectory. Finally, Section 7 closes with related work.

2   Model-Based Programming

Engineers like to reason about embedded systems in terms of state evolutions. However, embedded programming languages, such as Esterel[10] and Statecharts[11], interact with a physical plant by reading sensor variables and writing control variables (left, Figure 1). Constraint programming languages, such as the Timed Concurrent Constraint Language (TCC)[12], replace the traditional notion of a "store" as a valuation of variables with the notion of a store as a set of constraints on program variables. These languages interact with the store by "telling" and "asking" constraints at consecutive time points (middle, Figure 1). In both these cases, it is the programmer's responsibility to perform the mapping between intended state and the sensors and actuators. This mapping involves reasoning through a complex set of interactions under a range of

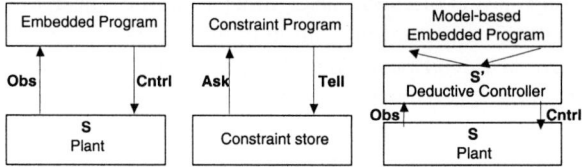

Fig. 1. Model of interaction for traditional embedded languages (left), concurrent constraint programming languages (middle) and model-based programming languages (right)

possible failure situations. The complexity of the interactions and the number of possible scenarios make this an error-prone process.

A model-based programming language leverages the benefits of both embedded programming and constraint programming, with the key difference that it interacts directly with the plant state (right, Figure 1). This is accomplished by allowing the programmer to *read or write constraints on "hidden" state variables in the plant,* i.e. states that are not directly observable or controllable. It is then the responsibility of the language's execution kernel to map between hidden states and the plant sensors and control variables. This mapping is performed automatically by employing a deductive controller that reasons from a common-sense plant model.

A model-based program is comprised of two components. The first is a *control program,* which uses standard programming constructs to codify specifications of desired system behavior. In addition, to execute the control program, the execution kernel needs a model of the system it must control. Hence the second component is a *plant model,* which includes models of the plant's nominal behavior and common failure modes. This model unifies constraints, concurrency and Markov processes.

A model-based program is executed by automatically generating a control sequence that moves the physical plant to the states specified by the control program (Figure 2). We call these specified states *configuration goals.* Program execution is performed using a *model-based executive,* such as Titan, which repeatedly generates the next configuration goal, and then generates a sequence of control actions that achieve this goal, based on knowledge of the current plant state and plant model.

The Titan model-based executive consists of two components, a *control sequencer* and a *deductive controller.* The control sequencer is responsible for generating a sequence of configuration goals, using the control program and plant state estimates. Each configuration goal specifies an abstract state for the plant to be placed in. The deductive controller is responsible for estimating the plant's most likely current state based on observations from the plant (*mode estimation*), and for issuing commands to move the plant through a sequence of states that achieve the configuration goals (*mode reconfiguration*).

3   A Model-Based Programming Example

Model-based programming enables a programmer to focus on specifying the desired state evolutions of the system. For example, consider the task of inserting a spacecraft into orbit around a planet. Our spacecraft includes a science camera and two identical redundant engines (Engines A and B), as shown in Figure 3. An engineer thinks about this maneuver in terms of state trajectories:

> Heat up both engines (called "standby mode"). Meanwhile, turn the camera off, in order to avoid plume contamination. When both are accomplished, thrust one of the two engines, using the other as backup in case of primary engine failure.

This specification is far simpler than a control program that must turn on heaters and valve drivers, open valves and interpret sensor readings for the engine. Thinking in terms of more abstract hidden states makes the task of writing the control program much easier, and avoids the error-prone process of reasoning through low-level system interactions. In addition, it gives the program's execution kernel the latitude to respond to failures as they arise. This is essential for achieving high levels of robustness.

As an example, consider the model-based program for spacecraft orbital insertion. The spacecraft dual main engine system (Figure 3) consists of two propellant tanks, two main engines and redundant valves. The system offers a range of configurations for establishing propellant paths to a main engine. When the propellants combine within the engine they produce thrust. The flight computer controls the engine and camera by sending commands. Sensors include an accelerometer, to confirm engine operation, and a camera shutter position sensor, to confirm camera operation.

Control Program – The RMPL control program, shown in Figure 4, codifies the informal specification we gave above as a set of state trajectories. The specific RMPL constructs used in the program are introduced in Section 4. Recall that, to perform orbital insertion, one of the two engines must be fired. We start by concurrently placing the two engines in standby and by shutting off the camera.

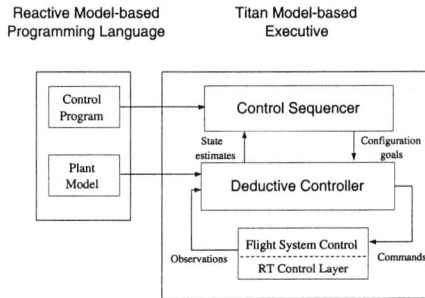

Fig. 2. Architecture for a model-based executive

This is performed by lines 3-5, where the comma at the end of each line denotes parallel composition. We then fire an engine, choosing to use Engine A as the primary engine (lines 6-9) and Engine B as a backup, in the event that Engine A fails to fire correctly (lines 10-11). Engine A starts trying to fire as soon as it achieves standby and the camera is off (line 7), but aborts if at any time Engine A is found to be in a failure state (line 9). Engine B starts trying to fire only if Engine A has failed, B is in standby and the camera is off (line 10).

Several features of this control program reinforce our earlier points. First, the program is stated in terms of state assignments to the engines and camera, such as "EngineB = Firing". Second, these state assignments appear both as assertions and as execution conditions. For example, in lines 6-9, "EngineA = Firing" appears in an assertion (line 8), while "EngineA = Standby," "Camera = Off" and "EngineA = Failed," appear in execution conditions (lines 7 and 9). Third, none of these state assignments are directly observable or controllable, only shutter position and acceleration may be directly sensed, and only the flight computer command may be directly set. Finally, by referring to hidden states directly, the RMPL program is far simpler than a corresponding program that operates on sensed and controlled variables. The added complexity of the latter program is due to the need to fuse sensor information and generate command sequences under a large space of possible operation and fault scenarios.

Plant Model – The plant model is used by a model-based executive to map sensed variables in the control program to queried states and asserted states to specific control sequences. The plant model is specified as a concurrent transition system, composed of probabilistic component automata[2]. Each component automaton is represented by a set of component modes, a set of constraints defining the behavior within each mode, and a set of probabilistic transitions between modes. Constraints are used to represent co-temporal interactions between state variables and inter-communication between components. Probabilistic transitions are used to model the stochastic behavior of components, such as failure and intermittency. Reward is used to assess the costs and benefits associated with particular component modes. The component automata operate concurrently and synchronously.

For example, we can model the spacecraft abstractly as a three component system (2 engines and a camera), by supplying the models depicted graphically

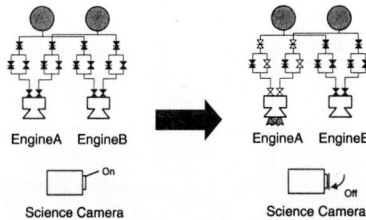

Fig. 3. Simple spacecraft for orbital insertion

```
1  OrbitInsert ()::{
2    do
3      { EngineA  = Standby,
4        EngineB  = Standby,
5        Camera = Off,
6        do
7          when  EngineA  = Standby AND Camera = Off
8            donext  EngineA  = Firing
9          watching  EngineA  = Failed,
10         when  EngineA  = Failed AND  EngineB  = Standby AND Camera = Off
11           donext  EngineB  = Firing}
12   watching  EngineA  = Firing OR  EngineB  = Firing
13 }
```

Fig. 4. RMPL control program for the orbital insertion scenario

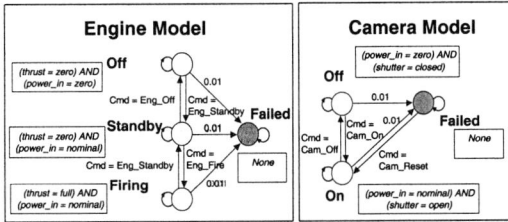

Fig. 5. State transition models for a simplified spacecraft

in Figure 5. Nominally, an engine can be in one of three modes: *off, standby* or *firing*. The behavior within each of these modes is described by a set of constraints on plant variables, namely *thrust* and *power_in*. In Figure 5 these constraints are specified in boxes next to their respective modes. The engine also has a *failed* mode, capturing any off-nominal behavior. We entertain the possibility of a novel engine failure by specifying no constraints for the engine's behavior in the *failed* mode[13].

Models include commanded and uncommanded transitions, both of which are probabilistic. For example, the engine has uncommanded transitions from *off, standby* and *firing* to *failed*. These transitions have a 1% probability, indicated as arcs labeled 0.01. Transitions between nominal modes are triggered on commands, and occur with probability 99%.

Executing the Model-Based Program – When the orbital insertion control program is executed, the control sequencer starts by generating a configuration goal consisting of the conjunction of three state assignments: "EngineA = Standby", "EngineB = Standby" and "Camera = Off" (lines 3-5). To determine how to achieve this goal, the deductive controller considers the latest estimate of the state of the plant. For example, suppose the deductive controller determines from its sensor measurements and previous commands that the two engines are already in standby, but the camera is on. The deductive controller deduces from the model that it should send a command to the plant to turn the camera off. After executing this command, it uses its shutter position sensor to confirm that the camera is off. With "Camera = Off" and "EngineA = Standby", the control sequencer advances to the configuration goal of "EngineA = Firing" (line 8).

The deductive controller identifies an appropriate setting of valve states that achieves this behavior, then it sends out the appropriate commands.

In the process of achieving goal "EngineA = Firing", assume that a failure occurs: an inlet valve to Engine A suddenly sticks closed. Given various sensor measurements (e.g. flow and pressure measurements throughout the propulsion subsystem), the deductive controller identifies the stuck valve as the most likely source of failure. It then tries to execute an alternative control sequence for achieving the configuration goal, for example, by repairing the valve. Presume that the valve is not repairable; Titan diagnoses that "EngineA = Failed". The control program specifies a configuration goal of "EngineB = Firing" as a backup (lines 10-11), which is issued by the control sequencer to the deductive controller.

4   The Reactive Model-Based Programming Language

RMPL is an object-oriented language, like Java. In general, RMPL constructs are conditioned on the current state of the physical plant, and they act on the plant state in the next time instant. State assertions are specified as constraints on plant state variables that should be made true. RMPL's model of interaction is in contrast to Esterel and TCC, which both interact with the program memory, sensors and control variables, but not with the plant state. Esterel interacts by emitting and detecting signals, while TCC interacts by *telling* and *asking* constraints on program variables. In contrast, RMPL constructs *ask* constraints on plant state variables, and request that specified constraints on state variables be *achieved* (as opposed to *tell*, which asserts that a constraint **is** true). State assertions in RMPL control programs are treated as *achieve* operations, while state condition checks are *ask* operations.

RMPL currently uses propositional state logic for its constraint system. In propositional state logic each proposition is an assignment, $x = v$, where variable x ranges over a finite domain $\mathbb{D}(x)$. Propositions are composed into formulae using the standard logical connectives: and ($\wedge$), or ($\vee$) and not ($\neg$). The constants **True** and **False** are also valid constraints. A constraint is *entailed* if it is implied by the plant model and the most likely current state of the physical plant.

We introduce RMPL by first highlighting its desired features. We then present the RMPL constructs used to encode control programs. These constructs are fully orthogonal, that is, they may be nested and combined arbitrarily. RMPL constructs are closely related to the TCC programming language constructs[12].

The orbital insertion example highlights five design features of RMPL. First, the program exploits full concurrency, by specifying parallel threads of execution; for example, the camera is turned off and the engines are set to standby in parallel (lines 3-5). Second, it involves conditional execution; for example, the control program must check for two conditions, prior to firing Engine A: that the engine to be fired is in standby mode, and that the camera is turned off (line 7). Third, it involves iteration; for example, line 7 says to iteratively test until Engine A is in standby and the Camera is off, and then to proceed. Fourth, the program involves preemption; for example, if the primary engine fails, the act of firing it should be preempted, in favor of firing the backup engine (lines 6-9). These four features are common to most synchronous reactive programming languages. As highlighted previously, the fifth and defining feature of RMPL is the ability to reference hidden states of the physical plant within assertions and condition checks, such as "**when** EngineA = Standby ∧ Camera = Off **donext** EngineA = Firing" (lines 7-8).

The RMPL constructs are defined as follows. We use lower case letters, like c, to denote constraints on variables of the physical plant, and upper case letters, like A and B, to denote well-formed RMPL expressions:

- g [**maintaining** m]. Asserts that the plant should progress towards a state that achieves g, while maintaining m throughout. If m does not hold at any point, then assertion of g terminates immediately. "maintaining m" is optional (defaults to **True**).
- **if** c **thennext** A_{then}[**elsenext** A_{else}]. Starts executing A_{then} in the next instant, if the most likely current plant state entails c. The optional expression A_{else} is executed starting in the next instant if c is *not* entailed by the most likely current state.
- **unless** c **thennext** A. Starts executing A in the next instant if the current theory does *not* entail c.
- A, B. Concurrently executes A and B, starting in the current instant.
- **always** A. Starts a new copy of A at each instant of time, for all time.
- $A; B$. Performs A until A is finished, then starts B.
- **when** c **donext** A. Waits until c is entailed by the most likely plant state, then starts A in the next instant.
- **whenever** c **donext** A. For every instant in which c holds for the most likely state, it starts a copy of A in the next instant.
- **do** A **watching** c. Executes A, but if c becomes entailed by the most likely plant state at any instant, it terminates execution of A.

The above-mentioned RMPL constructs are used to encode control programs. This subset is sufficient to implement most of the control constructs of the Esterel language[4]. Note that RMPL can also be used to encode the probabilistic transition models capturing the behavior of the plant components. The additional constructs required to encode such models are defined in [14].

5   Model-Based Program Execution Semantics

We define the execution of a model-based program in terms of legal state evolutions of a physical plant $\mathbb{P}$.

Plant Model – A plant $\mathbb{P}$ is modeled as a *partially observable Markov decision process* (POMDP) $M = \langle \Pi, \Sigma, \mathbb{T}, P_\Theta, P_\mathbb{T}, P_O, R \rangle$. Π is a set of *variables*, each ranging over a finite domain. Π is partitioned into *state variables* Π_s, *control variables* Π_c, *observable variables* Π_o, and *dependent variables* Π_d. A *full assignment* σ is defined as a set consisting of an assignment to each variable in Π. Σ is the set of all *feasible* full assignments over Π. A *state* s is defined as an assignment to each variable in Π_s. The set Σ_s, the projection of Σ on variables in Π_s, is the set of all feasible states.

$\mathbb{T}$ is a finite set of *transitions*. Each transition $\tau \in \mathbb{T}$ is a function $\tau : \Sigma \to \Sigma_s$, i.e. $\tau(\sigma_i)$ is the state obtained by applying transition τ to any feasible full assignment σ_i. The transition $\tau_n \in \mathbb{T}$ models the system's nominal behavior, while all other transitions model failures. The probability of transition τ, given full assignment σ_i, is $P_\tau(\sigma_i)$, for $P_\tau \in P_\mathbb{T}$. $P_\Theta(s_0)$ is the probability that the plant has initial state s_0. The reward for being in state s_i is $R(s_i)$, and the probability of observing o_j in state s_i is $P_O(s_i, o_j)$.

A *plant trajectory* is a (finite or infinite) sequence of feasible states S : $s_0, s_1, \ldots$ such that for each s_i there is a feasible assignment $\sigma_i \in \Sigma$ which agrees with s_i on assignments to variables in Π_s and $s_{i+1} = \tau(\sigma_i)$ for some $\tau \in \mathbb{T}$. A trajectory that involves only the nominal transition τ_n is called a *nominal trajectory*. A *simple* trajectory does not repeat any state.

Model-Based Program Execution – A model-based program for plant $\mathbb{P}$ consists of a model M, described above, and a control program CP, described as a deterministic automaton $CP = \langle \Sigma_{cp}, \theta_{cp}, \tau_{cp}, g_{cp}, \Sigma_s \rangle$. Σ_{cp} is the set of *program locations*, where $\theta_{cp} \in \Sigma_{cp}$ is the program's initial location. Transitions τ_{cp} between locations are conditioned on plant states Σ_s of M, i.e. τ_{cp} is a function $\tau_{cp} : \Sigma_{cp} \times \Sigma_s \to \Sigma_{cp}$. Each location $l_i \in \Sigma_{cp}$ has a corresponding *configuration goal* $g_{cp}(l_i) \subset \Sigma_s$, which is the set of legal plant target states associated with location l_i.

A *legal execution* of a model-based program is a trajectory of feasible plant states, $S : s_0, s_1, \ldots$ of M, and locations $L : l_0, l_1, \ldots$ of CP such that: (a) s_0 is a valid initial plant state, that is, $P_\Theta(s_0) > 0$; (b) for each s_i there is a $\sigma_i \in \Sigma$ of M that agrees with s_i and o_i on the corresponding subsets of variables; (c) l_0 is the initial program location θ_{cp}; (d) $\langle l_i, l_{i+1} \rangle$ represents a legal control program transition, i.e. $l_{i+1} = \tau_{cp}(l_i, s_i)$; and (e) if plant state s_{i+1} is the result of a nominal transition from σ_i, i.e. $s_{i+1} = \tau_n(\sigma_i)$, then either s_{i+1} is the least-cost state in $g_{cp}(l_i)$, or $\langle s_i, s_{i+1} \rangle$ is the prefix of a simple nominal trajectory that ends in a least-cost state $s_j \in g_{cp}(l_i)$.

Model-Based Executive – A model-based program is executed by a *model-based executive*. We define a model-based executive as a high-level *control sequencer* coupled to a low-level *deductive controller*.

A control sequencer takes as inputs a control program CP and a sequence $S : s^{(0)}, s^{(1)}, \ldots$ of plant state estimates. It generates a sequence $\gamma : g^{(0)}, g^{(1)}, \ldots$ of configuration goals. A complete definition of the control sequencer is given in Section 6.

A deductive controller takes as inputs the plant model M, a sequence of configuration goals $\gamma : g^{(0)}, g^{(1)}, \ldots$, and a sequence of observations $O : o^{(0)}, o^{(1)}, \ldots$. It generates a sequence of most likely plant state estimates $S : s^{(0)}, s^{(1)}, \ldots$ and a sequence of control actions $\mu : \mu^{(0)}, \mu^{(1)}, \ldots$.

The sequence of state estimates is generated by a process called *mode estimation* (ME). ME incrementally tracks the set of state trajectories that are consistent with the plant model, the sequence of observations and the control actions. The ME process is framed as an instance of POMDP belief state update, which computes the probability associated with being in state s_i at time $t + 1$ according to the following equations:

$$p^{(\bullet t+1)}[s_i] = \sum_{j=1}^{n} p^{(t\bullet)}[s_j] P_{\mathbb{T}}(\sigma_j \mapsto s_i)$$

$$p^{(t+1\bullet)}[s_i] = p^{(\bullet t+1)}[s_i] \frac{P_O(s_i, o_k)}{\sum_{j=1}^{n} p^{(\bullet t+1)}[s_j] P_O(s_j, o_k)}$$

where $P_{\mathbb{T}}(\sigma_j \mapsto s_i)$ is defined as the probability that M transitions from σ_j to state s_i, and the probability $p^{(\bullet t+1)}[s_i]$ is conditioned on all observations up to $o^{(t)}$, while $p^{(t+1\bullet)}[s_i]$ is also conditioned on the latest observation $o^{(t+1)}$. The tracked state with the highest belief state probability is selected as the most likely state $s^{(t)}$.

The sequence of control actions is generated by a process called *mode reconfiguration* (MR). MR takes as inputs a configuration goal and the most likely current state from ME, and it returns a series of commands that progress the plant towards a least-cost state that achieves the configuration goal. MR accomplishes this through two capabilities, the *goal interpreter* (GI) and *reactive planner* (RP). GI uses the plant model and the most likely current state to determine a reachable target state that achieves the configuration goal, while minimizing cost (or maximizing reward) $R(s)$. RP takes a target state and a current mode estimate, and generates a command sequence that moves the plant to this target. RP generates and executes this sequence one command at a time, using ME to confirm the effects of each command.

Since the size of the set of possible current states is exponential in the number of components, computational resource limitations only allow a small fraction of the state space to be explored in real time. ME tracks the most likely states using the OpSat optimal constraint satisfaction engine[15]. GI also uses OpSat to search for a minimum-cost target state. RP, also called *Burton*[3], is a sound, complete planner that generates a control action of a valid plan in average case constant time.

The deductive controller has been described extensively in [2, 3], in the remainder of this paper we focus on the technical details of the control sequencer.

6   Control Sequencer

The RMPL control program is executed by Titan's control sequencer. Executing a control program involves compiling it to a variant of hierarchical automata, called *hierarchical constraint automata (HCA)*, and then executing the automata in coordination with the deductive controller. In this section, we define HCA, their compilation and execution.

6.1   Hierarchical Constraint Automata

To efficiently execute RMPL programs, we translate each of the constructs introduced in Section 4 into an HCA. In the following we call the "states" of an HCA
locations, to avoid confusion with the physical plant state. An HCA has five key
attributes. First, it composes sets of concurrently operating automata. Second,
each location is labeled with a constraint, called a *goal constraint*, which the
physical plant must immediately begin moving towards, whenever the automaton marks that location. Third, each location is also labeled with a constraint,
called a *maintenance constraint*, which must hold for that location to remain
active. Fourth, automata are arranged in a hierarchy – a location of an automaton may itself be an automaton, which is invoked when marked by its parent.
This enables the initiation and termination of more complex concurrent and sequential behaviors. Finally, each transition may have multiple target locations,
allowing an automaton to have several locations marked simultaneously. This
enables a compact representation for iterative behaviors, like RMPL's **always**
construct.

Hierarchical encodings form the basis for embedded reactive languages like
Esterel[10] and State Charts[11]. A distinctive feature of an HCA is its use of
constraints on plant state, in the form of goal and maintenance constraints. We
elaborate on this point once we introduce HCA.

A *hierarchical, constraint automaton (HCA)* is a tuple $\langle \Sigma, \Theta, \Pi, \mathbb{G}, \mathbb{M}, \mathbb{T} \rangle$,
where:

- Σ is a set of *locations*, partitioned into *primitive locations* Σ_p and *composite locations* Σ_c. Each composite location denotes a hierarchical constraint
  automaton.
- $\Theta \subseteq \Sigma$ is the set of *start locations* (also called the *initial marking*).
- Π is the set of plant state variables, with each $x_i \in \Pi$ ranging over a finite
  domain $\mathbb{D}[x_i]$. $\mathbb{C}[\Pi]$ denotes the set of all finite domain constraints over Π.
- $\mathbb{G} : \Sigma_p \to \mathbb{C}[\Pi]$, associates with each location $\sigma_i^p \in \Sigma_p$ a finite domain
  constraint $\mathbb{G}(\sigma_i^p)$ that the plant progresses towards whenever σ_i^p is marked.
  $\mathbb{G}(\sigma_i^p)$ is called the *goal constraint* of σ_i^p. Goal constraints $\mathbb{G}(\sigma_i^p)$ may be
  thought of as "set points", representing a set of states that the plant must
  evolve towards when σ_i^p is marked.
- $\mathbb{M} : \Sigma \to \mathbb{C}[\Pi]$, associates with each location $\sigma_i \in \Sigma$ a finite domain constraint $\mathbb{M}(\sigma_i)$ that must hold at the current instant for σ_i to be marked.
  $\mathbb{M}(\sigma_i)$ is called the *maintenance constraint* of σ_i. Maintenance constraints
  $\mathbb{M}(\sigma_i)$ may be viewed as representing monitored constraints that must be
  maintained in order for execution to progress towards achieving any goal
  constraints specified within σ_i.
- $\mathbb{T} : \Sigma \times \mathbb{C}[\Pi] \to 2^{\Sigma}$ associates with each location $\sigma_i \in \Sigma$ a transition
  function $\mathbb{T}(\sigma_i)$. Each $\mathbb{T}(\sigma_i) : \mathbb{C}[\Pi] \to 2^{\Sigma}$, specifies a *set* of locations to be
  marked at time $t + 1$, given appropriate assignments to Π at time t.

At any instant t, the "state" of an HCA is the set of marked locations $m^{(t)} \subseteq
\Sigma$, called a *marking*. $\mathfrak{M}$ denotes the set of possible markings, where $\mathfrak{M} \subseteq 2^{\Sigma}$.

In the graphical representation of HCA, primitive locations are represented as circles, while composite locations are represented as rectangles. Goal and maintenance constraints are written within the corresponding locations, with maintenance constraints preceded by the keyword "maintain". Maintenance constraints can be of the form $\models c$ or $\not\models c$, for some $c \in \mathbb{C}[\Pi]$. For convenience, in our diagrams we use c to denote the constraint $\models c$, and $\bar{c}$ to denote the constraint $\not\models c$. Maintenance constraints associated with composite locations are assumed to apply to all subautomata within the composite location. When either a goal or a maintenance constraint is not specified, it is taken to be implicitly **True**.

Transitions are conditioned on constraints that must be entailed by the conjunction of the plant model and the most likely estimated state of the plant. For each location σ, we represent the transition function $\mathbb{T}(\sigma)$ as a set of transition pairs (l_i, σ_i), where $\sigma_i \in \Sigma$, and l_i is a set of labels (also known as *guard conditions*) of the form $\models c$ (denoted c) or $\not\models c$ (denoted $\bar{c}$), for some $c \in \mathbb{C}[\Pi]$. This corresponds to the traditional representation of transitions as labeled arcs in a graph, where σ and σ_i are the source and target of an arc with label l_i. Again, if no label is indicated, it is implicitly **True**.

Our HCA encoding has four properties that distinguish it from the hierarchical automata employed by the above-mentioned reactive embedded languages[10, 11]. First, multiple transitions may be simultaneously traversed. This permits an exceptionally compact encoding of the state of the automaton as a set of markings. Second, transitions are conditioned on what can be deduced from the estimated plant state, not just what is explicitly observed or assigned. This provides a simple, but general, mechanism for reasoning about the plant's hidden state. Third, transitions are enabled based on lack of information. This allows default executions to be pursued in the absence of better information, enabling advanced preemption constructs. Finally, locations assert goal constraints on the plant state. This allows the hidden state of the plant to be controlled directly.

Each RMPL construct maps to an HCA, as shown in Figure 6. For example, the RMPL code for orbital insertion (Figure 4) compiles to the HCA shown in Figure 7.

6.2   Executing HCA

To execute an HCA A, the control sequencer starts with an estimate of the current state of the plant, $s^{(0)}$. It initializes A using $m_F(\Theta(A))$, a function that marks the start locations of A and all subautomata of these start locations. It then repeatedly steps automaton A using the function $Step_{HCA}$, which maps the current state estimate and marking to a next marking and configuration goal. m_F and $Step_{HCA}$ are defined below.

Given a set of automata m to be initialized, $m_F(m)$ creates a *full marking*, by recursively marking the start locations of m and all their starting subautomata: $m_F(m) = m \cup \bigcup \{m_F(\Theta(\sigma)) \mid \sigma \in m, \sigma \text{ is composite}\}$.

$Step_{HCA}$ transitions an automaton A from the current full marking to the next full marking and generates a new configuration goal, based on the current

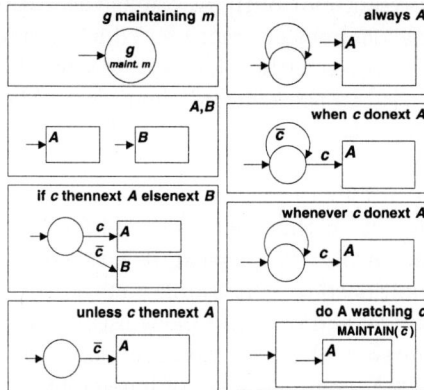

Fig. 6. Corresponding HCA for various RMPL constructs

state estimate. That is, $Step_{HCA}(A, m^{(t)}, s^{(t)}) \rightarrow \langle g^{(t)}, m^{(t+1)}, s^{(t+1)} \rangle$ is defined by the following algorithm:

1. **Check maintenance constraints for marked composites.** Unmark all subautomata of any marked composite location in $m^{(t)}$ whose maintenance constraint is not entailed by $s^{(t)}$.
2. **Setup goal.** Output, as the configuration goal $g^{(t)}$, the conjunction of goal constraints from currently marked primitive locations in $m^{(t)}$ whose maintenance constraints are entailed by $s^{(t)}$.
3. **Take action.** Request that mode reconfiguration issue a command that progresses the plant towards a state s that achieves the configuration goal $g^{(t)}$.
4. **Read next state estimate.** Once the command has been issued, obtain from mode estimation the plant's new most likely state $s^{(t+1)}$.

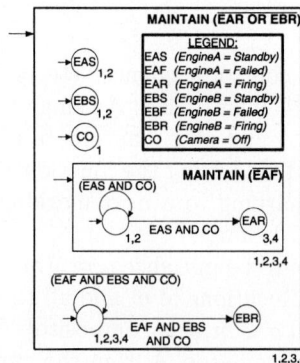

Fig. 7. HCA model for the orbital insertion scenario

5. **Await incomplete goals.** If the goal constraint of a primitive location marked in $m^{(t)}$ is not entailed by $s^{(t+1)}$, and its maintenance constraint was not violated by $s^{(t)}$, then include that location as marked in $m^{(t+1)}$.

6. **Identify enabled transitions.** A transition from a marked primitive location σ_i^p in $m^{(t)}$ is enabled if both of the following conditions hold true:
   (a) σ_i^p's goal constraint is satisfied by $s^{(t+1)}$, or its maintenance constraint was violated by $s^{(t)}$;
   (b) the transition's guard condition is satisfied by $s^{(t+1)}$.
   A transition from a marked composite location σ_i^c in $m^{(t)}$ is enabled if both of the following conditions hold true:
   (a) none of σ_i^c's subautomata are marked in $m^{(t+1)}$ and none of σ_i^c's subautomata have enabled outgoing transitions;
   (b) the transition's guard condition is satisfied by $s^{(t+1)}$.

7. **Take transitions.** Mark and initialize in $m^{(t+1)}$ the target of each enabled transition. Re-mark in $m^{(t+1)}$ all composite locations with subautomata that are marked in $m^{(t+1)}$.

A's execution completes at time τ if $m^{(\tau)}$ is the empty marking, and there is no $t < \tau$ such that $m^{(t)}$ is the empty marking.

6.3   Example: Executing the Orbital Insertion Control Program

The control sequencer interacts tightly with the mode estimation and mode reconfiguration capabilities of the deductive controller, which we demonstrate with a failure-free execution trace for the orbital insertion scenario. Markings for each execution cycle are represented in Figure 7 by the numerical labels associated with each location.

Initial State – Initially, all start locations are marked (locations labeled "1", Figure 7). We assume mode estimation provides initial plant state estimates *EngineA=Off, EngineB=Off, Camera=On.*

Execution will continue as long as the maintenance constraint on the outermost composite location, $\not\models$ *(EngineA=Firing OR EngineB=Firing)*, remains true. It terminates as soon as *(EngineA=Firing OR EngineB=Firing)* is entailed. Similarly, execution of the inner composite location terminates if ever *(EngineA=Failed)* is entailed.

First Step – Since none of the maintenance constraints are violated for the initial state estimate, all start locations remain marked. The goal constraints asserted by the start locations consist of *EngineA=Standby, EngineB=Standby* and *Camera=Off*. These state assignments are conjoined into a configuration goal, and passed to mode reconfiguration. Mode reconfiguration issues the first command in a sequence that achieves the configuration goal. In this example, mode estimation confirms that *Camera=Off* is achieved after a one-step operation.

The locations asserting *(EngineA=Standby)* and *(EngineB=Standby)* remain marked in the next execution step, because these two configuration goals have not yet been achieved. Since *Camera=Off* has been achieved and there are no specified transitions from the primitive location that asserted this state goal, this thread of execution terminates. The other two marked primitives correspond to "**when** ... **donext** ..." expressions in the RMPL control program, they both remain marked in the next execution step, since the only enabled transitions from these locations are self-transitions. The next execution step's marking includes locations labeled with a "2" in Figure 7.

Second Step – The maintenance constraints are confirmed to hold for the current state estimate. Next, the goal constraints of marked locations are collected, *EngineA=Standby* ∧ *EngineB=Standby*, and passed to mode reconfiguration. Mode reconfiguration issues the first command towards achieving this goal.

Assume that a single command is required to set both engines to standby, and that this action is successfully performed. Consequently, mode estimation indicates that the new state estimate includes *(EngineA=Standby)* and *(EngineB=Standby)*. This results in termination of the two execution threads corresponding to these goal constraint assertions. In addition, the transition labeled with condition *(EngineA=Standby AND Camera=Off)* is enabled, and hence traversed. Thus, after taking the enabled transitions, only two of the primitive locations remain marked, as shown by labels "3" in Figure 7.

Remaining Steps – The deductive controller issues and monitors a command sequence, given goal *(EngineA=Firing)*, until a flow of fuel and oxidizer are established, and mode estimation confirms that the engine is indeed firing. Since this violates the outer maintenance condition, the entire block of Figure 7 is exited.

7   Discussion

Titan is implemented in C++. The performance of its deductive controller is documented in [3, 15]. Titan is being demonstrated on the MIT SPHERES mission, and mission scenarios for NASA's ST-7 and MESSENGER missions.

Turning to related work, the model-based programming paradigm synthesizes ideas underlying synchronous programming, concurrent constraint programming, traditional robotic execution and POMDPs. Synchronous programming languages [10, 11] were developed for writing control code for reactive systems. Synchronous programming languages exhibit logical concurrency, orthogonal preemption, multiform time and determinacy, which Berry has convincingly argued are necessary characteristics for reactive programming. RMPL is a synchronous language, and satisfies all these characteristics.

Model-based programming and concurrent constraint programming share common underlying principles, including the notion of computation as deduction over systems of partial information[12, 16]. RMPL extends constraint programming with a paradigm for exposing hidden states, a replacement of the constraint store with a deductive controller, and a unification of constraint-based and Markov modeling. This provides a rich approach to managing discrete processes, uncertainty, failure and repair.

RMPL and Titan also offer many of the goal-directed tasking and monitoring capabilities of AI robotic execution languages, like ESL[17] and RAPS[18]. One key difference is that RMPL's constructs fully cover synchronous programming, hence moving towards a unification of a goal-directed AI executive with its underlying real-time language. In addition, Titan's deductive controller handles a rich set of system models, moving execution languages towards a unification with model-based autonomy.

Acknowledgments

This work was supported in part by the DARPA MOBIES program under contract F33615-00-C-1702, and by NASA's Cross Enterprise Technology Development program under contract NAG2-1466. The authors would like to thank Seung Chung, Paul Elliott, Lorraine Fesq, Vineet Gupta, Michael Pekala, Robert Ragno, Gregory Sullivan, John Van Eepoel, and David Watson.

References

[1] Young, T., *et al.*: Report of the Mars Program Independent Assessment Team. NASA Tech. Rep. (March 2000)

[2] Williams, B. C., Nayak, P.: A Model-Based Approach to Reactive Self-configuring Systems. In: Proceedings of AAAI-96, Vol. 2. AAAI Press, Menlo Park, CA, USA (1996) 971–978

[3] Williams, B. C., Nayak, P.: A Reactive Planner for a Model-Based Executive. In: Proceedings of IJCAI-97, Vol. 2. Morgan Kaufmann, San Francisco, CA, USA (1997) 1178–1185

[4] Ingham, M., Ragno, R., Williams, B. C.: A Reactive Model-Based Programming Language for Robotic Space Explorers. In: Proceedings of ISAIRAS-01. Montreal, Canada (2001)

[5] Chung, S., Van Eepoel, J., Williams, B. C.: Improving Model-Based Mode Estimation Through Offline Compilation. In: Proceedings of ISAIRAS-01. Montreal, Canada (2001)

[6] Kim, P., Williams, B. C., Abramson, M.: Executing Reactive Model-Based Programs Through Graph-Based Temporal Planning. In: Proceedings of IJCAI-01, Vol. 1. Morgan Kaufmann, San Francisco, CA, USA (2001) 487–493

[7] Bernard, D., *et al.*: Design of the Remote Agent Experiment for Spacecraft Autonomy. In: Proceedings of the IEEE Aerospace Conference. Snowmass at Aspen, CO, USA (1999)

[8] Ingham, M., *et al.*: Autonomous Sequencing and Model-Based Fault Protection for Space Interferometry. In: Proceedings of ISAIRAS-01. Montreal, Canada (2001)

[9] Goodrich, C., Kurien, J., Continuous Measurements and Quantitative Constraints - Challenge Problems for Discrete Modeling Techniques. In: Proceedings of ISAIRAS-01. Montreal, Canada (2001)

[10] Berry, G., Gonthier, G.: The Synchronous Programming Language ESTEREL: Design, Semantics, Implementation. Science of Computer Programming, Vol. 19, No.2. (1992) 87–152

[11] Harel, D.: Statecharts: A Visual Formulation for Complex Systems. Science of Computer Programming, Vol. 8, No. 3. (1987) 231–274

[12] Gupta, V., Jagadeesan, R., Saraswat, V.: Models of Concurrent Constraint Programming. In: Proceedings of the International Conference on Concurrency Theory (CONCUR 1996), Lecture Notes in Computer Science, Vol. 1119. Springer-Verlag, Berlin Heidelberg (1996) 66–83

[13] Davis, R.: Diagnostic Reasoning Based on Structure and Behavior. Artificial Intelligence, Vol. 24. (1984) 347–410

[14] Williams, B. C., Chung, S., Gupta, V.: Mode Estimation of Model-Based Programs: Monitoring Systems with Complex Behavior. In: Proceedings of IJCAI-01, Vol. 1. Morgan Kaufmann, San Francisco, CA, USA (2001) 579–590

[15] Williams, B. C., Ragno, R. J.: Conflict-Directed A* and its Role in Model-Based Embedded Systems. To appear: Journal of Discrete Applied Mathematics

[16] Di Pierro, A., Wiklicky, H.: An Operational Semantics for Probabilistic Concurrent Constraint Programming. In: Proceedings of the International Conference on Computer Languages (ICCL 98). IEEE Computer Society Digital Library (1998) 174–183

[17] Gat, E.: ESL: A Language for Supporting Robust Plan Execution in Embedded Autonomous Agents. In: Plan Execution: Problems and Issues. Papers from the 1996 Fall Symposium. AAAI Press, Menlo Park, CA, USA (1996) 59–64

[18] Firby, R. J.: The RAP Language Manual. In: Animate Agent Project Working Note AAP-6, University of Chicago. Chicago, IL, USA (March 1995)

The Adaptive Constraint Engine

Susan L. Epstein[1], Eugene C. Freuder[2], Richard Wallace[2],
Anton Morozov[1], and Bruce Samuels[1]

[1] Department of Computer Science
Hunter College and The Graduate School of The City University of New York,
New York, NY 10021, USA
susan.epstein@hunter.cuny.edu
[2] Cork Constraint Computation Centre, University College Cork
Cork, Ireland
{e.freuder,rwallaceo}@4c.ucc.ie

Abstract. The Adaptive Constraint Engine (ACE) seeks to automate the application of constraint programming expertise and the extraction of domain-specific expertise. Under the aegis of FORR, an architecture for learning and problem-solving, ACE learns search-order heuristics from problem solving experience. This paper describes ACE's approach, as well as new experimental results on specific problem classes. ACE is both a test-bed for CSP research and a discovery environment for new algorithms.

1   Introduction

The Adaptive Constraint Engine (*ACE*) is a program that learns from experience to be a better constraint programmer. A constraint satisfaction problem (*CSP*) involves a set of variables, a *domain* of values for each variable, and a set of *constraints* that specify which combinations of values are allowed. A *solution* to the problem assigns a value to each variable that satisfies all the constraints. Every (binary) CSP has an underlying *constraint graph*, where each variable is represented by a vertex whose possible labels are its domain values. An edge in the constraint graph appears between two vertices whenever there are constraints on the values of their corresponding vertices. One may think of an edge as labeled by the permissible pairs of values between its endpoints. The *degree* of a variable is the number of edges to it in the underlying constraint graph.

Currently, ACE learns search-order heuristics. We supply ACE with a set of primitive methods that characterize variables in the constraint graph, such as maximum domain size, minimum domain size, maximum degree, and minimum degree. These primitives are embedded in procedures called *Advisors* that collaborate on search-order decisions. For example, one Advisor, might recommend "choose the variable with maximum domain size" while another recommends "choose the variable with minimum domain size." As it solves problems, ACE learns which Advisors to value, and how to weight their advice. ACE relies upon an underlying Advisor-based architecture called *FORR* (FOr the Right Reasons), which has proved successful in other domains [1-4]. In an earlier paper, some of us used FORR to construct GC, a graph-

P. Van Hentenryck (Ed.): CP 2002, LNCS 2470, pp. 525-540, 2002.
© Springer-Verlag Berlin Heidelberg 2002

coloring program [5]. Here we extend the approach to general CSP's and incorporate the following advances:

- ACE can combine primitive Advisors to learn new Advisors.
- ACE demonstrates how learning on simple training instances can transfer to difficult test problems.
- ACE can learn different heuristics for different search stages (early, middle, late).
- ACE employs a new weight-learning algorithm.

ACE has demonstrated that it can not only rediscover classic heuristics, but also make new discoveries of equal or greater value. Specifically, ACE has discovered that maximizing the product of degree and forward-degree only in the early stage of search, and simply minimizing domain size thereafter, can be more effective in reducing the size of the search tree than minimizing the ratio of domain size to degree throughout the search. We also demonstrate that lessons learned by ACE can be applied in a more conventional context. In general, ACE provides a powerful testbed for exploring the nature of the search process with much greater ease and subtlety than has been heretofore available. The next section of this paper provides an overview of FORR. Subsequent sections describe ACE, the experimental design and results, and our ability to transfer ACE's discoveries to a more traditional context. The final discussion includes an analysis of our results and plans for future work.

2   FORR

FORR is a problem-solving and learning architecture for the development of expertise from multiple heuristics. To make a decision, FORR combines the output of a set of procedures called Advisors; each Advisor represents a general principle that may support expert behavior [1]. This approach is supported by evidence that people integrate a variety of strategies to accomplish problem solving [2,6,7]. A FORR-based application is constructed for a particular set of related tasks called a *domain*, such as path finding in mazes [3] or game playing [4]. A FORR-based program develops expertise during repeated solution attempts within a *problem class*, a set of problems in its domain (e.g., contests at the same game, or trips with different starting and ending points in the same maze). FORR-based applications often produce expert-level results after learning on as few as 20 problems in a class. Learning is relatively fast because a FORR-based application begins with the pre-specified, domain-specific knowledge of its Advisors.

FORR partitions its Advisors into a hierarchy of tiers, based upon their correctness and the nature of their response. A FORR-based program begins with a set of pre-specified Advisors intended to be *problem-class independent*, that is, relevant to most classes in the domain. Each Advisor represents some domain-specific principle likely to support expert behavior. An Advisor is represented as a time-limited procedure whose input is the current problem state and the legal actions in that state. An Advisor's output is a set of *comments* which indicate how its particular principle evaluates those actions. A comment has the form *<strength, action, Advisor>* where *strength* indicates the degree of support or opposition as an integer in [0, 10]. Comments may vary in their strength, but an Advisor may not comment more than once on any action in the current state.

During execution, a FORR-based application develops expertise for a new problem class as it learns *weights* (described in Section 3.3) to reflect the reliability and utility of Advisors for that particular set of problems. Thus far, ACE learns only from its own problem solving attempts, without examples solved by others. (Our description here does not cover the full scope of the FORR architecture, only those aspects which ACE currently uses. The interested reader can find further details in [8].)

3   ACE

ACE is a FORR-based program for the CSP domain. For ACE, a problem class is the set of problems produced by the generator under a particular set of specifications, as described in Section 4. Within any given class, problems are randomly generated.

3.1   Decision Making in ACE

A problem-solving state for ACE is a partially (or fully) solved CSP. A state description pairs each variable either with an assigned value or with a domain of possible values from which its value will be selected. ACE represents the solution to a CSP as a sequence of steps generated with the following algorithm:

While some variable has no assigned value
  Select an unassigned variable v
  Select a value a *for* v *from the domain of* v
  Assign a *to* v
  For each unassigned neighbor n *of* v
    Remove *any values in the domain of* n *inconsistent with* a
    While any unassigned variable has an empty domain
      Retract *the most recent value assignment*

From this perspective, a CSP on n variables requires at least $2n$ decision steps in its solution: n variable selections alternated with n value selections. Thus an error-free solution path will contain exactly $2n$ steps.

Given this framework, there are four key decision-making processes involved: propagation, retraction, variable selection, and value selection. ACE has a set of procedures to address each process. Propagation is done either with *forward checking*, where the domains of the neighbors (in the constraint graph) of the newly-valued variable are recalculated, based on the constraints from the newly-valued variable, or with *maintained arc consistency* (MAC3), where this process is extended repeatedly to every unassigned variable until no domain changes. Retraction is currently done only with *backtracking*, which returns to a node closer to the root in the search tree, where it retracts the value assignment that caused the empty domain and removes that value from the legal values that variable may subsequently assume in the current state. If necessary, additional variables are automatically "unvalued" as well. With either propagation method plus backtracking, ACE is *complete* (capable of finding a solution). The procedures for variable selection and value selection are represented in ACE by Advisors.

3.2   ACE's Advisors

In a domain with many heuristics, FORR's Advisor hierarchy promotes both efficiency and accuracy. First, *tier 1* isolates rationales expected to be correct from those that are merely heuristic. A FORR-based application begins decision making with a pre-sequenced list of tier-1 Advisors. When a tier-1 Advisor comments positively on an action, no subsequent Advisors are *consulted* (given the opportunity to comment), and the action is executed. When a tier-1 Advisor comments negatively on an action, that action is eliminated from consideration, and no subsequent Advisor may support it. If the set of possible actions is thereby reduced to a single action, that action is executed. ACE has two tier-1 Advisors, Victory and Later. If only one variable remains unvalued and has at least one legal value, *Victory* assigns it a value. If an iteration is for variable selection, *Later* limits that choice to variables whose degree is at least as large as the number of values remaining after propagation. (Although Later is always correct for graph coloring, it is not for general CSP's. We are currently addressing this notion of timing with an approach similar to that of Section 4.3)

Table 1. The concerns underlying ACE's tier-3 Advisors. All concerns are computed dynamically, except where noted. Sources are given where relevant

Concern	Definition
Variable selection	
Degree	Number of neighbors in the constraint graph (static)
Domain	Number of remaining possible values
Forward Degree	Number of unvalued neighbors
Backward Degree	Number of valued neighbors
Domain/Degree	Ratio of domain size to degree
Constraints	Number of constraint pairs on variable [9]
Edges	Edge degree, with preference for the higher/lower degree endpoint (static)
Reverse Edges	Edge degree, with preference for the lower/higher degree endpoint (static)
Dynamic Edges	Edge degree, with preference for the higher/lower degree endpoint
Dynamic Reverse Edges	Edge degree, with preference for the lower/higher degree endpoint
Value selection	
Common Value	Number of variables already assigned this value
Options Value	Number of constraints on selected variable that include this value
Conflicts Value	Resulting domain size of neighbors [10]
Domain Value	Minimal resulting domain size among neighbors [10]
Secondary Options Value	Number of constraints from neighbors to nearly-neighbors
Secondary Value	Number of values among nearly-neighbors
Weighted Domain Size Value	Domain size of neighbors, breaking ties with frequency [10]
Point Domain Size Value	Weighted function of the domain size of the neighbors, a variant on an idea in [10]
Product Domain Value	Product of the domain sizes of the neighbors

Typically with FORR, tier 1 does not identify an action, so control passes to *tier 2*. Tier-2 Advisors plan, and recommend sequences of actions, instead of a single action. (ACE does not yet incorporate tier-2 Advisors; they are a focus of current work.) Finally, if neither tier 1 nor tier 2 produces a decision, control passes to *tier 3*, where most decisions are made. Tier-3 Advisors are heuristic and consulted in parallel. A decision is computed as a weighted combination of their comments in a process called *voting*, described in the next section. The action that receives the most support during voting is executed, with ties broken at random. (ACE uses heuristics to search because the problem space in which it functions is NP-hard. Nonetheless, any solution it produces is complete.)

Each of ACE's tier-3 Advisors encapsulates a single primitive, naive approach to selecting a variable or selecting a value. To generate them, we identified basic properties (*concerns*) and formulated one procedure to minimize each concern and another to maximize it. Thus each concern gives rise to two Advisors. Some concerns were gleaned from the literature, some are common CSP lore, and others were naively hypothesized. For example, one traditional concern is the *degree* of a variable, the number of neighbors it has in the constraint graph. For variable selection, the tier-3 Advisor *Max Degree* supports the selection of unvalued variables in decreasing degree order, with comment strengths from 10 down. Although Max Degree is popular among CSP solvers, we also implemented its dual, *Min Degree*, which comments on variables in increasing degree order. Another example of a concern, this time a naïve one for value selection of an already-chosen variable, is *common value*, the number of variables already assigned this value. *Min Common Value* supports the selection of values less frequently in use; *Max Common Value* is its dual. The full complement of concerns that generate ACE's tier-3 Advisors is detailed in Table 1. There, *edge degree* is the sum of the degrees of the endpoints of an edge, and a *nearly-neighbor* is a variable at distance two in the constraint graph from the variable being assigned a value.

These 19 concerns generate 38 Advisors that correspond naturally to properties of the constraint graph and search tree associated with general CSP's. A skeptical reader might be concerned that, consciously or not, we have somehow "biased" our set of Advisors. Even if that were so, we would respond that it is still up to FORR to learn how to use the Advisors appropriately, and that the ability to incorporate our expertise into the FORR architecture by specifying appropriate Advisors is a feature, not a bug.

3.3   Voting and Weight Learning in ACE

Although a FORR-based program begins with problem-class-independent, tier-3 Advisors, they may not all be of equal significance or reliability in a particular problem class. Therefore, FORR is equipped with a variety of weight-learning algorithms. FORR permits the user to partition each task into *stages*, so that a weight-learning algorithm can learn weights for each stage in the solution process. For now, the number and definition of each stage is pre-specified by the user. The premise behind all weight learning in FORR is that the past reliability of an Advisor is predictive of its future reliability. We used a weight-learning algorithm called DWL in these experiments.

DWL (*Digression-based Weight Learning*) learns problem-class-specific weights for tier-3 Advisors; it is specifically designed to encourage short solution paths. After a problem has been solved successfully, DWL examines the trace of that solution. DWL extracts *training instances*, pairs of the form <*state, decision*>. The intuition behind DWL is suggested by Figure 1, which diagrams the search to a solution. The solid path is the *underlying perfect search path*; it includes exactly $2n$ correct decision steps, represented in Figure 1 as black circles. Those decisions should be maximally reinforced. The remainder of the search consists of *digressions*, subtrees rooted along the solid path, whose roots (represented as white circles in Figure 1) are eventually retracted. A decision at the root of a digression is an error that produces an *over-constrained* (i.e., unsolvable) sub-problem; it should be discouraged. Decisions at all but the root of a digression address an over-constrained problem, and should be reinforced in inverse proportion to the number of steps required to discover that the problem has no solution.

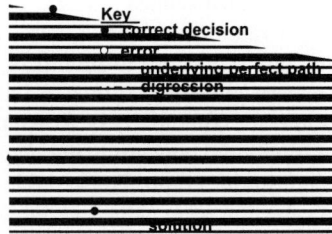

Fig. 1. A search tree for a CSP, as seen by DWL

Under DWL, all pre-specified tier-3 Advisors begin as equally significant. The comments of an often-correct Advisor gradually have more influence during voting, while those of an often-incorrect Advisor are soon overwhelmed. DWL learns weight w_i for Advisor i with the following algorithm:

For all i, $w_i \leftarrow 0.05$
For each training instance <s, d> with state s, decision a, and next state s'
  For each Advisor A_i that produces comments c_i on s
  $d_i \leftarrow d_i + 1$
  If s' was not the root of a digression
    then if c_i supports a, increase w_i else decrease w_i
    else if c_i supports a, decrease w_i else increase w_i

DWL also uses a *discount factor* of 0.1 to introduce each Advisor gradually into the decision process. When ACE makes a decision, tier 3 chooses the action with the greatest support, as follows:

$$\underset{j}{argmax}\left\{\sum_i \omega_i w_i c_{ij}\right\} \text{ where } \begin{cases} d_i = \text{number of opinions } i \text{ has generated.} \\ \omega_i = \begin{cases} 0.1 * d_i \text{ if } d_i < 10. \\ 1 \text{ otherwise.} \end{cases} \\ w_i = \text{weight of Advisor } i. \\ c_{ij} = \text{opinion of consulted Advisor } i \text{ on choice } j. \end{cases}$$

Note that an Advisor must be consulted and comment to figure in this computation. Although all Advisors are consulted during learning, only those that have earned a weight greater than that of *Anything* are consulted during testing. Anything is a non-voting baseline Advisor which comments with randomly-generated strength on n randomly-chosen actions $(0.5)^n$% of the time. Thus DWL fits ACE to correct decisions, learning to what extent each tier-3 Advisor reflects expertise.

3.4   An Example

The following example shows how ACE makes decisions. Figure 2 represents a constraint graph on five variables, each with domain {1, 2, 3, 4, 5}. If D were now assigned the value 3, D's immediate neighbors (A and C) have their own domains reduced: A can now be 1 or 4, while C can be 1 or 2. Under forward checking, ACE does not continue to remove values of variables more distant from D, so B and E would still have 5 possible values each, while A and C would have 2. ACE must now select another variable to value. Since the number of possible values for each of B and E is greater than their respective degrees, the Advisor Later will eliminate B and E from among the possibilities. The remaining unvalued variables, A and C, are then forwarded to the variable-selection Advisors in tier 3. For example, Min Degree would support the selection of variable C with a strength of 10, and the selection of variable A with a strength of 9. (In this simple example, Max Degree would counter those comments exactly. In a larger constraint graph, however, the dual pairs of Advisors typically address different choices.) Similarly, Max Forward Degree would support the selection of variable A, which has 2 unvalued neighbors, with a strength of 10, and variable C, which has one unvalued neighbor, with a strength of 9. ACE tallies the comments on A and C from all the tier-3 Advisors, multiplying each comment's strength by the weight of the Advisor that produced the comment, and then selects the variable with the most support.

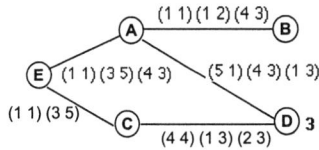

Fig. 2. A partially-valued problem on 5 variables. Edges are labeled by permissible value pairs, in alphabetical order

4   Experimental Design and Results

Because it breaks voting ties at random, ACE is non-deterministic. Its performance is therefore typically judged over a set of r runs. Each *run* consists of a learning phase and a testing phase. In the *learning phase*, the program learns weights while it attempts to solve each of l problems from the specified class. In the *testing phase*, weight-learning is turned off, and the program tries to solve a set of additional problems from the same class. Since ACE can get stuck in a "blind alley," where there are no successes from which to learn, new runs also present fresh opportunities for success. This is actually conservative, as we argue below that one could reasonably utilize the best result from multiple runs.

In all the experiments reported here, ACE used DWL. Rather than assume that selection heuristics are consistently reliable throughout the solution of a problem, we specified three distinct weight-learning stages, determined by the percentage of variables thus far assigned values: *early* (fewer than 20%), *middle* (at least 20% but no more than 80%), and *late* (more than 80%). (This is different from the graph coloring work in [5] which employed only a single stage.) Unless otherwise stated, ACE also used MAC3 for propagation and was permitted no more than s task steps per problem. A *task step* is either the selection of a variable, the selection of a value, or the retraction of a value or a variable. As discussed earlier, a CSP on n variables requires at least $2n$ steps. Data was averaged over 10 runs, each with a learning phase of 80 problems followed by a testing phase of 10 problems.

All problems were produced by a random problem generator available at http://www.cs.unh.edu/ccc/code.html. Although there is no guarantee that any particular set of problems was distinct, given the large size of the problem classes the probability that a testing problem was also a training problem is extremely small. Our generator defines *edge density* as the percentage of possible edges beyond the minimal n-1 necessary to connect the constraint graph on n vertices, and *tightness* as the percentage of possible value pairs that are forbidden by the constraints. When generating problems of a fixed size (number of variables, maximum domain size, and tightness), increasing the density eventually makes it more difficult to find problems with solutions. For example, with 50 variables, domain size 20, and tightness 0.6, no such problems could be generated with density 0.100 in 100 attempts, although they could be generated at density 0.080. We focus our attention here on densities where problems with at least one solution were readily generated. (Those reported upon here are guaranteed to have at least one solution, but ACE can work with over-constrained problems as well.)

Table 2. Performance of an ablated version of ACE under forward checking, averaged over 10 runs in different training environments. All problems had 30 variables, maximum domain size 5, tightness .4, and density .005. Power is percentage of backtrack-free solutions. Time is in seconds per solved problem. Also included are the number of steps in the longest solution during testing, and the percentage of learning problems unsolved due to the step limit

Learning step limit	Power	Time	Checks	Longest testing Solution	Unsolved learning problems
70	13%	.16	145.40	1639	32.38%
80	14%	.12	118.44	717	21.38%
100	18%	.13	167.77	1041	11.50%
200	12%	.17	163.34	2471	5.00%
400	10%	.13	125.41	837	1.25%
800	11%	.12	121.93	511	0.50%
1000	11%	.14	125.68	1035	0.38%

We evaluated ACE on its solutions: by computation time (in seconds), number of retractions (backtracks), and number of constraint checks. (A *constraint check* is a confirmation that a value in the domain of an unassigned variable is still possible given the current assigned values.) Cited differences are significant at the 95% confidence level.

4.1   Step-Limited Learning

The learning phase in a run gleans training instances from successful problem-solving experience, as described in Section 3.3. ACE's learning is, at the moment, *unsupervised*, that is, no outside expert is offering suggestions or corrections. The quality of its training instances is unpredictable — they may be good examples or they may simply have been lucky choices. To function as an expert, however, ACE needs to experience the sorts of decision situations that an expert would confront.

One way to enhance the quality of the training instances is to consider only those from good (i.e., short) solution traces. ACE can either abandon a problem after some fixed number of steps, or work until it is solved. The experiment described here sought to identify the best approach. We used forward checking with a primitive version of ACE that included only the first four concerns from Table 1, so that there would be room for improvement in the program's performance. We then limited the program to $s = 70, 80, 100, 200, 400, 800$, and 1000 steps for learning, but permitted it to work to solution during testing. The results appear in Table 2, where *power* is percentage of backtrack-free solutions. Although their size (30 variables, domain size 5) leaves room for inefficient solutions by naïve solvers, these are sparse problems (density .005, tightness .4), so one would expect an expert to solve them quickly. A perfect solution to such a problem would include 60 steps. Under a 70-step limit, however, ACE did not solve, and therefore could not learn from, nearly a third of the learning problems. Moreover, its performance after learning on the remaining two thirds offered no noteworthy improvement in time or number of constraint checks over higher s values. When the program was given many more than 100 steps in which to solve learning problems, the quality of its testing performance never consistently improved. We have therefore settled on a 100-step learning limit for problems on 30 variables; it is efficient during development and appears to provide examples as good as those from higher or lower limits. During testing, however, we let each program run until it solved the problem.

Table 3. ACE's performance, as averaged over 10 runs. All problems had maximum domain size 8, and tightness .5. Power is percentage of backtrack-free solutions

Variables	Density	Approach	Power	Time	Retractions	Checks
30	.075	Traditional	68%	0.43	0.41	7381.90
30	.075	ACE no learning	87%	0.99	0.19	6323.31
30	.075	ACE learning	70%	0.72	0.60	6884.24
30	.100	Traditional	19%	0.65	3.42	12216.55
30	.100	ACE no learning	61%	1.72	6.40	12945.50
30	.100	ACE learning	81%	0.96	1.24	8476.14
50	.045	Traditional	0%	0.16	3.50	39445.70
50	.045	ACE learning	42%	2.00	3.89	21599.17

4.2   The Value of Learning

The next set of problems, this time for the full version of ACE, all had a larger domain size of 8 and tightness .5. Densities of 0.075 and 0.100 for 30 variables and .045 for

50 variables were examined. For comparison, on 100 problems from each problem class, we also tested both ACE without weight-learning and *Traditional*, which minimizes the ratio of a variable's domain size to its degree and selects values at random [5]. (Traditional simply reduces ACE to a single tier-1 Advisor.)

Table 4. The number of runs during which an ACE tier-3 Advisor was active during early (1), middle (2), and late (3) stage testing on the last two problem sets in Table 3. Particularly consistent Advisors appear in bold, those that are significant without their dual appear in italics, and those that are infrequently relevant appear in parentheses

Advisor	n = 30			n = 50		
	1	2	3	1	2	3
Variable concerns						
Max Backward Degree		10	10		10	10
(Min Backward Degree)				2		
Max Constraints	10		2	10		
Max Degree	10	10	10	10	10	10
Min Domain	7	10	10	10	10	10
Min Domain/Degree	10	10	10	10	10	10
Max Dynamic Edges	10		7	10		
Max Dynamic Reverse Edges			7			10
Max Forward Degree	10		4	10		
Min Forward Degree			6			10
Max Reverse Edges	10	5	9	10		
Value concerns						
Max Common Value	3	7	4	1	8	8
Min Common Value	10	6	6	9	7	2
Max Conflicts Value		2	5		4	4
Min Conflicts Value	10	8	5	9	6	6
Max Domain Value	10	8	5	10	6	6
Min Domain Value		2	5		4	4
Max Options Value	10	8	5	9	6	6
Min Options Value		2	5		4	4
Max Point Domain Size Value		2	5		4	4
Min Point Domain Size Value	10	8	5	10	6	6
Max Product Domain Value	10	8	5	10	6	6
Min Product Domain Value		2	5		4	4
Max Secondary Options Value	10	8	5	10	6	6
Min Secondary Options Value		2	5		4	4
Max Secondary Value	10	8	5	10	6	6
Min Secondary Value		2	5		4	4
Max Weighted Domain Size Value	10	8	5	10	7	6
Min Weighted Domain Size Value	10	2	5	10	5	4

The results, in Table 3, show that weight learning substantially improved performance on the two more difficult sets of problems. With learning, ACE solved those test problems with fewer constraint checks, and in less time. ACE requires more elapsed time than Traditional because its decision calculation is more complex: it must compute the opinions of many Advisors, combine them with their current weights, and tally the results. The resultant decisions, however, are more likely to be correct, that is, not retracted later.

Recall that an Advisor active during testing is one whose weight has demonstrated that it consistently performs better than random advice (Anything). For each class, the Advisors that ACE relied on during testing appear in Table 4, along with the number of runs (out of 10) where their weight in a stage qualified them for use during testing. Together with their weights, the Advisors of Table 4 could be construed as an algorithm for variable selection and value selection within the problem class. Note that although every concern is represented in Table 4, 9 Advisors are absent. According to Table 4, both an Advisor and its dual (e.g., Max and Min Weighted Domain Size Value) can be relevant in a stage; it is the extremity of the concern, rather than its value, that is significant. Some Advisors, such as Max Constraints, are relevant only in a single stage. Others, such as Max Dynamic Edges, are relevant only early and late in problem solving, and not in the middle. Still others, such as Max Degree, appear consistently relevant. The active Advisors also display much greater consistency in the early stage of problem solving. Finally, there appear to be more heuristics that are consistently reliable in all stages for variable selection than there are for value selection.

It is interesting to compare ACE's learned weights with the performance predicted in the literature for some of these concerns. Min Domain/Degree [11] is confirmed as valuable in all problem-solving stages. Min Point Domain Size Value is confirmed for early and middle-stage solving, but relevant only about half the time for late-stage solving. Contrary to prediction, however, the Constraints concern functions well only in the early period, and as a maximum, not as a minimum. This may turn out to be a peculiarity of this class of problems, but one of ACE's advantages is that it automates the process of adapting heuristic processing to specific problem classes.

4.3   Learning New Advisors

Given a language in which to express them, FORR can learn new tier-3 Advisors [12]. Min Domain/Degree led us to wonder about the efficacy of other arithmetic combinations of concerns. We therefore formulated an *arithmetic variable language* in which an Advisor's concern would be either the product or the quotient of a pair of variable-selection concerns. (Sums and differences proved weaker in early testing and were eliminated.) Each expression in this language is of the form:

$$<function_1, function_2, attitude, stage>$$

where stage is early, middle, or late (as defined in Section 3.3), the two functions are any pair of distinct concerns (such as those in Table 1), and *attitude* is one of the following: maximize $function_1$* $function_2$, minimize $function_1$* $function_2$, maximize $function_1/ function_2$, and minimize $function_1/ function_2$.

To learn new Advisors within a language, FORR monitors how each possible expression would perform at problem solving. During weight learning, each expression is given the opportunity to comment on training instances from the underlying perfect search path, as if it were a tier-3 Advisor. For each expression, FORR tallies each attitude's frequency (number of times it discriminates) and accuracy (number of times it is correct) for each stage.

During problem solving, each expression in a language is either potential, active, spawned, or inactive. Initially, all expressions are *potential*, monitored for possible inclusion in decision making. After every t tasks ($t = 10$ here), FORR reevaluates each expression's status. Those that fail to discriminate or never comment are eventually made *inactive*, to speed subsequent computation. Potential expressions with an attitude that has been accurate at least 85% of the time are promoted to *active* status. Active expressions provide input to their language's *summary Advisor*, which combines their comments to structure its own. Once an active expression has tallied 95% accurate, it is *spawned*, that is, transformed into an individual Advisor, and the expression no longer participates in the summary Advisor's computation. Both the summary Advisor and the spawned Advisors are subject to the discount factor discussed in Section 3.3, so that they enter the decision process gradually. This permits ACE to maintain its performance level as it introduces new Advisors.

In our first experiment with learning new Advisors, we formulated a simple language for the concerns Domain, Degree, Forward Degree, and Backward Degree. As described earlier, each expression combined a pair of these concerns (e.g., Domain and Degree) and considered four computations on them: minimize their product, maximize their product, minimize their quotient, or maximize their quotient. We then removed the Domain/Degree concern from ACE's list in Table 1 (*ACE*–), and had ACE learn on 30 variables, maximum domain size 8, tightness .4, density .100. For comparison we also tested ACE– alone, and *MDD*, a program with Min Domain/Degree as its only Advisor.

Table 5. Performance of a variety of programs, with and without the ability to learn tier-3 Advisors. MDD is the program with Min Domain/Degree as its only Advisor. ACE– is the program without the Domain/Degree concern. The learning Advisors approach is an ablated version of ACE, as described in the text

Approach	Concerns	Power	Time	Retractions	Checks
MDD	—	19%	0.69	3.42	12216.55
ACE	all	81%	0.96	1.24	8476.14
ACE–	all but MDD	80%	0.96	1.17	8152.18
Learn Advisors	4 variable	80%	1.04	1.34	8048.66

The results, in Table 5, were startling. ACE outperformed MDD, as expected, but so did ACE–, suggesting that the Min Domain/Degree heuristic might not make a necessary contribution, despite its high weight. Indeed there was no statistically significant difference between ACE and ACE– along any metric. Furthermore, when ACE was permitted to learn new Advisors in a language capable of expressing Min Domain/Degree (the last line in Table 5), the expression for Min Domain/Degree never became active even once in 10 runs. Instead, on every run, exactly one expression ever became active, the same one every time: "maximize the product of degree and forward degree in the early stage." With this single learned Advisor, the learning-Advisors version of ACE performed just as well as ACE and as ACE–.

4.4   Learning Transfer

We have confirmed, outside of ACE and on fairly hard problems, that when the new "maximize the product of degree and forward degree" heuristic is used at the top of the search tree, subsequent use of Min Domain/Degree is comparable to the use of domain size alone. To accomplish this, we incorporated the new heuristic into a CSP algorithm coded in a conventional manner, and tested it on reasonably difficult 150-variable problems.

Our results, in Table 6, are significant for several reasons. They demonstrate that:

- Lessons learned with ACE can be transferred to a conventional algorithmic context.
- Lessons learned on easy problems can be relevant to hard problems.
- Our conventional understanding of search-order heuristics may be overly simplistic.

Table 6. Performance results in nodes per problem for MAC3 and three conventional heuristics, with and without the product heuristic learned by ACE. Data is averaged over 10 runs using code separate from ACE. Problems had 150 variables, domain size 5, density .05, and tightness .24

Conventional heuristic	Alone	Enhanced heuristic
Min domain (MD)	86,065	3,218
MDD	4,277	3,218
MD after degree preorder	12,602	3,218

Our initial tests ran three conventional heuristics: min domain (MD), min (domain/degree) (MDD), and MD after first ordering the variables by descending degree. Then we repeated the same tests, this time replacing the conventional heuristic by min (degree * forward-degree) in the top fifth of the search tree. It is admittedly odd that all the latter tests averaged to the same (rounded off) search tree size, but the top of the tree appears so dominant that, in most cases, the same nodes get visited, albeit in a different order. With this approach, the search tree is actually somewhat reduced, while processing time slightly increases due to the dynamic calculation of forward degree.

In general, the importance of the processing at the top of the search tree is not surprising, but ACE allows us to make progress on turning "folklore" (what you do at the top of the search tree is more important than what you do at the bottom) into science (or, at least, into engineering). The fact that domain size, the conventional bedrock of variable ordering, can be ignored at the critical top of the search tree is surprising, at least at first blush. On reflection it would seem to make perfect sense that domain size would be less critical at the top of the tree, before propagation from search choices has as much chance to effect domain size reduction, while forward degree would be critical at the top of the tree, where it is going to be relatively large, and help to determine the amount of propagation. ACE can inspire us to pose and help us to further evaluate such hypotheses.

5   Discussion

A traditional CSP heuristic for variable ordering uses secondary heuristics to break ties, or combines a few heuristics in crude mathematical combinations. The few attempts to automate the construction of constraint solvers, including Laurière's pioneering work, have thus far either tried to select a single method or tried to invent a special-purpose algorithm [13-17]. In contrast, ACE permits us to order such advice in a more flexible and subtle manner.

In experiments on a variety of problems, ACE regularly identifies heuristics previously considered essential by constraint researchers in a general CSP context: Min Domain, Max Degree, Min Domain/Degree, and Max Backward Degree. In particular, for ordinary CSP's, ACE has confirmed the importance of minimal domain size, often employed individually by constraint researchers in a general CSP context, as a variable ordering heuristic. ACE indicates, however, that in the early stage, when fewer than 20% of the variables have been valued, Min Domain is not necessarily productive.

With Advisor learning, ACE permits thorough empirical investigation not only of individual heuristics, but of combinations of them as well. ACE's ability both to confirm conventional wisdom and to provide further analysis is enticing. The emphasis on maximizing backward degree, for example, is puzzling until one realizes that, since these problems are so sparse, maximizing backward degree may push a significant number of degree-one variables to the end of the search, where forward checking will have ensured that they can be instantiated without any backtracking. This raises a further puzzle as to why minimizing backward degree does not figure prominently in the late stage; but then one realizes that this could risk switching over too early. Maximizing backward degree will do the "right "thing up to and including the time when the maximum backward degree is one, whenever that occurs. All this begins to seem awfully clever of ACE, though, of course, "clever" is not really the operative word here; the currently popular "emergent" may be more appropriate.

In general, ACE is able not only to "rediscover" useful heuristics, but also to explore more sophisticated combinations and timing patterns in applying these heuristics than an individual experimenter could easily consider. In this manner ACE can not only support but also instigate research. Our work with Domain/Degree in Section 4.3 is a good example.

To build ACE we did not have to tune FORR's learning parameters. The discount factor of 0.1 has been traditional in FORR, as have the initial Advisor weight of 0.05 and the constants employed in learning new Advisors (discussed in Section 4.3). The proportion of Anything's comments was devised to make few comments more likely than a single one, and again is standard in FORR. Only the stage designations (set rather arbitrarily at 20% and 80%) are new; in previous FORR-based, non-CSP applications there were only two stages, with 15% in the early stage.

Our current research plans include extension to over-constrained problems, as well as to other, more concrete classes of CSP's. We are also investigating a variety of propagation and retraction methods, and actively solicit empirically-validated suggestions for new Advisors from the CSP community. Furthermore, we are working to make stage designation more flexible, and to incorporate other weight learning algorithms, as well as planning Advisors for tier 2.

In summary, ACE is intended to become a comprehensive architecture for acquiring and controlling collaborative and adaptive constraint solving methods. It will establish a taxonomy of Advisors, from very problem-dependent to very general, languages in which to express them, and ways to combine them effectively. ACE should eventually be able to acquire uncodified expertise, to uncover new techniques, and to discover useful new solvers for specific classes of CSP's. In short, ACE is both a CSP-solver and a partner in CSP research.

Acknowledgements

We thank Francesca Rossi and Alessandro Sperduti for suggestions that led to DWL. We also thank the anonymous referees for their constructive suggestions. Eugene Freuder is supported by a Principal Investigator Award from Science Foundation Ireland.

References

1. Epstein, S. L.: For the Right Reasons: The FORR Architecture for Learning in a Skill Domain. Cognitive Science 18 (1994) 479-511
2. Ratterman, M. J. and Epstein, S. L.: Skilled like a Person: A Comparison of Human and Computer Game Playing. In Proceedings of Seventeenth Annual Conference of the Cognitive Science Society. Lawrence Erlbaum Associates, Pittsburgh (1995) 709-714
3. Epstein, S. L.: On Heuristic Reasoning, Reactivity, and Search. In Proceedings of Fourteenth International Joint Conference on Artificial Intelligence. Morgan Kaufmann, Montreal (1995) 454-461
4. Epstein, S. L.: Prior Knowledge Strengthens Learning to Control Search in Weak Theory Domains. International Journal of Intelligent Systems 7 (1992) 547-586
5. Epstein, S. L. and Freuder, G. Collaborative Learning for Constraint Solving. In: Walsh, T. (ed.): Principles and Practice of Constraint Programming – CP2001. Vol. 2239. Springer Verlag, Seattle WA (2001) 46-60
6. Biswas, G., Goldman, S., Fisher, D., Bhuva, B. and Glewwe, G. Assessing Design Activity in Complex CMOS Circuit Design. In: Nichols, P., Chipman, S. and Brennan, R. (eds.): Cognitively Diagnostic Assessment. Vol. Lawrence Erlbaum, Hillsdale, NJ (1995)
7. Crowley, K. and Siegler, R. S.: Flexible Strategy Use in Young Children's Tic-Tac-Toe. Cognitive Science 17 (1993) 531-561
8. Epstein, S. L.: Pragmatic Navigation: Reactivity, Heuristics, and Search. Artificial Intelligence 100 (1998) 275-322
9. Kiziltan, Z., Flener, P. and Hnich, B.: Towards Inferring Labelling Heuristics for CSP Application Domains. In Proceedings of KI'01. Springer-Verlag, (2001)
10. Frost and Dechter, R.: Look-ahead value ordering for constraint satisfaction problems. In Proceedings of IJCAI-95. Montreal (1995) 572-578
11. Bessiere, C. and Regin, J.-C. MAC and combined heuristics: Two reasons to forsake FC (and CBJ?) on hard problems. In: Freuder, E. C. (ed.): Principles and Practice of Constraint Programming - CP96, LNCS 1118. Vol. Springer-Verlag, (1996) 61-75
12. Epstein, S. L., Gelfand, J. and Lock, E. T.: Learning Game-Specific Spatially-Oriented Heuristics. Constraints 3 (1998) 239-253
13. Borrett, J., Tsang, E. P. K. and Walsh, N. R.: Adaptive constraint satisfaction: the quickest first principle. In Proceedings of 12th European Conference on AI. Budapest, Hungary (1996) 160-164

14.   Caseau, Y., Laburthe, F. and Silverstein, G. A Meta-Heuristic Factory for Vehicle Routing Problems. In: Principles and Practice of Constraint Programming – CP'99. Vol. LNCS 1713. Springer, Berlin (1999)
15.   Minton, S.: Automatically Configuring Constraint Satisfaction Programs: A Case Study. Constraints 1 (1996) 7-43
16.   Smith, D. R. KIDS: A Knowledge-based Software Development System. In: Lowry, M. R. and McCartney, R. D. (eds.): Automating Software Design. Vol. AAAI Press, (1991)
17.   Laurière, J. L.: ALICE: A Language and a Program for Solving Combinatorial Problems. Artificial Intelligence 10 (1978) 29-127

Indexical-Based Solver Learning

Thi Bich Hanh Dao, Arnaud Lallouet, Andrei Legtchenko, and Lionel Martin

Université d'Orléans — LIFO
BP 6759 — F-45067 Orléans cedex 2

Abstract. The pioneering works of Apt and Monfroy, and Abdennadher and Rigotti have shown that the construction of rule-based solvers can be automated using machine learning techniques. Both works implement the solver as a set of CHRs. But many solvers use the more specialized chaotic iteration of operators as operational semantics and not CHR's rewriting semantics. In this paper, we first define a language-independent framework for operator learning and then we apply it to the learning of partial arc-consistency operators for a subset of the indexical language of Gnu-Prolog and show the effectiveness of our approach by two implementations. On tested examples, Gnu-Prolog solvers are learned from their original constraints and powerful propagators are found for user-defined constraints.

Keywords: CSP; consistency; learning; rule-based constraint solver.

1 Introduction

Building a constraint solver is a notoriously complex task [12, 18, 16] and it has been recently demonstrated that — at least some parts of — this design can be automated by systematic search [4] or by using machine learning techniques [1, 2]. An automatic tool to generate solvers may help the solver designer by giving him a first implementation and letting him concentrate on non-trivial optimization. But it is also useful to the user who may, with little experience, develop a global constraint ad-hoc to his problem and get for free a propagator for it. We provide in this paper a formal framework to define finite domain solver learning and we propose a learning method which fits in this framework.

An efficient technique for computing consistencies in Constraint Satisfaction Problems (CSPs) is to use a data representation for the CSP and a set of operators whose common fixed-point models the expected consistency. The operators are then applied via chaotic iteration [13, 3] until reaching their common fixed-point. But solvers differ in the way they represent these operators: they can be written in the implementation language [18, 16] or in a higher-level language such as indexicals [21]. An indexical operator is written "X in r" where X is the name of a variable, and r is an expression which limits the range of possible values for X and which may depend on other variables' current domains. For example, the constraint $and(X, Y, Z)$, defined by the following table, yields three indexical operators, one for each variable:

P. Van Hentenryck (Ed.): CP 2002, LNCS 2470, pp. 541–555, 2002.
© Springer-Verlag Berlin Heidelberg 2002

X	Y	Z
0	0	0
0	1	0
1	0	0
1	1	1

and :

Gnu-Prolog indexicals:

```
X in min(Z) .. max(Z)*max(Y)+1-min(Y)
Y in min(Z) .. max(Z)*max(X)+1-min(X)
Z in min(X)*min(Y) .. max(X)*max(Y)
```

It is obvious that the expression for Z depending on X and Y is simple and intuitive whereas the expression for X depending on Y and Z is not. Building manually such expressions for arbitrary constraints is undoubtedly a challenge.

In this paper, we propose a framework to define the learning of such operators in three steps. We consider that a CSP is a set of n-ary constraints.

1. We define a notion of *semantic approximation* of a CSP, which consists in replacing the original problem by an approximate one, from the point of view of the data-structure and the solutions. For a CSP C composed of several n-ary constraints, its approximation K uses different, usually simpler constraints (for example, the domain of each variable), and the notion of solution is replaced by the weaker one of consistency. Operators are introduced to transform these CSPs and their closure defines a consistent state. A similar though more general framework is the one of [7] for semiring-based CSPs.
2. We define a notion of *syntactic approximation*. The choice of a representation language, both for the data and the operators, is of crucial importance since the language may not allow to represent all possible data or operators. This defines a second level of approximation but also a concrete representation. For example, intervals are a data representation for variable domains and indexicals for operators.
3. It is then possible to define a learning space of all possible operators and check the fitness of each candidate operator towards the definition of the constraint. Operator learning consists in an exploration of this learning space to look for the best candidate.

We propose a learning technique and two implementations of indexical operator learning specialized to the context of the partial arc-consistency of Gnu-Prolog [11] which consists in contracting the bounds of the variables domain, represented as intervals. The learned operator can be intuitively thought as the summary of the best possible reductions done by the constraint on every possible interval which could be encountered during the solving process.

The paper is organized as follows. In section 2, preliminaries on CSP solving are given. In section 3, we present our approximation framework, from which the learning problem is derived. In section 4, we specialize our framework for the learning of indexicals for partial arc-consistency and we present the language biases we used. Section 5 is devoted to the implementations and section 6 gives an illustration with some examples.

2   Preliminaries

Let V be a set of variables and $D = (D_X)_{X \in V}$ their domains. The domains we consider are finite and totally ordered sets. For $W \subseteq V$, we denote by D^W the set of tuples on W, namely $\Pi_{X \in W} D_X$. Therefore, we have $D^V = \Pi D$. Projection of a tuple or a set of tuples on a set of variables is denoted by $|$, natural join of two sets of tuples is denoted by $\bowtie$.

Definition 1 (Constraint).   *A constraint c is a pair (W, T) where*

- *$W \subseteq V$ is the* arity *of the constraint c and is denoted by $var(c)$.*
- *$T \subseteq D^W$ is the* solution *of c and is denoted by $sol(c)$.*

Definition 2 (Approximation ordering).   *A constraint $c' = (W', T')$ approximates $c = (W, T)$, denoted by $c \subseteq c'$, if $var(c') = var(c)$ and $sol(c) \subseteq sol(c')$.*

The join of two constraints is defined as a natural extension of the join of tuples: the *join* of c and c' is the constraint $c \bowtie c' = (var(c) \cup var(c'), sol(c) \bowtie sol(c'))$.

Definition 3 (CSP).   *A CSP is a set of constraints.*

Join is naturally extended to CSPs and a CSP C is identified to be the join of its constraints $\bowtie C$. This defines the *solutions* of the CSP. A direct computation of this join is too expensive to be tractable. This is why various methods have been considered so far to compute the solutions of a CSP. We present here a short description of some of them for a comparison with other works (the presentation order is not significant):

- *search methods*: basically, it amounts to try values for the variables and test the constraints for satisfiability. Almost all other methods are hybridized with search to get completeness.
- *symbolic transformations*: by this, we refer to a variety of syntactic transformations of the constraints in order to obtain a solved form, for example in the $CLP(\mathcal{R})$ [15] system. A further level of abstraction comes with the CHR language [14] which allows to describe rewriting-based solvers in a simple and versatile way. For example, here is a possible rule in the CHR language to simplify a boolean store:
$$\texttt{and(X,Y,Z)} \land \texttt{Z=1} \iff \texttt{X=1} \land \texttt{Y=1} \land \texttt{Z=1}$$
In our vision, the main characteristics of this language is that it uses first-order variables, or in other terms, that a variable represents an element of the domain.
- *approximations*: to be solved, constraints are represented not only by their syntactic form but also extensionally by their solutions. A state is an over-approximating CSP and transitions from a CSP to a smaller one are represented by correct, monotonic and contracting operators which are iterated until reaching a property called *consistency*. The contracting operators are most of the time written in the solver's implementation language (C++ for

Ilog Solver [18], Claire for The Choco System [16], ...) and this is probably the reason why this formalism is often perceived as only implementation-relevant.

There is however an exception with the "indexicals" language introduced in [21] and used in the Gnu-Prolog system [9, 11] or in the Sicstus Prolog system [8]. In this framework, variables are second-order and designate constraints instead of domain elements. It allows the description of operators of the form "X in r" where X represents the domain of the variable, "in" is the set inclusion and r is an expression of some set language. We believe that this paradigm is more general than it seems since it is parametrized by the language of r. This paradigm deserves further research since there is still no formalism having the same generality and expressive power to define indexical operators as the CHR formalism for the symbolic transformation point of view. A step towards this goal may be the so-called delay clauses of B-Prolog [23]. Indeed, the choice of the "r" language is of particular importance in a learning perspective.

– *other methods*: various other methods have been tackled to solve CSPs (see for example [20]).

3   A Model of Approximation for CSPs

In this section, we present a high-level model for the approximation made by consistency adapted from the more general framework of [7]. This set-theoretic formulation allows to describe very precisely the approximation process in a language-independent way. The basic idea is to clearly separate the CSP to be solved from its approximation (and more generally from the sequence of approximating CSPs).

3.1   Semantic Approximations

Let C be a CSP over a set of variables V. Since a CSP is somehow identified with its join constraint $\bowtie C$, it can be approximated by a CSP K over the same set of variables V and such that $\bowtie C \subseteq \bowtie K$. In this case and by extension, we write $C \subseteq K$.

Intuitively, the CSP K is intended to be physically represented, for example (but not exclusively) by sets of tuples. This is why C and K may be built on completely different constraints. When all constraints in K are unary, and thus represent the domain of variables, it yields to the well-known "domain reduction scheme" used in most solvers. We call K the *approximating* CSP. Here is an example of two different approximating CSPs:

Example 4. Let C be the CSP composed of one constraint: $c = (\{X, Y, Z\}, \{(0,0,0), (0,0,1), (0,1,0), (1,0,1)\})$. Here are two approximating CSPs $K_1 = \{x, y, z\}$ and $K_2 = \{x, yz\}$ which are represented in figure 1. Here $x = (\{X\}, \{(0), (1)\})$ is an unary constraint representing the domain of X and $yz = (\{Y, Z\},$

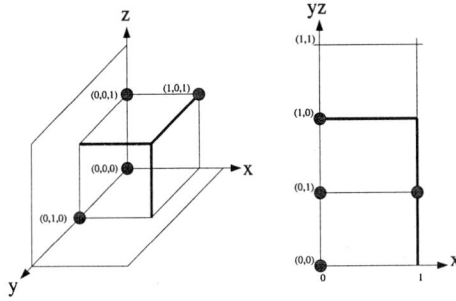

Fig. 1. Two different approximations for a CSP

$\{(0,0), (0,1), (1,0)\})$ is an arbitrary binary constraint. The constraints y and z are defined in the same straightforward way.

Most of the time, switching from C to K provides a gain in terms of memory consumption. For example, in the domain reduction approximation for n variables and a domain of size m, it boils down from m^n to $m * n$. But the trade-off is that representable approximations are less precise since they are limited to (the union of) cartesian products.

In the rest of the paper, C denotes the CSP to be solved, and K its approximating CSP. Moreover, we only use the domain reduction scheme. This means that the approximating CSP K is always composed of one unary constraint x for each variable $X \in var(C)$ (a lowercase letter designates the constraint while an uppercase designates the variable). Since our goal is to find the best approximation (in some sense), we call an approximating CSP K a *search state* and the set of such states is the *search space* $S = \Pi_{X \in V}\mathcal{P}(D_X)$. For $W \subseteq V$, we denote by $S_W = \Pi_{X \in W}\mathcal{P}(D_X)$ the search space restricted to W, hence $S = S_V$. We just indicate that this framework can be extended to approximations made with constraints of arbitrary arity but domain approximations help to keep simplicity to the notations.

3.2   Consistencies

In order to reach a certain degree of precision, approximations have to be refined: a sequence of over-approximating CSPs $(K_i)_{i \in \mathbb{N}}$ such that $\forall i \geq 0, K_i \supseteq K_{i+1}$ is built, until reaching a closure called *consistency*. Transitions between states are computed by operators. The nature of the operators determines the consistency and they are supposed to be correct, monotonic and contractant [3].

Example 5 (Projection operator).   Let $c = (W, T)$ and $X \in W$. The projection $c_X : S_{W-\{X\}} \rightarrow \mathcal{P}(D_X)$ is defined by $c_X(s) = \{t_X \in D_X \mid t \in T \text{ and } t|_{W-\{X\}} \in s\}$. Suitably extended to S in order to be an operator, it is used for arc-consistency.

A set of operators is associated to the CSP and is iterated until reaching their common closure. This is often done by chaotic iteration [13, 3]. We are concerned in this paper with the learning of such operators in the particular case of partial arc-consistency used for example in Gnu-Prolog. Variable domains are represented only as intervals and thus only their bounds are contracted. Usually, to each constraint is associated an operator for each variable it contains. Let R be the set of reduction operators for a CSP C. We write $R \downarrow K$ the closure of K by the operators of R, i.e., the greatest CSP $K' \subseteq K$ such that $\forall r \in R, K' = r(K')$. A search state K is R-consistent if $K = R \downarrow K$.

3.3 Correctness and Completeness

Correctness for an operator r means that no solution is lost, or in other terms, that $C \subseteq K \Longrightarrow C \subseteq r(K)$. This is a strongly needed property since an incorrect solver may discard a solution forever. Completeness, however, is not a required property at the operator's level since this is achieved by the search mechanism.

But often solvers require the operators to be *singleton complete*, i.e., complete only for singletons. Let us define this notion:

Definition 6 (Singletonic CSP).
An approximating CSP K is singletonic if $\forall k \in K, |sol(k)| = 1$.

Intuitively, a singletonic CSP K on the set of variables V represents a tuple of D^V, a potential solution of the CSP C.

Definition 7 (Singleton Completeness).
Let C be a CSP and R its associated set of operators. The set R is singleton complete if for any singletonic CSP K, we have

$$K \not\subseteq C \Longrightarrow |sol(R \downarrow K)| = 0$$

This means that a non-solution tuple must be rejected by (at least) *one* operator. On the other side, correctness for singletonic CSPs means that a tuple is solution if accepted by *all* operators.

Singleton completeness is the basis of the compilation scheme of Gnu-Prolog since the (high-level) constraints such as $X = Y + Z$ are replaced by an "equivalent" formulation in the indexical language. However, the compilation can be effective only if the operators are able to distinguish between a solution and a non-solution, at least at the tuple level. Operationally, it means that, when dealing with a candidate solution, the consistency check can be realized by the propagation mechanism itself. But an important remark is that singleton completeness is a global property and is thus highly complex to check for an arbitrary set of operators because two non-solution tuples may be rejected by two different operators. In contrast, correctness check for an operator remains a local verification which only involves this operator.

3.4   Syntactic Approximations: Intervals and Indexicals

The above formalism is language-independent but we still need to represent the domains and operators since learning is impossible without a representation. First, intervals are chosen for domain representation for their low space cost. This notion of approximation, different than consistency, comes from interval analysis and is presented for example in [3] where it is based on a family of subsets. This is an approximation of the domain while the consistency defines an approximation of the solutions. It defines the representable subsets of a variable's domain.

The indexical language introduced in [21] and used in Gnu-Prolog [11] and Sicstus Prolog [8] is a convenient language to define operators. An operator is expressed by a second-order constraint $x \subseteq r$ where x is a constraint of the approximating CSP K and r a constraint expression in a given language. Since we consider that all constraints in K are unary, the evaluation of r is a "range", i.e., another monadic constraint.

Example 8. For example, the high-level constraint X #= Y+C is compiled for partial arc-consistency by Gnu-Prolog into two indexical operators:

X in min(Y)+C .. max(Y)+C   and   Y in min(X)-C .. max(X)-C

For full arc-consistency, the same constraint is compiled to:

X in dom(Y)+C   and   Y in dom(X)-C

A subset of the Gnu-Prolog indexical language is given in figure 2.

c ::=	X in r	
r ::=	t_1 .. t_2	(interval)
	{ t }	(singleton)
	r_1 : r_2	(union)
	r_1 & r_2	(intersection)
t ::=	min(Y)	(indexical term *min*)
	max(Y)	(indexical term *max*)
	ct	(constant term)
	t_1+t_2 | t_1-t_2 | t_1*t_2 | t_1/$^<t_2$ | t_1/$^>t_2$	(integer operations)
ct ::=	n | infinity	(values)
	ct_1+ct_2 | ct_1-ct_2 | ct_1*ct_2 | ct_1/$^<ct_2$ | ct_1/$^>ct_2$	

Fig. 2. A subset of Gnu-Prolog indexical language

Yet, since the Gnu-Prolog indexical language does not contain conditional expressions, the formulation of some operators may be operationally inefficient. This is why Gnu-Prolog implements an ad-hoc delay mechanism by the syntax val(X) which represents the same value as dom(X) but delays until X is instanciated. It is the only guard of the language.

4   Description of the Learning Problem

In this section, we present the example space, the learning space and the learning algorithm. Semantic approximations of CSPs are a vast framework and many choices have to be made. Here we present as restrictions the main choices we made to get a tractable learning problem.

Let $c = (W, T) \in C$ be a constraint. The exact projection function c_X of c on a variable $X \in W$ has been defined in example 5. Our goal is to learn a function L_X^c which mimics the behavior of c_X and is at least correct. This means that $\forall s \in S_{var(c)-\{X\}}, L_X^c(s) \supseteq c_X(s)$. But we also want to be the closest possible to the projection function since the constant function $s \mapsto D_X$ is correct but useless.

Definition 9 (Example Set).   *The function c_X, or equivalently the set of pairs $Ex(c, X) = \{(s, c_X(s)) \mid s \in S_{var(c)-\{X\}}\}$ is called the* example set *for L_X^c.*

Learning is often made from an incomplete set of examples, and a part of the learning process consists in finding a suitable generalization. In solver learning, a missing example may yield an incorrect behavior, which contradicts the most crucially expected solver property.

Restriction 1 Since we want to get correct operators, we use the whole example set in the learning process.

The size of this example set is $2^{\Sigma_{X \in var(c)} |D_X|}$, which is in general far too large to be completely traversed. In contrast, the interval space has a size in $O(\Pi_{X \in var(c)} |D_X|^2)$. In order to shrink the search space, arbitrary subsets can be "rounded" to their next including interval.

Restriction 2 We compute with intervals.

Nevertheless, the output of an operator could be any subset. In order to further reduce the learning space, we set the following language bias:

Restriction 3 The output of the learned operator is a single interval.

Because of this restriction, the operator L_X^c is expressed in the indexical language by its minimal and maximal bounds $minL_X^c$ and $maxL_X^c$, which are arithmetic expressions not involving X. Note that the power of indexicals is not fully used but also that it is sufficient to represent the partial arc-consistency used in Gnu-Prolog.

Now we make these restrictions more formal in order to define the example set really used in the learning process. First, interval lattices are a particular case of lattice approximations:

Definition 10 (Lattice Approximation).   *Let E be a set and P a sub-lattice of $\mathcal{P}(E)$ such that $\emptyset \in P$ and $E \in P$. For $e \in \mathcal{P}(E)$, we define:*

$$up_P(e) = \inf\{p \in P \mid e \subseteq p\}$$

Let Int_X be the interval lattice of D_X. In order to define the input of the function to be learned, we need to define the search space in which the computation takes place. It consists of a unique interval for each variable. For $W \subseteq V$, let $Int_W = \Pi_{Y \in W} Int_Y$. The interval approximation can be extended to cartesian products by $up_{Int_W} : S_W \to Int_W$ defined by:

$$s \mapsto \Pi_{Y \in W}\ up_{Int_Y}(s_Y)$$

We denote by $[s]$ this interval approximation of s. Note that the approximation domain Int_W is omitted since there is no possible confusion. By computing in the interval lattice, we preserve the correctness:

Proposition 11.

$$\forall s \in S_{var(c)-\{X\}},\ c_X(s) \subseteq c_X([s])$$

Proof. By monotony of c_X.

Definition 12 (Approximate Example Set).
The approximate example set *for L_X^c is given by the function*

$$Ex^{Int}(c, X) : Int_{var(c)-\{X\}} \to Int_X$$

such that
$$Ex^{Int}(c, X)(s) = [c_X(s)]$$

The bounds of L_X^c can be learned separately from a separate example set. For example, for $minL_X^c$, the example set is given by the function $Int_{var(c)-\{X\}} \to \mathbb{N}$ defined by $s \mapsto min([c_X(s)])$. In the following, we focus on $minL_X^c$, but the other bound is obtained by the same method.

Now, we cannot be more precise without introducing a language to express operators. The remaining problem is to find a suitable expression in the sub-grammar of terms and constant terms (entries t and ct in figure 2) which mimics as closely as possible the behavior of the function $min([c_X(s)])$. In order to limit the complexity of the learning process, we use the following language bias. Since the sum is present in the language, our technique consists in fixing the general form of the function to be learned to a linear combinaison of terms, each one being expressed without the addition. Let $\mathcal{L}_1 = \{min(Y), max(Y) \mid Y \in W$ and $Y \neq X\}$, $\mathcal{L}_2 = \{t_1 * t_2 \mid t_1, t_2 \in \mathcal{L}_1\}$ and $\mathcal{L} = \mathcal{L}_1 \cup \mathcal{L}_2$.
Then we can express $minL_X^c$ as the following linear form:

$$minL_x^c = \Sigma_{w \in \mathcal{L}}\ \alpha_w * w + \alpha_0$$

The last part of the learning algorithm consists in finding the coefficients α_w, in order to meet the correction constraints. For each example s, the value of $minL_X^c(s)$ is correct if lesser or equal than the real value $min([c_X(s)])$.

In contrast, completeness cannot be ensured the same way because it would sometimes prevent the system to have a solution. Singleton completeness, which is not a local property, cannot be expressed at this level. Our approach consists in finding the most complete function in a certain sense, by minimizing a quality function for each candidate. We tried different quality functions and the results are presented in the next section. A typical quality function is to minimize the global error between the candidate and the real value. Hence we get the following linear program:

`minimize:`

$$\Sigma_{s \in Int_{var(c)-\{X\}}} \ min([c_X(s)]) - minL_X^c(s)$$

`subject to:`

$$\forall s \in Int_{var(c)-\{X\}} , \quad minL_X^c(s) \leq min([c_X(s)])$$

The correctness of the algorithm is ensured by construction.

One may wonder if the restrictions we made and the biases we used do not yield a too much restricted framework. Here are some answers:

- The formalism of semantic approximations we use is very general and allows us to test many hypotheses. Indeed, with our definition of semantic approximation, all kinds of consistencies can be formalized in a language independent way. However, indexicals are high-level enough to easily allow the handling of the many syntactic transformations necessary to the learning process.
- The results we present in section 6 show that the operators learned are of good quality. In particular on regular constraints, we are able to find the classical operators of Gnu-Prolog. On arbitrary constraints, we still obtain a good pruning power.
- The choices we made present a good balance between the complexity of the learning task and the size of the explored search space. In particular, the use of a strong language bias is a common feature in machine learning [22].
- The complete construction of a solver may probably not be fully automatic. But a collection of learning tools with different techniques and algorithms may be of great help. We rather think of these tools as being part of a solver design environment.

5   Implementations

We have built two systems implementing this framework. A first system handles constraints of arbitrary arity, uses the simplex algorithm and yields X in r in the form described above (a linear combinaison of elements of $\mathcal{L}$). The second one handles only binary constraints, uses a genetic algorithm, and proposes three different (but still fixed) forms of operators.

5.1 The Simplex Learner

The principle of this implementation is to solve the previous linear programming problem with the simplex algorithm: the simplex learner is a C program which calls the solver lp_solve[1].

The command-line user interface allows mainly to build minimal and maximal bounds for each variable with basic simplifications and to compute reductions obtained with these bounds.

5.2 The Genetic Learner: GA-ILearner

This second implementation uses genetic algorithms to improve the quality of a population of candidate solutions. This C++ application has a graphic interface which allows the user to "draw" his constraint with the mouse. The user constraint appears on screen as red dots (see figure 3). Only binary constraints are allowed in order to be representable on screen, but variable domains range up to 50×50. The user can learn the bounds of the functions separately, or specify them manually. Three fixed forms of functions are proposed for each bound: linear $(X_{min} = A * min(Y) + B * max(Y) + C)$, rational $(X_{min} = \frac{A}{min(Y)+1} + \frac{B}{max(Y)+1} + C)$ and quadratic $(X_{min} = A * min(Y)^2 + B * max(Y)^2 + C * min(Y) * max(Y) + D * min(Y) + E * max(Y) + F)$. An example of rational approximation is given in figure 3. The singletons which are

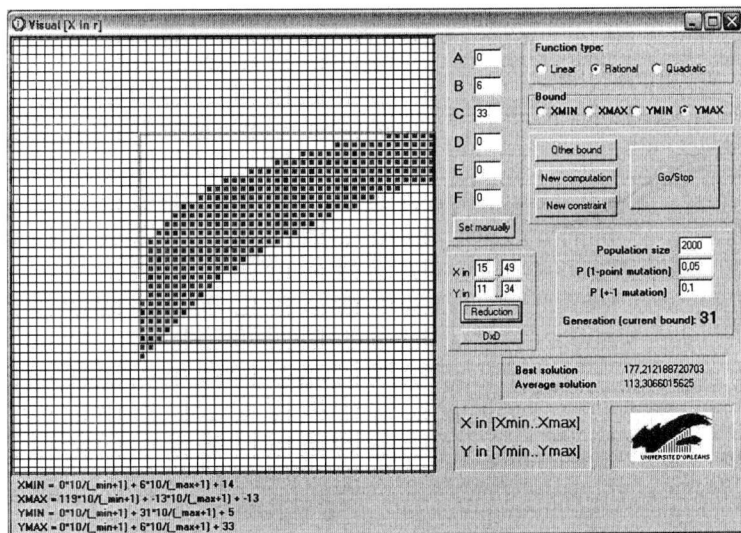

Fig. 3. Rational approximation of a cloud

---

[1] ftp://ftp.es.ele.tue.nl/pub/lp_solve ©

and$_3$:

X_0	X_1	X_2
0	0	0
0	0.5	0
0	1	0

X_0	X_1	X_2
0.5	0	0
0.5	0.5	0.5
0.5	1	0.5

X_0	X_1	X_2
1	0	0
1	0.5	0.5
1	1	1

Fig. 4. The constraint and$_3$

accepted by the indexicals appear on screen as grey dots. The user may then specify a domain, which appears as a red box, and visualize the reduced domain yield by his indexicals, which appears as a green box (in figure 3, the user box is $[0..49] \times [0..49]$ and the reduced domain is given by the inner box). Since the learned indexicals may not be monotonic, the reduced interval may be smaller than the singleton solutions. Sufficient conditions for the indexicals to be monotonic can be obtained with syntactic biases. However, correctness with respect to the constraint's solutions is ensured by construction. Singleton completeness is difficult (and sometimes impossible) to ensure. We tried a greedy algorithm to generate new indexicals from the non-covered examples but this does not solve all the cases.

The construction of the indexical is left to a genetic algorithm in which individuals are a sequence of bits representing the coefficients. The quality function is inversely proportional to the square of the error between the candidate and the example set. We tried as definition of error the simple sum of the individual errors on each intervals and the sum of individual errors relative to the size of the interval. Incorrect individuals are strongly penalized. Surprisingly, these notions of error, besides the complexity of their evaluation, exhibit a relatively flat search space with very deep and narrow local minimas. This sometimes causes a slow convergence of the population, which is usually of a few seconds.

6   Examples

We present in this section some examples of learned indexicals, illustrated by reductions using them. The results we present in this section have been obtained with the simplex implementation. First, we mention that the same indexicals as Gnu-Prolog are found for ordinary boolean constraints such as *And*, *Or* or *Xor*.

Three-valued logic.   Variables in three-valued logic can have one of the values 1, 0 and 0.5, which stand for true, false and unknown respectively. We present here the And$_3$ constraint defined in figure 4. From this constraint our algorithm generates the following indexicals:

```
X0 in [ Min(X2) ..   1.00 -   Min(X1)*Min(X1) + Min(X1)*Max(X2) ]
X1 in [ Min(X2) ..   1.00 -   Min(X0)*Min(X0) + Min(X0)*Max(X2) ]
X2 in [ Min(X0)*Min(X1) ..   Max(X0) - Max(X0)*Max(X0) + Max(X0)*Max(X1) ]
```

The reduction with $X_0 = 0$, $X_1 \in [0, 1]$ and $X_2 = 0.5$ gives:

```
X0 in [ 0.50 .. 0.00 ],  X1 in [ 0.50 .. 1.00 ],  X2 in [ 0.50 .. 0.00 ]
```

We notice that the first and the third indexicals represent the empty interval, which mean that all elements whose $X_0 = 0$ and $X_2 = 0.5$ are rejected by these indexicals. When $X_2 = 0.5$, these indexicals imply that X_0 and X_1 must not be 0, and when $X_2 = 1$, then X_0 and X_1 must be 1. These results are computed by the generated indexicals.

Other examples.   A more complete set of examples and experimentations can be found in [6]. For example, we found indexical expressions for the "full adder" constraint `fulladder(X0,X1,X2,X3,X4)` meaning $X_0 + X_1 + X_2 = 2 * X_3 + X_4$ or for the equivalence `equiv3(X0,X1,X2)` in three-valued logic among others.

An interesting point is that the propagator built by the system makes a user-defined constraint behave as an ad-hoc global constraint. Experiments have been made on the all-different constraint for the arity 3 and 4. The pruning power lies between the naive implementation as differences and a specialized implementation [19].

Integration in Gnu-Prolog.   When singleton complete indexicals are found, they can be fruitfully integrated in Gnu-Prolog, thus making a propagator for a user-defined global constraint. The main advantage is that the learned indexicals can replace the original indexicals generated by Gnu-Prolog in its compilation process. Moreover, since a global constraint replaces several atomic constraints and since Gnu-Prolog breaks long expressions into smaller ones, the result is that less indexicals have to be scheduled, yielding an increased propagation speed.

For example, for the constraint $0 \leq X - Y \leq 4$, our system generates the two following indexicals: `X in min(Y) .. max(Y)+4` and `Y in min(X)-4 .. max(X)`. In Gnu-Prolog, this constraint has to be written as two constraints $0 \leq X - Y$ and $X - Y \leq 4$, yielding 4 indexicals. Our test consists in trying all possible reductions for the intervals with bounds in $[0..20]$ for both variables. On a laptop Pentium III-m 1GHz, 256 Mb, the time of our indexicals is $35.0s$ while Gnu-Prolog's one is $36.8s$. There is only a difference of two indexicals on this example, hence we can expect better results for more complex expressions. As a comparison, the use of Gnu-Prolog's built-in predicate `fd_relation` with the set of tuples satisfying the constraint leads to a time of $193.9s$. This shows the utility of the method in the general case.

7   Conclusion

Related work.   Solver learning is an emerging technique which was pioneered by Apt and Monfroy in [4, 5] and Abdennadher and Rigotti [1, 2].

In [4] and [5], very simple rules of the form $x_1 = s_1, \ldots, x_n = s_n \rightarrow y \neq a$ are at first considered. They provide a notion of consistency weaker than arc-consistency. Then these rules are extended by replacing equality by membership to achieve arc-consistency. The learning algorithm generates every rule to check its validity, and redundant rules are eliminated. This framework is language-independent, but the rules have a very restrictive form.

The work of [1] extends the language issue to the far more expressive framework of CHRs. The PROPMINER algorithm consists in an exploration of a user-restricted learning space for the rule's lefthand side and a computation of the righthand side, leading to the choice of the best covering rules. In [2], this work has been extended to handle prolog-like definition of constraints. This work is based on CHR and its rewriting semantics. We propose in contrast to define lower-lovel operators which yield in general faster solvers. CHRs subsume indexicals in term of expressivity (and indexicals can be mimicked by CHRs) but their execution mechanism is different. In addition, our learning algorithm is not related to PROPMINER, which is mostly syntactic. Instead, it is rather closer to the learning of arithmetic functions for which a difficulty is the lack of suitable generalisation ordering on the hypothese space.

Other formalisms compute upper bounds at run-time, such as Generalized Constraint Propagation [17], or Constructive Disjuction [21, 10], but are not designed to statically build a solver.

Summary.   In this paper we have presented a general framework of semantic approximations for finite domains CSPs. We applied this framework to the learning of indexical operators [21, 10] which are at the core of the Gnu-Prolog system [11] and built two learning tools. The first one handles constraints of arbitrary arity and uses the simplex algorithm as optimization tool. The second is restricted to binary constraints but proposes a graphical user interface which allows the user to draw his constraint and to visualize the learned expressions. It uses internally a genetic algorithm to achieve the optimization. On regular constraints, such as arithmetic or boolean constraints, Gnu-Prolog indexicals are found. On user-defined constraints, the generated operators are of good quality in term of pruning power.

Acknowledgements

This work has benefited from discussion with Michel Bergère, AbdelAli Ed-Dbali, Gérard Ferrand and Christel Vrain.

References

[1] S. Abdennadher and C. Rigotti. Automatic generation of propagation rules for finite domains. In Rina Dechter, editor, *Constraint Programming*, volume 1894 of *LNCS*, pages 18–34, Singapore, 2000. Springer.

[2] S. Abdennadher and C. Rigotti. Towards inductive constraint solving. In Toby Walsh, editor, *Constraint Programming*, volume 2239 of *LNCS*, pages 31–45. Springer, Nov 26 - Dec 1 2001.

[3] K. R. Apt. The essence of constraint propagation. *Theoretical Computer Science*, 221(1-2):179–210, 1999.

[4] K. R. Apt and E. Monfroy. Automatic generation of constraint propagation algorithms for small finite domains. In *Constraint Programming CP'99*, 1999.

[5] K. R. Apt and E. Monfroy. Constraint programming viewed as rule-based programming. *Theory and Practice of Logic Programming*, 1(6):713 – 750, 2001.

[6] Michel Bergère, Thi Bich Hanh Dao, AbdelAli Ed-Dbali, Gérard Ferrand, Arnaud Lallouet, Andrei Legtchenko, Lionel Martin, and Christel Vrain. Learning interval bounds of indexical-based solvers. Research Report RR-LIFO-2002-07, LIFO, Université d'Orléans, BP 6759, F-45067 Orléans Cedex 2, 2002.

[7] Stephano Bistarelli, Ugo Montanari, and Francesca Rossi. Semiring-based constraint satisfaction and optimization. *Journal of the ACM*, 44(2):201–236, March 1997.

[8] Mats Carlsson, Greger Ottosson, and Björ Carlson. An open-ended finite domain constraint solver. In Hugh Glaser, Pieter H. Hartel, and Herbert Kuchen, editors, *Programming Languages: Implementations, Logics, and Programs*, volume 1292 of *LNCS*, pages 191–206, Southampton, UK, September 3-5 1997. Springer.

[9] Philippe Codognet and Daniel Diaz. A minimal extension of the wam for clp(fd). In David Scott Warren, editor, *International Conference on Logic Programming*, pages 774–790, Budapest, Hungary, June 21-25 1993. MIT Press.

[10] Philippe Codognet and Daniel Diaz. Compiling constraints in clp(fd). *Journal of Logic Programming*, 27(3):185–226, 1996.

[11] Daniel Diaz and Philippe Codognet. Design and implementation of the gnu prolog system. *Journal of Functional and Logic Programming*, 2001(6), 2001.

[12] Mehmet Dincbas, P. Van Hentenryck, H. Simonis, A. Aggoun, and A. Herold. The CHIP System: Constraint Handling in Prolog. In Ewing Lusk and Ross Overbeek, editors, *9th International Conference on Automated Deduction*, Argonne, May 1988. Springer.

[13] François Fages, Julian Fowler, and Thierry Sola. Experiments in reactive constraint logic programming. *Journal of Logic Programming*, 37(1-3):185–212, 1998.

[14] Thom Früwirth. Theory and practice of Constraint Handling Rules. *Journal of Logic Programming*, 37(1-3):95–138, 1998.

[15] Joxan Jaffar, Spiro Michaylov, Peter J. Stuckey, and Roland H. C. Yap. The *CLP(R)* language and system. *ACM Transactions on Programming Languages and Systems*, 14(3):339–395, 1992.

[16] François Laburthe and the OCRE project. Choco: implementing a CP kernel. In *TRICS, Techniques foR Implementing Constraint programming Systems, CP 2000 post-conference workshop*, Technical report TRA9/00, Singapore, sep 2000.

[17] Thierry Le Provost and Mark Wallace. Generalized constraint propagation over the CLP Scheme. *Journal of Logic Programming*, 16:319–359, 1993.

[18] Jean-Francois Puget and Michel Leconte. Beyond the glass box: Constraints as objects. In John W. Lloyd, editor, *International Logic Programming Symposium*, pages 513–527, Portland, Oregon, 1995. MIT Press.

[19] Jean-Charles Régin. A filtering algorithm for constraints of difference in csps. In *AAAI, National Conference on Artificial Intelligence*, pages 362–367, Seattle, WA, USA,, 1994. AAAI Press.

[20] Edward Tsang. *Foundations of Constraint Satisfaction*. Academic Press, 1993.

[21] P. van Hentenryck, V. Saraswat, and Y. Deville. Constraint processing in cc(fd). draft, 1991.

[22] V. N. Vapnik. *The Nature of Statistical Learning Theory*. Springer, New York, 1995.

[23] Neng-Fa Zhou. A high-level intermediate language and the algorithms for compiling finite-domain constraints. In Joxan Jaffar, editor, *Joint International Conference and Symposium on Logic Programming*, pages 70–84, Manchester, UK, 15-19 June 1998. MIT Press.

Learning the Empirical Hardness of Optimization Problems:
The Case of Combinatorial Auctions

Kevin Leyton-Brown, Eugene Nudelman, and Yoav Shoham*

Computer Science Department, Stanford University
Stanford CA 94305
{kevinlb;eugnud;shoham}@cs.stanford.edu

Abstract. We propose a new approach for understanding the algorithm-specific empirical hardness of $\mathcal{NP}$-Hard problems. In this work we focus on the empirical hardness of the winner determination problem—an optimization problem arising in combinatorial auctions—when solved by ILOG's CPLEX software. We consider nine widely-used problem distributions and sample randomly from a continuum of parameter settings for each distribution. We identify a large number of distribution-nonspecific features of data instances and use statistical regression techniques to learn, evaluate and interpret a function from these features to the predicted hardness of an instance.

1   Introduction

It is no secret that particular instances of $\mathcal{NP}$-Hard problems can be quite easy to solve in practice. In recent years researchers in the constraint programming and artificial intelligence communities have studied the *empirical* hardness of individual instances or distributions of $\mathcal{NP}$-Hard problems, and have often managed to find simple mathematical relationships between features of the problem instances and the hardness of the problem. The majority of this work has focused on decision problems: that is, problems that ask a yes/no question of the form, "Does there exist a solution meeting the given constraints?". The most successful approach for understanding the empirical hardness of such problems—taken for example in [3, 1]—is to vary some parameter of the input looking for a hard-easy-hard transition corresponding to a phase transition in the solvability of the problem. This approach uncovered the famous result that 3-SAT instances are hardest when the ratio of clauses to variables is about 4.3; it has also been applied to other decision problems such as quasigroup completion [7]. Another approach rests on a notion of backbone [17, 1], which is the set of solution invariants.

---

* We would like to acknowledge contributions by Rámon Béjar, Carla Gomes, Henry Kautz, Bart Selman, Lyle Ungar and Ioannis Vetsikas.

P. Van Hentenryck (Ed.): CP 2002, LNCS 2470, pp. 556–572, 2002.

1.1   Empirical Hardness of Optimization Problems

Some researchers have also examined the empirical hardness of optimization problems, which ask a real-numbered question of the form, "What is the best solution meeting the given constraints?". These problems are clearly different from decision problems, since they always have solutions and hence cannot give rise to phase transitions in solvability. One way of finding hardness transitions related to optimization problems is to transform them into decision problems of the form, "Does there exist a solution with the value of the objective function $\geq$ x?" This approach has yielded promising results when applied to MAX-SAT and TSP. Other experimentally-oriented work includes the extension of the concept of backbone to optimization problems [24], although it is often difficult to define for arbitrary problems and can be costly to compute.

A second approach is to attack the problem analytically rather than experimentally. For example, Zhang performed average case theoretical analysis of particular classes of search algorithms [25]. Though his results rely on independence assumptions about the branching factor and heuristic performance at each node of the search tree that do not generally hold, the approach has made theoretical contributions—describing a polynomial/exponential-time transition in average-case complexity—and shed light on real-world problems. Korf and Reid predict the average number of nodes expanded by a simple heuristic search algorithm such as A* on a particular problem class by making use of the distribution of heuristic values in the problem space [14]. As above, strong assumptions are required: e.g., that the branching factor is constant and node-independent, and that edge costs are uniform throughout the tree.

Both experimental and theoretical approaches have sets of problems to which they are not well suited. Existing experimental techniques have trouble when problems have high-dimensional parameter spaces, as it is impractical to manually explore the space of all relations between parameters in search of a phase transition or some other predictor of an instance's hardness. This trouble is compounded when many different data distributions exist for a problem, each with its own set of parameters. Theoretical approaches are also difficult when the input distribution is complex or is otherwise hard to characterize, but they also have other weaknesses. They tend to become intractable when applied to complex algorithms, or to problems with variable and interdependent edge costs and branching factors. Furthermore, they are generally unsuited to making predictions about the empirical hardness of individual problem instances, instead concentrating on average (or worst-case) performance on a class of instances.

1.2   Our Methodology

Some optimization problems do not invite study by existing experimental *or* theoretical approaches: problems characterized by a large number of apparently relevant features, the existence of many, highly parameterized distributions, significant variation in edge costs throughout the search tree and the desirability of predicting the empirical hardness of individual problem instances.[1] We propose a novel experimental approach for predicting the running time of a given algorithm on individual instances of such a problem, drawn from one of many different distributions. Our methodology follows:

1. An optimization algorithm is selected.
2. A set of problem instance distributions is selected. For each parameter of each distribution a range of acceptable values is established.
3. Problem size is defined and a size is chosen. Problem size will be held constant to focus on unknown sources of hardness.
4. A set of polytime-computable, distribution-independent features is selected.
5. To generate instances, a distribution is chosen at random and then the range of acceptable values for each parameter is sampled. This step is repeated until the desired number of problem instances have been generated.
6. For each problem instance the running time of the optimization algorithm is determined, and all features are computed.
7. Redundant or uninformative features are eliminated.
8. A function of the features is learned to predict running time (or some other measure of empirical hardness), and prediction error is analyzed.

The application of machine learning to the prediction of running time has received some recent study (see, eg., [12]); however, there is no other work of which we are aware that uses such an approach primarily in order to understand the empirical hardness of an $\mathcal{NP}$-Hard problem. Although our methodology applies to the broad class of problems described above, for concreteness we concentrate on one widely-studied problem that exemplifies the class. The winner determination problem (WDP) is a constraint programming optimization problem associated with combinatorial auctions. It has often been observed that WDP algorithms vary by many orders of magnitude in their running times for different problems of the same size—even for different instances drawn from the same distribution. However, little is known about what causes WDP instances to differ in their empirical hardness. Understanding what characteristics of data instances are predictive of long running times would be useful for predicting how long an auction will take to clear, tuning data distributions for hardness, constructing algorithm portfolios, designing package bidding rules to reduce the chances of long clearing times and possibly for improving the design of WDP algorithms.

1.3   Overview

In section 2 we give an introduction to combinatorial auctions in general, and previous work on the WDP in particular. We then survey nine of the most widely-studied combinatorial auction data distributions in section 3. (Because of space limitations we give the range of acceptable values we chose for each distribution on our website.) In section 4 we discuss holding the problem size

---

[1] We observe that these characteristics are not unique to optimization problems, but in this paper we limit our discussion to optimization.

constant in order to concentrate on unknown sources of hardness; in section 5 we describe our 25 distribution-independent features. Finally, our experimental results and analysis are presented in section 6.

2   Combinatorial Auctions

Combinatorial auctions have received considerable attention in computer science over the past several years because they provide a general framework for allocation and decision-making problems among self-interested agents: agents may bid for bundles of goods, with the guarantee that these bundles will be allocated "all-or-nothing". These auctions are particularly useful in cases where agents consider some goods to be *complementary*, which means that an agent's valuation for some bundle exceeds the sum of its valuation for the goods contained in the bundle. They may also allow agents to specify that they consider some goods to be *substitutable*, e.g., agents can state XOR constraints between bids, indicating that at most one of these bids may be satisfied.

2.1   Combinatorial Auction Winner Determination

The winner determination problem (WDP) is choosing the subset of bids that maximizes the seller's revenue, subject to the constraint that each good can be allocated at most once. A WDP instance consists of a set of bids: bid i is made up of a bundle of goods denoted b_i and a price offer p_i. If a set of bids are joined by an XOR constraint, the constraint is represented through the addition of a "dummy good" which is included in b_i. (A dummy good is an artificial good that exists only to enforce an XOR constraint; see [6].) The WDP may be formulated as an integer program, where indicator variables x_i encode the inclusion or exclusion of each bid i from the allocation:

$$\text{maximize:} \quad \sum_i x_i p_i$$

$$\text{subject to:} \quad \sum_{i|g\in b_i} x_i \leq 1 \qquad \forall g$$

$$x_i \in \{0,1\} \qquad \forall i$$

Although this problem is equivalent to weighted set-packing and is therefore $\mathcal{NP}$-Hard, there are cases where it is important to solve the WDP to optimality. There has been much discussion of the application of the Vickrey-Clarke-Groves mechanism to combinatorial auctions (e.g., a good survey of combinatorial auction research is [4]). This economic mechanism requires that a provably-optimal solution to the WDP be provided. Parkes and Ungar [19], among others, have proposed ascending auction mechanisms that also require provably-optimal solutions to the WDP. Also, it is known that the WDP is inapproximable within any constant factor: cf. [21].

Much recent work has concerned algorithms for solving the WDP to optimality. A very influential early paper was [20], but it focused on tractable subcases of the problem and addressed computational approaches to the general WDP only briefly. The first algorithms designed specifically for the general WDP were published at IJCAI-99 [6, 21]; these authors improved and extended upon their algorithms in [16, 22]. Other influential algorithmic work on the general WDP is [18, 8].

More recently, researchers have converged towards solving the WDP with branch-and-bound search, using a linear-programming relaxation of the problem as a heuristic. There has thus been increasing interest in the use of ILOG's CPLEX software to solve the WDP, particularly since the mixed integer programming module in that package improved substantially in version 6 (released 2000), and again in version 7 (released 2001). In version 7.1 this off-the-shelf software has reached the point where it is competitive with the best special purpose software, Sandholm's CABOB [22]. Indeed, CABOB makes use of CPLEX's linear programming package as a subroutine and uses branch-and-bound search. The combinatorial auction research community has thus seen convergence towards branch-and-bound search in general, and CPLEX in particular, as the preferred approach to optimally solving the WDP. In this paper we selected CPLEX 7.1 as our WDP algorithm.

3   Artificial Data Distributions

3.1   Legacy Data Distributions

The wealth of research into algorithms for solving the WDP has created a need for many instances on which to test these algorithms. Since to date computational hurdles have made real-world data scarce, researchers have generally turned to artificial distributions for the evaluation of WDP algorithms. Along with the first wave of algorithms for the WDP, seven distributions were proposed in [21, 6, 11] that have been widely used by other researchers including many of those cited above. Each of these distributions may be seen as an answer to two questions: what number of goods to request in a bundle, and what price to offer for a bundle. Given a required *number* of goods, all distributions select *which* goods to include in a bid uniformly at random without replacement. The following methods are used to select the number of goods in a bundle:

- **Uniform:** Uniformly distributed on $[1, num\_goods]$
- **Normal:** Normally distributed with $\mu = \mu_g$ and $\sigma = \sigma_g$
- **Constant:** Fixed at $constant\_goods$
- **Decay:** Starting with 1, increment the size of the bundle until $rand(0,1) > \alpha$
- **Binomial:** Request n goods with probability
  $p^n (1-p)^{num\_goods-n} C(num\_goods, n)$
- **Exponential:** Request n goods with probability $Ce^{-n/q}$

The following methods are used to select a price offer:

- **Fixed Random:** Uniform on $[low, hi]$
- **Linear Random:** Uniform on $[low \cdot n, hi \cdot n]$
- **Normal:** Draw from a normal distribution with $\mu = \mu_p$ and $\sigma = \sigma_p$

The seven legacy distributions follow:

- **[L1]** *Sandholm*: Uniform; Fixed Random: $low = 0$, $hi = 1$
- **[L2]** *Sandholm*: Uniform; Linear Random: $low = 0$, $hi = 1$
- **[L3]** *Sandholm*: Constant: $constant\_goods = 3$; Fixed Random: $low = 0$, $hi = 1$
- **[L4]** *Sandholm*: Decay: $\alpha = 0.55$; Linear Random: $low = 0$, $hi = 1$
- **[L5]** *Boutilier et al.*: Normal: $\mu_g = 4$, $\sigma_g = 1$; Normal: $\mu_p = 16$, $\sigma_p = 3$
- **[L6]** *Fujishima et al.*: Exponential: $q = 5$; Linear Random: $low = 0.5$, $hi = 1.5$
- **[L7]** *Fujishima et al.*: Binomial: $p = 0.2$; Linear Random: $low = 0.5$, $hi = 1.5$

3.2   CATS Distributions

Subsequent research has exposed a variety of problems with these legacy distributions: see, for example, [2, 4, 15]. Broadly, these concerns may be divided into challenges to the realism of these distributions as a model for bidding in CA's and claims that these distributions are not empirically hard. We attempted to address the first group of problems in previous work [15], proposing the Combinatorial Auction Test Suite (CATS). Indeed, the CATS distributions have been widely used, by many of the authors cited above and also for example by [10, 23, 13]. In this paper we consider four CATS distributions: **regions, arbitrary, matching, and scheduling.**[2] Although the available space does not permit the enumeration of each distribution's parameters, we give a high-level description of each distribution. *Regions* models an auction of real estate, or more generally of any goods over which two-dimensional adjacency is the basis of complementarity; bids request goods that are adjacent in a planar graph. *Arbitrary* is similar, but relaxes the planarity assumption and models arbitrary complementarities between discrete goods such as electronics parts or collectables. *Matching* applies to FAA airline take-off and landing rights auctions; each bid requests one take-off and landing slot bundle, and each bidder submits an XOR'ed set of bids for acceptable bundles. *Scheduling* models a distributed job-shop scheduling domain, with bidders requesting an XOR'ed set of resource time-slots that will satisfy their specific deadlines.

By modeling bidders explicitly and creating bid amounts, sets of goods and sets of substitutable bids from models of bidder valuations and models of problem domains, we aimed for the CATS distributions to serve as a step towards a

---

[2] We have not included the **paths** distribution because we are updating and extending it; we will include results concerning this distribution in the full version of this paper.

realistic set of test distributions. However, we made no efforts to tune the distributions to provide hard instances. In practice, many researchers have remarked that some CATS problems are comparatively easy. In section 6 we show experimentally that some CATS distributions are always very easy for CPLEX, while others can be extremely hard.

4   The Issue of Problem Size

Some sources of empirical hardness in $\mathcal{NP}$-Hard problem instances are well-understood. Our goal is to understand what *other* features of instances are predictive of hardness so we hold these parameters constant, concentrating on variations in other features.

For the WDP, it is well known that problems become harder as the number of goods and bids increases.[3] For this reason, researchers have traditionally reported the performance of their WDP algorithms in terms of the number of bids and goods of the input instances. While it is easy to fix the number of goods, holding the number of bids constant is not as straightforward as it might appear. Most special-purpose algorithms make use of a polynomial-time preprocessing step which removes bids that are strictly dominated by one other bid. More precisely, bid i is dominated by bid j if the goods requested by i are a (non-strict) superset of the goods requested by j, and the price offer of i is smaller than or equal to the price offer of j. (This is similar in flavor to the use of arc-consistency as a preprocessing step for a CSP or weighted CSP problem.) It is thus possible for the size of problems given as input to the WDP algorithm to vary even if all generated instances had the same number of bids.

It is not obvious whether domination ought to remove many bids, or whether the relationship between the average number of non-dominated bids and total bids ought to vary substantially from one distribution to another. No other work of which we are aware characterizes this relationship, so we set out to measure it. Figure 1 shows the number of non-dominated bids as a function of the total number of bids generated. In these experiments, with each line representing an average over 20 runs, bids were generated for an auction with 64 goods, and the program stopped after 2000 non-dominated bids had been made. We observe that some of the "legacy" distributions are considerably more likely than others to generate non-dominated bids; we do not show the CATS distributions in this graph as all four generated virtually no dominated bids.

Of course, many other polynomial-time preprocessing steps are possible, e.g., a check for bids that are dominated by a pair of other bids. Indeed, CPLEX employs many, much more complex preprocessing steps before initiating its own branch-and-bound search. However, our own experience with algorithms for the

---

[3] An exception is that problems generally become easier when the number of bids grows *very* large in distributions favoring small bundles, because each small bundle is sampled much more often than each large bundle, giving rise to a new distribution for which the optimal allocation tends to involve only small bundles. We consider much smaller numbers of bids here.

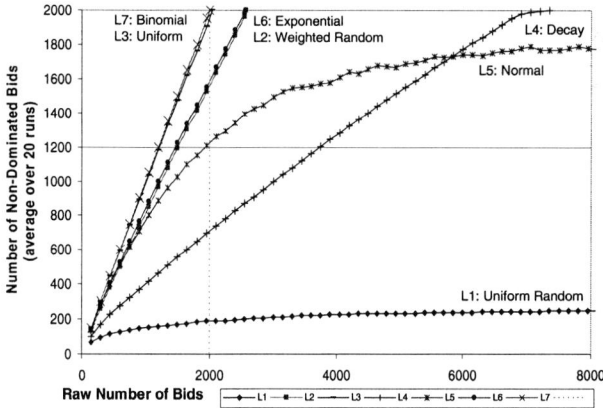

Fig. 1. Non-Dominated Bids vs. Raw Bids

WDP has suggested that other polynomial-time preprocessing steps offer much poorer performance in terms of the number of bids discarded in a given amount of time. The results above certainly suggest that the results of strict domination checking should not be disregarded, since distributions differ substantially in the ratio between the number of non-dominated bids and the raw number of bids. We thus defined the problem size as the pair (*number of goods, number of non-dominated bids*). We re-implemented the CATS software so that it generated instances for all CATS and legacy distributions with a specified number of *non-dominated* bids: the software iteratively generated bids and removed dominated bids until the specified target was reached. Our focus on the number of non-dominated bids forced us not to consider bids from the distributions L1 and L5 in the remainder of the paper, because they often failed to generate the specified number of non-dominated bids even after millions of bids were created. (We note that this helps explain why L1 and L5 have been found empirically easy by other researchers.)

5   Features

As described above, we characterize each problem instance with a set of features. There is no automatic way of constructing a feature set: researchers must use their domain knowledge to identify properties of the instance that appear likely to provide useful information about empirical hardness. We only consider features that can be generated from *any* problem instance, without knowledge of how that instance was constructed. Furthermore we restrict ourselves to those features that are computable in polynomial time, since the computation of the features should scale well as compared to solving the optimization problem. Although features must be manually selected, there are statistical techniques for identifying useless features. Identifying such features is important because highly

Bid-Good Graph Features:

1-3. **Bid nodes degree statistics:** max and min degree of the bid nodes, and standard deviations.

4-7. **Good nodes degree statistics:** average, maximum, minimum degree of the good nodes, and their standard deviations.

Bid Graph Features:

8. **Edge Density:** number of edges in the BG divided by the number of edges in a complete graph with the same number of nodes.

9-11. **Node degree statistics:** the max and min node degrees in the BG, and their standard deviation.

12-13. **Clustering Coefficient and Deviation.** A measure of "local cliqueness." For each node calculate the number of edges divided by $k(k-1)/2$, where k is the number of neighbors. We record average (the clustering coefficient) and standard deviation.

14. **Average minimum path length:** the average minimum path length, over all pairs of bids.

15. **Ratio of the clustering coefficient to the average minimum path length:** One of the measures of the smallness of the BG.

16-19. **Node eccentricity statistics:** The eccentricity of a node is the length of a shortest path to a node furthest from it. We calculate the maximum eccentricity of BG (graph diameter), the minimum eccentricity of BG (graph radius), average eccentricity, and standard deviation of eccentricity.

LP-Based Features:

20-22. L_1, L_2, L_∞ norms of the integer slack vector.

Price-Based Features:

23. **Standard deviation of prices among all bids:** $stdev(p_i)$

24. **Deviation of price per number of goods:** $stdev(p_i/|b_i|)$

25. **Deviation of price per square root of the number of goods:** $stdev(p_i/\sqrt{|b_i|})$.

Fig. 2. Four Groups of Features

correlated features can unnecessarily increase the dimensionality of the hypothesis space: this can degrade the performance of some regression algorithms and also makes the resulting formula harder to interpret.

For our WDP case study, we determined 35 features which we thought could be relevant to the empirical hardness of the optimization, ranging in their computational complexity from linear to cubic time. After feature selection we were left with 25 features: these are summarized in Fig. 2. We describe our features in more detail below, and also mention some of the features that were eliminated by feature selection.

There are two natural graphs associated with each instance. First, is the *bid-good graph* (BGG): a bipartite graph having a node for each bid, a node for each good and an edge between a bid and a good node for each good in the given bid. We measure a variety of BGG's properties: extremal and average degrees and their standard deviations for each group of nodes. The average number of goods per bid was perfectly correlated with another feature, and so did not survive our feature selection.

The *bid graph* (BG) represents conflicts among bids (thus it is the constraint graph for the associated CSP). As is true for all CSPs, the BG captures a lot of useful information about the problem instance. Our second group of features are concerned with structural properties of the BG.[4] We originally measured the first and third quartiles and the median of the BG node degrees, but they turned out to be highly correlated with edge density. We also measured the average number of conflicts per bid, but since the number of bids was held constant

---

[4] We thank Rámon Béjar for providing code for calculating the clustering coefficient.

this feature was always proportional to edge density. We considered using the number of connected components of the BG to measure whether the problem is decomposable into simpler instances, but found that nearly every instance consisted of a single component. Finally, it would be desirable to include some measure of the size of the (unpruned) search space. For some problems branching factor and search depth are used; for WDP neither is easily estimated. A related measure is the number of maximal independent sets of BG, which corresponds to the number of feasible solutions. However, this counting problem is hard, and to our knowledge does not have a polynomial-time approximation.

The third group of features is calculated from the solution vector of the LP relaxation of the WDP. We calculate the *integer slack* vector by replacing each component x_i with $min(|x_i|, |1-x_i|)$. These features appeared particularly useful both because the slack gives insight into the quality of CPLEX's initial solution and because CPLEX uses LP as its search heuristic. Originally we also included median integer slack, but excluded the feature when we found that it was always zero.

Our last group of features is the only one to explicitly consider the prices associated with bids. While the scale of the prices has no effect on hardness the spread is crucial, since it impacts pruning. We note that feature 25 was shown to be an optimal bid-ordering heuristic for branch-and-bound search on the WDP in [8].

6   Experimental Results

We generated three separate data sets of different problem sizes, to ensure that our results were not artifacts of one particular choice of problem size. The first data set contained runs on instances of 1000 bids and 256 goods each, with a total of 4500 instances (500 instances per distribution). The second data set with 1000 bids and 144 goods had a total of 2080 instances; the third data set with 2000 bids and 64 goods contained 1964 instances. Where we present results for only a single data set, the first data set was always used. All of our runtime data was collected by running CPLEX 7.1 with preprocessing turned off. We used a cluster of 4 machines, each of which had 8 Pentium III Xeon 550 MHz processors and 4G RAM and was running Linux 2.2.12. Since many of the instances turned out to be exceptionally hard, we stopped CPLEX after it had expanded 130,000 nodes (reaching this point took between 2 hours and 22 hours, averaging 9 hours). Overall, solution times varied from as little as 0.01 seconds to as much as 22 hours. We estimate that we consumed approximately 3 years of CPU time collecting this data. We also computed our 35 features for each instance. (Recall that feature selection took place after all instances had been generated.) Each feature in each data set was normalized to have a mean of 0 and a standard deviation of 1. Regression was performed using the open-source R package (see www.r-project.org).

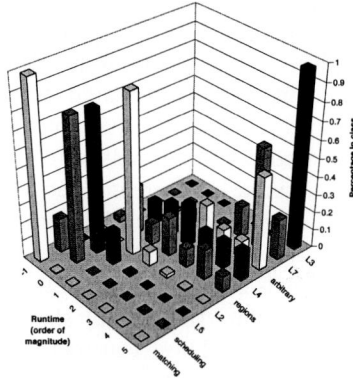

Fig. 3. Gross Hardness

6.1   Gross Hardness

Before attempting to characterize the hardness of our problems with machine learning techniques, we examined the gross hardness of each distribution. To our knowledge no previously published results show the *distribution* of hard and easy problems across different data distributions. Figure 3 shows the results of 500 runs for each distribution on problems with 256 goods and 1000 non-dominated bids, indicating the number of instances with the same order-of-magnitude runtime—i.e., $\lfloor \log_{10}(runtime) \rfloor$—for each of our nine distributions. Each instance of each distribution had different parameters, each of which was sampled from a range of acceptable values.

This figure illustrates that some data distributions were always easy for CPLEX, while others were nearly always hard. It is interesting that most distributions had instances that varied in hardness by several orders of magnitude, despite the fact that all instances had the same problem size. In the next sections we will describe our attempts to predict the order-of-magnitude hardness of data instances—effectively, to induce the hardness information in Fig. 3 without running CPLEX or identifying the distribution from which an instance was drawn.

6.2   Homing in on Sources of Hardness

Since we wanted to learn a continuous-valued model of the features, we used statistical regression techniques.[5] We chose the logarithm of CPLEX running time as our response variable—the value to be predicted—rather than absolute running time, for consistency with our original motivation of automatically reconstructing the gross hardness figure. We wanted the model to be penalized

---

[5] A large literature addresses the statistical techniques we used; for an introduction see, e.g., [9].

according to whether the predicted and actual values had the same order of magnitude: if we had tried to predict absolute running times then the model would have been penalized very little for dramatically mispredicting the running time of very easy instances, and would have been penalized heavily for slightly mispredicting the running time of the hardest instances. We performed regression on a training set consisting of 80% of each of our datasets, and then tested our model on the remaining 20% to evaluate its ability to generalize to new data.

Linear Regression One of the simplest and most widely-studied regression techniques is linear regression. This technique works by finding a hyperplane in the feature space that minimizes root mean squared error (RMSE), which is defined as the square root of the average squared difference between the predicted value and the true value of the response variable. Minimizing RMSE is reasonable because it conforms to the intuition that, holding mean absolute error constant, models that mispredict all instances equally should be preferred to models that vary in their mispredictions. Although we go on to consider nonlinear regression, it is useful to consider the results of linear regression for two reasons. First, one of our main goals was to understand the factors that influence hardness, and insights gained from a linear model are useful even if other, more accurate models can be found. Second, our linear regression model serves as a baseline to which we can compare the performance of more complex regression techniques.

In Fig. 4(a) we report both RMSE and mean absolute error, since the latter is often more intuitive. A third measure, adjusted R^2, is the fraction of the original variance in the response variable that is explained by the model, with a penalty for more complex models. Despite this penalty, adjusted R^2 is a measure of fit to the training set and cannot entirely correct for overfitting; nevertheless, it can be an informative measure when presented along with test set error. Overall, this table shows that our linear model would be able to do a good job of classifying instances into the bins shown in Fig. 3, despite the fact that it is not given the distribution from which each instance was drawn: 93% of the time the log running times of the data instances in our test set were predicted to the correct order of magnitude (i.e., with an absolute error of less than 1.0). Figures 4(b) and 4(c) show histograms of mean absolute and RMS error, with bin width 0.1. These histograms show that most instances are predicted very accurately, and few instances are dramatically mispredicted.

Data Point	Mean Abs Err	RMSE	Adj. R^2
1000 Bids/256 Goods	0.399	0.543	0.938
1000 Bids/144 Goods	0.437	0.579	0.909
2000 Bids/64 Goods	0.254	0.368	0.912

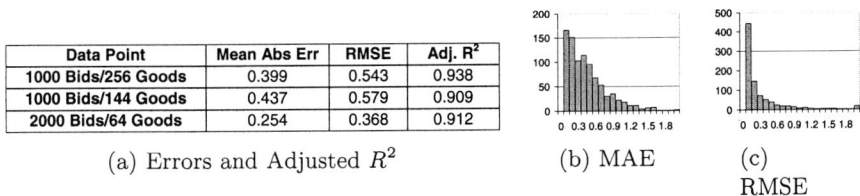

(a) Errors and Adjusted R^2 (b) MAE   (c) RMSE

Fig. 4. Experimental results for linear regression

Data Point	Mean Abs Err	RMSE	Adj. R^2
1000 Bids/256 Goods	0.183	0.297	0.987
1000 Bids/144 Goods	0.272	0.475	0.974
2000 Bids/64 Goods	0.163	0.272	0.981

(a) Errors and Adjusted R^2 (b) MAE   (c) RMSE

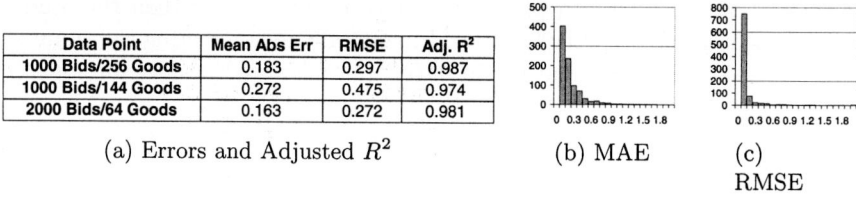

Fig. 5. Experimental results for 2nd degree polynomial regression

Nonlinear Models Although our linear model was quite effective, we expected that nonlinear interactions between our features would be important, and therefore looked to nonlinear models. A simple way of performing nonlinear regression is to compute new features based on nonlinear interactions between the original features, and then to perform linear regression on the union of both sets of features. We added all products of pairs of features to our linear model, including squares of individual features, which gave us a total of 350 features. This allowed us to fit a 2nd degree polynomial instead of our previous linear model. For all three of our datasets this model gave considerably better error measurements on the test set and also explained nearly all the variance in the training set, as shown in Fig. 5(a).

We also explored another nonlinear regression technique, Multivariate Adaptive Regression Splines (MARS) [5]. MARS models are linear combinations of the products of one or more basis functions, where basis functions are the positive parts of linear functions of single features. The RMSE on our MARS models differed from the RMSE on our second-order model only in the second decimal place; as MARS models can be unstable and difficult to interpret, we focus on the second-order model here.

Analysis The results summarized above demonstrate that it is possible to learn a model of our features that accurately predicts the log of CPLEX running time on novel instances. For some applications (e.g., predicting the time it will take for an auction to clear; building an algorithm portfolio) accurate prediction is all that is required. For other applications it is necessary to *understand* what makes an instance empirically hard. In this section we set out to interpret our models.

It is tempting to interpret a model by comparing the coefficients assigned to the different features; since all features have the same mean and standard deviations, more important features should tend to have larger coefficients. The reason that this does not work is that most features are at least somewhat correlated. Two perfectly correlated but entirely unimportant features can have large coefficients with opposite signs in a linear model; in practice, since imperfect correlation and correlations among larger sets of variables are common, it is difficult to untangle the effects of correlation and importance in explaining a given coefficient's magnitude. One solution is to force the model to have smaller coefficients and/or to contain fewer variables. Requiring smaller coefficients reduces interactions between correlated variables; two popular techniques are ridge regression and lasso regression. We evaluated these techniques using cross validation and found no significant effect on errors or on interpretability of the model, so we do not present these results here.

Another family of techniques allows interpretation without the consideration of coefficient magnitudes. These techniques select "good" subsets of the features, essentially performing exhaustive enumeration when possible and various greedy search techniques otherwise. Small models are desirable for analysis because they are easier to interpret directly and because a small, optimal subset will tend to contain fewer highly covariant features than a larger model. We plotted subset size (from 1 to the total number of variables) versus the RMSE of the best model built from a subset of each size. We then chose the smallest subset size at which there was little incremental benefit gained by moving to the next larger subset size. We examined the features in the model, and also measured each variable's cost of omission—the (normalized) difference between the RMSE of the model on the original subset and a model omitting the given variable. It is important to note that because of correlation between features many different subsets may achieve nearly the same RMSE, and that very little can be inferred from what *particular* variables are included in the best subset of a given size. This is of little concern, however, when subset selection is used only to gain a conceptual understanding of the features that are important for predicting empirical hardness; in this case the substitution of one feature for another covariant feature is irrelevant because the inclusion of either feature in the model has the same intuitive meaning. It is also worth noting that subset selection and cost of omission were both evaluated using the test set, but that all model selection was evaluated using cross validation, and all analysis was performed after our models had been learned.

Figure 6(a) shows the RMSE of the best subset containing between 1 and 25 features for linear models; since we had only 25 features in total we selected the best subsets by exhaustive comparison. We chose to examine the model with seven features because it was the first for which adding another feature did not cause a large decrease in RMSE. Figure 6(b) shows the seven features in this model and their respective costs of omission (scaled to 100). The most striking conclusion is that structural features are the most important. Edge density of BG is essentially a measure of the constrainedness of the problem, so it is not surprising to find that this feature is the most costly to omit. Clustering coefficient, the second feature, is a measure of average cliquiness of BG; this feature gives an indication of how local constraints in the problem are. All but one of the remaining features concern node degrees in BG or BGG; the final feature is the L_1 norm of the linear programming slack vector. The importance of this feature is quite intuitive: the L_1 norm is close to 0 for problems that are almost completely solved by LP, and larger for more difficult problems.

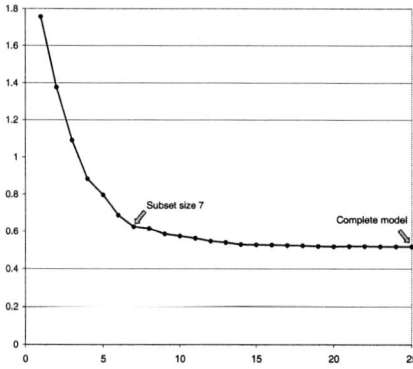

(a) Subset size vs. RMSE

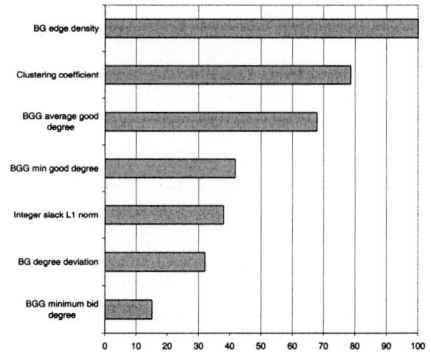

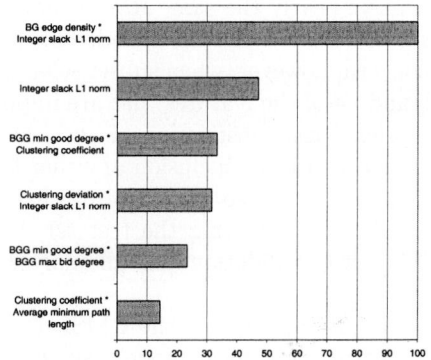

(b) Cost of omission for subset size 7

Fig. 6. Subset Selection in Linear Models

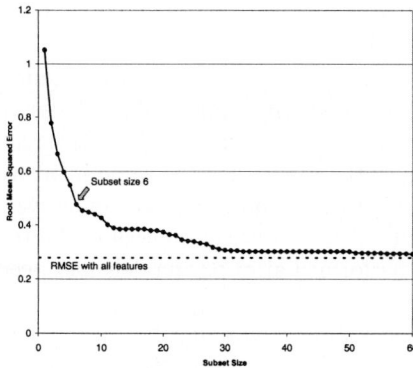

(a) Subset size vs. RMSE

(b) Cost of omission for subset size 6

Fig. 7. Subset Selection in Second-Order Models

Figure 7(a) shows the best subsets containing between 1 and 60 features for second-order models. In this case we had 350 features, making exhaustive exploration of features impossible; we instead used four different greedy subset selection methods and at each size chose the best subset among the four. The subsets shown in Fig. 7(a) are likely not the RMSE-minimizing subsets of the given sizes, but since our goal was only to understand what sorts of features are important this likely lack of optimality is not a serious problem. We observe that the interactions between features dramatically improved RMSE on very small subsets. Figure 7(b) shows the costs of omission for the variables from the best subset of six features. Again we observe that edge density of BG is a critically important feature, as are the clustering coefficient and node degrees. We observe that overall many second-order features were selected. The L_1 norm becomes more important than in the linear model when it is allowed to interact with other features; in the second-order model it is also sufficiently important to be included as the only first-order feature. It is striking that no price features were important in either our first- or second-order models. Although price-based features do appear in larger models, they seem not to be as critically important as structural or LP-based features. This may be partially explained by the fact that the removal of dominated bids eliminates the bids that deviate most substantially on price, and indeed caused us to eliminate the distribution (L1) in which average price per good varied most dramatically across bids.

7   Conclusion and Future Directions

This paper makes two main contributions. First, we performed an extensive experimental investigation into the hardness of the WDP. We contrasted widely-used WDP distributions with respect to their empirical hardness, and showed that the traditional definition of problem size as raw number of goods and bids can be misleading on some distributions. We identified structural, distribution-independent features of WDP instances and showed that they can be very closely related to CPLEX running time. Second and more importantly, we proposed a new, general methodology for understanding the empirical hardness of complex, high-dimensional $\mathcal{NP}$-Hard problems. We believe that our methodology, based on using machine learning techniques to identify hard regions of the feature space, is applicable to a wide variety of hard problems. Furthermore, it has many uses: straightforward prediction of running time; effective algorithm selection in algorithm portfolios; insight into the features that influence hardness to inform theoretical analysis; possibly, the design of improved optimization algorithms.

References

[1] D. Achlioptas, C. Gomes, H. Kautz, and B. Selman. Generating satisfiable instances. In *AAAI-00*, 2000.
[2] A. Anderson, M. Tenhunen, and F. Ygge. Integer programming for combinatorial auction winner determination. In *ICMAS*, 2000.
[3] P. Cheeseman, B. Kanefsky, and W. M. Taylor. Where the Really Hard Problems Are. In *IJCAI-91*, 1991.
[4] S. de Vries and R. Vohra. Combinatorial auctions: A brief survey. Unpublished, 2000.
[5] J. Friedman. Multivariate adaptive regression splines. *Annals of Statistics*, 19, 1991.
[6] Y. Fujishima, K. Leyton-Brown, and Y. Shoham. Taming the computational complexity of combinatorial auctions: Optimal and approximate approaches. In *IJCAI-99*, 1999.

[7] Carla P. Gomes and Bart Selman. Problem structure in the presence of perturbations. In *AAAI/IAAI*, 1997.

[8] R. Gonen and D. Lehmann. Optimal solutions for multi-unit combinatorial auctions: Branch and bound heuristics. In *ACM Conference on Electronic Commerce*, 2000.

[9] T. Hastie, R. Tibshirani, and J. Friedman. *Elements of Statistical Learning*. Springer, 2001.

[10] R. C. Holte. Combinatorial auctions, knapsack problems, and hill-climbing search. In *Canadian Conference on AI*, 2001.

[11] H. H. Hoos and C. Boutilier. Solving combinatorial auctions using stochastic local search. In *AAAI-00*, 2000.

[12] E. Horvitz, Y. Ruan, C. Gomes, H. Kautz, B. Selman, and M. Chickering. A bayesian approach to tackling hard computational problems, 2001.

[13] R. Kastner, C. Hsieh, M. Potkonjak, and M. Sarrafzadeh. On the sensitivity of incremental algorithms for combinatorial auctions, 2002. UCLA CS Tech. Report 020000.

[14] R. Korf and M. Reid. Complexity analysis of admissible heuristic search. *AAAI-98*, 1998.

[15] K. Leyton-Brown, M. Pearson, and Y. Shoham. Towards a universal test suite for combinatorial auction algorithms. In *ACM Conference on Electronic Commerce*, 2000.

[16] K. Leyton-Brown, Yoav Shoham, and Moshe Tennenholtz. An algorithm for multi-unit combinatorial auctions. In *Proceedings of AAAI-00*, 2000.

[17] R. Monasson, R. Zecchina, S. Kirkpatrick, B. Selman, , and L. Troyansky. Determining computational complexity for characteristic 'phase transitions'. *Nature*, 400, 1998.

[18] N. Nisan. Bidding and allocation in combinatorial auctions. In *ACM Conference on Electronic Commerce*, 2000.

[19] D. C. Parkes. iBundle: An efficient ascending price bundle auction. In *ACM Conference on Electronic Commerce*, 1999.

[20] M. H. Rothkopf, A. Pekec, and R. M. Harstad. Computationally manageable combinatorial auctions. *Management Science*, 44(8), 1998.

[21] T. Sandholm. An algorithm for optimal winner determination in combinatorial auctions. In *IJCAI-99*, 1999.

[22] T. Sandholm, S. Suri, A. Gilpin, and D. Levine. Cabob: A fast optimal algorithm for combinatorial auctions. In *IJCAI-01*, 2001.

[23] Dale Schuurmans, Finnegan Southey, and Robert C. Holte. The exponentiated subgradient algorithm for heuristic boolean programming. In *IJCAI-01*, 2001.

[24] J. Slaney and T. Walsh. Backbones in optimization and approximation. In *IJCAI-01*, 2001.

[25] W. Zhang. *State-Space Search: Algorithms, Complexity, Extensions, and Applications*. Springer, 1999.

Restart Policies with Dependence among Runs: A Dynamic Programming Approach

Yongshao Ruan[1], Eric Horvitz[2], and Henry Kautz[1]

[1] University of Washington
Seattle WA 98195, USA
{ruan,kautz}@cs.washington.edu
[2] Microsoft Research
Redmond WA 98052, USA
horvitz@microsoft.com

Abstract. The time required for a backtracking search procedure to solve a problem can be minimized by employing randomized restart procedures. To date, researchers designing restart policies have relied on the simplifying assumption that runs are probabilistically independent from one another. We relax the assumption of independence among runs and address the challenge of identifying an optimal restart policy for the dependent case. We show how offline dynamic programming can be used to generate an ideal restart policy, and how the policy can be used in conjunction with real-time observations to control the timing of restarts. We present results of experiments on applying the methods to create ideal restart policies for several challenging search problems using two different solvers.

1 Introduction

Combinatorial search algorithms in many domains exhibit high variance in running time over fixed sets of problems [23, 6, 19, 13, 7, 24]. In some cases, the probability distribution for the running time of a search algorithm over a problem set is *heavy-tailed*, having *infinite* mean and variance [8, 10, 9]. Investigators have pursued an understanding of the basis for such great variation in run-time, and have sought to exploit the uncertainty in execution time to develop more predictable and efficient procedures [3, 12].

Several investigators have explored the value of *randomized restarts* [11]. In this area of work, randomness is overlayed on the branching heuristic of a systematic search algorithm. If the search algorithm does not terminate within some number of backtracks, referred to as a *cutoff*, the run is halted and the algorithm is restarted with a new *random seed*. The randomized restart method has been demonstrated to reduce the total execution time on a wide variety of problems in scheduling, theorem-proving, circuit synthesis, planning, and hardware verification [22].

In Horvitz *et al.* (2001) [14], we introduced a general framework for building probabilistic models that predict a search algorithm's performance on a given

P. Van Hentenryck (Ed.): CP 2002, LNCS 2470, pp. 573–586, 2002.
© Springer-Verlag Berlin Heidelberg 2002

problem instance, on the basis of the algorithm's behavior during the first few search steps. We asserted that such Bayesian models provide a foundation for work on speed-up learning and control of problem solvers. In other related work, in Kautz *et al.* (2002) [17], we showed that predictive models could be used to design superior dynamic restart strategies for randomized problem solvers, for the case where runs are probabilistically independent. In this paper, we extend these results to the more general and more complex situation where runs are probabilistically *dependent*, where each run provides an update about the nature of the probability distribution that generated the problem instance.

We shall first review some details of prior work and define the problem of dynamic restarts with dependencies. We show that the optimal restart policy for the dependent case can be modeled as a dynamic programming (DP) problem. We present a method centering on the use of offline DP to generate an ideal restart policy. Then, we show how observations can be incorporated into the restart policy. Finally, we illustrate the efficacy of the restart policies with experiments on several representative problems.

2   Research on Restart Policies

The basis for using randomized restarts is straightforward: the longer a backtracking search algorithm runs without finding a solution, the more likely it is that the algorithm is exploring a barren part of the search space, rather than branching early on states of critical variables that will be necessary for a solution. The designers of restart policies must grapple with minimization of total run time given a tradeoff; as the cutoff time is reduced, the probability that any particular run will reach a solution is diminished, so runs become shorter but more numerous.

Previous theoretical work on the problem of determining an ideal cutoff has made two assumptions: first, that the only feasible observation is the *length* of a run; and second, that the runs are *independent*. Under these conditions Luby *et al.* [21] described provably optimal restart policies. In the case of complete knowledge of the distribution, the optimal policy is the fixed cutoff that minimizes $E(T_c)$, the expected time to solution restarting every c backtracks. In the case of no knowledge of the distribution, Luby *et al.* further showed that a universal schedule of cutoff values of the form

$$1, 1, 2, 1, 1, 2, 4, \ldots$$

gives an expected time to solution that is within a log factor of that given by the optimal fixed cutoff, and that no other universal schedule is better by more than a constant factor.

Although the results of Luby *et al.* were taken by many in the research community to have settled all open issues on restart strategies, many real-life scenarios violate both assumptions. In Horvitz *et al.* [14] and Kautz *et al.* [17] we demonstrated that features other than run time can be used in the restart control policy of backtrack solvers. We introduced a framework for constructing

Bayesian models that can predict the run time of problem solvers, and showed that observations of various features capturing the state of the solver during the first few steps of a run could be fused to predict the length of a run with a useful degree of accuracy. We described several approaches to apply the observation into restart control policies and showed that the dynamic restart policies with observations beat the static optimal policy of Luby *et al.* by 40% to 65%. However, these papers retained the limiting assumption that runs were probabilistically independent.

The assumption that runs are independent can be violated in a number of settings. Consider the case where we have knowledge of the existence of several different probability distributions over run time, $D_1, D_2, \ldots$. A problem instance is drawn from one of the distributions based on prior probabilities and each run is performed on that same instance. In this setting, observations about the time exhibited until a restart of one or more prior runs of the same instance provides a probabilistic update about the probability distribution over run time of current and future runs.

It is easy to see how restart policies for independent and dependent runs can differ. Consider the simple case of distributions based on point probabilities. Suppose in the independent case a run always ends in 10 or 100 steps with equal probability: $P(t_i = 10) = P(t_i = 100) = 0.5$. In this case the optimal policy is to always restart after 10 steps if the problem is not solved. On the other hand, consider the dependent case where in D_1 all runs take 10 steps and in D_2 all runs take 100 steps, and a fixed instance is chosen from one of the distributions with equal probability. Then the optimal policy is to run with a cutoff ≥ 100. If the problem is not solved after 10 steps then we know the problem *requires* 100 steps, so a solver should continue. Any fixed cutoff less than 100 gives a non-zero probability of never solving the problem—and thus an infinite expected run time.

Our paper addresses the challenge of designing restart policies for dependent runs. Our specific contributions include:

- Modeling the optimal restart policy for dependent runs as a DP problem
- Specification of different predictive models and showing how they are used in dynamic restart policies
- Evaluating the optimal restart policies empirically with and without runtime observations and comparing these results with the best fixed-cutoff policies and the universal restart policy of Luby *et al.*.

3   Dependent Restarts without Observations

To simplify the presentation, we will focus on dependent runs for the case of two run-time distributions (RTDs), which we shall denote as *source* distributions D_1 and D_2. The results can be extended in a straightforward manner to the case of n distributions. At the outset of problem solving, one of the distributions is chosen according to a given prior probability, but the choice is not revealed to the solver. For each run we specify a cutoff t, and a sample is drawn from the chosen RTD. If the sample's run time is less than t the problem is solved; otherwise, we perform another run with a new sample from the same distribution. Thus, with each unsuccessful run, we gain additional information about the distribution that was initially chosen.

This analysis characterizes several problem-solving scenarios, including the scenarios where (i) each D_i is the RTD for a single instance under a randomized solver; (ii) each D_i corresponds to an ensemble of instances with similar RTD's; or (iii) each D_i is the RTD of a heterogeneous ensemble, and the solver gets a new problem instance for each run. Another scenario of interest is where each D_i corresponds to a heterogeneous ensemble of instances, and the same problem instance is used for each run. The analysis of this *single-instance* scenario requires additional mathematical machinery that relates the RTD of an ensemble to the RTD's of its individual instances under a randomized solver, as we will explain in a forthcoming paper.

If we had perfect knowledge of the distribution that generated the instance, the problem would collapse to the independent case described by Luby *et al.* Let us consider the case where we are uncertain about the source distribution. Our goal is to find the optimal policy $(t_1, t_2, ...)$, where t_k is the cutoff for k-th run, such that the total number of steps to a solution is minimized. After each unsuccessful run, the solver's beliefs about the source distribution should be updated. We shall first consider the situation where we are limited solely to evidence about the time spent on prior runs. We formulate the problem of finding the optimal restart policy for the dependent case as a Markov decision process (MDP) ([15]).

Formally, the dependent restart problem can be described as a Markov decision process as follows: Let d_i be the prior probability of a run being chosen from distribution D_i, $p_i(t)$ the probability that a run will be selected from D_i stopping exactly at t, and $q_i(t) = \sum_{t' \leq t} p_i(t')$ the cumulative function of $p_i(t)$, where $i = 1, 2$. We will always assume that p_i is non-trivial in the sense that $p_i(\inf) < 1$. Each state is a tuple of (d_1, d_2) and the set of actions for all states is the set of all possible cutoffs. Given an action t (*i.e.*, cutoff $= t$) and state $S = (d_1, d_2)$, the next possible state is either that the problem is solved (the termination state), or $S' = (d'_1, d'_2)$, where d'_1 and d'_2 are the updated probabilities. Once the solver reaches the termination state, denoted $S_0 = (0, 0)$, it remains there at no further cost. An *optimal restart control policy* is one whose *expected cost* to reach the termination state is minimum.

Let T denote the event that a run has not found a solution in the cutoff t, and D_i denote the event that the instance is from distribution D_i, where $i = 1, 2$. In this analysis, we are only considering the prior run times in updating d_1 and d_2. So we have

$$d_i' = \frac{P(T, D_i)}{\sum_{j=1,2} P(T, D_j)}$$
$$= \frac{P(D_i)P(T|D_i)}{\sum_{j=1,2} P(D_j)P(T|D_j)}$$
$$= \frac{d_i(1 - q_i(t))}{\sum_{j=1,2} d_j(1 - q_j(t))}$$

where $i = 1, 2$.

The immediate cost of setting the cutoff to be t at state S (*i.e.*, the expected length of the run from state S with a cutoff t), denoted $R(S, t)$, is

$$R(S, t) = \sum_{i=1,2} d_i (\sum_{t' \le t} t' p_i(t') + t(1 - q_i(t))$$
$$= \sum_{i=1,2} d_i(t - \sum_{t' < t} q_i(t')) \tag{1}$$

Thus, the next state $S' = (d_1', d_2')$ depends only on the previous state $S = (d_1, d_2)$ and the corresponding cutoff t. The same is true for the immediate cost R. So the state space satisfies the Markov property. With this, finding the optimal restart policy for the dependent runs is an MDP.

Given a cutoff t, the transition probabilities from S to S' and the termination state S_0 are

$$P(S'|S, t) = \sum_{i=1,2} d_i(1 - q_i(t))$$
$$P(S_0|S, t) = \sum_{i=1,2} d_i q_i(t)$$

The transition probability from S to any state other than S' and S_0 is 0.

The optimal expected solution time from state $S = (d_1, d_2)$ is the optimized sum of the immediate cost $R(S, t)$ and the optimal expected solution time of the two possible future states, denoted $V^*(S)$, which is given by the following Bellman equation:

$$V^*(S) = \min_t \{R(S, t) + P(S'|S, t)V^*(S')$$
$$+ P(S_0|S, t)V^*(S_0)\}$$
$$= \min_t \{R(S, t) + P(S'|S, t)V^*(S')\}$$
$$= \min_t \{\sum_{i=1,2} d_i(t - \sum_{t < t} q_i(t'))$$
$$+ \sum_{i=1,2} d_i(1 - q_i(t))V^*(S')\}$$

where we use the relation of $V^*(S_0) = 0$ and Equation 1.

$V^*(S)$ can be computed using DP. We have experimented with both policy iteration and value iteration for DP. A restart policy is said to be *proper* if, for each state $S = (d_1, d_2)$, we only select a cutoff t such that $P(S_0|S, t) > 0$, *i.e.*, each state has a positive transition probability to the termination state. Both policy iteration and value iteration are proved to converge to the ideal optimal value in theory[2], with the assumption of proper restart policies. In our studies, we have found that policy iteration converges faster than value iteration. Thus, we choose policy iteration for the experiments presented below. Another practical problem is that the state space is continuous and we thus potentially must solve the problem for an infinite state space. For computational tractability, we transform the continuous space into a discrete state space and then apply finite-state DP methods. We shall review the experiments for the case of dependent runs without observation in Section 5. Before reviewing these results, we shall explore the case where we consider observations gathered during run time, in addition to the time taken by previous runs.

4   Dependent Restarts with Observations

Beyond run time, other evidence about the behavior of a solver may be valuable for updating beliefs about the source distribution. Indeed, watching a trace or visualization of a backtracking search engine in action can provide updates about run time. As mentioned above, our earlier work provides a general framework for constructing Bayesian models to predict the run time of problem solvers, and shows how probabilistic models can be used to create optimal dynamic restart policies for the case of independent runs [14, 17]. We now consider situations where the system can make observations that update beliefs about the current D_i.

Let us explore the case where an evidential feature F of the solver state is observed during a run. F can be taken to be a function of the initial trace of the solver, as calculated by a decision tree over low-level variables. F may be binary-valued—providing, for example, an update about whether the current run will last at least 10,000 steps or not. F can also be multi-valued; for example, the feature may indicate which leaf of predictive decision tree model should be used to infer the RTD associated with a set of features observed during the initial portion of the run. For simplicity of exposition, we shall consider the case where F is binary-valued, *i.e.*, 0 or 1.

Our analysis makes no assumptions about the *meaning* of F. In practice, we need to choose an F that helps us choose a better cutoff value for the run. One natural choice for F is the output of a decision tree that is trained to discriminate between instances from D_1 and D_2. We call such an F a *distribution predictor*. In the experiments below, we use a SAT/UNSAT distribution predictor which discriminates between satisfiable and unsatisfiable instances. Another natural choice is to base F on a decision tree trained to discriminate "short" (less than median run time) verses "long" (greater than median run time) runs from the prior-weighted union of D_1 and D_2. We call such an F a *run-time predictor*.

Intuitively, a distribution predictor provides us with probabilistic information that can be used to tune the cutoff to be good for the predicted distribution, while a run-time predictor would allow us to discard runs that are predicted to be long. However, it is important to understand that the dynamic programming procedure for calculating the optimal sequence of cutoff values does not rely on the explicit semantics of the predictive models: it simply determines the optimal cutoffs for any specified predictor. In Sec. 5, we compare the use of SAT/UNSAT distribution and run-time predictors on a benchmark test suite.

Thus, in addition to the run-time evidence, we now include information about the observation of F, which we include in the extended definition of a state. The extended state can now be described as (d_1, d_2, F), where d_1, d_2 are the same as those described in previous section. We define the transition probability, state transition, and the corresponding cost as follows: Besides T and D_i defined above, let F_n denote the feature observed at nth run, where F_n can be 0 or 1.

Before we can derive the transition probabilities and state transitions, we must compute the *interim probability* $P(D_i, F_{n+1}|F_n, T)$. The interim probability is the probability that the instance is generated by distribution D_i and F_{n+1} is observed in the $(n+1)$-th run, given that the n-th run had observation F_n and there is no solution for t steps.

$$P(D_i, F_{n+1}|F_n, T) = P(F_{n+1}|F_n, T, D_i)P(D_i|F_n, T)$$

We obtain the first part of the right side of the above formula (the probability of observing F_{n+1} in the next run) by conditioning on the assumptions that the instance is from distribution D_i, F_n is observed in the n-th run, and no solution is found within t steps:

$$P(F_{n+1}|F_n, T, D_i) = P(F_{n+1}|D_i)$$

We assert that the probability of observation F is independent of the previous observations and the selected cutoff, conditioned on the assumption that the instance is drawn from D_i.

The second part of the right side of the formula, *i.e.*, $P(D = D_i|F_n, T)$, is the probability that the instance is from distribution D_i, assuming that F_n is observed and no solution is found within t steps.

$$P(D = D_i|F_n, T) = \frac{P(T|F_n, D_i)P(D_i|F_n)}{P(T|F_n)}$$
$$= \frac{d_i P(T|F_n, D_i)}{P(T|F_n)}$$

Combining the two parts, we have

$$P(D_i, F_{n+1}|F_n, T) = \frac{d_i P(T|F_n, D_i)P(F_{n+1}|D_i)}{P(T|F_n)}$$

We note that $P(T|F_n, D_i)$, $P(F_{n+1}|D_i)$, and $P(T|F_n)$ can be derived from the data.

Thus, the transition probability from state $S_n = (d_1, d_2, F_n)$ with action t to $S_{n+1} = (d'_1, d'_2, F_{n+1})$ is

$$
\begin{aligned}
P(S_{n+1}|S_n, T) \\
&= P(F_{n+1}|F_n, T) \\
&= \sum_{i=1,2} P(D_i, F_{n+1}|F_n, T) \\
&= \frac{\sum_{i=1,2} d_i P(T|F_n, D_i) P(F_{n+1}|D_i)}{P(T|F_n)}
\end{aligned} \tag{2}
$$

For the next state $S_{n+1} = (d'_1, d'_2, F_{n+1})$, we have

$$
\begin{aligned}
d'_i &= P(D_i|F_n, T, F_{n+1}) \\
&= \frac{P(D_i, F_{n+1}|F_n, T)}{P(F_{n+1}|F_n, T)} \\
&= \frac{d_i P(T|F_n, D_i) P(F_{n+1}|D_i)}{\sum_{i=1,2} d_i P(T|F_n, D_i) P(F_{n+1}|D_i)}
\end{aligned}
$$

With a binary-valued F, from state $S_n = (d_1, d_2, F_n)$ with cutoff $= t$, we know that a solver will be in one and only one of the three states: a solution is found and the solver will be in the termination state S_0, no solution is found but F is true, or no solution is found and F is false. Let $S'_{n+1} = (d'_1, d'_2, F_{n+1} = 1)$ and $S''_{n+1} = (d''1, d''_2, F_{n+1} = 0)$ denote the last two states respectively. The transition probability from S_n to any other states is 0.

The immediate cost $R(S_n, t)$, i.e., the expected length of the nth run, associated with setting the cutoff to t at state S_n, is given by Equation 1. Similar to no-observation analysis, the optimal expected solution time from state $S_n = (d_1, d_2, F_n)$, denoted $V^*(S_n)$, is the optimized sum of the immediate cost $R(S_n, t)$ plus the optimal expected solution time of the three possible future states, which is given by the following Bellman equation:

$$
\begin{aligned}
V^*(S_n) \\
&= \min_t \{ R(S_n, t) + P(S_0|S_n, t) V^*(S_0) \\
&\quad + P(S'_{n+1}|S_n, t) V^*(S'_{n+1}) \\
&\quad + P(S''_{n+1}|S_n, t) V^*(S''_{n+1}) \} \\
&= \min_t \{ R(S_n, t) + P(S'_{n+1}|S_n, t) V^*(S'_{n+1}) \\
&\quad + P(S''_{n+1}|S_n, t) V^*(S''_{n+1}) \} \\
&= \min_t \{ R(S_n, t) + P(T)(P(S'_{n+1}|S_n, T) V^*(S'_{n+1}) \\
&\quad + P(S''_{n+1}|S_n, T) V^*(S''_{n+1})) \} \\
&= \min_t \{ \sum_{i=1,2} d_i (t - \sum_{t'<t} q_i(t'))
\end{aligned}
$$

$$+ \ (1 - \sum_{i=1,2} d_i q_i(t))(P(S'_{n+1}|S_n, T)V^*(S'_{n+1})$$

$$+ \ P(S''_{n+1}|S_n, T)V^*(S''_{n+1}))\}$$

where $P(S'_{n+1}|S_n, T)$ and $P(S''_{n+1}|S_n, T)$ can be computed by Equation 2.

Similar to the case with no observation, the dynamic dependent restart policy for the case with run-time observations can be computed with the use of DP as described in Section 3.

5   Experiments and Results

We performed a set of experiments to explore our approach to finding optimal restart policies with and without observations. We investigated the dependent restart policies for the multiple-instance problem-solving scenario described as Case iii in Section 3. For the multiple-instance situation, we choose an instance from $D_i, i = 1, 2$ according to prior probabilities. Then, for each run, a new instance from the same distribution D_i is randomly selected. We can draw and attempt to solve as many instances as we would like, but the goal is to solve one instance as soon as possible.

We considered as benchmark domains the quasigroup completion problem [7, 1, 18] and the graph coloring problem. Experiments performed in earlier work by Horvitz et al. [14] only considered satisfiable problems. In the experiments performed for this paper, we considered distributions containing unsatisfiable as well as satisfiable problem instances. As described in Section 3, we investigated dependent restart policies for the multiple-instance problem-solving scenario (that is, a heterogeneous ensemble with a new instance drawn for each run). As we noted, a forthcoming paper will explore the more complex case of a fixed instance drawn from a heterogeneous ensemble.

5.1   Background on Benchmark Domains

A quasigroup is an ordered pair $(L, \cdot)$, where L is a set and $(\cdot)$ is a binary operation on L such that the equations $a \cdot x = b$ and $y \cdot a = b$ are uniquely solvable for every pair of elements a, b in L. The order N of the quasigroup is the cardinality of the set L. An incomplete or partial Latin Square P is a partially filled N by N table such that no symbol occurs twice in a row or a column. The Quasigroup Completion Problem (QCP) is the problem of determining whether the remaining entries of the table can be filled in such a way that we obtain a complete Latin Square. For our studies, we generated a total of 10,000 instances, of which 6,062 were satisfiable. The instances are of order 30 with 337 unassigned variables or "holes."

The second problem domain we explored is solving propositional satisfiability (SAT) encodings of the Graph Coloring Problem (GCP). Graph coloring problem is a well-known combinatorial problem from graph theory. Given a graph $G = (V, E)$, where V$=\{v_1, v_2, ..., v_n\}$ is the set of vertices and E the set of edges connecting the vertices, we seek to find a coloring $C : V \rightarrow N$, such that connected vertices always have different colors. The challenge is to decide whether a coloring of the given graph exists for a particular number of colors.

We use the following strategy for encoding graph coloring problem instances into SAT: Each assignment of a color to a single vertex is represented by a propositional variable; each coloring constraint (edge of the graph) is represented by a set of clauses ensuring that the corresponding vertices have different colors. Two additional sets of clauses ensure that valid SAT assignments assign exactly one color to each vertex. The instances used in our studies are generated using Culberson's flat graph generator [5]. The challenge is to decide whether the instances are 3-colorable. The instances contain 5,000 satisfiable instances and 5,000 unsatisfiable instances. The instances are generated in such a way that all 3-colorable instances are 2-uncolorable and all 3-uncolorable instances are 4-colorable.

As a third domain, we explored a planning problem in the logistics domain. Kautz and Selman [16] showed that propositional SAT encodings of STRIPS-style planning problems could be efficiently solved by SAT engines. The logistics domain involves moving packages on trucks and airplanes among locations in different cities. In the logistics domain, a state is a particular configuration of packages and vehicles. We generated instances with 5 cities, 15 packages, 2 planes, and 1 truck per city. We generated a total of 7,900 instances, where 3,618 of the instances were satisfiable. To decrease the variance among instances, all of the satisfiable instances can be solved with 12 parallel steps but cannot be solved with 11 steps. All of the unsatisfiable instances cannot be solved with 12 steps but can be solved with 13 steps.

5.2   Learning Predictive Models

We used the Satz-Rand [11] randomized backtracking search engine for the problems encoded as SAT. Satz-Rand is a randomized version of the Satz system of Li and Anbulagan [20]. For QCP problems, we experimented with a specialized randomized CSP solver built using the ILOG constraint programming library.

We implemented the methods described by Horvitz *et al.* to learn predictors for run time based on observations (the feature F described in Section 4). The solvers were instrumented so that low-level observational variables could be collected over an observational horizon of up to 100 solver choice points. (A *Choice point* is a state in the backtracking search procedure where the algorithm makes a variable assignment heuristically, rather than making an assignment that is forced via propagation of previously set values. Types of value propagation include unit propagation, backtracking, lookahead, and forward-checking. We employed Bayesian learning procedures developed by Chickering, Heckerman, and Meek [4] to induce predictors in the form of decision trees built from the summary statistics of the low-level variables, from training sets generated from approximately 10,000 runs. As mentioned in Sec. 4, we experimented with two kinds of predictors: SAT/UNSAT distribution predictors, classifying an instance as a satisfiable or unsatisfiable instance, and run-time predictors, classifying a run as short or long, depending on whether the run time was less than or greater than the median time for the training set. Details about the procedure for learning predictive models are described in [17].

5.3   Comparing Policies for Dynamic Dependent Restarts

As described earlier, the optimal restart policy for dependent runs can be constructed offline by using policy iteration for DP, where we transform the continuous and infinite state space into a discrete state space and then apply finite-state DP methods. For all of the experiments, we quantitized the search space uniformly into 10,000 segments, taking into consideration the tradeoff between computational efficiency and accuracy. Policy construction via DP with policy iteration required about one hour on a Pentium-800 machine with 1 gigabyte of memory.

To characterize the improvements associated with the dynamic dependent restart policies, we ran comparative experiments with a fixed cutoff restart policy, where the same cutoff is used for every run. The *optimal fixed cutoff* restart policy selects the fixed cutoff which minimizes the expected solution time:[1]

$$\min_{t} \frac{d_i(t - \sum_{t' < t} q_i(t'))}{q_i(t)}$$

Beyond the case for the universal restart policy of Luby *et al.*[2], we constructed optimal restart policies from training data and tested the policies on test data that had not been used for training. Results comparing the optimal restart policy of the two predictive models and the optimal restart policy without observation with the best fixed cutoff restart policy are shown in Table 1. For the problem domains studied, we found that the expected run time of both of the dynamic restart policies with observation are lower than that of the optimal dynamic restart policy without observations. We attribute the improvement in solution time, ranging from about 10% to 30% for the domains, to effectively harnessing the predictive models for differentiating runs. For all of the problems, we found that the run-time predictive model yields faster solution times than the SAT/UNSAT distribution predictive model. We believe that this is based in differentiating short runs from long runs, which endows the solver with an ability to avoid expending time on non-promising long runs.

6   Summary and Directions

We described the challenge of relaxing the assumption of independence in randomized restart procedures for backtracking search. We defined the dynamic

---

[1] Note that the cutoff is usually different from the optimal cutoffs for distributions D_1 and D_2.

[2] Luby *et al.*'s universal restart policy does *not* change from distribution to distribution.

Table 1. Comparative results of optimal policies with and without observation with the best fixed cutoff and Luby *et al.*'s universal restart policy, where ERT is the expected run time (choice points) and improvements are measured over Luby *et al.*'s universal policy

	QCP		Graph Coloring		Planning	
Restart Policy	ERT	Improve-ment(%)	ERT	Improve-ment(%)	ERT	Improve-ment(%)
Optimal, no predictor	33,895	86.8	45,960	87.4	25,948	79.5
Optimal, run-time	26,423	89.7	31,012	91.5	18,418	85.4
Optimal, distribution	26,564	89.6	36,272	90.0	23,724	81.2
Best fixed cutoff	33,926	86.8	48,276	86.7	26,058	79.4
Luby *et al.*universal	257,363	0	363,626	0	126,383	0

dependent restart problem and showed how we can employ dynamic programming in offline procedures to generate ideal real-time restart policies. We first explored the case where a solver only considers information about the execution time of previous runs and then extended the analysis to include evidence about problem-solving behavior observed during runs. Finally, we presented the results of experiments in three domains, including quasigroup completion, graph coloring, and logistics-planning problems.

We are pursuing several extensions to the results presented here. Our ongoing work includes the development of dynamic dependent restart procedures for the single-instance scenario. In this setting, we seek to relate the RTD of an ensemble to the RTD's of its individual instances under a randomized solver. We are also studying the generalization of the methods to scenarios that make weaker assumptions about the nature of the underlying RTD. As part of this work, we are exploring the use of methods from reinforcement learning to infer the underlying distribution from previous search trajectories.

We believe that there is great opportunity in continuing to take a Bayesian perspective in tackling combinatorial problems, where we develop machinery and methods that allows solvers to be *believers* that take into consideration evidential observations about problem solving, and that can consider probabilistic dependencies among multiple solving sessions.

References

[1] Dimitris Achlioptas, Carla P. Gomes, Henry A. Kautz, and Bart Selman. Generating satisfiable problem instances. In *AAAI/IAAI*, pages 256–261, 2000.

[2] D. P. Bertsekas and J. N. Tsitsiklis. *Neuro-Dynamic Programming*. Athena Scientific, 1996.

[3] Hubie Chen, Carla Gomes, and Bart Selman. Formal models of heavy-tailed behavior in combinatorial search. *Lecture Notes in Computer Science*, 2239:408ff, 2001.

[4] David Maxwell Chickering, David Heckerman, and Christopher Meek. A Bayesian approach to learning Bayesian networks with local structure. In *Proceedings of the Thirteenth Conference On Uncertainty in Artificial Intelligence (UAI-97)*, pages 80–89, Providence, RI, 1997. Morgan Kaufman Publishers.

[5] Joseph C. Culberson and Feng Luo. Exploring the k-colorable landscape with iterated greedy. In David S. Johnson and Michael A. Trick, editors, *Dimacs Series in Discrete Mathematics and Theoretical Computer Science, Vol. 36*, pages 245–284, 1996.

[6] I. Gent and T. Walsh. Easy Problems are Sometimes Hard. *Artificial Intelligence*, 70:335–345, 1993.

[7] Carla P. Gomes and Bart Selman. Problem Structure in the Presence of Perturbations. In *Proceedings of the Fourteenth National Conference on Artificial Intelligence (AAAI-97)*, pages 221–227, New Providence, RI, 1997. AAAI Press.

[8] Carla P. Gomes, Bart Selman, and Nuno Crato. Heavy-tailed Distributions in Combinatorial Search. In Gert Smolka, editor, *Principles and practice of Constraint Programming (CP97) Lecture Notes in Computer Science*, pages 121–135, Linz, Austria., 1997. Springer-Verlag.

[9] Carla P. Gomes, Bart Selman, Nuno Crato, and Henry Kautz. Heavy-tailed phenomena in satisfiability and constraint satisfaction problems. *J. of Automated Reasoning*, 24(1–2):67–100, 2000.

[10] Carla P. Gomes, Bart Selman, and Henry Kautz. Boosting Combinatorial Search Through Randomization. In *Proceedings of the Fifteenth National Conference on Artificial Intelligence (AAAI-98)*, pages 431–438, New Providence, RI, 1998. AAAI Press.

[11] Carla P. Gomes, Bart Selman, and Henry A. Kautz. Boosting combinatorial search through randomization. In *AAAI/IAAI*, pages 431–437, 1998.

[12] Aaai-2000 workshop on leveraging probability and uncertainty in computation, 2000.

[13] T. Hogg, B. Huberman, and C. Williams (Eds.). Phase Transitions and Complexity (Special Issue). *Artificial Intelligence*, 81(1–2), 1996.

[14] Eric Horvitz, Yongshao Ruan, Carla Gomes, Henry Kautz, Bart Selman, and Max Chickering. A Bayesian approach to tackling hard computational problems. In *Proceedings the 17th Conference on Uncertainty in Artificial Intelligence (UAI-2001)*, pages 235–244, Seattle, USA, 2001.

[15] R. A. Howard. *Dynamic Programming and Markov Processes*. MIT Press, 1960.

[16] H. Kautz and B. Selman. Pushing the envelope: planning, propositional logic, and stochastic search. In *Proceedings of the Thirteenth National Conference on Artificial Intelligence (AAAI-96)*, pages 1188–1194, Portland, OR, 1996. AAAI Press.

[17] Henry Kautz, Eric Horvitz, Yongshao Ruan, Bart Selman, and Carla Gomes. Dynamic randomized restarts: Optimal restart policies with observation. To appear in AAAI, 2002.

[18] Henry Kautz, Yongshao Ruan, D. Achlioptas, Carla P. Gomes, Bart Selman, and Mark Stickel. Balance and filtering in structured satisfiable problems. In *Proceedings of the Sixteenth International Joint Conference on Artificial Intelligence (IJCAI-01)*, pages 351–358, 2001.

[19] S. Kirkpatrick and B. Selman. Critical behavior in the satisfiability of random Boolean expressions. *Science*, 264:1297–1301, 1994.

[20] Chu Min Li and Anbulagan. Heuristics based on unit propagation for satisfiability problems. In *Proceedings of the International Joint Conference on Artificial Intelligence*, pages 366–371. AAAI Pess, 1997.

[21] M. Luby, A. Sinclair, and D. Zuckerman. Optimal speedup of las vegas algorithms. *Information Process. Letters*, pages 173–180, 1993.

[22] Matthew W. Moskewicz, Conor F. Madigan, Ying Zhao, Lintao Zhang, and Sharad Malik. Chaff: Engineering an efficient SAT solver. In *Design Automation Conference*, pages 530–535, 2001.

[23] B. Selman, H. Kautz, and B. Cohen. Local search strategies for satisfiability testing. In D. Johnson and M. Trick, editors, *Dimacs Series in Discrete Mathematics and Theoretical Computer Science, Vol. 26*, pages 521–532. AMS, 1993.

[24] T. Walsh. Search in a Small World. In *Proceedings of the International Joint Conference on Artificial Intelligence*, pages 1172–1177, Stockholm, Sweden, 1999.

Visopt ShopFloor:
On the Edge of Planning and Scheduling

Roman Barták*

Charles University in Prague, Faculty of Mathematics and Physics
Malostranské námestí 2/25
118 00 Praha 1, Czech Republic
bartak@kti.mff.cuni.cz

Abstract. Visopt ShopFloor is a complete system for solving real-life scheduling problems in complex industries. In particular, the system is intended to problem areas where traditional scheduling methods failed. In the paper we describe the heart of the Visopt system, a generic scheduling engine. This engine goes beyond traditional scheduling by offering some planning capabilities. We achieved this integrated behaviour by applying Constraint Logic Programming in a less standard way - the definition of a constraint model is dynamic and introduction of constraints interleaves with search.

1 Introduction

Scheduling is one of the strongest application areas of constraint programming [18]. The reason of such success can be found in a similar static character of both scheduling problems and constraint satisfaction problems. First, the problem structure is fully described in advance. In case of scheduling it means that all the activities and all the relations between the activities are known in advance. In case of standard constraint satisfaction problem (CSP) it means that all the variables, their domains, and the constraints are known in advance. The problem solving then consists merely of searching the space of alternative combinations of activity locations or variables' values respectively. Search is also a core technology in the close area of planning. However, the main difference from scheduling is the dynamic character of planning [14]. The structure of the plan is so variable that it can be hardly encoded in variables, domains, and constraints defined before the problem solving starts. Thus, planning typically uses ad-hoc algorithms even if there exist approaches based on general concepts like CSP. These approaches either try to fit a planning problem into a static concept of CSP [7,15] or they are based on generalisations of the CSP framework like Dynamic CSP [12] or Structural CSP [13].

---

* The research is supported by the Grant Agency of the Czech Republic under the contract no. 201/01/0942.

P. Van Hentenryck (Ed.): CP 2002, LNCS 2470, pp. 587–602, 2002.

588   Roman Barták

To solve the problems on the edge of planning and scheduling we propose to use an existing technology of Constraint Logic Programming (CLP) in the way this framework was originally defined [9]. Note that since CSP has been formalised, the same static approach is applied to solve the problems in CLP as well, i.e., first define the variables, the domains, and the constraints and then do search/labelling [16]. In particular, it means that the alternatives should be resolved at the level of constraints rather than at the level of CLP rules. For example, the following CLP program:

```
p(X):- X#=<1 #\/ X#>=2.
```

is assumed to be better than the program:

```
p(X):- X#=<1.
```

```
p(X):- X#>=2.
```

As argued in [17], the second CLP model of disjunction is less efficient because it requires backtracking over the CLP rules (problem formulation) when labelling discovers that X>1. If the structure of alternatives in the problem looks like the left part of Figure 1 then the alternatives should be definitely modelled as a disjunctive constraint. However, in many problems the structure looks more like the right part of Figure 1, i.e. the alternatives are more complex. It means that in different branches of the CLP search tree, we get different sets of variables and constraints, i.e. different CSPs. Then the advantages of CLP becomes more evident because in a single CLP program we can express several (in some sense similar) constraint satisfaction problems and thus to reduce the exponential grow of the number of constraints in the planning-like problems. Our basic idea is to return to the roots, i.e., to use constraints in CLP in the same way as unification is used [9]. It means that constraints are introduced during search and thus different sets of constraints are active in different branches of the search tree. In some sense, it implies that labelling/search interleaves with CSP formulation, i.e. deciding the value of some variable determines the remaining set of variables and constraints.

Fig. 1. A structure of the CSP formulation in CLP - problem is formulated from left to right, nodes express alternative rules (Prolog choice points). In the left part, the alternatives are "independent" so they can be modelled as disjunctive constraints. In the right part, one choice determines what will be the next alternatives

We believe that CLP approach is sufficient to model and solve mixed planning and scheduling problems. To demonstrate this attitude we have implemented a generic scheduling engine for the Visopt ShopFloor system. The main difference of our solver from other scheduling systems is full integration of the planning component i.e. the solver does both planning and scheduling tasks. We can say that planning is resolved at the level of CLP rules while labelling of variables solves the scheduling task.

The paper summarises our work on the scheduling engine for the Visopt ShopFloor system [20]. We first introduce the problem area and discuss its description (Section 2). Then we present some details of the internal architecture of the scheduler, in particular we describe a dynamic constraint model and a basic scheduling strategy (Section 3). We conclude with some results and lessons learned (Section 4).

2   Problem Area and Its Description

Visopt ShopFloor is not another academic planner/scheduler but its design has been driven completely by a commercial area, i.e. by existing problems in real-live factories. The emphasis has been put to complex areas where the traditional scheduling techniques failed because they were not able to cover whole complexity of the problem. In particular, we concentrate on scheduling problems in food, chemical, and pharmaceutical industries. Nevertheless, the original goal was to design a generic scheduling engine applicable to other areas as well. So, from the beginning we accommodate the engine by rich modelling interface for problem description.

2.1   Order-Driven Production

Basically, the goal is to generate a plan/schedule of production for a given time period. It means that notions like makespan are not used there directly because the scheduled period is fixed.

The production is driven by *orders*, i.e., the user specifies a set of orders to be scheduled. Each order is described by a set of ordered items together with requested quantities. It is also possible to describe alternative items that can be delivered if the ordered item is not available (provided that the total ordered quantity is fulfilled). Moreover, the ordered quantity can be relaxed as well so we can deliver more or less than the user requested (if the customer allows it). Thus the ordered quantity is not necessarily a constant number - it could be an interval with one number inside the interval indicating the ordered quantity. We use a penalty mechanism to describe how good the quantity requirement is fulfilled. Basically, the penalty is increasing (linearly) if we deliver quantity different from the ordered quantity (see Figure 2). For the alternative items, the ordered quantity is zero, i.e. if we deliver alternative items instead of the ordered items then we pay the penalty. Thus no special mechanism to distinguish between the ordered items and the alternative items is necessary.

Finally, for each order the user describes the delivery time, the acceptable delivery time, and the latest delivery time. The delivery must be realised in the interval ⟨delivery time, latest delivery time⟩, in particular we do not allow to deliver before the delivery time and after the latest delivery time. Nevertheless, the latest delivery time can be set to supreme and it such a case we can postpone production for the order if there is not enough capacity to produce for the order. This technique is useful to model the forecast orders that are satisfied only if there is free production capacity (i.e. the real orders are preferred). If we deliver no later than the acceptable delivery time then no penalty is applied, otherwise a penalty for lateness is used (see Figure 2). Earliness is not modelled as a penalty for the orders (recall that no early deliveries are allowed); we model it as a cost of storing of the item. We believe that the above penalty/cost framework makes the model closer to reality.

Using intervals instead of constant numbers for the item quantities and the delivery times is the way of introducing the soft constraints into the model. Satisfaction of such constraints is measured by a uniform penalty/cost mechanism that allows us to express various optimisation criteria. We discuss optimisation issues later in the paper (Section 2.4).

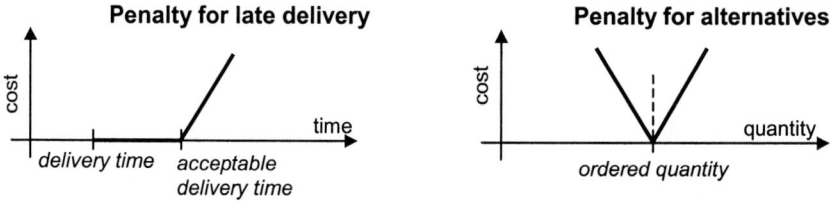

Penalty for late delivery

Penalty for alternatives

Fig. 2. Penalty mechanism for orders

2.2   Complex Resources

A typical feature of our problem area is using *resources (machines) with complex behaviour*. This behaviour is described via *states* and *transitions* between the states. At each time, the resource can be at one state only or the resource is in the transition between two states (we allow a non-negative transition time to be assigned to each transition). The transition scheme is typically described by a directed graph (Figure 3) or by a transition table. Note also that the transition scheme can naturally model set-ups, changeovers, and similar features of the resources.

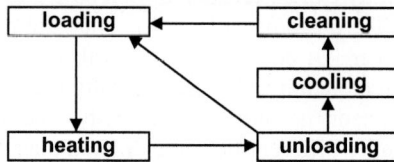

Fig. 3. A simple transition scheme for the resource

Currently, we concentrate on batch production primarily so the schedule of the resource is described by a sequence of non-overlapping batches[1]. Each batch belongs to one of the resource states and the user may restrict the length of the batch sequence in the state. For example a minimal number of five batches and a maximal number of ten batches of some state S can be in sequence. It means that we cannot change the state S of the resource until at least five batches of this state have been processed and we have to change the state S to another state (following the transition scheme) if ten batches of the state S have been processed. In addition to this min batch/max batch

---

[1] Continuous process can be decomposed into a sequence of batches. Parallel processing can also be modelled via batches using a timetabling concept (but this is less efficient).

constraint and the transition scheme, the user may specify other sequencing constraint that we call a *counter*. The counter says that after a given number of batches of specific states there must be a batch of a given state, e.g. after ten processing batches there must be a cleaning batch. Our transition scheme with counters is one of the advantages of the Visopt system because the traditional scheduling systems (usually based on task-centric models [2,8]) can hardly model such complexity of resources.

For each state the user specifies (process) *duration* of batches of this state. The location of the batch in time can be further restricted by using *time windows*, i.e., the batch must start and complete in specified time intervals. Like duration, the time windows are common for all the batches of the given state, i.e., the user specifies the time windows for states rather than for particular batches. The user may set the batches (states) to be either non-interruptible (the batch must run within a time window) or interruptible (the batch can start in one time window and complete in another time window). In case of interruptible batches we distinguish between the processing duration, i.e., time spent in time windows, and the idle duration, i.e., time spent out of time windows. The total duration of the batch equals to the sum of the processing duration and the idle duration. Note also that the batch stays in the resource from the beginning to the end of processing so even if the batch is in idle time no other batch can be processed by the same resource (Figure 4).

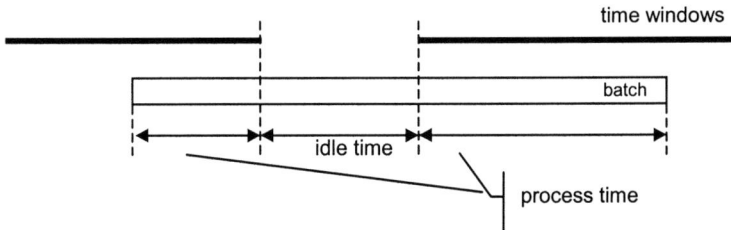

Fig. 4. Interruptible batch occupies the resource out of time windows too

To make the concept of interruptible/non-interruptible batches more general, we allow the user to express the maximal ratio between the idle duration and the processing duration. If this maximal ratio is zero, then the batch is non-interruptible. If maximal ratio is one then the batch is interruptible but the idle duration cannot be longer than the processing duration etc. Thus, the user may describe a full scale of interruptibility.

Note also, that the concept of interruptibility is different from pre-emptiveness used in traditional scheduling. A pre-emptive activity may be stopped in the middle, another activity (activities) is processed and then the original activity is re-started (perhaps on different resource). In our concept, the pre-emptive activities can simply be modelled by a set of batches (see Figure 6 for example).

The *capacity* of the batch can be constant or it can be variable: for example a single heating batch may be used to heat two to five tons of the item. Typically, the user describes some minimal capacity processed by the batch (e.g., two tons), maximal capacity processed by the batch (e.g., five tons), and the increment in capacity (e.g., one ton so two, three, four, or five tons of the item can be processed in the batch).

2.3   Resource Dependencies

Typically, there are more resources involved in the problem and these resources interact in a predefined way. We describe this interaction by *supplier-consumer dependencies*. It particular, each batch has some input items that are consumed and some output items that are produced (in some batches, there are only the input items or only the output items or no items at all). There must be a supplier for the input items, i.e., there must exist some batches that produce the item, and there must be a consumer for the output items. For each item that appears in the model, the user specifies all possible connections between the supplying resources and the consuming resources. Every such connection describes a flow of the item from one resource to another resource. The user specifies the delay between the end of the supplying batch and the start of the consuming batch (constant or variable in a specified range) as well as a quantum of the item moved through the dependency (Figure 5).

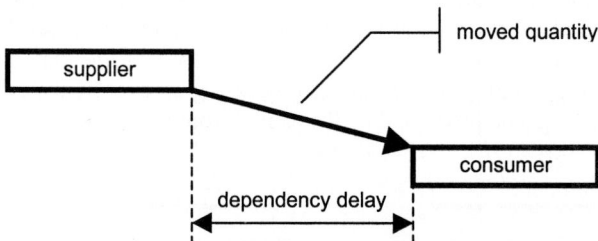

Fig. 5. Batches are connected via dependencies

The main difference of the supplier-consumer dependency from a precedence relation is moving some quantity through the dependency. Assume that we have a batch consuming ten tons of some item. This batch must be connected to enough supplying batches in such a way that the sum of quantities in dependencies (supplied quantities) is equal to ten tons (consumed quantity). Note also that the structure of dependencies may vary significantly: we can have one supplying batch providing ten tons or we can use five batches, each one provides two tons etc. (Figure 6). Moreover, many-to-many relations between the batches are allowed. Recall that the user describes just which dependencies are allowed between the batches and what are their parameters. The decision about how to connect the batches is done during scheduling. Actually, this is a way of introducing the planning features to the system.

Supplier-consumer dependencies may also mimic behaviour of some resources like movers and stores. If there are no other constraints on the mover (like limited capacity) then the mover can be fully modelled using the dependencies. Otherwise a mover should be described as a resource. Also, it is possible to model some stores like buffers using dependencies with variable dependency delay. The variability of the delay describes the minimal and the maximal storing time for the item.

Note finally that the custom orders behave like a consumer in supplier-consumer dependencies. Using this technique, the user describes which items can be ordered and what resources supply these items. In a similar way, the user can define purchase as the supplier for some items. It means that some items may be purchased from

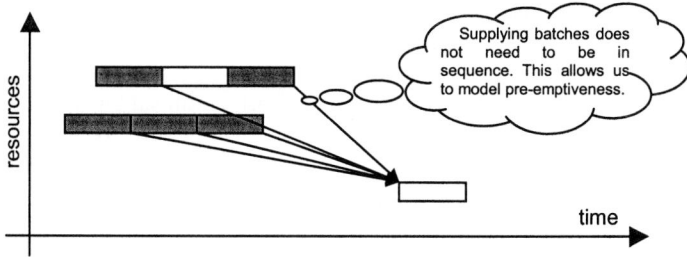

Fig. 6. One consuming batch can be connected to several supplying batches spread over more resources (shadow rectangles). The only restriction is that the requested quantity must be supplied and the time distance between the supplying batches and the consuming batch satisfies the dependency delay

external suppliers. Thanks to generality of the dependency mechanism there is no problem to define items which can be both produced on site or which can be purchased. It is up to the solver to decide how the item is acquired.

Using the above dependency mechanism we can capture arbitrary process flow in the factory including re-cycling, many-to-many relations between resources etc. This is usually very hard or even impossible in the existing scheduling systems where typically only the precedence relations can be defined.

2.4   Objectives

As we have already mentioned, the basic task is to generate a feasible schedule for the fixed period of time. Some users prefer to minimise the number of set-ups, others like to minimise the storing time or to maximise the satisfaction of customers (to minimise the sum of penalties in orders). Quite often *multi-criteria optimisation* is required.

Our opinion about optimisation in scheduling is that all the optimisation criteria substitute what the user really needs - to maximise the profit. Thus we decided to use optimisation based on the cost in the Visopt system. It means that the optimisation criterion is shifted from the solving level to the modelling level (to the definition of costs/penalties). In addition to penalty mechanism described above (Section 2.1), the user may put cost to batches (dependent on duration and processed quantity), to transitions, and to dependencies. The optimisation task is then to minimise the total sum of costs and penalties in the schedule. Another criterion asked by the customers is schedule robustness, i.e., small sensitivity to flaws during production. It can be modelled using penalties or more tighten constraints; small flaws are solved at the production level, e.g., using a frozen flavour if the fresh one is not available.

We believe that our unified cost model can cover most real-life optimisation criteria. In Section 2.1 we already showed how to model lateness and earliness using the penalty mechanism. If the objective is to minimise the number of set-ups then the user may put the cost only to the batches/transitions describing the set-ups. Minimisation of makespan is widely used but it seems to be rather artificial objective. We can model it by putting a delay penalty to the virtual order that is scheduled after all other orders. The important feature of the Visopt system is that all the above (and many other) criteria can be combined together. So using a single optimisation parameter - the cost - also removes the difficulties of multi-criteria optimisation.

Note finally, that a typical user does not require finding an optimal solution - a good enough solution is accepted as well. Cost optimisation is used to get good schedules but it is the user who decides if the solution is "good enough". Typically, the quality of the schedule is measured by savings achieved when the schedule is applied to production. In many cases, a small improvement of the schedule over the existing schedule is assumed to be a "good enough" solution. If the user finds the schedule "no-good" then he or she can modify the cost parameters in such a way that the bad part of the schedule is penalised. Then a new schedule is generated by the system.

To summarise the discussion about the optimisation: the main point is that we are not required to prove optimality or the distance from the optimal solution - we should simply produce a good schedule.

3   Realisation of the Solver

Visopt ShopFloor system consists of two independent parts: the ShopFloor (SF) user interface and the scheduling engine. The user describes the problem in SF and he or she gets the results in the form of a Gantt chart there. The problem description is very intuitive; the user just specifies what resources are used including their parameters, what are the dependencies between the resources (what is the item flow in the factory), and what are the actual orders (the demands). This description can be done manually or it can be generated automatically from an ERP system. When the problem is fully specified, the SF module generates a text file called a *factory model* with all the parameters. Basically, the factory model consists of three parts:

- description of resources, i.e., states, their attributes, and transitions,
- description of item flow, i.e., supplier-consumer dependencies,
- description of orders.

The factory model forms the only input to the scheduling engine. There are no constraints explicitly described in the factory model which makes the solver independent of the problem specification. Thus, the scheduling engine first generates a constraint model according to the problem specification. Note that this constraint model is dynamic, i.e., at the beginning only the objects and the constraints that are known are introduced and as the search progresses, the new objects and constraints are generated (see Introduction for a general description of this process). We describe the constraint model in Section 3.1. The second part of the solver is the scheduling strategy. It is basically a labelling procedure that decides about the values of variables in the constraint model. Again, this procedure must take in account that the constraint model is dynamic, i.e., assigning a value to the variable may introduce new variables and new constraints to the system. We describe the labelling procedure in Section 3.2.

3.1   Constraint Representation

There exist approaches trying to represent the dynamic problems in a static way using
the dummy variables [7,15]. Unfortunately, we cannot use these approaches because
the number of dummy variables is huge in planning-like problems. Thus we decided
to use a representation where some variables and constraints are introduced
dynamically during search [3]. The basic idea is as follows: at the beginning we
introduce only the objects that are known, i.e., the custom orders. As these custom
orders should be satisfied, we also start dependencies to the resources that can
produce the ordered items. When the actual supplier is found (this is usually decided
during labelling), we need to find suppliers for this supplier etc. To summarise it: if
there is a planning decision, i.e. the decision about what objects should be part of the
plan/schedule, we introduce all of them (via dependencies). Together with these
objects, the relevant constraints are posted so we can exploit the power of constraint
propagation. In some sense, this is a realisation of the idea of active decision
postponement [10].

Slots. Basically, the Visopt solver uses a resource-centric model [2,8] i.e. the
activities are grouped per resources rather than per tasks. The reason for choosing this
model is large complexity of the resource constraints in comparison with the
dependency constraints. The resource centric model is realised via *slots*. The slot is a
shell filled by a batch during scheduling. For each resource we have a chain of slots
and during scheduling these slots are being filled by batches according to demand
form other resources. The difference from the slots in timetabling is time location of
slots. In timetabling, the slots represent fixed time intervals. In the Visopt solver, the
slots may slide in time. Still, the order of slots is fixed but the slots may be shifted in
time, e.g., if the slot is moved to later time then all the successive slots must be moved
as well (Figure 7).

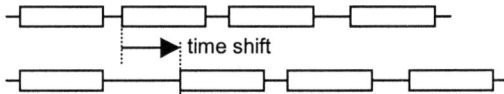

Fig. 7. Slots can move in time provided that the ordering of slots is preserved

Because the slots are not fixed in time, there are two finite domain (FD) variables in
each slot representing the *start time* and the *end time* of the slot. As described in
Section 2.2, we distinguish between the *process and idle duration* so there are two
more FD variables representing these durations. Recall that decomposition of duration
into process and idle parts depends on the time windows (Figure 4), i.e., on the state
of the resource. So the next FD variable describes what is the *state* of the resource in
the slot. Together, the semantic of the constraint that connects all these variables can
be described in the following way:

```
start_time in TimeWindows(state)
end_time in TimeWindows(state)
process_duration =
ProcessDuration(state,start_time,end_time)
idle_duration = IdleDuration(state,start_time,end_time)
```

```
start_time + process_duration + idle_duration =
end_time
```

The first two constraints above are realised using tabular constraints, i.e., the binary constraints where the domain is expressed as a table of compatible pairs [4] and the last three constraints are realised using a dedicated global constraint with a special filtering algorithm working with the time windows.

Transitions. Note that the ordering of slots is fixed so the next slot must start after the end of the previous slot. The exact distance between the slots can be derived from the transition scheme defined for the resource. Basically, this distance depends on the states of the slots so the following formula describes the transition time constraint:

```
end_time_i + TransitionTime(state_i, state_i+1) = start_time_i+1
```

where the index indicates the ordering number of the slot.

To complete the description of the transition scheme, we need to specify the relation between the states in two consecutive slots. Recall that for each state the user describes the minimal and the maximal number of batches. Thus, for each slot we should know how many slots right before have the same state. Thus we introduce a new FD variable called a *serial number* that indicates a relative position of the slot in the longest continuous sequence of the slots with the same state (Figure 8).

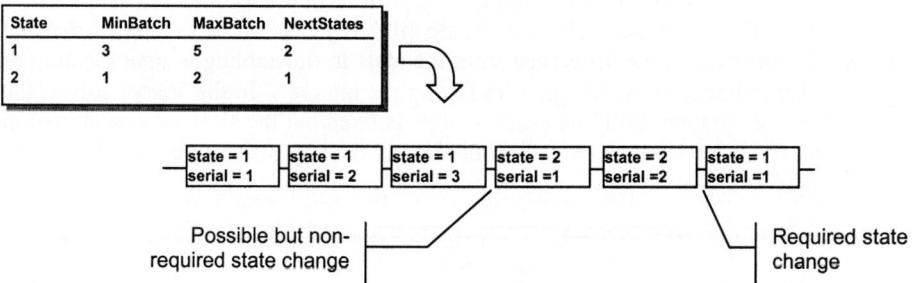

Fig. 8. The serial numbers in the slots indicate the position of the batch (slot) in the sequence of slots of the same state

The semantics of the transition constraint can then be described using the following formulas:

```
∀i serial_number_i in 1..MaxBatches(state_i)
state_i+1 in {state_i} ∪ NextStates(state_i)
state_i=state_i+1 ⇒ serial_number_i+1 = serial_number_i+1
state_i≠state_i+1 ⇒ serial_number_i+1 = 1
serial_number_i<MinBatches(state_i) ⇒ state_i=state_i+1
```

It is possible to implement the transition constraints exactly as specified above but to get better pruning we use a special global constraint describing the transition [7]. Note also, that the transition constraint can be seen as a special version of the counters (Section 2.2) so counters are implemented in a very similar way.

Introducing the Slots. There are two ways how to introduce the slots to the system. First, it is possible to estimate the maximal number of slots using the transition scheme, duration of batches etc. and to generate all necessary slots in advance. The disadvantage of this approach is that it may introduce a huge number of dummy slots that will not be used in the final schedule. The only advantage could be better propagation because the slot variables are known and the constraints among them are posted before we start labelling. However, we do not need propagation in far future slots that will not be used in the final schedule (moreover, the propagation is weak there and it slows down the system). Therefore we generate the slots dynamically on demand. It means that if we find that some batch could be allocated to the resource then we generate a slot for it. So slots are added due to a transition scheme (restricted transition time) or due to a demand from other resources (asking for the supplier/consumer). Note also that even if we introduce the slot it does not mean that it will be filled by the batch that caused this introduction. Perhaps some other batch overhauls it or the slot stays empty. Still, the ordering of slots is fixed so it is not possible to introduce a new slot in-between two existing slots (because the transition constraints have already been posted). Thus, deciding to which slot the batch is allocated corresponds to the decision about the absolute ordering of batches in the resource. This view is similar to the idea of permutation based scheduling presented in [19]. The main difference of our approach is that we can solve problems where the appearance of batch depends on allocation of other batches. In particular, the structure of batches in the resource depends on demands from other resources as well as on the transition scheme for the resource (using intermediate batches for set-ups etc.).

Filling the Slots. There is another difference between slots and batches. The batch describes also the input and the output quantities of the processed items so for each item there is a FD variable describing its quantity. If the number of items is large, it is not efficient to include such variables into the slot until the batch (state) in the slot is known. Thus, these variables (and the corresponding constraints, e.g., the capacity limit) will be introduced dynamically when the state in the slot is known, i.e., when the domain of the state variable becomes singleton. In our constraint model, such introduction is done automatically using event-driven programming.

Dependencies. Dependencies form the most dynamic part of the model. Recall that the dependency describes a supplier-consumer relation between two batches so the dependency will connect two slots filled by respective batches. Because the dependency is closely related to the item we cannot introduce the dependency until we know the item and its quantity. As described in the previous paragraph, the variable specifying the item quantity is introduced as soon as we know the batch - the state - in the slot. At the same time we can start dependencies from the given slot.

Assume that we have an input item defined for the batch in the slot. Dependencies should connect this batch with all the supplying batches. It is possible to post dependency to every slot that can be filled by a supplying batch. However, this eager method has huge memory consumption when applied to large-scale problems with hundreds or thousands of slots. Thus, we use a more lazy method that posts a minimal number of dependencies covering the required quantity. Typically, these dependencies go to the first possible slot of the supplying resources. If we find later that these slots cannot be filled by a supplying batch then we move the dependency to the next slot and so on. If there is no slot found in the resource, the dependency is made empty. Other dependencies can be introduced as soon as we find that the dependencies generated so far are not enough (e.g. because some of them have been made empty). For each slot, the system maintains links to all non-empty dependencies going to this slot. These links are then used during scheduling when deciding what batch will be filled in the slot (see Section 3.2).

Dependency Constraints. Dependency connects the supplying batch with the consuming batch and it posts a constraint between the end time of the supplying batch and the start time of the consuming batch (Figure 5). Moreover, there is some quantity of the item going through the dependency so the sum of all such quantities per item must be equal to the processed quantity in the batch. In addition to these basic constraints we can post some redundant constraints to reduce symmetries, to improve domain pruning etc.

First, it should be said that the dependency can be started both from the supplying batch as well as from the consuming batch. To remove this symmetry we can use a first-come-first-serve principle so the first dependency will connect two batches and the dependency in the reverse direction will be made empty.

Note also that dependencies make demands for batches in the resource. Thus, if we decide about ordering of dependencies going to a particular resource then, in fact, we determine the ordering of batches in the resource. There exist filtering algorithms doing such decisions using information about time, like edge-finding [1]. However, the global constraints representing these constraints are usually static in the sense that they can be defined only over a known set of demands. Because the dependencies are introduced dynamically we need a dynamic version of such global constraints [5]. In the Visopt solver we use a simple dynamic version of the edge-finding algorithm. Unfortunately, the edge-finding like methods are less effective there because the domains of time variables are not very restricted. Methods based on ordering of batches, e.g. [11], are more appropriate there. We use a global constraint that orders the dependencies going to the resource using information about the ordering of batches in the resource where from the dependencies have been started. A detail description of this constraint is out of scope of this paper; Figure 9 shows the basic idea.

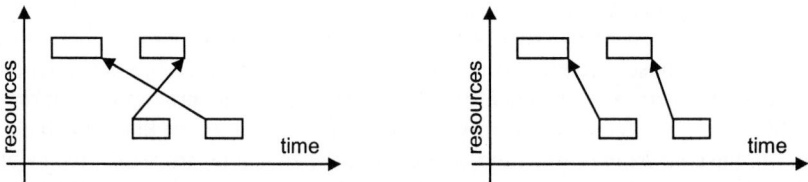

Fig. 9. A global constraint for ordering the dependencies may forbid the order of dependencies on the left and may force the ordering on the right depending on the dependency delay and the distance of consuming batches (the arrow shows a direction from the batch that posted the dependency)

3.2   Labelling Strategy

The constraint model is dynamic but autonomous. It means that the variables and the constraints are introduced automatically when the system finds out that they are necessary. Typically, new variables and new constraints are introduced when a domain of some variable becomes singleton. For example, if the domain of the state variable in the slot becomes singleton, then the variables for item quantities in the slot are introduced and the dependencies for these items are started. The labelling strategy must only be aware about the incomplete character of the constraint model i.e. the new variables may appear during labelling.

Basically, the labelling strategy is responsible for filling the slots by batches and for finding connections between the batches/slots. This task is fulfilled in two steps:

1. the slot that is not yet filled by a batch is selected,
2. the state/batch in this slot is decided (the slot is closed).

Recall that the slots are introduced dynamically from left to right so we should close the leftmost slot in the resource first. Of course, it is reasonable to close the slots in the resource where some demand exists. This demand is modelled via dependencies going to the resource. Recall that the dependencies are started in the custom orders first so we should close the resource closest to the custom order before we can continue to next resources. To summarise the above discussion, the labelling strategy closes the slots in the order-to-purchase left-to-right order. This interleaved ordering is realised via a borderline called *frontier* that is moving in steps from left (past) to right (future) in the schedule. At each step, only the slots starting before the frontier are closed in the order-to-purchase ordering (see Figure 10).

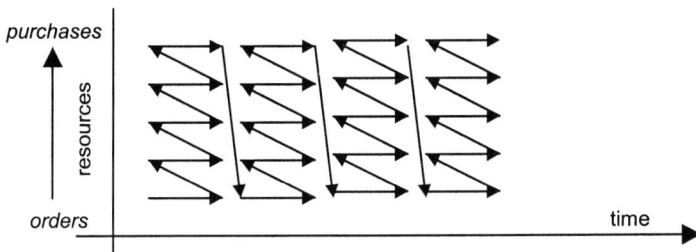

Fig. 10. Ordering used in the labelling strategy

The second decision of the scheduling strategy is about the batch in the selected slot. The labelling strategy first selects the "best" dependencies and connects them to the slot. This is done via setting the quantity variable in the dependency to be greater than zero (maximal possible value is tried first). We use a heuristic defining the relation "better" between the dependencies. This heuristic takes in account the time of the dependency (the earlier dependencies are better), the cost increment when choosing the dependency (the smaller cost is better), and other criteria. Note that when some dependencies are fixed to the slot, the rest dependencies are moved to the next possible slot. Thus, the decision about the ordering of dependencies is equivalent to the decision about the ordering of batches in the slots. After selecting the dependencies in the slot, the labelling strategy assigns the value to the state variable and to the item quantities variables. At the end of each scheduling step, the time variables in the closed slots are labelled - the earlier times are preferred.

Currently the Visopt scheduling engine uses backtracking-based search driven by the above described variable and value selection criteria. The basic search strategy is enhanced by user defined backjumping, i.e., we selected some significant variables to which the system backtracks upon failure.

4   Results and Conclusions

Visopt ShopFloor system has been tested in several pilot projects in one of the biggest chemical enterprises in Europe, one of the biggest and famous candy producers in The Netherlands, and one of the biggest dairies in Israel among others. The feedback from the companies is very positive - Visopt ShopFloor is the only system, among the systems that they tested, that can fully cover the complexity of production in these enterprises via offering rich modelling capabilities supported by a new solving technology. The unique features of Visopt, that the other scheduling systems cannot cover, include modelling of complex transition schemes for resources, modelling of arbitrary dependency structure of the factory, modelling of set-ups, cleaning, and maintenance including by-products, and modelling of process and item alternatives.

For purposes of this paper we use the results of scheduling for the candy producer which was the most complex model among the above mentioned pilot projects (we can schedule the other models in seconds or minutes). This problem requires many of the unique features of Visopt including groups of alternative but not identical resources with time windows, item dependent set-up times, and many-to-many relations between the resources leading to many alternative production routes. It is also a large-scale problem as Table 1 shows. In particular, notice the resolution of time and quantity that determines roughly the size of the domains for time and quantity variables.

Table 1. Problem size

Number of resources	34
Total number of resource states	991
Size of scheduled period	1 week (10 080 minutes)
Time resolution	1 minute
Number of items	294
Number of orders	45
Total quantity in orders	88.5 tons (88 485 kg)
Quantity resolution	1 kilogram

Table 2 shows the size of the schedule and the time of scheduling. We use SICStus Prolog 3.8.7 for implementation of the scheduling engine, all our global constraints are implemented in clpfd library of SICStus Prolog.

Table 2. Solution size

Number of batches	5946
Number of dependencies	9325
Runtime	53 minutes (Pentium 4/1700 MHz)

For comparison, the traditional schedulers handle about 20.000 batches [personal communication to Wim Nuijten from ILOG] but all these batches are known in advance. In planning, the size of plans is measured in tens of actions [AIPS02 planning competition]. Recall that the input to the Visopt engine consists of the model of the factory and the list of demands. All the batches are introduced (planned) during the problem solving and allocated to resources (scheduling). Thus, we are basically solving a (limited) planning problem under time and resource constraints. As Table 2 shows, Visopt ShopFloor system can generate plans in the size close to the size of the traditional scheduling problems but with a more complex and tied structure.

References

1. Baptiste, P. and Le Pape, C.: Edge-finding constraint propagation algorithms for disjunctive and cumulative scheduling, in *Proceedings of the Fifteenth Workshop of the U.K. Planning Special Interest Group* (1996).
2. Barták, R.: Conceptual Models for Combined Planning and Scheduling. *Electronic Notes in Discrete Mathematics,* Volume 4, Elsevier (1999).
3. Barták, R.: Dynamic Constraint Models for Planning and Scheduling Problems. *Proceedings of the ERCIM/CompulogNet Workshop on Constraint* Programming, LNAI Series, Springer Verlag (2000).
4. Barták, R.: Filtering Algorithms for Tabular Constraints, in *Proceedings of CP2001 Workshop CICLOPS*, Paphos, Cyprus (2001), 168-182.
5. Barták, R.: Dynamic Global Constraints in Backtracking Based Environments, in *Annals of Operations Research*, Kluwer (2002), to appear.
6. Barták, R.: Modelling Transition Constraints. The ECAI Workshop on Modelling and Solving Problems with Constraints (2002).
7. Beck, J.Ch. and Fox, M.S.: Scheduling Alternative Activities. *Proceedings of AAAI-99*, USA (1999), 680-687.
8. Brusoni, V., Console, L., Lamma. E., Mello, P., Milano, M., Terenziani, P.: Resource-based vs. Task-based Approaches for Scheduling Problems. *Proceedings of the 9th ISMIS96*, LNCS Series, Springer Verlag (1996).
9. Gallaire, H.: Logic Programming: Further Developments, in: IEEE Symposium on Logic Programming, Boston, IEEE (1985).
10. Joslin, D. and Pollack M.E.: Passive and Active Decision Postponement in Plan Generation. *Proceedings of the Third European Conference on Planning* (1995).
11. Laborie P.: Algorithms for Propagating Resource Constraints in AI Planning and Scheduling: Existing Approaches and New Results. In *Proceedings of 6th European Conference on Planning,* Toledo, Spain (2001), 205-216.

12. Mittal, S. and Falkenhainer, B.: Dynamic Constraint Satisfaction Problems. *Proceedings of AAAI-90*, USA (1990), 25-32.
13. Nareyek, A.: Structural Constraint Satisfaction. *Proceedings of AAAI-99 Workshop on Configuration* (1999).
14. Nareyek, A.: AI Planning in a Constraint Programming Framework. Proceedings of the Third International Workshop on Communication-Based Systems (2000).
15. Pegman, M.: Short Term Liquid Metal Scheduling. *Proceedings of PAPPACT98 Conference*, London (1998), 91-99.
16. van Hentenryck, P.: *Constraint Satisfaction in Logic Programming*, The MIT Press, Cambridge, Mass. (1989).
17. Van Hentenryck, P., Deville, Y.: The Cardinality Operator: A new Logical Connective for Constraint Logic Programming. *Proceedings of the International Conference on Logic Programming* (1991), 745-759.
18. Wallace, M.: Applying Constraints for Scheduling, in: *Constraint Programming*, Mayoh B. and Penjaak J. (eds.), NATO ASI Series, Springer Verlag (1994).
19. Zhou, J.: A Permutation-Based Approach for Solving the Job-Shop Problem. *Constraints*, vol. 2 no. 2 (1997), 185-213.
20. Visopt B.V. http://www.visopt.com

Constraint Programming Contribution
to Benders Decomposition: A Case Study

Thierry Benoist, Etienne Gaudin, and Benoît Rottembourg

Bouygues e-lab, 1 av. Eugène Freyssinet
78061 St Quentin en Yvelines Cedex, France
{tbenoist,egaudin,brottembourg}@bouygues.com

Abstract. The aim of this paper is to demonstrate that CP could be a better candidate than MIP for solving the master problem within a Benders decomposition approach. Our demonstration is based on a case study of a workforce scheduling problem encountered in a large call center of Bouygues Telecom, a French mobile phone operator. Our experiments show that CP can advantageously replace MIP for the implementation of the master problem due to its greater ability to efficiently manage a wide variety of constraints such as the ones occurring in time tabling applications.

1   Introduction

J.F. Benders initially introduced the eponymous decomposition method [1] for solving large-scale Mixed Integer Programming (MIP) problems. The partitioning consisted in separating integer variables and real variables in order to gain efficiency and to treat larger instances via decomposition. Benders decomposition has also been successfully used in a different way to take advantage of underlying problem structures for various optimization problems such as network design [2,3], hose or power supply planning [4] or stochastic optimization [5]. It is especially well suited when assignment of a subset of variables yields easily solvable disconnected and convex slave problems, such as flows for example. More recently, Benders decomposition has been used by the Constraint Programming (CP) community in order to hybrid linear programming with other kinds of algorithms [6,7,8,9].

The aim of this paper is to demonstrate that CP can be a better choice than MIP for solving some large-scale optimization problems with a decomposition based on problem structure. We do not propose a new framework based on Benders decomposition, but adapt classic Benders decomposition, where CP plays the role of MIP within the master problem solving. Our demonstration is based on a case study of a workforce scheduling problem encountered in a large call center of a French mobile phone operator, Bouygues Telecom, subsidiary of Bouygues. This problem will be referred to as the WORKFORCE SMOOTHING PROBLEM (WSP) in the rest of this paper. We applied Benders decomposition to this problem to take advantage of its network flow under-

P. Van Hentenryck (Ed.): CP 2002, LNCS 2470, pp. 603-617, 2002.
© Springer-Verlag Berlin Heidelberg 2002

lying structure in order to treat large instances of call center scheduling. Even if the resulting master problem has a linear underlying structure, we show that CP, equipped with a flow global constraint with its greater ability to efficiently manage a wide variety of constraints, could advantageously replace MIP as a master solver. The article is structured as follows. In section 2, WSP will be introduced and modeled as a Mixed-Integer Program with an underlying flow structure. Section 3 will be devoted to a brief presentation of Benders decomposition. In section 4, the Benders decomposition for WSP will be introduced, presenting the master and the slave problems induced by the variable partitioning. Section 5 will describe its implementation. We will present in section 6 the main lines of the global constraint "flow", branching guide for the master problem in CP. Finally, section 7 will point out the benefit of using a CP framework within a Benders decomposition when additional constraints are concerned.

2   Workforce Smoothing Problem

We first encountered the WSP after the introduction of the French "35 heures" labor rule in 2000, reducing weekly hours from 39 to 35. This new rule, stating that each employee must work 35 hours a week (on a yearly basis in our case) was particularly challenging for workforce management in call centers. Bouygues Telecom, the third largest French mobile operator with more than 6 million customers, relies almost exclusively on its call centers to keep contact with its customers. Those centers gather 2500 agents and provide a broad spectrum of services (up to 30 different activities). Agent timetables must be scheduled in order to cover the "expected work load per activity": ensuring that, at each time period, enough skilled employees are present in order to answer expected calls. A service level is defined for each activity yielding a strict minimum staffing requirement. The combinatorial scheduling problems at stake have obvious economical issues for telecom operators: avoiding understaff (to limit the amount of delayed calls thus ensure a sufficient quality of service (QoS)) and of course overstaff. This problem must be solved on different time horizons: from minutes to year. In this paper we will introduce WSP to model the long-term horizon problem.

The activity of a call center heavily depends on the season (Christmas gifts yields new customers, Valentine's day is an opportunity to promote new offers...). Consequently, one has to smooth agents weekly hours on a yearly basis ensuring that each agent reaches a total amount of hours (typically 1600) and that workload requirements for each skill are satisfied as much as possible.

2.1   Model

During P periods, we consider N agents for which:

- Ω: $[1,N] \to Z^+$ gives the total number of hours per agent,
- C_n^{max} : $[1,N] \to Z^+$ and C_n^{min} : $[1,N] \to Z^+$ are the maximum and minimum number of hours over any period for an agent.

Agents can work on K different skills, $S \subseteq [1,N] \times [1,K]$ denoting the set of feasible pairs. Workload requirements per period and per skill are given by $Q:[1,P] \times [1,K] \to Z^+$.

With these notations the WORKFORCE SMOOTHING PROBLEM can be written with $N \times P \times K$ integer variables $\omega_{n,p,k}$ representing the amount of work performed by agent n, during period p, on skill k.

maximize Δ
subject to:

$$\sum_{\substack{p \leq P \\ k \in K_n}} \omega_{n,p,k} \leq \Omega_n \qquad\qquad \forall\, n \leq N \qquad\qquad (1)$$

$$C_n^{\min} \leq \sum_{k \in K_n} \omega_{n,p,k} \leq C_n^{\max} \qquad \forall\, p \leq P,\, n \leq N \qquad (2)$$

$$\Delta \leq \sum_{n \in N_k} \omega_{n,p,k} - Q_{k,p} \qquad\qquad \forall\, p \leq P,\, k \leq K \qquad (3)$$

where $K_n = \{k \leq K, (n,k) \in S\}$ and $N_n = \{n \leq N, (n,k) \in S\}$

K_n denotes the set of skills that agent n can potentially perform and N_k, conversely, represents the set of agents that can potentially perform skill k. Constraints (1) set that each agent does not exceed its workload objective. Constraints (2) are derived from each agent contract; it limits the minimum and maximum work duration per period (typically a week or a set of consecutive weeks). Constraints (3) define Δ as the lower bound of the workload satisfaction gap. Maximizing Δ is equivalent to minimizing the worst understaffed skills for all periods, which is a commonly used criterion to represent QoS in call center scheduling tools. An optimum with $\Delta \geq 0$ ensures a QoS of 100%.

1.2   Problem Structure

The WSP has an underlying flow structure. It differs from a maximum flow problem only by its objective function. Finding a feasible solution for a fixed objective value is equivalent to solving a feasible flow problem in the graph described in Fig. 1 (on each edge the interval $[l,u]$ represents the lower and upper bound of the flow going through the edge). This graph has three layers. There is one node per agent in the first one, one node per agent and per period in the second one and finally one node per period and per skill in the last one. The incoming flow of a first layer node is equal to the total number of hours of the corresponding agent (minimum edge flow = maximal edge flow = Ω_n). This flow is dispatched per period through the second layer and then per skills through the last layer. The outgoing flow on each node of the third layer is bounded from below by the workload of the corresponding skill/period pair $Q_{n,p}$ plus Δ. The flow passing from the second to the third layer is a feasible solution of a WSP, the so-called $\omega_{n,p,k}$ variables.

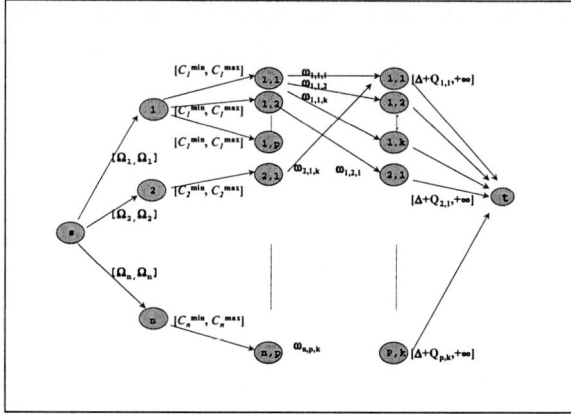

Fig. 1. WSP layered graph

One can imagine a pseudo polynomial algorithm based on a dichotomic search of the objective Δ for the WSP. The efficiency of this trivial algorithm depends on the complexity of the feasible flow algorithm. For basic WSP, it consists of a simple feasible flow problem (which is equivalent to a maximum flow problem [10]), which can be efficiently implemented using standard flow algorithms [17] or Linear Programming. Unfortunately, this straightforward tractability is far less obvious for real life problems with additional constraints such as restricted domain for the working duration (some values in $[C_n^{min}, C_n^{max}]$ may be forbidden, for example due to prohibit shift combinations within a week, see section 7.2), patterns of working duration (the number of consecutive periods at C_n^{max} may be restricted), or equity on the skills distribution, to name a few. According to those enriched domains or constraints, the "feasibleFlow" sub-problem can become NP-hard in the general case.

These constraints frequently occur in real life problems, depending on legislation or trade union agreements and advocate the need for a more flexible approach than pure flow algorithms. Unfortunately, our experiments with basic approaches with CP or MIP solvers exceeded the computational time limit stated by the operational context. A typical call center WSP gathers hundreds of agents, a dozen of skills with a time horizon of at least 15 weeks. The problem size may exceed millions of variables with hundreds of thousands of constraints. This size is not out of reach for off-the-shelf MIP tools, as we shall see in the following, but we will highlight how the use of Benders decomposition can drastically speed up the process.

3   Classical Benders Decomposition

Benders Decomposition is a variable partitioning procedure used for solving complex mathematical programming problems [1]: at each iteration of this algorithm, a master problem is solved to fix values of a subset of variables, and a slave solver both completes this assignment and produces a duality based "Benders cut" that is added to the master problem. We refer the reader to either [1] for a general introduction and convergence properties of Benders decomposition, or [7] for a presentation of the method closer to the CP formalism.

Benders decomposition can be applied when problem P has the following structure:

P: **minimize** $f(x)+cy$
Subject to: $Ax+Gy \geq b$ where $x \in D$ and $y \geq 0$

y variables are typically continuous variables and D encompasses discrete domains.

For any assignment x^*, the slave problem reads as follow:

SP: **minimize** cy
Subject to: $Gy \geq b -Ax^*$ where $y \geq 0$ and Ax^* constants

A solution of the dual of this linear problem is a linear combination of its inequalities [11] whose left-hand side is smaller than cy (i.e. u such that $uG \leq c$) and thus leading to a lower bound: $cy \geq u(b-Ax^*)$. The duality theorem claims that for u^* minimizing $u(b-Ax^*)$, this bound is the optimum[1] of SP.

It shall be noted that dual feasibility is independent of x^*, thus the inequality $cy \geq u^*(b-Ax)$ is valid for all x. Therefore, each time a new x_i^* is considered, the corresponding inequality can be added to the master problem defined after I iterations by:

MP: **minimize** z
Subject to: $z \geq f(x)+ u_i^*(b-Ax)$ $\forall$ $i<I$ where $x \in D$

Each iteration i consists of:

1. finding a solution x_i^* of MP (optimal unless MP is unbounded)
2. finding an optimal solution y_i^* of SP and an optimal solution u_i^* of its dual
3. adding the corresponding Benders cut into MP

The algorithm stops once no more improving solution can be produced by the master problem. This will occur at least once all x^* have been tried, and much sooner in practice. In other words, at each iteration z_i^* is a lower bound of the original problem and (x_i^*, y_i^*) is a solution of the problem with cost γ_i^*: the procedure stops once $z_i^* = \min_i(\gamma_i^*)$.

From a practical point of view, Benders decomposition can be efficiently applied if the slave problem SP is easy to solve or specially structured (for instance composed of independent slave problems as in section 4) and if cuts yield to a quick convergence of the Master Problem. Nevertheless, it is important to notice that Benders decomposition has the reputation of being time consuming, partially because of the amount of cuts to be introduced in the process before convergence, partially because of the difficulty of the master problem at stake for MIP solvers.

To our knowledge, two main streams of research have been proposed in the literature to combine MIP and CP approaches for Benders decomposition schemes. Hooker, Jain & Grossmann and Thorsteinsson [resp. 6,9,8] keep MIP engines for the master solver and generate "feasibility" (or "no good") cuts through CP slave solvers. They focus on problems where the master fixes cost-based abstract decisions such as task assignment on machines. The slave solvers - one per resource -, then typically

---

[1] In case of unbounded dual, another Benders cut can be added (see [])

checks the feasibility of the assignments yielding cuts in case of contradiction. It takes into account local symbolic constraints like time windows or "occur" constraints.

In Eremin & Wallace [7], the approach is closest to ours even though the benefit of using CP as a master solver does not appear clearly in their experiments. It is frequent in telecom network design problems for instance that intricate constraints can couple the investment variables together. On the contrary, the subproblems that are generated by the master can be linear programs as they represent flows or assignments. Our approach aim at keeping the symbolic constraint at the master level (hence using CP) and makes use of (linear) duality as a set of cost indicators for the master.

4   Benders Decomposition for the WSP

How could the variables of WSP be partitioned? The answer is not trivial as there is only one type of variables. Therefore, we introduce a set of intermediate variables $w_{n,p}$ representing the working hours per agent per period, hence the sum of all working hours, on any skill for agent n during period p.

Theses variables should be linked to the $\omega_{n,p,k}$ ones through the following constraints:

$$\sum_{k \in K_n} \omega_{n,p,k} = w_{n,p} \quad \forall p \leq P, n \leq N \qquad (4)$$

Constraints (1) and (2) could be rewritten using $w_{n,p}$

$$\sum_{p \leq P} w_{n,p} \leq \Omega_n \quad \forall n \leq N \qquad (5)$$

$$C_n^{min} \leq w_{n,p} \leq C_n^{max} \forall p \leq P, n \leq N \qquad (6)$$

The new formulation of WSP with constraints (6), (5), (4) and (3) has now a similar structure as the "Benders friendly" one described in section 3.

If we decompose with $w_{n,p}$ variables on one side and $\omega_{n,p,k}$ on the other side, the resulting decomposition is a mono-skill WSP for the master problem and a set of independent one-period WSP for slave problems.

4.1   Master Problem:

The master problem can be written
MP-WSP: **maximize** Δ
subject to:

$$\sum_{p \leq P} w_{n,p} \leq \Omega_n \quad \text{with } C_n^{min} \leq w_{n,p} \leq C_n^{max} \quad \forall n \leq N \qquad (7)$$

For any solution of this master problem we define SP-WSP slave problems, described in the following section. This initial master problem is unbounded but will be enriched with constraints on Δ at each step of the algorithm.

4.2   Slave Problem for Period p:

Writing $W_n = w_{n,p}$ the result of the master problem for agent n, and period p and $Q_k = Q_{p,k}$ the workload on skill k for period p, the pth slave problem can be written with $N \times K$ integer variables $x_{n,k}$ playing the role of $\omega_{n,p,k}$:

SP-WSP: **maximize** δ_p
subject to:

$$\sum_{k \in K_n} x_{n,k} \leq W_n \quad \forall n \leq N \tag{8}$$

$$\delta_p \leq \sum_{n \in N_k} x_{n,k} - Q_k \quad \forall k \leq K \tag{9}$$

Given a solution of the master problem (MP-WSP), and solutions of the induced *slave* problems (SP-WSP), $\omega_{n,p,k}$ is a solution of the WSP where Δ is equal to the minimum of all slave objectives (δ_p).

4.3   Dual Slave Problem

Although SP-WSP is a MIP, we will use the dual of its *continuous relaxation* to extract Benders cuts. A formulation of this dual is the following:

DSP-WSP: **Minimize** $\sum_{n=1}^{N} y_n W_n - \sum_{k=1}^{K} z_k Q_k$

subject to:

$$\sum_{k=1}^{K} z_k \geq 1 \tag{10}$$

$$y_n - z_k \geq 0 \quad \forall (n,k) \in S \tag{11}$$

For any dual solution, the objective value is an upper bound of δ_p (objective of the primal problem) and (12) is a valid inequality for the MP-WSP.

$$\Delta \leq \sum_{n=1}^{N} y_n W_{n,p} - \sum_{k=1}^{K} z_k Q_{p,k} \tag{12}$$

For all critical slave problems (those with the highest dual lower bound) the optimal dual solution yields Benders cut (12) for the master problem.

4.4   Termination

In classical Benders decomposition, what ensure termination is the following rationale: if an assignment x^* is considered a second time by the master solver, its cost will be *perfectly* estimated thanks to the corresponding Benders Cut (duality theorem), thus x^* will be rejected because it will not improve the value of the master problem.

On the contrary, in our case, the above Benders cut merely *approximately* estimate the cost of the re-considered x^* assignment because it is extracted from the continuous *relaxation* of the slave (see section 4.3). We prove in the next paragraph that this integrality gap is bounded by 1, and use this bound to prove Benders termination in this case.

As soon as the continuous relaxation of SP-WSP has an optimal solution of cost δ^* then the integrality theorem [17] ensures the existence of an integer solution of cost $\lceil\delta^*\rceil$ (flow with less stringent *integer* capacities). Once this solution is found (the first time x^* is considered) an improvement cut $\Delta \leq \lceil\delta^*\rceil$-1 can be added to the master problem. Finally the δ^* estimation of the Benders cut will be sufficient to prevent x^* from being considered a second time ($\delta^* \geq \lceil\delta^*\rceil$-1).

4.5   Benders Cuts Interpretation

A trivial dual solution (satisfying (10) and (11)) is $z_k=1/K$ $\forall k \geq K$ and $y_n=1/K$ $\forall n \geq N$. It produces inequality $K\Delta \leq \Sigma w_{n,p} - \Sigma Q_{p,k}$ that merely express the fact that the ideal dispatch of the global gap Δ_{total} (total number of worked hours minus workload) would lead to a maximum of Δ_{total}/K. The same reasoning is valid for any subset of skills with the associated subset of agents able to works on these skills. These $P\times2^K$ redundant constraints could be posted *a priori* but the Benders process will select only the necessary ones. Indeed a look at complementary slackness equations shows that for each x^* the Benders cut is the constraint issued from the subset of *saturated* skills.

5   Implementation of the Basic WSP

In this section we describe the Benders procedure and the master and slave algorithms. The MIP part is based on Xpress-MP, the MIP solver of Dash [12]. The CP implementation uses CHOCO, the finite domain CP solver of F. Laburthe [13]. These two solvers were piloted through the Claire language of Yves Caseau [14].

5.1   Benders Algorithm

The Benders algorithm consists of:

1. Solving the master problem (infeasibility means that the current best solution is optimal).
2. Solving the P induced slave problems and post the corresponding Benders cuts in the master problem.
3. If the corresponding global solution is better than the best solution so far, post the improvement cut $\Delta \geq \Delta_{best} + 1$ to the master problem.

The combination of Benders and improvement cuts prevents any master solution to be generated twice, hence the algorithm completes within a finite number of iterations (c.f. section 4.4).

5.2   Master Problem

The MIP program is quite straightforward, it is the direct implementation of the model described in section 4.1. We add the initial cut $K\Delta \leq \Sigma w_{n,p} - \Sigma Q_{p,k}$ (see section 4.5) to the MP-WSP to prevent this MIP from being unbounded for the first iteration.

The CP implementation is based on the flow constraint described in section 6. It uses a flow structure similar to the one described in section 2.1, simplified since MP-WSP is a mono skilled WSP. The search algorithm is an adaptation of the trivial one describe in section 0. We first label the value of the Δ variable using a dichotomy search, then we enumerate the $w_{n,p}$ variables implied in the Benders cuts. The order of processing of theses variables is based on the "first fail" principle [18]. We choose first the $w_{n,p}$ variable implied in the greatest number of constraints with the smallest domain size. The assigned values are chosen accordingly to the support structure of the flow constraint (see section 6.4).

5.3   Slave Problems

We have tested a CP and a LP approach for the slave problems: initially, we supposed that we could get optimal dual solutions by solving the primal slave problem and using complementary slackness equations. This approach is limited by the nature of our primal CP algorithm. It is based on maximum flow algorithms (see section 6.2), which works only on discrete variables. This is quite efficient for basic WSP because most of the slave problem optimal solutions are integer so we were able to generate enough cuts in practice. Unfortunately, we loose convergence if we put additional constraints on the master problem.

We could have introduced general duality principles as in [6] but using LP techniques seems to be more accurate as slave problems have an adapted linear structure.

6   Flow in Constraint Programming

A standard way to overcome limitation of CP engines is to introduce specific constraints, the so-called global constraints [15], which can handle efficient dedicated state-of-the-art algorithms. Network Flow is one of the most studied graph problems but, surprisingly, constraint solvers did not have Flow constraint until recently [16], though matching constraints have been added with success to almost every CP solver. We present in this section a flow constraint developed as an extension to CHOCO, in order to efficiently handle the flow aspect of our master problem. First, we describe the semantic of the constraint, then its algorithmic principles.

6.1   Semantic

Lets note $G=(N,A)$ a graph with N nodes and A arcs. The following equations model a feasible flow problem on G between the source node s and the sink node t:

$$\sum_{j:(i,j)\in A} x_{ij} - \sum_{j:(j,i)\in A} x_{ij} = \begin{cases} v & \text{for } i=s \\ 0 & \forall i \in N-\{s,t\} \\ -v & \text{for } i=t \end{cases} \tag{13}$$

$$l_{ij} \leq x_{ij} \leq u_{ij} \quad \forall (i,j) \in A \tag{14}$$

The flow between s and t is equal to v. Equations (13) ensure flow conservation at each node, (14) impose that the flow on each arc is between its lower and upper bounds.

The flow constraint interface is a direct translation of this model. The following call choco/flow(G,s,t,v) in a CHOCO program [13] defines a flow on G between s and t of value v where:

- G is a list formulation of the graph with one element per node; edge from the ith node to the jth node is defined by a couple (C$_{ij}$:IntVar, j:integer) in the list $G[i]$ where C$_{ij}$ denotes the domain of the flow on the edge, i.e. C$_{ij}$=$[l_{ij}..u_{ij}]$ with $x_{ij} \in [l_{ij},u_{ij}]$ (see example below),
- s is the index of the source node in the list G,
- t is the index of the sink node in the list G,
- v is the domain of the flow between source and sink.

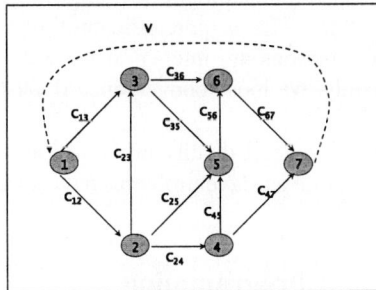

Fig. 2. Flow problem on a simple oriented graph

The flow problem described in figure 2 is obtained by the following CHOCO call:

```
choco/flow([  [[C₁₂,2],[C₁₃,3]],              // node 1
             [[C₂₃,3],[C₂₄,4],[C₂₅,5]],       // node 2
             [[C₃₅,5],[C₃₆,6]],               // node 3
             [[C₄₅,5],[C₄₇,7]],               // node 4
             [[C₅₆,6]],                       // node 5
             [[C₆₇,7]],                       // node 6
             nil],                            // node 7
          1,7,V)
```

6.2   Propagation Principles

There are two types of propagation algorithms implemented in the flow constraint:

- The first one is local to each node, it insures the flow conservation constraint (13) by applying the standard (in CP solver) bound propagation rules of linear constraints [18]
- The second one is global to the graph, it checks the existence of a feasible flow and maintains the minimal and the maximal value of the flow in the graph[2], i.e. the domain of the v variable.

All global propagation rules are based on a maximum flow algorithm. It is obvious for the computation of the maximal value of the flow in the graph but we use also a maximum flow algorithm to find a feasible flow and to compute the minimum flow:

- To find a feasible flow, we solve a maximum flow problem on a modified graph, using a standard transformation proposed in [10];
- Computing minimal flow is done by solving, from any feasible flow, a maximum flow problem on the reverse graph of G (i.e. same nodes as G but with reverse edges).

As we intensively use maximum flow algorithm, we implemented a Highest-label preflow–push algorithm of [19]. It has one of the lowest complexity ($O(n^2m^{1/2})$ with $n=|N|$ and $m=|A|$) and probably the best efficiency in practice [17].

6.3   Reaction to Events/Incrementality

The main difficulty of the implementation of a global constraint lies in the dynamic nature of CP solvers. Constraints must react to solver events, i.e. any modification of the domain of their variables, in order to check their feasibility and deduce some domain reductions or inconsistency. So, a good constraint implementation must trigger as less propagation rules as possible. To do so, the solution consists in maintaining a support structure and use incremental propagation algorithms.

The support structure used by the flow constraint to filter solver events is a maximum feasible flow, named Φ, represented by the corresponding residual flow in G.

The flow constraint reacts only to bound modification events of its variables. These events correspond to an increase/decrease of the lower/upper bound of an arc capacity or an increase/decrease of the minimum/maximum global flow. Events trigger two different reactions according to the support structure:

- The new domain bounds are consistent with current support flow Φ, i.e. x_{ij} is still in the reduced domain $C_{ij}=[l_{ij}, u_{ij}]$. Triggering a global propagation rule is useless, it is only necessary to update the structure used to memorize Φ (a residual graph is used to represent this flow).
- It is incompatible with current flow Φ. First, we must find a new feasible flow (or trigger a contradiction if such a flow does not exist) and then compute the new minimal/maximum flow.

---

[2] Note that this bound consistency is only maintains on the flow variable v and not on arcs C_{ij}.

Finding a new feasible flow is done incrementally with the use of a graph transformation similar to the one used for finding a feasible flow. Computing the new minimum and maximum flow is also done incrementally, as the preflow push algorithm is intrinsically incremental.

6.4   Using Support Structure as a Branching Oracle

The support structure of the flow constraint maintains at any step (precisely, at any fix-point of the CP solver) a feasible maximum flow. As other constraints than the flow constraint co-exist within the model, this flow might not be a solution for the global problem. This flow contains a value for each arc and for the global flow. This value is in the domain of the arc and flow variables but it could be incompatible according to other constraints like Benders cut or even with the flow constraint if some enumerated domains are used as the flow constraint is only bound consistent. As this value could be a good oracle value for a search algorithm, we offer the `choco/getFlow(C:FlowConstraint,varIdx:integer)` API function to retrieve it with O(1) computational cost.

Note that with this method, we can use the constraint solver as an incremental flow algorithm. For example, the dichotomy search algorithm described in section 0 could be implemented using the following principles:

1.   fix the Δ variable to a value `maxGap`,
2.   update the lower bound of the incoming arcs of the sink node (see   constraint (3) and figure 1) according to current Δ value,
3.   then try to find a feasible flow by calling the CHOCO propagation engine.

If the solver triggers a contradiction, there is no solution with Δ=`maxGap`, otherwise `maxGap` is a feasible value and the `getFlow` values are a solution of the problem.

To our knowledge, it is the first time that global constraint gives Oracle according to its internal structure. With this innovative feature, flow problems of more than 1 million arcs variables had been already solved in CHOCO for workforce scheduling.

7   Experimental Results

Two situations have been studied:

1. the basic WSP,
2. a WSP with a limited domain for the working hours per period.

On both situations we compared the CP master/LP slaves and the MIP master/LP slaves approach. The first case study is also used to compare our Bender decomposition approach with pure CP and pure MIP methods.

Benchmarking instances are inspired from real instances provided by Bouygues Telecom call center sites. They have the following common features:

- all agents have the same working hours bounds per period with $C_I^{min} = 33$ and $C_I^{max} = 42$;
- the skill distribution is non uniform, there are ten skills at all;

- the workload objectives for all the agents are uniformly distributed between $P* C_I^{min}$ and $P* C_I^{max}$ (P is the number of periods).
- A total of 50 instances were generated, involving 50 to 500 agents (see **Table 1**).

7.1   Case Study 1: Basic WSP

The first result of this study is that Benders decomposition is much faster than pure CP or pure MIP approach, as soon as the number of agents exceeds 100 (more than 10 times faster with 500 agents). This speed up is due to the few number of iterations, that is always smaller than 3 (**Table 2**). The second remark is that the master solving technique (CP or LP) has little effect on performances for this basic WSP.

Table 1. Average computing duration in seconds for case study 1

Problem size	CP/LP	MIP/LP	Pure CP	Pure MIP
50	1.2	1.9	5.4	1.3
100	1.1	1.1	21.3	3.8
200	3.2	1.8	74.6	15.8
300	3.4	2.6	197.0	22.0
500	6.1	4.8	X	63.7

Table 2. Distribution of the MIP/LP number of iterations for case study 1

Problem size	1	2	3	4 and more
50	50%	40%	10%	0%
100	60%	30%	10%	0%
200	80%	10%	10%	0%
300	80%	20%	0%	0%
500	70%	30%	0%	0%

7.2   Case Study 2: Working Hours in a Domain with Holes

For each agent and each period, we require the number of worked hours to belong to {33, 35, 37, 39, 41, 42}. This kind of constraints should be added when agent shifts and combination of shifts are predefined. Forbidden combinations of shifts occur frequently in call centers to compensate for unstructured shifts and weekly working hours, following trade unions requirements.

This domain constraint has no impact at all on the slave problems, but the master solver has to be adapted. New variables and new constraints have to be added to the MIP. For each variables $w_{n,p}$, we create six binary variables variables $v_{n,p,i}$ constrained by equations (15) and (16).

$$w_{n,p}=33*v_{n,p,1}+35*v_{n,p,2}+37*v_{n,p,3}+39*v_{n,p,4}+41*v_{n,p,5}+42*v_{n,p,6} \quad \forall n \le N, \forall p \le P \qquad (15)$$

$$v_{n,p,1}+v_{n,p,2}+v_{n,p,3}+v_{n,p,4}+v_{n,p,5}+v_{n,p,6} = 1 \quad \forall n \le N, \forall p \le P \qquad (16)$$

No constraints need to be added to the CP model; only the type of domain variables has to be changed, using enumerated domain variables instead of bound variables. As the flow constraint is only bound consistent (see section 6.2), we must label all the $w_{n,p}$ variables and not only the ones implied in Benders cuts as for the basic WSP.

This domain-constrained problem is harder than the basic one for both methods: we were not able to find the optimum of problems with more than 100 agents. But the CP/LP can optimally solve twice as many problems as the MIP/LP (see table 3). Beside the average solving duration is smaller for CP/LP whereas the number of iterations is larger. Our experiments seem to indicate that CP stabilizes the computational time of the decomposition.

Table 3. Percentage of optimally solved problems in less than 30 minutes for case study 2

Problem size	Nb Instances	CP/LP			MIP/LP		
		% solved	avg. time	avg. nbIter	% solved	avg. time	avg. nbIter
50	10	80%	11s	4.4	40%	90s	1.6
75	10	90%	20s	4	60%	42s	2
100	10	70%	35s	3.3	30%	39s	1.5

8   Conclusions

We have presented a successful Benders decomposition for a time tabling problem occurring in call center scheduling with annualization. Not surprisingly, our preliminary experiments show that additional constraints like domain holes, handicap classic Benders implementation with MIP tools as master solvers, and advocate the use of CP instead. The global constraint "flow" captures a good share of the structure of the QoS satisfaction problem and its support facilitates the branching strategy of the master.

The domain constraints are a preliminary step towards the implementation of richer and more symbolic constraints like working hours patterns issued from shift combinations present in call center legacy.

To our knowledge, the proposed CP-master/LP-slave implementation is the first competitive example of such a Benders decomposition compared to classical MIP-master/LP-slave scheme. These promising results stress the relevance of hybridizations strategies posting the symbolic constraints to a CP solver while using Linear Programming to tackle linear aspects.

Acknowledgement

The authors would like to thank F. Buscaylet and F. Pernias for their preliminary experiments on the 35 weekly hours problem at e-lab.

References

[1] J. F. Benders. Partitioning procedures for solving mixed-variables programming problems. Numerische Mathematik, 4:238-252, 1962.
[2] A. M. Geoffrion and G. W. Graves. Multicomodity distribution system design by Benders decomposition. Management Science, 20:822-844, 1974.
[3] M. Minoux. Network Synthesis and Optimum Network Design Problems: Models, Solution Methods and Applications. Network, 19:313-360, 1989.
[4] N. Kagan and R. N. Adams. A Benders' Decomposition Approach To The Multi-Objective Distribution Planning Problem. International Journal of Electrical Power & Energy Systems, 15(5):259-271, 1993.
[5] R.M. Wollmer. Two stage linear programming under uncertainty with 0-1 first stage variables. Mathematical Programming, 19:279-288, 1980.
[6] J.N. Hooker and G. Ottosson. Logic-based Benders decomposition. Mathematical Programming, to appear in November 2001.
[7] A. Eremin and M. Wallace. Hybrid Benders decomposition algorithms in constraint logic programming. CP 2001, LNCS, 2239:1-15, 2001.
[8] E. S. Thornsteinsson. Branch-and-Check: a Hybrid Framework Integrating Mixed Integer Programming and Constraint Logic Programming. In Proceedings of CP-01, Lecture Notes in Computer Science, 2239:16-30. Springer-Verlag, November 2001.
[9] V. Jain, I. E. Grossmann. Algorithms for Hybrid MILP/CP Models for a Class of Optimization Problems. In Informs Journal On Computing, 13:258-276, 2001.
[10] C. Berge and A. Ghouila-Houri. Programming, Games and Transportation Networks. Wiley, New York, 1962.
[11] V. Chvatal. Linear Programming. W. H. Freeman, New York, 1983.
[12] XPRESS-MP. http://www.dash.co.uk, 2002.
[13] F. Laburthe and the OCRE project team. CHOCO: Implementing a CP kernel. CP 2000 Workshop Program, 2000.
[14] Y. Caseau , F.-X. Josset, F. Laburthe. Claire: Combining Sets, Search and Rules to Better Express Algorithms. Proceeding of ICLP'99, MIT Press, New Mexico, 1999.
[15] N. Beldiceanu and E. Contejean. Introducing Global Constraints in CHIP. Mathematical and Computer Modeling, 20(2):97-123, 1994.
[16] A. Bockmayr, N. Pisaruk and A. Aggoun. Network Flow Problems in Constraint Programming. CP 2001, LNCS, 2239:196-210, 2001.
[17] R.K. Ahuja, T.L. Magnanti and J.B. Orlin. Network Flows : theory, algorithms and applications. Prentice Hall, 1993.
[18] P. Van Hentenryck. Constraint Satisfaction in Logic Programming. The MIT Press, 1989.
[19] A.V. Goldberg and R.E. Tarjan. A new approach to the maximum flow problem. *Proceedings of the 18th ACM symposium on Theory of Computing*, 1986.

Modeling Camera Control
with Constrained Hypertubes

Marc Christie, Éric Languénou, and Laurent Granvilliers

IRIN, Université de Nantes
B.P. 92208, 44322 Nantes Cedex 3, France

Abstract. In this paper, we introduce a high-level modeling approach to camera control. The aim is to determine the path of a camera that verifies given declarative properties on the desired image, *e.g.*, location or orientation of objects on the screen at a given time. The path is composed of elementary movements called hypertubes, based on established cinematographic techniques. Hypertubes are connected by relations that guarantee smooth transitions. Interval consistency techniques and quantified constraint solving algorithms are used to compute and propagate solutions between consecutive hypertubes. Preliminary experimental results from a prototype show a great improvement in time and quality of animations with respect to former approaches.

1 Introduction

Much research in computer animation has led to realistic movements for objects or characters. For instance, some delicate tasks such as animating hair or tissue are now automated in modelers. áHowever, few effort has focussed on camera control, which is an important task in story telling. The aim is to assist the control of the camera parameters in order to ease the creation of camera paths. The rightmost scene in Fig. 1 presents a possible camera path derived from three pictures: the camera must follow the cowboy during a linear movement and then turn around the indian such that both characters appear in the image when the camera is behind the indian.

Early works in computer graphics use low-level spline interpolation and smooth transitions [6]. However, computed paths are generally non-realistic and far from the user's mind. Moreover, the user has to determine a set of points that compose the trajectory of the camera, thus spending precious time in a tedious generate-and-test process (place the camera and check the result). Fig. 2 presents some problems inherent to such interpolation methods: between Key 1 and Key 2, there is no guarantee that the character stays on the screen (if ever he moves faster/slower than the camera). Moreover, there is no guarantee that the interpolation of the angle of the camera is correctly done between Key 2 and Key 3. A possible solution is to insert intermediate keyframes in order to verify such properties.

Other works are based on constrained optimization [5] for computing optimal camera positions. For this category of algorithms, it may be difficult to determine

P. Van Hentenryck (Ed.): CP 2002, LNCS 2470, pp. 618–632, 2002.

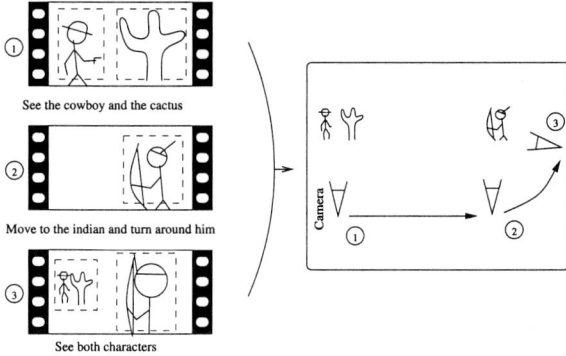

Fig. 1. A simple shot

objective criteria and such methods are very sensitive to starting points. An interesting declarative approach [4] offers high-level control over the camera. The proposed framework automatically generates predefined camera positions considering character events in the 3D scene (start, stop, turn, pick-up) and user-defined properties. Yet, camera positions are computed via vector algebra and cannot manage complex properties on the screen.

Further approaches rely on differential equations [12, 7]. The camera parameters are expressed through the relationship linking the motion of objects in the 3D scene and the motion of their projected images on the 2D screen. However, these approaches are well suited for real-time environments but they do not provide a global control on the camera path.

Recently, several constraint-based approaches [9, 1, 8] have been investigated. In this framework, the aim is to give the user declarative tools for animation modeling. The main problem here is the size and the under-constrained nature of constraint systems. We may recall that a camera has seven degrees of freedom (translation, rotation and focus) and each property of the desired image, *e.g.*, the location of an object on the screen, leads to a set of constraints over all

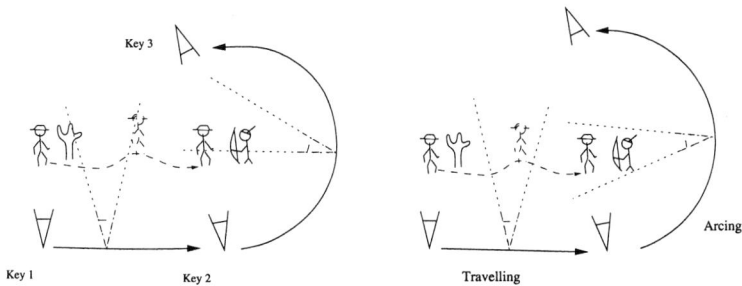

Fig. 2. Classical interpolation method (left) vs. hypertube approach (right)

these degrees. Moreover, to animate the camera, the constraint system should be solved for every frame, *i.e.*, 24 times per second or more likely for every keypoint composing the camera's path, *i.e.*, 28 variables for a basic spline involving four keypoints. Classical constraint programming techniques such as propagation cannot directly handle these problems within a reasonable computational cost.

In this paper, we propose to describe trajectories of cameras as sequences of parameterized elementary movements, called *hypertubes*: linear movement (traveling), rotation of a camera around its horizontal or vertical axes (panoramic), zoom-in, zoom-out and arcing that allows one to turn around objects. The user has to fix the sequence of elementary camera movements as well as the desired properties on objects, then the constraint programming system has to compute the parameters of hypertubes. Our solver implements the following algorithms: (1) interval-based filterings [11, 3] to remove inconsistencies and to isolate inner boxes for each hypertube; (2) given a hypertube, choice of a solution among the set of inner boxes with respect to an optimization criterion in order to determine starting conditions for the next hypertube; (3) backtracking for inconsistent hypertubes. Moreover, properties can be stated for time intervals using an universally quantified time variable [2]. Preliminary experiments show efficient constraint solving processes. Note that backtracking is not much used due to the under-constrained nature of constraint systems, and the computed paths are natural (see rightmost Fig. 2).

The outline of this paper is as follows. The next section recalls CSP and camera control background. Section 3 describes our main contribution, namely the hypertube model. Section 4 presents the experimental results.

2   Preliminaries

In this section, we briefly introduce the necessary background on Numeric Constraint Satisfaction Problems (NCSPs) [11] and camera control.

2.1   Numeric CSPs

In the following, we consider the set of closed intervals whose bounds are floating-point numbers. An interval is canonical if it contains no more than two floating-point numbers. A n-ary box $\mathbf{B}$ is a Cartesian product of intervals $B_1 \times \cdots \times B_n$. A box is canonical if each of its component is canonical.

A NCSP is a triple $\langle \mathcal{C}, \mathcal{V}, \mathcal{B} \rangle$ where $\mathcal{C}$ is a set of constraints over the real numbers, $\mathcal{V}$ is the set of variables occurring in $\mathcal{C}$ and $\mathcal{B}$ is a union of boxes representing the variable domains. Given a NCSP P with n variables, the set of solutions of P is the set

$$Sol(P) = \{r \in \mathbb{R}^n \mid r \in \mathcal{B} \wedge \forall c \in \mathcal{C} \ (r \text{ verifies } c)\}.$$

A box $\mathbf{B}$ is an *outer box* for P if $Sol(P) \subseteq \mathbf{B}$, and $\mathbf{B}$ is an *inner box* for P if $Sol(P) \supseteq \mathbf{B}$. Given a NCSP $\langle \mathcal{C}, \mathcal{V}, \mathcal{B} \rangle$, an *outer operator* is an algorithm that computes a union of boxes $\mathcal{B}^o$ such that $Sol(P) \subseteq \mathcal{B}^o \subseteq \mathcal{B}$, and an *inner operator* is an algorithm that computes a union of inner boxes $\mathcal{B}^i$ for P.

2.2   Camera Control

The aim of camera control is to assist the user in the computation of the camera parameters. Many approaches calculate a single solution depending on a chosen optimization function and therefore do not provide a general control on the camera movement.

Our research follows Jardillier and Languénou's work [9]. Their approach is based on the following ideas: (1) the user provides a high-level cinematograhic-based description; (2) each property given in this description is written as a constraint; (3) a constraint solver, which implements pure interval methods [13, 15], computes consistent solution sets in which the animator navigates.

The main feature of [9] is the specification of camera movements by a high-level intelligent process. However, a number of drawbacks can be identified. The path of the camera is restricted to very basic movements, namely a hyperbola for each parameter. The whole problem is modeled by one "global" and under-constrained constraint system, which requires expensive computations. In fact, increasing the number of variables and constraints exponentially increases computation time. Finally, navigation in the set of solutions is not very satisfactory: too many similar solutions are computed in an undefined order and no classification assists the animator.

The hypertube approach introduced in Section 3 overcomes these main lacks, namely expensive computations, restricted movements and poor interactivity.

3   The Hypertube Model

The hypertube model is a new constraint-based approach to camera control. In this framework, the user acts as a film director. He provides (1) a sequence of elementary and generic camera movements to model the shot, and (2) properties such as locations or orientations of objects on the screen. The goal is to instantiate the given camera movements that verify the desired properties. The geometrical description of the scene (dynamic of characters and objects) is generally given by a modeler and is an input to our system.

3.1   From Cinema to Constraints

Movements. We introduce a set of elementary camera movements, the cinematographic primitives called *hypertubes*, that allow the modeling of arbitrary movements by composition (see Fig. 3). Each movement depends on a set of parameters, as follows[1].

---
[1] Note that in this paper we do not consider the rolling axis of the camera.

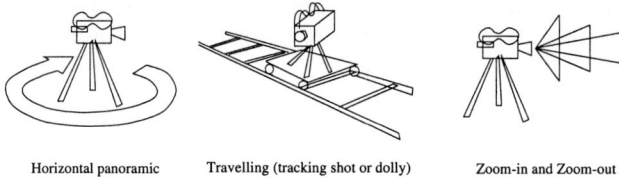

Horizontal panoramic   Travelling (tracking shot or dolly)   Zoom-in and Zoom-out

Fig. 3. Elementary camera movements

- Traveling (see Fig. 4) is a linear movement of the camera for both descriptive or object tracking purposes. Dolly and track are specific travelings where the point of view of the camera is respectively parallel or orthogonal to the movement. In our tool, traveling is parameterized by two points: the initial camera location (variables T_{X1}, T_{Y1}, T_{Z1}) and the final location (variables T_{X2}, T_{Y2}, T_{Z2}). The orientation of the camera is constant during this movement; thus two variables are necessary, respectively T_θ and T_ϕ for the pan and the tilt angle. The zoom factor is represented by one variable (T_γ).
- Panoramic (see Fig. 5) realizes a rotation of the camera around its horizontal axis (tilt) or vertical axis (pan). Similar to traveling, a pan is used for descriptive or tracking purposes. Panoramic is parameterized by a fixed camera location (variables P_X, P_Y, P_Z), the initial camera angles ($P_{\theta1}$ and $P_{\phi1}$) and final camera angles (variables $P_{\theta2}$ and $P_{\phi2}$). The zoom factor is given by $P\gamma$.
- Zoom-in and zoom-out play on the focal distance of the camera. The parameters are a camera location (Z_X, Z_Y, Z_Z), orientation (Z_θ, Z_ϕ) and two variables standing for the initial and final zoom factors, $Z_{\gamma1}$ and $Z_{\gamma2}$.
- Arcing (see Fig. 6) allows the camera to swivel around an object or group of objects. This movement is parameterized by the center of arcing (variables A_X, A_Y, A_Z), the initial and final locations of the camera in polar coordinates (the radius A_r and the angles $A_{\theta1}, A_{\theta2}$), and a zoom factor A_γ.

Each parameter is associated with an interval domain. The default values are the size of the 3D scene for locations and the interval $[-\pi, \pi]$ for orientations.

Any other movement may be defined as a merge of elementary movements, e.g., doing a panoramic while the camera is executing a traveling. Furthermore, we have introduced the notion of *local* movements, which are movements defined

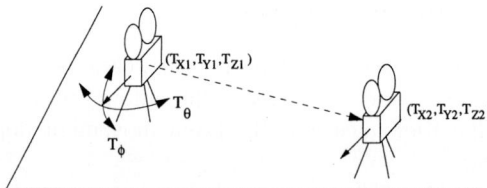

(T_{X1}, T_{Y1}, T_{Z1})

T_θ

T_ϕ

(T_{X2}, T_{Y2}, T_{Z2})

Fig. 4. A traveling primitive

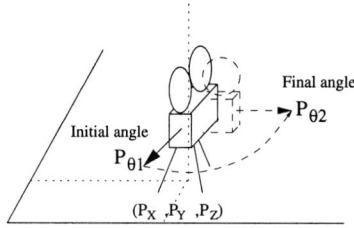

Fig. 5. A horizontal panoramic primitive

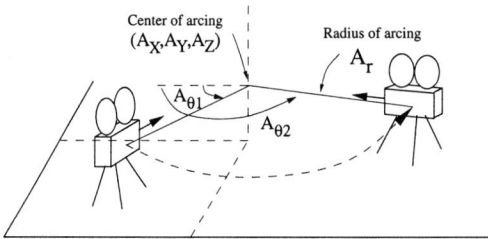

Fig. 6. An arcing primitive

in the local basis of an object. In other terms, the camera moves along with an object, typically when a camera is attached to a car.

Properties. In our modeling framework, classical cinematographic properties are made available. In the following, we describe two of them, namely location and orientation of objects on the screen.

During the creation of cinematographic scenes, the artist may specify the location of objects on the screen as in Fig. 1. More precisely, location areas are defined by rectangles called frames (see Fig. 7). Frames restrain the projection

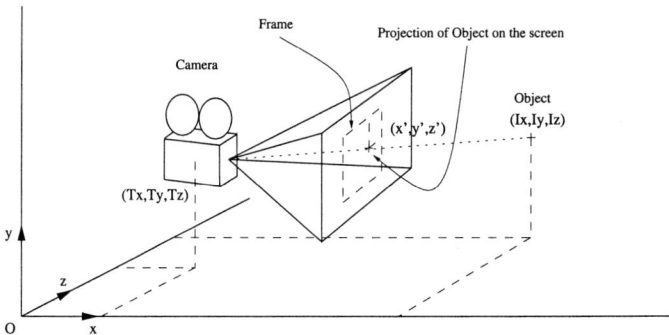

Fig. 7. Projection of a $3D$ point in a frame through a pinhole camera

zone of objects, which are represented by points, or more generally by spheres. Let us illustrate this notion with the introductory example. Screen #2 represents the indian framed in the left hand side of the screen, at the end of the traveling. The indian's location is defined by (I_X, I_Y, I_Z) and the frame is given with two intervals $[F_{X1}, F_{X2}]$ and $[F_{Y1}, F_{Y2}]$. Such a property leads to the following constraint system on the variables of the traveling primitive:

$$\begin{cases} z' & \geqslant 0 \\ x'/(z'/T_\gamma) \geqslant F_{X1} \\ x'/(z'/T_\gamma) \leqslant F_{X2} \\ y'/(z'/T_\gamma) \geqslant F_{Y1} \\ y'/(z'/T_\gamma) \leqslant F_{Y2} \end{cases}$$

The intermediate variables (x', y', z') define the indian's coordinates (object I) in the local basis of the camera. These variables are defined as follows:

$$\begin{cases} x' = -(I_X - T_{X2})\sin T_\theta + (I_Y - T_{Y2})\cos T_\theta \\ y' = -(I_X - T_{X2})\cos T_\theta \sin T_\phi + (I_Y - T_{Y2})\sin T_\phi \sin T_\theta + (I_Z - T_{Z2})\cos T_\phi \\ z' = -(I_X - T_{X2})\cos T_\theta \cos T_\phi + (I_Y - T_{Y2})\sin T_\theta \cos T_\phi + (I_Z - T_{Z2})\sin T_\phi \end{cases}$$

These constraints express the nonlinear relationship between the location of an objet in the $3D$ scene and its projection through a camera (see Fig. 7); therefore constraining the projection area of an object constrains the parameters of the camera. This location property allows correct camera placements for photographic composition.

Orientation properties correspond to notions such as *"seeing the front of an object"* or *"seeing an object upside-down"*. Let us illustrate this notion with an *over the shoulder* shot (see screen #3 in Fig. 1). Suppose that the cowboy and the indian characters are respectively located on the left and right sides of the screen. The camera is located behind the indian just over his shoulder, thus seeing his back. The property *"see the back of the indian"* may be rewritten in the following constraint system on the parameters of the arcing:

$$\begin{pmatrix} I_X - (A_X + A_R \sin A_{\theta2}) \\ I_Y - (A_Y + A_R \cos A_{\theta2}) \\ I_Z - A_Z \end{pmatrix} \cdot \begin{pmatrix} -V_X \\ -V_Y \\ -V_Z \end{pmatrix} \leqslant 0$$

where vector (V_X, V_Y, V_Z) represents the orientation of the indian character.

Finally, powerful modelers need properties to be verified for a given time interval [9], e.g., *"The cowboy must be seen on the left-hand side of the screen during the traveling"*. Computed parameters of the camera must respect the constraint system within this time interval, which requires an interval solver that manages universally quantified constraints [2].

3.2 From Constraints to Hypertube Modeling

A *hypertube* is a NCSP associated with an elementary movement, a set of properties and a duration. The path of the camera is defined by a sequence of hypertubes interlaced with *intertubes*, namely relations between two successive hypertubes that guarantee continuity of movements. In a hypertube, the speed of the camera is generally constant but may be modified for starting and ending a shot. Fig. 8 shows the link between a horizontal traveling hypertube and an arcing hypertube. Continuity is guaranteed by the following relations:

$$\begin{cases} A_r = \|A_X - T_{X2}\| \\ A_{\theta 1} = \arctan\left(\frac{A_X - T_{X2}}{A_Y - T_{Y2}}\right) \\ A_Z = T_{Z2} \end{cases}$$

Now, suppose that the traveling has already been computed and the center of arcing has been defined by the user. In this case, the variables A_r and $A_{\theta 1}$ can be directly evaluated. Therefrom, the remaining variable for the arcing movement, namely $A_{\theta 2}$, can be determined. Hypertube solving clearly operates through intertubes.

More formally, an *intertube* between two hypertubes $\mathcal{H}$ and $\mathcal{H}'$ is a set of equations "v = e" where v is a variable from $\mathcal{H}'$ and e is an expression over variables from $\mathcal{H}$ and $\mathcal{H}'$.

Two categories of intertubes have been introduced: *point intertubes* and *box intertubes* (see Fig. 9). Point intertubes join directly two consecutive hypertubes to ensure continuity. They are typically used between arcings or traveling and arcing. Box intertubes introduce a very small path section in order to realize smooth transitions over movement and speed. This is implemented as a simple interpolation between camera parameters of consecutive already-instanciated hypertubes. Intertubes may be seen as specific hypertubes that do not require any solving process.

A camera shot is therefore defined by the sequence

$$\mathcal{H}_1, \mathcal{I}_{1,2}, \mathcal{H}_2, \mathcal{I}_{2,3}, \ldots, \mathcal{I}_{p-1,p}, \mathcal{H}_p,$$

where each $\mathcal{H}_i$ is a hypertube and each $\mathcal{I}_{i,i+1}$ is an intertube between $\mathcal{H}_i$ and $\mathcal{H}_{i+1}$. Let $\langle \mathcal{C}_i, \mathcal{V}_i, \mathcal{B}_i \rangle$ denote $\mathcal{H}_i$, $\mathcal{C}$ be $\bigcup_i \mathcal{C}_i$, $\mathcal{V}$ be $\bigcup_i \mathcal{V}_i$, $\mathcal{B}$ be $\bigcup_i \mathcal{B}_i$ and $\mathcal{I}$ be $\bigcup_i \mathcal{I}_{i,i+1}$. Let $\mathcal{H}$ be the NCSP $\langle \mathcal{C} \cup \mathcal{I}, \mathcal{V}, \mathcal{B} \rangle$. In this work, we are interested in

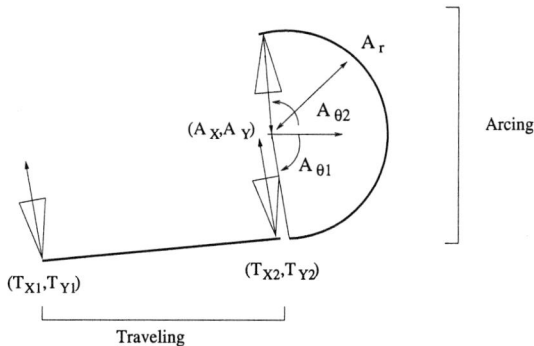

Fig. 8. Linking traveling and arcing

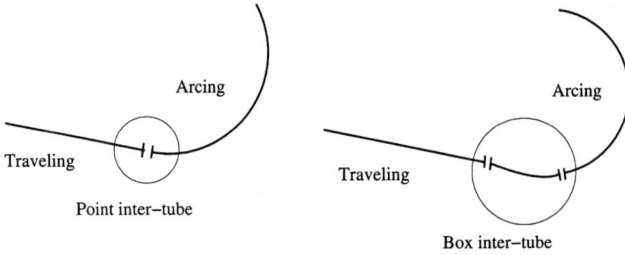

Fig. 9. Point intertube vs. box intertube

determining approximate solutions of $\mathcal{H}$. The sequence of hypertubes/intertubes will be used to implement efficient search algorithms. For efficiency reasons, the set of variables $\mathcal{V}$ can be divided in four sets:

- Fixed variables. In most cases, these variables are fixed by the user, *e.g.*, to specify the center of an arcing.
- Linked variables. These variables appear in intertubes. If we refer to our first example (see Fig. 8), A_r and $A_{\theta 1}$ are linked variables.
- Constrained variables. This is the set of non-fixed variables occurring in at least one constraint. These variables correspond to usual variables in the CSP framework.
- Free variables. This set contains the rest of the variables. These variables generally cause $\mathcal{H}$ to be under-constrained and are involved in the quality assessment.

3.3   Constraint Solving

We define a search algorithm[2] that combines constraint propagation, quantified constraint solving and enumeration to compute one verified solution of the global NCSP $\mathcal{H}$. The sequence

$$\mathcal{H}_1, \mathcal{I}_{1,2}, \mathcal{H}_2, \mathcal{I}_{2,3}, \ldots, \mathcal{I}_{p-1,p}, \mathcal{H}_p$$

is used to tune the search. Given $i \in \{1, \ldots, p-1\}$, suppose that the hypertube $\mathcal{H}_i$ is such that $\mathcal{B}_i$ is composed of a nonempty set of inner boxes $\mathcal{B}_i^i$ and a set of outer boxes $\mathcal{B}_i^o$. The computation for $\mathcal{H}_{i+1}$ is illustrated in Fig. 10.

The search follows a DFS strategy. The choice function selects and extracts some best canonical inner box $\mathbf{B}_i^{(j)}$ in the set $\mathcal{B}_i^i$, which is propagated through the next intertube $\mathcal{I}_{i,i+1}$. A local consistency-based propagation step then computes new domains for the linked variables shared by $\mathcal{I}_{i,i+1}$ and the next hypertube $\mathcal{H}_{i+1}$. If some domain becomes empty, the algorithm backtracks towards the

---

[2] Due to a lack of space, only a rough version of the constraint solving algorithm is presented. A more formal description is the subject of another paper. Note that this paper is mainly devoted to the modeling aspect of our work.

$$\mathcal{H}_i : \langle \mathcal{C}_i, \mathcal{V}_i, \mathcal{B}_i^i \cup \mathcal{B}_i^o \rangle$$

Choice of solution $\qquad\qquad\qquad\qquad\cdots\qquad\qquad\cdots$

$$\mathcal{H}_i^{(1)} : \langle \mathcal{C}_i, \mathcal{V}_i, \{\mathbf{B}_i^{(1)}\}\rangle \qquad \mathcal{H}_i^{(j)} : \langle \mathcal{C}_i, \mathcal{V}_i, \{\mathbf{B}_i^{(j)}\}\rangle$$

Propagation via intertubes $\qquad\qquad\qquad\cdots\qquad\qquad\cdots$

$$\mathcal{I}_{i,i+1}^{(j)}$$

Instanciation of hypertube $\qquad\qquad\qquad\cdots\qquad\qquad\cdots$

$$\mathcal{H}_{i+1}^{(j)} : \langle \mathcal{C}_{i+1}, \mathcal{V}_{i+1}, \mathcal{B}_{i+1}^{(j)} \rangle$$

Inner/outer computation $\qquad\qquad\qquad\cdots\qquad\qquad\cdots$

$$\mathcal{H}_{i+1}^{(j)} : \langle \mathcal{C}_{i+1}, \mathcal{V}_{i+1}, \mathcal{B}_{i+1}^{i\,(j)} \cup \mathcal{B}_{i+1}^{o\,(j)} \rangle$$

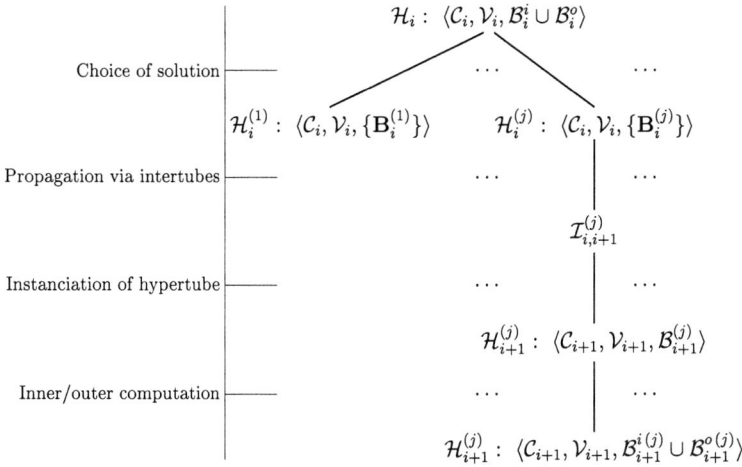

Fig. 10. Enumeration tree for solving hypertubes

node $\mathcal{H}_i$. Otherwise, the set of boxes of $\mathcal{H}_{i+1}$ is updated with the new domains of the linked variables, which gives $\mathcal{B}_{i+1}^{(j)}$. A quantified constraint solving method is applied on $\mathcal{H}_{i+1}^{(j)}$, which generates a set of inner boxes and a set of outer boxes for this problem. If the set of inner boxes is empty then the algorithm backtracks towards the node $\mathcal{H}_i$.

The general algorithm Solve is given in Table 1. The argument of the first call is the whole sequence ($i = 1$). Prop. 1 states that Solve may loose solutions of the global NCSP $\mathcal{H}$ (incompleteness due to the quantified constraint solving algorithm, see [2]), but every computed box is included in the solution set of the NCSP (soundness).

Proposition 1. *Alg.* Solve *is sound and incomplete.*

An implementation of the choice function ChooseBestInner will be presented in the next section, and we refer the reader to [2, 14] for quantified constraint solving methods.

4   Experimental Results

We have implemented a prototype engine for camera control. Constraint solving is implemented by the OpAC C++ library with an extension to manage universally quantified constraints [2]. The experiments were conducted on a PC Pentium II/350MHz under Linux.

Table 1. General search algorithm

```
1  Solve (ℋᵢ, ℐᵢ,ᵢ₊₁, ..., ℋₚ)  returns inner box
2  begin
3       Bᵣ := empty box
4       found := false
5       Bⁱ ∪ Bᵒ := QuantifiedConstraintSolving(ℋᵢ)
6       while (Bⁱ ≠ ∅ and not (found))  do
7           B := ChooseBestInner(Bⁱ)        % Bⁱ is modified
8           if (i = p) then
9               found := true
10              Bᵣ := B
11          else
12              ℋ'ᵢ₊₁ := PropagateViaIntertube(ℋᵢ₊₁, ℐᵢ,ᵢ₊₁, B)
13              Bᵣ := B×Solve(ℋ'ᵢ₊₁, ℐᵢ₊₁,ᵢ₊₂, ℋᵢ₊₂, ..., ℋₚ)
14              found := (Bᵣ ≠ empty box)
15          end
16      end
17      return (Bᵣ)
18 end
```

4.1   Implementation Details

Alg. **Solve** is driven by the **ChooseBestInner** function, which chooses some canonical box among a set of computed inner boxes $\mathcal{B}^i$. There are two levels of choice. During backtracking, $\mathcal{B}^i$ is managed by a tabu strategy in order to select some inner box $\mathbf{B}^i$. Each chosen box at a given step then becomes tabu for a given number of steps which avoids consecutive propagations of similar solutions. Among the set of nontabu inner boxes, the canonical box is computed as follows:

1. Each inner box is assigned a quality value, which is given by quality functions. The objective is to select the best inner box by qualifying the *goodness* of a camera movement. For example, a *good* travelling should keep close to the object it follows (distance between the camera and the shooted object) and the size of the object on the screen should remain relatively constant all along the shot.
2. Inside the best inner box $\mathbf{B}^i$ w.r.t. quality values, the best canonical box $\mathbf{B}$ is computed by a recursive splitting method that selects the best splitted box at each step. This process ends when any of maximum execution time, maximum number of splittings or minimal splitting size is reached. The canonical interval at the middle of the last computed box is then returned.

4.2   Benchmarks

In Table 2 the results for three benchmarks are reported, which shows the computation time w.r.t. the size of models. Due to a lack of space, only the second benchmark is described.

Table 2. Execution times for 3 different examples

Problem	Hypertubes	Variables	Constraints	First solution (ms)
Example #1	2	18	9	3940
Example #2	3	22	12	5290
Example #3	6	48	24	9880

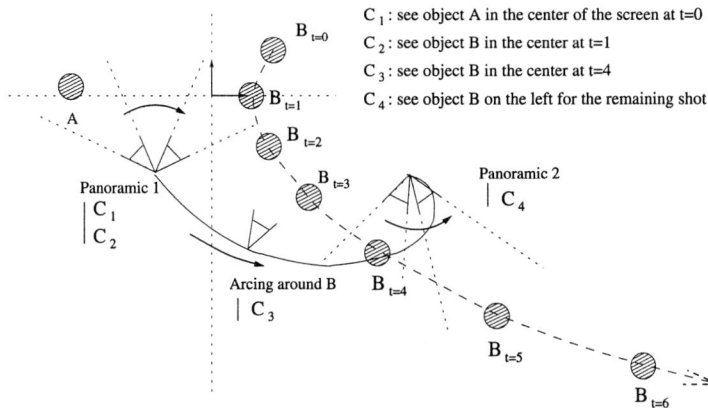

C_1: see object A in the center of the screen at t=0
C_2: see object B in the center at t=1
C_3: see object B in the center at t=4
C_4: see object B on the left for the remaining shot

Fig. 11. Example based on a pan, a local arcing and a second pan

Example #2 (see Fig. 11) relies on a 3D scene that is composed of two objects A and B. Object A is static and object B moves along a predefined path. The shot is composed of three basic movements: a first horizontal panoramic from A to B, an arcing around mobile object B and finally a horizontal panoramic to follow B.

The first hypertube has been defined with two projection properties: objects A and B must project in the center of the screen respectively at the beginning and the end of the panoramic. At the end of the second hypertube (arcing), a projection property constrains object B to be in the center of the screen too. Finally, a property specifying that object B should lay on the left hand part of the screen during the panoramic ends the shot. All the projection constraints are drawn as frames on Fig. 12. An up-view image illustrating a set of computed camera paths is presented in Fig. 13.

4.3   Discussion

The results in Table 2 show that the computation time grows linearly w.r.t. the number of hypertubes. The execution time for Example #2 is around 5 seconds for a 6 seconds animation. Note that most of the time is spent in the computation of inner boxes for the first hypertube. An interesting feature is that each hypertube contains a list of possible solutions, which can be proposed to the animator (see Fig. 13).

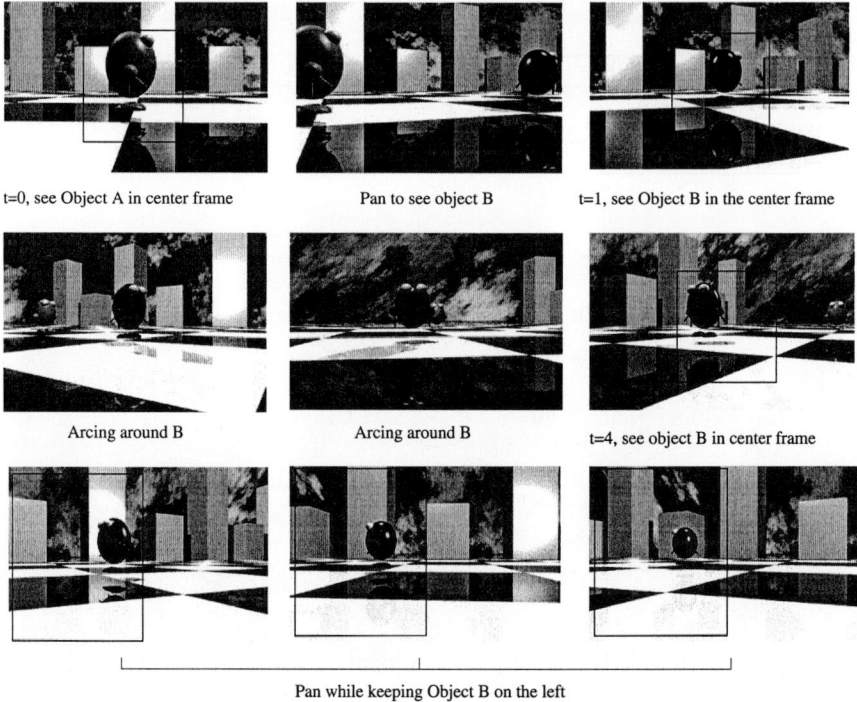

Fig. 12. Evaluation: Object A is light-colored and object B is dark-colored

A precise comparison with the former approach [9] is difficult: the paths computed by the hypertube approach are more complex; the solutions are *natural* since established camera movements are used; and good quality solutions are propagated. Nevertheless we can state that our results are very encouraging: the previous approach needs important execution times (more than 10 minutes for the first solution) for problems defined over more than 7 variables. Our examples range from 18 to 48 variables with first solutions computed in 4 to 10 seconds.

Concerning this former approach, carried out experiments had shown that the quantified constraint solving process is computationally expensive, especially with numerous variables and large variable domains. Our efforts have then focussed on reducing the number of variables by means of hypertubes, and directing the solving process with propagation of good canonical solutions through intertubes. Consequently, constraint solving is applied on hypertubes in which most variables have been instantiated, thus providing high performances. A similar process, *i.e.* NCSP decomposition and interNCSP propagation, may be found in [10] and provides efficient results for solving rigid geometric systems.

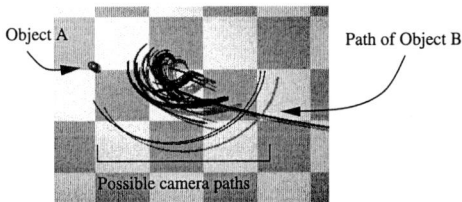

Fig. 13. Evaluation: Upview – An overview of possible camera paths

4.4   Direct Manipulation of the Camera Path

The authors believe that the aim of declarative modeling is to assist the user in his task, but will never be powerful enough to represent one user's mind. Thus our tool, alike classical approaches, allows direct and indirect manipulation of the computed camera paths, while maintaining the user's properties.

For example the user may not be satisfied by the computed radius of an arcing; any domain modification on this variable is first checked for consistency in the local hypertube and then propagated to previous and next hypertubes, thus updating the whole path if necessary.

Furthermore the user may modify locations or orientations of objects in the 3D space, thus recomputing the camera path. If inconsistency is detected while manipulating the path, the user's modification is simply deleted. In the future, we intend to work on a smoother approach, looking for the *closest solution* to the user's modification.

5   Conclusion

This paper has proposed a new CSP approach to camera control based on established cinematographic techniques. A specific algorithm to improve computation and quality of solutions has been introduced. Experimental tests have shown very encouraging results thereby enforcing the choice of our hypertube model. This opens exciting perspectives for our application, especially regarding visual occlusion (avoiding camera positions where objects hide the ones we want to see), a complex problem many people tackle.

We now intend to pursue in the direction of real-time environments where the path of the camera, *i.e.*, the hypertubes, will be generated on the fly considering events in the 3D scene such as entering a room or meeting each other. Furthermore, we aim at searching and implementing other constraint satisfaction problems that may be expressed by the means of CSP decomposition and variable linking, and that may hopefully benefit of these results.

References

[1] W. Bares, S. McDermott, C. Bourdreaux, and S. Thainimit. Virtual 3D camera composition from frame constraints. In *Proceedings of the eighth ACM international conference on Multimedia*, pages 177–186, Marina del Ray, California, United States, 2000. ACM Press New York.

[2] F. Benhamou and F. Goualard. Universally quantified interval constraints. In *Proceedings of the 6th Int. Conf. on Principles and Practice of Constraint Programming (CP'2000)*. LNCS, Springer, 2000. Singapour.

[3] F. Benhamou, F. Goualard, E. Languénou, and M. Christie. An algorithm to compute inner approximations of relations for interval constraints. In *Proceedings of the third International Ershov memorial Conference on Perspectives of system informatics (PSI'99)*, *LNCS*, Novosibirsk, Russia, 1999. Springer.

[4] D. Christianson, S. Anderson, L. He, D. Salesin, D. Weld, and M. Cohen. Declarative camera control for automatic cinematography (video). In *Proceedings of the Thirteenth National Conference on Artificial Intelligence and the Eighth Innovative Applications of Artificial Intelligence Conference*, pages 148–155, Menlo Park, August 4–8 1996. AAAI Press / MIT Press.

[5] S. Drucker and D. Zelter. Intelligent camera control in a virtual environment. In *Proceedings of Graphics Interface '94*, pages 190–199, Banff, Alberta, Canada, May 1994. Canadian Information Processing Society.

[6] J. Foley, A. Dam, S. Feiner, and J. Hughes. *Computer Graphics: Principles and Practice*. Addison-Wesley Publishing Co., Reading, MA, 2nd edition, 1990. T 385.C587.

[7] M. Gleicher and A. Witkin. Through-the-lens camera control. In Edwin E. Catmull, editor, *Computer Graphics (SIGGRAPH '92 Proceedings)*, volume 26-2, pages 331–340, July 1992.

[8] N. Halper, R. Helbing, and T. Strothotte. A camera engine for computer games: Managing the trade-off between constraint satisfaction and frame coherence. In *Proceedings of the Eurographics'2001 Conference*, volume 20, 2001.

[9] F. Jardillier and E. Languénou. Screen-space constraints for camera movements: the virtual cameraman. In N. Ferreira and M. Göbel, editors, *Eurographics'98 proceedings*, volume 17, pages 175–186. Blackwell Publishers, 108 Cowley Road, Oxford OX4 IJF, UK, 1998.

[10] C. Jermann, G. Trombettoni, B. Neveu, and M. Rueher. A constraint programming approach for solving rigid geometric systems. In *Proceedings of the 6th Int. Conf. on Principles and Practice of Constraint Programming (CP'2000)*. LNCS, Springer, 2000. Singapour.

[11] O. Lhomme. Consistency techniques for numeric CSPs. In Ruzena Bajcsy, editor, *Proceedings of International Joint Conference on Artificial Intelligence (IJCAI-93)*, pages 232–238, Chambery, France, August 1993. Morgan Kaufmann.

[12] E. Marchand and N. Courty. Image-based virtual camera motion strategies. In *Graphics Interface Conference, GI 2000*, May 2000.

[13] R. Moore. *Interval Analysis*. Prentice-Hall, Englewood Cliffs, N. J., 1966.

[14] S. Ratschan. Approximate Quantified Constraint Solving by Cylindrical Box Decomposition. *Reliable Computing*, 8(1):21–42, 2002.

[15] J. Snyder. Interval analysis for computer graphics. In Edwin E. Catmull, editor, *Computer Graphics (SIGGRAPH '92 Proceedings)*, volume 26-2, pages 121–130, July 1992.

Robust and Parallel Solving
of a Network Design Problem

Claude Le Pape, Laurent Perron,
Jean-Charles Régin, and Paul Shaw

ILOG SA
9 rue de Verdun, F-94253 Gentilly Cedex
{clepape,lperron,jcregin,pshaw}@ilog.fr

Abstract. Industrial optimization applications must be "robust," *i.e.*, must provide good solutions to problem instances of different size and numerical characteristics, and continue to work well when side constraints are added. This paper presents a case study in which this requirement and its consequences on the applicability of different optimization techniques have been addressed. An extensive benchmark suite, built on real network design data provided by France Telecom R&D, has been used to test multiple algorithms for robustness against variations in problem size, numerical characteristics, and side constraints. The experimental results illustrate the performance discrepancies that have occurred and how some have been corrected. In the end, the results suggest that we shall remain very humble when assessing the adequacy of a given algorithm for a given problem, and that a new generation of public optimization benchmark suites is needed for the academic community to attack the issue of algorithm robustness as it is encountered in industrial settings.

1 Introduction

In the design and development of industrial optimization applications, one major concern is that the optimization algorithm must be robust. By "robust," we mean not only that the algorithm must provide "good" solutions to problem instances of different size and numerical characteristics, but also that the algorithm must continue to work well when constraints are added or removed. This expectation is heightened in constraint programming as the inherent flexibility of constraint programming is often put forward as its main advantage over other optimization techniques. Yet this requirement for robustness is rarely recognized as the top priority when the application is designed. Similarly, the benchmark problem suites that are used by the academic community generally do not reflect this requirement. In practice, it has important effects on the reinforcement of problem formulation, search management, the advantages of parallel search, the applicability of different optimization techniques including hybrid combinations, *etc.* This paper presents a specific case study in which such questions have been addressed.

P. Van Hentenryck (Ed.): CP 2002, LNCS 2470, pp. 633–648, 2002.

An extensive benchmark suite, presented in Section 2, has been built on the basis of real network design data provided by France Telecom R&D [2]. The suite includes three series of problem instances corresponding to different characteristics of the numerical data. In each series, seven instances of different size are provided. In addition, six potential side constraints are defined, leading to 64 versions of each instance. The goal is to design an algorithm which provides the best results on average when launched on each of the $3 * 7 * 64 = 1344$ instances with a CPU time limit of 10 minutes. Indeed, the network designer wants to get a good cost estimate in a few minutes. In some cases, this estimate will be refined through an overnight run. The differences between the 1344 instances make it hard to design an algorithm that performs well on all instances. Notice that in the context of the current application, both the introduction of new technologies and the evolution of network usage can have an impact on problem size, numerical characteristics, and side constraints. It is believed that an optimization technique which applies well to all of the 1344 problem instances is more likely to remain applicable in the future than an optimization technique which performs particularly well on some instances, but fails to provide reasonable solutions on some others.

Three rounds of design, implementation, and experimentation have been performed while the benchmark was in construction. The aim of the first round (Section 3) was to select a few basic optimization techniques for the problem. This round was focused on the easiest versions of rather small instances. This enabled a detailed examination of the behavior of several algorithms and led to a better understanding of the complex nature of the base problem. The second round (Section 4) extended the study to middle-size instances with different numeric characteristics and side constraints. We selected, improved, and compared three basic algorithms, based on constraint programming, mixed integer programming, and column generation. At the end of this round, the constraint programming algorithm appeared as the most robust (which does not mean that the other algorithms can no longer be improved). Finally, the third round (Section 5) aimed at improving this algorithm. The algorithm which currently performs best on the overall benchmark combines constraint programming and local search.

2   The Network Design Benchmark

The benchmark problem consists in dimensioning the arcs of a telecommunications network, so that a number of commodities can be simultaneously routed over the network without exceeding the chosen arc capacities. The capacity to be installed on an arc must be chosen in a discrete set and the cost of each arc depends on the chosen capacity. The objective is to minimize the total cost of the network.

In practice, two main variants of the problem can be considered. In the "mono-routing" variant, each commodity must be routed along a unique path, while in the "multi-flow" variant, each commodity can be split and routed along many paths. We have focused on the mono-routing variant which has been less studied in the literature. Rothlauf, Goldberg, and Heinzl [9] have worked on a similar problem (data from Deutsche Telekom) but require the resulting network to be a tree, which makes mono-routing equivalent to multi-flow. Gabrel, Knippel, and Minoux [5] and Bienstock and Günlük [3] have developed an exact method for network design problems with a discrete set of possible arc capacities and multi-flow routing. To our knowledge, these studies are the closest to the one we report in this paper.

Given are a set of n nodes and a set of m arcs (i, j) between these nodes. A set of d demands (commodities) is also defined. Each demand associates to a pair of nodes (p, q) an integer quantity Dem_{pq} of flow to be routed along a unique path from p to q. In principle, there could be several demands for the same pair (p, q), in which case each demand can be routed along a different path. Yet, to condense notation and keep the problem description easy to read, we will use a triple (p, q, Dem_{pq}) to represent such a demand.

For each arc (i, j), K_{ij} possible capacities $Capa_{ij}^k$, $1 \leq k \leq K_{ij}$, are given, to which we add the null capacity $Capa_{ij}^0 = 0$. One and only one of these $K_{ij} + 1$ capacities must be chosen. However, it is permitted to multiply this capacity by an integer between a given minimal value $Wmin_{ij}^k$ and a given maximal value $Wmax_{ij}^k$. Hence, the problem consists in selecting for each arc (i, j) a capacity $Capa_{ij}^k$ and an integer coefficient w_{ij}^k in $[Wmin_{ij}^k, Wmax_{ij}^k]$. The choices made for the arcs (i, j) and (j, i) are linked. If capacity $Capa_{ij}^k$ is retained for arc (i, j) with a non-null coefficient w_{ij}^k, then capacity $Capa_{ji}^k$ must be retained for arc (j, i) with the same coefficient $w_{ji}^k = w_{ij}^k$, and the overall cost for both (i, j) and (j, i) is $w_{ij}^k * Cost_{ij}^k$.

Six classes of side constraints are defined. Each of them is optional, leading to 64 variants of each problem instance, identified by a six-bits vector. For example, "011000" indicates that only the second constraint *nomult* and the third constraint *symdem*, as defined below, are active.

- The security (*sec*) constraint states that some demands must be secured. For each node i, an indicator $Risk_i$ states whether the node is considered "risky" or "secured." Similarly, for each arc (i, j) and each k, $1 \leq k \leq K_{ij}$, an indicator $Risk_{ij}^k$ states whether the arc (i, j) in configuration k is considered risky or secured. When a demand must be secured, it is forbidden to route this demand through a node or an arc which is not secured.
- The no capacity multiplier (*nomult*) constraint forbids the use of capacity multipliers. For each arc (i, j), two cases must be considered: if there is a k with $Wmin_{ij}^k \geq 1$, the choice of $Capa_{ij}^k$ with multiplier $w_{ij}^k = Wmin_{ij}^k$ is imposed; otherwise, the choice of $Capa_{ij}^k$ is free, but $w_{ij}^k \leq 1$ is imposed.
- The symmetric routing of symmetric demands (*symdem*) constraint states that for each demand from p to q, if there exists a demand from q to p, then the paths used to route these demands must be symmetric. (Similarly, if there are several demands between the same nodes p and q, these demands must be routed on the same path.) In practice, this constraint reduces (in

most cases divides by 2) the number of routes to be constructed for the given demands.

- The maximal number of bounds ($bmax$) constraint associates to each demand (p, q, Dem_{pq}) a limit $Bmax_{pq}$ on the number of bounds (also called "hops") used to route the demand, *i.e.*, on the number of arcs in the path followed by the demand. In particular, if $Bmax_{pq} = 1$, the demand must be routed directly on the arc (p, q).
- The maximal number of ports ($pmax$) constraint associates to each node i a maximal number of incoming ports Pin_i and a maximal number of outgoing ports $Pout_i$. For each node i, the constraint imposes $\sum_{j,k} w_{ij}^k \leq Pout_i$ and $\sum_{j,k} w_{ji}^k \leq Pin_i$.
- The maximal traffic ($tmax$) constraint associates to each node i a limit $Tmax_i$ on the total traffic managed by i. This includes the traffic that starts from i ($\sum_{q \neq i} Dem_{iq}$), the traffic that ends at i ($\sum_{p \neq i} Dem_{pi}$), and the traffic that goes through i (the sum of the demands Dem_{pq}, $p \neq i$, $q \neq i$, for which the chosen path goes through i). Notice that it is possible to transform this constraint into a limit on the traffic that enters i (which must be smaller than or equal to $Tmax_i - \sum_{q \neq i} Dem_{iq}$) or, equivalently, into a limit on the traffic that leaves from i (which must be smaller than or equal to $Tmax_i - \sum_{p \neq i} Dem_{pi}$).

Twenty-one data files, organized in three series, are available. Each data file is identified by its series (A, B, or C) and an integer which indicates the number of nodes of the considered network. Series A includes the smallest instances, from 4 to 10 nodes. The optimal solutions to the 64 variants of A04, A05, A06, and A07, are known. At this point, proved optimal solutions are available for only 44 variants of A08, one variant of A09, and one variant of A10. Series B and C include larger instances with 10, 11, 12, 15, 16, 20, and 25 nodes. Proved optimal solutions are available only for 12 variants of C10. The instances of series B have more choices of capacities than the instances of series A, which have more choices of capacities than the instances of series C. So, in practice, instances of series B tend to be harder because the search space is larger, while instances of series C tend to be harder because each mistake has a higher relative cost.

3   Application of Multiple Optimization Techniques to the Base Problem

In the first round, five algorithms were developed and tested on the simplest instances of the problem: series A with only the *nomult* and *symdem* constraints active. Focusing on simple instances enabled us to compute the optimal solutions of these instances and trace the behavior of algorithms on the base problem, without noise due to side constraints. The drawback is that focusing on simple instances does not allow for the anticipation of the effect of side constraints. The same remark holds for problem size: it is easier to understand what algorithmically happens on small problems, but some algorithmic behaviors show up on large problems which are not observable on smaller problems. Five algorithms were tested:

- CP: a simple constraint programming algorithm, based on ILOG Solver[12] integer and set variables, developed by France Télécom R&D.
- CP-PATH: a more complex algorithm which combines classical constraint programming with a shortest path algorithm.
- MIP: the CPLEX[4] mixed integer programming algorithm, with the emphasis on finding feasible solutions, applied to a minor variant of the MIP formulation given in [2].
- CG: a column generation algorithm, which consists in progressively generating possible paths for each demand and possible capacities for each arc. At each iteration, a linear programming solver is used to select paths and capacities and guide the generation of new paths and new capacities. In addition, a mixed integer version of the linear program is regularly used to generate legal solutions.
- GA: an ad-hoc genetic algorithm.

Attempts to use local search to improve the solutions found by the CP-PATH algorithm were also made, with two distinct neighborhoods: (1) reroute one demand, (2) decrease the capacity of an arc, allow the capacity of another arc to increase, reroute all demands with CP-PATH. In practice, these combinations of CP-PATH and local search did not provide better solutions than CP-PATH alone.

Optimal solutions were found using the CPLEX algorithm, version 7.5, with no CPU time limit. For the A10 instance, however, the CPLEX team at ILOG suggested a different parameterization of the CPLEX MIP (emphasis on optimality, strong branching) which resulted in many less nodes being explored. With this parameterization, the first integer solution was found in more than three hours, far above the time limit of 10 minutes. The optimal solution was found in more than six days. Further work, with intermediate (beta) versions of CPLEX, showed that this could be reduced to a few hours. Yet at this point we do not believe the problem can be exactly solved in 10 minutes or less.

Table 1 provides, for each instance, the optimal solution and the value of the best solution found by each algorithm within the CPU time limit. The last column provides the mean relative error (MRE) of each algorithm: for each algorithm, we compute for each instance the relative distance $(c - o)/o$ between the cost c of the proposed solution and the optimal cost o, and report the average value of $(c - o)/o$ over the 7 instances.

4 Extensions and Tests with Side Constraints

In the second round, the study was extended to the mid-size instances (10 to 12 nodes) and, most importantly, to the six side constraints. We decided to focus mostly on three algorithms, CP-PATH, CG, and MIP. Indeed, given the previous results, CP-PATH and CG appeared as the most promising. The MIP algorithm

Table 1. Initial results on series A, parameter 011000

	A04	A05	A06	A07	A08	A09	A10	MRE
Optimum	22267	30744	37716	47728	56576	70885	82306	
CP	22267	30744	37716	49812	74127	97386	104316	14.2%
CP-PATH	22267	30744	37716	47728	56576	70885	83446	0.2%
MIP	22267	30744	37716	47728	56576	73180	99438	3.4%
CG	22267	30744	37716	47728	57185	72133	87148	1.2%
GA	22267	30744	37716	48716	60631	75527	88650	3.4%

was a priori less promising, but different ideas for improving it had emerged during the first round, and it had also provided us with optimal solutions, although with much longer CPU time. This section describes the main difficulties we encountered in extending these algorithms to the six side constraints of the benchmark.

4.1   Column Generation

The six side constraints are integrated in very different ways within the column generation algorithm:

- The *symdem* constraint halves the number of routes that need to be built. Therefore, the presence of this constraint simplifies the problem.
- The *bmax* constraint is directly integrated in the column generation subproblem. For each demand Dem_{pq}, only paths with at most $Bmax_{pq}$ arcs must be considered.
- Similarly, the *nomult* constraint is used to limit the number of capacity levels to consider for each arc.
- The *pmax* and *tmax* constraints are directly integrated in the master linear program. They cause no particular difficulty for the column generation method *per se*, but make it harder to generate integer solutions.
- The *sec* constraint is the hardest to integrate. Constraints linking the choice of a path for a given demand and the choice of a capacity level for a given arc can be added to the master linear program when the relevant columns are added. But, before that, the impact of these constraints on the significance of a path cannot be evaluated, which means that many paths which are not really interesting can be generated. This slows down the overall column generation process. Also, just as for *pmax* and *tmax*, the addition of the *sec* constraint makes integer solutions harder to generate.

The first results were very bad. In most cases, no solution was obtained within the 10 minutes. This was improved by calling the mixed integer version of the master linear program at each iteration, each time with a CPU time limit evolving quadratically with the number of performed iterations. This enabled the generation of more solutions, but sometimes resulted in a degradation of the quality of the generated solutions (MRE of 2.1% in place of 1.2% for the seven instances used in the first round). Also, the current version of the algorithm is still unable to find a solution to A10 with parameter "100011" in less than 10 minutes. This is precisely the parameter for which the *sec, pmax*, and *tmax* constraints are active, while the *nomult, symdem*, and *bmax* constraints, which tend to help column generation, are not active. Over B10, B11, B12, C10, C11 and C12, 128 such failures occur. The *pmax* constraint is active in 126 of these cases. In the others, both *sec* and *tmax* are active.

4.2   Mixed Integer Programming

Various difficulties emerged with the first tests of the MIP algorithm. First, no solution was found in 10 minutes on A10 with parameters "010111" and "110111," *i.e.*, when *nomult, bmax, pmax*, and *tmax* are active, and *symdem* (which divides the problem size by 2) is not. On the A series, the results also show a degradation of performance when *bmax* and *tmax* are active.

Numerous attemps were made to improve the situation. First, we tried to add "cuts," *i.e.*, redundant constraints that might help the MIP algorithm:

- For each demand and each node, at most one arc entering (or leaving) the node can be used.
- For each node, the sum of the capacities of the arcs entering (or leaving) the node must be greater than or equal to the sum of the demands arriving at (or starting from) the node plus the sum of the demands traversing the node.
- For each demand and each arc, the routing of the demand through the arc excludes, for this arc, the capacity levels strictly inferior to the demand.

In general, these cuts resulted in an improvement of the lower bounds, but did not allow the generation of better solutions within the time limit of 10 minutes. We eventually removed them.

A cumulative formulation of arc capacity levels was also tested. Rather than using a 0-1 variable y^k for each level k, this formulation uses a 0-1 variable δ^k to represent the decision to go from a capacity level to the next, *i.e.*, $\delta^k = y^{k+1} - y^k$. As for the cuts, the main effect of this change was an improvement of lower bounds.

We also tried to program a search strategy inspired by the one used in the CP-PATH algorithm. This allowed the program to generate solutions more often in less than 10 minutes, but the solutions were of a poor quality.

Hence, the results are globally not satisfactory. However, the MIP algorithm sometimes finds better solutions than the CP-PATH algorithm. For example, on C11, there are only 31 variants out of 64 on which the MIP algorithm (with the cumulative formulation) generates solutions in 10 minutes, but out of these 31 variants, there are 18 for which the solution is better than the solution obtained by CP-PATH. It might be worthwhile applying both algorithms and keeping the best overall solution.

4.3   Constraint Programming with Shortest Paths

A Graph Extension to Constraint Programming To simplify the implementation, we basically introduced a new type of variable representing a path from a given node p to a given node q of a graph. More precisely, a path is represented by two set variables, representing the set of nodes and the set of arcs of the path, and constraints between these two variables.

- If an arc belongs to the path, its two extremities belong to the path.
- One and only one arc leaving p must belong to the path.
- One and only one arc entering q must belong to the path.
- If a node i, $i \neq p, i \neq q$, belongs to the path, then one and only one arc entering i and one and only one arc leaving i must belong to the path.

Several global constraints have been implemented on such path variables to determine nodes and arcs that must belong to a given path (*i.e.*, for connexity reasons), to eliminate nodes and arcs that cannot belong to a given path, and to relate the path variables to other variables of the problem, representing the capacities and security levels of each arc.

Solving the Network Design Problem with Graph Library At each step of the CP-PATH algorithm, we chose an uninstantiated path for which the demand Dem_{pq} was greatest. We then determined the shortest path to route this demand (to this end, we solved a constrained shortest path problem). A choice point was then created. In the left branch, we constrained the demand to go through the last uninstantiated arc of this shortest path. In case of backtrack, we disallowed this same arc for this demand. Once a demand was completely instantiated, we switched to the next one. A new solution was obtained when all demands were routed. The optimization process then continued in Discrepancy-Bounded Depth-First Search (DBDFS[1]) with a new upper-bound on the objective.

First experiments exhibited the following difficulties: (1) Performances deteriorated when the *tmax* constraint was active.(2) For 3 sets of parameters on the A10 instance, the algorithm was unable to find a feasible solution in less than 10 minutes. In fact, it turned out that the combination of the maximal number of ports constraint (*pmax*) and the maximal traffic constraint (*tmax*) made the problem quite difficult. (3) Bad results on B10 stemmed from a quite asymmetric traffic. For instance, between the first two nodes of the B10 instance, the traffic was equal to 186 in one direction and 14 in the other. (4) Performance was unsatisfactory in the presence of the maximal number of bounds constraint (*bmax*).

Several modifications of the program were thus made necessary. First, a "scalar product"-like constraint was implemented. This constraint directly links the traffic at each node with the paths used for the routing. This constraint propagates directly from the variable representing the traffic at each node to the variables representing the demands, and vice-versa, without the intermediate use of the traffic on each arc. This allowed more constraint propagation to take place and solved difficulties (1) and (2), even though the combination of the $pmax$ and $tmax$ constraints remains "difficult."

The third difficulty (3) was partly resolved by modifying the order in which the various demands are routed. In the initial algorithm, the biggest demand was routed first. Given a network with 6 nodes and the demands $Dem_{01} = 1800$, $Dem_{10} = 950$, $Dem_{23} = 1000$, $Dem_{32} = 1000$, $Dem_{45} = 1900$ and $Dem_{54} = 50$, the previous heuristic behaved as follows:

- In the case of symmetrical routing, ($symdem = true$), the demands are routed in the following order: Dem_{01} and Dem_{10}, then Dem_{23} and Dem_{32}, then Dem_{45} and Dem_{54} .
- In the case of nonsymmetrical routing, ($symdem = false$), the order is Dem_{45}, Dem_{01}, Dem_{23}, Dem_{32}, Dem_{10}, Dem_{54}.

In the case of symmetrical routing, it is a pity to wait so long before routing Dem_{45}, since a large capacity will be needed to route this demand.

Likewise, in the case of nonsymmetrical routing, it could be worthwhile to route Dem_{10} before Dem_{23} and Dem_{32}, given that the routing of Dem_{01} has created a path which is probably more advantageous to use for Dem_{10} than for Dem_{23} and Dem_{32}.

The heuristic was therefore modified:

- In the case of symmetrical routing, the weight of each demand is the sum of twice the biggest demand plus the smallest demand. The demands are then ordered by decreasing weight. This results in the following order: Dem_{01} and Dem_{10}, then Dem_{45} and Dem_{54}, and finally Dem_{23} and Dem_{32}.
- In the case of nonsymmetrical routing, the weight of each demand is the sum of twice the considered demand plus the reverse demand. This results in the following order: Dem_{01}, Dem_{45}, Dem_{10}, Dem_{23}, Dem_{32}, Dem_{54}.

The average gain on the B10 instance is 3%. On the C instances, however, this change deteriorated performances by roughly 1%. The new heuristic was therefore kept, although it was not a complete answer to the previous problem.

The last difficulty was solved by strengthening constraint propagation on the length of each path. The following algorithm was used in order to identify the nodes and the arcs through which a demand from p to q needs to be routed:

- We use the Ford algorithm (as described in [6]) to identify the shortest admissible path between p and each node of the graph, and between each node of the graph and q.
- We use the path lengths computed in this way (i) to eliminate nodes through which no path of length less than $Bmax_{pq}$ arcs can pass and (ii) to mark nodes such that the demand can be routed around the node by a path of length less than $Bmax_{pq}$ arcs.
- We use the Ford algorithm again on each unmarked node to determine if there exists a path from p to q with less than $Bmax_{pq}$ arcs not going through the node.

Using this algorithm was finally worthwhile, although its worst case complexity is $O(nmBmax_{pq})$, $O(n^4)$. The most spectacular improvement was of 1.73% on the 64 variations of the B12 problem, meaning an improvement of 3.46% on the 32 variations where $bmax$ is active. On average, this modification also improved the results on the C series. Nevertheless, on the C12 problem, the results were worse by a factor of 0.4%.

4.4   Experimental Results

Tables 2 and 3 summarize the results on series A and on the instances with 10, 11, and 12 nodes of series B and C. There are four lines per algorithm. The "Proofs" line indicates the number of parameter values for which the algorithm found the optimal solution and made the proof of optimality. The "Best" line indicates the number of parameter values for which the algorithm found the best solution known to date. The "Sum" line provides the sum of the costs of the solutions found for the 64 values of the parameter. A "Fail" in this line signifies that for f values of the parameter, the algorithm was not able to generate any solution within the 10 minutes. The number of failures f is denoted within parentheses. Finally, the "MRE" line provides the mean relative error between the solutions found by the algorithm and the best solutions known to date. Notice that the MRE is given relative to the best solutions known to date, found either by one of the four algorithms in the table or by other algorithms, in some cases with more CPU time. These reference solutions may not be optimal, so all the four algorithms might in fact be farther from the optimal solutions. Note also that each algorithm is the result of a few modifications of the algorithm initially applied to the instances of series A with parameter "011000." Similar efforts have been made for each of them. Yet it is obvious that further work on each of them might lead to further improvements.

The differences with the results of Section 3 are worth noticing: a large degradation of performance with the introduction of side constraints and with an increase in problem size; and important variations with the numerical characteristics of the problem as shown by the differences between A10, B10, and C10.

Table 2. Solutions found in 10 minutes, series A, for 64 parameter values

Algorithm		A04	A05	A06	A07	A08	A09	A10	Total
CP-PATHS	Proofs	64	64	64	33	7	0	0	232
	Best	64	64	64	62	43	23	25	345
	Sum	1782558	2351778	2708264	3290940	4076785	5027246	5934297	25171868
	MRE	0.00%	0.00%	0.00%	0.01%	0.69%	1.25%	1.57%	0.50%
MIP	Proofs	64	64	64	27	1	0	0	220
	Best	64	64	64	27	13	2	0	234
	Sum	1782558	2351778	2708264	3318572	4219647	5640421	Fail (2)	Fail (2)
	MRE	0.00%	0.00%	0.00%	0.88%	4.20%	13.62%	33.11%	7.29%
CUMULATIVE MIP	Proofs	64	64	64	7	0	0	0	199
	Best	64	64	64	31	4	0	0	227
	Sum	1782558	2351778	2708264	3337284	4417611	5934187	Fail (3)	Fail (3)
	MRE	0.00%	0.00%	0.00%	1.42%	9.06%	19.44%	29.02%	8.28%
CG	Proofs	64	64	36	20	0	0	0	184
	Best	64	64	64	45	12	2	1	252
	Sum	1782558	2351778	2708264	3310007	4263830	5621264	Fail (1)	Fail (1)
	MRE	0.00%	0.00%	0.00%	0.60%	5.11%	12.85%	22.09%	5.77%

Table 3. Solutions found in 10 minutes, series B and C, for 64 parameter values

Algorithm		B10	B11	B12	C10	C11	C12
CP-PATH	Proofs	0	0	0	10	0	0
	Best	4	1	2	20	0	0
	Sum	1626006	3080608	2571936	1110966	2008833	2825499
	MRE	7.96%	10.67%	8.71%	5.77%	11.60%	14.95%
MIP	Proofs	0	0	0	0	0	0
	Best	3	6	1	6	0	0
	Sum	Fail (16)	Fail (20)	Fail (39)	Fail (10)	Fail (24)	Fail (63)
	MRE	23.68%	22.28%	19.24%	12.82%	51.20%	17.42%
CUMULATIVE MIP	Proofs	0	0	0	0	0	0
	Best	3	1	0	1	1	0
	Sum	Fail (14)	Fail (26)	Fail (29)	Fail (15)	Fail (33)	Fail (42)
	MRE	14.16%	14.05%	20.27%	10.92%	12.83%	26.61%
CG	Proofs	0	0	0	0	0	0
	Best	0	0	0	1	0	1
	Sum	Fail (26)	Fail (24)	Fail (19)	Fail (32)	Fail (10)	Fail (17)
	MRE	27.27%	35.49%	47.67%	28.75%	79.42%	27.49%

5 Scaling

The results of the second stage have shown that the constraint programming algorithm which calculates the shortest paths is the strongest. As already mentioned, it is obvious that all algorithms can be improved. Yet we decided to focus mostly on improving the CP-PATH algorithm.

5.1 Analysis of Previous Results

Two important elements were acknowledged. First, an analysis of the explored search trees showed that during the search almost all the improving solutions (especially in the B series) questioned one of the first routing decisions that had been taken in order to build the previous solution. This suggested, on the one hand, the construction of a parallel search on a multiprocessor, and, on the other hand, the questioning of the decisions made in the upper part of the tree first. Besides, an analysis of the first found solution demonstrated that the algorithm had a tendency to build networks having a large number of low-capacity arcs. This turned out to be quite unfortunate as better solutions could be constructed quite easily from them using a smaller number of arcs, but with greater capacities. In the case of bigger instances with homogeneous demands, such mistakes were common and took quite some time to be corrected as the absence of big demands does not help the propagation of the constraints involved in this benchmark. This suggested a postoptimization phase implemented using local search. This was the most natural way of correcting these mistakes as it was lightweight both in term of code and performances. Any other tentative correction of these mistakes through the modification of the heuristics resulted in deteriorated overall quality as specializing the heuristic for one particular instance of the problem had the tendency to make it less robust on the average.

5.2 Extending and Refining the Previous Framework

Exploiting Parallel Computing ILOG Parallel Solver is a parallel extension of ILOG Solver [12]. It was first described in [7]. It implements *or*-parallelism on shared memory multi-processor computers. ILOG Parallel Solver provides services to share a single search tree among workers, ensuring that no worker starves when there are still parts of the search tree to explore and that each worker is synchronized at the end of the search.

First experiments with ILOG Parallel Solver were actually performed during the first and second round. These experiments are described in [8] and [2]. Switching from the sequential version to the parallel version required a minimal code change of a few lines, and so we were immediately able to experiment with parallel methods.

It should also be noted that the parallel version uses four times more processing power than the sequential on the machine we used.

Changing the Search Tree Traversal CP-PATH uses the DBDFS[1] search procedure to explore the search tree. As described in [7], open nodes of the search tree are evaluated and stored in a priority queue according to their evaluation. The DBDFS strategy evaluates nodes by counting the number of right moves from the root of the search tree to the current position in the search tree. Two variations have been implemented to change this evaluation and to add weights to discrepancies (*cf.* [2]). Both variations rely on the depth of the search tree. The first one tries a fixed weight schema, while the second adapts the weight mechanism to focus even more on the top of the search tree in case of a deep search tree.

Adding Local Search The analysis of the second round suggested that the search procedure should be split in three. The first part consists of a search for a feasible solution where the search would be penalized if it took the decision to open a new arc (by doubling the cost of the arc).

The second phase consists of a postoptimization of this first solution based on local search. This local search phase is implemented on top of the ILOG Solver Local Search framework[10, 11]. This framework is built upon the essential principles of local search: those of a current solution, a neighborhood structure, ways of exploring this neighborhood structure, move acceptance criteria, and metaheuristics. Each of these concepts translates into one or more Solver objects which can be naturally instantiated for the problem at hand. Like ILOG Solver's other fundamental objects such as constraints and goals, new local search objects, such as neighborhoods, can be defined or refined by users, resulting in a close match between the solving methods and the problem structure. Importantly, local moves are made in ILOG Solver by the application of search goals, in the same manner as for complete search. This facilitates combinations of local and tree-based search, which is in fact what we used here.

In our case we created a neighborhood which had as neighbors the removal of each arc from the graph. Such a destructive move requires some rerouting to maintain feasibility of the solution. As local and tree-based search mechanisms can be combined in Solver, at each such move we used traditional tree-based search to reroute paths in order to attempt to maintain feasibility. The neighborhood and tree searches are naturally combined in the same search goal.

The local search process we employed was entirely greedy. At each stage, we removed the arc from the graph which decreased the cost by the greatest amount (after rerouting), stopping when there was no arc we could remove without being able to legally reroute the traffic.

This whole mechanism was coded in less than fifty lines of code.

The last phase is the original optimization tree-based search, but with an improved upper bound.

5.3 Results

Table 4 gives the results of the four new algorithms, compared to CP-PATH, on the instances of size 10, 11, and 12 of the B and C series. It also provides the results of CP-PATH + LS executed in parallel with four processors. Globally, the best improvement comes from parallelism, closely followed by local search. The two search procedures (variations 1 and 2) which were promising on eight variants of the problems as described in [2] turned out to be not robust enough. They improved the results on the B series but worsened them on the C series.

Table 4. Solutions found in 10 minutes, series B and C, for 64 parameters values

Algorithm		B10	B11	B12	C10	C11	C12
CP-PATH	Best	4	1	2	20	0	0
	Sum	1626006	3080608	2571936	1110966	2008833	2825499
	MRE	7.96%	10.67%	8.71%	5.77%	11.60%	14.95%
CP-PATH Parallel	Best	6	1	1	36	0	0
	Sum	1597793	3009386	2548122	1084577	2002557	2794864
	MRE	5.98%	8.00%	7.73%	3.28%	11.13%	13.65%
CP-PATH + Variation 1	Best	1	0	4	10	0	0
	Sum	1608752	3015921	2563522	1133098	2024920	2862054
	MRE	6.80%	8.28%	8.32%	7.80%	12.43%	16.42%
CP-PATH + Variation 2	Best	2	2	3	10	0	0
	Sum	1601555	3018046	2547425	1123779	2034917	2838541
	MRE	6.27%	8.32%	7.66%	6.87%	12.99%	15.44%
CP-PATH + LS	Best	4	3	2	20	0	0
	Sum	1610770	3023086	2555469	1110966	2003101	2801849
	MRE	6.91%	8.39%	7.81%	5.77%	11.30%	13.97%
CP-PATH + LS Parallel	Best	4	4	0	34	0	0
	Sum	1592778	2967717	2535516	1085266	2005714	2777129
	MRE	5.55%	6.53%	7.12%	3.36%	11.29%	12.91%

We applied the CP-PATH + LS algorithm to the A series and the results were exactly identical to those of CP-PATH, $i.e.$, local search brought no improvement on this series. We also applied CP-PATH and CP-PATH + LS on the larger instances with 15 to 25 nodes. The MRE ranges from 6.24% (on C16) to 38.03% (on B25) for CP-PATH and from 4.99% (on B25) to 23.53% (on B15) for CP-PATH + LS. We believe that these figures underestimate the deviation from the optimal solutions as fewer algorithms provided reasonably good solutions on the larger instances. It is interesting to notice that local search had a significant impact mostly on series B, when the number of possible capacity levels for each arc is the highest.

Table 5. Effect of each constraint on the MRE

	B10	B11	B12	C10	C11	C12
sec = 0	5.52%	10.50%	9.43%	2.04%	10.39%	14.94%
sec = 1	5.58%	2.57%	4.81%	4.67%	12.20%	10.88%
nomult = 0	6.75%	8.91%	8.13%	3.26%	11.97%	13.54%
nomult = 1	4.35%	4.16%	6.12%	3.45%	10.61%	12.29%
symdem = 0	7.72%	7.91%	9.58%	4.74%	12.23%	12.50%
symdem = 1	3.38%	5.16%	4.67%	1.97%	10.35%	13.32%
bmax = 0	5.38%	6.23%	6.38%	3.87%	10.71%	15.76%
bmax = 1	5.72%	6.84%	7.86%	2.84%	11.87%	10.06%
pmax = 0	5.88%	7.48%	6.65%	6.69%	12.79%	12.85%
pmax = 1	5.21%	5.59%	7.60%	0.03%	9.79%	12.97%
tmax = 0	4.14%	6.87%	7.48%	2.32%	7.22%	13.03%
tmax = 1	6.95%	6.20%	6.76%	4.40%	15.36%	12.80%

Table 5 shows the effect of the presence of each constraint on the results. For each optional constraint, it provides the MRE obtained with CP-PATH + LS in Parallel when the constraint is inactive (parameter set to 0) and when the parameter is active (parameter set to 1). Hence, each percentage in the table is the average of 32 numbers. Once again, these figures should be taken with care as the MRE is computed with respect to best known solutions. However, when the MRE is significantly greater when a parameter is set to 1 than when it is set to 0, it indicates that the performance of the algorithm is affected by the presence of the constraint. This occurs with *tmax* on B10, C10 and C11, and to a lesser extent with *sec*. On the other hand, *nomult* and *symdem* tend to make the problem easier to solve.

6 Conclusion

In this paper, we have presented a case study based on a benchmark aimed at evaluating and improving the robustness of algorithms. The results do not suggest that we have found the ultimate algorithm for this benchmark. On the contrary, we believe that all the algorithms we tried can still be improved, and that there are many other algorithms to design and test on this benchmark. We note that most of the work was done by developers mostly acquainted with constraint programming, but with direct feedback from mixed integer programming specialists, and significant time spent on each approach, so all of the developed algorithms are equally hard to improve. Branch-and-price and large neighborhood search algorithms, developed by Alain Chabrier and Laurent Perron, are currently under test.

Our aim in this paper was to show the type of performance discrepancies that can occur when industrial optimization applications are developed and some types of corrections that can be applied: (1) put more or less emphasis on the generation of admissible solutions; (2) strengthen problem formulation; (3) strengthen constraint propagation; (4) adapt variable selection heuristics to symmetries or asymmetries in the problem; (5) use *or*-parallelism; (6) adapt the tree search traversal strategy to the characteristics of the problem; (7) use local search to improve the first solution(s) found by a tree search algorithm.

One of the most important aspects of this study has been the ability to implement and test such corrections with minimal development effort.

The results, and our everyday industrial practice, compel us to be modest when stating that an algorithm is appropriate for a given problem. The differences between our initial results on A10 and the results obtained even on instances of the same size like B10 and C10 show that we ought to be cautious.

As mentioned, the benchmark suite we used is public. Instances are available at http://www.prism.uvsq.fr/Rococo. We believe other benchmark suites of a similar kind are needed for the academic community to attack the issue of algorithm robustness as it is encountered in industrial settings, where data are neither random nor uniform and where the presence of side constraints can necessitate significant adaptations of the basic models and problem-solving techniques found in the literature.

7   Acknowledgments

This work has been partially financed by the French MENRT, as part of RNRT project ROCOCO. We wish to thank our partners in this project, particularly Jacques Chambon and Raphaël Bernhard from France Télécom R&D, Dominique Barth, Bertrand Le Cun and Thierry Mautor from the PRiSM laboratory, and Claude Lemaréchal from INRIA Rhône-Alpes. The very first CP program was developed by Olivier Schmeltzer, the very first CG program by Alain Chabrier, and the very first MIP program by Philippe Refalo. We thank Alain and Philippe and the CPLEX team for many enlightening discussions over the course of the ROCOCO project.

References

[1] J. Christopher Beck and Laurent Perron.   Discrepancy-Bounded Depth First Search. In *Proceedings of CP-AI-OR 00*, March 2000.

[2] Raphaël Bernhard, Jacques Chambon, Claude Lepape, Laurent Perron, and Jean Charles Régin.   Résolution d'un problème de conception de réseau avec parallel solver. In *Proceeding of JFPLC*, 2002. (In French).

[3] Daniel Bienstock and Oktay Günlük. Capacitated network design: Polyhedral structure and computation. *ORSA J*, 1996:243–260, 1996.

[4] Cplex. *ILOG CPLEX 7.5 User's Manual and Reference Manual*. ILOG, S.A., 2001.

[5] V. Gabrel, A. Knippel, and M. Minoux. Exact solution of multicommodity network optimization problems with general step cost functions. *Operations Research Letters*, 25:15–23, 1999.

[6] Michel Gondran and Michel Minoux. *Graphes et algorithmes*. Eyrolles, 1995.

[7] Laurent Perron. Search procedures and parallelism in constraint programming. In Joxan Jaffar, editor, *Proceedings of CP '99*, pages 346–360. Springer-Verlag, 1999.

[8] Laurent Perron. Practical parallelism in constraint programming. In *Proceedings of CP-AI-OR 2002*, pages 261–276, March 2002.

[9] Franz Rothlauf, David E. Goldberg, and Armin Heinzl. Network random keys: A tree representation scheme for genetic and evolutionary algorithms. *Evolutionary Computation*, 10(1):75–97, 2002.

[10] P. Shaw, V. Furnon, and B. de Backer. A lightweight addition to CP frameworks for improved local search. In Ulrich Junker, Stefan E. Karisch, and Torsten Fahle, editors, *Proceedings of CP-AI-OR 2000*, 2000.

[11] Paul Shaw, Vincent Furnon, and Bruno De Backer. A constraint programming toolkit for local search. In Stefan Voss and David L. Woodruff, editors, *Optimization Software Class Libraries*, pages 219–262. Kluwer Academic Publishers, 2002.

[12] Solver. *ILOG Solver 5.2 User's Manual and Reference Manual*. ILOG, S. A., 2001.

Connections Reservation with Rerouting for ATM Networks: A Hybrid Approach with Constraints

Muriel Lauvergne[1], Philippe David[2], and Patrice Boizumault[3]

[1] France Telecom R&D
F-22300 Lannion, France
muriel.lauvergne@rd.francetelecom.fr
[2] Ecole des Mines de Nantes
BP 20722, F-44307 Nantes Cedex 3, France
philippe.david@emn.fr
[3] Université de Caen
GREYC UMR 6072, Campus 2 bat Sciences 3
F-14032 Caen Cedex, France
patrice.boizumault@info.unicaen.fr

Abstract. This paper presents a hybrid method developed at France Telecom R&D to solve a difficult network problem. It takes place in an ATM network administration context and consists in planning connection demands over a period of one year.

We introduce a new framework for solving this problem within the allowed computing time. This framework is based on two major elements: first a hybrid method which mixes shortest path algorithms, constraint propagation and repairing principles, then a model for the time dimension which is a critical issue in this ATM network administration problem.

We compare our method with a greedy method (without rerouting) presently used in FTR&D upon realistic problems. The results of our experiments show that the difficult problem of rerouting can be solved with our method. Moreover, rerouting leads to accept of 46% of connections that are rejected with the greedy algorithm.

This paper is a revised version of [14].

1 Introduction

ATM (Asynchronous Transfer Mode) is a high speed network which can fulfill various communication services. The basic concept of an ATM communication is that all users can send traffic to any node, at a chosen rate called bandwidth. One of its main characteristics is that all information relative to a demand have to be routed on the same path: we are not in a flow context.

Our application takes place in a network administration context, and is close to a QoS routing problem [18]. QoS routing is a key issue for multi-commodity broadband networks. It consists of selecting routes with sufficient resources for

P. Van Hentenryck (Ed.): CP 2002, LNCS 2470, pp. 649–663, 2002.
© Springer-Verlag Berlin Heidelberg 2002

the required QoS parameters. Those parameters depend on networks and services. They concern several characteristics, e.g.: bandwidth, path size, delays, costs, cell loss ratio. The computation complexity is determined by the composition rules of the metrics used to characterise a route weight: additive (i.e., the route weight is the sum of links weights, e.g., delay is an additive metric), multiplicative (i.e., the route weight is the product of links weights, for example loss ratio is a multiplicative metric) or concave (i.e., the route weight only depends on the minimum weight, e.g., bandwidth is a concave metric) [3].

Our problem is a quality of service (QoS) routing problem with many concave metrics and an additive metric, for which we permit rerouting. Our aim is to plan resources used by allocated connections, and to use this information when admitting new connection demands. The admission of a new connection demand ensures that a route can be found for this new demand, so that all requirements are satisfied within the network availability. Reservations are planned for a period of one year, and their acceptation or reject must be computed within a given time of one minute per demand.

To improve reservation, we allow the rerouting of some connections that have already been accepted. This proposition creates a complex problem because of both its size and the exponential number of potential reroutings that can be generated. Our method uses:

- an efficient time representation to deal with calendar size (one year),
- classical graph algorithms to compute routes,
- repair principles to compute a solution within the allowed computing time (anytime problems),
- heuristics and constraints propagation to improve the resolution.

Section 2 describes the resource allocation problem and proposes a calendar model. Section 3 motivates the choice of our method and section 4 details this method. An example is depicted in section 5. In section 6, we give experimental comparative results, and finally, we conclude with comments about our realization and with further works.

2   Problem

2.1   Description

A network is composed of nodes and links; links are characterized by a connection type and a bandwidth capacity. Several connections may be routed through the same link subject to its bandwidth availability. Each demand is described by:

- a source node and a destination node,
- a connection type which specifies the links that can be used,
- an ATM Transfer Capability (ATC) parameter, depending on the QoS required,
- a traffic calendar.

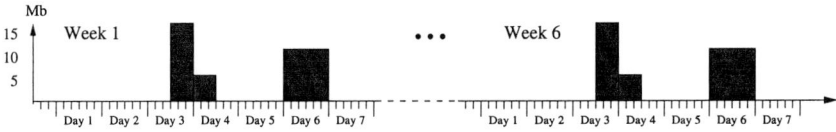

Fig. 1. Calendar for C3

Depending on the service he needs, the user chooses one ATC. For each ATC, rules depict how to add the demand on links. The traffic contract describes the traffic characteristics and the guaranteed Quality of Service (QoS). Moreover, because of technological limitations, it is impossible to share a connection amongst multiple routes: this is mono-routing.

In this paper we call "connection" a demand that has been accepted on the network. A connection has all characteristics of a demand, together with a list of links from source to destination, called "route". The only QoS parameters considered are the capacity, the route length, and some ATM links attributes. Capacity parameters can be considered as one concave metric per slot of time. The route length is the number of nodes of the route: it is an additive metric. A link attribute is a parameter that is considered individually to determine if a given link is acceptable or not. This application only takes into account types of links, that are required to depict the hierarchical structure of the ATM network.

The user asks for a non-permanent connection, during at most one year. The required traffic must be constant on slots, and may be periodic. For example, one can ask for those calendars:

- C_1: 15 Mb from 6.15.00 at midnight, to 8.15.00 at midnight and 10 Mb from 9.1.00 at mid-night, to 9.15.00, at midnight;
- C_2: 5 Mb every Monday and Tuesday, from 5 am to 6.45 am, and 3 Mb every Saturday from 11 pm to 0.45 am;
- C_3: From week 1 to week 6, 15 Mb on Wednesday from noon to midnight, 5 Mb on Thursday from midnight to noon, and 10 Kb on Saturday, all day long (illustrated figure 1).

For our application, we consider that an accepted connection can be rerouted (i.e., its route can be modified) with respect to some constraints. On this one-slot time example, figure 2, the demand "5 between A and B" is refused without rerouting, and is admitted after connection 2 is rerouted.

The aim of the application is to find, within the allowed time, a way to accept the current demand that respects its QoS requirements. This way can be a single route, if it exists, or a set of routes including the rerouting of several connections. A connection cannot be rejected, but a demand can. The major criterion to respect is the minimization of the number of refused demands. The secondary criteria taken into account are:

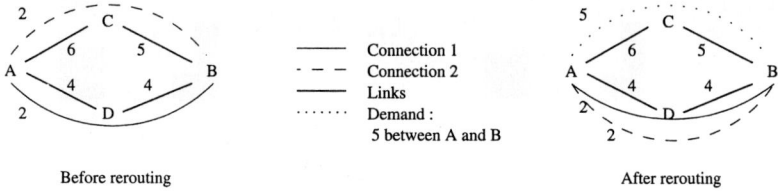

Fig. 2. Rerouting interest

- minimizing the number of rerouted connections: so we are looking for stable solutions;
- minimizing the global length of routes;
- balancing the network availabilities.

2.2   Time Processing

An important difficulty comes from the time dimension. Indeed the reservation is computed for a year, divided into quarters: 35,000 slots of time have to be considered for each demand and each link.

We have proposed [13] a hierarchical structure close to the BDD [2] that permits us to represent the availability of a link, as well as the bandwidth calendar of a demand on a compact tree. This structure is called Restricted Nary Tree (RNT).

Superfluous data due to periodic demands are suppressed by creating a hierarchical level for each type of periodicity.

Superfluous data due to long constant slots are suppressed by gathering together consecutive and similar subtrees. Figure 3 presents such a modeling for the calendar of C_3 depicted before. Experimental results show that this compact representation works fine, especially in case of periodic demands. Having an efficient representation of time is absolutely necessary in our context.

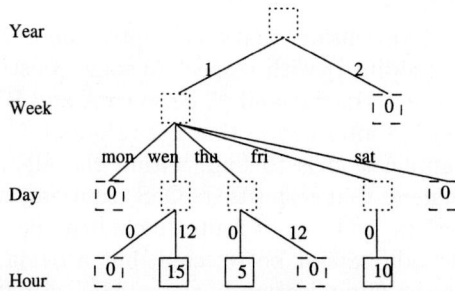

Fig. 3. Calendar for C3

3   Choice of a Method

3.1   Characteristics of the Problem

This problem is dynamic. Actually, resource availability evolves with time, and because of rerouting, we have to reconsider routes that have already been allocated. This often brings superfluous work, and moreover, gives unstable results. In this application, we would like to limit this superfluous work, by looking for stable solutions that generate few modifications of routes, when rerouting is required.

This problem is "anytime". A solution has to be computed within a given time (i.e., less than one minute per new demand). Afterwards, the demand is rejected.

This is a hard problem. The complexity of this problem is a consequence of the complexity of routing several demands.

This is a large-scale problem, especially on its time dimension. Currently, the reservation is computed for a year, divided into quarters. There are then about 35.000 slots of time. The size of the network is about 100 nodes, 800 links and about 700 connections are routed for a year.

3.2   Related Problems

For ATM networks, real time routing is achieved by PNNI[1], but the routing algorithm used for this hierarchical protocol is specific.

Routing problems complexity depends on what types of metrics are involved. When there are many additive or multiplicative QoS metrics for a QoS routing problem, [3] have shown that the allocation of every single demand is NP-complete. An overview of QoS routing algorithms is given in [18], but all those algorithms only consider one demand, without any rerouting.

Resource Allocation In Networks (RAIN) problems are design problems where capacity assignment is already achieved. It consists in finding one route for each demand, so that the bandwidth requirements of most demands are satisfied within the resource capacities of the links. It is close to a routing problem, except that all demands are known prior to the resolution. When rerouting is authorized, the RAIN problem is closer to the reservation problem. In fact, rerouting can be managed by selecting a set of connections and routing them like in a RAIN problem. When demands cannot be divided among multiple routes, like in an ATM context, the RAIN problem is NP-complete [6]. Christian Frei [5] introduced a "blocking island" paradigm, based on a hierarchy of bandwidth availabilities. This approach allows to formulate and solve the RAIN problem as a CSP problem. Unfortunately, because of the time dimension, this hierarchy of bandwidth availabilities cannot be applied to our reservation problem. The "blocking island" paradigm has been extended in case of multiple concave metrics [6]. This can be applied to our problem, where the bandwidth description for each quarter can be considered as a concave metric. However dealing

---
[1] Private Network-to-Network Interface

with 35,000 metrics seems to be unrealistic with the "blocking island" extended paradigm.

3.3   Selecting a Method

Four main categories of methods can be used to solve our problem:

- Constructive methods, based upon backtracking or branch and bound techniques. Constraint programming can be classified in this category [7] [20].
- Local search methods start from an initial solution (often randomly generated). From this initial solution, exchanges between components are performed and results are evaluated. The exchange producing the best solution is retained and the procedure continues until a stopping test. The exchange process depends on the method (e.g., simulated annealing [11] [10], tabu search [9] [8], repair-based methods [16] [4]...) and on the neighborhood system used. The choice of a neighborhood generating mechanism should be driven by the structure of the problem.
- Greedy methods construct a solution from scratch with no backtracking mechanism. These methods are obviously very fast, but they can be used only on problems with very specific properties.
- Systematic constructive methods could not be used because of the size of the problem that must be solved on a given time. Local search seems to be interesting, but for our problem it is difficult to value and compare neighbors, and then to guide the search.

Hybrid methods, can be obtained by combining methods [17] [19] [12]. For each category, methods can be systematic or not, and can provide an optimal solution or not. A hybrid technique, combining shortest path algorithms, constraint propagation and repairing principles [16] [1] appeared to be well suited for solving this problem.

4   Resolution

With our method, this problem is solved as a satisfaction problem, and search is induced by the optimisation parameters.

4.1   General Algorithm

The general algorithm is presented below. First, a route is searched for the connection demand using shortest path algorithms. If such a route does not exist, various conflicts are computed: a conflict is composed of a correct route and a set of connections in conflict with the demand for this route. Then, for each conflict, a CSP (restricted to the area of the network that can be modified by solving this conflict) is built in order to determine a new allocation accepting the demand: the current solution is locally repaired. Such CSPs are small. The search space is pruned by the propagation of connectivity constraints. Moreover, thanks to variable and value ordering heuristics, the resolution can be guided to a good solution, in terms of stability and path length.

Restricted CSPs (RCSPs [13]) corresponding to various conflicts are successively treated. Indeed, if a solution to one RCSP is found within the allowed computing time, the demand is accepted. If not, the demand will be rejected. We can expect to manage several conflicts in the allowed computing time because the size of RCSPs is small, and their resolution time limited by an inner timeout.

Algorithm :

```
solving (Demand, Network)
OkRoutes <- routing-whitout-rerouting(Demand, Network)

IF OkRoutes != {}
THEN    ;;; a solution without rerouting exists
   Solution <- choose-OkRoute(OkRoutes, Demand, Network)
   RETURN admitting-notification(Demand)

ELSE    ;;; there is no solution without rerouting
   NotOkRoutes <- preliminary-step(Demand, Network)

   ;;; for each NotOkRoute, build and solve the relative RCSP
   WHILE ( NotOkRoutes != {} AND More-solving-time != 0 )
   DO
     Conflict <- choose-NotOkRoute(NotOkRoutes)
     Rcsp <- rcsp-building(Conflict, Demand, Network)
     solving(Rcsp)
   END WHILE

   RETURN rejecting-notification(Demand)
END IF
```

Next sections depict the principal steps of this method.

4.2   Preliminary Step

The aim of this step is to provide a route for a demand without rerouting, or, in case of failure, a set of conflicts. A conflict consists in a route proposed for the new demand, and a set of connections, that we can try to reroute to admit the demand.

We use a shortest path algorithm close to Dijkstra's one, that takes into account the residual bandwidth. We also identify reasons why a link is rejected, and memorize this link if its rejection is caused by bandwidth availability problems. A memorized link, that belongs to a correct route for a demand, is a conflict link. On each conflict link, we select connections that are in conflict with the demand (i.e., that are active on at least one common slot of time), and that respect conditions for rerouting.

As a consequence, we often obtain many conflicts for a demand: althought some of these are redundant and we order them according to the number and the capacity of connections. A selection allows us to reject sub-conflicts, and the ordering enables us to try to repair first the easiest conflicts. If there are still too many conflicts, we only consider the easiest.

Moreover, all ATM attributes have been taken into account during this preliminary work by selecting only suitable links and connections.

4.3   Building Restricted CSPs

After the preliminary step, we have got for each conflict, a set of demands to reroute. This problem looks like a design problem, and a natural way to model it, is to introduce boolean variables to represent the passage of a connection across a link. This choice allows to write connectivity constraints thanks to Kirchoff rules, and capacity constraints as sums. Moreover, the mono-routing and the objective function of routing every demand can easily be expressed. So this choice fits, but doesn't suffice to solve the problem, because of the difficulty to benefit from the connectivity constraints structure (which would permit to trim the search tree and to build efficient variables ordering strategy). Therefore our representation is based on the position of links for each connection.

A RCSP is defined by the tuple (V, D, C), where each variable of the set V describes which link is allocated for a rerouted connection at a certain position on its route. That is why, for each demand d_i, we introduce n_d variables: $d_{i,1}$, $d_{i,2}$, ..., d_{i,n_d}, where n_d is the maximum size admitted for the route of d. The maximum size n_d takes into account the shortest size of a path without capacity constraints, and a "freedom degree", that express how much the size can differ from the shortest size.

Domains D of the variables are sets of links. On a first step, for each demand, a double labeling is computed for every link of the network, that gives how far this link stands from source and from destination. Then, thanks to this double labeling, we can limit the domains by keeping only those links that are on a correct route (i.e., not too long, and which verify ATM attributes). To represent routes shorter than n_d links, a stop value is added to domains.

An example of domains building is given in figure 4, for a network with twelve links: a_1, ...,a_{12}, and a demand between A and E (in bold).

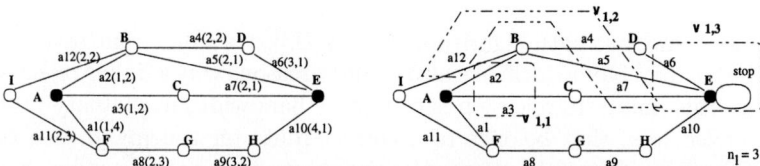

Fig. 4. Distances and domains building for C1

Moreover, when their residual capacity are inferior to the corresponding demand being rerouted, values are removed from the domains[2].

There are two kinds of constraints in C: connectivity constraints, between variables created for the same connection, and capacity constraints, between variables created for distinct connections, and which have at least one common link in their domains.

4.4   Solving RCSPs

The search method used to solve each RCSP is based on backtrack (with a timeout) that is made efficient thanks to adequate order heuristics and specific propagation of constraints.

At first, our variable ordering takes variables created for the demand, that are instantiated to the values of the repair route. Then, variables related to the largest connection are selected with a first fail heuristic. To yield a profit from the connectivity constraints structure, we select variables of each connection from destination to source. Value ordering enables to guide the search towards a good solution in terms of length (by instantiating first to the stop value) and to a good solution regarding stability (by instantiating first to the previous value).

Constraint Propagation: The characteristics of this problem lead us to define a specific and appropriate propagation scheme:

- (1): Connectivity constraints are always relative to two successive variables that belong to the same connection.
- (2): Because of the time dimension, testing a capacity constraint is much more expensive than testing a connectivity constraint.
- (3): As a connection cannot use a link twice, the result of a capacity test on a variable $v_{i,j}$ does not depend on instantiated variables $v_{i,k}$, $k > j$, but only on instantiated variables $v_{h,l}$, $h \neq i$.

Note: Because of (3), we could remove some values from the domains *a priori*, before starting with a new connection. This would prune the search tree, but it could generate some capacity constraint tests that are not helpful. Because of (2), we ignored it. Then, we define the following propagation scheme:

- (a) We first make the domains being arc-consistent for the connectivity constraints.
- (b) During the resolution, we create a list L of modified links, whose residual capacity is modified because of the current partial allocation. This list is kept up to date when we start to instantiate variables relative to a new connection (i:e:, after the instantiation of avariable $v_{i,1}$), and when we backtrack to a variable relative to an older connection (i:e:,when we backtrack to a variable $v_{i,1}$). This is sufficient because of (3).

---

[2] To limit the number of comparisons between calendars, this filtering is not applied dynamically as variables are instantiated.

- (c) When we instantiate $v_{i,j}$ to the value a, we test connectivity constraints between $v_{i,j}$ and $v_{i,j-1}$ if $j > 1$ (forward), and the capacity constraint relative to a if $a \in L$.
- (d) If the capacity constraint fails when we instantiate $v_{i,j}$ to a, we remove a from all the domains of variables $v_{i,k}$, and we propagate connectivity constraints. Because of (1),it is enough to propagate them by testing successively arc-consistency between each variable and its neighbor, and to limit this propagation to variables $v_{i,k}$, relative to $v_{i,j}$. The forward propagation (variables $v_{i,k}$, $k < j$) cuts dead sub-trees. The backward propagation (variables $v_{i,k}$, $k > j$) has sense because of (3), and prevents from redundant search.
- (e) we up date deleted values only when we backtrack to a variable relative to an older connection (and not for each backtrack).

5   Example

5.1   Description

To illustrate our method, we present the resolution of a problem restricted as follows. At first we do not take into account types of connections and links, ATC, and QoS. Secondly, we consider that time dimension is restricted to three slots of time, and we note (b_1, b_2, b_3) a calendar, where b_1, b_2, and b_3 are the values of capacities for each slot. Moreover each demand is treated before those three slots of time. At least, we decide to build only routes whose size is equal to the shortest size, or one additional link (i:e:, the freedom degree is one).

The network at the beginning of this example deals with three connections :

- C_1, between A and E, has for calendar $(0, 6, 6)$, and for route (a_3, a_7).
- C_2, between E and F, has for calendar $(0, 4, 0)$, and for route (a_7, a_3, a_1).
- C_3, between A and D, has for calendar $(5, 0, 0)$, and for route (a_2, a_4).

This network is described in figure 5, a. Each link has for label its name: a_i, its capacity, and its current reservations: a matrix with a line per connection and a column per slot of time.

When repairing steps are described, letters are refering to contraint propagation scheme, on last section.

5.2   First Demand

A first demand occurs between A and I, with a calendar $(0, 4, 0)$. It can be accepted without rerouting, so, it is, and this first demand becomes connection C_4, on the route (a_2, a_{12}). The network reservations are then depicted in figure 5, b.

5.3   Second Demand

A second demand occurs between A and E, with a calendar $(0, 7, 0)$. This demand can not be accepted without rerouting...

Preliminary Step

Correct shortest routes for the demand, without taking into account availability constraints, are the routes $r_1 = (a_2, a_5)$ and $r_2 = (a_3, a_7)$. Conflict links on those routes are a_2, that supports connections C_3 and C_4, and a_7, that supports connections C_1 and C_2. Calendar of C_3 is not in conflict with the demand, so, there are two conflicts: cf_1, composed of the route r_1 and connection C_4 and cf_2, composed of the route r_2 and connections C_1 and C_2.

As cf_1 concerns only one connection, we begin with this conflict.

Resolution of the First Conflict

To solve this conflict, we first remove the connection C_4, and consider that the demand is accepted on the route r_1. The associated network is depicted in figure 5,c.

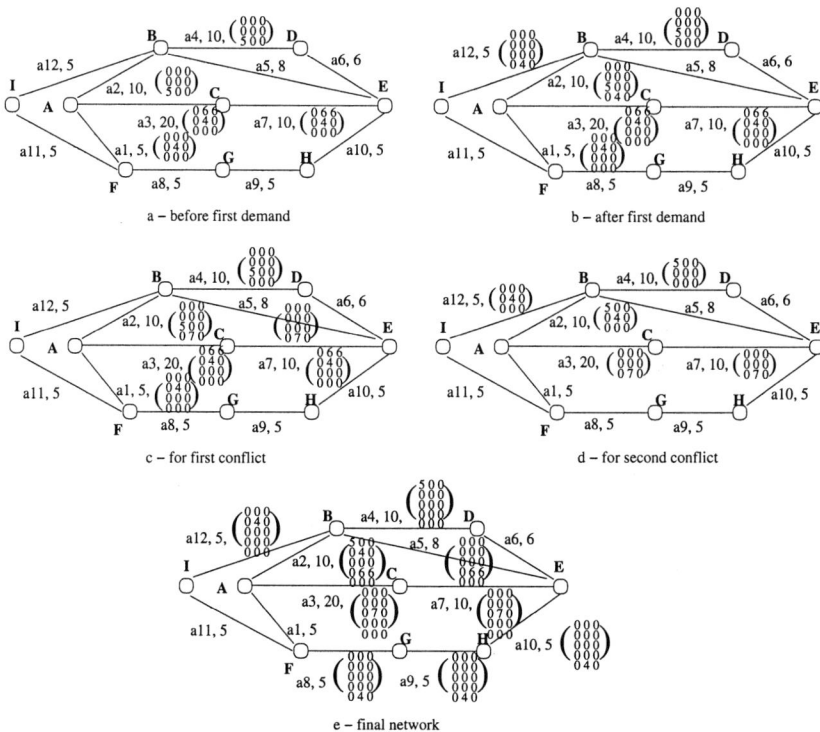

Fig. 5. States of the network

Without taking into account availability constraints, C_4 has got a shortest route of two links. As it has not got any route of size three, we only consider routes of two links to build RCSP. So, we introduce two variables: $v_{4,1}$ for the link in first position and $v_{4,2}$ for the link in second position. Respective domains are $\{a_1, a_2\}$ and $\{a_{11}, a_{12}\}$. Because of availability, $v_{4,1}$ can not be instantiated to a_1 or a_2. So, this first conflict has no solution, modifications are removed and the network is like before solving, as depicted in figure 5, b.

Resolution of the Second Conflict

To solve this conflict, we first remove connections C_1 and C_2, and consider that the demand is accepted on the route r_2. The associated network is depicted in figure 5, d.

Without taking into account any availability constraints, C_1 has got a shortest route of two links, and three links long routes exist. Because of the freedom degree, we do consider longer paths. So, we introduce three variables: $v_{1,1}$, $v_{1,2}$, and $v_{1,3}$ for the connection C_1. C_2 has got a shortest route of three links, and four links long routes exist. So, we introduce four variables: $v_{2,1}$, $v_{2,2}$, $v_{2,3}$ and $v_{2,4}$ for the connection C_2.

We have detailed domains building for the connection C_1 on figure 4. Double labeling is computed for each link, and according to it, the link may belong to a domain or not.

Some values can already be deleted from domains because their residual availibility is inferior to the corresponding connection: a_6 for $v_{1,3}$, a_7 and a_12 for $v_{1,2}$, a_{12} for $v_{2,3}$ and $v_{2,2}$ and a_7 for $v_{2,1}$.

There are two types of constraints: connectivity constraints, that are binary constraints, and capacity constraints, with one global constraint per link.

A preliminary arc-consistency step on connectivity constraints removes values that have no support in a domain. It removes a_4 from the domain of $v_{1,2}$, a_3 from the domain of $v_{1,1}$, a_{11} from the domains of $v_{2,4}$ and $v_{2,3}$, and a_3, a_5 and a_{10} from the domain of $v_{2,2}$, a_3 and a_9 from the domain of $v_{2,3}$ and a_8 from the domain of $v_{2,4}$.

We order domains and values with the heuristics depicted section 4.4: at first the Stop value, then the previous value, and the other values according to their link number. Finally, ordered variables and domains are:

$v_{1,3}$: *Stop*	$v_{2,4}$: *Stop*, a_1
$v_{1,2}$: a_5	$v_{2,3}$: a_1, a_2, a_8
$v_{1,1}$: a_2	$v_{2,2}$: a_2, a_4, a_9
	$v_{2,1}$: a_5, a_6, a_{10}

When we solve this RCSP with our method, we test consistency of the partial solution after each instantiation. We only propagate connectivity constraints when a capacity constraint fails. The solving tree is depicted in figure 6.

We first instantiate $v_{1,3}$ to *Stop*, $v_{1,2}$ to a_5 and $v_{1,1}$ to a_2 without failure. L is up to date with $L = \{a_5, a_2\}$ (b). We instantiate $v_{2,4}$ to *Stop*, $v_{2,3}$ to a_1 and $v_{2,2}$ to a_2: $a_2 \in L$ (c), so we test the capacity constraint, that fails. So we remove a_2 from the domains of $v_{2,2}$ and $v_{2,3}$ (d), and we propagate to next variables that belong to the current connection C_2. The next variable is $v_{2,1}$ and its domain is

Domains

$Dv_{1,3}$ = {Stop}

$Dv_{1,2}$ = {a5}

$Dv_{1,1}$ = {a2}

$Dv_{2,4}$ = {Stop, a1}

$Dv_{2,3}$ = {a1, a2, a8}

$Dv_{2,2}$ = {a2, a4, a8}

$Dv_{2,1}$ = {a5, a6, a10}

Stop

a5

a2

L= {a5, a2}

Stop

a1   a8

a2

$Dv_{2,2}$ = {a4, a9}
$Dv_{2,3}$ = {a1, a8}
$Dv_{2,1}$ = {a6, a10}

a4   a9   a4   a9

a6   a10

L= {a5,a2, a8, a9, a10}

ai connectivity failure
ai capacity failure

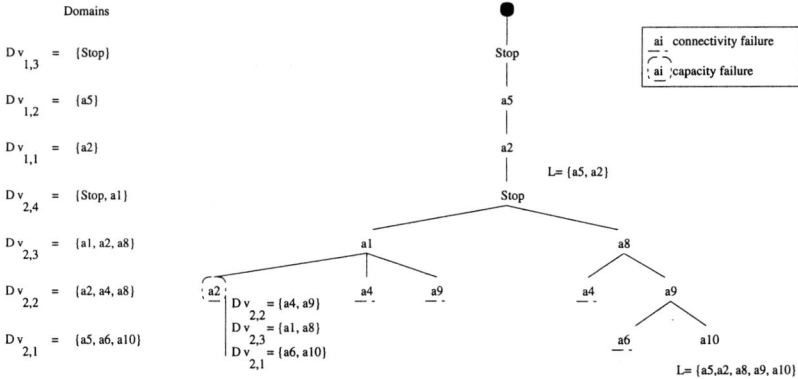

Fig. 6. Resolution of the second conflict

$\{a_5, a_6, a_{10}\}$. As a_5 has only got a_2 for support, it is removed from the domain of $v_{2,1}$; a_6 and a_{10} have other value than a_2 for support so we keep them. There is no more variables to propagate forward the failure, and backward propagation do not remove any value. Those removals are kept until we have to backtrack to a variable relative to a connetion before C_2, so, never in this case.

So we backtrack and re-instantiate $v_{2,2}$ successively to a_4, and a_9: there are always connectivity failures (c). We backtrack and re-instantiate $v_{2,3}$. a_2 has been removed from the domain of $v_{2,3}$, then we try a_8: it is right. a_2 has been removed from the domain of $v_{2,2}$, and because of connectivity (c) we can not instantiate $v_{2,2}$ to a_4, but to a_9. The value a_5 has been removed from the domain of $v_{2,1}$ and connectivity constraints (c) fail instantiating it to a_6.

So we instantiate $v_{2,1}$ to a_{10}: there is no more failure, and this solution is kept. The final network is illustrated in figure 5, e.

6   Experimental Results

Rerouting is of particular interest when many demands are rejected. It was not yet the case for France Telecom R&D. So we have built test examples based on the structure of the real network and with a set of demands close to real demands: we have considered every demand many times, by modifying their capacity.

First experimentations [13], show that in this context it is useless to permit too large freedom degree. In fact, if we admit demands on too long routes, the network will reach a stalemate for the next demands. It gives best results with a freedom degree equal to one.

In this paper, we present different series of evaluations. Each serie is defined by its set of demands: from 1349 demands for the first serie, to 2879 demands for the last one. For each serie we give average results made of fourteen differ-

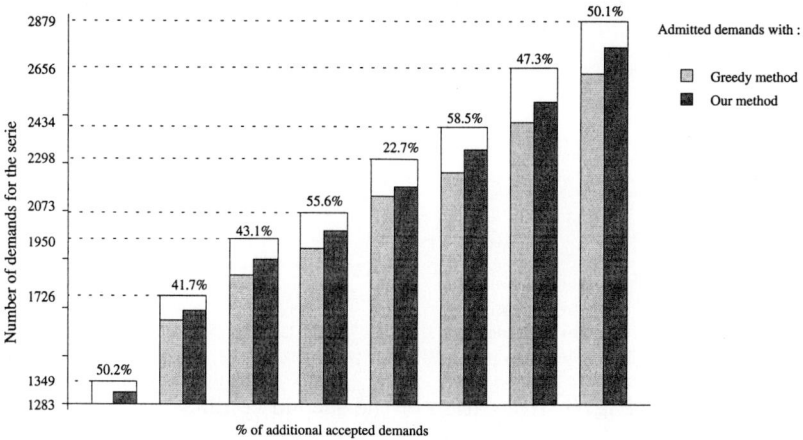

Fig. 7. Additional admitted demands

ent experimentations. Experimentations were made within a global time of one minute per new demand.

Figure 7 shows the comparison between the numbers of admitted demands without rerouting, and with rerouting. The method without rerouting is the greedy method used at France Telecom, improved by our time processing. The other method, with rerouting, is the method described in this paper.

To sum up figure 7, rerouting with our method allows one to admit on average 46% of demands that would be rejected otherwise, without increasing noticeably the length of the routes.

7   Conclusion and Further Work

In this paper we have presented an incomplete hybrid method to solve a large scale real problem within a given computing time. Our experiments have shown that, with such a method, rerouting is efficient for planning connections demands.

This application has been selected as a pilot application for a RNRT[3] project: EOLE[4], and in this context, the method will be improved by taking more precisely into account the resolution of CSP on a given time [15].

To end, we would like to notice that this problem is part of a larger problems family, for which we have to modify some of the affectations within a given time, but not all the affectations. An approach like our's, seems to be well suited for solving these problems.

---

[3] French national network of research for Telecommunications

[4] "Environement d'Optimisation en LignE pour des problemes telecom": *www.telecom.gouv.fr/rnrt/projets/res_d45_ap99.htm*

References

[1] Boizumault, P., David, P, Djellab, D.: Resource allocation in a mobile telephone network: A constructive repair algorithm. In G. Finke, J. F. Maurras, and P. Tolla, editors, RAIRO Recherche Operationnelle, special issue. Hermes. 2000.

[2] Bryant, RE.: Graph-based algorithms for boolean function manipulation. IEEE, Transaction on Computers, C-35(8):677-691. 1986.

[3] Crowcroft, J., Wang, Z.: Quality of service routing for supporting multimedia applications. IEEE Journal on Selected Areas in Communications, 17(7):1228-1234. 1996.

[4] David, P.: A constraint-based approach for examination timetabling using local repair techniques. N 1408 in LNCS, pages 169-186. Springer Verlag. Selected papers (extended version) from the Second International Conference on the Practice And Theory of Automated Timetabling. 1997.

[5] Frei, C., Faltings, B.: Resource allocation in networks using abstraction and constraint satisfaction techniques. CP-99, LNCS 1713, pages 204-218. Springer. 1999.

[6] Frei, C.: Abstaction Techniques for Resource Allocation in Communication Networks. PhD thesis, Ecole Polytechnique Federale de Lausanne. 2000.

[7] Freuder, EC.: Partial constraint satisfaction. Artificial Intelligence, 58(1-3):21-70. 1989.

[8] Glover, F.: Tabu search. I. ORSA Journal of Computing, 1(3):190-206. 1989.

[9] Glover, F.: Tabu search. II. ORSA Journal on Computing,, 2(1):4-32. 1990.

[10] Kirkpatrick, S.: Optimization by simulated annealing: quantitative studies. Journal of Statistical Physics, 34(5). 1984.

[11] Kirkpatrick, S., Gelatt, CD., Vecchi, MP.: Optimization by simulated annealing. Science, (220). 1983.

[12] Laburthe, F., Caseau, Y.: SALSA, a language for search algorithms. In CP'98, LNCS 1520, pages 310-324. Springer. 1998.

[13] Lauvergne, M.: PhD Thesis : Connections Reservation with Rerouting for ATM Networks: a hybrid approach with constraints. Ecole des Mines de Nantes. 2002.

[14] Lauvergne, M., David, P., Boizumault, P.: Resources Allocation in ATM networks: A Hybrid Approach. Integration of AI and OR Techniques for Combinatorial Problems (CPAIOR). 2001.

[15] Loudni, S., Boizumault, P.: A new hybrid method for solving on constraint optimization problems on anytime contexts. ICTAI. 2001.

[16] Minton, S., Johnston, MD., Philips, AB., Laird, P.: Minimizing conflicts: a heuristic repair method for constraint satisfaction and scheduling problems. Artificial Intelligence, 58(1-3):161-205. 1992.

[17] Pesant, G., Gendreau, M.: A view of local search in constraint programming. In CP-96, LNCS 1118, pages 353-366. Springer. 1996.

[18] Nahrstedt, K., Chen, S.: An overview of quality of service routing for the next generation high-speed networks: Problems and solutions. IEEE Special issue on transmission and distribution of digital video. 1998.

[19] Schaerf, A.: Combining local search and look-ahead for scheduling and const raint satisfaction problems. In Proc. of the 15th International Joint Conference on Artificia l Intelligence (IJCAI-97), pages 1254- 1259, Nagoya, Japan. Morgan Kaufmann. 1997.

[20] Verfaillie, G., Schiex, T.: Solution reuse in dynamic constraint satisfaction problems. In AAAI'94, pages 307-312, Seattle, WA. 1994.

Communication and Computation in Distributed CSP Algorithms*

Cèsar Fernàndez[1], Ramón Béjar[1], Bhaskar Krishnamachari[2], and Carla Gomes[2]

[1] Departament d'Informàtica i Enginyeria Industrial, Universitat de Lleida
Jaume II, 69, E-25001 Lleida, Spain
{ramon,cesar}@eup.udl.es
[2] Department of Computer Science, Cornell University
Ithaca, NY 14853, USA
{bhaskar,gomes}@cs.cornell.edu

Abstract. We introduce SensorDCSP, a naturally distributed benchmark based on a real-world application that arises in the context of networked distributed systems. In order to study the performance of Distributed CSP (DisCSP) algorithms in a truly distributed setting, we use a discrete-event network simulator, which allows us to model the impact of different network traffic conditions on the performance of the algorithms. We consider two complete DisCSP algorithms: asynchronous backtracking (ABT) and asynchronous weak commitment search (AWC). In our study of different network traffic distributions, we found that, random delays, in some cases combined with a dynamic decentralized restart strategy, can improve the performance of DisCSP algorithms. More interestingly, we also found that the *active introduction of message delays by agents can improve performance and robustness, while reducing the overall network load.* Finally, our work confirms that AWC performs better than ABT on satisfiable instances. However, on unsatisfiable instances, the performance of AWC is considerably worse than ABT.

1 Introduction

In recent years we have seen an increasing interest in Distributed Constraint Satisfaction Problem (DisCSP) formulations to model combinatorial problems arising in distributed, multi-agent environments [2, 14, 16, 17, 18, 20]. There is a rich

---

* Research supported by AFOSR, grant F49620-01-1-0076 (Intelligent Information Systems Institute) and F49620-01-1-0361 (MURI grant on Cooperative Control of Distributed Autonomous Vehicles in Adversarial Environments), CICYT, TIC2001-1577-C03-03 and DARPA, F30602-00-2-0530 (Controlling Computational Cost: Structure, Phase Transitions and Randomization) and F30602-00-2-0558 (Configuring Wireless Transmission and Decentralized Data Processing for Generic Sensor Networks). The views and conclusions contained herein are those of the authors and should not be interpreted as necessarily representing the official policies or endorsements, either expressed or implied, of AFOSR, DARPA, or the U.S. Government.

P. Van Hentenryck (Ed.): CP 2002, LNCS 2470, pp. 664–679, 2002.
© Springer-Verlag Berlin Heidelberg 2002

set of real-world distributed applications, such as in the area of networked systems, for which the DisCSP paradigm is particularly useful. In such distributed applications, constraints among agents, such as communication bandwidth and privacy issues, preclude the adoption of a centralized approach.

We propose SensorDCSP, a benchmark inspired by one of such distributed applications that arise in networked distributed systems [1, 8]. SensorDCSP is a truly distributed benchmark, a feature not present in many prior benchmark problems used to study the performance of DisCSP algorithms, such as N-Queens and Graph Coloring. SensorDCSP involves a network of distributed sensors simultaneously tracking multiple mobile nodes. The problem underlying SensorDCSP is NP-complete. We show that the SensorDCSP domain undergoes a phase transition in satisfiability, with respect to two control parameters: the level of sensor compatibility and the level of the sensor visibility. Standard DisCSP algorithms on our SensorDCSP domain exhibit the easy-hard-easy profile in complexity, peaking at the phase transition, similarly to the pattern observed in centralized CSP algorithms. More interestingly, the relative strength of standard DisCSP algorithms on SensorDCSP is highly dependent on the satisfiability of the instances. This aspect has been overlooked in the literature due to the fact that, so far, the performance of DisCSP algorithms has been evaluated mainly on satisfiable instances. We study the performance of two well known DisCSP algorithms – asynchronous backtracking (ABT) [18], and asynchronous weak commitment search (AWC) [17]– on SensorDCSP. Both ABT and AWC use agent priority ordering during the search process. While these priorities are static in ABT, AWC allows for dynamic changes in the ordering, and was originally proposed as an improvement over ABT. One of our findings is that although AWC does indeed perform better than ABT on satisfiable instances, its performance is not as good on unsatisfiable problem instances.

Our SensorDCSP benchmark also allows us to study other interesting aspects specific to DisCSPs that are dependent on the physical characteristics of the distributed environment. For example, while the underlying infrastructure or hardware is not critical in studying CSPs, we argue that this is not the case for DisCSPs in communication networks. This is because the traffic patterns and packet-level behavior of networks, which affect the order in which messages from different agents are delivered to each other, can significantly impact the distributed search process. To investigate these kinds of effects, we implemented our DisCSP algorithms using *a fully distributed discrete-event network simulation environment* with a complete set of communication oriented classes. The network simulator allows us to realistically model the message delivery mechanisms of varied distributed communication environments ranging from wide-area computer networks to wireless sensor networks.

We study the impact of communication delays on the performance of DisCSP algorithms. We consider different link delay distributions. Our results show that the presence of a random element due to the delays can improve the performance of AWC. For the basic ABT, even though link delay deteriorates the performance of the standard algorithm, a decentralized restart strategy that we developed for

ABT improves its solution time dramatically, while also increasing the robustness of solutions with respect to the variance of the network link delay distribution. These results are consistent with results on successful randomization techniques developed to improve the performance of CSP algorithms [4]. Another novel aspect of our work is the introduction of a mechanism for *actively* delaying messages. The active delay of messages decreases the communication load of the system, and, somewhat counter-intuitively, can also decrease the overall solution time.

The organization of the rest of the paper is as follows. In Section 2 we formalize our model of DisCSP. In Section 3 we describe SensorDCSP and model it as a DisCSP. In Section 4 we describe two standard DisCSP algorithms and the modifications we have incorporated into the algorithms. In Section 5 we present our experimental results on the active introduction of randomization by the agents and, in Section 6, we present results on delays caused by different traffic conditions in the communication network. Finally, we present our conclusions in Section 7.

2 Distributed CSPs

In a distributed CSP, variables and constraints are distributed among the different autonomous agents that have to solve the problem. A DisCSP is defined as follows: (1) A finite set of agents $A_1, A_2, \cdots, A_n$; (2) A set of local (private) CSPs $P_1, P_2, \cdots, P_n$, where the CSP P_i belongs to agent A_i; A_i is the only agent that can modify the value assigned to the variables of P_i; (3) A global CSP defined among variables that belong to different agents.

In general in DisCSP algorithms each agent only controls one variable. We extended the single-variable approach by making every agent consist of multiple virtual agents, each corresponding to one local variable. In order to distinguish between communication and computation costs in our discrete event simulator, we use different delay distributions to distinguish between messages exchanged between virtual agents of a single real agent (intra-agent messages) and those between virtual agents of different real agents (inter-agent messages).

3 SensorDCSP – A Benchmark for DisCSP Algorithms

The availability of a realistic benchmark of satisfiable and unsatisfiable instances, with tunable complexity, is critical for the study and development of new search algorithms. In the DisCSP literature one cannot find such a benchmark. SensorDCSP, the sensor-mobile problem, is inspired by a real distributed resource allocation problem [13] and offers such desirable characteristics.

In SensorDCSP we have multiple sensors $(s_1, \ldots s_m)$ and multiple mobiles $(t_1, \ldots t_n)$ which are to be tracked by the sensors. The goal is to allocate three distinct sensors to track each mobile node, subject to two sets of constraints: visibility constraints and compatibility constraints. Figure 1 shows an example with six sensors and two mobiles.

Each mobile has a set of sensors that can possibly detect it, as depicted by the bipartite visibility graph in the leftmost panel of Figure 1. Also, it is required that each mobile be assigned three sensors that satisfy a compatibility relation with each other; this compatibility relation is depicted by the graph in the middle panel of Figure 1. Finally, it is required that each sensor only track at most one mobile. A possible solution is shown in the right panel, where the set of three sensors assigned to every mobile is indicated by connecting them to the mobile with the light edges of the figure.

This problem is NP-complete since we can reduce it from the problem of partitioning a graph into cliques of size three [1, 6]. However, the boundary case where every pair of sensors is compatible, is polynomially solvable, since we can reduce that case to a feasible flow problem in a bipartite graph [7].

We define a random distribution of instances of SensorDCSP. An instance of the problem is generated from two different random graphs, the visibility graph and the compatibility graph. Apart from the parameters number of mobiles and number of sensors, we also specify a parameter that controls the edge density of the visibility graph (P_v) and a second one that controls the edge density for the compatibility graph (P_c). These parameters specify the independent probability of including a particular edge in the corresponding graph. As these two graphs model the resources available to solve the problem, P_v and P_c control the number of constraints in the generated instances.

We have developed an instance generator for these random distributions that generates DisCSP-encoded instances. We believe that SensorDCSP is a good benchmark problem because of the simplicity of the generator, and because, as we shall show, one can easily generate easy/hard, unsatisfiable/satisfiable instances by tuning the parameters P_v and P_c appropriately.

We encoded SensorDCSP as a DisCSP as follows: each mobile is associated with a different agent. There are three different variables per agent, one for each sensor that we need to allocate to the corresponding mobile. The value domain of each variable is the set of sensors that can detect the corresponding mobile. The intra-agent constraints between the variables of one agent are that the three sensors assigned to the mobile must be different and must be pair-wise compatible. The inter-agent constraints between the variables of different agents are that a given sensor can be selected by at most one agent. In our implementation

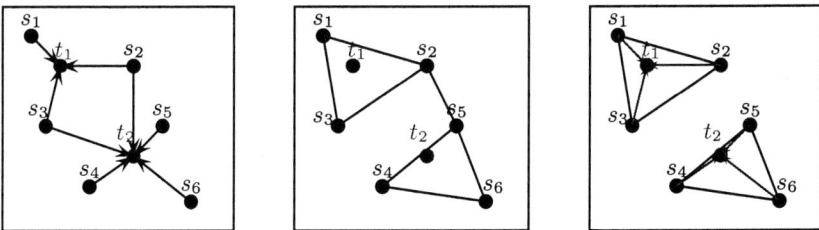

Fig. 1. A SensorDCSP problem instance

of the DisCSP algorithms this encoding is translated to an equivalent formulation where we have three virtual agents for every real agent, each virtual agent handling a single variable.

4   DisCSP Algorithms

In the work reported here we considered two specific DisCSP algorithms, Asynchronous Backtracking Algorithm (ABT), and Asynchronous Weak-Commitment Search Algorithm (AWC). We provide a brief overview of these algorithms but refer the reader to [20] for a more comprehensive description. We also describe the modifications that we introduced to these algorithms. As mentioned before, we assume that each agent can only handle one variable. The neighbors of an agent A_i refer to the set of agents that share constraints with A_i.

The **Asynchronous Backtracking Algorithm (ABT)** is a distributed asynchronous version of a classical backtracking algorithm. This algorithm needs a static agent ordering that determines an ordering between the variables of the problem. Agents use two kinds of messages for solving the problem – *ok* messages and *nogood* messages. Agents initiate the search by assigning an initial value to their variables. An agent changes its value when it detects that it is not consistent with the assignments of higher priority neighbors, and so it maintains an agent view, which consists of the variable assignments of its higher priority neighbors.

Each time an agent assigns a value to its variable, it issues the *ok* message to inform its set of lower priority neighbors about this new assignment. When an agent is not able to find an assignment consistent with its higher priority neighbors, it sends a *nogood* message to the lowest priority agent among the agents that have variables in the *nogood*. A *nogood* message consists of a subset of the agent view that does not permit the agent to find a consistent assignment for itself. A *nogood* message causes the receiver agent to record the received *nogood* as a new constraint and to try to find an assignment consistent with its higher priority neighbors and with all the recorded constraints. If the top-priority agent is forced to backtrack, because it cannot fix the problem by asking a higher priority neighbor to change its assignment, this means that the problem has no solution. On the other hand, when the system reaches a state where all agents are happy with their current assignments (no *nogood* messages are generated), this means that the agents have found a solution.

The **Asynchronous Weak-Commitment Search Algorithm (AWC)** can be seen as a modification of the ABT algorithm. The primary differences are as follows. A priority value is determined for each variable, and the priority value is communicated using the *ok* message. When the current assignment is not consistent with the agent view, the agent selects a new consistent assignment that minimizes the number of constraint violations with lower priority neighbors. When an agent cannot find a consistent value and generates a new *nogood*, it sends the *nogood* message to all its neighbors, and increases its priority one unit over the maximal priority of its neighbors. Then, it finds a value consistent with higher priority neighbors and informs its neighbors with *ok* messages. If no new *nogood* can be generated, the agent waits for the next message.

The most obvious way of introducing randomization in DisCSP algorithms is by randomizing the value selection strategy used by the agents. In the ABT algorithm this is done by performing a uniform random value selection, among the set of values consistent with the agent view and the *nogood* list, every time the agent is forced to select a new value. In the AWC algorithm, we randomize the selection of the value among the values consistent with the agent view and the nogood list, and that minimize the number of violated constraints. This form of randomization is analogous to the randomization techniques used in backtrack search algorithms.

A novel way of randomizing the search, relevant in the context of DisCSP algorithms, is by introducing forced delays in the delivery of messages. Delays introduce randomization because the order in which messages arrive to the target agents determines the order in which the search space is traversed. More concretely, every time an agent has to send a message, it follows the following procedure:

1. **With** probability p:
   $d := r$;
   else (with probability $(1 - p)$)
   $d := 0$;
2. deliver the message with delay d

By delivering a message with delay d we mean that the agent informs its communication interface that it should wait d seconds before delivering the message through the communication network. The parameter r is the fraction of the mean communication delay added by the agent. In our implementation of the algorithms, this strategy is performed by using the services of the discrete event simulator that allow specific delays to be applied selectively in the delivery message queue of each agent.

We have also developed the following decentralized restarting strategy suitable for the ABT algorithm: the highest priority agent uses a timeout mechanism to decide when a restart should be performed. It performs the restart by changing its value at random from the set of values consistent with the *nogoods* learned so far. Then, it sends *ok* messages to its neighbors, thus producing a restart of the search process, but without forgetting the *nogoods* learned. This restart strategy is different from the restart strategy used in centralized procedures, such as rand-satz [4], because the search is not restarted from scratch, but rather benefits from prior mistakes since all agents retain the *nogoods*.

5 Complexity Profiles of DisCSP Algorithms on SensorDCSP

As mentioned earlier, when studying distributed algorithms it is important to factor in the physical characteristics of the distributed environment. For example, the traffic patterns and packet-level behavior of networks can affect the order in which messages from different agents are delivered to each other, significantly impacting the distributed search process. To investigate these kinds of effects, we have developed an implementation of the algorithms ABT and AWC using the Communication Networks Class Library (CNCL) [5]. This library provides a discrete-event network simulation environment with a complete set of communication oriented classes. The network simulator allows us to realistically model the message delivery mechanisms of varied distributed communication environments ranging from wide-area computer networks to wireless sensor networks.

The results shown in this section have been obtained according to the following scenario. The communication links used for communication between virtual agents of different real agents (inter-agent communication) are modeled as random negative exponential distributed delay links, with a mean delay of 1 time unit. The communication links used by the virtual agents of a real agent (intra-agent communication) are modeled as fixed delay links, with a delay of 10^{-3} time units. We use fixed delay links because we consider that a set of virtual agents work inside a private computation node that allows them to communicate with each other with dedicated communication links. This scenario could correspond to a heavy load network situation where inter-agent delay fluctuations obey to the queuing time process on intermediate systems. The factor of 1000 difference between the two delays reflects that usually intra-agent computation is less expensive that inter-agent communication. In the last section of the paper we will see how different delay distribution models over the inter-agent communication links can impact the performance of the algorithms.

For our experimental results, we considered different sets of instances with 3 mobiles and 15 sensors, with every set generated with different values for the parameters P_c and P_v, ranging from 0.1 to 0.9. Every set contains 19 instances, giving a total number of 81 data points. Each instance has been executed 9 times with different random seeds. The results reported in this section were obtained using a sequential value selection function for the different algorithms.

Figure 2 shows the ratio of satisfiable instances as a function of P_c and P_v. When both probabilities are low, the instances generated are mostly unsatisfiable. On the other hand, for high probabilities most of the instances are satisfiable. The transition between the satisfiable and unsatisfiable regions occurs

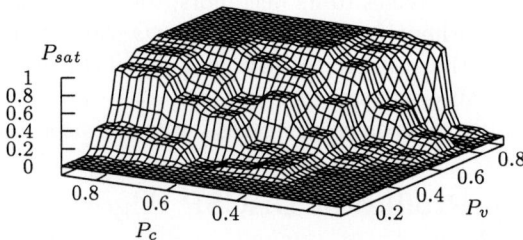

Fig. 2. Ratio of satisfiable instances depending on the density parameter for the visibility graph (P_v) and the density parameter for the compatibility graph (P_c)

within a relatively narrow range of these control parameters, analogous to the phase transition in CSP problems, e.g., in SAT [10].

Also consistent with general CSP problems, we observe that the phase transition coincides with the region where the hardest instances occur. Figure 3 shows the mean solution time with respect to the parameters P_c and P_v. As can be noted, the hardest instances lie on the diagonal that defines the phase transition zone, with a peak for instances with a low P_c value. The dark and light solid lines overlaid on the mesh depict the location of the iso-lines for $P_{sat} = 0.2$ and $P_{sat} = 0.8$, respectively, as per the phase transition surface of Figure 2. As mentioned before, the SensorDCSP problem is NP-complete only when not all the sensors are compatible between them ($P_c < 1$) [7], so the parameter P_c could separate regions of different mean computational complexity, as in other mixed P/NP-complete problems like 2+p-SAT [10] and 2+p-COL [15]. This is particularly visible in the mean time distribution for AWC in Figure 3.

We observe that the mean times to solve an instance appear to be larger by an order of magnitude for AWC than for ABT. At first glance, this is a surprising result considering that the AWC algorithm is a refinement of ABT and results reported for satisfiable instances in the literature [19, 20] conclude on a better performance for AWC. The explanation for such a discrepancy is the fact that our results deal with both satisfiable and unsatisfiable instances. Our further investigations showed that while AWC does indeed outperform ABT on satisfiable

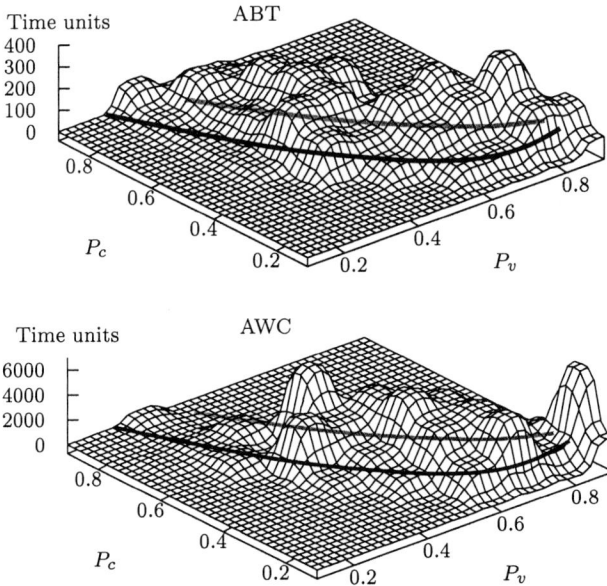

Fig. 3. Mean solution time with respect to P_v and P_c for ABT and AWC algorithms

instances, it is much slower on unsatisfiable instances. This result seems consistent with the fact that the agent hierarchy on ABT is static, while for AWC, such a hierarchy changes during problem solving, taking more time to inspect all the search space when unsatisfiable instances are considered.

5.1   Randomization and Restart Strategies

In this section we describe experimental results that demonstrate the effect of adding a restart strategy to ABT. The introduction of a randomized value selection function was directly assumed in [19]. In extensive experiments we have performed with our test instances, we noticed that the randomized selection function is indeed better than a fixed selection function. However, as the randomization can introduce more variability in the performance, ABT should be equipped with a restart strategy. We have not defined a restart strategy for AWC, because, as we will see in the last section, the dynamic priority strategy of AWC can be viewed as a kind of built-in partial restart strategy. In the results reported in the rest of the paper both ABT and AWC use randomized value selection functions.

To study the benefits of the proposed restart strategy for ABT, we have solved hard satisfiable instances with ABT with restarts, using different cutoff times. Figure 4 shows the mean time needed to solve a hard satisfiable instance with the corresponding 95% confidence intervals for different cutoff times. We observe clearly that there is an optimal restart cutoff time that gives the best performance. As we will discuss in the last section, when considering the delays of real communication networks, the use of restart strategies becomes a requirement, given the high variance in the solution time due to randomness of link delays in the communication network.

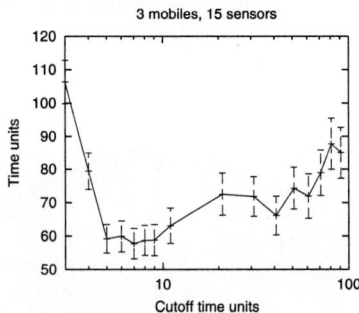

Fig. 4. Mean time to solve a hard satisfiable instance by ABT using restarts with different cutoff times

5.2   Active Delaying of Messages

A novel way of randomizing a DisCSP algorithm corresponds to introducing delays in the delivery of the agents' outgoing messages, as we described in Section 4. In this section we describe our experimental results using AWC, where the amount of delay added by the agents is a fraction r (from 0 to 1) of the fixed delay on the inter-agent communication links. In other words, we consider that all the inter-agent communication links have fixed delays, of 1 time unit, in contrast to what we did in the previous sections, because we want to isolate the effect of the delay added by the agents.

Figure 5 shows the results for a hard satisfiable instance from our SensorD-CSP domain, for different values of p, the probability of adding a delay, and r, the fraction of delay added with respect to the delay of the link. We have that the difference in performance in number of messages can be as high as 3 times between the best case and the worst case. The horizontal plane cutting the surface shows the median time needed by the algorithm when we consider no added random delays ($p = 0, r = 0$). We see that agents can indeed improve the performance by actively introducing some additional random delays, when exchanging messages. We also observe that the performance in number of messages is almost always improved when agents add random delays. Perhaps more surprisingly, in terms of the total solution time, the performance can also improve, if the increase in delay r is not too high. The reason could be the ability of AWC to exploit randomization during the search process due to its inherent restarting strategy.

6   The Effect of the Communication Network Data Load

As described in the previous section, when working on a communication network with fixed delays, the performance of AWC can be improved, depending on the amount of random delay addition that the agents introduce into the message delivery system. However, in real networks, the conditions of data load present in the communication links used by the agents cannot always be modeled with

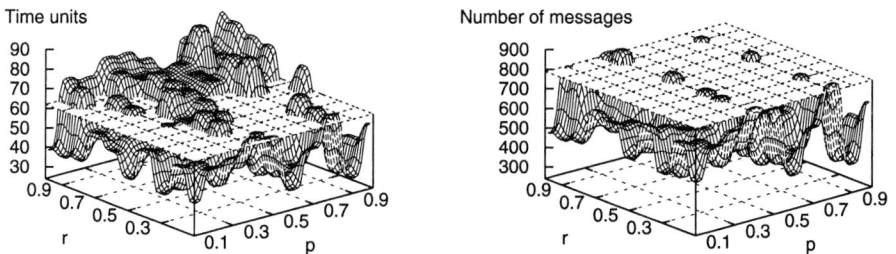

Fig. 5. Median time and number of messages to solve a hard satisfiable instance when agents add random delays in outgoing messages. The horizontal plane represents the median time when no delay is added ($p = 0$)

674   Cèsar Fernàndez et al.

fixed delay links. It is worthwhile understanding how different communication
network environments can impact the performance of the algorithms. In this
section we study the effect produced in the performance of DisCSP algorithms
by considering delay distributions corresponding to different traffic conditions.

For the results of Section 5.2 we considered inter-agent communication links
with random exponentially distributed delays. To study how exponentially distributed delays affect the performance with respect to fixed delays, we can consider intermediate situations in which some of the inter-agent links have a fixed
delay and the rest are exponentially distributed.

Figure 6 shows the median number of messages and time needed by AWC for
solving a hard satisfiable instance with 4 mobiles and 15 sensors, when we vary
the percentage of inter-agent communication links with a fixed delay. The rest of
the inter-agent communication links are assumed to have random exponentially
distributed delays.

The performance of AWC is worst when 100% of the links have a fixed delay,
indicating that the conditions of the network clearly affect the performance of the
algorithm: a element of randomness in the delay distributions clearly improves
the performance of AWC. Observe that we have a clear correlation between the
number of messages and time needed, meaning that the increase or decrease
in the time needed is mainly because of the change in the number of messages
exchanged.

We now examine various link delay distributions that can be used to model
communication network traffic. Traditionally, exponential negative distributed
inter-arrival times have been used to model data traffic due to their attractive
theoretical properties, but in the past decade it has been shown that, although
these models are able to capture single user sessions properties, they are no
longer suitable for modeling aggregate data links in local or wide area network
scenarios[3, 9, 11]. Facing this fact, we simulate network delays according to

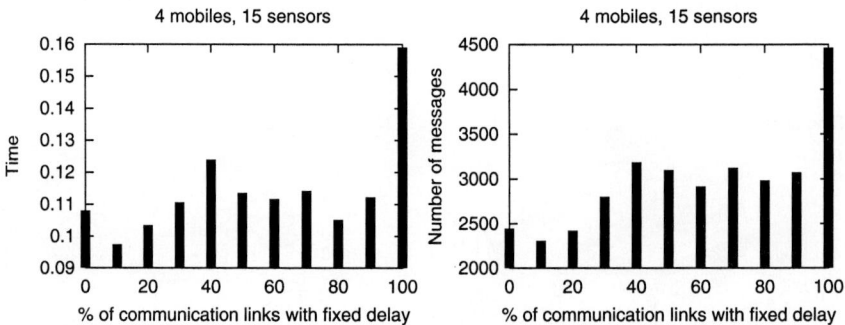

Fig. 6. Median number of messages and time exchanged to solve a hard satisfiable instance by AWC when the data load is not homogeneous among all the
inter-agent communication links

three different models for the inter-arrival time distribution; the above mentioned exponential negative distribution, the log-normal distribution and the Fractional Gaussian Noise (FGN)[12].

The log-normal distribution is useful to obtain distributions with any desired variance, whereas FGN processes are able to capture crucial characteristics of the Internet traffic as long-range dependence and self-similarity that are not suited by other models. We synthesize FGN from α-stable distributions with parameters $H = 0.75$ and $d = 0.4$,

Figure 7 shows the cumulative density functions (CDF) of time required to solve hard instances for AWC, ABT, and ABT with restarts, when all the inter-agent communication links have delays modeled as fixed, negative exponential, and log-normal, with identical mean and different variances.

Table 1 and 2 show the estimated mean and variance of the number of messages exchanged as well as the solution time for the different cases when the same instance is used for three algorithms.

The results in Figure 7 and Tables 1 and 2 show that the delay distributions have an algorithm-specific impact on the performance of the basic ABT and on AWC.

For the basic ABT, on hard instances, the solution time becomes worse when channel delays are modeled by random distributions as opposed to the fixed delay case. The greater the variance of the link delay, the worse ABT performs. However, introducing the restart strategy has the desirable effect of improving

Table 1. Statistics estimated from the distributions of number of messages with different inter-agent link delay models

Delay distribution	Mean			Variance		
	ABT	ABT-rst	AWC	ABT	ABT-rst	AWC
Fixed	$1.8 \cdot 10^5$	$1.2 \cdot 10^5$	$8.2 \cdot 10^2$	$3.6 \cdot 10^{10}$	$1.3 \cdot 10^{10}$	$3 \cdot 10^5$
Negative expon. ($\sigma^2 = 1$)	$1.7 \cdot 10^5$	$1.5 \cdot 10^5$	$3.5 \cdot 10^2$	$2.8 \cdot 10^{10}$	$0.9 \cdot 10^{10}$	$4.5 \cdot 10^5$
Log-normal ($\sigma^2 = 5$)	$2.2 \cdot 10^5$	$1.3 \cdot 10^5$	$3.5 \cdot 10^2$	$5.0 \cdot 10^{10}$	$1.7 \cdot 10^{10}$	$4.8 \cdot 10^5$
Log-normal ($\sigma^2 = 10$)	$2.6 \cdot 10^5$	$1.6 \cdot 10^5$	$3.5 \cdot 10^2$	$7.1 \cdot 10^{10}$	$2.4 \cdot 10^{10}$	$4.9 \cdot 10^5$

Table 2. Statistics estimated from the distributions of time to solve in time units with different inter-agent link delay models

Delay distribution	Mean			Variance		
	ABT	ABT-rst	AWC	ABT	ABT-rst	AWC
Fixed	98	69	53	8562	3600	1230
Negative expon. ($\sigma^2 = 1$)	111	71	28	10945	3947	266
Log-normal ($\sigma^2 = 5$)	157	103	28	21601	8438	288
Log-normal ($\sigma^2 = 10$)	188	131	28	30472	13423	402

the performance of ABT. Furthermore, ABT with restarts is fairly robust and insensitive to the variance in the link delays.

AWC behaves differently from the basic ABT. On hard instances, having randomization in the link delays improves the solution time compared to the fixed delay channel. Further, the mean solution time for AWC is extremely robust to the variance in communication link delays, although the variance of solution time is slightly affected by this.

Experiments run with FGN delay models show no significant differences in performance for the three algorithms in relation to other traffic models with the same variance.

In general, we found that on satisfiable instances, AWC always performs significantly better than ABT, even ABT with restart. Thus AWC appears to be a better candidate in situations when most instances are likely to be satisfiable.

7   Conclusions

We introduce SensorDCSP, a benchmark that captures some of the characteristics of real-world distributed applications that arise in the context of distributed networked systems. The two control parameters of our SensorDCSP generator, sensor compatibility (P_c) and sensor visibility (P_v), result in a zero-one phase transition in satisfiability.

We tested two complete DisCSP algorithms, synchronous backtracking (ABT) and asynchronous weak commitment search (AWC). We show that the phase transition region of SensorDCSP induces an easy-hard-easy profile in the solution time, both for ABT and AWC, which is consistent with CSPs. We found that AWC performs much better than ABT on satisfiable instances, but worse on unsatisfiable instances. This differential in performance is most likely due to the fact that on unsatisfiable instances, the dynamic priority ordering of AWC slows the completion of the search process.

In order to study the impact of different network traffic conditions on the performance of the algorithms, we used a discrete-event network simulator. We found that random delays can improve the performance and robustness of AWC. In contrast, on hard satisfiable instances, the performance of the basic ABT deteriorates dramatically when subject to random link delays. However, we developed a decentralized dynamic restart strategy for ABT, which results in an improvement and shows robustness with respect to the variance in link delays. *Most interestingly, our results also show that the active introduction of message delays by agents can improve performance and robustness, while reducing the overall network load.*

These results validate our thesis that when considering networking applications of DisCSP, one cannot afford to neglect the characteristics of the underlying network conditions. The network-level behavior can have an important, algorithm-specific, impact on solution time. Our study makes it clear that DisCSP algorithms are best tested and validated on benchmarks based on real-world problems, using network simulators. We hope our benchmark domain will be of use for the further analysis and development of DisCSP methods.

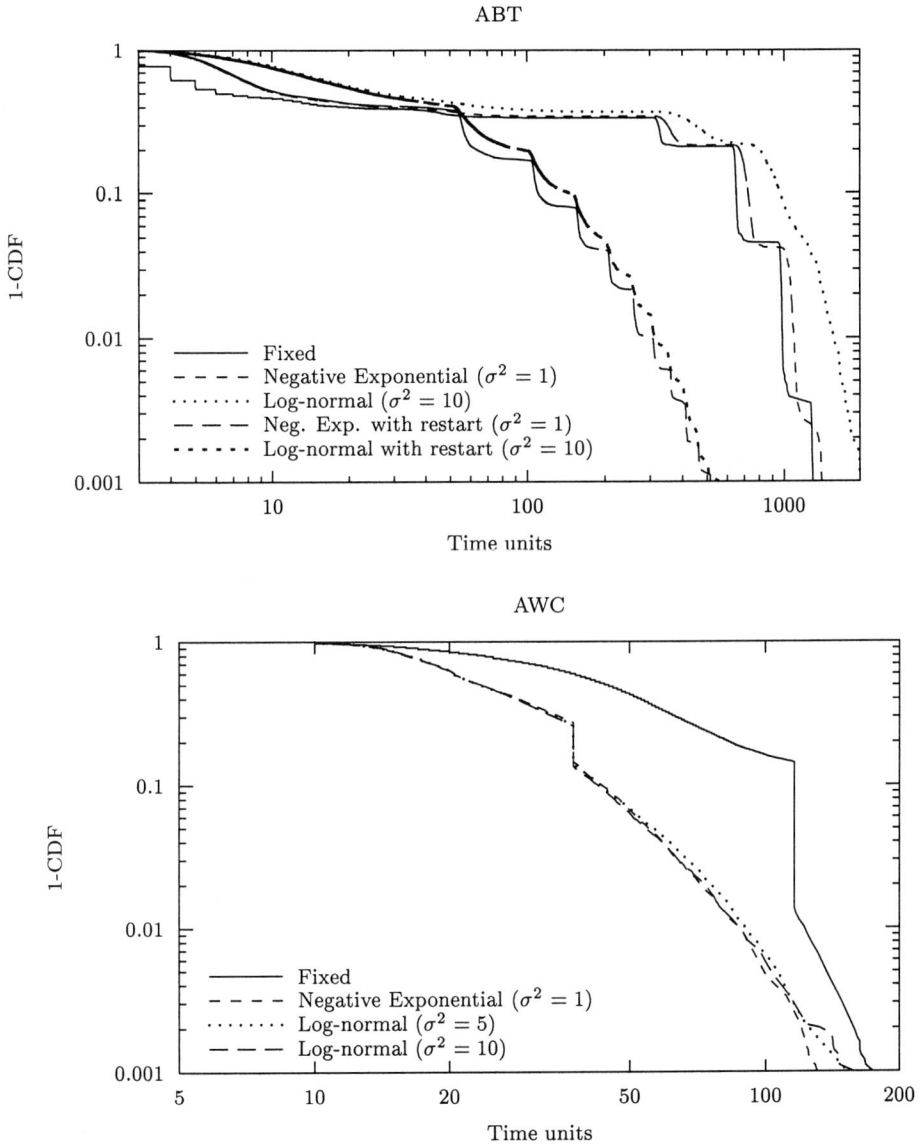

Fig. 7. Cumulative density functions (CDF) of time to solve hard instances for their respective algorithms, AWC, ABT and ABT with restarts under different link delay models

678   Cèsar Fernàndez et al.

References

[1] R. Béjar, B. Krishnamachari, C. Gomes, and B. Selman. Distributed constraint satisfaction in a wireless sensor tracking system. In *Workshop on Distributed Constraint Reasoning, International Joint Conference on Artificial Intelligence*, Seattle, Washington, August 2001. http://liawww.epfl.ch/ silaghi/proc_wsijcai01.html.

[2] S. E. Conry, K. Kuwabara, V. R. Lesser, and R. A. Meyer. Multistage negotiation for distributed constraint satisfaction. *IEEE Transactions on Systems, Man, and Cybernetics (Special Section on DAI)*, 21(6):1462–1477, 1991.

[3] M. Crovella and A. Bestavros. Self-Similarity in World Wide Web Traffic: Evidence and Possible Causes. *IEEE Transactions on Networking*, 5(6):835–846, December 1997.

[4] C. P. Gomes, B. Selman, and H. A. Kautz. Boosting combinatorial search through randomization. In *AAAI/IAAI*, pages 431–437, 1998.

[5] M. Junius, M. Büter, D. Pesch, et al. CNCL. Communication Networks Class Library. Aachen University of Technology. 1996.

[6] D. Kirkpatrick and P. Hell. On the complexity of general graph factor problems. *SIAM Journal of Computing*, 12(3):601–608, 1983.

[7] B. Krishnamachari. *Phase Transitions, Structure, and Complexity in Wireless Networks*. PhD thesis, Electrical Engineering, Cornell University, Ithaca, NY, May 2002.

[8] B. Krishnamachari, R. Béjar, and S. B. Wicker. Distributed problem solving and the boundaries of self-configuration in multi-hop wireless networks. In *Hawaii International Conference on System Sciences (HICSS-35)*, January 2002.

[9] W. Leland, M. Taqqu, W. Willinger, and D. Wilson. On the Self-Similar Nature of Ethernet Traffic (Extended Version). *IEEE Transactions on Networking*, 2(1):1–15, February 1994.

[10] R. Monasson, R. Zecchina, S. Kirkpatrick, B. Selman, and L. Troyansky. Determining computational complexity from characteristic 'phase transitions'. *Nature*, 400:133–137, July 1999.

[11] V. Paxson and S. Floyd. Wide area traffic: the failure of Poisson modeling. *IEEE/ACM Transactions on Networking*, 3(3):226–244, 1995.

[12] G. Samorodnitsky and M. S. Taqqu. *Stable Non-Gaussian Random Processes*. Chapman & Hall, 1994.

[13] Sanders and Air Force Research Lab. ANTs challenge problem. *http://www.sanders.com/ants/overview-05-09.pdf*, 2000.

[14] K. Sycara, S. Roth, N.Sadeh, and M. Fox. Distributed constrained heuristic search. *IEEE Transactions on Systems, Man and Cybernetics*, 21(6):1446–1461, 1991.

[15] T. Walsh. The interface between P and NP: COL, XOR, NAE, 1-in-k, and Horn SAT. *APES Report*, APES-37-2002, 2002.

[16] M. Yokoo. Weak-commitment search for solving constraint satisfaction problems. In *Proceedings of the 12th Conference on Artificial Intelligence (AAAI-94)*, pages 313–318, 1994.

[17] M. Yokoo. Asynchronous weak-commiment search for solving distributed constraint satisfaction problems. In *Proceedings of the First International Conference on Principles and Practice of Constraint Programming (CP-95)*, pages 88–102, 1995.

[18] M. Yokoo, E. H. Durfee, T. Ishida, and K. Kuwabara. Distributed constraint satisfaction for formalizing distributed problem solving. In *Proccedings of the Twelfth IEEE International Conference on Distributed Computing Systems*, pages 614–621, 1992.

[19] M. Yokoo, E. H. Durfee, T. Ishida, and K. Kuwabara. The distributed constraint satisfaction problem: Formalization and algorithms. *IEEE Transactions on Knowledge Data Engineering*, 10(5):673–685, 1998.

[20] M. Yokoo and K. Hirayama. Algorithms for distributed constraint satisfaction: A review. *Autonomous Agents and Multi-Agent Systems*, 3(2):198–212, 2000.

Continuous First-Order Constraint Satisfaction with Equality and Disequality Constraints

Stefan Ratschan[*]

Institut d'Informatica i Aplicacions, Universitat de Girona, Spain
stefan.ratschan@risc.uni-linz.ac.at

Abstract. In an earlier paper we have shown, how one can successfully use constraint satisfaction techniques for proving and solving formulae in the first-order predicate language over the real numbers (i.e., real first-order constraints). This approach was restricted to inputs that contain inequality symbols such as $\leq$, but no equality symbols ($=$) or disequality symbols ($\neq$). In this paper we lay the basis for extending this approach to inputs that contain (dis)equalities. This considerably widens the practical applicability of numerical constraint satisfaction methods.

1 Introduction

Let a real first-order constraint be a formula in the first-order predicate language with predicate symbols $=, \neq, \leq, <$, function symbols such as $+, \times, \sin, \exp$, and their usual interpretation over the real numbers. The problem of solving real first-order constraints is of fundamental importance—we have created a web-page [4] that lists more then 50 papers with applications. In an earlier paper [5] we have shown how one can extend constraint satisfaction techniques to solve real first-order constraints that do not contain equalities or disequalities—removing some of the problems of the classical quantifier elimination algorithms [2]. In this paper we set the basis for extending this approach to the case with equalities and disequalities.

The main difficulty for introducing equalities in this context is, that the solution set of equality constraints does not have volume, which can make it very difficult to find elements in such a solution set. However, it is often quite easy to find a small interval that provably contains a solution. For example, the expression $x^2 - 2$ is negative for $x = 0$ and positive for $x = 4$. Hence, by elementary analysis (Boltzmann intermediate value theorem), the interval $[0, 4]$ contains a solution of $x^2 - 2 = 0$, and $\exists x \; x^2 - 2 = 0$ is true. Note that this approach fails if we use the larger interval $[-4, 4]$, where the function is positive also for $x = -4$.

By applying first-order constraint satisfaction [5, 1] one can find intervals that enclose the solutions of the occurring equalities tightly. But, up to now it was unclear, how to extend the approach sketched above to general first-order constraint for which all the variables ranges over small closed intervals.

---

[*] This work has been supported by a Marie Curie fellowship of the European Union under contract number HPMF-CT-2001-01255.

P. Van Hentenryck (Ed.): CP 2002, LNCS 2470, pp. 680–685, 2002.

2   Main Idea

In this section we demonstrate the main idea of how to (dis)prove first-order constraints (short: constraints) with small quantifier bounds. For this we employ a semi-formal style. In the following section we will then describe the formal details.

We fix a totally ordered set $\mathcal{V} = \{x_1, \ldots, x_{|\mathcal{V}|}\}$ of variables. For any constraint ϕ and constants $a_1, \ldots, a_{|\mathcal{V}|}$, we denote by $\phi(a_1, \ldots, a_{|\mathcal{V}|})$ the result of substituting $a_1, \ldots, a_{|\mathcal{V}|}$ into ϕ (note that this only changes the free variables). For an interval I, we denote by $\underline{I}$ its lower bound, and by $\overline{I}$ its upper bound. Given a box $B \subseteq \mathbb{R}^{|\mathcal{V}|}$ and a variable $u \in \mathcal{V}$, we denote by $B(u)$ the coordinate of B corresponding to u according to the order on $\mathcal{V}$.

We proceed recursively according to the structure of constraints. For example, for a constraint of the form $\exists x \in I_x \; \forall y \in I_y \; \exists z \in I_z \; x^2yz = 0 \; \wedge \; xy^2z - 1 = 0$, we first compute some information for the atomic sub-constraints $x^2yz = 0$ and $xy^2z - 1 = 0$, then for $x^2yz = 0 \wedge xy^2z - 1 = 0$, $\exists z \in I_z \; x^2yz = 0 \wedge xy^2z - 1 = 0$, and so on. Along the way we try prove existential quantifiers or disprove universal quantifiers using this information.

Which information allows us to do this? Let us first consider a constraint of the form $\exists x \in I \; \phi$. In this case, knowing that ϕ has a solution in I suffices to prove the constraint However, information about one solution for all atomic sub-constraints is not enough: Consider a constraint of the form $\exists x \in I_x \exists y \in I_y \; \phi_1 \wedge \phi_2$. From knowing that both ϕ_1 and ϕ_2 have a solution within $I_x \times I_y$, we cannot infer that $\phi_1 \wedge \phi_2$ has a solution in $I_x \times I_y$, because the respective solutions might be different.

Thus we have to propagate more information for proving existentially quantified conjunctions. In the example above, from knowing that *for all y in I_y there is an x in I_x such that ϕ_1* and that *for all x in I_x there is a y in I_y such that ϕ_2*, and furthermore knowing that the solution for the existentially quantified variable depends continuously on the universally quantified one, we can prove $\exists x \in I_x \exists y \in I_y \; \phi_1 \wedge \phi_2$ (in other words, on the left-hand side of Figure 1, there is a line going from left to right, and a line going from top to bottom, and therefore there is a point on both lines).

One might think that information similar to the above is enough. But while it would be sufficient in the example above, in general, it does not propagate. For illustrating this, we assume that in the above example both ϕ_1 and ϕ_2 contain an additional parameter p, and assume that we have the information *for all p in I_p for all y in I_y there is an x in I_x such that ϕ_1* and *for all p in I_p for all x in I_x there is a y in I_y such that ϕ_2*. This information allows us to prove $\forall p \in I_p \exists x \in I_x \exists y \in I_y \; \phi_1 \wedge \phi_2$, but it does *not* allow us to propagate the according continuity information: In general, the x- and y-coordinates of solutions of $\phi_1 \wedge \phi_2$ might not depend continuously on p! For example, the p- and x-coordinates of the solution might look like the right-hand side of Figure 1, where for all p we can find an according x in the solution, but this solution can not be described by a continuous function.

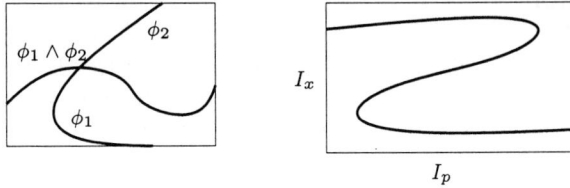

Fig. 1. Information propagation

In order to deal with this problem we use even more general information to describe such solutions: Given a constraint ϕ, a variable set $\{u_1, \ldots, u_k\} \subseteq \mathcal{V}$ and a box $B \subseteq \mathbb{R}^{|\mathcal{V}|}$, the information that we propagate is the predicate "there exist continuous $F_{x_1}, \ldots, F_{x_{|\mathcal{V}|}}$ (*witness functions*) in $\mathbb{R}^k \to \mathbb{R}$ such that for all $(s_1, \ldots, s_k) \in [0, 1]^k$,

- for all $i \in \{1, \ldots, k\}$, $s_i = 0$ implies $F_{u_i}(s_1, \ldots, s_k) = \underline{B(u_i)}$,
- for all $i \in \{1, \ldots, k\}$, $s_i = 1$ implies $F_{u_i}(s_1, \ldots, s_k) = \overline{B(u_i)}$,
- for all $i \in \{1, \ldots, |\mathcal{V}|\}$, $F_{x_i}(s_1, \ldots, s_k) \in B(x_i)$,
- $\phi(F_{x_1}(s_1, \ldots, s_k), \ldots, F_{x_{|\mathcal{V}|}}(s_1, \ldots, s_k))$ is true."

The first item guarantees that there is a witness on the lower bound (in the right-hand side of Figure 1, the solution touches the box on the left-hand side). The second item does the same for the upper bound (the solution touches the box on the right-hand side). The third item requires the witness function to stay within the box, and the fourth item requires the witness function to describe a solution.

In the following we denote the above predicate by $M_\forall(\{u_1, \ldots, u_k\}, \phi, B)$. We call such a predicate *witness predicate*, and k its *dimension*. This predicate implies the first-order predicate $\forall u_1 \in B(u_1) \ldots \forall u_k \in B(u_k) \exists v_1 \in B(v_1) \ldots \exists v_l \in B(v_l) \phi$, where $\{v_1, \ldots, v_l\} = \mathcal{V} \setminus \{u_1, \ldots, u_k\}$. Moreover, for a closed constraint ϕ, a set of variables U and box B, $M_\forall(U, \phi, B)$ implies that ϕ holds. So this is the information we want to compute for proving the total constraint.

For disproving universal quantifiers, we take the negation of the input constraint, and apply the above procedure to the resulting existential quantifiers.

Note that the above approach will fail if the involved intervals are too large: First, the solution of the constraint might behave too wildly, making it impossible to describe it by witness functions (e.g., for the constraint $x^2 + y^2 = 1$ within $[-2, 2] \times [-2, 2]$ no witness predicate with dimension higher than 0 holds). And second, the larger a box, the higher is the effort to find such witness functions

3   Computing and Propagating Witness Predicates

In this section we show formally how one can propagate witness predicates over the logical symbols $\wedge$, $\vee$, $\exists$, and $\forall$.

Theorem 1.

- If $M_\forall(U_1, \phi_1, B)$, $M_\forall(U_2, \phi_2, B)$, and $U_1 \cup U_2 = \mathcal{V}$, then $M_\forall(U_1 \cap U_2, \phi_1 \wedge \phi_2, B)$.
- If $M_\forall(U_1, \phi_1, B)$ and $M_\forall(U_2, \phi_2, B)$ then $M_\forall(U_1, \phi_1 \vee \phi_2, B)$ and $M_\forall(U_2, \phi_1 \vee \phi_2, B)$.
- If $M_\forall(U, \phi, B)$ then $M_\forall(U \setminus \{x\}, \exists x \in B(x)\ \phi, B)$.
- If $M_\forall(U, \phi, B)$ where U contains all the free variables of ϕ then $M_\forall(U, \forall x \in B(x)\ \phi, B)$.

Proof. We just show the first case, the rest is easy. The idea of the proof is that whenever the witness functions of ϕ_1 and of ϕ_2 have the same value, then this is a solution for $\phi_1 \wedge \phi_2$, and so the fourth property necessary for witness functions is fulfilled. We will prove that there exist such values and construct witness functions from them that fulfill the remaining properties.

We assume that in the order on $\mathcal{V}$ the elements of $U_1 \cap U_2$ appear first. Let $F^1_{x_1}, \ldots, F^1_{x_{|\mathcal{V}|}}$ be the witness functions of ϕ_1, and let $F^2_{x_1}, \ldots, F^2_{x_{|\mathcal{V}|}}$ be the witness functions of ϕ_2. For all $i \in \{1, \ldots, |\mathcal{V}|\}$, let $\mathcal{F}^1_{x_i} : [0, 1]^{|U_1|+|U_2|} \to \mathbb{R}$ be such that $\mathcal{F}^1_{x_i}(r_1, \ldots, r_{|U_1|+|U_2|}) := F^1_{x_i}(r_1, \ldots, r_{|U_1|})$ and let $\mathcal{F}^2_{x_i} : [0, 1]^{|U_1|+|U_2|} \to \mathbb{R}$ be such that $\mathcal{F}^2_{x_i}(r_1, \ldots, r_{|U_1|+|U_2|}) := F^2_{x_i}(r_{|U_1|+1}, \ldots, r_{|U_1|+|U_2|})$.

Let $\mathcal{G} : [0, 1]^{|U_1|+|U_2|} \to \mathbb{R}^{|\mathcal{V}|}$ be the function for which the i-th component is $\mathcal{F}^1_{x_i} - \mathcal{F}^2_{x_i}$, where $i \in \{1, \ldots, |\mathcal{V}|\}$. For all elements $(r_1, \ldots, r_{|U_1|+|U_2|})$ of the solution set of $\mathcal{G} = 0$, $\phi_1(\mathcal{F}^1_{x_1}(r_1, \ldots, r_{|U_1|+|U_2|}), \ldots \mathcal{F}^1_{x_{|\mathcal{V}|}}(r_1, \ldots, r_{|U_1|+|U_2|}))$ and $\phi_2(\mathcal{F}^1_{x_1}(r_1, \ldots, r_{|U_1|+|U_2|}), \ldots, \mathcal{F}^1_{x_{|\mathcal{V}|}}(r_1, \ldots, r_{|U_1|+|U_2|}))$ hold. So for these values $\phi_1 \wedge \phi_2$ holds, too. Now we show that such solutions of $\mathcal{G} = 0$ exist, and that we can describe them by witness functions.

Observe that the dimension of the co-domain of $\mathcal{G}$ is $|\mathcal{V}| = |U_1 \cup U_2| = |U_1| + |U_2| - |U_1 \cap U_2|$, which allows us to interpret the first $|U_1 \cap U_2|$ variables of $\mathcal{G}$ as parameters. Now we apply a parametric version of Miranda's theorem (Theorem 5.3.7 of Neumaier [3]). It suffices to prove that there is a bijection C between the variables $x_1, \ldots, x_{|\mathcal{V}|}$ and the coordinates of $\mathcal{G}$ that are no parameters, such that for an arbitrary, but fixed $i \in \{1, \ldots, |\mathcal{V}|\}$, for all $(r_1, \ldots, r_{|U_1|+|U_2|}) \in [0, 1]^{|U_1|+|U_2|}$,

$$r_{C(i)} = 0 \text{ implies } \mathcal{F}^1_{x_i}(r_1, \ldots, r_{|U_1|+|U_2|}) - \mathcal{F}^2_{x_i}(r_1, \ldots, r_{|U_1|+|U_2|}) \leq 0, \text{ and} \quad (1)$$

$$r_{C(i)} = 1 \text{ implies } \mathcal{F}^1_{x_i}(r_1, \ldots, r_{|U_1|+|U_2|}) - \mathcal{F}^2_{x_i}(r_1, \ldots, r_{|U_1|+|U_2|}) \geq 0. \quad (2)$$

Here we have two cases:

- $x_i \in U_2$: In this case, let $C(i) := |U_1| + k$, where k is the number of x_i in U_2 according to the order on $\mathcal{V}$. Therefore $C(i)$ points into the witness functions of ϕ_2, and according to the properties of these witness functions $r_{C(i)} = 0$ implies $\mathcal{F}^2_{x_i}(r_1, \ldots, r_{|U_1|+|U_2|}) = \underline{B(i)}$, and $r_{C(i)} = 1$ implies $\mathcal{F}^2_{x_i}(r_1, \ldots, r_{|U_1|+|U_2|}) = \overline{B(i)}$. As a consequence, since $\mathcal{F}^1_{x_i}(r_1, \ldots, r_{|U_1|+|U_2|}) \in B(i)$, the Inequalities 1 and 2 hold.

– Otherwise ($x_i \in U_1$ but not in U_2): In this case let $C(i)$ be the number of x_i in U_1. Since all variables in $U_1 \cap U_2$ appear before in the order, $C(i) > |U_1 \cap U_2|$, and it points to the coordinates of $\mathcal{G}$ that are no parameters. So according to the properties of these witness functions $r_{C(i)} = 0$ implies $\mathcal{F}^1_{x_i}(r_1, \ldots, r_{|U_1|+|U_2|}) = \underline{B(i)}$, and $r_{C(i)} = 1$ implies $\mathcal{F}^1_{x_i}(r_1, \ldots, r_{|U_1|+|U_2|}) = \overline{B(i)}$. As a consequence, since $\mathcal{F}^2_{x_i}(r_1, \ldots, r_{|U_1|+|U_2|}) \in B(i)$, the Inequalities 1 and 2 hold (up to a insignificant change of signs).

Now by the parametric Miranda's theorem there is a continuous function $S : [0,1]^{|U_1 \cap U_2|} \to [0,1]^{|\mathcal{V}|}$ such that for all $(p_1, \ldots, p_{|U_1 \cap U_2|}) \in [0,1]^{|U_1 \cap U_2|}$, $\mathcal{G}(p_1, \ldots, p_{|U_1 \cap U_2|}, S(p_1, \ldots, p_{|U_1 \cap U_2|})) = 0$. Therefore, the functions $\lambda p_1, \ldots, p_{|U_1 \cap U_2|} \cdot \mathcal{F}^1_{x_i}(p_1, \ldots, p_{|U_1 \cap U_2|}, S(p_1, \ldots, p_{|U_1 \cap U_2|}))$, where $i \in \{1, \ldots, |\mathcal{V}|\}$, provide the witness functions for $M_\forall(U_1 \cap U_2, \phi_1 \wedge \phi_2, B)$. It is easy to show that they fulfill the necessary properties. □

It is easy to check that the above theorem is optimal in the sense that in general $M_\forall$ does not hold for supersets of the ones provided.

Given a first-order constraint with small quantification bounds we can now compute witness predicates for atomic constraints, and use Theorem 1 to propagate this information to witness predicates for the total constraint. Any witness predicate for then total constraint proves it. For disproving a constraint we do the same on the negation of the constraint. Whenever we succeed to compute a witness predicate for the negation, we have disproven the original constraint.

4   Conclusion

In this paper we have lain the basis for using constraint programming techniques for solving first-order constraints that contain (dis)equalities. For building a successful solver it remains to combine the result with continuous first-order constraint satisfaction [5], which can compute a constraint that is equivalent to the input, but for which the variables range over small intervals. The main problem is, to determine how small the intervals of which variables should be, such that one can efficiently compute the necessary witness functions.

The author thanks Arnold Neumaier for important suggestions.

References

[1] F. Benhamou and F. Goualard. Universally quantified interval constraints. In *Proc. of the Sixth Intl. Conf. on Principles and Practice of Constraint Programming (CP'2000)*, number 1894 in LNCS, Singapore, 2000. Springer Verlag.

[2] G. E. Collins. Quantifier elimination for the elementary theory of real closed fields by cylindrical algebraic decomposition. In B. F. Caviness and J. R. Johnson, editors, *Second GI Conf. Automata Theory and Formal Languages*, volume 33 of *LNCS*, pages 134–183. Springer Verlag, Wien, 1975.

[3] A. Neumaier. *Interval Methods for Systems of Equations*. Cambridge Univ. Press, Cambridge, 1990.

[4] S. Ratschan. Applications of real first-order constraint solving — bibliography. http://www.risc.uni-linz.ac.at/people/sratscha/appFOC.html, 2001.

[5] S. Ratschan. Continuous first-order constraint satisfaction. In *Artificial Intelligence, Automated Reasoning, and Symbolic Computation*, number 2385 in LNCS. Springer, 2002.

A Relaxation of the Cumulative Constraint

John N. Hooker[1] and Hong Yan[2]

[1] Graduate School of Industrial Administration, Carnegie Mellon University
Pittsburgh, PA 15213 USA
jh38@andrew.cmu.edu
[2] Department of Management, Hong Kong Polytechnic University
Hung Hom, Kowloon, Hong Kong, China
mshyan@inet.polyu.edu.hk

Abstract. Hybrid methods that combine constraint programming with
mathematical programming make essential use of continuous relaxations
for global constraints. We state a relaxation for the *cumulative* constraint.
In particular we identify facet-defining inequalities for problems in which
some jobs have the same duration, release time, and resource consumption rate. We also identify a much larger class of valid inequalities that
exist in all problems.

The *cumulative* constraint [1, 2] represents a scheduling problem in which total rate of resource consumption must not exceed a maximum level at any one
time. We propose a continuous relaxation for the *cumulative* constraint for use
in hybrid systems that combine constraint programming and mathematical programming (MP). A more complete exposition, with proofs and examples, may
be found at http://ba.gsia.cmu.edu/jnh.

Recent research [3, 4, 5, 7, 8, 9, 17] suggests that hybrid methods can improve
over the modeling and solution capabilities of pure CP or MP, particularly for
optimization problems. A key element of hybrid methods is to combine constraint
propagation with the solution of a continuous relaxation of the problem. The
resulting bound on the optimal value can be used to prune the search in a
branch-and-bound (branch-and-relax) scheme.

Continuous relaxations have recently been developed for several constraints,
sometimes resulting in substantial speedups in computation. These include the
all-different [8, 18], *element* (used to implement variable indices, such as y in
the expression x_y) [10, 13], piecewise linear constraints [10, 14, 15], and logical
expressions that involve cardinalities [18, 19].

A continuous relaxation for the *cumulative* constraint appears even more
promising in a hybrid methods that use logic-based Benders decomposition [6,
11]. Jain and Grossmann [12] applied this method to a machine scheduling problem in which the master problem assigns jobs to machines, and the subproblem
schedules the jobs. The master problem is an MILP. The subproblem decomposes into 1-machine scheduling feasibility problems with time windows. Each
of these 1-machine problems is a special case of *cumulative* and was solved by
a commercial CP routine. This hybrid method led to dramatic speedups relative to commercial MILP and CP solvers acting alone. It is shown in [16] that

P. Van Hentenryck (Ed.): CP 2002, LNCS 2470, pp. 686–690, 2002.

these were possible because Jain and Grossmann added a simple relaxation of the 1-machine *cumulative* constraint to the master problem, even though the relaxation is quite weak. This suggests that a relaxation for the general *cumulative* constraint, as well as other global constraints, could be very useful in hybrid methods based on decomposition.

1   The Form of the Relaxation

The *cumulative* constraint may be written

$$\text{cumulative}(t, d, r, L) \tag{1}$$

where $t = (t_1, \ldots, t_n)$ is a vector of start times for jobs $1, \ldots, n$, $d = (d_1, \ldots, d_n)$ is a vector of job durations, $r = (r_1, \ldots, r_n)$ a vector of resource consumption rates, and scalar L the amount of available resources. The domain of each t_j is given as $[a_j, b_j]$, which defines an earliest start time a_j and a latest start time b_j for job j. The *cumulative* constraint requires that

$$\sum_{\substack{j \\ t_j \le t < t_j + d_j}} r_j \le L, \quad \text{all } t$$

and $a \le t \le b$.

We analyze the problem in two parts: the "lower" problem, in which the upper bounds $b_j = \infty$, and the "upper" problem, in which the lower bounds $a_j = -\infty$. Relaxations for the upper and lower problem can then be combined to obtain a relaxation for the entire problem. We will study the upper problem. The analysis of the lower problem is closely parallel.

Assume $a_1 \le \cdots \le a_n$. The relaxation consists of valid constraints (cuts) of the form

$$t_{j_1} + \cdots + t_{j_k} \ge h \tag{2}$$

for the upper problem, where $j_1 < \cdots < j_k$. The inequalities are valid in the sense that for any $t = (t_1, \ldots, t_n)$ satisfying *cumulative*, $(t_{j_1}, \ldots, t_{j_k})$ satisfies (2). A valid right-hand side h can be found for (2) by minimizing the left-hand side of (2) subject to the upper problem. Note that the inequalities (2) do not involve integer variables as is typical in MILP. There is no practical MILP formulation for the *cumulative* constraint unless one discretizes time, in which case a large number of variables can result.

2   Valid Inequalities

We first identify some valid inequalities (2) that are facets of the convex hull of the feasible set of *cumulative*. These facets exist when there are subsets of jobs with the same release time, duration, and resource consumption rate.

Theorem 1. *Suppose jobs $j_1, \ldots, j_k$ satisfy $a_{j_i} = a_0$, $d_{j_i} = d_0$ and $r_{j_i} = r_0$ for $i = 1, \ldots, k$. Let $Q = \lfloor L/r_0 \rfloor$ and $P = \lceil k/Q \rceil - 1$. Then the following defines a facet of the convex hull of the upper problem.*

$$t_{j_1} + \cdots + t_{j_k} \geq (P+1)a_0 + \frac{1}{2}P[2k - (P+1)Q]d_0 \tag{3}$$

provided $P > 0$. Furthermore, bounds of the form $t_j \geq a_j$ define facets.

We now identify valid inequalities that are in general non-facet-defining but exist in all problems. Given a set of jobs $j_1, \ldots, j_k$, split each job j_i into $n_{j_i} = \lfloor d_{j_i}/\Delta d \rfloor$ segments of equal duration $\Delta d \leq \min_{i'}\{d_{j_{i'}}\}$. If part of a job is left over (i.e., $d_{j_i} > \lfloor d_{j_i}/\Delta d \rfloor \Delta d$), simply ignore the excess. Let $k' = \sum_{i=1}^{k} n_{j_i}$ be the total number of segments, and let each segment j of job j_i have resource consumption $r'_j = r_{j_i}$ and weight $w_j = 1/n_{j_i}$.

Theorem 2. *Given any subset of jobs $j_1, \ldots, j_k$, the inequality $t_{j_1} + \cdots + t_{j_k} \geq h_{relax}$ is valid for the upper problem, where*

$$h_{relax} = \sum_{j=1}^{k'} w_j \left(p_j - 1 - (p_j - p_{j-1}) \frac{(p_j - 1)L - R_{j-1}}{r'_j} \right) \Delta d - E$$

and

$$p_j = \left\lfloor \frac{R_j}{L} \right\rfloor + 1 \qquad R_j = \sum_{\ell=1}^{j} r'_\ell \qquad E = \sum_{i=1}^{k} \tfrac{1}{2}(n_{j_i} - 1)\Delta d$$

$\Delta d \in [0, \min_{i'}\{d_{j_{i'}}\}]$ is chosen to result in a tight relaxation. If one sets $\Delta d = 0$, the inequality simplifies as follows.

Corollary 1. *Renumber the jobs $j_1, \ldots, j_k$ using indices $q = 1, \ldots, k$ so that the products $r_q d_q$ occur in nondecreasing order. The following is a valid inequality for the upper problem when $\Delta d \to 0$:*

$$t_{j_1} + \cdots + t_{j_k} \geq \sum_{q=1}^{k} \left((k - q + \tfrac{1}{2})\frac{r_q}{L} - \tfrac{1}{2} \right) d_q \tag{4}$$

The value of Δd that yields the best cut may be zero, the smallest d_{j_i}, or something in between. These cases are illustrated respectively by Figs. 1–3.

Figure 1 shows a plot of h_{relax} versus Δd for an example in which $d = (2, 3, 5)$, $r = (5, 4, 6)$ and $L = 10$. Here $\Delta d = \min_i\{d_{j_i}\} = 2$ yields the strongest cut, with $h_{relax} = 1$. The asymptotic value of h_{relax} as $\Delta d \to 0$ is 0.8.

Figure 2 illustrates a 3-job problem in which $d = (1.1, 2, 2)$, $r = (5, 4, 6)$, and $L = 6$. Here $\Delta d = 0$ yields the strongest cut, with $h_{relax} = 2.742$.

Figure 3 shows a 5-job problem in which $d = (1.1, 2, 3, 4, 5)$, $r = (5, 5, 4, 4, 6)$, and $L = 12$. Here $\Delta d = 1$ yields the strongest cut, with $h_{relax} = 3.287$. The asymptotic value of h_{relax} as $\Delta d \to 0$ is 3.179.

Since h_{relax} is easily computed, one can in practice do a line search on Δd to approximate its maximum value. Note that the maximum value of h_{relax} occurs at a value of Δd that evenly divides at least one of the durations d_{j_i} (or at $\Delta d = 0$).

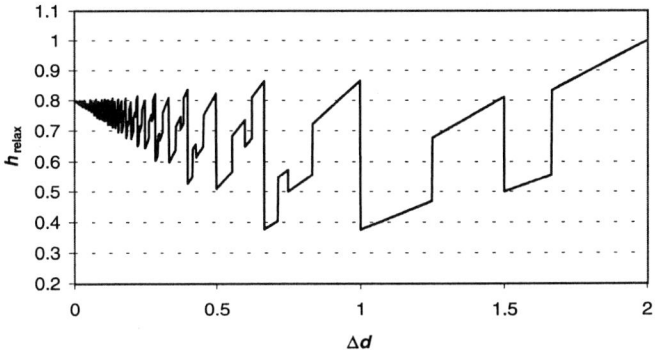

Figure 1

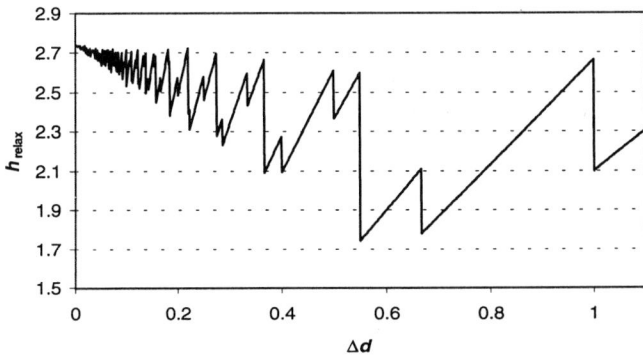

Figure 2

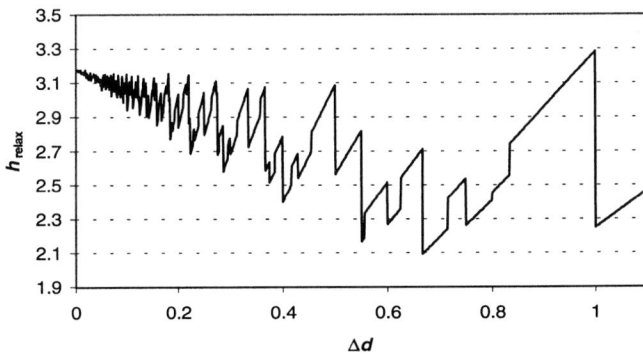

Figure 3

References

[1] Aggoun, A., and N. Beldiceanu, Extending CHIP in order to solve complex scheduling and placement problems, *Mathematical and Computer Modelling* **17** (1993) 57–73.

[2] Baptiste, P., and C. Le Pape, Constraint propagation and decomposition techniques for highly disjunctive and highly cumulative project scheduling problems. *Principles and Practice of Constraint Programming (CP 97)*, Springer-Verlag (Berlin, 1997) 375–89.

[3] Bockmayr, A., and T. Kasper. 1998. Branch and infer: A unifying framework for integer and finite domain constraint programming, *INFORMS Journal on Computing* **10** 287–300.

[4] Demassey, S., C. Artigues and P. Michelon, A hybrid constraint propagation-cutting plane algorithm for the RCPSP, *4th International Workshop on Integration of AI and OR techniques in Constraint Programming for Combinatorial Optimisation Problems (CPAIOR'02)*, Le Croisic, France (2002) 321-331.

[5] Heipcke, S. 1999. Combined Modelling and Problem Solving in Mathematical Programming and Constraint Programming, Ph.D. Thesis, University of Buckingham.

[6] Hooker, J. N. 1995. Logic-based Benders decomposition, presented at INFORMS 1995.

[7] Hooker, J. N. 1997. Constraint satisfaction methods for generating valid cuts, in D. L. Woodruff, ed., *Advances in Computational and Stochasic Optimization, Logic Programming and Heuristic Search*, Kluwer (Dordrecht) 1–30.

[8] Hooker, J. N. 2000. *Logic-Based Methods for Optimization: Combining Optimization and Constraint Satisfaction*, Wiley (New York).

[9] Hooker, J. N. 2001. Logic, optimization and constraint programming, to appear in *INFORMS Journal on Computing*.

[10] Hooker, J. N., and M. A. Osorio. 1999. Mixed logical/linear programming, *Discrete Applied Mathematics* **96-97** 395–442.

[11] Hooker, J. N., and G. Ottosson, Logic-based Benders decomposition, to appear in *Mathematical Programming*.

[12] Jain, V., and I. E. Grossmann. 1999. Algorithms for hybrid MILP/CLP models for a class of optimization problems, *INFORMS Journal on Computing*, to appear.

[13] Ottosson, G., and E. Thorsteinsson. 2000. Linear relaxations and reduced-cost based propagation of continuous variable subscripts, CP'AI'OR'00.

[14] Ottosson, G., E. Thorsteinsson, and J. N. Hooker. 1999. Mixed global constraints and inference in hybrid CLP-IP solvers, *CP99 Post-Conference Workshop on Large Scale Combinatorial Optimization and Constraints*, http://www.dash.co.uk/wscp99, 57–78.

[15] Réfalo, P. 1999. Tight cooperation and its application in piecewise linear optimization, in J. Jaffar, ed., *Principles and Practice of Constraint Programming*, Lecture Notes in Computer Science **1713**, Springer (Berlin), 373-389.

[16] Thorsteinsson, E. S. 2001. Branch-and-check: A hybrid framework integrating mixed integer programming and constraint logic programming, *CP01*.

[17] Williams, H. P., and J. M. Wilson. 1998. Connections between integer linear programming and constraint logic programming–An overview and introduction to the cluster of articles, *INFORMS Journal on Computing* **10** 261–264.

[18] Williams, H. P., and Hong Yan. 2001. Representations of the all-different predicate, *INFORMS Journal on Computing*, to appear.

[19] Yan, H., and J. N. Hooker. 1999. Tight representation of logical constraints as cardinality rules, *Mathematical Programming* **85** 363–377.

Improving GSAT Using 2SAT

Peter J. Stuckey and Lei Zheng

Dept. of Computer Science & Software Engineering
The University of Melbourne
VIC 3010, Australia
{pjs,zhengl}@cs.mu.OZ.AU

Abstract. GSAT has been proven highly effective for solving certain
classes of large SAT problems. It starts from a randomly generated truth
assignment and tries to reduce the number of violated clauses by iteratively flipping some variables' truth value. GSATs effectiveness arises
from the speed of a single flip, since this allows a large space of possible solutions to be explored. It does not examine any inter-relationship
between the clauses of the problem it attacks.
2SAT problems are highly tractable (linear time solvable), and some SAT
problems, such as graph colouring, contain a high proportion of 2SAT
information. In this paper we show how we can alter GSAT to take into
account the 2SAT clauses, so that it never investigates truth assignments
that violate a binary clause. This reduces the search space considerably.
We give experimental results illustrating the benefit of our new approach
on hard 3SAT problems involving a substantial 2SAT component.

1 Introduction

Propositional satisfiability (SAT) is the problem of deciding if there is an assignment for the variables in propositional formula that makes the formula true.
Traditionally, systematic complete algorithms based on backtracking were used
to solve SAT problems. However, randomized local search procedures for SAT,
such as GSAT [3], WalkSAT [2], and DLM [5], although incomplete, have been
proven highly effective for solving certain classes of large SAT problems.

Arguably, the simplest of these successful local search algorithms is GSAT [3].
GSAT starts with some randomly generated truth assignment, and tries to increase the number of satisfied clauses by iteratively flipping some variables' truth
value. The process ends up when either a solution is found, or a local minima
of satisfied clauses is detected, or a preset maximum number of flips is reached.
A key to the effectiveness of GSAT is the incremental data structures that are
used to determine which variable to flip, that is which variable when flipped will
lead to the maximum increase in satisfied clauses. These incremental data structures mean that each flip is very fast, and hence a large part of the search space
can be explored. GSAT has been shown to outperform backtracking procedures
on several classes of SAT problems.

Previous work [6] has shown that taking account of 2SAT information can
substantially improve DP backtracking procedures. In this paper, we propose

P. Van Hentenryck (Ed.): CP 2002, LNCS 2470, pp. 691–695, 2002.
© Springer-Verlag Berlin Heidelberg 2002

extending GSAT, obtaining GSATB, a method that only examines truth assignments that satisfy the binary clauses that occur in the SAT problem under consideration. The method is simple. Whenever a variable is flipped, we also flip all the variables that would otherwise violate a binary clause. Effectively we incorporate a 2SAT solution procedure into the GSAT flip mechanism. The benefit of this is that the search space is considerably reduced. The disadvantage is that at each flip we need to do considerably more work. We attempt to ameliorate this disadvantage by building efficient incremental data structures for determining which variable when flipped will, after all consequent flips have taken place, lead to the maximum increase in satisfied clauses. We show how for 3SAT problems with significant numbers of binary clauses GSATB improves upon GSAT, both in terms of number of flips and search time.

2 The GSAT Procedure

GSAT is a random greedy hill-climbing procedure. It starts with a randomly generated truth assignment and refines this assignment by flipping the truth value of a variable which leads to the largest increase in the number of satisfied clauses. Such flips are repeated until either a satisfying assignment is found, a local minima is found, or the preset maximum number of flips (MAX-FLIPS) is reached. This process is repeated up to MAX-TRIES times at the most. It is clear that GSAT is incomplete.

To facilitate the selection of the next variable to flip, an array $diff1$ is used. The value of $diff1$ for each variable in the given SAT problem equals (the number of satisfied clauses after flipping that variable) − (the number of currently satisfied clauses). The key to GSAT's speed is the fast incremental evaluation of the $diff1$ array [3].

3 Modifying GSAT to Maintain 2SAT Consistency

GSATB performs exactly the same greedy local search as that in GSAT except that the current valuation maintained by GSATB always satisfies the 2SAT subproblem. That is, in order to maintain 2SAT satisfiability, whenever a variable is flipped, we also flip all the variables that would otherwise violate a binary clause. We call the resulting step a $flip2$. Hence for any variable p in the formula, we record the $flipset$ for p, the set of variables (including p) which need to be flipped, if p is flipped, to maintain 2SAT satisfiability.

Example 1 Given the 3SAT problem $\{[\bar{p}q], [\bar{q}r], [\bar{p}r], [\bar{q}\bar{r}s]\}$ together with current valuation $\{\bar{p}, \bar{q}, \bar{r}, s\}$ then $flipset[p] = \{p, q, r\}$ since flipping p requires that we also flip q and r to satisfy the binary clauses. A flip2 of p results in the valuation $\{p, q, r, s\}$, and note now that $flipset[p] = \{p\}$.

Just as in GSAT, GSATB chooses to flip one of the variables for which the resulting state has the least number of unsatisfied (non-binary) clauses. In order to choose which variable to flip, we define another array *diff2*. The value of *diff2* for each variable in the given 3SAT problem under current assignment equals (the number of satisfied clauses after flipping that variable and all the remaining variables in its *flipset*) − (the number of current satisfied clauses). We will choose to flip the variable with the maximal value of *diff2*.

Since GSATB takes advantage of binary clauses it is useful to extract as many binary clauses from the original formulation as possible. We employ three techniques: binary resolution closure, Krom subsumption resolution and the binary implication rule. Brafman [1] has already demonstrated how such preprocessing can improve GSAT.

Similarly to GSAT, the key to the efficiency of GSATB is the fast incremental recalculation of *diff2* values. It might seem that the value of *diff2* for each variable equals the sum of *diff1* of all the variables in its *flipset* (calculating the *diff1* values on the non-binary clauses only, since the binary clauses will never be violated). The following example illustrates that this is not correct.

***Example* 2** Consider the formula $\{[p\bar{q}], [p\bar{r}], [\overline{qrs}]\}$, where the current assignment is $\{p, q, r, s\}$. The non-binary clause $\{[\overline{qrs}]\}$ is not satisfied by the current assignment. We have $diff1[p] = 0$, and $diff1[q] = diff1[r] = diff1[s] = 1$, since flipping any one of these variables will satisfy the non-binary clause. Now $flipset[p] = \{p, q, r\}$. Clearly $diff2[p] \neq 2$. The reason for the error is that we count the clause $[\overline{qrs}]$ twice, once for each of q and r.

The correct definition of *diff2* (for 3SAT problem) includes adjustments to correct the duplicate countings that occur in the simple sum. We need to adjust for clauses in which two or three variables will be flipped simultaneously. See [4] for a full definitions of the adjustments.

Updating *diff2* is much more complicated than updating *diff1*. All the elements in the *flipset* of one variable contribute to the value of the *diff2* of that variable. When flips are made, the dependencies between variables are broken and the *flipset* can completely change. Hence incremental update of *diff2* values requires extra data structures, and a complex two stage process, first updating the *flipsets*, and then incrementally recalculating the adjustments and *diff2* values. See [4] for details.

4   Experimental Evaluation

GSATB is written in standard C. It takes the standard conjunctive normal form (CNF) file as its input. We use flat graph colouring and **parity-8** problems from **http://www.intellektik.informatik.tu-darmstadt.de/satlib/** to illustrate the performance of GSATB under different circumstances. We compare against the publicly available GSAT (version 41) code also from the above web site. We execute both GSAT and GSATB on the problem resulting after 2SAT preprocessing. Note that only the **parity-8** benchmarks are modified by the simplification.

All the experiments described here were conducted on a 1GHz Dell Pow-
erEdge 2500 running Solaris 8/x86 with 2×9GB memory. All executions use
MAX-FLIPS equal to 5 times the number of variables, for both GSAT and
GSATB, and MAX-TRIES of 10000 for GSAT and 1000 for GSATB. All runs
succeed in finding a solution, except the examples for GSAT marked $\gg$ in which
none do, and par-2 where GSAT succeeds only 50% of the runs.

4.1   Performance on Flat Graph Colouring Problems

Graph Colouring is a well-known combinatorial problem from graph theory. Instances in this class contain 90% binary clauses. None of the 2SAT simplification
methods extract further binary clauses. The flat-50 suite contains 1000 instances,
while other suites contain 100 instances each. The results in Table 1, show the
size of the problem in terms of number of variables and binary (2SAT) and
ternary (3SAT) clauses. The table also shows the average time (in milliseconds)
and flip2s and flips (the total number of flips including flipping variables in
flipset) over each suite of graphs. Each flip2 step on average involves flipping 2
variables. As the problem size increases the advantage of GSATB becomes more
and more marked, as the search space reduction leads to quicker solutions.

4.2   Performance on Parity Problems

Parity problems are significantly simplified by 2SAT simplification techniques,
sizes for compressed problems in the original form are $(\approx 70, \approx 30, \approx 250)$,
while the uncompressed problems are $(\approx 350, \approx 370, \approx 800)$. Table 2 gives the
average results of 1000 executions of both GSAT and GSATB on 2SAT simplified
versions of the problem. Note the cost for flips is now 20 times greater than in
GSAT, since we need to recalculate *adjust2* and *adjust3* values often. Still for
the uncompressed problems the reduction in search space overhauls this extra
cost.

5   Conclusion and Future Work

GSAT is a simple yet powerful approach to solving SAT problems. By treat-
ing the binary clause information of the SAT problem specially we can modify

Table 1. Comparative performance on flat graph colouring problem

Benchmark Suite				GSAT		GSATB		
Name	#vars	2SAT	3SAT	time(ms)	flips	time(ms)	flip2s	flips
flat-30	90	270	30	1.9	1057	3.2	272	530
flat-50	150	495	50	27.1	14209	23.7	1917	3777
flat-75	225	765	75	288.0	151553	209.3	13752	27179
flat-100	300	1017	100	3069.2	1624535	355.3	20793	41082
flat-125	375	1278	125	19326.4	10127842	3627.2	188987	373703
flat-175	525	1776	175	$\gg$515150.0	$\gg$262500000	22049.9	965900	1910127

Table 2. Comparative performance on 2SAT simplified Parity-8 problems.
⋆ indicates average over 50% successful runs

Name	2SAT simp #vars	2SAT	3SAT	GSAT time(ms)	flips	GSATB time(ms)	flip2s	flips
par-1-c	64	565	167	13.5	4661	94.0	1625	4298
par-1	143	2865	167	2675.5	854984	206.0	9434	10850
par-2-c	68	465	195	22.5	8334	102.5	2087	5297
par-2	151	2716	195	⋆7082.0	⋆2347531	796.0	29824	36509
par-3-c	75	465	223	29.5	10126	164.5	4640	9174
par-3	155	3161	223	4326.0	1385096	1657.0	74153	84356
par-4-c	67	465	191	24.5	9592	211.5	4046	11005
par-4	153	2538	191	3428.5	1164284	544.5	24392	29770
par-5-c	75	638	208	39.0	13697	117.0	3426	6123
par-5	156	5555	208	2700.0	607710	1150.0	48550	54842

GSAT to only ever investigate valuations that satisfy the 2SAT subproblem. This substantially reduces the search space that needs to be explored. GSATB is uniformly better than GSAT in terms of numbers of flips, but each flip is substantially more expensive, so it is not universally beneficial in terms of time. We hope to be able to further improve the data structures, and update algorithms for GSATB to improve this relative performance.

We intend to similarly modify other local search procedures such as WalkSAT and DLM to maintain 2SAT satisfiability. For WalkSAT this should be straightforward since it simply involves translating the upwards moves capabilities for flip2s. For DLM it will be substantially more complicated since the Lagrange multipliers are in effect penalties for each clause, thus adjustments not need to take into account clause penalties, in order to correctly compute *diff2*.

References

[1] Ronen I. Brafman. A simplifier for propositional formulas with many binary clauses. In *Procs. of IJCAI-2001*, pages 515-522, 2001.
[2] B. Selman and H. Kautz. Domain-independent extensions to GSAT: Solving large structured satisfiability problems. In *Procs. of IJCAI-93*, pages 290–295, 1993.
[3] B. Selman, H. Levesque, and D. G. Mitchell. A new method for solving hard satisfiability problems. In *Procs. of AAAI-92*, pages 440–446. AAAI Press/MIT Press, 1992.
[4] P. J. Stuckey and L. Zheng. Improving GSAT using 2SAT. Technical report, Department of Computer Science and Software Engineering, The University of Melbourne, 2002. `www.cs.mu.oz.au/~pjs/papers/gsatb.ps.gz`
[5] Z. Wu and B. W. Wah. An efficient global-search strategy in discrete lagrangian methods for solving hard satisfiability problems. In *Procs. of AAAI-2000*, pages 310–315, 2000.
[6] L. Zheng and P. J. Stuckey. Improving SAT using 2SAT. In *Pros. of ACSC-2002*, pages 331–340, Melbourne, 2002.

A Relational Constraint Solver
for Model-Based Engineering

Jakob Mauss, Frank Seelisch, and Mugur Tatar

DaimlerChrysler Research, Knowledge-Based Engineering
Alt-Moabit 96a, D-10559 Berlin,
{jakob.mauss,frank.seelisch,mugur.tatar}@dcx.com

Abstract. Model-based applications in engineering, such as diagnosis, configuration or interactive decision-support systems, require embedded constraint solvers with challenging capabilities. Not only *consistency checking* and *solving*, but also the computation of (minimal) *conflicts* and *explanations* are required. Moreover, realistic models of engineered systems often require the usage of very *expressive constraint languages*, which mix continuous and discrete variable domains, linear and non-linear equations, inequations, and even procedural constraints. A positive feature of the models of typical engineered systems is, however, that their corresponding constraint problems have a bounded and even relatively small density (induced width).

We present here our relational constraint solver RCS that has been specifically designed to address these requirements. RCS is based on variable elimination, exploiting the low-density property. To analyze a set of constraints, RCS builds a so-called *aggregation tree* by joining the input constraints and eliminating certain variables after every single join. The aggregation tree is then used to compute solutions, as well as explanations and conflicts. We also report some preliminary experimental results obtained with a prototype implementation of this framework.

1 Introduction

Constraint solving is a key technology required to develop knowledge-based applications in engineering, such as diagnosis, configuration or interactive decision-support systems. In most of the cases the constraint solvers are just embedded tools in a larger environment and the whole problem-solving process cannot be specified as a single constraint satisfaction problem. Other (software or human) agents are usually responsible for the dynamic (re)formulation of the constraint problems to be solved, and the space of problems that has to be investigated often depends on the results obtained at previous steps. The computation of solutions in case of consistency has to be complemented by the computation of (minimal) conflicts in case of inconsistency and by the computation of explanations. These additional services play a central role

P. Van Hentenryck (Ed.): CP 2002, LNCS 2470, pp. 696-701, 2002.

in supporting conflict-driven search, in maintaining and debugging large knowledge bases, and in interactive applications. Beside the additional services related to the computation of conflicts and explanations, typical applications require the solver to support a rich, expressive constraint language with, for instance, mixing continuous and discrete variables, linear and non-linear constraints, etc. To summarize, the applications addressed here require a constraint solver with the following challenging properties:

- **Rich Language**: ability to process linear and non-linear equations, disequations, inequalities, variables with discrete and continuous domains, procedurally defined constraints, user-defined structured data types, arrays, and sets.
- **Conflicts and Explanations**: ability to compute small if not minimal conflicts from a given inconsistent set of constraints, and explanations of variable solutions.
- **Reasonable Completeness and Efficiency**: ability to solve variables and detect inconsistency for the expressive modeling language, without requiring the human user to add redundant constraints (e.g. to solve algebraic loops) in order to compensate for the weakness of the solver.

On the other hand, there are some positive features common to many model-based applications that can be exploited by the constraint solver:

- **Low Density**: The set of constraints to be analyzed is typically derived from a compositional model of a technical system. Although the overall system model may contain hundreds of components and thousands of variables, every component of the system interacts with only few neighboring components. In effect, the resulting set of constraints to be analyzed has a low density (induced width w^* in [1]), i.e. every variable occurs in only few constraints.
- **Similarity of the Constraint Problems**: During search, e.g. in the space of possible diagnoses or configurations, the constraint solver has to analyze a sequence of different constraint problems (contexts). However, successive instances in this sequence differ in only few constraints. Similarity can be exploited by *incremental* solving techniques.

Most of the constraint solvers currently available, either commercially or from academic research, do not simultaneously address all of the above requirements. Usually they focus on specific problem classes, such as finite domains or linear algebraic constraints, where they achieve high degrees of completeness thanks to special-purpose algorithms, but violate the rich-language requirement. Few solvers deliver minimal conflicts and explanations.

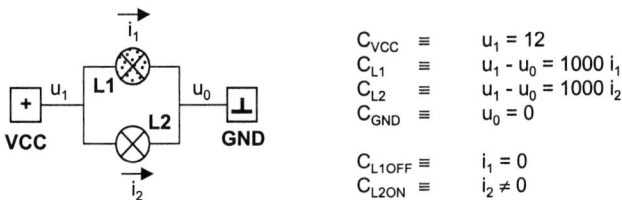

$$C_{VCC} \equiv u_1 = 12$$
$$C_{L1} \equiv u_1 - u_0 = 1000\, i_1$$
$$C_{L2} \equiv u_1 - u_0 = 1000\, i_2$$
$$C_{GND} \equiv u_0 = 0$$

$$C_{L1OFF} \equiv i_1 = 0$$
$$C_{L2ON} \equiv i_2 \neq 0$$

Fig. 1. A circuit model with four component models and two observations

In this paper, we present the relational constraint solver RCS. RCS has been specifically designed to meet the requirements and to exploit the useful properties listed above. RCS has been implemented in Java and its integration into various model-based applications (such as MDS, cf. [3]) is under way.

To get an idea of the principles underlying RCS, consider the simple circuit shown in Fig. 1. Assume the circuit's nominal behavior is modeled by four component models, i.e. four constraints C_{VCC}, C_{L1}, C_{L2}, C_{GND}. Additionally, in a diagnosis scenario, there may be constraints C_{L2ON}, C_{L1OFF} representing the observation that bulb L2 is lit, while at the same time L1 is not lit. One can see that (a) the six constraints shown in Fig. 1 are inconsistent and (b) contain two minimal conflicts, i.e. two minimal inconsistent subsets

1. $\{C_{L1}, C_{L1OFF}, C_{VCC}, C_{GND}\}$
2. $\{C_{L1}, C_{L1OFF}, C_{L2}, C_{L2ON}\}$

In a consistency-based diagnostic framework (cf. [5]), one might conclude that probably L1 is broken or the observation 'L1 not lit' is wrong, since suspending any of the corresponding constraints C_{L1} and C_{L1OFF} will restore consistency. There are four double faults, such as 'VCC and L2 both broken', each of which explains both conflicts as well.

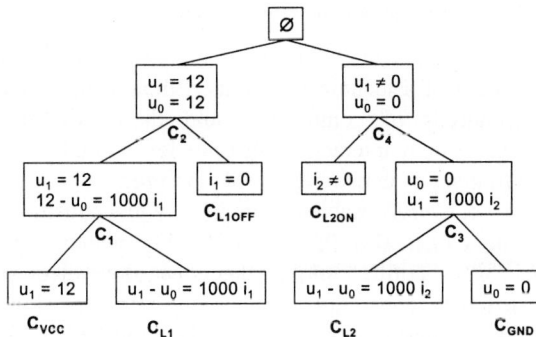

Fig. 2. Aggregation tree for proving the inconsistency of six constraints

Using RCS, the above context can be analyzed as shown in Fig. 2. To check the consistency of a given set of constraints, RCS builds a binary tree, called an *aggregation tree*, as shown in Fig. 2. Every node of the aggregation tree holds a constraint. The tree is constructed bottom-up, starting from the leaf nodes that hold the six given constraints. Every non-leaf node holds the constraint resulting from aggregating the constraints at its left and right sub-node. Two constraints are aggregated by first joining them (conjunction) and then eliminating all variables from the result that do only occur in the left and right sub-tree. For instance, in order to aggregate C_1 and C_{L1OFF}, first C_1 and C_{L1OFF} are joined, then i_1 is eliminated, leading to the constraint C_2. In contrast, the variable u_1 is not eliminated from C_2 because u_1 occurs in C_{L2}, which is not contained in the two sub-trees of C_2. In general, the root of an aggregation tree holds the empty constraint (falsity), if and only if the set of constraints of its leaf nodes is inconsistent. These ideas lead to a framework for constraint solving that addresses the previously mentioned requirements. There are generic algorithms (cf. [2]) based on aggregation trees for consistency checking (from scratch and incremental), variable solving, computing minimal conflicts and minimal explanations (minimal constraint sets that imply the variable solution). All those algorithms require a number of joins linear in the number of constraints.

2   Experimental Results

To give an idea of the runtime performance achieved by the current implementation of RCS, we consider the spacecraft propulsion system shown in Fig. 3.

The helium pressurizes two propellant tanks, forcing the contained oxidizer and fuel to flow into the engine, where it reacts and produces heat and thrust. This system contains 45 components (including sensors for pressure, temperature and valve positions not shown in Fig. 3). Every component model is of the form $\vee\ (mode = m_k \wedge r_k)$ where *mode* is a discrete variable representing a behavioral mode (e.g. nominal or broken) of the component, and r_k is a relation representing the component's behavior in mode m_k. The pressure regulators are modeled using non-linear equations. The engine is modeled by a procedurally defined relation that uses given characteristic lines to compute the chamber pressure and temperature as a function of fuel and oxidizer pressure. The remaining components are modeled by and/or-junctions of propositions and linear equations. See [4] for details.

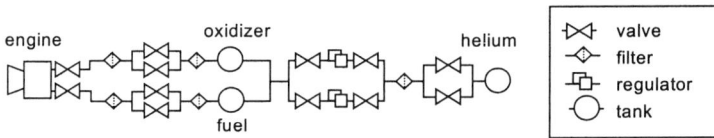

Fig. 3. Propulsion system with 45 components

We defined 100 consistent contexts (4 specific valve settings × 1 no-fault + 24 single-faults) in an arbitrary but fixed ordering. Neighboring contexts differed mostly by 2 relations, a few times by 1 or 3. Each context had 459 variables and 447 relations, each of which had 2.3 variables on average, at most 4 disjuncts and 8 atoms.

The task for RCS was then to sequentially check consistency and derive solutions for all variables, in all 100 contexts. The two following experiments have been run 100 times on a PC with 500 MHz and 128 MByte RAM, and our results show rather small variances. For each run, we permuted the order of the input relations which resulted in different structures of the derived aggregation trees. First, RCS did non-incremental consistency checking. In the second experiment, RCS deployed the incremental check, recomputing only few paths in the aggregation tree.

consistency check	agg	t [msec]	t / agg	arity	disjuncts	atoms
non-incremental	446.0	494.4	1.1	2.7	4.01	13.9
incremental	23.1	29.9	1.2	2.8	4.08	15.3

Fig. 4. Experimental results

In the table, *agg* denotes the average number of aggregations required to check one context, and *t* gives the average runtime for checking one context. The last three columns give average properties of the derived non-leave relations. While *arity* denotes the average arity of all derived non-leave relations, *disjuncts* and *atoms* denote the average of the maximum that occurred in each context.

First, we point out that the average arity of non-leave relations almost equals the average for leaf relations (2.7 resp. 2.8 as opposed to 2.3). This supports our assumption concerning bounded induced width in compositional system models.

Second, the average number of aggregations for an incremental consistency check remains bounded and seems to relate to the theoretical result of *O(log(n))*. Note that our greedy aggregation strategy does not aim at balanced trees. Still, we achieved a considerably small average number of aggregations (about 23) for incrementally updating an aggregation tree with 447 leaves.

In both experiments, we also ran the procedure for solving all variables. On average, this took 689 msec for incrementally derived aggregation trees, and 538 msec for non-incrementally derived trees. Solving itself is not currently incremental in RCS. We also analyzed the same 100 contexts with our old TMS-based solver used in MDS [3]. The MDS solver was 3 to 5 times faster for this task, mainly due to the non-incremental solving currently used by RCS. Incremental solving (or speed up by solving only for required variables) is subject of further investigation.

We also validated the performance of RCS for computing minimal conflicts (algorithm XC1, cf. [2]) with conflict computation by constraint suspension. For details, see [2].

3   Conclusion

We presented a relational framework for consistency-checking, solving, and computing minimal conflicts and explanations. The framework aims at *decomposing* the above tasks into join and project operations involving relations with small arity *n*, while the overall problem may contain hundreds of variables. Keeping *n* small is essential, since many elimination algorithms are exponential in *n*. Our framework keeps *n* small provided that (1) the given problem allows such a decomposition, and that (2) the control strategy used to build the underlying aggregation tree is smart enough to find such a decomposition. We argued that (1) holds for a relevant class of problems occurring in knowledge-based engineering. Regarding (2), the experimental results given in section 2 indicate that good decompositions can be found using relatively simple greedy control strategies.

References

[1]   R. Dechter: Bucket Elimination: a Unifying Framework for Reasoning. *Artificial Intelligence*, 113, pp. 41 - 85, 1999.
[2]   J. Mauss, M. Tatar: Computing Minimal Conflicts for Rich Constraint Languages. *15th European Conference on Artificial Intelligence ECAI 2002*, Lyon, France, 2002.

[3]   J. Mauss, V. May, M. Tatar: Towards Model-based Engineering: Failure Analysis with MDS. *ECAI-2000 Workshop W31 on Knowledge-Based Systems for Model-Based Engineering,* http://www.dbai.tuwien.ac.at/event/ecai2000-kbsmbe/papers, 2000.

[4]   M. Tatar, P. Dannenmann: Integrating Simulation and Model-based Diagnosis into the Life Cycle of Aerospace Systems. *Principles of Diagnosis Dx99,* Loch Awe, 1999.

[5]   W. Hamscher, J. de Kleer, L. Console: *Readings in Model-Based Diagnosis.* Morgan Kaufmann, 1992.

Conflict-Based Repair Techniques for Solving Dynamic Scheduling Problems

Abdallah Elkhyari[1], Christelle Guéret[1,2], and Narendra Jussien[1]

[1] École des Mines de Nantes
4, rue Alfred Kastler, F-44307 Nantes Cedex 3, France
{aelkhyar,gueret,jussien}@emn.fr
[2] IRCCyN – Institut de Recherche en Communications et Cybernétique de Nantes

1 Introduction

Scheduling problems have been studied a lot over the last decade. Due to the complexity and the variety of such problems, most work consider static problems in which activities are known in advance and constraints are fixed. However, every schedule is subject to unexpected events (consider for example a new activity to schedule or a machine breakdown). In these cases, a new solution taking these events into account is needed in a preferably short time and as close as possible to the current solution.

Constraint Satisfaction Problems (CSP) are increasingly used for solving scheduling problems: many global temporal and resource constraints have been developed [1, 2, 3]. However, dynamic CSP (an extension of the CSP framework where the set of variables or/and constraints evolves throughout computation [4]) have not been used for solving dynamic scheduling problems. Moreover, dynamic scheduling problems are themselves seldom studied [5]. Two classical methods are used to solve such problems are: recomputing a new schedule from scratch each time an event occurs (a quite time consuming technique) or constructing a partial schedule and completing it progressively as time goes by (like in on-line scheduling problems – this is not compatible with planning purposes).

Extending work on dynamic arc-consistency [6], the use of *explanations* (a set of constraint justifying solver actions) have been introduced for solving dynamic problems [7]. However, no application of such a technique have been made to scheduling problems. In this paper, we introduce the integration of explanation capabilities within scheduling-related global constraints and show how using such techniques speeds up the solving of dynamic problems (compared to solving a series of static problems).

2 Solving Dynamic Problems Using Explanations

Solving dynamic problems requires incremental addition and retraction of constraints. Even though incremental constraint addition is naturally handled by modern constraint solvers, incremental retraction of constraints is often performed using trace/undo recorded information [6, 7]. Such an information is used to determine past effects of a removed constraint that need to be undone [8].

P. Van Hentenryck (Ed.): CP 2002, LNCS 2470, pp. 702–707, 2002.

Explanations [7] are a generalization of that information. An explanation is a set of constraints that justifies an action of the solver (classically value removals) *i.e.* as long as each constraint that appears in the explanation remains active (not removed) the value removal (in our example) is valid (no valid solution can be built from this partial assignment). An explanation for the removal of value a from variable x is denoted `expl(`$x \neq a$`)`.

Several explanations may exist for a given removal. Providing precise and short explanations for solver actions is a key issue to the interest of using explanation-based techniques within constraint programming: upon undoing past effects of a constraints only the necessary modifications are to be done. A good compromise between precision and ease of computation is to use the solver-embedded knowledge to provide interesting explanations [7]. When considering global constraints, an easy way of providing explanations is to merely consider the whole set of variables involved in that constraint. However, efficient explanations need a more precise study of the algorithms used to propagate those constraints as we will see in the next section.

Explanations can also be used to efficiently guide the search. Indeed, most classical backtracking-based searches only proceed by backtracking to the last choice point when encountering failures. Explanations can be used to improve standard backtracking and to exploit information gathered to improve the search: to provide intelligent backtracking, to replace standard backtracking with a jump-based approach [9] *à la Dynamic Backtracking*, or even to develop new local searches on partial instantiations [10]. More information on these topics is available on `www.e-constraints.net`.

3 Explanations for Scheduling-Related Global Constraints

The Resource Constrained Project Scheduling Problem (RCPSP) is a general scheduling problem. It consists of a set of activities $A = \{1, 2, \ldots, n\}$ and a set of renewable resources $R = \{1, \ldots, r\}$. Each resource k is available in a given constant amount R_k. Each activity i has a duration p_i and requires a constant amount a_{ik} of resource k to be processed. Preemption is not considered. Activities are related by two sets of constraints: temporal constraints modelled through precedence constraints (*i.e.* mathematical binary relations), and resource constraints that state that for each time period and for each resource, the total demand cannot exceed the resource capacity. The objective considered here is the minimization of the makespan (total duration) of the project. This problem is *NP-hard* [11].

Providing explanation for temporal binary constraints is straightforward (consider the associated mathematical relations – see [7]). Explanations for resource management constraints are not that easy. It is necessary to study the algorithms used for propagation. Classical techniques for maintaining resource limitations for scheduling problems include: *resource-histogram* [1, 2], *core-times* [3] and *task-interval* [1, 2].

3.1   Resource-Histogram Constraints

The principle of the *resource-histogram* technique [1, 2] is to associate to each resource k an array `level`(k) in order to keep a timetable of the resource requirements. This histogram is used for detecting a contradiction and reducing the time-window of activities.

The *core-times* technique [3] is used for computing lower bounds using a destructive method. A *core-time* $CT(i)$ is associated to each activity i. It is defined as the interval of time during which a portion of an activity is always executed whether it starts at its earliest or latest starting time. A lower bound of the schedule is obtained when considering only the *core-time* of each activity. If a resource-conflict is detected then some lower bounds can be upgraded.

Combining these two techniques provides an efficient resource-conflict detecting constraint. A timetable for each resource is computed as follows: for each activity i, its *core-time* $CT(i) = [f_i, r_i + p_i)$ (f_i is the latest starting time of i and r_i its earliest starting time) is computed and the amount a_{ik} of resource k for each time interval $[f_i, f_i+1), \ldots, [r_i+p_i-1, r_i+p_i)$ is reserved. We associate to each *timetable constraint* two histograms (see Fig. 1):

- a *level histogram* which contains the amount of resource required at each time interval $[t-1, t)$.
- an *activity histogram* which contains the sets S_t of activities which require any amount of resource for each time period $[t-1, t)$. It will essentially be used for providing explanations.

These histograms are used in the following ways:

- detecting resource conflicts when the required level of a resource k in a given time period t exceeds the resource capacity. The conflict set associated to this contradictory situation is constituted from the set of activities (S_t) stored in slot t of the activity histogram. We use the following equation (c being the histogram constraint itself): $\left(\bigwedge_{v \in S_t} \left(\bigwedge_{a \in d(v)} \mathrm{expl}(v \neq a) \right) \right) \wedge c.$
- tightening the time-window of an activity. It may occur that the current bounds of the time-window of an activity are not compatible with the other activities. In that situation, the tightening of the time-window will be explained by the set S_t of activities requiring the resources during the incompatible time-period $[t-1, t)$. The following equation is used (c being the histogram constraint itself): $\left(\bigwedge_{v \in S_t} \left(\bigwedge_{a \in d(v)} \mathrm{expl}(v \neq a) \right) \right) \wedge c.$

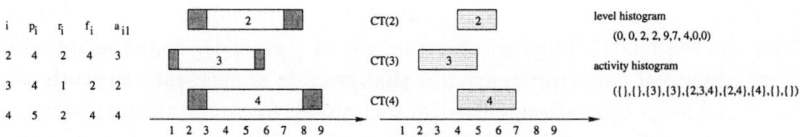

Fig. 1. Example of timetable

3.2   Task-Interval Constraints

Using *task-intervals* for managing cumulative resources provides different services [1, 2]: conflict detection, precedence deduction and time-window tightening. A *task-interval* $T = [i, j]$ is associated to each pair of activities (i, j) which require the same resource k. It is defined as the set of activities ℓ which share the same resource and such that $r_i \leq r_\ell$ and $d_\ell \leq d_j$ (r_i being the earliest starting time of the activity i and d_i its due date) *i.e.* that need to be scheduled between tasks i and j. The set $\texttt{inside}(TI)$ represents the set of activities constituting the *task-interval*, while $\texttt{outside}(TI)$ contains the remaining activities. Let define $\texttt{energy}(TI) = \sum_{\ell \in \texttt{inside}(TI)} (d_\ell - r_\ell) \times a_{\ell k}$ the total *energy* required by a *task-interval*.

Several propagation rules can be defined upon *task-intervals* [1, 2]. We consider here the following two:

Integrity rule If $\texttt{energy}(TI)$ is greater than the total *energy* available in the task-interval $[i, j]$ (*i.e.* $(d_j - r_i) \times R_k$) then a conflict is detected. The conflict explanation set is built from the set of activities *inside* the *task-interval*: (c being the constraint associated to this rule) $\left(\bigwedge_{v \in \texttt{inside}(TI)} \left(\bigwedge_{a \in d(v)} \texttt{expl}(v \neq a) \right) \right) \wedge c$.

Throw rule This rule consists in tightening the time-window of an activity intersecting a given *task-interval* TI. This is done by comparing the necessary energy shared with the activities in TI and energy available during the *task-interval*. The explanation of this update is built from the set of activities *inside* the *task-interval*: (c being the constraint associated to this rule) $\left(\bigwedge_{v \in \texttt{inside}(TI)} \left(\bigwedge_{a \in d(v)} \texttt{expl}(v \neq a) \right) \right) \wedge c$.

4   Experiments on Dynamic RCPSP

We developed a branch and bound search using the presented explanation-based techniques and based upon a branch and bound algorithm from [12]. This interactive system accepts several types of modification on the scheduling problem: temporal events (adding/removing precedence/overlapping/disjunctive relations, modifying time-windows), activity related events (adding/removing), resource related events (adding/removing/modifying).

Table 1 presents some first results on dynamic RCPSP. In this table, we report the relative time speed-up obtained using explanation-based dynamic constraint solving compared to solving each problem from scratch. The table reports results considering 4 consecutive modifications from an original problem. As we can see, those results are quite promising. Even bad results (instance 4) get better in the long run. However, notice that some results (not reported here) show that dynamic handling is not always the panacea and rescheduling from scratch can be very quick. Obviously, further experiments need to be done.

706   Abdallah Elkhyari et al.

Table 1. Some Kolish, Sprecher and Drexl instances (4 consecutive dynamic events). (`www.wior.uni-karlsruhe.de/RCPSP/ProGen.html`). Relative speed-up (in %)

12 act./4 res.	Modif. 1	Modif. 2	Modif. 3	Modif. 4
# 1	46.24	54.92	62.68	63.13
# 2	3.81	26.38	46.62	55.92
# 3	22.13	10.64	21.08	22.21
# 4	-29.21	-0.35	15.74	30.27
# 5	32.01	67.90	75.15	75.65
# 6	46.72	52.58	47.75	49.27
# 7	12.76	26.09	35.84	35.58
# 8	35.88	44.12	45.82	45.87

5   Conclusion

In this paper, we presented the integration of explanations within scheduling-related global constraint and its interest for solving dynamic scheduling problems. We presented first experimental results of a system that we developed using those techniques. These results demonstrate that incremental constraint solving for scheduling problems is really useful.

We are currently improving our system with user-interaction capabilities still using explanations. Moreover, we are conducting high scale experiments (larger problems, easy/medium/hard problems, ...) to validate our approach.

References

[1] Caseau, Y., Laburthe, F.: Improving clp scheduling with task intervals. In Hentenryck, P. V., ed.: Proceedings of ICLP'94, MIT Press (1994) 369–383
[2] Caseau, Y., Laburthe, F.: Cumulative scheduling with task-intervals. In: Joint International Conference and Symposium on Logic Programming (JICSLP). (1996)
[3] Klein, R., Scholl, A.: Computing lower bounds by destructive improvement: an application to Resource-Constrained Project Scheduling Problem. European Journal of Operational Research **112** (1999) 322–345
[4] Dechter, R., Dechter, A.: Belief maintenance in dynamic constraint networks. In: AAAI'88, St Paul, MN (1988) 37–42
[5] Artigues, C., Roubellat, F.: A polynomial activity insertion algorithm in a multi-resource schedule with cumulative constraints and multiple modes. European Journal of Operational Research **127** (2000) 297–316
[6] Bessière, C.: Arc consistency in dynamic constraint satisfaction problems. In: Proceedings AAAI'91. (1991)
[7] Jussien, N.: e-constraints: explanation-based constraint programming. In: CP01 Workshop on User-Interaction in Constraint Satisfaction, Paphos, Cyprus (2001)
[8] Debruyne, R., Ferrand, G., Jussien, N., Lesaint, W., Ouis, S., Tessier, A.: Correctness of constraint retraction algorithms. Research Report 2002-09, LIFO Orléans, France (2002) `www.emn.fr/jussien/publications/debruyne-LIFO2002-09.ps`
[9] Jussien, N., Debruyne, R., Boizumault, P.: Maintaining arc-consistency within dynamic backtracking. In: Proceedings CP'00. LNCS 1894, Springer-Verlag (2000) 249–261

[10] Jussien, N., Lhomme, O.: Local search with constraint propagation and conflict-based heuristics. Artificial Intelligence **139** (2002) 21–45
[11] Blazewicz, J., Lenstra, J., Rinnoy Kan, A.: Scheduling projects subject to resource constraints: classification and complexity. Discrete Applied Mathematics **5** (1983) 11–24
[12] Brucker, P., Knust, S., Schoo, A., Thiele, O.: A branch and bound algorithm for the Resource-Constrained Project Scheduling Problem. EJOR **107** (1998) 272–288

Scaling Properties of Pure Random Walk on Random 3-SAT

Andrew J. Parkes

CIRL, 1269 University of Oregon, Eugene OR 97404, USA
http://www.cirl.uoregon.edu/parkes/

Abstract. Experimental results are given on the scaling of the Pure Random Walk version (PRWSAT) of WalkSAT. PRWSAT is very simple because of the absence of heuristics: not only the clause is selected at random, but also the literal within that clause. The main result is that, despite the simplicity and absence of heuristics, it has nontrivial behavior on Random 3-SAT. There appears to be a threshold at a clause/variable ratio of about 2.65. Below the threshold, problems are solved in a tightly-distributed and linear number of flips. Above the threshold scaling appears to be non-polynomial. The simplicity and the nontrivial threshold make it a good candidate for theoretical analysis.

1 Introduction

Random k-SAT problems are interesting because of their sharp phase transitions (PTs) [1, 2, and others]. For Random k-SAT, given n variables, we select c clauses uniformly at random from the set of all clauses with k literals. The relevant order parameter is $\alpha = c/n$. For $\alpha < \alpha_k$ instances are almost always satisfiable, and for $\alpha > \alpha_k$ they are almost always unsatisfiable. The case $k = 2$ can be analysed exactly giving $\alpha_2 = 1.0$ (for example [3]). However, no known methods can determine α_k for $k \geq 3$, though empirical work on Random 3-SAT suggests that $\alpha_3 \approx 4.24$ [1, 4]. The best that exact analysis can do is to provide upper and lower bounds. Upper bounds are determined by "moment methods." Lower bounds are obtained by analysing a sufficiently simple algorithm and demonstrating a high probability of finding a solution up to some threshold value of α. The best such bound, $\alpha_3 \geq 3.26$, [5] is obtained from constructive greedy algorithms based on extending partial assignments (usually augmented with some very limited heuristics). However, such algorithms are not particularly effective close to the PT. Instead, for satisfiable instances of Random 3-SAT it is often better in practice to use a local search (iterative repair) algorithm. Of this class, one of the most effective is "WalkSAT" (WSAT) [6]. Hence, a possible avenue towards obtaining better lower-bounds is to develop better methods to analyze average-case behavior of local search algorithms. Better analysis methods should also be developed because local search algorithms are often used on practical constraint problems but are generally poorly understood.

In general, it seems that algorithms amenable to analysis of average-case scaling often have properties P1 and P2:

P. Van Hentenryck (Ed.): CP 2002, LNCS 2470, pp. 708–713, 2002.
© Springer-Verlag Berlin Heidelberg 2002

P1: Non-trivial behavior when limited to polynomial running time. The successful analyses in [7, 5] are all polynomial time. Generally, attempts at analysis
are unsuccessful when the average runtimes are exponential; presumably because too much variance accrues. (Worst-case, rather than average-case, is
different, *e.g.* [8]). Non-triviality means at least some problems are solved.

P2: "Distributions should be tight" or "runtime characteristics should be highly
predictable". Usually, as the algorithm progresses, properties of the search
state follow a course that is "tightly distributed about the mean." For example, in [5] different runs exhibit very little variation in the structure of
the unsatisfied clauses. Apparently, average-case analysis techniques cannot
handle algorithms that exhibit large variations between runs or instances.

In this paper we do not attempt to improve theoretical analysis, but instead
identify a simple local search algorithm that experimentally shows these properties, and is a good candidate for developing theoretical analyses. The algorithm
we consider is "Pure Random WalkSAT" (PRWSAT) of Papadimitriou [9]:

> $P :=$ a randomly generated truth assignment
> **for** $j := 1$ to MAX-FLIPS {
>   **if** (P is a solution)   **then** return P
>   **else**
> $c :=$ a randomly selected unsatisfied clause
>   flip a random literal from c }
>   **return** failure

This algorithm is $O(n^2)$ on 2-SAT but the arguments used do not extend to 3-
SAT [9]. Also, the absence of heuristics means it will generally be very ineffective.
However, here we summarize experimental studies indicating that, on Random
3-SAT, it does have interesting nontrivial behaviors: Solving problems in linear
time, with tight distributions of flips used.

2   Empirical Results for PRWSAT

The experimental methods we follow are close to those of [10]. Over a range
of values of α we measure the median number of flips needed to solve Random
3-SAT instances. The median is selected due to its resilience against outliers.
We chose to rescale the flips by the number of clauses that are initially expected
to be unsatisfied, that is, by $c/8$ for Random 3-SAT. The rescaled flips give a
measure of flip efficiency. Also, since the rescaling factor is $\Theta(n)$, it makes it
easier to read the graphs.

The main result is given in Figure 1. There appears to be a threshold at
$\alpha_L \approx 2.65$. For $\alpha < \alpha_L$ the scaling is $\Theta(n)$ (that is, the rescaled flips appears
not to grow with n). Figure 1(b) shows that although it is linear, it is still
quantitatively worse than WSAT. Above the threshold, Figure 1(c), it appears
that the growth is worse than a power-law (indicated by ever-increasing gaps
on the logarithmic y-axis). Secondly, Figure 2 gives results on the nature of the

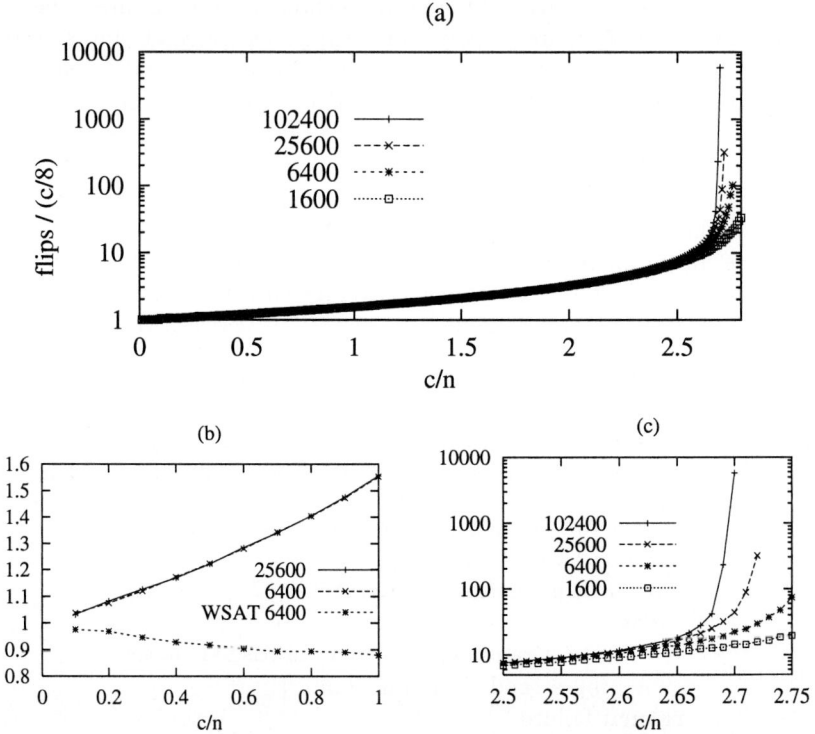

Fig. 1. PRWSAT on Random 3-SAT for indicated values of n. The y-axis is median flips rescaled by a $\Theta(n)$ factor. (a) gives a broad picture. (b) and (c) zoom the end ranges. In (b) the extra (lower) curve is the standard (heuristically-enabled) WSAT

distribution of flips needed to solve instances. Figure 2(a), shows that below the threshold, at $\alpha = 2.6$, the distribution of flips becomes very tight. In the limit, there is little variance between instances and runs. In contrast, above the threshold, at $\alpha = 2.7$, Figure 2(b) shows that the scaling is not linear, and also that the distribution does not appear to become tight for large n. At $\alpha = 2.7$, the medians did not fit a simple power-law, but did give a good fit (not shown) to $f_1 n^{f_2 + f_3 \log(n)}$, a "power-law with growing exponent," as also found useful in [11, 10].

These results indicate (subject to the obvious caveats of empirical studies) that below a threshold at $\alpha \approx 2.65$ the scaling is $\Theta(n)$ and flips used are "tightly clustered about the mean", but above the threshold scaling is (mildly) super-polynomial and the variance is high. The threshold also appears to be sharp.

An early result on thresholds [7] was for an algorithm based on the pure literal rule. If a literal appears, but not its complement, then enforcing that literal cannot affect satisfiability. Once enforced then some clauses become satisfied, can be

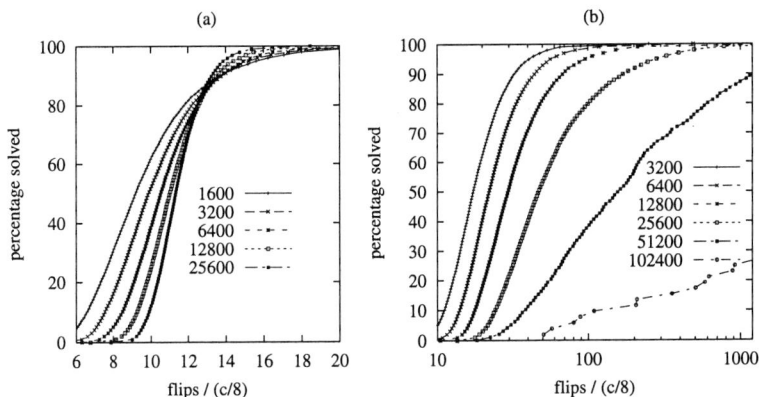

Fig. 2. (Rescaled) flip distributions for PRWSAT on Random 3-SAT. (a) $\alpha = 2.6$ (b) $\alpha = 2.7$

removed, and more pure literals might be enforceable. For Random 3-SAT with $\alpha < 1.63$ iterating this procedure almost always leads to a solution. However, PRWSAT also favors pure literals: once a pure literal is valued correctly then it will never occur in an unsatisfied clause and so can never be flipped back, and once so fixed, other literals can become effectively pure. The challenge is that it is not clear how many flips are needed before some pure literal is flipped to the correct value. Recent theoretical work has been able to show that PRWSAT does have polynomial scaling below 1.63 [12]. However, we remark that Figure 1 does not appear to show any significant changes at 1.63. Presumably, in practice, PRWSAT often finds a solution before having found all pure literals.

Similar experiments (omitted due to lack of space) on a direct parallel version of PRWSAT (following [13]) show a slightly lower threshold, $\alpha \approx 2.55$, below which parallel scaling is good, $O(\log(n))$, and distributions are tight.

2.1   PRWSAT on Random 2-SAT

For completeness we also summarize results on Random 2-SAT. Recall that the satisfiability phase transition (PT) is at $\alpha = 1$. Firstly, Figure 3(a) suggests that the scaling is $\Theta(n)$ even up to close to the PT. Below the PT, for example, at $\alpha = 0.8$ of Figure 3(b), we see a sharp distribution, and scaling that is $\Theta(n)$. Exactly at the PT, $\alpha = 1.0$, scaling must be still $O(n^2)$, but results (not shown) were inconclusive as to whether the scaling is better than $O(n^2)$. However, this is already sufficient to see a strong contrast to Random 3-SAT where linear scaling held only up to 2.65 which is far from the satisfiability PT at 4.25.

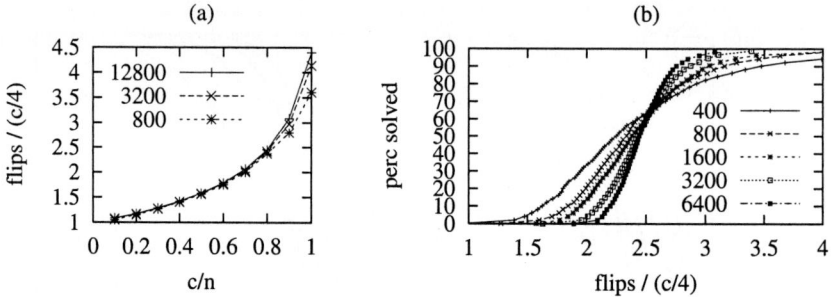

Fig. 3. PRWSAT on Random 2-SAT. (a) Rescaled flips for various n. (b) Distribution of rescaled flips at $\alpha = 0.8$

3   Conclusion

For Random 3-SAT, and $\alpha < 2.65$, PRWSAT solves problems in linear flips, and with tight distributions. This, and the absence of complicated heuristics, mean it a good candidate for formal theoretical analyses.

4   Acknowledgments

This work was sponsored in part by grants from Defense Advanced Research Projects Agency (DARPA), number F30602-98-2-0181, and DARPA and Air Force Research Laboratory, Rome, NY, under agreement numbered F30602-00-2-0534. The U.S. Government is authorized to reproduce and distribute reprints for Government purposes notwithstanding any copyright annotation thereon. The views and conclusions contained herein are those of the authors and should not be interpreted as necessarily representing the official policies or endorsements, either expressed or implied, of DARPA, Rome Laboratory, or the U.S. Government.

References

[1] Kirkpatrick, S., Selman, B.: Critical behavior in the satisfiability of random boolean expressions. Science **264** (1994) 1297–1301

[2] Friedgut, E.: Sharp thresholds of graph properties, and the k-SAT problem. Journal of the American Mathematical Society **12** (1999) 1017–1054

[3] Goerdt: A remark on random 2-SAT. DAMATH: Discrete Applied Mathematics and Combinatorial Operations Research and Computer Science **96** (1999)

[4] Crawford, J. M., Auton, L. D.: Experimental results on the crossover point in random 3-SAT. Artificial Intelligence **81** (1996) 31–57

[5] Achlioptas, D., Sorkin, G. B.: Optimal myopic algorithms for random 3-SAT. In: IEEE Symposium on Foundations of Computer Science (FOCS 00). (2000) 590–600

[6] Selman, B., Kautz, H., Cohen, B.: Local search strategies for satisfiability testing. In Johnson, D. S., Trick, M. A., eds.: Cliques, Coloring and Satisfiability, American Mathematical Society (1996) 521–531

[7] Broder, A. Z., Frieze, A. M., Upfal, E.: On the satisability and maximum satisability of random 3-CNF formulas. In: Proc. 4th Ann. ACM-SIAM SODA. (1993) 322–330

[8] Hirsch, E. A.: SAT local search algorithms: Worst-case study. Journal of Automated Reasoning **24** (2000) 127–143

[9] Papadimitriou, C.: On selecting a satisfying truth assignment. In: Proc. IEEE symposium on Foundations of Computer Science. (1991) 163–169

[10] Parkes, A. J.: Easy predictions for the easy-hard-easy transition. In: Proceedings of the Eighteenth National Conference on Artificial Intelligence (AAAI-2002). (2002)

[11] Parkes, A. J., Walser, J. P.: Tuning Local Search for Satisfiability Testing. In: Proceedings of AAAI-96, Portland, OR (1996) 356–362

[12] Ben-Sasson, E.: Personal communication (2002)

[13] Parkes, A. J.: Distributed local search, phase transitions, and polylog time. In: Proc. "Stochastic Search Algorithms" workshop, IJCAI-01". (2001)

Criticality and Parallelism in Structured SAT Instances

Andrea Roli

DEIS – Università degli Studi di Bologna, Italia
aroli@deis.unibo.it

Abstract. In this work we address the question of whether and how parallel local search exhibits the *criticality and parallelism* phenomenon when performed on structured instances. We experimentally show that also for structured instances there exists an optimal value of parallelism which enables the algorithm to reach the optimal performance and, by analyzing the frequency of node degree of the graphs associated with the SAT instances, we observe that an asymmetric and not regular distribution strongly affects the algorithm performance with respect to the parallelism.

1 Introduction

The phenomenon called *criticality and parallelism* has been observed in the context of local search algorithms applied to combinatorial optimization problems [4, 3], where local search is modified by applying τ local moves in parallel. The most important results observed so far can be summarized in the following properties: (i) the algorithm performance increases as parallelism increases, up to a parallelism degree (τ_{opt}) at which it starts to decrease, (ii) the optimal parallelism depends on a parameter which measures the connectivity of the system, and (iii) when the decrease in performance for $\tau > \tau_{opt}$ is abrupt, the behavior is accompanied by a phase transition.

The same phenomenon has been discovered in parallel local search for SAT [5] and MAXSAT [6], where a parallel version of GSAT [7] (called PGSAT) has been applied. In PGSAT, variables are divided in τ subsets and, for each subset, we flip the variable that, if flipped, decreases the greatest number of unsatisfied clauses. For satisfiable SAT instances it has been experimentally shown that the best global performance (time, iterations, fraction of solved instances) is achieved with an optimal parallelism degree τ_{opt}. Furthermore, τ_{opt} is monotonically non increasing with the connectivity among variables.

Recent studies [9] investigate the different distribution of node degree of the graphs associated with random and structured CSPs and its impact on search. The authors show that real world problems frequently have a connectivity distribution strongly different from that of random instances and they point out how this topological characteristic may affect the search effectiveness.

P. Van Hentenryck (Ed.): CP 2002, LNCS 2470, pp. 714–719, 2002.

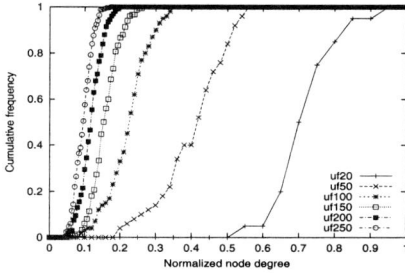

Fig. 1. Cumulative frequency vs. normalized node degree for Uniform Random 3-SAT instances in the threshold region

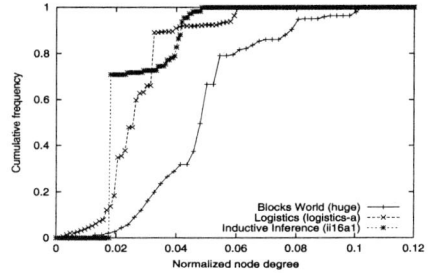

Fig. 2. Cumulative frequency vs. normalized node degree in structured instances: Blocks World (*huge*), Logistics (*logistics-a*) and Inductive Inference (*ii16a1*)

The aim of this work is to investigate the effects of problem structure on the parallelization of local search for SAT problems, and compare them with previous results concerning random instances [5, 6].

2 Structured SAT Instances

In this section we first define the node degree distribution of graphs associated with random and structured SAT instances. Then we show and discuss results of PGSAT, run with different values of τ, on two representative structured SAT instances.

The graph associated with a SAT instance is an undirected graph $\mathcal{G} = (\mathcal{V}, \mathcal{A})$, where each node $v_i \in \mathcal{V}$ corresponds to a variable and edge $(v_i, v_j) \in \mathcal{A}$ $(i \neq j)$ if and only if variables v_i and v_j appear in a same clause. In an instance with n variables, each node v_i, $i = 1, \ldots, n$, has a degree $q_i \in \{0, 1, \ldots, n-1\}$. We define the *average connectivity* of the instance as the average node degree of the corresponding graph, i.e., $q = \frac{1}{n} \sum_{i=1}^{n} q_i$. Moreover, to make direct comparisons among instances with different number of variables, we also introduce the normalization of q: $\bar{q} = \frac{q}{n-1}$. In order to compare the node degree distribution between instances, we consider the cumulative frequency $Freq(j) =$ frequency of a node connected to not more than j nodes. Fig.1 shows the cumulative frequency vs. the normalized node degree for random 3-SAT instances retrieved from SATLIB [2]. Note that the curves are quite regular and, as the number of variables increases, they converge to a step function located at the average node degree.

Structured instances are characterized by the presence of some regularity in their components, for example graph problems based on ring or lattice topology, SAT problems obtained by encoding logic problems (circuit testing, inductive inference, planning, etc.). Fig.2 shows the curve of cumulative frequency for structured SAT instances taken from SATLIB. The plotted curves show apparent

716   Andrea Roli

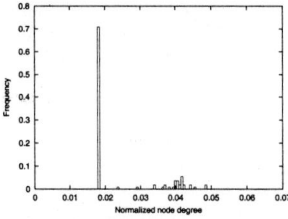

Fig. 3. Frequency vs. normalized node degree in the instance *ii16a1*

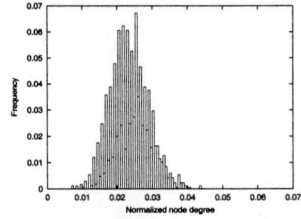

Fig. 4. Frequency vs. normalized node degree in the instance *3sat1650*

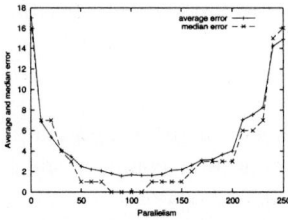

Fig. 5. Average and median error against τ for PGSAT on the instance *ii16a1*

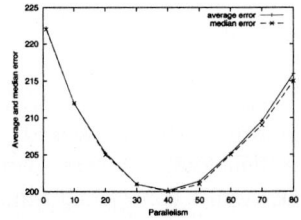

Fig. 6. Average and mcdian error against τ for PGSAT on the instance *3sat1650*

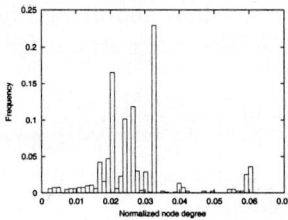

Fig. 7. Frequency vs. normalized node degree in the instance *logistics-a*

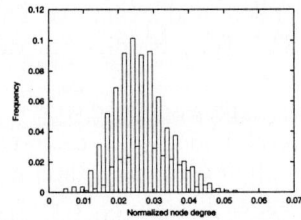

Fig. 8. Frequency vs. normalized node degree in the instance *3sat828*

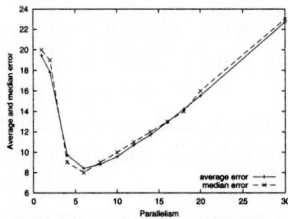

Fig. 9. Average and median error against τ for PGSAT on the instance *logistics-a*

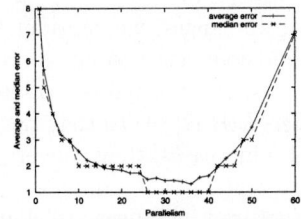

Fig. 10. Average and median error against τ for PGSAT on the instance *3sat828*

differences with those of random SAT problems. They are not as regular as random ones and they have gaps and plateaus, thus structured instances have a more spread and non-uniform connectivity distribution. The instance *ii16a1* has 1650 variables and a normalized average connectivity $\overline{q}_{ii16a1} = 0.0239$. Its frequency of node degree is shown in Fig.3, along with that of a random 3-SAT instance of the same size and normalized connectivity (instance *3sat1650*) in Fig.4. We can note that the node degree frequency of the structured instance is highly asymmetric and has a peak close to 0.018, corresponding to the large gap in the cumulative frequency. Therefore, *ii16a1* has a very large number of nodes with lower connectivity than the average. Conversely, the node degree frequency of the random instance is regular and the highest peak in frequency is very close to the mean. Fig.5 and Fig.6 show the average and median error (number of unsatisfied clauses) respectively on *ii16a1* and *3sat1650* for PGSAT with different values of τ. Results are averaged over 500 trials. We first observe that also for the structured instance there exists an optimal value of τ. Nevertheless, despite the fact that the two instances have the same average connectivity, the optimal parallelism is higher for *ii16a1* than for *3sat1650*. We conjecture that the high number of nodes with low degree present in the instance *ii16a1* is the cause of higher optimal parallelism. We performed the same kind of experiments on the *logistics-a* instance, by comparing it with a random 3-SAT instance of the same size (828 variables) and normalized average connectivity $\overline{q} = 0.0275$ (instance *3sat828*). Fig.7 and Fig.8 show the respective node degree frequency. Note that the distribution of *logistics-a* is not regular and has a high peak at normalized node degree 0.0326. The results of PGSAT performance with respect to τ are plotted in Fig.9 and Fig.10. The results are analogous, but dual, to the previous ones on *ii16a1*. We can observe that also for this structured instance there is a value of τ leading to a minimum average error, but in this case the optimal parallelism for *logistics-a* is lower than that of the random instance. This difference may be explained by observing that the highest peak in *logistics-a* node degree frequency corresponds to a node degree higher than the average value, which characterizes the random instance.

We can conclude this section by considering that the results obtained clearly show that an optimal parallelism value exists also for structured instances. Nevertheless, not surprisingly, this value is strongly affected by the asymmetric frequency of node degree. In particular, we observe that the highest peaks location seem to be the most relevant characteristic influencing the optimal parallelism.

3   Morphing from Random to Structure

The results of the previous section show that for structured instances, characterized by asymmetric frequency distribution, the optimal parallelism is mostly affected by the highest peaks of node degree distribution. To investigate more deeply this difference, we generated instances with a controlled amount of *structure*, by means of a technique called *morphing* [1]. We generated instances gradually morphing from a satisfiable random 3-SAT instance to a structured one (namely, *ii16a1*). We observed[1] that the more similar the node degree frequency distributions of two instances (especially peaks location), the closer is their optimal parallelism degree.

4   Conclusion and Future Work

In this work we have compared the connectivity distribution of random and structured SAT instances and observed its impact on the parallelization of local search. We first showed that also in the case of structured instances there is a critical value of parallelism τ_{opt} that optimizes the average solution quality. Secondly, we observed that in structured instances τ_{opt} is strongly affected by the highest peaks in the node degree distribution. The definition of an automatic procedure to set τ to a near-optimal value is subject of ongoing work, along with the use of parallelization as a mechanism to adapt the balance between intensification and diversification.

We are currently exploring different ways of parallelizing local search, for example by probabilistic flips, such that each variable flips with a probability which depends on the increase of number of satisfied clauses. Moreover, we are studying the relations between SAT/MAXSAT instance connectivity and properties of the search landscape and we are configuring experiments to check whether a phase transition exists also in the case of PGSAT on SAT/MAXSAT problems.

There are several open issues to explore, like the exploitation of graph properties to define the subsets of strongly connected variables (instead of dividing variables at random), the investigation of the relation between criticality and parallelism and the introduction of noise in local search, the study of other graph characteristics, like diameter, clustering and *small world* properties [8].

Acknowledgments

I thank Michela Milano for her support, helpful discussions and suggestions. I also thank the anonymous reviewers for useful comments.

References

[1] I. P. Gent, H. H. Hoos, P. Prosser, and T. Walsh. Morphing: Combining structure and randomness. In *Proceedings of AAAI99*, pages 654–660, 1999.

[2] H. Hoos and T. Stützle. SATLIB: An online resource for research on SAT. In I. Gent, H. van Maaren, and T. Walsh, editors, *SAT2000: Highlights of Satisfiability Research in the Year 2000*, pages 283– 292. IOS Press, 2000.

[3] S. A. Kauffman and W. Macready. Technological evolution and adaptive organizations. *Complexity*, 26(2):26–43, March 1995.

---

[1] Due to lack of space, graphs are omitted. A longer version of this paper is available as LIA Technical report at www.lia.deis.unibo.it/research/TechReport.html.

[4] W. G. Macready and S. A. Kauffman A. G. Siapas. Criticality and parallelism in combinatorial optimization. *Science*, 271:56–59, January 1996.

[5] A. Roli. Criticality and parallelism in GSAT. *Electronic Notes in Discrete Mathematics*, 9, 2001.

[6] A. Roli and C. Blum. Critical Parallelization of Local Search for MAX–SAT. In *AI*IA2001: Advances in Artificial Intelligence*, volume 2175 of *Lecture Notes in Artificial Intelligence*, pages 147–158. Springer, 2001.

[7] B. Selman, H. J. Levesque, and D. Mitchell. A new method for solving hard satisfiability problems. In *Proceedings of the Tenth National Conference on Artificial Intelligence*, pages 440–446, 1992.

[8] T. Walsh. Search in a small world. In *proceedings of IJCAI99*, pages 1172–1177, 1999.

[9] T. Walsh. Search on high degree graphs. In *Proceedings of IJCAI-2001*, 2001.

Characterizing SAT Problems
with the Row Convexity Property*

Hachemi Bennaceur[1] and Chu Min Li[2]

[1] LIPN, Institut Galilée, Université Paris 13
Av. J.B. Clément 93240 Villetaneuse, France
hachemi.bennaceur@lipn.univ-paris13.fr
[2] LaRIA, Université de Picardie Jules Verne
5 Rue du Moulin Neuf, 80000 Amiens, France
cli@laria.u-picardie.fr

Abstract. Using the literal encoding of the satisfiability problem (SAT) as a binary constraint satisfaction problem (CSP), we relate the path consistency concept and the row convexity of CSPs with the inference rules in the propositional logic field. Then, we use this result to propose a measure characterizing satisfiable and unsatisfiable 3-SAT instances. The correlation between the computational results allows us to validate this measure.

1 Introduction

The relationship between constraint satisfaction problems (CSPs) and propositional satisfiability (SAT) is explored by studying the mappings between them [7]. In this paper, we extend this connection by relating some concepts used in this two frameworks, and propose a measure characterizing satisfiable and unsatisfiable 3-SAT instances. This work is based on the literal encoding of the satisfiability problem (SAT) as a binary constraint satisfaction problem (CSP) [1]. Using this encoding, it is shown that arc consistency is equivalent to unit resolution [7, 2]. In the first part of this paper, we generalize this result by relating the path consistency concept with unit and binary resolution rules (unit and binary resolutions will be defined later) in the propositional logic. In the second part of this paper, we relate the row convexity property of CSPs with the pure literal rule and then we use this result to propose a measure characterizing satisfiable and unsatisfiable 3-SAT instances. The correlation between the computational experiment results allows us to validate this measure. CSP and SAT formalisms and some basic definition are described in [3], which also contains all the proofs of our results.

---

* This work is partially supported by French CNRS under grant number SUB/2001/0111/DR16

2   Path Consistency and Inference Rules

In this section, we relate the unit and binary resolution rules with the path consistency. Let S denotes a SAT problem and $P(S)$ its associated CSP.

Definition 1. *We call Unit (resp. Binary) Resolution the resolution rule applied to two clauses of which at least one is unary (resp. binary).*

Let UR(S) denote the Unit Resolution closure of S. It is shown that:

Theorem 1. *[7] Computing $UR(S)$ allows to achieve arc consistency on $P(S)$.*

Let $BUR(S)$ denote the Binary and Unit Resolution closure of S. We have the following result generalizing Theorem 1 and relating strong path consistency to unit and binary resolution.

Theorem 2. *Computing $BUR(S)$ allows to achieve strong path consistency on $P(S)$, i.e., if $BUR(S)$ does not contain empty clause, after removing the value $\bar{l}$ from all domains in $P(S)$ for each unit clause l in $BUR(S)$, and after removing the pair (l_1, l_2) from all relations in $P(S)$ for each clause $\bar{l}_1 \vee \bar{l}_2$, $\bar{l}_1$ or $\bar{l}_2$ in $BUR(S)$, $P(S)$ becomes strongly path consistent.*

3   Characterization of Satisfiable and Unsatisfiable 3-SAT Instances

We first relate the row convexity property of CSPs with the pure literal rule and then we present a measure characterizing satisfiable and unsatisfiable 3-SAT instances.

3.1   Row Convexity

Van Beek and Dechter have identified a tractable class of CSPs for which a solution can be found using a path consistency algorithm [6]. The result is based on the row convexity property. A binary relation between two variables X_i and X_j of a CSP may be represented as a (0-1)-matrix with $|D_i|$ rows and $|D_j|$ columns by imposing an ordering on the domains of the variables. A zero at the intersection of row r and column c means that the pair consisting of the rth element of D_i and the cth element of D_j is not allowed; a one at this intersection means that the pair is allowed. A (0-1)-matrix is row convex if in each row there is no two 1 separated by 0. A relation is row convex if its associated matrix is row convex.

Definition 2. *[6] Given an ordering of the variables $X_1, ..., X_n$, a binary CSP is directionally row-convex if each of the (0,1)-matrices of R_{ij}, where variable X_i occurs before variable X_j in the ordering, is row convex.*

Theorem 3. *[6] Let P be a path consistent binary CSP. If there exists an ordering of the variables $X_1, ..., X_n$ and of the domains $D_1, ..., D_n$ of P such that P is directionally row convex, then a solution can be found without backtracking using a path consistency algorithm.*

Corollary 1. *The satisfiability problems containing only binary clauses (2-SAT) can be solved using a path consistency algorithm.*

3.2   Row Convexity and the Pure Literal Rule

The following result relates the row convexity property with the pure literal rule using the literal encoding of a 3-SAT instance.

Lemma 1. *Let S be a 3-SAT instance and $P(S)$ its associated CSP. If $P(S)$ is directionally row convex then there exists in S a pure literal.*

Theorem 4. *Let m be the number of clauses of S. $P(S)$ is directionally row convex iff there exists a partition $S_1, ..., S_k : (1 \le k \le m)$ of the set of clauses S such that S contains a pure literal which occurs only in the clauses of S_1, and each set of clauses $S - (S_1 \cup ... \cup S_i) : (1 \le i < k)$ contains a pure literal.*

3.3   Measure Characterizing Satisfiable and Unsatisfiable 3-SAT Instances

We are searching for the relationship between the satisfiability of a SAT instance and its (directional) row convexity. If the SAT instance S is unsatisfiable, $P(S)$ is necessarily non directionally row convex. We are interested in the question: what is the non convexity point beyond which S is unsatisfiable (if the point exists)?

In order to answer the question, we define the minimal row non-convexity NC of a 3-SAT instance to be the smallest number of row non-convex $(0,1)$-matrices representing the constraints for any variable and value ordering. We use a simple heuristic shown in figure 1 to estimate NC for a 3-SAT instance.

The MinimalRowNonConvexity procedure essentially computes an ordering of clauses in the initial S and of literals in each clause. If $P(S)$ is directionally row convex, the procedure returns 0 and is similar to the FindOrder procedure in [6], otherwise it computes the number of row non-convex $(0,1)$-matrices under the ordering. To see this, it is sufficient to note that only the $(0,1)$-matrices between clauses removed at the same stage of the algorithm can have zeros separating two ones, because of the complementary literal in the middle position (if any). The counting of the number of occurrences of variables can be done in $O(n+m)$ time, where m and n are respectively the number of clauses and variables in S. So the complexity of the MinimalRowNonConvexity procedure is $O(n(n+m))$.

Procedure MinimalRowNonConvexity(S)
Begin
NC:=0;
repeat
    let $neg(x)$ and $pos(x)$ denote the number of positive and negative
    occurrences of variable x in the current S;
    select x such that $neg(x) * pos(x)$ is the smallest,
    break tie by choosing x such that $neg(x) + pos(x)$ is the largest;
    remove all clauses containing x or $\bar{x}$ from S,
    for every removed clause c, record its removing time $f(c)$;
    Order the literals of the removed clauses such that x or $\bar{x}$
    is in the middle position;
    NC:=$NC + neg(x) * pos(x)$;
until S becomes empty;
put all removed clauses in order of $f(c)$;
return NC;
End

Fig. 1.

4   Experimentation

We try to estimate the satisfiability of a 3-SAT instance using its NC. Before
being able to do this, we use the MinimalRowNonConvexity procedure to estimate NC for a large sample of random 3-SAT instances. We vary n from 300
to 450 incrementing by 50 and m so that $m/n = 4, 4.1, 4.2, 4.25, 4.3, 4.4, 4.5$ respectively. Empirically, when the ratio m/n is near 4.25, S is unsatisfiable with
the probability 0.5 and is the most difficult to solve [5]. The number of instances
included in our study at each point $(m/n, n)$ are as follows : 3000 instances for
$m/n = 4$ and n varying from 300 to 450, 1000 instances for m/n varying from
4,1 to 4,5 and n=300 and n=350. 600 and 400 instances are solved respectively
for n=400 and n=450, and m/n varying from 4,1 to 4,5.

    In order to compare the minimal row non-convexity NC of satisfiable and
unsatisfiable instances, we solve these instances using Satz [4] and divide the
instances at each point into satisfiable class and unsatisfiable class. In the sequel,
we directly denote by NC the average estimated minimal row non-convexity of a

Table 1. Ratio NC/n for satisfiable (left) and unsatisfiable (right) instances at
each point $(m/n, n)$

	300	350	400	450	300	350	400	450
4	3.35 (2983)	3.34 (2998)	3.34 (2999)	3.34 (2999)	3.47 (17)	3.55 (2)	3.43 (1)	3.55 (1)
4.1	3.58 (944)	3.57 (972)	3.56 (582)	3.57 (392)	3.69 (56)	3.64 (28)	3.65 (18)	3.64 (8)
4.2	3.80 (715)	3.79 (746)	3.79 (452)	3.79 (307)	3.88 (285)	3.86 (254)	3.86 (148)	3.84 (93)
4.25	3.90 (551)	3.91 (547)	3.90 (319)	3.90 (224)	3.99 (449)	3.98 (453)	3.96 (281)	3.95 (176)
4.3	4.02 (370)	4.02 (353)	4.01 (197)	4.00 (128)	4.10 (630)	4.08 (647)	4.08 (403)	4.08 (272)
4.4	4.24 (128)	4.25 (85)	4.22 (46)	4.23 (27)	4.34 (872)	4.32 (915)	4.32 (554)	4.32 (373)
4.5	4.51 (32)	4.49 (11)	4.43 (5)	4.45 (4)	4.59 (968)	4.58 (989)	4.58 (595)	4.58 (396)

Table 2. Ratio NC/n for satisfiable (left) and unsatisfiable (right) instances at each point $(m/n, n)$. At points (360, 4) and (380, 4), none of the 1000 solved instances is unsatisfiable

	220	240	260	280	320	340	360	380	220	240	260	280	320	340	360	380
4	3.36	3.36	3.35	3.35	3.35	3.34	3.34	3.34	3.47	3.47	3.51	3.46	3.45	3.53	-	-
4.1	3.59	3.58	3.57	3.58	3.57	3.56	3.56	3.56	3.70	3.69	3.69	3.65	3.65	3.66	3.69	3.61
4.2	3.81	3.81	3.80	3.80	3.80	3.79	3.79	3.79	3.89	3.89	3.89	3.88	3.86	3.86	3.86	3.85
4.25	3.92	3.91	3.90	3.91	3.92	3.89	3.90	3.90	4.00	4.00	3.99	3.99	3.99	3.97	3.97	3.96
4.3	4.03	4.02	4.02	4.02	4.02	4.00	4.00	4.01	4.12	4.11	4.10	4.09	4.09	4.07	4.08	4.07
4.4	4.26	4.23	4.26	4.25	4.24	4.22	4.23	4.24	4.35	4.35	4.34	4.34	4.33	4.31	4.32	4.31
4.5	4.51	4.47	4.43	4.48	4.43	4.44	4.43	4.51	4.61	4.60	4.60	4.59	4.59	4.57	4.57	4.57

class of instances. It is clear that satisfiable instances have smaller NC. Table 1 shows the ratio NC/n in boldface (and the number of instances averaged between parentheses) at each point $(m/n, n)$ for satisfiable and unsatisfiable instances.

We have empirically observed from table 1 that the ratio NC/n tends to be a constant for a given value m/n and a class, except for the points where few instances are solved (e.g. unsatisfiable instances for $m/n = 4$, satisfiable instances for $m/n = 4.5$). This is particularly true for satisfiable instances when $m/n \leq 4.25$ and for unsatisfiable instances when $m/n > 4.25$. The difference of NC/n between satisfiable and unsatisfiables classes tends to become larger when $m/n < 4.2$ and $m/n > 4.3$ (except the point $m/n = 4$ where there are few unsatisfiable instances and the point $m/n = 4.5$ where there are few satisfiable instances), which can be used to explain the threshold phenomenon.

To verify the phenomenon, we solve a large sample of instances at other points from $n = 220$ to $n = 380$ increasing by step 20 (excluding $n = 300$). 1000 instances are solved at each point. Table 2 shows the ratio NC/n at these points. Note that there are always few unsatisfiable instances when $m/n = 4$ and few satisfiable instances when $m/n = 4.5$.

It appears that the ratio NC/n could be used to estimate the satisfiability of a given random 3-SAT instance. For example, we know that an instance near the threshold $(m/n = 4.25)$ is satisfiable with an empirical probability 0.5. However if $NC/n < 3.90$, it should be more likely satisfiable. One might also think that a reason for the unsatisfiability of an instance is the large number of its row non-convex (0-1)-matrices.

For random 3-SAT, NC/n gives a more precise indication for the satisfiability of an instance than the simple ratio m/n. Following this indication, different strategies can be applied to solve the instance. Furthermore, NC/n might be helpful for the branching heuristic: branching variable should be chosen so that the two generated subproblems are more likely unsatisfiable [4]. Finally, we are especially interested in the relationship between NC/n and the number of the solutions of a SAT instance.

References

[1] Bennaceur H., *The Satisfiability problem regarded as constraint-satisfaction problem*, In the proceeding of the 12th European Conference on Artificial Intelligence, Page 125-130, Budapest, Hungary, August 1996.

[2] Bennaceur H. *A comparison between SAT and CSP techniques*, Research Report LIPN 2001-10.

[3] Bennaceur H., Li C. M., *Characterizing SAT Problems with the Row Convexity Property*, Research report LaRIA-2002-08, June 2002. See http://www.laria.u-picardie.fr/~cli

[4] Li C. M., *A constraint-based approach to narrow search trees for satisfiability*, Information Processing Letters, 71:75–80, 1999.

[5] Mitchell, D, Selman, B., Levesque H., *Hard and Easy Distributions of SAT Problems*, In Proceedings of AAAI'92, pages 459-465, San Jose, CA, 1992.

[6] Van Beek P., Dechter R., *On the Minimality and Global Consistency of Row-Convex Constraint Networks*, Journal of the ACM, 42:543-561, 1995.

[7] Walsh T., *SAT v CSP*, in Proceedings of CP-2000, pages 441-456, Springer-Verlag LNCS-1894, 2000.

Interchangeability in Soft CSPs

Stefano Bistarelli[1], Boi Faltings[2], and Nicoleta Neagu[2]

[1] Istituto di Informatica e Telematica (IIT), CNR, Pisa, Italy
Stefano.Bistarelli@iit.cnr.it
[2] Artificial Intelligence Laboratory (LIA), EPFL, Ecublens, Switzerland
boi.faltings,nicoleta.neagu@epfl.ch

Abstract. Substitutability and interchangeability in constraint satisfaction problems (CSPs) have been used as a basis for search heuristics, solution adaptation and abstraction techniques. In this paper, we consider how the same concepts can be extended to *soft* constraint satisfaction problems (SCSPs).

We introduce the notions of *threshold* α and *degradation* δ for substitutability and interchangeability. In $_\alpha$interchangeability, values are interchangeable in any solution that is better than a threshold α, thus allowing to disregard differences among solutions that are not sufficiently good anyway. In $^\delta$interchangeability, values are interchangeable if their exchange could not degrade the solution by more than a factor of δ.

Theorems, algorithms to compute $(^\delta/_\alpha)$interchangeable sets of values, and a more general treatment of all the ideas presented in this paper can be found in [2].

1 Introduction

Substitutability and interchangeability in CSPs have been introduced by Freuder ([8]) in 1991 with the intention of improving search efficiency for solving CSP.

Interchangeability has since found other applications in abstraction frameworks ([10, 15, 8, 5]) and solution adaptation ([14, 11]). One of the difficulties with interchangeability has been that it does not occur very frequently.

In many practical applications, constraints can be violated at a cost, and solving a CSP thus means finding a value assignment of minimum cost. Various frameworks for solving such soft constraints have been proposed [9, 6, 12, 7, 13, 3, 4, 1]. The soft constraints framework of c-semirings [3, 1] has been shown to express most of the known variants through different instantiations of its operators, and this is the framework we are considering in this paper.

The most straightforward generalization of interchangeability to soft CSP would require that exchanging one value for another does not change the quality of the solution at all. This generalization is likely to suffer from the same weaknesses as interchangeability in hard CSP, namely that it is very rare.

Fortunately, soft constraints also allow weaker forms of interchangeability where exchanging values may result in a degradation of solution quality by some measure δ. By allowing more degradation, it is possible to increase

P. Van Hentenryck (Ed.): CP 2002, LNCS 2470, pp. 726–731, 2002.
© Springer-Verlag Berlin Heidelberg 2002

the amount of interchangeability in a problem to the desired level. We define $^{\delta}$substitutability/interchangeability as a concept which ensures this quality. This is particularly useful when interchangeability is used for solution adaptation.

Another use of interchangeability is to reduce search complexity by grouping together values that would never give a sufficiently good solution. In $_{\alpha}$substitutability/interchangeability, we consider values interchangeable if they give equal solution quality in all solutions better than α, but possibly different quality for solutions whose quality is $\leq \alpha$.

Just like for hard constraints, full interchangeability is hard to compute, but can be approximated by neighbourhood interchangeability which can be computed efficiently and implies full interchangeability. We define the same concepts for soft constraints.

2 Background

2.1 Soft CSPs

A soft constraint may be seen as a constraint where each instantiations of its variables has an associated value from a partially ordered set which can be interpreted as a set of preference values. Combining constraints will then have to take into account such additional values, and thus the formalism has also to provide suitable operations for combination ($\times$) and comparison ($+$) of tuples of values and constraints. This is why this formalization is based on the concept of c-semiring $S = \langle A, +, \times, \mathbf{0}, \mathbf{1} \rangle$, which is just a set A plus two operations[1].

Constraint Problems. Given a semiring $S = \langle A, +, \times, \mathbf{0}, \mathbf{1} \rangle$ and an ordered set of variables V over a finite domain D, a *constraint* is a function which, given an assignment $\eta : V \to D$ of the variables, returns a value of the semiring.

By using this notation we define $\mathcal{C} = \eta \to A$ as the set of all possible constraints that can be built starting from S, D and V.

Consider a constraint $c \in \mathcal{C}$. We define his support as $supp(c) = \{v \in V \mid \exists \eta, d_1, d_2.c\eta[v := d_1] \neq c\eta[v := d_2]\}$, where

$$\eta[v := d]v' = \begin{cases} d & \text{if } v = v', \\ \eta v' & \text{otherwise.} \end{cases}$$

Note that $c\eta[v := d_1]$ means $c\eta'$ where η' is η modified with the association $v := d_1$ (that is the operator $[\,]$ has precedence over application).

Fig. 1 shows the graph representation of a fuzzy CSP[2]. Variables and constraints are represented respectively by nodes and by undirected (unary for c_1 and c_3 and binary for c_2) arcs, and semiring values are written to the right of the corresponding tuples. Here we assume that the domain D of the variables contains only elements a and b and c.

---

[1] In [3] several properties of the structure are discussed. Let us just remind that it is possible to define a partial order $\leq_S$ over A such that $a \leq_S b$ iff $a + b = b$.

[2] Fuzzy CSPs can be modeled in the SCSP framework by choosing the c-semiring $S_{FCSP} = \langle [0,1], max, min, 0, 1 \rangle$.

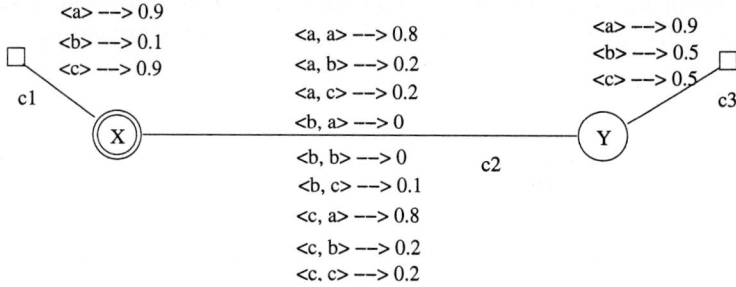

Fig. 1. A fuzzy CSP

Combining soft constraints. When there is a set of soft constraints $\mathcal{C}$, the combined weight of the constraints is computed using the operator $\otimes : \mathcal{C} \times \mathcal{C} \to \mathcal{C}$ is defined as $(c_1 \otimes c_2)\eta = c_1\eta \times_S c_2\eta$.

For instance, consider again the fuzzy CSP of Fig. 1. For the tuple $\langle a, a \rangle$ (that is, $x = y = a$), we have to compute the minimum between 0.9 (which is the value assigned to $x = a$ in constraint c_1), 0.8 (which is the value assigned to $\langle x = a, y = a \rangle$ in c_2) and 0.9 (which is the value for $y = a$ in c_3). Hence, the resulting value for this tuple is 0.8.

2.2   Interchangeability

Interchangeability in constraint networks has been first proposed by Freuder [8] to capture equivalence among values of a variable in a discrete constraint satisfaction problem. Value $v = a$ is *substitutable* for $v = b$ if for any solution where $v = a$, there is an identical solution except that $v = b$. Values $v = a$ and $v = b$ are *interchangeable* if they are substitutable both ways.

3   Interchangeability in Soft CSPs

In soft CSPs, there is no crisp notion of consistency. In fact, each tuple is a possible solution, but with different level of preference. Therefore, in this framework, the notion of interchangeability become finer: to say that values a and b are interchangeable we have also to consider the assigned semiring level.

More precisely, if a domain element a assigned to variable v can be substituted in each tuple solution with a domain element b without obtaining a worse semiring level we say that b is full substitutable for a.

Definition 1 (Full Substitutability (FS)). *Consider two domain values b and a for a variable v, and the set of constraints C; we say that b is Full Substitutable for a on v ($b \in FS_v(a)$) if and only if $\bigotimes C\eta[v := a] \leq_S \bigotimes C\eta[v := b]$*

When we restrict this notion only to the set of constraints C_v that involve variable v we obtain a local version of substitutability.

Definition 2 (Neighborhood Substitutability (NS)). *Consider two domain values b and a for a variable v, and the set of constraints C_v involving v;*

we say that b is neighborhood substitutable for a on v ($b \in NS_v(a)$) if and only if $\bigotimes C_v \eta[v := a] \leq_S \bigotimes C_v \eta[v := b]$

When the relations hold in both directions, we have the notion of Full/Neighborhood interchangeability of b with a.

Definition 3 (Full and Neighborhood Interchangeability (*FI* and *NI*)). *Consider two domain values b and a, for a variable v, the set of all constraints C and the set of constraints C_v involving v. We say that b is Full interchangeable with a on v ($FI_v(a/b)$) if and only if $b \in FS_v(a)$ and $a \in FS_v(b)$. We say that b is Neighborhood interchangeable with a on v ($NI_v(a/b)$) if and only if $b \in NS_v(a)$ and $a \in NS_v(b)$.*

This means that when a and b are interchangeable for variable v they can be exchanged without affecting the level of any solution.

As an example of interchangeability and substitutability consider the fuzzy CSP represented in Fig. 1. The domain value c is neighborhood interchangeable with a on x ($NI_x(a/c)$); in fact, $c_1 \otimes c_2 \eta[x := a] = c_1 \otimes c_2 \eta[x := c]$ for all η.

The domain values c and a are also neighborhood substitutable for b on x ($\{a, c\} \in NS_v(b)$). In fact, for any η we have $c_1 \otimes c_2 \eta[x := b] \leq c_1 \otimes c_2 \eta[x := c]$ and $c_1 \otimes c_2 \eta[x := b] \leq c_1 \otimes c_2 \eta[x := a]$.

3.1 Degradations and Thresholds

In soft CSPs, it is possible to obtain more interchangeability by allowing degrading the solution quality when values are exchanged. We call this $^{\delta}$interchangeability, where δ is the *degradation* factor.

When searching for solutions to soft CSP, we can gain efficiency by not distinguishing values that could in any case not be part of a solution of sufficient quality. In $_{\alpha}$interchangeability, two values are interchangeable if they do not affect the quality of any solution with quality better than α. We call α the *threshold* factor.

Both concepts can be combined, i.e. we can allow both degradation and limit search to solutions better than a certain threshold ($^{\delta}_{\alpha}$interchangeability).

Thus we define:

Definition 4 ($^{\delta}/_{\alpha}$Full Substitutability ($^{\delta}/_{\alpha}FS$)). *Consider two domain values b and a for a variable v, the set of constraints C and the semiring levels δ and α; we say that b is $^{\delta}$full Substitutable for a on v ($b \in {}^{\delta}FS_v(a)$) if and only if for all assignments η, $\bigotimes C\eta[v := a] \times_S \delta \leq_S \bigotimes C\eta[v := b]$.*

We say that b is $_{\alpha}$full substitutable for a on v ($b \in {}_{\alpha}FS_v(a)$) if and only if for all assignments η, $\bigotimes C\eta[v := a] \geq \alpha \implies \bigotimes C\eta[v := a] \leq_S \bigotimes C\eta[v := b]$

Similar to the plain version, *neighbourhood*$^{\delta}_{\alpha}$substitutability is obtained by only evaluating the definition on the neighbourhood of a variable, and $^{\delta}_{\alpha}$interchangeability is defined as substitutability both ways.

As an example consider Fig. 1. The domain values c and b for variable y are $_{0.2}$Neighborhood Interchangeable. In fact, the tuple involving c and b only differ for the tuple $\langle b, c \rangle$ that has value 0.1 and for the tuple $\langle b, b \rangle$ that has value 0. Since we are interested only to solutions greater than 0.2, these tuples are excluded from the match.

In [2], we present a number of useful theorems relating to $^\delta_\alpha$interchangeability, in particular that $neighbourhood^\delta_\alpha$interchangeability implies $full^\delta_\alpha$interchangeability, and results on transitivity and limit cases.

4   Conclusions

Interchangeability in CSPs has found many applications for problem abstraction and solution adaptation. In this paper, we give hints to extend the concept of Interchangeability to soft CSPs in a way that maintains the attractive properties already known for hard constraints.

The two parameters α and δ allow us to express a wide range of practical situations. The threshold α is used to eliminate distinctions that would not interest us anyway, while the allowed degradation δ specifies how precisely we want to optimize our solution.

References

[1] Bistarelli, S.: Soft Constraint Solving and programming: a general framework. PhD thesis, Dipartimento di Informatica, Università di Pisa, Italy (2001) TD-2/01

[2] Bistarelli, S., Faltings, B., Neagu, N.: A definition of interchangeability for soft csps. In: Proc. of the Joint Workshop of the ERCIM Working Group on Constraints and the CologNet area on Constraint and Logic Programming on Constraint Solving and Constraint Logic Programming. (2002) Selected papers will be published in LNCS series

[3] Bistarelli, S., Montanari, U., Rossi, F.: Semiring-based Constraint Solving and Optimization. J. ACM **44** (1997)

[4] Bistarelli, S., Montanari, U., Rossi, F.: Semiring-based Constraint Logic Programming: Syntax and Semantics. TOPLAS ACM **23** (2001)

[5] Choueiry, B. Y.: Abstraction Methods for Resource Allocation. PhD thesis, EPFL PhD Thesis no 1292 (1994)

[6] Dubois, D., Fargier, H., Prade, H.: The calculus of fuzzy restrictions as a basis for flexible constraint satisfaction. In: Proc. IEEE International Conference on Fuzzy Systems. (1993)

[7] Fargier, H., Lang, J.: Uncertainty in constraint satisfaction problems: a probabilistic approach. In: Proc. European Conference on Symbolic and Qualitative Approaches to Reasoning and Uncertainty (ECSQARU). Volume 747 of LNCS. (1993)

[8] Freuder, E. C.: Eliminating interchangeable values in constraint satisfaction problems. In: Proc. of AAAI-91. (1991)

[9] Freuder, E., Wallace, R.: Partial constraint satisfaction. AI Journal **58** (1992)

[10] Haselbock, A.: Exploiting interchangeabilities in constraint satisfaction problems. In: Proc. of the 13th IJCAI. (1993)

[11] Neagu, N., Faltings, B.: Exploiting interchangeabilities for case adaptation. In: In Proc. of the 4th ICCBR01. (2001)

[12] Ruttkay, Z.: Fuzzy constraint satisfaction. In: Proc. 3rd IEEE International Conference on Fuzzy Systems. (1994)

[13] Schiex, T., Fargier, H., Verfaille, G.: Valued Constraint Satisfaction Problems: Hard and Easy Problems. In: Proc. IJCAI95. (1995)

[14] Weigel, R., Faltings, B.: Interchangeability for case adaptation in configuration problems. In: Proc. of the AAAI98 Spring Symposium on Multimodal Reasoning, Stanford, CA. (1998) TR SS-98-04

[15] Weigel, R., Faltings, B.: Compiling constraint satisfaction problems. Artificial Intelligence **115** (1999)

On Constraint Problems with Incomplete or Erroneous Data

Neil Yorke-Smith and Carmen Gervet

IC–Parc, Imperial College, London, SW7 2AZ, U.K.
{nys,cg6}@icparc.ic.ac.uk

Abstract. Real-world constraint problems abound with uncertainty. Problems with incomplete or erroneous data are often simplified at present to tractable deterministic models, or modified using error correction methods, with the aim of seeking a solution. However, this can lead us to solve the wrong problem because of the approximations made, an outcome of little help to the user who expects the right problem to be tackled and correct information returned. The certainty closure framework aims at fulfilling these expectations of correct, reliable reasoning in the presence of uncertain data. In this short paper we give an intuition and brief overview of the framework. We define the certainty closure to an uncertain constraint problem and show how it can be derived by transformation to an equivalent certain problem. We outline an application of the framework to a real-world network traffic analysis problem.

1 Motivation

Real-world Large Scale Combinatorial Optimisation problems (LSCOs) have inherent data uncertainties. The uncertainty can be due to the dynamic and unpredictable nature of the commercial world, but also due to the information available to those modelling the problem. In this paper we are concerned with the latter form of uncertainty, which can arise when the data is not fully known or is even erroneous. This work is motivated by practical issues we faced when working on two real-world applications, the first in energy trading [4] and the second in network traffic analysis [5].

In both applications the data information is incomplete or erroneous. In the energy trading problem, the demand and cost profiles have evolved due to market privatisation; the only data available is the profiles from previous years. Thus the existing simulation or stochastic data models would not help address the actual problem after market deregulation. In the network traffic analysis problem, we are forced to use partial data due to the overwhelming amount of information. Further, the data can be erroneous due to unrecorded packet loss or time gaps between readings of router tables.

In such cases, to grasp the actual complexity of the LSCO and bring useful feedback to the user, it is crucial to deal with real data despite its incompleteness or intrinsic errors. The core question is how to ensure that the correct problem is formulated and that correct information is derived.

P. Van Hentenryck (Ed.): CP 2002, LNCS 2470, pp. 732–737, 2002.

We propose a formal framework, based on the CSP formalism, that can be applied to the heterogeneous constraint classes and computation domains found in real-world LSCOs. The contribution of the certainty closure framework is three-fold:

- **Data as a primary concept.** We complete the CSP-based description of a LSCO by bringing data as a primary concept into the CSP formalism. We model explicitly what is known about the uncertain data (for instance, by an interval of values) in terms of an *Uncertain Constraint Satisfaction Problem*. The absence of approximation and data correction allows us to separate the data issues from those related to the constraint model.
- **Closure of a UCSP.** We introduce the *certainty closure*, a correct set of solutions to the UCSP that excludes no solution possible given the present knowledge of the data. We do not attempt to compute an unwarranted single 'solution'. Rather, the certainty closure can provide useful insight into the uncertain problem, for instance by identifying actual reasons for unsatisfiability.
- **Correctness and tractability.** The paradigm we follow is model accuracy: correctness of the information derived without approximations or assumptions. We propose two resolution forms to derive the certainty closure: enumeration and transformation. The latter, central to our contribution, aims at reasoning about the UCSP by transforming it into an equivalent CSP.

Our purpose in essence consists of introducing to constraint programming concepts and properties that enable us to reason about these classes of problems. In order to ensure the practical value of the framework, we address specifically how the closure of an uncertain constraint problem can be derived in a tractable way.

2 Uncertain CSP: Intuition

We give an intuition of the certainty closure framework by applying it to an example of the networking problem. Consider the fragment of an IP network shown in Fig. 1. Four nodes, corresponding to routers and designated A to D, are shown, together with the bidirectional traffic flow on each link. Each router makes decisions on how to direct traffic it receives, based on a routing algorithm and local flow information. The problem is to determine guaranteed bounds for the traffic flow between end-points from measurements made at routers [5].

The network can be modelled as a CSP. The variables are the volume of traffic, $V_{ij} \in \mathbb{R}^+$, entering at node i and leaving at node j. The constraints state that the volume of traffic through each link in each direction is the sum of the traffic entering the link in that direction. There is also an upper bound on the flows that use only a single link, such as V_{ab} and V_{ad}.

Due to the volume of information required to represent the traffic data exactly, and to the time gap between reading router tables, it is not possible to sample the true traffic in an entire network at one instant. Instead, we measure

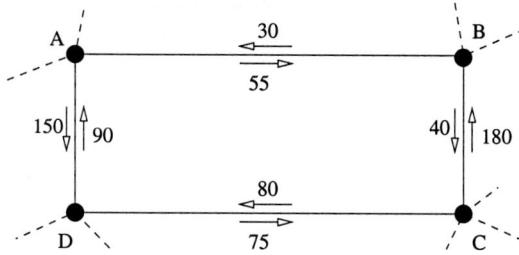

Fig. 1. Traffic flow in a network fragment

the aggregated flow volume on a link over a given time interval, and derive the volume of traffic on the link as the difference between end and start measurements. The result is that the data information obtained is inevitably incomplete and erroneous. On the link D→C, for example, the flow might measure as 70 at D and as 80 at C, whereas the true value, equal at both nodes, is presumably somewhere between. Classically, we might choose one value in the possible range to work with: the median, for instance.

Secondly, when there are two paths of equal cost (from the perspective of the routing algorithm), the traffic is split equally between them in 90% of cases. This is true for flows from A to C, for example. To simplify the model, the current approach assumes that the traffic is split equally in all such cases. Supposing these modelling decisions, consider the traffic flow problem. There are eight traffic constraints:

A→D $V_{ad} + 0.5V_{ac} + 0.5V_{bd} = 150$

D→C $V_{dc} + 0.5V_{db} + 0.5V_{ac} = 75$

C→B $V_{cb} + 0.5V_{ca} + 0.5V_{db} = 180$

B→A $V_{ba} + 0.5V_{bd} + 0.5V_{ca} = 30$

(the other four similarly in the clockwise direction).

Unfortunately, the CSP is unsatisfiable. The current approach to the problem uses a data correction procedure (minimising deviation on the link volumes) in order to reach a satisfiable model. Another common interpretation would be that the problem is simply over-constrained. But could the lack of solution be due to the assumptions and approximations made? Suppose we do not attempt error correction and, further, model the actual dispatching of traffic, known to be anywhere between 30–70% between two paths. The more accurate CSP that results is again unsatisfiable.

At this point the erroneous approximation to the traffic flow data becomes clear. Let us remove all approximations and represent the uncertain flow measurements explicitly. Modelling the problem as an uncertain CSP, we have:

A→D $V_{ad} + [0.3, 0.7]V_{ac} + [0.3, 0.7]V_{bd} = [135, 160]$

D→C $V_{dc} + [0.3, 0.7]V_{db} + [0.3, 0.7]V_{ac} = [70, 80]$

$$C \rightarrow B \qquad V_{cb} + [0.3, 0.7]V_{ca} + [0.3, 0.7]V_{db} = [180, 190]$$
$$B \rightarrow A \qquad V_{ba} + [0.3, 0.7]V_{bd} + [0.3, 0.7]V_{ca} = [25, 40]$$

We cannot hope to give a single value assignment and declare it to be 'the' true solution; however we can give an interval for each variable and assert that any possible solution lies within. Hence the best information we can produce based on the new traffic flow model is: $V_{ac} \in [0, 150], V_{ad} \in [30, 64], V_{db} \in [32, 200], V_{dc} \in [0, 40], V_{ca} \in [0, 133], V_{cb} \in [17, 64], V_{bd} \in [0, 133]$, and $V_{ba} \in [0, 20]$ (and the four single-link flows in the clockwise direction). This is the certainty closure. The system tells us that there is a solution to the problem that corresponds to at least one possible realisation of the data. If more information about the data becomes available to us, then it will be possible to refine the closure.

This illustrative introduction to uncertain constraint problems highlights the main aspects of uncertain constraint models and benefits of the certainty closure framework. It shows in particular that model accuracy and reliable quantitative results can be more valuable than seeking a solution at the cost of correctness. Further, representing incomplete or erroneous data adequately can reveal the true reason for model unsatisfiability.

In the sequel we outline how the closure can be obtained in a tractable manner.

3   Finding the Closure: Overview

Informally, an *uncertain CSP* is a simple extension to a classical CSP with an explicit description of the data. The *certainty closure* of an uncertain CSP P is the union of solutions to P such that every solution that is feasible under one or more realisations of P is contained in the closure. A *realisation* of the data is the selection of one value for each data coefficient from its *uncertainty set* of possible values; each realisation gives rise from P to a classical, certain CSP. While the examples here use intervals for the uncertainty set, since this is the form of the data in the networking problem, in general the data may be represented in any way — a set of values, an interval, an ellipsoid, or otherwise — as fits the computation domain.

We have identified two resolution forms to derive the certainty closure: enumeration and transformation. The first is to consider every data realisation: each gives rise to a certain CSP, which we solve, and the closure is then formed from all the solutions to the satisfiable CSPs. Unfortunately this approach can be exponential in the number of CSPs generated and is not suited to handling continuous data. The second form is to transform the uncertain CSP into a single, equivalent certain CSP. The objective is to ensure both correctness and tractability by seeking a CSP which can be solved efficiently using existing techniques, and whose complete solution set coincides with the certainty closure of the UCSP. For space reasons we will only outline the transformation method.

Solving an Equivalent CSP This resolution form consists of transforming the uncertain constraint problem to an equivalent certain problem, solvable by existing resolution techniques. The transformation aims at deriving a standard CSP model that has (or contains, in the worst case) the same set of solutions as the UCSP. The theoretical issues related to the approach are: (i) the identification of the constraint classes that allow us to find a transformation operator, and (ii) the definition of the transformation operator and its properties such that the two problems are solution-equivalent.

Without describing in details the properties of the operator, we briefly outline the transformation operation we have implemented for the networking problem. The UCSP corresponding to the problem has linear network flow constraints with positive real intervals as coefficients; it is an instance of a *positive orthant interval linear system*[1]. We illustrate the transformation on linear constraints over two variables X_1 and X_2 with domains in $\mathbb{R}^+$. Suppose uncertain constraints of the form $\mathbf{a_1} X_1 + \mathbf{a_2} X_2 \leq \mathbf{a_3}$, where $\mathbf{a_i} = [\underline{\mathbf{a_i}}, \overline{\mathbf{a_i}}]$ are real, closed intervals. Then the operator transforms each constraint separately in the following way:

$$\mathbf{a_1} X_1 + \mathbf{a_2} X_2 \leq \mathbf{a_3} \rightarrow \begin{cases} \underline{\mathbf{a_1}} X_1 + \underline{\mathbf{a_2}} X_2 \leq \overline{\mathbf{a_3}} & \text{if } \underline{\mathbf{a_2}} \geq 0 \\ \underline{\mathbf{a_1}} X_1 + \overline{\mathbf{a_2}} X_2 \leq \underline{\mathbf{a_3}} & \text{if } 0 \in \mathbf{a_2} \\ \overline{\mathbf{a_1}} X_1 + \overline{\mathbf{a_2}} X_2 \leq \underline{\mathbf{a_3}} & \text{if } \overline{\mathbf{a_2}} < 0 \end{cases}$$

We can prove that the transformation is generic to any system of linear constraints, and that it correctly and tightly yields the certainty closure. The transformed constraint problem can be solved by using linear programming. The upper and lower bounds on the possible values for each variable X_i are found by solving two linear programs, with objective $\max X_i$ and $\min X_i$ respectively. We thus obtain the projection of the certainty closure onto the domain of each variable. This gives guaranteed bounds for each end-to-end traffic flow.

4   Discussion

We have introduced the certainty closure as a generic framework to reason about constraint problems with data uncertainty, focusing on incomplete and erroneous data. The framework is complementary to stochastic data models (e.g. [6]). Our current research looks at finding uncertain constraint classes and their corresponding tractable transformation operators.

Existing approaches to data uncertainty in CP come from a different perspective. Most authors consider uncertainty due to a dynamic and unpredictable environment and thus seek robust solutions that hold under the most possible realisations of the data. We are not aware of any work in CP aimed at building correct solution sets in the presence of erroneous data, the closest being work on interval CSPs in the presence of universally quantified variables [2]. Our work in concept is more closely related to that in operational research [1] and control theory [3].

---

[1] In 2D, for instance, the positive orthant is the upper-right quadrant.

Acknowledgements

This work was partially supported by the EPSRC under grant GR/N64373/01. The authors thank the anonymous reviewers for their suggestions.

References

[1] Ben-Tal, A. and Nemirovski, A. Robust convex optimization. *Mathematics of Operations Research*, **23** (1998).

[2] Benhamou, F. and Goualard, F. Universally quantified interval constraints. In: *CP-2000*.

[3] Elishakoff, I. Convex modeling — a generalization of interval analysis for nonprobabilistic treatment of uncertainty. In: *Proc. of the Intl. Workshop on Applications of Interval Computations (APIC'95)*, El Paso, TX, 76–79 (1995).

[4] Gervet, C., Caseau, Y. and Montaut, D. On refining ill-defined constraint problems: A case study in iterative prototyping. In: *Proc. of PACLP'99*, London, 255–275 (1999).

[5] Gervet, C. and Rodošek, R. RiskWise-2 problem definition. IC–Parc Internal Report (2000).

[6] Walsh, T. Stochastic constraint programming. In: *Proc. of AAAI'01 Fall Symposium on Using Uncertainty within Computation*, Cape Cod, MA, 129–135 (2001).

Heuristic Constraint Propagation[*]

Meinolf Sellmann[1] and Warwick Harvey[2]

[1] University of Paderborn, Department of Mathematics and Computer Science
Fürstenallee 11, D-33102 Paderborn
sello@uni-paderborn.de
[2] IC-Parc, Imperial College
Exhibition Road, London SW7 2AZ, UK
wh@icparc.ic.ac.uk

Abstract. For NP-hard constraint satisfaction problems the existence
of a feasible solution cannot be decided efficiently. Applying a tree search
often results in the exploration of parts of the search space that do not
contain feasible solutions at all. Redundant constraints can help to detect
inconsistencies of partial assignments higher up in the search tree. Using
the social golfer problem as an example we show how complex redundant
constraints can be propagated incompletely using local search heuristics.

Keywords: redundant constraints, local search, incomplete propagation, social golfer problem

1 Introduction

Assume we are given an NP-hard constraint satisfaction problem (CSP). Even
though there is no proof that we cannot solve the problem efficiently, there is
strong empirical evidence that we cannot compute a solution in polynomial time.
The common approach is to explore the search space in some sophisticated manner that tries to consider huge parts implicitly. For CSPs, e.g. when performing
tree search, that means we try to cut off preferably large parts of the tree that
do not contain any feasible solutions through domain filtering algorithms. If we
find that the search expands too many nodes, we may wish to spend more time
at each node in an attempt to reduce the number of nodes explored. A common
way to do this is to add redundant constraints; these can result in inconsistencies
being detected higher up in the search tree. However, since checking whether a
given partial assignment is extendible to a full solution is usually of the same
computational complexity as the original problem, redundant constraints typically still only enforce a relaxation of the actual problem. We propose adding
tight redundant constraints that may be hard to verify exactly, but that can be
checked by applying some heuristic. The intention is to achieve more propagation than could be obtained using only those constraints which are (relatively)

---

[*] This work was partly supported by the German Science Foundation (DFG) project
SFB-376. An earlier version of this paper appeared as [8].

easy to propagate completely, but at a cost lower than would be needed by a complete and deterministic algorithm.

For a recent overview on the integration of constraint programming and local search of we refer to the recent tutorial by Focacci et al. [4]. As with other methods, constraint programming forms the basis of our approach. However, our use of local search is quite different to any of the methods considered so far. For a given model for a problem, we suggest considering the addition of complex redundant constraints, and then using local search to perform (incomplete) propagation of these constraints.

We illustrate this using the *Social Golfer Problem* as an example: 32 golfers want to play in 8 groups of 4 each week, in such way that any two golfers play in the same group at most once. How many weeks can they do this for? [1] The problem can be generalized by parameterizing it to g groups of s players each, playing for w weeks, which we write as g-s-w. There are two main aspects to the problem that make it challenging to solve even small instances in reasonable time: the social golfer problem is highly symmetric, and the clique structure of the constraints ensuring that any two golfers do not play together more than once makes it hard to judge the feasibility of a partial assignment.

In [3, 5, 6, 10], different methods for the efficient handling of symmetries in the social golfer problem have been presented. In this paper we use SBDD [3] and focus on the problems caused by the constraint structure of the problem.

2   Heuristic Constraint Propagation

In a tree search for the social golfers, it is hard to decide whether a partial assignment is extendible to a complete solution; i.e. it may not be obvious when there is no solution in a given subtree. When using the model in [8], many searches only backtracked when the assignments for an entire week are almost complete or even after having started to do assignments in the last week only. To improve the situation for the social golfer problem (as for many other CSPs) we can try to formulate necessary constraints for partial assignments to be extendible to complete, feasible solutions. Here we have a choice: choose a weak redundant constraint that can be propagated efficiently, or pick a condition that is more accurate but maybe much harder to verify. For the latter, we may consider applying a heuristic to perform incomplete domain filtering or pruning. Note that the incompleteness of this filtering does not affect either the soundness or the completeness of the search since the added constraints are redundant; it may just mean that the tree searched may be larger than strictly necessary.

Due to space considerations we only present one of the two types of additional constraints we added to our model; full details and examples can be found in [8].

---

[1] Problem 10 in CSPLib [2]. Since this work was done, it has been pointed out that the social golfer problem may not have been the best example to use. It seems there may be good non-heuristic propagators for tight redundant constraints for this problem. For example, it is closely related to the problems studied in [1]; indeed, one of the specific problems there is equivalent to golf 6-6-3.

Table 1. A partial instantiation of the 5-3-2 social golfer problem

	group 1			group 2			group 3			group 4			group 5		
week 1	1	2	3	4	5	6	7	8	9	10	11	12	13	14	15
week 2	1	4	7	2	5	8	3	*	*	*	*	*	*	*	*

Consider the example in Table 1, searching for a two-week schedule for 15 golfers playing in 5 groups of 3.

For the given partial assignment, suppose we add player 6 to group 3. Observe that players 10, 11 and 12 must be separated in week 2. As there are only three more groups that have not yet been filled completely, the third player in group three must be one of players 10, 11 and 12. Now there are only two groups left that have not been completed yet, but players 13, 14 and 15 must still be separated. Therefore, the current partial assignment is inconsistent, and we can backtrack.

We can generalize this observation. For a given incomplete week, we define a residual graph R that consists of a node for each unassigned player and an edge for each pair of such players that have already been assigned to play together in some other week. An example of a very simple residual graph, corresponding to week two from Table 1, is shown in Figure 1. Then, for the given week we count the number of groups that are not closed yet and compare that number with the size of the biggest clique in R. If the first number is smaller than the latter, then there is no way to extend the current assignment to the rest of the week, and the assignment is inconsistent.

Thus a clique exceeding a certain cardinality is a sufficient condition to prove inconsistency, allowing us to backtrack immediately. Finding a clique of size k is known to be NP-hard for arbitrary graphs, and while the residual graphs we are dealing with have special structure that may allow the efficient computation of such a clique, we chose not to try to find a polynomial-time complete method. Instead we apply a heuristic search to find a sufficiently large clique, an approach which, as we shall see, has advantages over one which simply returns the largest possible clique.

Reconsider the situation given in Table 1. We can add neither player 6 nor player 9 to group 3 for the same reason: the members of group 4 and group 5

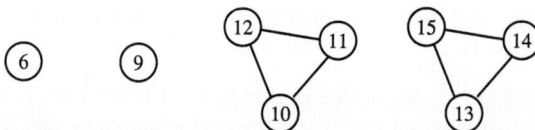

Fig. 1. The residual graph of week 2 from Table 1

Table 2. The CPU time needed to compute all unique solutions (in seconds), and in brackets the number of choice points visited when computing all unique solutions

	4-3-3	4-3-4	4-3-5	5-4-3	5-4-4	5-4-5	5-4-6	5-3-6	5-3-7
PI	0.32	0.71	0.98	46.63	83.24	132	143	>5 days	>5 days
	(102)	(182)	(227)	(7430)	(5392)	(6409)	(17129)		
H	0.23	0.43	0.31	40.19	43.2	43.74	33.80	13933	13311
	(76)	(87)	(90)	(6205)	(2829)	(2823)	(2818)	(266140)	(266268)
V	0.36	0.62	0.47	57.30	90	98.25	46.69	85855	1815
	(100)	(173)	(116)	(7415)	(5282)	(5574)	(3300)	(1075165)	(153697)
HV	0.25	0.4	0.26	47.78	47.45	44.18	23.21	6771	394
	(76)	(75)	(74)	(6205)	(2750)	(2791)	(1770)	(165238)	(85790)

of week 1 must be separated, and to do so we require the two open positions in group 3 of week 2. When checking the redundant constraint described above, assume we have set up the residual graph and suppose the heuristic we apply finds the two disjoint cliques of size three ($\{10, 11, 12\}$ and $\{13, 14, 15\}$). Since the sizes of these cliques are equal to the number of incomplete groups, we have not found a witness showing that the current partial assignment cannot be extended to a full schedule — indeed, the schedule can still be completed. However, since group 3 has only two open positions left, we can conclude that group 3 must be a subset of $\{3\} \cup \{10, 11, 12\} \cup \{13, 14, 15\}$. That is, we can use heuristic information for domain filtering.

We conclude that finding a witness for unsatisfiability is a complex task, but it can be looked for by applying a heuristic. Moreover, even if we do not find such a witness, we may find other "good" witnesses (namely some fairly large cliques) and their information can be combined and used for domain filtering. Therefore, it is advantageous to use a heuristic that not only provides us with good solutions quickly, but that also gives us several solutions achieving almost optimal objective values. Local search heuristics seem perfectly suited for this purpose.

To confirm our theoretical discussion, we implemented the model as described in [8] in C++, compiled by gcc 2.95 with maximal optimization (O3). All experiments were performed on a PC with a Pentium III/933MHz-processor and 512 MB RAM running Linux 2.4. We present a comparison of four different parameter settings: The plain implementation without redundant constraints (PI), PI plus horizontal constraints only (H), PI plus vertical constraints only (V) (see [8]), and PI plus horizontal and vertical constraints (HV).

In Table 2, the variants are evaluated on several social golfer instances. To make the comparison fair and reduce the impact of other choices such as the variable and value orderings used, we compute all unique solutions of an instance (or prove that there are none, for the 4-3-5 and 5-4-6 instances), counting the number of choice points and measuring the CPU time required.

Clearly, using both types of additional constraints result in the biggest reduction of choice points, though for small numbers of weeks the vertical constraints do not give any benefit when horizontal constraints are used (and little benefit even when they are not). A similar trend can be seen in the effectiveness of the horizontal constraints: while they are useful for small numbers of weeks, their effectiveness improves as the number of weeks increases.

Using the (HV) setting, we have been able to compute all unique solutions for all instances with at most 5 groups and 5 players per group [8]. To the best of our knowledge, this is the first computational approach that has been able to compute these numbers for instances of this size. Moreover, we found solutions for many previously unsolved (at least by constraint programming) larger instances, such as the 10-6-6 and the 9-7-4 instances.[2] Finally, using the methods described in this paper, we were able to compute a six week solution for the six groups of five instance, to prove that there are exactly two such unique solutions, and to prove that these solutions are optimal by showing that no seven week solution exists.

3   Conclusions

Using as an example the social golfer problem, we have introduced the idea of heuristic constraint propagation for complex redundant constraints. We proposed two different types of additional constraints, so called horizontal and vertical constraints. Propagating both types of constraints exactly would require the computation of all the maximal cliques in residual graphs with certain structural properties. Instead, we perform an incomplete propagation using a local search method to find a number of maximal cliques (but perhaps not all of them and perhaps not the largest possible). We have shown how such sets of cliques can be used for domain filtering and pruning. The experiments clearly show that adding tight redundant constraints to the problem can be of benefit, even when they are only propagated incompletely.

References

[1] N. Beldiceanu. An Example of Introduction of Global Constraints in CHIP: Application to Block Theory Problems, *ECRC Tech. Report TR-LP-49*, May 1990.

[2] *CSPLib: a problem library for constraints*, maintained by I. P. Gent, T. Walsh, B. Selman, http://www-users.cs.york.ac.uk/~tw/csplib/

[3] T. Fahle, S. Schamberger, M. Sellmann. Symmetry Breaking, *Proc. of CP'01*, LNCS 2239, pp. 93–107, 2001.

[4] F. Focacci, F. Laburthe, A. Lodi. Local Search and Constraint Programming, *Handbook of Metaheuristic*, Kluwer Academic Publishers, to appear.

[5] F. Focacci and M. Milano. Global Cut Framework for Removing Symmetries, *Proc. of CP'01*, LNCS 2239, pp. 77–92, 2001.

---

[2] An overview of solutions found by constraint programming can be found at [7].

[6] I. P. Gent and B. M. Smith. Symmetry Breaking During Search in Constraint Programming, *Proc. of ECAI'2000*, pp. 599-603, 2000.

[7] W. Harvey. *Warwick's Results Page for the Social Golfer Problem*, http://www.icparc.ic.ac.uk/~wh/golf/

[8] M. Sellmann and W. Harvey. Heuristic Constraint Propagation, *Proc. of CPAIOR'02*, Le Croisic, France, pp. 191–204, March 2002.

[9] ILOG. ILOG SOLVER. Reference manual and user manual. V5.0, ILOG, 2000.

[10] B. Smith. Reducing Symmetry in a Combinatorial Design Problem, *Proc. of CPAIOR'01*, Wye, UK, pp. 351–360, April 2001.

An Arc-Consistency Algorithm for the Minimum Weight All Different Constraint

Meinolf Sellmann

University of Paderborn, Department of Mathematics and Computer Science
Fürstenallee 11, D-33102 Paderborn
sello@uni-paderborn.de

Abstract. Historically, discrete minimization problems in constrained logical programming were modeled with the help of an isolated bounding constraint on the objective that is to be decreased. To overcome this frequently inefficient way of searching for improving solutions, the notion of *optimization constraints* was introduced. Optimization constraints can be viewed as global constraints that link the objective with other constraints of the problem at hand. We present an arc-consistency (actually: hyper-arc-consistency) algorithm for the *minimum weight all different constraint* which is an optimization constraint that consists in the combination of a linear objective with an all different constraint.

Keywords: optimization constraint, cost based filtering, all different constraint, minimum weight all different constraint, MinWeightAllDiff, IlcAllDiffCost

1 Introduction

In recent years, a joint effort of the constraint programming (CP) and operations research (OR) community has yield new concepts that can improve approaches for discrete optimization problems which are hard both in terms of feasibility and optimality. An important contribution is the idea of *optimization constraints* [10]. Though never explicitly stated as constraints, in the OR world optimization constraints are frequently used for bound computations and variable fixing. From a CP perspective, they can be viewed as global constraints that link the objective with some other constraints of the problem.

The constraint structure of many discrete optimization problems can be modeled efficiently using all different constraints. As a matter of fact, the all different constraint was one of the first global constraints that were considered [11]. Regarding the combination of the all different constraint and a linear objective, in [3], Y. Caseau and F. Laburthe introduced the *MinWeightAllDiff* constraint. In first applications [4], it was used for pruning purposes only. In [8, 9], F. Focacci et al. showed how the constraint (they refer to it as the *IlcAllDiffCost constraint*) can also be used for domain filtering by exploiting reduced cost information.

In this paper, we present an arc-consistency algorithm for the minimum weight all different constraint. It is based on standard operations research algorithms for the computation of minimum weighted bipartite matchings and

P. Van Hentenryck (Ed.): CP 2002, LNCS 2470, pp. 744–749, 2002.

shortest paths with non-negative edge weights. We show, that arc-consistency can be achieved in time $O(n(d + m \log m))$, where n denotes the number of variables, m is the cardinality of the union of all variable domains, and d denotes the sum of the cardinalities of the variable domains.

The remaining paper is structured as follows: In Section 2, we formally define the minimum weight all different constraint. The arc-consistency algorithm for the constraint is presented in Section 3. Finally, we conclude in Section 4.

2   The Minimum Weight All Different Constraint

Given a natural number $n \in \mathbb{N}$ and variables $X_1, \ldots, X_n$, we denote with $D_1 := D(X_1), \ldots, D_n := D(X_n)$ the domains of the variables, and let $D := \{\alpha_1, \ldots, \alpha_m\} = \bigcup_i D_i$ denote the union of all domains, whereby $m = |D|$. Further, given costs $c_{ij} \geq 0$ for assigning value α_j to variable X_i (whereby c_{ij} may be undefined if $\alpha_j \notin D_i$), we add a variable for the objective $Z = Z(X, c) = \sum_{i, X_i = \alpha_j} c_{ij}$ to be minimized. Note, that the non-negativity restriction on c can always be achieved by setting $\hat{c}_{ij} := c_{ij} - \min_{i,j} c_{ij}$, which will change the objective by the constant $n \min_{i,j} c_{ij}$.

In the course of optimization, once we have found a feasible solution with associated objective value β, we are searching for improving solutions only, thus requiring $Z < \beta$. Then, we define:

Definition 1. *The* minimum weight all different constraint *is the conjunction of an all different constraint on variables $X_1, \ldots, X_n$ and a bound constraint on the objective Z, i.e.:*

$$\text{MinWeightAllDiff}(X_1, \ldots, X_n, c, \beta) := \text{AllDiff}(X_1, \ldots, X_n) \wedge (Z < \beta).$$

Because otherwise there exists no feasible assignment, in the following we will assume $m \geq n$. There is a tight correlation between the minimum weight all different constraint and the *weighted bipartite perfect matching problem* that can be formalized by setting $G := G(X, D, c) := (V_1, V_2, E, c)$ where $V_1 := \{X_1, \ldots, X_n\}$, $V_2 := \{\alpha_1, \ldots, \alpha_m\}$ and $E := \{\{X_i, \alpha_j\} \mid \alpha_j \in D_i\}$. It is easy to see that any perfect matching[1] in G defines a feasible assignment of all different values to the variables. Therefore, there is also a one-to-one correspondence of cost optimal variable assignments and minimum weighted perfect matchings in G.

For the latter problem, a series of efficient algorithms have been developed. Using the *Hungarian method* or the *successive shortest path algorithm*, it can be solved in time $O(n(d + m \log m))$, where $d := \sum_i |D_i|$ denotes the number of edges in the given bipartite graph. For a detailed presentation of approaches for the weighted bipartite matching problem, we refer to [1].

Because there are efficient algorithms available, there is no need to apply a tree search to compute an optimal variable assignment if the minimum weight all different constraint is the only constraint of a discrete optimization problem.

---

[1] With the term "perfect matching" we refer to a subset of pairwise non-adjacent edges of cardinality $n \leq m$.

However, the situation changes when the problem consists of more than one minimum weight all different constraint or a combination with other constraints. Then, a tree search may very well be the favorable algorithmic approach to tackle the problem [3].

In such a scenario, we can exploit the algorithms developed in the OR community to compute a bound on the best possible variable assignment that can still be reached in the subtree rooted at the current choice point. Also, it has been suggested to use reduced cost information to perform cost based filtering at essentially no additional computational cost [9].

In the following, we describe an algorithm that achieves arc-consistency in the same worst case running time as is needed to compute a minimum weighted perfect matching when using the Hungarian method or the successive shortest path algorithm.

3   An Arc-Consistency Algorithm

To achieve arc-consistency of the minimum weight all different constraint, we need to remove all values from variable domains that cannot be part of any feasible assignment of values to variables with associated costs $Z < \beta$. That is, in the graph interpretation of the problem, we need to compute and remove the set of edges that cannot be part of any perfect matching with costs less than β.

For any perfect matching M, we set $\text{cost}(M) := \sum_{\{X_i,\alpha_j\} \in M} c_{ij}$. Further, we define the *corresponding network* $N^M := (V_1, V_2, A, c^M)$ whereby

$$A := \{(X_i, \alpha_j) \mid \{X_i, \alpha_j\} \in M\} \cup \{(\alpha_j, X_i) \mid \{X_i, \alpha_j\} \notin M\},$$

and $c_{ij}^M := -c_{ij}$ if $\{X_i, \alpha_j\} \in M$, and $c_{ij}^M := c_{ij}$ otherwise. That is, we transform the graph G into a directed network by directing matching edges from V_1 to V_2 and all other edges from V_2 to V_1. Furthermore, the cost of arcs going from V_1 to V_2 is multiplied by -1.

In the following, we will make some key observations that we will use later to develop an efficient arc-consistency algorithm. For a cycle C in N^M, we set $\text{cost}(C) := \sum_{e \in C} c_e^M$. Let M denote a perfect matching in G.

Lemma 1. *Given an edge $e \notin M$, and assume that there exists a minimum cost cycle C_e in N^M that contains e.[2]*

a) *There is a perfect matching M_e in G that contains e, and it holds that $\text{cost}(M_e) = \text{cost}(M) + \text{cost}(C_e)$.*

b) *The set M is a minimum weighted perfect matching in G, iff there is no negative cycle in N^M.*

c) *If M is of minimum weight, then for every perfect matching M_e that contains e it holds that $\text{cost}(M_e) \geq \text{cost}(M) + \text{cost}(C_e)$.*

---

[2] Here and in the following we identify an edge $e \in G$ and its corresponding arc in the directed network N^M.

Proof. a) Let C_e^+ and C_e^- denote the edges in E that correspond to arcs in C_e that go from V_2 to V_1, or from V_1 to V_2, respectively. We define $M_e := (M \setminus C_e^-) \cup C_e^+$. Obviously, $e \in M_e$, and because of $|C_e^+| = |C_e^-|$, M_e is a perfect matching in G. It holds: $\text{cost}(M_e) = \text{cost}(M) - \text{cost}(C_e^-) + \text{cost}(C_e^+) = \text{cost}(M) + \text{cost}(C_e)$.

b) Follows directly from (a).

c) It is easy to see that the symmetric difference $M \oplus M_e = M \setminus M_e \cup M_e \setminus M$ forms a set of cycles $C_1, \dots, C_r$ in G that also correspond to cycles in N^M. Moreover, it holds that $\text{cost}(M_e) = \text{cost}(M) - \text{cost}(M \setminus M_e) + \text{cost}(M_e \setminus M)$, and thus $\text{cost}(M_e) = \text{cost}(M) + \sum_i \text{cost}(C_i)$. Without loss of generality, we may assume that $e \in C_1$. Then, because of (b) and $\text{cost}(C_e) \leq \text{cost}(C_1)$, we have that $\text{cost}(M_e) \geq \text{cost}(M) + \text{cost}(C_1) \geq \text{cost}(M) + \text{cost}(C_e)$. ☐

Theorem 1. *Let M denote a minimum weight perfect matching in G, and $e \in E \setminus M$. There exists a perfect matching M_e with $e \in M_e$ and $\text{cost}(M_e) < \beta$, iff there exists a cycle C_e in N^M that contains e with $\text{cost}(C_e) < \beta - \text{cost}(M)$.*

Proof. Let C_e denote the cycle in N^M with $e \in C_e$ and minimal costs.

$\Rightarrow$ Assume that there is no such cycle. Then, either there is no cycle in N^M that contains e, or $\text{cost}(C_e) \geq \beta - \text{cost}(M)$. In the first case, there exists no matching M_e that contains e.[3] And in the latter case, with Lemma 1(c), we have that $\text{cost}(M_e) \geq \text{cost}(M) + \text{cost}(C_e) \geq \beta$, which is a contradiction.

$\Leftarrow$ We have that $\text{cost}(C_e) < \beta - \text{cost}(M)$. With Lemma 1(a) this implies that there exists a perfect matching M_e that contains e, and for which it holds that $\text{cost}(M_e) = \text{cost}(M) + \text{cost}(C_e) < \beta$. ☐

With Theorem 1, now we can characterize values that have to be removed from variable domains in order to achieve arc-consistency. Given a minimum weight perfect matching M in G, infeasible assignments simply correspond to arcs e in N^M that are not contained in any cycle C_e with $\text{cost}(C_e) < \beta - \text{cost}(M)$.

Of course, if $\text{cost}(M) \geq \beta$ we know from Lemma 1(b) that the current choice point is inconsistent, and we can backtrack right away. So let us assume that $\text{cost}(M) < \beta$. Then, using empty cycles C_e with $\text{cost}(C_e) = 0 < \beta - \text{cost}(M)$ we can show that all edges $e \in M$ are valid assignments. Thus, we only need to consider $e \notin M$. By construction, we know that the corresponding edge in N^M is directed from V_2 to V_1, i.e. $e = (\alpha_j, X_i)$. Denote with $\text{dist}(X_i, \alpha_j, c^M)$ the shortest path distance from X_i to α_j in N^M. Then, for the minimum weight cycle C_e with $e \in C_e$ it holds: $\text{cost}(C_e) = c_{ij} + \text{dist}(X_i, \alpha_j, c^M)$. Thus, it is sufficient to compute the shortest path distances from V_1 to V_2 in N^M.

We can ease this work by eliminating negative edge weights in N^M. Consider potential functions $\pi^1 : V_1 \to \mathbb{R}$ and $\pi^2 : V_2 \to \mathbb{R}$. It is a well known fact, that the shortest path structure of the network remains intact if we change the cost function by setting $\bar{c}_{ij}^M := c_{ij}^M + \pi_i^1 - \pi_j^2$ for all $(i, j) \in M$, and $\bar{c}_{ij}^M := c_{ij}^M - \pi_i^1 + \pi_j^2$ for all $(i, j) \notin M$. Then, $\text{dist}(X_i, \alpha_j, c^M) = \text{dist}(X_i, \alpha_j, \bar{c}^M) - \pi_i^1 + \pi_j^2$. If the network does not contain negative weight cycles (which is true because M is a

---

[3] Note, that this observation is commonly used in domain filtering algorithms for the all different constraint [11].

perfect matching of minimum weight, see Lemma 1(b)), we can choose potential functions such that $\bar{c}^M \geq 0$. This idea has been used before in the all-pairs shortest path algorithm by Johnson [6].

In our context, after having computed a minimum weight perfect matching, we get the node potential functions π^1 and π^2 for free by using the dual and negative dual values corresponding to the nodes in V_1 and V_2, respectively. As a matter of fact, the resulting cost vector $\bar{c}^M$ is exactly the vector of reduced costs $\bar{c}$.

We summarize: To achieve arc-consistency, first we compute a minimum weight perfect matching in a bipartite graph in time $O(n(d + m \log m))$. We obtain an optimal matching M, dual values π^1, π^2, and reduced costs $\bar{c}$. If $\text{cost}(M) \geq \beta$, we can backtrack. Otherwise, we set up a network $N = (V_1, V_2, A, \bar{c})$ and compute n single source shortest paths with non-negative edge weights, each of them requiring time $O(d + m \log m)$ when using Dijkstra's algorithm in combination with Fibonacci heaps [6]. We obtain distances $\text{dist}(X_i, \alpha_j, \bar{c})$ for all variables and values. Finally, we remove value α_j from the domain of X_i, iff

$$\bar{c}_{ij} + \text{dist}(X_i, \alpha_j, \bar{c}) = c_{ij} + \text{dist}(X_i, \alpha_j, \bar{c}) - \pi_i^1 + \pi_j^2$$
$$= c_{ij} + \text{dist}(X_i, \alpha_j, c^M) = \text{cost}(C_{\{i,j\}}) \geq \beta - \text{cost}(M),$$

where $C_{\{i,j\}}$ is the shortest cycle in N^M that contains $\{i,j\}$. Obviously, this entire procedure runs in time $O(n(d + m \log m))$.

Interestingly, the idea of using reduced cost shortest path distances has been considered before to strengthen reduced cost propagation [9]. For an experimental evaluation of this idea, we refer to that paper. Now we have shown that this enhanced reduced cost propagation is powerful enough to guarantee arc-consistency for the minimum weight all different constraint.

4   Conclusions

We have introduced an arc-consistency algorithm for the minimum weight all different constraint that runs in time $O(n(d + m \log m))$. At first sight this sounds optimal, because it is the same time that is needed by algorithms for the weighted bipartite perfect matching problem such as the Hungarian method or the successive shortest path algorithm. However, two questions remain open: 1. Can we base a cost based filtering algorithm on the cost scaling algorithm that gives the best known time bound for assignment problems that satisfy the similarity assumption? And 2. Can the above filtering method be implemented to run incrementally faster?

References

[1] R. K. Ahuja, T. L. Magnati, J. B. Orlin. *Network Flows*. Prentice Hall, 1993.
[2] N. Barnier and P. Brisset. Graph Coloring for Air Traffic Flow Management, *Proc. of CPAIOR'02*, Le Croisic, France, pp. 133–147, March 2002.
[3] Y. Caseau and F. Laburthe. Solving Various Weighted Matching Problems with Constraints, *Proc. of CP'97*, LNCS 1330, pp. 17–31, 1997.

[4] Y. Caseau and F. Laburthe. Solving Small TSPs with Constraints, *Proc. of ICLP'97*, The MIT Press, 1997.

[5] Y. Caseau and F. Laburthe. Heuristics for large constrained routing problems, *Journal of Heuristics*, 5:281–303, 1999.

[6] T. H. Cormen, C. E. Leiserson, R. L. Rivest. *Introduction to Algorithms*. The MIT Press, 1990.

[7] T. Fahle. Cost based Filtering vs. Upper Bounds for maximum Clique, *Proc. of CPAIOR'02*, Le Croisic, France, pp. 93–107, March 2002.

[8] F. Focacci, A. Lodi, M. Milano. Solving TSP through the Integration of OR and CP Techniques, *Workshop on Large Scale Combinatorial Optimization and Constraints, CP'98*, Electronic Notes in Discrete Mathematics, 1998.

[9] F. Focacci, A. Lodi, M. Milano. Integration of CP and OR methods for Matching Problems, *Proc. of CPAIOR'99*, Ferrara, Italy, 1999.

[10] F. Focacci, A. Lodi, M. Milano. Cost-Based Domain Filtering. *Proceedings of the CP'99* Springer LNCS 1713:189–203, 1999.

[11] J. C. Regin. A Filtering Algorithm for Constraints of Difference in CSPs, *Proc. of AAAI*, pp. 362–367, 1994.

Algebraic Properties of CSP Model Operators[*]

Y. C. Law and Jimmy H. M. Lee

Department of Computer Science and Engineering
The Chinese University of Hong Kong
Shatin, N.T., Hong Kong SAR, China
{yclaw,jlee}@cse.cuhk.edu.hk

1 Introduction

The task at hand is to tackle *Constraint Satisfaction Problems* (CSPs) defined
in the sense of Mackworth [4]. This paper aims to take a first step towards a
CSP-based *module systems* for constraint programming languages and modeling
tools. The call for such a system is two-fold. First, most existing constraint programming languages have some sort of module systems, but these systems are
designed for the underlying languages. Thus these module systems facilitate the
construction of large constraint programs in a particular language, but not of
CSP models. Second, a module system designed for CSP models with clear and
clean semantics should allow us to reason the properties of CSP models declaratively without actually solving the CSPs. As a first attempt, we introduce six
operators for manipulating and transforming CSP models: namely intersection,
union, channeling, induction, negation, and complementation. For each operator,
we give its syntactic construction rule, define its set-theoretic meaning, and also
examine its algebraic properties, all illustrated with examples where appropriate. Our results show that model intersection and union form abelian monoids
respectively among others.

The rest of the paper is organized as follows. Section 2 provides the basic
definitions relating to CSP models. In Section 3, we examine the definitions and
properties of the six operators in details. Section 4 gives further algebraic properties, which allow us to identify possible algebraic structures of the operators. We
summarize and shed light on possible future direction of research in Section 5.

2 From Viewpoints to CSP Models

There are usually more than one way of formulating a problem P into a CSP.
Central to the formulation process is to determine the variables and the domains (associated sets of possible values) of the variables. Different choices
of variables and domains are results of viewing the problem P from different angles/perspectives. We define a *viewpoint* to be a pair (X, D_X), where

---

[*] The work described in this paper was substantially supported by a grant from the
Research Grants Council of the Hong Kong Special Administrative Region (Project
no. CUHK4183/00E).

P. Van Hentenryck (Ed.): CP 2002, LNCS 2470, pp. 750–754, 2002.

$X = \{x_1, \ldots, x_n\}$ is a set of variables, and D_X is a set containing, for every $x \in X$, an associated domain $D_X(x)$ giving the set of possibles values for x.

A viewpoint $V = (X, D_X)$ defines the possible assignments for variables in X. An *assignment* in V (or in $U \subseteq X$) is a pair $\langle x, a \rangle$, which means that variable $x \in X$ (or U) is assigned the value $a \in D_X(x)$. A *compound assignment* in V (or in $U \subseteq X$) is a set of assignments $\{\langle x_{i_1}, a_1 \rangle, \ldots, \langle x_{i_k}, a_k \rangle\}$, where $\{x_{i_1}, \ldots, x_{i_k}\} \subseteq X$ (or U) and $a_j \in D_X(x_{i_j})$ for each $j \in \{1, \ldots, k\}$. *Note* the requirement that *no* variables may be assigned more than one value in a compound assignment. Given a set of assignments θ, we use the predicate $cmpd(\theta, V)$ to ensure that θ is a compound assignment in V. A *complete assignment* in V is a compound assignment $\{\langle x_1, a_1 \rangle, \ldots, \langle x_n, a_k \rangle\}$ for all variables in X.

When formulating a problem P into a CSP, the choice of viewpoints is not arbitrary. Suppose $sol(P)$ is the set of all solutions of P (in whatever notations and formalism). We say that viewpoint V is *proper* for P if and only if we can find a subset S of the set of all possible complete assignments in V so that there is a one-one mapping between S and $sol(P)$. In other words, each solution of P must correspond to a distinct complete assignment in V. We note also that according to our definition, any viewpoint is proper with respect to a problem that has no solutions.

A *constraint* can be considered a predicate that maps to *true* or *false*. The *signature* $sig(c) \subseteq X$, which is the set of variables involved in c, defines the scope of c. We abuse terminology by saying that the compound assignment $\{\langle x_{i_1}, a_1 \rangle, \ldots, \langle x_{i_k}, a_k \rangle\}$ also has a signature: $sig(\{\langle x_{i_1}, a_1 \rangle, \ldots, \langle x_{i_k}, a_k \rangle\}) = \{x_{i_1}, \ldots, x_{i_k}\}$. Given a compound assignment θ such that $sig(c) \subseteq sig(\theta)$, the *application* of θ to c, $c\theta$, is obtained by replacing all variables in c by the corresponding values in θ. If $c\theta$ is *true*, we say θ *satisfies* c, and θ *violates* c otherwise. In addition, the negation $\neg c$ of a constraint c is defined by the fact that $(\neg c)\theta = \neg(c\theta)$ for all compound assignments θ in $X \supseteq sig(c)$. We overload the $\neg$ operator so that it operates on both constraints and boolean expressions.

A *CSP model M* (or simply *model* hereafter) of a problem P is a pair (V, C), where V is a proper viewpoint of P and C is a set of constraints in V for P. Note that, in our definition, we allow two constraints to be on the same set of variables: $c_i, c_j \in C$ and $sig(c_i) = sig(c_j)$. A *solution* of $M = (V, C)$ is a complete assignment θ in V so that $c\theta = $ *true* for every $c \in C$. Since M is a model of P, the constraints C must be defined in such a way that there is a one-one correspondence between $sol(M)$ and $sol(P)$. Thus, the viewpoint V essentially dictates how the constraints of P are formulated (*modulo* solution equivalence).

3   Operators over CSP Models

We are interested in operators in the space of CSP models. In this section, we introduce several such operators and give the set-theoretic semantics and properties of these operators. In the rest of the presentation, we assume $M_1 = (V_1, C_{X_1})$ and $M_2 = (V_2, C_{X_2})$, $V_1 = (X_1, D_{X_1})$ and $V_2 = (X_2, D_{X_2})$.

Model intersection forms *conjuncted models* by essentially conjoining constraints from constituent models. A solution of a conjuncted model must thus also be a solution of all of its constituent models. More formally, the conjuncted model $M_1 \cap M_2$ is $((X_1 \cup X_2, D_{X_1 \cup X_2}), C_{X_1} \cup C_{X_2})$, where for all $x \in X_1 \cup X_2$,

$$D_{X_1 \cup X_2}(x) = \begin{cases} D_{X_1}(x) & \text{if } x \in X_1 \wedge x \notin X_2 \\ D_{X_2}(x) & \text{if } x \notin X_1 \wedge x \in X_2 \\ D_{X_1}(x) \cap D_{X_2}(x) & \text{otherwise} \end{cases}$$

We overload the $\cap$ operator so that it operates on CSP models as well as sets. A consequence of the definition is that every solution of a conjuncted model must satisfy all constraints in its constituent models.

Model union deals with choices in constraint processing. The result is a *disjuncted model*, which allows solutions of any one of the constituent models to be extended to solutions of the disjuncted model. More formally, the disjuncted model $M_1 \cup M_2$ is $((X_1 \cup X_2, D_{X_1 \cup X_2}), \{c_1 \vee c_2 | c_1 \in C_{X_1} \wedge c_2 \in C_{X_2}\})$, where for all $x \in X_1 \cup X_2$,

$$D_{X_1 \cup X_2}(x) = \begin{cases} D_{X_1}(x) & \text{if } x \in X_1 \wedge x \notin X_2 \\ D_{X_2}(x) & \text{if } x \notin X_1 \wedge x \in X_2 \\ D_{X_1}(x) \cup D_{X_2}(x) & \text{otherwise} \end{cases}$$

We overload the $\cup$ operator so that it operates on CSP models as well as sets. The strength of the combined whole may well be more than the sum of the strength of the individuals. This is the case with the solution set of a disjuncted model with respect to its constituent models.

Cheng *et al.* [1] define a *channeling constraint* c to be a constraint, where $sig(c) \not\subseteq X_1$, $sig(c) \not\subseteq X_2$, and $sig(c) \subseteq X_1 \cup X_2$. We note in the definition that the constraints in the two models are immaterial. Channeling constraints relate actually viewpoints but not models. Suppose there is a set C_c of channeling constraints connecting the viewpoints V_1 and V_2. *Model channeling* combines M_1 and M_2 using C_c to form a *channeled model*, which is $M_1 \cap M_2$ plus the channeling constraints C_c. More formally, the channeled model $M_1 \overset{C_c}{\bowtie} M_2$ is $((X_1 \cup X_2, D_{X_1 \cup X_2}), C_{X_1} \cup C_{X_2} \cup C_c)$, where for all $x \in X_1 \cup X_2$,

$$D_{X_1 \cup X_2}(x) = \begin{cases} D_{X_1}(x) & \text{if } x \in X_1 \wedge x \notin X_2 \\ D_{X_2}(x) & \text{if } x \notin X_1 \wedge x \in X_2 \\ D_{X_1}(x) \cap D_{X_2}(x) & \text{otherwise} \end{cases}$$

Given two models M_1 and M_2. The channeled model $M_1 \overset{C_c}{\bowtie} M_2$ is more constrained than the conjuncted model $M_1 \cap M_2$. A solution of $M_1 \overset{C_c}{\bowtie} M_2$ must satisfy all constraints in M_1 and M_2 plus the channeling constraints C_c.

Model induction [3] is a method for systematically generating a new model from an existing model, using another viewpoint and channeling constraints. We note that a model M_1 contains two types of constraints: the explicit constraints as stated in C_{X_1} and the implicit constraints for enforcing valid variable assignments. Given a set of channeling constraints defining a total and injective function f from the possible assignments in V_1 to those in V_2. The core of model induction is a *meaning-preserving* transformation from constraints in model M_1, both implicit and explicit (C_{X_1}), using f to generate constraints C_{X_2} in viewpoint V_2. Due to space limitation, readers are referred to Law and Lee [3] for the detailed definition of model induction.

Model negation takes a model as input and generates a *negated model* by negating all constraints in the original model. Given a model $M = (V, C)$, the viewpoint of the negated model remains unchanged. For each constraint $c \in C$, the negated constraint $\neg c$ is in the negated model. Thus $\neg M = (V, \{\neg c | c \in C\})$. We overload also the $\neg$ operator so that it operates on CSP models as well as boolean expressions. Since we negate all constraints, solutions of the negated model $\neg M$ consist of all complete assignments that violate all constraints in M. Unfortunately, solutions of $\neg M$ cannot be constructed from solutions of M, but negation does neutralize each other by the fact that $(\neg(\neg c))\theta = \neg((\neg c)\theta) = \neg(\neg(c\theta)) = c\theta$.

Model complementation provides an alternative means to handle negative information. The *complemented model* $\overline{M}$ of a model M contains the same viewpoint as M. The only constraint in $\overline{M}$ is the negation of the conjunction of all constraints in M. Solutions of $\overline{M}$ thus violates at least one constraint in M. More formally, if $M = (V, C)$, then $\overline{M} = (V, \{\neg(\bigwedge C)\})$, where $\neg(\bigwedge C)$ is equivalent to $\bigvee\{\neg c | c \in C\}$. Solutions of M and $\overline{M}$ partition the set of all possible complete assignments for (the viewpoint of) M. By definition, complementation also annihilates the effect of another.

4   Algebraic Structures

In this section, we identify the algebraic structures of some of the introduced operators. In the following, $M = (V, C)$, M_1, and M_2 denote CSP models. $E_\emptyset = ((\emptyset, \emptyset), \emptyset)$ is the *empty CSP*, which consists of no variables and no constraints. $E_\perp = ((\emptyset, \emptyset), \{false\})$ is the *contradictory CSP*, which has also no variables and only the constant $false$ as constraint. The empty CSP is a satisfiable CSP with the *empty assignment* $\emptyset$ as its solution, while the contradictory CSP is unsatisfiable with no solutions. A *monoid* [2] $(G, \odot)$ is a nonempty set G together with a binary operation $\odot$ on G which is associative, and there exists an identity element $e \in G$ such that $a \odot e = e \odot a = a$ for all $a \in G$. A monoid is said to be *abelian* if $\odot$ is commutative. Let $\mathcal{M}$ be the set of all CSP models.

Table 1 summarizes the common algebraic properties of some of the introduced model operators. Except for the distributivity of union over intersection, we skip the proof of the other straightforward properties. As we can see, $(\mathcal{M}, \cap)$ forms an abelian monoid with the empty CSP $E_\emptyset$ as the identity element. Model intersection is also idempotent since $M \cap M = M$. Similarly, $(\mathcal{M}, \cup)$ forms also an abelian monoid with the contradictory CSP $E_\perp$ as the identity element. Besides, taking the union of any model and the empty CSP $E_\emptyset$ vanishes the constraints in the disjuncted model, which has all complete assignments as solutions. Both intersection and union fail to be a group due to the lack of inverse elements.

Table 1. Algebraic Properties of Some Model Operators

• $M_1 \cap M_2 = M_2 \cap M_1$	• $M_1 \cup (M_2 \cap M_3) = (M_1 \cup M_2) \cap (M_1 \cup M_3)$
• $(M_1 \cap M_2) \cap M_2 = M_1 \cap (M_2 \cap M_3)$	
• $M \cap E_\emptyset = M$	• $M_1 \overset{C_c}{\bowtie} M_2 = M_2 \overset{C_c}{\bowtie} M_1$
• $M \cap M = M$	• $(M_1 \overset{C_{c_1}}{\bowtie} M_2) \overset{C_{c_2}}{\bowtie} M_3 = M_1 \overset{C_{c_1}}{\bowtie} (M_2 \overset{C_{c_2}}{\bowtie} M_3)$
	• $M_1 \overset{\emptyset}{\bowtie} M_2 = M_1 \cap M_2$
• $M_1 \cup M_2 = M_2 \cup M_1$	
• $(M_1 \cup M_2) \cup M_3 = M_1 \cup (M_2 \cup M_3)$	• $\neg(M_1 \cap M_2) = \neg M_1 \cap \neg M_2$
• $M \cup E_\perp = M$	
• $M \cup E_\emptyset = (V, \emptyset)$	

5 Concluding Remarks

A good module system should be compositional and be based on a rich algebra of model operators. We introduce six such operators and examine their properties. The work as reported is insufficient to form a practical model algebra, but should serve to shed light on the design of future CSP-based module systems.

We believe that we are the first to propose a systematic study of model operators and their algebraic properties. It is a purpose of the paper to arouse interest in this important new direction of research. There is plenty of scope for future work. First, it would be interesting to look for other useful operators, and even perhaps to refine the definition of the proposed operators. In particular, we focus on satisfiable models, and relatively little is known about the negation and complementation operators. Second, much work is needed to design a practical and yet versatile module system, based on an algebra (even if there is one), in constraint-based interactive problem-solving tools and constraint programming languages. Third, the work suggests the possible notions of "reusable model components" and "model patterns," which can serve as the brick and mortar for and save much effort in the construction of huge and complex CSP models.

References

[1] B. M. W. Cheng, K. M. F. Choi, J. H. M. Lee, and J. C. K. Wu. Increasing constraint propagation by redundant modeling: an experience report. *Constraints*, 4(2):167–192, 1999.

[2] T. W. Hungerford. *Algebra*. Springer-Verlag, 1974.

[3] Y. C. Law and J. H. M. Lee. Model induction: a new source of CSP model redundancy. In *Proceedings of the 18th National Conference on Artificial Intelligence*, 2002.

[4] A. K. Mackworth. Consistency in networks of relations. *AI Journal*, 8(1):99–118, 1977.

AC-3$_d$ an Efficient Arc-Consistency Algorithm with a Low Space-Complexity

Marc R. C. van Dongen

CS Department UCC/Cork Constraint Computation Centre
Western Road, Cork, Ireland
dongen@cs.ucc.ie

Abstract. Arc-consistency algorithms prune the search-space of Constraint Satisfaction Problems (CSPs). They use *support-checks* to find out about the properties of CSPs. Their *arc-heuristics* select the constraint and their *domain-heuristics* select the values for the next support-check. We shall combine AC-3 and DEE and equip the resulting hybrid with a *double-support* domain-heuristic. The resulting hybrid AC-3$_d$ is easy to implement and requires the same data structures as AC-3 thereby improving on AC-7's space-complexity. We shall present experimental results which indicate that AC-3 can compete with AC-7.

1 Introduction

Arc-consistency algorithms are widely used to prune the search-space of Constraint Satisfaction Problems (CSPs). They use *support-checks* to find out about the properties of CSPs. Their *arc-heuristics* select the constraint and their *domain-heuristics* select the values for the next support-check. We shall integrate AC-3 and DEE and equip the resulting hybrid with a *double-support* domain heuristic thereby creating an arc-consistency algorithm called AC-3$_d$, which can compete with AC-7 in time and which has a space-complexity which improves on that of AC-7.

One reason for the increased performance of AC-3$_d$ is that it uses a double-support heuristic and not the most commonly used *lexicographical* domain-heuristic.

We shall present experimental results which indicate that AC-3$_b$ can compete with AC-7 both in time on the wall and in the number of support-checks.

2 Constraint Satisfaction

A *Constraint Satisfaction Problem* (or CSP) comprises a set of n variables, a function D that maps each of these variables to its domain, and a collection of e constraints.

Let α and β be two variables, let $D(\alpha) = \{1, \ldots, a\} \neq \emptyset$, and let $D(\beta) = \{1, \ldots, b\} \neq \emptyset$. In this paper binary constraints are matrices. The set containing all a by b zero-one matrices is denoted $\mathbb{M}^{ab}$. Let $M \in \mathbb{M}^{ab}$ be a constraint

between α and β. A value $i \in D(\alpha)$ is *supported* by $j \in D(\beta)$ if $M_{ij} = 1$.
Similarly, $j \in D(\beta)$ is supported by $i \in D(\alpha)$ if $M_{ij} = 1$. Matrices, rows and
columns are *non-zero* if they contain more than zero ones, and *zero* otherwise.
M is *arc-consistent* if for each $i \in D(\alpha)$ the i-th row of M is non-zero and for
each $j \in D(\beta)$ the j-th column of M is non-zero. A CSP is *arc-consistent* if
its domains are non-empty and its constraints are arc-consistent. A variable is
a *neighbour* of another variable if there is a binary constraint between them.
The *degree* $\deg(\alpha)$ of α is the number of neighbours of α. The *density* of a
(connected) CSP is defined as $2e/(n^2 - n)$. The *tightness* of $M \in \mathbb{M}^{ab}$ is defined
as $1 - \frac{1}{ab} \sum_{i=1}^{a} \sum_{j=1}^{b} M_{ij}$.

The *row-support* (*column-support*) of a matrix is the set containing the indices of its non-zero rows (columns). The *support-check* $M_{ij}^?$ is a test to find
the value M_{ij}. We shall write checks$_\mathcal{A}(M)$ for the number of support-checks
required by arc-consistency algorithm $\mathcal{A}$ to compute the row-support and the
column-support of M.

$M_{ij}^?$ *succeeds* if $M_{ij} = 1$. $M_{ij}^?$ is a *single-support check* if, just before it was
carried out, the row-support status of i was known and the column-support status of j was unknown, or vice versa. $M_{ij}^?$ is a *double-support check* if, just before
the check was carried out, both the row-support status of i and the column-support status of j were unknown. A domain-heuristic is a *double-support heuristic* if
it prefers double-support checks. The potential payoff of a double-support check
is twice as large as that of a single-support check. This is an indication that
arc-consistency algorithms should prefer double-support checks. Another indication is that to minimise the total number of support-checks one has to maximise
the number of successful double-support checks [6].

3   Related Literature

Mackworth presented the AC-3 arc-consistency algorithm [4]. With Freuder he
presented a lower bound of $\Omega\left(ed^2\right)$ and an upper bound of $\mathbf{O}\left(ed^3\right)$ for its
worst-case time-complexity [5]. As usual, d is the maximum domain size. AC-3
has a $\mathbf{O}\left(e + nd\right)$ space-complexity. Experimental results indicate that arc-heuristics influence the average performance of arc-consistency algorithms [8].

Bessière, Freuder and Régin present an arc-consistency algorithm called AC-7
[1, 2]. AC-7 has an optimal upper bound of $\mathbf{O}\left(ed^2\right)$ for its worst-case time-complexity and has been reported to behave well on average. AC-7's space-complex-
ity is $\mathbf{O}\left(ed\right)$.

Results from an experimental comparison between the support-checks required by AC-7 and AC-3_b are presented in [6]. AC-3_d is a cross-breed between
AC-3 and DEE [6, 4, 3]. Both AC-7 and AC-3_b were equipped with a lexicographical arc-heuristic. AC-3_b used a double-support and AC-7 a lexicographical domain-heuristic. AC-3_b was more efficient than AC-7 for the majority of
the $30,420$ random problems. Also AC-3_b was more efficient on average. These
are surprising results because AC-3_b, unlike AC-7, repeats support-checks. The

results are also interesting because AC-3$_b$ has a space-complexity of $\mathbf{O}\,(e + nd)$ which is better than that of AC-7. These results were the first indication that domain-heuristics can improve arc-consistency algorithms.

4   The AC-3$_d$ Algorithm

In this section we shall study AC-3$_d$ and its domain-heuristic $\mathcal{D}$. Space constraints led to a minimal presentation. The reader is referred to [6, 7] for proof and further details.

AC-3$_d$ is inspired by AC-3 and DEE [4, 3]. AC-3$_d$ uses a queue of arcs just like AC-3. If AC-3$_d$'s arc-heuristics select the arc (α, β) from the queue and if (β, α) is not in the queue then AC-3$_d$ proceeds like AC-3 by *revising* $D(\alpha)$ using the constraint M between α and β. Here, to revise a domain using constraint M, means to remove its unsupported values using the constraint M. AC-3$_d$ uses Mackworth's revise to revise $D(\alpha)$ with M [7]. If $D(\alpha)$ was changed due to the revision then for each neighbour $\gamma \neq \beta$ of α the arc (γ, α) is added to the queue if it was not in the queue. The difference between AC-3 and AC-3$_d$ becomes apparent if (β, α) is also in the queue. If this is this case then AC-3$_d$ also removes (β, α) from the queue and uses $\mathcal{D}$ to *simultaneously* revise $D(\alpha)$ and $D(\beta)$. Arcs are added to the queue in a similar way as described before. AC-3$_d$ inherits its space-complexity and worst-case time-complexity from AC-3.

$\mathcal{D}$ does not repeat support-checks. It will first find its row-support in the lexicographical order on its rows. When it tries to find support for row r it will first use double-support checks and then single-support checks until the support-status of r is known. Finally, $\mathcal{D}$ will use single-support checks for the unsupported columns.

For sufficiently large domain sizes a and b the average *time-complexity* of $\mathcal{D}$ is less than $2\max(a, b) + 2$. This is almost optimal and if $a \approx b$ then $\mathcal{D}$ is about twice as efficient as the average time-complexity of a lexicographical heuristic [6].

5   Experimental Results

We have taken results from Bessière, Freuder and Régin as published in [2] and compared them against our own results. We divided their times by 5 because their algorithms were run on a machine which was 5 times slower [2, 7].

The problem set consists of Radio Link Frequency Assignment Problems (RLFAPs) and random problems. The RLFAP problems were obtained from `ftp://ftp.cs.unh.edu/pub/csp/archive/code/benchmarks`. The objective for each CSP is that it be made arc-consistent or to decide that this is not possible. To generate the random problems, we used Frost, Dechter, Bessière and Régin's random constraint generator, which is available from `http://www.lirmm.fr/~bessiere/generator.html`. The generator was run with seed 0.

The random CSPs consist of four groups. Each group contains 50 random CSPs and is uniquely determined by a tuple $\langle n, d, p_1, p_2 \rangle$. Here, n is the number

Table 1. Average Results for Random Problems

	$\langle 150, 50, 0.045, 0.500 \rangle$ underconstrained		$\langle 150, 50, 0.045, 0.940 \rangle$ overconstrained	
	checks	time	checks	time
AC-3 BFR	100,010	0.016	514,973	0.074
AC-7 BFR	94,030	0.038	205,070	0.058
AC-3	99,959	0.022	135,966	0.013
AC-3_d	50,862	0.019	69,742	0.007
	$\langle 150, 50, 0.045, 0.918 \rangle$ phase-transition/sparse		$\langle 50, 50, 1.000, 0.875 \rangle$ phase-transition/dense	
	checks	time	checks	time
AC-3 BFR AC	2,353,669	0.338	2,932,326	0.382
IC	4,865,777	0.734	8,574,903	1.092
AC-7 BFR AC	481,878	0.154	820,814	0.247
IC	535,095	0.184	912,795	0.320
AC-3 AC	2,254,058	0.162	4,025,746	0.302
IC	2,602,318	0.196	6,407,079	0.491
AC-3_d AC	1,734,362	0.140	2,592,579	0.245
IC	2,010,055	0.171	4,287,835	0.394

of variables, d is the (uniform) size of the domains, p_1 is the density of the constraint-graph, and p_2 is the (uniform) tightness of the constraints. The groups are $\langle 150, 50, 0.045, 0.500 \rangle$ under-constrained CSPs (easy), $\langle 150, 50, 0.045, 0.940 \rangle$ over-constrained CSP (easy), $\langle 150, 50, 0.045, 0.918 \rangle$ low density CSPs at the phase-transition (difficult), and finally $\langle 50, 50, 1.000, 0.875 \rangle$ high density CSPs at the phase-transition (very difficult).

The algorithms that were compared are AC-7 (called AC-7 BFR from here on) as presented in [2], AC-3 (called AC-3 BFR from here on) as presented in [2], our implementation of AC-3, and our implementation of AC-3_d. AC-3 was equipped with a lexicographical domain-heuristic. The arc-heuristic that was used for AC-3 and AC-3_d prefers arc (α, β) to (α', β') if $s_\alpha < s_{\alpha'}$, if $s_\alpha = s_{\alpha'} \wedge d_\alpha < d_{\alpha'}$, if $s_\alpha = s_{\alpha'} \wedge d_\alpha = d_{\alpha'} \wedge s_\beta < s_{\beta'}$, or if $s_\alpha = s_{\alpha'} \wedge d_\alpha = d_{\alpha'} \wedge s_\beta = s_{\beta'} \wedge d_\beta \leq d_{\beta'}$, where $S_x = |D(x)|$ and $d_x = \deg(x)$. This very expensive heuristic is better for AC-3_d than a lexicographical heuristic with which it almost "degenerates" to AC-3.

The results for the random problems are listed in Table 1. The columns "checks" and "time" list the average number of support-checks and the average time. For the phase-transition we separated results for problems that could be made arc-consistent (marked by "AC") and problems that could not (marked by "IC").

It is difficult to explain the differences between AC-3 BFR and AC-3. Sometimes AC-3 BFR is better and sometimes AC-3. We don't know anything about AC-3 BFR's implementation, but we believe that the differences are solely caused by arc-heuristics.

AC-3$_d$ is better than both AC-3 BFR and AC-3. Only for underconstrained problems does it require slightly more time than AC-3 BFR. This is consistent with the literature [7]. It is interesting to notice that AC-3$_d$ is a lot better than AC-3 BFR and AC-3 for the overconstrained problems.

Outside the phase-transition region AC-3$_d$ outperforms AC-7 BFR in time and checks. AC-3$_d$ is much better than AC-7 BFR for the overconstrained problems. In the phase-transition region AC-3$_d$ requires more checks than AC-7 BFR. For the sparse problems in the phase-transition region AC-3$_d$ saves time. AC-7 should be preferred for dense problems in the phase-transition region.

The results for the RLFAP Problems are presented in Table 2. AC-3$_d$ does better in checks than AC-3 BFR and AC-3. AC-3 BFR performs better in time than AC-3$_d$ for Problems 3, 5, and 11. This is consistent with our findings for the random problems because these problems are relatively easy [7]. AC-3$_d$ does significantly better than AC-3 BFR for RLFAP#8 both in time and checks. This is also consistent with our findings for the overconstrained problems because RLFAP#8 cannot be made arc-consistent and is relatively easy.

AC-3$_d$ performs better in time and checks than AC-7 BFR for all problems. Again, the results for RLFAP#8 are consistent with our findings for the overconstrained problems. The results for the other problems are also consistent with the other results because the RLFAP Problems are not in the phase-transition region and are relatively easy.

6 Conclusions and Recommendations

In this paper we have presented a general purpose arc-consistency algorithm called AC-3$_d$ which can compete with AC-7 in time and whose $O(e + nd)$ space-complexity improves on AC-7's $O(ed)$ space-complexity. We have presented experimental results of a comparison between AC-7 and AC-3$_d$. For the problems under consideration AC-3$_d$ performs better in time on the wall and in the number of support-checks outside the phase-transition region. In the phase-transition region AC-7 always requires fewer checks. Only for dense problems in the phase-transition region does it require less time.

One reason for the performance of AC-3$_d$ is its double-support heuristic. We should like to extend our comparison with AC-3$_d$ to include other arc-consistency algorithms.

Table 2. Average Results for RLFAP Problems

	AC-3 BFR		AC-7 BFR		AC-3		AC-3$_d$	
	checks	time	checks	time	checks	time	checks	time
RLFAP#3	615,371	0.050	412,594	0.138	615,371	0.124	267,532	0.092
RLFAP#5	1,735,239	0.126	848,438	0.232	833,282	0.252	250,797	0.136
RLFAP#8	2,473,269	0.168	654,086	0.168	1,170,748	0.420	25,930	0.040
RLFAP#11	971,893	0.072	638,932	0.212	971,893	0.268	406,247	0.186

References

[1] C. Bessière, E. C. Freuder, and J.-C. Régin. Using inference to reduce arc consistency computation. In C. S. Mellish, editor, *Proceedings of the Fourteenth International Joint Conference on Artificial Intelligence (IJCAI'95)*, volume 1, pages 592–598, Montréal, Québec, Canada, 1995. Morgan Kaufmann Publishers, Inc., San Mateo, California, USA.

[2] C. Bessière, E. G. Freuder, and J.-C. Régin. Using constraint metaknowledge to reduce arc consistency computation. *Artificial Intelligence*, 107(1):125–148, 1999.

[3] J. Gaschnig. Experimental case studies of backtrack vs. Waltz-type vs. new algorithms for satisficing assignment problems. In *Proceeding of the Second Biennial Conference, Canadian Society for the Computational Studies of Intelligence*, pages 268–277, 1978.

[4] A. K. Mackworth. Consistency in networks of relations. *Artificial Intelligence*, 8:99–118, 1977.

[5] A. K. Mackworth and E. C. Freuder. The complexity of some polynomial network consistency algorithms for constraint satisfaction problems. *Artificial Intelligence*, 25(1):65–73, 1985.

[6] M. R. C. van Dongen. *Constraints, Varieties, and Algorithms*. PhD thesis, Department of Computer Science, University College, Cork, Ireland, 2002.

[7] M. R. C. van Dongen. AC-3$_d$ an efficient arc-consistency algorithm with a low space-complexity. Technical Report TR-01-2002, Cork Constraint Computation Centre, 2002.

[8] R. J. Wallace and E. C. Freuder. Ordering heuristics for arc consistency algorithms. In *AI/GI/VI '92*, pages 163–169, Vancouver, British Columbia, Canada, 1992.

Integrating Search Objects in Asynchronous Constraint Solving

Georg Ringwelski

Fraunhofer FIRST, Kekuléstraße 7, 12489 Berlin, Germany
georg.ringwelski@first.fhg.de

Asynchronous Constraint Solving (ACS) integrates dynamic constraint processing into concurrent Object Oriented Programming. Cooperating constraint solvers run in parallel to the application program and infer actual variable domains incrementally from constraints that are added or retracted in the application thread. Constraint addition starts a chaotic iteration on the variable domains leading to a fixed point where no more domain reductions can be deduced from the constraint implementations. Constraint retraction removes all consequences of a constraint from the knowledge represented in the variables and can thus be considered the inverse operation to constraint addition.

Inconsistencies, that occur during propagation, are posted as event objects to handlers that define a reaction on the failure. Such an inconsistency event handler should be provided in every application, to define the desired behavior. ACS itself provides, like most CLP systems, a standard handler method that prints "no" to stdout and retracts the failed constraint.

Search, which is in difference to CLP not system inherent in OOP, is integrated in ACS as a separated object. The search algorithm is defined in the propagation methods of a constraint object, that can semantically be described as "every variable is instantiated". The integration as objects allows the use of arbitrary algorithms that implement a given search-interface. The algorithms can use an encapsulated search space without propagation of the non-deterministically determined assignments by using boolean consistency-check functions provided by the constraints. Alternatively the search algorithms can use regular propagation and check the consistency during chaotic iteration in domain reduction methods and variables. In these algorithms the search constraint posts instantiation constraints and provides an event listener that reacts on inconsistencies by retracting instantiations and re-posting them with changed values.

In interactive or continuous applications new constraints may be posted after a solution has been found by a search constraint. If the defined solution is not consistent with the new constraint, search has to be re-started in order to keep all constraints (including search) satisfied. This is done by an inconsistency event listener of the search constraint. If such an inconsistency occurs, the search is retracted, the new constraint is added to the CSP and search is re-posted in order to find an new solution. To improve the performance of the adaption of search to new constraints we plan to implement incremental search constraints in future work. The idea of such constraints is to remain a part of the solution and to retract and change only some instantiations in order to find an new solution.

P. Van Hentenryck (Ed.): CP 2002, LNCS 2470, p. 761, 2002.
© Springer-Verlag Berlin Heidelberg 2002

Distributed Constraint-Based Railway Simulation

Hans Schlenker

Fraunhofer FIRST, Kekuléstraße 7, 12489 Berlin, Germany
`hans.schlenker@first.fraunhofer.de`

In Railway Simulation, given timetables have to be checked against various criteria, mainly correctness and robustness. Most existing approaches use classical centralized simulation techniques. This work goes beyond that in two main aspects: I use Constraint Satisfaction to get rid of dead lock problems and the simulation is done distributed. This should make it possible to solve a Railway Simulation problem, never solved before in its complexity: the German railway network. In all existing simulation approaches, physical systems are described in terms of states and (mostly discrete) events. In Constraint-Based Simulation, we use a modeling that is completely different to classical approaches: The system to be simulated is described as one complex Constraint Satisfaction Problem (CSP). This CSP is solved using the well-known propagation and search techniques. In our application, the railway network is mapped into an abstract discrete model: It is divided into *blocks*, while each *real track section* may belong to more than one block. A block is then the atomical exclusion unit: In no event, one block may be occupied by more than one train at the same time. The way of a train through the network is divided into parts such that each part refers to exactly one block and the concatenation of all parts makes up the whole way of the train from its source to its destination. Assigning start and duration times to each part wrt. its block then gives directly a solution to the simulation problem. The big advantage of this approach is that dead lock situations are detected very early: constraint propagation does this for us. Distributed Railway Simulation (DRS) is Railway Simulation in a distributed manner: The simulation problem is cut into several pieces, which are simulated in several nodes. A meta-algorithm conducts the distributed simulation process: (1) Decompose problem (2) Start simulators (3) Distribute problem parts (4) Main loop: (4a) Let parts be simulated, *minimizing trains' delays* (4b) Try merging parts; where necessary to fit solutions: re-do simulation of parts, *minimizing differences to previous run* (5) Merge partial results into global result. The simulation problem is decomposed along the following criteria: *space* (e.g. the Berlin area), *time* (e.g. morning or afternoon), *train type* (e.g. national trains or regional trains only), and simulation granularity. We define an ordering between simulation parts: For each criterion, a separate ordering is defined, e.g. morning $\sqsubseteq$ afternoon, Europe $\sqsubseteq$ Germany $\sqsubseteq$ Bavaria $\sqsubseteq$ Munich , international trains $\sqsubseteq$ national trains $\sqsubseteq$ regional trains, abstract $\sqsubseteq$ detailed. These orderings are combined or extended to simulation *parts*, defining a partial ordering. The simulation is then conducted such that for each two parts p and q, if $p \sqsubseteq q$, then p must be computed *before* q.

P. Van Hentenryck (Ed.): CP 2002, LNCS 2470, p. 762, 2002.
© Springer-Verlag Berlin Heidelberg 2002

Symmetry Breaking in Peaceably Coexisting Armies of Queens

Karen E. Petrie

School of Computing & Engineering, University of Huddersfield, U.K.
k.e.petrie@hud.ac.uk

The "Peaceably Coexisting Armies of Queens" problem [1] is a difficult optimisation problem on a chess-board, requiring equal numbers of black and white papers to be placed on the board so that the white queens *cannot* attack the black queens (and necessarily vice versa).

The problem has the usual symmetry of the chess-board, as in the familiar n-queens problem; in addition, in any solution we can swap all the white queens for all the black queens, and we can combine these two kinds of symmetry. Hence the problem has 16 symmetries.

CSPs are often highly symmetric. Given any solution, there are others which are equivalent in terms of the underlying problem being solved. This can give rise to redundant search, since subtrees may be explored which are symmetric to subtrees already explored. To avoid redundant search, constraint programmers try to exclude all but one in each equivalence class of solutions.

Here I break symmetry during search using SBDS, developed by Gent and Smith [2]. SBDS works by taking a list of symmetry functions, provided by the programmer, and placing constraints derived from these symmetry functions on backtracking to a choice point and making the alternative choice.

I investigate how SBDS integrates with traditional CSP modelling techniques, such as reformulating the problem and modelling variable/value ordering heuristics, compared to other symmetry breaking methods.

Symmetry breaking is a vital to solving this problem in reasonable time: it gives a 5-fold improvement over the basic model. Moreover, it allows us to enumerate just non-isomorphic solutions. By combining SBDS with other CSP techniques, we can reduce run time still further. The use of these CSP techniques would be difficult if we had broken the symmetry by adding constraints or by reformulating the problem.

References

[1] R. A. Bosch. Peaceably Coexisting Armies of Queens *Optima*, 62:6-9. 1999.
[2] I. Gent and B. M. Smith. Symmetry breaking in constraint programming. In *ECAI-2000*, 599-603, 2000.

P. Van Hentenryck (Ed.): CP 2002, LNCS 2470, p. 763, 2002.
© Springer-Verlag Berlin Heidelberg 2002

Batch Processing with Sequence Dependent Setup Times

Petr Vilím

Charles University, Faculty of Mathematics and Physics
Malostranské náměstí 2/25, Praha 1, Czech Republic
vilim@kti.mff.cuni.cz

Abstract. Batch processing with sequence dependent setup times is a new extension of the disjunctive scheduling (scheduling on a unary resource). There are several successful filtering algorithms for solving disjunctive scheduling problem in a constraint programming framework. I adapted two of these algorithms (namely edge-finding and not-first/not-last) for the new extended problem and developed other three algorithms (not-before/not-after, precedence-graph-based filtering, sequence composition). Each of these algorithms filters out a different type of inconsistent values so they can be used together to achieve the maximum filtering.

The batch processing problem consists of a set of activities which have to be scheduled on a given resource. Each activity can be processed only in a given time interval (so called time window). The resource (unlike the unary resource, see [1]) can process several activities simultaneously, but the sum of their required capacities cannot exceed the capacity of the resource. Moreover, only the activities of the same family (type) can be processed together. The processing is done in batches: activities processed simultaneously start together and complete together, their processing time depends only on the family of the batch (*i.e.* the family of all activities in the batch). When one batch completes, the resource have to be adjusted for the next batch. Time needed for that (*i.e.* the setup time) depends on the families of both adjacent batches.

More information about these filtering algorithms, as well as experimental results, can be found in [2] and [3].

References

[1] Baptiste, P., Le Pape, C.: Edge-Finding Constraint Propagation Algorithms for Disjunctive and Cumulative Scheduling. In proceedings of the Fifteenth Workshop of the U. K. Planning Special Interest Group (1996)

[2] Vilím, P., Barták, R.: Filtering Algorithms for Batch Processing with Sequence Dependent Setup Times. In proceedings of the 6th International Conference on AI Planning and Scheduling, AIPS'02 (2002)

[3] Vilím, P.: Batch Processing with Sequence Dependent Setup Times: New Results. In proceedings of the 4th Workshop of Constraint Programming for Decision and Control, CPDC'02 (2002)

P. Van Hentenryck (Ed.): CP 2002, LNCS 2470, p. 764, 2002.

Interactive Heuristic Search Algorithm

Tomáš Müller

Department of Theoretical Computer Science, Charles University
Malostranské náměstí 2/25, Praha 1, Czech Republic
muller@kti.mff.cuni.cz

Abstract. We present a hybrid heuristic search algorithm for constraint satisfaction problems, which was proposed as a mixture of two basic approaches: local search and backtrack based search. One of its major advantages is interactive behaviour in the sense of changing the task during the search. Some results are presented using the well known n-queens problem.

In the current personal computing environment, the interactive behaviour of software is a feature requested by many users. Interactivity manifests itself in two directions: the user can observe what is happening inside the system and he or she can immediately influence the system. Naturally, this requires a special algorithm that is building the solution step by step and that can present a feasible (sub-) result at anytime. Moreover, such algorithm can be exposed to a task change, so it should not restart solving from scratch after such a change but the new solution should be built on top of the former solution.

The presented algorithm is a generalization of an interactive algorithm we designed for solving timetabling problems. Description of this timetabling algorithm and some achieved results on a real lecture timetabling problem are presented in papers [1, 2].

We propose an interactive algorithm that works in iterations. The algorithm uses two basic data structures: a set of variables that are not assigned and a partial feasible solution. At each iteration step, the algorithm tries to improve the current partial solution towards a complete one: the algorithm heuristically selects an un-assigned variable and chooses its value. Even if the best value is selected (whatever the best means), it may cause some conflicts with already assigned variables. Such conflicting variables are removed from the solution (become unassigned) and they are put back to the list of non-assigned variables.

We also present some results of the described algorithm on the N-queens problem, for example the algorithm needs 558 milliseconds to solve the problem with 1000 queens (on Intel Pentium III 1GHz, 256MB RAM, Windows 2000, JDK 1.4.0).

References

1. T. Müller and R. Barták. *Interactive Timetabling.* In Proceedings of the ERCIM workshop on constraints, Prague, 2001.
2. T. Müller and R. Barták. *Interactive Timetabling: Concepts, Techniques, and Practical Results.* In Proceedings of the PATAT'02 conference, Gent, 2002.

P. Van Hentenryck (Ed.): CP 2002, LNCS 2470, p. 765, 2002.

On Constraint Problems with Incomplete or Erroneous Data*

Neil Yorke-Smith

IC–Parc, Imperial College, London, SW7 2AZ, U.K.
nys@icparc.ic.ac.uk

Real-world Large Scale Combinatorial Optimisation problems (LSCOs) have inherent data uncertainties. The uncertainty can be due to the dynamic and unpredictable nature of the commercial world, but also due to the information available to those modelling the problem. We are concerned with the latter form of uncertainty, which can arise when the data is not fully known or is even erroneous. Our work is motivated by practical issues faced in real-world applications, for instance in energy trading [1]. Here, the demand and cost profiles have evolved due to market privatisation; thus the existing simulation or stochastic data models would not help address the actual problem.

In such cases, to grasp the actual complexity of the LSCO and bring useful feedback to the user, it is crucial to deal with real data despite its incompleteness or intrinsic errors. The core question is how to ensure that the correct problem is formulated and that correct information is derived.

We propose a formal framework that can be applied to the heterogeneous constraint classes and computation domains found in real-world LSCOs. The aim is to provide the user with reliable insight by: (1) enclosing the uncertainty using what is known for sure about the data, (2) guaranteeing the correctness of the model so described, and (3) deriving the closure to an uncertain constraint problem. We define the *certainty closure* and show how it can be derived by transformation to an equivalent certain problem. The closure describes all feasible solutions that hold under at least one satisfiable realisation of the data.

Practical usage of the framework — applied to a real-world network traffic analysis problem with uncertainty [2] — has shown that, in addition to the correct solution set, it provides us with insight into the constraint network. Our current research looks at finding uncertain constraint classes and their corresponding tractable transformation operators.

References

[1] Gervet, C., Caseau, Y., Montaut. D. On Refining Ill-Defined Constraint Problems: A Case Study in Iterative Prototyping. In: *Proc. of PACLP-99*, London (1999) 255–275
[2] Yorke-Smith, N., Gervet, C. Data Uncertainty in Constraint Programming: A Non-Probabilistic Approach. In: *Proc. of AAAI'01 Fall Symposium on Using Uncertainty within Computation*, Cape Cod, MA (2001) 146–152

---

* This work was partially supported by the EPSRC under grant GR/N64373/01.

P. Van Hentenryck (Ed.): CP 2002, LNCS 2470, p. 766, 2002.

Design of a New Metaheuristic for MAXSAT Problems

Andrea Roli

DEIS – Università degli Studi di Bologna

Iterated Local Search for MAXSAT

Metaheuristics [1] are approximate algorithms which effectively and efficiently exploit search space characteristics to find near-optimal solutions. Their combination with CP [2] is also very successful. In this work we present a new metaheuristic for tackling large MAXSAT instances. A survey of the state of the art of metaheuristics for MAXSAT can be found in [4]. The algorithm we designed is based on Iterated Local Search strategy [3] and combines the most effective local search strategies for SAT problems. Its high level scheme is the following:

s_0 = Generate_Initial_Solution_Randomly()
s^* = Parallel_MAX–GSAT(s_0, stop condition)
repeat
    s' = WalkSAT_Perturbation(s^*, *number of non_improving moves*)
    Adapt_tabu_length(*number of non_improving moves*)
    $s^{*'}$ = Tabu_Search(s')
    if $F(s^{*'}) > F(s^*)$ **then** set $s^* = s^{*'}$ [accept $s^{*'}$ if it is better than s^*]
while termination condition met

The most important property of *ILS-MAXSAT* is to achieve a dynamic balance between intensification and diversification, crucial in the exploration of large search spaces. The algorithm has been proven very effective on large unweighted MAXSAT instances and extensive comparisons with the best available algorithms is subject of ongoing work.

References

[1] C. Blum and A. Roli. Metaheuristics in combinatorial optimization: Overview and conceptual comparison. Tech. Rep. IRIDIA/01-13, IRIDIA, Université Libre de Bruxelles, 2001.
[2] F. Focacci, F. Laburthe, and A. Lodi. Local search and constraint programming. In *In Proceedings of MIC'2001*, pages 451–454, 2001.
[3] H. Ramalhino Lourenco, O. Martin, and T. Stützle. Iterated Local Search. In *Handbook of Metaheuristics*. To appear. Also available at http://www.intellektik.informatik.tu-darmstadt.de/~tom/pub.html.
[4] T. Stützle, H. Hoos, and A. Roli. A review of the literature on local search algorithms for MAX-SAT. Tech. Rep. AIDA–01-02, Intellectics Group, Darmstadt University of Technology, 2001.

P. Van Hentenryck (Ed.): CP 2002, LNCS 2470, p. 767, 2002.
© Springer-Verlag Berlin Heidelberg 2002

Disjunctive and Continuous Constraint Satisfaction Problems

Miguel A. Salido and Federico Barber

Departamento de Sistemas Informáticos y Computación
Universidad Politécnica de Valencia, Spain
{msalido,fbarber}@dsic.upv.es

Abstract. In this work, we extend the class of Horn constraints to include disjunctions with an arbitrary number of linear inequalities, linear disequations and non-linear disequations. We propose a preprocess step in which two algorithms are carried out. The first algorithm called *Constraint Selection Algorithm (CSA)* translates the disjunctive non-binary CSP into a non-disjunctive one. This algorithm selects the more appropriate set of atomic constraints that is more likely to be consistent. The second algorithm called *Constraint Ordering Algorithm (COA)* classifies the resultant constraints from the most restricted to the least restricted one. Then, a CSP solver carries out the search through the non-disjunctive and ordered problem.

Koubarakis, in [1], has studied the class of *Horn Constraints* which includes disjunctions with an unlimited number of disequations and *at most one* inequality per disjunction. (e.g., $3x_1 - 4x_2 - 2x_3 \leq 4 \lor x_1 + 3x_2 - x_4 \neq 6 \lor x_1 + x_3 + x_4 \neq 9$). We extend the class of Horn constraints to include disjunctions with an arbitrary number of linear inequalities, linear disequations and non-linear disequations. For example: $2x_1 + 3x_2 - x_3 \leq 6 \lor x_1 + 5x_4 \leq 9 \lor 2x_1 - x_3 \neq 3 \lor x_2^3 - \sqrt[3]{x_3} \neq 2$.

The resulting class will be called the class of *Extended Horn Constraints*. Our objective is mainly to decide global consistency, and also to obtain one o several solutions, and the solution that optimizes an objective or multi-objective function. To achieve these objective, we propose two algorithms: the *Constraint Selection Algorithm (CSA)* that selects the non-disjunctive problem that is more likely to be consistent and the *Constraint Ordering Algorithm (COA)* that classifies the resultant constraints in order to study the more restrict constraints in first place. These algorithms can be applied to general CSP solvers like *HSA* [2] in order to manage the class of extended Horn constraints.

Extended version in: http://www.math.unipd.it/~frossi/cp2002-doctoral.html

References

[1] Koubarakis, M.: Tractable Disjunction of Linear Constraints. In Proceedings of Principles and Practice of Constraint Programming, CP-96, (1999) 297–307
[2] Salido, M. A., Giret, A., Barber, F.: Constraint Satisfaction by means of Dynamic Polyhedra. In Operational Research Proceedings. Springer-Verlag, (2002) 405–412

P. Van Hentenryck (Ed.): CP 2002, LNCS 2470, p. 768, 2002.
© Springer-Verlag Berlin Heidelberg 2002

Tuning Randomization
in Backtrack Search SAT Algorithms

Inês Lynce and João Marques-Silva

Technical University of Lisbon, IST/INESC/CEL, Portugal
{ines,jpms}@sat.inesc.pt

Propositional Satisfiability (SAT) is a well-known NP-complete problem, being fundamental in solving many application problems in Computer Science and Engineering. Recent work on SAT has provided experimental and theoretical evidence that the use of randomization can be quite effective at solving hard instances of SAT. First, randomization was used in local search SAT algorithms, where the search is started over again to avoid getting *stuck* in a locally optimal partial solution. Moreover, in the last few years randomization has also been included in systematic search algorithms. As a result, backtrack search is given more freedom either to find a solution or to prove unsatisfiability. Indeed, backtrack search algorithms, randomized and run with restarts, were shown to perform significantly better on specific problem instances.

A complete backtrack search SAT algorithm can be *randomized* by introducing a fixed or variable amount of randomness in the branching heuristic. The amount of randomness may affect the value of the selected variable or which variable is selected from the set of variables with the highest heuristic metric (or even within $x\%$ of the highest metric).

A *restart strategy* consists of defining a *cutoff* value in the number of backtracks, and repeatedly running a randomized complete SAT algorithm, each time the limiting cutoff value is reached. If restarts are used with a fixed cutoff value, then the resulting algorithm is *not* complete. On the other hand, if there is a policy for increasing the cutoff value (e.g. by a constant amount after each restart), then the algorithm is complete, and thus able to prove unsatisfiability.

More recently, the introduction of randomization in the backtrack step has also been proposed. Here, the conflict clause is used for *randomly* deciding which decision assignment variable is to be toggled. This contrasts with the usual non-chronological backtracking approach, in which the most recent decision assignment variable is selected as the backtrack point.

Nonetheless, the use of randomization entails, by definition, an unpredictable behavior. Consequently, tuning the use of randomization is not only a key aspect, but can also be a difficult and challenging task. The analysis of experimental results obtained for different configurations of randomized algorithms can certainly bring some key insights on this topic [1].

References

[1] I. Lynce and J. P. Marques-Silva. Tuning randomization in backtrack search SAT algorithms. Technical Report RT/05/2002, INESC, June 2002.

P. Van Hentenryck (Ed.): CP 2002, LNCS 2470, p. 769, 2002.
© Springer-Verlag Berlin Heidelberg 2002

Constraint Solving in Test-Data Generation

Yuan Zhan

Department of Computer Science, University of York
York, YO10 5DD, UK
yuan@cs.york.ac.uk

Abstract. Test data generation is the most labor-intensive work for software testing. As a result, automatic test case generation is a way forward. It is typical to denote the conditions of searching the test input that can cause a particular action to occur into constraint problems. Consequently, practical method for solving the constraints is desired.

Software testing is an important process that is performed to support quality assurance. The testing activities usually include designing test cases, executing the software with the test cases and then examining the results produced by the executions. Studies indicate that testing consumes more than half of the labor expended to produce a working program [4]. Of all the activities consisted in testing, test cases generation is the most labor-intensive and time-consuming work. Hence, practical ways to automate the test-data generation is a way forward.

Since complete test is impossible [4], we have to find ways to generate the most effective test-data that can cover all the error prone points and, the most important, can detect the faults. A variety of coverage criteria [3] have been developed to judge the sufficiency of the test set. These criteria can also act as the directions for generating test cases. A simple example of these criteria that is based on the program is statement coverage, which requires every statement in the program being executed at least once. Thus to satisfy the coverage requirement, we need to generate test-data that can execute some particular statements or execute some particular paths. These requirements are usually denoted into constraint satisfaction problem. By solving the constraints, we can get the test-data [1].

Other than generating tests from the program, we may also try to generate test cases from the speciation or architecture. Constraint solving can be applied in a similar way.

References

[1]   Rich DeMillo and Jeff Offutt. Constraint-Based Automatic Test Data Generation. IEEE Transactions on Software Engineering, 17(9): 900-910, September 1991.

[2]   J. King. Symbolic Execution and Program Testing. Communications of the ACM, 19(7): 385-394, 1976.

P. Van Hentenryck (Ed.): CP 2002, LNCS 2470, pp. 770-771, 2002.

[3]   H. Zhu, P. A. V. Hall and J. H. R. May. Software Unit Test Coverage and Adequacy.

[4]   B. Beizer. Software Testing Techniques. Thomson Computer Press, 2nd edition, 1990.

Improving Cost Calculations for Global Constraints in Local Search

Markus Bohlin

SICS Västerås, Sweden
markus.bohlin@sics.se

Local search for constraint satisfaction is usually performed by local minimization of a cost function. Traditionally, the cost function used is simply the number of violated constraints for a given assignment. When introducing global constraints in local search[1], use of this cost function will give the effect that practically no global constraints will be satisfied. The reason for this is that global constraints in general are much harder to satisfy than other constraints, and are as a consequence of this also hard to satisfy within the limited neighborhood of the current assignment. Another reason is that the value of satisfying a global constraint is as low as for any other constraint. Specific cost functions for global constraints have been proposed[1,2] to amend this. The total cost of an assignment using this scheme is the sum of the costs of the constraints present.

Instead of using a specific cost function for each global constraint, we propose to use a generic cost function, based on a formal definition of the specific global constraint used. We use a framework based on set reasoning regarding certain basic constraints to formally define global constraints. From this definition, we then calculate a fair *virtual* cost, based on the number of basic constraints that are violated. In addition to using the virtual cost to guide local search, we can use this cost function for labeling heuristics, such as the *most constrained first* strategy found in many traditional constraint programming systems.

We have given formal definitions and virtual costs for the global constraints *alldifferent*, *serialize*, and two variants of *cumulative*. As a basis for our calculations, we use *basic constraints*, which are in our system disjunctions of linear constraints. We have also invented and implemented algorithms based on sweep, which can for the scheduling constraints above calculate the virtual cost in linear time in the number of tasks in the constraint. The framework we propose can also be used for other techniques that can take advantage of the increased granularity. For example, we can perform dynamic weighting and tabu search on the specific basic constraints that are violated in a global constraint.

We intend to investigate inclusion of more global constraints in our framework, and to prove the connection between theoretical cost and the sweep algorithm. We will also investigate the correctness of the cost calculations on real-world problems in timetabling, dynamic scheduling and planning.

[1] Alexander Nareyek. Using Global Constraints for Local Search. *Proc. DIMACS Workshop on Constraint Programming and Large Scale Discrete Optimization*, 1998.
[2] P. Galinier and J. Hao, A General Approach for Constraint Solving by Local Search, *Proc. Second International Workshop on Integration of AI and OR Techniques in Constraint Programming for Combinatorial Optimization Problems*, 2000.

P. Van Hentenryck (Ed.): CP 2002, LNCS 2470, p. 772, 2002.
© Springer-Verlag Berlin Heidelberg 2002

A Modeling Framework for Constraints

Gerrit Renker

School of Computing, RGU Aberdeen, UK
gr@scms.rgu.ac.uk

Abstract. This paper reports on the MACRON (*Modeling and Acquiring Constraints Reusing Object Notation*) project, which defines a modeling framework for CSPs compliant to available standards.

1   Introduction and Objectives

Modeling is widely used in database design and traditional software engineering. A broad range of both methodologies and (visual) support tools exist for these disciplines. In constraint solving, modeling support is less ubiquitous. The MACRON project aims at achieving a high level of modeling support for the (re-) formulation of CSPs. This involves (visual) notation, tools and a methodology.

2   Modeling in Macron

We use a visual representation in form of UML [1] diagrams, complemented by a textual constraint notation using the Object Constraint Language (OCL) of UML. OCL is fully integrated into the UML standard and can access all parts of a UML diagram. An explanation of OCL is beyond scope here, see [3].

Traditionally, CSPs are represented as a triple of variables, domains and constraints. The figure below illustrates this notion in UML .

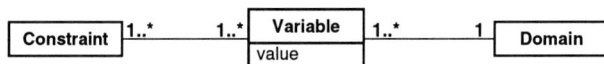

Considering that domains are a special case of unary constraints, the traditional CSP definition comprises only single-attribute entities (variables) and its relationships are restricted to just one type (constraints). In many real-life problems, however, constituting entities may exhibit multiple attributes, domains may be structured and relationships may be nested in complex ways. To allow this kind of complexity, we use an OO representation of the problem, similar to the use of semantic data modeling in database design. Briefly, the most important reasons for using an OO representation lie here in the ability to differentiate several types of relationships and to consider a problem at various levels of abstraction. It is important to point out that the OO representation is primarily used for modeling purposes. It is not imperative to actually implement each entity as an object.

P. Van Hentenryck (Ed.): CP 2002, LNCS 2470, pp. 773–774, 2002.
© Springer-Verlag Berlin Heidelberg 2002

3   A Sketch: N-queens Problem

The n-queens problem is sufficiently well-known to present a model and a few
OCL features. We do not consider diagonal attacks here. The following OCL
constraints relate to the structural model via the class context.

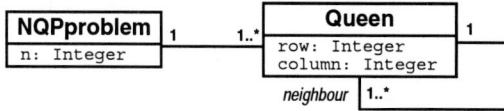

Shown below are the multiplicity constraint and the uniqueness constraints for
the rows and columns.

```
context NQProblem inv:
    queen->size() = self.n and --multiplicity
    queen->isUnique(row) and
    queen->isUnique(column)
```

The isUnique() construct is similar to the alldifferent global constraint, which
is implemented in several constraint programming languages.

4   Discussion and Further Work

We have performed case studies on a variety of known CSPs. The results show
that UML/OCL facilitate the expression of CSPs and that the visual model aids
structuring the problem. The next step is a critical assessment of this approach
and comparison with languages such as OPL [2]. For instance, unaltered OCL
does not supply high-level expressions such as atmost() constraints and does not
have any constructs to specify the search process. Without additions, OCL can
only help to build static and abstract CSP models at the moment. On the other
hand, OPL does not employ visual models. Further, OCL (as also OPL) does not
have a published formal semantics yet. Resolving these issues is ongoing work.

References

[1] James Rumbaugh, Ivar Jacobson, and Grady Booch. *The Unified Modeling Language Reference Manual.* Addison-Wesley, 1999.
[2] Pascal Van Hentenryck. *The OPL Optimization Programming Language.* The MIT Press, January 1999.
[3] Jos B. Warmer and Anneke G. Kleppe. *The Object Constraint Language: Precise Modeling with UML.* Addison Wesley, 1999.

A Linear Programming Based Satisfiability Solver Using a New Horn-Driven Search Tree Design

Linda van Norden and Hans van Maaren

Technical University Delft, Faculty of Information Technology and Systems
Mekelweg 4 2628 CD Delft, P.O. Box 5031 2600 GA Delft, The Netherlands
L.vanNorden@its.tudelft.nl

We will present an algorithm for the satisfiability problem, which finds its origin in the Integer Programming area, and therefore will also generalize to more general constraint programming problems. This algorithm is based on single-lookahead unit resolution ([2]), linear programming and a new search tree design based on a tree design by ([1]). The special aspect of the tree is that it is not a binary search tree. The advantage of our algorithm over a standard integer programming approach, is that we need to solve a linear program only in a very limited number of nodes in the search tree. In every node in the search tree we first apply single-lookahead unit resolution. The unit propagation algorithm we used in our implementation is based on the watched literal strategy. Only in case the unit resolution does not lead to the conclusion that the formula in the node is unsatisfiable or has a satisfying assignment, we solve a linear program. The solution of the linear program is used to split the part of the search into subparts. This splitting aims for getting a formula close to a Horn formula.

Horn clauses are clauses in which at most one variable occurs in negated form. Therefore, formulae with only Horn clauses of size two or larger are always satisfied if all variables are set to true. After unit resolution, all clauses have length two or more. The linear programming algorithm finds a feasible solution that is as close as possible to the all-ones vector. An almost Horn formula will therefore yield linear programming solutions that are closer to an integer-valued solution. By construction, conflicts are likely to be close to the linear programming solution. Preprocessing is applied to make formulae closer to Horn formulae. Below we give a brief overview of our algorithm

1. Apply single look-ahead unit propagation in order to simplify the formula
2. Apply an heuristic to make the formula more Horn-like
3. If the formula is not proved to be unsatisfiable or satisfiable, transform the simplified CNF-formula to a set of linear constraints
4. Solve the linear program, this gives a solution vector ω
5. Use ω to partition the search space.

P. Van Hentenryck (Ed.): CP 2002, LNCS 2470, pp. 775–776, 2002.

References

[1] Van Maaren, H., Dang, C., Simplicial pivoting algorithms for a tractable class of integer programs. *Journal of Combinatorial Optimization, 6.* 2002, 133-142

[2] Franco, J., *Relative size of certain polynomial time solvable subclasses of satisfiability. DIMACS Series Discrete Math. Theoret. Computer Science, volume 35.* Amer.Math.Soc., Piscataway, NJ, 1997, 211-233

A Concurrent Constraint Programming Approach for Trajectory Determination of Autonomous Vehicles*

Luis Quesada and Peter Van Roy

Catholic University of Louvain, Louvain-la-Neuve, Belgium
{luque,pvr}@info.ucl.ac.be

Abstract. We present trajectory determination of Autonomous Vehicles as an extension of the open-path asymmetric Traveling Salesman Problem with Time Windows.

In this work we shows an approach to model trajectory determination, using concurrent constraint programming, for autonomous multi-agent systems in charge of automatically managing the mission of an uninhabited vehicle.

In the approach suggested by [GP01] and [BGP99], the task of the constraint solver is to automatically generate a plan for autonomous vehicles according to changes in the environment. The generation of the plan considers the constraints associated with the trajectory of the vehicle, the scheduling of the mission goals and the management of resources. Thus, the task of the solver is to find a solution (a plan) that satisfies all those constraints.

We extend their approach by introducing the notion of elimination of irrelevant variables and considering a more sophisticated search strategy based on the structure of the environment. The environment, which is represented by a directed graph, can be defined by demand by using virtual edges that are expanded when it is inferred that the vehicle could use those edges.

When the constraints of the generation of the plan are considered, Trajectory determination turns out to be an open-path asymmetric generalization of the Traveling Salesman Problem with Time Windows [PGPR96], where nodes are allowed to be optional and cumulative constraints have to be considered.

References

[BGP99] E. Bornschlegl, C. Guettier, and J. Poncet. Automatic planning for autonomous spacecrafts constellation. In *PDCS'99*, 1999.

[GP01]   C. Guettier and J. Poncet. Multi-levels planning for spacecraft autonomy. In *i-sairas 2001*, 2001.

[PGPR96] G. Pesant, M. Gendreau, J. Potvin, and J. Rousseau. An exact constraint logic programming algorithm for the travelling salesman with time windows, 1996.

---

* This research is partially funded by the PIRATES project of the Walloon Region (Belgium) and the PEPITO project of the European Union

P. Van Hentenryck (Ed.): CP 2002, LNCS 2470, p. 777, 2002.
© Springer-Verlag Berlin Heidelberg 2002

Using Constraint Propagation to Accelerate Column Generation in Aircraft Scheduling*

Mattias Grönkvist

Department of Computing Science, Chalmers University of Technology
Eklandagatan 86, S-412 96 Göteborg, Sweden

Abstract. We discuss how the use of Constraint Programming can help speed up a *Column Generation* process for the *Tail Assignment* problem. A generalized preprocessing technique based on constraint propagation is presented that can remove up to 98% of the connections of the flight network, much more than methods currently in use. The result is substantial speed-up and increased solution quality for the column generator. We also show how propagation can be used within fixing heuristics, and present a heuristic propagation-based preprocessing method taking cost into consideration. Computational results on data from several airlines is presented.

The *Tail Assignment* problem is the problem of constructing individual maintenance feasible routes for a set of aircraft, while covering a set of flights. Our formulation of the problem is more general than typical tail assignment formulations, making it suitable for long-term tail assignment including re-fleeting and crew integration, while considering all operational constraints. Long-term tail assignment makes the transition from planning to operations smoother than with the procedures currently used at many airlines.

It is our experience that constraint programming is very strong from a feasibility point of view, but is less suited to the type of heavy-duty optimization needed in e.g. airline scheduling. For column generation, a well-known solution method in operations research, the situation is the opposite − it is very powerful for optimization, but it is weaker when it comes to feasibility. Integrating the two for tail assignment is interesting because the problem has a strong feasibility component, as no extra aircraft exist and all flights must be covered exactly once, while optimization is essential for long-term planning. We show how constraint propagation can dramatically improve the performance of the column generation process, both runtime and quality-wise. Constraint propagation is used in a preprocessing step, to reduce the complexity of the problem, and in fixing heuristics, making the heuristics more stable. There are several other possibilities for integration, some of which are discussed briefly. The overall conclusion is that there is great potential for integrating constraint propagation and column generation for problems similar to tail assignment, e.g. crew scheduling problems.

---

* Research partly funded by Carmen Systems AB, http://www.carmen.se

P. Van Hentenryck (Ed.): CP 2002, LNCS 2470, p. 778, 2002.
© Springer-Verlag Berlin Heidelberg 2002

Solving and Learning Soft Temporal Constraints; Ceteris Paribus Statements Represented as Soft Constraints Problems

Kristen B. Venable

University of Padova, Italy
kvenable@math.unipd.it

Abstract. Soft temporal constraints problems (TCSPs) allow to describe in a natural way scenarios where events happen over time and preferences are associated to event distances and durations. However, sometimes such local preferences are difficult to set, and it may be easier instead to associate preferences to some complete solutions of the problem. The Constraint Satisfaction framework combined with Machine learning techniques can be useful in this respect. Soft constraints are useful in general for manipulating preferences. In particular it is possible to approximate CP nets, a graphical representation of ceteris paribus conditional preference statements, with semiring based soft constraints problems.

I have worked on the development of a machinery for both solving and learning simple TCSPs, where each constraint is represented as a single interval and a function associating a preference to each point of the interval. The main results achieved are [3]: 1) some theoretical results on tractability of some sub classes of problems; 2) two solvers that are able to deal with simple TCSP with a particular shape of the preference functions; 3) a random simple TCSP generator; 4) a learning module which learns convex quadratic preference functions. Recently I have worked on building a relation between CP nets [2] and semiring based soft constraints [1]. Soft constraints allow to modify CP nets adding a quantitative representation of preferences. This is interesting since such an approximation allows to overcome some complexity deficiencies that the two models have when faced with dominance queries and optimal solution search.

References

[1] S. Bistarelli, U. Montanari, and F. Rossi. Semiring-based Constraint Solving and Optimization. Journal of the ACM, 44(2):201–236, March 1997.
[2] Craig Boutilier, Ronen I. Brafman, Holger H. Hoos, and David Poole. Reasoning with ceteris paribus preference statements. Proceedings of the Fifteenth Conference on Uncertainty in Artificial Intelligence, pages 71-80, Stockholm, 1999.
[3] F. Rossi, A Sperduti, K. B. Venable, L. Khatib, R. Morris, and Paul Morris. Solving and Learning Soft Temporal Constraints: Experimental Setting and Results. Proceedings of Constraint Programming Conference CP 2002, Ithaca, NY, 2002.

P. Van Hentenryck (Ed.): CP 2002, LNCS 2470, p. 779, 2002.
© Springer-Verlag Berlin Heidelberg 2002

A Partially Solved Form for Heterogeneous Constraints in Disjunctive Normal Form

Frank Seelisch

DaimlerChrysler AG
Research Information & Communication, Knowledge-based Engineering
Frank.Seelisch@DaimlerChrysler.com

In order to support constraint solving for challenging engineering applications, as e.g. accomplished by the *Relational Constraint Solver* (see [MST]), we need to implement *join* and *project* operators (see e.g. [AHV] or [M]) for heterogeneous constraints. The heterogeneity is due to finite domain and real-valued variables, linear and non-linear arithmetic constraints, (dis-)equations and inequalities.

In such a framework, it turns out advantageous to spend reasonable effort on the computation of "convenient representations" of intermediate constraints, especially in view of subsequent projection steps. A constraint is "conveniently represented" if it is in a so-called *partially solved form*. The equivalence

$$z = x \cdot y \quad \Leftrightarrow \quad (x = z \div y \ \land \ y \neq 0) \ \lor \ (z = 0 \ \land \ y = 0)$$

relates an atomic constraint in solved form for z to a disjunction in solved form for x. Although more complex, the right-hand side representation is more useful when we are about to eliminate variable x, since it provides a substitute for x.

In our implementation of a *Relational Constraint Solver*, we have realised a *partially solved form* to speed up the computation of projections, which is based on and extends known normal forms (see e.g. [HG], [I]). Establishing our *partially solved form* may involve the reformulation of non-linear constraints, as exemplified above. Therefore, our approach goes beyond the postponement of non-linear constraints until they have simplified to linear ones, as e.g. deployed in CLP($\mathbb{R}$).

References

[MST]   J. Mauss, F. Seelisch, M. Tatar: A Relational Constraint Solver for Model-based Engineering, *Principles and Practice of Constraint Programming - CP2002*, Conference Proceedings, 2002.

[AHV]   S. Abiteboul, R. Hull, V. Vianu: Foundations of Databases, *Addison-Wesley*, 1995, ISBN 0-201-53771-0.

[M]   D. Maier: The theory of relational databases, *Computer Science Press*, Rockville, MD, 1986.

[HG]   P. Van Hentenryck and T. Graf: Standard Forms for Rational Linear Arithmetics in Constraint Logic Programming, *Annals of Mathematics and Artificial Intelligence*, 5(2-4), 1992.

[I]   J.-L. Imbert: Solved Forms for Linear Constraints in CLP Languages, *Proceedings of the Sixth International Conference on Artificial Intelligence*, AIMSA'94, pp. 77-90, World Scientific, Sofia, Bulgaria, 1994.

P. Van Hentenryck (Ed.): CP 2002, LNCS 2470, p. 780, 2002.

Models of Injection Problems*

Brahim Hnich[1] and Toby Walsh[2]

[1] Computer Science Division, Department of Information Science, Uppsala University
Uppsala, Sweden
Brahim.Hnich@dis.uu.se
[2] Cork Constraint Computation Center, University College Cork, Ireland
tw@4c.ucc.ie

There are many problems that can be modelled as injection problems. These problems can be scheduling problems, combinatorial graph problems, cryptarithmetic puzzles, etc. Injection problems can be modelled as constraint satisfaction problems. The straightforward formulation would be to have as many variables as the elements of the source set that range over the target set, which captures a total function. To enforce that the function is injective, we would need to state an alldifferent constraint among all the variables. Dual variables can also be used along with the primal ones and linked through channeling constraints. We propose three different ways of achieveing this, as well as we add some implied constraints. The proposed models of injection problems are compared using the constraint tightness parameterized by the level of local consistency being enforced [2]. We proved that, with respect to arc-consistency a single primal alldifferent constraint is tighter than channeling constraints together with the implied or the dual not-equals constraints, but that the channeling constraints alone are as tight as the primal not-equals constraints. Both these gaps can lead to an exponential reduction in search cost when MAC or MGAC are used. The theoretical results showed that occurs constraints on dual variables are redundant, so we can safely discard them. The asymptotic analysis added details to the theoretical results. We conclude that it is safe to discard some of the models because they achieve less pruning than other models at the same cost. However, we keep a model employing primal and dual variables even though it achieves the same amount of pruning as a primal model at a higher cost because it might allow the development of cheap value ordering heuristics. Experimental results on a sport scheduling problem confirmed that MGAC on channeling and implied constraints outperformed MAC on primal not-equals constraints, and could be competitive with maintaining GAC on a primal alldifferent constraint.

References

[1] B. Hnich and T. Walsh. Models of Injection Problems. In *Proc. of the ECAI'02 Workshop on Modelling and Solving Problems with Constraints*. 2002.
[2] T. Walsh. Permutation Problems and Channeling Constraints. In *Proc. of the IJCAI'01 Workshop on Modelling and Solving Problems with Constraints*. 2001.

---

* Full version of this work can be found at [1].

P. Van Hentenryck (Ed.): CP 2002, LNCS 2470, p. 781, 2002.

Partial Symmetry Breaking

Iain McDonald

University of St Andrews, Fife, Scotland
iain@dcs.st-and.ac.uk

Abstract. In this paper I define *partial symmetry breaking*, a concept that has been used in many previous papers without being the main topic of any research.

1 Introduction and Motivation

We are now at a point in constraint programming research where there are many methods of both recognizing symmetries and breaking symmetries in CSPs. A symmetry breaking **method** for CSPs, can be broken into two parts, the symmetry breaking **technique** and the symmetry **representation**. The technique is how we apply the symmetry breaking. The symmetry representation is concerned with how the descriptions of symmetries are implemented and how we use this implementation to apply the symmetry breaking technique. Symmetry breaking can be improved by reducing the number of symmetries we need to consider. This affects the *representation* of the symmetries but not the *technique*.

In [1] it is shown that where there is a large number of symmetries, we can discard some of them and by doing so reduce run-time greatly. By only describing a subset of symmetries we are performing *partial symmetry breaking* (PSB) i.e. performing some redundant search because the symmetry breaking technique is too costly or even impossible to perform.

Acknowledgments

The author is funded by an EPSRC studentship. He would like to thank his supervisors Ian Gent and Steve Linton as well as Tom Kelsey, Barbara Smith, Toby Walsh and all the other members of the APES research group.

References

[1] Iain McDonald and Barbara Smith. Partial symmetry breaking. Technical Report APES-49-2002, APES Research Group, May 2002. Available from http://www.dcs.st-and.ac.uk/~apes/apesreports.html.

P. Van Hentenryck (Ed.): CP 2002, LNCS 2470, p. 782, 2002.
© Springer-Verlag Berlin Heidelberg 2002

Automatic Generation
of Implied Clauses for SAT

Lyndon Drake, Alan Frisch, and Toby Walsh

Artificial Intelligence Group, Department of Computer Science, University of York
York YO10 5DD, United Kingdom
{lyndon,frisch,tw}@cs.york.ac.uk,
http://www.cs.york.ac.uk/~{lyndon,frisch,tw}

Propositional satisfiability (SAT) is the archetypal NP-complete problem [1]. A great deal of recent SAT research, particularly on the performance of SAT solvers, has been driven by structured instances, which are obtained by mapping other problem classes into SAT. It is possible to efficiently solve a wide range of problems by mapping them into SAT and solving the SAT representation of the problem.

Currently, the most effective complete method for solving SAT instances is backtracking search. Logical inference can be used to reduce the size of the search space a SAT solver must explore. Unfortunately, inference often consumes so much time and memory that these costs outweigh the benefit gained by pruning the search space. The challenge is to limit this overhead while still pruning enough of the search space to make the inference worthwhile.

Existing techniques for combining inference with search include unit propagation [2], conflict learning [3], and resolution-based methods [4, 5]. Some ways to reduce the overhead of inference include: using data structures that make fast inference operations possible; allowing inference only during preprocessing; and heuristics for determining when inference is worthwhile. We are working on explaining why some inference techniques are more beneficial to search than others, and using that information to select other beneficial inference techniques.

References

[1] S. A. Cook. The complexity of theorem-proving procedures. In *Proceedings of the Third ACM Symposium on Theory of Computing*, pages 151–158, 1971.
[2] Martin Davis, George Logemann, and Donald Loveland. A machine program for theorem-proving. *Communications of the ACM*, 5:394–397, 1962.
[3] João P. Marques Silva and Karem A. Sakallah. Conflict analysis in search algorithms for satisfiability. In *Proceedings of the IEEE International Conference on Tools with Artificial Intelligence*, Nov 1996.
[4] Irina Rish and Rina Dechter. Resolution versus search: Two strategies for SAT. In Ian Gent, Hans van Maaren, and Toby Walsh, editors, *SAT2000: Highlights of Satisfiability Research in the Year 2000*, volume 63 of *Frontiers in Artificial Intelligence and Applications*, pages 215–259. IOS Press, 2000.
[5] Allen van Gelder. Satisfiability testing with more reasoning and less guessing. In D. S. Johnson and M. Trick, editors, *Cliques, Coloring, and Satisfiability: Second DIMACS Implementation Challenge*, DIMACS Series in Discrete Mathematics and Theoretical Computer Science. American Mathematical Society, 1995.

P. Van Hentenryck (Ed.): CP 2002, LNCS 2470, p. 783, 2002.
© Springer-Verlag Berlin Heidelberg 2002

Bridging the Gap between SAT and CSP*

Carlos Ansótegui and Felip Manyà

Department of Computer Science, Universitat de Lleida, Spain

Our research program is aimed at bridging the gap between propositional satisfiability encodings and constraint satisfaction formalisms. The challenge is to combine the inherent efficiencies of SAT solvers operating on uniform satisfiability encodings with the much more compact and natural representations, and more sophisticated propagation techniques of CSP formalisms. Our research objective is to define a new language —MV-SAT— that incorporates the best characteristics of the existing many-valued languages [1,2], as well as to develop fast MV-SAT solvers. MV-SAT is formally defined as the problem of deciding the satisfiability of MV-formulas. An MV-formula is a classical propositional conjunctive clause form based on a generalized notion of literal, called MV-literal. Given a domain T ($|T| \geq 2$) equipped with a total ordering $\leq$, an MV-literal is an expression of the form $S : p$, where p is a propositional variable and S is a subset of T which is of the form $\{i\}$, $\uparrow i = \{j \in T \mid j \geq i\}$, or $\downarrow i = \{j \in T \mid j \leq i\}$ for some $i \in T$. The informal meaning of $S : p$ is "p is constrained to the values in S".

In our talk, (i) we discuss the logical and complexity advantages of MV-SAT compared to SAT and other many-valued problem modeling languages; (ii) we show that MV-SAT encodings of some combinatorial problems are much more compact and natural than SAT encodings; for instance, while a SAT encoding of a quasigroup of order n uses n^3 variables and $O(n^4)$ clauses, an MV-SAT encoding uses n^2 variables and $2n^2$ clauses; (iii) we describe MV-WalkSAT, a local search solver that incorporates advanced heuristics to escape from local optima; and (iv) we provide experimental evidence that MV-WalkSAT outperforms WalkSAT in all the benchmarks we have tried (graph coloring, quasigroup completion, all interval series, round robin, and social golfer). The table shows the experimental results obtained for hard instances of the quasigroup completion problem.

	order 33			order 36		
algorithm	ω	flips	seconds	ω	flips	seconds
WalkSAT	30	$9.41 \cdot 10^6$	21.49	22	$89.61 \cdot 10^6$	255.52
MV-WalkSAT	20	$1.63 \cdot 10^6$	3.09	18	$10.59 \cdot 10^6$	18.78

* Research partially supported by the project CICYT TIC2001-1577-C03-03.

P. Van Hentenryck (Ed.): CP 2002, LNCS 2470, pp. 784–785, 2002.
© Springer-Verlag Berlin Heidelberg 2002

References

[1] R. Béjar, A. Cabiscol, C. Fernández, F. Manyà, and C. P. Gomes. Capturing structure with satisfiability. In *CP-2001*, pages 137–152, 2001.
[2] A. M. Frisch and T. J. Peugniez. Solving non-boolean satisfiability problems with stochastic local search. In *IJCAI-2001*, 2001.

Reducing Symmetry in Matrix Models[*]

Zeynep Kiziltan

Department of Information Science,Uppsala University, Sweden
Zeynep.Kiziltan@dis.uu.se

Symmetry in a CSP is a permutation of variables, or the values in the domains, or both which preserve the state of the search: either all of them lead to a solution or none does. Hence, elimination of symmetry is essential to avoid exploring equivalent branches in a search tree. An important class of symmetries in constraint programming arises from matrices of decision variables where any two rows can be interchanged, as well as any two columns. Eliminating all such symmetries is not so easy as the effort required may be exponential. We are thus interested in reducing significant amount of row and column symmetries in matrix models with a polynomial effort. In this respect, we have shown that lexicographically ordering both rows and columns of a matrix model reduces much of such symmetries[1]. For an $n \times n$ matrix model with row and column symmetry, $O(n)$ lexicographic constraints between adjacent rows and columns are imposed. We have shown that decomposing a lexicographic ordering constraint between a pair of vectors carries a penalty either in the amount or the cost of constraint propagation. We have therefore developed a linear-time global-consistency algorithm which enforces a lexicographic ordering between two vectors[2]. Our experiments confirm the efficiency and value of this new global constraint. As a matrix model has multiple rows and columns, we can treat such a problem as a single global ordering constraint over the whole matrix. Alternatively, we can decompose it into lexicographic ordering constraints between all or adjacent pairs of vectors. Such decompositions hinder constraint propagation in general. However, we identify the special case of a lexicographical ordering on 0/1 variables where it does not.

Towards reducing much of row and column symmetries in an efficient way, one can lexicographically order one dimension, and insist that the vectors of the other dimension are ordered by their sums, as well as break ties between the vectors with equal sums lexicographically. Alternatively, the vectors of the latter dimension can be viewed as multisets, and multiset ordering can be applied. Multiset ordering would be stronger than row-sum ordering. This is because two vectors may have the same sum, whereas two vectors treated as multisets are never equal unless they are identical. Currentlly, we are investigating how multiset ordering can be achieved effectively and efficiently.

---

[*] I am very grateful to Pierre Flener, Alan Frisch, Brahim Hnich, Ian Miguel, Barbara Smith, and Toby Walsh for the development of the work presented here.

[1] P. Flener, A. Frisch, B. Hnich, Z. Kiziltan, I. Miguel, J. Pearson, and T. Walsh. Breaking row and column symmetries in matrix models. In *Proc. of CP'02*, 2002.
[2] A. Frisch, B. Hnich, Z. Kiziltan, I. Miguel, and T. Walsh. Global constraints for lexicographic orderings. In *Proc. of CP'02*, 2002.

P. Van Hentenryck (Ed.): CP 2002, LNCS 2470, p. 786, 2002.
© Springer-Verlag Berlin Heidelberg 2002

Studying Interchangeability
in Constraint Satisfaction Problems

Nicoleta Neagu

Artificial Intelligence Laboratory (LIA)
Computer Science Department, Swiss Federal Institute of Technology (EPFL)
CH-1015 Ecublens, Switzerland
neagu@lia.di.epfl.ch
http://liawww.epfl.ch/

Abstract. Most work in constraint satisfaction has concentrated on computing a solution to a given problem. In practice, it often happens that an existing solution needs to be modified to satisfy additional criteria or changes in the problem. For example, a schedule or plan might have to be adjusted when a resource is missing. The concept of *interchangeability* characterizes the possibilities for making local changes to CSP solutions.

Keywords: constraint satisfaction problem, interchangeability, soft constraint satisfaction problems.

In certain settings, it is important not to generate solutions, but to modify an existing solution so that it satisfies additional or revised objectives. The general problem is to change certain variable assignments of a given CSP solution to satisfy new criteria. In the CSP literature, the possibilities of exchanging variable values in a CSP is known as *interchangeability*, concept first introduced by Freuder [1].

We have studied interchangeability for classic Constraint Satisfaction Problems, and developed algorithms for computing minimal and minimum partial interchangeabilities in a static CSP. [2].

Further we have defined interchangeability for soft Constraint Satisfaction Problems [3] and propose algorithms for computing interchangeabilities in soft CSPs [3]. In valued constraint satisfaction problems, constraints may be violated at a certain cost. Every way of violating a constraint carries with it a cost of that violation, and the cost of a solution is a combination of the costs of each constraint violation it implies. Following the work of Bistarelli, Montanari and Rossi ([4]), we consider combination functions that imply a semiring structure. This includes in particular taking the sum (also known as partial constraint satisfaction) and the maximum (also known as fuzzy constraint satisfaction) of the violation costs. We have considered how the same concepts can be extended to *soft* constraint satisfaction problems ([3]) and further we propose algorithms for computing substitutability and interchangeabilities for soft CSPs ([3]). For that, we had introduced ([3]) two notions: α- and δ-substitutability/interchangeability,

P. Van Hentenryck (Ed.): CP 2002, LNCS 2470, pp. 787–788, 2002.

and showed ([3]) that they satisfy analogous theorems to the ones already known for hard constraints. We gave ([3]) a general algorithm for soft constraint satisfaction as well as more efficient versions for special cases.

We defined the same concepts for soft constraints, and prove that neighbourhood implies full $(^\delta/_\alpha)substitutability/interchangeability$. We gave algorithms for neighbourhood $(^\delta/_\alpha)substitutability/interchangeability$, and we proved several interesting and useful properties of the concepts ([3]).

References

[1] Eugene C. Freuder. Eliminating Interchangeable Values in Constraint Satisfaction Problems. In *In Proc. of AAAI-91*, pages 227–233, Anaheim, CA, 1991.
[2] Nicoleta Neagu and Boi Faltings. Exploiting Interchangeabilities for Case Adaptation. In *In Proc. of the 4th ICCBR-01*, pages 422–437, Vancouver, CA, 2001.
[3] Stefano Bistarelli, Boi Faltings, and Nicoleta Neagu. Interchangeability in Soft CSPs. In *Proc. of the 8th CP-2002.*, Ithaca, NY, USA, 2002.
[4] Stefano Bistarelli, Ugo Montanari, and Francesca Rossi. Semiring-based Constraint Solving and Optimization. *Journal of ACM.*, 44, n.2:201–236, 1997.

Constraint Modeling in the Context of Academic Task Assignment

Robert Glaubius and Berthe Y. Choueiry

Computer Science and Engineering, University of Nebraska-Lincoln
{glaubius,choueiry}@cse.unl.edu

We explore fundamental issues of the modeling, implementation, and processing of non-binary constraints. General techniques for reformulating non-binary constraints (i.e., hidden variable, dual graph [1]) are not practical for high-arity constraints [4]. In our study, we motivate our need to express practical requirements as non-binary constraints, then we explore reformulation methods to deal with them since the conventional methods [1] become impractical. Our work builds on the work of Gent et al. [2], while we motivate and anchor our investigations in the practical context of a real-world application. This is the assignment of graduate teaching assistants to courses in our department. This task is a critical responsibility that our department's administration has to drudge through every semester. The idea for this particular application is borrowed from Rina Dechter, at the UC Irvine. We model this application using 4 types of unary constraints, one type of binary constraint, and 3 types of non-binary constraints. Since in our application problems are over-constrained, a satisfactory assignment is one that maximizes the number of courses covered. For this purpose, we adopt a new consistency checking mechanism that allows variables to be assigned a null value during search. For two assignments that cover the same number of courses, we further discriminate between them by choosing the one of highest quality, obtained by a combination of the value of the preferences in each assignment. We experiment with two different criteria to maximize preferences. We establish that two of our non-binary constraints are decomposable into equivalent networks of binary constraints, which significantly improves the performance of search [3]. Our efforts have resulted in a prototype system under field-test since August 2001. This system has effectively reduced the number of conflicts, thus yielding a commensurate increase in course quality. It has also decreased the amount of time and effort spent on making the assignment and gained the approval and satisfaction of our staff, faculty and student body.

References

[1] F. Bacchus and P. van Beek. On the conversion between non-binary and binary constraint satisfaction problems. In *AAAI/IAAI*, pages 310–318, 1998.
[2] I. P. Gent, K. Stergiou, and T. Walsh. Decomposable constraints. In *New Trends in Constraints*, pages 134–149, 1999.
[3] R. Glaubius and B. Y. Choueiry. Constraint Constraint Modeling and Reformulation in the Context of Academic Task Assignment. In *Working Notes of the Workshop Modelling and Solving Problems with Constraints, ECAI 2002*, Lyon, France, 2002.
[4] J-C. Régin. Usenet message posted on comp.constraints, 1998.

P. Van Hentenryck (Ed.): CP 2002, LNCS 2470, p. 789, 2002.
© Springer-Verlag Berlin Heidelberg 2002

Design Tradeoffs
for Autonomous Trading Agents

Ioannis A. Vetsikas

Computer Science Dept., Cornell U., Ithaca, NY 14853
vetsikas@cs.cornell.edu

We examine several issues associated with the design of agents trading in e-marketplaces. We use an adaptive, robust agent architecture combining principled methods and empirical knowledge. The agent needs to solve an optimization problem in order to maximize its gain. Deciding the optimal quantities to buy and sell is only part of the problem. The desired prices and the time of bid placement is also important. Bid aggressiveness must be balanced against the cost of obtaining increased flexibility.

Conclusions We used the Trading Agent Competition problem [10] to examine bidding in simultaneous auctions. As expected there is no optimal strategy, but rather best responses to the strategies of the competing agents. Nonetheless empirical results lead to some interesting conclusions. We demonstrate how to maximize the flexibility (actions available, information etc.) of the agent while minimizing the cost that it has to pay for this benefit, and show that by using simple knowledge (like modeling prices) of the domain it can make this choice more intelligently and improve its performance even more. We also show that bidding aggressively is not a panacea and establish that an agent, who is just aggressive enough to implement its plan efficiently, outperforms overall agents who are either not aggressive enough or who are too aggressive. Finally we show that even though generating a good plan is crucial for the agent to maximize its utility, the greedy algorithm that we use is more than capable to help the agent produce comparable results with other agents that use a slower provably optimal algorithm. One of the primary benefits of our architecture is that it is able to combine seamlessly both principled methods and methods based on empirical knowledge, which is the reason why it performed so consistently well in the TAC. Overall our agent is adaptive, versatile, fast and robust and its elements are general enough to work well under any situation that requires bidding in multiple simultaneous auctions.

References

[1] P. Anthony, W. Hall, V. Dang, and N. R. Jennings. Autonomous agents for participating in multiple on-line auctions. In *IJCAI Workshop on E-Business and Intelligent Web*, 2001.
[2] Y. Fujishima, K. Leyton-Brown, and Y. Shoham. Taming the computational complexity of combinatorial auctions. In *Proc of IJCAI-99*, pages 548–553, Aug. 1999.

P. Van Hentenryck (Ed.): CP 2002, LNCS 2470, pp. 790–791, 2002.
© Springer-Verlag Berlin Heidelberg 2002

[3] A. Greenwald and P. Stone. Autonomous bidding agents in the trading agent competition. *IEEE Internet Computing, April*, March/April 2001.

[4] A. R. Greenwald and J. Boyan. Bid determination for simultaneous auctions. In *Proc of the 3rd ACM Conference on Electronic Commerce*, pages 115–124 and 210–212, Oct. 2001.

[5] A. R. Greenwald, J. O. Kephart, and G. J. Tesauro. Strategic pricebot dynamics. In *Proceedings of the ACM Conference on Electronic Commerce (EC-99)*, Nov. 1999.

[6] P. Klemperer. Auction theory: A guide to the literature. *Journal of Economic Surveys Vol13(3)*, July 1999.

[7] C. Preist, C. Bartolini, and I. Phillips. Algorithm design for agents which participate in multiple simultaneous auctions. *In Agent Mediated Electronic Commerce III (LNAI), Springer-Verlag, Berlin*, pages 139–154, 2001.

[8] T. Sandholm and S. Suri. Improved algorithms for optimal winner determination in combinatorial auctions. In *Proc 7th Conference on Artificial Intelligence (AAAI-00)*, July 2000.

[9] P. Stone, M. L. Littman, S. Singh, and M. Kearns. ATTac-2000: an adaptive autonomous bidding agent. In *Proc 5th International Conference on Autonomous Agents*, May 2001.

[10] M. P. Wellman, P. R. Wurman, K. O'Malley, R. Bangera, S. de Lin, D. Reeves, and W. E. Walsh. Designing the market game for tac. *IEEE Internet Computing*, March/April 2001.

Author Index

Lecture Notes in Computer Science

For information about Vols. 1–2371
please contact your bookseller or Springer-Verlag

Vol. 2407: A.C. Kakas, F. Sadri (Eds.), Computational Logic: Logic Programming and Beyond. Part I. XII, 678 pages. 2002. (Subseries LNAI).

Vol. 2408: A.C. Kakas, F. Sadri (Eds.), Computational Logic: Logic Programming and Beyond. Part II. XII, 628 pages. 2002. (Subseries LNAI).

Vol. 2409: D.M. Mount, C. Stein (Eds.), Algorithm Engineering and Experiments. Proceedings, 2002. VIII, 207 pages. 2002.

Vol. 2410: V.A. Carreño, C.A. Muñoz, S. Tahar (Eds.), Theorem Proving in Higher Order Logics. Proceedings, 2002. X, 349 pages. 2002.

Vol. 2412: H. Yin, N. Allinson, R. Freeman, J. Keane, S. Hubbard (Eds.), Intelligent Data Engineering and Automated Learning – IDEAL 2002. Proceedings, 2002. XV, 597 pages. 2002.

Vol. 2413: K. Kuwabara, J. Lee (Eds.), Intelligent Agents and Multi-Agent Systems. Proceedings, 2002. X, 221 pages. 2002. (Subseries LNAI).

Vol. 2414: F. Mattern, M. Naghshineh (Eds.), Pervasive Computing. Proceedings, 2002. XI, 298 pages. 2002.

Vol. 2415: J.R. Dorronsoro (Ed.), Artificial Neural Networks – ICANN 2002. Proceedings, 2002. XXVIII, 1382 pages. 2002.

Vol. 2416: S. Craw, A. Preece (Eds.), Advances in Case-Based Reasoning. Proceedings, 2002. XII, 656 pages. 2002. (Subseries LNAI).

Vol. 2417: M. Ishizuka, A. Sattar (Eds.), PRICAI 2002: Trends in Artificial Intelligence. Proceedings, 2002. XX, 623 pages. 2002. (Subseries LNAI).

Vol. 2418: D. Wells, L. Williams (Eds.), Extreme Programming and Agile Methods – XP/Agile Universe 2002. Proceedings, 2002. XII, 292 pages. 2002.

Vol. 2419: X. Meng, J. Su, Y. Wang (Eds.), Advances in Web-Age Information Management. Proceedings, 2002. XV, 446 pages. 2002.

Vol. 2420: K. Diks, W. Rytter (Eds.), Mathematical Foundations of Computer Science 2002. Proceedings, 2002. XII, 652 pages. 2002.

Vol. 2421: L. Brim, P. Jančar, M. Křetínský, A. Kučera (Eds.), CONCUR 2002 – Concurrency Theory. Proceedings, 2002. XII, 611 pages. 2002.

Vol. 2422: H. Kirchner, Ch. Ringeissen (Eds.), Algebraic Methodology and Software Technology. Proceedings, 2002. XI, 503 pages. 2002.

Vol. 2423: D. Lopresti, J. Hu, R. Kashi (Eds.), Document Analysis Systems V. Proceedings, 2002. XIII, 570 pages. 2002.

Vol. 2425: Z. Bellahsène, D. Patel, C. Rolland (Eds.), Object-Oriented Information Systems. Proceedings, 2002. XIII, 550 pages. 2002.

Vol. 2426: J.-M. Bruel, Z. Bellahsène (Eds.), Advances in Object-Oriented Information Systems. Proceedings, 2002. IX, 314 pages. 2002.

Vol. 2430: T. Elomaa, H. Mannila, H. Toivonen (Eds.), Machine Learning: ECML 2002. Proceedings, 2002. XIII, 532 pages. 2002. (Subseries LNAI).

Vol. 2431: T. Elomaa, H. Mannila, H. Toivonen (Eds.), Principles of Data Mining and Knowledge Discovery. Proceedings, 2002. XIV, 514 pages. 2002. (Subseries LNAI).

Vol. 2435: Y. Manolopoulos, P. Návrat (Eds.), Advances in Databases and Information Systems. Proceedings, 2002. XIII, 415 pages. 2002.

Vol. 2436: J. Fong, C.T. Cheung, H.V. Leong, Q. Li (Eds.), Advances in Web-Based Learning. Proceedings, 2002. XIII, 434 pages. 2002.

Vol. 2438: M. Glesner, P. Zipf, M. Renovell (Eds.), Field-Programmable Logic and Applications. Proceedings, 2002. XXII, 1187 pages. 2002.

Vol. 2439: J.J. Merelo Guervós, P. Adamidis, H.-G. Beyer, J.-L. Fernández-Villacañas, H.-P. Schwefel (Eds.), Parallel Problem Solving from Nature – PPSN VII. Proceedings, 2002. XXII, 947 pages. 2002.

Vol. 2440: J.M. Haake, J.A. Pino (Eds.), Groupware: Design, Implementation and Use. Proceedings, 2002. XII, 285 pages. 2002.

Vol. 2442: M. Yung (Ed.), Advances in Cryptology – CRYPTO 2002. Proceedings, 2002. XIV, 627 pages. 2002.

Vol. 2443: D. Scott (Ed.), Artificial Intelligence: Methodology, Systems, and Applications. Proceedings, 2002. X, 279 pages. 2002. (Subseries LNAI).

Vol. 2444: A. Buchmann, F. Casati, L. Fiege, M.-C. Hsu, M.-C. Shan (Eds.), Technologies for E-Services. Proceedings, 2002. X, 171 pages. 2002.

Vol. 2445: C. Anagnostopoulou, M. Ferrand, A. Smaill (Eds.), Music and Artificial Intelligence. Proceedings, 2002. VIII, 207 pages. 2002. (Subseries LNAI).

Vol. 2446: M. Klusch, S. Ossowski, O. Shehory (Eds.), Cooperative Information Agents VI. Proceedings, 2002. XI, 321 pages. 2002. (Subseries LNAI).

Vol. 2447: D.J. Hand, N.M. Adams, R.J. Bolton (Eds.), Pattern Detection and Discovery. Proceedings, 2002. XII, 227 pages. 2002. (Subseries LNAI).

Vol. 2448: P. Sojka, I. Kopeček, K. Pala (Eds.), Text, Speech and Dialogue. Proceedings, 2002. XII, 481 pages. 2002. (Subseries LNAI).

Vol. 2451: B. Hochet, A.J. Acosta, M.J. Bellido (Eds.), Integrated Circuit Design. Proceedings, 2002. XVI, 496 pages. 2002.

Vol. 2453: A. Hameurlain, R. Cicchetti, R. Traunmüller (Eds.), Database and Expert Systems Applications. Proceedings, 2002. XVIII, 951 pages. 2002.

Vol. 2454: Y. Kambayashi, W. Winiwarter, M. Arikawa (Eds.), Data Warehousing and Knowledge Discovery. Proceedings, 2002. XIII, 339 pages. 2002.

Vol. 2455: K. Bauknecht, A M. Tjoa, G. Quirchmayr (Eds.), E-Commerce and Web Technologies. Proceedings, 2002. XIV, 414 pages. 2002.

Vol. 2456: R. Traunmüller, K. Lenk (Eds.), Electronic Government. Proceedings, 2002. XIII, 486 pages. 2002.

Vol. 2469: W. Damm, E.-R. Olderog (Eds.), Formal Techniques in Real-Time and Fault-Tolerant Systems. Proceedings, 2002. X, 455 pages. 2002.

Vol. 2470: P. Van Hentenryck (Ed.), Principles and Practice of Constraint Programming – CP 2002. Proceedings, 2002. XVI, 794 pages. 2002.

Vol. 2483: J.D.P. Rolim, S. Vadhan (Eds.), Randomization and Approximation Techniques in Computer Science. Proceedings, 2002. VIII, 275 pages. 2002.